# ENCYCLOPEDIA OF AMERICAN FOREIGN POLICY

Glenn Hastedt

Facts On File, Inc.

**Encyclopedia of American Foreign Policy**

Copyright © 2004 by Glenn Hastedt

Facts On File, Inc.
132 West 31st Street
New York NY 10001

**Library of Congress Cataloging-in-Publication Data**

Hastedt, Glenn P., 1950–
Encyclopedia of American foreign policy / by Glenn Hastedt.
p. cm.
Includes bibliographical references and index.
ISBN 0-8160-4642-5
1. United States—Foreign relations—Encyclopedias. I. Title.
E183.7.H28 2003
327.73'003—dc21          2003049186

Text design by Joan M. Toro
Cover design by Cathy Rincon
Illustrations by Jeremy Eagle

Printed in the United States of America

VB Hermitage 10  9  8  7  6  5  4  3  2  1

This book is printed on acid-free paper.

# Contents

LIST OF ENTRIES
iv

INTRODUCTION
vii

ENTRIES A TO Z
1

SELECTED BIBLIOGRAPHY
539

INDEX
544

# List of Entries

★ ─────────────────────────────────

Acheson, Dean
Act of Chapultepec
Adams, John
Adams, John Quincy
Afghanistan
Africa
Agriculture, Department of
Alaska, purchase of
Algeria
Alliance for Progress
alliances
America First Committee
American Civil War
*American Insurance Co. v. Canter*
American national style
American Revolution
Angola
Antiballistic Missile System Treaty
ANZUS Pact
Arab-Israeli conflict
Argentina
arms control
Arms Control and Disarmament Agency
arms transfers
Articles of Confederation
Asian financial crisis
Atlantic Charter
Baker Plan
ballistic missile defense
Baltic states
*Banco National de Cuba v. Sabatino*
Barbary pirates
Baruch Plan

Bay of Pigs
Berlin crisis, 1948
Berlin crisis, 1958
Berlin crisis, 1961
bin Laden, Osama
bipolarity
Blaine, James
bomber gap
Borah, William E.
Bosnia and Herzegovina
bracero program
Brady Plan
Brazil
Bretton Woods system
Brezhnev Doctrine
Bricker Amendment
brinksmanship
Bryan, William Jennings
Bullitt, William
bureaucracy
bureaucratic-politics decision-making model
Bush, George H. W.
Bush, George W.
Byrnes, James
Calhoun, John C.
Cambodia
Camp David accords
Camp David II
Canada
Caribbean Basin Initiative
Carter, Jimmy
Carter Doctrine
Central Asian republics
Central Intelligence Agency
Central Treaty Organization

Chile
China
Church Committee
civil-military relations
clandestine collection
Clay, Henry
Clayton-Bulwer Treaty
Cleveland, Grover
Clinton, Bill
cold war
collective security
Colombia
Commerce Department
communism, Soviet
Comprehensive Test Ban Treaty
conference diplomacy
Conference on Security and Cooperation in Europe
Congo
Congress, U.S.
Constitution, U.S.
containment
Coolidge, Calvin
Coordinating Committee for Multilateral Controls
counterintelligence
covert action
Croatia
*Crosby v. Foreign Trade National Council*
Cuba
Cuban-American National Foundation
Cuban missile crisis
Czechoslovakia

*Dames & Moore v. Regan*
Dayton Accords
debt crisis
Defense Department
Defense Intelligence Agency
Democratic Party
democratic peace
democratization
demographics, global
détente
deterrence failures
deterrence strategies
diplomacy
director of central intelligence
disarmament
dollar diplomacy
domestic influences on U.S. foreign policy
Dominican Republic
domino theory
doves
drug trafficking
dual containment
Dulles, John Foster
Earth Summit, Rio de Janeiro
economic sanctions
Egypt
Eisenhower, Dwight D.
Eisenhower Doctrine
elections
elite decision-making theory
El Salvador
embassy

enlargement
Enterprise for the Americas
    Initiative
environment
Eritrea
espionage
Ethiopia
European Union
executive agreements
fast-track authority
Federal Bureau of
    Investigation
Federalist Papers
Federalist Party
filibustering
first ladies and American
    foreign policy
Florida, acquisition of
Food for Peace
Ford, Gerald
foreign aid
Foreign Service Officers
    Corps
Formosa Resolution
Fourteen Points
France
Franklin, Benjamin
Frelinghuysen, Frederick
French and Indian War
Fulbright, J. William
Gadsden Purchase
Gaither Committee Report
General Agreement on
    Tariffs and Trade
Germany
globalization
*Goldwater et al. v. Carter*
Goldwater-Nichols Defense
    Reorganization Act
Grant, Ulysses S.
Great Britain
Greece
Grenada, invasion of
Guatemala
guerrilla warfare
Gulf War Syndrome
Haig, Alexander
Haiti
Hamilton, Alexander
Harding, Warren G.
Hawaii, annexation of
hawks
Hay, John

Helms, Jesse
Helms-Burton Act
Hickenlooper Amendment
HIV/AIDS
*Holmes v. Jennison*
Homeland Security,
    Department of
Hoover, Herbert
House, Edward Mandell
Hughes, Charles Evans
Hughes-Ryan Amendment
Hull, Cordell
human rights
humanitarian intervention
Hungary
idealism
immigration
*Immigration and
    Naturalization Service
    v. Chadha*
imperialism
India
Indonesia
Insular Cases
intelligence
intelligence community
interest groups
Intermediate-Range
    Nuclear Forces Treaty
international-affairs budget
International Criminal
    Court
international crises
internationalism
international law
International Monetary
    Fund
international organization
international system
International Trade
    Organization
Iran
Iran-contra initiative
Iranian hostage crisis
Iran-Iraq War
Iraq
Iraq War
Ireland
Islam, political
isolationism
Israel
Italy
Jackson, Andrew

Jackson-Vanik Amendment
Japan
Jay's Treaty
Jefferson, Thomas
Johnson, Lyndon
Joint Chiefs of Staff
Jordan
Kellogg-Briand Pact
Kennan, George
Kennedy, John F.
Kennedy Round
Kissinger, Henry
Korean War
Kosovo
Kuwait
Kyoto Protocol
land mines
Laos
Law of the Sea conferences
League of Nations
Lebanon
legalism
Lend-Lease
Liberia
Libya
Lincoln, Abraham
Lippmann gap
Lodge, Henry Cabot
Logan Act
London Naval Conferences
Louisiana Purchase
MacArthur, Douglas
Madison, James
Madrid accords
Manifest Destiny
Mariel boatlift
Marshall, George C.
Marshall Plan
massive retaliation
McCarthyism
McNamara, Robert S.
media
Mexican War
Mexico
military-industrial complex
missile gap
*Missouri v. Holland*
Monroe Doctrine
Montreal Protocol
moral pragmatism
Morgenthau Plan
Morocco
most-favored-nation status

multinational corporations
    and American foreign
    policy
multipolarity
MX missile
Namibia
national intelligence
    estimates
national interest
National Reconnaissance
    Office
National Security Act, 1947
National Security Advisor
National Security Agency
National Security Council
Native Americans
Netherlands
neutrality legislation, 1930s
*New York Times
    v. United States*
Nicaragua
Nigeria
Nixon, Richard
Nixon Doctrine
nongovernmental
    organizations
North American Free
    Trade Agreement
North Atlantic Treaty
    Organization
North Korea
Northern Ireland
NSC-68
nuclear compellence
nuclear deterrence strategy:
    Soviet Union
nuclear deterrence strategy:
    United States
nuclear war
nuclear weapons arsenal
nuclear winter
Nye Committee
Office of Strategic Services
oil
Olney, Richard
Open Door policy
Open Skies
Operation Desert Shield
Operation Desert Storm
Operation Just Cause
Operation Uphold
    Democracy
Oregon Territory

Organization of American
      States
Organization of Petroleum
      Exporting Countries
Ostend Manifesto
Pakistan
Palestine Liberation
      Organization
Panama
Panama Canal,
      acquisition of
Panama Canal Treaties
Partnership for Peace
peacekeeping and
      peacemaking
peace movements
Pentagon Papers
Persian Gulf War
personality
Philippines
Pierce, Franklin
Pike Committee
Pinckney's Treaty
Platt Amendment
pluralism
Point Four Program
Poland
Polk, James
population policy
Potsdam Conference
power
preemption
president
Prize Cases
public diplomacy
public opinion
Puerto Rico
al-Qaeda
Radio Free Europe
RAND Corporation
Rapacki Plan
rational-actor decision-
      making model
Reagan, Ronald
Reagan Doctrine
realism
Reciprocal Trade
      Adjustment Acts
refugees

religion
Republican Party
revisionism
Rio Pact
rogue states
Roosevelt, Franklin D.
Roosevelt, Theodore
Roosevelt Corollary
Root, Elihu
Rush-Bagot Agreement
Russia
Rwanda
Saudi Arabia
secretary of defense
secretary of state
sectionalism
September 11, 2001
Seward, William
single integrated
      operational plan
small-group decision-
      making model
Smithsonian Agreement
Smoot-Hawley Tariff
Somalia
South Africa
Southeast Asia Treaty
      Organization
South Korea
Spain
Spanish-American War
*Sputnik*
State Department
Stimson, Henry
Strategic Arms Limitation
      Talks
Strategic Arms Limitation
      Talks I (SALT I)
Strategic Arms Limitation
      Talks II (SALT II)
Strategic Arms Reduction
      Talks
Strategic Arms Reduction
      Treaty I
Strategic Arms Reduction
      Treaty II
Strategic Arms Reduction
      Treaty III

Strategic Defense
      Initiative
Strategic Offensive
      Reductions Treaty
Sudan
Suez crisis
summit conferences/
      diplomacy
Sumner, Charles
Supreme Court
Syria
Taft, William
Taiwan
Tehran Conference
Teller Amendment
terrorism
Texas, annexation of
Thailand
think tanks
Tibet
Tokyo Round
Tower Commission
trade policy
Treasury Department
Treaty of Ghent
Treaty of Paris
Treaty of Portsmouth
Treaty of Versailles
Trilateral Commission
tripolarity
Truman, Harry
Truman Doctrine
Tunisia
Turkey
Tyler, John
U-2 incident
*Underhill v. Hernandez*
unilateralism
unipolarity
United Nations
United States Agency
      for International
      Development
United States Information
      Agency
United States Institute of
      Peace

United States Trade
      Representative,
      Office of the
*United States v. Belmont*
*United States v. Curtiss-
      Wright Export Corp.*
Uruguay Round
USA PATRIOT Act
Vance, Cyrus
Vandenburg, Arthur
Venezuela
Venezuelan boundary
      dispute
verification
Vietnam
Vietnam War
Vladivostok accords
Wallace, Henry
*Ware v. Hylton*
War of 1812
War Powers Resolution
Warsaw Pact
Washington, George
Washington Conference
weapons of mass
      destruction
Webster, Daniel
Whig Party
Wilmot Proviso
Wilson, Woodrow
Wilsonianism
women and American
      foreign policy
World Bank
World Summit on
      Sustainable
      Development
World Trade Organization
World War I
World War II
Wye River accords
Yalta Conference
*Youngstown Sheet & Tube
      Company v. Sawyer*
Yugoslavia
Zimbabwe
Zimmermann Telegram

# Introduction

American foreign policy is an evolving subject of inquiry. Not only do new issues and challenges appear on the policy-making agenda, but historians and political scientists are constantly reevaluating the past in order to better understand the present and future. This volume appears at a particularly apropos time. We have now begun to put some distance between ourselves and the cold war, permitting us to evaluate it with a more measured eye. We are also far enough into the post–cold war era that the many early speculative debates about its character have been replaced by more focused inquiries into concrete problem sets, such as peacekeeping, globalization, and terrorism. We have also experienced the terrorist attacks of September 11, 2001. Not only did they transform the presidency of George W. Bush, but, along with the American response, they appear to have ushered in a new era of American foreign policy.

At the same time that American foreign policy can be seen as constantly evolving, we can also identify four consistent points that underlie the conduct of American foreign policy over time. First, it is outward looking. Foreign policy is made with an eye to opportunities and challenges that lay beyond America's borders. Second, foreign policy is about choices. While we tend to speak of countries being forced to respond to developments abroad with military power, economic sanctions, or declarations of resolve, the reality is quite different. Policy makers have a surprisingly wide range of options open to them. *National interest* and *national security* are not self-defining terms. They take on meaning only after goals and values are established. If the goals or values deemed important change, so, too, do the menu of options before policy makers. Third, foreign policy is heavily influenced by domestic considerations. It is outward looking, but the choices made reflect not only an evaluation of the external environment within which the United States operates but also the pull of personalities, institutions, and societal forces. Fourth, American foreign policy is influenced by the past. Decisions are not made in a vacuum. Previously undertaken policies always cast a shadow over the present and future. The past influences the present even at those times when American foreign policy makers seem blind to what has already transpired. In those cases history exerts its hidden influence by structuring how Americans view the world and how others respond to American foreign policy. Each of these themes is elaborated below.

In looking outward, American foreign policy seeks to position the United States in such a manner that its core values and goals are protected from threat and advanced when the opportunity presents itself. These core goals and values are deeply embedded in the American historical experience and combine to constitute an American worldview and national style. Among the key ideas that have helped Americans define their position in the world are a sense of uniqueness or exceptionalism, a penchant for unilateral action, and legalistic definitions of world problems and their solutions. One of the interesting questions about the future of American foreign policy is the extent to which the traditional American worldview will continue to shape American foreign policy as new voices are added to the policy-making process from groups such as women, African Americans, and Hispanic Americans who do not identify as closely with this legacy.

The world beyond the United States's borders can be conceptualized in any number of different ways. It can be viewed as threatening or supportive, stable or unstable, simple or complex or as encroaching on the United States's freedom of action or as distant and of little concern. A reading of the historical record shows that all of these views have been held by American foreign-policy makers at one time or another. More systematically, we can characterize the world beyond the United States by the manner in which power is organized. The most common starting point for thinking in these terms is with the distribution of military power. Here we speak of the international system as unipolar (when only one major power center exists), bipolar (when two competing power centers exist), and multipolar (when power is relatively evenly distributed among five or more power centers). For much of its history American foreign policy benefited greatly from the existence of a multipolar world in which the great powers of Europe were repeatedly at war with one another. The cold war was a bipolar international system and greatly limited the United States's range of options. The contemporary era appears to be unipolar in nature, with the United States emerging from the cold war as the sole remaining superpower. It is also possible to think of the global distribution of power in economic terms. Here we encounter the concepts of free trade, interdependence, dependency, and globalization. For much of its history the United States sought to take advantage of a free-trade international system that had been organized by the British. After World War II it fell upon the United States to maintain such a system. One consequence was increased economic interdependence and a loss of unilateral control over key economic decisions. The Organization of Petroleum Exporting Countries (OPEC) oil crisis and trade wars with Japan and Western Europe reflected this new reality. One of the major challenges to American foreign policy today is adjusting to and operating in a globalized international economy. Its potential for further limiting American power appears great, but many commentators assert that it also provides the United States with great opportunities to exert its will and influence in world politics. Key to this debate is the ability of soft power to replace economic and military power as an instrument of foreign policy.

The most fundamental choice that the United States or any country makes in orienting itself to the world is its selection of a grand strategy. Grand strategy is more than just a statement of goals and values. By defining a state's place in the world, it provides policy makers with guidance on such challenging questions as defining core values, identifying what opportunities should be exploited and what situations are threatening, determining its relationship to the international community as a whole, and deciding how its power should be used. Agreement on a grand strategy does not guarantee success in foreign policy. In the period leading up to World War II, America's grand strategy was isolationism. Today few view that policy as having been attuned to the emerging realities of interwar world politics. For most of the last half of the 20th century, American foreign policy operated within the context of a single grand strategy that is viewed more positively: containment. The primary challenge facing the United States was defined as the Soviet Union. It was a global challenge that threatened all aspects of American society and was best met by the application of counterpressure, especially military counterpressure. Over time this cold war competition between the United States and the Soviet Union came to appear quite manageable, and the Soviet Union became a predictable—and in many ways comfortable—enemy to deal with as formal and informal rules of conduct for both sides emerged. All of this has changed. With the end of the cold war and the breakup of the Soviet Union, U.S. grand strategy lost its focal point. A wide-ranging debate ensued in which policy makers, analysts, and citizens put forward alternative grand strategies for guiding U.S. foreign policy into the 21st century. They included returning to isolationism, democratizing the world, and pursuing global hegemony. The terrorist attacks of September 11, 2001, brought a temporary halt to this debate. The principal threat to the United States now seemed clear, and support for a foreign policy structured around a war against terrorism was widespread. In 2002, however, the debate over grand strategy began again. The George W. Bush administration was focusing on Iraq as the principal security threat to the United States and as one that had to be met with military power. To this end it put forward a new grand strategy: preemption. Both the new grand strategy and the possibility of war with Iraq were met with intense debate. Disagreement over the proper grand strategy to follow is nothing new in the evolution of American foreign policy. We can witness debates over the merits of isolationism and internationalism in the early years of the republic. A grand strategy of continental expansionism had both supporters and detractors, especially as the question of slavery came into focus. Not all supported America's entry into global politics as an imperialist power at the turn of the 20th century. Woodrow Wilson and Henry Cabot Lodge clashed over American grand strategy at the end of World War I.

Grand strategy only sets the broad parameters within which a country formulates its foreign policy. It must also design specific lines of action with particular countries and regions in mind. This may require nothing more than a minor adjustment from the norm in how the United States deals with a given state. In other circumstances it may require that a country be treated as an exception to the rule. We see this in the fact that revelations of human-rights violations or the possession of weapons of mass destruction are not always viewed in the same light by American officials. While policy makers may view such adjustments as prudent and in the national interest or as short-term accommodations, the inconsistencies they bring about always present the danger of overwhelming grand strategy to the point where it becomes unrecognizable. An important contributing factor to the complexity and richness of American regional and bilateral foreign policy is that they entail a two-way flow of influence. Not only is the United States dealing with another state in trying to achieve its foreign-policy goals, but that state is trying to realize its own set of goals in dealing with the United States. The reality for many states is that they do not appear on the radar screen of American foreign policy. Relations with them are minimal and uncomplicated. For these states their primary point of interaction with the United States often comes from their joint participation in regional and international organizations. Following the Senate's rejection of the League of Nations, the United States was not an active participant in international organizations prior to the end of World War II. Since then, the number of these organizations has skyrocketed, and the United States has come to see participation in these bodies as serving the national interest. This does not mean that U.S. participation in international organizations is free from controversy.

Disagreement continues to exist over the benefits of multilateral versus unilateral action and the associated political and economic costs, as was reflected in American diplomacy at the United Nations and with North Atlantic Treaty Organization (NATO) states in early 2003. It was also visible earlier as the Bush administration decided not to participate in the Kyoto Protocol on protecting the environment and in the establishment of the International Criminal Court. The newest targets and partners of American bilateral diplomacy are nongovernmental organizations. Once largely restricted to an advocacy role in international politics, they are now often found on the operational front lines of such highly visible and controversial international undertakings as peacekeeping missions, de-mining projects, and responding to the HIV/AIDS pandemic.

One of the enduring challenges faced by states is to translate strategic principles into concrete actions. In theory a wide array of choices are open to states, but in reality the effective range of choice is restricted by power considerations. States may engage in persuasion, offer bribes or make promises, make threats, or seek to force their will upon another state. The instrument chosen for doing so may entail the use of diplomacy, economic power, military power, arms control and disarmament, or covert action. No exercise of power is cost-free. It is easy to pay too much to obtain the cooperation of others or to deter an unwanted action. Another danger that states constantly face is the possibility of becoming trapped into supporting a failing regime. Even success presents difficulties. The security dilemma holds that the end result of succeeding in making oneself more secure or powerful is to provoke others into taking compensating action that will negate one's gains. One possible outcome of this situation is a destructive and uncontrollable arms race.

The United States is no stranger to the decisions that need to be made in conducting its statecraft. In its formative years, U.S weakness greatly constrained what policy makers could do. Its foreign-policy behavior was not much different from that of newly independent states in the late 20th century. At the same time its geographic position and ongoing conflicts among the great powers in Europe offered it the opportunity to secure foreign policy objectives at relatively little cost. In the latter part of the 19th century and first part of the 20th century, the United States possessed the raw ingredients to play the role of a major world power but chose not to do so. It is only with the advent of the cold war that the United States began to conduct a foreign policy that made use of the full array of policy instruments at its disposal. In doing so, however, the dangers noted above appeared. Foreign aid was given freely but (according to its critics) produced minimum security dividends. The United States became embroiled in a war in Vietnam from which it could not escape, and it allied itself with failing dictators in Latin America, Iran, and the Philippines. And one of the defining features of the cold war was the nuclear arms race with the Soviet Union.

Turning to the domestic side of American foreign policy, a great deal of debate exists over the proper role of the public voice in making American foreign policy. The temptation is great, especially on the part of policy makers, to assume that American foreign policy is too important to be left to the whims of the public. For advocates of this position, foreign policy and domestic policy are two very different arenas, and the American response to foreign challenges and opportunities ought to be left to professionals. They recite President John Kennedy's admonition that domestic-policy failures can defeat us while foreign-policy failures can kill us. Standing opposed to this school of thought is one that stresses that the essence of democracy is popular control and accountability. Foreign policy is no different from domestic policy. Advocates of this perspective would also question whose professional expertise is to be heeded, because the history of American foreign policy is replete with disagreements between professionals over how to proceed. Which school of thought wins is more than an academic question. Studies have shown that consistent policy differences exist between the mass public and elites over their attitudes to the importance of foreign aid, membership in the United Nations, protectionist trade legislation, and the use of troops abroad.

One problem that both groups must face is deciding where to look for expressions of the public's view on foreign policy. One way in which it can be expressed is through public opinion polls. Elections are another way in which the public has input into making foreign policy. Special interest groups are a common way in which the American public seeks to influence foreign-policy decisions. Economic, ethnic, and ideological groups all have organized to lobby for their causes. Think tanks also play a prominent role in the domestic foreign-policy debate by providing information and policy options. Perhaps most controversial of late is the role of the media. In the eyes of some, the media have come to exert a domineering and distorting influence on foreign-policy decision making. The "CNN effect" refers to the presumed ability of the media to force policy makers into action by shining the spotlight of news coverage on an event or to force them to abandon a course of action by presenting images of wounded and dead soldiers and anti-Americanism abroad. Others see the media as having a less powerful voice in policy making. In this view the media remains heavily dependent upon policy makers for guidance on where to find a story and how to frame issues. Determined policy makers who know what they want to accomplish will not be swayed by the media but will use it to their advantage.

Domestic influences on American foreign policy extend beyond the manner and extent to which the public raises its voice. Also important are the institutions that make American foreign policy and the operation of the policy-making process. With regard to the institutional context of American foreign policy, it has long been observed that the Constitution is an invitation to struggle for control of the content of U.S. foreign policy. It is a struggle among the three branches of the American national government: Congress, the presidency, and the Supreme Court. It is the president who speaks for the United States, and historically it is the president who has won this struggle. It is not a struggle that is always engaged and victory cannot be assumed, as Wilson discovered with the Treaty of Versailles. Compromise is often necessary on trade legislation, appointments, and the content of treaties. The Supreme Court has typically sought to remove itself from the center of the struggle, although its decisions often have had far-reaching effects on the ability of the two other bodies to compete against one another. Congress, too, has not always acted as a challenger. At times it has been disinterested in foreign policy, and other times a spirit of bipartisanship has prevailed. Beneath the surface lies yet another important institutional actor, the bureaucracy. They play an influential role in foreign policy making by providing policy makers with information, defining problems, and implementing the selected policy. Bureaucracies are not neutral in carrying out these tasks. As with the other institutions that help make foreign policy, their positions are heavily influenced by internal norms, standard operating procedures, personalities, and a desire to control the situation.

The people and institutions that make American foreign policy do not come together in a haphazard fashion. Patterns exist, and analysts have developed a number of models of the policy process to explain how decisions are made. All highlight different aspects of reality and have their own strengths and weaknesses. The most frequently employed is the rational-actor model. It makes the least data demands on the observer and treats the decision-making unit as a black box, assuming for analytical purposes that a unity in outlook characterizes decision makers as they respond to external threats and opportunities. Quite often American foreign policy can be understood from the perspective of rational-actor decision-making models, but on other occasions the decisions fail to conform. In those circumstances other models are needed. Among the most frequently employed are bureaucratic models that emphasize the role of bureaucratic actors in decision making and small-group decision-making models that focus on the influence of group dynamics on policy outcomes. Also receiving considerable attention are elite models that stress the common ties and outlooks among those who make decisions and how these bonds overcome differences rooted in institutional settings and partisan political affiliations. Finally, some analysts employ pluralist models. Viewed from this perspective, foreign-policy decisions represent the balance of political power among domestic interest groups with the government acting as an umpire.

Finally, we turn to the influence of the past. Earlier foreign-policy undertakings by the United States, the debates that surrounded them, and the ideas about the United States's place in the world that informed them provide an invaluable source of insight into the present. They constitute streams of thought and action into which contemporary decisions flow. Sometimes these streams are hospitable to new undertakings, and policy initiatives move ahead smoothly. At other times these streams are fraught with peril. They contain hidden boulders and treacherous rapids that hold the potential for undermining and frustrating well-laid plans. Successful policy making thus requires an understanding of the past if these streams are to be navigated successfully. Yet, for reasons that are not difficult to understand, American foreign policy tends to be present- and future-oriented. It is the present that defines the challenges and opportunities being faced. It is the future that will judge whether the decisions made are wise. The past tends to get ignored in large measure because of our uncertainty over how to approach it. We are attracted to it out of a desire to avoid repeating its failures and to duplicate its successes. We want no more Vietnams, Bay of Pigs, or Cuban missile crises. We also yearn for the development success of another Marshall Plan and the prospect of establishing warm relations with former enemies, as we did with Germany and Japan following World War II. At the same time we seek to distance ourselves from the past out of the fear that the present and the future will bear little resemblance to it. President George W. Bush spoke to this feeling when, following the September 11, 2001, terrorist attacks, he spoke of a war against terrorism that would be unlike any the United States had fought before. Looking to the past for answers is also complicated by the fact that our understanding of the past is never complete. Not only do we bring conceptual blinders and biases to its study, but we are constantly uncovering new information. As such, the history of American foreign policy has not been written so much as it is constantly being rewritten and rediscovered.

These four broad themes constitute the major point of reference for selecting entries into this volume. No single volume, or even multiple volumes, on a topic so broad in scope as American foreign policy can hope to provide entries to cover every possible research interest. What I have ventured to do here is to provide much more than a starting place for inquiry. Either standing alone or in cross-reference to other entries, the hope is that the articles contained here will provide accounts of American foreign policy that will meet the needs of most readers. My selection of entries plus the information they provide reflects both a sense of what is standard coverage of American foreign policy as well as my approach to these subjects in teaching and research. The suggested readings that accompany many entries plus the other fine volumes related to American foreign policy published by Facts On File, such as those on the cold war and espionage, provide ready-made and easily accessible places from which to explore subjects in more depth. For additional information on contemporary events, academic journals are an important source of commentary and analysis. *Current History, Foreign Affairs, Foreign Policy, National Interest, Orbis, Washington Quarterly,* and *World Policy Journal* all contain well-written articles pitched at a broad audience of readers. Taken together these journals cover virtually the full spectrum of contemporary thinking on American foreign policy.

## A

### Acheson, Dean (1893–1971) *secretary of state*

In his roles as undersecretary of state (1945–47) and SEC-RETARY OF STATE (1949–53) Dean Gooderham Acheson was involved in many of the key decisions in transitioning U.S. foreign policy from the uncertainty over how to proceed after the end of WORLD WAR II to the COLD WAR. Prior to assuming these positions he had been actively involved in administering the LEND-LEASE program and negotiating the establishment of such postwar international economic organizations as the INTERNATIONAL MONETARY FUND and the WORLD BANK in his role as assistant secretary of state for economic affairs in the Roosevelt administration.

As undersecretary of state, Acheson first served under James Byrnes, who HARRY TRUMAN had defeated for the DEMOCRATIC PARTY presidential nomination. Relations between Byrnes and Truman were not close, and Acheson found himself playing the role of mediator and chief STATE DEPARTMENT contact for Truman. During this period Acheson advocated a policy of international control and management of nuclear power. In 1946 he cochaired a committee with David Lillienthal and Robert Oppenheimer that wrote a report calling for the establishment of an international atomic development agency. Their report became the foundation for the BARUCH PLAN that was presented to the UNITED NATIONS, where it encountered crippling opposition from the Soviet Union.

Under Secretary of State GEORGE MARSHALL, Acheson played a significant role in both managing the State Department and formulating policy. He endorsed GEORGE KENNAN's strategy of containment and was instrumental in constructing the TRUMAN DOCTRINE, under which the United States pledged support for GREECE and TURKEY and other states threatened by international COMMUNISM. He also proposed the outlines of what would become the MARSHALL PLAN, through which the United States sought to bring about the economic recovery of Europe and stop the spread of communism.

Acheson emerged as a staunch anticommunist but one who was Eurocentric. This outlook would embroil him in great political conflict as secretary of state. He successfully argued against aid for Jaing Jieshi's (Chiang Kai-shek) Nationalist forces in CHINA to prevent their defeat by Mao Zedong (Mao Tse-tung) in the Chinese civil war in 1949. One month after the Communist victory, Acheson delivered an address to the National Press Club in which he omitted any reference to SOUTH KOREA as a part of the U.S. defense

Dean Acheson *(Library of Congress)*

1

perimeter in Asia. Six months later, in June 1950, North Korean forces invaded South Korea. Acheson now reversed himself and recommended that U.S. forces be sent to South Korea to prevent its defeat. Even now, however, he continued his Eurocentric view on U.S. security interests, asserting that such a move was necessary to reassure America's European allies of its willingness to come to their defense. Acheson argued for supporting the French effort to reestablish control over VIETNAM for similar reasons. It was necessary to secure French support for what he saw as the crucial need to unite and rearm GERMANY.

Acheson's failure to adopt the same uncompromising attitude toward communist expansion in Asia that he did in Europe left him open to charges of being soft on communism from the Republican right. Acheson and the State Department became prime targets of Senator Joseph McCarthy, who referred to Acheson as the "Red Dean."

Acheson often spoke out on foreign-policy issues after leaving office. He criticized President Eisenhower's MASSIVE RETALIATION policy and advised President JOHN KENNEDY on the BERLIN and CUBAN MISSILE CRISES. During the latter he advocated air strikes against Soviet missiles in CUBA, a policy that most acknowledge in all probability would have led to a nuclear war.

See also MCCARTHYISM; RUSSIA; TAIWAN.

**Further reading:** Acheson, Dean. *Present at the Creation: My Years in the State Department.* New York: Norton, 1969.

## Act of Chapultepec (Inter-American Reciprocal Assistance and Solidarity)

In February 1945 the United States and its Latin American allies met at Chapultepec, in Mexico City. The document that emerged from the Inter-American Conference on Problems of War and Peace was not a formal treaty but rather a set of principles. It was agreed that an attack on any one American state would be considered an attack on all. Furthermore, it was agreed that the inter-American system of consultation and periodic meetings needed to be revised and organized on the basis of a written constitution.

The Act of Chapultepec of March 6, 1945, is significant because of the two organizations that were established to implement these principles. The RIO PACT was created to implement the COLLECTIVE-SECURITY principles, and the ORGANIZATION OF AMERICAN STATES (OAS) was created to provide a constitutionally based system of relations.

An important impetus for the Act of Chapultepec was wartime diplomacy within the Western Hemisphere. Two days after Pearl Harbor the United States called a meeting of the ministers of foreign affairs of the American republics. Meeting in January 1942 the United States hoped to get all of the states of the region to break off diplomatic relations with the Axis powers. ARGENTINA and CHILE refused. Over the course of the next several months relations between the United States and Argentina became strained, and the United States sought to isolate Argentina politically and economically. In October 1944 Argentina requested a meeting of foreign ministers to address the failure of other states in the region to recognize the new government dominated by Juan Perón. Washington opposed the meeting but agreed to it under pressure from other Latin American states on the conditions that Argentina not attend and that the conference examine ways to strengthen hemispheric solidarity.

**Adams, John** (1735–1826) *president of the United States*
John Adams served as the second president of the United States. The political conflicts within his administration, which centered in large part on foreign-policy issues, helped promote partisan politics in the new republic. One early political battle came over the appointment of James Madison, a Republican, to be special envoy to FRANCE. When a member of his cabinet threatened to resign over the prospect of a pro-British Federalist administration having a pro-French Republican as its representative to France, Adams changed his position and did not offer Madison the post.

The most significant conflict in his administration involved a "quasi-war" with France. Relations with France had deteriorated at the end of the Washington administration. A major problem involved French actions against American commercial shipping interests. The French justified their actions on the grounds that JAY'S TREATY had violated the commercial treaty signed with the United States in 1778. Adams sought a navy with strong coastal defenses and a small increase in the size of the army. Congress, however, supported Secretary of the Treasury ALEXANDER HAMILTON's proposal for a larger regular army.

Congress did approve Adams's request for funds to send a diplomatic mission to Paris to resolve the crisis. The mission proved to be anything but a success. Not only did French officials refuse to meet with the American delegation, but they also sought a bribe of $250,000 for allowing them the privilege of presenting their case. The request for such a "loan" was not totally unexpected. But the request occurred at the conclusion of negotiations. Without instructions permitting them to pay such a fee, two of the three Americans, John Marshall and Charles Pinckney, returned to the United States. The third, Elbridge Gerry, would leave a few months later. To prove to doubtful pro-French Republicans that the U.S. delegation had been mistreated, Adams released correspondence detailing these charges, substituting the letters XYZ for the real names. Congress responded to news of the XYZ AFFAIR by estab-

John Adams, second president of the United States. Painting by E. Savage in 1800 *(Library of Congress)*

lishing a Navy Department, abrogating two existing treaties with France, increasing the size of the army, and authorizing naval action against French pirates.

French officials were taken back by the depth of the American anti-French response. In 1799 Adams sent a peace mission to Paris over the objections of influential members of the FEDERALIST PARTY. The American's terms called for payment of reparations for damages done to U.S. shipping and French acceptance of the unilateral U.S. termination of the treaties of 1778 and 1788. The French resisted, and ultimately a compromise was worked out. Known as the Convention of 1800, the French agreed to the termination of the two treaties and the United States dropped its claims against France and agreed to pay any claims filed by U.S. citizens against France.

The Convention of 1800 is cited as a factor contributing to his loss at the hands of THOMAS JEFFERSON in the presidential election of 1800 and the demise of the Federalist Party. It is also cited as an indirect factor that made the LOUISIANA PURCHASE possible because it put U.S.-French relations on a better footing.

During the AMERICAN REVOLUTION, Adams played a key role in the earliest U.S. foreign policy initiatives. In 1778 Congress appointed him to serve as commissioner to France, where he assisted BENJAMIN FRANKLIN and Arthur Lee in improving Franco-American relations. In 1782 he negotiated a treaty of recognition and loans from the Dutch

government. Along with Benjamin Franklin and John Jay, Adams negotiated the TREATY OF PARIS (1783) that ended the Revolutionary War. Adams remained in Europe to serve as the first U.S. minister to GREAT BRITAIN but was unable to negotiate a commercial treaty with Great Britain due to its lack of interest in dealing with its former colony as an equal.

**Further reading:** Brown, Ralph A. *The Presidency of John Adams.* Lawrence: University Press of Kansas, 1975.

### Adams, John Quincy (1767–1848) *secretary of state, president of the United States*

John Quincy Adams was the sixth president of the United States, and he held a number of important diplomatic posts prior to that. They included SECRETARY OF STATE (1817–25), minister to GREAT BRITAIN, minister to RUSSIA, minister to the NETHERLANDS, and a member of the delegation sent by President James Madison to negotiate the TREATY OF GHENT (1814). While occupying this post the United States began negotiations on what became the RUSH-BAGOT TREATY that demilitarized the Great Lakes. At the end of the WAR OF 1812 both the United States and Great Britain had begun a naval buildup on the Great Lakes and Lake Champlain. The Treaty of Ghent had not addressed this issue, thus setting the stage for a naval arms race. In November 1815 Adams was instructed to raise the possibility of a mutual disarmament treaty to the British. British foreign minister Robert Stewart, Viscount Castlereagh agreed to the negotiations in April 1816. Negotiations were transferred to Washington, where an agreement was reached and signed by Secretary of State Richard Rush and British minister Charles Bagot. The treaty restricted the United States and Great Britain to naval forces that were sufficient only for police and customs operations and allowed each side to withdraw after giving six months notice. Land fortifications were unaffected by the agreement, and it was only with the Treaty of Washington in 1871 that fortifications were effectively removed from the U.S.-Canadian border.

Adams's most significant contributions to American foreign policy came as secretary of state. He is generally considered to be the best secretary of state of the 19th century. As secretary of state he secured the FLORIDA Territory from Spain through the Adams-Onís Treaty (1819). This treaty, sometimes referred to as the Transcontinental Treaty, was significant because it resolved several territorial disputes with Spain. The exact boundaries of the territory that came to the United States with the LOUISIANA PURCHASE were not clear. Spain and the United States held conflicting claims to TEXAS and West Florida. The United States had also made several unsuccessful attempts to acquire all of Florida since the WAR OF 1812. In this treaty

Spain ceded control over the Floridas to the United States and gave up its claims to the Pacific Northwest. In return the United States gave up its very questionable claim that Texas was part of the Louisiana Territory and agreed to assume the responsibility for settling claims against SPAIN by U.S. citizens for up to $5 million. Lastly, a boundary line separating the United States and MEXICO was agreed to; it ran from the Sabine River at the Gulf of Mexico northwest to the 42nd parallel and then across to the Pacific Ocean. This effectively established the southern boundary of the OREGON Territory.

John Quincy Adams's best-remembered contribution to American foreign policy as secretary of state was in helping craft the MONROE DOCTRINE that became, and continues to be, a touchstone for U.S. foreign policy in Latin America. Rejecting calls from Great Britain for a joint declaration over the future of Latin America, the Monroe Doctrine unilaterally declared the region to be off-limits to any further attempts at colonization by European powers. Future presidents routinely cited the Monroe Doctrine as a rationale for taking military action to force unfriendly governments from power or restore the peace.

**Further reading:** Bemis, Samuel F. *John Quincy Adams and the Foundations of American Foreign Policy.* New York: Norton, 1949; Weeks, William E. *John Quincy Adams: American Global Empire.* Lexington: University of Kentucky Press, 1992.

## Afghanistan

Located at the crossroads of Central Asia, Afghanistan is about the size of Texas, with an area of 252,000 square miles. In July 2000 it had an estimated population of 28.85 million people, with an additional 4 million living outside its borders, primarily in IRAN and PAKISTAN. Afghanistan's location placed it at the center of the "great game" played between GREAT BRITAIN, the imperial power in INDIA, and RUSSIA in the 1800s, as each sought to use Afghanistan as a buffer to protect its interests. Afghanistan's modern boundaries were set by agreements between Britain and Russia between 1880 and 1901. These agreements also called for Great Britain to give up control over Afghanistan's domestic affairs but not its foreign policy. This did not happen until August 9, 1919, which is the day Afghanistan uses to officially date its independence. In 1964 Mohammad Zahir Shah instituted a series of liberal reforms that permitted extremist groups to organize. They included the People's Democratic Party of Afghanistan, which had ties to the Soviet Union. On April 28, 1978, it would lead a bloody coup that transformed Afghanistan into a communist state. Fighting continued, and in 1979 Soviet forces would enter Afghanistan to prop up its failing ally.

The 1979 Soviet invasion of Afghanistan marked a turning point in U.S.-Soviet relations. After VIETNAM the watchword in U.S. foreign policy toward the SOVIET UNION was DÉTENTE. The confrontational policies and harsh rhetoric of containment were replaced by policies that rested upon a presumption that cooperation was possible. Though points of tension continued to mark the U.S.-Soviet relationship, particularly in regard to human-rights violations and Soviet support for insurgency groups in Africa throughout the 1970s, the assumption remained that U.S.-Soviet relations had moved into a new and more stable pattern. This ended with the Soviet invasion of Afghanistan. In its wake the Carter administration adopted a tougher line, and its successor, the Reagan administration, resurrected the confrontational rhetoric and policies of the COLD WAR era.

The roots of the Soviet invasion of Afghanistan and the ensuing guerrilla war go back to the 1973 coup d'etat that overthrew King Zahir Shah. The Soviet Union did not engineer this coup but did give it its tacit support. Very soon the new regime came under attack from two different wings of the Marxist People's Democratic Party. One (Khalq) was Maoist, and the other (Parcham) was pro-Moscow in orientation. In April 1978 Khalq led a bloody coup, and in December a 20-year treaty of friendship and cooperation was signed with the Soviet Union that ended Afghanistan's formal neutrality.

Upon taking power Khalq sought to transform Afghanistan's largely tribal society through a series of radical social, educational, and economic reforms. Rioting and armed opposition emerged throughout the country, and the Soviet Union urged the new leaders to slow the pace of their reform agenda. The Soviet Union found it necessary to step up the shipment of military supplies and send in combat personnel to help the new government in the rapidly escalating civil war. In September a rival Khalq faction seized power, but it, too, refused to heed Moscow's advice and actually stepped up the pace of the reforms. Once again the Soviet Union stepped up its military presence. On December 27 the Soviet Union sent in more than 50,000 troops to prevent what appeared to be the impending military triumph of Islamic forces known as the Mujahideen. Babrak Kamal, head of the Parcham faction, was installed as the new president.

The original Soviet military plan called for the Afghan army to bear the bulk of the responsibility for defeating the Mujahideen. Wholesale defections changed this policy. Before the 1980 coup the Afghan army had 100,000 troops. By the end of 1980 it was effectively down to 10,000–15,000 fighting troops. As a result, within one year of the Soviet occupation the Soviet army grew to 110,000, with several thousand more reserves stationed just north of the Afghan border. Initially Soviet forces tried to conduct a conventional-style military operation against the Mujahideen. After sustaining heavy losses, the Mujahideen retreated into the mountains and began to conduct a classical guerrilla war. The Soviet Union's strategy relied heavily upon search and destroy missions and establishing strategic hamlets much as the United States did during the VIETNAM WAR. The results were the same, as the Soviet Union had 24-hour control only over about 10 percent of the country.

An important contributing factor to the Mujahideen's success was U.S. aid that was provided under the aegis of the REAGAN DOCTRINE. American military aid to the Mujahideen rose from $120 million in 1984 to $630 million in 1987, bringing the accumulated total of U.S. military aid to $2.1 billion. Additional U.S. aid was funneled through allies such as SAUDI ARABIA, CHINA, and PAKISTAN. Pakistan was a key player. It was a major conduit for U.S. arms, a recruiting ground for the Mujahideen,

and the destination of some 3.5 million Afghan refugees who fled the fighting.

Military defeats were accompanied by political defeats. Kamal was unable to unify the various factions of the Afghan Marxist Party or generate popular support for his government. In 1986, in yet another effort to engineer an end to the war, the Soviet Union replaced him with Najibullah, a KGB-trained former head of the secret police. He, too, failed to solidify political control over Afghanistan.

During the early 1980s Soviet leaders became increasingly disillusioned with the costs of the military stalemate in Afghanistan and began to explore the possibility of a negotiated settlement. Informal peace talks had been under way in Afghanistan since 1982, but it was 1988 before an agreement was worked out between Afghanistan and Pakistan. The United States and the Soviet Union acted as guarantors of the Geneva accords. Both superpowers promised not to intervene in Afghanistan's internal affairs and the

Soviet Union agreed to a timetable for withdrawing its forces by February 15, 1989. An estimated 14,500 Soviet soldiers and 1 million Afghanis lost their lives in the fighting that raged between 1979 and 1989. Also absent from these peace negotiations were the Mujahideen, who refused to accept the Geneva accords. The civil war thus continued, and from the fighting emerged the Taliban. They were former Mujahideen of Pashtun background. They were supported by Pakistan and dedicated themselves to removing the feuding warlords from power and establishing a fundamentalist Islamic state. By 1998 they had taken control over all of Afghanistan except for a small corner in the northeast and the Panjshir Valley.

The Taliban initially were supported by the United States. They were seen to provide a solution to the TERRORISM, GUERRILLA WARFARE, and DRUG TRAFFICKING that were taking place in Afghanistan. One STATE DEPARTMENT official noted that "the United States should actively assist the Taliban because even though it is fundamentalist, it does not practice anti-U.S. style fundamentalism." Within one month after its seizure of power this assessment changed. Promised aid did not arrive, and the United States began criticizing the Taliban's HUMAN-RIGHTS record as it embarked on a program of draconian reforms designed to bring into existence the promised Islamic state. Beginning in the mid-1990s the Taliban also began to give sanctuary to OSAMA BIN LADEN and his AL-QAEDA terrorist group. It was this organization that was responsible for the SEPTEMBER 11, 2001, terrorist attacks on the World Trade Center and the Pentagon.

After the September 11th terrorist attacks President GEORGE W. BUSH demanded that the Taliban expel Osama bin Laden and al-Qaeda and sever its ties with international

An F/A-18 Hornet prepares for launch on November 14, 2001, while aboard the USS *Kitty Hawk*. The ship was supporting bombing missions over Afghanistan in Operation Enduring Freedom. *(Woods/U.S. Navy)*

terrorism in general. When this did not happen, on October 7, 2001, 26 days after the attacks on the Pentagon and World Trade Center, the United States and its allies began aerial strikes against terrorist facilities and Taliban military targets inside Afghanistan. Ground forces were supplied largely by the Northern Alliance, a coalition group that had opposed Taliban rule. Their efforts were aided and guided by the CENTRAL INTELLIGENCE AGENCY (CIA). Reportedly the CIA presence in northern Afghanistan consisted of about 150 nonuniformed paramilitary personnel. On November 13, the Northern Alliance retook Kabul, Afghanistan's capital city, which the Taliban had captured from it in 1996. Taliban forces fled to the south, where U.S. Special Forces had been operating. The first U.S. Special Forces had entered Afghanistan on October 19. It was the first such commando operation since 1993 in SOMALIA. About 100 Special Forces were present in the south and another 200 in the north. In both areas the U.S. strategy was to rely on the indigenous anti-Taliban forces to take the lead in finding and fighting the Taliban and al-Qaeda forces. Conventional forces, the U.S. Marines, arrived on November 25. They were to engage in sustained assaults against enemy targets, prevent reinforcements from reaching these forces, and block their lines of escape. On December 6, the Taliban agreed to surrender their southern stronghold of Kandahar. This left only one major region within Afghanistan that was holding out against the American-led coalition. It was the White Mountain region, and, on December 13, U.S.-backed Afghani guerrilla forces attacked under the cover of U.S. air support. These forces claimed victory on December 16. However, Osama bin Laden, who was one of the major targets of the military campaign from the outset, remained at large. The heavy American reliance on the Northern Alliance and other indigenous groups to take the lead in locating and fighting Taliban and al-Qaeda forces emerged as the major critique of the U.S. war plan.

In conjunction with the military campaign to defeat the Taliban, diplomatic negotiations were taking place to shape the future Afghan government. In late November the UNITED NATIONS sponsored a meeting of Afghanistan's four main anti-Taliban political groups. They represented the Northern Alliance, the exiled king Mohammed Zahir Shah, a Pashtun exile group affiliated with Pakistan, and a Pashtun exile group affiliated with Iran. Only the Northern Alliance controlled territory in Afghanistan. On December 5 they agreed to create a multiethnic interim government. Hamid Karzai, a Pashtun, was selected to head this body, which would take power on December 22 as the Afghan Interim Authority. Elections were scheduled to be held within two years. It was also agreed that an international PEACEKEEPING force would be sent to Kabul.

Since its creation the Afghan Interim Authority coalition has struggled to maintain its unity and expand its power beyond Kabul. In January 2003, U.S. troops in Afghanistan numbered about 8,000, and their primary mission remained capturing and defeating the Taliban and its allies. Nation-building and reconstruction remain secondary objectives. Operation Anaconda held in spring 2002 inflicted sufficient damage on Taliban and al-Qaeda forces that they have not been able to mount significant attacks on government forces. This has not prevented them from engaging in propaganda campaigns, assassination, terrorism, and guerrilla warfare. Controversy also came to surround U.S. military activity when it was revealed that U.S. forces were engaging in hot pursuit of Taliban and al-Qaeda fighters into Pakistan. The United States claimed Pakistan had given its approval to these missions while Pakistan equivocated on the matter.

With American support, Hamid Karzai was installed as president after the defeat of the Taliban in 2001. American attention to the situation in Afghanistan lessened as momentum for the IRAQ WAR built. While this was happening, and without great fanfare, warlordism and the Taliban made a significant political comeback. Increasingly the U.S. is finding itself entangled in a war between private armies of warlords that claim loyalty to the American cause and who Karzai's government cannot stop. In 2003, U.S. Agency for International Development officials only traveled with heavily armed escorts, and U.S.-supported educational programs worked effectively in only 10 of Afghanistan's 34 provinces, due to security issues. Antigovernment violence continued to escalate through 2003.

**Further reading:** Arnold, Anthony. *Afghanistan.* Palo Alto, Calif.: Stanford University Press, 1985; Kakar, M. Hassar. *Afghanistan: The Soviet Invasion and the Afghan Response.* Berkeley: University of California Press, 1995; Woodward, Bob. *Bush at War.* New York: Simon and Schuster, 2002.

## Africa

U.S. foreign policy toward Africa intensifies with the post–WORLD WAR II era. Prior to that, meaningful contact would date back to its dealings with the BARBARY PIRATES between 1800 and 1815. Piracy was commonplace along Africa's north coast, and the United States followed the European practice of paying tribute to the pirates in return for free passage. American policy changed after an 1800 incident in which a higher tribute was demanded from the United States than had been agreed to. Fighting continued intermittently until 1805, when an agreement was reached that was to end hostilities. However, fighting continued through the WAR OF 1812, and it was not until 1815 that the conflict was truly terminated.

America's initial cold war foreign policy toward Africa centered on the Islamic states of the Sahara. In large measure this was because much of the rest of Africa was still colonial territory. But it also reflected the central position that containing COMMUNISM played in American foreign-policy thinking. The proximity of Saharan Africa to southern Europe made it an area of concern. It had been the danger of communism spreading to GREECE and TURKEY that had prompted the TRUMAN DOCTRINE in 1947. The emergence of EGYPT's Gamal Abdel Nasser as a leader of the Arab world also drew American attention to Saharan Africa. For the United States at this time, Arab nationalism was seen as a threat to the stability of the Middle East and a force to be exploited by the Soviet Union. Nasser was the leading spokesperson for Arab nationalism, and American foreign policy sought to contain and isolate him.

In the late 1950s and early 1960s American foreign policy was redirected to sub-Saharan Africa. The challenges presented by Arab nationalism continued, but by now the problem was clearly defined as a Middle Eastern issue and not an African one. For the United States the African foreign-policy problem was one of responding to and directing the pro-independence demands emerging from the states of the old colonial empires of its European allies. Fearful that rapid decolonialization would be destabilizing and desirous of solidifying European support for the NORTH ATLANTIC TREATY ORGANIZATION (NATO) American foreign policy tended to follow the lead of its European allies on African matters. Generally, this meant that it opposed independence movements and favored a go-slow policy. FRANCE and Portugal, who, along with Belgium, strongly resisted decolonialization, used American military aid to try and hold on to their colonies in ALGERIA, ANGOLA, and Mozambique.

American foreign policy toward the newly independent states of sub-Saharan Africa continued to be formulated within the context of global rather than regional or national considerations. Anticommunist African regimes and GUERRILLA movements were supported with little concern for their corruption or brutality. In some cases, such as Zaïre (now the Democratic Republic of the CONGO) and Angola, the United States became deeply involved in civil wars. President JOHN KENNEDY broke with this pattern somewhat in that he sought to identify the United States in a positive fashion with the aspirations of the newly independent states and their leaders. The PEACE CORPS, which had a heavy presence in Africa, was perhaps the most visible symbol of this policy.

The same anticommunist global logic also led the United States to support South Africa and other white minority governments. This policy position was especially pronounced in the first part of HENRY KISSINGER's tenure in the Nixon-Ford White House as NATIONAL SECURITY ADVISOR and SECRETARY OF STATE and then during the Reagan administration. The United States moved away from its close support of white regimes and confrontation with procommunist guerrilla forces in 1976. The Reagan administration never really wavered in its support of the white minority government of South Africa or anticommunist guerrillas. It was largely due to pressure from CONGRESS and the public that U.S. foreign policy began to push SOUTH AFRICA to end apartheid. Even then this pressure was tempered by a concern for strategic stability as put forth in the Reagan administration's doctrine of constructive engagement.

In between the Nixon-Ford administrations and that of Reagan was JIMMY CARTER's presidency. Carter entered office pledging to free the United States from its obsession with communism. In Africa his commitment to HUMAN RIGHTS and liberal INTERNATIONALISM led the United States to publicly embrace causes advocated by black African states. Nowhere was this more pronounced than in American efforts to end white minority rule in Rhodesia (now ZIMBABWE). At the same time U.S. foreign policy toward Africa did not completely free itself from larger concerns. In the 1970s yet another external dimension was added to the United States's Africa policy. A concern for continued access to Middle East OIL led to the development of the CARTER DOCTRINE and the acquisition of military bases around the Horn of Africa. In the process the United States became partner to a regional conflict between ETHIOPIA and SOMALIA. During the 1970s and 1980s the United States provided humanitarian aid to the drought-stricken Sahel and the war-torn Horn of Africa, but even there larger geostrategic considerations on occasion stopped the needy from receiving assistance.

The end of the COLD WAR promised an opportunity to view African problems in their own light. It is an opportunity that largely went by without being seized. In part this was due to the failure of the American PEACEKEEPING operation in Somalia. The strongly negative public reaction to this effort virtually guaranteed that no administration would send American troops to Africa to restore order, as they would be called to do in RWANDA and LIBERIA. Post–cold war administrations also turned a deaf ear to African developmental, environmental, and health problems. To the extent that these problems were addressed by American officials, they were handled within the context of the American domestic political debate over the merits of GLOBALIZATION, protecting the ENVIRONMENT, HIV/AIDS prevention, and family-planning practices. Far less attention was given to democratization efforts in Africa than was given to developments in East Europe or RUSSIA. American foreign policy changed direction somewhat in

2003. In his 2003 State of the Union address, President George W. Bush announced that the United States would begin a $15 million, five-year program to combat AIDS in Africa. In May 2003 the Senate approved funding for the program. Major support for the initiative came from pharmaceutical companies hoping to profit by the program.

During his campaign for the presidency GEORGE W. BUSH indicated that Africa did not fit into the national strategic interests of the United States. After the SEPTEMBER 11, 2001, terrorist attacks on the United States, American foreign policy rediscovered Africa to a degree. As in the past, however, African policy was made in a global context. This time it was the war against TERRORISM and those states with a history of supporting Islamic terrorism, such as SUDAN and Somalia, that were identified as potential targets for American military action.

See also CONFERENCE ON SUSTAINABLE DEVELOPMENT; IMPERIALISM; POINT FOUR PROGRAM; POPULATION POLICIES; RUSSIA.

**Further reading:** Laidi, Zaki. *The Superpowers and Africa.* Chicago: University of Chicago Press; Schraeder, Peter. *United States Foreign Policy toward Africa.* Cambridge, UK: Cambridge University Press, 1994.

## Agriculture, Department of (United States Department of Agriculture)

Founded in 1862, the U.S. Department of Agriculture (USDA) is a relative newcomer and junior partner to the STATE DEPARTMENT as a member of the foreign-affairs BUREAUCRACY. Its emergence as a foreign-policy actor is significant because it reflects the changing agenda of world politics as it moves away from an exclusive concern with military and political issues to one that includes economic problems. It is a role that promises to become more significant as GLOBALIZATION intensifies. This will bring added challenges to the State Department's traditional role as the lead foreign-affairs bureaucracy and require that ways be found of effectively integrating Agriculture's voice into foreign policy-making deliberations. One move suggested by some is the creation of a national economic security council that is truly the equal in importance to the military-oriented NATIONAL SECURITY COUNCIL.

USDA's primary foreign-policy activities lie in the areas of helping to ensure open markets for American agricultural products and providing food aid to needy people overseas. It is also a key force in ensuring the health and safety of American farm products and in this role actively prevented the outbreak of foot-and-mouth disease that swept through Europe in 2001 from infecting American livestock.

A principal force within the USDA for promoting American agricultural sales abroad is the Foreign Agriculture Service, which operates out of U.S. embassies, consulates, and field offices. By monitoring market conditions and the global competitiveness of American agriculture, the Foreign Agriculture Service seeks to promote trade policies that will provide market access for American farmers. A major area of concern in this regard has been obtaining access to the European Union. The long-standing goal of the Common Agricultural Policy has been to help Europe's politically powerful small farmers withstand foreign competition. The conflict between Europe and the United States has often produced heated language and threats of trade wars.

The Foreign Agriculture Service also administers a number of export promotion, technical, and food assistance programs in cooperation with other U.S. government agencies, international organizations, and the private sector. For example, the Office of Agriculture Export Assistance provides buyer alerts that help farmers target their overseas advertising, a foreign buyers list that contains a country and product specific listing of agricultural importers around the world, and a trade leads service that offers farmers up-to-date information on requests for bids by foreign firms.

The best-known foreign-policy activity of the USDA is administering FOREIGN-AID food programs, and the best-known food aid program is Public Law (PL) 480 or "FOOD FOR PEACE." This program is divided into three parts: Title I is administered by the USDA, while Titles II and III are administered by the Agency for International Development. Under Title I the USDA is authorized to engage in government-to-government sales of agricultural products to friendly developing counties under the umbrella of long-term credit arrangements of 30 years with a seven-year grace period. Repayment may be made using either U.S. dollars or local currencies. This is important because the ability to use local currencies to purchase foods allows foreign countries to use scarce U.S. dollars or other hard currencies to purchase products needed for economic development in international markets.

Under the terms of PL 480 and related pieces of legislation, no agricultural commodity can be made available to a foreign country if doing so would reduce domestic U.S. supplies below an acceptable level unless it is for pressing humanitarian reasons. Countries that engage in violations of HUMAN RIGHTS are ineligible. A requirement also exists that at least 75 percent of all U.S. food-aid tonnage be shipped on U.S. flag vessels.

While clearly of great value to developing countries, the Food for Peace program has been characterized as foreign aid for American farmers and firms due to the cargo preference requirement and the requirement that the food being sold or donated abroad be obtained through price-support programs.

See also GATT; TRADE POLICY; WORLD TRADE ORGANIZATION.

## al-Qaeda    See under letter Q.

## Alaska, purchase of

Alaska was purchased from RUSSIA in 1867. It marked the last piece of continental expansionism by the United States. Unlike the earlier acquisitions of the FLORIDA, TEXAS, or OREGON Territories or the Mexican cession that brought California into U.S. possession, there was no popular or elite pressure to acquire Alaska. Rather, it was the work of one person, Secretary of State WILLIAM SEWARD. Seward was a committed expansionist who had tried unsuccessfully to acquire basing rights for the United States in the Caribbean Sea following the end of the AMERICAN CIVIL WAR.

At this point in time, the United States and RUSSIA had friendly relations. Alaska, or Russian America, as it was known at the time, marked an extension of Russia's Siberian possessions, and there were no significant issues of contention between the two countries. Russia knew that Alaska contained gold but was interested in ridding itself of the territory for two reasons. First, it was then an unprofitable area. Russian America was administered through the Russian-American Company. This was a trading company whose charter had expired in 1862 and was now facing bankruptcy. Russia would either have to rule the territory itself or subsidize the company. Second, it was difficult to defend. Russian leaders fully expected to lose Alaska to the British in a future war. Rather than have this happen, Russian leaders contemplated offering Alaska to the United States.

In 1860 Russian diplomats reported that President James Buchanan was willing to pay $5 million for Alaska. Russian leaders temporized and did not seize the offer. The Civil War then broke out, putting an end to the negotiations.

With the Civil War over, and Russia now determined to rid itself of Alaska, in 1867 Edouard de Stoeckl, the Russian minister to the United States, let it be known that Alaska could be purchased. Seward seized the opportunity and agreed to buy Alaska for $7.2 million. This was $2.2 million above the minimum selling price that de Stoeckl had been instructed to accept. Few in the United States shared Seward's enthusiasm for the Alaskan purchase, and many had not even heard of it.

The purchase ran into such strong opposition in the Senate that Senator CHARLES SUMNER, chairman of the Senate Foreign Relations Committee and longtime critic of

Seward, suggested to de Stoeckl that he withdraw the treaty rather than face an embarrassing defeat. Instead, both Seward and de Stoeckl began a strenuous and expensive lobbying campaign that included subsidies to the press and bribes. Sumner was an important convert to their cause, and the Senate voted to approve the treaty by a vote of 37-2. Opposition in the House continued, and more than a year later it approved the appropriations needed to purchase Alaska by a vote of 113-43. By that time, the United States had already taken possession of Alaska, raising the American flag on October 18, 1867.

**Further reading:** Holbo, Paul S. *Tarnished Expansion.* Knoxville: University of Tennessee Press, 1983.

## Algeria

The second-largest country in Africa, Algeria is more than three times the size of TEXAS, with an area of 919,590 square miles. It has a population of 31,736,000 people. Situated on the coast of northern Africa, Algeria has attracted a host of foreign invaders. The Arab invasions of the eighth and 11th centuries had the greatest impact on Algeria's culture, bringing Islam and the Arabic language. The major European presence in Algeria's history was France. It imposed a naval blockade in the 1820s and followed this up with an invasion in 1830. Algerian forces held out until 1847, at which time Algeria became a French territory. In 1871 Algeria became an overseas department of FRANCE. This elevated its status from a colony to an integral part of France. Still, there was very little mixing of the European and Muslim populations, and Europeans controlled the political and economic life of Algeria.

A proindependence movement formed after WORLD WAR I. The Liberation Front (FLN), a splinter group formed in 1954, became the leading opponent of French rule. Its aggressive military tactics and guerrilla war strategy brought harsh French reprisals that further polarized public opinion in France and Algeria. Fear that France might agree to independence brought about a political crisis that ended with Charles de Gaulle's return to power and the founding of the Fifth French Republic. Fighting continued between French forces and the FLN until March 18, 1962, when a cease-fire was signed at Evian, France.

The Evian accords called for a referendum to be held to determine Algeria's future. French voters supported the agreement in a referendum. Elements of the French army stationed in Algeria continued to oppose the prospect of independence and staged a revolt that was crushed in June. On July 1 Algerians overwhelmingly voted for independence. France granted independence on July 3. By year's end most of the European "colonists" had left. An estimated 100,000 Muslims and 10,000 French soldiers were killed in the seven-year war for independence.

After independence Algeria adopted an activist foreign policy that placed it in the forefront of Arab and developing nation causes. It provided political support to the Arabs in the 1967 and 1973 Arab-Israeli wars, and in 1971 it nationalized without compensation French energy firms. Historically the Soviet Union was Algeria's largest supplier of weapons, and it continues to be a leading military power in the region. Algeria's anti-United States and anti-Western stance became so pronounced that diplomatic relations were disrupted between 1967 and 1974. Tensions continued after relations were resumed due to Algeria's support of the freedom fighters' bid to create an independent state out of Western Sahara. This put it into conflict with the United States, which was sympathetic to Morocco's desire to annex it.

Relations with the United States warmed in the 1980s as Algeria played an important role in securing the release of the American hostages in IRAN in 1981. Beginning around 2000 there was a noticeable increase in the level of U.S.-Algerian cooperation. The two sides worked together in seeking a solution to the conflict between ETHIOPIA and ERITREA. Algeria publicly condemned the September 11, 2001, terrorist attacks, and contacts between the two military establishments accelerated, including a modest military training program. Economic ties were also strengthened. The Export-Import Bank has an active program in Algeria guaranteeing $1.9 billion in investments, the U.S.–North American Economic Partnership provides Algeria with $1.2 billion in technical assistance, and the DEPARTMENT OF AGRICULTURE provides Algeria with a loan program valued at $50 million for the purchase of American agricultural products.

At the same time that its foreign relations with the United States were improving, Algeria was also undergoing domestic unrest. Political parties other than the FLN were legalized in 1989, and one of the strongest to emerge was the militant Islamic Salvation Front (FIS). In December 1991 it won the first round of elections for delegates to the National People's Assembly. Rather than risk a FIS victory in the second round that was scheduled for January 1992, the government cancelled the election. Sparked by this decision a costly civil war began that resulted in more than 100,000 deaths before fighting diminished in 1999, when the FIS renounced the use of force and the government followed with a blanket pardon to FIS forces.

See also ARAB-ISRAELI CONFLICT; RUSSIA.

**Further reading:** Stone, Martin. *The Agony of Algeria.* New York: Columbia University Press, 1997.

## Alliance for Progress

The Alliance for Progress was a Kennedy administration initiative intended to bring about social, economic, and political reform in Latin America through an infusion of FOREIGN AID. It left a mixed record, failing to achieve most of its goals. It is one of a series of development programs that have been put forward by the United States. President HARRY TRUMAN'S POINT FOUR PROGRAM preceded it, and President RONALD REAGAN'S CARIBBEAN BASIN INITIATIVE followed it.

When President JOHN KENNEDY assumed office in 1961, American economic interests in Latin America were well established. So too was American neglect of these states. Between 1948 and 1958, only 2.4 percent of U.S. economic aid went to Latin America. While the MARSHALL PLAN was funneling large amounts of reconstruction economic aid to Europe, Latin American states received less aid than did Belgium and Luxembourg. A by-product of this neglect was mounting poverty that fueled anti-American revolutionary movements. Particularly disturbing to U.S. policy makers was the rise to power of Fidel Castro in CUBA in 1959. The Kennedy administration employed a variety of policy instruments to remove him from office, including a covert invasion, the BAY OF PIGS. Kennedy also sought to prevent future Castro's from gaining power by championing a regional economic development plan, the Alliance for Progress.

The Alliance for Progress was launched in August 1961 at a meeting of the United States and Latin American states (minus Cuba) at Punta del Este, Uruguay. It was to be an alliance of free states dedicated to the elimination of tyranny and poverty from the Western Hemisphere. Its central feature was to be a massive influx of capital that would generate peaceful social and economic reforms. A 10-year plan calling for combining $20 billion in foreign capital with $80 billion in local funds was envisaged. Of the $20 billion in external funds, $10 billion would come from the U.S. government and $300 million would come from U.S.-based investors.

The results of the Alliance for Progress were mixed, with few of its goals realized. Regional economic growth in the 1960s was significant, growing at 2.4 percent per capita, only slightly behind the goal of 2.5 percent. Seven Latin American states met this target figure, 12 fell short, and two experienced declining gross national products. Foreign assistance from the Alliance for Progress, however, appears to have played only a small part in these economic successes. Agrarian and social reform continued to lag. Adult illiteracy rates and infant mortality rates remained high, and land reform was virtually absent, as less than 1 million of the 15 million peasant families in Latin America benefited from alliance-inspired reforms. The most glaring failure of the alliance lay in promoting democracy. The year 1962–63 saw six military coups. The political situation in the region was such that in 1966 a State Department official declared that "no preference would be shown for representative democratic institutions in distributing Alliance funds."

Overall judgments regarding its accomplishments depend heavily upon the analytical perspective adopted. Revisionist scholars see in the Alliance for Progress not a desire for economic, social, and political reform on the part of the United States, but a concern for protecting Washington's position of economic and political preeminence. From this perspective the true goal of the Alliance was to head off social reform in the interest of securing a positive investment climate for American business, subsidizing American firms, and ensuring politically compliant states in the region. As evidence of the first two points, revisionists cite the HICKENLOOPER AMENDMENT, which suspended foreign aid to any state nationalizing U.S. property without prompt and just compensation, and the fact that of the $1.5 billion in U.S. funds distributed to Latin America in the first two years of the Alliance for Progress, $600 million was for the purchase of U.S.-made goods and $150 million was for surplus food available under the FOOD FOR PEACE program.

More traditional scholars, those who focus less on the significance of economic factors in the making of U.S. foreign policy, assert that the Alliance for Progress is typical of American foreign policy initiatives in Latin America. They see in it a familiar three-part cycle. First, after a period of neglect, U.S. policy makers rediscover Latin America and set out to reform the region. Second, Latin American leaders resist. Third, the United States becomes frustrated, turns to the military (or covert action) as its policy instrument of choice, thus supplanting a concern for reform with a desire for stability. Washington then forgets about the region again.

**Further reading:** Levinson, Jerome, and Juan de Onis. *The Alliance That Lost Its Way.* Chicago: Crown Publishing, 1970.

## alliances

Alliances are a staple of international politics. They are formal agreements between states in which they pledge to use their military resources in a coordinated fashion in specially designated circumstances. At the most basic level alliances may be classified as either bilateral (involving two states) or multilateral (involving more than two states). Alliances also may be defensive or offensive in their basic orientation. They are generally entered into in order to accomplish one or more of the following goals: to increase one's power, restrain other states, promote

international stability, or provide security for the government in power. Because alliance members may have contradictory goals, managing alliances can be a difficult proposition. Political disputes can lead to paralysis or the withdrawal of support by key members.

The realization that considerable political, economic, and military resources will have to be devoted to alliance management is an argument against entering into them. Larger states frequently come to feel that they are being exploited by smaller free-riding states that gain greatly from the alliance but pay little for those benefits. To limit their costs larger states call for greater equality in burden sharing. Another danger to be avoided by larger states is being trapped into supporting the foreign policies or the political survival of the government in a smaller state. Smaller states are also leery of losing their freedom of action by joining an alliance.

In addition to the debate over whether joining an alliance is advisable, controversy also surrounds the place of alliances in world politics. Realists tend to look at alliances in a positive light. They are seen as an important instrument for maintaining the balance of power. Alliances are created to counter an aggressive rival or set of rivals and are expected to dissolve when the threat has passed. Idealists take exception to this assessment. They see the creation of an alliance as far more likely to lessen state security and international stability. This is because the creation of the alliance will be seen as a provocative move by nonmembers and will produce a countervailing action. It may take the form of creating a counteralliance, unilaterally increasing one's power, or a preemptive strike.

Alliances were long anathema in American foreign policy. President GEORGE WASHINGTON gave expression to this view in his farewell address when he warned against entering into entangling alliances. This unilateralist tendency in the American national style supported such important foreign policy initiatives as the MONROE DOCTRINE and the OPEN DOOR POLICY. In the latter case it also manifested itself in the unwillingness of the United States to join in any form of coordinated military action to protect Chinese sovereignty from Japanese aggression. The rejection of alliances was never total. During the AMERICAN REVOLUTION and the AMERICAN CIVIL WAR, American envoys were sent abroad in hopes of finding allies and obtaining military support.

The first formal break with the American reluctance to enter into alliances came in Latin America and culminated in the founding of the ORGANIZATION OF AMERICAN STATES (OAS) in 1948. The United States had long acted unilaterally in the Western Hemisphere, and the OAS was the culmination of efforts dating back to the 1920s to provide a multilateral structure within which to continue exercising this power. The more significant break soon followed, with the establishment of the NORTH ATLANTIC TREATY ORGA-NIZATION (NATO) in 1949. With it the United States was permanently involving itself in the affairs of Europe. Troops would be stationed there and a standing political and military decision-making structure established. NATO also moved the United States away from a defense policy centered on collective security against unnamed threats, as was implied by the OAS, to one that was intended to deal with a specific enemy in the context of balance of power thinking.

There followed in the 1950s and early 1960s a spate of bilateral and multilateral alliance-building efforts. Notable among them were the SOUTHEAST ASIA TREATY ORGANIZATION, the CENTRAL TREATY ORGANIZATION, the ANZUS PACT, and mutual defense treaties with JAPAN, TAIWAN, and the PHILIPPINES. Collectively these alliances were unified and given common purpose by the strategy containment. In reality they constituted something far less than a coherent alliance system. American power was their only common denominator, and the pull of the particularistic interests of their members limited the value they added to American national security. Over time, one by one, they lost their vitality. Only NATO endured and prospered until the end of the COLD WAR, when it too began to reexamine the rationale for its existence.

In the post–cold war INTERNATIONAL SYSTEM, some commentators have come to question the continued relevance of alliances for managing the international system or adding to state security. The principal concern is not so much with their military capabilities as it is with the slowness of their decision-making processes and the likelihood that any decision reached will be heavily compromised, robbing the alliance of the clarity of political purpose it needs to act effectively. In this view it is preferable to abandon standing alliances in favor of ad hoc posses or coalitions that are put together to deal with specific problems and have little formal bureaucratic structure to them. This was the approach followed by President GEORGE H. W. BUSH in the PERSIAN GULF WAR versus IRAQ and by President GEORGE W. BUSH in the opening moves in the war against TERRORISM in AFGHANISTAN. In the IRAQ WAR the Bush administration followed a similar strategy. It worked outside of NATO and the UN system to put together a "coalition of the willing." Prominent among its members were the former Communist states of East Europe that were seeking membership in NATO. Secretary of Defense Donald Rumsfeld collectively referred to them as the "new Europe." Shortly after the war began, the administration claimed that the coalition of the willing had grown to 46 states, exceeding the number of states that supported the United States in the Persian Gulf War. The extent of many of these contributions, however, was quite limited. Six coalition states—Palau, Costa Rica, Iceland, the Marshall Islands, Micronesia, and the Solomon Islands—had no army.

**Further reading:** Osgood, Robert E. *Alliances and American Foreign Policy.* Baltimore: Johns Hopkins University Press, 1968; Riker, William H. *The Theory of Political Coalitions.* New Haven, Conn.: Yale University Press, 1962; Walt, Stephen. *The Origins of Alliances.* Ithaca, N.Y.: Cornell University Press, 1987.

## America First Committee

The America First Committee was a short-lived and vocal noninterventionist organization that was dedicated to keeping the United States out of WORLD WAR II. It was founded in September 1940 around four central principles. First, the United States must build an impregnable defense. Second, if it is prepared, no foreign power or group of states can successfully attack the United States. Third, American democracy is best preserved by keeping out of the war in Europe. Fourth, "aid short of war" only weakens America's national defense and threatens to involve the United States in foreign wars.

While the American First Committee was national in scope, its center of operations was in the Midwest and its core group of supporters came from the business community. Robert Douglas Stuart, Jr., the son of the first vice president of Quaker Oats, was its founder. Other key business members included General Robert E. Wood, chairman of the board of Sears Roebuck, H. Richardson Smith of the Vick Chemical Company, and Jay Hormel, president of Hormel Meat Packing Company. Among the prominent political figures to join its ranks was Robert La Follette, a former governor of Wisconsin. Future president GERALD FORD was a member as was future member of Congress Jonathan Bingham. Famed aviator Charles A. Lindbergh was its leading orator and speech giver. Lindbergh had moved to GREAT BRITAIN in 1935 following the kidnapping of his son. While abroad he developed an interest in German aviation and close ties with leading German political figures. In 1938 Hermann Goering, head of the Luftwaffe, presented Lindbergh with the German Service Cross for his contributions to aviation. Lindbergh returned to the United States in 1939 as an advocate of ISOLATIONISM.

Perhaps the most controversial speech given by Lindbergh on behalf of the America First Committee was the one he gave in Des zq, Iowa, on September 11, 1941. In it he asserted that "the three most important groups who have been pressing the country toward war are the British, the Jewish, and the Roosevelt administration. Behind these groups, but of lesser importance, are a number of capitalists, Anglophiles, and intellectuals who believe that the future of mankind depends upon the domination of the British Empire." In speaking of "the Jewish" he stated, "no person with a sense of dignity of mankind can condone the persecution of the Jewish race in Germany . . . their greatest danger to this country lies in their large ownership and influence on our motion pictures, our press, our radio, and our government." He concluded by saying: "[W]e are on the verge of war, but it is not yet too late to stay out. . . . It is not yet too late to retrieve and to maintain the independent American destiny that our forefathers established in the new world." Lindbergh's anti-Semitic views were not shared by all those who supported the America First Committee, and this speech caused great consternation within its ranks.

On the eve of Pearl Harbor, however, the America First Committee remained strong. It had about 450 chapters. At its height it counted more than 800,000 members committed to preserving American neutrality. Its chief lobbying opponent was the Committee to Defend America by Aiding the Allies. This group shared the America First Committee's desire to keep the United States out of war but felt the best way to do so was by giving aid to the British. The Japanese attack on Pearl Harbor brought an end to its activities. The America First Committee pledged its support for the war and officially disbanded on April 22, 1942.

See also INTERNATIONALISM; PEACE MOVEMENTS.

## American Civil War

The first shots of the American Civil War were fired by Confederate forces at Fort Sumter, South Carolina, on April 12, 1861. By that time, the first diplomatic salvo had already been proposed. Seven Southern states had seceded upon ABRAHAM LINCOLN's election to the presidency in 1860. With little experience in foreign affairs, Lincoln announced that Secretary of State WILLIAM H. SEWARD would take the lead in this area. Seward was a prominent Republican and the leading Northern candidate for the presidential nomination but also the prime target of Republican radicals who hoped to replace him with CHARLES SUMNER. Seward felt that one way to reunite the country was by provoking a foreign war, and he suggested this strategy to President Lincoln in a memo on April 1, 1861. Lincoln declined.

With the Civil War now a reality and his "wrap-the-world-in-fire" strategy rejected, the primary challenge facing Seward was to keep GREAT BRITAIN on the sidelines. No serious disputes separated the United States (the North) from Great Britain when the Civil War began, and opinion in the latter was divided over how to proceed. Members of the aristocracy tended to support secession out of their general opposition to the American experiment in democracy. A number of journals were supportive of the South as the underdog and dismayed that Lincoln publicly stated that his purpose was to preserve the Union and not to end slavery. Self-interest also led Great Britain to support the South. A fragmented United States would be less of an economic and diplomatic competitor. About 80 percent of the cotton used by the British textile industry came from the South. Freed from the need to address mercantile interests in the North, an independent Confederacy promised the British a less hostile trading partner. Aligned against these views were several noninterventionist ones, including a desire not to unleash destabilizing forces in the international system, support by the working class for the North, and large profits that were being made in dealing with both the North and the South.

The first test of U.S. diplomacy in this regard came quickly. One week after the Civil War began, Lincoln imposed a maritime blockade on the Confederacy. Doing so elevated the dispute to the status of an international war since a blockade can be imposed only against a belligerent state. In May the British responded by issuing a proclamation of neutrality. This angered the North but stopped short of recognizing Southern independence. In granting the South the same legal standing as the North, the British action did boost Southern morale. It also permitted them to seek loans abroad and employ privateers and commerce destroyers in order to capture Northern ships. The British balanced their action by denying either side the right to bring captured vessels into British ports where they could be sold as prizes of war. This restriction hurt the Confederacy far more than it did the North because the South had few commercial ships that the North could capture.

Late 1861 brought a second diplomatic crisis with the *Trent* affair. In an effort to win foreign recognition and condemnation of the Northern blockade, the Confederacy sent James Mason and John Slidell to Great Britain and France, respectively. They successfully ran the Northern blockade and made their way to Cuba, where they boarded the British steamship *Trent*. The USS *San Jacinto* under the command of Captain Charles Wilkes intercepted the *Trent*, bordered the ship, and removed Mason and Slidell. It then allowed the *Trent* to continue. Wilkes had acted without orders and in violation of international law, which mandated that he should have seized the *Trent* and brought it before a prize court for adjudication rather than simply taking the contraband from it.

Having had precious little to cheer about so far in the Civil War, the incident was greeted with cheers in the North. It was condemned in Great Britain as an insult, and the British Foreign Office insisted upon release of the prisoners and a suitable apology from the United States. The slowness of international communication allowed tempers to cool, and in December Seward issued a statement acknowledging that Wilkes had acted in error but that he was glad to see that Great Britain now supported the principles for which the United States had fought the WAR OF 1812, namely, the illegality of seizing goods from neutral ships.

THE PENDING CONFLICT.

A print reflecting grave Northern fears of British and French interference on behalf of the Confederacy in the Civil War (*Harper's Weekly*)

With the end of the *Trent* affair the first major diplomatic crisis of the Civil War passed peacefully. The next time the specter of British intervention seemed imminent was in September and October 1862. The North's defeat at the Second Battle of Bull Run led many in the British government to conclude that the time was right for mediation that would result in separation. Before it could act on this impulse, news reached London of the Confederate defeat at the Battle of Antietam. Pushing mediation now it was feared might provoke the North into war. The theme of mediation and division was picked up by Napoleon III of France. He had just established a puppet empire in Mexico, and a divided United States would pose less of a threat to his expansionist plans. Congress passed a resolution declaring that any attempt at mediation would be considered an unfriendly act.

The North scored a major diplomatic triumph during these diplomatic maneuverings with the Emancipation Proclamation. It firmly placed the North on high moral ground by transforming the Civil War from a struggle over political unity into one over slavery. Lincoln had proposed making the proclamation earlier but had been counseled against doing so by Seward, who argued that unless announced on the heals of a military victory, freeing slaves would be seen by European leaders as a desperate act intended to incite a slave uprising. Antietam provided that opportunity. While European leaders reacted with skepticism, the public embraced the announcement, making it harder for prointerventionist forces to gain the political upper hand.

The final diplomatic crisis of the Civil War centered on efforts by Northern diplomats to stop the construction of a Confederate navy. Lacking naval vessels of their own, the Confederacy turned to British shipyards. The British Neutrality Act of 1819 prohibited the construction of warships for belligerents, but the Confederacy and British builders easily circumvented the spirit of the law by having weapons put on ships after they left Great Britain. Three Confederate commerce destroyers, as they were called, the *Florida, Alabama,* and *Shenandoah* burned, sank, or incapacitated about 250 Northern merchant ships. Also constructed in Great Britain for the Confederacy were the *Georgia* and *Rappahannock. Charles Francis Adams, the U.S. minister in London, protested the construction of these ships to British authorities, documenting their true purpose and submitting a bill for damages. The British refused to act since technically no British law had been broken.

In 1863 Congress expressed its anger by passing a bill authorizing the president to commission Northern privateers. In as much as there were no Southern merchant ships for these privateers to target, it was clear to all that British merchants were now endangered. British authorities responded by seizing the *Alexandra* while it was under construction. The British government lost the court case that resulted from this action and was forced to release the vessel to the Confederacy, but by then it was of little military value.

Even more threatening to the North than the construction of Confederate commerce destroyers was the construction of two "Laird rams." These were ships built with wrought-iron "piercers" that were designed to break a naval blockade. When armed they would have the potential of laying siege to Northern ports. Commentators suggest that had they been built, there is good reason to believe that the South could have won the Civil War and the North would have declared war against Great Britain. Adams threatened as much, as the sailing date for the rams approached. The British government had already reached a similar conclusion and two days before receiving Adams's warning ordered the rams held.

The United States continued to press its claims resulting from losses inflicted by the Confederate navy. In the 1871 Treaty of Washington Great Britain expressed its regret for not having exercised "due diligence" to prevent the construction and arming of these ships. The treaty also established a commission to determine how much compensation should be provided. Known as the *Alabama Claims*, it rejected the U.S. demand for "indirect damages" associated with the costs of fighting the Civil War. A British estimate put the total resulting figure at $8 billion. Instead, the commission agreed that Great Britain should pay $15.5 million to the United States. This was the first arbitration treaty entered into by the United States.

**Further reading:** Crook, Franklin. *Diplomacy of the Civil War.* New York: Random House, 1975; Ferris, Norman B. *The Trent Affair: A Diplomatic Crisis.* Knoxville: University of Tennessee Press, 1977; Fishel, Edwin C. *The Secret War for Union: The Untold Story of Military Intelligence in the Civil War.* Boston: Houghton Mifflin, 1996.

## *American Insurance Co. v. Canter* (1828)

The CONSTITUTION was not clear on every question concerning the distribution of power between the federal government and the states or between the various branches of the federal government. One area of uncertainty was whether or not the federal government had the right to acquire additional territory via treaty and thus not be required to obtain the consent of the states. This was a significant domestic political question, since these new territories could over time expect to become states and thus alter the distribution of political power within the United States.

In the *American Insurance Co. v. Canter* the SUPREME COURT ruled that the permission of states was not needed. Chief Justice John Marshall justified the Court's ruling by introducing the concept of "resulting powers." He asserted that even though the power to acquire new territories was not explicitly mentioned in the Constitution, it followed logically from the "the aggregate powers of the national government" to make war and enter into treaties, and from the power to acquire treaties comes the right to govern over them.

At issue was the 1819 treaty with SPAIN by which the United States acquired the territory of FLORIDA. Three years later Congress passed legislation creating a government for Florida. A ship, the *Point à Petre*, which was wrecked off the Florida coast and its cargo of cotton sent to FRANCE, was saved and brought ashore. Canter purchased the cotton at an auction that was held pursuant to Florida law in order to pay salvage claims. The American Insurance Co., which insured the cargo, brought suit in court to recover the cotton, claiming that the original acquisition of Florida and the subsequent establishment of a judicial system was unconstitutional. In its decision the Supreme Court sided with Canter.

## American national style

The American national style consists of the reoccurring patterns of thought and action that typify the American approach to world politics. It provides a conceptual starting point for studying American foreign policy that emphasizes the role of societal and historical influences rather than government structures, personality, or the demands of the international system.

The sources of the American national style are found in the conditions under which earlier generations of American policy makers operated and the ideas that guided their thinking. Between the mid-1600s and the mid-1800s the United States grew from a series of isolated settlements into an economic power. Just as important for the development of the American national style is the fact that this growth took place without any master plan. Individual self-reliance, flexibility, and improvisation were the cardinal virtues in developing America. The United States was a "how-to-do-it" society where energies were directed at the problem at hand and where long-range considerations received scant attention. This growth occurred against a period of relative international calm. Closer to home the defense of American borders did not require the creation of a large standing army or navy. Peace and security seemed to come naturally, and Americans drew a direct connection between peace, democracy, and economic growth. The dynamics of the marketplace and the power of governments were seen to be in direct competition with one another. Americans embraced the former and rejected the latter, favoring a system of limited government. Rejecting war as a means of providing for national security, Americans embraced trade and enlightened self-interest as forces for promoting the peaceful settlement of disputes. It was a short step from viewing the American historical experience as unique to embracing the concept of American exceptionalism and the belief that whereas other countries pursued national interests, the United States was motivated by a higher sense of mission in conducting its foreign policy.

Three patterns of thought and action provide the building blocks from which the American national style emerges. The first pattern is UNILATERALISM, or a predisposition to act alone in addressing foreign policy problems. ISOLATIONISM, INTERNATIONALISM, and NEUTRALITY are all consistent with this basic orientation to world affairs. The second pattern is MORAL PRAGMATISM. The American sense of morality has two elements. First, it assumes that the behavior of states can be judged by moral standards. Second, it is assumed that the American definition of morality provides that standard. American pragmatism takes the form of an engineering approach to foreign-policy problems. U.S. involvement is typically put in terms of "setting things right." The third pattern to U.S. foreign policy is LEGALISM. Foreign policy problems are to be solved in the name of legal principles and the establishment of international rules rather than primarily through the use of brute force.

These three patterns come together to support the two dominant orientations Americans have adopted to international affairs: internationalism and isolationism. It is this shared foundation that makes it possible for Americans to shift between these two orientations so effortlessly. One study suggests that movement between the two has not been haphazard but occurs regularly in 25–30-year cycles. Disagreement exists among scholars as to the triggering mechanism that sets off a new cycle. Factors suggested include the arrival of a new generation of policy makers, the health of the economy, and domestic-policy failings.

Commentators have suggested that the American national style holds a number of consequences for the overall conduct of American foreign policy regardless of whether internationalism or isolationism is the dominant orientation. One consequence is a tendency to "win the war and lose the peace." It stems from the American tendency to see war and peace as polar opposites rather than as part of a continuum. The absence of a conceptual link between the two means that war plans tend to be drawn up in a political vacuum, and they do not serve as an instrument of statecraft. A second consequence is the existence of a double standard in judging the behavior of states. Convinced of its righteousness and predisposed to act unilaterally, the United States has often engaged in actions it condemns on the part of others. Soviet interventions in CZECHOSLOVAKIA, HUNGARY, and POLAND are condemned as acts of IMPERIALISM, but U.S. interventions in GRENADA, PANAMA, and the DOMINICAN REPUBLIC are held to be morally defensible. The third consequence is an ambivalence to DIPLOMACY. In the abstract, diplomacy is valued as a means of settling disputes, but the product of diplomacy is viewed with skepticism. If the U.S. position is the morally correct one than any compromise involves a rejection of those principles and a potential triumph for evil. A last consequence is impatience. Optimistic at the start of an undertaking and convinced of the correctness of its position, Americans tend to want quick results. They become impatient when positive results are not forthcoming and turn away in frustration.

Two key questions are asked of the American national style today. First, is it well-suited to world politics in the 21st century? Many fear that the pull of the past has become counterproductive and the need is for a new outlook on world politics, one that stresses shared experiences rather than historical uniqueness. A case in point is the IRAQ WAR. All three traits were present and in combination produced an American approach to dealing with Saddam Hussein that left it politically isolated in world politics. The Bush administration acted outside of the UNITED NATIONS (UN) and treated the NORTH ATLANTIC TREATY ORGANIZATION (NATO) as irrelevant. It also made it clear to all that the "coalition of the willing" would not control American decisions about how to prosecute the war. This would be a unilateral American undertaking supported by others. Legalism was evident. The rationale for war was Iraq's refusal to comply with UN resolutions. The centerpiece of the solution for rebuilding Iraq put forward after the war was the creation of a democratic system where the rule of law would be supreme. The conduct of the war also was consistent with the principles of moral pragmatism. President Bush did not hesitate to invoke the rightness of the American cause and the obligation that the United States had to act. With the justness of its cause firmly established in their minds, the administration turned to the task of constructing the war plan for removing Saddam Hussein from power. Little interest was shown in exploring alternative lines of action or delay as advocated in the UN. Moreover, little attention was given by these planners to the task of providing emergency supplies in the immediate postwar period or the problems of postwar reconstruction and rule. These were issues beyond the scope of the blueprint for military action. Second, can it change? One possible mechanism for change is the arrival into power of policy makers who do not share this "American experience." Ethnic minorities and women are most frequently mentioned as comprising two leadership groups for whom the American experience has been quite different.

**Further reading:** Dallek, Robert. *The American Style of Foreign Policy.* New York: New American Library, 1983; Goldstein, Judith. *Ideas, Interests, and American Foreign Policy.* Ithaca, N.Y.: Cornell University Press, 1993; Perkins, Dexter. *The American Approach to Foreign Policy.* Cambridge, Mass.: Harvard University Press, 1962.

## American Revolution

American DIPLOMACY during the American Revolution was conducted by CONGRESS. Several months prior to the Declaration of Independence, it had established a "secret committee of correspondence" to carry out its foreign policy. Secret envoys were sent to Europe, where they met a cold reception. European states, fearful of provoking an angry British response, wanted little to do with these uninvited representatives of the fledgling American republic. Not only were American diplomats unwanted, they lacked diplomatic skills and had great difficulty obtaining instructions from Congress. It could take two months for written instructions to arrive and about one-third of all correspondence failed to reach Europe.

The first phase of U.S. diplomacy during the American Revolution dealt with FRANCE. France was a logical target because it was GREAT BRITAIN's main rival and had just experienced a humiliating defeat at its hands in the FRENCH AND INDIAN WAR (also known as the Seven Years' War, 1756–63). As a result of this war France had lost its North American holdings. Thanks largely to the prodding of Pierre-Augustin Caron de Beaumarchais, French officials gradually came to see the revolt of the American colonists as a means for inflicting harm on their British rivals. On May 2, 1776, two months prior to the declaration of independence, France decided to secretly provide military aid to the colonists through the establishment of a fictitious company.

Not until September 1776 did the United States send official diplomatic representatives to Paris. The U.S. mission consisted of Arthur Lee, Silas Deane, and BENJAMIN FRANKLIN. It was only after the U.S. victory at Saratoga in October 1777 that the French were willing to go beyond providing secret help. In large measure they were motivated by the fear that the United States and Great Britain might arrive at some type of reconciliation that would

American statesman Benjamin Franklin *(center)* arriving in Paris, where he served as the first American ambassador *(Hulton/Archive)*

reunite the two and perhaps threaten French holdings in the West Indies. The French were restrained in their ability to move on these concerns by alliance ties with SPAIN. Unlike France, Spain had little interest in a formal declaration of war against Great Britain. Frustrated by Spain's reticence and fearful of reconciliation, France signed a treaty of amity and commerce with the United States on February 8, 1778. The treaty was based on the American plan of 1776 wherein the Continental Congress set forward the self-styled American principles for dealing with Europe. This treaty signaled the formal diplomatic recognition of the United States by France. As expected, Great Britain responded with a declaration of war against France. This led to the signing of a Franco-American Treaty of ALLIANCE in which both sides pledged to fight until American independence was "formally or tactically assured." Both states also agreed not to sign a separate peace with Great Britain.

American diplomatic efforts now turned to Spain, which was offended that France would enter into an agreement with the United States without its consent. Spain viewed the situation in North America differently from France. It still possessed colonies there and was fearful that a successful revolution by the Americans could threaten the stability of its holdings. John Jay was sent to Spain in hopes of securing an alliance and obtaining funds. The mission has been described as "one long purgatory," as Spanish officials showed little inclination to talk with Jay. The U.S. defeat at Charleston hardened Spanish resistance to an alliance so much that Madrid rejected Jay's offer to abandon all U.S. claims for navigation rights on the Mississippi River. In the end, Jay did succeed in borrowing a small sum from Spain.

The NETHERLANDS was the next target of U.S. diplomacy. JOHN ADAMS was sent to The Hague from his post in France in 1780. Great Britain would soon declare war on the Netherlands for its aggressive pursuit of new trade opportunities with the rebellious American colonies and its trade with France. The United States hoped to take advantage of the growing dispute between them. In April 1782 Adams was able to obtain a formal recognition of American independence by the Netherlands. More important, he was then able to secure a loan that averted the bankruptcy of the U.S. government, followed by a treaty of amity and commerce.

Setbacks in the Revolutionary War culminating in the defeat at Yorktown took their toll on British interest in fighting the colonists. A change in government in 1782 led the British to explore the possibility of a peace agreement with Franklin, who went so far as to propose that Great Britain cede CANADA to the United States. Because of declining health, Franklin turned over the negotiations to Jay, who was suspected of French motives. Spain had formally become a French ally against Great Britain in 1779. The price tag was the return of Gibraltar. American interest in signing a peace agreement put the French in a quandary. The Franco-Spanish agreement pledged France (and through its treaty with the United States, the United States) to fight Great Britain until Gibraltar was returned to Spain. While a U.S.–British peace treaty would have violated the terms of the Franco-American treaty, it would save France the expense of a continued war simply to meet Spanish war aims. On the other hand, France desired to see a weak United States emerge from the Revolutionary War, one that would be dependent upon it. This required continued fighting and not a peace agreement.

Acting without consulting France, the United States signed a preliminary peace agreement with Great Britain on November 30, 1782. It was then necessary to explain to French officials why a separate peace had been negotiated. Not only did Franklin successfully accomplish this task, but he also received an additional loan from France. The formal peace treaty, the TREATY OF PARIS, was signed on September 8, 1783, with the approval of France. It differed little from the preliminary agreement.

**Further reading:** Bemis, Samuel F. *The Diplomacy of the American Revolution.* 4th ed. New York: Peter Smith, 1957; Dull, Johnathan. *A Diplomatic History of the American Revolution.* New Haven, Conn.: Yale University Press, 1985.

## Angola

About twice the size of TEXAS, with an area of 480,400 square miles, Angola has a population of 10.5 million people. Portugal first established a bridgehead in Angola in 1482 and was the dominant foreign power until November 11, 1975, when Angola became independent. Portugal arrived in search of gold but instead exploited Angola as a source of slaves for its Brazilian colony. Rather than grant Angola independence after WORLD WAR II, Portugal designated Angola an overseas province in 1951 and encouraged white immigration.

Three different independence movements challenged continued Portuguese rule. In 1956 a Marxist guerrilla force, the Popular Movement for the Independence of Angola (MPLA), was established in Zambia and attracted Angolan intellectuals. In 1962 the Front for the Liberation of Angola (FNLA) was established in the CONGO, and its fighters had significant support from the Organization of African Unity and from the Bakongo region in northern Angola. The final group was established in 1966. It was the National Union for the Total Independence of Angola (UNITA) and drew support from the Ovimbundo region in the center of Angola.

In April 1974 the dictatorship was overturned, and an anticolonialist military government seized power in Portugal. It arranged for a cease-fire with the rebel forces and announced its intention to grant Angola its independence. A coalition government was formed among the three independence movements, but it quickly broke down. The MPLA became the ruling party and turned to the SOVIET UNION and CUBA for aid. The United States gave its support first to the FNLA and then to UNITA. SOUTH AFRICA also supported UNITA as part of its strategy of defeating the Namibian liberation group—the South-West Africa People's Organization (SWAPO)—that was operating out of Angola.

The United States had supported Portugal's policy of continued rule over Angola. After the 1974 coup it moved quickly to involve itself in the civil war. Angola became a key and symbolic battleground in the United States's foreign policy after VIETNAM. The Nixon administration sought to organize its relations with the Soviet Union around the concept of DÉTENTE. According to this strategy the United States and the Soviet Union would act less as protagonists and more as partners. ARMS CONTROL agreements, such as those emerging from the STRATEGIC ARMS LIMITATIONS TALKS, and increased trade were examples of détente in action. The Nixon administration also expected the Soviet Union to refrain from challenging Western interests in the Third World. Soviet leaders, however, did not share this interpretation of détente. From their point of view the Third World remained a legitimate area of contestation between the superpowers. Angola became the place where these two interpretations of détente collided.

The principal vehicle for American involvement in Angola was the CENTRAL INTELLIGENCE AGENCY (CIA). In June 1974 the CIA began supporting the FNLA, even though the Forty Committee, which was charged with approving covert action, had not done so. Soon the Forty Committee would give its support, and in 1975 President GERALD FORD authorized a $14 million program to help the FNLA. It proved to be insufficient as the MPLA, with the aid of Cuban forces and Soviet arms, defeated the FNLA and UNITA forces. The Ford administration refused to recognize the MPLA government and sought congressional approval for additional funding. In December 1975 CONGRESS refused to pass the Clark Amendment, which prohibited American involvement in Angola.

The question of what to do about Angola was rejoined by the Reagan administration. President JIMMY CARTER had continued Ford's policy of nonrecognition but refrained from involving Washington in Angola's ongoing civil war. UNITA continued to receive support from South Africa during this period. RONALD REAGAN placed Angola in both a global context and a regional one. According to

Chester Crocker, assistant SECRETARY OF STATE for Africa, the U.S. policy was one of constructive engagement. The objective was to link the withdrawal of Cuban and South African forces from Angola with Namibian independence. The Clark Amendment was repealed in 1985, opening the way for the Reagan administration to begin providing covert military aid to UNITA. Fighting escalated in 1987 and 1988, but no clear-cut victor emerged. In December 1988 Crocker achieved his long-sought goals as a result of complex negotiations between Angola, South Africa, Cuba, the Soviet Union, and the United States. In 1989 the George Bush administration helped engineer the withdrawal of all foreign forces from Angola. In turn, this led the way to the Bicesse accord of 1991, which established an electoral process that would determine the legitimate government of Angola.

Jonas Savimbi, UNITA's longtime leader, failed to win the first round of the 1992 election. While the United Nations declared the election to be fair, Savimbi refused to accept the results and resumed fighting. The Clinton administration began to distance itself from Savimbi and, in 1993, recognized the MPLA as the legitimate government of Angola. A peace agreement was signed in 1994 in Lusaka, Zambia, but it collapsed in 1998. Prior to that, in August 1997, the United Nations imposed economic sanctions on UNITA. A 1999 Angolan military offensive inflicted heavy damage on UNITA's forces. Savimbi, however, continued to fight and returned to GUERRILLA WARFARE. Additional UN sanctions were added in 2001 that were designed to limit UNITA's access to money. Much of its activity was financed through the sale of diamonds mined from the Angolan territory still under its control. Estimates placed the value of these sales at $500 million annually. Savimbi died in combat in 2002, and another cease-fire agreement was reached.

The United States gave approximately $89 million in aid to Angola in fiscal year 2001. Some $55 million consisted of development and humanitarian assistance. The STATE DEPARTMENT also provided $3.5 million for demining programs. The United States has also developed a major stake in Angola's oil industry. More than one-half of Angola's total oil production goes to the United States.

See also LAND MINES; RUSSIA.

**Further reading:** Marcum, John. *The Angolan Revolution.* Cambridge, Mass.: MIT Press, 1978; Stockwell, John. *In Search of Enemies: A CIA Story.* New York: Norton, 1978.

## Antiballistic Missile Treaty

The Antiballistic Missile (ABM) Treaty was negotiated between the United States and the Soviet Union (see RUSSIA) at the first STRATEGIC ARMS LIMITATION TALKS (SALT). These talks began in Helsinki in November 1969 and concluded on May 26, 1972. They produced one treaty, the ABM Treaty, and one executive agreement. Initially more attention was focused on the executive agreement, since it contained the number of weapons that the two sides agreed could be contained in their respective nuclear arsenals. The ABM Treaty was approved by the Senate by a vote of 88-2 in August 1972. As a result of the political battle over ratification, it was understood by both the White House and CONGRESS that the numbers of NUCLEAR WEAPONS agreed upon in any SALT II agreement would be included in a treaty rather than an executive agreement so that Congress could vote on it.

The ABM Treaty limited each side two antiballistic missile sites, with 200 antiballistic missiles per site. Each side was permitted one anti-ballistic missile site dedicated to protecting an intercontinental ballistic missile (ICBM) site, which was dedicated to protecting a city. This formula was necessary since the Soviet ABM system was a city system and the American ABM system that was under construction was an ICBM system. In 1974 an additional agreement limited each side to one deployed ABM system. In 1975 work on the one U.S. site was terminated by the Senate. One reason the ABM Treaty was not as controversial as the interim agreement at the time was that considerable doubt existed in the U.S. national security community about the value or desirability of an ABM system.

The first ABM system under serious discussion in the United States was the Nike-Zeus system, which was designed to shoot down supersonic bombers. Work on it began in 1956. In 1963 the Pentagon put forward the Nike-X system. SECRETARY OF DEFENSE ROBERT MCNAMARA opposed the deployment of an ABM system because he felt it was not technologically sound and feared it would result in an arms race with the Soviet Union. Pressure mounted on the Johnson administration to go forward with an ABM because the Soviet Union had begun construction of an ABM around Moscow. McNamara felt that any Soviet ABM system would be easily overwhelmed by the continued development of Multiple Independently Targeted Reentry Vehicle (MIRV) technology by the United States. MIRV technology allowed the United States to place several warheads on a missile that could be directed at different targets, thus greatly complicating the task that any ABM system had in identifying, tracking, and destroying incoming missiles. The ABM was also opposed on the grounds that it was destabilizing. A nuclear peace was seen to rest on the existence of mutual assured destruction, which held that since both the United States and the Soviet Union had the ability to withstand a nuclear attack, they could inflict a devastating retaliatory strike. An ABM system could serve as a nuclear shield, offering an attacker the possibility of escaping nuclear destruction.

In 1966 Congress approved funds for an ABM even though LYNDON JOHNSON had not requested any monies. In 1967 the Johnson administration included funding for the ABM in its budget request but also indicated that it would seek an arms control agreement with the Soviet Union to ban such systems. In June 1967 a summit conference was held at Glassboro State Teachers College, located approximately one-half way between Washington and New York, where Soviet leader Alexei Kosygin was attending a meeting at the UNITED NATIONS. The talks failed to produce an ARMS CONTROL agreement when Kosygin proclaimed the Soviet ABM defensive and unobjectionable. The Johnson administration had little choice but to proceed with an ABM. To minimize its size and strategic impact, in September 1967 McNamara announced that the United States would begin constructing an anti-Chinese ABM system. CHINA had only exploded its first nuclear device in 1964.

President RICHARD NIXON had little interest in an anti-Chinese ABM system but did need a weapons system to trade away in his planned arms control talks with the Soviet Union. MIRV technology was considered too valuable so Nixon redesignated the anti-Chinese ABM system (Sentinel) as an anti-Soviet ABM system (Safeguard).

Of far more lasting significance than the numeric limitations agreed to in the ABM Treaty was the stipulation that neither side could develop, test, or deploy ABM components. This prohibition placed a major obstacle in the way of President RONALD REAGAN's STRATEGIC DEFENSE INITIATIVE and the national BALLISTIC MISSILE DEFENSE system proposed in the 1990s. Advocates of these systems claimed that the ABM Treaty was an anachronism from an early nuclear period. Defenders of the ABM Treaty saw it as the centerpiece of all COLD WAR nuclear arms control agreements and feared that, if ignored, a new arms race would result. In a turnabout, it was now American strategists who held ABM systems to be defensive and unobjectionable and the Soviets and others around the world who argued it was destabilizing. What had changed was who possessed the ABM (or was ahead in its development) and who did not.

President GEORGE W. BUSH strongly supported development of a national ballistic missile defense system and, in December 2002, officially gave notice that the United States was withdrawing from the ABM Treaty. The United States withdrew from the ABM Treaty in June 2003.

**Further reading:** Lindsay, James M., and Michael O'Hanlon. *Defending America: The Case for a Limited National Missile Defense System.* Washington, D.C.: Brookings, 2001.

## ANZUS Pact

The ANZUS (Australia–New Zealand–United States) Pact was signed on September 1, 1951, and became operational on April 9, 1952. By its terms, these three states agreed that an armed attack in the Pacific against any one of them would endanger the peace and security of all of them. Unlike the NORTH ATLANTIC TREATY ORGANIZATION (NATO), the ANZUS Pact did not create a unified standing military capability. Rather, the partners pledged to consult with one another in such an eventuality and respond in accordance with their respective constitutional processes, a phrase that weakened any automatic response. As was also the case with other ALLIANCES put in place in the 1950s, members joined for differing reasons. The United States was primarily concerned with stopping communist expansion in the region. Australia and New Zealand were primarily concerned with the possibility of a rearmed JAPAN seeking to extend its domination over the Pacific.

The alliance system survived into the 1980s. A major change took place following New Zealand's decision to bar nuclear-powered vessels or those carrying NUCLEAR WEAPONS from its ports. This decision reflected growing concern in New Zealand with nuclear testing in the Pacific. It created a crisis because the U.S. Navy did not disclose which ships carried nuclear weapons. As a result, in 1986 the United States suspended its treaty obligations to New Zealand. However, the treaty remains formally in existence. Also as a result of this decision, joint-training exercises with the United States have been severely restricted, as has intelligence sharing. In 1991 President GEORGE H. W. BUSH announced that under normal conditions American surface ships do not carry nuclear weapons. They are restricted to submarines. His announcement brought U.S. and New Zealand policy closer together, but it did not end the ban. New Zealand's current defense policy stresses the need to maintain only a credible minimum force. With that in mind in 1999 it cancelled a lease-to-buy agreement for 28 F-16 aircraft from the United States, and in 2000 it ended plans to upgrade its P3-C aircraft.

Following the suspension of U.S. defense commitments to New Zealand, the United States and Australia have held annual bilateral meetings. The first took place in Canberra in 1985. It was at the second meeting in San Francisco that the change in the status of ANZUS was announced. Although it took a less defiant stand than New Zealand, Australia was also critical of U.S. nuclear policy in the Pacific. It wanted the United States to sign the South Pacific Nuclear Free Zone Treaty and criticized French nuclear testing in the region.

The issue that has created the most bilateral tension between the United States and Australia in recent years is agricultural trade policy. Australia opposes two sets of U.S. actions. First, it opposes American protectionist trade barriers on the importation of wheat, wool, meats, dairy products, lead, zinc, and uranium. An estimated 40 percent of Australia's foreign earnings come from agricultural exports. Second, Australia opposes the U.S. practice of imposing third-party economic sanctions against states doing business with CUBA, LIBYA, or IRAN. For its part, the United States objects to Australia's barriers on the importation of cooked chicken, fresh salmon, and fruit. It also opposes Australia's government procurement policies that discriminate against foreign companies and what it sees as inadequate laws protecting intellectual property rights.

## Arab-Israeli conflict

ISRAEL and its Arab neighbors have been in a constant state of conflict since its independence in 1948. The United States was an active partner in some of these conflicts and has been actively involved in peace negotiations almost from the outset. While no formal "war" has been fought since 1973, peace remains elusive.

The first Arab-Israeli conflict coincides with the creation of the state of Israel. Palestine was under a British mandate dating back to the LEAGUE OF NATIONS. Throughout British rule Arab nationalists and Zionists had clashed over the region's future. GREAT BRITAIN had publicly endorsed the idea of a separate Jewish state in Palestine with the Balfour Declaration of 1918. During the interwar period and WORLD WAR II, it backed away from this position by limiting the flow of European Jews into Palestine. This was done out of concern for maintaining access to Middle East OIL and good relations with Arab leaders. In February 1947 Great Britain announced that it was terminating its mandate and turning the matter over to the UNITED NATIONS (UN). In August a UN commission, the United Nations Special Commission on Palestine, recommended partition and the creation of both a Jewish and a Palestinian state. Zionists supported the proposal while Arabs rejected it, seeking only one state. The full UN endorsed that report by a vote of 33-13, with 10 abstentions, on November 29.

Low-level fighting broke out between Jewish and Arab forces almost immediately and continued into early 1948. Israel declared its independence on May 14, 1948, one day before British forces withdrew from Jerusalem. By that time Jewish forces had taken control of virtually all of the territory that was to become Israel. In the process some 300,000 Arabs became refugees. On May 15 Arab forces from Egypt, Transjordan, SYRIA, and LEBANON attacked Israel. From then until June 11 Israeli forces engaged in a defensive campaign. In July they took the offensive, inflicted heavy blows on Arab forces, and captured additional territory. A cease-fire was put in place on July 19, but fighting did not end. Israel went on the offensive again, taking territory in the Negev that was still under Arab control but was designated as part of Israel by the UN plan. Its forces also took territory away from Syrian and Lebanese forces that the UN plan had not assigned to Israel. UN-sponsored armistice agreements signed in 1949 brought the war to an end. The first was signed with EGYPT on February 25 and the last with Syria on July 20. The war left Israel in control of one-half more land than it was to have had according to the UN plan. The remaining Arab land was taken over by Transjordan (which then changed its name to JORDAN). The net result of these land transfers was to turn half of Palestine's prewar 1.3 million Arabs into refugees.

The United States recognized Israeli independence immediately but did not come to its aid during the war. After the war the United States worked largely through the UN to bring about an accommodation between the Arabs and Israelis. Along with FRANCE and TURKEY the United States sat on a UN Conciliation Commission that was set up in December 1948. Its work ended in failure. Next, the United States, Great Britain, and France announced the Tripartite Declaration in May 1950. The three states promised to limit arms sales to the Arabs and Israelis in hopes of bringing about a political resolution of the conflict.

That agreement soon unraveled as Israel rearmed with weapons purchased from France. Egypt, under the leadership of Gamal Abdel Nasser, then requested weapons from the United States. President DWIGHT EISENHOWER rejected the bid, and on September 27, 1955, Egypt signed an agreement with the Soviet Union (see RUSSIA) for weapons. In turn, this agreement raised security concerns in Israel and created pressure for preemptive military action. Great Britain and France joined with Israel in planning for such an attack. Great Britain did so in hopes of regaining control of the SUEZ Canal. France was fearful of the spillover effect of Arab nationalism on its unresolved crisis in ALGERIA.

The attack unfolded on October 29, 1956. Israel attacked Egypt and sent forces toward the Suez Canal. The next day France and Great Britain issued an ultimatum calling upon both sides to respect a cease-fire and accept British and French forces along the Suez Canal to guarantee its continued operation. Israel quickly accepted these terms. Egypt rejected them, and fighting between Egyptian and French and British forces took place. Egyptian forces left the Sinai to defend the Suez Canal, at which point Israeli forces captured the Sinai. To the surprise and dismay of the British, French, and Israelis, the United States publicly opposed their actions and pressed for an early cease-fire. The Eisenhower administration had little love for Nasser, so although Washington was not consulted, American acquiescence was expected. In July 1955 the United States had given voice to its dissatisfaction with

Nasser's growing ties with communist states and hostility toward Israel by refusing to make available financing that already had been promised for the Aswan Dam. Israel was forced to unconditionally withdraw from the Sinai and Gaza Strip. A United Nations Emergency Force (UNEF) was placed in the Sinai on the Egyptian side of the armistice line in November 1956.

War came again to the region in 1967. Tensions had been rising for several years. One contributing factor was Israel's decision to divert water from the Sea of Galilee. It produced calls from Syria for united Arab action against Israel. A second development was the founding of the PALESTINE LIBERATION ORGANIZATION (PLO) in 1964 along with calls for the "liberation of Palestine." On June 5 Israeli unleashed a devastating preemptive attack against Egyptian, Syrian, Jordanian, and Iraqi airfields. The resulting air superiority allowed Israeli ground forces to achieve their objectives with little difficulty. The war ended with Israel in control of the Sinai, Gaza Strip, Golan Heights, and West Bank.

One consequence of the 1967 war was that it led to a more pronounced involvement of the United States and the Soviet Union in the conflict. Each had become the primary arms supplier—the United States for Israel and the Soviet Union for the Arab states. The most immediate product of their deepened involvement was UN Resolution 242, passed on November 22, 1967. It asserted the "inadmissibility of the acquisition of territory by war and the need to work for a just and lasting peace in which every state can live in security." In operational terms its key provisions called for Israel to return the land it captured in return for the acknowledgment of its right to exist and its territorial integrity.

Resolution 242 failed to end the conflict. Instead a "war of attrition" broke out. Thanks to an influx of Soviet weaponry, Egypt's military was stronger in the summer of 1968 than it had been before the war, and Nasser used it to attack Israeli positions in the Sinai. Israel countered by undertaking bombing raids deep into Egyptian territory. Nasser now countered by asking for additional Soviet help, including Soviet advisers. The United States sought to break this circle of rising violence with the Rogers Plan. SECRETARY OF STATE William Rogers called for a cease-fire that included acceptance of Resolution 242. Egypt and Jordan accepted the plan, but Israel did not. It changed its position only after the United States promised continuing military aid and agreed that Israel would not have to withdraw completely to its pre-1967 boundaries. A cease-fire took place on August 8, 1970.

In 1973 it would be the Arabs that struck first. Anwar Sadat was now president of Egypt. He had become convinced that the status quo in the Middle East was not tenable but could not be changed through diplomacy. Even though the odds of success in war were slight, he found them preferable to inaction. On October 6, 1973, on Yom Kippur, Egypt and Syria launched their attacks. In spite of good intelligence, Israel was caught by surprise and incurred heavy casualties. The tide of battle turned in mid-October. On October 22 a cease-fire went into effect that was orchestrated by the United States and the Soviet Union. Israel did not stop fighting, however, and the Soviet Union protested to the United States, threatening to send in its own troops. President RICHARD NIXON responded by placing U.S. nuclear forces on a heightened state of worldwide alert. The crisis passed on October 25 when Israel concluded military operations.

The months following the end of the 1973 war found NATIONAL SECURITY ADVISOR HENRY KISSINGER engaging in shuttle diplomacy. He alone held sufficient trust in Israel and Egypt to negotiate agreements reducing the level of tension in the region. Traveling back and forth between these two states, Kissinger secured an agreement on October 28 that freed the Egyptian Third Army from the encircling grip of Israeli forces. A November 11 agreement committed both states to respecting UN Resolution 242. And, on January 18, 1974, a Disengagement of Forces Agreement was reached that created valuable breathing space between Egyptian and Israeli forces. Kissinger then turned his attention to obtaining an agreement between Syria and Egypt.

Kissinger succeeded in obtaining still another agreement in September 1975. Known as Sinai II it produced an agreement on Israel's part for a further withdrawal of its forces and the establishment of a new cease-fire line. Egypt agreed to open the Suez Canal to Israeli commerce. The political price of this agreement was high. In side memorandums Kissinger agreed to provide continued economic and military assistance to Israel and not to "recognize or negotiate with the PLO so long as the PLO does not recognize Israel's right to exist." This last agreement was prompted by an October 1974 Arab Summit in Morocco that identified the PLO as the sole legitimate representative of the Palestinian people. While this side agreement made Sinai II possible, it also temporarily brought to an end the American role as Middle East peacemaker.

The next American peace initiative would wait until 1978, after a stunning move by Sadat. On November 9, 1977, Sadat announced that he would go to Israel in search of peace. And so he did. Israeli prime minister Menachem Begin reciprocated with a December visit to Egypt. Negotiating committees formed in the wake of these two historic visits failed to make progress on a peace agreement. To break the deadlock President JIMMY CARTER invited both leaders to CAMP DAVID. The meetings began on September 5, 1978, and concluded with two agreements on September 17. The first agreement dealt with issues

A Palestinian man walks past a caravan of Israeli armored personnel carriers near a checkpoint in the West Bank. *(Getty Images)*

dividing Israel and Egypt and would lead to a peace treaty on March 26, 1979. The second dealt with the future of the West Bank and Gaza and involved both of these states as well as the United States. This part of the agreement settled little. What it did was provide a framework for negotiating an agreement. Talks began on the West Bank–Gaza framework on May 25, 1979, but they did not succeed. Instead, war again came to the region.

On March 14, 1978, Israel invaded LEBANON. The goal was to create a security zone in southern Lebanon that would stop PLO attacks on Israel. American diplomacy now shifted to deal with this problem. Special envoy Philip Habib succeeded in negotiating a cease-fire between Israel and the PLO in July 1981. Israeli leaders, however, found the cease-fire to have created an unacceptable situation because the PLO remained based in Lebanon and was still seen as a threatening force. Accordingly, on June 6, 1982, Israel invaded Lebanon again. Operation Peace for Galilee sought to destroy the PLO leadership and infrastructure and bring about the election of a pro-Israeli government that would sign a viable peace treaty. Only the first goal was realized. With the PLO surrounded in Beirut, Lebanon's capital, Habib negotiated a cease-fire and an agreement that ensured the PLO would leave Lebanon. Israel failed to reach its other goals as Lebanon fell into chaos and civil war.

With the PLO weakened the Reagan administration sought to break the ongoing stalemate with a Jordanian peace option announced on September 1, 1982. Carter had failed to involve Jordan in the Camp David process. Reagan now hoped to do so by publicly opposing any new Israeli settlements in the West Bank or Gaza and calling for self-government by the Palestinians under some form of political affiliation with Jordan. RONALD REAGAN's plan was dead on arrival. Israel rejected it as deviating from Camp David.

An Arab summit held a few days later took a hard-line stance and reaffirmed the position that the PLO was the sole representative of the Palestinian people.

Matters took a turn for the worse on the ground for the United States in Lebanon. The same month that Reagan announced his peace plan, the United States joined France, Italy, and Great Britain in sending peacekeeping force to Lebanon. Welcomed at first these forces soon became identified with Israel and came under attack from terrorists. On April 18 a bombing of the U.S. EMBASSY killed 63 people. Then, on October 23, 1983, 241 U.S. Marines were killed in a terrorist attack on their barracks. By March 1984 the United States had ended its presence in Lebanon.

It would be 1988 before another American peace initiative was undertaken. By now, the character of the Arab-Israeli conflict had changed again. In late 1987 a sustained and widespread uprising known as the intifada, which employed the tactics and strategies of TERRORISM and GUERRILLA WARFARE began in the occupied territories of Gaza and the West Bank. Secretary of State George Shultz traveled to the Middle East in hopes of speeding up negotiations. He failed, but events were moving in unexpected directions. On November 5, 1988, PLO chairman Yasser Arafat announced the formation of an independent Palestinian state, and on December 14 he announced its acceptance of UN Resolution 242. On its way out of office the Reagan administration then announced it would enter talks with the PLO.

Both the Bush and Clinton administration (the MADRID ACCORDS and CAMP DAVID II, respectively) attempted to engineer Arab-Israeli peace agreements. Neither succeeded in stopping the violence, and the failure of Camp David II in 2000 appears to have contributed to the onset of the second intifada, or uprising. President GEORGE W. BUSH vacillated in his response to the steadily worsening situation. At the outset of his administration he was not inclined to take an activist role in the peace process but was prepared to recognize a Palestinian state. Later he would wholeheartedly endorse the Israeli position that Arafat was an obstacle to peace and must be removed before talks could begin and any Israeli concessions were needed. Bush did not involve himself again in the Arab-Israeli dispute until after the IRAQ WAR when he put forward his "road map for peace." It has three phases. The first focuses on ending the violence. The Palestinians are to stop terrorist attacks and Israel is to freeze building new settlements in Palestinian territories. In the second phase a Palestinian state will be created by 2005. In the third phase the final borders between the two states will be settled, and the fate of Jerusalem will determined. The road map immediately encountered difficulties as a result of a new wave of Palestinian terrorist attacks and Israeli reprisals.

Commentators make several points in summarizing the history of the American participation in the Arab-Israeli conflict. First, the United States has emerged as Israel's major ally and protector even though no formal agreement binding them together exists. Second, the United States has been an active participant in most of the major peace negotiations that have occurred. This is because only the United States is seen as being capable of persuading Israel to give up any of the land it acquired in 1967 in return for a peace agreement. Third, the American role has varied widely over time. It has been a facilitator, mediator, energizer, and messenger to name but a few roles it has played. Fourth, while fundamental issues, such as the status of Jerusalem, the fate of Palestinian refugees, and the disposition of the occupied territories, remain unresolved the context of the negotiations has changed repeatedly. Israeli and Arab policy makers have changed, and they come to the negotiating table with varying degrees of domestic support. Large-scale warfare has given way to the intifada, and the COLD WAR has ended.

**Further reading:** Laqueur, Walter, and Barry Rubin. *The Israel-Arab Reader: A Documentary History of the Middle East.* Durham, N.C.: Duke University Press, 1984; Oren, Michael, B. *Six Days of War: June 1967 and the Making of the Modern Middle East.* New York: Oxford University Press, 2002; Spiegel, Steven L. *The Other Arab-Israeli Conflict: Making America's Middle East Policy from Truman to Reagan.* Chicago: University of Chicago Press, 1985.

## Argentina

Argentina is the second-largest country in South America. It has an area of 1.1 million square miles that is equivalent to the size of the United States east of the Mississippi. It has a population of approximately 37 million people. Argentina was visited by Spanish navigator Juan Diaz de Solias in 1516, and SPAIN established a permanent colony here in 1580. Argentina declared its independence in 1816, and the United States established diplomatic ties in 1822.

American-Argentine relations have been marked by periods of controversy that in large measure have been fueled by Argentine concerns about the United States's true intentions in promoting regional unity and American fears that Argentina would become a spearhead for foreign influence within the Western Hemisphere. On Argentina's side these concerns became manifest at the first International (Pan) American Conference in 1889. SECRETARY OF STATE JAMES BLAINE had proposed such a conference in 1881, but it was not until he returned to the proposition in 1889 that the conference was held. Its focus shifted from war prevention to trade promotion. From Argentina's point of view, proposals for low tariffs, compulsory arbitration of disputes, and reciprocal trade agreements constituted but a cover for making Latin America into an American market and the states of the region into "tributaries." Argentina's skepticism of American hemispheric leadership continued into the next century. On the economic front it resented American tariffs on Argentine beef and grain. Argentine anger reached the point that in 1940 it placed an embargo on all American imports. Tempers cooled shortly thereafter, and in October 1941 a new trade agreement was reached between the two nations.

On the political front Argentina continued to resist calls for regional unity. It remained neutral during WORLD WAR II. At the Eighth International Conference of American States at Lima, Peru, in 1938 Argentina left the conference before it unanimously endorsed a declaration supporting common action to meet common dangers. In January 1942 Argentina, along with CHILE, blocked a U.S. effort at a ministers of foreign affairs conference to obtain binding agreements on the part of Latin American states to break diplomatic relations with the Axis powers. In the end the proposed agreement was left as a recommendation. Of particular concern to the United States at this time was Argentina's fascist orientation. A military coup in 1943 brought the colonel's clique into power led by Juan Perón, who American officials saw as being a neo-Nazi. Argentina belatedly declared war on Germany and JAPAN. It did so March 27, 1945. In January 1944, under pressure from the Allies, it had reluctantly broken off diplomatic relations with the Axis powers. The half-hearted nature of this decision was reflected in public accusations by the United States that in spite of this act Argentina had "deserted the Allied cause."

Argentina had also been absent at the Inter-American Conference on Problems of War and Peace held at Chapultepec in early 1945. This conference endorsed the concept of regional security and pledged all states to support the MONROE DOCTRINE. With its declaration of war Argentina also signed the ACT OF CHAPULTEPEC. This both cleared the way for Argentina to join the UNITED NATIONS and for the United States to lift the economic sanctions it had imposed after the coup and to recognize the Argentine government.

The uneasy nature of U.S.-Argentine relations did not change after the war. The United States tried to block Perón's election as president by publicly circulating a "blue book" that chronicled Argentina's wartime pro-Nazi leanings. The move failed and only helped cement Perón's standing as a strong nationalist. Relations improved in the 1950s and 1960s, only to become strained again when President JIMMY CARTER criticized Argentina's HUMAN-RIGHTS policy and later when the United States supported British claims to the Falkland Islands in the 1982 Falkland Islands/Islas Malvinas War.

Over the past decade the most significant issues in U.S.-Argentine relations have centered on Argentina's financial situation and its ability to repay its international debt. The Argentine debt problem was one of the major forces propelling the United States to put forward the BAKER and BRADY PLANS in an effort to stabilize international financial relations.

See also DEBT CRISIS.

**Further reading:** Tulchin, Joseph. *Argentina and the United States.* New York: Macmillan, 1990.

## arms control

Arms control approaches the problem of curbing international violence from a different perspective from that of DISARMAMENT, its major conceptual competitor. It does not focus on reducing or eliminating the number of weapons in existence per se but tries to place restraints on the use of force. The guiding assumption behind arms control is that the root causes of international conflict lie in the political realm. Weapons aggravate tensions between states, but they do not cause them. Proponents of arms control further assume that in spite of their differences, potential enemies have an interest in cooperating so that the most damaging and disruptive features of a conflict will not come to pass.

Two principal forms of arms control agreements have been negotiated. The first involves agreements that are intended to avoid or to control crisis situations. One example is the Hot Line and Modernization Agreements (1963) that established direct radio, wire-telegraph, and satellite communications between the United States and the Soviet Union. A second example is the Conference on Confidence and Security Building Measures (1984) that produced an agreement requiring all states to give two years' advance notice of any large-scale military exercise, provide a calendar of out-of-garrison military maneuvers to which observers could be sent, and accept three verification challenges per year.

The second type of arms control agreement addresses the size and composition of military forces. The STRATEGIC ARMS LIMITATION TALKS (SALT I and II) are examples. Other examples include the 1963 Limited Test Ban Treaty that banned nuclear testing in the atmosphere, outer space, and underwater and placed restrictions on underground testing; the 1968 Non-Proliferation Treaty that sought to stop the spread of nuclear weapons to nonnuclear states; and the COMPREHENSIVE TEST BAN TREATY (1996) that has been signed but was rejected by the U.S. Senate.

Arms control agreements need not take the form of formally negotiated treaties. They may also consist of informally agreed upon "traffic rules" and unilateral actions undertaken in the spirit of self-restraint. An example of the former would be the mutual announcements made by the United States and Russia after the COLD WAR that they would "detarget" their nuclear weapons. Examples of unilateral actions include General Secretary Mikhail Gorbachev's announcement that the Soviet Union would suspend its nuclear testing and Christmas bombing moratoriums by the United States during VIETNAM.

From about 1946–57, disarmament proposals rather than arms control dominated the American foreign policy agenda. Although a change in outlook had already begun, the severity of the CUBAN MISSILE CRISIS caused policy makers to look beyond disarmament to arms control as a vehicle for reducing the threat of nuclear war between the United States and the Soviet Union. The high and low point of arms control were the SALT treaties. They were ambitious treaties to cap the number of nuclear missiles and warheads, but they did not bring about any real reduction in the size of the two nuclear arsenals. Compliance and verification problems in the management of arms control agreements also produced a sense of disenchantment with the products of lengthy arms control negotiations. Led by President RONALD REAGAN, American officials began a two-pronged search for an alternative to arms control. One path led in the direction of renewed interest in disarmament and an effort to produce real reductions in nuclear arsenals. The STRATEGIC ARMS REDUCTION TALKS (START) symbolized this effort. The second path led in the direction of pursuing a viable defense against nuclear weapons. The STRATEGIC DEFENSE INITIATIVE (SDI), or "Star Wars," symbolized this quest.

Nuclear arms control has had a checkered history. In the words of one longtime observer it has had a series of "wins, losses, and draws." Advocates credit it with having slowed the global arms race, helped avoid crises, and saved significant amounts of money. Critics argue that it served only to weaken the United States, making the country more vulnerable to Soviet pressure, and failed to stop the spread of nuclear weapons. The debate rages as strong as ever in the post–cold war era as arms control is forced to address new issues, such as the Chinese nuclear threat, the increased importance of multilateral over bilateral agreements, the proliferation of weapons of mass destruction, dual-use technologies, and the need to place curbs on the proliferation of conventional weapons. May 2003 saw Russia and the United States take a new step forward in arms control. That month the Russian parliament's lower house ratified the STRATEGIC OFFENSIVE REDUCTIONS TREATY (also known as the Moscow Treaty), which was signed by U.S. president Bush and Russian president Vladimir Putin on May 24, 2002. The U.S. Senate had approved the treaty in March, but Russia delayed action due to its opposition to the IRAQ WAR.

See also DETERRENCE; NUCLEAR DEFENSE STRATEGY; RUSSIA; WEAPONS OF MASS DESTRUCTION.

**Further reading:** Dunn, Lewis. *Controlling the Bomb: Nuclear Proliferation in the 1980s.* New Haven, Conn.: Yale University Press, 1982; George, Alexander, et al. *U.S.-Soviet Security Cooperation: Achievements, Failures, Lessons.* New York: Oxford University Press, 1988; Haley, Edward P. et al., eds. *Nuclear Strategy, Arms Control, and the Future.* Boulder, Colo.: Westview, 1983; Schelling Thomas, and Morton Halperin. *Strategy and Arms Control.* New York: Pergamon-Brassey's Classic, 1985.

## Arms Control and Disarmament Agency

The Arms Control and Disarmament Agency (ACDA) was created in 1961 with the mission of strengthening American national security by "formulating, advocating, negotiating, implementing, and verifying effective arms control, non-proliferation, and disarmament policies." President JOHN KENNEDY saw a need for such an agency as a political counterweight to what he and others had come to perceive as the routine and overly zealous advocacy of new weapons systems by the DEFENSE DEPARTMENT. ACDA was integrated into the STATE DEPARTMENT on April 1, 1999, as part of a general reorganization that also brought the U.S. Information Agency into the State Department.

The ACDA was typically regarded as a fringe bureaucratic player in the national security policy process, but it was not without influence. Its influence reached its highest point with the STRATEGIC ARMS LIMITATION TALKS (SALT) I TREATY. Its influence declined as HENRY KISSINGER, who at different times served as both SECRETARY OF STATE and NATIONAL SECURITY ADVISOR for the Nixon-Ford administrations, took control over arms control negotiations. ACDA's influence rebounded somewhat during the Carter administration but fell out of favor in the Reagan administration with its early emphasis on building up military power rather than restraining it. Reagan's second-term interest in arms control provided a boost for ACDA's fortunes, but it acted under considerable guidance from the White House. President GEORGE H. W. BUSH, who succeeded Reagan, preferred to rely upon his own White House staff and the National Security staff for ARMS CONTROL advice.

Noticeable pressure began to build to shut down ACDA in the early 1990s with the end of the COLD WAR. A December 1992 report by the inspector general's office of the State Department concluded that ACDA "has lost ground to other agencies in recent years and its use as an instrument of government has declined." It concluded that no consensus existed on what role ACDA should play in the future or if there even was a role for it. Vice President Al Gore identified reforming the State Department as an important goal in his plan to reinvent government and the absorption by State of ACDA was included in that plan.

Still, little might have come from the idea had Senator JESSE HELMS (R-N.C.), chair of the Senate Foreign Relations Committee, not been a vociferous opponent of the ACDA as well as the UNITED STATES AGENCY FOR INTERNATIONAL DEVELOPMENT. The need to placate Helms became the final impetus to implementing the reorganization.

In its last years ACDA operated with four bureaus: Intelligence, Verification and Information Management; Multilateral Affairs; Nonproliferation; and Strategic and Eurasian Affairs. Upon its termination and incorporation into the State Department, the key functions of the ACDA were placed under the policy oversight of the under secretary of state for arms control and international security. This official also serves as the senior adviser to the president and secretary of state on arms control, nonproliferation, and disarmament. There are four bureaus specifically designated to carry out this work: Arms Control, Nonproliferation, Political-Military Affairs, and Verification and Compliance. This last bureau produces the president's annual report to Congress on adherence to and compliance with arms control agreements.

See also CARTER, JIMMY; DISARMAMENT; FORD, GERALD; NIXON, RICHARD; REAGAN, RONALD.

## arms transfers

Arms transfers, a category that includes but is not limited to arms sales, play a significant role in American foreign policy because they have become a standard instrument by which the United States seeks to exert its influence in world affairs. The Arms Export Control Act of 1974 requires that all arms transfers valued at more than $25 million be reported to CONGRESS. A 1980 study showed that more than 100 cases each year were reported. The same study showed that the United States received nearly 10,000 requests per year from foreign governments for military equipment and that more than 20,000 requests per year were received from private companies seeking to obtain export licenses.

States seek to sell and acquire weapons for a variety of purposes, and the lack of fit between the goals of the sellers and buyers often results in tension and conflict. For arms sellers three strategic reasons for the sale are most commonly advanced. First, arms transfers can provide leverage over the recipient. They serve as a visible sign of support for the recipient. Second, they can be used to advance specific security objectives. These security goals may relate to the specific state receiving weapons or be geared to promoting regional stability. Third, arms transfers can be used as part of a bargaining process to obtain specific concessions, such as access to military bases.

None of these rationales is without problems. Leverage tends to be fleeting and diminishes over time. In fact, one can speak of situations in which "reverse leverage" is created. The foreign supplier becomes trapped in its support of a government. South VIETNAM is an example. Regardless of how poorly the war effort went forward, the United States came to feel that it had little choice but to continue to prop up and support the government of the day. IRAN and the PHILIPPINES are also good examples. In each case the government, that of the shah in Iran and Ferdinand Marcos in the Philippines, was a loyal ally of the United States that became corrupt and isolated from the public. The United States was so closely identified with these regimes due to arms transfers that it came to be seen as part of the problem. In Iran the United States never succeeded in distancing itself from the shah. It was able to do so in the Marcos case but only with great difficulty. Iran is also an example of how efforts to promote regional stability or the security of a specific state may backfire. The United States provided arms to Iran in hopes that it would help contain the spread of communism. The shah accepted these weapons as a way of making Iran a regional superpower. Rather than bring about stability these arms sales helped fuel a regional arms race. TURKEY illustrates the difficulty of using arms sales as part of a bargaining strategy to obtain basing rights. Once a military base is established, the host state and not the arms provider gains the bargaining advantage. Turkey demanded increased access to American markets as the price for renewing basing rights in 1985. It also suspended or threatened to suspend these rights in retaliation for what it saw as anti-Turkish policies over Cyprus and Armenian rights.

To these strategic reasons can be added an economic imperative. Producing modern weapons systems is expensive. One way of holding down costs is to produce for export. Assembly lines stay "hot," and the per unit price goes down. In some cases the economic rationale leads to situations in which some weapons systems are produced by American firms solely for export. The F-15 fighter by McDonnell Douglas is one example. The M-1A2 tank by General Dynamic Corporation is another. The economic and strategic rationales behind arms transfers are not always compatible with one another. Security concerns may call for limiting the availability of a weapons system while economic considerations point in the opposite direction.

There have been five major turning points in the development of U.S. arms transfer policy. The first came in the early 1960s when the Kennedy administration began promoting arms sales to U.S. allies as a means of narrowing the size of the growing U.S. balance of payments problem. President JOHN KENNEDY felt that a major reason for the balance of payments problem was the high cost the United States incurred in stationing troops abroad. Arms purchases would help balance the ledger. The second turning point came in RICHARD NIXON's administration when it sought to use arms sales and arms transfers as a means of shifting the primary responsibility for stopping communism from the United States to key regional states. Significantly, this shift largely coincided with the 1973 OIL crisis that greatly increased the buying power of America's Middle East allies. No longer did they have to settle for obsolete military technologies. They could demand and purchase state-of-the-art equipment. U.S. arms transfers increased 150 percent from 1968 to 1977. In 1970 sales to Iran were valued at $13.3 million. In 1974 they had reached $3.9 billion.

The third turning point in the evolution of U.S. arms transfer policy came with the Carter administration. President JIMMY CARTER sought to make arms transfers an exceptional tool of foreign policy rather than a normal instrument. In the first 15 months after this policy shift was put in place, 614 requests from 92 states for more than $1 billion in weapons were turned down. Pakistan, Taiwan, and Iran were among those who had requests denied. It was not long before the Carter administration found it difficult to work within its own guidelines. Major exceptions included the sale of seven AWACs to Iran and a $1.8 billion arms deal with SOUTH KOREA that compensated it for a reduction in the size of U.S. forces stationed there. Even the CAMP DAVID ACCORDS, Carter's major diplomatic triumph, required arms transfers to cement the deal. ISRAEL was given $2.2 billion in new arms credits, and EGYPT was given $1.5 billion.

The Reagan and Bush administrations embraced the Nixon viewpoint that arms transfers were an acceptable and normal instrument of foreign policy. Reagan used them as a tool in the global struggle against communism, and Bush used them to solidify relations with key allies. In its first three months in office the Reagan administration offered some $15 billion in weapons and other forms of military assistance to other states. Reagan's most controversial arms transfer occurred early in his administration when he approved an $8.5 billion arms deal with SAUDI ARABIA that critics argued gave that country an offensive capability that threatened Israel.

A fifth phase began after the PERSIAN GULF WAR. The unique feature of this period is not the approach taken by the United States but rather the global context in which arms sales are made. First, the overall value of arms traded has declined significantly. Between 1991 and 1995 arms sales averaged $32.3 billion. This is down 45 percent from its 1985 level. In the Middle East, along with other countries, the United States called for an end to arms transfers to the region. Second, the demise of the Soviet Union means that one of the world's major arms exporters, and one that often was a key supplier in regional arms races with the United States, is no longer a major force. In some respects this has made the United States the world's leading arms exporter by default.

Both the BILL CLINTON and GEORGE W. BUSH administrations have continued to view arms transfers as normal instruments of foreign policy with the result that the United States now dominates the world market, accounting for almost one-half of all weapons exported. In the 1990s the United States exported more than $96 billion worth of weapons. In 1998 the Clinton administration sold more than $31 billion in weapons to more than 140 states. In 1995 it opposed a congressional plan that would have limited arms sales to democratically elected governments that respected HUMAN RIGHTS. Clinton said this proposal intruded on the president's authority to conduct foreign policy and that no single set of criteria should take precedence over others in making arms transfer decisions. After the SEPTEMBER 11, 2001, terrorist attacks, Bush asked CONGRESS for the authority to waive all restrictions on American military aid and weapons exports for five years as part of the war against TERRORISM.

Critics of arms transfers as an instrument of American foreign policy assert that they have done little to enhance American global security and that they have had a harmful effect on developing states by distorting their spending patterns. From 1960 to 1987 military spending among developing countries rose from $24 billion to $145 billion, an average of 7.5 percent per year. In 1990 it rose to $242 billion. Accompanying this economic cost is also a human cost that is measured in the lives lost due to wars and the use of antipersonnel mines. Critics also contend that while arms exports provide jobs in the United States in the short run, they do little to address the more fundamental problem of economic adjustment that the defense industry faces in an era of smaller defenses budgets.

See also MILITARY-INDUSTRIAL COMPLEX; RUSSIA.

**Further reading:** Markusen, Ann R., and Sean Costagan, eds. *Arming the Future: A Defense Industry for the 21st Century.* New York: Council on Foreign Relations, 1999; Neuman, Stephanie, and Robert Harkavey, eds. *Arms Transfers in the Modern World.* New York: Praeger, 1980; Pierre, Andrew J. *The Global Politics of Arms Sales.* Princeton, N.J.: Princeton University Press, 1982.

## Articles of Confederation

After declaring its independence from GREAT BRITAIN and prior to writing and ratifying the CONSTITUTION, the United States was governed at the national level by the Articles of Confederation. It provided for a league of sovereign states rather than for a strong central government. No executive power existed. CONGRESS was given the traditional foreign policy powers of the British Crown: to make war and peace, to send and receive ambassadors, to enter into treaties, and to conduct Indian affairs. States were prohibited from conducting foreign policy, engaging in war without the consent of Congress, or maintaining anything but a militia by way of armed forces. The division of labor created by the Articles of Confederation left states in full control of their domestic affairs. Congress had no power to legislate internally, tax, or regulate commerce.

The absence of any concrete domestic powers soon became a major foreign policy liability. The TREATY OF PARIS that ended the AMERICAN REVOLUTION called for the United States to repay its debts and money owed to Great Britain for confiscated property. Yet, Congress under the Articles of Confederation could not force states to do so. Intent upon receiving payment, Great Britain threatened to intervene militarily. Uncertainty over the ability of the United States to meet its international commitments led the NETHERLANDS and FRANCE to hesitate to enter into treaties. The constitutional convention addressed this problem through the Supremacy Clause that established treaties, including those already entered into, as "the supreme law of the land." The Supreme Court invoked the Supremacy Clause in *WARE V. HYLTON*, a decision that required Virginians to pay their Revolutionary War–era debts to Great Britain.

See also AMERICAN REVOLUTION.

**Further reading:** Giunta, Mary A., ed. *The Emerging Nation: A Documentary History of Foreign Relations under the Articles of Confederation, 1780–1789.* 3 vols. Washington, D.C.: National Historical Publications and Records Commission, 1996.

## Asian financial crisis

The Asian financial crisis of 1997–98 represented a new and serious threat to the stability of the international financial system. Up until this point, the principal financial threat to the health of the international economy was seen as residing in the inability of the governments of developing nations to repay their debts. The Asian financial crisis was different—it was rooted in the new mobility of privately held money and the failure of governments and international organizations to develop a capacity for monitoring and managing these capital flows.

Beyond its strictly financial impact, the Asian financial crisis had a major psychological effect because the stunning economic growth of Asian states had spawned talk of a "Pacific Century." JAPAN was the leading economy in the region. In 1981 the U.S. balance of trade deficit with Japan was $18.5 billion. In 1987 it had jumped to $56.3 billion. Between 1960 and 1986, the share of world trade accounted for by SOUTH KOREA, TAIWAN, Hong Kong, and Singapore grew from 6 to 18 percent. Collectively they accounted for more than 60 percent of manufactured exports from developing states.

The crisis began in THAILAND in July 1997 when foreign investors, fearing that a devaluation of the Thai currency would undermine the profitability of their loans, began selling their Thai currency holdings. The Thai government tried but failed to maintain the value of its currency in the face of this sell-off and ended up running out of foreign exchange reserves. Between July 1997 and March 1998, Indonesian, South Korean, and Thai exchange rates dropped between 36 and 72 percent. In South Korea unemployment jumped from 2.5 percent in 1997 to 7.6 percent in August 1998, a level not experienced for 30 years.

The root causes of the Asian financial crisis are complex. In part they are rooted in the questionable domestic economic foundations on which the rapid growth of these economies had been built. Commonly referred to as "crony capitalism," a close association had developed between banks, governments, and private firms that permitted wasteful and nonproductive investments and borrowing. Root causes are also found in the volume of private funds being invested worldwide by large institutional investors managing pension and mutual funds. The depth of the financial crisis also was in part due to the actions of the INTERNATIONAL MONETARY FUND (IMF). It insisted that the same remedies used to deal with the Third World DEBT CRISIS be applied here. Critics asserted that these remedies were self-defeating because economic austerity measures increased the likelihood of slow short-term economic growth and would encourage investment managers to move their funds elsewhere in search of greater immediate profits.

The Asian financial crisis is important on several levels. First, as with the debt crises of the 1980s, the United States was once gain confronted with a situation in which it could not escape leadership responsibilities if the international financial system was to avert collapse. Second, it brought forward calls for reforming the IMF's lending policies and raised doubts about the wisdom of concentrating so much economic power in international organizations that to a degree were beyond the control of governments and citizens. Third, it raised the possibility that international financial relations were entering a new and dangerous era. Alan Greenspan, chair of the U.S. Federal Reserve, observed that along with the Mexican crisis of 1995, the Asian crisis may be the model for a new high-tech international financial system. He noted that it was a system that appeared fully stable but then will behave as if a dam has burst. The problem, he admitted, is that we do not yet really understand how the system works or why the dam breaks.

See also MEXICO.

**Further reading:** Hunter, William C. et al., eds. *The Asian Financial Crisis: Origins, Implications, and Solutions.* Boston: Kluwer Academic Press, 1999.

## Atlantic Charter

The Atlantic Charter was a statement of British and American war aims that came out of a secret meeting between President FRANKLIN ROOSEVELT and Prime Minister Winston Churchill. The conference took place in Placentia Bay, Newfoundland, on August 9–13, 1941. It was the first of the wartime conferences between Roosevelt and Churchill. The Soviet Union, which had been invaded by GERMANY in June 1941, was not invited. The conference produced one clear-cut military commitment on the part of the United States. The American navy would now convoy British ships across the Atlantic as far as Iceland. The continued attachment of CONGRESS to a neutral foreign policy led Roosevelt to delay announcing this policy until September 11 when a German submarine torpedoed the USS *Greer.* Roosevelt did not mention that the *Greer* had been shadowing a German U-boat for three hours prior to the attack.

The most enduring accomplishment of the meeting was the signing of Atlantic Charter. This document constituted a statement of Anglo-American war aims. It contained eight points. First, neither the United States nor Great Britain sought to acquire new territory through the war. Second, there were to be no territorial changes made against the wishes of the people involved. Third, the right of all people to choose their own form of government was recognized. Fourth, they favored free access to trade and raw materials. Fifth, they wished to see improved collaboration among all states to improve labor standards, economic advancement, and social security. Sixth, they wanted a peace that would secure the freedom of all peoples from fear and want. Seventh, they sought freedom of the seas. And, eight, they advocated a peace that rejected the use of force and favored disarmament with the ultimate establishment of a permanent system of general security.

Reaction in the United States to the announcement of the Atlantic Charter at the end of the conference was one of disappointment. Advocates of intervention into the war hoped for more than this list of vague statements that were reminiscent of WOODROW WILSON'S FOURTEEN POINTS and Roosevelt's New Deal rhetoric. Roosevelt's isolationist opponents correctly pointed out that the Atlantic Charter was a major step toward open support of Great Britain and participation in the war against Germany.

The Atlantic Charter became an important propaganda tool in the war against Germany and JAPAN. Forty-six states would sign the document. The SOVIET UNION officially gave its support to the Atlantic Charter as well but made it clear that it intended to acquire territory from POLAND and reacquire the BALTIC STATES. Foreshadowing future U.S.-Soviet disagreements about the shape of the post–WORLD WAR II world, in December 1941 Joseph Stalin commented: "I thought the Atlantic Charter was directed against those people who were trying to establish world domination. It now looks as if the Charter was directed against the USSR."

See also AMERICA FIRST COMMITTEE; ISOLATIONISM; NEUTRALITY ACTS; RUSSIA.

# B

## Baker Plan

The Baker Plan was put forward in September 1985 by Secretary of the Treasury James Baker at a meeting of the WORLD BANK as the Reagan administration's strategy for addressing the international DEBT CRISIS that had begun in the early 1980s. Developing nations had become heavily dependent on short-term loans from commercial banks as a source of development funds. Slow growth and high interest rates in economically advanced states plus high energy prices conspired to create a global recession in which demand for their exports had seriously weakened, leaving these states without adequate funds to service their debts. At first the United States worked with the INTERNATIONAL MONETARY FUND and commercial banks to provide countries with an infusion of money to help them over the initial crisis period. By 1985 it had become clear that this ad hoc approach to addressing the problem was not producing economic growth nor reducing the level of Third World indebtedness.

The Baker Plan contained three elements: (1) debtor countries were expected to pursue structural adjustment policies that would increase the efficiency of their economies and make them more attractive to foreign investment, (2) commercial banks would lend new money to debtor states, and (3) international institutions would provide additional loans. By 1987–88 it was clear that the Baker Plan had not helped countries grow out of their debt. Many were becoming even more indebted.

Observers have identified several problems that the Baker Plan was not able to overcome. It was not able to generate enough new money to produce real growth in debtor states. The plan had envisioned an additional $20 billion from commercial banks and $9 billion from international lending agencies, such as the International Monetary Fund. While the actual amount of new money provided by commercial banks is subject to debate, studies suggest that between 1986 and 1988, the amount of new financing provided by commercial banks did not exceed the money they received in interest payments. Also, the Baker Plan was not able to guarantee that debtor states would undertake a consistent pattern of economic reforms. Without a positive record of reform, investors lacked confidence in the ability of local economies to generate growth even with new money being made available.

The overall record of the Baker Plan was mixed. Some debtor states made progress in reducing the size of their indebtedness, and the threat to the stability of the international financial system receded. Still, not enough growth was generated to push the debt problem off of the international agenda. In 1989 the United States put forward the BRADY PLAN as a further attempt to address this problem. The Baker Plan is significant because of the leadership role that the United States assumed in international economic matters. Up until this point the Reagan administration had shown little evidence of any interest in exercising such leadership; without it, serious disruptions in international financial relations may have occurred. At the time some commentators saw the debt crisis as the most severe challenge to the international financial system since the Great Depression of the 1930s.

See also BUSH, GEORGE H. W.; REAGAN, RONALD.

## ballistic missile defense

The purpose of a ballistic missile defense (BMD) system is to protect a society against an adversary's offensive missiles. The desirability and feasibility of BMD systems have been debated by American policy makers and strategists since the 1960s. The debate has often been intense because a BMD system negates one of the key principles behind MUTUAL ASSURED DESTRUCTION. It holds that stability (and peace) in the nuclear age are best ensured when neither side has the ability to prevent a retaliatory strike. In essence, each society's population is held hostage, and neither side can make the first move.

BMD systems were proposed as far back as the Eisenhower era. Conceptually they were extensions of the air defense systems developed in WORLD WAR II to shoot down attacking enemy aircraft. The first extensive public debate centered around the antiballistic missile (ABM) system proposed in the Johnson administration by SECRETARY OF DEFENSE ROBERT MCNAMARA. At issue was the construction of an anti-Soviet system. McNamara opposed such a system in large measure because he feared that it would set off an expensive arms race. Others opposed it because of its cost and its destabilizing effect on the nuclear balance. McNamara lost the political battle within the Johnson administration but was able to introduce the ABM in 1967 as a "light" system designed to protect against an emerging Chinese nuclear force. He warned against expanding it into an anti-Soviet system.

President RICHARD NIXON had little interest in an anti-Chinese ABM system. A central feature of his foreign policy was DÉTENTE with the Soviet Union (see RUSSIA). ARMS CONTROL played a key part in the design of this strategy. Negotiating agreements required that Nixon have something to trade. The Soviet Union had already begun construction of an ABM system, so Nixon transformed the U.S. system into an anti-Soviet ABM and then concluded the 1972 ANTI-BALLISTIC MISSILE SYSTEM TREATY that prohibited either side from developing and testing ABM technology or constructing new ABM systems beyond the two permitted in the treaty.

The construction of a BMD next emerged as a controversial issue when President RONALD REAGAN proposed the STRATEGIC DEFENSE INITIATIVE (SDI) as a means of freeing the United States from the threat of NUCLEAR WAR. As proposed by Reagan SDI was to be a long-term research agenda that was to bear fruit in the 1990s. Instead, in early 1987 the Reagan administration began exploring the possibility of an early deployment of such a system. The GEORGE H. W. BUSH administration that followed it declared that SDI as a leak-proof system had been oversold but continued pursuing a BMD system. Bush's version was called "brilliant pebbles" and involved stationing missiles in space that would ram and destroy attacking enemy missiles thousands of miles from the United States. President BILL CLINTON's administration officially terminated SDI when in May 1993 the SDI Office was closed and replaced by a Ballistic Missile Defense Office that would develop follow-on missiles to the Patriot system used in the PERSIAN GULF WAR.

The death of SDI did not mark the end of efforts to build a BMD. The Republican Party's Contract with America called for building a BMD system by 2003, and REPUBLICAN PARTY legislators introduced legislation to this effect. In 1995 Clinton vetoed it but did agree in 1996 to a 3+3 system in which his administration would spend three years designing and testing BMD systems and three years

deploying one. Missile tests in 1998 by IRAN and NORTH KOREA created new pressures for a BMD system, and in 1999 both the House and Senate passed legislation calling upon the United States to deploy a BMD as soon as technologically feasible, with 2005 being set as the target date.

Clinton's proposed BMD plan constituted a significant departure from those that preceded it. He rejected a space-based system in favor of one that relied heavily upon ground-based interceptors supported by a network of ground-based radars and space-based infrared sensors. The first deployments were expected to be made in Alaska with 20 high-speed interceptors capable of shooting down a limited number of incoming warheads. That number was expected to grow to as many as 100 in the first phase and 250 in the second. In 2000 Clinton announced that he would leave the decision on building a BMD system to his successor.

A payload launch vehicle carrying a prototype exoatmospheric kill vehicle is launched from Meck Island at the Kwajalein Missile Range on December 3, 2001, for a planned intercept of a ballistic missile target over the central Pacific Ocean. *(Department of Defense)*

President GEORGE W. BUSH campaigned as an ardent supporter of a BMD system. Once in office he moved swiftly to have a rudimentary system in place by 2004 but did not commit his administration to a specific plan. Early indications were that he would proceed with an Alaska basing plan but include space- and sea-based interceptors. The Bush administration formally unveiled its national ballistic missile defense strategy in May 2003 with the release of a brief document entitled "National Policy on Ballistic Missile Defense." The document was essentially a public version of the National Security Presidential Directive 23 that Bush signed in December 2002 and offered no new details on administration plans. It called for stationing long-range missile interceptors in Alaska and California by September 2004.

The terms of the debate over the merits of a BMD system have changed little since the 1960s. And, in a sense, the debate has come full circle since, after the end of the COLD WAR in 1989, BMD systems are again being touted as "light" systems designed to protect the United States from emerging nuclear threats by ROGUE STATES rather than a massive Soviet launch.

Critics raise a number of objections. First, they question its technological feasibility. In 1999 the success rate was four hits in 18 tests. There were 10 consecutive failures beginning in 1991 Even Clinton's less technologically ambitious BMD system succeeded in only one of its first three tests and even then the tracking system failed. Cost is a second factor. More than $60 billion was spent on various BMD programs between 1980 and 2000. The General Accounting Office estimated that it could cost more than $28 billion to deploy a single BMD site by 2006. A third complaint involves the lack of clarity over what threat is being defended against. Rogue states and terrorist organizations do not need to use ballistic missiles to deliver warheads against the United States. There is also concern about the strategic impact of a BMD system. As McNamara feared it could fuel an arms race as all parties seek to gain a BMD system as well as sufficient offensive missiles to overwhelm one.

Advocates of a BMD concede that we might not know precisely the nature of the threats facing the United States but that we must take steps to protect ourselves. A flexible BMD system does this. Further, they assert that without a BMD, rogue states and other adversaries will be emboldened by vulnerability to their threats of attack against the United States or its allies. The lack of such a system might also prevent American officials from taking necessary action against such states. Citing the cost factor in building a BMD, advocates challenge the notion that other states could construct offsetting BMD systems.

Much of the controversy over building a BMD has centered on the ABM Treaty. Proceeding with a BMD requires abrogating the treaty, since it prohibits the development of such a system. To its defenders the ABM Treaty is the cornerstone of the network of nuclear arms control agreements put into place during the cold war. Its value is both symbolic and practical. Opponents hold it to be an anachronism from an earlier nuclear era that stands as an impediment to legitimate efforts at nuclear defense. Many also prefer unilateral efforts at security national security to those based on international agreements. In 2000 the UNITED NATIONS General Assembly voted 88–5 with 66 abstentions for a resolution calling for strict adherence to the treaty. The United States was one of the five states opposing the resolution. Of America's allies only Israel joined in supporting this position. RUSSIA and CHINA both supported adherence to the ABM Treaty. This UN vote reflected the Bush administration's determination to terminate American adherence to the treaty. Bush gave formal notice of his intent to withdraw in 2002.

**Further reading:** Carter, Ashton, and Daid Schwartz, eds. *Ballistic Missile Defense.* Washington, D.C.: Brookings, 1984.

## Baltic states

The Baltic states are comprised of three relatively small states that lie at the northwestern edge of eastern Europe and border on the Baltic Sea. Estonia has a population of 1.4 million people and is about the size of New Hampshire and Vermont with an area of 17,462 square miles. Lithuania has a population of 3.47 million and an area of 26,080 square miles, making it about the size of West Virginia. Latvia has a smaller population, 2,366,000 people, but is also about the size of West Virginia, with an area of 25,640 square miles. Because of their small size and proximity to Russia, the Baltic states have been a frequent target for foreign armies as well as for colonization by and political union with larger European states, including GERMANY, Sweden, POLAND, and RUSSIA.

A major turning point in the history of the Baltic states came with WORLD WAR I. The collapse of the czarist system in Russia combined with an invasion by the German army created political conditions that allowed each of these states to gain their formal independence and membership in the LEAGUE OF NATIONS. The United States recognized Estonia on July 22, 1922, and Latvia and Lithuania on July 28. Independence lasted some 22 years and effectively came to an end with the signing of the Molotov-Ribbentrop Nonaggression Pact between Nazi Germany and the Soviet Union on August 23, 1939. It gave Russia control over most of the Baltic states and in return gave Germany control over most of Poland. Estonia was occupied by Soviet forces in June 1940 and admitted into the Soviet Union as the Estonian Socialist Republic on August 6, 1940. Latvia was annexed by the Soviet Union the day before, and Latvia entered the Soviet Union on August 3. In each of the three Baltic republics mass deportation campaigns soon followed.

It was not surprising then that when Nazi Germany invaded Russia on June 22, 1941, many in the Baltic states welcomed the development in hopes of gaining back their independence. History documents all too clearly that this was not to be. German rule was as oppressive as Soviet rule. Thousands were sent to concentration camps, and hundreds of thousands were massacred. After the end of WORLD WAR II the Soviet Union reestablished control over the Baltic states and instituted yet another wave of mass deportations. It is estimated that between 1941 and 1952 some 30,000 Lithuanian families were exiled to Siberia, some 120,000 people were deported, and 300,000 were made political prisoners. Anti-Soviet GUERRILLA movements sprang up in the region and unsuccessfully challenged Stalin's rule. To speed the region's incorporation back into the Soviet Union, ethnic Russians were encouraged to immigrate into these states.

The United States never recognized the forced incorporation of the Baltic states into the Soviet Union after World War II. It did nothing of consequence to alter this situation because, unlike neighboring client states that remained outside of the Soviet Union, the Baltic states were formally part of it. The major symbolic move was to continue to recognize their embassies in Washington.

Momentous political change came to the Baltic states with Mikhail Gorbachev's ascension to power. Perestroika and glasnost spurred the development of nationalist feelings and dissident political parties. Estonia, Lithuania, and Latvia became leading forces in the dissolution of the Soviet Union. Attempts by the Soviet Union to reverse the pro-independence movement that was developing in the region through the use of military force failed. Lithuania declared its independence in March 1990, and the final Soviet troops left in 1993. Estonia declared its independence in 1991, and the last Soviet troops were withdrawn in August 1994. Virtually all Russian troops left Latvia at the same time. Its citizens passed a referendum on independence in March 1991.

Relations between Russia and the Baltic states are cordial, but a strong undercurrent of tension exists. A major contributing factor is the presence of a large ethic Russian minority in these countries that faces serious discrimination in the form of language laws that restrict their ability to obtain key positions in the government and businesses. Also of concern to Russia is the entry of these states into the NORTH ATLANTIC TREATY ORGANIZATION (NATO). By doing so they bring the armed forces of a historical enemy (and perhaps a future one) to Russia's doorstep, a condition

that czarist and Soviet leaders had long considered unacceptable. Finally, geography presents a problem. The Russian city of Kaliningrad is cut off from Russia by the Baltic states. Once belonging to Germany, Kaliningrad is strategically valuable to Russia because it gives that country a port city on the Baltic Sea.

The major U.S. diplomatic initiative with Lithuania, Latvia, and Estonia is the U.S.-Baltic Charter. This partnership is designed to promote the full integration of these states into Europe and establish the basis for economic, political, and security cooperation. Bilateral working groups have been established that focus on these issues. More broadly, this "Charter of Partnership" is part of the U.S.–Northern Europe Initiative, whose purpose it is to promote regional cooperation in northern Europe and strengthen U.S.-Nordic ties. One concrete goal is to integrate the Baltic states and northwest Russia into northern Europe by developing cross-border linkages.

**Further reading:** Birthe, Hansen, and Bertel Heurlin, eds. *The Baltic States in Global Politics.* New York: St. Martin's 1999; Ole, Norguard et al. *The Baltic States after Independence.* Williston, Vt.: Edward Elgar, 1996.

## *Banco Nacional de Cuba v. Sabbatino* (1964)

Jurisdictional struggles within the federal government to control the conduct of American foreign policy frequently pit CONGRESS against the PRESIDENT. Sometimes, however, they involve the judiciary. Unlike Congress the judiciary has not actively sought out confrontation, preferring instead to find avenues of cooperation. Two such avenues lie in the Act of State doctrine and the concept of "political questions." The case of *Underhill v. Hernandez* (1897) is a prime example of the SUPREME COURT employing the Act of State doctrine to withdraw itself from a foreign-policy dispute; *Banco Nacional de Cuba v. Sabbatino* is an example of how this doctrine can generate political controversy.

This case involved the nationalization of American sugar interests by Fidel Castro after he came to power in 1959. In early 1960 an American broker contracted to buy Cuban sugar. Before the sugar could be shipped President DWIGHT EISENHOWER cut the amount of sugar that could be imported into the United States as part of his administration's policy of trying to force Fidel Castro from power in CUBA. The Cuban government retaliated by nationalizing the property of firms in which Americans held a financial interest. The firm from which the sugar was bought was one such firm. The American broker then entered into a new contract with the now nationalized firm for the sugar. However, when the sugar was sold, the American broker did not send payment to the now nationalized Cuban firm but to Sabbatino, who was acting on behalf of the original

American owners. Banco Nacional de Cuba brought suit to recover its money, but a U.S. district court ruled that since the expropriation was carried out without compensation it violated international law and ruled against the Cuban government.

The Supreme Court overruled this decision. It acknowledged that the Act of State doctrine, which requires that every sovereign state is bound to respect the independence of every other sovereign state and not allow its courts to sit in judgment over the acts of other governments, is not required by the CONSTITUTION. But Justice John Harlan observed that it does have constitutional underpinnings and that it expresses "a strong sense of the judicial Branch that its engagement in the task of passing on the validity of foreign acts of states may hinder rather than further this country's pursuit of goals." Justice Harlan's opinion also rejected arguments that upholding the decision and ignoring the Act of State doctrine would contribute to U.S. foreign-policy objectives in Cuba.

Angered by the Court's decision, Congress passed the HICKENLOOPER AMENDMENT to prevent the courts from applying the Act of State doctrine unless instructed to do so by the executive branch. The case is also significant because it deals with Cuba and with issues involving nationalization of American property. The most recent effort to address these long-standing grievances is the HELMS-BURTON ACT that pitted Congress against the president and angered U.S. allies by bringing them into the battle of wills between Castro and Congress.

## Barbary pirates

The U.S. encounter with the Barbary pirates is significant for two reasons. First, it was instrumental in building the U.S. Navy. Second, it illuminated the problems of constructing foreign policy under the ARTICLES OF CONFEDERATION.

The Barbary pirates operated out of four northern African states: MOROCCO, Algiers, Tripoli, and Tunis. Only one, Morocco, was truly independent. The others were part of the Turkish Ottoman Empire. The rulers of these states made large sums of money by preying upon commercial traffic in the Mediterranean Sea—capturing ships, seizing their cargo, and holding it and their crews for ransom. Seafaring states could forestall such attacks by paying protection money. European states led by GREAT BRITAIN chose to pay because it was cheaper than going to war. The American colonies had benefited from such protection but lost it upon independence. Too poor to pay blackmail and too weak to defeat the Barbary pirates, American shipping was virtually forced out of the Mediterranean Sea.

Between the late 1780s and early 1790s, Algiers captured more than a dozen American ships and held more than 100 Americans as slaves. In March 1794 CONGRESS responded to this situation by authorizing the construction of six frigates to protect American ships in the Mediterranean. These ships formed the nucleus of the U.S. Navy. The United States also signed a peace treaty with Algiers wherein the United States agreed to pay ransom and an annual tribute. The following years treaties were signed with Tripoli and Tunis. Neither one called for the payment of annual tributes. These treaties proved to be largely worthless, and in 1801 Tripoli repudiated its treaty and declared war on the United States.

President THOMAS JEFFERSON, who had just been elected, responded to this challenge by increasing the size of the U.S. Navy and authorizing it to undertake defensive measures against the Barbary pirates. The United States signed a peace treaty in 1805, but the agreement did not put an end to acts of piracy against U.S. vessels. Nonetheless, in 1807 Jefferson withdrew the U.S. Navy from the Mediterranean Sea in order to deal with problems closer to home. It was only in 1815 that Congress took decisive action. Commodore Stephen Decatur was sent to the Mediterranean to defeat the Barbary pirates and dictate peace terms.

## Baruch Plan

The Baruch Plan is significant because it was the first official American plan put forward to deal with the problem of NUCLEAR WEAPONS. It was presented to the UNITED NATIONS (UN) in 1946 and named in honor of Bernard Baruch, a trusted adviser of President HARRY TRUMAN. The plan grew out of deliberations on the part of a committee headed by SECRETARY OF STATE DEAN ACHESON and Chairman of the Tennessee Valley Authority David Lilienthal.

The Baruch Plan called for international control of all phases of the development and use of atomic energy. The specific instrument was to be an International Atomic Development Authority that would operate under the supervision of the UN but whose actions would not be subject to a Security Council veto. Baruch envisioned the authority as responding with "immediate, swift, and sure punishment" to any state that tried to acquire nuclear weapons. The Soviet Union's (see RUSSIA) counterproposal stressed that international safeguards against the spread of atomic energy could only come into existence after the United States destroyed its (monopoly of) nuclear weapons. The Soviet Union also insisted that any international authority had to be subject to a Security Council veto. After three years of deliberation, efforts to implement the Baruch Plan were halted. This occurred some two months after the Soviet Union detonated its first atomic bomb on September 23, 1949.

The Baruch Plan is rooted in neo-Wilsonian INTERNATIONALISM and lies very much within the AMERICAN NATIONAL STYLE of conducting foreign policy. It emphasized a universal and legal solution to a politicomilitary problem by proposing the creation of an international body that would establish global rules for atomic power. Although a failure, the Baruch Plan served as a model for thinking about how to control atomic energy for the next decade. It stands in sharp contrast to the national security thinking that would arise in the 1960s, which emphasized the deterrent role of nuclear weapons and the maintenance of large nuclear inventories.

Doubt continues to exist today whether the United States was really serious about the proposal and whether it could have been implemented. CONGRESS was not interested in sharing U.S. atomic knowledge or placing it under international control. The McMahon Act permitted the armed forces to build atomic weapons. The military services had lobbied for this power. They had been largely excluded from the development of the Baruch Plan and were reluctant to relinquish control over atomic weapons technology. Implementation of the Baruch Plan faced a major theoretical and practical hurdle. Atomic energy was to be put under international control, but states were to retain full sovereignty in all other aspects of their foreign and domestic policies. Many observers noted that the inherent contradiction between these two positions made effective implementation highly unlikely.

See also ARMS CONTROL; COLD WAR; DISARMAMENT; WILSON, WOODROW.

## Bay of Pigs

The Bay of Pigs invasion of CUBA generally is viewed as one of the most significant American foreign blunders of the COLD WAR. Its roots lay in cold war hubris regarding the scope of American power, stereotyping of the enemy, and pathologies associated with SMALL-GROUP DECISION MAKING. Because the locale was the same and the policy makers in the United States largely were the same, the Bay of Pigs invasion is also linked with one of the major American foreign-policy successes of the cold war: the October 1962 CUBAN MISSILE CRISIS.

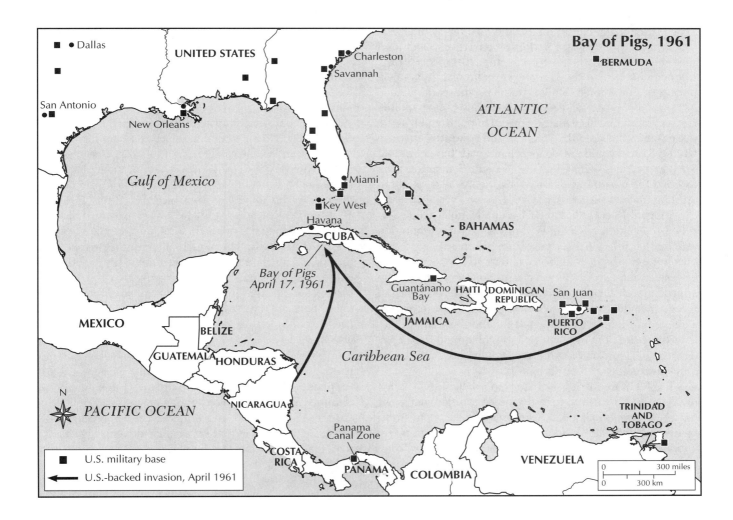

Although carried out by the Kennedy administration, planning for the Bay of Pigs dates back to the Eisenhower administration. Fidel Castro came to power in 1959, overthrowing longtime pro-American dictator Fulgencio Batista, whose rule had grown increasingly corrupt and repressive. Upon seizing power Castro quickly moved to initiate a series of economic and social reforms designed to lessen America's economic dominance of the Cuban economy. Among the actions he took was confiscating American sugar mills and other property without compensation. He also turned to RUSSIA for economic aid and, by so doing, declared that the MONROE DOCTRINE was dead. Gradually Castro's rhetoric, which was always nationalistic and anti-American, took on a harsh Marxist-Leninist tone.

Dating back at least to the PLATT AMENDMENT, the United States had always viewed Cuba as an integral element in its hemispheric national security system. The Eisenhower administration shared this view and, in March 1960, it ordered the CENTRAL INTELLIGENCE AGENCY (CIA) to organize Castro's removal from power. The vehicle was to be a band of Cuban exiles organized and trained by the CIA in GUATEMALA. Just before leaving the presidency Eisenhower cut off diplomatic relations with Cuba.

Foreign policy was a major issue in the presidential race between RICHARD NIXON and JOHN KENNEDY. Kennedy hit hard at the Eisenhower administration's permitting a "communist satellite" to be established in Cuba. As he would in BERLIN, President Kennedy came to define Cuba as a test of wills with the Soviet Union. Kennedy gave the go-ahead to the CIA's plan on the condition that the United States would not be associated with the operation. Such assurances were given and accepted in spite of the fact that the upcoming invasion was openly talked about in Washington and the press.

In April 1961 the 1,400 CIA-trained Cuban exile guerrilla force landed in Cuba. Within two days the operation was in shambles. Stiffer resistance than expected was encountered, the invasion force and its air support was less effective than expected, and no uprising took place. The approximately 1,000 surviving members of the invasion force surrendered and were sent to prisoner-of-war camps. They would later be exchanged for food and medicine. There was no denying America's involvement, and condemnation from even America's staunchest allies was quick in coming.

President Kennedy took full responsibility for the failed invasion and instituted a study to determine what went wrong. Among its major conclusions was the danger incurred by new administrations in undertaking major foreign-policy initiatives when high-ranking personnel did not know each other's strengths and weaknesses and when inherent tensions existed between "new" political leaders and "old" bureaucratic interests and ways of doing business.

Others acknowledge the importance of these points but place greater emphasis on a general failure of American policy makers to understand the limits of their own power and the true character of their opponents. Still others point to a phenomenon known as groupthink in which policy makers participating in a small group, such as those who approved and oversaw the Bay of Pigs invasion, lose contact with reality and make poor quality decisions.

See also EISENHOWER, DWIGHT; REVISIONISM.

**Further reading:** Blight, James, and Peter Kornbluh. *The Politics of Illusion: The Bay of Pigs Invasion Reexamined.* Boulder, Colo.: Lynne Rienner, 1997.

## Berlin crisis, 1948

Berlin was a divided city within a divided country. WORLD WAR II summit conferences, most notably at YALTA, had divided GERMANY into four occupation zones. Berlin, the capital of the Third Reich, was located 110 miles inside of the Russian control zone and was similarly divided into four zones. Informal agreements among the four occupying powers specified the routes that could be used to supply the forces stationed in the Western three sectors.

In December 1947 a Four Power meeting on the future of Germany ended in a deadlock. From this point forward the United States, GREAT BRITAIN, and FRANCE met to discuss Germany's future without Russian participation. A conference in London, in January 1948 that the Soviet Union did not attend, produced calls for rapid movement forward on the establishment of West German political institutions, including a constitution. Relations among the Four Powers deteriorated further when Russia withdrew from the allied Control Council in Berlin in March 1948 and declared that it no longer existed. In April Moscow stopped the shipment of military supplies to Western units in Berlin. On June 18 a common currency was introduced for the three Western zones. The Soviet Union responded the same day by declaring that the Western powers had no right to be in Berlin. All road traffic in and out of Berlin to the West was stopped and within days electricity, coal, food, and other supplies coming from the West were halted.

The Western powers rejected the Soviet claim that they had no right to be in Berlin and began a massive airlift of supplies to the city. At one point, planes landed every two minutes. Sixty long-range bombers capable of delivering atomic weapons were moved from the United States to Great Britain as a sign of resolve. Evidence suggests that Joseph Stalin hoped to use the Berlin crisis as a lever to force the West to negotiate a settlement of the German question on terms favorable to Moscow. In particular, he sought to reassert Four Power control over Germany and stop the

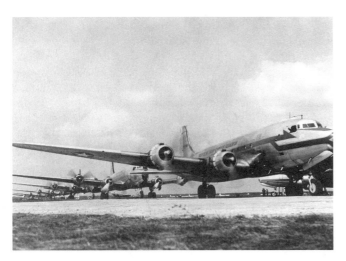

U.S. Air Force C-54s are lined up awaiting takeoff from Rhein-Main Air Base in Frankfurt for Berlin during the airlift in which the Allies flew thousands of tons of food, coal, and other supplies to the western sectors of Berlin daily. *(United States Air Force)*

movement toward the emergence of a West German state. The blockade was lifted in May 1949 after 324 days. During the crisis the Soviet Union attempted but failed to negotiate a delay in the formation of West Germany.

The Berlin crisis of 1948 was the first in a series of Soviet-American crises that centered on this city. It is significant as an early test of American resolve in the face of Soviet challenges and as one that helped reassure America's European allies of its commitment to their defense, thus pushing images of Munich and appeasement further into the past. As evidence of this commitment, in April 1949, the NORTH ATLANTIC TREATY ORGANIZATION (NATO) was established. It is also significant because of the shadow cast by nuclear weapons and long-range delivery systems that altered the local balance of military power that so favored the Soviet Union. Finally, it indicated how difficult it would be to change the geographic status quo in the COLD WAR.

See also BERLIN CRISIS, 1958; BERLIN CRISIS, 1961; BRINKMANSHIP; DETERRENCE; INTERNATIONAL CRISES; RUSSIA; WORLD WAR II.

**Further reading:** Clay, Lucius. *Decision in Germany.* Garden City, N.J.: Doubleday, 1950.

## Berlin crisis, 1958

The second Berlin crisis began in November 1958 when the Soviet Union announced that in six months it would end the Four Power occupation of Berlin. RUSSIA would sign a peace treaty with East Germany and turn control of East Berlin over to it. After the West's withdrawal, Berlin would technically become a free city, but it would be entirely beholden to the Communist East German government for its survival. Through this ultimatum Moscow once again hoped to curb West Germany's integration into West Europe and sow doubts about America's reliability as an ally.

A very real problem for the Soviet Union and its East German ally from the very outset had been the ability of East Germans to use Berlin as an exit route to the West. Since 1949 approximately 3 million had fled to the West. Numbered among them were many of East Germany's most skilled citizens. West Berlin had also come to serve as a key element of West Germany's espionage and propaganda network. Soviet leaders were also angry that the United States continued to call for unifying GERMANY through free elections and refused to recognize the East German government and that it was rearming West Germany.

The 1958 crisis was not an exact replay of the 1948 crisis because the military balance in Europe had shifted in Russia's favor since then. As before, the Soviet Union enjoyed a military advantage on the ground. U.S. atomic power was also negated through the world's first successful testing of an intercontinental missile and the launching of SPUTNIK in 1957. Now both the United States and the Soviet Union possessed the means to deliver nuclear weapons to each other's homeland.

President DWIGHT EISENHOWER rejected the advice of SECRETARY OF STATE DEAN ACHESON and others to challenge the Soviet position militarily by sending American military troops to West Berlin. Instead he turned to diplomacy. A May 1959 foreign ministers meeting yielded little. Eisenhower next invited Soviet leader Nikita Khrushchev to visit the United States in September 1959. At the Camp David meeting Khrushchev withdrew his threat to solve the "Berlin problem" unilaterally in return for an American promise to negotiate the matter at a Four Power Summit. The summit was set for May 1960. However, the Soviet downing of a U-2 spy plane on the eve of the summit plus the refusal of Eisenhower to apologize for the espionage led to the summit's collapse. Khrushchev announced that he would wait until the new American administration took office to take up the question of Berlin again.

See also BERLIN CRISIS, 1948; BERLIN CRISIS, 1961; BRINKSMANSHIP; COLD WAR; DETERRENCE; INTERNATIONAL CRISES; WORLD WAR II.

## Berlin crisis, 1961

The 1961 Berlin crisis was the last of the COLD WAR Berlin crises. This time it centered on the construction of the Berlin Wall. Its creation symbolized to all that the cold war would not be a passing phenomenon in world politics. For this reason the destruction of the Berlin Wall in 1989 is seen as the symbolic ending point of the cold war. It ushered in a particularly tense period in U.S.-Soviet relations that culminated in the CUBAN MISSILE CRISIS, a conflict that many in the West incorrectly thought was linked to the imminent onset of yet another Berlin crisis.

Soviet leader Nikita Khrushchev first met President JOHN F. KENNEDY in June 1961 in Vienna. The agenda included Berlin, Laos, and a nuclear test-ban treaty. As he had at the outset of the 1958 Berlin crisis, Khrushchev insisted that Berlin become a free city and that if the West refused to leave Berlin, making this possible, he would sign a separate peace treaty with East Germany. Kennedy refused, asserting that the West had a legitimate presence in Berlin by virtue of having defeated Nazi Germany. Although Kennedy thought he had stood firm against Khrushchev, the conventional wisdom holds that he did not and that Khrushchev came away from Vienna convinced that Kennedy could be intimidated.

Even before the summit conference began Kennedy and Khrushchev were ensnarled in a test of wills. Two weeks before the summit Kennedy, in a message entitled "On Urgent National Needs," asked CONGRESS for a significant increase in the defense budget and authority to construct a civil defense fallout shelter system. Khrushchev responded to this move in early July by announcing that the Soviet Union would increase its defense expenditures. Kennedy countered in late July with the public statement that "we cannot and will not permit the Communists to drive us out of Berlin." Kennedy followed with a specific request that called for increased defense spending together with doubling the draft and calling up reserve units.

On August 13, 1961, Khrushchev played his final cards. A barbed wire fence was erected between the two Berlins. It was followed by the construction of a concrete wall. In addition to international politics, the ongoing population flow from East to West Germany continued to alarm Soviet and East German officials. Approximately 200,000 East Germans had passed through Berlin to the West in 1961 before the wall was erected. These numbers had increased steadily as tensions rose. They joined almost 2.5 million Germans who fled to the West between 1948 and 1960.

There was nothing the West could do to tear the wall down. The best it could do was to send a contingent of troops from West Germany through East Germany to West Berlin as a show of its resolve. The troops arrived without incident. In June 1963 Kennedy traveled to Berlin for a show of continued support for the West Berlin people. Speaking to a large crowd he told them *"Ich bin ein Berliner"* (I am a Berliner).

According to some the larger significance of the third Berlin crisis is that by stemming the population flow out of East Germany the construction of the Berlin Wall actually led to the long-term reduction in tensions in Central Europe because it created a situation that the Soviet Union could live with: two Germanys with stable frontiers and populations each held in check by their protecting superpower. Also of significance is the fact that this stability would cause cold war competition to move out of Europe to points in the Third World, including CUBA and VIETNAM.

See also BERLIN CRISIS, 1948; BERLIN CRISIS, 1958; BRINKSMANSHIP; DETERRENCE; INTERNATIONAL CRISES; SUMMIT DIPLOMACY; WORLD WAR II.

**Further reading:** Smith, Jean. *The Defense of Berlin.* Baltimore: Johns Hopkins University Press, 1963.

**bin Laden, Osama** (1957–  ) *terrorist leader*
Believed to have been born in 1957, Osama bin Laden is the acknowledged head of the AL-QAEDA terrorist organization that was responsible for the SEPTEMBER 11, 2001, terrorist attacks on the World Trade Center and the Pentagon. He was placed on the FEDERAL BUREAU OF INVESTIGATION's 10 Most Wanted List in 1999. His capture or death was one of the main objectives of the January 2002 U.S. military campaign in AFGHANISTAN. He apparently survived that operation and is rumored to be alive in the mountainous region along the Afghanistan-PAKISTAN border. Osama bin Laden appeared in video clips and voice clips following the Afghan campaign but has not been seen in person.

Osama bin Laden was born in SAUDI ARABIA and is the youngest son of a wealthy Yemeni-born businessman. In school he was trained to become an engineer and was expected to work in his father's construction business. Osama bin Laden became radicalized in the 1970s with the Soviet invasion of Afghanistan. At that time he went to Pakistan to help organize and finance non-Afghan resistance forces to the Soviet occupation. In 1988 he founded al-Qaeda. Its goal is to build a transnational and strictly fundamentalist Islamic state. Osama bin Laden became further radicalized during the PERSIAN GULF WAR when Saudi Arabia allowed the United States to station troops in that country. He objected to allowing Western forces so close to Muslim sacred sites. Osama bin Laden was caught smuggling arms in 1991 and went to SUDAN, where he financed terrorist training camps.

His Saudi citizenship was revoked in 1994, and in 1996 he was expelled from Sudan after he was linked to the attempted assassination of Egyptian president Hosni Mubarak. From Sudan he fled to Afghanistan, where he joined forces with the Taliban and declared war against the United States. In 1998 he was linked to the bombings of U.S. EMBASSIES in Kenya and Tanzania. In retaliation for these attacks the Clinton administration launched cruise missile attacks on his camps in Afghanistan. Subsequent to

Osama bin Laden *(Getty Images)*

those attacks, Osama bin Laden has been linked to the attack on the USS *Cole* in Yemen in 2000. Following this attack the CENTRAL INTELLIGENCE AGENCY was authorized to undertake COVERT ACTION programs against him. At first this authorization was limited to capturing him. Later it was expanded to include the use of lethal force. Because of limited and spotty information no attack against him took place.

**Further reading:** Bodansky, Yossef. *Bin Laden: The Man Who Declared War on America.* New York: Forum, 1999; Reeve, Simon. *The New Jackels: Ramzi, Yousef, Osama bin Laden and the Future of Terrorism.* Boston: Northeastern University Press, 1999.

## bipolarity

A bipolar international or regional system is one in which power is concentrated at two "poles." These poles may be ALLIANCES or individual states. Bipolarity as a form of INTERNATIONAL SYSTEM structure is significant because according to the logic of international systems analysis,

each type of international system has certain rules for survival. States are free to disregard these rules, but they do so at their own peril. The COLD WAR was a bipolar international system, and much of the cold war conflict between the United States and the Soviet Union can be understood in terms of its inner logic and rules.

Because of the distribution of power into two competing poles, each of the dominant states comes to see the other as an adversary that must be kept in check at all times and at all costs. Failure to do so, allowing the other superpower to gain an upper hand, may place the state in a position of permanent inferiority and domination because there is no other state in the system powerful enough to help preserve its independence. Counteraction is thus inevitable. The logic of bipolarity also makes true neutrality on the part of any significant state impossible. Neither superpower can be sure that a neutral state will remain neutral should conflict break out. The prudent course of action is to bring that state into one's alliance structure before the enemy succeeds in doing so.

The essential rules for a bipolar system can be summarized as follows. First, a state must increase its capabilities compared to those of the opposing dominant state. Second, a state must engage in a major war rather than permit the rival to achieve a position of preponderance. Third, a state must try to eliminate its rival. Fourth, a state should act to conserve its resources. It should negotiate rather than fight, fight a small war rather than a large war, and fight rather than fail to eliminate its rival.

The KOREAN WAR is an excellent example of how the rules of bipolarity influenced state behavior. No matter how unimportant the United States had declared SOUTH KOREA to be, once the North Koreans attacked, the United States felt compelled to respond with military force. Similarly, so long as the U.S. goal was to reestablish the status quo, the Communist bloc could stand on the sidelines. But once the stated goal became reunification, the rules of bipolarity demanded that the Communists take counteraction and intervene. VIETNAM is also understandable in the context of bipolarity. It did not matter how inconsequential Vietnam appeared to be in the larger context of bipolar competition. No rival can be permitted to gain an advantage of any size for fear that it will lead to permanent superiority. The Eisenhower administration's phrase *falling dominoes* speaks to this very concern.

Analysts have identified a variant bipolarity, loose bipolarity, which has its own rules and logic. Power remains concentrated in two poles, and each superpower continues to view the other with suspicion and counters any move it may make. Three key differences emerge. First, there is an increased possibility that important states may exist as neutrals due to the prohibitive costs of contesting for their allegiance. Second, there is a decreased ability of the two leading states to control their respective alliance systems. Command is replaced by negotiation. Third, international organizations become more important as each superpower sees them as a potentially low cost way of exercising its influence on the fringes of the system.

Many observers believe that by the late 1960s and 1970s the international system had become a loose bipolar one. The Soviet Union was having difficulty controlling CHINA and was forced to intervene militarily in CZECHOSLOVAKIA in 1968. Strains within the NORTH ATLANTIC TREATY ORGANIZATION (NATO) over burden sharing and the proper amount of cooperation with the Soviet Union and Eastern Europe became more pronounced. Many European states also questioned the wisdom of the VIETNAM WAR.

Bipolarity in either form is seen as having come to end with the conclusion of the cold war. This does not mean it will not reappear at the regional or global level. The two most frequently identified rivals for the United States in a new bipolar era are a resurgent RUSSIA or a bellicose China.

See also MULTIPOLARITY; UNIPOLARITY.

**Further reading:** Dougherty, James E., and Robert L. Pfaltzgraff, Jr. *Contending Theories of International Relations.* 4th ed. New York: Longman, 1997; Kaplan, Morton. *System and Process in International Politics.* New York: Wiley, 1962; Mearshimer, John. *The Tragedy of Great Power Politics.* New York: Norton, 2001.

## Blaine, James (1830–1893) *secretary of state*

James Blaine was SECRETARY OF STATE twice, first in 1881 and then again from 1889 to 1892. In each case the position was seen as a consolation prize. Blaine was a strong-willed and powerful figure within the REPUBLICAN PARTY who was repeatedly passed over as a presidential candidate in favor of less controversial figures. Blaine's lack of a background in DIPLOMACY or INTERNATIONAL LAW did not stop him from being an extremely active secretary of state, but when combined with his often arrogant personality, it did significantly limit his successes.

In his first tour of duty as secretary of state, Blaine tried unsuccessfully to renegotiate the CLAYTON-BULWER TREATY of 1850. It was an impediment to constructing an American canal because it provided for joint British and American protection of an interoceanic canal. Blaine told his British counterpart that conditions had changed and the agreement violated the spirit of the MONROE DOCTRINE, adding that the agreement weakened "our rightful and long established claim to priority on the American continent." He followed up this failed effort with similarly unsuccessful efforts to mediate border disputes between MEXICO and GUATEMALA and CHILE and Peru. This last venture caused

particular problems for American diplomacy because Blaine openly sided with Peru against the victorious Chilean demands for territory following a war between them. Blaine's last major act as secretary of state in 1881 was to issue invitations for an International (Pan) American Conference to examine ways of preventing war. The incoming Cleveland administration canceled the conference.

Blaine was more successful in his involvement in Venezuelas's financial crisis. Since 1864 European powers had been threatening to intervene if Venezuela did not signal its intent to make good on foreign debts. By 1881 FRANCE was prepared to go one step further and actually use military force for this purpose. Blaine intervened and proposed instead that the United States collect revenues in Venezuela and distribute the funds to claimants. Implementing negotiations were incomplete when Blaine left office. His successor, FREDERICK FRELINGHUYSEN, objected to the agreement, and it was dropped.

Such was the slow pace of Cleveland's diplomacy that when Blaine returned to the position of secretary of state in 1889 he was able to chair the first meeting of this very conference. Failure, however, continued to follow him. He sought but did not achieve a hemispheric-wide customs union or a system for arbitrating international disputes. The best he could accomplish was an agreement to pursue bilateral pacts. Only six states agreed, and they did so with threats of American economic sanctions hovering over their heads.

Beyond Latin America, Blaine also ventured into the Asia-Pacific region. A dispute involved seal hunting in the Bering Sea. In 1886 U.S. ships began to size Canadians schooners in the Bering Sea beyond the traditional three-mile limit that defines territorial waters. The British, who still handled CANADA's foreign policy matters, protested. Pushed by an angry CONGRESS, Blaine issued a defiant rebuttal. In his response Blaine did not claim the area as an American sea but did assert that sealing was against good public morals and that the Canadian policy was one step removed from piracy. Finally, an arbitration treaty was agreed to in February 1892. Its decisions, reached in 1893, rejected the American position on all major counts.

Blaine also became involved in establishing an international protectorate over Samoa. The United States for some time had been interested in establishing a presence in Samoa for economic and security reasons. Its harbors provided a convenient coaling station for transoceanic traffic. The Berlin Conference of 1889 established a British-German-American protectorate over the islands. Blaine opposed a permanent division of the islands or outright annexation.

## bomber gap

The "bomber gap" was a political controversy that erupted in the United States in the mid-1950s over the strength of the Soviet bomber fleet. It produced an outcry among the public for additional defense spending and pitted the air force and CENTRAL INTELLIGENCE AGENCY (CIA) in a bureaucratic battle over the content of intelligence estimates. It was determined that the bomber gap never existed. Had it existed, the bomber gap would have represented a major challenge to the DWIGHT EISENHOWER administration's NUCLEAR DETERRENCE STRATEGY.

By 1954 intelligence had established that the SOVIET UNION had built a prototype bomber, "the Bison," that had intercontinental capabilities. Such a bomber could reach the United States and would represent a threat to America's nuclear forces and its population. Original estimates place the number in production at 25 to 40 planes. On Aviation Day, July 13, 1955, the Bison was unveiled by the Soviet military in a series of flyovers. U.S. military attachés counted 28 planes. Working on the basis of presumed production capacity and the Soviet Union's hostile intent, the air force now concluded that far more Bisons were being produced than was first thought. The national intelligence estimate (NIE) for 1956 placed the projected number of Bisons at 600 to 800.

CIA analysts examining economic data reached a different conclusion. A key point of debate was over how many Bison were being produced in one "batch." The air force said 10; the CIA said five. By 1957 it was clear to many in the national security bureaucracy that the CIA was correct, but the air force refused to adjust its estimates downward. The existence of a large Soviet strategic bomber force would ensure the existence of a large American strategic bomber force. For similar reasons the army and navy supported the CIA's estimate. They hoped that a smaller Soviet force would allow more money to go into their budgets. The stalemate between these positions was broken by the Soviet Union when it launched SPUTNIK into orbit and began testing an intercontinental missile (ICBM). Missiles rather than bombers became the focal point of concern, and the bomber gap turned into concern about a MISSILE GAP. The bomber gap is significant because it typifies the worst-case thinking that has been common to U.S. responses to Soviet military developments. The missile gap and the window of vulnerability cited by the RONALD REAGAN administration also fit into this pattern. The bomber gap controversy also shows the interplay of organizational self-interest and threat response that is central to the BUREAUCRATIC POLITICS interpretation of how U.S. foreign policy is made.

See also COLD WAR; NUCLEAR WEAPONS; RUSSIA.

## Borah, William E. (1865–1940) senator
Senator William E. Borah, Republican from Idaho, served in the U.S. Senate from 1907 to 1940. He was a member of the Foreign Relations Committee from 1913 to 1940 and served as its chair from 1924 to 1932. Borah was a powerful spokesperson for ISOLATIONISM and neutrality in U.S. foreign policy.

Borah opposed the TREATY OF VERSAILLES and U.S. membership in the LEAGUE OF NATIONS. He was a leader of the "irreconcilables," a group of about 14 senators who agreed to support reservations to the treaty while at the same time promising to vote against it no matter how it was modified. Borah asserted that he had supported entry into WORLD WAR I in order to defeat GERMANY and little else: "I join no crusade; I seek or accept no alliance; I obligate this Government to no other power. I make war alone for my countrymen and their rights, for my country and its honor." Borah would later oppose U.S. membership in a proposed World Court on the grounds that it represented a backdoor attempt to get the United States to join the League of Nations.

In place of membership in the League of Nations as a means to fostering U.S. security, Borah advanced the idea of DISARMAMENT. In December 1920, one month after President WARREN HARDING's election, he introduced a resolution for such a conference. Harding objected to the idea, but public support for it made it impossible to ignore, and the WASHINGTON NAVAL CONFERENCE was held in 1921–22. Consistent with his isolationist principles Borah objected to one of the agreements that came out of this conference, the Four Power Treaty. It pledged the United States, GREAT BRITAIN, FRANCE, and JAPAN to respect each other's rights to island possessions in the Pacific, call a conference if disputes arose, and communicate with one another. Borah argued that this was a thinly disguised ALLIANCE designed to involve the United States in the Asian balance of power. CONGRESS approved the treaty by a four-vote margin but with a reservation that there was no U.S. commitment to use force.

Borah advanced the cause of disarmament again in 1923 when he introduced a resolution in the Senate calling for a universal treaty that would make war "a public crime under the law of nations." This support for the "outlawry of war" became the basis for the 1928 KELLOGG-BRIAND PACT that sought to accomplish this very aim. In the 1930s his support for isolationism led Borah to oppose President FRANKLIN ROOSEVELT's efforts to amend the neutrality laws so that the United States could ship arms to France and Great Britain. Borah feared that doing so would allow the British to manipulate U.S. foreign policy for its own purposes.

See also NEUTRALITY ACTS; RUSSIA.

**Further reading:** Maddox, Robert. *William E. Borah and American Foreign Policy.* Baton Rouge: University of Louisiana Press, 1969.

## Bosnia and Herzegovina

Bosnia and Herzegovina is about the size of West Virginia. It has an area of 19,741 square miles and a population of 3.5 million people. It became an independent state on April 11, 1992, following a referendum in which the Bosnian Muslims and Bosnian Croats voted overwhelmingly to secede from YUGOSLAVIA. They followed CROATIA and Slovenia, both of which had declared their independence in 1991. Bosnia's Serbs, however, did not support independence. In defiance of international recognition of Bosnia and Herzegovina's independence, the Bosnian Serbs declared their own state: the Serb Republic of Bosnia. Their actions were motivated in part by fears raised by extremist Bosnian Serbs and their allies in Serbian-controlled Yugoslavia that the Muslim Bosnians would persecute them and establish a fundamentalist Islamic state.

Compared to the Muslim Bosnians, the Serb Bosnians were well armed, having access to weapons from the Yugoslav military. They quickly set out on a campaign to liberate Serbs living in Muslim-dominated areas. It is from these military campaigns that the term *ethnic cleansing* originated. Murder, torture, and rape were common. Reports also surfaced of Nazi-style concentration camps. By the end of 1993 the Muslim Bosnian government controlled little of Bosnia and Herzegovina. Seventy percent was under the control of the Serbian Bosnians.

The Western response was muted. The GEORGE H. W. BUSH administration had little desire to intervene militarily. Chairman of the JOINT CHIEFS OF STAFF COLIN POWELL argued that it would be a war with no clearly defined objectives. The British and French were concerned that an expanded war with a Western military presence would threaten the safety of peacekeepers elsewhere in the former Yugoslavia. RUSSIA also opposed strong international action. Nationalists there argued that a historical affinity existed between Russia and Serbia, since both were Slavic peoples. Economic sanctions were imposed across the board. In theory the sanctions were to be neutral, equally felt by all. In practice they hurt the Muslim Bosnians more than they did the Serbian Bosnians since the later had access to military weapons through Yugoslavia. The UNITED NATIONS launched a peace initiative that became known as the Vance-Owen Plan after its two principal authors, former U.S. SECRETARY OF STATE CYRUS VANCE and David, Lord Owen of Britain. It called for dividing Bosnia into three largely autonomous districts that would each be ethnically homogeneous. The Bosnian Serbs rejected the plan, although Yugoslavia favored it. By now the economic sanctions put in place by the United Nations were taking their toll on its economy and Serbian president Slobodan Milošević wished to secure peace. The United Nations also took steps to investigate allegations of war crimes and atrocities in the fighting. In October 1992 it set up a War Crimes Commission. Evidence it accumulated led to the February 1993 decision to convene a war crimes trial in The Hague, Netherlands. The major military action taken was the establishment of six safe zones where Muslims would not be attacked and where there would be a UN presence.

In 1994 the international political landscape began to favor the Muslim Bosnians, and grounds began to be laid for an American peace initiative. In March 1994 Muslim Bosnians and Croat Bosnians agreed to a federated Bosnian state. In late 1994 the United States renewed its pressure on Milošević for an agreement. In 1995 it also courted Croatia. Illegal arms shipments to Croatia were not stopped, and military advice was given to its army in advance of a highly successful campaign by Croatia to recapture territory that had fallen under the control of Serbian Croats. The situation on the ground, however, remained perilous for the Bosnian Muslims. In 1995 Bosnian Serb forces attacked UN safe zones, and a massive ethnic cleansing campaign was directed at the Muslim population of Srebrenica.

The culmination of this political pressure was to bring Milošević, Croatian president Franjo Tudjman and (Muslim) Bosnian president Alija Izetbegović to Dayton, Ohio, for a SUMMIT CONFERENCE in November 1995. The agreement reached there, the DAYTON ACCORDS, was ratified in Paris in December and became the basis for all subsequent attempts to bring peace to Bosnia. Among other things, it provided for the continued existence of a single Bosnia and Herzegovina and for the presence of a NORTH ATLANTIC TREATY ORGANIZATION (NATO) peacekeeping force that was to remain in place until June 1998.

A key stumbling block to the full implementation of the Dayton Accords within Bosnia and Herzegovina has been Radovan Karadzić, the president of the renegade Serb

U.S. Marines escort Serbian detainees to the Kosovo-Serbia border, July 3, 1999. *(Department of Defense)*

Republic of Bosnia. Karadžić had been indicted for war crimes by the international tribunal set up to investigate the situation in the former Yugoslavia. In theory he could be arrested by NATO forces, but such action risks destabilizing the political situation inside Bosnia. Karadžić used his ties with local police forces and organized crime to thwart any implementation of the Dayton Accords within Serb-controlled territory. In March 2002 NATO made its first attempt to arrest Karadžić and failed; the move angered Bosnian Serbs. This Bosnian Serb noncooperation produced a situation in which few REFUGEES had been able to return to their homes. Before the fighting Srebrenica's population was 70 percent Muslim. In 1999 it was still 100 percent Serb.

Other stumbling blocks also existed. The Muslim Bosnians were taking action that contradicted the terms of the Dayton Accords. In 1998 they began a secret program of military training and arms procurement in preparation for the day when NATO peacekeepers left Bosnia. For a time in 2001–02 it looked as if this might be about to happen. The GEORGE W. BUSH administration had made no secret of its dislike for PEACEKEEPING operations, and in 2001 the American participation in the NATO force was reduced to 3,100 people. In 2002 the Bush administration threatened to withdraw U.S. peacekeepers from Bosnia as part of its dispute with the UN and other states over the creation of a permanent INTERNATIONAL CRIMINAL COURT. Also in 2001 hard-line nationalist forces within the Bosnian Croat community began lobbying for a separate Croat state within Bosnia as opposed to federation with the Muslim Bosnians.

**Further reading:** Burg, Steven L., and Paul S. Shoup. *The War in Bosnia-Hercegovina: Ethnic and International Intervention.* New York: M.E. Sharpe, 1999; Gow, James. *Triumph of the Lack of Will: International Diplomacy and the Yugoslav War.* New York: Columbia University Press, 1997; Woodward, Susan. *The Balkan Tragedy: Chaos and Dissolution after the Civil War.* Washington, D.C.: Brookings, 1995.

## bracero program

Also known as the Mexican Contract Labor Program, the bracero program ran from 1942 to 1964. Originally intended to be a temporary measure, the bracero program quickly established itself as a permanent feature of the American labor market. Some observers liken it to government-administered labor insurance for American farmers. Beyond its direct economic impact, the bracero program helped establish the basic outlines of contemporary Mexican IMMIGRATION flows into the United States along with the cultural, economic, social, and political issues that figure prominently in U.S.-Mexican relations.

The immigration of Mexican labor into the United States did not begin with the bracero program in 1942. In 1909 President WILLIAM HOWARD TAFT signed an executive agreement with Mexican president Porfirio Díaz that permitted thousands of Mexican contract workers to harvest sugar beets in Colorado and Nebraska. When the United States entered WORLD WAR I, provisions banning contract labor were waived to allow some 73,000 Mexican workers into the United States. For its part the Mexican government was concerned with the treatment being received by Mexican workers. The Mexican constitution of 1917 contained a provision that sought to safeguard the rights of emigrant workers, and the Mexican government attempted to discourage workers from going to the United States unless they already had contracts that provided such protections. These efforts were largely ineffective. In 1929, with the Great Depression underway in the United States and large numbers of Mexicans returning home due to the lack of jobs, the Mexican government sought but failed to obtain a bilateral agreement with the United States that would allow them to jointly manage the flow of workers across the border.

While some braceros worked in the railroad industry, most were employed in agriculture. The unpredictability of agricultural harvests due to weather conditions and other factors created a demand for large quantities of temporary workers who could move from place to place on short notice and remain for as long as needed. The economics of farming also emphasized the need for maintaining as small a full-time labor force as possible in nonharvest times. As early as 1940 American farming interests were warning of labor shortages even though in the bigger picture many Americans remained unemployed due to the Great Depression. U.S. involvement in WORLD WAR II further tightened the labor market and added support to the farmer's demand for a new influx of migrant workers.

On August 4, 1942, Mexico and the United States signed an agreement that permitted the large-scale and sustained recruitment of temporary workers in Mexico for work in the United States. The wartime years actually produced the smallest migrant flow in the history of the bracero program. Mexican and American data disagree on the exact number of migrants during the years 1943–46, but the range is between 49,000 to 82,000 per year. From 1947 to 1954 the average annual migration was between 116,000 and 141,000 per year. In the last 10 years of the bracero program the average annual number of migrant worker contracts recorded was 333,000.

At the outset of the bracero program, MEXICO possessed significant bargaining strength, which allowed it to insert provisions protecting migrant rights, such as insisting that the braceros be paid the prevailing wage in the community in which they were working, and prohibiting Mexicans from being rejected at "white" restaurants and other facilities in the American South. Mexico blacklisted Texas because of its discrimination policies and would not allow braceros to go there. Gradually, however, Mexico's leverage began to weaken. Contributing factors included U.S. legislation, the growing power of American farm organization, the perception that migration to the United States provided a safety valve for the Mexican economic and political system, and the growing phenomenon of illegal, or wetback, immigration into areas, such as Texas, where demand for migrant labor was great. In 1943 Congress passed Public Law 45 that gave legal status to the agreement reached with Mexico in 1942. One of its key provisions was that the United States could unilaterally declare an "open border" if need be. This power was used in May 1943 to grant one-year entrance permits. Texas farmers rushed into Mexico and began recruiting migrants and in the process undermined the orderly bilateral recruitment of workers. Lax border control enforcement in the early 1950s further contributed to the flow of illegal migrant workers. An attempt of sorts was made to bring order back to the bracero program in 1951 with the passage of Public Law 78. It placed responsibility for enforcing terms of the Bracero Program on the U.S. government. The weakness of the Mexican government's position is revealed in the fact that it was now the U.S. secretary of labor who would determine what the prevailing wage to be paid braceros actually was.

In the late 1940s and early 1950s the United States sought to deal with the problem of illegal migrant labor by transforming it into legal labor. This was done by mass deportations and mass legalizations. The scope of the problem was immense. From 1955 to 1959, 18 percent of all seasonal farm laborers were braceros. In New Mexico, braceros made up 70 percent of the seasonal labor force. Between 1947 and 1949 the President's Commission on Migratory Labor estimated that 142,000 deportable Mexicans in the United States were legalized as braceros. In 1950 slightly more than 19,800 new bracero contracts were awarded, but an estimated 96,200 illegal Mexicans were working in the United States.

Pressures that would bring the bracero program to an end began to surface in the late 1950s. American agricultural worker organization became seriously concerned about the wage-depressing effects that the braceros had on farm labor. A study by Ernesto Galarza, entitled *Strangers in Our Fields,* published in 1956, highlighted the deplorable conditions that governed the lives of migrant workers and led to demands that the provisions of Public Law 78 be enforced and that farm groups not be given primary responsibility for the program's oversight. Within CONGRESS pressures also began to build. In 1960 an extension of the bracero program was not voted on until the last

day of the session, and in 1962 the Kennedy administration openly opposed its renewal. A final extension in 1963 was obtained only after it was made known that Mexico opposed it termination.

Conditions in the farming industry also contributed to the demise of the bracero program. Braceros had been welcomed because they were more efficient than domestic labor. A 1959 study found them to be 30 percent more productive. The value of their labor was lessened by the increased mechanization of farm work. By 1964, for example, three-quarters of cotton was mechanically harvested.

The legacy of the bracero program is found in many areas. It reinforced the pre–World War II migration pattern of Mexicans to the United States and provides the context within which more recent migration has occurred. Seasonal and regional concentrated agricultural jobs became the norm for Mexicans coming to the United States as opposed to establishing permanent residences. Part of the Mexican government's response to the end of the bracero program was to create jobs along the U.S. border for returning migrants. This became the border industrialization, or maquiladora, program. It has not worked as expected since these firms have preferred to hire young Mexican women rather than returning braceros. Within the United States the end of the bracero program has not ended the debate over how to address the problem of illegal Mexican workers in the United States or how to provide sanctioned labor to employers. The Reagan administration proposed a pilot program whereby 50,000 Mexicans would be given permits each year for temporary work in the United States. The GEORGE W. BUSH administration floated the idea of a massive amnesty program for illegal Mexican migrants in the months prior to the SEPTEMBER 11, 2001, terrorist attacks. His move was widely criticized as a politically motivated one to attract Hispanic voters to the REPUBLICAN PARTY. Recognizing that this proposal was now no longer a high priority or one compatible with fears of homeland security in the United States, in March 2002 Mexican president Vicente Fox called for establishing a new guest worker program.

**Further reading:** Calavita, Kitty. *Inside the State: The Bracero Program, Immigration, and Inside the INS.* New York: Routledge, 1992.

## Brady Plan

The Brady Plan was the third U.S. initiative to deal with the Third World DEBT CRISIS of the 1980s. The first response was a rapid transfer of funds to MEXICO in 1982 to avoid default on its loans. This was accompanied by additional funds from international lending sources, such as the INTERNATIONAL MONETARY FUND (IMF) and an agreement by banks to postpone debt repayments. In return, states agreed to implement austerity measures. This ad hoc approach prevented an international financial crisis, but it did not provide the basis for economic growth. It was replaced in 1985 by the BAKER PLAN, which sought, but failed, to engineer a new inflow of money and additional domestic economic reforms.

Introduced by Secretary of the Treasury Nicholas Brady in 1989, the Brady Plan continued to stress a case-by-case approach to solving the debt crisis. It also embraced the ongoing principles of domestic economic reforms and increased funding by private and public creditors. Its major innovation was to move from debt repayment to debt reduction by emphasizing principal write-downs and interest reduction. In essence, instead of simply providing debtor states with new money, banks would voluntarily reduce their debt claims in return for increased repayment guarantees on the remaining money owed them. From the debtors' perspective, this amounted to having part of their debt bought back and the remainder of their debts restructured.

The central goal of the Brady Plan was to reduce the level of a country's indebtedness to manageable proportions. On balance the plan was successful. It did not succeed in generating a significant amount of new money for debtor states than did earlier approaches to the debt crisis. The Brady Plan did succeed, however, in lengthening the time horizon used by banks and debtor states to resolve their problems. This is significant because it gave debtor states the opportunity to break out of a time-consuming cycle of loan refinancing negotiations. It also allowed them to concentrate more fully on domestic economic reforms, making them more attractive to foreign investors.

Not all "Brady countries" have been equally successful in taking advantage of these new conditions. Mexico was the first state to do so, and up until 1995 it was the most successful. NIGERIA and the PHILIPPINES are examples of states that have not been successful.

## Brazil

Brazil is slightly smaller than the United States and occupies almost half of South America. With an area of 3.29 million square miles, it has an estimated population of 177 million people. It ranks sixth in size of total population in the world. Brazil was claimed for Portugal in 1500 and remained a Portuguese colony until 1808 when the Portuguese rulers fleeing from Napoleon's forces established the seat of government there. Brazil officially became independent in 1822. The United States was the first country to recognize Brazil's independence.

U.S. foreign relations with Brazil traditionally have been cordial but not particularly close, with most accounts describing Brazil as a traditional American friend. It publicly supported the United States during the SPANISH-AMERICAN WAR and the ROOSEVELT COROLLARY to the MONROE DOCTRINE. Along with ARGENTINA and CHILE, Brazil played mediator in the U.S.-Mexican standoff that followed President WOODROW WILSON's decision to send U.S. Marines into MEXICO in April 1914 during the Mexican Revolution. The ABC powers—Argentina, Brazil, and Chile—served as mediators at a meeting between American and Mexican representatives held at Niagara Falls, Canada, in May 1914. A plan was agreed to but never implemented.

American interest in Brazil has tended to parallel rising concerns about hemispheric security. During WORLD WAR I Brazil was one of eight states in Latin America to declare war on GERMANY. The most notable other states to do so were states dominated by Washington: PANAMA, NICARAGUA, HAITI, and CUBA. In WORLD WAR II Brazil was the first Latin American state to declare war. Particularly important to the war effort was its use as a staging area for flying reinforcements to North Africa. Brazil was also the only Latin American state to send military forces to the European theater. During the war the United States supplied Brazil with large amounts of LEND-LEASE supplies and substantial loans.

This same concern with security led the United States to be supportive of Brazil's right-wing governments during the COLD WAR. In return Brazil broke relations with Fidel Castro's Cuba and voted with the United States to block Communist CHINA's membership in the UNITED NATIONS. President JIMMY CARTER broke with this pattern of support, and he singled out Brazil for its HUMAN-RIGHTS violations.

The most enduring aspect of the Brazilian-American relationship has been the economic relationship. In the later half of the 1800s, Brazil and Cuba were the two leading Latin American trading partners of the United States. In 1893–94 U.S. economic interests in Brazil led the United States to send a naval squadron to break a rebel blockade of Rio de Janeiro. By the end of World War I, the United States controlled 40 percent of Brazil's foreign trade. Today the United States is the largest foreign investor in Brazil. From 1994 to 2000 the level of this investment increased from $19 billion to $35 billion. Over the past decade some conflicts have emerged to cloud U.S.–Brazilian economic relations. They center for the most part on questions of trade competition, technology transfer, and debt repayment.

See also MULTINATIONAL CORPORATIONS; REVISIONISM.

**Further reading:** Black, Jan. *United States Penetration of Brazil*. Philadelphia: University of Pennsylvania Press, 1977; Smith, Joseph. *Unequal Giants*. Pittsburgh, Pa.: University of Pittsburgh Press, 1991.

## Bretton Woods system

The Bretton Woods system consists of three institutions established after WORLD WAR II for the purposes of bringing about global economic recovery and managing the international economic system. Such a system was seen as necessary because, in the eyes of many, the nationalist economic policies followed by most states in the 1930s had prevented global economic cooperation and caused the Great Depression to have been more severe and to have lasted longer than it should have. The Bretton Woods system never functioned in the manner expected by its founders, but the institutions it created continue to serve as the key international organizations in managing global economic relations. Moreover, it was in the context of the Bretton Woods system and through its institutions that the United States came to exercise global economic leadership after World War II.

In July 1944, representatives from 44 states met at Bretton Woods, New Hampshire, to establish institutions for regulating the post–World War II international economy. They set up the INTERNATIONAL MONETARY FUND (IMF) and the International Bank for Reconstruction and Development (IBRD), better known as the WORLD BANK. These two institutions, along with the GENERAL AGREEMENT ON TARIFFS AND TRADE (GATT), which was set up as a temporary body following the 1947 Havana Charter meeting, constitute the core of the Bretton Woods system that lasted for nearly two decades.

As originally conceived, the Bretton Woods system was to be based on fixed exchange rates. The IMF would supervise this system. The World Bank was created to facilitate economic recovery by making loans to needy states. By 1947 the Bretton Woods system was on the verge of collapse. Economic recovery in Europe was proving to be more difficult than expected to bring about, and the COLD WAR was heating up. At this point the United States stepped forward and took over de facto management responsibilities in the Bretton Woods system. Most notably the U.S. dollar became the international currency of choice, replacing gold and the British pound. The MARSHALL PLAN and military expenditures through the NORTH ATLANTIC TREATY ORGANIZATION (NATO) placed large quantities of U.S. dollars in the hands of other states, facilitating economic recovery and international trade.

U.S. unilateral management ended around 1960 when the constant outflow of dollars from the United States began to undermine confidence in the health of the U.S. economy. This produced a run on the dollar as currency speculators converted dollars into gold. The United States withstood this challenge but from this point forward required the cooperation of other states to maintain the integrity of the Bretton Woods system. Management now took place through a series of smaller groups. A key body was the Group of Ten, established in 1961, which was made up of the finance ministers of 10 leading industrial countries. The Bretton Woods system collapsed in August 1972 when, without consulting other states, President RICHARD NIXON announced that the U.S. dollar would no longer be convertible into gold and that the United States would impose a 10 percent surcharge on foreign goods in an effort to push JAPAN and GERMANY to change the values of their currencies.

The "Nixon shock" set off a wave of crisis management undertakings that continues today. Though no longer the unchallenged dominant economic power, the United States continues to be at the center of ad hoc regional and global responses to international economic problems brought on by debt and currency crises, such as those that befell MEXICO in the early 1980s and Asia in the late 1990s.

See also ASIAN FINANCIAL CRISIS; INTERNATIONAL ORGANIZATIONS.

**Further reading:** Gardner, Richard. *Sterling Diplomacy: The Origins and Prospects of Our International Economic Order.* New York: Columbia University Press, 1969; Grieco, Joseph, and G. John Ikenberry. *State Power and World Markets.* New York: Norton, 2003.

## Brezhnev Doctrine

The Brezhnev Doctrine served as the legal or political justification for the WARSAW PACT's August 20, 1968, invasion of CZECHOSLOVAKIA. It takes its name from Leonid Brezhnev, who was head of the Soviet Communist Party at the time. It formally introduced the idea of limited sovereignty for socialist states. In theory the Brezhnev Doctrine spoke to a responsibility to all socialist states. In practice it established the Soviet Union (see RUSSIA) as the judge of how far reform efforts could progress in communist states. Some saw it as the equivalent to the DOMINO THEORY that gripped American foreign policy during much of the COLD WAR in which the defection of any ally was unacceptable because of the spillover effect that it could have on other states. Others have likened it to the MONROE DOCTRINE, which claimed a special role for the United States in determining the domestic policies of Latin American states.

The Brezhnev Doctrine had a lengthy pedigree. Joseph Stalin had sent a letter to Josip Broz, Marshal Tito and the Yugoslav Communist Party in 1948 making a somewhat similar point. In July 1968, Brezhnev delivered a 2,000-word manifesto that was published on July 19. It warned of the dangers facing Czechoslovakia should it continue on its reformist path. The Warsaw letter spoke of the common obligation of all socialist states not to allow the "loss of revolutionary gains already achieved." After this came the Bratislava Manifesto of early August, whose key sentence stated: "[I]t is the common international duty of all socialist states to support, strengthen, and defend these gains [the establishment of communism], which have been achieved at the cost of every people's heroic efforts and selfless labor."

The invasion of Czechoslovakia succeeded in stabilizing the political situation in East Europe and produced only a brief setback in U.S.-Soviet relations. President LYNDON JOHNSON cancelled a trip to the Soviet Union and postponed ARMS CONTROL talks. The long-term fallout was greater in the communist world, where CHINA found new reasons to suspect Soviet leadership. Repeal of the Brezhnev Doctrine by Mikhail Gorbachev was an important step toward normalizing relations with East Europe before the fall of communism.

## Bricker Amendment

Put forward by Senator John Bricker (R-Ohio) the Bricker Amendment was a constitutional amendment that would have required Senate approval of all EXECUTIVE AGREEMENTS. The amendment failed by the slim margin of one vote in the Senate in 1954 and thus did not go to the states for their approval. In the absence of this requirement executive agreements continue to exist beyond the reach of the legislative branch. Such is not the case with treaties. They cannot go into force unless ratified by a two-thirds majority in the Senate. The Case-Zablocki Act of 1972 picked up the theme of congressional oversight of executive agreements but only required that the PRESIDENT inform CONGRESS of all executive agreements that had been entered into.

Advocates of the Bricker Amendment were motivated primarily by two different sets of concerns. Conservative Republicans had become angered by what they saw as the excessively internationalist and unilateralist tendencies of FRANKLIN ROOSEVELT and HARRY TRUMAN. Bricker stated that he wanted to prevent another YALTA, referring to the WORLD WAR II summit conference attended by President Franklin Roosevelt, British prime minister Winston Churchill, and Soviet leader Joseph Stalin at which Roosevelt was seen by conservative critics as having turned Eastern Europe over to the Communists. Other supporters cited Truman's decision to send U.S. forces to KOREA and to fight that war without a congressional declaration of war.

A second source of support came from state's rights southern Democrats. They viewed with suspicion a series of SUPREME COURT decisions that provided an activist federal government with a means of circumventing Congress should it wish to change conditions within states, such as segregation. *MISSOURI V. HOLLAND* (1920) had established the supremacy of treaties over state law. *U.S. V. BELMONT* (1934) had extended that principle to include executive agreements.

Had it become part of the CONSTITUTION, the Bricker Amendment would have served to reduce significantly presidential foreign-policy power. Executive agreements are a favored tool of presidents when entering into agreements with foreign states, and they are used in a variety of policy areas. Especially after VIETNAM, treaties have proven to be especially problematic instruments of foreign policy. In the area of international trade, presidents have sought, but not always received, FAST-TRACK authority to speed the consideration of treaties by the Senate and, by so doing, improve the odds of a treaty emerging in a form acceptable to other signatory states.

**Further reading:** Tananbaum, Duane. *The Bricker Amendment Controversy.* Ithaca, N.Y.: Cornell University Press, 1988.

## brinksmanship

*Brinksmanship* is a term coined during the Eisenhower administration. It represented a type of general operating principle of American COLD WAR foreign policy during the 1950s and 1960s and pointed to a specific strategy for managing international crises. Simply put, the Soviet Union could be contained by raising the stakes of U.S.–Soviet confrontations to the point at which the cost of success would be prohibitively high. According to the logic of brinksmanship, only by pushing the adversary to the brink of war could war be avoided. As practiced by Eisenhower's SECRETARY OF STATE JOHN FOSTER DULLES, the strategy of brinksmanship had a clear and visible nuclear dimension as on more than one occasion Dulles raised the possibility of using nuclear weapons if the Soviet Union or CHINA did not back down.

The foreign policy crises and confrontations most associated with brinksmanship during the Eisenhower administrations include the KOREAN WAR, the Jinmen and Mazu (Quemoy and Matsu) crises, and the BERLIN CRISIS, 1958. A reliance on brinksmanship continued in the Kennedy administration as evidenced by its handling of the BERLIN CRISIS, 1961, and the CUBAN MISSILE CRISIS.

Brinksmanship has also been studied outside the context of American cold war containment policy as a general strategy for managing INTERNATIONAL CRISES. Evidence suggests that it is most frequently employed when a leader is politically vulnerable and seeks to draw attention away from his or her domestic problems. The domestic weakness of policy makers employing brinksmanship also means that it is not a policy that can be easily controlled once set in motion.

In 2002–03, NORTH KOREA engaged in a form of brinksmanship with the United States. North Korea announced that it was a nuclear power and that only if the

United States entered into direct negotiations with it would it stop movement in this direction. North Korea was worried both about its rapidly deteriorating economic condition and the prospect of military action against it by the United States. Preoccupied with the IRAQ WAR the GEORGE W. BUSH administration sought to diplomatically isolate North Korea. This strategy failed. Talk of military action that would be consistent with the administration's new policy of PREEMPTION only scarred America's Asian allies. Ultimately multilateral talks were begun that brought in key regional states that had an interest in stability on the Korean Peninsula.

See also EISENHOWER, DWIGHT; KENNEDY, JOHN; RUSSIA.

## Bryan, William Jennings (1860–1925) *secretary of state*

William Jennings Bryan was a three-time DEMOCRATIC PARTY presidential candidate who served as SECRETARY OF STATE (1913–15) during the administration of WOODROW WILSON. In his 1900 campaign against WILLIAM MCKINLEY, Bryan spoke out against American IMPERIALISM and opposed the annexation of the PHILIPPINES. Interestingly, as a senator he had urged ratification of the treaty to end the SPANISH-AMERICAN WAR in spite of his personal opposition to imperialism in the apparent hope of making it a campaign issue in 1900.

Bryan helped Woodrow Wilson win the Democratic presidential nomination in 1912 and was rewarded with the post of secretary of state. Wilson largely acted as his own secretary of state and gave Bryan a relatively free hand to use his office as a pulpit for promoting world peace and international arbitration as a means for settling disputes. He did so largely by negotiating a series of peace treaties wherein each state agreed that disputes would be submitted to an international commission for investigation and that states would not go to war until this process was completed. Popularly known as "cooling-off treaties," Bryan negotiated 30 Treaties for the Advancement of Peace, 22 of which went into effect. The first was signed with EL SALVADOR; GREAT BRITAIN, FRANCE, and ITALY also signed treaties. GERMANY refused.

Bryan resigned as secretary of state in protest over Wilson's handling of the sinking of the *Lusitania* by a German submarine in 1915. The *Lusitania* was a British passenger ship that was carrying 4,200 cases of rifle cartridges. On May 7, 1915, it was attacked by a German submarine, killing 1,198 people, 128 of whom were Americans. Wilson responded by sending two diplomatic notes to Germany. Bryan objected to the harsh tone of the second note and the failure of the Wilson administration to reprimand Great Britain for its wartime obstruction of U.S. shipping. Once the United States entered WORLD WAR I, however, Bryan supported U.S. participation and became a strong advocate for the TREATY OF VERSAILLES and the LEAGUE OF NATIONS.

**Further reading:** Clements, Kendrick. *William Jennings Bryan: Missionary Isolationist*. Knoxville: University of Tennessee Press, 1982.

## Bullitt, William C. (1891–1967) *diplomat*

William C. Bullitt was an American diplomat who specialized in Russian affairs. His career spanned two world wars, and his shifting views on the nature of COMMUNISM epitomized the conflicting views Americans have held about Soviet communism and the difficulty of reconciling them into a coherent policy.

Bullitt joined the STATE DEPARTMENT in 1917 as a member of its West European Affairs division. He soon moved on to be chief of its Division of Current Intelligence, and in 1919 he became a member of the U.S. delegation to the Paris Peace Conference. President WOODROW WILSON sent Bullitt on a fact-finding mission to RUSSIA, where he made contact with the Bolshevik forces and Vladimir Lenin. Bullitt turned the mission into more than what Wilson had envisioned. He returned to Paris with a peace proposal advocating that the Western powers recognize the Communist government. According to Bullitt's plan, the Western powers would withdraw their troops from the Russian civil war, stop supporting the White (anti-Bolshevik) forces, and lift their economic blockade. In return the Bolsheviks would implement a cease-fire and allow the White forces to hold the territories they occupied. The British opposed Bullitt's plan, and Wilson ignored it. His advice was rejected, and Bullitt would speak out against the TREATY OF VERSAILLES.

Bullitt spent the 1920s in Paris but returned in 1932 to work on FRANKLIN ROOSEVELT's presidential campaign as an expert on European affairs. He was rewarded for his efforts with an appointment as a special assistant to Secretary of State CORDELL HULL. His task was to explore ways of improving relations with the Soviet Union. Largely because of his efforts a treaty between the two states was reached, ending their diplomatic isolation. Bullitt was rewarded in 1933 by being named the first U.S. ambassador to the Soviet Union. It was not long, however, before Bullitt's attitude changed, and he became staunchly anti-Soviet. He attributed most of the problems in U.S.-Soviet relations to the Soviet Union and its leaders' intransigent position on foreign policy matters. He left his post in 1936 to help in Franklin Roosevelt's reelection campaign. Bullitt would leave the administration in 1943 after serving as ambassador to France and holding other less significant positions. After the end of WORLD WAR II, Bullitt attacked

Roosevelt's handling of Soviet leader Joseph Stalin and his failure to take a hard line against the Soviet Union at YALTA.

## bureaucracy

Public attention tends to focus on the actions of the PRESIDENT, deliberations within CONGRESS, or struggles between these two institutions when looking for answers to questions about the content and conduct of U.S. foreign policy. Yet, largely out of public view, several bureaucracies have long played an equally important role. Most notable among them have been the STATE DEPARTMENT, DEFENSE DEPARTMENT, and CENTRAL INTELLIGENCE AGENCY (CIA). Recently they have been joined, at least periodically, by the OFFICE OF U.S. TRADE REPRESENTATIVE and the DEPARTMENTS of TREASURY, COMMERCE, and AGRICULTURE.

These bureaucracies exercise influence throughout the policy process. They are a source of ideas about how to solve problems and often are the first to point out the existence of a problem. They are the instruments used to solve problems and the source of information about the extent to which a policy is succeeding or failing. Bureaucracies are also a source of almost endless frustration to policy makers moving more slowly to implement policies then they would like or failing to respond to their directives.

These two faces of bureaucracy are not accidental. They are deeply embedded in its very nature. On the one hand bureaucracy possesses machine-like qualities. It is a neutral tool purposefully created to carry out specific tasks, such as promoting trade, protecting territory, negotiating with other countries, and gathering intelligence. One-time SECRETARY OF STATE and NATIONAL SECURITY ADVISOR HENRY KISSINGER spoke to this side of bureaucracy when he stated, "the purpose of bureaucracy is to devise standard operating procedures that can effectively cope with most problems." Bureaucracy thus frees policy makers to concentrate on the unexpected and exceptional problems and allows them to pursue policy innovations.

The essence of the bureaucratic machine is captured in its organizational chart that identifies key tasks and their relationship to one another. As the goals change, so too should the organizational chart as new priorities—promoting HUMAN RIGHTS, PEACEKEEPING, counterterrorism, and building democracy—receive their own organizational home or move up in prominence in the organizational hierarchy. When it fails to identify meaningful options to deal with routine problems, bureaucracy becomes a hindrance, forcing policy makers to direct their attention away from creative problem solving in order to supervise and manage the routine.

The other side of bureaucracy, the one that frustrates presidents, is found in the informal system of unwritten rules of conduct, fundamental assumptions about an organization's mission, and ways of approaching one's work that spring up spontaneously around the formal system of organizational charts and legal lines of authority. The informal system is not outward looking and concerned with the demands of those who established the organization or who now run it. It is inward looking and protective of the careers and interests of those who are employed in the organization.

The two faces of bureaucracy often do collide, but by definition they are not hostile to one another. They are both vital contributors to its success. The formal structure places boundaries on activities and promotes predictability and consistency in performance. The informal system provides redundancy to ensure that tasks will be accomplished in a predictable manner and allows the organization to cope with contingencies and problems that were not anticipated when the formal system was set up.

Presidents have resorted to several different strategies to manage the foreign-affairs bureaucracy. One is to insist that those who are employed in the bureaucracy—be they military officers, diplomats, or CIA analysts—adhere to strict professional standards. A second is to place political appointees in key positions of authority within the bureaucracy. A third strategy has centered on devising a system for managing relations between the White House and the foreign-affairs bureaucracies. The central instrument relied upon by presidents is the NATIONAL SECURITY COUNCIL and the national security advisor. More recently Congress has entered the picture. Unhappy with bureaucratic (and presidential) performance it created an OFFICE OF THE U.S. TRADE REPRESENTATIVE in the White House, mandated a reorganization of the Defense Department through the GOLDWATER-NICHOLS ACT, and integrated the ARMS CONTROL AND DISARMAMENT AGENCY and the U.S. INFORMATION AGENCY into the State Department.

See also BUREAUCRATIC-POLITICS DECISION-MAKING MODEL.

**Further reading:** Kaufman, Herbert, *The Limits of Organizational Change.* University: University of Alabama Press, 1971; Thompson, James. *Organizations in Action.* New York: McGraw Hill, 1967; Warwick, Donald. *A Theory of Public Bureaucracy: Politics and Organization in the State Department.* Cambridge, Mass.: Harvard University Press, 1975; Wilensky, Harold. *Organizational Intelligence.* New York: Basic Books, 1967.

## bureaucratic-politics decision-making model

Bureaucratic politics is the process by which people inside governmental administrative structures bargain with one another over how to respond to policy problems. Unlike the RATIONAL-ACTOR DECISION-MAKING MODEL that sees policy as a rational response to a situation or ELITE-DECISION-MAKING THEORY and pluralist models that see policy as a product of societal forces, the bureaucratic-politics decision-making model sees policy making as a political process. Conflict resolution, not problem solving, is the order of the day for policy makers.

Politics dominates the decision-making process because no individual is in a position to determine policy alone. Power is shared, and the individuals who share power disagree in large measure because they are located at different places within the government and see different faces of the problem. In fact, there is no single definition of the problem because each part of the government views policy problems through a lens heavily colored by organizational self-interest and past experience. Moreover, policy problems rarely enter or leave the policy process in a clearly definable manner. According to the bureaucratic-politics decision-making model, more frequently they flow through it in a fragmented state and become entangled with other ongoing policy problems. The cumulative result is that policy is not formulated with respect to any underlying conception of the American NATIONAL INTEREST but by the way in which the problem surfaces and the path it takes through the policy process.

Not everyone in the government is a participant in a particular policy-making "game." Action channels link individuals and organizations together. They are formed out of organizational routines as well as formal and informal rules that determine how a policy is to be decided. Is it to be by committee, consensus, or majority vote, or does someone have a veto over what is to be done? Deadlines exist that speed up the tempo of a decision or slow it down. They may also force a decision regardless of how prepared policy makers are to act.

Bargaining is a time consuming and expensive process. For this reason, the bureaucratic-politics perspective holds that the product of these deliberations will differ only marginally from what is already in place. All, or most, participants will need to be able to claim that their position has prevailed. The inflexible and blunt nature of organizational routines and standard operating procedures reinforces the tendency for policy to change only at the margins. Administrative feasibility is a constant check on the ability of policy makers to produce unique and innovative responses to the problems confronting them. In sum, the best predictor of future policy is not the policy that maximizes U.S. national interests but one that is only incrementally different from current policy, regardless of how the policy problem has changed.

The bureaucratic-politics decision-making model makes important contributions to understanding U.S. foreign policy by highlighting the political and organizational nature of policy making. It directs our attention away from Congress as the institution where politics happens and toward the bureaucracy. By doing so we cease to view bureaucracy as a machine and see it as a political force that looks inward to its own interests in addressing problems. Moreover, by focusing on bureaucracy, the bureaucratic-politics model extends our definition of the decision-making process so that it does not stop with the choice of an option but includes the process of implementation and evaluation. This decision-making model has been most influential in framing our understanding of long-running policy problems, such as those involving TRADE, aid, the ENVIRONMENT, and weapons procurement and strategic issues.

INTERNATIONAL CRISIS situations are seen as ill-suited for this type of analysis since the speed with which they unfold tends to short-circuit bureaucratic participation. This does not mean that the representatives of important bureaucracies do not participate in crisis decisions but, as the small-group decision-making model suggests, when they do participate the influence of bureaucratic self-interest on the decision is minimized by the dynamics of group decision making.

The heavy data demands of the bureaucratic decision-making model limit its utility in terms of both the range of issues that can be studied and the number of countries whose foreign policies can be studied. Several pointed criticisms also have been raised concerning its interpretation of how U.S. foreign policy is made. The most serious is that the model underestimates the power of the PRESIDENT to shape the policy process and the decisions that flow from it. A related criticism is that the presumed interests of participants in the policy process are drawn too literally from their organizational positions. Not enough consideration is given to the way in which broader societal trends and domestic politics influence how problems are viewed.

**Further reading:** Allison, Graham, and Philip Zelikow. *Essence of Decision: Explaining the Cuban Missile Crisis.* 2d ed. Boston: Addison Wesley Longman, 1999; Destler, I. M. *Presidents, Bureaucrats, and Foreign Policy.* Princeton, N.J.: Princeton University Press, 1972; Halperin, Morton. *Bureaucratic Politics and Foreign Policy.* Washington, D.C.: Brookings, 1974.

## Bush, George H. W. (1924– ) *president of the United States*

George Herbert Walker Bush was the 41st president of the United States. A Republican, he served one term as president (1989–93). Bush brought with him an extensive background in foreign affairs. He served as U.S. representative to the UNITED NATIONS (1971–73), first chief of the U.S. Liaison Office in the People's Republic of CHINA

President George H. W. Bush (*third from right at table*) gives a press conference with his National Security Council to announce that Iraq has invaded Kuwait. *(George Bush Presidential Library)*

(1974–75) and director of the CENTRAL INTELLIGENCE AGENCY (1975–77). On the political front he had served as chairman of the REPUBLICAN PARTY, had served two terms in the House of Representatives, and was a failed presidential candidate in 1980. He was selected by RONALD REAGAN as his vice presidential candidate and served two terms in that office under Reagan.

Bush's first foreign-policy moves can be seen as an effort to tie up the loose ends of Reagan's foreign policy. He moved quickly to terminate the controversy over support for the contras. CONGRESS agreed to authorize nonmilitary aid for the contras through the upcoming election, but Congress could terminate the aid. In PANAMA, Bush inherited a failed policy of economic sanctions and covert action designed to force Manuel Noriega out of power. His involvement in drug trafficking had transformed him from an ally into a liability. In December 1989 Bush ordered U.S. forces to invade Panama and remove him from power. The ORGANIZATION OF AMERICAN STATES condemned the move, but Bush justified it as consistent with American

rights under the PANAMA CANAL TREATIES. Bush and Russian leader Mikhail Gorbachev signed a STRATEGIC ARMS REDUCTION TREATY (START I) in June 1991. A second START treaty was agreed to with Boris Yeltsin in 1992. Reagan had set the START process in motion in 1981, but no agreement had been reached. Finally, Bush broke through the impasse on how to end the international DEBT CRISIS by sponsoring the BRADY PLAN.

Gorbachev's reform efforts presented the Bush administration with a series of unexpected foreign-policy challenges involving unilateral ARMS CONTROL and disarmament proposals, demands for democratic reform in Eastern Europe, the breakup of the Soviet Union (see RUSSIA), and the disintegration of YUGOSLAVIA. Bush adopted a wait-and-see policy toward most of these developments. The Bush administration's indecision in how to respond to the end of the COLD WAR era also characterized its policy toward China. On June 4, 1989, Chinese troops attacked demonstrators on Tiananmen Square, killing hundreds. Protests had been building for some time, demanding prodemocracy reforms. Bush responded by imposing economic sanctions and suspending high-level contacts between the two governments. By the end of the year, however, the administration lost much of its enthusiasm for punishing China for its HUMAN-RIGHTS violations and became more concerned with protecting America's long-term economic and strategic interests in the region and began taking steps to normalize relations.

The defining moment of the Bush administration's foreign policy was the PERSIAN GULF WAR. Responding to IRAQ's invasion of KUWAIT, Bush organized a global military and diplomatic coalition to compel Saddam Hussein's forces to leave Kuwait. A UNITED NATIONS (UN) resolution gave Iraq until January 15, 1991, to do so. On January 12 both houses of Congress authorized Bush to use force against Iraq. On January 16, with the UN headline having passed, Bush unleashed OPERATION DESERT STORM. On February 23, allied forces invaded Iraq, and 100 hours later Bush declared that Kuwait was liberated. At a joint session of Congress on March 6, Bush announced that the war was over. Tension in the region did not end. Saddam Hussein now turned his remaining forces against Kurds in northern Iraq and Shi'ite Muslims in the south. Bush announced that the United States would not act to either support these forces or bring down Saddam Hussein's government.

In the area of international economic relations, Bush advanced two major initiatives. First, he promoted the URUGUAY ROUND GENERAL AGREEMENT ON TARIFFS AND TRADE (GATT) talks that had begun in 1986 as a cornerstone of the post–cold war international economic system. Second, he worked to establish a regional free-trade area through the NORTH AMERICAN FREE TRADE AGREEMENT (NAFTA). He had hoped to complete this initiative prior to the 1992 presidential election but failed to do so. Instead it became embroiled in electoral politics, and it fell to President BILL CLINTON to finalize the agreement.

After his defeat in the 1992 presidential election, Bush continued to conduct an activist foreign policy. In early December he began consulting with European allies over ways of stopping Serbian aggression in BOSNIA AND HERZEGOVINA. That same month he also ordered U.S. troops to SOMALIA as part of Operation Restored Hope. In early January 1993 he signed the START II treaty.

The hallmark of Bush's foreign policy was its pragmatism. As such, it is not surprising that evaluations of it differ largely over the relative merits of such a foreign policy. Some see this pragmatism as being especially well suited to cleaning up the debris of the cold war era but as having blinded Bush to the opportunities in the unchartered waters of the emerging post–cold war era. Pragmatism in the post–cold war era, however, has its defenders. They argue that since the INTERNATIONAL SYSTEM was then undergoing a transition, it was unlikely that any over-arching strategic vision could have proven effective. Under these circumstances pragmatism was the wisest course of action.

**Further reading:** Hybel, Alex. *Power over Rationality: The Bush Administration and the Gulf War.* Albany: State University of New York Press, 1993; Woodward, Bob. *The Commanders.* New York: Touchstone, 1991.

## Bush, George W. (1946– ) *president of the United States*

George Walker Bush is the 43rd president. Son of George Herbert Walker Bush, the 41st president, he was elected president over the DEMOCRATIC PARTY candidate Al Gore in 2000 in one of the most closely contested and controversial presidential elections in American history. Prior to being elected president Bush was a two-time governor of Texas, elected in 1994 and 1998.

Bush's approach to foreign policy emerged early in his administration and remained consistent over time. Four traits are paramount. First, it is unilateralist in orientation. CONGRESS is not seen as an equal partner or even a junior one. Foreign policy is treated as the president's reserve, and Bush has used the power of public pronouncements to set the direction of American foreign policy and force other foreign-policy actors, at home or abroad, to adapt. Second, it is partisan. Bush values loyalty and teamwork. Foreign policy is made in open discussion among those he trusts. Moreover, Bush has delegated a greater amount of foreign-policy power to his associates than has been the case with previous presidents. Third, it is absolutist in orientation. Bush has led with maximum demands and portrayed issues in black-and-white terms. Finally, it has been dogged. Bush has set an agenda and stuck with it regardless of any opposition he has encountered. While compromises have been necessary, they have not diminished the perception that he and his administration are in charge and have a foreign-policy agenda.

While consistent in its approach to foreign-policy making, the content of Bush's foreign policy has evolved. It can be divided into three phases. The first phase spanned the time from his inauguration until the tragic events of SEPTEMBER 11, 2001. During this period the Bush administration sought to differentiate itself from BILL CLINTON's foreign policy by demonstrating a willingness to say no and by going against what its predecessor had done or what U.S. allies wanted done. The administration rejected the KYOTO PROTOCOL as flawed, embraced a NATIONAL BALLISTIC MISSILE SYSTEM, and abandoned the ANTIBALLISTIC MISSILE SYSTEM TREATY. The new Bush administration also made it clear that it was not inclined to undertake an activist foreign policy that embraced HUMANITARIAN INTERVENTION as a key element.

The most significant foreign policy challenge faced by Bush during this first phase was a conflict with CHINA over the downing of an American spy plane. Concern was expressed by some observers that while the administration handled the details of the INTERNATIONAL CRISIS adroitly enough, Bush's public comments displayed a lack of understanding of the complex relationship between the United States, China, and TAIWAN. His statements made it appear that the United States had changed its one China policy in favor of support for Taiwanese statehood. The Bush administration quickly reaffirmed the existing policy.

September 11 ushered in a second phase. President Bush transformed from a reluctant internationalist with strong unilateralist leanings to a fervent internationalist who embraced the rhetoric of MULTILATERALISM. While global in scope, the focus of his attention in this phase was narrow: defeating TERRORISM.

Terrorism had not moved to the top of the Bush administration's policy agenda prior to September 11. Bush administration officials were reportedly unhappy with the Clinton administration's approach to dealing with AL-QAEDA, but action had not progressed far beyond a second tier of advisers who were working on a national security presidential directive. It was taken up by cabinet officials on September 4 and called for a phased escalation of pressure against the Taliban to force them to abandon al-Qaeda. In concrete terms, Bush's antiterrorism policy showed more continuity than change, and where there was change it was not always in the direction of a more assertive stance. For example, Bush did not resume Clinton's policy of covert deployment of cruise missile submarines or gunships near AFGHANISTAN that would have allowed short notice attacks on al-Qaeda leadership targets. Bush did not speak publicly of the dangers of terrorism prior to September 11 except in the context of the ballistic missile defense system. Internal wrangling within the TREASURY DEPARTMENT crippled efforts at implementing policies designed to identify and interrupt secret terrorist financial systems of support. Twice the Bush administration informed the Taliban that it would hold them responsible for an al-Qaeda attack but took no military action.

The Bush administration's first terrorist target after September 11 was Afghanistan. The goal was to remove the Taliban from power and, if possible, destroy al-Qaeda and its leader OSAMA BIN LADEN. The Bush administration portrayed the struggle against terrorism as a new type of warfare, global in scope and uncertain in duration. Bush soon found that the rhetoric of a global war against terrorism came more easily than did designing a strategy to deal with terrorism. The largest divide was between those who supported a narrow definition of the immediate task that entailed only strikes against

Afghanistan and those who had a broader vision that included war with Iraq. The issue was settled in favor of an Afghanistan-only strategy in large part because those favoring war with Iraq were not able to present a strategy for accomplishing its objectives.

Once the war began in Afghanistan, it was a very conventional war, and one that on the whole brought a great deal of credit to the Bush administration. The CENTRAL INTELLIGENCE AGENCY (CIA) engaged in covert action by providing financial and material support to dissident forces in Afghanistan. The military undertook highly successful air strikes against targets inside Afghanistan. U.S. troops on the ground engaged in limited military action with much of the search-and-destroy efforts being carried out by local allied forces. The mission was also a success in the conventional sense that it brought down the Taliban government. The total cost of the operation was modest: 110 CIA officers, 315 Special Forces personnel, massive air power, and $70 million in CIA-funded bribes and inducements.

The Bush administration's foreign policy entered a third phase following the end of the Afghan operation. The battlefield victory appeared complete, and the question to be answered was "what next?" The Bush administration now began to define its sense of purpose in broader terms. Terrorism was still the preeminent issue on the foreign-policy agenda but was not the only one. It found itself struggling to provide a coherent response to escalating conflicts in South Asia and the Middle East, ARMS CONTROL initiatives with RUSSIA, and trade issues with European allies. Freedom and its defense emerged as the defining watchwords of Bush's foreign policy in this third phase.

Bush defined the enemies of freedom in his 2002 State of the Union address as an axis of evil consisting of IRAQ,

President George W. Bush addresses the audience during the Pentagon memorial service on October 11, 2001, in honor of those who perished in the terrorist attack on the building one month earlier. *(Department of Defense)*

NORTH KOREA, and IRAN. Iraq had been a potential target of American forces earlier, and it now reemerged as the principal American enemy because of its support of international terrorism and pursuit of WEAPONS OF MASS DESTRUCTION. As in the days and weeks following the September 11 terrorist attacks, a debate again broke out in the administration over the wisdom of war with Iraq. SECRETARY OF DEFENSE Donald Rumsfeld and his staff and Vice President Dick Cheney were the principal advocates of war. SECRETARY OF STATE COLIN POWELL was not convinced of the wisdom of war. This time, supporters of war with Iraq held the day.

In September 2002 the administration openly and vehemently began to talk about the need to bring about a "regime change" in Iraq. The Bush administration was prepared to act unilaterally. It put forward a new strategic doctrine of PREEMPTION to justify such action. It asserted that deterrence does not work against terrorists and that the United States must be prepared to take decisive military action to thwart such threats. Domestic and global opposition to the possibility of war forced President Bush to delay and obtain congressional and UNITED NATIONS support for military action. Having secured support from Congress and the United Nations, the Bush administration continued its military buildup in the Persian Gulf as weapons inspectors returned to Iraq.

Inspectors had last been in Iraq in 1998. Through the summer Iraq and the United Nations quarreled over if and how these inspections might be resumed. The Bush administration considered these discussions to be little more than a delaying tactic on the part of Iraq. President Bush spoke at the United Nations on the one-year anniversary of the September 11 terrorist attacks and challenged the world organization to face up to the "grave and gathering danger" of Iraq or stand aside and allow the United States to act.

Bush's address set off a period of intense diplomatic maneuvering at the United Nations over the language of a new UN resolution demanding that Iraq disarm and permit inspections. FRANCE and RUSSIA led the opposition to such a resolution. In October the United States put forward a revised draft resolution. On November 8, 2002, the UN Security Council unanimously approved Resolution 1441, giving Iraq 30 days to produce a "currently accurate, full, and complete declaration of all aspects of its programmes to develop chemical, biological, and nuclear weapons, ballistic missiles. . . ." UN weapons inspectors were to update the Security Council in 60 days.

The Bush administration and the UN Security Council continued to spar over the extent of Iraqi compliance and the need for another resolution that would justify American military action. On January 28, President Bush gave his State of the Union address in which he indicated to Saddam Hussein that he had missed his "final chance" by not cooperating with UN weapons inspectors. On February 24 the United States and Great Britain indicated that they would soon introduce a new resolution that would declare Iraq to be in "further material breach" of UN orders to disarm. This announcement brought forward renewed opposition from GERMANY, RUSSIA, CHINA and France. President Bush reiterated that the United States was prepared to go ahead without UN support. On March 16 the U.S. and its major Security Council allies, GREAT BRITAIN and SPAIN, held a one-hour summit conference. The following day President Bush issued an ultimatum to Saddam Hussein to go into exile or face military action. The next day the sponsors announced that they would pull their resolution authorizing military force against Iraq because they had reached the conclusion that "Council consensus will not be possible." That night President Bush addressed the nation and gave Saddam Hussein 48 hours to leave Iraq. On Tuesday, March 18, Saddam Hussein rejected Bush's ultimatum.

The ground war began early in the evening on March 20 as United States and British troops crossed into Iraq from Kuwait. It was preceded by a decapitation air strike against the Iraqi leadership. The forward movement of coalition ground forces was uneven. U.S. troops met with little effective resistance, and the British encountered stiffer resistance, especially around Basra. The invasion supply line eventually grew to more than 250 miles and became subject to GUERRILLA and terrorist attacks. In late March a week-long pause in the ground offensive took place. When it resumed, U.S. ground forces rapidly advanced on Baghdad. The United States made another attempt to kill Saddam Hussein, dropping four 2,000-pound "bunker buster" bombs on one of his fortified underground command centers. On April 9, Baghdad fell to U.S. forces. On May 1, aboard the USS *Abraham Lincoln,* President Bush declared victory in the war in Iraq. The postwar period has been marked by two controversies. First, Bush was charged with misusing intelligence on the existence of Iraqi weapons of mass destruction in making the U.S. government's case for war. Second, the reconstruction of Iraq went poorly with many protests and repeated attacks on U.S. forces with casualties.

**Further reading:** Woodward, Bob. *Bush at War.* New York: Simon and Schuster, 2002.

## Byrnes, James (1879–1972) *secretary of state*

James F. Byrnes had an expansive career as a public servant. In addition to serving as SECRETARY OF STATE under President HARRY TRUMAN (1945–47) Byrnes also was a senator and congressperson from South Carolina, an associate justice of the SUPREME COURT, and presidential adviser. He ended his career as governor of South Carolina, where he opposed integration. Byrnes was frequently mentioned as a vice presidential candidate in 1944 but lost out to Harry Truman.

Byrnes played a key role in early COLD WAR American foreign policy. Prior to being picked by Truman to replace Edward Stettinius, Jr., as secretary of state, Byrnes had been a confident of FRANKLIN ROOSEVELT and took a lead role in politically "selling" the YALTA agreement to conservatives in CONGRESS. Byrnes also was instrumental in the American decision to drop the atomic bomb on Hiroshima. He served as Truman's personal representative on a top secret interim committee that was studying the issue. Byrnes argued against inviting the Soviets to view the first test explosion in New Mexico and for using it in WORLD WAR II. Byrnes hoped that using the bomb would shorten the war and prevent the Soviet Union (see RUSSIA) from gaining concessions from JAPAN with its promised entry into the Pacific theater after Germany was defeated.

As secretary of state Byrnes met frequently with Joseph Stalin and other high-ranking Soviet officials at POTSDAM, London, Paris, New York, and Moscow. Soon, Byrnes's position began to change, and for a brief period of time he became a champion of good relations with the Soviet Union. He supported its domination over Eastern Europe and looked favorably on the international control of atomic energy. Truman apparently became convinced that Byrnes was "babying" the Soviets and was critical of him. By 1946, Byrnes's position on the Soviet Union changed back to a more aggressive stance. Byrnes resigned as secretary of state in January 1947. Truman had failed to protect him from critics who felt his pragmatic approach to dealing with the Soviet Union was out of step with the increasingly ideological nature of U.S.-Soviet COLD WAR relations.

# C

## Calhoun, John C. (1782–1850) *secretary of state, secretary of war*

Longtime congressperson and senator, John Caldwell Calhoun served as both SECRETARY OF STATE (1844–45) and secretary of war (1817–25). During the WAR OF 1812 Calhoun was a leading nationalist "war hawk" who pushed for war with GREAT BRITAIN and westward expansion. After the war he would become a fervent advocate of states' rights, advancing the concept that a state could revoke or nullify federal legislation that it ruled did not apply to it.

As a senator, Calhoun was an important political force in the controversy over the OREGON Territory that waged in the early 1840s. Both the United States and Great Britain had overlapping claims to part of it. In 1841 proposals surfaced in the Senate to build forts along the route to Oregon and to make generous grants of land to American settlers who traveled there. Calhoun opposed forcing the issue and advocated a policy of "wise and masterly inactivity." He was convinced that over time normal American migration of the region would settle the issue in favor of U.S. land claims and avoid the need for a diplomatic or military confrontation with Great Britain. Calhoun continued to adhere to this position when in 1844 as secretary of state under President John Tyler he turned down a British proposal for settling the dispute through arbitration.

Also as secretary of state, Calhoun signed a treaty of annexation with TEXAS on April 12, 1844. The Upshur-Calhoun Treaty was submitted to the Senate for ratification on April 22. In the intervening days Calhoun sent a note to the British minister in Washington in which he not only defended Texas annexation but also praised slavery and stated that annexation was necessary to prevent it from falling under the influence of the British who would abolish slavery there. The Senate voted on the treaty on June 8. Both presidential candidates, HENRY CLAY for the WHIGS and MARTIN VAN BUREN for the DEMOCRATS, opposed immediate annexation. Coupled with Calhoun's defense of slavery, the treaty went down to defeat by a vote of 35-16.

**Further reading:** Lander, Ernest, Jr. *Reluctant Imperialist: Calhoun, the South Carolinians, and the Mexican War.* Baton Rouge: University of Louisiana Press, 1980.

## Cambodia

Cambodia is about the size of Missouri. It is 69,900 square miles in size and has a population of 12.3 million people. Modern-day Cambodia traces its roots back to the Hindu state of Funan and the Kingdom of Angkor. In the sixth century the Khmer forces of the Kingdom of Angkor conquered Funan and established themselves as the dominant power in the region. However, with the fall of the Khmer Empire in the 15th century, Cambodia became a target for foreign domination. In 1854 the king of Cambodia sought out French protection. A French protectorate was formally established in 1863, and Cambodia joined the Indochina Union in 1887. It remained under French control until WORLD WAR II when it fell under Japanese occupation.

Cambodian pro-independence forces led by King Norodom Sihanouk took advantage of JAPAN's 1945 decision to dissolve the French Vichy colonial administration to declare independence in March of that year. This independence was short-lived, since in October 1945 Allied forces regained control and returned Southeast Asia to French colonial control. In January 1946 FRANCE granted Cambodia a measure of self-government within the French Union, but Sihanouk and his followers were not satisfied with this limited grant of autonomy and continued to press for independence. France granted independence in 1953 but Cambodia was soon invaded by communist forces from Vietnam. Under terms of the Geneva peace agreement of 1954, these troops agreed to leave and Cambodia pledged itself to a policy of neutrality.

Neutrality was difficult to sustain in the context of an ever-escalating war in VIETNAM and internal political divisions at home that included an insurgency by the local communist party known as the Khmer Rouge. Sihanouk, who had resigned as king to head the Popular Socialist Party, refused to join the SOUTHEAST ASIA TREATY ORGANIZATION (SEATO) but did agree to a military aid agreement with the United States. He broke diplomatic relations with the United States in 1965. A few years earlier, in 1963, he had accused it of supporting antigovernment activities and rejected American FOREIGN AID. Between 1955 and 1963 the United States had supplied Cambodia with $409.6 million in economic aid and $83.7 million in military aid. At the same time, however, the CENTRAL INTELLIGENCE AGENCY (CIA) was providing support to one of his main opponents, Son Ngoc Thamh.

The U.S. opposition to Sihanouk was based in part on the fact that by the mid-1960s Cambodia's eastern provinces had become sanctuaries and staging areas for the North Vietnamese army and the Vietcong. In spring 1969 the United States began a secret bombing campaign against communist strongholds in Cambodia as part of its effort to win the war in Vietnam. Interestingly that same year Cambodia and the United States resumed diplomatic ties. The increasing strength of the Communists in Cambodia had pushed Sihanouk back into the pro-American camp. Estimates placed the number of North Vietnamese forces in Cambodia at more than 50,000. Further escalation occurred in 1970. Between April and June American and South Vietnamese forces invaded Cambodia in an attempt to destroy their bases and supply lines.

During the period 1970–75, when Cambodia was known as the Khmer Republic, the United States provided it with $1.18 billion in military assistance and $503 million in economic aid. Corruption, political infighting, and military inefficiencies, however, plagued the military and political apparatus of the pro-American government led by General Lon Nol, who had ousted Sihanouk in March 1970. By 1973 the Khmer Rouge controlled nearly 60 percent of the country. Their military strength grew from about 3,000 to more than 30,000. CONGRESS ordered an end to the bombing in 1973. By that time some 540,000 tons of bombs had been dropped on Cambodia. On January 1, 1975, the Khmer Rouge launched a major offensive. Congress refused to permit additional aid for the Cambodian government, and on April 17 it fell. Khmer leader Pol Pot renamed the country Kampuchea and unleashed one of the most extensive reigns of terror in history. Cities and towns were evacuated and public executions were common. Estimates of those who died between 1975 and 1979 range from 1 million to 3 million.

In 1979 Vietnam invaded Kampuchea and forced Pol Pot's government to leave the capital of Phnom Penh. The UNITED NATIONS continued to recognize Pol Pot's government as the legitimate government and a civil war continued until a peace treaty was signed on October 31, 1991. As part of the agreement the United Nations assumed governing responsibility for Cambodia and set in motion the process of holding free elections. One major consequence of the war was a massive REFUGEE flow. It is estimated that at one point some 500,000 Cambodians had sought refuge along the Cambodian-Thai border. The United States, working through the United Nations International Children's Emergency Fund (UNICEF) and the World Food Program, provided more than $100 million in aid to these people between 1979 and 1982.

Following the peace treaty the United States and Cambodia have taken small steps to normalize their relations. In 1992 a U.S. TRADE embargo was lifted, and the United States ended its opposition within international lending agencies to providing Cambodia with loans. Full diplomatic relations were reestablished on September 24, 1993, following the holding of elections supervised by the United Nations in May 1993.

**Further reading:** Haas, Michael. *Cambodia, Pol Pot, and the United States.* New York: Praeger, 1991; Shawcross, William. *Sideshow: Kissinger, Nixon, and the Destruction of Cambodia.* New York: Pocket, 1972.

## Camp David accords (A Framework for Peace in the Middle East Agreed at Camp David; Framework for a Peace Treaty between Egypt and Israel)

The Camp David accords of 1978 represented a dramatic breakthrough in efforts to achieve a peace agreement between Israel and its Arab neighbors. President JIMMY CARTER invited Israeli prime minister Menachem Begin and Egyptian president Anwar Sadat to the presidential retreat at Camp David; after 13 days of intensive negotiations, two agreements were signed.

The Camp David meeting was not Carter's first attempt at arranging a Middle East peace. Initially he had hoped to seek a comprehensive peace settlement through a Geneva conference that would be cosponsored by the Soviet Union. This plan evoked opposition within the United States because it had been long-standing U.S. policy to keep the Soviet Union out of the region. Such a conference would have legitimized their presence. ISRAEL opposed a Geneva peace conference because it feared that it would be outvoted by a coalition of Arab and Soviet states.

The impasse over how to proceed was broken in dramatic fashion in November 1977 when Sadat announced that he would be willing to go to Jerusalem to talk with Begin. The psychological impact of Sadat's trip was immense because it established the principle of face-to-face negotiations. However, no agreement was reached, and talks between the two sides had reached an impasse

President Jimmy Carter *(left)* meets with Egyptian president Anwar Sadat at Camp David, Maryland, September 1978. *(Hulton/Archive)*

by the summer of 1978. Carter sought to break the deadlock by inviting the two leaders to Camp David in October of that year.

Carter's vision of a Middle East peace agreement was based on the 1967 UNITED NATIONS Resolution 242 whereby the Arabs would recognize Israel's right to exist in return for Israel's withdrawal from territories it seized during war. Begin refused to accede to Carter's requests that Israel accept its 1967 borders, and fearful of losing support from Jewish voters in the United States, he pressed Sadat to make concessions. Both sides were promised and received large amounts of U.S. FOREIGN AID in return for signing the Camp David accords.

Two agreements comprise the Camp David accords. The first consisted of a statement of goals. They dealt with negotiations leading to self-government for the West Bank and Gaza and the future participation of JORDAN and the Palestinians in the peace process. The second agreement was a "framework for peace." It called for Israel to withdraw from the Sinai in return for Egyptian diplomatic recognition. This peace treaty was to be signed within three months of the conclusion of Camp David.

Arab reaction was intense and negative. Jordan, SAUDI ARABIA, SYRIA, IRAQ, LIBYA, ALGERIA, and South Yemen all condemned Sadat. When the negotiations resumed deadlock set in again. This time Carter flew to the Middle East to try to restart the peace process. A peace treaty was signed on March 26, 1979, providing for a phased Israeli withdrawal from the Sinai to be completed by 1982, full diplomatic recognition, the stationing of UN troops as a buffer along the Egyptian-Israeli border, and the opening of negotiations with the Palestinians. By the end of 1979 the geopolitical landscape of the Middle East had changed dramatically, and nothing came of the peace agreement. The shah fell from power in IRAN, and Americans were taken hostage at the U.S. EMBASSY. The Soviet Union invaded AFGHANISTAN and Israeli forces, and PALESTINE LIBERATION ORGANIZATION forces were fighting in LEBANON.

See also ARAB-ISRAELI CONFLICT; EGYPT; RUSSIA.

**Further reading:** Quandt, William. *Peace Process: American Diplomacy and the Arab-Israeli Conflict.* Washington, D.C.: Brookings, 1993.

## Camp David II

Carried out over several weeks in July 2000, Camp David II was a summit conference between Israeli prime minister Ehud Barak and Palestinian Authority chairman Yasser Arafat. It was arranged by President BILL CLINTON near the end of his term in office and marked an attempt to bring closure to the peace process begun at the MADRID CONFERENCE in 1991. The conference is significant because it was both an end and a beginning. It ended a series of peace initiatives and conferences that began with Camp David in 1978. It marked the beginning of a new era because of the violence that followed. Future negotiations would address the same issues but in a very different context. Arafat had been a fixture at Arab-Israeli negotiations, but the escalating violence and TERRORISM that followed produced public calls by President GEORGE W. BUSH in June 2002 for his removal from power. The violence had transformed American foreign policy on the Arab-Israeli conflict from that of mediator and arbitrator to one of firm support for the Israeli position.

Four issues, none of which were new to Arab-Israeli peace negotiations, dominated the agenda. The first was the transfer of territory on the West Bank from ISRAEL to the Palestinian Authority. The key exchange involved Israel's agreement to give up unpopulated territory inside Israel for Israeli settlements in the occupied West Bank. A second issue involved the timing of Palestinian statehood. The Oslo accords expired in September, and Arafat threatened to unilaterally declare Palestinian independence at that time if an agreement was not reached. A third issue was the status of Jerusalem. Israel was willing to allow Palestinian sovereignty over Palestinian neighborhoods in Jerusalem in return for allowing Israeli settlements outside its current boundaries to be incorporated into the city. This proposal left unaddressed the status of the Old City that both sides claimed exclusive sovereignty over. The final issue involved the fate of Palestinian REFUGEES. The crux of the problem here involved the ability of Palestinians who had fled Israel in 1948 to return home. Their numbers were placed as high as 4 million people. The total Jewish population of Israel has been placed at 5.2 million people. Barak declared he would not accept any agreement permitting these Palestinians to return. Arafat insisted that they must have this right.

While no real agreement was reached on the refugee issue, it was the failure to reach an agreement on Jerusalem that deadlocked the negotiations and caused them to fail. Clinton sought to remove the issue from the negotiating table by proposing it should be deferred. Barak agreed but Arafat refused. Clinton publicly blamed Arafat, and the PALESTINE LIBERATION ORGANIZATION (PLO) for the failure of Camp David II. Arab commentators argued that the Camp David II agreement as it was emerging was doomed to failure. Only a complete Israeli withdrawal that results in two viable states could ensure peace. They characterized the Israeli territorial exchange agreement as one based on a policy of separation, which would create isolated pockets of Palestinian settlements that would be physically and politically isolated from one another and under Israeli economic domination.

See also ARAB-ISRAELI CONFLICT; CAMP DAVID ACCORDS; WYE RIVER ACCORDS.

## Canada

Canada is the second-largest country in the world. Canada has a population of approximately 30 million. It shares almost 9,000 kilometers of border with the United States. As the longest undefended border in the world, it reflects the closeness of the Canadian-American relationship and highlights a continental focus on a shared security. Likewise, today Canada and the United States are each other's most important trading partners.

The relationship was not always so cordial, though; it reflected the tensions of the American-British relationship through much of the 19th century. Canada was not granted dominion status until 1867, and it was not until the 1931 Statute of Westminster that it gained legal jurisdiction over its own internal and external affairs. In fact, until the 1940s, the American-Canadian relationship was very much dependent on British-American relations.

Long after the AMERICAN REVOLUTION, Canada remained a colony of GREAT BRITAIN and prided itself on a rejection of American republicanism. American United Empire Loyalists, supporters of King George III against GEORGE WASHINGTON and the Continental Congress, found safe haven in Canada after the British surrender. Most of the 40,000 to 50,000 Loyalists who fled from the thirteen colonies after the official victory of 1783 had experienced the fury of what they viewed as mob rule, and they sought a different path in Canada. In these early years, the distrust between the people of the two states ran deep.

When Great Britain went to war with Napoleon I's FRANCE, its navy attempted to lock Europe in an extensive blockade. The broad terms of this led the Royal Navy (RN) to board and seize many American ships they suspected of carrying contraband. Likewise, the British arrested and pressed British-born American sailors into service with the RN. In response, the United States launched an attack against British North America (Canada) in what became known as the WAR OF 1812. These attacks were repelled by a coalition of British troops, French-Canadian militiamen, and Native-American tribes, while the Royal Navy, in turn, bombarded Washington. Much of the capital was burned to the ground. The outcome of the conflict produced a tenuous balance. Both sides then knew not only that the meager British forces in North America could not protect Canadian territories from American invasion but also that the United States could not prevent the RN from bombarding its key cities on the eastern seaboard. This situation remained largely unchanged until the mid-1860s.

The British were determined to improve relations with the United States, wishing to eliminate its expensive commitments in North America. Though Canada was granted dominion status in 1867, and the last British garrison was removed by 1871, Britain still controlled Canada's foreign affairs, and London used the opportunity to gain favor with the United States. A key example of this is the ALASKA boundary dispute. While boundary disputes had been going on since the 18th century, most of the firm agreements like the "54-40" were made very peaceably and without great dissent. Regarding Alaska, however, the United States purchased the territory from RUSSIA in 1867, according to maps of what Russia believed to be its territory, but which entailed more land than stipulated in an 1825 agreement. From this discrepancy, the dispute arose. In 1898, after repeated requests to survey the land went unheeded, the United States and British Columbia agreed to compromise on the land—except that news of this compromise became public knowledge and western American states objected. Thus, the 1898 claim went unsettled until 1903, when an international, six-member tribunal was assembled to resolve the matter. President THEODORE ROOSEVELT successfully convinced the British that they would lose American goodwill over the matter, and, ironically, a British judge cast the deciding vote in favor of the American position. Canadian discontent with the decision led the British to grant Canada more autonomy in its relations with the United States, and in the first decade of the 20th the two grew closer.

Bonds between Canada and the United States first strengthened over trade and commerce. WORLD WAR I accelerated the process, since the war also severely injured the British economy. By 1919, British investment in Canada amounted to 57 percent of total foreign investment in the country, whereas American investment amounted to 39 percent of the total, which was already a significant change from the prewar levels. By 1922, Britain was still struggling with the cost of the war, and American investment reached 50 percent—and then an astonishing 60 percent in 1939. Similarly, in 1901, exports from Canada to the United States were less than half of those to the United Kingdom, but by 1918 they had reached four-fifths of the British total, even while Canada supplied great amounts of food and munitions to the British war effort. Imports from the United States to Canada were 250 percent of those from the United Kingdom in 1901, and only two decades later in 1918 they were 1,000 percent greater. In 1923, American investors controlled 41 percent of the Canadian steel industry, 45 percent of the electrical industry, 52 percent of copper smelting, 52 percent of drugs and chemicals, and 70 percent of the auto industry.

Canada gained legal jurisdiction over its external as well as internal affairs under the Statute of Westminster, passed by the British Parliament in 1931. Even then, however, it was tempting for the United States to consider Canada a subsidiary of Britain. This arrangement did not change until WORLD WAR II, for Canada declared war against Nazi GERMANY in September 1939 at Great Britain's side, two years before the United States officially engaged in hostilities. As a result, Canada's increasingly close economic and geographic ties with the United States served as an important link between the neutral Americans and important belligerents, such as Britain.

During this conflict, military cooperation between Canada and the United States began in earnest. President FRANKLIN ROOSEVELT and Prime Minister William Lyon Mackenzie King met in Ogdensburg, New York, on August 17, 1940, to discuss matters of mutual defense. The result was the Ogdensburg Declaration, creating the Permanent Joint Board on Defense (PJBD) that was to provide recommendations to the countries' respective governments on matters of continental security. The board continues to provide policy-level consultation on bilateral defense matters today. Canada and the United States were both founding members of the NORTH ATLANTIC TREATY ORGANIZATION (NATO) and thereby share security commitments. In addition, in response to the Soviet threat, the United States and Canada formed the North American Aerospace Defense Command (NORAD) in 1958, coordinating continental air defense.

During both world wars, Canada and the United States enjoyed the buffer zones of security afforded them by the Atlantic and Pacific Oceans. However, in the COLD WAR, bomber and missile threats posed by the Soviets were not bound by the same limitation; geographic realities stipulated that bomber approach routes and missiles would target the continental United States over Canada's Arctic. This imminent threat, security agreements, and close economic ties ensured that Canada and the United States would largely cooperate through the course of the COLD WAR. For example, both states' troops fought together in the United Nations Emergency Force (UNEF) to protect South Korea in 1950. President HARRY TRUMAN wished to fight COMMUNISM in Asia in accordance with his newly established TRUMAN DOCTRINE, and Canadian politicians were willing to send troops to protect South Korean democracy, though they were hesitant to cross the 38th parallel. The results were not entirely successful, and NORTH KOREA was lost to the Communists. Soon after, Canada participated in the UNITED NATIONS (UN) International Control Commission for Indochina, along with INDIA and POLAND, beginning in 1954, but little more than a decade later, in 1968, Canada was just one of many countries calling upon the United States to halt its bombing campaign over VIETNAM. Close relations did not always suggest consensus.

In the late 1960s and early 1970s Canada embarked upon a series of foreign-policy reviews and even considered withdrawing from NATO as well as from other organizations. Although it remained a member, the country did pull back on its commitments in favor of other pursuits, including UN PEACEKEEPING. This served as a point of tension between Canada and the United States, exacerbated by the fact that at the same time, the two countries engaged in a dispute regarding jurisdiction over the important Northwest Passage. On August 25, 1969, the American tanker *Manhattan* left the eastern seaboard en route for the Alaskan North Slope, where significant OIL reserves had recently been discovered. The ship was charged with the responsibility of testing the feasibility of a route to deliver oil from Prudhoe Bay once the oil fields had been tapped. The *Manhattan*'s voyage brought into question Canada's sovereignty over its northern territories, also challenging its newly developed pollution laws. To the Americans' disappointment, Canada took a firm stand on the matter, and the United States was forced to find alternative means of delivering the oil to the continental states.

Today the two countries work in close cooperation on a variety of environmental issues. The International Joint Commission (IJC), established as part of the 1909 Boundary Waters Treaty to mediate boundary water issues, and the Great Lakes Water Quality Agreement (1972) serve as excellent examples of cooperation in controlling transboundary water pollution. The two states meet twice a year to consult on matters of air pollution under the terms of the Air Quality Agreement (1991), aimed at controlling acid rain and other problems related to air pollution.

The Canadian-American economic relationship is one of the closest in the world. Today it is estimated that the equivalent of $1.4 billion per day in goods, services, and investment cross the border, along with more than 200 million people per year. This reality is largely the result of the Canada–United States Free Trade Agreement (FTA), the terms of which were negotiated in the early 1980s and was signed into effect on January 1, 1989. In 1990, MEXICO was included in talks regarding a free trade agreement, and on January 1, 1994, the NORTH AMERICAN FREE TRADE AGREEMENT (NAFTA) was implemented, creating a free trade area between Canada, the United States, and Mexico.

The war on TERRORISM has been a slightly contentious issue at times, some feeling that Canadian prime minister Jean Chrétien did not pledge Canadian support quickly enough after SEPTEMBER 11, 2001. However, Canadians were included in the World Trade Center casualties, and its proximity to the United States and its shared culture made the terrorist attacks personal to Canadians as well. Relations between the two countries grew closer when Canada sent part of its small military forces to AFGHANISTAN to take part in the ground war there, stretching thin its already overworked, underresourced army. Sadly, four soldiers from the Princess Patricia's Canadian Light Infantry on training exercises were killed in a friendly fire incident by U.S. National Guard Airmen on April 18, 2002. On the official level, this has not affected DIPLOMACY, with both sides ready to recognize that the incident is a tragedy, and that suitable punishment will be administered, if necessary. The U.S. inquiry is ongoing. Canada's commitment to this new war stays true.

**Further reading:** Doran, Charles F. *Forgotten Partnership.* Baltimore: Johns Hopkins University Press, 1984; Granastein, J. L., and Norman Hillmer. *Canada and the United States in the 1990s: For Better or for Worse.* New York: Addison-Wesley Longman, 1992; Lipset, Seymour Martin. *Continental Divide.* New York: Routledge and Taylor, 1990.

—Stephanie Cousineau

## Caribbean Basin Initiative

The Caribbean Basin Initiative (CBI) was announced by President RONALD REAGAN in a speech to the ORGANIZATION OF AMERICAN STATES on February 24, 1982. Although more narrow in its geographic scope, the CBI followed in the line of such initiatives as the POINT FOUR PROGRAM under President HARRY TRUMAN and the ALLIANCE FOR PROGRESS under President JOHN KENNEDY as an American plan to bring about economic, political, and social progress in Latin America.

As presented by President Reagan, the CBI contained six elements. First and most important, it was to be a one-way free-trade zone that would allow Caribbean goods to enter the United States duty-free. Second, a series of tax incentives would be put into place to encourage investment in the region. Third, increased emergency financial and military aid would be made available. Fourth, private sector training and technical assistance would be provided. Fifth, an emphasis would be placed on developing a coordinated regional development plan. Sixth, specific side promises were made to PUERTO RICO that were not made to other states. Eligibility was limited to those states within the Caribbean basin that were not designated by the

United States as communist and which did not discriminate against U.S. exports or nationalize U.S. property without compensation.

An interim assessment published in 1990 found that while the CBI did help American corporations, "it is fairly clear that greater U.S. economic involvement in the Caribbean has done little to solve the economic problems of the region or enhance the standard of living of a majority of the Caribbean people." Several factors were cited as limiting the effectiveness of the CBI. First, CONGRESS amended the CBI several times in response to protectionist pressures from U.S. firms and constituents. Second, the CBI allowed firms to play Caribbean states against one another in pursuit of their investments, thereby limiting its economic impact. For example, Barbados's exports to the United States fell from $202 million to $51 million as manufacturers went elsewhere in search of cheaper labor. Third, because the CBI focused on stimulating export sales, little attention was paid to creating backward linkages to other elements of local economies or reinvesting profits.

The dispersal of funds within the Caribbean basin was also limited in its economic impact. Several of the poorest states in desperate need of help received little. HAITI secured only 1.2 percent of CBI funds. Key national security allies of the United States received more than their fair share. EL SALVADOR was to receive 36 percent of all funds before congressional action reduced this figure. Jamaica, which had just voted out of office a socialist government, received 14 percent of CBI funds. Costa Rica and Honduras, two states that were key players in the U.S. anti-Sandinista policy, received 20 percent and 10 percent of these funds, respectively.

As with other economic development initiatives in Latin America, such as the Alliance for Progress, the CBI is typically viewed in the context of either revisionist accounts that stress the importance of protecting and furthering American economic interests in formulating U.S. policy toward Latin America or security-focused accounts that stress the role that economic aid has played in U.S. efforts to shore up friendly governments.

**Further reading:** Deere, Carmen. *In the Shadows of the Sun: Caribbean Development Alternatives and U.S. Policy.* Boulder, Colo.: Westview, 1990; Newfarmer, Richard, ed. *From Gunboats to Diplomacy: New U.S. Policies for Latin America.* Baltimore: Johns Hopkins University Press, 1984.

**Carter, Jimmy** (1924–    ) *president of the United States, Nobel Peace Prize recipient*
James Earl Carter was the 39th president of the United States. Running as a Washington outsider, he came from political obscurity to capture the DEMOCRATIC PARTY pres-

idential nomination in 1980 and served one term as president (1977–81).

Consistent with his status as a Washington outsider, Carter promised to bring about major changes in the tone and direction of U.S. foreign policy. Above all else, he promised to bring a renewed sense of moral purpose to U.S. foreign policy by stressing HUMAN RIGHTS. Carter centralized decision making in the White House relying heavily upon NATIONAL SECURITY ADVISOR Zbigniew Brzezinski for advice and relegating to SECRETARY OF STATE CYRUS VANCE the task of administering the STATE DEPARTMENT. This led to clashes between the two that contributed to the inconsistency in foreign policy that plagued the administration.

Even though foreign policy had not played a major role in the presidential campaign, Carter plunged quickly into making changes in it. His first NATIONAL SECURITY COUNCIL decision directive involved the determination to pursue a new Panama Canal Treaty. He followed this up with a decision to abandon the Vladivostok formula that the Ford administration had negotiated as the basis for STRATEGIC ARMS LIMITATION TALKS (SALT II) in favor of an agreement that specified deeper cuts in the U.S. and Soviet NUCLEAR WEAPONS arsenal. The PANAMA CANAL TREATIES were realized but at great political cost. The Soviet Union (see RUSSIA) resented Carter's attempt to lessen its relevance to U.S. foreign policy and when finally agreed to the details of the SALT II Treaty closely resembled that which Carter had rejected as inadequate.

Carter's major foreign-policy success came in September 1978 when he hosted Israeli prime minister Menachem Begin and Egyptian president Anwar Sadat to a summit conference at the presidential retreat at Camp David. The resulting CAMP DAVID ACCORDS broke a cycle of war and violence that had characterized the region since the end of WORLD WAR II. Carter was less successful in his efforts to end conflict in Central America, particularly in NICARAGUA. Initially his administration supported the Sandinista government that replaced longtime U.S. ally Anastasio Somoza. By the time it left office, however, Carter had authorized CENTRAL INTELLIGENCE AGENCY (CIA) support for anti-Sandinista forces.

By the end of his term, U.S. foreign policy was returning to its COLD WAR logic. The triggering event was the 1979 Soviet invasion of AFGHANISTAN. Carter responded by halting the SALT II ratification process and stopping the sale of high technology to the Soviet Union—part of what is now called the CARTER DOCTRINE. In his 1980 State of the Union address he warned that any attempt by outside forces to gain control of the Persian Gulf region would be repelled by any means, including military force. The international politics of confrontation soon spread to IRAN. There, opposition forces led by the exiled Ayatollah Khomeini deposed the U.S.–backed shah. Responding angrily to the U.S. decision to permit the shah to come to the U.S. for medical treatment, a mob seized the U.S. EMBASSY. Both diplomacy and a military rescue effort failed to win the release of the hostages. The crisis dragged on for 444 days before they were released on RONALD REAGAN's inauguration day in 1981.

Both those on the political left and right have criticized Carter's foreign policy. Liberal critics found much to like in his emphasis on human rights but faulted him for an inability to carry through on his reformist agenda. His strategic incoherence and erratic tactics led some to characterize his foreign policy as a "hell of good intentions." Conservative critics were not as charitable. They condemned Carter for having an immature vision of world politics that was inconsistent with its underlying power dynamics. Jeane J. Kirkpatrick, who would go on to serve as UNITED NATIONS ambassador under President Reagan, asserted that Carter's human-rights policy was fundamentally flawed because it did not recognize the differences between left- and right-wing governments. Right-wing governments could make the transition to democracy, while left-wing governments could not. A final perspective on Carter's foreign policy argued that its limitations were not due to his vision of the world or inconsistent policies. They were a product of the fact that his administration governed in a period of adjustment, which lacked the symbols and doctrines within which earlier presidents could frame their policies and garner public support.

After leaving the White House Carter continued to take an active role in world affairs. He undertook a personal diplomatic mission to NORTH KOREA, where he helped broker an agreement with the United States that ended the international controversy over North Korea's nuclear weapons program. In 1989 he attempted unsuccessfully to mediate the civil war in ETHIOPIA. Carter went to HAITI and helped arrange a peaceful transfer of power to Jean-Bertrand Aristide when it appeared that a military conflict with the United States was imminent. Carter also led missions to Nicaragua (1990) and PANAMA (1989) to monitor elections in those countries. Carter was awarded the Nobel Peace Prize for his efforts toward promoting international peace in 2002.

**Further reading:** Carter, Jimmy. *Keeping Faith.* New York: Bantam, 1982; Garthoff, Raymond. *Détente and Confrontation: American-Soviet Relations from Nixon to Reagan.* Rev. ed. Washington, D.C.: Brookings, 1994; Vance, Cyrus. *Hard Choices: Critical Years in American Foreign Policy.* New York: Simon and Schuster, 1983.

## Carter Doctrine

The Carter Doctrine is the name given to the policy announced by President JIMMY CARTER in response to the Soviet Union's (see RUSSIA) December 1979 invasion of AFGHANISTAN. He stated that the United States would treat an "attempt by any outside force to gain control of the Persian Gulf region as an assault on the vital interests of the United States and such force will be repelled by any means necessary, including military force."

The Carter Doctrine represented a virtual about-face for Carter's foreign policy toward the Soviet Union. Carter had campaigned on a platform that rejected power politics and promised to replace it with an emphasis on HUMAN RIGHTS and morality. The inevitable consequence of his foreign policy was to deemphasize the importance of the Soviet Union to U.S. foreign policy and to draw attention to how it treated its citizens. Both moves offended Soviet leaders who continued to view world politics through a prism that emphasized the importance of power politics and traditional security concerns.

For the Soviet Union, unrest in Afghanistan represented a classic threat to their security and could not be tolerated. When repeated efforts to bolster the authority of the local pro-Moscow Communist Party proved futile, the Soviet Union sent in its own forces. The Soviet action caught the Carter administration off guard and called into question the wisdom of his foreign-policy agenda. As part of his response Carter requested a 5 percent increase in annual defense spending (up from the 3 percent he had been requesting) and expanded the American naval and air presence in the Persian Gulf. Though generally applauded, some commentators criticized Carter's response as overreacting and motivated by domestic political concerns. They argued that while deplorable, the Soviet invasion of Afghanistan did not represent a calculated Soviet move to control the Persian Gulf. This debate was soon overshadowed by the Iranian hostage crisis and the Carter administration's inability to secure the release of the Americans taken hostage.

**Further reading:** Smith, Gaddis. *Morality, Reason, and Power: An American Diplomacy in the Carter Years.* New York: Hill and Wang, 1986.

## Central Asian republics

Five states make up the Central Asian republics (CARS). All achieved their independence in 1991 following the collapse of the Soviet Union. While united by history, culture, and geography, they also constitute a diverse set of states. Kazakhstan is the largest state. It is four times the size of Texas, with an area of 1.048 million square miles. Turkmenistan and Uzbekistan are each about the size of California, with areas of 188,407 square miles and 172,696 square miles, respectively. The two smallest states are Kyrgyzstan, which is about the size of South Dakota, and Tajikistan, which is about the size of Wisconsin. Uzbekistan's population is the largest at 24.1 million, and it has the smallest percentage of ethnic Russians. Turkmenistan has the smallest population with 4.3 million people. Within the borders of Kazakhstan, Turkmenistan, and Uzbekistan can be found vast OIL and natural gas reserves, making them prime targets for foreign investors. Tajikistan and Kyrgyzstan remain largely agricultural economies and have few natural resources on which to base economic growth strategies. Militarily, Uzbekistan possesses the largest and most competent military force in the region.

The central political reality for the CARS remains the legacy of their membership in the Soviet Union. Politically they tend to be autocracies whose rulers are holdovers from the Soviet era. Their economies continue to be shaped by years of central planning. RUSSIA also remains the most significant foreign presence in the region. The CARS recognize the need to maintain good relations with Russia but are also fearful of attempts by Moscow to reassert dominance over the region.

The two extremes in relations between Russia and the CARS are represented by Tajikistan and Kazakhstan. Russian involvement in Tajikistan has been the most pronounced. As a result of a civil war between Islamic conservatives and the government that lasted from 1992 to 1997 and the resulting Russian PEACEKEEPING efforts, by the mid-1990s Tajikistan was for all practical purposes a Russian satellite. By February 1993 there were some 3,500 Russian troops and 20,000 military support personnel in Tajikistan, and by 1994 Russia was paying nearly 70 percent of the Tajik budget. Of particular concern to Russia was the influence of the Taliban regime in neighboring AFGHANISTAN on Tajik politics. Even prior to their coming to power, an estimated 65,000 Tajik GUERRILLAS were training in Afghanistan. Russian relations with Kazakhstan revolve around three realities. First, about 40 percent of the Kazakh population is ethnic Russian. Second, Kazakhstan was the site of Russian nuclear weapons deployments. Third, Kazakhstan possesses extensive oil reserves. It is also an exporter of wheat and coal. The second and third points have made Kazakhstan an important regional state in Western eyes and give it negotiating leverage vis-à-vis Russia that other CARS lack. The United States has provided Kazakhstan with more than $78 billion in aid to remove and dismantle its nuclear forces. It has sealed 181 nuclear test tunnels and turned over to the United States more than a half ton of weapons-grade uranium. The last of its warheads were removed in 1995. Since 1993 the UNITED STATES AGENCY FOR INTERNATIONAL DEVELOPMENT (USAID) has administered more than $273 million in technical assistance programs to Kazakhstan, and American companies have invested more than $5 billion there since 1993. In contrast, between 1992 and 1998 Tajikistan and Kyrgyzstan received only $3 and $70 million in economic aid from USAID.

Prior to the terrorist attacks of SEPTEMBER 11, 2001, the United States's primary interest in Central Asia was the lure of oil and natural gas. Those attacks shifted America's attention to national security issues. Uzbekistan's location in the geographic center of Central Asia has made it an important ally. It granted the United States' request for access to military air bases in southern Uzbekistan as part of the preparation for war in Afghanistan against the Taliban. Following the terrorist attacks visits by American officials have become more common. SECRETARY OF STATE Colin Powell and SECRETARY OF DEFENSE Donald Rumsfeld as well as numerous congresspeople have visited there.

Incidents of TERRORISM in Central Asia actually became more noticeable in the late 1990s. The group that has garnered the most attention is the Islamic Movement of Uzbekistan (IMU). Its goal is to establish an Islamic state in the Ferghana valley that borders Kyrgyzstan, Tajikistan, and Uzbekistan. Founded in 1998 it is considered to be the most dangerous Central Asian terrorist force. In August 1999 it launched attacks against Kyrgyzstan from Tajikistan that resulted in the declaration of a state of emergency and the payment of between $3 and $5 million in ransom to obtain the release of hostages, which included American and Japanese citizens. Estimates also place IMU control over the flow of narcotics entering Kyrgyzstan at 70 percent.

Because the region borders Iran and Afghanistan it is not surprising that the activities of radical Islamic groups in Central Asia are of concern to the United States. Some commentators, however, urge caution in organizing American foreign policy toward the region around this threat, noting that POLITICAL ISLAM in the region is a complex force with many faces. For example, operating alongside the IMU in the Ferghana valley is the Hizb-ut-Tahrir (Hu T). Founded in 1952 it has surged into prominence as a political force that emphasizes grassroots activity rather than violence as the most appropriate means for establishing an Islamic state. They also note the existence of other dimensions to the security problem. These include the presence of millions of Afghan REFUGEES who fled Taliban rule, poverty, HUMAN RIGHTS violations, and governmental corruption that is tied to DRUG TRAFFICKING.

It has also been noted that the CARS states have foreign-policy agendas that may place them at odds with the United States. The Clinton administration exerted pressure on the Kazakh government to cancel the sale of 40 MIG jets to NORTH KOREA. In 1997 Turkmenistan opened an oil pipeline to Iran in opposition to the American preference that no Caspian Sea oil flow through that country. Kyrgyzstan is in a long-running conflict with CHINA involving ethnic policy. The CARS states also have yet to cooperate effectively with one another on a sustained basis. Border disputes divide them, and Uzbekistan is suspected by the others of desiring to dominate the region. Russia remains the lynchpin for regional security and the fulcrum for cooperative efforts. Its interests in the region set limits to the scope of American influence.

Finally, although its full potential and consequences are not yet clear, the domestic politics of American foreign policy toward Central Asia is undergoing change. This is symbolized by the establishment of a bipartisan and bicameral congressional Silk Road Caucus in fall 2001. Its goal is to foster economic, political, and cultural ties with Central Asia. It also provides a focal point for CARS lobbying efforts with the U.S. government.

**Further reading:** Anderson, John. *The International Politics of Central Asia.* New York: St. Martin's 1997; Atabaki, Touradji, and John O'Kane, eds. *Post-Soviet Central Asia.* New York: St. Martin's, 1998.

## Central Intelligence Agency (CIA)

The Central Intelligence Agency (CIA) was created by the 1947 NATIONAL SECURITY ACT. It assigned the CIA the following tasks: (1) to advise the NATIONAL SECURITY COUNCIL (NSC) on intelligence matters related to national security; (2) to make recommendations to the NSC for the coordination of departmental and agency intelligence activities; (3) to correlate, evaluate, and disseminate intelligence; (4) to perform for the benefit of existing intelligence agencies such additional services as the NSC determines; and (5) to perform "other functions and duties" relating to national security intelligence as the NSC may direct. Absent in this listing of tasks is any explicit authorization to engage in covert action or to collect its own information. Both of these tasks, however, quickly, became part of its organizational mission.

Two intelligence organizations preceded the CIA. Its immediate predecessor was the Central Intelligence Group that was established by presidential directive in January 1946. Headed by a DIRECTOR OF CENTRAL INTELLIGENCE (DCI), the Central Intelligence Group was responsible for the coordination, planning, evaluation, and dissemination of intelligence. It was also given the authority to engage in the overt collection of intelligence. The National Intelligence Authority, composed of the secretaries of state, war, and navy, and a personal representative of the PRESIDENT was created to serve as a supervisory body. The budget and personnel in the Central Intelligence Group also were provided by these three executive departments. Through this approach to national security intelligence, the existing departments tried to guarantee that they would continue to have control over their intelligence operations. Advocates of centralizing intelligence had hoped that the Central Intelligence Group could provide independent intelligence analysis that would minimize the impact of what was perceived as the all-too frequently biased analysis being carried out by the STATE DEPARTMENT and military services. The hope also existed that as a coordinator of intelligence the Central Intelligence Group could limit the amount of duplication built into the existing system of intelligence collection.

The United States's first independent intelligence agency was the OFFICE OF STRATEGIC SERVICES (OSS) established by executive order in June 1942. Headed by William J. Donovan, it was established in WORLD WAR II and was heavily influenced by its contacts with British intelligence. The goal was to place within a single intelligence agency the responsibility for intelligence collection, analysis, espionage, sabotage, and propaganda. At the war's end President HARRY TRUMAN disbanded the OSS and distributed its resources among the State Department and the military services. The CIA would share many of the operational problems encountered by the OSS in its brief history. Other intelligence organizations challenged its role in intelligence collection and analysis. It competed with other intelligence organizations in presenting its views to the president and other policy makers. And, internally, its clandestine side tended to dominate over its analytic side.

The head of the CIA is the director of central intelligence (DCI) who simultaneously serves as the head of the INTELLIGENCE COMMUNITY. This dual role is testimony to the fact that the CIA continues to exist as one of many intelligence agencies and that many intelligence resources exists beyond its reach.

CIA is divided into a series of functional directorates. Two have emerged as particularly important for the conduct of U.S. foreign policy. The Directorate of Intelligence was created in 1952 and is the largest directorate. It is the primary producer of government intelligence documents that range in frequency from daily briefs to weekly, quarterly, and yearly assessments. It also conducts occasional special reports, the best known of which is the NATIONAL INTELLIGENCE ESTIMATE (NIE). The purpose of the NIE is to present the intelligence community's best judgment on a problem. Using 1982 as an example, 67 NIEs were produced. During the COLD WAR most NIEs focused on the Soviet Union (see RUSSIA).

The other directorate that has acquired special standing is the Directorate for Operations. Also created in 1952 it is the most controversial directorate within the CIA and the one that is often targeted for abolition by critics of the CIA. The Directorate for Operations has three main missions: the clandestine collection of INTELLIGENCE, COUNTERINTELLIGENCE, and COVERT ACTION. This last mission has produced some of the CIA's most notable successes and stunning failures. Numbered among the early successes are the overthrow of Mohammad Mossadegh in IRAN that allowed the shah to return to power and the overthrow of

Jacob Arbenz Guzmán in GUATEMALA. Notable failures included an attempt to overthrow President Sukarno of Indonesia and the BAY OF PIGS invasion of CUBA that was intended to remove Fidel Castro from power. By the 1970s, the cumulative effect of two decades of covert action was to produce a popular image of the CIA as a "rogue elephant" that was out of control. Rather than just rely upon executive-branch oversight, CONGRESS moved to create two special committees, one in each chamber, to oversee intelligence. It also insisted that covert actions be accompanied by an explicit "Presidential Finding" that they were in the national interest.

The end of the cold war and the fall of COMMUNISM in the Soviet Union robbed the CIA of its central intelligence and covert action focus. In 1991 President GEORGE H. W. BUSH issued National Security Directive 29, calling for a top-to-bottom examination of the mission, roles, and priorities of the intelligence community. In addition to having to justify its continued existence, the CIA found its performance in many areas under attack. On the intelligence side, the most fundamental questions centered on why it had failed to predict these two momentous events. A major counterintelligence embarrassment occurred when it was revealed that Aldrich Ames, who had joined the CIA in 1962 and worked on Soviet counterintelligence operations, had been on the Soviet payroll since 1985 and received more than $1.5 million to serve as a spy. Covert action programs continued, but they also became more public and visible. A case in point was the congressional funding for Iraqi resistance groups dedicated to overthrowing Saddam Hussein. The CIA also has found itself charged with new missions, such as helping to try to broker an Arab-Israeli peace agreement in the closing weeks of the Clinton administration. The CIA's role expanded again following

the SEPTEMBER 11, 2001, terrorist attacks on the World Trade Center and the Pentagon. The Bush administration relied upon it heavily to organize resistance forces to the Taliban in northern AFGHANISTAN. This made it a major force in the war against the Taliban and required the coordination of CIA and military activity in a context reminiscent of the covert action activities undertaken by the Office of Strategic Services during WORLD WAR II.

After the September 11 terrorist attacks the CIA's intelligence estimating abilities and procedures came into question. So too did its cooperation with the FEDERAL BUREAU OF INVESTIGATION (FBI) and other members of the intelligence community. Congress pressed for the creation of an independent panel to review the performance of intelligence agencies with regard to September 11. President GEORGE W. BUSH opposed the creation of this body. He then relented but placed bureaucratic obstacles in its way.

**Further reading:** Colby, William. *Honorable Men, My Life in the CIA.* New York: Simon and Schuster, 1978; Hulnick, Arthur. *Fixing the Spy Machine.* Westport, Conn.: Praeger, 1999; Johnson, Loch. *The Central Intelligence Agency: History and Documents.* New York: Oxford University Press, 1989; Ranelagh, John. *The Agency, the Rise and Decline of the CIA.* New York: Simon and Schuster, 1987.

## Central Treaty Organization (CENTO)

The Central Treaty Organization (CENTO) was formed in 1959 for the purposes of containing communist expansion into the Middle East. It was one of a series of ALLIANCES created by the Eisenhower administration to encircle and contain the Soviet Union. Overly identifying nationalism with COMMUNISM, CENTO did more to isolate the United States from the Arab world than protect it from communism.

CENTO was a successor organization to the Baghdad Pact, also known as the Middle East Treaty Organization. This organization was founded in April 1955, and its members were GREAT BRITAIN, TURKEY, IRAQ, IRAN, and PAKISTAN. Loosely speaking, they formed a northern tier of states that would block the SOVIET UNION from expanding into the Arab world. The United States did not join the Baghdad Pact largely out of a concern for its relationship with Israel.

It was not long before the volatile mixture of nationalism and communism came to challenge this attempt at securing the Middle East status quo. Egyptian president Gamal Abdel Nasser saw the Baghdad Pact as neocolonial meddling and as a threat to his POWER. Contributing to this perception were the facts that Iraq was a traditional rival of EGYPT's for regional dominance and the CENTRAL INTELLIGENCE AGENCY had only recently helped engineer the overthrow of the anti-Western and nationalist leader

CIA director George Tenet *(left)* and Secretary of State Colin Powell talk following Powell's address to the UN Security Council on February 5, 2003, in New York City.

Mohammad Mossadegh in Iran. In September 1955 he signed an arms agreement with the Soviet Union as a means of offsetting the U.S. move. This set in motion a series of conflicts involving the Western powers and Israel on one side and Egypt and Arab nationalist forces on the other. In 1956 the SUEZ CRISIS marked a failed British-French-Israeli effort to wrest control of the Suez Canal from Egypt and undermine Nasser's attempt to build up pan-Arabism in the region. In 1958 the United States sent Marines into LEBANON in response to that government's call for help to put down a domestic rebellion and "indirect aggression."

As these events unfolded the United States sought to bolster the resolve and military power of the Baghdad Pact states without formally joining the alliance. In 1956 they were assured by the United States that an attack on any of them would be viewed "with the utmost gravity." In 1957 the EISENHOWER DOCTRINE was announced, pledging the United States to defend the Middle East against Soviet aggression. In 1958 the United States went even further in signing a declaration of collective security with the Baghdad Pact states. After the overthrow of King Faisal II in 1958 Iraq had been steadily moving closer to the Soviet Union. In late March it officially withdrew from the Baghdad Pact. Separate bilateral peace agreements were signed with Turkey, Pakistan, and Iran that same month. In August at a meeting in Turkey the alliance officially changed its name to CENTO. The alliance was further weakened when in 1962 Pakistan, a member of both SOUTHEAST ASIA TREATY ORGANIZATION (SEATO) and CENTO, indicated that it might withdraw. Pakistani leaders had been angered by the American decision to supply arms to its neighbor and enemy INDIA during a regional crisis involving CHINA. CENTO formally dissolved in September 1979. In March of that year Iran withdrew following the revolution that ended the shah's rule, and Pakistan also withdrew, asserting that CENTO no longer contributed to its defense.

See also NORTH ATLANTIC TREATY ORGANIZATION; RUSSIA.

## Chile

Chile is located in South America. It is nearly twice the size of California with an area of 302,778 square miles. It has a population of 15.3 million people. The first Europeans arrived in Chile in 1541, and Chile was conquered by Pedro de Valdivia in 1550 and made part of the Viceroyalty of Peru. Chile declared its independence in 1810 when its leaders proclaimed it to be an autonomous republic within the Spanish monarchy. Total independence was proclaimed in 1818. The United States recognized Chile in 1832.

The United States has deeply involved itself in Chilean affairs on three occasions, each of which spawned feelings of suspicion and resentment within Chile. The first was during the War of the Pacific, 1879–84. This conflict pitted Chile against Peru and Bolivia. Chile emerged victorious and demanded territory from Peru as compensation for war expenses. SECRETARY OF STATE JAMES BLAINE opposed the demand, but the United States was unable to prevent it. There was little support in the United States for military action to block Chile, and American diplomats were divided, with some backing Peru and others supporting Chile. As a result of the war Chile expanded its northern territory by almost one-third.

The second ill-fated involvement soon followed. Civil war broke out in Chile in 1891 when the Congressionalists revolted against the Chilean president, who was seeking dictatorial powers. In the span of less than one year five highly inflammatory events occurred that alienated the winning side, the Congressionalists. The first involved the Chilean steamer *Itaca*. The rebels had purchased rifles and ammunition in New York for their cause. They were shipped to California and ultimately placed on the *Itaca*. The Chilean government lobbied the United States to stop the transaction. With U.S. naval forces in hot pursuit the *Itaca* safely arrived in Chile with its cargo. In the interests of maintaining good relations with the United States but resenting the U.S. position, the Congressionalists turned the ship and its cargo over to American authorities who sent it back to California.

The second incident involved hostile actions by a U.S. company that implicitly acted with the support of the U.S. Navy. The U.S.-based Central and South American Telegraph Company cut international telegraph lines used by the Congressionalists but arranged for government communications to continue. The line in question lay submerged off of the Chilean coast and was cut under the protection of the USS *Baltimore*. It was cut because the company was unable to reach a satisfactory agreement with the Congressionalists over protecting its investments.

The third incident in the civil war occurred when a U.S. communiqué relayed information to Washington about 8,000 Congressionalist forces landing north of Quinteros Bay. The story was released by supporters of the president and was viewed by Congressionalists as evidence that the United States had been spying on them. The fourth incident occurred just as the civil war was ending. Supporters of the president took refuge in the U.S. legation, and the Congressionalists took steps to prevent them from fleeing. An incorrect report that was widely circulated in the press and originated with an American indicated that President Balmaceda was one of them and that he had been rescued by the U.S. Navy.

The final incident came when some 120 sailors from the USS *Baltimore* took shore leave in October 1891. A brawl resulted in which two U.S. sailors were killed, 17 were injured, and many others were arrested. The United States demanded an apology from the new Constitutionalist government, but when none was forthcoming President Benjamin Harrison threatened to intervene. Chilean officials responded angrily and publicly, and sentiment for war rose in both countries. In January 1892 the United States sent an ultimatum to Chile demanding an apology and threatening to break diplomatic relations. Chile capitulated and apologized and provided financial compensation to the injured and to the families of the deceased. Although the Chilean apology was expected, President Harrison went forward and delivered a special message to Congress that in effect amounted to a declaration of war. Harrison came under heavy political criticism in the United States for his address.

The third controversial involvement of the United States with Chile occurred during the COLD WAR. In 1970 Senator Salvador Allende, founder of Chile's Socialist Party, led a leftist coalition composed of Marxists, radicals, and socialists to a narrow electoral victory and he was named president by the Chilean congress. His reform agenda included the nationalization of most of the remaining private industries and banks as well as agricultural reforms, including land appropriation and collectivization.

Allende was seen as a threat by the Nixon administration on several levels. Politically, his leftist leanings and electoral popularity were seen as setting a dangerous precedent that might open the Western Hemisphere to communism. Economically, Allende's reforms threatened many of America's leading economic interests. In response RICHARD NIXON unleashed a broadly constructed program of covert action. Its clandestine support of anti-Allende political leaders succeeded in denying him electoral victories in 1958 and 1964. Between 1964 and 1969 the CENTRAL INTELLIGENCE AGENCY (CIA) spent almost $2 million on training anticommunist organizers in slums and rural areas.

Allende governed for three tumultuous years. He was overthrown on September 11, 1973, by a military coup, and a new government led by General Augusto Pinochet took power. Since his election in 1970, the CIA had organized a series of COVERT ACTIONS to remove him from office. Focusing on the death of Chilean chief of staff General René Schneider in 1970, this covert action became a principal focal point during congressional investigations into CIA assassination attempts by the CHURCH COMMITTEE.

Neither of the three candidates for the presidency in the 1970 election won a majority of votes in the election; according to Chilean law, a runoff was scheduled to be held in a joint session of the Chilean congress. Tradition held that the top vote getter in the general election, Allende with 36.6 percent, would be selected. The Nixon adminis-

tration found this unacceptable. Allende had run with the backing of both socialists and communists and, as with previous social reformers who took power in the DOMINICAN REPUBLIC and GUATEMALA, his domestic agenda was considered to be anti-American.

NATIONAL SECURITY ADVISOR HENRY KISSINGER brought together the 40 Committee, which oversaw CIA covert action programs. A two-track strategy was put into place designed to prevent Allende from becoming president. Track I consisted of behind-the-scenes political maneuvering within Chile, including labor stoppages, propaganda, and withholding of American credit, that would permit outgoing president Eduardo Frei, who could not serve another consecutive term as president, to continue in office after only a brief exit from power. The 40 Committee approved $250,000 for bribes to bring this about, although evidence now suggests that no bribes were paid. Track II consisted of a campaign of social and economic disruption and included support for a military coup and was kept secret even within the U.S. government. One way this was to be brought about was by "making the economy scream." Eight million dollars would be spent on Track II–type initiatives between 1970 and 1973. Although not accepted by the CIA, the International Telephone and Telegraph Company offered $1 million to help prevent Allende from becoming president. General Schneider opposed a coup. The CIA made plans to assassinate him or kidnap him. During a kidnap attempt carried out by a group of officers not affiliated with the CIA, Schneider was killed. His death cemented Allende's victory as his right-wing opponent Jorge Alessandri now called for his selection as president.

With Allende's election, President Richard Nixon's administration now concentrated on destabilizing the domestic situation in Chile. An "invisible" economic blockade was put in place whereby U.S. foreign-aid funds and monies from international organizations and private investment were halted or hindered. Anti-Allende political forces within Chile received financial assistance from the CIA. More than $1 million was approved by the 40 Committee for supporting parties in various local elections. Evidence also points to CIA support for truckers' strikes. The deteriorating economic situation helped opposition forces win 56 percent of the vote in the March 1973 midterm election.

Matters soon came to a head. General Augusto Pinochet, a hard-line conservative, assumed control of the military in August. That same month the Chilean congress passed a resolution denouncing Allende's government for its habitual violation of the constitution and called for the military to "put an end" to his rule. On September 11 the coup began, and late that day the military announced that Allende had committed suicide. More than 3,000 people were killed or disappeared in violence following the coup organized by the military and directed at eliminating the "cancer of Marxism" from Chile.

U.S. involvement in Chile between 1970 and 1973 left deep scars on U.S. foreign policy. The CIA was the institution most deeply affected. Its past record of success and failure in both covert operations and intelligence gathering along with its possible involvement in other assassinations became the subject of major House and Senate investigations, the most famous of which was led by Senator Frank Church (D-Idaho). The coup against Allende along with the violence that followed also served as an important stimulus to the passage of HUMAN RIGHTS legislation by CONGRESS that sought to deny U.S. funds to any government that engaged in gross violations of human rights.

Pinochet's rule, which lasted until 1988, was marked by serious and widespread human-rights abuses that were criticized by President JIMMY CARTER. Even prior to his becoming president, anger at Pinochet's human-rights policies were building in the United States. In June 1976 the Kennedy Amendment cut off all U.S. military aid to Chile until human-rights conditions improved. The assassination of Orlando Letelier in Washington complicated relations further. He had been Allende's ambassador to the United States and was killed by Chilean intelligence agents. The Reagan administration was more sympathetic to Pinochet, but it too urged democratic reforms on the reluctant Chilean leader. In 1986 the United States sponsored a resolution at the UNITED NATIONS Human Rights Commission expressing "profound concern" over the situation in Chile.

Along with these largely hostile and unwelcomed interactions, Chile has also had more traditional diplomatic interactions with the United States. Along with ARGENTINA and BRAZIL, Chile played mediator in the U.S.–Mexican standoff that followed President WOODROW WILSON's decision to send U.S. Marines into MEXICO in April 1914 during the Mexican Revolution. The ABC— Argentina, Brazil, and Chile—powers served as mediators at a meeting between American and Mexican representatives held at Niagara Falls, Canada, in May 1914. A plan was agreed to but never implemented. In January 1942 Chile, along with Argentina, blocked a U.S. effort at a ministers of foreign affairs conference to obtain binding agreement on the part of Latin American states to break diplomatic relations with the Axis powers. In the end it was left as a recommendation.

U.S.-Chilean relations deteriorated during the IRAQ War. Chile was a member of the UN Security Council that deliberated over whether or not to issue a resolution supporting U.S. military activity against Saddam Hussein. Chile opposed such a move, and after the war ended the United States made known its displeasure by slowing down negotiations that would have led Chile to join the NORTH AMERICAN FREE TRADE ASSOCIATION (NAFTA).

See also MULTINATIONAL CORPORATIONS; REVISIONISM.

**Further reading:** Sater, William. *Chile and the United States.* Athens: University of Georgia Press, 1993; Sigmund, Paul E. *The United States and Democracy in Chile.* Baltimore: Johns Hopkins University Press, 1993.

## China

China is located in Asia and its population was estimated to be 1.284 billion people in 2002. It has an area of 3.7 million square miles, making it larger than the land area of the United States, which is 3.5 million square miles. The first American contact with China came in 1784 when the *Empress of China* sailed from New York to Canton. Fifteen months later it returned, and the China trade was born. In the coming years the volume of trade between the United States and China fluctuated widely and did not constitute a significant portion of the U.S. global trade balance. By 1801, 34 American ships made the crossing to China. Trade relations were curtailed by the WAR OF 1812 and then grew again in the 1830s and 1840s. By 1870, 50 American commercial firms had set up operations in China. This number fell to 31 in the 1880s. By 1900 American investments in China amounted to less than $20 million.

The China trade of the 1800s operated against the backdrop of a number of important social and political developments in both countries. One of these was the presence of American missionaries in China. The first missionaries came in the 1830s. By the turn of the 20th century an estimated 1,000 missionaries were in China. Their presence in China produced some converts to Christianity and helped boost American commerce. Their writings also became the primary source of information about China for most Americans.

Pressures in the opposite direction came from the Chinese government's desire to limit trade with the West. Canton was the only port open to such trade. In 1832 Edmund Roberts was sent on a mission to sign trade agreements with several Asian states. He was able to sign two with China that removed some restrictions on American commerce. Additional commercial opportunities were opened up to American merchants following the 1839 Opium War. The Treaty of Nanjing in 1842 ended that war with GREAT BRITAIN, which obtained Hong Kong, opened access to five additional ports for the British, and established the principle of extraterritoriality. Caleb Cushing was appointed as the first American commissioner to China. He was instructed to obtain by means of DIPLOMACY the same terms for American merchants that the British had won in the Opium War. In 1844 he signed the Treaty of Wanghia (Wangxia) that accomplished these goals.

The next major event in U.S.-Chinese relations was the Burlingame Treaty of 1868. Anson Burlingame was appointed U.S. minister to China in 1861. On the surface it was a fairly mundane treaty dealing with commerce, residence rights, and travel. The treaty's broader significance is found in the inclusion of a clause by SECRETARY OF STATE WILLIAM SEWARD that guaranteed unrestricted Chinese IMMIGRATION to the United States. By 1880, an estimated 75,000 Chinese lived in California. Initially Chinese immigrants had been welcomed on the West Coast as a source of cheap labor, but as the boom in railroad construction passed their presence became a source of economic and social conflict, California passed a series of highly discriminatory laws.

CONGRESS took up calls from the West Coast to exclude Chinese immigration by passing a series of legislative measures that were vetoed by various presidents. In 1879 it passed a law limiting how many Chinese could travel on a ship to the United States. President Rutherford B. Hayes vetoed the measure. The Angell Treaty of 1881 gave the United States the right to circumvent the Burlingame Treaty by suspending Chinese immigration to the United States. In 1882 Congress passed legislation that suspended Chinese immigration for 20 years. President Chester Arthur vetoed it. Congress then rewrote the act to suspend Chinese immigration for 10 years. Arthur signed this bill. The Geary Act of 1892 renewed this suspension, and legislation passed in 1904 went one step further by excluding Chinese immigration.

The Sino-Japanese War of 1894–95 set the stage for the next significant American diplomatic engagement in China. The Sino-Japanese War had demonstrated to everyone China's domestic and international weaknesses. The speed of China's defeat accelerated and intensified foreign pressure for economic concessions. One manifestation of China's weakness was the creation of exclusive spheres of economic influence. In 1898 and 1899 the British approached the United States about joint action to keep China open to all foreign traders and curb the spread of spheres of influence. The United States did not respond favorably as it continued to hold an isolationist-unilateralist orientation toward international matters. The British call for an OPEN DOOR did, however, meet with a favorable response in American policy-making circles. On September 6, 1899, Secretary of State JOHN HAY sent diplomatic notes to RUSSIA, GERMANY, and Great Britain calling upon them to not discriminate against commercial interests from other states in their spheres of influence.

The Boxer Rebellion of 1900 brought additional instability to China. Led by nativist forces its targets initially included both foreigners and the Manchu dynasty but soon focused only on foreigners. Hay, fearing that European powers would seek to carve up China politically as well as economically, now issued a second round of OPEN DOOR notes. On July 3, 1900, he asked these same states to pledge their support for the territorial and political integrity of China as well as support for a policy of equal and impartial trade.

The first two decades of the 20th century found the United States pursuing a dual policy of economic engagement and political detachment. DOLLAR DIPLOMACY was advanced by President WILLIAM HOWARD TAFT as a means of allowing the United States to play a major role in world politics without having to engage in military undertakings. Taft encouraged bankers, investors, and merchants to go abroad in search of profits. Their economic success would pave the way for American political domination and make military domination of foreign countries unnecessary. Latin America and China were singled out as two areas of special importance. His administration, however, experienced difficulty in convincing American banking interests to invest in China either alone or as part of international consortiums. One particularly notable venture was investment in railroad construction across Manchuria. This move angered both Japan and Russia, which had come to see Manchuria and northern China as falling within their spheres of influence. President WOODROW WILSON announced that since the terms of the loan to China to finance the railroad project might be seen as threatening its sovereignty, he could not promise U.S. government support for the plan. The next day the American bankers, who had been pressured into participating in the plan by the Taft administration, announced that they were withdrawing from it.

The core political problem was Japan's military ascendancy in the region at the expense of China. President THEODORE ROOSEVELT sought to stabilize matters through the Root-Takahira Agreement of November 30, 1908. In it the United States and Japan agreed to uphold the open door in China, respect each other's possessions, and maintain the status quo in the Pacific. WORLD WAR I demonstrated the weakness of this policy. Not only did Japan seize many of GERMANY's holdings in China, but also it issued the 21 Demands to China in January 1915 that would have established a virtual Japanese protectorate over the country. Secretary of State WILLIAM JENNINGS BRYAN and the Wilson administration refused to recognize Japan's territorial gains, but they did concede that Japan had special interests in the region. This position became codified on November 2, 1917, when Secretary of State Lansing and Japanese viscount Kikujiro Ishii signed an agreement acknowledging that "territorial propinquity creates special relationships . . . and Japan has special interests in China." Lansing came under attack for his agreement and sought to defend himself by arguing that he was referring to economic interests. Japan, however, endorsed a more expansive definition of the concept. Two additional diplomatic attempts were undertaken in the 1920s to try to stabilize the relationship between China and Japan. They both occurred as part of the WASHINGTON CONFERENCE of 1921. In the Four Power Treaty of December 13, the United States, Great Britain, Japan, and Russia agreed to respect each other's rights in the Pacific. A February 6, 1922, Nine Power Treaty pledged signatory states to "respect the sovereignty, independence, and the territorial and administrative integrity of China."

Diplomacy, however, could not save China. It gradually sank into civil war and constantly faced the specter of Japanese domination. American foreign policy did little to stabilize the situation. Sun Zhongshan (Sun Yat-sen) had spearheaded the movement that succeeded in ousting the Manchu dynasty from power in 1913. Wilson quickly recognized his government, but Sun Zhongshan was soon forced from power. It would be 1928 before political power was again centralized in China, this time in the hands of General Jiang Jieshi (Chiang Kai-shek) who headed the Nationalist (Guomindang; Kuomintang) Party. That year the United States signed a treaty restoring tariff autonomy to China and granting it most favored nation status.

Jiang faced two serious threats to his ability to rule China. The first came from within. In consolidating his power Jiang had defeated the Communists, but he had not succeeded in destroying them. From 1935 to 1937, led by Mao Zedong (Mao Tse-tung), the remaining Communists embarked upon a 6,000-mile "Long March." The second threat came from outside China as Japan continued to move toward regional supremacy. In September 1931 an incident was staged in Manchuria that served as a pretext for the Japanese occupation of that region. An explosion damaged a section of the Japanese-controlled South Manchurian railway, and Japanese forces rushed to protect the property. The United States took no actions to reverse the Japanese seizure of Manchuria and contented itself with a statement of nonrecognition of Japan's territorial gains known as the Stimson Doctrine that was issued by Secretary of State HENRY STIMSON in 1937. On July 7 Chinese and Japanese forces fought at the Marco Polo Bridge. Intense fighting with a terrible loss of civilian life spread throughout China, and Japanese forces occupied Shanghai and Nanjing.

It was only now that the United States and others began to take active measures to block continued Japanese advancement in China. The Soviet Union had helped engineer a truce between the Communists and Nationalists in early 1937. Unwilling to take on isolationist opposition, President FRANKLIN ROOSEVELT did not take direct action against Japan. He instead delivered a "Quarantine Speech" on October 5, 1937, in which he called for global action against states promoting international anarchy. Roosevelt refused to invoke the NEUTRALITY ACT because it would have prevented him from giving China any aid whatsoever. It did so mainly through providing loans. Still, by the end of 1938, Japan controlled virtually all of China's ports.

WORLD WAR II in China was a three-sided affair with Japanese forces fighting a coalition of Chinese Communist and Nationalist forces that were as interested in contesting each other as they were in defeating the Japanese. The United States's official position announced at the Cairo Conference of 1943 was to return to China all territory taken from it by Japan, including Manchuria and Formosa. Actions, however, did not match rhetoric. The United States's primary objective once it entered the war was to defeat Nazi Germany. Victory in the Pacific would have to wait. This set up an uneasy relationship between the United States and Jiang. He was disappointed that the United States offered more military advice than matériel and clashed frequently with General Joseph Stilwell, who represented the United States. For its part, the United States was frustrated by the corruption in Jiang's government and military apparatus and the poor battlefield performance of its troops. The United States had comparatively little contact with the Communist forces. In late 1944 General Patrick Hurley sought to bring the two sides together in a true coalition government. The effort failed miserably. Jiang rejected the agreement that the Communists had agreed to and convinced Hurley to adopt a hard-line stance toward the Communists.

The United States would make one more try at bringing the Communists and Nationalists together. After Japan's surrender General GEORGE C. MARSHALL made a trip to China for this purpose. The Marshall mission lasted from December 1945 to January 1947. Neither side was willing to concede, and the civil war resumed. Jiang's government had become thoroughly corrupt and isolated from the peasantry. Mao was confident of victory and angered by Joseph Stalin's decision to sign a treaty of friendship with Jiang's Nationalist government in August 1945. Less than three years after Marshall's mission ended in failure, Jiang's Nationalist forces retreated to Formosa (TAIWAN), and Mao announced the establishment of the People's Republic of China (PRC) on September 21, 1949.

By 1948 the Truman administration had made the decision not to intervene further militarily or politically to try to save Jiang. In August, Secretary of State Marshall informed the American embassy in China that the United States would not support a coalition government with the Communists, nor would it seek to mediate a settlement to the conflict. In December of that year it reacted coolly to a request for an additional $3 billion in aid. Already, it had airlifted Jiang's forces to territories being abandoned by the Japanese in an effort to prevent them from falling into Communist hands. The United States had also continued wartime military aid to his government. In July 1949 the STATE DEPARTMENT issued a 1,054-page White Paper that placed the blame for Jiang's defeat squarely on his shoulders and absolved the United States of any responsibility for permitting the impending Communist victory. The White Paper settled little in the United States as for months Republicans had lobbied the Truman administration for action to prevent Mao's victory. HARRY TRUMAN's "loss of China" would provide the raw material for Senator Joseph McCarthy's charges that China had fallen due to the treacherous actions of Communists within the State Department.

The United States soon came into conflict with China in an unexpected setting. On June 25, 1950, North Korean troops invaded SOUTH KOREA. U.S. forces were caught off guard, and a crushing defeat was only averted through an inspired military campaign led by General DOUGLAS MACARTHUR that landed U.S. troops at Inchon, behind NORTH KOREA's advancing line. The flow of combat now changed, and it was American forces, fighting under the UNITED NATIONS' flag, which found themselves in a position to capture all of North Korea and unite the two countries. South Korean troops entered North Korea on October 1, 1950. That day the Chinese asked the Indian ambassador to China to inform the United States that the Chinese would regard the presence of American troops north of the 38th parallel that divided North and South Korea as a justification for sending Chinese troops into the war. The Truman administration and General MacArthur discounted this and other warnings of Chinese concern and resolve.

U.S. troops crossed into North Korea on October 7 but did not encounter Chinese forces. It was only on October 26, with the U.S. forces on the verge of reaching the Yalu River that separated North Korea from China, that this happened. Heavy fighting ensued, only to be broken off on November 7. MacArthur called for bombing China, but his request was denied. On November 25 the Chinese launched a counterattack that drove American forces out of North Korea.

China's entry into the KOREAN WAR was not interpreted as an act of self-defense or as one provoked by MacArthur's actions. Rather, it was taken as proof of Chinese hostility and the existence of a Sino-Soviet alliance that had spread the COLD WAR to Asia. Just as did the fall of China a few years earlier, the Korean War spawned a major political controversy in the United States. This one pitted Truman against MacArthur, whom he had relieved of his command on April 11, 1951, for insubordination.

For the next two decades the conflict between Taiwan (Formosa) and the PRC would provide the most serious point of confrontation between the PRC and the United States. The conflict proceeded at two levels. Diplomatically, the United States was now closely aligned with Jiang and his Nationalist regime, which maintained that it was still the official government of China. The PRC also maintained that only one Chinese government existed and that Taiwan was part of China. This set up an unavoidable and reoccurring conflict at the United Nations, where China had been given a permanent seat on the Security Council. On a yearly basis the United States would beat back efforts to replace the Nationalists with a PRC representative. In the Pacific it set up a war of words between the Nationalists and Communists over which was the legitimate government of China. Officially the United States spoke of "unleashing" Jiang's forces against the PRC, but unofficially it had secured promises from him not to undertake any military action without U.S. approval. Just as in Europe, the Eisenhower administration had no intention of pairing its rhetoric of rolling back the iron curtain with concrete military action.

Periodically, in 1954–55, 1958, and 1961–62, however, this diplomatic conflict did escalate, bringing the United States close to fighting with the PRC. American domestic politics required a firm and tough response, but neither the Eisenhower nor Kennedy administrations ever sought a military confrontation. The 1954 crisis was ignited by the U.S. decision to remove the Seventh Fleet from the Taiwan Strait and rumors of an impending alliance between the United States and Taiwan. In 1953 Taiwan and the United States had signed a mutual defense agreement. The PRC sought to deter further moves in this direction by shelling the Jinmen (Quemoy) and Mazu Islands. These islands were located off the coast of the mainland and controlled by the Nationalist government. The move failed to have its desired effect of intimidating the United States, as President Dwight Eisenhower secured the FORMOSA RESOLUTION from CONGRESS, which gave him the authority to act in any manner he saw fit to protect Taiwan. The shelling also did not stop the United States from going ahead with creating the SOUTHEAST ASIA TREATY ORGANIZATION (SEATO) as part of its global CONTAINMENT strategy. The PRC also initiated the 1958 crisis out of concerns over the United States's growing interest in pursuing a two-China policy. As was the case with the other two Formosa crises, this crisis petered out and ended in a stalemate that reaffirmed the status quo. The final crisis was precipitated by the Nationalists who had been threatening to use Jinmen and Mazu as launching pads for an invasion of the PRC. President JOHN F. KENNEDY made it known to the PRC through diplomatic intermediaries that the United States would not permit any such attack.

It had been an article of faith in American foreign policy that China and the Soviet Union were like-minded allies who together threatened the United States around the world. Evidence to the contrary had been building

President Richard Nixon, with his wife, Pat *(foreground, right),* and Secretary of State William Pierce Rogers, at the Great Wall of China *(Hulton/Archive)*

since the early 1960s, but the implications of a Sino-Soviet split were slow to make their way into U.S. foreign-policy thinking. This changed as the United States looked to the post-VIETNAM era. With U.S. power significantly weakened by the war in Vietnam, President RICHARD NIXON and his NATIONAL SECURITY ADVISOR HENRY KISSINGER sought to replace containment with a policy of DÉTENTE. This policy treated the Soviet Union more as an ally than as an adversary, but it also required that the United States find an insurance policy that would block any attempt by the Soviet Union to exploit the United States's weakened power position.

The answer seized upon was improved relations with China. The United States moved publicly and quietly to bring this about. President Nixon publicly referred to China by its official name, the People's Republic of China, rather than employing the familiar "Communist China."

In 1970 the United States made it known through diplomatic channels to the PRC that is was willing to declare that the Taiwan issue was one that the Chinese should decide for themselves, thus removing it as an issue that stood in the way of better relations between them. On April 21, 1971, the PRC extended a secret invitation for a high-ranking member of the Nixon administration to visit China and discuss how to improve relations between the two countries. In July 1971 Kissinger made a secret visit to China, and it was announced that President Nixon would make an official visit the following year. In October the United States supported the PRC's takeover of the Chinese seat in the United Nations.

Nixon's famous trip took place in February 1972 and ended with the Shanghai Communiqué in which both states declared their opposition to any power achieving hegemony in Asia. It was clear to all that, although unnamed, the power in question was the Soviet Union. Here was the first visible attempt to play the "China card" and block the Soviet Union's expansionist moves. The opening to China did not have the immediate or far-reaching impact that Nixon and Kissinger had hoped for. Domestic political problems hampered both sides. In the United States the Nixon administration became consumed and politically crippled by Watergate. In China, Mao Zedong and Zhou Enlai (Chou En-lai) died, and a power struggle ensued.

Official diplomatic relations between the United States and the PRC were not established until the Carter administration. President JIMMY CARTER announced on December 15, 1978, that the United States would establish official diplomatic relations with China effective January 1, 1979. This decision brought forward immediate protests from supporters of Taiwan. Senator Barry Goldwater unsuccessfully brought a suit to the SUPREME COURT, GOLDWATER V. CARTER, trying to block the move. RONALD REAGAN promised to reverse the decision in his 1980 presidential campaign. Upon becoming president, however, Reagan let it stand.

Three broad sets of issues have been contested by the United States and the PRC since official diplomatic relations were established. They involve HUMAN RIGHTS, TRADE POLICY, and security. Policies formulated to address problems in one issue area often spill over and affect the other two. As a result PRESIDENTS often have come under intense domestic political cross pressures in formulating China policy, and the policies adopted have often been plagued with internal contradictions.

The most politically visible human-rights conflict resulted from the Tiananmen Square incident of June 4, 1989. Dissatisfaction with the pace of economic and political reforms on the part of many in China had been building for some time. The death of Hu Yaobang, a former reform-minded head of the Communist Party, led to pro-democracy demonstrations by Chinese students at Tiananmen Square. Early in the morning on June 4 Chinese troops attacked the crowds and set off a nationwide campaign to reestablish political orthodoxy in China. President GEORGE H. W. BUSH responded to the Tiananmen Square attacks by suspending high-level political contacts between the two countries, imposing economic sanctions, including suspending ARMS TRANSFERS, and calling for international organizations to postpone consideration of Chinese loan applications. Bush soon, however, moved U.S. foreign policy in the opposite direction. In July he sent a secret delegation to China to make sure that broader U.S. security and economic interests were not permanently harmed. He would also veto congressional legislation allowing Chinese citizens to extend their legal stay in the United States, lifted a congressional ban on loans doing business in

China, and announced the sale of three communications satellites to the PRC.

Beyond the matter of political rights associated with democratization, several other human-rights issues are on the U.S.-PRC agenda. Religious freedom, especially in Tibet, has been a reoccurring point of conflict. The "religious right" in the United States has made this a major point of their political lobbying campaigns, along with opposition to China's family-planning practices that seek to limit the size of families. Forces on the political left have championed the rights of Chinese workers, including prison laborers, who produce products for export to the West and often work in foreign-owned plants. The low pay and harsh working conditions in these plants greatly complicated China's bid to normalize trade relations with the United States and join the WORLD TRADE ORGANIZATION.

The major reoccurring trade issue in U.S.-PRC relations was China's attempt to obtain MOST-FAVORED-NATION (MFN) STATUS. For 20 years Congress held yearly votes on the terms under which Chinese goods would enter the United States. The granting of MFN status had been conceived of as a tool to force the Soviet Union to improve its human-rights policies in the early 1970s, but following Tiananmen Square, it was also directed at China. Congress had routinely sought to link the two policy areas, and presidents worked to keep them separate. During his presidential campaign Bill Clinton had promised to tie MFN status to improvements in China's human-rights record. After taking office his administration was targeted by some 800 business and trade associations that feared any such move would cripple their businesses and cost thousands of American jobs. As had presidents before him, once in office Clinton reversed his position. In September 2000 Clinton secured one of his most significant legislative victories when the Senate voted to permanently grant China normal trade status (the term *MFN* had been changed in hopes of reducing the political symbolism attached to the vote). This vote was doubly significant since it cleared the way for the PRC to join the World Trade Organization.

In the security area the United States has been troubled by a number of Chinese foreign-policy initiatives, the most vexing of which has been its active involvement with arms sales of sophisticated weapons or components to states that the United States has viewed with suspicion. Foremost among these are PAKISTAN (prior to SEPTEMBER 11, 2001), SYRIA, and IRAN. For its part the PRC has been angered by continued U.S. arms sales to Taiwan. President GEORGE W. BUSH conducted the largest arms sale to Taiwan since 1992 in his first year in office. It followed on the heels of an incident in which the PRC had downed an American surveillance aircraft and held its crew for several days after it collided with a Chinese military aircraft in international air space over the South China

Sea on March 31, 2001. In an attempt not to be overly provocative, Bush held back on some of the more controversial aspects of the deal, such as providing destroyers equipped with sophisticated Aegis radar systems, but he did not rule out future arms sales to Taiwan.

As this episode illustrates, the support of the United States for Taiwan remains very much an irritant in U.S.–PRC relations. In 1995 Taiwan's president Lee Teng-hui made a high-profile "unofficial" trip to the United States during which Congress treated him as if he were a head of state. The PRC responded by recalling its ambassador to the United States and refusing to accept the credentials of the new U.S. ambassador.

The United States's relations with China became somewhat tense in late 2002 and 2003. Three issues contributed principally to this condition. The first was the announcement by NORTH KOREA that it had acquired a NUCLEAR WEAPONS ARSENAL. The Bush administration's doctrine of PREEMPTION, if applied here, would have created a major regional crisis. Second, China opposed the United States at the UN in its desire for a resolution permitting it to use force against IRAQ. China viewed the IRAQ WAR as dangerous because it illustrated the extent to which American power now exceeded that of other states in the INTERNATIONAL SYSTEM. Finally, China took offense at U.S. accusations that Chinese firms were helping IRAN acquire nuclear capability.

See also ECONOMIC INSTRUMENTS; ESPIONAGE; INTEREST GROUPS; RELIGION.

**Further reading:** Cohen, Warren I. *America's Response to China.* New York: Columbia University Press, 1990; Johnston, Alastair Ian. *Cultural Realism: Strategic Culture and Grand Strategy in Chinese History.* Princeton, N.J.: Princeton University Press, 1995; Shambaugh, David. *Beautiful Imperialist: China Perceives America, 1972–1990.* Princeton, N.J.: Princeton University Press, 1991.

## Church Committee

The Church Committee, also known as the Senate Select Committee to Study Government Operations with Respect to Intelligence Activities, was formed in 1975 in the wake of revelations of wrongdoings by the CENTRAL INTELLIGENCE AGENCY (CIA). Its work represents a watershed in the way in which CIA oversight is conducted.

The Church Committee, so named after its chairperson, Senator Frank Church (D-Idaho), was created following a December 1974 article in the *New York Times* detailing extensive—and illegal—domestic activities, such as wiretappings, break-ins, and mail openings, by the CIA. While many of these actions were related to VIETNAM, others preceded it, dating back to the 1950s. The list of transgressions was actually the result of efforts by the head of the INTELLIGENCE COMMUNITY and DIRECTOR OF CENTRAL INTELLIGENCE, James Schlesinger, to find out the extend of the CIA's involvement in illegal activities following revelations of CIA involvement in the Watergate burglary.

Both the Senate Armed Forces and Appropriations Committees responded to these revelations by holding hearings. President GERALD FORD established a committee chaired by Vice President Nelson Rockefeller to investigate CIA behavior. Both houses of CONGRESS also established special committees to investigate the CIA. The counterpart committee in the House to the Church Committee became the Pike Committee.

The Church Committee concluded operations in April 1976 after 15 months of work. Most of its hearings were held in private, and the committee worked closely with executive branch officials, including representatives from the CIA, most notably Director of Central Intelligence William Colby. It concentrated its efforts on uncovering questionable activities that the CIA had carried out. Among its most stunning revelations was the existence of the Track II program designed to remove Salvadore Allende from power in CHILE and assassination plots against Fidel Castro in CUBA and other foreign leaders. With regard to assassinations, the Church Committee reached the conclusion that "no foreign leaders were killed as a result of assassination plots initiated by officials of the United States."

One of the starting assumptions of the Church Committee was that the CIA had been, in the words of its chair, "a rogue elephant," running around the world out of control. In actual fact, the opposite proved to be the case. The committee concluded that "PRESIDENTS and administrations have made excessive . . . use of COVERT ACTION." It documented 81 projects that were approved by the director of central intelligence between 1949 and 1952 and that this number grew to 163 in the Kennedy administration and 142 in the Johnson administration. It was even revealed that Representative Lucien Nedzi, who was chair of the CIA subcommittee of the House Armed Services Committee, had been briefed about CIA covert actions. Nedzi was the chair of the House's first special committee. This revelation led to its termination and replacement by a new committee chaired by Otis Pike (D-N.Y.).

To tighten oversight of the CIA the Church Committee recommended that two steps be taken. First, each house should establish permanent intelligence oversight committees rather than rely upon the current system of oversight by subcommittees of the Appropriations and Armed Services Committee of the House and Senate. Second, a legislative charter should be written clearly establishing what type of behavior was permissible and what was not. Without such a charter the intelligence community would continue to be governed solely by largely secret orders and directives coming from the executive branch. The first goal was quickly realized as each house set up permanent select committees on intelligence. The second has not been. Efforts to do so bogged down during the Carter administration and have not been resurrected. Still, the principle of legislative oversight has been firmly established, and as the conflict over NICARAGUA and the Boland Amendment illustrate, Congress is willing to defend its prerogatives and hold presidents accountable for the conduct of covert actions.

**Further reading:** Johnson, Loch. *A Season of Inquiry: Congress and Intelligence.* Chicago: Dorsey, 1988.

## civil-military relations

The central problems encompassed by the phrase *civil-military relations* are those of establishing a clear distinction between political and military spheres of responsibility in making foreign-policy decisions and ensuring that civilian authority is superior to military authority. For much of its history these problems did not play a significant role in U.S. military thought because geography had provided the United States with a formidable buffer separating it from Europe and giving it neighbors that presented few national security challenges. Consequently, the American military establishment was small, and troops were deployed largely in the sparsely populated West, which was isolated from most of American society. This changed after WORLD WAR II when the United States assumed a global role and the American military establishment became large and permanent.

A starting point of assessing the pattern of civil-military relations in the United States is the nature of the American military tradition. Three strands are seen as providing its foundation. The first is technicism, the belief that a military officer should possess a technical or mechanical skill of some type. The second strand is populism, the belief that national defense is the responsibility of all citizens. This is embodied in the idea of a militia or national guard made up of citizen-soldiers. The third strand is professionalism. This is the belief that there exists a science of war and body of knowledge on how to fight wars.

The first two strands are firmly embedded in the broader American political tradition of liberalism. The third is not. One of the hallmarks of these professions is that they are self-governing. Another is that the members of the professions stand apart from society and have a responsibility to it. This sense of separateness and special calling can easily translate into challenges to civilian control as it did during the KOREAN WAR when General DOU-GLAS MACARTHUR came into open conflict with President HARRY TRUMAN.

Establishing the dividing line between the civilian and military spheres of authority is hampered by the nature of the U.S. political system. The Constitution does not speak directly to this question. It denotes the PRESIDENT as commander in chief, but it does not specify what that entails. The Constitution is far more concerned with establishing and distributing powers among the president and CONGRESS. These divided powers, while providing for a system of checks and balances, also tend to draw the military into political conflicts. Nowhere was this more evident than in the VIETNAM WAR. The American military emerged from VIETNAM estranged from both its civilian overseers and society at large.

One important question debated today is whether the military is more aggressive than its civilian counterparts when it comes to the use of force. Contrary to popular images, this appears not to be the case. Civilians and the military part company over how and when to use force. The military prefers to use force quickly, massively, and decisively, and it is skeptical of making bluffs that involve the use of force. Civilians, especially diplomats, tend to see the use of force as an admission of failure and prefer to hold back from using it for longer periods of time, but they are more predisposed to making threats involving force.

Care must be taken to avoid treating the "military" as if it is a single entity. Differences in outlook exist among the military services and within them on using force. More generally, it is said that the three services have their own personalities and cultures. The navy, it is said, worships at the altar of tradition, the army at the altar of country and duty, and the air force at that of technology. The navy is the most concerned with protecting its independence; the air force sees itself as the guarantor of national security in the nuclear age; and the army views itself as the artisan of the traditional craft of warfare.

Several challenges confront the professional military and threaten to create problems for American civil-military relations today. One is the degree to which the military should reflect the broader values of American society. Most commonly this question is directed at the gender and ethnic makeup of the military and its officer corps. Another dimension to this issue centers on the values adhered to the military. Evidence suggests that the office corps is far more conservative in its political outlook than its civilian overseers. A second challenge comes from the revolution in military affairs, the wide-ranging impact that modern technology has had on the preparation, organization, and conduct of war. The ability to see battlefields in real time in Washington threatens to rob military commanders of their unique sphere of influence and expertise. A third challenge lies in the evolving nature of modern warfare. The more warfare resembles that found in VIETNAM, SOMALIA, and BOSNIA AND HERZEGOVINA and the less it resembles OPERATION DESERT STORM during the PERSIAN GULF WAR, the more blurred becomes the dividing line between war and peace, which has been central to American thinking about the dividing line between military and civilian authority. The IRAQ WAR also showed evidence of this tension, as SECRETARY OF DEFENSE Donald Rumsfeld and career military officers clashed over the merits of his strategy for moving ground forces forward that relied upon speed and small numbers. During the war Rumsfeld publicly defended himself from his critics, and after the war senior officers resigned or were removed from their posts. Finally, the pattern of American civil-military relations will be challenged by the changing nature of the tasks assigned to the military. War fighting is being replaced by PEACEKEEPING. The skills and expertise associated with one are not necessarily those needed for the other, and the proper role played by civilians may differ.

**Further reading:** Betts, Richard. *Soldiers, Statesmen and Cold War Crises.* Cambridge, Mass.: Harvard University Press, 1977; Builder, Carl. *The Masks of War.* Baltimore: Johns Hopkins University Press, 1989; Janowitz, Morris. *The Professional Soldier.* New York: Free Press, 1960.

## clandestine collection

INTELLIGENCE is a key ingredient in the formation of a successful foreign policy. Intelligence is not the same thing as raw data or information. Rather, it is information that has been analyzed and evaluation. The information that is transformed into intelligence is obtained either through overt or clandestine means. Overt information is obtained from public sources, such as newspapers, journals, the media, and meetings with key individuals. Clandestine information is collected secretly. *Espionage* is a commonly used synonym for the clandestine collection of information.

The collection of information is driven by "intelligence requirements" that specify the type of information that is needed. Requirements can be set by policy makers who have identified a problem of concern or by intelligence analysts who need a piece of information to complete or clarify their analysis. Once a requirement is in place the next task is to determine who is in possession of that information or where it can be obtained. The final component to clandestine collection is to determine what resources to employ. When dealing with relatively open political systems overt collection methods may suffice. The opposite tends to be true when the target is a closed society or "denied" area. During the COLD WAR the principal targets of the U.S. INTELLIGENCE COMMUNITY were the Soviet Union (see RUSSIA) and its allies. Because they were denied areas,

clandestine means of intelligence collection assumed great importance in U.S. intelligence. The CENTRAL INTELLIGENCE AGENCY (CIA) is the preeminent intelligence organization in the area of clandestine collection, but it is not the only one.

Clandestine collection techniques can be grouped under two broad headings. The first is human intelligence (HUMINT). As its name implies, HUMINT is collected by people. The person collecting the information is not necessarily an intelligence professional. Typically CIA personnel stationed abroad operate under cover. That is, their employment with the CIA or other intelligence agency is disguised. Cover can be provided by a diplomatic post, apparent employment by another U.S. government agency, or by a corporation. Particularly controversial has been the use of academic or media positions as cover. The intelligence officer, or "case officer," most often works through "agents" who engage in the actual collection of information. Agents are selected because of their potential access to needed information, reliability, and willingness to work secretly. At other times the intelligence officer will work with the host country's intelligence services to obtain information. Among the most frequently employed HUMINT techniques include breaking and entering offices and homes, opening mail, bugging or using hidden microphones, listening to wiretaps, and intercepting fax and printer communications.

The second broad category of clandestine collection techniques is technical intelligence. Technical collection programs are said to account for some 90 percent of the intelligence collection budget. Signals intelligence (SIGINT) encompasses several different types of clandestine intelligence activities. Communications intelligence (COMINT) involves intercepting and decoding the communications of other governments. Electronic intelligence (ELINT) consists of intercepts of electromagnetic radiations from radars and other special communications systems. Telemetry intelligence (TELINT) is a special category of ELINT and focuses on information gained by intercepting missile telemetry. SIGINT is obtained in a variety of ways. One method is through fixed installations along the border of denied areas. A second is through "ferret" flights, which are flights by specially designed planes that skirt the borders of the target state in order to determine how its defense systems function under specified circumstances. A third SIGINT platform is the high performance aircraft that flies at high altitudes and great speed. The first such plane was the U-2. A major international incident occurred in 1960 when a U-2 was shot down over the Soviet Union and its pilot, Gary Francis Powers, was captured. The SR-71 now performs this function.

Imagery intelligence is a broad category within technical intelligence. It may be collected using the same planes that are used to collect SIGINT. More often, however, imagery intelligence is associated with overhead reconnaissance satellites. Two different types of reconnaissance satellites are used. Geosynchronous satellites are "parked" in a fixed position above the Earth so that they may keep a designated area under constant surveillance. A second type of satellite is placed in a near polar elliptical orbit around the earth that allows most of the Earth to pass beneath it. Reconnaissance satellites are capable of doing more than just taking high-resolution photographs—when equipped with infrared sensors they can also detect missile firings.

The clandestine collection of information through technical means played an important role in the evolution of ARMS CONTROL agreements. One of the major impediments to arms control agreements is the fear that the other side is cheating. By using national technical means (NTMs) of verification both the United States and the Soviet Union were in a position to reassure themselves that cheating was not taking place in the treaties signed as a result of the STRATEGIC ARMS LIMITATION TALKS (SALT). Each side agreed that certain forms of NTM verification was needed and that neither would interfere with these efforts.

**Further reading:** Burrows, William. *Deep Black: Space Espionage and National Security.* New York: Random House, 1986; Richelson, Jeffrey T. *A Century of Spies: Intelligence in the Twentieth Century.* New York: Oxford University Press, 1995.

**Clay, Henry** (1777–1852) *statesperson, secretary of state*
One of the leading statespeople in the era after the AMERICAN REVOLUTION, Henry Clay was a strong nationalist who exerted a powerful influence over the American political scene in the first half of the 19th century. Clay's active participation in U.S. foreign policy is most evident in four episodes. First, in the years leading up to the WAR OF 1812, Clay was a prominent "war hawk" urging the United States to go to war with GREAT BRITAIN. He also served on the U.S. delegation that negotiated the TREATY OF GHENT that ended the war. Second, in the period after the War of 1812, Clay became an advocate for the "American System." This economic development program emphasized banking reforms and large-scale public spending on railroads, roads, and canals that would hasten the development of a national economy. It also called for high tariffs to protect this developing market from foreign competition. This plan was supported by the West and Northeast but opposed by the South. Third, Clay opposed the annexation of TEXAS. He did so fearing that annexation would lead to war with MEXICO. Clay supported the war once it began, even though he was concerned that the United States had initiated the con-

test solely for the purpose of taking Mexican territory. Both of these last two positions—support for high tariffs and opposition to Texas annexation—are seen as having contributed to his defeat in the presidential elections of 1832 and 1844. Finally, Clay's political stature was such that not only was he repeatedly elected by his colleagues to serve as Speaker of the House of Representatives, but he was also the first speaker to use this position as a political weapon. Clay used his power of committee appointments to ensure that key committees, such as foreign affairs and military affairs, were started by men who shared his views.

Clay served an undistinguished term as SECRETARY OF STATE under President JOHN QUINCY ADAMS. Clay had supported Adams over the more popular ANDREW JACKSON and the objections of the Kentucky state legislature in the electoral runoff conducted in the House of Representatives. Charges abounded that Clay and Adams had entered into a "corrupt bargain." No conclusive evidence points to such a deal, although the charge plagued both men for the remainder of their political careers.

**Further reading:** Remini, Robert V. *Henry Clay: Statesman for the Union.* New York: Norton, 1991.

## Clayton-Bulwer Treaty

This controversial agreement was negotiated by John Clayton, who served as SECRETARY OF STATE from March 1849 to July 1850, and the British minister to the United States Sir Henry Bulwer. The agreement signed on April 19, 1850, provided that both the United States and GREAT BRITAIN would forsake unilateral action on an interoceanic canal. They agreed to cooperate in its construction and not seek unilateral control over the canal once it was built or try to fortify the canal. While this provision of the treaty was clear, others were not. Article I stated that neither country would "occupy" or "colonize" or exercise "domination" over any part of Central America. Great Britain interpreted this provision to mean an end to new occupations. Clayton interpreted it be retroactive in its coverage, thus forcing Great Britain to abandon positions it currently held. The Senate ratified the treaty with little debate by a vote of 42-11. The margin of support was deceptive, as the treaty soon came under attack. Where defenders saw it as having halted British expansion in Latin America, opponents felt that its terms violated the spirit of the MONROE DOCTRINE by pledging the United States not to take unilateral action in constructing a canal. Concrete instances of dispute arose over the British failure to withdraw from the Mosquito Coast, British establishment of a crown colony on Honduran Bay in 1852 (British Honduras, now Belize), and the efforts of American filibusters to annex NICARAGUA to the United States.

As interest in an interoceanic canal for both economic and security reasons grew in the United States, it fell to later secretaries of state to seek either the repeal of the Clayton-Bulwer Treaty or its revision. Neither JAMES BLAINE nor FREDERICK FRELINGHUYSEN succeeded. JOHN HAY would have success. Acting on the heels of the second Walker Commission report that favored a canal route through Nicaragua, Hay and British ambassador to the United States Julian Pauncefote concluded an agreement abrogating the Clayton-Bulwer Treaty. The British position changed largely in recognition of the new balance of power in the region. American influence was ascending, and the British government found it increasingly costly to maintain its Central American presence.

## Cleveland, Grover (1837–1908) *president of the United States*

Stephen Grover Cleveland served as the 24th and 26th president. He is the only president to serve two nonconsecutive terms. In his first term he emphasized civil-service reform and lower tariffs that hurt labor. In his second term economic problems and social unrest plagued his administration, and he proved incapable of forging a compromise with the many diverse elements of the DEMOCRATIC PARTY to successfully address these problems.

In making foreign policy, a leading principle embraced by Cleveland was a resistance to acquiring territory or establishing U.S. protectorates abroad. In his first term he withdrew a treaty from consideration by the Senate that would have made NICARAGUA a protectorate of the United States. He also opposed commercial treaties with Latin America for fear that they would become economic protectorates. Interestingly, he supported a commercial treaty with HAWAII. In his second term, however, Cleveland moved away from endorsing close ties with Hawaii, withdrawing from Senate consideration a treaty that would have annexed it, asserting that annexation would violate "a high standard of honor and mortality." His administration also denounced the actions of the U.S. consul in Samoa, who, without consulting Washington, announced the establishment of a U.S. protectorate there to forestall a similar move by GERMANY.

Cleveland's most serious foreign-policy problem involved the Venezuelan boundary dispute between VENEZUELA and Great Britain, the colonial power in British Guiana. The Cleveland administration's insistence that the MONROE DOCTRINE gave it the right to intervene in the dispute brought forward talk of the possibility of war between the United States and GREAT BRITAIN. The conflict was resolved by the establishment of an arbitration panel, which ruled largely in favor of Great Britain.

The Cleveland administration also had ongoing conflicts with CANADA over fishing and seal hunting rights.

Resolution of a fishing dispute along the coastal Northeast became embroiled in partisan politics. Cleveland signed a compromise treaty to settle the dispute just before the 1888 election, but Republicans in the Senate refused to act on it so as to deny Cleveland and the Democrats credit. Cleveland responded with a request from CONGRESS to give him the power to prohibit the transit of goods across the Canadian border as a means of forcing an agreement. Republicans, fearing the economic consequences of such action, denied him the authority but gave him a public relations coup.

**Further reading:** Campbell, Charles S. *The Transformation of American Foreign Relations, 1865–1900.* New York: Harper and Row, 1976; May, Ernest. *Imperial Democracy: The Emergence of America as a Great Power.* New York: Harper and Row, 1961.

## Clinton, Bill (1946– ) *president of the United States*

William (Bill) Jefferson Clinton was the 42nd president. He served two terms (1993–2001). Clinton was a five-term governor of Arkansas. He began his presidency with little foreign-policy experience and professing little interest in foreign affairs. His was to be a domestic-policy presidency. Clinton found, however, that world events would not give him the luxury of simply pursuing a domestic agenda. As Clinton's first DIRECTOR OF THE CENTRAL INTELLIGENCE AGENCY, R. James Woolsey, noted, the post–COLD WAR world might have lacked the single dangerous dragon of Soviet COMMUNISM, but it contained plenty of dangerous snakes. SOMALIA, BOSNIA AND HERZEGOVINA, HAITI, and KOSOVO would provide a series of constant short-term and immediate challenges for the Clinton administration's foreign-policy team. During his second term Clinton was only the second president to be impeached. He was acquitted by the Senate on February 12, 1999, but the impeachment proceedings and the political fallout from his relationship with White House intern Monica Lewinsky seriously compromised his administration's ability to conduct much more than a reactive foreign policy.

Clinton's initial attempts at directing American foreign policy provoked controversy and disappointment. This was largely due to the considerable amount of vacillation in words and deeds that accompanied it. In Bosnia, for example, he quickly rejected the Vance-Owens Peace Plan that was underway only to propose a plan very similar to it. Two months after advancing this plan Clinton abandoned it for a stronger response that might involve force. The conditions laid out as a precondition for using force, however, were unlikely to be met. They included an exit strategy, public support, and the likelihood of success in stabilizing the situation. Before the end of the year, three

STATE DEPARTMENT officials would resign, criticizing Clinton's Bosnia policy as "misguided, vacillating, and dangerous." Somalia and Haiti also provided their share of setbacks as local leaders successfully defied U.S. POWER. In Somalia General Mohammed Farah Aidid eluded capture, and his forces killed 18 U.S. soldiers and wounded 84 others. In Haiti, an agreement to transfer power to exiled president Jean-Bertrand Aristide collapsed. A U.S. Navy vessel with forces whose job it would be to reform the Haitian security services turned back from Haiti rather than meet an angry mob.

In the midst of these events the Clinton administration sought to regain control over American foreign policy through a series of addresses that sought to lay out its vision. The key concept that emerged from these presentations was "enlargement." It entailed expanding the community of democratic nations and market economies and countering the aggression of backlash states. These speeches and their message failed to accomplish their objectives as the vacillation of the Clinton administration continued. Matters improved somewhat during the second administration, although its conduct of the war in Kosovo was still marked by political and military inconsistencies.

International trade and monetary policy proved to be areas in which the Clinton administration enjoyed considerable success. Early in the first term the most pressing issues were the need to bring the NORTH AMERICAN FREE TRADE AGREEMENT (NAFTA) negotiations to a conclusion and to approve the URUGUAY ROUND/GENERAL AGREEMENT ON TARIFFS AND TRADE (GATT) treaty establishing the WORLD TRADE ORGANIZATION. Clinton succeeded on

President Bill Clinton shakes hands with soldiers at the Tuzla air field, Bosnia and Herzegovina, on December 22, 1997. *(Department of Defense)*

both counts but failed in his bid to obtain FAST-TRACK AUTHORITY. Clinton was also successful in meeting the Mexican peso crisis that threatened to undermine support for NAFTA. Clinton's greatest accomplishment came in convincing CONGRESS to grant CHINA MOST-FAVORED-NATION (MFN) status. As a presidential candidate Clinton had vowed to deny China MFN status, but he came to embrace the Bush administration's argument for decoupling HUMAN RIGHTS and trade issues by holding out hope that improved economic conditions in China would lead to increased respect for human rights.

Clinton's record in nuclear diplomacy was decidedly mixed. NORTH KOREA's withdrawal from the International Atomic Energy Agency in 1994 presented Washington with a major challenge and plunged it into controversial negotiations with that country over its nuclear program. An agreement was reached in October whereby North Korea agreed to freeze its nuclear program and allow for international inspections. It did not have to dismantle its existing nuclear facilities. For its part, the United States agreed both to provide North Korea with advanced nuclear technologies and to relax trade restrictions. In 1996 Clinton negotiated a COMPREHENSIVE TEST BAN TREATY. It was hailed as the "longest sought, hardest fought prize in ARMS CONTROL history." Clinton submitted it to the Senate for ratification in 1997. There it became hostage to Senator JESSE HELMS's (R-N.C.) hostility to Clinton's foreign-policy agenda. On October 13, 1999, the treaty finally came up for a vote; the Senate rejected it by a vote of 51-48. Finally, the Clinton administration was unable to control pressure for a national BALLISTIC MISSILE DEFENSE system. After a third test of the proposed technology failed on July 8, 2000, it announced that it would pass on to its successor the controversial decision on whether or not to proceed.

Early evaluations of Clinton's foreign policy were almost uniformly negative. The harshest commentaries came from isolationists who argued that American national interests did not extend to PEACEKEEPING operations. Liberal and conservative critiques focused on his inexperience and repeated policy zig-zags. Typical of this critical outlook was a tendency to downgrade accomplishments, such as the administration's involvement in the peace process in NORTHERN IRELAND that led to the signing of the Good Friday Peace Agreement. By the end of Clinton's second term a more balanced assessment had emerged. Many critiques now focused on Clinton's continued lack of vision and his overreliance on personal diplomacy, such as in his last-minute efforts to arrange an Arab-Israeli peace agreement. Defenders argued that for all of its problems, Clinton's foreign policy had succeeded in reducing the threat of war, fostering an open economy, and spreading American values. One commentator asserted it was a foreign policy "well-suited to an era where there is little to gain and much to lose" through foreign involvement.

See also ARAB-ISRAELI CONFLICT; RUSSIA; VANCE, CYRUS.

**Further reading:** Steel, Ronald. *Temptations of a Superpower.* Cambridge, Mass.: Harvard University Press, 1995.

## cold war

The cold war was the defining feature of the international system between the end of WORLD WAR II and the fall of the Berlin Wall in 1989. It was a period of competition, hostility, and tension between the Western powers and the communist bloc states. While frequently intense, the cold war never escalated into direct and open warfare between the United States and the Soviet Union (see RUSSIA), the two leaders. At any point in time, U.S.-Soviet interactions with each other and in other parts of the globe were characterized by a combination of political maneuvering, diplomatic wrangling, psychological warfare, ideological competition, economic coercion, arms races, and proxy wars.

The conventional starting point for dating the beginning of the cold war is the period immediately following the conclusion of World War II. It is also possible to use other starting points, depending upon which aspect of the cold war interaction between the United States and the Soviet Union is considered most important. The earliest starting point that has considerable support among scholars is the period between 1917 and 1920. On March 15, 1917, the new Communist government that came into power with the Russian Revolution of the same month signed the Treaty of Brest-Litovsk with GERMANY, ending their participation in WORLD WAR I. Western powers, including the United States, responded by sending troops to Russia under the pretext of stopping Japanese expansion into Siberia. A more fundamental goal was to aid the anticommunist forces in hopes of bringing Russia back into the war. Even though World War I ended on November 11, 1918, Western troops remained until early 1920.

The interwar period is a second possible starting point for the cold war. The Soviet Union felt slighted over American refusal to grant it diplomatic recognition, something that did not happen until 1933. For its part the United States was suspicious of Soviet intentions. It saw the Soviet Union as pursuing a dual foreign policy marked at the official level by seeking normal relations with the West and at a second level by trying to spread revolution and overthrow capitalism. The specific vehicle for this was the COMINTERN. Created in 1919 it was an international organization of Communist parties headquartered in Moscow whose stated purpose was to undermine capitalist societies from within.

Animosity and distrust between the West and the Soviet Union reached new heights in the late 1930s. The Soviet Union rejected the British and French claim that the Munich Agreement of 1938 that gave Adolf Hitler's Germany control over the Sudetenland offered "peace in our time." In the Soviet's eyes it had the effect of inviting a German attack on the Soviet Union and provided Germany with a gateway to carry it out. Western fears were fueled the following year with the signing of the Molotov-Ribbentrop Pact, which established neutrality between the Soviet Union and Germany in the event of war with a third power. A secret protocol to this agreement gave the Soviet Union rights to eastern POLAND and the Baltic.

Hitler's surprise attack on the Soviet Union in June 1941 instantly transformed it into an American ally but did little to bring a greater degree of trust to this relationship. The Soviet Union saw the West's repeated delays in opening a western front as an attempt to lock itself and Germany into a series of military battles that would leave them both exhausted. For its part, the West saw Moscow's refusal to enter the war against Japan as a major irritant. Of all the war-related controversies, it is the decision to drop the atomic bomb on Hiroshima that has emerged as one of the most fundamental points of disagreement among revisionist and orthodox interpretations of the cold war. Orthodox histories see the use of the atomic bomb as a military necessity directed against JAPAN. Revisionists view it as part of an emerging U.S. cold war maneuver with Russia in which its use was meant to signal American technological superiority and power.

Those who date the cold war as beginning in the post–World War II period place the greatest emphasis on the short period between the concluding months of World War II and the outbreak of the KOREAN WAR in 1950. During World War II the United States, the Soviet Union, and GREAT BRITAIN met several times to work out the details of the postwar international order. These attempts, particularly those at YALTA and POTSDAM, failed, and this contributed to the distrust and acrimony that came to divide the victors. All three states had different agendas. Great Britain's principal interest was to secure a buffer zone in Germany that would protect FRANCE from future attacks and stop Soviet expansion into Poland. The Soviet Union wanted reparations (compensations for war damages) from Germany so that it could rebuild its economy. The Soviet Union also sought domination over Poland, a weakened Germany, and possessions in Asia. The United States also had multiple objectives. President FRANKLIN ROOSEVELT wanted to see the UNITED NATIONS established, have the Soviet Union enter the war against Japan, and reduce Soviet influence over Poland. These conflicting concerns guaranteed that any decision reached at Yalta and Potsdam would have to be arrived at through a process of diplomatic give-and-take. They also would be heavily influenced by

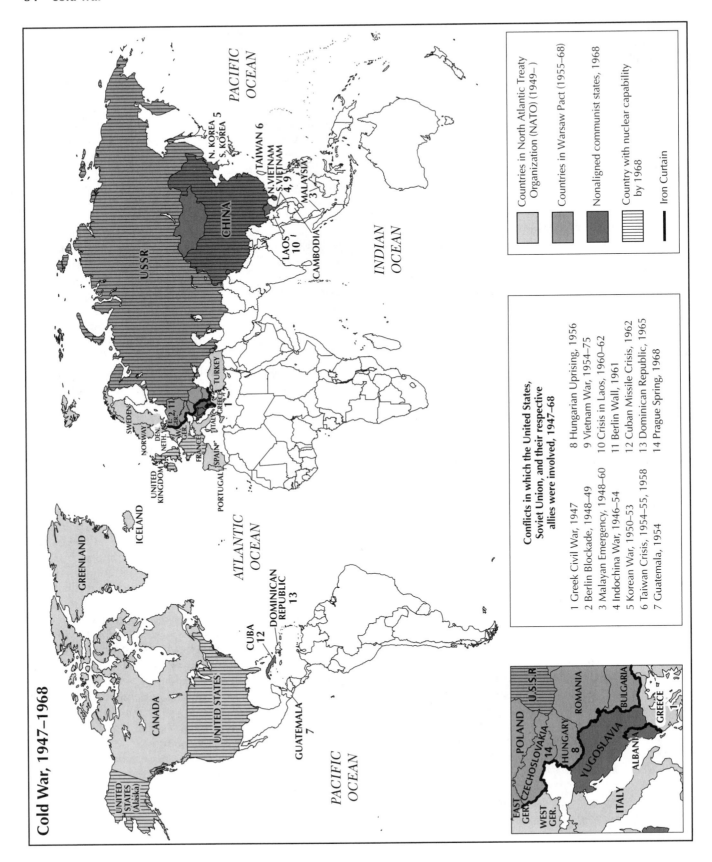

# Cold War, 1947–1968

PACIFIC OCEAN

ATLANTIC OCEAN

INDIAN OCEAN

PACIFIC OCEAN

USSR

CHINA

N. KOREA 5
S. KOREA 5
TAIWAN 6
N.VIETNAM
S.VIETNAM
4, 9
MALAYSIA 3
LAOS 10
CAMBODIA

SWEDEN
NORWAY
DEN.
NETH.
UNITED KINGDOM
PORTUGAL SPAIN
FRANCE
BEL.
LUX.
W. GER.
ITALY
GREECE 1
TURKEY

ICELAND

GREENLAND

CANADA

UNITED STATES

UNITED STATES (Alaska)

CUBA 12
DOMINICAN REPUBLIC 13
GUATEMALA 7

Countries in North Atlantic Treaty Organization (NATO) (1949– )

Countries in Warsaw Pact (1955–68)

Nonaligned communist states, 1968

Country with nuclear capability by 1968

Iron Curtain

**Conflicts in which the United States, Soviet Union, and their respective allies were involved, 1947–68**

1 Greek Civil War, 1947
2 Berlin Blockade, 1948–49
3 Malayan Emergency, 1948–60
4 Indochina War, 1946–54
5 Korean War, 1950–53
6 Taiwan Crisis, 1954–55, 1958
7 Guatemala, 1954

8 Hungarian Uprising, 1956
9 Vietnam War, 1954–75
10 Crisis in Laos, 1960–62
11 Berlin Wall, 1961
12 Cuban Missile Crisis, 1962
13 Dominican Republic, 1965
14 Prague Spring, 1968

EAST GER.
WEST GER.
POLAND
CZECHOSLOVAKIA 14
HUNGARY 8
U.S.S.R.
ROMANIA
YUGOSLAVIA
BULGARIA
ALBANIA
ITALY
GREECE 1

the military realities of the moment, that is, what territory the British, American, and Soviet troops occupied. Soviet occupation of Eastern Europe all but guaranteed that they would prevail in political decisions affecting these states. American and British occupation of ITALY and GREECE meant Soviet exclusion from these areas.

One of the first cold war trouble spots was IRAN. Historically, it had been under British domination. Because it was an important source of OIL in 1941 Soviet and British forces sent troops there in an effort to prevent Hitler from gaining access to it. American forces also entered Iran to supervise the shipment of wartime LEND-LEASE aid to the Soviet Union. By agreement, all of these forces were to leave Iran within six months of the war's end. U.S. and British forces complied with the agreement, but the withdrawal date of March 2, 1946, came and went with Soviet forces firmly encamped in northern Iran. The issue was brought to the United Nations, and President HARRY TRUMAN issued an ultimatum to Joseph Stalin demanding the withdrawal of Soviet forces. The crisis ended when Iranian troops defeated the pro-Soviet forces.

Conflict also broke out over the Dardanelles. Under a 1936 international agreement, TURKEY controlled the navigation of the Bosporus and Dardanelles. In 1945 the Soviet Union demanded that unilateral Turkish control be replaced by a system of joint Soviet-Turkish governance that would provide it with naval and land bases in the straits. Turkey rebuffed these advances with the help of the United States. To show his seriousness, Truman sent the Sixth Fleet to the eastern Mediterranean Sea. The crisis eased in late 1946 but came to life again in 1947 as a result of renewed Soviet pressures in the region. On February 21, 1947, Great Britain informed the United States that it could no longer afford to meet its traditional obligations to protect Greece and Turkey. Less than one month later, on March 12, 1947, Truman addressed a joint session of CONGRESS and requested $400 million in economic and military FOREIGN AID for Greece and Turkey. Just as important as this request for aid was the language Truman used to justify U.S. support for these two governments. Known as the TRUMAN DOCTRINE, he argued that the United States "must support free peoples who are resisting attempted subjugation by armed minorities or by outside pressure."

Three months later the United States took another step in linking its defense with that of Europe. SECRETARY OF STATE GEORGE MARSHALL announced that the United States was prepared to underwrite a plan for European economic recovery. The MARSHALL PLAN offered U.S. financing to European states if they would first agree among themselves on a recovery plan. All European states were invited to participate in the drafting of a collective plan. The Soviet Union chose not to participate and pre-vented the East European states from joining as well. This effectively served to divide postwar Europe into two parts.

In 1949 the economic division of Europe was reinforced by its military partition with the establishment of the NORTH ATLANTIC TREATY ORGANIZATION (NATO). The United States, Great Britain, France, CANADA, the NETHERLANDS, Belgium, Luxembourg, Denmark, Iceland, Norway, Italy, and Portugal were charter members. Greece and Turkey joined in 1952. West Germany followed in 1955. This last act prompted the Soviet Union to organize its European allies, or satellites, into the WARSAW PACT Treaty Organization. The lone East European communist state not to join was YUGOSLAVIA. The Yugoslav Communists under the leadership of Josip Broz, Marshal Tito was fiercely independent and stubbornly resisted Stalin's demands that Yugoslavia subordinate its foreign-policy goals to those of the Soviet Union. Because of this independent attitude in 1948 Stalin expelled Yugoslavia from the international communist movement.

Tito's expulsion coincided with the first of the BERLIN CRISES. When World War II ended Berlin became a divided city within a divided country. It lay 110 miles inside the Soviet occupation zone. In 1948 the Soviet Union cut off the western sectors of Berlin from the remainder of occupied Germany. The United States responded to this attempt to force the West out of Berlin with an around-the-clock airlift of supplies that continued for 324 days. Confronted with the reality that their efforts had failed, Soviet leaders called off the blockade in May 1949.

It was also during the late 1940s that the conceptual basis for the U.S. cold war policy of CONTAINMENT emerged. In 1947 GEORGE KENNAN wrote an article in *Foreign Affairs* in which he argued that "the main element of any United States policy toward the Soviet Union must be that of a long-term, patient but firm and vigilant containment of Russian expansionist tendencies." The Marshall Plan and the creation of NATO were logical applications of this containment policy and had the effect of placing a ring around the Soviet Union's European border. In the early 1950s, U.S. policy makers extended this ring around the remainder of the Soviet Union. Bilateral agreements were signed with Japan, TAIWAN, SOUTH KOREA, and the PHILIPPINES. A mutual defense treaty, the ANZUS PACT, was signed between Australia, New Zealand, and the United States in 1951. After the French withdrew from Indochina in 1954 the United States joined with France, Great Britain, New Zealand, Australia, PAKISTAN, the Philippines, and THAILAND in creating the SOUTHEAST ASIA TREATY ORGANIZATION (SEATO). The final piece of the encirclement puzzle was put in place in 1955 when the United States, Great Britain, Turkey, Iran, IRAQ, and Pakistan formed the CENTRAL TREATY ORGANIZATION (CENTO, also known as the Baghdad Pact).

The final chapter of the cold war in the 1940s and the first chapter in the 1950s were played out in Asia. Initially, the United States and Soviet Union expected Jiang Jieshi (Chiang Kai-shek) and his Nationalists to defeat Mao Zedong (Mao Tse-tung) and his Communists in the civil war that was being fought for control of CHINA. Instead Mao triumphed handily. In 1948 his forces launched a major offensive that ultimately brought all of Manchuria and northern China under Communist control. In September 1949, Mao announced the formation of the People's Republic of China (PRC), and by year's end Jiang Jieshi and his followers had fled to the island of Taiwan located 100 miles off the Chinese coast. Mao promptly aligned China with the Soviet Union, a move that the United States viewed as significantly increasing Soviet power.

In June 1950 North Korean forces crossed the 38th parallel into South Korea. The invasion caught the United States by surprise. Statements by U.S. policy makers had given the impression that the Korean Peninsula was not regarded as a central national security concern, but once the attack began, the United States reversed its position and sent in forces under the UN flag. It took UN forces three months to stop the North Korean advance and reclaim South Korea. Once on the offensive they continued their advance and crossed into NORTH KOREA. Chinese warnings that this would cause them to intervene were discounted. The United States was surprised a second time when, in November, Chinese troops crossed the Yalu River en masse. It was not until March 1951 that Chinese forces were pushed back behind the 38th parallel and a stalemate in the fighting was reached. Peace talks began that July, but a truce in the KOREAN WAR was not signed until 1953.

American and Russian cold war policies in Europe in the early and mid-1950s largely were directed at shoring up their respective ALLIANCES. Tangible gains were made in West Europe as the European allies took the first steps toward greater economic cooperation with the establishment of the European Common Market in 1957, but efforts to extend West European military cooperation beyond the framework set out in NATO repeatedly met with failure. Alliance politics in Eastern Europe were of a quite different nature. Joseph Stalin's death in March 1953 set in motion a prolonged power struggle in Moscow and the capitals of Eastern Europe. Within months rioting broke out in East Germany to protest the continuation of harsh Communist rule. The help of the Russian army was required to put down the rebellion. Nikita Khrushchev, who emerged victorious in Moscow, contributed to the next series of East European uprisings with his 1956 secret speech at the 20th Party Congress at which he denounced Stalin's excesses. Designed to help him consolidate his power base in Russia, the speech also undermined the legitimacy of most East European leaders who had served as loyal lieutenants of Stalin. Rioting soon broke out in HUNGARY and Poland as old Communist leaders were swept away and replaced by

Nationalists. The political situation stabilized in Poland but not in Hungary. In the face of declarations that Hungary was withdrawing from the Warsaw Pact, Soviet forces invaded the country and reestablished Communist Party control. It should be noted that the United States was just as concerned about the loyalty of states in Latin America and just as committed to preventing defections. The CENTRAL INTELLIGENCE AGENCY (CIA) organized a covert action to restore a pro-American regime in GUATEMALA in 1956, and President LYNDON JOHNSON cited the threat of COMMUNISM as his rationale for sending U.S. Marines to the DOMINICAN REPUBLIC in 1964.

The East-West cold war in Europe returned with dramatic suddenness in 1958. The site was Berlin and centered around a Soviet ultimatum to turn it into a free city. The timing of Khrushchev's ultimatum was closely tied to the October 1957 launching of the first satellite, SPUTNIK, and the successful testing of the first intercontinental ballistic missile (ICBM). Together they signaled that for the first time the Soviet Union possessed the ability to launch military strikes directly at the United States from the Soviet Union. As in 1948 the United States weathered the storm, and the status quo over Berlin continued.

The 1950s also witnessed a brief thaw in U.S.-Soviet relations. DWIGHT EISENHOWER and Khrushchev met at a summit conference in Geneva in 1955 that produced good feelings and a relaxation of tensions. The "Spirit of Geneva" was short-lived. A summit conference set for Paris in 1957 ended in disaster. The Soviet Union had shot down a U-2 spy plane over Soviet territory, capturing its pilot, Gary Francis Powers. The United States denied allegations of spying, claiming a weather observation plane had strayed over Soviet airspace. The Russians produced Powers, denounced the United States, and stormed out of Paris.

The 1960s began with yet another crisis over Berlin. Between 1948 and 1960, 2.5 million East Germans had fled to West Germany using Berlin as an escape route. To end this exodus the Soviet Union constructed a wall dividing the city in two. Shortly after the 1961 BERLIN CRISIS, CUBA became the focus of cold war tensions. The United States had become obsessed with removing Fidel Castro from power in Cuba shortly after he assumed power in 1959. The CIA drew up plans for his "elimination," and Eisenhower approved a plan for sending a small group of Cuban exiles back to Cuba for purposes of conducting a GUERRILLA WARFARE campaign against him. This plan evolved into a larger operation, the BAY OF PIGS invasion, which was authorized by President JOHN F. KENNEDY and took place on April 17, 1961. The results were disastrous. Some 1,400 Cuban exiles landed at the Bay of Pigs and quickly were surrounded by 20,000 well-equipped soldiers loyal to the regime. On the third day, the 1,200 survivors were marched off to prison camps.

A little more than one year later, the United States and the Soviet Union became locked in a test of wills over the presence of Soviet missiles in Cuba. Rumors that offense missiles were being built there had started circulating in the summer of 1962, but conclusive evidence of the buildup was not obtained until October 14 when a U-2 overflight produced pictures of construction sites that matched those of missile installations observed in the Soviet Union. Kennedy announced the discovery of the missiles and the imposition of a naval blockage on national television on October 22. He also set a deadline for a Soviet response. The crisis ended on October 29 when Khrushchev agreed to remove Soviet missiles in return for a U.S. pledge not to intervene in Cuba, but this solution was not easily reached. Perhaps at no time was the world closer to a NUCLEAR WAR than it was during the CUBAN MISSILE CRISIS in October 1962. President Kennedy put the odds of avoiding war at one out of three. Khrushchev later observed that "the smell of burning hung in the air."

The cold war took on still an additional dimension in the late 1950s and early 1960s. It entered the Third World. In particular it descended upon the newly independent states of AFRICA and Asia that were just emerging from colonial rule. Many of these began as battlegrounds in which the United States and Soviet Union supported competing indigenous leaders, hoping to make states allies or at least deny them to the other. Some newly independent states joined with more established independent states, such as EGYPT, INDIA, and INDONESIA, to create a neutral pathway between the two superpowers. The nonaligned movement did not fully succeed in this goal in large part because its nationalist rhetoric was interpreted by many in the United States as anti-American. In the logic of the bipolar cold war INTERNATIONAL SYSTEM, this made most nonaligned states procommunist.

A positive offshoot of the Cuban missile crisis was a burst of ARMS CONTROL efforts. In 1963 the "hot line" was set up between the United States and the Soviet Union to permit secure and direct communication between the two capitals. That same year a test ban treaty was signed, in 1967 an outer space treaty was agreed to, and in 1968 a non-proliferation treaty was approved. Progress in arms control was halted by the Soviet invasion of CZECHOSLOVAKIA and the deepening U.S. presence in VIETNAM.

Antonin Novotny, a loyal Soviet ally, was replaced by Alexander Dubček as head of the Czech Communist Party in 1968. Under his leadership, the party sought to shed its rigid Stalinist past and began to experiment with free-market economic reforms and democratic principles. Fearing that the "Prague Spring" might spill over and infect other East European states, the Soviet Union orchestrated an invasion of Czechoslovakia by Warsaw Pact troops. In justifying its actions the Soviet Union put forward the BREZH

NEV DOCTRINE, which asserted the right of the Soviet Union to determine when communism was threatened by counterrevolutionary forces and take corrective actions.

America's involvement in Vietnam began in the 1950s. After the end of World War II, France sought with little success to reestablish its rule over Indochina. The Eisenhower administration provided financial support for the French but refused to commit U.S. troops to the French cause. In 1954 the French were forced to negotiate a withdrawal. The Geneva Peace accords envisioned a country temporarily divided at the 17th parallel with Communist forces in control of the North and pro-Western forces in control of the South. An election was scheduled for 1956 to unify the country. The United States did not participate in these negotiations but pledged not to use force to disturb them. Its policies soon followed a different path. South Vietnam was put under the protective cover of SEATO, and elections were not held. North Vietnam, under the leadership of Ho Chi Minh, and communist allies in South Vietnam now began a military campaign to unify all of Vietnam.

When Eisenhower left office there were 1,000 American military advisers present. Kennedy authorized an additional 15,000 advisers. Under Johnson, the war became increasingly Americanized as U.S. forces carried out sustained and massive bombing campaigns against the North and U.S. ground troops began fighting in the South. Nixon sought to reverse this, at least on the ground, by implementing a policy of Vietnamization. It was designed to create conditions such that by 1972 the South Vietnamese army would be able to hold its own when supported by U.S. air and sea power. To prevent North Vietnam from attacking before Vietnamization could be implemented the Nixon administration designed a two-part strategy. Cambodia was invaded with the hope of cleaning out North Vietnamese sanctuaries and the bombing of North Vietnam was increased. The strategy failed. In spring 1972 North Vietnam attacked across the demilitarized zone, forcing Nixon to re-Americanize the war. By the time the war ended in 1975, 55,000 Americans had lost their lives in Vietnam; as many as 541,000 Americans were fighting there at its height; $150 billion were spent on the war effort; hundreds of thousands of Vietnamese died or were wounded; millions of tons of bombs were dropped; and 20 million craters were left behind.

Another positive note in the cold war during the 1960s for the United States was the Sino-Soviet split. In the early 1950s China and the Soviet Union each had supported the other's foreign-policy initiatives giving rise to the image of a monolithic Communist bloc. By the mid-1960s it was clear that this was no longer the case, if it ever was. Three reasons stand out as especially important for why this split occurred. First, the Chinese and Russians disagreed about the political value of Soviet nuclear weapons. The Chinese were far more willing to take risks and bring the specter of nuclear war into its confrontations with the United States. Ideological differences constituted a second contributing factor to the Sino-Soviet split. Each saw the other as having deviated from the true path of Marxism-Leninism. A third factor behind the Sino-Soviet split involved a series of conflicts of NATIONAL INTEREST. The most serious of these contested territorial claims resulted in a series of military clashes along their border. China claimed that Russian czars had imposed nine unequal treaties on previous regimes, causing China to loose some 580,000 square miles of territory.

Convinced that neither the American public nor CONGRESS was likely to support future prolonged military campaigns, Nixon redirected American foreign policy. A first change was to augment U.S. POWER with that of other states. The goal was to make it more difficult for the Soviet Union to challenge the United States without forcing the United States to maintain a large military establishment or global presence. The key state in this scenario was China. U.S. policy makers came to see the threat of improved relations with China as a trump card that could be held in reserve and played at a crucial point in the future. A prerequisite for playing the China card was diplomatic recognition of China. The United States has never recognized the Communist government as the legitimate rulers of China. The Nixon administration took the first steps in that direction when in July 1971 Nixon announced to a stunned world that it would "seek the normalization of relations" with China and he would soon visit there.

A second policy change sought to minimize future Soviet challenges by treating the Soviet Union less as a rival and more as a partner in the international system. Known as DÉTENTE, the goal was to create a framework of limited cooperation between the two superpowers within the context of ongoing competition and conflict. At its center stood a strategy of linkages that sought to substitute a network of linked rewards and punishments for the application of military power as the primary means of containing the Soviet Union. Détente's greatest success came in the area of arms control, most notably with the signing of the SALT I and SALT II agreements. Détente's greatest failing was an inability to establish agreed upon rules to govern U.S.–Soviet competition in the Third World. Matters came to a head in ANGOLA, ETHIOPIA, SOMALIA, and the Middle East, where Soviet support for procommunist and nationalist forces was seen by the United States as unwarranted adventurism and by the Soviet Union as a legitimate exercise of its power. In spite of this desire to establish a better working relationship with the Soviet Union, the United States continued to see Latin America as an area of special significance and one that was off-limits to Soviet influence. In CHILE the United States used COVERT ACTION to under-mine the government of Salvador Allende and reestablish a strong pro-American regime.

The cold war in the 1980s was a decade of reversal, with Soviet activism replaced by American activism. President RONALD REAGAN promised to reestablish American credibility and restore American military power. He rejected the notion common to the latter half of the 1970s that American power had declined. He also rejected the notion that the United States could cooperate or work with the Soviet Union. For the Reagan administration the world remained very much the same as it had been for the past several decades: a world of conflict in which the main protagonist was a Communist Soviet Union. The purpose of American power as expressed in the REAGAN DOCTRINE was not only to check the spread of communism but also to assist in bringing down communist rulers. Many of the early foreign policy initiatives of the Reagan administration were low-risk, high-profile, short-term undertakings designed to highlight this change in outlook, such as the invasion of GRENADA and the bombing of LIBYA.

Two prominent long-term examples of the Reagan administration's commitment to reversing the fortune of communism were its support for anticommunist forces in NICARAGUA and AFGHANISTAN. In Nicaragua 40 years of arbitrary, oppressive, and corrupt family rule came to an end in July 1979 when the pro-U.S. dictator Anastasio Somoza Debayle went into exile. At first the United States adopted a tolerant attitude toward the new Sandinista government, but this began to change as the Sandinistas delayed free elections, reimposed press censorship, and began assisting rebels in El Salvador who were trying to bring down another pro-U.S. right-wing government. In November 1981 Reagan signed a presidential finding authorizing the spending of $19 million to transform this small and largely ineffective fighting force into one (the contras) that would be capable of stopping the flow of Sandinista weapons into EL SALVADOR.

Congress suspected that the real purpose for organizing a 5,000-person contra force was to overthrow the Sandinista regime. To prevent this from happening it passed the Boland Amendments that barred the use of CIA or DEFENSE DEPARTMENT funds for the purpose of overthrowing the Nicaraguan government or provoking a military exchange between it and Honduras. Chafing under this restriction the Reagan administration devised a covert plan for increasing the amount of funds available to the contras. At the heart of the administration's plan was a scheme to divert money to the contras from the covert sale of weapons to Iran as part of a plan to free American hostages (the IRAN-CONTRA INITIATIVE). When it became public the plan produced a storm of controversy. Nicaragua remained a visible item on the American foreign-policy agenda until the Bush administration was able to negotiate a deal with Congress to keep aid flowing to the contras through internationally supervised elections scheduled for February 1990. To the surprise of virtually everyone, the Sandinistas lost this election.

The Soviet Union became actively involved in Afghanistan when a 1973 coup removed King Zahir Shah from power. Infighting between pro-Russian and pro-Maoist forces within the new Communist government caused the situation to deteriorate to the point that in December 1979 the Soviet Union sent in a 50,000-troop invasion force to restore order. The original Soviet plan called for the Afghan army to bear the bulk of the responsibility for pacifying the Afghan population. Wholesale defections quickly negated this strategy; as a result, within one year the Soviet Union occupation army grew to 110,000, and it had to bear the primary responsibility for fighting the guerrillas, or Mujaheddin, who were supported by U.S. funds. American military aid to the Mujaheddin rose from $120 million in 1984 to $630 million in 1987.

At the same time that the Soviet Union was trying to extricate itself from Afghanistan, even more fundamental challenges were confronting it. Abroad, its East European buffer zone was collapsing. The first signs of a crack in the iron curtain that separated Eastern Europe from the rest of the continent came with the birth of the Solidarity trade union movement in Poland in 1981. By decade's end Solidarity-led protests again would spring up, setting off a wave of prodemocracy movements in the rest of East Europe that culminated in the fall of the Berlin Wall in 1989. The greatest challenge, however, came at home. The Soviet political, economic, and social order had become stagnant and incapable of generating the resources necessary for the Soviet Union to act as a great power. A last attempt at innovation and renewal came when Mikhail Gorbachev became head of the Communist Party. His foreign policy, based on the principles of New Thinking, helped move the Soviet Union out of purely confrontational posture with the United States to one that included the START arms control initiatives. He also put Soviet–East European relations on a more positive footing by renouncing the Brezhnev Doctrine in 1989 and achieving a withdrawal from Afghanistan. Still, this was not enough. His policies of perestroika (restructuring) and glasnost (openness) failed to energize the Communist Party or the Soviet Union. Demands for increased autonomy and then independence on the part of the Soviet Union's many constituent republics could not be constrained, and on December 26, 1991, the Soviet Union collapsed and the Russian Republic assumed control over its embassies and its seat in international bodies, such as the United Nations.

The reasons for this turn of events are the subject of great controversy. Three major lines of thought exist. The first gives credit to President Ronald Reagan's military buildup

(*From left to right*) Mikhail Gorbachev, Ronald Reagan, and George H. W. Bush at the close of the cold war era, New York Harbor. *(Ronald W. Reagan Library)*

and ideological assertiveness. The second stresses the important influence that liberal Western ideas about the nature of international politics had on Mikhail Gorbachev and the Soviet elite. The third explanation places greatest emphasis on the long-term decay of the Soviet economy and sees American ideas and actions as playing only a secondary role.

**Further reading:** Flemming, D. F. *The Cold War and Its Origins, 1917–1950.* Garden City, N.Y.: Doubleday, 1961; Gaddis, John L. *The United States and the Origins of the Cold War.* New York: Columbia University Press, 1972; ———. *The Long Peace: Inquiries into the History of the Cold War.* New York: Oxford University Press, 1987; Lebow, Richard Ned, and Jancie Gross Stein. *We All Lost the Cold War.* Princeton, N.J.: Princeton University Press, 1994; Williams, William A. *The Tragedy of American Diplomacy.* Rev. ed. New York: World, 1962.

## collective security

Collective security is a system for preserving global peace that was advanced as an alternative to the balance of power by WOODROW WILSON and became one of the fundamental operating principles of the LEAGUE OF NATIONS. Although it proved unsuccessful in the case of the latter, it continues to be advanced as a means for securing peace in the post–COLD WAR international system.

Collective-security systems start from the premise that an attack on one member is considered an attack on all members. Unlike traditional ALLIANCES that are created with an eye toward countering the power of a specific state, collective security seeks to counter potential aggression from any quarter. The assumption is that confronted with the combined power of all other states in the international system, aggression will fail, and knowing this, any potential aggressor will be deterred.

The requirements for a successful operation of a collective-security system are many. First, no one state can be powerful enough to resist the combined power of the rest of the international community. Second, the primary loyalty of other states must be to the international community and not to aggressor states. Unless this happens the aggressor can count on allies in its cause. Third, the response of the international community must be rapid. Lengthy delays increase the possibility that the gains obtained through aggression can be solidified and protected. Fourth, collective security assumes that the aggressor can be easily identified. This requirement has come under heavy scrutiny as GUERRILLA WARFARE, TERRORISM, and other forms of unconventional warfare become more prominent. The difficulty of identifying the aggressor in these types of conflict situations is compounded by the fact that many post–cold war conflicts begin as civil or ethnic wars rather than international wars.

The League of Nations failed to implement an effective collective-security system. JAPAN's aggression against Manchuria and CHINA went unchecked, as did ITALY's invasion of ETHIOPIA and GERMANY's moves against CZECHOSLOVAKIA and Austria. The reasons can be found in the inability of the League of Nations to establish the necessary requirements for success. The United States refused to join the League of Nations. FRANCE did join, but Paris was concerned principally with stopping German aggression and not aggression in the abstract. And when confronted with German aggression, it joined GREAT BRITAIN in deciding that the costs of countering Germany's moves were too high.

The creation of the UNITED NATIONS (UN) after WORLD WAR II revived interest in a collective-security system. However, the decision to give the permanent members of the Security Council a veto over the use of force by the UN meant that a true collective-security system would not be created. In time, the UN would develop an alternative set of principles for preserving peace in the INTERNATIONAL SYSTEM. They included preventive DIPLOMACY and PEACEKEEPING.

In the post–cold war era three great experiments in collective security have taken place. The first involved the successful construction of a global coalition against Saddam Hussein in response to IRAQ's invasion of KUWAIT. The boldness of the move plus the potential threat to international OIL flows facilitated a coordinated international response. The second involves the effort to recast the NORTH ATLANTIC TREATY ORGANIZATION (NATO) from a defensive alliance that was created to stop Soviet aggression into a collective-security organization. NATO's performance in the Balkans and its reluctance to make RUSSIA a member make it unclear whether this transformation is possible. European efforts to create a military capability separate from NATO may or may not make collective security a reality. Problems of political will remain. The third attempt at constructing a collective-security system came in the wake of the SEPTEMBER 11, 2001, terrorist attack on the World Trace Center and the Pentagon. In the aftermath of the attack global unity against OSAMA BIN LADEN's terrorist organization was quickly achieved, but disagreements soon emerged over tactics and the effort to expand the war against terrorism to other groups.

**Further reading:** Claude, Inis. *Swords into Plowshares.* 4th ed. New York: Random House, 1971; Weiss, Thomas, ed. *Collective Security in a Changing World.* Boulder, Colo.: Westview, 1993.

## Colombia

Colombia is the fourth-largest country in South America. It has an area of 440,000 square miles, making it about the size of Texas, New Mexico, and Arkansas. It has a population of 42 million people. The first permanent Spanish settlement in Colombia was established in 1525. In 1549 the areas became a Spanish colony, and in 1717 the Viceroyalty of New Granada was created. It encompassed the current countries of Colombia, PANAMA, VENEZUELA, and Ecuador. Colombia became independent in 1810, and the United States was one of the first countries to recognize it in 1822.

Until recently by far the most significant interaction in the United States had with Colombia involved negotiations that led to the construction of the PANAMA CANAL. American interest in an interoceanic canal had been piqued by the SPANISH-AMERICAN WAR and the earlier discovery of gold in California. Both events brought home the need for a waterway that would reduce the sailing time around South America. While the actual physical construction of such a waterway was challenging, the recent opening of the Suez Canal established that it could be done. More significant were a series of diplomatic and political obstacles.

The initial set of diplomatic obstacles centered on obtaining the rights to build and defend a canal. The CLAYTON-BULWER TREATY of 1850 pledged the United States and GREAT BRITAIN to neither build nor fortify a canal without the other's consent. In 1901 SECRETARY OF STATE JOHN HAY negotiated two treaties with the British ambassador to the United States, Sir Julian Paunceforte. The first treaty recognized the United States's right to build a canal, and the second treaty recognized its right to control and fortify a canal. While these treaties cleared the way for the construction of an interoceanic canal, the question of where to build the canal remained.

Two routes were eyed. One would pass through NICARAGUA. The second would pass through PANAMA, territory then under the control of Colombia. The Nicaraguan route had long been preferred and was endorsed by the Walker Commission that had been set up by President WILLIAM MCKINLEY to examine possible routes. President THEODORE ROOSEVELT, however, came to favor the Panama route as a result of heavy pressure by Philippe Bunau-Varilla, who had financial interests in and represented a Panama Canal company, and Mark Hanna, chair of the REPUBLICAN PARTY National Committee. After much debate CONGRESS also endorsed the Panama route in 1902.

Hay moved quickly to conclude a treaty with Colombia's representative to the United States, Tomás Herrán. The Hay-Herrán Treaty signed on January 22, 1903, transferred a six-mile stretch of land to the United States, which was granted control in perpetuity. In return Colombia received $10 million plus an annual fee of $250,000. Three days after the agreement was signed Herrán received instructions from Colombia not to sign an agreement. The U.S. Senate ratified the treaty on March 17, but seeking better financial terms, Colombia's Senate rejected the pact on August 12. The United States responded angrily. Roosevelt drafted but did not sent a message to Congress in which he suggested the land needed for the Panama Canal be taken by force. Hay sent what amounted to an ultimatum to the Colombian government.

The United States now turned its attention directly to Panama, where Bunau-Varilla was seeking to organize a revolt. Armed with the knowledge that a U.S. warship would arrive in Panama on November 2, plans for the revolt were put into place. As expected, on that date the *Nashville* reached Panama. The next day the revolt broke out, and on November 4 independence was declared. The United States recognized Panama as a sovereign state on November 6. The American response had been complicated by an 1846 treaty between the United States and New Granada. According to its terms the United States was given transit rights through the Panamanian isthmus but pledged itself to a policy of "perfect neutrality."

Angered by the U.S. action Colombia sought to block it by taking the issue to international arbitration. The United States objected. Roosevelt refused to admit any wrongdoing. His successor, President WILLIAM HOWARD TAFT, did make peace overtures to Colombia, but it was not until the administration of WOODROW WILSON that concrete steps were taken to placate Colombia. A treaty was signed in 1914 in which the United States expressed its "sincere regret" for the events in Panama and agreed to pay an additional $25 million. Opposition within the Senate held up action for seven years. It was revived under President WARREN HARDING. The expression of regret was removed, but the $25 million payment was retained. The Senate approved the treaty in April 1921 by a vote of 69-19. The discovery of OIL reserves in Colombia rather than a change in conscience appears to have been the major factor in this belated action.

The dawning of a new century again finds the United States deeply involved with Colombia. Colombia is the world's leading supplier of refined cocaine and a major source of heroin. More than 90 percent of the cocaine that enters the United States is produced, processed, or shipped though Colombia. The foreign-policy problem of reducing the flow of illegal drugs into the United States is complicated by the fact that within Colombia the drug problem is enmeshed in a complex civil war that involves the government, right-wing paramilitary forces, drug dealers, and leftist guerrillas.

The principal point of involvement for the United States in combating the DRUG TRAFFICKING problem is Plan Colombia, an international plan that was introduced by the Colombian government in 1999. Its stated objectives are to promote peace, combat the narcotics industry, revive the Colombian economy, improve respect for HUMAN RIGHTS, and strengthen democracy. Responding to Plan Colombia, Congress approved a $1.3 billion FOREIGN-AID package in 2000. This came in addition to some $300 million in aid already in place for the fiscal year 2000. American participation in Plan Colombia and its overall posture toward the drug problem in Colombia has been widely criticized for its heavy emphasis on using the military and police forces to address the problem. Twin fears exist that not only does this strategy place insufficient emphasis on the economic, political, and human-rights issues involved in Colombia's ongoing civil war and therefore that it will fail but also that U.S. military personnel will become active participants in the war against drugs.

**Further reading:** Lael, Richard A. *Arrogant Diplomacy.* Wilmington, Del.: Scholarly Resources, 1987; Randall, Stephen J. *Colombia and the United States.* Athens: University of Georgia Press, 1992.

## Commerce Department (United States Department of Commerce)

Established in 1903 as the Department of Commerce and Labor, the Department of Commerce became a separate entity in 1913. It is a relative newcomer to the foreign-affairs bureaucracy along with the DEPARTMENT OF AGRICULTURE and the TREASURY DEPARTMENT. In 1945 an Office of International Trade was established, and in 1980 the International Trade administration was set up. Along with the Bureau of Export Administration, it is the focal point for the Commerce Department's international activities.

The International Trade Administration is dedicated to opening markets for American products and providing information and assistance to U.S. exporters. It does so by providing three services. First, through its U.S. and Foreign Commercial Service, it helps maintain a series of domestic and overseas offices that provide general export counseling and assistance. A primary focal point of their efforts is to help small and medium-sized businesses promote their goods abroad. Second, through its Trade Development unit, the International Trade Administration acts as an advocate for firms seeking foreign procurement contracts. It does this through direct appeals and direct contacts with foreign decision makers and by promoting U.S. exports at trade shows. The Trade Development unit also monitors economic trends in the United States and abroad. Third, its office of Import Administration and the Trade Compliance Center works to ensure that laws and agreements are enforced to prevent unfair trading practices that harm U.S. firms and weaken the competitive strength of U.S. businesses. In 1998, for example, the Import Administration initiated 47 antidumping or countervailing duty investigations into foreign practices that unfairly harmed U.S. firms.

The Trade Development and Import Assistance units also work with representatives from other agencies, such as the OFFICE OF THE UNITED STATES TRADE REPRESENTATIVE, to provide policy makers with advice in international trade negotiations. Import Assistance offices have participated in negotiations on a multilateral steel agreement, an international shipbuilding agreement, and a subsidies and antidumping agreement.

The Bureau of Export Administration is charged with advancing U.S. national security, foreign policy, and economic interests by regulating exports of critical goods and technologies, enforcing compliance with these regulations, and monitoring the U.S. industrial base to ensure that it remains strong. One key office within the Bureau of Export Administration includes the Office of Nonproliferation Controls and Treaty Compliance, which is charged with administering U.S. responsibilities under the Nuclear Suppliers Group agreement, the Missile Technology Control Regime agreement, and the Chemical Weapons Convention. The Office of Strategic Trade and Foreign Policy Controls is responsible for implementing multilateral export controls in the area of conventional weapons and dual-use technologies. It also has responsibility for export controls to terrorist countries. A third office, the Office of Strategic Industry and Economic Security, implements programs that are designed to ensure that the needs of U.S. defense industries are met, and it provides advocacy assistance to U.S. defense exporters.

The Department of Commerce's economic promotion and monitoring activities place it at the intersection of powerful domestic- and foreign-policy pressures. As with the Department of Agriculture and Treasury Department, Commerce tends to have an "America first" perspective in which domestic interests are given greater weight than foreign considerations. This often places it at odds with the STATE DEPARTMENT and DEFENSE DEPARTMENT, which tend to be more sensitive to foreign concerns. These tensions have become especially acute with the establishment of the WORLD TRADE ORGANIZATION and the perception that many of its rulings disadvantage U.S. firms. Similar tensions are found in the promotion of arms sales. The United States is a global leader in arms sales, but their volume, character, and destination are often the subject of intense political controversy.

## communism, Soviet

During the COLD WAR the principal threat to American foreign policy was defined as the spread of communism. The Soviet Union was seen as the center of international communism, and containment of Soviet expansionism was the policy adopted to achieve this objective. The close identification between the Soviet Union's goals and the goals of international communism led American officials to use them interchangeably in characterizing national security threats. This practice created problems for American foreign policy as leaders in developing countries began pledging their allegiance to communism. The United States sought to counter and defeat these political forces without fully appreciating the extent to which they were motivated by historical and domestic factors rather than by an underlying affinity with the Soviet Union's goals. This same critique can be leveled against Soviet leaders who overly committed themselves and Soviet POWER resources to aiding these movements even when they added little to Soviet security in a narrow sense.

This blurring of the threat posed by the Soviet Union and the threat posed by communism in other states was due in large measure to the fact that the language of Marxist-Leninist writings became the language of Soviet foreign policy. According to Marxist theory the structure of relationships in a society are determined by its economic system. In any society there exists a dominant mode of production that determines property relations. In capitalism the owners of the means of production are the bourgeoisie who seek to maximize their profits by exploiting the work of labor by paying it less than it is due. The state is an instrument of the dominant class and oppresses others in society. Conflict is inevitable, and eventually the workers will seize control of the means of production and establish a socialist economic order. Under socialism class antagonisms will disappear, and gradually the state will wither away because it is not needed. Similarly, state boundaries will become irrelevant. They were created by capitalists to keep people of the same economic class apart. For Marx there was a historical inevitability in all of this. The triumph of communism was inevitable.

Lenin extended the Marxist analysis to include a global dimension. The modification was necessary because the revolution predicted by marxism had not taken place. Lenin argued that capitalism had temporarily saved itself by entering into a stage of IMPERIALISM. Exploiting foreign labor allowed capitalists to buy off portions of the working class. For Lenin, revolution would occur only where there existed both exploitation and political consciousness. This directed attention to the most advanced portions of the developing world where exploitation existed alongside an educated class. Robbed of its ability to exploit workers in other countries, the dynamics identified by Marx would run their predetermined course.

Soviet leaders used this language because their rule was born in a revolution and because at one level the Communist Party's right to rule depended upon its ability to fulfill the Marxist promise. In the realm of foreign policy, communist rhetoric allowed the Soviet Union to portray its foreign policy as inherently peaceful due to its class character. At the same time the opposition and hostility of capitalist states could be taken as a given, as could the global nature of the struggle.

As a consequence the domestic political role played by communist ideology in the language of Soviet foreign policy tended to be quite rigid at any one time. There was a correct way to interpret Marx and Lenin. Over time, however, modifications did occur. In 1924 Joseph Stalin advanced the idea of socialism in one country. It replaced the concept of permanent revolution that had been favored by Leon Trotsky, whom he had defeated in the political struggle to succeed Lenin as head of the Communist Party after his death. In Trotsky's formulation communism in the Soviet Union could succeed only in the context of a global revolutionary uprising. Stalin's view held that because of the Soviet Union's immense resources it could establish a socialist system in the face of global hostility. Nikita Khrushchev adjusted official Soviet thinking again in 1956 when he proclaimed the concept of peaceful coexistence. In doing so he moved away from Stalin by allowing for the peaceful establishment of socialism and denying the inevitability of war with capitalist states. Khrushchev did not announce the end of conflict between capitalism and socialism but proclaimed its movement away from a direct U.S.-Soviet conflict to safer forms of combat, such as competition in the Third World.

A 1968 poster for the Soviet Communist Party declaring, "We are building communism!" *(Library of Congress)*

A more radical adjustment in Soviet rhetoric came when Mikhail Gorbachev put forward his New Thinking. According to some observers it marked the end of revolutionary faith on the part of Soviet leaders. Gorbachev replaced the class struggle with interdependence as the central feature of Soviet foreign policy. In the process he moved Soviet foreign policy away from the pursuit of security through military means to the pursuit of security through ARMS CONTROL. This change in outlook led to arms control talks between Gorbachev and RONALD REAGAN at a hastily called Reykjavík SUMMIT CONFERENCE in 1986, which, at one point, appeared to be on the verge of producing an agreement to ban all ballistic missiles.

It should be noted that while the basic principles of Soviet communism were often quite rigid, this was not true around the world. In CHINA, Mao Zedong adapted communism to Asian conditions. He placed rural peasants at the center of the revolutionary process instead of urban workers. Similar adjustments were made in AFRICA and Latin America as these states emerged from colonial rule. What especially appealed to communists in these settings was Lenin's theory of a vanguard party. Because Lenin held that revolution required political consciousness as well as exploitation, a revolutionary elite was necessary to organize and instill this consciousness and lead the revolution. In Europe communism also evolved. In West Europe communist parties were often discredited for employing Soviet communist rhetoric. In its place a less antagonistic version of communism, Eurocommunism, evolved that looked to electoral victory as the road to power. In East Europe communism took on a more nationalist face, although there were limits to the degree that the Soviet Union would tolerate deviation from Moscow's ideological line as shown by the interventions led or supported by the Soviet Union into HUNGARY, POLAND, EAST GERMANY, and CZECHOSLOVAKIA.

See also RUSSIA.

**Further reading:** Berdyaev, Nicholas. *The Origin of Russian Communism.* London: Geoffrey Bless, 1955; Tucker, Robert. *The Soviet Political Mind.* New York: Praeger, 1963.

## Comprehensive Test Ban Treaty

The Comprehensive Test Ban Treaty (CTBT) was signed on September 24, 1996. It was hailed by President BILL CLINTON as the "longest sought, hardest fought prize in ARMS CONTROL history." The U.S. Senate did not, however, give its consent to the treaty.

Between 1945 and 1962 the United States and the Soviet Union conducted 355 atmospheric nuclear tests. Following the CUBAN MISSILE CRISIS the two states begin arms control talks designed to produce a comprehensive test ban treaty. Their efforts fell short, and in 1963 only a limited test ban treaty was signed that banned testing in the atmosphere, outer space, and underwater. Underground testing continues to be permitted. The Senate gave its consent to this treaty. This situation continued essentially unchanged until 1991 when the Soviet Union, the United States, FRANCE, and GREAT BRITAIN agreed to self-imposed moratoriums on nuclear testing. CHINA, the only other acknowledged nuclear power, refused to join in the moratorium.

In 1993 the Conference on Disarmament received a mandate from the nuclear powers to begin negotiations on a comprehensive test ban treaty. Negotiations began in 1994. These talks soon bogged down as each of the nuclear powers pursued its own agenda. France and Great Britain wanted safety tests permitted under any new treaty. China wanted the right to conduct peaceful nuclear explosions. The United States, RUSSIA, France, and Great Britain all wanted to be allowed to conduct small nuclear tests.

In January 1995 the United States made the decision to pursue a permanent test ban rather than one that would be limited to 10 years as had been considered. In June France announced it would resume nuclear testing prior to signing any CTBT. In August the United States, along with France and Great Britain, agreed to a zero-yield CTBT. France announced the end of its testing program in January 1996. That same month, INDIA announced that it would support a test ban treaty only in the context of a time-bound agreement rather than one of unlimited duration. India and IRAN continued to block final agreement on a treaty until September when an agreement was reached. On September 10, the UNITED NATIONS approved the treaty, and on September 24 the treaty was opened for signatures, with President Clinton being the first to sign. A total of 2,046 nuclear tests had been conducted by that date.

On October 13, 1999, the Senate rejected the treaty by a vote of 51-48 with Senate Minority Leader Robert Byrd (D-W.Va.) voting "present." The vote fell largely along party lines with only four Republicans joining the 44 Democrats to support it. The treaty had been submitted to the Senate in September 1997 where it sat hostage. Senator JESSE HELMS (R-N.C.), chairman of the Senate Foreign Relations Committee that had jurisdiction over the treaty, opposed it. He wanted two other treaties submitted for ratification first. They were a 1996 treaty with RUSSIA that would permit the deployment of a limited antiballistic missile defense system under the existing ANTIBALLISTIC MISSILE TREATY and the 1997 KYOTO PROTOCOL on global climate control. Helms opposed both treaties; consequently, the Clinton administration was unwilling to help bring them to a vote. There matters stood until 1999. Fearful that the Democrats would make the Republican-controlled Senate's refusal to act on the CTBT a campaign issue, Senate Majority Leader Trent Lott (R-Miss.) arranged for the CTBT to be voted out of Helms's committee so that it might be voted on and defeated by the full Senate. It soon became apparent to the Clinton administration and treaty supporters that they lacked the necessary votes to gain the Senate's consent. Clinton unsuccessfully sent a letter to the Senate urging a postponement of the vote.

**Further reading:** Carter, Ralph, ed. *Contemporary Cases in U.S. Foreign Policy.* Washington, D.C.: Congressional Quarterly Press, 2002.

## conference diplomacy

Conference diplomacy is a form of multilateral DIPLOMACY that is a staple of modern diplomacy. Multilateral diplomacy is contrasted with bilateral diplomacy. In the latter only two countries participate. In the former many states may be present. Three factors have given rise to conference diplomacy and help distinguish it from classical forms of multilateral diplomacy. First, conference diplomacy rests on the principles of universal participation and equality. All countries may participate, and formal equality exists among all parties. In the period of classical diplomacy attendance at multilateral conferences would be restricted to the great powers, and within that group a hierarchy of power would be recognized. Second, the hallmark of conference diplomacy is its focus on addressing shared global concerns rather than advancing narrowly defined national interests, as was the case with multilateral diplomacy in the classical period. This does not mean, however, that countries do not try to advance their own interests in conducting conference diplomacy. Third, conference diplomacy within an issue area, such as the ENVIRONMENT, TRADE, or HUMAN RIGHTS, has become an institutionalized ongoing process. Not only do negotiating sessions last for long periods of time, but regular follow-up sessions are built in or there is the expectation that future conferences will be held on the subject. This contrasts with earlier multilateral efforts that tended to be called to resolve specific issues.

Perhaps the longest-running case of conference diplomacy engaged in by the United States is the GENERAL AGREEMENT ON TARIFFS AND TRADE (GATT) talks. Occurring over several decades and conducted in negotiating "rounds," the GATT talks have been the principal vehicle for managing an open international trade system since WORLD WARD II. The URUGUAY ROUND GATT talks produced the WORLD TRADE ORGANIZATION that has taken over this management responsibility. Another important example of conference diplomacy is the Helsinki accords, which came out of the CONFERENCE ON SECURITY AND COOPERATION IN EUROPE, 1973–75. This 1975 agreement legitimized the borders that emerged in Europe at the end of World War II and laid out basic principles of human rights. Follow-up conferences mandated by the Helsinki accords became a key instrument by which the West pressured the Soviet Union and its East European allies for improvement in the treatment of its citizens. Global environmental issues have also been addressed at conferences. Numbered among them are the LAW OF THE SEA conferences, the ozone depletion conferences, the Rio Earth Summit, the Kyoto Summit, and world population summits.

What is significant about conference diplomacy is that despite the United States's overwhelming military, economic, and diplomatic resources, it has often struggled to achieve is objectives. Painful compromises have often been necessary; on occasion, outright rejection of an agreement has occurred. This happened in 2001 when the GEORGE W. BUSH administration made known its intention not to abide by the Kyoto Protocol. It has led to the search for new means to influence decisions and given

rise to the importance of "soft power" as a means of accomplishing goals. Soft power relies on the manipulation of values, information, and symbols rather than the employment of force.

Conference diplomacy has also been challenging to the United States at a conceptual level. The AMERICAN NATIONAL STYLE favors legalistic solutions to problems and ones that emphasize formula-based solutions. Yet, the American national style also contains a strong belief that the American solution to problems is the correct one, making compromise unnecessary. PRESIDENTS have often negotiated agreements based on the first set of principles while CONGRESS has often questioned the product of these negotiations using the second set of principles.

In May 2003 the Bush administration announced a surprising reversal in U.S. policy. Only days after rejecting a global pact that would curb tobacco use worldwide, it came out in support of the agreement without reservations. Earlier the United States had insisted on an opting-out clause. The treaty contains a ban on cigarette advertising (except where that would be unconstitutional as in the United States) as well as requires health warnings and urges high taxes on tobacco products. The treaty took three years to negotiate, and negotiations were conducted under the auspices of the World Health Organization.

## Conference on Security and Cooperation in Europe  (CSCE)

The Conference on Security and Cooperation in Europe (CSCE) that took place from 1973 to 1975 served as a surrogate for a WORLD WAR II peace treaty. Negotiations occurred in three stages. First, there was an opening meeting of foreign ministers. Second, there was a period of detailed negotiations. The CSCE culminated in the signing Final Act of the CSCE, also known as the Helsinki accords.

The very existence of the CSCE was a reflection of the changed relations between the United States and the Soviet Union (see RUSSIA) in the early 1970s. Gone was the COLD WAR competition between the two superpowers. In its place was DÉTENTE, or a relaxation of tensions. In Europe détente was joined by a new attitude on the part of West GERMANY. Under the leadership of Chancellor Willy Brandt, it adopted a policy of Ostpolitik that sought to bring about a reconciliation between East and West Germany and a normalization of West German relations with East Europe in general.

An agreement accepting the post–World War II boundaries of Europe and the legitimacy of the governments of East Europe were high-priority items for the Soviet Union. Soviet leader Leonid Brezhnev actively sought an agreement by 1976 when the 25th Party Congress was set to meet. Neither President RICHARD NIXON nor SECRETARY OF STATE HENRY KISSINGER attached the same practical or symbolic importance to the CSCE, and it was not until 1975 that the United States reciprocated the Soviet's seriousness about the negotiations. This change of heart roughly coincided with the fall of South VIETNAM and the more general fear that détente would collapse.

The negotiations leading up to the CSCE and those that took place there have been characterized as a "bazaar" in which states negotiated on a broad array of issues and entered into a complex set of trade-offs and subsidiary agreements. While 35 states participated in the conference the key deals were negotiated between the United States and the Soviet Union. As a price for calling the CSCE the United States obtained Soviet agreement on completing a four-power agreement on Berlin, the convening of the MUTUAL AND BALANCED FORCE REDUCTION TALKS, and the inclusion of HUMAN RIGHTS on the agenda. During the negotiations at the conference the American position hardened, falling into line with its West European allies who shared the Soviet Union's view that the CSCE agreement would be a defining feature of their future relations with the Soviet Union and wanted to craft a tightly worded agreement. The final agreement was arrived at by way of what was in effect a "take it or leave it" Western proposal to deal with all of the unresolved points in the area of humanitarian issues. The Soviet Union resisted but placed greater value on the completion of the CSCE negotiations.

The Helsinki accords are broken down into three baskets. Basket I dealt with security and confidence-building measures. It contained a reference to the inviability of international frontiers as well as respect for human rights and freedoms. Basket II dealt with measures to increase trade, economic, scientific, and environmental cooperation among European states. Basket III addressed humanitarian issues, including the free flow of information, cultural and educational exchanges, and improving the conditions for "human contacts." Apart from these three baskets the Helsinki accords also made reference to increased cooperation in the Mediterranean.

The American public and Congress were unprepared for the signing of the Helsinki Final Act. The Nixon and Ford administrations had consistently downplayed the importance of the negotiations, and CONGRESS had not been consulted to any significant degree. Moreover, the Helsinki accords were defined as neither a treaty nor an agreement and thus not subject to Senate ratification. Congress responded by establishing a CSCE Commission to oversee the extent of progress in promoting human rights in Eastern Europe and the Soviet Union. Ethnic groups with strong ties toward Eastern Europe and the Baltic region objected strongly to what they saw as a capitulation to the Soviet's claim of legitimacy in these regions.

In subsequent years, American evaluations of the Helsinki accords became more positive as they were seen as an important instrument for bringing about domestic reform in the Soviet Union and Eastern Europe. The principal vehicle for doing so was periodic follow-up conferences. The idea of such a conference was introduced by the West midway through the negotiations as a compromise attempt to deal with the question of implementation. As originally agreed upon there was to be a single follow-up conference in Belgrade two years after the Helsinki accords were signed. At Belgrade (1977–78) the West insisted that further review conferences be held, and after objecting the Soviet Union agreed. The second follow-up conference was held at Madrid (1980–83).

## Congo (Democratic Republic of the Congo)

Most recently known as Zaire, Congo (officially, Democratic Republic of the Congo) is about the size of the United States east of the Mississippi River, with an area of 905,000 square miles. It has a population of 52 million people. The Portuguese were the first Europeans to arrive in 1482. Belgium began to colonize the region in the late 1870s. In 1885 King Leopold II of Belgium made the region his personal colony as the Congo Free State. In 1908 it came under the control of the Belgian government and was renamed the Belgian Congo. By that time mining had become the key economic activity of the colony, and the most important mining region was Katanga Province. After WORLD WAR II proindependence pressures built in the Belgian Congo, but they were resisted by Belgium. Two of the leading proponents of independence were Joseph Kasavubu and Patrice Lumumba. In early 1960 Belgium relented and announced that it would grant the Belgian Congo its independence later that year. It had done little, however, to prepare the country for independence either politically or economically, and the Republic of the Congo, established on June 30, 1960, quickly succumbed to civil unrest.

Lumumba became the Congo's first prime minister and Kasavubu its first head of state. On July 11, in a move that was encouraged by Belgian economic interests, Moise Tshombe declared Katanga independent. Belgium sent in troops to protect its citizens and economic interests, a move that had the de facto effect of helping the secessionist forces of Tshombe. The UNITED NATIONS sent in PEACEKEEPING forces, but they were not allowed to interfere in domestic affairs. Lumumba responded to these developments by seeking help from the Soviet Union (see RUSSIA). He was dismissed as prime minister by Kasavubu on September 5, and a little more than one week later, on September 14, Lieutenant Colonel Joseph Mobutu led an army coup. On December 1, Lumumba was arrested by the army and reportedly died trying to escape in February 1961.

Lumumba's death was one of five that the CHURCH COMMITTEE investigated in the mid-1970s in its study of alleged CENTRAL INTELLIGENCE AGENCY (CIA) involvement in assassination plots. The committee concluded that in the cases of Lumumba and Fidel Castro the CIA was involved in plots to kill foreign leaders. CIA officials in the Congo had urged his "permanent disposal," and steps were underway to bring this about. Events, however, outpaced CIA planning, and Lumumba was captured by Mobutu's forces. There is no evidence that the CIA was involved in his death.

Fighting continued in the Congo until 1965 when Mobutu again seized power. In 1971 he renamed the country Zaire and adopted the name Mobutu Sese Seko. Mobutu was a firm ally of the United States during his long reign and actively supported the American position in the Angolan civil war. He also sent troops to Chad in 1983 as part of a U.S.-supported military show of force intended to prevent a Libyan take over attempt. The corruption and inefficiency of his government along with exorbitant personal spending practices bankrupted the Congolese economy and involved the United States and other Western powers in repeated financial rescue efforts. The domestic situation in the Congo deteriorated to the point that the United States withdrew its ambassador from March 1993 to November 1995. Earlier, in 1991, Congolese soldiers protesting unpaid wages began rioting, and 2,000 French and Belgian troops with the aid of U.S. air transports were sent in to evacuate 20,000 foreign nationals from the Congo.

With Mobutu out of the country under treatment for cancer, Laurent Kabila was sworn in as president on May 29, 1997, and he changed the country's name from Zaire to the Democratic Republic of the Congo. Kabila was the leader of a rebel force that received support from Zambia, ANGOLA, RWANDA, and Uganda. Just over a year later, in July 1998, Kabila ordered all foreign troops out of the

Africans demonstrate in Dar es Salaam, Tanzania, against American aid to the Tshombe regime in the Congo. *(Hulton/Archive)*

Congo. His order was largely ignored, setting the stage for further external involvement in the Congo's affairs. Rwandan and Ugandan troops sought to overthrow Kabila's government, but they were stopped from doing so by Angolan, Zimbabwean, and Namibian troops. Rwanda, however, remained in control of much of eastern Congo. This chaotic state of affairs reflects both the absence of effective governing institutions in the Congo and the spilling over of the genocidal civil war in Rwanda into the Congo.

In July 1999 a peace accord was agreed to by the six warring governments at Lusaka, Zambia. Later the two principal Congolese rebel groups also gave their consent. Part of the plan called for sending in a United Nations peacekeeping force, but they never arrived due to the continued violence and insecurity that existed within the country. Kabila was held to be principally responsible for the accord's failure. He was assassinated on January 16, 2001, and his son, Joseph, took power. While some foreign troops have been withdrawn, little progress has been made in establishing a legitimate political order. Indirect American foreign aid resumed that year. The UNITED STATES AGENCY FOR INTERNATIONAL DEVELOPMENT provided local and international nongovernmental agencies with $100 million for relief and development programs.

**Further reading:** Kelly, Sean. *America's Tyrant: The CIA and Mobutu of Zaire.* Washington, D.C.: American University Press, 1993.

## Congress, U.S.

From a presidential perspective Congress is a hostile obstacle course through which foreign-policy proposals must be maneuvered. It is one that cannot be avoided because the CONSTITUTION gives Congress a voice in ratifying treaties, approving appointments, spending money, and regulating commerce. In the words of Edwin Corwin the Constitution is an "invitation to struggle." It is not surprising then that throughout the course of the history of American foreign policy major initiatives have been cast as a struggle of wills between the PRESIDENT and key congressional figures: WOODROW WILSON versus HENRY CABOT LODGE, LYNDON JOHNSON versus J. WILLIAM FULBRIGHT, HARRY TRUMAN versus Joseph McCarthy. The invitation to struggle is one that Congress frequently took up prior to the COLD WAR. At least four policy areas that often placed it in conflict with the president can be identified. The first involved expansionism. The acquisition and incorporation of TEXAS and the OREGON TERRITORY found Congress at odds with Presidents JOHN TYLER and JAMES POLK. U.S. GRANT encountered congressional opposition in his efforts to obtain HAITI. A second area of conflict involved IMMIGRATION into the United States. Congress adopted exclusionary legisla-

tion that severely limited immigration from Asia. The third involved the use of force. Most notable here were the NEUTRALITY ACTS, passed by Congress in the interwar years, that handcuffed President FRANKLIN ROOSEVELT in his efforts to aid GREAT BRITAIN against Nazi GERMANY. Finally, the president and Congress frequently clashed on economic matters over tariff rates and approving reciprocal trade agreements. The high tariffs of the 1920s are a good example of Congress exercising its prerogatives in the former area, and its refusal to approve reciprocal trade agreements with SPAIN, BRAZIL, Germany, and Austria-Hungary in the 1890s are examples of the later.

Today, Congress's influence in foreign policy is due to more than just the presence of strong individuals. We can begin to understand the congressional voice in foreign-policy making by examining the means by which it speaks. Congress expresses its voice in one of four basic ways. The first is by passing a resolution. This is a statement made by one or both houses and signed by the president. The second is a legislative bill that becomes a law when it is signed by the president or passed over the president's veto. The number of pieces of legislation that bear on foreign policy has increased dramatically with the expansion of the foreign-policy agenda to include a significant nonmilitary dimension. For example, the 1960 edition of *Legislation on Foreign Relations* was 519 pages long. In 1985 it ran 2,698 pages.

In the battle for control over foreign policy, presidential initiatives generally are phrased as bills, and congressional initiatives are expressed as resolutions. Congress seeks to influence presidential foreign-policy legislation in several ways. One is by attaching "barnacles" or amendments to them. These amendments may direct foreign-aid funding for specific countries or purposes, such as aid for ISRAEL or security assistance. Another type of amendment that has become popular is to require that the STATE DEPARTMENT issue an annual evaluation on a country's policy in areas such as HUMAN RIGHTS, religious freedom, the ENVIRONMENT, DRUG TRAFFICKING, or nonproliferation in order to remain eligible for FOREIGN AID. Typically an escape hatch exists, allowing presidents to certify a country for aid if it is in the "national interest" to do so. A second way has been to employ a legislative veto. In this case the legislation is written in broad strokes that gives the executive branch the authority to implement the legislation as it sees fit unless Congress objects. Legislative vetoes have been used in arms sales legislation and the WAR POWERS RESOLUTION. In the *IMMIGRATION AND NATURALIZATION SERVICE V. CHADHA* case, the SUPREME COURT ruled the legislative veto to be unconstitutional.

A third mechanism that Congress employs to exercise its voice in foreign policy matters is oversight of the implementation of foreign policy by the executive branch. Here the battle engaged is over access to information and public support for American foreign policy. During the VIETNAM WAR, J. William Fulbright chaired the Senate Foreign Relations Committee and used it to hold hearings into the conduct of the war. During the Reagan administration the Senate Intelligence Committee was angered by the failure of the CENTRAL INTELLIGENCE AGENCY (CIA) to inform the committee it had mined harbors in NICARAGUA. President GEORGE W. BUSH and Congress clashed over the creation of an independent body to investigate the performance of the INTELLIGENCE COMMUNITY prior to the SEPTEMBER 11, 2001, terrorist attacks. Bush opposed the creation of the panel, but he then agreed. Congressional figures charged that his administration then blocked its creation by behind-the-scenes stalling. In seeking to exercise its oversight powers Congress makes heavy use of the legislative amendments that require the State Department to report on sensitive issues. The 1986 Anti-Apartheid Act required information on 10 key issues concerning SOUTH AFRICA.

The final way in which Congress regularly interacts with the president in making foreign policy is through its budgetary powers. As with the other means of influencing foreign policy, congressional budgetary powers are blunt in nature and are not fine-tuned to the particulars of a problem. Cutting of funding is difficult. Efforts to end funding for the Vietnam War routinely failed. Only after the peace agreement had been reached was funding cut off. Ending funding for the contras in Nicaragua was highly controversial and led the Reagan administration to pursue the IRAN-CONTRA initiative as a way of circumventing this ban. Control over how funds are spent has been equally problematic. In 1971, Congress allocated funds for a manned bomber. President RICHARD NIXON opposed the project and did not spend the money. Prior to the PERSIAN GULF WAR Congress allocated funds for sea lift vessels. The money was diverted by SECRETARY OF DEFENSE Dick Cheney to other projects, and the ships were not available when needed. Finally, budgetary controls do little to offset the president's unilateral ability to commit the United States to a course of action by announcing policy decisions such as the EISENHOWER DOCTRINE or a war on TERRORISM.

Further insight into the manner in which Congress influences American foreign policy comes through an examination of its processes and structures and the attitudes of its members. Individuals have been able to play a dominant role in shaping foreign policy because traditionally the work of Congress is done in committees and subcommittees. Added to this are the long-established operating principles of seniority and deference. In the past this allowed key members of the Senate Foreign Relations Committee and the House Foreign Affairs Committee to dominate foreign-policy deliberations for long periods of time. The great expansion in the scope of foreign policy has altered this picture by giving more senators and congresspeople the opportunity to take center stage and influence policy. In the process it has also made it more difficult for Congress to speak with a single voice on foreign-policy matters. For example, in 1976 the DEFENSE DEPARTMENT spent 77,556 witness hours before Congress, and some dozen Senate committees are involved in economic foreign-policy making and oversight.

Contemporary legislators who hold powerful influence over the conduct of American foreign policy are often referred to as either gadflies or policy entrepreneurs, depending on their motives. Gadflies are seen as motivated by a desire to influence long-term policy trends. Policy entrepreneurs are seen as motivated by short-term electoral considerations. Prominent recent gadflies include Senator JESSE HELMS and Senator George McGovern. Congressman and later senator Richard Torrecelli is seen by many as a policy entrepreneur for his allegiance to the CUBAN-AMERICAN NATIONAL FOUNDATION and its anti-Castro policies. Senator Henry "Scoop" Jackson (R.-Wash.) exhibited characteristics of each. He was firmly anti-Soviet and opposed DÉTENTE on these grounds, but he was also known as the "Senator from Boeing" for his support of military spending programs that benefited Boeing Aircraft in his home state of Washington.

The burgeoning foreign-policy agenda has also caused senators and congresspeople to rely more and more heavily on their individual staff, committee staff, and THINK TANKS for information. This dependence has created concern for whether staffers are serving Congress or pursuing their own agendas. In some instances it has led to situations in which staffers become as powerful as those they serve. This occurred in the 1970s when Richard Pearle was a staff aid to Senator Jackson who opposed détente with the Soviet Union and successfully linked Soviet immigration policy to MOST FAVORED NATION STATUS through the JACKSON-VANIK AMENDMENT over the objection of President Richard Nixon.

Staff aids and think tanks not only provide congresspeople with information, but they also offer guidance on how to vote. In doing so they compete with two other well-established sources of influence. One is party. Loyalty to the DEMOCRATIC PARTY or the REPUBLICAN PARTY is important both to a congressperson's reelection chances and to his or her ability to assume positions of importance within Congress. Party loyalty does not translate into uniformity in outlook or prevent significant intraparty conflicts from developing. Within the Republican Party today an important divide exists between traditional foreign-policy hawks and deficit hawks. Within the Democratic Party one finds a divide between the protectionist wing of the party and free-trade liberals. Geography also offers guidance on how to vote. Regardless of party affiliation, legislators from regions threatened with the loss of jobs and income by globalization and free trade are likely to support protectionist measures while those from regions that will benefit will promote free-trade policies.

Finally, in judging the role and impact that Congress has on American foreign policy, it is important to recognize that we are dealing with a dynamic situation rather than a static one. Change occurs both within issue areas and over time. For example, congressional involvement in ARMS CONTROL policy has changed with the end of the cold war. No longer is arms control concerned with questions of American weakness or strength vis-à-vis the Soviet NUCLEAR WEAPONS ARSENAL. Now, the issue stresses the need to address weaknesses in the Russian command and control system and the possibility that Russian scientists might be aiding terrorist groups. It has also expanded to include WEAPONS OF MASS DESTRUCTION that exist on a global scale.

We can see change in the congressional-executive relationship even within a relatively short time span, such as the early years of the COLD WAR through the Vietnam War. The first years of the cold war were ones of accommodation between the two branches. Bipartisanship was the key phrase as presidents and Congress sought to present a united front to the world in foreign-policy matters. This was followed by a period of antagonism as the two branches argued over who lost CHINA and who was responsible for the stalemate in the KOREAN WAR. It was the period of MCCARTHYISM and the BRICKER AMENDMENT. The decade from the mid-1950s to the mid-1960s saw the relationship change again. With containment agreed upon as the centerpiece of American foreign policy, Congress became acquiescent. Foreign-policy debates dealt with implementing containment, and this was a matter for the executive branch. This was an era of supportive resolutions, such as the Gulf of Tonkin Resolution, that backed an expansion of the war in Vietnam. During the Vietnam War congressional-executive relations were ambiguous. Congress as a whole was reluctant to challenge the president, but individuals such as J. William Fulbright, Wayne Morse, and Mark Hatfield did.

Since Vietnam, Congress has sought to redefine its relationship with the president in two ways. First, it has sought to place limits on presidential power. The WAR POWERS RESOLUTION, the Jackson-Vanik Amendment, the insistence on amendments to the PANAMA CANAL TREATIES, and the insistence on amendments to the NORTH AMERICA FREE TRADE AGREEMENT are prominent examples. Second, it has sought to take the initiative by promoting its own foreign-policy agenda. This was evident in its antiapartheid stance, its support for the prodemocracy and religious freedom groups in China, its interest in denuclearization in Russia, and its support for the nuclear freeze movement during the Reagan administration.

Congress was relatively acquiescent in its dealings with President Bush leading up to the IRAQ WAR. As late as August 2003 signs from the Bush administration suggested that it did not feel that the formal support of Congress was necessary in order to conduct a war against IRAQ. Bush's public statements only went so far as to indicate the he would consult with legislators, something that falls short of obtaining their approval. Such support was not guaranteed. The concerns expressed by the public over Bush's failure to justify the war and his inclination to act unilaterally also existed in Congress. In early September, Senator Larry Craig, chair of the Senate Republican Policy Committee and a strong Bush supporter, indicated that he was not prepared to vote for war at the time. Classified briefings by DIRECTOR OF CENTRAL INTELLIGENCE George Tenet and SECRETARY OF STATE Colin Powell failed to convince key Democratic leaders. Under pressure from both parties to obtain Congressional approval for military action, President Bush asked for such authorization on September 19. The White House–drafted resolution authorized the president to "use all means that he determines, including force," in order to enforce the United Nations Security Council resolutions, defend the national interest of the United States against the threats posed by Iraq, and restore international peace and security in the region.

Congress was supportive of the proposal, but voices of opposition were heard. Many felt it was far too open-ended an endorsement of presidential war-making powers, similar to those approved by the Gulf of Tonkin Resolution in 1964, which authorized the use of military force in Vietnam. On the Democratic side, Senator Edward Kennedy (Mass.) and Senator John Edwards (N.C.) came out in opposition of the resolution. Republican Senators Chuck Hagel (Nebr.) and Richard Lugar (Ind.) called for a multilateral approach to the war. President Bush rejected efforts to try and force him to work through the United Nations. In early October the Bush administration reached a compromise with Congress. The revised resolution was passed on October 10 by a vote of 77-23 in the Senate and 296-139 in the House. The resolution supported efforts by the president to obtain action by the Security Council but then authorized the use of force. Borrowing language from the War Powers Resolution it requires the president to notify Congress no later than 48 hours after exercising this authority and requires that he report at least once every 60 days to the Congress.

See also RUSSIA; SECTIONALISM.

**Further reading:** Robinson, James A. *Congress and Foreign Policy: A Study in Legislative Influence.* Homewood, Ill.: Dorsey, 1962; Spanier, John, and Joseph Nogee, eds. *Congress, the Presidency, and Foreign Policy.* New York: Pergamon, 1981; Weisman, Stephen R. *A Culture of Def-*

*erence: Congress's Failure of Leadership in Foreign Policy.*
New York: Basic Books, 1995.

## Constitution, U.S.

Long ago the constitutional scholar Edward Corwin described the constitutional division of power between the PRESIDENT and CONGRESS as an "invitation to struggle over the privilege of directing U.S. foreign policy." This struggle continues today as these two institutions vie for leadership in four areas: treaty-making power, appointment power, war power, and commerce power.

The Constitution states that the president, by and with the advice and consent of the Senate, has the power to make treaties. The president's role in the treaty-making process has not been the source of serious controversy. He or she nominates the negotiators, issues instructions to them, and submits the treaty to the Senate for its advice and consent. If consent is given she or he then makes a decision on whether to ratify the treaty. Most of the controversy surrounding the treaty-making power has focused on the nature of senatorial advice and consent. According to the Constitution a two-thirds yes vote is needed in order to give consent. Virtually from the outset senatorial advice and consent have been given at the same time. The Constitution does not require that it be done this way, and presidents have developed a number of informal ways of obtaining senatorial advice. Following the Senate's rejection of the TREATY OF VERSAILLES that established the LEAGUE OF NATIONS, presidents have routinely included key members of the Senate on negotiating teams as a means of obtaining input. While statistically the Senate has rejected few treaties outright, presidents have learned that its approval is far from automatic. In 1999 the Senate rejected the COMPREHENSIVE TEST BAN TREATY. It has made changes in 69 percent of the treaties that came before it between 1789 and 1963. On several occasions its known opposition caused presidents to not even submit a treaty or to withdraw it from consideration. The Havana Charter that would have established the INTERNATIONAL TRADE ORGANIZATION is an example of the former, and the STRATEGIC ARMS LIMITATIONS TREATY (SALT II) is an example of the latter.

The Senate's power of advice and consent has been somewhat negated over time by two developments that have strengthened presidential power. The first is the president's increased reliance on EXECUTIVE AGREEMENTS over treaties as a means of entering into agreements with other states. Unlike treaties, executive agreements do not require the consent of the Senate before becoming law. Second, since 1974 Congress began granting FAST-TRACK authority to presidents in international trade negotiations. In doing so Congress agreed to expeditiously vote on trade agreements and not attach any amendments to them. Both

these developments have not gone unchallenged. In the 1950s the Senate almost passed the BRICKER AMENDMENT, a constitutional amendment that would have given the Senate a voice in approving executive agreements. Post–COLD WAR presidents have struggled to obtain fast-track authority, which was once granted almost automatically, and its use was denied to President BILL CLINTON. A second area of contestation is over the appointment of ambassadors and other government officials. This power is not limited to foreign affairs–related appointments, but they have been among the most heavily contested. In theory, by exercising a voice in treaty negotiations, the Senate is able to influence its content. In practice this linkage has never been fully put into place. The Senate has failed to systematically exercise its confirmation power. Those without diplomatic credentials but with political connections are routinely approved for ambassadorships. When the Senate has raised its voice in opposition, the intent has been to make a policy statement rather than comment on the qualifications of the nominee. This was the case when JIMMY CARTER nominated Theodore Sorensen to head the Central Intelligence Agency and RONALD REAGAN nominated Ernest Lefever to be assistant SECRETARY OF STATE for HUMAN RIGHTS. Presidents have also turned the confirmation power into something less than intended by making heavy use of personal representative as negotiators. FRANKLIN ROOSEVELT, for example, relied heavily on Harry Hopkins in making international agreements and not Secretary of State CORDELL HULL.

The war powers of the constitution are split into three parts. Congress has the power to declare war. It also has the power to raise and maintain armed forces. The president is designated as commander in chief. As with the other distribution of powers what in theory fits together nicely runs into problems in practice. A first problem is with the question of when a state of war comes into existence. The United States has only declared war five times: the WAR OF 1812, the SPANISH-AMERICAN WAR, the MEXICAN WAR, WORLD WAR I, and WORLD WAR II. According to the SUPREME COURT in the PRIZE CASES (1862) a state of war is determined by prevailing conditions and not legal declarations. America's global responsibilities and the need to maintain forces limit Congress's power to control a president's use of force by denying him or her an army or navy. The congressional-presidential struggle over war making powers came to a head during the VIETNAM era and led to the passage of the WAR POWERS RESOLUTION over President RICHARD NIXON's veto. It requires that presidents notify congress within 48 hours after introduction of military forces if there is no declaration of war and that the president remove them within 60 days if Congress does not either declare war or adopt a joint resolution approving the action. No president has recognized its constitutionality, though none has openly challenged it. The Supreme Court in its *IMMIGRATION AND NATURALIZATION SERVICE V. CHADHA* decision raised doubts about its constitutionality by rejecting the legitimacy of the legislative veto around which the War Powers Resolution is built.

The fourth area of joint power is commerce power. The Constitution gives Congress the power to regulate commerce with foreign countries. Power sharing is necessary here because only the president can negotiate treaties. Conflict in this area has highlighted the differing political perspectives that the two branches bring to bear on international trade and financial relations. Where presidents have sought to use trade as an inducement to change or reinforce desired behavior in other states, legislators have seen trade as a means of protecting the economic interests of their constituents or advancing other constituent interests. This was the case during the period of DÉTENTE when the Nixon and Ford administrations sought to use MOST-FAVORED-NATION (MFN) status as a means of getting the Soviet Union to cooperate on ARMS CONTROL and Third World issues. Led by Senators Henry "Scoop" Jackson and Richard Vanik, Congress used MFN status to pressure the Soviet Union to change its treatment of Soviet Jews by passing the JACKSON-VANIK AMENDMENT.

The foreign-policy struggle between the two branches continues in part because there are gaps in the Constitution's coverage of key questions. Nowhere is there mention of who has the power to terminate a treaty. This is the key constitutional question in deciding the fate of the ANTIBALLISTIC MISSILE TREATY. It also continues because Supreme Court decisions have the potential to redefine powers. Thus, the Constitution is best seen as a starting point for the debate over what branch controls American foreign policy rather than as a definitive statement of powers granted in perpetuity.

**Further reading:** Crabb, Cecil, and Pat Holt. *Invitation to Struggle: Congress, the President and Foreign Policy.* 2d ed. Washington, D.C.: Congressional Quarterly Press, 1984; Henkin, Louis. *Foreign Affairs and the Constitution.* Mineola, N.Y.: Foundation Press, 1972; Smith, Jean E. *The Constitution and American Foreign Policy.* St. Paul, Minn.: West Publishing, 1989.

## containment

Containment was the overarching strategic framework for U.S. foreign policy during the COLD WAR. In theory it was a multifaceted program that entailed the use of economic, diplomatic, and military instruments of American foreign policy to hold Soviet expansionism in check, but in reality military instruments dominated. It is important to recognize that no single line of action was in place over this 40-year period.

Instead, we can identify two broadly constructed strategic postures. They were symmetrical containment and asymmetrical containment. Under symmetrical containment the United States sought to contain the Soviet Union (see RUSSIA) and COMMUNISM by applying an equal and proportionate amount of counterforce at the location where the attempted expansion took place. Under asymmetrical containment the United States sought to accomplish the same objective by responding to Soviet aggression on its own terms. It would choose the place of retaliation or counterpressure. Significantly, these two strategies of containment did not occur randomly but alternated throughout the cold war.

The first cold war containment strategy was embodied in the X article authored by GEORGE KENNAN. It was an asymmetrical containment strategy. This article, "The Sources of Soviet Conduct," appeared in *Foreign Affairs.* It drew upon a cable he sent to Washington from the U.S. embassy in Moscow in which he outlined a theory of Soviet foreign-policy behavior and the proper U.S. response. Kennan called for a policy of strong point defense in which the United States would not respond to Soviet aggression everywhere in the world but would apply counterpressure at carefully selected locations. The second containment strategy was contained in NATIONAL SECURITY COUNCIL (NSC) document-68. NSC-68 was produced before the KOREAN WAR but was not endorsed because of its budgetary implications. After fighting began it became the strategic blueprint for containing Soviet expansion. NSC-68 called for a policy of perimeter defense in which Soviet aggression would be resisted at all breakout points. It was a policy of symmetrical containment.

The third containment policy was the New Look. Adopted by the Eisenhower administration it was a policy of asymmetrical containment. Under the New Look the United States would respond to Soviet aggression at places and means of its own choosing. The key military capability wielded under the New Look was nuclear retaliation, with the Soviet Union being the target of choice. The Kennedy administration replaced the New Look with a strategy of flexible response. This was a symmetrical containment strategy. It called for meeting Soviet aggression wherever it occurred and with an equivalent amount of force. Under flexible response the United States developed a GUERRILLA WAR–fighting capability to complement the U.S. conventional capability and developed a series of graduated nuclear options that would permit the use of nuclear weapons at different levels of intensity.

The fifth containment strategy was DÉTENTE. It was an asymmetrical containment strategy that employed a policy of economic-military linkages to hold Soviet aggressiveness in check. This strategy was adopted out of a realization that after VIETNAM the American public would not support a large military establishment or the placing of troops in combat. It was hoped that U.S. economic strength could compensate for this weakness and be used as a carrot and stick to reward or punish the Soviet Union for its overall conduct of foreign policy. Détente was the policy of the Nixon, Ford, and Carter administrations. It ended with the Soviet invasion of AFGHANISTAN in 1979. The sixth and final containment strategy was embodied in the REAGAN DOCTRINE. According to it the goal of American foreign policy was not only to contain the spread of communism but also to actively work to remove communism from power in countries where it ruled. Thus, the Reagan Doctrine was a symmetrical containment policy.

Commentators make three points in evaluating the alteration between symmetrical and asymmetrical containment strategies. First, the switch from one to the other had little to do with changes in Soviet foreign policy. Because of this, little learning is evident in U.S. cold war foreign policy. Second, domestic factors appear to be most responsible for the alternating pattern. Often the change occurred because a new administration came into office and wanted to distance itself from its predecessor. More important were economic considerations. Symmetrical containment is expensive and difficult to sustain financially. The New Look, for example, sought to substitute technology for soldiers, and détente sought to substitute economic power for military power. Third, with each passing alteration inconsistencies in applying these containment strategies became more pronounced. Reagan, for example, while trying to stop European states from helping finance a Russian OIL pipeline that would bring oil to Europe, dropped a grain embargo against POLAND. He spent his first term referring to the Soviet Union as the "evil empire" and building up U.S. military power only to turn around in the second term and enter into discussions at the Reykjavík SUMMIT CONFERENCE with Soviet leader Mikhail Gorbachev that would have done away with the intercontinental BALLISTIC MISSILES that formed the backbone of the U.S. nuclear deterrent force.

**Further reading:** Gaddis, John L. *Strategies of Containment: A Critical Appraisal of Postwar National Security Policy.* New York: Oxford University Press, 1993; Kennan, George. *American Diplomacy, 1900–1950.* New York: New American Library, 1951; Lukacs, John. *A New History of the Cold War.* Garden City, N.Y.: Anchor, 1966.

## Coolidge, Calvin (1872–1933) *president*

Calvin Coolidge was the 30th president of the United States, succeeding to the presidency on the death of WARREN HARDING. Coolidge is best known for his 1925 remark that "the business of America is business" and his detached operating style that included long afternoon naps. Although

he makes no mention of foreign policy in his autobiography, Coolidge's term as president (1923–29) did find the United States actively involved in world affairs.

One area of great activity was Latin America. WOODROW WILSON's policy of being the "policeman of the Caribbean" had come under attack in the 1920 presidential campaign, and the Harding administration took steps to put U.S.–Latin American relations on a more conciliatory path. A particularly troublesome case was NICARAGUA. In 1925 U.S. Marines ended a 13-year presence there but returned in 1926 as instability and the threat of rebellion returned. The Coolidge administration sided with the right-wing government, and when the rebels seemed on the verge of victory it dispatched several thousand marines to Nicaragua. The intervention occurred without congressional approval, and critics, principally Democrats, liberals, and anti-imperialists, called this Coolidge's "private war." Coolidge defended his actions as designed to protect American lives and property and prevent foreign infiltration of the region. In 1927 Coolidge sent HENRY STIMSON as his special envoy to Nicaragua in an attempt to end the crisis. Stimson succeeded in getting both sides to agree to an American-supervised election. This election satisfied both left-wing and right-wing elements in Nicaragua.

Coolidge's concern for protecting American property reappeared elsewhere in his foreign policy. In 1927 he insisted upon compensation from CHINA for American property destroyed in rioting in Nanjing. He also sent a special envoy to Mexico to defuse a tense political standoff over the rights of American OIL companies. Coolidge was also unsympathetic to European calls for reducing the debt they owed to the United States, commenting at one point, "they hired the money, didn't they?" Believing that German economic recovery was central to the stability of post–WORLD WAR I Europe, Coolidge did support efforts to reduce its war debts. The most notable initiative was the Dawes Plan that provided Germany with an infusion of private investment funds in return for a rescheduled debt repayment program.

## Coordinating Committee for Multilateral Export Controls

The Coordinating Committee for Multilateral Export Controls (COCOM) was a 1949 agreement between all members of the NORTH ATLANTIC TREATY ORGANIZATION (NATO), except for Iceland, and JAPAN on a program for denying technology and equipment to the Soviet Union (see RUSSIA) and its allies that held military potential. Coordination was not easily or fully achieved because the United States tended to have a broader definition of strategic goods than did the Europeans or Japanese. COCOM is significant because its history highlights the difficulty of achieving joint action and the unilateralist tendencies of American foreign policy.

For the United States, COCOM was paralleled by a unilateral effort to achieve the same goal of strategic denial. Trade with communist states was controlled by the Export Control Act of 1949 and the Battle Act of 1950. At the outset virtually every item that might be considered to have some military value was placed on the COMMERCE DEPARTMENT's Commodity Control List. Beyond seeking to deny the Soviet Union sensitive technology and products, the Battle Act also sought to push U.S. allies into a greater degree of cooperation. It denied defense assistance to any state that reexported American goods on the restricted list. During the KOREAN WAR this list ran to more than 1,000 items.

Particularly revealing of COCOM's problems was a 1976 incident in which the United States denied a U.S. firm an export license to sell its product to the Soviet Union because the item was on the restricted list. The company appealed the decision, pointing out that a French firm was already selling similar equipment to the Soviet Union. The United States went to COCOM to get the item exempted from the embargo only to have FRANCE deny that French firms were selling such equipment. Later Paris admitted it but stated that the goods were nonstrategic. In the end, the United States denied the export license to the American firm.

Long dormant, new life was breathed into COCOM by RONALD REAGAN. The first high-level meeting since the 1950s was held in 1982. Disunity continued to be a problem. Of particular concern to the Reagan administration was Europe's willingness to provide technology to the Soviet Union for building an OIL pipeline that would link Siberian fields to consumers in West Europe. The Europeans rejected the argument that such a pipeline would make them dependent on the Soviet Union and vulnerable to political pressure. They saw it as an economic opportunity to reduce their energy dependence on the Middle East and stimulate their economies. As earlier, the United States responded to European reluctance to join with it by imposing unilateral sanctions. This time the target was American firms. They would be prohibited from participating in the pipeline and punished if U.S. technology was used by European firms in the project.

With the end of the COLD WAR, COCOM lost its rationale, and efforts began to pare down the number of restricted items. The pattern of U.S.-European and U.S.-Japanese conflict continued, with America's allies pushing for a more rapid action than the United States was willing to take. In 1995 COCOM was allowed to lapse. It was replaced by a new looser arrangement, the New Forum. The focus of their joint efforts was now directed at limiting the sale of weapons and dual-use technologies to RUSSIA.

## counterintelligence

The purpose of counterintelligence (CI) is to detect and cope with threats. It is a hybrid concept incorporating a number of different dimensions. At least five members of the INTELLIGENCE COMMUNITY have responsibility for CI: the CENTRAL INTELLIGENCE AGENCY (CIA), the FEDERAL BUREAU OF INVESTIGATION (FBI), and the intelligence agencies of the army, navy, and air force. Because different agencies and different policy makers will vary in the importance they attach to each, it is difficult to incorporate CI into national security policy.

One common view is to treat CI as a law enforcement problem. The analogy is made to police work, especially as it relates to investigating crimes. The analogy is incomplete, however. One great difference between police work and CI is that police officers are investigating a crime. In CI there is no certainty that an act of espionage has taken place. Not only is the starting point to their investigations different but so too is the ultimate purpose of their efforts. The purpose of police work is to obtain a conviction. This is not the purpose of CI. Bringing the situation to light or terminating the activity may not be desirable. CI does seek to prevent the loss of secret material, but having accomplished this CI may also attempt to exploit the situation in order to accomplish other national security goals.

A second dimension to CI is as an adjunct to INTELLIGENCE analysis. CI is capable of obtaining information that is central to determining the severity of threats to national security. At a minimum, knowledge of where an adversary is attempting to penetrate one's government is highly revealing of its intentions. CI operations may also provide valuable information about the capabilities of an enemy or its plans. Viewed in this light the product of CI requires the same type of critical evaluation and analysis that other information is subjected to. Critics of CI maintain that this was not always the case for two reasons. First, there exists a strong tendency within the intelligence community to ascribe greater truth and importance to secretly obtained information than to that obtained through public sources. Second, there is a tendency to treat one's intelligence colleagues as above suspicion, making the intelligence community vulnerable to penetration by foreign intelligence agencies.

A third and fourth dimensions to CI are its uses as a security program and as counterespionage. CI as a security program is largely passive in nature and is concerned with limiting the potential success of future penetration programs. Measures taken include security education initiatives, technological surveillance countermeasures, and threat or vulnerability assessments. CI as counterespionage seeks to counter an ongoing penetration or other hostile activity (neutralization) and possibly turn it to one's own advantage (manipulation). The latter goal can be achieved by feeding disinformation into the system in hopes that it is treated as legitimate or by "turning" a spy into a "double agent."

As is the case with other aspects of intelligence, the failures of CI are more visible than its successes. Throughout the COLD WAR and into the post–cold war era a string of foreign penetrations of U.S. intelligence services and other critical national security agencies have made headlines and produced demands for reform. What these incidents reveal is that the SOVIET UNION has not been the only foreign power seeking to gain clandestine access to American secrets. Major penetrations organized by Chinese and Israeli intelligence have also been uncovered. Among the penetrations that have gained the most notoriety are those involving Aldrich Ames, Robert Hanssen, Ronald Pelton, and Jonathan Jay Pollard.

One of the most troubling aspects of CI to most Americans involves the potential for abuse of power, especially as it relates to violations of the rights of Americans. These dangers are highlighted by CIA and FBI CI programs in the 1960s and 1970s. In 1967 the CIA undertook a special overseas CI program at the direction of the White House that investigated links between Soviet propaganda themes and the positions advanced by anti-VIETNAM WAR protesters. Concluded in 1972, Operation CHAOS found no evidence of Soviet manipulation. In the course of this CI program the CIA created about 13,000 files, with a computerized index of more than 300,000 names. From 1955 to 1975, the FBI conduced 740,000 investigations into possible acts of subversion and 190,000 investigations into "extremist matters" in the United States. By 1975 it had approximately 6.5 million files. The best known FBI CI program was COINTELPRO, which took place at the same time the CIA was conducting Operation CHAOS. Under COINTELPRO not only did the FBI investigate radical groups and individuals in the United States, but it also acted as an agent provocateur within these groups, attempting to discredit key individuals and produce internal conflict within them.

Steps were taken to address this potential for abuse in 1978 with the passage of the Foreign Intelligence Surveillance Act, which permitted electronic surveillance on Americans but required presidential authorization and that the action be reported to CONGRESS. The act did not address physical surveillance on Americans. President JIMMY CARTER issued an executive order the same year on this subject. It stated that the CIA could not engage in CI operations inside the United States and that the FBI could do so only "in the course of a lawful investigation." This language has been modified somewhat by subsequent presidential orders. President RONALD REAGAN's executive order, for example, permits physical surveillance on Americans abroad if significant information can be obtained that "cannot reasonably be acquired by other means."

See also COVERT ACTION; RUSSIA.

**Further reading:** Barron, John. *Breaking the Ring.* Boston: Houghton Mifflin, 1987; Mangold, Tom. *James Jesus Angleton, the CIA's Master Spy Hunter.* New York: Simon and Schuster, 1991; Riebling, Mark. *Wedge: The Secret War between the FBI and CIA.* Rev. ed. New York: Knopf, 2002.

## covert action

Covert action seeks to achieve U.S. foreign-policy objectives by altering the internal balance of power in a foreign state. In popular usage covert action is all but synonymous with CENTRAL INTELLIGENCE AGENCY (CIA) paramilitary undertakings, but this is not always the case. Nor is it the case that covert action came to an end with the end of the COLD WAR. It remains perhaps the most controversial and difficult to control of all policy instruments.

At least five distinct activities fall under this heading. The most common form of covert action is clandestine support for individuals and organizations. It may be financial or technical or involve the training of personnel. Common targets are politicians, unions, political parties, church groups, and professional associations. This form of covert action was the major form of early CIA covert-action programs in FRANCE, ITALY, and West GERMANY. Between 1948 and 1968 it is estimated that the CIA spent more than $65 million on these types of programs in Italy alone. A widely publicized case of CIA clandestine support involved efforts to block the election of Salvador Allende in CHILE. Another form of clandestine support involves the provision of security assistance and intelligence training to foreign governments. According to one account in 1983 the governments of Chad, PAKISTAN, LIBERIA, PHILIPPINES, and LEBANON were all receiving such covert assistance.

A second form of covert action is propaganda. The best-known covert radio broadcasting systems were Radio Free Europe and Radio Liberty, directed at Eastern Europe and the Soviet Union (see RUSSIA), respectively. At its peak the CIA had more than 800 propaganda and public information organizations and individuals engaged in this form of covert action. Particularly controversial has been the involvement of American journalists and academics in propaganda activities.

A third category of covert action involves economic sabotage. Comparatively few economic operations have been undertaken by the CIA, and they have not been very successful. The most frequent target appears to have been Fidel Castro's government in CUBA. One of the most famous economic sabotage operations that has come to light is Operation Mongoose. Authorized by President JOHN KENNEDY in November 1961 it was to involve the destruction of railroad yards and bridges. The plan was called off when the saboteurs were spotted approaching Cuba by boat. While Operation Mongoose was cancelled in

January 1963 economic sabotage against Cuba continued when, in October, President Kennedy approved 13 economic sabotage operations. Targets included OIL tanks, copper mines, and electric power grids.

The fourth category of covert action involves paramilitary undertakings. In the immediate post–WORLD WAR II period these operations were directed at the SOVIET UNION and Eastern Europe. They were almost always failures. In the 1950s the most significant CIA covert paramilitary operations took place in developing nations. In 1953 the United States and GREAT BRITAIN undertook a joint operation in IRAN to bring down Prime Minister Mohammad Mossadegh and replace him with the shah. In 1954 the CIA helped bring down the government of Jacobo Arbenz Guzmán in GUATEMALA. The 1960s saw the failed BAY OF PIGS operation. This put a temporary dent into the use of paramilitary operations. The major paramilitary operation of the 1970s was in ANGOLA. In the 1980s NICARAGUA became one of the CIA's most controversial and visible covert paramilitary operations. Along with the paramilitary operation in AFGHANISTAN, the Nicaraguan operation raised serious questions about how covert such efforts could be and whether they should remain under CIA control given their increasingly public nature.

The final form of covert action is assassination. The existence of a unit for planning "special operations" can be traced back to the earliest days of the CIA. By all accounts no actual assassination operations or planning was ever done. The most thorough investigation into U.S. involvement in assassination plots was conducted by the CHURCH COMMITTEE in the 1970s. It investigated five cases in which the United States was alleged to have been involved in assassination plots. The Church Committee concluded that in two cases (Fidel Castro of Cuba and Patrice Lumumba of the CONGO) the United States did conceive assassination plots. It found evidence of at least eight plots to kill Castro. In one case (that of Rafael Trujillo of the DOMINICAN REPUBLIC) it concluded that the United States did not initiate the plot but did give aid to dissidents knowing that assassination was among their goals. There was no evidence to suggest that the United States wanted to kill Ngo Dinh Diem in VIETNAM, although it did want him out of power. General Rene Schneider was killed as a consequence of the covert operation undertaken by the Nixon administration in Chile, but the Church Committee found no direct U.S. link to his death.

Covert action did not disappear with the end of the cold war. One major "overt" covert action took place against IRAQ between 1992 and 1996. The goal was to remove Saddam Hussein from power by encouraging a military coup and reducing his control over outlying areas, such as Iraqi Kurdistan. The cost of the program was estimated to be $100 million. Little was achieved as in June 1996 Saddam Hus-

sein arrested and executed more than 100 Iraqis that he believed were involved in the plot. Infighting between Kurd opposition groups contributed to the failure and presented the CIA with a problem at home. Its disenchantment with the Iraqi resistance forces ran counter to CONGRESS's interest in funding them. As the GEORGE W. BUSH administration began planning for war with Iraq in 2002 the CIA's work with these groups once again became highly visible.

CIA covert action also played a significant role in the war against TERRORISM in Afghanistan following the SEPTEMBER 11, 2001, terrorist attacks in the United States. It was active in both the northern and southern regions of Afghanistan, organizing opposition forces and urging Taliban supporters to defect. The first American casualty in the war was a CIA official who died while interrogating a pro-Taliban prisoner. Even prior to these attacks the CIA had been involved in efforts to target OSAMA BIN LADEN and his AL-QAEDA network. After the bombing of the U.S. EMBASSIES in Nairobi, Kenya, and Dar es Salaam, Tanzania, President BILL CLINTON issued a finding consistent with the provisions of the HUGHES-RYAN AMENDMENT that authorized funding covert operations against Osama bin Laden. The presidential finding would be modified to allow the CIA to move from capturing him to using lethal force if necessary, including shooting down aircraft. The CIA recruited Pakistanis and Afghanis as part of this covert action, but little came of it, and no attack on bin Laden took place.

**Further reading:** Godson, Roy. *Dirty Tricks or Trump Cards: U.S. Covert Action and Counterintelligence*. Washington, D.C.: National Defense University, 1995; Prados, John. *The President's Secret Wars: CIA and Pentagon Covert Operations from World War II through Iranscam*. New York: William Morrow, 1986; Rositzke, Harry. *CIA's Secret Operations: Espionage and Counterespionage and Covert Action*. Boulder, Colo.: Westview, 1988; Treverton, Gregory. *Covert Action: The Limits of Influence in the Postwar World*. New York: Basic Books, 1987.

## Croatia

Croatia is about the size of West Virginia and became an independent state on June 25, 1991, with former general Franjo Tudjman as president. It has a population of 4.8 million people. Along with Slovenia, it was the first to break away from YUGOSLAVIA. Unlike Slovenia, Croatia did not possess an ethnically homogeneous population. It contained a Serb minority of about 600,000, and this provided an entry point for Serb-dominated Yugoslavia to try to block Croatian independence. Movement toward independence began in April 1990 when the Croatian Republic of Yugoslavia elected a noncommunist government and sought more autonomy within Yugoslavia.

Fighting began almost immediately between Croatian troops and Serb (Yugoslav) forces who aligned themselves with Serbian Croats concentrated in southern Croatia. Serbian-Croats began demanding greater autonomy for themselves in 1990 when it became clear that Croatia was moving toward independence. Many feared a return of Croat prejudices that surfaced during WORLD WAR II when Croatia became a German puppet state and fought against the Serbs. Croatia's new government rejected calls for a referendum as unconstitutional and asserted that sufficient protections existed within the current political system. Still, a referendum was held in August 1990, and 99 percent of the Serbs voted in favor of autonomy. This was followed by an October 1990 declaration by the Serb National Council that declared territory that was predominantly Serb to be autonomous from the Croat republic government. Croat authorities responded by sending police into Serb-controlled areas.

Fighting came under control in February 1992 when the UNITED NATIONS sent in a PEACEKEEPING force. The cease-fire froze the territorial status quo then in place that gave Serbs control of 30 percent of Croatia (East Slavonia). The EUROPEAN UNION had already recognized Croatia's independence in January 1992, and it became a member of the UNITED NATIONS in 1993. From the outset the new state of Croatia faced a major problem with displaced populations. Large numbers of Croats had fled Serb-controlled land during the war or were expelled as part of the Serbs campaign of ethnic cleansing. A new wave of REFUGEES was created in 1993 when Croatia began a military campaign to retake Serb-controlled lands. Some 300,000 Serbs fled to Bosnia and Yugoslavia as a result of this military action, which included a strong element of ethnic cleansing on the part of the Croats.

Croatia soon involved itself in BOSNIA AND HERZEGOVINA's civil war that started in 1992 by helping the Croat Bosnians in this multisided affair. Part of Croatia's motivation lay in reacquiring territory lost to the Serbian Croats in 1991. It accomplished this goal with an agreement signed in conjunction with the DAYTON PEACE ACCORDS that returned East Slavonia to Croatian rule following a transition period in which United Nations peacekeepers would supervise the region. Croatia took control of this region in January 1998 but has been slow to implement other aspects of the Bosnian peace agreement, such as facilitating the return of Serbian refugees, addressing HUMAN-RIGHTS abuses, and curtailing freedom of the press. Many were critical of U.S. foreign policy during this period because the CLINTON administration quietly began backing Croatia in order to obtain its support for an end to fighting in Bosnia. The United States permitted Croatia to acquire arms in violation of the overall arms embargo in place and provided military advice to the Croatian army. As a result it was a far more effective fighting force in 1995 when it retook Serb-controlled regions of Croatia.

Tudjman's autocratic rule and hopes of creating a greater Croatia led to Croatia's isolation in world politics in the late 1990s as it revived fears of a rebirth of its fascist past. Both NATO and the European Union were cool on the possibility of Croatian membership, and the Clinton administration blocked a $30 million WORLD BANK loan because of its human-rights violations and failure to implement the Dayton Accords. In 1999 the ORGANIZATION OF SECURITY AND COOPERATION IN EUROPE issued a report critical of Croatia's human-rights abuses and its failure to cooperate with the international tribunal investigating war crimes in the former Yugoslavia. Tudjman had steadfastly rejected the tribunal's jurisdictional authority in Croatia. Tudjman's death on December 10, 1999, lessened Croatia's international isolation somewhat. The new government expressed a willingness to cooperate with The Hague war crimes tribunal. This decision sparked political opposition within the legislature and riots in the streets. One key area of cooperation between the United States and Croatia today is removing land mines. The United States has provided Croatia with almost $5 million since 1999 to remove land mines. Croatia hopes to have almost 1 million mines removed by 2010.

**Further reading:** Glenny, Misha. *The Fall of Yugoslavia: The Third Balkan War.* 3d ed. New York: Penguin, 1997; Gow, James. *Triumph of the Lack of Will: International Diplomacy and the Yugoslav War.* New York: Columbia University Press, 1997.

### *Crosby v. National Foreign Trade Council* (2000)

This case resurrected the long-dormant issue of rights held by states to make foreign policy. This question had been addressed as early as *WARE V. HYLTON* (1796). At issue was the 1996 Massachusetts Burma Act that prohibited Massachusetts government agencies from making purchases from companies operating in Burma (Myanmar). The act was designed to protest Burma's HUMAN-RIGHTS policy and place pressure on companies to lend their voices to those demanding change. Along with Massachusetts 14 states and some local governments had enacted such restrictive legislation. Targeted states included NORTHERN IRELAND, CUBA, NIGERIA, and INDONESIA. Similar types of state and local legislation had been used in the 1980s to pressure SOUTH AFRICA to end its policy of apartheid.

Then, as with this case, business interests brought lawsuits challenging the legality of these prohibitions. None, however, reached the SUPREME COURT. In the Massachusetts case business interests led by the Foreign Trade Council and the U.S. Chamber of Commerce also successfully challenged the law in the lower courts. Seventy-eight members of Congress filed briefs supporting the Massachusetts law. Whereas the Justice Department argued that the Massachusetts law usurped CONGRESS's power to "regulate commerce with foreign nations," Massachusetts asserted that it was only choosing how to spend its own money.

In a unanimous verdict, the Supreme Court overturned the Massachusetts Burma Act. Speaking for the Court, Justice David Souter returned to traditional arguments heard in *U.S. V. CURTISS WRIGHT EXPORT CORPORATION* (1936) in supporting the power of the national government over states in foreign policy. He stated: "[I]t is not merely that the differences between the state and federal acts in scope and type of sanctions threaten to complicate discussion; they compromise the very capacity of the president to speak for the nation with one voice in dealing with other governments." He continued, "if the Massachusetts law is enforceable, the president has less to offer and less economic and diplomatic leverage as a consequence." He also observed that the apartheid cases offered no guidance to the Court since the Supreme Court never ruled on the constitutionality of those laws.

The Court's ruling is significant not only because it flies in the face of renewed state activism in international economic relations but also because many question the validity of the traditional distinction made between foreign and domestic policy in an era of increased interdependence and GLOBALIZATION. The Supreme Court's decision also embodied a paradox similar to that found in the 1930s. At that time, the Supreme Court, which had rejected most of Franklin Roosevelt's New Deal legislation, affirmed vast presidential powers in foreign policy. In this case, the Supreme Court, which had generally taken a pro–state's rights position, reaffirmed vast presidential powers in foreign policy.

## Cuba

The island of Cuba is located some 90 miles off the south coast of FLORIDA. It has an area of 44,200 square miles, making it about the size of Pennsylvania. It has a population of 11 million people. Cuba was the last major Spanish colony to gain its independence, doing so in 1902 following a 50-year struggle. The United States recognized Cuba that same year and broke diplomatic relations in 1961. Since 1977 each country has maintained an "interests section" in the other's capital that operates under the protection of the Swiss embassy.

Virtually from the outset Cuba has played a prominent role in American foreign policy. It was assumed by many of the first generation of American leaders that Cuba was destined to be annexed by the United States. After failing

to purchase West Florida from SPAIN, President THOMAS JEFFERSON remarked, "We must have both the Floridas and Cuba." In 1823 SECRETARY OF STATE JOHN QUINCY ADAMS wrote, "the annexation of Cuba to our federal republic will be indispensable to the continuance and integrity of the Union." Still, until the MEXICAN WAR of 1848, the American approach to Cuba was largely defensive and protective, with the goal being as much to keep the French and British out of Cuba as it was to actively work for its annexation.

After the Mexican War the United States adopted a more aggressive approach to annexation. Westward economic expansion made Cuba an attractive port for vessels on their way around South America to the Pacific Ocean. More important, however, Cuban annexation came to be seen by some Southerners as necessary to offset the growing number of free states in the Union. Slavery was not abolished in Cuba until 1886, and the expectation was that out of annexation would come one or two proslavery states.

President JAMES POLK tried to buy Cuba from Spain in 1848 for $100 million, but Spain refused, and the British and French expressed their disapproval of such a purchase. Upon becoming president in 1853 FRANKLIN PIERCE renewed American efforts to acquire Cuba. In 1854 he instructed his minister to Spain, Pierre Soule, to purchase Cuba for $130 million or less. Failing that, he was to seek Cuban independence. This offer came on the heels of an incident that incited American public opinion against Spain. Cuban (Spanish) authorities seized the American merchant ship *Black Warrior* for violating port regulations. The ship had entered and left Cuban waters on numerous occasions without incident. Pierce demanded a $100,000 indemnity from Spain. Ultimately Spain agreed to pay a small fee.

Later in 1854 Soule along with JAMES BUCHANAN, minister to GREAT BRITAIN, and John Mason, minister to FRANCE, met at the direction of Secretary of State William Macy in Ostend, Belgium, to discuss the annexation of Cuba. In the OSTEND MANIFESTO they recommended the purchase of Cuba and, failing that, "wrestling it from Spain if we possess the power." James Buchanan became president in 1857 and urged annexation. The Senate Foreign Relations Committee supported the idea and recommended $30 million be set aside for this purpose.

Parallel to U.S. efforts to annex Cuba came forays from filibusters and private adventurers. The key figure was General Narciso López, who attempted to invade Cuba and free it in 1849, 1850, and again in 1851 with the ultimate goal of incorporating it into the United States. After López met his death at the hands of a Spanish military court, John Quitman, a former governor of Mississippi, took up the challenge of freeing Cuba, but he abandoned his crusade in 1855.

The AMERICAN CIVIL WAR deflected attention away from Cuba, but interest returned during the administration of General ULYSSES S. GRANT, when in 1868 Cuban revolutionaries began to press for independence. The Grant administration was under political pressure to recognize the independence fighters as belligerents but ultimately adopted a hands-off policy to the conflict. An important force lobbying for recognizing the Cubans rebels were Cuban exiles who had moved to the United States. The potential for U.S. involvement in the revolution spiked in 1873 with the *Virginius* incident. The *Virginius* was a Cuban gun-running ship that illegally flew an American flag. Intercepted by a Spanish warship and brought back to Santiago, Cuba, more than 50 of its crew were shot as pirates. Some of those killed were Americans. With tensions rising, Secretary of State Hamilton Fish worked out a compromise that averted military confrontation when Spain agreed to pay an indemnity to the families of those killed.

War would not be averted in 1898. The situation in Cuba had taken a turn for the worse when in 1896 the Spanish government sent General Valeriano Weyler y Nicolau to Cuba. As part of his program of pacification, reconcentration camps were set up in the country where civilians were sent in an effort to cut off support for the rebels. The conditions in these camps were such that thousands died. CONGRESS responded by passing a resolution favoring recognizing Cuban belligerency. President GROVER CLEVELAND sidestepped the matter, but his administration and that of his successor WILLIAM MCKINLEY came under increasing pressure from the yellow press, which enflamed public opinion about Cuba as part of a strategy to increase circulation and profits.

In January 1898 the USS *Maine* arrived in Havana as a display of force intended to protect American property and lives. Not long thereafter, on February 15, 1898, an explosion sunk the *Maine,* killing more than 250 men. On March 9 with war hysteria building, Congress unanimously passed a measure providing for $50 million in war preparations. Before the month ended, on March 28, an American court of inquiry ruled that the *Maine* had been sunk by a submarine mine.

Initially McKinley tried to avert war by negotiating a settlement with Spain. An agreement was reached whereby Spain would revoke the policy of reconcentration and grant an armistice. Agreeing to these terms was not easy for the Spanish government. While it recognized the hopelessness of its position in Cuba, Spanish public opinion remained opposed to abandoning it. The Spanish capitulation did not end the crisis as political pressure on McKinley continued to build. Two days after the Spanish government made known its position, on April 11, 1898, McKinley asked Congress for the authority to use military force to end the conflict in Cuba. On April 19, Congress passed a resolution equivalent to a declaration of war. Of most significance

in the congressional resolution was the TELLER AMENDMENT that stipulated that annexation of Cuba was not an American objective. On April 25 a state of war was officially declared to have existed between Spain and the United States since April 21.

Victory came quickly to the United States, and by the Treaty of Paris in 1898 control over Cuba passed to the United States. The American military occupation began in January 1899 and continued for the next three and a half years. As a condition of granting independence Cuba had to agree to the PLATT AMENDMENT in 1901. The Platt Amendment would become part of the Cuban constitution and achieve treaty status in 1903.

The American military presence in Cuba did not end in 1903 when independence was achieved. Armed interventions took place in 1906, 1912, and 1917. The motivating factor in each was a perceived need to protect American property and economic interests. These interests had grown quite large and would continue to do so. By the 1890s almost 94 percent of Cuban sugar was sold in American markets, and soon thereafter Cuban imports from the United States represented nearly one-half of all U.S. exports to Central and South and America. In the 1940s and 1950s American firms controlled about 70 percent of all the petroleum brought into Cuba and 42 percent of its sugar production. American firms enjoyed near monopolies in the telephone, electrical, and railroad industries. By the late 1950s American foreign investment in Cuba was valued at nearly $1 billion.

Not surprisingly, accompanying an American concern with stability in the Cuban economy was a growing sense of nationalist frustration with American economic and political dominance. Steps were taken in the 1930s to reduce these tensions. The Platt Amendment was abrogated in 1934. The same year the Jones-Costigan Act lowered American protective tariffs on sugar imports. However, problems remained. Corruption and mismanagement were commonplace, and in the early 1950s violence mounted against the regime of Colonel Fulgencio Batista y Zaldívar, who had ruled Cuba directly or indirectly since 1934.

One of Batista's leading opponents was Fidel Castro, who headed the 26th of July Movement. Castro succeeded in uniting nationalist forces under his leadership. Batista's ability to counter Castro was limited not only by the corruption of his government but by American foreign policy. In the late 1950s the United States had come to the conclusion that Batista would not make the necessary political reforms and therefore could not ensure political stability in Cuba. It began taking steps to distance itself symbolically from Batista. An arms embargo was imposed, and the American ambassador was recalled for consultations.

Castro assumed power in January 1959, and his economic and social reform agenda soon brought him into

Fidel Castro *(National Archive)*

conflict with the United States. Given America's position of economic dominance in Cuba, American firms and properties became a primary target for nationalization, labor reform, and price adjustments. Matters took a further turn for the worse in 1960 when Soviet aid began to flow into Cuba and economic ties between the two were cemented. There then began a series of tit-for-tat measures. Castro's government began to expropriate American property. The United States cut the Cuban sugar quota. Cuba nationalized more American property. The United States placed a trade embargo on Cuba that only made exceptions for food and medicine. Cuba continued to nationalize American holdings. In January 1961 the United States broke diplomatic relations.

The United States did more than just sever diplomatic ties. It also tried to overthrow Castro by sponsoring an invasion by Cuban exiles in April 1961. The Eisenhower administration had conceived the original plan in April 1960, but it fell to the new Kennedy administration to implement the plan. What had once been thought of as a means of infiltrating dissident Cubans back into Cuba was transformed over time into a full-scale invasion. The Cuban exiles landed at the BAY OF PIGS, but instead of over-

whelming a dispirited army and inciting a popular uprising, the Cuban exiles were quickly and soundly defeated, and Castro used the occasion to cement his hold on power by cracking down on remaining dissidents. The episode also drove Castro further into the Soviet camp.

A little more than one year later, in October 1962, the United States again found itself confronting Cuba. This time, however, the issue was not Castro per se but the discovery of Soviet offensive missiles in Cuba. Over a tense span of 13 days the United States and the Soviet Union (see RUSSIA) moved to the edge of NUCLEAR WAR and back again. As part of the agreement that produced the withdrawal of these missiles, the United States promised not to invade Cuba. Deterring such an invasion had been given by the Soviet Union as a reason for placing missiles in Cuba.

The United States may have pledged not to invade Cuba, but the CUBAN MISSILE CRISIS did not mark the end of the Kennedy administration's attempts to drive Castro from power. President JOHN KENNEDY and his successors now acted through more indirect, covert, means. Operation Mongoose was intended to bring all U.S. assets together to accomplish this end. Economic sabotage played a central role in these plans. Authorized in 1961 Operation Mongoose was cancelled in 1963, but economic COVERT ACTION continued into the 1970s with weather modification programs and programs to infect Cuban livestock with a flu virus. The CENTRAL INTELLIGENCE AGENCY (CIA) was also authorized to engage in assassination as part of its covert-action program against Castro. At least eight assassination attempts directed at Castro are documented between 1960 and 1965. Most never went beyond the planning stage, but twice poison pills were sent to Cuba, and once weapons were provided to a Cuban dissident.

U.S. relations with Cuba moved in two different directions in the 1970s. At first relations showed signs of improvement. In 1973 Cuba signed an antihijacking agreement with the United States. In 1975 the ORGANIZATION OF AMERICAN STATES, with American support, lifted the hemispheric-wide economic blockade that was in place. HENRY KISSINGER even went to Cuba to explore what other positive steps might be taken to improve relations. Limited diplomatic relations through the establishment of interest sections was reestablished in 1977.

Relations were also worsening. Castro began to send Cubans abroad to help other revolutionary movements. In some cases this took the form of teachers, construction workers, and physicians. In others, such as ANGOLA, ETHIOPIA, SOMALIA, and South Yemen, Cuban troops were dispatched. Angola became the key COLD WAR battleground, with the United States supporting one set of forces and Cuba and the Soviet Union supporting another. At one point Kissinger complained that there were "8,000 Cubans running around." The exit of Cuban forces was finally achieved as apart of a broader agreement involving the fate of Angola and Namibia that was agreed to in 1988. Cuban troops left Angola prior to the July 1991 deadline that had been established.

By the 1980s the core issues in Cuban-American relations had shifted back to the Western Hemisphere. One set of issues centered on President RONALD REAGAN's assertion that Cuba was seeking to export COMMUNISM throughout the Americas. Direct or indirect U.S. military involvement in EL SALVADOR, NICARAGUA, and GRENADA all drew their inspiration from this reading of Cuban foreign policy.

A second set of issues centered on large-scale Cuban refugee flows to the United States. These flows had become a reoccurring feature in American-Cuban relations. A first wave of REFUGEES fled Cuba after Castro seized power. Some 10,000 arrived between January 1959 and December 1960. A second wave began in 1962 and continued through the MARIEL BOATLIFT of April 21, 1980. Cubans in the first wave overwhelmed relief agencies, but they were welcomed as signs of the failure of communism. The second wave was manageable in scope, and most Cubans had relatives in the United States and were defined as "consumer refugees." Beginning with the Mariel boatlift things changed. Economic conditions in Cuba had worsened. An estimated 130,000 Cubans fled before the Mariel boatlift was ended in September. These Cubans were not welcomed, as the American public perceived the situation as one in which Castro was "dumping" the poor and other undesirable elements of Cuban society on the United States.

Around this time U.S.-Cuban relations had also become more complicated politically for American presidents. Cuban refugees had by now become an effective lobbying force. The most notable group was the CUBAN-AMERICAN NATIONAL FOUNDATION (CANF). It advocated a tough hard line toward Castro with the clear objective of forcing him from power. An early lobbying success was the Reagan administration's decision to establish Radio Martí. Modeled loosely on Radio Free Europe, it was a vehicle for broadcasting anti-Castro news and propaganda back to Cuba. A second success came in 1992 with the passage of the Torricelli bill. Then member of Congress Robert Toricelli (R-N.J.) had become a strong supporter of CANF and a major recipient of its financial support. His bill tightened existing trade restrictions that the Reagan administration had put into place and prohibited subsidiaries of American firms from doing business with Cuba through other countries. It also permitted the president to withhold foreign aid, debt relief, and other forms of economic assistance to countries that provided assistance to Cuba.

In the mid-1990s worsening economic conditions in Cuba helped spark yet another refugee exodus to the United States. The numbers had been building steadily from 467 in 1990 to 3,656 in 1993. In August 1994 Castro indicated that he would no longer try to stop Cubans from leaving. A dramatic surge in Cubans attempting to reach the United States by boat and raft ensued. President BILL CLINTON tried to stem the tide by revoking the long-standing official U.S. policy of granting political asylum to those fleeing communism. He then ordered the U.S. Navy to intercept these vessels and take their occupants to Guantánamo Bay. By the end of September more than 21,000 Cubans had been brought there. An agreement negotiated that month brought the crisis to an end and established an orderly outflow of 20,000 Cubans per year to the United States.

The year 1996 was an election year, and it saw the passage of new legislation intended to remove Castro from power. The HELMS-BURTON ACT, also known as the Cuban Liberty and Democracy Act, authorized lawsuits against foreign companies that had purchased property once owned by Americans and nationalized by Castro. Clinton opposed the bill but threw his support behind it as the election neared and political pressure mounted. As a concession to the White House, the legislation was revised to contain language allowing the PRESIDENT to waive this provision if he or she felt American national security interests would be enhanced by doing so. From the point of view of the politics of American foreign policy, the most significant aspect of the Helms-Burton bill was that it codified into law all previous executive orders relating to Cuba. This meant that it would now require congressional action to change them.

Part of the political pressure building support for the Helms-Burton Act was an incident in February 1996 when two planes flown by the Brothers to the Rescue, an anti-Castro exile organization, were shot down by the Cuban air force for violating Cuban air space.

**Further reading:** Dominguez, Jorge. *To Make the World Safe for Revolution.* Cambridge, Mass.: Harvard University Press, 1989; Kaplowitz, Donna. *Anatomy of a Failed Embargo.* Boulder, Colo.: Lynn Rienner, 1998; Perez, Louis, Jr. *Cuba and the United States.* Athens: University of Georgia Press, 1997.

## Cuban-American National Foundation

Founded in Florida in 1981 the Cuban-American National Foundation (CANF) has established itself as the most politically powerful lobbying force on CUBA in the United States. CANF's own literature describes it as delivering an "organized and powerful Cuban-American voice in Washington," where it has built "bridges of communication with the executive and legislative branches." Beyond the United States CANF claims to have raised "awareness of Cuba's plight with world leaders and in capitals around the globe."

Officially CANF supports a nonviolent transition to a pluralistic market-based democracy in Cuba. In practice its stance is staunchly anti-Castro. Opponents charge that through the years it has intimidated and harassed those members of the Cuban community who would open a dialogue with Fidel Castro rather than work to force him from power. CANF was founded by Jorge Mas Canosa, who served as its chairman until his death on November 23, 1997. Born in Cuba, Mas Canosa was forced into exile twice, once for opposing Batista and later for opposing Castro. He participated in the BAY OF PIGS invasion in April 1961. Under President RONALD REAGAN, Mas Canosa served as chair of the President's Advisory Board for Cuba Broadcasting that oversaw Radio Martí. He also served PRESIDENTS GEORGE H. W. BUSH and BILL CLINTON in this capacity. At the state level he served under Republican and Democratic governors on the Government Commission on a Free Cuba.

CANF's Free Cuba Political Action Committee evolved into a force to be reckoned with. Between 1979 and 1997 CANF channeled more than $3 million into congressional and presidential campaigns. In 1992 it had contributed to 26 congressional candidates and "maxed out" on its contribution to Representative Robert Torricelli (R-N.J.), who represents a large Cuban-American community and authored the 1992 Cuban Democracy Act. Passed in an election year and endorsed by both Bush and Clinton in an effort to gain the electoral support of Cuban-American voters, it has been described as an economic declaration of war against Castro. It prohibits foreign affiliates of U.S. firms from trading with Cuba. CANF flexed its political muscles again in 1994 when over the objection of more moderate Cuban-American forces it convinced the Clinton administration to change its existing policy and prohibit Cuban-Americans from wiring money back to their families in Cuba and ending family reunification flights.

Other forms of influence were also documented. In 1995 an investigation by the UNITED STATES INFORMATION AGENCY brought forward allegations that Jorge Mas Conosa in his role of overseeing Radio Martí had deliberately misreported American foreign policy toward Cuba and in the process undermined U.S. immigration initiatives. Allegations of wrongdoing also shadowed Mas Canosa's business dealings, in which a grand jury investigated charges that $58 million in paving contracts for work never done had been awarded to his firm. Another report questioned the awarding of more than $280 million in federal funds to CANF.

The dynamics of Cuban-American lobbying changed with the death of Mas Canosa in 1997 and Pope John Paul II's 1998 trip to Cuba. The pope's trip created a climate that invited outreach rather than confrontation while Mas Canosa's death set off a power struggle within CANF between older hard-liners and a younger generation of leaders who had never lived in Cuba and did not necessar-

ily harbor hopes of returning. It would be the older generation that would leave as Jorge Mas Santos, 37, took over as chairman of CANF. In all 22 directors of CANF would resign, including several who were founding members. Many of the old guard founded a new organization—the Cuban Council for Liberty. Among other points of disagreement was a decision by the new CANF leadership to reach out beyond the Cuban exile community and establish links with other political groups.

In many ways the catalyst for this change in outlook was the Elian Gonzalez episode. On Thanksgiving night 1999, six-year-old Elian Gonzalez was rescued from an inner tube floating in the Atlantic. Along with his mother, who drowned, he was fleeing Cuba for the United States. Attorney General Janet Reno asserted that he should be reunited with his father, who remained in Cuba. An often vicious public relations and court fight ensued. Joining CANF in the attempt to keep Elian in the United States were several members of Congress. One of them, Dan Burton (D-Ind.), received 600 percent more money from CANF than he did from his Indiana constituents for his reelection bid. Both of the leading Republican presidential candidates, GEORGE W. BUSH and John McCain, supported its cause. For its part, Castro labeled it a case of kidnapping. In the end Elian Gonzalez was returned, and CANF's political clout suffered a serious symbolic setback.

See also DOMESTIC INFLUENCES ON U.S. FOREIGN POLICY; ELECTIONS; INTEREST GROUPS.

## Cuban missile crisis

In reflecting on the Cuban missile crisis Soviet leader Nikita Khrushchev observed that "the smell of burning hung in the air." More so than any other single event during the COLD WAR, it was the Cuban missile crisis that brought the two superpowers to the brink of war. In a sense the crisis had been building for years, running through GREECE and TURKEY in 1947, the establishment of communist governments in Eastern Europe, the KOREAN WAR, and a growing number of Third World battlegrounds, the latest of which was CUBA. Most immediately, the crisis came on the heels of the failed BAY OF PIGS invasion by which the United States had hoped to remove Fidel Castro from power.

The crisis began on October 14, 1962, when a U-2 spy plane photographed medium-range missile sites under construction in Cuba. President JOHN KENNEDY was informed on October 16 and created the Executive Committee (ExCom) of the NATIONAL SECURITY COUNCIL (NSC) to manage the crisis. From Kennedy's perspective the goal was clear: to remove the missiles from Cuba. The Soviet reason for putting the missiles in Cuba was puzzling and remains so. The Kennedy administration saw it primarily as an effort by Khrushchev to alter the nuclear balance by obtaining a communist counter to American missiles stationed in Turkey that threatened RUSSIA. Another scenario considered was that Khrushchev intended to use missiles in Cuba as a bargaining ploy to force the West out of BERLIN. Recent Soviet accounts point to an explanation discounted by ExCom, namely, to protect Cuba from an American invasion.

Initial deliberations in ExCom focused heavily on military options. DEAN ACHESON, a former SECRETARY OF STATE, argued for an air strike. The Joint Chiefs of Staff favored an invasion. The possibilities of a secret overture to Castro or an overture to Khrushchev of "missiles in Turkey for missiles in Cuba" were rejected as giving too much legitimacy to Khrushchev's actions and as rewarding him for his boldness, thus threatening future challenges to the United States. Time was not on the side of the United States. The Soviets had shown little concern for camouflaging their actions, and construction of the offensive missile bases continued through the crisis. The absence of Soviet efforts to conceal their actions (versus the secrecy with which they managed to get the missiles to Cuba) remains one of the mysteries of the missile crisis. Divided organizational responsibilities and standard bureaucratic operating procedures are among the most frequently cited explanations.

The policy option chosen by ExCom involved a naval quarantine of weapons shipments to Cuba. The choice's most positive virtues were that it constituted a middle ground between a costly military response and inaction and

Picture from a spy satellite showing a missile launch site in Cuba *(John F. Kennedy Library)*

it singled the intent to take further action. Its major negatives were that it did nothing to stop the construction of missiles or get them out and it left opened the possibility of retaliation in Berlin. Once operational the 42 Russian missiles had a range of 1,100 miles and could strike targets along the East Coast.

Kennedy went on national television on October 22 to take his case to the American people and the world. The blockade was announced, as was support by the ORGANIZATION OF AMERICAN STATES. Tensions ran incredibly high as the next wave of Soviet ships approached the blockade line composed of more than 180 ships. To demonstrate his seriousness Kennedy ordered an invasion force to FLORIDA and a B-52 bomber force loaded with nuclear weapons was sent aloft. In the end, the Soviet ships stopped and permitted an American force to search them for weapons. The ship stopped and searched had been carefully selected and deemed "safe" by U.S. authorities beforehand. Not so carefully orchestrated was the location of the quarantine line. It was not where Kennedy thought. Bureaucratic and organizational factors thus affected both sides as they worked their way through the crisis.

As the crisis progressed a troubling series of personal communications came from Khrushchev that were both conciliatory and hostile in tone. A first communication contained a promise to disarm the missiles for a public promise not to invade Cuba. A second communication linked the removal of missiles in Cuba to the removal of missiles in Turkey. This last offer presented the Kennedy administration with a real dilemma. Kennedy had order the missiles out of Turkey prior to the crisis because he perceived them to lack military value. This had not been done out of fear of alienating Turkey. Taking the missiles out now, however, was seen as politically unacceptable. Robert Kennedy suggested that the first offer should be accepted and the second one treated as if it was never made. This diplomatic ploy provided the basis for settling the crisis on October 28 when Khrushchev agreed to remove the missiles on these terms.

Up until then it was not clear that diplomacy would prevail. An offer of a summit conference was rejected by Kennedy until after the missiles were removed. On October 27, a U-2 was shot down over Cuba. President Kennedy had given orders that if this were to occur, the United States would retaliate with military action. On the 27th, however, he changed his mind, giving diplomacy added time to work. To compound matters, the day before another U-2 had accidentally entered Soviet air space. This move easily could have been interpreted as a provocation or last minute attempt at reconnaissance before hostilities began.

The Cuban missile crisis is still widely examined as a case study of crisis management. Particular attention is paid to the interaction of personality, organizational interests, bureaucratic inertia, small group decision dynamics, and strategic principles. It is generally treated as an example of successful crisis management, although many question the Kennedy administration's willingness to engage in public confrontation rather than private diplomacy and the influence of domestic political considerations that placed on extraordinarily high value on toughness.

The Cuban missile crisis left a mixed legacy for U.S.–Soviet nuclear relations. On the one hand, it ushered in a period of ARMS CONTROL that led to the 1963 Nuclear Test Ban Treaty. On the other hand, at least circumstantial evidence points to a Soviet decision to undertake a major expansion in its nuclear forces so that, in the words of one Soviet leader, "we will never be caught like this again."

See also COLD WAR; COVERT ACTION; INTERNATIONAL CRISES; NUCLEAR STRATEGY; SMALL-GROUP DECISION-MAKING MODEL.

**Further reading:** Graham, Alison, and Philip Zeikow. *Essence of Decision: Explaining the Cuban Missile Crisis.* 2d ed. New York: Addison Wesley Longman, 1999; Fursenko, Aleksandr, and Timothy Naftali. *One Hell of a Gamble: Khrushchev, Castro, and Kennedy, 1958–1964.* New York: Norton, 1997; Garthoff, Raymond. *Reflections on the Cuban Missile Crisis.* Washington, D.C.: Brookings, 1989.

## Czechoslovakia

Czechoslovakia was dissolved on January 1, 1993, when the Czech Republic and Slovakia separated to become two independent nations. The Czech Republic is about the size of Virginia and has a population of 10.2 million people. The two countries had first been united as one in 1918 when the Czech and Slovak Federal Republic was established out of the defeated Austrian-Hungarian Empire following WORLD WAR I. Economic disparities between the Czech lands and Slovakia and ethnic conflicts created political tensions for the new democracy, which was built around a highly centralized government. The most significant ethnic challenge came from Germans, who made up more than 20 percent of the population and were geographically concentrated in the Sudetenland. Backed by Adolf Hitler, extreme nationalists within the German community demanded annexation and union with GERMANY. BRITAIN and FRANCE acceded to these demands at the 1938 Munich Conference. The agreement was hailed by the Western powers as securing peace for a generation, but it was not to be, and the policy of appeasement followed at Munich became one of the most vilified in history. After the Munich Conference, POLAND also obtained territorial concessions and what was left of the state was renamed Czecho-Slovakia.

In March 1939 Czecho-Slovakia was further dismembered by Germany. Two provinces, Bohemia and Moravia, were made German protectorates, while Slovakia was granted independence and made a German satellite state. A fourth province, Ruthenia, was given to HUNGARY. During WORLD WAR II a pro-Western government in exile was set up in London under the leadership of former president Edvard Beneš. Soviet and American forces liberated Czecho-Slovakia in 1945. Its pre-Munich boundaries were more or less restored by the 1945 Potsdam Conference. Elections in 1946 produced a Communist-dominated coalition government.

The Communists used their position in the government to affect Czechoslovakia's foreign and domestic policies. It blocked Czechoslovakia's participation in the Marshall Plan in June 1947. In March 1948 Jan Masaryk, the noncommunist foreign minister, died under suspicious circumstances, his death officially declared a suicide. The Communists also maneuvered to gain complete control over the government, which they did in February 1948. Purge trials were conducted in the early 1950s as the Soviet-backed Communist Party consolidated its hold on power.

Communist rule in Czechoslovakia was marked by periodic waves of reform and liberalization. The two most important were the Prague Spring of 1968 and the Velvet Revolution of 1989. In 1968 Communist reformers led by Alexander Dubček sought to democratize the political and economic systems. The stated goal was to give socialism a "human face." In spite of pledges of loyalty to Moscow, Dubček's moves were seen as threatening by the Soviet Union (see RUSSIA). With the BREZHNEV DOCTRINE as is justification, WARSAW PACT troops invaded Czechoslovakia in August 1968, and the reforms were reversed. November 1989 brought forward large-scale antigovernment demonstrations in Prague. The reform movement that gave birth to these protests had begun more than a decade earlier in 1977 when HUMAN-RIGHTS supporters released Charter 77 that criticized the government for its human-rights record and failure to live up to the terms of the Helsinki accords. At first the police squashed the protests, but eventually the Communist government resigned and in December a new government was formed under the leadership of the former dissident Václav Havel. The transition from Communist state to a democratic and capitalist one was completed in May 1991 when the last Soviet troops departed. Separatist pressures from Slovakia quickly overwhelmed the new political order, and on August 26, 1992, it was announced that the Czech Republic and Slovak Republic would be split into two states on January 1, 1993.

As was the case with the other East European satellite states during the COLD WAR, U.S. relations with Czechoslovakia were not accorded a high priority. Bilateral issues were always of secondary importance to the broader question of U.S.-Soviet relations. The United States, for example, did little more than protest the Soviet invasion of 1968. The VIETNAM WAR and the desire of America's European allies for stability on the continent precluded it from doing much more. In terms of bilateral relations the failure to compensate Americans for property nationalized by the Communists was an irritant in U.S.-Czech relations for many years as was the American refusal to turn over to Czechoslovakia some 18.4 tons of gold held in Fort Knox. These issues were mutually resolved in 1982 when the United States agreed to release the gold and Czechoslovakia agreed to pay $81.5 million in claims to Americans.

At first the United States opposed the dissolution of Czechoslovakia, fearing that it might aggravate regional tensions and spark the breakup of additional states in Eastern Europe. Today this is no longer an issue. Since its creation the Czech Republic has taken several steps to integrate itself into the broader European community of states. It became a member of the NORTH ATLANTIC TREATY ORGANIZATION on March 12, 1999. In 2002 the Czech Republic completed talks for joining the EUROPEAN UNION, a process that is scheduled to be completed in 2004.

**Further reading:** Bradley, John. *Post Communist Czechoslovakia.* New York: Columbia University Press, 1997; Brzezinski, Zbigniew. *The Soviet Bloc: Unity and Conformity.* Cambridge, Mass.: Harvard University Press, 1967; Valenta, Jiri. *Soviet Invasion of Czechoslovakia: Anatomy of a Decision.* Baltimore: Johns Hopkins University Press, 1979.

# D

## Dames & Moore v. Regan (1981)

This case centers on President JIMMY CARTER's November 1979 declaration of a national emergency in response to the seizure of American hostages at the American EMBASSY in Tehran, IRAN. Citing the International Emergency Economic Powers Act (IEEPA), Carter blocked the removal or transfer of Iranian assets that were being held under the jurisdiction of U.S. authorities. Dames & Moore was a consulting firm doing business with the Iranian government that claimed it was owed a large sum of money. A district court issued an attachment against Iranian property in the United States so that Dames & Moore might be paid.

As part of the agreement that produced the release of the hostages, the United States agreed to drop legal claims against IRAN and that all attachments would be nullified. A special Iran–United States Claims Tribunal was set up to settle all outstanding claims against Iran through a process of binding arbitration. Dames & Moore brought suit against Secretary of the Treasury Donald Regan to block any enforcement of this agreement so that they might get all of the money owed them.

Unlike *YOUNGSTOWN SHEET AND TUBE CO. V. SAWYER* (1952), in which the SUPREME COURT ruled that President HARRY TRUMAN had overstepped his powers in dealing with the private sector, in this case the Supreme Court supported the PRESIDENT. In effect, it ruled that in the name of national security a president could deny an American with claims against a foreign government access to the courts. In part, this ruling was based on the fact that, unlike the 1952 steel seizure case in which Congress had indicated its clear intent through the Taft-Hartley Act that nationalization could not be used to settle a labor dispute, here the Court read congressional action in passing the IEEA and the Hostage Act as signaling "a strong willingness that the President have broad discretion when responding to the hostile acts of foreign sovereigns. . . . [W]e cannot ignore the general tenor of Congress' legislation in this area."

The IEEPA thus provides a broad umbrella under which the president can take unilateral economic action against other states. President RONALD REAGAN did so when he issued an executive order severing economic relations with LIBYA over its support for international TERRORISM. Similarly President GEORGE H. W. BUSH froze KUWAIT's assets in the United States to prevent IRAQ from confiscating them after it invaded that country.

## Dayton Accords  (Dayton Peace Accords)

The Dayton Accords are the 1995 peace agreement brokered by the United States to bring peace to BOSNIA AND HERZEGOVINA. Bosnia was one of several republics to break away from YUGOSLAVIA in the early 1990s. Slovenia and CROATIA declared their independence in 1991, and Bosnia and Herzegovina followed in 1992. Immediately the Bosnian Serbs resisted the move and declared their own independent state, the Serb Republic of Bosnia. Intense fighting followed. The Bosnian Serbs were aided by the Yugoslav army, which was Serb-controlled. The Muslim Bosnians not only lost a great deal of territory but also became the victims of a vicious and massive ethnic cleansing campaign by the Bosnian Serbs. The international community did little to stop the fighting beyond imposing economic sanctions on all sides, establishing safe zones within Bosnia for the Muslims to flee to, and placing diplomatic pressure on Yugoslavia and Croatia to help end the fighting. The one concrete peace plan, the Vance-Owen Plan, put forward in 1992 would have created 10 ethnically homogeneous provinces. It was rejected.

A cease-fire was arranged in Bosnia on October 10, 1995. In November 1995 the United States brought together Yugoslav president Slobodan Milošević, Croatian president Franjo Tudjman, and (Muslim) Bosnian president Alija Izetbegović to Wright-Patterson Air Force Base, Dayton, Ohio, for a summit conference. The agreement reached on November 21 provided for maintenance of the territorial integrity and independence of Bosnia and Herzegovina. A central government was to be established that would hold jurisdiction over foreign affairs. Beneath the national level, Bosnia and Herzegovina was to be divided into two administrative units of approximately equal size, with 51 percent going to the Muslim-Croat Federation and the remainder to the Bosnian Serbs. Both Bosnian and Bosnian Serb military forces would withdraw to agreed upon positions so that a NORTH ATLANTIC TREATY ORGANIZATION (NATO) PEACEKEEPING force known as IFOR could be inserted. IFOR took over for a UNITED NATIONS protection force (UNPROFOR) that had been supervising the safe zones on December 20. NATO troops were to stay until June 1998 and deal only with military-related matters. The United States agreed to provide one-third of the 60,000-person force.

As part of the Dayton Accords it was agreed that elections would be held in nine months and that each of the administrative units would respect HUMAN RIGHTS and the right of displaced persons to regain their property. Former Swedish prime minister Carl Bildt was placed in charge of overseeing the nonmilitary aspects of the agreement. He had no direct liaison with NATO forces but was expected to help construct a police force and ensure the right to free travel throughout Bosnia.

Implementation of the Dayton Accords has not gone smoothly. It has been resisted and undermined by ultranationalist Bosnian Serbs. Bosnian Croats and Muslim Bosnians have also taken steps to undermine the agreement, leaving a pervading sense of ethnic distrust in the country. However, successes were realized. IFOR did succeed in separating the combatants, and elections were held on schedule. Prisoners of war were exchanged.

The agreement itself has been criticized for being little more than a bundle of compromises that do not constitute a coherent strategy. It has produced what some refer to as a silent occupation of Bosnia. Moreover it is an occupation that began before any of the warring factions had accomplished their objectives. Izetbegović wanted the agreement to reestablish Bosnia and Herzegovina's prewar independence status of having a strong central government. Tudjman and Milošević favored a loose association in hopes that the Bosnian Croats and Bosnian Serbs might at some point in the future be annexed by Croatia and Yugoslavia, respectively.

The United States provided more than $14 billion in foreign aid to Bosnia in an effort to spur economic recovery. The United States's commitment to the Bosnian peacekeeping operation is limited. The GEORGE W. BUSH administration is not in favor of such operations and threatened to block the continuance of the mission in 2002 as part of its dispute with the United Nations over the establishment of an INTERNATIONAL CRIMINAL COURT.

**Further reading:** Burg, Steven L., and Paul S. Shoup. *The War in Bosnia-Hercegovina: Ethnic and International Intervention.* New York: M.E. Sharpe, 1999; Gow, James. *Triumph of the Lack of Will: International Diplomacy and the Yugoslav War.* New York: Columbia University Press, 1997; Woodward, Susan. *The Balkan Tragedy: Chaos and Dissolution after the Civil War.* Washington. D.C.: Brookings, 1995.

## debt crisis

In the 1980s many developing countries were rocked by a major debt crisis. The crisis had its roots in the 1970s when a combination of factors led to a surge of investment in these states. Foremost among these factors was the rise in OIL prices brought on by the actions of the ORGANIZATION OF PETROLEUM EXPORTING COUNTRIES (OPEC). The combination of price hikes and denial not only led to a huge inflow of money to these states but recession and declined investment opportunities in the advanced economies. Developing nations that seemed on the verge of economic take-off became the recipients of much of this money. It was not long, however, before the impact of recession in the advanced economies and high oil prices affected the economies of these states in the form of reduced demand for their products, higher operating costs, and reduced foreign aid. The net result was that these states now found it increasingly difficult to pay back the debts they had incurred. Compounding the problem was the fact that most of these debts were now owed to commercial banks, who had lent at higher interest rates and with shorter payback periods than is the case with loans from international lending agencies, such as the WORLD BANK. As a result, by 1982 the external debt of developing nations had risen 264 percent above the 1975 level, and 76 percent of the debt owed by the highly indebted countries was now held by commercial sources compared to 60 percent in 1975.

The debt crisis hit full force in August 1982 when MEXICO announced that it could not service its foreign debts. A Mexican default on its debts threatened the stability of the international financial system. Not only was Mexico a large debtor state, owing more than $85 billion, but other highly indebted states faced similar problems. At the end of 1982, ARGENTINA, Mexico, BRAZIL, VENEZUELA, and CHILE owed a combined total of $260 billion. Private banks, especially U.S. banks, stood to loose considerable amounts of money, shaking investor confidence and threatening their very solvency. As the leading state in international economic matters, it fell to the United States to take the lead in averting this impending crisis.

Within two days of Mexico's announcement, the United States sent Mexico $2 billion as prepayment for oil and as credits for the purchase of U.S. agricultural products. Foreign banks agreed to postpone debt service fees for three months, and the INTERNATIONAL MONETARY FUND (IMF) agreed to enter into negotiations with Mexico on a long-term arrangement for financing its debt. This agreement was reached in November. It provided Mexico with an additional $3.8 billion in credits and required Mexico to undertake a series of domestic austerity measures. Commercial banks also agreed to lend Mexico an additional $5 billion as a condition for the IMF loan. This combination of new IMF and commercial loans coupled with austerity measures proved to be a temporary fix. A global financial meltdown had been averted, but new growth was not forthcoming. If anything, austerity programs had made growth more difficult by reducing domestic demand for goods and reducing investment.

The United States intervened again in September 1985 when Secretary of the Treasury James Baker put forward a three-part plan to promote economic growth in debtor states, something Baker identified as the key to ending the debt crisis. Debtor states would implement market-oriented reforms designed to stimulate growth, commercial banks would provide $20 billion in new loans over the next three years, and multilateral lending agencies such as the World Bank would increase their lending by $3 billion per year. The BAKER PLAN did not produce the desired effect. Most debtor states fell into an economic recession, and both debtors and lenders succumbed to debt fatigue as their respective commitments to making the Baker Plan work steadily lessened. Pressures began to build from U.S. allies and debtor states for a new approach to the debt crisis, one that placed debt reduction rather than repayment at its center. President-elect GEORGE H. W. BUSH indicated his support for such an initiative in December 1988. In March 1989, Secretary of the Treasury Nicholas Brady unveiled the new U.S. plan that embraced this shift in priorities.

It would be inaccurate to say that the debt problem no longer exists; for example, Argentina faced several international debt crises in the first years of the 21st century. There now exists a clear division in which some states are defined as highly indebted poor countries with little hope of escaping their condition and others are defined as market-oriented developing countries that might. The attention of the international financial community also shifted in the 1990s from developing-nation indebtedness to problems caused by the rapid movement of privately held money that spurred the ASIAN FINANCIAL CRISIS.

**Further reading:** Amuzegar, Jahangir. "Dealing with Debt." *Foreign Policy* 68 (1987); Birdsell, Nancy, and John Williamson. *Delivering on Debt Relief: From IMF Gold to a New Aid Architecture.* Washington, D.C.: Institute for International Economics, 2002; Riley, Stephen, ed. *The Politics of Global Debt.* New York: St. Martin's 1993.

## Defense Department (United States Department of Defense)

For most of its history the military services of the United States were organized under the separate commands of the War Department and the Navy Department. No political or military authority other than the PRESIDENT existed above these two departments to coordinate and direct their efforts. During WORLD WAR II the ineffectiveness of this system laid the groundwork for the creation of a national military establishment as part of the 1947 NATIONAL SECURITY ACT. This act also established the cabinet-rank position of the SECRETARY OF DEFENSE and the Department of the Air Force and converted the War Department into the Department of the Army. The military services were placed directly under the control of the secretary of defense. In 1949 an amendment to the 1947 National Security Act transformed the National Military Establishment into the Department of Defense, and the three military departments were stripped of their cabinet-level status. A chairman of the JOINT CHIEFS OF STAFF was also established by this piece of legislation.

Together, the president and the secretary of defense are referred to as the National Command Authority. The secretary of defense is charged with carrying out the directives of the president. At the heart of the secretary's office are four key undersecretaries in charge of policy, finance, force readiness, and purchasing. The chairman of the Joint Chiefs of Staff, the military departments, and the unified commands are tasked with implementing these policies. Each has a specific set of responsibilities. The chairman of the Joint Chiefs of Staff plans and coordinates the deployment of American forces, the unified commands conduct these operations, and the military services train and equip the necessary forces.

There are nine unified commands today. Each is composed of forces from two or more services. Five have geographic responsibility: the European Command (extending into most of Africa and ISRAEL, LEBANON, and SYRIA), the Central Command (covering parts of Africa, most of the Middle East, and West Asia), the Southern Command (Central America, South America, and the Caribbean), the Pacific Command (Southwest Asia, Australia, and Alaska), and the Joint Forces Command (the North Atlantic and Arctic Oceans). Four commands have worldwide responsibility: the Space Command, the Special Operators Command, the Transportation Command, and the Strategic Command. The Office of the Chairman of the Joint Chiefs of Staff has responsibility for U.S. forces in RUSSIA and military issues involving CANADA and MEXICO. Each unified command is headed by a commander in chief (CINC) who is in a chain of command running directly from the president and the secretary of defense.

Since the 1980s a dominant reform issue within the Defense Department has been improving the operational efficiency of the armed forces. The failed 1979 hostage rescue effort, the 1983 terrorist attack on the Marines in Beirut, Lebanon, and the problems encountered in the 1983 invasion of GRENADA gave rise to these concerns. Over the objections of the executive branch and the military, CONGRESS passed two pieces of legislation in 1986 designed to remedy perceived performance shortcomings. The GOLDWATER-NICHOLS ACT strengthened the position of the Joint Chiefs of Staff relative to the individual services and strengthened those parts of the Defense Department that have an interservice perspective. The Cohen-Nunn Act established a unified command for special operations and created an assistant secretary of defense for special operations and low-intensity conflict.

Today a concern for operational efficiency has been joined by a concern for cost. The Defense Department's annual budget was approximately $280 billion in 2000. Almost one-half goes for salaries and one-quarter for operating and maintaining military forces. About one-sixth goes for purchasing material, and another one-sixth goes for research and development. Between the end of the COLD WAR and the end of the century, the Defense Department experienced a loss of about one-quarter of its budget and a reduction of more than one-third of its full-time positions. The problem of cost can also be approached from another perspective. As originally planned the U.S. Air Force was going to purchase 132 B-2 Stealth bombers at a cost of $500 million each. In 1991 that figure was reduced to 75 planes at a cost in excess of $2 billion each.

The twin concerns for efficiency and cost have been combined in three debates that take as their point of departure the reality that the end of the cold war has not produced a noticeable end to global violence. In the first decade after the end of the cold war, the Defense Department estimates that it engaged in 99 major commitments. One debate is over the existence of a peace dividend. This debate pits defense hawks who see a need for increased defense spending to ensure U.S. security against deficit hawks who wish to reduce all areas of government spending. A second debate involves the impact defense cuts have made on military readiness. The key question is, have they resulted in "hollow forces," a military establishment that looks robust on paper but is sorely lacking in training, modern weapons, and effectiveness? The third debate concerns the significance of the revolution in military affairs on U.S. combat capabilities. This refers to the impact of modern technology on how we organize, prepare for, and fight wars.

## Defense Intelligence Agency

The Defense Intelligence Agency (DIA) was created on August 1, 1961, by Department of Defense Directive 5105.21. DIA is significant to the study of American foreign policy as an example of organizational reform and for the highly charged role it played in the politics of producing INTELLIGENCE estimates in the 1960s and 1970s.

DIA was given four tasks by its founding document. First, DIA was to organize, direct, manage, and control all Department of Defense intelligence resources assigned to DIA. Second, it was to review, coordinate, and supervise those defense intelligence functions retained by the military services. Third, it was to obtain maximum efficiency and economy in managing these resources. Fourth, it was to respond directly to priority requests from the United States Intelligence Board and the major components of the DEFENSE DEPARTMENT. In addition to these tasks DIA was given three functions: to produce all Department of Defense intelligence estimates and contributions to national estimates, set all Department of Defense intelligence priorities, and carry out miscellaneous functions related to intelligence.

In 1964–65 four additional intelligence functions were assigned to DIA. First, it was made responsible for photographic intelligence formerly carried out by the military services. Second, by way of consolidating the dissemination of intelligence, DIA became responsible for communicating both raw and finished intelligence between Defense Department and non-Defense Department agencies. Third, DIA was put in charge of all automated data handling projects within the Defense Department. Finally, DIA was charged with a program of "extraordinary military services" that were not publicly specified.

DIA came into existence as the culmination of a trend toward centralization and consolidation within the Department of Defense that began in the Eisenhower administration. The NATIONAL SECURITY ACT OF 1947 had left intact the intelligence units of the military services. The services defended the existence of separate intelligence agencies in terms of their own unique needs for tactical intelligence that would not be met by a single intelligence unit. The Eisenhower administration, however, became increasingly frustrated by the tendency of each of the military services to use their intelligence units to produce intelligence estimates that advanced their own budgetary goals over national goals. The classic example was the air force's discovery of a BOMBER GAP followed by a MISSILE GAP. The CENTRAL INTELLIGENCE AGENCY (CIA) and the STATE DEPARTMENT were ambivalent over the creation of the DIA. Bargaining over intelligence estimates with multiple military intelligence services had been time-consuming and frustrating, but there was also the realization that a single Defense Department intelligence agency could become a formidable bureaucratic opponent.

DIA did, in fact, become the CIA's major institutional competitor within the INTELLIGENCE COMMUNITY. The two frequently were on opposing sides on major intelligence estimates related to the prospects for victory in VIETNAM and assessments of Soviet military power. The DIA was slow to match its bureaucratic clout with a reputation for high-quality analysis. DIA was routinely accused of producing "intelligence to please." Its work was often characterized as sloppy and frequently inaccurate. These assessments reflected the pull of three realities governing its existence. First, DIA was serving two masters: the unified military as embodied by the Office of the Secretary of Defense and the JOINT CHIEFS OF STAFF and the three separate services. Second, intelligence work has not been considered a major route for career advancement within the military, so it has difficulty attracting high-quality personnel. Third, military officers serving in DIA are on loan from their home services and will return there when their tour of duty is completed. This creates an ever-present incentive to protect the interests of one's military service over those of the military as a whole.

See also NUCLEAR WEAPONS ARSENAL; RUSSIA.

## Democratic Party

It is commonplace to find American foreign-policy debates in the press reported in terms of the competing positions held by the REPUBLICAN PARTY and Democratic Party. While it is true that foreign policy often divides them, it is also true that they are often internally divided over what foreign policy to pursue. In part this is due to the fact that in a parliamentary democracy, party loyalty is necessary to maintain the government in power. The separate election of the PRESIDENT in the United States relieves American political parties of some of the need to support the party line at all costs. American parties are also less ideological in makeup than many European parties. First and foremost American political parties exist to win elections. Foreign-policy disputes also exist within American parties because of the impact of SECTIONALISM. Economic factors often produce regional variations in how political parties view foreign-policy issues.

The Democratic Party is the oldest continuously operating political party in the United States. It can trace its roots back to the administration of GEORGE WASHINGTON, when factions emerged. One group, led by ALEXANDER HAMILTON, favored a strong central government, an economy based on manufacturing, and close foreign relations with GREAT BRITAIN. They became the FEDERALIST PARTY. The other faction, led by THOMAS JEFFERSON, favored states' rights, envisioned an America dominated by small farmers, and a foreign policy aligned with FRANCE. They were known as the Democratic-Republicans or Republicans. The term *Democratic Party* did not become common until 1828 with ANDREW JACKSON's victory.

If one considers America's frontier policy as foreign policy, then foreign-policy issues often divided the Democratic Party as much as they separated the parties of the day. In an interesting twist, Jefferson and his political allies switched their position and endorsed the idea of a strong central government in pursuing the LOUISIANA PURCHASE in 1803. Because of the popularity of the Louisiana Purchase in the American West, Jefferson's party secured a large domestic political payoff from the acquisition. Prior to the WAR OF 1812 a new generation of party leaders emerged that advocated war against Great Britain. Known as the "war hawks," they were led by HENRY CLAY and JOHN CALHOUN. The American victory in that war spelled doom for the Federalist Party, which had opposed the war from its New England political stronghold. Disagreements soon emerged in the party over the wisdom of protective tariffs. They were favored by the northern wing of the party but opposed by its southern wing. In the 1840s the Democratic Party became identified with continental expansionism, but beneath the surface unity of this goal lurked a growing dispute over slavery. On the eve of the AMERICAN CIVIL WAR three positions had emerged within the Democratic Party. One group favored a policy of popular sovereignty that would allow the incoming states to determine whether they would be slave states or free states. Other Democrats, also in the North, opposed slavery. They were known as "barnburners." A third group of Southern Democrats favored protecting slavery in the territories. Jefferson Davis was a leader of this faction.

In the period after the civil war foreign-policy issues both united and divided the Democrats. Most Republicans favored protective tariffs, and Democrats tended to oppose them. Likewise, the Democratic GROVER CLEVELAND administration adopted a less interventionist foreign policy than had Republican administrations of the era. However, most Democrats supported the imperialist policies at turn of the 20th century. An important exception to this was WILLIAM JENNINGS BRYAN, who emerged as a spokesperson for the pacifist and isolationist wing of the party. Bryan became WOODROW WILSON's SECRETARY OF STATE but resigned when he felt Wilson was abandoning a policy of neutrality and leading the United States into WORLD WAR I. Most Democrats supported Wilson on the LEAGUE OF NATIONS, but Republican opposition and his unwillingness to compromise led to its defeat.

The influx of European immigrants into the Democratic Party in the first decades of the 20th century created a complex tapestry against which party leaders sought to construct a foreign policy. FRANKLIN ROOSEVELT favored an internationalist policy largely out of strategic considerations. Other party leaders, responding to the anti-British sentiments of German and Irish immigrants, advocated a policy of neutrality. One ethnic group within the Democratic Party group that did support a pro-British foreign policy were Jewish Americans. They were motivated out of a desire to create a Jewish homeland in the Middle East. The immediate post–WORLD WAR II era saw the Democratic Party split over how to deal with the Soviet Union. Franklin Roosevelt's policy had been predicated on the assumption that a working accommodation with Joseph Stalin could be reached. HENRY WALLACE built upon this foundation and argued for a policy of accommodation. President HARRY TRUMAN moved in the opposite direction to a policy based on hostility toward RUSSIA and COMMUNISM. Strategic arguments such as those made by GEORGE KENNAN plus domestic political concerns related to keeping and attracting immigrant groups to the party combined to steer him in this direction.

During the first decades of the COLD WAR, Democrats and Republicans united behind Kennan's policy of CONTAINMENT in a show of bipartisanship. Still, throughout the cold war the Democratic Party consistently had to rebut charges that it was soft on communism, weak on defense, and could not be trusted with the nation's security. For that reason, it has been argued that only a Republican president such as Richard Nixon could go to CHINA or enter into ARMS CONTROL talks with the Soviet Union. In the post–cold war era Democrats have suffered under the related charges that the party is naïve about the true nature of world politics and prone to engage in costly HUMANITARIAN INTERVENTIONS or sacrifice American NATIONAL INTERESTS in pursuing multilateral international agreements.

Wallace's legacy is one factor contributing to this image of suspicion. It was soon reinforced by the picture of the Democrats produced by MCCARTHYISM and congressional investigation into Soviet ESPIONAGE in the early 1950s. Another key factor was the internal conflict that ripped apart the Democratic Party during the VIETNAM WAR. While President JOHN KENNEDY had been the first to commit American military personnel to Vietnam as advisers, it was under LYNDON JOHNSON that the American military presence expanded to include combat troops. President LYNDON JOHNSON's handling of the war was challenged in and outside the party. Republicans led by Barry Goldwater charged that he was not pursuing the war vigorously enough. Democrats led by Eugene McCarthy, Robert Kennedy, George McGovern, and J. WILLIAM FULBRIGHT charged that the war was a mistake. This left wing of the party would emerge as dominant in foreign policy and would obscure from view the position taken by conservative Democrats, such as Senator Henry "Scoop" Jackson, who led the opposition to Nixon's policy of DÉTENTE. One result of this perception of weakness is an attempt by party leaders to articulate a centrist foreign policy that speaks to the importance of national strength but does not abandon the interest in HUMAN RIGHTS and similar causes that are important to the party's liberal wing.

Democratic senators J. William Fulbright *(left)* and Eugene McCarthy *(LBJ Library Collection)*

National security policy is not the only divisive foreign-policy issue confronting the Democratic Party today. Trade also presents a problem. Long identified as the party of free trade, important elements in the party have now embraced protectionism. The shift has come about due to the changing economic fortunes of key party constituencies. Once workers and manufacturing centers in the Northeast benefited from the ability to enter foreign markets and did not fear competition at home, but this is no longer the case. Foreign competition costs Americans jobs, and aged industries cannot compete abroad. President BILL CLINTON had to rely heavily on Republican congressional support in order to obtain approval for the NORTH AMERICAN FREE TRADE AGREEMENT and obtaining permanent MOST-FAVORED-NATION STATUS for China, since a majority of Democrats opposed these agreements.

See also CONGRESS; DOMESTIC INFLUENCES ON FOREIGN POLICY; ELECTIONS; INTEREST GROUPS; PUBLIC OPINION.

## democratic peace

The democratic peace is an age-old concept that since the end of the COLD WAR has come to be treated by many as a fundamental truth of world politics. It holds that democracies do not go to war with other democracies. The logical conclusion that follows from this argument is that by enlarging the sphere of democracy, creating more and more democratic states, one reduces the chances of international violence. Peace results. The democratic peace serves as a powerful argument in favor of an American foreign policy centered on promoting DEMOCRATIZATION.

Several different arguments are given for why democratization encourages peace. Immanuel Kant put forward the idea of a "perpetual peace" in which citizens in a democracy are able to constrain policy makers through their right to vote and the policy makers' need to provide information that justifies war. A second factor that prevents democracies from going to war are institutional constraints on executive action. No single leader is in a position to make the decision to go to war. A third factor is the existence of liberal norms. Central to these norms is the belief that military and political power must be checked and that civil rights and liberties must be respected. Fourth, Kant argued that commerce is inconsistent with war. The more interdependent states become, the less likely they are to go to war with one another. Free-trade economic systems and political democracies are not identical, but they are supportive of one another and frequently do coexist.

History does not show that democracies are inherently more peaceful than other types of political systems, and the democratic peace does not make this argument. The argument is more narrowly drawn. Democracies do not go to war with other democracies. On the surface the evidence supports this argument. We are hard pressed to find examples of democracies going to war with one another.

Critics of the democratic peace argument raise four objections. First, what is being argued is the peacefulness of liberal democracies and not democracies in general. Critics maintain that because liberal democracies are not the only type of democracy in the post–cold war era, the value of the democratic peace argument is compromised. A second critique is that the democratic peace is inconsequential. The argument here is that from a statistical perspective the odds that any two states would be locked into combat in a given year are slight. The fact that they are democratic adds little predictive value. A third and related critique is that the validity of the democratic-peace argument depends heavily on how democracy is defined. ISRAEL's 1981 invasion of LEBANON could be classified as a war between two democracies. So too could the AMERICAN CIVIL WAR and the WAR OF 1812, since in each case both sides (the Confederacy and the Union, and the United States and GREAT BRITAIN) claimed they were democracies. A final critique is made by realist commentators who maintain that a close reading of cases where democracies pulled back from going to war with one another point to balance of power and security considerations as being the determining factors in why war was averted. One example cited is the *Trent* affair, which threatened to involve the United States and Great Britain in a war due to the latter's potential support for the Confederacy.

**Further reading:** Kegley, Charles, Jr., ed. *Controversies in International Relations Theory: Realism and the Neoliberal Challenge.* New York: St. Martin's, 1995; Layne, Christopher. "Kant or Cant: The Myth of the Democratic Peace." *International Security* 19 (1994); Thompson, William R., and Richard Tucker. "A Tale of Two Democratic Peace Critiques." *International Studies Quarterly* 41 (1997): 41.

## democratization

During the COLD WAR the primary focal point of American foreign policy was largely negative: containing the spread of COMMUNISM. With its end many advocated adopting a more positive posture, one that sought to reestablish American moral leadership in world affairs. The foreign-policy goal that both ends of the political continuum found agreement on was advancing the cause of democracy. This did not mean, however, that putting this policy into practice was not controversial or without detours.

The first strands of this theme began to emerge in the Reagan administration with its support for anticommunist movements in NICARAGUA, AFGHANISTAN, and elsewhere. President RONALD REAGAN's continued support for right-wing anticommunist governments struck many as counter to the ideal of democratization. President GEORGE H. W. BUSH gave verbal support to the idea of advancing democracy but pulled back when confronted with the confusing situation in RUSSIA and the Tiananmen Square crackdown in CHINA. He was criticized for his failure to advance democracy in both these cases. President BILL CLINTON made enlarging the area of democracy a central tenet of his foreign policy. Even so, his supporters often criticized his foreign policy for its inconsistency. Conservative critics claimed that Clinton was not engaged in democratization but in social work by engaging in HUMANITARIAN INTERVENTIONS. President GEORGE W. BUSH pledged to end his predecessor's interventionist foreign policy and protect more narrowly defined American NATIONAL INTERESTS. Following the SEPTEMBER 11, 2001, terrorist attacks Bush did not hesitate to define the war on TERRORISM as one involving the global defense of freedom and democracy.

A considerable amount of writing exists on building democracy from which American policy makers can draw in constructing a foreign policy centered on democratization. Three major themes can be identified that are of relevance to this task. The first centers on the difficulty of defining democracy. Americans respond almost instinctively to questions about the nature of democracy in terms of free elections and then stop. It has become commonplace to have American or UNITED NATIONS election observers in attendance in newly established democracies to certify elections as fair. As much as free elections are an essential element in the operation of a democracy, they do not capture its full essence. Among others, respect for the rule of law, guarantees of civil liberties, the principle of majority rule and the protection of minority rights, political equality, and the accountability of elected officials to the public can be cited as integral elements of democracy. When building democracy is seen as involving all of these tasks and not just holding free elections the task facing American foreign policy becomes considerably more complex. There is also a danger of an overly expansive definition of democracy. American foreign policy has come to treat the expansion of democracy and the expansion of free-enterprise capitalism as inseparable. Critics of this policy argue that whereas economic growth may be a prerequisite for the growth of democracy, free-market capitalism is not, and by making it so the United States has unduly complicated the democratization process.

As just noted, economic growth is seen by many as a prerequisite for democracy. It is not the only factor cited. A second frequently mentioned prerequisite is political culture. To succeed, it is argued that democratic institutions and procedures must be embedded in a set of political values that are supportive of active political participation, civic trust, the rule of law, and accountability. For some commentators a third prerequisite is a supportive INTERNATIONAL SYSTEM. This is one in which there is relatively little international conflict or economic distress. It is also one in which international actors are predisposed to and capable of providing assistance to fledgling democratic governments. A focus on prerequisites provides a caution to American foreign policy on two points. First, building democracy is a lengthy process, since these prerequisites are not put into place easily. Second, building democracy may require the assistance of other states. Neither of these requirements, long-term commitment or multilateralism, have been enduring features of American foreign policy.

In addition to a concern for definitions and prerequisites, the literature on building democracy has also addressed the question of process. Is democracy best created by a revolution from below, or must it be guided and brought into existence by elites? During the cold war American foreign policy all but ruled out bringing democracy to communist states as a definitional impossibility. Jeane Kirkpatrick, who served as ambassador to the United Nations in the Reagan administration, argued that history showed no instances of communist governments being replaced by democratic ones. Therefore, communist movements had to be stopped from seizing power. Moreover, she held it quite possible that authoritarian governments could evolve into democratic governments and opposed the Carter administration's policy of pressuring them to bring about changes in their HUMAN-RIGHTS policies.

Foreign policy analysts often distinguish between possession and milieu goals. The former are goals such as allies and markets that can belong to one state and denied to others. Milieu goals are different. They are not the property of any one state but are part of the environment in which the foreign-policy actions of all states are conducted. For

the United States, promoting democracy has been both a possession and a milieu goal. Cold war competition with the Soviet Union made it a possession goal. Countries were either pro-American or pro-Soviet. While in the developing world being pro-American did not automatically translate into being democratic, the two were virtually identical in the industrialized world. Promoting democracy has served as a milieu goal when it is cast in the light of traditional thinking about America's role in the world. During the cold war American policy makers rejected the isolationist argument for withdrawal from world affairs and embraced a vision in which American values could only flourish in a world whose beliefs and values mirrored those of the United States. Democracy was a key component of this international system.

The dual nature of efforts to promote democracy carried a number of implications for American foreign policy during the cold war. First, it led policy makers to devote considerable resources to promoting democratic governments. It was the perceived need to bolster pro-Western Italian political parties in the face of communist challenges that led to the first CENTRAL INTELLIGENCE AGENCY (CIA) COVERT ACTION undertakings in 1948. In the following decades the CIA would become a covert supporter of numerous political parties, candidates, labor unions, student groups, and newspapers. Second, because rhetoric about promoting democracy often conflicted with what the United States was actually doing, considerable inconsistency occurred in American foreign policy. For example, the Eisenhower administration openly spoke of "rolling back the iron curtain," but it did not come to the aid of Hungarian freedom fighters in 1956 when they rose up against the Communist authorities. The problem of consistency in promoting democracy was especially pronounced in America's dealings with Third World regimes. The United States seldom, if ever, pressed a pro-American authoritarian government to move toward democracy when it feared that leftist groups might triumph. Finally, the rhetorical importance given to building democracy caused it to become part of the domestic political debate over the broader conduct of American foreign policy that was ushered in by the VIETNAM WAR. Conservative internationalists saw military POWER and covert action as legitimate means for building democracy. Liberal internationalists rejected this assertion in favor of economic development and human-rights initiatives.

The dualistic nature of promoting democracy as a goal in American foreign policy continues in the post–cold war world. With the fall of communism and the establishment of a democratic political order in RUSSIA, a wave of optimism engulfed those active in the democratization process. Russia was not alone. BRAZIL, PAKISTAN, SOUTH KOREA, and Uruguay, among others, also took steps toward democratization in the 1980s. In the 1990s more than half of all African states had begun to explore political reforms that might lead to the establishment of democracy. More generally, commentators again argued that a democratic world would be a peaceful world, since the historical record showed that democracies did not go to war against one another.

By the first years of the 21st century some of this optimism had faded. Backsliding was evident in many areas. In Latin America states such as ARGENTINA and Brazil struggled with economic problems. In COLOMBIA democracy was caught up in a civil war in which long-standing social and political grievances were joined with DRUG TRAFFICKING. In VENEZUELA challenges from the military reappeared. Russian democracy continued to struggle against a backdrop of deteriorating social and economic conditions together with a war in Chechnya. Around Russia, in the CENTRAL ASIAN REPUBLICS and Eastern Europe, communist parties were making electoral comebacks, and ruling elites were described as having become tired of democracy. The ASIAN FINANCIAL CRISIS of the 1990s carried spillover effects into domestic politics as political parties long in power struggled to counter charges of corruption and economic mismanagement. With their actions at Tiananmen Square, Chinese authorities made it clear that they saw economic reform and political reform as two distinct processes. In addition to the traditional economic problems found in Africa, attempts to build democracy there now also had to deal with the long-term impact of the HIV/AIDS pandemic and renewal of widespread civil and ethnic violence.

Democratization is a policy goal that commands widespread support among the American public. For that reason, it will continue to enjoy a prominent place on the foreign-policy agenda. One significant consequence of the emergence of these varied challenges to democratization has been to highlight the need to place democratization strategies in a regional context and move away from the "one size fits all" democratization strategies of the cold war. The American response to the SEPTEMBER 11, 2001, terrorist attacks both promote and hinder democratization. It promotes it by identifying democracy building as a key component in the war on TERRORISM. It threatens to hinder it by demonstrating in AFGHANISTAN and IRAQ how difficult this process can be.

See also DEMOCRATIC PEACE; RUSSIA.

**Further reading:** Carothers, Thomas. *Aiding Democracy Abroad: The Learning Curve.* Washington, D.C.: Carnegie Endowment, 1999; Ikenberry, John G. *After Victory: Institutions, Strategic Restraint and the Rebuilding of Order after Major Wars.* Princeton, N.J.: Princeton University Press, 2000.

## demographics, global

Global demographic trends exert an important influence on the conduct of foreign policy. At base, population is an important ingredient in a country's inventory of national POWER resources. Population is also a complex and multidimensional policy area, involving subthemes such as aging, health, and migration. Finally, population is an issue that intersects with other problems, such as environmental degradation, poverty, and economic development.

It is common to speak of the world experiencing a population explosion; in fact, the 20th century has had the fastest population growth in history. The world's population grew to about 1 billion by 1700. It did not reach 1.6 billion until 1900. In 2000 the world's population had grown to some 6 billion people. The actual rate of growth peaked in the 1970s and has slowed since then. Several key trends exist beneath the surface of these figures. First, whereas in 1950 RUSSIA and Europe made up 22 percent of the world's population, today they make up 13 percent, and it is estimated that in 2050 they will make up 7.5 percent. In 1950 six of the 10 most populous states were in the developed world. By 2020 only the United States and Russia will remain on the top 10 list. By 2050 the global 65+ age cohort will triple in size to about 16 percent of the world's population. At the other end of the age continuum, several developing states will experience a youth bulge. AFGHANISTAN, PAKISTAN, SAUDI ARABIA, Yemen, and IRAQ will be most affected by this phenomenon.

The significance of these demographic trends can be seen by looking at the aging and youth bulge problem in closer detail. By 2050 nearly 1.5 billion people will be over the age of 65. As noted above, this is about 16 percent of the world's population. In the United States only 6.9 percent of the population is 65 or older. ITALY is already at the 19 percent level, with FRANCE expected to reach that mark by 2003, JAPAN in 2005, and GREAT BRITAIN in 2021. The United States is not expected to reach this point until 2023. The aging trend also affects two potential U.S. rivals, Russia and CHINA. By 2050 China is projected to have 300 million people over the age of 65. This is larger than the current size of the population in the United States. Not only is the Russian population aging, but it is also shrinking. The Russian population stood at 148.7 million in 1992. By 2050 it is expected to shrink to 118 million, approximately its 1960 population.

Taken as a whole the aging structure of the global population is likely to create a situation in which the United States will face a heavier burden in the areas of PEACEKEEPING and military interventions because its allies will have smaller armies and will be less able to accept global responsibilities. There is also concern that demographic trends will add to the number of humanitarian and military interventions the United States may be asked to make. High fertility states with few health resources available, such as Sierra Leone and LIBERIA, can be the source of famines and epidemics that require international intervention. Divergent fertility rates between feuding ethnic groups could affect regional balances of power and create tensions.

The aging population also will present challenges for continued global economic prosperity, as key developed states will have fewer citizens in the working age group and will face significant expenditure increases in the social-service sector. In particular the aging challenge will work to reduce the economic power of China and Japan because fewer resources will be available for investing in new technologies and infrastructure. Some speculate that the declining size of Russia's workforce will force it to import labor from neighboring states, create ethnic tensions, and perhaps breed a sense of vulnerability on the part of military officials.

The world's youth bulge presents another set of foreign-policy challenges for the United States. It refers to those in the 15-to-29 age cohort. Most of the states expected to experience a youth bulge lack the economic, political, or bureaucratic resources to effectively integrate these people into society. In the Middle East, unemployment is a major problem for the young, semieducated, urban dwellers. In sub-Saharan Africa, HIV/AIDS is a major problem for this age group. The youth bulge may also become a source of challenges to government authority. The Kurdish insurgency against Turkey has been propelled forward by a youth bulge. In Sri Lanka, the Sinhalese national insurgency in 1970 and the Tamil rebellion in the 1980s fed off a youth bulge. During this period more than 20 percent of the population was in the 15–24 age group. The government sent 14,000 youths to rehabilitation centers. By the mid-1970s, a time of heightened anti-American sentiment, half of Iran's population was under 16 and two-thirds was under 30. Some estimates suggest that the Palestinian population on the West Bank will grow from 1.8 million in 1990 to 4.7 million in 2020. Israel's population will only grow from 4.6 million to 6.7 million during this time period.

Forecasters fear that the youth bulge may thus have the effect of destabilizing key American allies in the developing world and also serve as fertile recruiting ground for radical and terrorist movements. One common method to relieve the population pressure brought on by a youth bulge is migration. But large-scale migration brings with it its own problems. As these youth move to jobs in other countries, they create diasporas that will lobby governments, including that of the United States, to intervene to protect their countrypeople in times of need. They also risk becoming the targets of discrimination in their adopted homelands and the focal point of international tensions.

Finally, it should be noted that predicting demographic trends is not easy. Population figures can be altered by any number of factors. War, civil and international, is the most common. Health problems are second. The United States Census Bureau had predicted that SOUTH AFRICA would gain 6 million people by 2025. Now it estimates that South Africa will lose almost 9 million people by that year. The reason for the change is the high prevalence of AIDS in that country.

See also POPULATION POLICY.

**Further reading:** Bailey, Ronald, ed. *The True State of the Planet.* New York: Free Press, 1995; Central Intelligence Agency. *Long Term Demographic Trends: Reshaping the Geopolitical Landscape.* Washington, D.C.: U.S. Government Printing Office, July 2001; Lutz, Wolfgang. "The Future of World Population." *Population Bulletin* 49 (1994).

## détente

*Détente* is the term used to describe American foreign policy roughly from the end of the VIETNAM WAR until the 1979 Soviet invasion of AFGHANISTAN. It marked a significant change in direction from the military-oriented and confrontational nature of CONTAINMENT. It was predicated on the need to reach an accommodation with the other major powers rather than dominate or isolate them. Disagreement exists as to whether détente is best seen as a successor foreign-policy strategy to containment or merely a means of implementing containment under changed circumstances. The principal changes were a reduction in American military power after VIETNAM and the absence of a societal consensus on the proper direction of American foreign policy.

The intellectual foundation for détente is found in the work of HENRY KISSINGER, who served first as NATIONAL SECURITY ADVISOR to President RICHARD NIXON and then as SECRETARY OF STATE to Nixon and President GERALD FORD. To Kissinger, a stable INTERNATIONAL SYSTEM could exist only if it was seen as legitimate by all of the major powers. This was not the case in the post–WORLD WAR II international system. The Soviet Union and CHINA were revolutionary powers whose principal foreign-policy goals included imposing their views on others. Kissinger was careful to note that legitimacy was not the same thing as justice or peace. A concern for legitimacy focused solely on devising agreed upon international arrangements managing global affairs and on establishing permissible aims and methods for the conduct of foreign policy. The key was that the major powers would recognize each others' rights and national interests, and violations of these basic operating principles would be punished.

The tactical centerpiece of détente was a strategy of linkages whereby the Nixon-Ford-Carter administrations sought to accomplish two objectives. First, Soviet foreign-policy behavior in one area would be linked with its behavior in another. Second, American power in one area could be used to compensate for weaknesses in another. Thus, undesirable Soviet military behavior could be punished or rewarded by addressing its economic policy, thus substituting American economic power for American military power. An important aspect of this linkage strategy in Kissinger's formulation was that it applied only to Soviet foreign policy. U.S. foreign-policy initiatives were not linked to Soviet domestic policy. This view was not shared by all within the United States, and the JACKSON-VANIK AMENDMENT to the 1974 Trade Reform Act explicitly linked the granting of MOST-FAVORED-NATION trade status to the Soviet Union's willingness to allow Jews to emigrate.

Most commentators identify three international agreements as lying at the heart of détente. The first is the 1972 STRATEGIC ARMS LIMITATION TALKS (SALT) I ARMS CONTROL agreement that sought to place limits on the U.S.–Soviet nuclear arms race. The second is the 1972 Shanghai Communiqué, which ended the more than 30-year policy of attempting to isolate Communist China and deny it a legitimate place in the international community. The third agreement is the 1975 HELSINKI ACCORDS, which are seen as closing the book on WORLD WAR II by recognizing that European boundaries were, in fact, permanent. It called for the peaceful resolution of disputes and respect for HUMAN RIGHTS.

Détente failed to establish an enduring basis on which to build a new relationship with China and the Soviet Union. A fundamental problem lay in differing perceptions of what détente meant. While Kissinger recognized its limits, détente was sold to the American public as the equivalent of peace. When Soviet-sponsored aggression continued in Africa and as charges of arms control violations mounted, détente lost much of its credibility. Evidence suggests that the Soviet Union and China embraced definitions of détente closer to Kissinger's original formulation, a formulation that recognized continued conflict but sought to make it safer.

Within the United States, both conservatives and liberals criticized détente. Each objected to its status quo orientation and lack of any clear moral purpose. Liberals tended to argue that détente was an outmoded foreign policy based on balance of power principles in an era that demanded a new forward-looking foreign policy based on a recommitment to traditional American values. Conservatives took exception to détente's willingness to accept the Soviet Union as a full partner. To them this was tantamount to ideological surrender. They saw nothing as having changed in Soviet foreign-policy behavior. The Soviet invasion of Afghanistan served as a vindication of this belief and laid the foundation for a return to a cold war orientation under President RONALD REAGAN.

See also CARTER, JIMMY; RUSSIA.

**Further reading:** Bell, Coral. *The Diplomacy of Détente: The Kissinger Era.* New York: St. Martin's, 1977.

## deterrence failures

Deterrence is a strategy in which the threat of military force is used in an attempt to prevent an opponent from taking a hostile action. Deterrence may involve nuclear weapons or conventional forces. A significant body of literature has developed on how to construct deterrence strategies. Its key elements are the possession of a capability to carry out the threatened action, credibility in making the threat, and the ability to communicate the threat clearly to the opponent. Far less attention has been given to the questions of how and why deterrence may fail. And deterrence does fail. Just looking at the post–COLD WAR era, the United States failed to deter IRAQ from invading KUWAIT and repeatedly failed in its efforts to deter escalations in the fighting in the Balkans. It has also experienced mixed success, at best, in using military force to deter terrorist attacks. More often than not U.S. military attacks on terrorists have been putative and retaliatory in nature. To the extent that the United States plays the role of peacekeeper or policeman of the post–cold war era, policy makers must be sensitive to the constant possibility of failure and the means by which it may come about.

When deterrence fails one of two general conditions results. The first is appeasement. Here the objectionable action occurs and is accepted because no military action is forthcoming. This is the situation that took place in interwar Europe when GERMANY's expansionist moves into CZECHOSLOVAKIA and Austria went unchallenged. The second outcome is war. This occurred in the PERSIAN GULF when the United States refused to accept the Iraqi invasion of Kuwait as legitimate.

There is no single path to war growing out of a deterrence failure. One possibility is a surprise attack, where the state that is the target of the deterrent strategy launches an unexpected military offensive. This is not a bolt-out-of-the-blue strike in which no warning exists but rather a military action that catches the deterring state off-guard in terms of objective, timing, scale, or purpose. Iraq's attack on Kuwait fits this category. The United States was carefully watching Iraq's preparations for war but was convinced up until the final hours that its military movements were designed to intimidate Kuwait rather than conquer it. The root cause here may either lay with the improper design of the deterrence strategy—it was not implemented in such a way that it could accomplish its goals—or with fundamental miscalculations regarding the enemy's power, intentions, resolve, or strategy.

A second possibility is that deterrence fails through a process of crisis escalation. Here each side has engaged in a series of competitive countermoves designed to establish their credibility and demonstrate their capability. At first, these moves are carefully orchestrated and controlled, but over time they take on a life of their own. Instead of behaving as if they were engaged in a chess match, rival policy makers act more like tired prizefighters who instinctively counterpunch but no longer have a strategy for winning the fight. The outbreak of WORLD WAR I fits this mold. It came about through a series of prescribed moves and countermoves made by Europe's great powers that were undertaken with little appreciation for the direction they were taking Europe.

A third way in which deterrence can fail is accidentally. This type of deterrence failure received a great deal of attention during the cold war. Much popular attention was given to the possibility of an authorized attack. Far more problematic was the possibility of a deterrence failure resulting from the inability of early warning systems to perform properly. Two types of failures were identified. A type I error was the failure to recognize that an attack had been launched against the United States. A type II error was the incorrect conclusion that such an attack had been launched. The type II error was most relevant for deterrence failures since it would lead to inappropriate and escalatory actions. Type II errors have taken place in the United States. During the 1950s a flock of Canada geese were read by the Distant Early Warning (DEW) line of radars as a Soviet missile attack. In 1960 meteor showers and lunar radar reflections led the Ballistic Missile Early Warning System (BMEWS) to conclude an attack was under way. In 1980 a computer chip malfunctioned, causing about 100 B-52 bombers to be readied for takeoff. A year earlier human error caused U.S. missiles and submarines to go on a heightened alert status.

See also BALLISTIC MISSILE DEFENSE; DETERRENCE STRATEGIES; NUCLEAR WEAPONS.

**Further reading:** George, Alexander, and Richard Smoke. *Deterrence in American Foreign Policy: Theory and Practice.* New York: Columbia University Press, 1974.

## deterrence strategies

Deterrence strategies are designed to prevent an opponent from undertaking an objectionable course of action. The most intensive studies of deterrence have focused on strategies that will prevent the use of NUCLEAR WEAPONS. Deterrence cannot be willed into existence or simply assumed to exist through the possession of a large nuclear arsenal.

Nuclear deterrence depends upon the successful integration of three elements: a nuclear arsenal capable of carrying out one's strategy, credibility, and the ability to communicate one's seriousness and intentions to the enemy.

A traditional starting point used in distinguishing between deterrence strategies is with the type of nuclear capability needed. This debate usually focused on the possession of a first- or second-strike posture. In a first-strike strategy a state seeks to deter a potential attacker through the threat of attacking first. It envisions a massive use of force such that the enemy will be unable to inflict serious damage with its surviving nuclear forces. In a second-strike strategy a state seeks to deter an attack by possessing the capability to absorb an enemy's nuclear attack and retaliate with so much force that it can inflict an unacceptable level of damage on its society. Harold Brown, SECRETARY OF DEFENSE under President JIMMY CARTER, defined a second-strike capability in terms of the ability to destroy the 200 largest Soviet cities. A third option also appears to exist. Known as minimum deterrence it asserts that a state will be deterred from launching a nuclear attack by the possession of a small nuclear force capable of destroying a carefully selected target list.

The selection of a target list logically follows from the selection of a first- or second-strike strategy. By their very nature first-strike strategies must concentrate on destroying an enemy's offensive forces and their associated command-and-control systems. This is known as counterforce targeting. To allocate too many nuclear weapons to any other set of targets runs the risk that enough of the opponents nuclear weapons will survive and inflict serious damage on one's own society. Second-strike strategies must adopt a countervalue targeting policy in which they direct their nuclear weapons against population and industrial targets. Here, the potential attacker's population is held "hostage." Countervalue targeting is objected to by many on moral grounds. In 1983 the National Conference of Catholic Bishops spoke out strongly against this policy. The hostage effect is defended on the grounds that there is nothing that can be done to escape this situation so long as nuclear weapons exist. Going second and targeting military sites would amount to blowing up empty silos, something unlikely to deter an attacker. Civilians are the only possible targets. Some strategists have sought to escape this dilemma by advocating a policy of limited strategic options that would allow for flexibility in nuclear retaliatory plans between the extremes of doing nothing and targeting civilians. Stability in the COLD WAR was seen as existing when each side adopted a second-strike strategy, producing a situation of MUTUAL ASSURED DESTRUCTION (MAD).

Also following from the selection of a first- or second-strike strategy are the characteristics of the nuclear weapons needed. A first-strike strategy requires highly accurate high-speed weapons that are capable of destroying hardened targets. Survivability is not a concern. Land-based intercontinental ballistic missiles (ICBMs) fit this description. A second-strike nuclear force above all else must be survivable. Given its target set, accuracy, large payloads, and speed are not crucial. Manned bombers and submarine-launched ballistic missiles (SLBMs) are the most appropriate choices.

Another major debate is whether or not to add a defensive component of a deterrence strategy. Such a move is advocated by those who endorse the concept of a BALLISTIC MISSILE DEFENSE system or the STRATEGIC DEFENSE INITIATIVE proposed by President RONALD REAGAN. Their advocates see the defense system as a means of escaping from the hostage effect. Opponents question its technical feasibility and desirability. They assert that any move to lessen the certainty of the hostage effect that lies at the heart of MAD is destabilizing and increases the temptation to use nuclear weapons.

The fundamental credibility problem in deterrence is making one's threat to unleash a first- or second-strike believable. A complicating factor here is that not all deterrence situations are alike. We can distinguish between immediate deterrence, in which the threat of war is a real and distinct possibility, and general deterrence, in which the principal fear is that the opponent might use force to gain an advantage should the opportunity arise. Most analysts focus on the challenges inherent in immediate deterrence. How do you convince another state that you will not back down? The problem is seen as especially acute the farther away the point of conflict is from your homeland, a situation referred to as extended deterrence. A commonly used tactic is to create a trip wire, or line in the sand, that, when crossed, produces an automatic response. Troops will often be dispatched to defend an ally in an effort to make deterrence credible. Written guarantees and highly visible public pledges of support, such as President JOHN KENNEDY's trip to Berlin at the height of the BERLIN CRISIS, 1961, are also employed.

Two different types of communication problems must be addressed in the construction of a successful deterrence strategy. First, one must be able to communicate with an opponent who may not share one's language or culture. Signals must be understood. It does no good to draw a line in the sand if it is not recognized as such. Second, one must be able to communicate with one's own nuclear forces. This problem is especially great the more one embraces a policy of limited strategic options. In simple terms what is needed is a shoot-look-shoot capability. This problem is often referred to as the command, control, communication, and intelligence (C3I) problem and involves overcoming both bureaucratic and technical obstacles to communication.

Finally, it needs to be noted that deterrence is not the only use to which nuclear weapons can be put. Some have asserted that nuclear weapons can also be used to fight a nuclear war. Official U.S. deterrence strategy has never embraced this position, but Soviet strategy did for a time. Still another possibility is to use them to compel another state. Here nuclear weapons would be used as a strategy designed to force an opponent to reverse a course of action already undertaken.

**Further reading:** Eden, Lynn, and Steven Miller, ed. *Nuclear Arguments: Understanding the Strategic Nuclear Arms and Arms Control Debates.* Ithaca, N.Y.: Cornell University Press, 1989; Green, Philip. *Deadly Logic.* Columbus: Ohio State University Press, 1966; Mearsheimer, John J. *Conventional Deterrence.* Ithaca, N.Y.: Cornell University Press, 1983; Morgan, Patrick. *Deterrence: A Conceptual Analysis.* Beverly Hills, Calif.: Sage, 1977.

## diplomacy

Diplomacy is a process of communication between governments. It is the central means by which states seek to protect and promote their interests in world politics. Diplomacy is associated with the STATE DEPARTMENT and EMBASSIES, but it is a far more all-encompassing activity. Because of its military, political, and economic power, the United States is deeply involved in diplomatic activity. Important controversies surround the pluses and minuses of each of the major forms of modern diplomacy that are noted below.

Diplomacy is commonly thought of as a two-pronged undertaking. Under normal circumstances it is concerned with managing the day-to-day affairs of the state. When conflict is present it is assumed that diplomacy is a problem-solving exercise in which states seek to resolve their differences on mutually favorable terms. As a communication process, however, diplomacy can advance a number of goals. Diplomacy can be concerned primarily with obtaining information. Diplomacy can be used to stall for time until political or military conditions permit a state to act. It can also be used to impose on other states a solution to a problem. Mutual benefit need not be present. Finally, diplomacy can be used for propaganda purposes to either put one's own state in a positive light or make others look bad.

At the time of America's independence diplomacy had acquired a distinctive character reflecting its distant roots in ancient GREECE and Rome and its more recent roots in the 1648 Treaty of Westphalia. Today we refer to the diplomacy of this period as classical diplomacy. It was European-centered and conducted in secret. Diplomacy was the province of elites who shared a common cultural background and was conducted for the purpose of promoting national or state interests and not global causes. It had developed its own inner logic of formal rules of etiquette and protocol that facilitated and regularized international state-to-state communications. American involvement in diplomacy can be dated to the Second Continental Congress that established a Committee of Secret Correspondence to engage in communications with friendly political forces abroad. On March 3, 1776, it sent Silas Deane as its secret agent to FRANCE for the purpose of purchasing weapons and exploring the possibility of an alliance. Deane has been described as a "scheming politician." After independence America's diplomatic core grew in stature with the addition of THOMAS JEFFERSON, JOHN ADAMS, and John Jay.

WOODROW WILSON helped usher in the period of modern diplomacy when he put forward his FOURTEEN POINTS. Numbered among them was a call for "open covenants, openly arrived at." This demand challenged one of the core principles of classical diplomacy, and the increased role of the public is one of the defining features of modern diplomacy. This role is evident in several ways. Legislatures now more actively debate the pros and cons of potential agreements. PUBLIC OPINION has become an important controlling factor in the bargaining and negotiating process. In fact, it has become so important that an entire area of diplomacy, public diplomacy, has emerged that is concerned with shaping the views of the public concerning the advantages and disadvantages of agreements.

Modern diplomacy is also characterized by an expansion and diversification in scope and coverage. No longer is diplomacy European-centered or carried out by elites from common backgrounds. Moreover, diplomacy is no longer concerned solely with promoting narrowly defined state interests. Transnational interests and universal standards are now major elements of many negotiations. These changes have also brought an expansion in the formal settings within which diplomacy is carried out. Traditional diplomacy was largely conducted on a bilateral basis except for a select few major European conferences, and even then only the great powers attended. CONFERENCE DIPLOMACY, in which most of the states of the world are represented, has become a prominent feature of modern diplomacy. So too has summit diplomacy, in which the heads of government interact directly with one another. Modern transportation and communication technologies play a central role in this change. Woodrow Wilson was the first American president to go overseas. RICHARD NIXON would leave for Europe 33 days after taking office. GEORGE H. W. BUSH had meetings with 135 other leaders in his first year in office. He spoke on the phone with foreign leaders some 190 times that year, giving rise to the phrase "rolodex diplomacy." One noticeable consequence of this trend to greater personal involvement in diplomacy by government leaders is a decline in the importance of the ambassador and the State Department in the diplomatic process.

**Further reading:** George, Alexander. *Forceful Persuasion: Coercive Diplomacy as an Alternative to War.* Washington, D.C.: United States Institute of Peace, 1991; Ikle, Fred. *Every War Must End.* New York: Columbia University Press, 1971; Putnam, Robert. "Diplomacy and Domestic Politics: The Logic of Two-Level Games." *International Organization* 42 (1988).

## director of central intelligence

The position of director of central intelligence (DCI) was established by the 1947 NATIONAL SECURITY ACT. According to it, the DCI is the primary adviser to the president and the NATIONAL SECURITY COUNCIL on national INTELLIGENCE. The DCI also serves as head of the CENTRAL INTELLIGENCE AGENCY (CIA). Executive orders have granted the DCI the power to develop a consolidated national intelligence budget and to direct the analytic and collection tasking efforts of all members of the INTELLIGENCE COMMUNITY. These members include the CIA, the DEFENSE INTELLIGENCE AGENCY, the NATIONAL SECURITY AGENCY, the FEDERAL BUREAU OF INVESTIGATION, the TREASURY DEPARTMENT, the ENERGY DEPARTMENT, the STATE DEPARTMENT, and army, navy, air force, and marine intelligence.

Few DCIs have sought, and none have truly achieved, real managerial control over the intelligence community. The most recent to try was Stansfield Turner, President JIMMY CARTER's DCI, who ran into strong opposition from SECRETARY OF DEFENSE Harold Brown. DCIs have not given priority to their role as head of the intelligence community because they face significant obstacles in trying to exercise this power. Only the CIA is a separate organization. All other elements of the intelligence community are parts of larger organizations, most often the DEFENSE DEPARTMENT. This results in a situation in which most members of the intelligence community are more responsive to departmental positions and priorities than they are to the orders of the DCI. As a result, the DCI's budgetary authority over them remains largely unrealized, and the ability to direct intelligence collection efforts is imperfect.

In defining their role as head of the CIA, DCIs have professed three different outlooks: managerial, covert action, and intelligence estimating. Only Jon McCone has given primacy to the intelligence estimating role, and he was largely an outsider to intelligence before his appointment. Alan Dulles and Richard Helms, two men who headed the CIA for long periods of time, stressed the COVERT ACTION side of the agency's mission. Since Helms was replaced by James Schlesinger, DCIs have attended to adopt a managerial orientation. A common theme to these managerial efforts is to increase White House control over the CIA. This was particularly evident in the actions of Turner and

William Casey, who served as DCI under President RONALD REAGAN. One consequence of this trend is the charge that intelligence estimating has become politicized, as its conclusions often appear to be driven by the concerns and values of senior management rather than intelligence professionals. This was a charge heard frequently about the CIA under Casey and his successor, William Gates. The charge of politicalization has also extended to covert action. The charge of politicizing intelligence was also leveled at the GEORGE W. BUSH administration for its portrayal of IRAQ as being in possession of weapons of mass destruction in the period leading up to the IRAQ WAR in spite of warnings by the CIA that this was not the case.

See also COUNTERINTELLIGENCE.

## disarmament

All disarmament proposals are based upon a single premise: Weapons are the primary cause of war. Thus, they share a single concern: Remove these weapons. Disarmament is significant because, along with arms control, it represents one way of pursuing national security without relying upon the possession of a balance or preponderance of military power.

Historically, disarmament has been practiced in two different ways. First, after a war, disarmament has been imposed upon the defeated state by the victor. The TREATY OF VERSAILLES limited the post–WORLD WAR I German army to 100,000 troops in hopes of preventing it from possessing an offensive capability. The victors have rarely been able to remain united and act together to enforce such limitations. The other type of disarmament is voluntary disarmament in which states seek to negotiate a mutually acceptable framework within which to reduce the size of military establishments. The Hague Conferences and the WASHINGTON NAVAL CONFERENCE are pre–WORLD WAR II examples of efforts to institute voluntary disarmament. Both were limited in the scope of their agreement and duration.

The ultimate logic of disarmament points to the total elimination of all weapons. This is known as general and complete disarmament. Such proposals draw their inspiration from a number of sources, the most important of which are deeply felt moral and ethical objections to war as an instrument of foreign policy, fears about the influence of the military over society, and concerns over the economic costs of war. Efforts to institute worldwide bans on the production and use of chemical and biological weapons fall into this category of disarmament proposals.

The far-reaching nature of this type of disarmament causes conservative defense planners to dismiss it as utopian. Yet, PUBLIC OPINION over complete and general disarmament proposals tends to be positive, leaving it to the state that declines to participate to explain why it is opposed to peace and favors arms races. An example of a complete and general disarmament proposal that resonated well with the public but created strategic problems is the proposal Secretary-General Mikhail Gorbachev made at the 1986 Reykjavík Summit. He proposed eliminating all nuclear armed ballistic missiles by 1996. President RONALD REAGAN accepted the plan only to turn on it when Gorbachev insisted that the price was abandoning the STRATEGIC DEFENSE INITIATIVE, or "Star Wars." Former SECRETARY OF DEFENSE James Schlesinger complained that in accepting Gorbachev's offer for total strategic disarmament Reagan had "jettisoned twenty five years of deterrence doctrine" and left it with little military power to protect its vital interests.

Often, disarmament proposals are more concrete and limited in scope. One type is referred to as disarmament to the lowest level of domestic safety. This is what President WOODROW WILSON hoped to achieve with his FOURTEEN POINTS and the limits it placed on GERMANY's army. The underlying assumption is that the public does not want war and that a sending a small army to war leaves a leader vulnerable to unrest at home. A second type of more limited disarmament is regional disarmament. It seeks to reduce or eliminate weapons in a specific area. A major form of such agreements is the creation of nuclear-free zones. In 1967 the Treaty of Tlatelolco created a nuclear-free zone in Latin America by prohibiting the possession, deployment, or testing of nuclear weapons in the region. The United States was not a party to the agreement, but along with the Soviet Union (see RUSSIA) and GREAT BRITAIN it has endorsed it. The Antarctic Treaty of 1959 bans the use of Antarctica for military purposes, including military testing. A 1971 treaty forbids placing nuclear weapons on the seabed, and the 1967 Outer-Space Treaty prohibits placing weapons in Earth orbit or stationing them in outer space.

Historically, disarmament proposals have not been endorsed as widely as has ARMS CONTROL, which starts from the premise that the true source of national security problems can be found in the political realm rather than with weapons themselves. They have been seen more as propaganda exercises than as true efforts in security building. Beginning in the Reagan administration, however, this began to change as Reagan and many Americans became disillusioned with the pace and success of arms control efforts symbolized by the STRATEGIC ARMS LIMITATION TALKS (SALT). Reagan announced that he wished to produce real cuts in weapons and not just set limits on their numbers and launched the STRATEGIC ARMS REDUCTION TALKS (START). An offshoot of these talks produced the first agreement between the United States and the Soviet Union—the INTERMEDIATE NUCLEAR FORCES (INF) TREATY that actually led to the reduction in number and placement of missiles.

A particularly important and controversial innovation in disarmament occurred in 1991 when Congress passed the Nunn-Lugar Act, also known as the Cooperative Threat Reduction Program. It was cosponsored by Senators Sam Nunn (D-Ga.) and Richard Lugar (R-Ind.). The legislation provided funds to help identify, destroy, and dispose of nuclear and chemical weapons in Russia. The disintegration of the Soviet Union had created a situation where many feared that terrorists could obtain access to these weapons or that Russian authorities might use them without the proper authority. It is estimated that Nunn-Lugar funds resulted in the deactivation of 5,014 warheads and 384 ICBMs. The program was opposed by groups such as the neo-isolationist THINK TANK the Cato Institute because it was providing assistance to a state that was still at least potentially an enemy and did little to advance U.S. national security interests. Funding for Nunn-Lugar began to lapse and be reduced over the decade since it was passed but the program received new interest following the SEPTEMBER 11, 2001, terrorist attacks.

Though on the ascendancy, the principle of disarmament continues to be challenged. During the Reagan administration the Star Wars defense system would have placed defensive weapons, such as laser beams, in outer space. While they are technically not WEAPONS OF MASS DESTRUCTION and therefore not prohibited by the Outer-Space Treaty, introducing them would have violated the spirit of the pact and represented a militarization of space. The shift in focus from the bilateral U.S.-Soviet nuclear relationship to a multilateral one in which proliferation is the central problem also presents major challenges to disarmament. It takes us back to the pre–World War II conferences when disarmament agreements required the consent of many states. The presence of multiple parties to an agreement also dramatically increases the political and technological problems of monitoring and verifying that these agreements are being adhered to. These problems have been met with considerable success in the area of ballistic missiles but less so in the area of chemical and biological weapons, as evidenced by the difficulties of monitoring IRAQ's compliance with UNITED NATIONS–mandated disarmament following the PERSIAN GULF WAR.

**Further reading:** Freedman, Lawrence. *The Evolution of Nuclear Strategy.* New York: St. Martins, 1983; Myrdal, Alva. *The Game of Disarmament: How the United States and Russia Run the Arms Race.* New York: Pantheon, 1977.

## dollar diplomacy

Dollar diplomacy is the name given to the early 20th-century American foreign policy that sought to use American economic strength rather than military POWER to guarantee U.S. national security and economic interests. It is most associated with the administration of WILLIAM HOWARD TAFT and its policy toward Latin America.

Taft held the view that the United States was a major commercial and banking power; along with his SECRETARY OF STATE Philander Knox, he promoted a vision of American foreign policy centered on the concept of a "traveling salesman." The United States would actively encourage and support American bankers and industrialists in their efforts to secure profit abroad. To Taft this was not economic IMPERIALISM because the United States was not trying to exploit others. Rather, American investments were seen as bringing prosperity to both the local population and American investors.

There was, however, an important national security dimension to dollar diplomacy. The United States had become concerned that Latin American states might become dependent on European capital for their economic development. This would provide European powers with a foothold in the region from which they could exert political influence over the internal affairs of these states and ultimately manipulate them for their own purposes. Taft's strategy was to force Latin American governments not to do business with European financiers. They were to reject new European funds in favor of American funds and replace existing European loans with American loans. With U.S. help these governments would be reorganized and put on a sounder financial footing. A key step in this process was the American takeover of customs houses, a favorite and profitable target of revolutionaries. The assumption was that once under American control revolutionaries would be less likely to challenge the government. The end result from the Taft administration's perspective would be a stable economy and peaceful political order that would attract additional American firms, thus earning profits for U.S. investors.

The clearest example of dollar diplomacy came in NICARAGUA. The Taft administration was particularly sensitive to events there because of its proximity to the PANAMA CANAL. In 1909 Nicaragua's entire debt was financed through a syndicate of European investors. Nicaragua's customs income was put up as payment for the loan. A revolution broke out in 1909 directed at removing the anti-American Nicaraguan leader José Santos Zelaya from power. By August 1910 the revolutionaries led by the pro-American Adolfo Díaz were in control of the country. Díaz turned to the United States for financial help to stabilize the economy. The United States refused to recognize the new government until it arranged for a new American loan to pay off and replace the existing European loan. Nicaragua also agreed to turn over control of its customs revenues and customs operation to the United States during the life of the loan.

Economic conditions continued to deteriorate and caused U.S. banks to exert unofficial control over Nicaragua's finances. The Senate rejected the proposed Knox-Castrillo Convention in May 1912, and this unofficial relationship continued. In July 1912 a revolt broke out against Díáz, and the Taft administration sent some 2,500 Marines to restore order. The main body of troops were removed that year, but a contingent remained until 1925. In an effort to quiet criticism in the region Knox made a good-will tour through the states surrounding the Caribbean in March 1912. He said, "I beg to assure you . . . that my Government does not covet an inch of territory south of the Rio Grande."

Dollar diplomacy continued in a fashion under Taft's successor, WOODROW WILSON. This was somewhat surprising since Wilson had denounced dollar diplomacy soon after taking office and promised a new policy for the region, going so far as to speak of a "spiritual union." His administration did not, however, act on this missionary rhetoric when given the opportunity. Rather than obtaining better terms from the Wilson administration when he sought to renegotiate the terms of the earlier failed treaty, Díáz emerged with a treaty that contained roughly the same provisions. Moreover, the Bryan-Chamorro Treaty also gave the United States the right to intervene in Nicaragua's internal affairs in a manner similar to that permitted by the PLATT AMENDMENT regarding CUBA's affairs.

Dollar diplomacy also played a minor role in America's foreign policy to CHINA, where it was viewed as the "financial expression" of John Hay's OPEN-DOOR policy. The primary focal point was on securing an American economic interest in the South Manchurian Railway as part of a larger plan to construct a transcontinental railway link that would connect with steamer traffic to create a global system of transport. The plan had the backing of the Taft administration but never came to fruition. The initiative was terminated early in the Wilson administration.

**Further reading:** Munro, Daniel G. *Intervention and Dollar Diplomacy in the Caribbean, 1900–1921.* Princeton, N.J.: Princeton University Press, 1964.

## domestic influences on U.S. foreign policy

Studies of U.S. foreign policy typically classify the forces that influence its content and conduct in terms of their relationship to decision makers. The most commonly used organizing frameworks locate these influences in the INTERNATIONAL SYSTEM, the BUREAUCRACY and the individual, and the domestic setting. Domestic influences on U.S. foreign policy include such factors as INTEREST-GROUP lobbying, PUBLIC OPINION, ELECTIONS, the activities of THINK TANKS, and the MEDIA. One of the major

debates in the study of U.S. foreign policy centers on the relative importance of these three sets of influences.

The most popular conceptual frameworks used to study U.S. foreign policy vary in the explanatory weight they accord domestic influences. REALISM emphasizes the primacy of power considerations and the struggle for survival in an anarchic international system. Thus, for the realist, external factors are most important. REVISIONISM, with its neo-Marxian roots, emphasizes the importance of capitalism. This leads revisionists to emphasize the role played by business groups and others that may profit from U.S. foreign policy and to deemphasize institutional factors, personality, and elections. Liberalism emphasizes shared values and common purpose in studying U.S. foreign policy. Often, liberal accounts of U.S. foreign policy emphasize the nature of the problems confronting the United States or the existence of a special U.S. mission as much as they do domestic political forces that promote peace and cooperation.

A second approach to determining the impact of domestic influences on U.S. foreign policy proceeds by examining different issue areas. The assumption is that no single answer exists but that the influence of domestic factors varies with the nature of the policy. The public's influence appears greatest concerning issues in which security and economic issues are present and where the problem has been on the political agenda for a long period of time. As these conditions are removed the influence of domestic forces lessens. Thus, self-contained, "one shot" foreign-policy undertakings are unlikely to be heavily influenced by domestic factors because of the lack of public awareness of the issue, the president's ability to control the flow of information, and the absence of sufficient time for interest groups to mobilize. This is true whether the issue is a crisis or not.

The weight accorded to the public's voice in foreign policy decision making has practical and normative consequences. Viewed from a practical perspective, it is not unrealistic to expect PRESIDENTs to seek out foreign-policy initiatives that minimize the influence of domestic factors. The greater the influence of public opinion, elections, the media, interest groups, and think tanks, the more difficult it is to control the direction that policy will take. Under these conditions the administration is forced to engage in a time consuming and complex "two-level bargaining" process in which it must simultaneously negotiate with foreign governments and the American public.

At the normative level, the issue of how much weight to attach to the public's voice in making foreign-policy decisions cuts to the heart of democratic theory. Should policy decisions reflect the views of the public, whom policy makers are pledged to represent, or should it reflect the professional views of experts in international affairs? Evidence suggests that most policy makers do not share the view that the public voice on foreign policy should prevail. Public attitudes are seen as something to be formed or shaped by a knowledgeable elite rather than something to be obeyed. At its most benign level this is reflected in the belief that the public needs to be educated about foreign-policy issues. At its worst, it takes the form of a manipulative attitude that sees public support as little more than a resource to be used in the political battle over whose policy preferences should prevail.

See also SECTIONALISM.

**Further reading:** Ikenberry, G. John. *American Foreign Policy: Theoretical Essays.* 4th ed. New York: Longman, 2002; Kull, Steven, and I. M. Destler. *Misreading the Public: The Myth of the New Isolationism.* Washington, D.C.: Brookings, 1999; Yankelovich, Daniel, and I. M. Dester, eds. *Beyond the Beltway: Engaging the Public in U.S. Foreign Policy.* New York: Norton, 1994.

## Dominican Republic

The Dominican Republic is located in the Caribbean Sea. It occupies the eastern two-thirds of the island of Hispaniola. HAITI occupies the remainder of the island. It has a population of some 8 million people and an area that is approximately the size of Vermont and New Hampshire combined (18,704 square miles). For much of its early history the Dominican Republic was known as Santo Domingo, its capital city.

The area occupied by the Dominican Republic was visited by Columbus on his first voyage in 1492. Brutal rule by earlier colonizers drastically reduced the size of the indigenous Taino population, and in 1503 Spaniards began bringing African slaves to Hispaniola in order to ensure labor for their plantations. In 1697 Spain ceded the western portion of the island to FRANCE. In 1804 this became the Republic of Haiti. Haitian forces conquered the whole island in 1822 and held it until 1844, when the Dominican Republic gained its independence. In 1861 the Dominican Republic voluntarily retuned to the Spanish Empire. Independence was restored in 1865 and in 1866 was recognized by the United States. The United States has a strong economic presence in the Dominican Republic. A total of 65 percent of the Dominican Republic's imports comes from the United States. The United States receives a similar proportion of its exports.

The Dominican Republic had become an object of U.S. attention in the 1850s. In late 1853 the FRANKLIN PIERCE administration sent an unofficial envoy to the Dominican Republic in hopes of arranging for a lease on a naval base at Samana Bay. An agreement was reached in 1854, but at the urging of the French and British who opposed an American naval presence in the Caribbean Sea the Dominican government added a clause to the agreement requiring that Dominicans "of all complexions" be treated "on the same footing" as citizens of the United States. This clause effectively killed the agreement.

Renewed American interest in the Dominican Republic did not return until after the AMERICAN CIVIL WAR. SECRETARY OF STATE WILLIAM SEWARD traveled to the Dominican Republic in 1866. This was the first trip ever made by a secretary of state outside of the United States. Not only did he agree to recognize Dominican independence, but he authorized negotiations that would lead to its absorption by the United States. These negotiations produced an annexation agreement in 1869. To the surprise of President ULYSSES GRANT, his cabinet objected to the agreement. Grant sent his envoy back to the Dominican Republic, where two new treaties were signed. The first provided for annexation. The second provided for a naval base at Samana Bay. Opposition was not limited to Grant's cabinet, and in 1870 the Senate Committee on Foreign Relations recommended that the annexation treaty be rejected, and the full Senate followed suit with a 28-28 vote that fell well short of the necessary two-thirds majority. In a face-saving gesture the Senate agreed to establish a commission to investigate the matter. It reported back favorably, but no further congressional action was forthcoming. Grant responded by supporting a lease agreement at Samana Bay that was negotiated by a private firm. The agreement reached in 1873 provided for a 100-year lease with virtual sovereignty over the region. An insurrection later that year nullified the lease.

The Dominican Republic next plays a major role in American foreign policy in the administration of TEDDY ROOSEVELT. In the latter half of the 19th century the economy of the Dominican Republic gradually became refocused from European markets to American ones. Its financial situation also deteriorated as large foreign debts were accumulated. In an effort to force the issue and as a show of force, European warships sailed into Dominican waters in 1900 and 1903. In 1904 France threatened to take over Dominican customs houses as a way of obtaining repayment of money owed. Roosevelt responded in December 1904 by putting forward the ROOSEVELT COROLLARY to the MONROE DOCTRINE. In it he reserved for the United States the role of policeman of the Western Hemisphere. He followed this up in 1906 by having the United States take over the job of customs collection in the Dominican Republic. His unilateral action followed some two years of wrangling with the Senate over a proposed Dawson-Sanchez Treaty that would have provided for a U.S. guarantee of the Dominican Republic's territorial integrity and procedure for collecting the Dominican debt. A coalition of Democrats and antiimperialists blocked action on a formal treaty until 1907.

When an insurrection in the Dominican Republic led to the closure of several customs houses in 1912 President

WILLIAM HOWARD TAFT sent in 750 marines to restore order. Domestic unrest continued, however, and in 1916 President WOODROW WILSON dispatched army and naval forces to the Dominican Republic and formally established military rule over the country. It would be 1920 before the United States announced plans to withdraw its occupying army. Negotiations continued into 1922 before the Hughes-Peynado Plan was accepted by both the United States and the Dominican Republic. At issue was whether the U.S. forces would simply leave or if the Dominican government had to formally acknowledge the customs and loan agreements that had been put into place. This latter interpretation was incorporated into the Hughes-Peynaldo Plan, and American forces completed their withdrawal in 1924. Financial sovereignty did not return to the Dominican Republic, however, until 1947, when its foreign debt was paid off.

American officials often touted the Dominican occupation as a model for efforts elsewhere in the hemisphere. In reality it was anything but trouble free. Within the Dominican Republic opposition came from rural peasants and workers and urban intellectuals. American economic interests solidified their hold on the country's economy during this period. In particular, American financial interests came to dominate the sugar industry and much of the agricultural land. An important part of the U.S. occupation was the creation of a national guard. Rafael Trujillo rose rapidly through the ranks of the national guard, becoming chief of staff of the national army in 1928. In 1930 he captured the presidency in a fraudulent election and ruled over the Dominican Republic, either directly or indirectly, until his assassination in 1961.

During the early COLD WAR period Trujillo was treated as a staunch and loyal ally in the struggle against COMMUNISM. By the end of the 1950s this began to change. Now, Trujillo's corrupt and oppressive rule was viewed as a point of vulnerability in the United States's efforts to contain the spread of communism in the hemisphere. It appeared to many that the next Fidel Castro would emerge in the Dominican Republic. A period of domestic instability followed Trujillo's assassination as forces on the political left and right sought to gain and hold power. In 1965 President LYNDON JOHNSON sent some 22,000 U.S. troops to the Dominican Republic to prevent what his administration described as the further spread of communism in the Western Hemisphere. The roots of the crisis that precipitated the invasion date back to the decades of poverty and political oppression under the rule of Rafael Trujillo, who had ruled as a dictator for 31 years. Juan Bosch, a social reformer who had been in exile for 20 years, was elected president to succeed him in 1962. From the outset the Kennedy administration had been skeptical of Bosch's political skills and continued to maintain good relations with the military.

Seven months after taking office, in 1963 just prior to JOHN KENNEDY's assassination, his government was overthrown by the military that announced that it would reestablish a "rightest state." A fragile government was put into office. The United States turned down requests for aid by the Dominican government. Its preference was for installing a new military government that would hold elections that would be won by someone other than Bosch.

In April 1965 pro-Bosch supporters within the military led a revolt against the new military government. Their stated goal was to reestablish constitutional government. They were opposed by pro-Trujillo elements within the military that wanted to reestablish a more conservative military dictatorship. Acting with a great sense of urgency and on the basis of incomplete information that the pro-Bosch forces were controlled by Communists, the Johnson administration quickly ordered 500 marines to the Dominican Republic to prevent "a Moscow-financed, Havana-directed plot to take over the Dominican Republic." Within 10 days more than 22,000 U.S. forces arrived. This was almost half the U.S. presence in VIETNAM. The rapid military build up was a legacy of the BAY OF PIGS invasion and the belief that inadequate forces had contributed greatly to that disaster. Evidence gathered after the invasion provided little support for the claim of a Communist-controlled revolt.

The fear of a Fidel Castro–type figure coming into power in the Dominican Republic had led the Eisenhower administration to consider supporting a coup against Trujillo in 1960. It saw in Trujillo's rule the same excesses that led to Batista's downfall in CUBA. The new Kennedy administration gave its support to anti-Trujillo forces but backed off following the failed Bay of Pigs invasion. The day prior to the coup, the United States sent a cable to the U.S. EMBASSY stating that it would not condone political assassination but implying that it would support a new government. To prevent Trujillo's sons from seizing power, Kennedy sent almost 40 ships to patrol off the coast of the Dominican Republic as a sign of U.S. concern. Along these lines, most commentators of the invasion of the Dominican Republic assert that it documents the extent to which American policy makers have been unable to distinguish between nationalist social reformers and communists, as well as shows their long-standing obsession with preventing a "second Castro" from coming to power. Other examples include the 1954 overthrow of Jacobo Arbenz Guzmán in GUATEMALA, RICHARD NIXON's efforts to remove SALVADOR ALLENDE from power in CHILE, and RONALD REAGAN's invasion of GRENADA.

The 1965 invasion is also significant because it highlights the contradictions inherent in the recently launched ALLIANCE FOR PROGRESS, hailed by the Kennedy and Johnson administrations as a major American foreign-policy initiative designed to bring democracy and prosperity to the region. Critics assert that the invasion of the Dominican Republic demonstrated how easily the rhetoric of the alliance was superceded by traditional America national security concerns and how little had changed in U.S.–Latin American relations since THEODORE ROOSEVELT's "Big Stick" policy. President Johnson also sought and received the support of the ORGANIZATION OF AMERICAN STATES (OAS) for the invasion, and its credibility in the region is seen as having been seriously impaired as a result.

Today one of the most important foreign-policy links uniting the Dominican Republic and the United States is the REFUGEE and IMMIGRATION flow between them. One of the most significant sources of foreign exchange for the Dominican Republic is tourism. In 1985 almost one-third of these tourist dollars were generated by Dominicans living abroad. It is further estimated that migrants abroad or those who have returned have purchased more than 60 percent of the housing stock in the Dominican Republic. Dominicans are the largest single ethnic group living in New York City. Estimates placed the number anywhere from 225,000 to more than 500,000 in 1990. The interconnections come through clearly when the Dominican Republic passed a constitutional amendment granting dual citizenship to Dominican immigrants living abroad. Up to 15 percent of the money raised in recent elections has come from New York City residents, making it a frequent campaign stop for Dominican candidates.

**Further reading:** Atkins, G. Pope, and Larmen C. Wilson. *The Dominican Republic and the United States.* Athens: University of Georgia Press, 1998; Calder, Bruce, J. *The Impact of Intervention.* Austin: University of Texas Press, 1984; Lowenthal, Abraham. *The Dominican Intervention.* New York: Columbia University Press, 1972.

## domino theory

The domino theory was an operating rule of American COLD WAR foreign policy that was derived from the broader strategic principle of containment. It was introduced into the language of American foreign policy by President DWIGHT EISENHOWER in an April 7, 1954, news conference on VIETNAM. He explained the American commitment to the noncommunist forces in the South this way: "[Y]ou have a row of dominoes set up. You knock over the first one, and what will happen to that last one is the certainty that it will go over very quickly." The Reagan administration would employ similar imagery decades later in justifying its policy of opposition to the Sandinistas in NICARAGUA and the invasion of GRENADA.

While introduced by Eisenhower, American policy makers had long been employing images that evoked the same mechanistic interpretation of world politics. It reflected a long-standing American conviction that it is both possible and necessary to realize a condition of absolute security. WOODROW WILSON spoke of bad revolutionary regimes that would infect neighboring countries in justifying U.S. interventions in MEXICO's and RUSSIA's civil wars. Speaking out in support of the TRUMAN DOCTRINE and military aid to GREECE and TURKEY, one-time isolationist senator Arthur Vandenberg predicted a "Communist chain reaction from the Dardenelles to the China Sea and westward to the rim of the Atlantic."

There was also an important domestic dimension to the domino theory that both helped and threatened American policy makers. On the positive side the domino theory offered policy makers a shorthand way of conveying to the American public the need for action without having to explain the details of a conflict. On the negative side it trapped American policy makers into taking action and made them vulnerable to charges of having been "soft on communism" or having "lost" a particular country. Used in this latter sense it drew on the European policy of appeasement at Munich that emboldened rather than stopped Adolf Hitler's advance.

**Further reading:** Ninkovich, Frank. *Modernity and Power.* Chicago: University of Chicago Press, 1994.

## doves

From the late 1960s into the 1980s the most important debates in American COLD WAR foreign policy can be characterized as those between HAWKS and doves for control over American military policy. At stake were the content of both the structure and size of U.S. conventional and nuclear forces and American military strategy. It was a debate that became intensely political and continued until the fall of COMMUNISM and the end of the cold war altered the American foreign-policy agenda.

Doves rejected the argument that communism was the principal source of America's foreign-policy problems. In VIETNAM and elsewhere in the Third World, the primary problem lay in such domestic political conditions as political oppression, poverty, hunger, and inequality. Their presence created a receptive audience for the communist message of American IMPERIALISM. Defining the problem this way made doves skeptical of the ability of conventional military power to promote American security. Economic FOREIGN AID and political reform instead topped their agenda.

Doves were just as skeptical of the ability of nuclear weapons to provide for American security. Instead, they placed their faith in the ARMS CONTROL agreements with the Soviet Union, such as the ANTIBALLISTIC MISSILE TREATY and the STRATEGIC ARMS LIMITATION TALKS. Where doves parted company with the Nixon administration was in their philosophical starting point for supporting these policies. RICHARD NIXON and HENRY KISSINGER saw themselves as REALISTS who were working to manage and balance POWER in world politics. Most doves were idealists or Wilsonians who had great faith in the ability of reason and shared interests to serve as the basis of national security policy. Doves were not so much worried about the threat posed by the Soviet Union (see RUSSIA) as they were by the threat posed by the global presence of large NUCLEAR WEAPONS ARSENALS.

In thinking about the causes of war doves held that provocation was the danger that needed to be avoided at all costs. Using the Japanese attack on Pearl Harbor as their model, doves cautioned that the buildup of military power did not deter aggression. It only served to incite a challenger into attacking before the unbalance of power grew even worse. What was needed was a strategy structured around accommodation and conciliation. Hawks countered that the dove prescription for keeping the peace amounted to appeasement. Citing Munich, the pre–WORLD WAR II conference at which GREAT BRITAIN and FRANCE tried to prevent war by recognizing Nazi Germany's claims to part of CZECHOSLOVAKIA, they argued that appeasement invited aggression and that only military superiority could deter it.

**Further reading:** Allison, Graham, et al., eds. *Hawks, Doves, and Owls: An Agenda for Avoiding Nuclear War.* New York: Norton, 1985.

## drug trafficking

Traditionally the foreign-policy agenda of states focused on issues related to national security and high DIPLOMACY. TRADE POLICY issues only occasionally were important. Other issues, such as international copyright statutes, protecting the environment, and international drug trafficking, were relegated to a secondary status. They were specialized issues that could be dealt with in nonpolitical settings and by midlevel officials.

This is no longer the case. The foreign-policy agenda has expanded so that these issues and others occupy a prominent place in bilateral and multilateral negotiations. CONGRESS now mandates annual reports on the prevention of drug trafficking and production efforts of states. Failure to be certified threatens the continuance of U.S. aid. Drug trafficking is a controversial issue on the foreign-policy agenda because it bridges domestic and international politics. Approached from a foreign-policy perspective, the drug trade is a supply problem that is addressed by limiting production and curtailing the amount of drugs coming into the United States. Approached from a domestic-policy perspective, the drug trade is a demand problem that is addressed by

improved law enforcement measures, education, treatment programs, and decriminalization.

Drug trafficking into the United States is carried out by diverse groups and enters through a variety of portals. One drug smuggled into the United States is cocaine. In 2001 the street value of a kilogram of cocaine ranged from $12,000 to $35,000. That same year U.S. authorities seized more than 111 metric tons of cocaine. Cocaine trafficking into the United States is carried out primarily by Colombian and Mexican organizations. The U.S.-MEXICO border is the main point of entry, and about 65 percent of the cocaine smuggled into the United States comes across the southwestern border. Colombian groups control the worldwide supply of cocaine and work with Mexican smugglers who bring the drug into the United States. They control the wholesale distribution of cocaine in the West and the Midwest. On the East Coast, Colombian groups continue to control the wholesale distribution of cocaine, but here too alliances with other groups are emerging. Dominican drug-trafficking organizations are playing an increasingly prominent role in the street-level distribution of cocaine in some areas.

A second drug smuggled into the United States is heroin. There are four major sources of supply: Mexico, South America (COLOMBIA), Southeast Asia (mainly Burma), and South Asia/Middle East (mainly AFGHANISTAN). Each has dominated the American market at some point over the past 30 years. Over the past 10 years the American market has shifted from one dominated by heroin from Southeast Asia to one in which heroin arrives from South America. On the West Coast, Mexican heroin remains most prevalent. Nearly all of the heroin produced in Mexico and Colombia is distributed in the United States. Colombian heroin arrives both on direct commercial flights from Colombia and through other South American states, principally Costa Rica, the DOMINICAN REPUBLIC, Ecuador, PANAMA, Mexico, ARGENTINA, and VENEZUELA. Heroin from Mexico frequently is smuggled into the United States in small quantities by illegal immigrants and migrant workers. Evidence from large seizures of heroin indicates that this is changing.

Southeast Asian heroin dominated the American market in the late 1980s and early 1990s. This heroin makes its way into the United States in a chain of relations that begin with independent brokers shipping through overseas Chinese criminal groups that connect with ethnic Chinese criminal groups in the United States. Shipments may go through any of a number of states, including the PHILIPPINES, Malaysia, Singapore, TAIWAN, and SOUTH KOREA. West African groups, mainly from NIGERIA, smuggle both Southeast Asian and Southwest Asian heroin into the United States. Of late they are most active in smuggling Southwest Asian heroin because it is cheaper. The cost of heroin in Pakistan that is produced in Afghanistan is about one-half the price of heroin in Bangkok. Much of the heroin produced in Southwest Asia is consumed in West Europe, PAKISTAN, and IRAN. Its distribution in the United States is concentrated among ethnic groups who have emigrated from the region. Criminal groups from LEBANON, Pakistan, TURKEY, and Afghanistan play central roles in the trafficking of heroin here.

In 2000 the price of a kilogram of heroin in the United States varied considerably by source. South African heroin ranged in price from $50,000 to $200,000 per kilogram. Mexican heroin, the least pure heroin, cost between $13,200 and $175,000 per kilogram. In between these two price levels was Southwest Asian heroin. It cost between $40,000 and $190,000 per kilogram.

The most readily available illegal drug in the United States is marijuana. There are an estimated 11.5 million current users. Most of the marijuana used in the United States is smuggled in from Mexico or other Latin American states. Organized crime groups have smuggled marijuana in from Mexico since the early 1970s. CANADA is becoming a major source of indoor-grown, high potency marijuana. Prices range between $400 and $2,000 per pound with one Canadian import from British Columbia going for between $5,000 and $8,000 per pound.

Other illicit drugs smuggled into the United States include ecstasy, LSD, PCP, flunitrazepam, GHB/GBL, steroids, and methamphetamine.

International drug trafficking raises a number of important issues for American foreign policy. One involves the use of military force as an antidrug instrument. Proponents see its use as capable of breaking the link between the international drug trade and the terrorist groups who protect them and profit from this activity through their presence in a producing state and by training local military and police forces to deal with the drug trade problem. Critics see it as a misdirected policy tool because it does not focus on the social-economic factors that give rise to drug production in other states or its consumption in the United States. They are also concerned that often in the past when the U.S. military has gone into developing countries it has sided with repressive regimes against the poorer groups in society who are often involved in producing drugs. Third, the international drug trade operates in conjunction with a large-scale international money-laundering system. The INTERNATIONAL MONETARY FUND estimates that roughly $600 million per year flows through this system. Disabling this system has become a high-priority item in the war against TERRORISM. Fourth, the international drug trade has raised questions about the role of drug cultivation in development strategies. Drug crops are cheaply grown. Convincing poor farmers to abandon them in favor of more expensive crops is not easily accomplished. Finally, concerns exist that drug production and trafficking represent

U.S. Drug Enforcement Agency Black Hawk helicopter begins landing in the Magdalena Medio region northwest of Bogotá, Colombia, moments before an antidrug operation was started on a cocaine laboratory in the mountains here, November 8, 2000. *(Photo by Piero Pomponi/Newsmakers)*

a potentially explosive ingredient, raising regional tensions as this activity expands across state borders. Such regional instability may threaten U.S. security interests, thus involving American military forces in PEACEKEEPING operations.

**Further reading:** Bagley, Bruce M., and William O. Walker, eds. *Drug Trafficking in the Americas.* Coral Gables, Fla.: North-South Center, University of Miami, 1996; Carpenter, Ted Galen. *Bad Neighbor Policy: Washington's Futile War on Drugs in Latin America.* New York: Macmillan, 2003.

## dual containment

Dual containment is the policy instituted by the Clinton administration in 1993 to deal with the threats posed by IRAN and IRAQ. It seeks to isolate each simultaneously without the aid of the other. Iraq is to be contained because it is considered a "criminal regime." Iran is to be contained because of its foreign policy that supports international TERRORISM, opposes the Arab-Israeli peace process, subverts Arab governments friendly to the United States, seeks to acquire WEAPONS OF MASS DESTRUCTION, and aims to acquire a conventional military capability aimed at dominating the region.

Dual containment represents the continuation of a trend in American foreign policy toward an increasingly direct American strategic role in the Persian Gulf. The central goal of this policy is to prevent any state from effectively challenging the United States as the dominant political-military presence in the region. Initially this meant keeping the Soviet Union (see RUSSIA) out of the Persian Gulf by bolstering the military power of regional allies. Later it meant insuring that a rough balance of power existed between Iraq and Iran. In practical terms this meant supporting Iraq in the IRAN-IRAQ WAR. Dual containment places the United States in a more central role as a unilateral manager of regional relations in the Persian Gulf. A secondary goal of dual containment is to provide for the continued security of SAUDI ARABIA and the smaller gulf monarchies.

Dual containment has been criticized on a number of grounds. In terms of practicality three issues are raised. It is questioned whether it is possible to contain either Iraq or Iran without the help of the other. The isolation of Iraq and Iran sought by dual containment also requires the active support of the other Arab states in the region. Finally, it is questioned whether regional politics can be essentially frozen in time through a policy of dual containment. On strategic grounds it is questioned whether dual containment threatens to bring about a strategic situation that is particularly harmful to American interests; namely, the political collapse of the Iranian and Iraqi regimes. An analogous strategic concern is that American influence in the region is being effectively challenged by states that do not fully abide by the international sanctions placed on these states.

President GEORGE W. BUSH initially supported dual containment by identifying Iran and Iraq as part of an axis of evil that also included NORTH KOREA. He then effectively ended the policy by seeking war with Iraq while leaving CONTAINMENT in place against Iran.

See also IRAQ WAR; PERSIAN GULF WAR.

## Dulles, John Foster (1888–1959) *secretary of state*

John Foster Dulles was SECRETARY OF STATE (1953–59) during the Eisenhower administration. The combination of Dulles's high visibility and blunt statements regarding the COLD WAR issues and the tendency of President DWIGHT EISENHOWER to avoid the limelight and delegate authority led many early cold war historians to assign great importance to Dulles as the main force behind U.S. foreign policy in these years. More recent scholarship suggests that Eisenhower was much more involved in foreign-policy making and that Dulles rarely acted without his support. Moreover, it now appears that Dulles held a much more complex image of world affairs than emerged in his public pronouncements. In either case, Dulles was one of the main architects of U.S. foreign policy at a time when U.S.-Soviet competition expanded from the confines of Europe and became truly global in nature.

Dulles began his foreign-policy career as a member of the U.S. delegation to the PARIS PEACE CONFERENCE, where he worked on the reparations section of the VERSAILLES TREATY, putting forward language that was less harsh than advocated by America's European allies. Out of government during the interwar period, Dulles often wrote on foreign-policy matters, emphasizing the key role played by international trade, the need for international reform, and antiinterventionism. He saw little value in challenging GERMANY and JAPAN if the sole purpose was to reestablish the old international order. His internationalist orientation made him a key political ally of the Truman administration as it sought to put forward a bipartisan foreign policy, and he represented the United States at many international meetings. This pattern of cooperation continued even after HARRY TRUMAN defeated Thomas Dewey for the presidency in 1948. Dulles had been Dewey's chief foreign-policy adviser and was expected to be his secretary of state.

Dulles was to achieve this post in 1953 when Dwight Eisenhower won the presidency. Along with Eisenhower he had made the Democrat's handling of foreign policy (the loss of CHINA, the KOREAN WAR, and the "immoral" policy of CONTAINMENT) major campaign issues. By this time, Dulles had made the transition from reforming internationalist to fervent anticommunist cold warrior. His record as secretary of state was mixed. Competition with the Soviet Union (see RUSSIA) was pursued with a renewed feeling of vigor and brashness that injected a sense of forcefulness and mission to U.S. foreign policy. Talk of MASSIVE RETALIATION, rolling back the iron curtain, and BRINKSMANSHIP did not, however, translate into an unbroken string of foreign-policy triumphs. Communist ideology and the Soviet Union's approach to development and successes, symbolized by *SPUTNIK* and the launching of an intercontinental ballistic missile, continued to inspire Third World resistance to U.S. military power. By the end of the Eisenhower administration its handling of foreign-policy issues had become the subject of widespread debate and a campaign issue in the 1960 presidential election. John Foster Dulles resigned as secretary of state one month before his death in 1959.

**Further reading:** Immerman, Richard, ed. *John Foster Dulles and the Diplomacy of the Cold War.* Princeton, N.J.: Princeton University Press, 1990; Marks, Frederic, III. *Power and Peace: The Diplomacy of John Foster Dulles.* Westport, Conn.: Praeger, 1993.

# E

## Earth Summit, Rio de Janeiro

The UNITED NATIONS Conference on Environment and Development (UNCED), also known as the Rio Earth Summit, met in Rio de Janeiro on June 3–12, 1992. A total of 180 states attended, and some 40,000 people were present either as delegates or observers. The Rio Earth Summit did not in and of itself produce any binding international agreements on the ENVIRONMENT, although two conventions were put forward for signature at the conclusion of the Rio Earth Summit. Instead, the Rio Earth Summit was viewed as a call to action. It produced Agenda 21, which presented a broadly constructed blueprint for achieving the goal of sustainable development. As in other international environmental SUMMIT CONFERENCES, the United States found itself on the defensive and was often in a minority position.

The Rio Earth Summit owed its inspiration to two different events. First, it was held on the 20th anniversary of the United Nations Conference on Human Development in Stockholm held in 1972. This was the first international meeting devoted to examining the intersection of global environmental and development concerns. That conference produced a set of nonbinding guiding principles and resulted in the creation of the UN Environment Programme. Second, the Rio Earth Summit was inspired by the publication of the Brundtland Commission's 1987 report, "Our Common Future." It introduced and popularized the concept of sustainable development, which it defined as "development that meets the need of present generations without compromising the ability of future generations to meet their own needs."

By the time the Rio Earth Summit convened most of the hard work had been completed. Separate negotiations had produced a Framework Convention on Climate Change and a Convention on Biological Diversity. All that remained was for the documents to be signed. The Rio Declaration had been largely agreed upon, as had the bulk of Agenda 21. Both of these were nonbinding guidelines on environment and development issues for states to follow in the 21st century. The conference itself was divided into two main parts. Work on completing Agenda 21 and the Rio Declaration was completed in the conference phase that ran from June 3 to 11. Among the most contentious remaining issues were those involving finance and technology transfer. The summit phase took place on June 12 and 13 when 102 notables and heads of states addressed the gathering. The documents were signed on June 14.

The Bush administration did not devote significant resources to the Rio Earth Summit, and President GEORGE H. W. BUSH was a reluctant participant in the summit phase of the meeting. In his address he announced that his goal was to "protect taxpayers" while at the same time protecting the environment. In a conciliatory gesture he stated that the United States would spend more than $1.2 trillion in the next decade on ecological concerns. The Bush administration objected to provisions in the Biodiversity Treaty that required states to protect endangered animals and plants on the grounds that the treaty did not provide patent protection of U.S. biotechnology firms. Election-year pressures and a slow economy were important factors that contributed to the hard line taken by the Bush administration. Bush confronted a strong challenger in BILL CLINTON and faced pressure from conservative third-party candidate Ross Perot.

The 120 action proposals of Agenda 21 can be broken down into seven major themes. They include improving the quality of life by more efficiently using the Earth's natural resources; protecting the global commons, developing more coherent ways for managing urban areas; addressing the problem of waste management, including chemicals; promoting sustainable development; and ensuring the active participation of all groups in society in the decision-making process on these topics. Additionally, a key component of Agenda 21 was the agreement to create the United Nations Commission on Sustainable Development to review and report on the progress made in implementing these principles.

The United States was the only major power not to sign the Biodiversity Treaty, although the Clinton administration eventually did sign it in 1994. The Climate Treaty pledged states to work toward reducing dangerous greenhouse gas emissions, but it did not set any particular levels of commitment. These were set in the KYOTO PROTOCOL. The Clinton administration signed this agreement while expressing concern over its terms. President GEORGE W. BUSH declared the agreement fundamentally flawed and withdrew the U.S. signature.

As the experience of these two agreements reveals, the Rio Earth Summit is best viewed as part of a stream of international environmental and development agreements and not as an isolated negotiation. Subsequent negotiations on related issues include the 1994 International Conference on Population and Development, the 1996 World Food Summit, and the 2002 Conference on Sustainable Development.

See also MONTREAL PROTOCOL.

**Further reading:** Choucri, Nazli, ed. *Global Accord: Environmental Challenges and International Response.* Cambridge, Mass.: Harvard University Press, 1993; Sitarz, Daniel, ed. *Agenda 21: The Earth Summit Strategy to Save Our Planet.* Boulder, Colo.: Earthpress, 1993.

## economic sanctions

In responding to international challenges and opportunities American foreign-policy makers have a variety of options to choose from. They may engage in DIPLOMACY, COVERT ACTION, or military undertakings. They may also engage in economic statecraft. It entails the deliberate manipulation of economic policy to achieve political objectives.

Several policy tools fall under the category of economic statecraft. The first is a tariff. This is a tax on foreign-made goods. Tariffs can be used to raise money, or they can be used to affect the behavior of other states. As part of the political-military strategy of DÉTENTE, the United States sought to use access to the American market as a tool to modify the Soviet Union's (see RUSSIA) military policies. The granting of MOST-FAVORED-NATION status was the vehicle for getting around high tariffs. A variant of this strategy is the manipulation of nontariff barriers to trade (NTBs). They take the form of labeling requirements, health and safety standards, buy-American legislation, and requirements that goods be shipped on American vessels.

A second economic policy tool is an embargo. This is a refusal to sell a commodity to another state. Examples include the 1917 Trading with the Enemy Act, the Battle Act, and the Export Control Act of 1949. All have been used to limit trade with Communist states. Embargoes have become a highly favored policy instrument of late.

Embargoes have been placed on trade with CUBA, are contained in the HELMS-BURTON ACT, and have been imposed against the military government in HAITI as part of the effort to return Jean-Bertrand Aristide to power. An arms embargo was put into place against the combatants in the Bosnian civil war. While neutral in language this embargo hurt Bosnian Muslims more so than it did Bosnian Serbs. The United States also worked with the UNITED NATIONS to put a near total embargo in place against IRAQ following its refusal to comply with the conditions of the PERSIAN GULF WAR cease-fire. After the IRAQ WAR ended one of the first moves undertaken by the Bush administration was to ask the United Nations to end its sanctions against Iraq. The Security Council voted unanimously (with Syria absent) to end the 13 years of sanctions on May 22, 2003. The move was somewhat controversial in that FRANCE and RUSSIA and other states were concerned with the amount of freedom that the new UN resolution would give the United States in dispersing money from Iraqi OIL production.

The popularity of embargoes have made them the subject of three lines of criticism. First, they are overused. Policy makers seem attracted to them out of a desire to show that they are doing something about a problem when no other policy instruments hold the promise of success. Second, embargoes have become weapons in domestic political disputes. Anti-Castro Cubans in the United States were strong advocates of the Helms-Burton Act, and they used their electoral and financial resources to build broad support for it in spite of objections by U.S. allies to its terms. CONGRESS passed the Iran-Libyan Sanctions Act in 1996 to punish these states for their support of TERRORISM. One victim was the American petroleum industry, and they lobbied the GEORGE W. BUSH administration to end the sanctions. Third, embargoes are morally wrong because they work indirectly by creating pain and suffering in the society at large in the hopes that this will force those in power to change their policies.

A third economic policy tool is the boycott. This is a refusal to buy the products of a given state. In 1995 the Clinton administration imposed a boycott against IRAN for its efforts to acquire nuclear technology and expertise. Its success was limited by the nonparticipation of other states. Much earlier, in the late 1960s and early 1970s, the United States joined a United Nations boycott of Rhodesia (ZIMBABWE) in an effort to force the white minority government to accept the principle of majority rule. The U.S. participation was compromised by a congressional move that permitted key Rhodesian natural resources to enter the U.S. market.

Quotas are the fourth policy instrument that is available to policy makers. This is a quantitative restriction on goods coming from another state. Because of the GENERAL AGREEMENT ON TARIFFS AND TRADE (GATT), quotas have not played a large role in the postwar era. A modern variant of the quota is the voluntary export restrictions (VER). The United States negotiated several of these with JAPAN. Today, quotas continue to attract support from protectionists seeking to provide relief for industries threatened by foreign competition. The American auto industry has often sought such support. Because of this link with protectionism quotas have been rejected on ideological grounds by advocates of free trade, such as policy makers in the Reagan administration. Threats of using quotas, however, continue. In 1994 President BILL CLINTON threatened to place a quota on Canadian grain entering the United States as part of an effort to gain bargaining leverage with CANADA over trade in agriculture.

**Further reading:** Haas, Richard N., ed. *Economic Sanctions and American Diplomacy.* New York: Council on Foreign Relations, 1998; Hufbauer, Jeffrey, et al. *Economic Sanctions Reconsidered.* Washington, D.C.: Brookings, 1990; Shambaugh, George E. *States, Firms and Power: Successful Sanctions in United States Foreign Policy.* Albany: State University of New York Press, 1999.

## Egypt

Egypt is the most populous country in the Arab world and the second most populous country in Africa, with a population of 68 million. It is about the size of Texas and New Mexico combined. All of its territory except for the Sinai Peninsula is in Africa. Egypt has existed as a unified political unit for more than 5,000 years. Egypt was a quasi-independent protectorate under Ottoman rule from 1517 to 1882. At that time it fell under British domination. GREAT BRITAIN formally granted Egypt independence in 1922, but a British protectorate continued in place until 1936. Egypt was officially neutral during WORLD WAR II, and although it did provide the British with access to its military facilities, the United States refused to provide it with LEND-LEASE funds.

Egypt and the United States were divided on a series of foreign-policy issues in the first years after World War II. Most notably, Egypt opposed the partition of Palestine and the creation of ISRAEL. It contributed forces to the Arab side in the 1948 war. U.S.–Egyptian relations took a turn for the worse following a 1952 military coup led by the Free Officers, who ousted King Farouk. One of the key participants in the coup was Colonel Gamal Abdel Nasser. He seized power in November 1954 and quickly established himself as a spokesperson for the Arab world. Nasser resisted American pressures that he join U.S.-sponsored regional defense organizations, such as the Middle East Defense Organization and the Baghdad Pact, that were directed at stopping Soviet expansion into the Middle East.

Instead, he turned to the Soviet Union (see RUSSIA) and became an ally as a source of military aid. In 1955 Egypt purchased weapons from CZECHOSLOVAKIA, marking the first Soviet ARMS TRANSFER to an Arab state. Nasser also pursued an active role in the nonaligned movement and played a leadership role in the 1955 meeting of nonaligned states in Bandung, INDONESIA.

In late 1955 DWIGHT EISENHOWER offered to extend aid to construct the Aswan Dam on the Nile River as part of a strategy to separate Egypt from the Soviet Union. Negotiations broke down when Egypt refused to agree to British and American terms for the loan and stepped up negotiations with Communist states for additional weapons. The Eisenhower administration now switched strategies and denied Egypt funding for the Aswan Dam in an attempt to lower Nasser's standing in the Arab world. The stratagem failed when Nasser, in defiance of Great Britain and FRANCE, nationalized the SUEZ CANAL in order to acquire the money needed to build the dam.

Soon thereafter, ISRAEL, Great Britain, and France joined in a venture designed to reopen the canal and reduce the Arab security threat to Israel and French colonial holdings in North Africa. In October 1956 Israeli forces advanced on the Suez Canal. According to a prearranged plan France and Great Britain demanded that they stop and announced that they would send PEACEKEEPING forces to the Suez Canal to keep it open. The net effect of these military undertakings was intended to be the destruction of the Egyptian military apparatus. Much to the surprise of these three states the United States demanded that they stop. A UNITED NATIONS Emergency Force (UNEF) was dispatched to the Egyptian side of the 1948 Sinai cease-fire line, where it remained until forced to leave in 1968.

The improvement in U.S.-Egyptian relations brought on by Eisenhower's stand was short-lived. Nasser turned to the Soviet Union for funding for the Aswan Dam. He also turned to them for economic and technical assistance for Egypt's industrialization program. On the foreign-policy front Egypt and SYRIA merged to form the United Arab Republic in February 1958. Although it lasted only until 1961, when a coup in Syria brought about its demise, the United Arab Republic reinforced Nasser's stature as a powerful independent force in the Middle East. Also in 1958 Nasser sponsored a coup in IRAQ that brought down a pro-Western government. Nasser was less successful in other foreign-policy endeavors. In early 1957 the United States put forward the EISENHOWER DOCTRINE in which it promised to work with states in the region to resist the spread of COMMUNISM. Nasser and other Arab nationalists saw it as a thinly veiled move directed at containing the spread of Arab nationalism. In September 1962 Egyptian forces entered Yemen, where they supported military officers, who with Egyptian support had overthrown the conservative government. They then helped defend the new government against Saudi Arabian- and American-backed opposition forces. Egypt incurred heavy losses and withdrew its forces from Yemen in 1967.

Nasser's biggest setback came in 1967 when Israel struck boldly against Egypt and its allies in what became known as the Six-Day War. In the process of routing Arab forces it seized the Golan Heights, the Sinai, and the Gaza Strip. The Six-Day War also produced a massive Palestinian REFUGEE flow that continues to complicate the settlement of the ARAB-ISRAELI CONFLICT. Nasser contributed to the near total defeat of the Arab militaries by employing provocative anti-Israeli rhetoric and engaging in menacing actions in the months leading up to the attack. The most dangerous of these was demanding that the UNEF leave the Sinai and closing the Strait of Tiran to Israeli shipping.

Nasser died on September 28, 1970, as he was about to try to mediate a dispute between JORDAN and the PALESTINE LIBERATION ORGANIZATION (PLO). He was replaced as president by Anwar Sadat, his first vice president and a fellow Free Officer. Sadat's first foreign-policy moves were directed at the Soviet Union. After failing to obtain all the weapons he sought from Moscow, Sadat expelled Soviet military advisers in July 1972. He followed this up with a stunning military offensive against Israel, starting the October 1973 Yom Kippur War. Arab forces could not sustain their initial successes, and by war's end Israel had effectively counterattacked. When Israeli forces continued advancing after a cease-fire was arranged, the Soviet Union threatened to send troops to the Middle East to defend its beleaguered ally. The United States responded by placing some of its nuclear forces on a heightened alert status.

In defeat, Sadat had succeeded in accomplishing one of his primary objectives: upsetting the status quo (in which Egypt was locked into a losing position) so that movement might be possible. The most visible form of movement took the shape of NATIONAL SECURITY ADVISOR HENRY KISSINGER's shuttle diplomacy that resulted in the signing of a cease-fire and military disengagement agreement. It also led to Sadat's reestablishing diplomatic relations with Israel that had been cut off following the 1967 war. Sadat's willingness to do so was heavily influenced by the United States's willingness to resume foreign-aid flows to Egypt. By 1977 the United States was providing more than $1 billion per year. Between 1975 and 2000 the United States Agency for International Development has provided Egypt with more than $24 billion in economic and development assistance.

Sadat would again shock the world in November 1977 by going to Jerusalem to seek peace with Israel. This trip was reciprocated with a trip by Israeli prime minister Menachem Begin to Egypt. With the peace process showing no signs of movement President JIMMY CARTER brought the two leaders to CAMP DAVID for a series of meetings in September 1978 that culminated in the signing of two historic agreements. The first was "A Framework for Peace in the Middle East." The second was "A Framework for the Conclusion of a Peace Treaty between Israel and Egypt." The peace treaty was signed in Washington on March 26, 1979. It resulted in a Nobel Peace Prize for Begin and Sadat and in sanctions against Egypt by Arab states. Cairo was expelled from the Arab League, and ECONOMIC SANCTIONS were placed against the country. On October 6, 1981, Sadat was assassinated by Muslim extremists who considered him to be a traitor. PRESIDENTS Nixon, Ford, and Carter attended his funeral, but no Arab head of state was present.

Hosni Mubarak, vice president and an air force commander in the 1973 war, succeeded Sadat. Mubarak remained committed to the peace process initiated by Sadat and played a key role in arranging the 1991 MADRID PEACE CONFERENCE that brought Israel and the PLO together. Mubarak, however, has also been critical of Israel. In June 1982 he protested Israel's invasion of Lebanon (although he took no military steps to counter it), and in September he recalled the Egyptian ambassador to protest the massacre of Palestinians in refugee camps that had been created by Israel and turned over to its Lebanese Christian allies. Overall the Egyptian-Israeli relationship during Mubarak's rule has been characterized both as an "angry peace" and a "cold peace."

Egypt was a key supporter of the United States in the PERSIAN GULF WAR. Egypt provided 35,000 troops to the cause, the third-largest contribution after the United States and Great Britain. Ten days after the invasion Egypt hosted an Arab League summit conference out of which grew the decision by Arab states to oppose IRAQ. (Egypt had been readmitted to the Arab League in 1989). After the war the United States forgave $7 billion in debts owed by Egypt for arms purchased in the 1970s. Military cooperation between the two states has also increased. Each year it hosts Operation Bright Star, the largest military exercise in the world. The United States also provides Egypt with an array of sophisticated weapons, including the F-4 jet, F-16 fighter, Apache helicopters, antiaircraft missile batteries, and surveillance aircraft.

Following the SEPTEMBER 11, 2001, terrorist attacks, the United States identified Egypt as a key supporter in the war against TERRORISM. However, during summer 2002 the GEORGE W. BUSH administration criticized Egypt for its HUMAN-RIGHTS violations. This complaint was voiced around the same time that criticisms were leveled against SAUDI ARABIA for its lack of aggressiveness in pursuing the war against terrorism. At issue is Mubarak's crackdown on antigovernment opposition groups. Included among them is the Muslim Brotherhood, which was founded in 1928 and is defined by the Egyptian government as an illegal organization.

**Further reading:** Aronson, Gregory. *From Sideshow to Center Stage.* Boulder, Colo.: Lynne Rienner, 1986; Quandt, William. *The United States and Egypt.* Washington, D.C.: Brookings, 1990.

## Eisenhower, Dwight D. (1890–1969) *president of the United States*

Dwight David Eisenhower was the 34th president of the United States. The presidency was Eisenhower's first elected office. Prior to this, Eisenhower had an illustrious career in the U.S. Army. He was an assistant to General DOUGLAS MACARTHUR in the PHILIPPINES in the 1930s, and during WORLD WAR II he commanded Allied forces in the invasions of North Africa, Sicily, and Italy. He was supreme Allied commander of the Allied invasion at Normandy. After the war he served as commanding officer of U.S. occupation forces in GERMANY and then as army chief of staff. Later he would serve as the first supreme commander of the NORTH ATLANTIC TREATY ORGANIZATION (NATO).

Eisenhower was elected in 1952. In that campaign he criticized President HARRY TRUMAN's policy of CONTAINMENT as both passive and immoral. In its place the Republicans promised a policy of liberation. Eisenhower also promised to go to Korea to help bring an end to that stalemated war. Although he suffered a heart attack in 1955, Eisenhower ran for reelection and won a landslide victory in 1956. Eisenhower gained a great deal of notoriety for his 1961 farewell address in which he warned against the dangers of a MILITARY-INDUSTRIAL COMPLEX. In his view the informal ALLIANCE that had developed between business and military interests in the United States had coalesced into a powerful lobby that threatened to distort the American economy and undermine democracy and American civil liberties.

Eisenhower's foreign-policy record was decidedly mixed. He sought to achieve a balance in ends and means that often had opposite effects from those intended. A case in point was his New Look defense policy. Eisenhower feared that a containment policy that gave the initiative to the Soviet Union as to where and how to challenge the United States was too expensive and threatened to undermine the American economy. Eisenhower sought to modify containment by reducing its reliance on U.S. conventional forces that were expensive to maintain and replacing it with a reliance on U.S. technology. He also sought to seize the advantage and not place the United States in a position of simply responding to acts of Soviet aggression. Eisenhower's answer was the strategy of massive retaliation that threatened the Soviet Union with nuclear attack. A similar paradox can be found in the area of COVERT ACTION. Eisenhower embraced it as an inexpensive means of removing communist challenges in the Third World. Yet, the initial successes in IRAN and GUATEMALA gave way to an uncritical embrace of covert action, led to its overuse in Indonesia, and set the stage for the BAY OF PIGS operation in CUBA in the Kennedy administration.

The foreign-policy rhetoric of the Eisenhower administration painted a world in terms of black and white. It aggressively defined U.S. interests by raising the specter that any falling "domino" might set off a chain reaction of defeats that would pose a threat to U.S. national security. Thus, social reformers were identified as communists, and U.S. Marines were sent to LEBANON to save a government from "international communism" when the true threat came from Arab nationalists aligned with Gamal Abdel Nasser in EGYPT. This rhetoric also helped build the impression of declining American power and foreign-policy failures. For example, in 1956 the Eisenhower administration was forced to "abandon" Hungarian freedom fighters in spite of talk of liberating East Europe and rolling back the iron curtain. Having labeled Nasser as a threat, the Eisenhower administration found itself supporting him and opposing its British, French, and Israeli allies for attempting to manufacture the SUEZ CRISIS.

President Dwight D. Eisenhower *(Dwight D. Eisenhower Library)*

The most debated question about Eisenhower's presidency is the degree of control he exercised over foreign policy. Early accounts pictured Eisenhower as passive, uninformed, and disinterested. SECRETARY OF STATE JOHN FOSTER DULLES was credited with being the true driving force behind U.S. foreign policy. It was Dulles's views of international politics and the Soviet Union and not Eisenhower's that mattered. Recent scholarship paints Eisenhower as a much more involved, "hidden hand" leader who was very much in charge, being briefed regularly by Dulles and giving his approval for major initiatives. In this interpretation of his presidency, Eisenhower is portrayed as deliberately fostering a public image of ignorance and disinterest as a device for freeing him from political constraints.

In the final analysis, commentators find more points of continuity with the Truman administration's foreign policy than they do deviations from it. Eisenhower held the line against communist expansion but little more. This left the Republicans vulnerable to Democratic charges in the 1960 presidential election that the purpose of foreign policy ought to be victory and that imagination and military strength were needed to achieve it.

See also EISENHOWER DOCTRINE; RUSSIA.

**Further reading:** Ambrose, Stephen. *Eisenhower.* 2 vols. New York: Simon and Schuster, 1983, 1984; Greenstein, Fred. *The Hidden Hand Presidency: Eisenhower as Leader.* New York: Basic, 1982.

## Eisenhower Doctrine

In 1958 the Eisenhower Doctrine provided the rationale for sending 14,000 troops to LEBANON to stop a coup by pro-Nasser Arabs. In the mid-1950s, the United States was drawn to the Middle East due to a combination of collapsing British colonial power and the fear of communist expansion. In 1953 the CENTRAL INTELLIGENCE AGENCY (CIA) orchestrated the overthrow of Mohammed Mossadegh in IRAN, bringing the shah back into power. In 1955 it helped put together the Baghdad Pact, an alliance of states designed to help encircle the Soviet Union (see RUSSIA) and prevent COMMUNISM from spreading into the region. In 1954 it offered aid to President Gamal Abdel Nasser to build the Aswan Dam in EGYPT. As a display of anger over Nasser's growing anti-Western policies it rescinded this offer in 1956 and helped spark the 1957 SUEZ CRISIS.

Fearing that the Soviet Union would be able to parlay the crisis into a greater presence in the region, Republican president DWIGHT EISENHOWER asked CONGRESS to approve a special program of military and economic aid for the Middle East. He asked Congress to approve, in advance, "the use of armed force to assist any nation or group of such nations requesting assistance against aggression from any national controlled by international communism." The DEMOCRATIC-controlled Congress refused. It was only after Eisenhower promised not to cut off U.S. aid to ISRAEL in retaliation for its participation in the Suez Crisis that Congress agreed to pass the Middle East resolution, better known as the Eisenhower Doctrine.

The Eisenhower Doctrine is significant for three reasons. First, it marked part of the general expansion of American CONTAINMENT policy into the developing world. Second, it is consistent with and reflects the AMERICAN NATIONAL STYLE of conducting foreign policy that emphasizes universal principles, moralism, and legalism. Third, it was part of a general trend in presidential-congressional relations in which Congress ceded authority to the PRESIDENT to carry out foreign policy without its specific consent by passing "area resolutions."

**Further reading:** Divine, Robert A. *Eisenhower and the Cold War.* New York: Oxford University Press, 1981.

## elections

It is an article of faith among most citizens that elections, especially presidential elections, are important because they determine the shape of future policy decisions. Rarely do we find an election in which the winning candidate does not cite election results in claiming a mandate for their policy program. Yet, is this the case? Evidence suggests that in and of themselves elections do not change the direction of foreign policy and that the claims for a mandate are overstated. For elections to confer a mandate upon the winner the voter must be knowledgeable about the issues, cast their ballots in accordance with their preferences, and be able to distinguish between parties or candidates.

Evidence on the first point is not encouraging. Most Americans appear to lack both a knowledge of and an interest in foreign affairs. In 1964 only 38 percent of Americans surveyed knew that RUSSIA was not a member of the NORTH ATLANTIC TREATY ORGANIZATION (NATO). In 1972 only 63 percent properly identified CHINA as a Communist country. In 1993 only 43 percent knew that SOMALIA was in Africa. Evidence also suggests that voters do not cast their ballots on the basis of foreign-policy positions. Primarily they are influenced by party affiliation, candidate image, and incumbency. And compared to domestic issues, foreign-policy issues have not been considered a good issue on which to run a campaign. Yet, we can find instances in which foreign-policy issues appear to have played a role in elections. Votes on foreign-policy issues can easily be taken out of context or used to place an incumbent on the defensive. Foreign-aid votes and treaty votes are often used in this way. For example, in the fiscal year 1980 foreign-aid bill, a complicated amendment was introduced that the administration objected to because one of its provisions would have created problems with American allies. Two congresspeople who voted against the amendment then found themselves attacked during the campaign for favoring aid to communist states that would have been barred by another provision of the amendment.

Candidates often do not disagree on major issues. In 1964 both LYNDON JOHNSON and Barry Goldwater campaigned on a platform that promised victory in VIETNAM. In 1968 both Hubert Humphrey and RICHARD NIXON promised to get the United States out of Vietnam. In their 1976 presidential campaigns both JIMMY CARTER and GERALD FORD spoke the language of DÉTENTE. In 1980 both Carter and RONALD REAGAN promised to stand firm against communist aggression and Islamic radicalism.

Some commentators assert that the impact of elections on U.S. foreign policy lies not in their ability to change policies directly but rather through the manor in which elections structure political behavior. A common refrain from foreign leaders is that foreign-policy making grinds to a halt every four years. Moreover, U.S. foreign policy tends to take on a nationalistic and militant quality.

It is argued that an election cycle exists that dominates noncrisis foreign-policy decision making. It begins in the presidential primary season when candidates present foreign-policy issues in oversimplified and stark terms in order to draw attention to themselves and separate themselves from the pack. In the general election presidential candidates seek to avoid offending any constituency, so they restrict themselves to such safe platitudes as being "strong on defense" and "protecting American business interests from unfair foreign trading practices." The absence of sustained and careful attention to foreign-policy issues produces a first year foreign policy that is long on clichés but short on a sensitivity to the perspectives of foreign states or the complexity of the problems being confronted. Under such conditions missteps and embarrassing about-faces are commonplace. Foreign policy becomes more pragmatic the second year of a president's term as experience builds and concern for midterm elections mount. In the third year a president's attention begins to focus on reelection as opposition candidates emerge. Foreign-policy issues are now looked at in the context of their impact on the election. The objectives are to clean up loose ends and minimize loses on the one hand and to produce victories no matter what the cost on the other. Viewed from this perspective the most promising year in which to undertake foreign-policy initiatives is a president's fifth year in office. Here, the president enjoys the twin advantages of popularity due to reelection and experience with foreign affairs. After that, the focus once again shifts in intensified fashion to the next presidential election as both parties now seek the office.

**Further reading:** Aldrich, John H., et al. "Foreign Affairs and Issue Voting." *American Political Science Review* 83 (1989); Foyle, Douglas C. *Counting the Public In: Presidents, Public Opinion, and Foreign Policy.* New York: Columbia University Press, 1999; Hughes, Barry. *The Domestic Context of American Foreign Policy.* San Francisco: Freeman, 1978; Pomper, Gerald. *Elections in America: Control and Influence in Democratic Politics.* New York: Dodd, Mead, 1968.

## elite decision-making theory

During the 1960s and early 1970s an intense debate existed over whether elite theory or PLURALISM best explained the process by which American foreign policy was made. These models have been overtaken by the RATIONAL ACTOR, BUREAUCRATIC POLITICS, and SMALL-GROUP DECISION-MAKING MODELS in popularity, but they continue to provide important insights into the dynamics of policy making.

Elite theory is not overly concerned with the details of action within the policy-making process, and it also rejects the idea that the state can be treated as a unitary actor responding to external stimuli. Of greatest importance to elite decision-making theory are the identities of those individuals making foreign policy and the underlying dynamics of national power, social myth, and class interests. According to elite theory, foreign policy is formulated as a response to demands generated by the domestic political and economic order. Key for elite theorists is the assertion that not all demands received equal attention. Some are more privileged than others. Those interests that receive special consideration and become embodied in policy advance the economic and political well-being of only a small sector of society.

These special interests are transformed into NATIONAL INTERESTS through the pattern of office holding and the structure of influence that exists within the United States. Thus, the need to protect American business interests from Third World social reformers is cast in terms of anticommunism. Elite theory sees policy makers in and out of government as being a stable and cohesive group who share common goals, interests, and values. Disagreement exists only at the margins and surface most frequently in disputes over how to implement policy and not over the ends of that policy. Those outside the elite group are held to be powerless. They react to policy rather than shape it. Furthermore, public reactions are often orchestrated and manipulated by elites. Ideas that do not build upon the relatively narrow range of value assumptions shared by the elite and that are supported by the underlying socioeconomic structure of American society will fail to become embodied in policy. Elite theory thus expects that the basic directions of U.S. foreign policy will change little, if at all.

Within this broad consensus elite theorists disagree on a number of points. First, disagreements exists over the ability of the public to short-circuit elite policy making by injecting its voice into the policy process. A key point of debate here is the influence of the MEDIA in the making of foreign policy. Adherents of the "CNN effect" assert that the media has made major inroads into the elite control of foreign policy through the ways foreign-policy issues are portrayed and how the public reacts to it. A second point of disagreement exists over how conspiratorial the elite consensus is. Proponents of the idea of a MILITARY-INDUSTRIAL COMPLEX see active and purposeful elite collaboration, whereas others base their analysis on more broad-based social forces.

Most recent administrations have been subject to elite-theory analysis. In the case of the Carter administration the object of attention was the large number of members of the Trilateral Commission who held high-ranking policy positions. In the Reagan administration attention was drawn to the links between Reagan appointees and the Committee on the Present Danger. In the Clinton administration many appointees were drawn from the Council on Foreign Relations and the Aspin Group.

Elite decision-making theory is a valuable source of insight into U.S. foreign policy because it stresses the ties that bind policy makers together rather than the issues that separate them.

See also CARTER, JIMMY; REVISIONISM; REAGAN, RONALD.

**Further reading:** Kolko, Gabriel. *The Roots of American Foreign Policy.* Boston: Beacon. 1969; Mills, C. Wright. *The Power Elite.* New York: Oxford University Press, 1956.

## El Salvador

El Salvador is located in Central America. It is about the size of Massachusetts, with an area of 8,260 square miles. It has a population of 6.2 million people. El Salvador became independent from Spain in 1821. It resisted a union with MEXICO in 1822 and asked the United States for statehood in 1823. A revolution in Mexico changed the dynamics of regional politics; instead of absorption into Mexico, the states of Central America formed the United Provinces of Central America. This federation ended in 1838, and El Salvador became an independent republic. The United States recognized El Salvador in 1863.

El Salvador's most significant politico-military interaction with the United States began in the 1970s. A fraudulent 1972 ELECTION denied victory to reform candidate José Napoleon Duarte and energized a leftist opposition. By 1979 GUERRILLA WARFARE broke out, setting in motion 12-year civil war. Support for the guerrillas came from NICARAGUA, where the Sandinistas had seized power.

Widespread HUMAN-RIGHTS violations occurred during the El Salvadoran civil war by both leftist forces and right-wing death squads supported by the government. In October 1979 the right-wing government of General Carlos Humberto Romero was overthrown by centrist opponents. The new government undertook an economic and political reform agenda, but guerrilla warfare continued. The Farabundo Martí National Liberation Front (FMNL) emerged as the government's primary leftist opponent. The murder of three American nuns by right-wing forces galvanized American public opinion against the government and led the JIMMY CARTER administration to suspend economic FOREIGN AID.

U.S. foreign policy shifted abruptly when RONALD REAGAN became president. His administration placed the conflict squarely in the context of communist aggression and employed the early COLD WAR image of falling dominoes. The Sandinista revolution in Nicaragua marked a first expansion of COMMUNISM beyond CUBA. By supplying arms to guerrillas in El Salvador a second domino was threatened. After that, all of Central American would be vulnerable, and then Reagan asked: "[W]hat would the consequence be for our position in Asia, Europe, and for alliances such as NATO?" In February 1981 the new administration released a STATE DEPARTMENT White Paper claiming that "definitive evidence [existed] of clandestine military support given by the Soviet Union, Cuba, and their communist allies to Marxist-Leninist guerrillas" bent on overthrowing the government of El Salvador. SECRETARY OF STATE ALEXANDER HAIG stated that his "externally managed and orchestrated intervention" would be dealt with at "the source." This represented a significant reversal from the policy of the Carter administration, which had curtailed economic aid due to the continuing human-rights abuses of the El Salvadoran government. The report met with controversy. References were made to a dissenting report within the State Department, and doubts as to the accuracy of the INTELLIGENCE used in writing it. A second attempt to bolster public support for an active U.S. role against the guerrillas came in 1982 when, on the eve of an El Salvadoran election, some intelligence reports were declassified. Haig pronounced the evidence as "overwhelming and unrefutable." However, in the days that followed, information emerged that contradicted it.

Domestic turmoil in El Salvador had long roots. Exploitative rule by the military and landowners had produced a situation in the mid-1970s in which 40 percent of the peasants had no land. This figure had risen from 12 percent in 1960. The Christian Democratic Party under the leadership of José Napoleon Duarte challenged these forces. Rather than allow an election in 1972 that Duarte might have won, the military took power and imprisoned and tortured Duarte. Left-wing forces now organized into a revolutionary opposition movement known as the Farabundo Martí Liberation Front (FMLN).

In 1979 junior military officers led a successful coup, bringing down the government of General Carlos Humberto Romero. While pledging to implement social reforms the new government continued a policy of political repression, with as many as 1,000 people being killed each month. In March 1980 the archbishop of San Salvador, who had spoken out against the violence, was assassinated, and in December four U.S. churchwomen were killed. Duarte emerged as head of this government, and the FLMN became its major opponent, leading a failed January 1981 military offensive against the government.

Beginning in early June 1981 Haig unsuccessfully sought NATIONAL SECURITY COUNCIL (NSC) approval for a blockade and other military action against Cuba as a means for dealing with the FLMN challenge to Duarte's government. SECRETARY OF DEFENSE Caspar Weinberger spoke out against these recommendations, citing fears of another VIETNAM. In fact, by this point in time, the struggle in El Salvador was not so much between the government and leftist forces as it was between the government and rightest forces allied with the military. These forces read into Haig's rhetoric an endorsement of its violence in the name of social order. Right-wing leader Roberto D'Aubuisson went so far as to assert that based on his meetings with the Reagan administration there would be no opposition from Washington to removing Duarte and the Christian Democrats from the ruling junta. The State Department responded by endorsing Duarte, but the White House stated, "[W]e just don't have a view on that."

Modernizing and supporting the military did not have the desired effect. Rather than getting weaker, the FLMN grew stronger. The Reagan administration placed the blame on Nicaragua and increasingly directed its attention there. Within El Salvador fighting crippled the economy. The gross national product declined 25 percent in eight years. By 1986, more than 40,000 people were killed or disappeared as a result of the actions of right-wing death squads. A U.S. Senate Intelligence Committee report concluded that "numerous Salvadoran and security forces and other officials organizations have been involved in encouraging or conducting death squad activity or violent abuses."

Gradually the administration shifted its focus to Nicaragua, and El Salvador became a less visible foreign-policy topic. In 1990 a UNITED NATIONS–brokered peace conference ultimately led to an agreement between the government and the guerrillas in 1991, with a cease-fire taking effect on February 1, 1992. The official end of the conflict occurred on December 15, 1992.

**Further reading:** America's Watch. *El Salvador's Decade of Terror.* New Haven, Conn.: Yale University Press, 1991; Diskin, Martin, and Kenneth Sharpe. *The Impact of U.S. Policy in El Salvador, 1979–1986.* Berkeley: University of California Press, 1986.

## embassy

In 2001 there were 191 countries in the world. The United States had diplomatic relations with 180 of them and maintained nearly 260 diplomatic and consular posts around the world. The embassy is the primary vehicle for representing American interests abroad. Embassies (which are typically located in the capital cities of foreign countries), consulates (which are found in large cities), and American diplomatic postings at international organizations are collectively referred to as U.S. missions. In some cases where the United States does not have full diplomatic relations with a country, it is represented by a liaison office or U.S. interests section.

Embassies are staffed by personnel from throughout the executive branch. In fact, it is not uncommon for STATE DEPARTMENT employees to account for less than one-half of the mission staff. Also typically found at missions are representatives from the Departments of COMMERCE, AGRICULTURE, DEFENSE, Justice (the Immigration and Naturalization Service, the Drug Enforcement Agency, and the FEDERAL BUREAU OF INVESTIGATION), the CENTRAL INTELLIGENCE AGENCY (CIA), and the U.S. AGENCY FOR INTERNATIONAL DEVELOPMENT. State Department officials at missions include political appointees, career FOREIGN SERVICE OFFICERS, and local nationals.

Missions are formally organized into "country teams" and headed by a chief of mission who is considered to be the president's personal representative. Normally ambassadors hold the title of chief of mission, but in some cases it may fall to a chargé d'affaires or minister. This individual is responsible for providing the PRESIDENT and SECRETARY OF STATE with expert guidance, directing and coordinating the activities of all executive-branch personnel, except for those under a U.S. area military commander, and cooperating with U.S. legislative and judicial branches to ensure that U.S. goals are advanced.

The country team is assigned several responsibilities. First are consular affairs. Officials assigned this task provide emergency services to Americans traveling abroad. These include emergency loans, searching for missing Americans, acting as a liaison with local police officials, and reissuing lost or stolen passports. Second are commercial, economic, and financial affairs. Officials working in this area provide assistance to American businesses. They provide advice on local trade policies, tariff laws, investment trends, financial developments, government procurement procedures, and potential joint-venture partners. These officials also help resolve trade disputes and issue reports

A Tanzanian policeman walks past a row of cars destroyed by a car bomb blast near the U.S. embassy in Dar es Salaam, August 1998. *(Reuters/Juda Ngwenya/Archive Photos)*

on economic matters that affect U.S. interests. Third are scientific and agricultural matters. These officials report on developments in these areas and are responsible for animal and plant inspections. Fourth are political, labor, and defense assistance issues. Political and labor officers and defense attachés analyze developments in their respective areas of jurisdiction and seek to promote the adoption of policies in the host country that advance U.S. interests. Fifth are administrative support and security functions. Officials working in this area are responsible for ensuring the routine functioning of the mission and ensuring its security.

Several concerns have been raised about the operation of U.S. embassies. One centers on the skills and outlooks possessed by ambassadors. There are two types of ambassadors, those who rise through the ranks of the Foreign Service and those who serve as political appointees. Whereas the former possess a thoroughgoing understanding of how a mission operates, the latter typically have lit-

tle experience in the day-to-day operation of a mission and little incentive to learn. At the end of President GEORGE H. W. BUSH's administration 20 percent of the ambassador corps consisted of political noncareer appointments. About 30 percent of President BILL CLINTON's ambassadorial appointments could be classified as political.

The first concern links directly to a second concern: the extent to which a country team truly functions as a team. Coordination problems are commonplace, and representatives from different agencies and bureaus are far more responsive to directives from their home offices in Washington than they are to instructions from the chief or the deputy chief of mission. To some extent these coordination problems simply reflect the difficulties of reaching a consensus at higher levels of policy making in Washington, but they are compounded by the differing linkages these officials establish with offices in the host government. Historically a particularly vexing problem has been coordinating with the CIA, whose officers operate under the cover of holding other positions within the embassy in carrying out their assignments and who often feel little need to keep the chief of mission or country team informed of their actions.

The third concern is the shrinking American presence abroad. The combination of limited funds for international activities plus an expanding foreign-policy agenda in some instances has required that embassies and consulates be closed or consolidated, raising questions about the ability of the United States to gather information abroad and effectively advance American interests.

A final concern is with the safety of American embassies. Responsibility for overseas embassies, the secretary of state, and high-ranking foreign officials when they visit the United States falls upon the Bureau of Diplomatic Security. Their task is a challenging one because American embassies and affiliated offices are highly visible symbolic targets for dissident groups to attack. It was not uncommon during the cold war years to see pictures of libraries and reading rooms attached to American embassies being attacked by student protestors. The current concern is with terrorist attacks. Major attacks were directed at the U.S. embassies in Nairobi, Kenya, and Dar es Salaam, Tanzania, in 1998. In May 2003, following terrorist attacks inspired by AL-QAEDA against foreigners in SAUDI ARABIA after the IRAQ WAR, the United States closed its embassies for a time.

See DIPLOMACY; TERRORISM.

## enlargement

Enlargement was the defining foreign-policy concept of the presidency of BILL CLINTON. PRESIDENT Clinton was the first true post–COLD WAR president. One of the most important tasks facing his administration was the formulation of a new foreign policy to replace CONTAINMENT. The GEORGE H. W. BUSH administration had not developed a new vision of American foreign policy. Commentators described its pre–PERSIAN GULF WAR approach to foreign policy as consisting largely of cleaning up the debris of the cold war.

In formulating its strategy of enlargement the Clinton administration worked from the concept of a DEMOCRATIC PEACE that was rooted in a WOODROW WILSON's vision of world politics. According to it, peace was best guaranteed by expanding (enlarging) the number of democratic states in the international system, increasing the level of trade between them, and promoting membership in international organizations (see DEMOCRATIZATION).

Clinton's policy did not represent a total break with recent American foreign-policy initiatives. RONALD REAGAN had also advocated spreading democracy, and George H. W. Bush was also an advocate of free trade. Clinton's

stress on multilateralism was new and became the object of criticism by Republicans. They charged that the United States's involvement in PEACEKEEPING activities in places such as HAITI, SOMALIA, and BOSNIA, as well as other HUMANITARIAN interventions, amounted to little more than international social work and prevented the United States from addressing more important national security issues.

## Enterprise for the Americas Initiative

On June 27, 1990, President GEORGE H. W. BUSH presented his Enterprise for the America's Initiative (EAI). He did so while negotiations to conclude the URUGUAY ROUND of GENERAL AGREEMENT ON TARIFFS AND TRADE (GATT) negotiations and NORTH ATLANTIC FREE TRADE AGREEMENT (NAFTA) negotiations were underway. President Bush asserted that the time had come for a new economic partnership in the hemisphere based "on trade, not aid." The EAI was endorsed by foreign ministers at a meeting at the General Assembly of the ORGANIZATION OF AMERICAN STATES in Santiago, CHILE, in June 1991.

The EAI is built around three pillars. The first is trade. The president declared his goal to be to create a "free trade zone from the port of Anchorage to the Tierra del Fuego." To this end, the United States was prepared to enter into a series of free-trade agreements with other market economies in Latin America and the Caribbean. Recognizing that not all states were prepared for such a step, Bush announced a willingness to negotiate bilateral framework agreements with states that would open markets and develop closer trade ties with the United States.

The second pillar is increased investment. This would be brought about by working with the Inter-American Development Bank and WORLD BANK to create new lending programs and investment funds for states that undertake market-oriented reforms that remove impediments to international investment.

The third pillar is debt relief. Citing the success of the BRADY PLAN but noting that more needs to be done, President Bush called for additional efforts to reduce commercial bank debt and official debt owed to the U.S. government. He proposed forgiving concessional loans that were used to purchase FOOD FOR PEACE aid and selling outstanding commercial loans to facilitate debt-for-nature swaps in countries where they have been established.

By mid-1993 uneven progress had been realized. The NAFTA agreement with MEXICO was signed, and bilateral framework agreements were in place with all regional states except CUBA, HAITI, and Suriname. The investment fund for the Inter-American Development Bank was not yet functioning, and funds were less than hoped for. The United States pledged $500 million for fiscal year 1993, but CONGRESS only appropriated $90 million, and the House of

Representatives only proposed spending $75 million in fiscal year 1994. Through June 1993 $875 million of official debt had been forgiven, out of $1,625 million.

See also ALLIANCE FOR PROGRESS; CARIBBEAN BASIN INITIATIVE; DEBT RELIEF.

## environment

Today, environmental problems are well-established features of the foreign-policy agenda of states and international organizations. This was not always the case. Traditional ways of thinking about foreign policy and international politics routinely led to the exclusion of environmental issues from consideration under all but the most extreme conditions. Environmental issues were seen either as domestic issues or as technical issues. They were not international political issues. The increased visibility and legitimacy has not translated into global solutions for environmental issues. Because of its political, economic, and technological resources the United States has become a key player in international environmental DIPLOMACY. However, Washington has often found itself in the minority in international deliberations.

The international politics of the environment are as complex as any in the field of world politics. Six critical problem areas can be identified. First, there is the issue of the quality of the Earth's atmosphere. It is being threatened by many of the by-products of modern and traditional society. Emissions of sulfur dioxide and nitrous oxide produce acid rain. The accumulation of carbon dioxide has led to the greenhouse effect in which world weather patterns are altered as a result of rising temperatures. Unwise agricultural practices increase the amount of atmospheric dust. The second critical issue is the depletion of freshwater supplies. At the root of the problem is the combination of ever-increasing demands made upon water resources due to population growth and agricultural and industrial development strategies. More than 200 river basins are international in scope, and 13 major rivers have five or more countries located within their watersheds. The situation is most dangerous in the Middle East.

The third environmental concern is the loss of soil productivity. In 1984 it was estimated that since 1977 desertification had increased at the rate of about 25.6 million acres per year. Starting in the 1990s, world farmers began losing an estimated 24 billion tons of topsoil from their crop lands annually. Although all countries face the problem of soil erosion it is particularly troubling in Africa, where much of the population still depends upon agriculture for food. The fourth concern is the loss of genetic diversity. Habitat destruction and poaching are recognized as major threats to the continued existence of many plants and animals. So too is modern technology. The development of hybrid seeds and synthetic materials has had a negative impact on the survivability of many genetic species found in the developing world.

The fifth environmental concern is tropical deforestation. The widespread harvesting of trees for fuel burning and the clearing of land for agriculture has resulted in the destruction of tropical rain forests. In the mid-20th century Ethiopia registered a 30 percent forest cover. In the 1980s this figure fell to 4 percent. Deforestation is both a problem in its own right and one that contributes to other problems, such as the loss of genetic diversity, the destruction of the atmosphere, and slowed economic development. The final environmental problem is the disposing of contaminated and hazardous wastes. One dimension of the problem involves the need to develop strategies for controlling the ongoing discharge of such materials into the atmosphere and coping with their long-term negative effects. A second dimension involves the need to control the international trade in waste. Short of hard currency, developing countries have become the depository for as much as one-fifth of the world's hazardous waste materials.

Overall, the United States's international environmental policy is best seen as a reflection of and extension of its domestic environmental programs. The first major piece of federal legislation dealing with air pollution came in 1955. The Air Pollution Control Act did little more than set up research and development programs. The 1970 Clean Air Act set up uniform national goals. This evolution mirrored that which took place in the area of water pollution. The 1948 Federal Water Pollution Control Act authorized the federal government to engage in research. The Water Quality Act of 1965 mandated that states establish standards, and the 1972 Federal Water Pollution Control Act sought to establish specific goals.

Washington's approach has been gradual, moving incrementally from authorizing research to setting goals, and American international environmental proposals have sought to minimize the cost that would be borne by the American public while working to convince other states to adopt American standards. They have also been coupled with economic or energy proposals. For this reason they are often referred to as convenient policies. This stands in contrast to a committed international environmental policy that would put forward proposals advancing tougher standards and high-priced penalties.

Convenience characterized the American position at the first major international environmental conference in Stockholm in 1972. The Stockholm Conference sought to address the economic, political, and social dimensions of global environmental problems in an integral fashion. At the conference, the United States was one of the strongest advocates of a 10-year ban on commercial whaling. This was an issue in which Washington had few economic interests. American delegates sought to weaken provisions of a proposed registrar of potentially toxic chemicals and abstained from voting on a resolution condemning NUCLEAR WEAPONS testing. Both of these were policy areas in which the United States had a major interest.

The Reagan administration was actively involved in the area of hazardous-waste disposal. President RONALD REAGAN rescinded President JIMMY CARTER's executive order restricting the export of hazardous materials on the grounds that each state had the right to decide its own standards. His administration also fought unsuccessfully to weaken international controls in this area. The United States cast the lone negative vote in international forums on a hazardous-waste resolution (146-1) and a World Charter for Nature (111-1).

The United States appeared to take a more cooperative and aggressive position in the negotiations over the MONTREAL PROTOCOL that sought to bring coordinated global action to bear on protecting the atmosphere. The United States supported reducing chloroflourocarbon (CFC) emissions. However, this support continued to represent a policy of environmental convenience. One of the most important sources of CFC emissions is aerosol spray cans, and these had been banned in the United States for 10 years. Moreover, Dupont and other major firms, which had already begun to develop substitutes for CFCs, supported the treaty.

The major international environmental-policy initiative of the Bush administration was the EARTH SUMMIT held in Rio de Janeiro in June 1992. GEORGE H. W. BUSH gave the initiative low priority and was most attracted to the domestic political issues raised by the proposed treaty. On the eve of his trip to address the conference Bush announced that the American environmental record was "second to none" but that it would be "counterproductive" to promote new environmental initiatives at the expense of the U.S. economy. Consistent with earlier domestic environmental initiatives Bush called both for passing a nonbinding set of principles and targets and for funding research and development programs. The Bush administration opposed a plan for sharing biotechnology with developing states because it might hurt the growing U.S. biotechnology industry. It also opposed setting legally binding targets for reducing global warming because of America's heavy dependence on fossil fuels and the fear that carbon dioxide controls might slow down the U.S. economy.

Controversy next arose over Washington's handling of the KYOTO PROTOCOL. The United States was again in the minority opposing key treaty provisions. At the last minute President BILL CLINTON agreed to have the United States sign the agreement in hopes of altering it during future deliberations. By this point CONGRESS had signaled its opposition to the treaty, which made ratification highly doubtful. GEORGE W. BUSH considered the treaty to be fatally flawed and withdrew from it. His actions, taken early in his administration, produced worldwide complaints about American UNILATERALISM.

**Further reading:** Caldwell, Lynton, K. *International Economic Policy: Emergence and Dimensions.* Rev. ed. Durham, N.C.: Duke University Press, 1996; Pinstrup-Anderen, Per, and Rajul Pandya-Lorch. *The Unfinished Agenda: Perspectives on Overcoming Hunger, Poverty, and Environmental Degradation.* Washington, D.C.: International Food Policy Research Institute, 2001; Porter, Garth, and Janet Brown. *Global Environmental Politics.* Boulder, Colo.: Westview, 1991.

## Eritrea

The size of Pennsylvania, with an area of 48,000 square miles and a population of 3.5 million people, Eritrea became independent on May 24, 1993. Prior to that time Eritrea had been ruled over by many different states. Historically it had been part of the ancient Ethiopian kingdom of Aksum, and it was on the basis of such ties that ETHIOPIA laid claim to Eritrea. GREAT BRITAIN and ITALY were the two major European powers to lay claim to it in the 19th century. Italy established a colonial presence in the 1880s. In 1935 Benito Mussolini used Eritrea as his base of operations for conquering Ethiopia. Great Britain captured it during WORLD WAR II and ruled it under a UNITED NATIONS mandate until 1952. In 1950 with U.S. support the United Nations had determined that Ethiopia and Eritrea should be joined in a federated state for 10 years. The decision was made over the objections of Eritrean nationalists.

Ethiopian emperor Haile Selassie formally annexed Eritrea in 1962. This decision set in motion a rebellion led by the Eritrean Liberation Front. After Selassie's overthrow in 1974 the Eritrean Liberation Front joined forces with the Eritrean Popular Liberation Front, and together these forces almost succeeded in pushing Ethiopia out of Eritrea. They were prevented from doing so by an infusion of military aid from the Soviet Union and the presence of Cuban forces on the side of Ethiopia. The rebellion in Eritrea continued to smolder through the 1980s. In 1991 the Eritrean rebels gained control over the region, and the United Nations organized a referendum on independence, which passed.

Since its independence the United States has provided substantial assistance to Eritrea. In fiscal year 2001, $50 million in humanitarian aid was given. It also gave another $10.2 million in development assistance. The need for foreign economic assistance is considerable due to the toll taken by Eritrea's involvement in two border struggles. The first was with Yemen over the control of islands in the Red

Sea. The second was with Ethiopia over a disputed border. Yemen prevailed in the first dispute. In the second the UNITED NATIONS sent in PEACEKEEPING forces as part of the cease-fire agreement, and an international tribunal ruling in 2002 gave both sides some of the disputed territory.

See also CUBA; RUSSIA; SOMALIA.

## espionage

Espionage is the act of secretly collecting information. More commonly we refer to it as spying. For most observers the history of American espionage begins after WORLD WAR II when the United States abandoned its staunch isolationist outlook on world affairs and entered into the COLD WAR with the Soviet Union. A closer look reveals that a much longer legacy exits.

Several notable cases of espionage occurred during the period surrounding the AMERICAN REVOLUTION. After the Boston Tea Party a group of some 30 Americans formed the Revere Gang, also known as the "Mechanics," to secretly gather information about British troop movements. It was information they obtained that provided warning to the minutemen of the pending British advance on Lexington. In 1776, with his retreating forces threatened by superior British firepower, General GEORGE WASHINGTON enlisted the services of Nathan Hale to spy on the British. His mission lasted only from September 1 to 22, 1776. Captured, he was executed without a trial. Several notable spy rings were organized and run by the Continental army during the American Revolution. One, the Culper Net, operated in the New York City and Long Island area. It played a key role in exposing General Benedict Arnold as a British spy. Benedict Arnold was a "walk-in": Rather than being recruited as a spy he volunteered his services to the British.

Up until World War II the history of American espionage is written in terms of the daring actions of individuals. It now begins to take on an organizational dimension. A first step involved the creation of the OFFICE OF STRATEGIC SERVICES (OSS). Its Secret Intelligence Branch (SI) conducted espionage throughout Europe. One of the most successful SI station chiefs was Allen Dulles, who would become a future head of the CENTRAL INTELLIGENCE AGENCY (CIA). One of his agents worked in the German Foreign Office and delivered more than 1,600 diplomatic cables. A second organizational development was the increased attention given to the use of technology as a means of spying on the enemy. The first great figure in American cryptanalysis was Herbert Yardley. His Black Chamber succeeded in breaking the codes of ARGENTINA, CHINA, CUBA, GREAT BRITAIN, FRANCE, GERMANY, JAPAN, and others before it was shut down in 1929 because, according to SECRETARY OF STATE HENRY STIMSON, "gentlemen do not read each other's mail."

The value of reading each other's mail became apparent during World War II as the United States and its allies experienced two great triumphs in cryptanalysis. The first involved the war with Japan. Code-named MAGIC, this effort allowed the United States to read key diplomatic traffic between the government of Japan and its EMBASSIES. The second cryptanalytic triumph was realized by the British, who successfully broke the code of one of Germany's key cipher machines. Code-named ULTRA, it provided the Allies with key information regarding German land, sea, and air campaigns in Europe and North Africa.

In the post–World War II era quantum leaps were made in the area of espionage through technological means. A first breakthrough was the development of the U-2 spy plane. It was a high-speed plane equipped with a high-definition camera. U-2 flights ended after the May 1960 downing of the plane piloted by Francis Gary Powers. Later breakthroughs would be made in satellite reconnaissance that permitted the interception of signal and electronic communications as well as the taking of high-resolution photographs.

Human espionage also accelerated with the onset of the cold war, when both the United States and the Soviet Union spied on each other. Among the most notable spy cases in the United States were those involving Robert Hanssen, the Johnny Walker spy ring, and Aldrich Ames. Respectively, these were Soviet spies in the FBI, U.S. Navy, and CIA. In February 2001, Robert Hanssen, a 27-year FBI veteran who specialized in COUNTERINTELLIGENCE, was arrested and charged with having spied for RUSSIA since 1985. He was the third FBI agent ever charged with espionage. Hanssen had received some $600,000 in cash and diamonds along with $800,000 escrowed in Russian bank accounts for his efforts. Included among the charges leveled at Hansen were 14 that were punishable by death.

John Walker began spying for the Soviet Union in 1968, apparently out of boredom and depression over the state of his marriage and career as a communications watch officer. He was the classic "walk-in," appearing at the Soviet embassy in January of that year and announcing that he wished to speak with someone from security. To prove his seriousness and value to the Soviets, Walker brought with him the key lists for the past 30 days to the KL-47 cipher machine. The heart of a cipher machine is a mathematical formula that is used to transform a plain-text message into an encrypted one. The logic is so sophisticated that there will be no one-to-one correspondence between the real letter and the letter that appears in the encrypted text. That is, no single letter will represent the letter o throughout the encrypted text. To further ensure the security of the communication system a key was required to read the encrypted message. The key is a one-time card that is used to engage the cipher machine. In essence it sets the staring point for the mathematical formula. Keys are changed every 24 hours. For the next two years, Walker provided the Soviet Union with information that for all practical purposes allowed Moscow to read all messages to and from American submarines and supporting ships. He also proceeded to organize his own spy ring. Walker's activities as a spy and spy master went unnoticed for more than 15 years.

A third major cold war case of espionage involves the activities of Aldrich Ames. His spying activities for the Soviet Union are widely considered to be the single most damaging breach of security in the CIA's history, costing at least 10 agents their lives and compromising more than 55 INTELLIGENCE operations over nearly a decade. Ames began working in the CIA's Directorate of Operations in 1968. On April 16, 1985, Ames walked into the Soviet embassy and presented the guard with a letter addressed to the resident KGB officer. Information in an envelope given by Ames to embassy officials provided the Soviet Union with the descriptions of two CIA moles operating within the embassy. Along with those names he provided the Soviets with information that established his identity as chief of the Soviet counterintelligence branch of the CIA. In return Ames sought $50,000.

Just as the onset of the cold war did not mark the beginning of espionage by and against the United States, so its passing in 1989 did not mark the end of espionage. Evidence on the continued relevance of espionage surfaces regularly. In 1996 CIA officer Harold Nicholson was arrested and charged with spying for RUSSIA. He pled guilty and is serving a 23-year sentence. In 1997 Edward Pitts, a 13-year FBI agent, was charged with spying for Russia. In 2000 army reserve colonel George Trofimoff was arrested for spying for Russia for more than 25 years. He is the highest-ranking military officer ever charged with espionage.

Turning to non-Russian hostile spying we find that in 2002 the DEFENSE INTELLIGENCE AGENCY's senior Cuban analyst, Ana Belán Montes, pled guilty to spying for CUBA for more than 16 years. Two years earlier Mariano Faget, a senior immigration official based in Miami, was charged with spying for Cuba. Also in 2002 a federal grand jury indicted Brian Regan, a retired air force master sergeant, with trying to spy for IRAQ, LIBYA, and CHINA. He wrote encrypted letters to leaders of Iraq and Libya offering them American INTELLIGENCE reports on their countries, satellite spy photographs, and related information.

The United States was not without its espionage successes. The most famous one involves KGB colonel Oleg Penkovsky, who provided the United States with key information on the CUBAN MISSILE CRISIS. Penkovsky first tried to defect in August 1960 but did not succeed until his third attempt because Western intelligence did not believe him.

After his recruitment Penkovsky was sent back to the Soviet Union with a tiny camera and instructions on what types of information were desired. In the coming months Penkovsky would pass additional information to his Western handlers, including a Soviet transcript of the Khrushchev-Kennedy SUMMIT CONFERENCE in Vienna. The KGB had begun to suspect Penkovsky of being a spy at least as early as January 1962. Penkovsky was arrested on October 31, during the Cuban missile crisis. It has been suggested that the timing of Penkovsky's arrest during the crisis signaled to the United States that the information Penkovsky gave them was correct.

See also INTELLIGENCE COMMUNITY.

**Further reading:** Hastedt, Glenn. *Espionage: A Reference Handbook.* Santa Barbara, Calif.: ABC-Clio, 2004; Hughes, John, and Harvey Klehr, *VENONA: Decoding Soviet Espionage in America.* New Haven, Conn.: Yale University Press, 1999; O'Toole, G. J. A. *Encyclopedia of Espionage.* New York: Facts On File, 1988.

## Ethiopia

Located on the Horn of AFRICA, Ethiopia is about the size of Texas, Oklahoma, and New Mexico combined, with an area of 472,000 square miles. It has a population of 68 million people, most of whom are engaged in subsistence farming. Ethiopia is the oldest independent state in Africa. The first sustained European presence came in 1493 when the Portuguese arrived. Bitter civil wars and hostility to foreigners contributed to a lengthy period of isolation from which Ethiopia, then known as Abyssinia, only emerged in the mid-19th century. Italy emerged as the dominant foreign power in the region in the late 1800s and in 1895 launched a failed invasion of Ethiopia that was designed to turn it into a protectorate. Following defeat at the battle of Adowa, Italy recognized Ethiopia's independence in 1896 but continued to hold on to its colony in ERITREA. Under Benito Mussolini, ITALY again invaded Ethiopia in 1935. The imposition of ECONOMIC SANCTIONS by the LEAGUE OF NATIONS had little effect, and on June 1, 1936, the king of Italy was made the emperor of Ethiopia, replacing Haile Selassie, who went into exile. British and South African forces liberated Ethiopia during WORLD WAR II, and in 1945 it again became an independent state.

Under Emperor Haile Selassie Ethiopia's post–World War II foreign policy was strongly pro-Western. Ethiopia received considerable foreign aid from the United States, and the United States was able to use Ethiopia's strategic location as a communications post. Between 1953 and 1974 Ethiopia received $197 million in military assistance. An important factor cementing their strategic partnership was American support for a 1950 UNITED NATIONS plan that united Ethiopia and Eritrea in a 10-year federation beginning in 1952.

In 1974 Haile Selassie was overthrown, and a revolutionary military government known as the Derg (the committee) came into power. The Derg turned toward the Soviet bloc for aid, signing a military assistance agreement in April 1975. Estimates place the amount of money owed by Ethiopia to the Soviet Union (see RUSSIA) for weapons at more than $3.5 billion. It followed these arms purchases up by expelling American military advisers and closing the Kagnew Station communications base. Domestically it imposed a purge in which thousands of suspected opponents of the Derg were tortured or killed.

SOMALIA sought to take advantage of the political chaos in Ethiopia by invading the Ogaden Desert region in July 1977 in order to advance its irredentist aims. It was only with an infusion of Soviet weapons and Cuban military forces that Ethiopia was able to hold on to the Ogaden. Somali forces were forced out in March 1978. Guerrilla activity by the Western Somali Liberation Front continued. The Ogaden National Liberation Front would later take the lead in GUERRILLA WARFARE.

The United States remained largely neutral in this struggle. It did not provide Somalia with weapons to offset the Communist support being received by Ethiopia. American neutrality ended following the Soviet invasion of AFGHANISTAN and the seizure of the American EMBASSY in Tehran. President JIMMY CARTER sold defensive weapons to Somalia. Later the United States cut off all economic assistance except for humanitarian and disaster aid under the terms of the 1985 International Security and Development Act, which makes such aid conditional on progress toward democracy and HUMAN RIGHTS.

The 1990s brought both an end to the COLD WAR and a new government. Ethiopia turned back to the West for aid, and relations with the United States have improved considerably. Addis Ababa supported economic sanctions against IRAQ in the PERSIAN GULF WAR as well as the use of military force. In fiscal year 1997 the United States aid to Ethiopia amounted to $77.2 million, including $39.9 million in food aid. President GEORGE H. W. BUSH also sought to mediate the conflict between Ethiopia and Eritrea, but by then Ethiopia had little chance of holding on to this region. Eritrean nationalists had risen up to challenge Ethiopia's rule in 1974. They temporarily succeeded in pushing Ethiopia out of Eritrea but were prevented from doing so by the same infusion of Communist military aid that turned the tide of battle against Somalia. In May 1993 Eritrea declared its independence. Fighting broke out between the two states in 1998, and in May 2000 Ethiopia launched a major invasion. A cease-fire agreement was signed in June 2000 and a treaty was agreed to in December.

**Further reading:** Korn, David A. *Ethiopia, the United States, and the Soviet Union.* Carbondale: Southern Illinois University Press, 1986.

## European Union

The founding steps toward creating the European Union (EU) took place in 1950 when on May 9 French foreign minister Robert Schuman proposed creating an INTERNATIONAL ORGANIZATION to coordinate the production of coal and steel. FRANCE and GERMANY had already fought two wars in the 20th century, and Schuman's plan would bind them together in the prospect of mutual economic gain. At the strategic level, the Schuman Plan marked a change in French thinking about how to deal with Germany. The idea of ALLIANCES replaced the traditional answer of seeking counterweights to it, namely RUSSIA. On April 8, 1951, France, Germany, ITALY, the NETHERLANDS, Luxembourg, and Belgium signed the Treaty of Paris establishing the European Coal and Steel Community. The six states agreed to create common external tariffs and a set of institutions to manage the new organization. In 1957 the six states expanded the depth and scope of their cooperation by signing the Treaty of Rome and creating the European Economic Community (EEC), also known as the Common Market.

Conspicuously absent from these economic efforts was GREAT BRITAIN. It valued its sovereignty, bilateral ties with the United States, and multilateral ties with the commonwealth more than it did the potential benefits of economic union with the Continent. The economic success of the EEC, however, was hard to deny, and attempts by Great Britain to fashion a rival, the European Free Trade Association, paled in comparison. Great Britain applied for admission to the EEC in 1963 only to be rejected by France. President Charles de Gaulle feared that British membership would dilute French influence. He again vetoed British membership in 1967. Great Britain did not enter the EEC until 1973.

The Treaty of Rome that created the EEC not only established a common market, but also it called for steps to move the member states down the road to political union. The next major step taken in this direction occurred in 1979 when France and Germany proposed establishing a European Monetary System. The immediate goal was to provide financial stability in the post–BRETTON WOODS international economic system by controlling fluctuations in exchange rates among EEC members. In the long run the goal was to establish a single European currency and monetary union. The first steps in this direction were taken without Great Britain, which did not want the value of the pound tied to other currencies.

The next major step toward political union came in 1985 with the decision to amend the Treaty of Rome.

Jacques Delors had become president of the European Commission that year, and he skillfully guided the members of the EEC down the path of integration. The Single European Act signed on February 17, 1986, formally replaced the EEC with the European Community (EC). Beyond the change in name came other important changes. One involved a change in decision-making rules. No longer were national governments to have vetoes over European Community decisions. In its place a system of qualified voting majorities was established to protect the interests of both large and small members. In economic terms the goal of the Single European Act was to remove nontariff barriers to trade. Enforcing this policy required shifting regulatory powers from national governments to the European Community level.

A combination of economic success and political crisis brought the next change in the political and economic structure of Europe. The Single European Act having been a success, talk now returned to the goal of establishing a common European currency. The crisis came in the form of the fall of the Berlin Wall and the impending possibility of German reunification. A united Germany, it was feared by some, might seek to establish an independent role for itself in Europe outside of existing European institutions. Preventing the future emergence of a "German Europe" required tying Germany more deeply into the role of a "European Germany." The answer to these challenges was the Treaty on European Union, or the Maastricht Treaty, signed in December 1991.

Once again a name change took place. The European Community became the European Union (EU). Under the terms of the Maastricht Treaty EU policies were separated into three pillars: economic and monetary union, common foreign and security policy (CFSP), and justice and home affairs. The Treaty on European Union was formally enacted on November 1, 1993. One of the goals identified in the first pillar was the creation of a monetary union and common currency. This goal was realized when on January 1, 2002, Euro bills and coins began to circulate in EU member states in place of national currencies of those states belonging to the European Monetary Union. Great Britain, Denmark, and Sweden opted not to participate.

The logic of integration that the EU followed in expanding to its present size is based on the notion of spillover. Success in one area was expected to spark interest and support for integration in another. The logic of spillover was to work at two levels. First, economic integration was to deepen. Second, economic integration was to lead toward political and security integration. Spillover has been far more successful in the first instance than in the second.

Because of its economic successes the EU has emerged as a major economic competitor (and partner) with the United States. The EU and United States account for about one-fifth of each other's merchandise exports and one-third of the trade in services. The EU accounts for 59 percent of all foreign investments in the United States, and the United States accounts for 51 percent of foreign investments in the EU. The two have often clashed over the conduct of international trade policy. More often than not agricultural issues have been at the core of these disputes. Farmers represent a small but politically powerful voting bloc in key EU states, most notably France, and virtually from the beginning European leaders have taken steps to protect the farmers' incomes and shield them from foreign competition as well as enhance their ability to compete in foreign markets. The key policy in this regard has been the Common Agricultural Policy (CAP). The CAP included subsidies and a tax on imports.

The Kennedy administration raised concerns about the CAP while it was still under discussion in 1961. The CAP went into effect in 1962 and immediately led to a "chicken war" as American exports of chickens to the EEC fell by two-thirds in a matter of weeks. Threats of retaliation were not long in following. The United States unsuccessfully sought to get the EEC to address the CAP in trade negotiations at both the KENNEDY and TOKYO ROUND negotiations carried out under the auspices of the GENERAL AGREEMENT ON TARIFFS AND TRADE (GATT). From the European perspective the CAP was nonnegotiable, and they were able to sustain this position throughout the 1960s. The EEC did agree in the Tokyo Round to make some concessions, such as lowering the tariffs on meat and dairy products.

Agriculture again topped the European-American negotiating agenda in November 1982 when U.S. trade representative William Brock proposed a new round of GATT talks that would become the URUGUAY ROUND. France reacted coolly to the prospects of trade talks that might jeopardize the CAP. The prospects of trade talks became more complicated in January 1986 when President RONALD REAGAN demanded compensation from the EC for $500 million in lost farm exports when SPAIN and Portugal joined the EC. A compromise was not reached until January 1987. Six months later the United States proposed eliminating all farm export subsidies by both the United States and the EU by 2000. Again the EU objected and in the process threatened to undermine the Uruguay Round negotiations. A December 1990 GATT negotiating meeting in Brussels produced a demonstration by 30,000 European farmers who opposed eliminating the CAP. Momentum was restored in November 1992 following the presidential election. Outgoing president GEORGE H.W. BUSH arranged for a meeting at Blair House in Washington at which the EC agreed to a 21-percent reduction in agricultural subsidies over a six-year period. This agreement was short-lived, and in December 1993 President BILL CLINTON sent a delegation consisting of the heads of the STATE DEPARTMENT, AGRICULTURE DEPARTMENT, and OFFICE OF THE U.S. SPECIAL TRADE REPRESENTATIVE to meet with EU leaders and arrange a compromise, which they did.

While the EU and the United States were able to come to an agreement on the CAP issue in 1993, disagreements have continued. Two of the most highly visible have involved beef hormones and bananas. Problems over beef hormones arose in 1985 when the EC announced it would ban the importation of animals and the meat from animals fed growth hormones. This is a standard practice in the United States and is part of the movement toward employing biotechnology to improve food yields and growth rates. In Europe it has raised concerns about the safety of the food supply and brought forward demands for action. The United States argues that no scientific evidence exists supporting these fears. It failed to get the EC to accept GATT mediation of the conflict but did agree to postpone implementation of the ban for one year under threat of retaliation. The impasse continued, and on January 1, 1989, the EC ban went into effect. In 1995 the United States approached the WORLD TRADE ORGANIZATION (WTO) and requested it settle the dispute. At first the EU succeeded in blocking this move, but on May 28, 1998, the WTO ruled in favor of the United States and CANADA, which had filed a suit of its own in 1996. The WTO instructed the EU to drop its ban on beef hormones. When the EU refused it authorized the United States to retaliate against $116.8 million in EU exports to the United States.

The conflict over bananas involves preferential treatment given by the EU to bananas imported from former European colonies in Africa, the Caribbean, and Pacific (ACP). Such preferences have been in place since the 1970s and fall under the rubric of the Lomé accords. The banana provisions were negotiated in the early 1990s. The United States protested the preferential duty-free treatment given to large quantities of bananas from ACP states in October 1995. Complaints from Latin American banana exporting states began in 1993 and in 1994 American-owned bananas companies lodged complaints with the Office of the U.S. Trade Representative under section 301 of the 1974 Trade Act. In 1997 the WTO ruled against the EU. An unsuccessful EU appeal was followed by an attempted compromise policy that the United States judged to be inadequate. In spring 1999 the WTO ruled that the United States could retaliate to the level of $191.4 million against EU imports to the United States.

The EU is not without its complaints or its successes in appealing to the WTO regarding what it sees as violations of free trade on the part of the United States. A particularly politically sensitive issue involves American attempts to protect its domestic steel industry from foreign competition. The Byrd Amendment, named after its primary sponsor

Senator Robert Byrd (D-W.V.) requires that any penalties collected from foreign steel companies found dumping their product in the United States must be turned over to the injured companies as opposed to going to the federal government. It is estimated that $470 million has been collected under the provisions of the Byrd Amendment. In January 2003 the WTO ruled against the United States.

Integration spillover into other policy areas came more slowly. A first move at some form of military integration came in the early 1950s following the outbreak of the KOREAN WAR. The United States was concerned that without the participation of German forces, Europe could not be defended in case of a Soviet attack. The NORTH ATLANTIC TREATY ORGANIZATION (NATO) had been created in 1949 but without Germany as a member. German rearmament, however, was opposed by many in Europe, especially the French. The outlines of a solution were presented by French foreign minister André Plevin. The Plevin plan called for creating a European army. All German forces would be subordinated to it, and other states would designate specific forces to be included in it. Initially the United States opposed the plan as militarily impractical, but it relaxed its opposition, and the six members of the ECSC signed the European Defense Community agreement in May 1952. French public opinion and French political leaders still could not accept the prospect of German rearmament, however, and the French General Assembly rejected the treaty in August 1954. The crisis in European unity was resolved when Great Britain proposed that the 1948 Brussels Treaty Organization that linked Great Britain, France, and the Benelux countries together be expanded to include Germany and Italy. This was agreed to, and the Western European Union (WEU) was created.

For all practical purposes, the WEU stagnated and all but disappeared until 1991 when it was reactivated by the Maastricht Treaty and designated as the foundation for a defensive capability of the EU. Since then its potential role has been clarified, but its capacity to act independently as an EU defense arm remains in doubt. The Amsterdam Treaty that came into effect in 1999 identified five objectives for an EU Common Foreign and Security Policy. They are to safeguard the common values, fundamental interests, independence, and integrity of its members; strengthen the security of the EU in all ways; preserve peace and strengthen international security in accordance with the principles of the United Nations and the HELSINKI ACCORDS; promote external cooperation; and develop and consolidate democracy, the rule of law, respect for HUMAN RIGHTS, and fundamental freedoms.

Operationally, the WEU can use military resources that its members have set aside for use by NATO. Several factors complicate the use of these forces independent of NATO. Among the most significant is the fact the WEU membership and NATO membership are not identical. Moreover, moving decision making out of NATO into the WEU does not end disagreements over how to use those forces. France and Germany have been the major advocates of building the WEU into a potential military force that could be used independently of the United States, while Great Britain remains more wedded to NATO. These disagreements prevented the WEU and by extension the EU, from which it is technically separate, from acting effectively on the ground to stop the fighting in BOSNIA AND HERZOGOVINA, KOSOVO, or CROATIA in the former YUGOSLAVIA. Some commentators have suggested that a possible division of labor is to have NATO undertake "hard security" problems and let the WEU handle "soft security" matters.

**Further reading:** Armstrong, David, et al. *From Versailles to Maastricht: International Organization in the Twentieth Century.* New York: St. Martin's, 1996; Park, William, and G. Wyn Rees. *Rethinking Security in the Post-Cold War Europe.* New York: Addison-Wesley Longman, 1998; Unwin, Derek W. *The Community of Europe: A History of European Integration since 1945.* New York: Longman, 1991.

## executive agreements

Executive agreements are international agreements entered into by PRESIDENTS. Unlike treaties, executive agreements do not need senatorial consent before taking force. Presidents have come to rely upon them heavily as a means for conducting foreign policy, and their use has come to symbolize the declining influence of CONGRESS on foreign policy.

Between 1946 and 1977 presidents entered into 451 treaties but signed more than 7,200 executive agreements. The overwhelming majority of these, 87 percent, were statutory agreements, agreements made with prior congressional approval. Tariff reductions are an example. However, others were entered into without congressional consent or even knowledge and were potentially significant. Ninety-nine established military bases overseas. In 1947 President HARRY TRUMAN entered into an agreement with the king of SAUDI ARABIA, in which he stated: "[O]ne of the basic policies of [the] U.S. is unqualifiedly to support

[the] territorial integrity of Saudi Arabia." Truman promised to take "energetic measures" through the UNITED NATIONS to ward off aggression against it.

Congress has taken several steps to try to curb the presidential use of executive agreements. In the 1950s it debated and nearly passed the BRICKER AMENDMENT. This was a proposed constitutional amendment that would have given the Senate the same consent powers in executive agreements that it has in treaties. In 1972 it passed the Case-Zablocki Act. This act required that Congress be informed of all executive agreements. The purpose was to give Congress the opportunity to take blocking action. Senator Clifford Case (D-N.J.) had estimated that there were at least 4,000 executive agreements in effect that Congress did not know about. The Case-Zablocki Act did not end the problem or practice of secret executive agreements. In 1975 it was estimated that some 400 to 600 agreements had still not be reported to Congress because the White House claimed they were verbal understandings, promises, or statements of intent rather than executive agreements. Included among these were a 1973 secret message RICHARD NIXON sent to North VIETNAM promising reconstruction aid if they accepted a peace agreement and the 1975 HELSINKI ACCORDS, which were defined as a statement of intent.

In its ruling in *UNITED STATES V. BELMONT*, the SUPREME COURT has held that executive agreements carry the same legal force as treaties. The primary restraint on the presidential use of executive agreements is political, the threat of congressional retaliation on part of the president's legislative agenda. An example of this occurred during the debate over the treaty enacted following the STRATEGIC ARMS LIMITATION TALKS (SALT I). The core of that treaty dealt with placing curbs on antiballistic missile systems. The agreed upon numbers for the U.S. and Soviet NUCLEAR WEAPONS ARSENALS were contained in an accompanying executive agreement. In order to secure passage of the SALT I Treaty the Nixon administration promised congressional critics that the "numbers" would be included in the SALT II Treaty so that they Senate could vote on them.

**Further reading:** Margolis, Lawrence. *Executive Agreements and Presidential Power in Foreign Policy.* New York: Praeger, 1986.

# F

## fast-track authority

Fast-track authority is a congressional grant of power to the PRESIDENT to negotiate trade agreements with other countries. The key feature to fast-track authority is that it requires CONGRESS to act quickly, restricting members to a single yes or no vote when the results of those negotiations are placed before them. Amendments cannot be added. This is held to be of the utmost significance by advocates of free trade because it strengthens the confidence of other states that the United States will abide by the terms of the trade agreement.

Presidents possess the constitutional authority to negotiate agreements with other states. Negotiating trade agreements is complicated by three factors. First, the CONSTITUTION gives Congress the power to control commerce. Second, the congressional politics of trade have been dominated historically by protectionist forces eager to limit foreign competition. Raising tariffs rather than lowering them was the objective of most legislators. Modern trade agreements have had the opposite goal. Politically, fast-track authority has served as a means for insulating legislators from protectionist pressures in their districts or states. Third, when a treaty requires changes in U.S. statutory law it must be submitted to Congress so that it may pass "implementing legislation." The impact of trade agreements on U.S. statutory law can be far-reaching. The NORTH AMERICAN FREE TRADE AGREE-MENT (NAFTA) required changes in 11,000 different tariff rates.

Congress first granted presidents broad powers to negotiate tariff reductions in 1934 with the passage of the Reciprocal Trade Agreements Act. This grant of authority has to be renewed periodically, and in 1974 fast-track authority was added to it in order to facilitate the TOKYO ROUND GENERAL AGREEMENT ON TARIFFS AND TRADE (GATT) talks. Congress agreed not to place legislative amendments on the trade agreement and to vote within 90 days. Congressional interests were protected by a manda-tory process of consultations between the executive branch and Congress before and during the negotiations.

Fast-track authority was renewed in 1979, 1988, and 1993. Among the notable agreements negotiated under fast-track authority are the 1979 Tokyo Round Agreement, the 1985 U.S.-Israeli Free Trade Agreement, the U.S.-Canada Free Trade Agreement of 1988, NORTH AMERI-CAN FREE TRADE AGREEMENT (NAFTA) in 1993, and the URUGUAY ROUND Agreements in 1994. Once seemingly routine the granting of fast-track authority is now quite controversial. The 1974 legislation passed by a vote of 323-6. It was extended in 1988 by a vote of 376-45, and in 1993 it passed by a vote of 295-126. The president's grant of fast-track authority expired when Congress passed the neces-sary implementing legislation for the WORLD TRADE ORGANIZATION that was created at the Uruguay Round. President BILL CLINTON sought and failed in 1997 to obtain a new grant of fast-track authority until at least 2001 in order to negotiate an expansion of NAFTA. Clinton's efforts failed for a combination of economic and political reasons. The principal economic reason was the uncertain impact of NAFTA on the U.S. economy. Clinton encoun-tered political opposition from a coalition of labor and envi-ronmental groups who wanted protection in these areas inserted into the body of the agreement. These groups had earlier mobilized against NAFTA, and their actions led to the insertion of side provisions in the agreement by the Clinton administration in order to gain congressional approval. President GEORGE W. BUSH also sought fast-track authority in order to negotiate a new round of WTO agree-ments and expand free trade within the Western Hemi-sphere. The request was made prior to the SEPTEMBER 11, 2001, terrorist attacks on the World Trade Center and the Pentagon. Even with the public show of congressional-legislative unity that followed this tragedy, when the House Ways and Means Committee voted its approval of the request in October, only two Democrats endorsed the mea-sure, and significant numbers of Republican members of the House were known to oppose it. Bush obtained fast-track authority in 2002.

## Federal Bureau of Investigation

Conventional accounts of American foreign policy do not accord the Federal Bureau of Investigation (FBI) a great deal of coverage. It is a recognized and established member of the INTELLIGENCE COMMUNITY, but until the SEPTEMBER 11, 2001, terrorist attacks on the United States this role was not considered significant. The war against TERRORISM catapulted the FBI into the limelight but also brought it criticism for its failure to cooperate more effectively with the CENTRAL INTELLIGENCE AGENCY (CIA). Due to these shortcomings and its inability to transition from a law enforcement agency into a counterterrorism unit, in late 2002, the GEORGE W. BUSH administration began to explore the possibility of creating a new domestic spy agency charged with INTELLIGENCE gathering and analysis against terrorism. This move was opposed by the FBI.

The forerunner of the FBI was created in 1908 when Attorney General Charles Bonaparte established a force of special agents to investigate federal crimes. On March 16, 1909, these agents were given an organizational identity when they formed the nucleus for the newly constituted Bureau of Investigation. During WORLD WAR I the bureau was assigned responsibility for the ESPIONAGE, Selective Service, and Sabotage Acts. This expansion in task was significant because historically one of the principal dilemmas that the FBI has faced in carrying out its mission is determining the dividing line between legitimate dissent and espionage or other illegal activities directed against the U.S. government. The dividing line was crossed quickly. During the war the attorney general encouraged the organization of private volunteer citizen groups to uncover disloyalty and aid the FBI in its new charge. Singled out for high praise in the report was the American Protective League (APL). The APL infiltrated leftist labor groups, such as the International Workers of the World, and anarchist groups in search of traitors and spies. Once these perceived threats had been squelched, it directed its attention to draft evaders.

Once the war ended a concern for countering foreign espionage remained, even though officially the FBI returned to its prewar role of investigating federal crimes. The focal point was the Red Scare of 1919–20. Attorney General A. Mitchell Palmer announced that the United States was being consumed by a "blaze of revolution." He placed J. Edgar Hoover in charge of a newly created General Intelligence Division within the Bureau of Investigation with orders to compile a listing of radical organizations and individuals. Palmer's raids of January 2, 1920, resulted in the arrest of practically every leader of the Communist Party in America or allied labor organizations. Often carried out without warrants, these raids resulted in many innocent people being arrested and a public outcry over their excesses.

With the movement toward war in Europe in the late 1930s and early 1940s, the FBI once again officially began to investigate subversion. In 1936 President FRANKLIN ROOSEVELT issued a presidential directive to this effect, and in 1940 CONGRESS gave the FBI additional authorization when it passed the Smith Act, which made advocacy of the violent overthrow of the U.S. government a crime. Using this authority the FBI uncovered several major espionage rings in the United States. In 1942 alone, it uncovered three. One involved a group of eight saboteurs recruited and led by George John Dasch. They tried to land by sea and conduct sabotage in Florida and Long Island. His handler was Lieutenant Walter Kappe of German intelligence. A second espionage ring involved three individuals. At its center was Count Anastase Andreievitch Vonsiatsky, the self-proclaimed führer of American fascism. Evidence indicates that at no time did these three individuals actually make contact with German agents or pass intelligence to them. The third Nazi espionage ring involved 33 members and was headed by Frederick Joubert Duquesne. On January 2, 1942, they were sentenced to a total of more than 300 years in prison. Duquesne was a naturalized American citizen born in South Africa. Much of the information that he obtained and tried to pass on to Germany involved industrial and technological matters that he acquired through correspondence with American business concerns in which he pretended to be a student. The key to uncovering the espionage ring was William Sebold, a German-born naturalized American citizen who acted as a double agent.

During World War II the FBI also acquired an overseas presence. A small group of special agents were split off to form the Secret Intelligence Service. They were stationed in Latin America, and their job was to provide information about Axis activities in the Western Hemisphere. Their establishment foreshadows future bureaucratic conflicts within the intelligence community. As part of the bureaucratic battle that led to the creation of the OFFICE OF STRATEGIC SERVICES (OSS), the forerunner of the CIA, J. Edgar Hoover obtained an agreement that prohibited the OSS from carrying out activities in Latin America.

After WORLD WAR II, the FBI turned its attention from Nazi-led espionage to communist espionage. Of particular concern was the possibility of communist spies having infiltrated the U.S. government. Executive orders by both DWIGHT EISENHOWER and HARRY TRUMAN gave the FBI responsibility for investigating allegations of disloyalty by federal employees. Particularly sensational were the arrests of Julius and Ethel Rosenberg, Klaus Fuchs, and Alger Hiss as Soviet spies. Questions about the validity of the allegations against them were laid to rest only in 1995 when the CIA released signals and intelligence intercepts that identified them as spies. Along with others they constituted a Soviet "atom spy" ring that penetrated the Manhattan Project and passed secret information about the atomic bomb to the Soviets.

Unfortunately, much excess was also present in the hunt for communist spies. Most notable in this regard was J. Edgar Hoover's Counter Intelligence Program (COINTELPRO). Originally targeted on the Communist Party and designed to carry out "dirty tricks" as much as it was to gather intelligence on espionage activities, COINTELPRO's operations were expanded to include leftist groups, such as the Black Panthers. All totaled, between 1955 and 1975 the FBI conducted 740,000 investigations into subversive matters and 190,000 investigations into extremist matters.

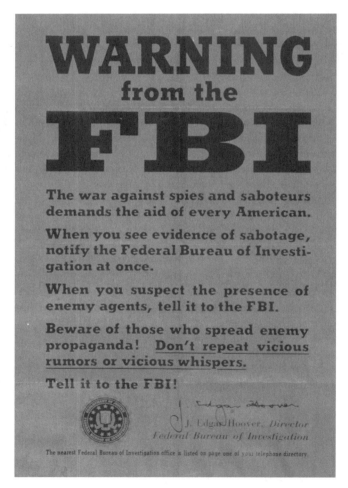

During World War II the FBI poster shown here warned Americans to be on the lookout for evidence of sabotage or rumor mongering. *(National Archives)*

After the end of the COLD WAR, the FBI's mission changed somewhat. The concern was still with protecting American national security interests, but the focus shifted from defending against the aggressive actions of hostile foreign intelligence agencies to protecting U.S. information and technologies. This redefinition was part of the 1991 National Security Threat List produced by the White House. With the passage of the U.S. PATRIOT ACT on October 26, 2001, the FBI's mission expanded again as it was now charged with defending the United States from future terrorist attacks.

See also COUNTERINTELLIGENCE; HOMELAND SECURITY, DEPARTMENT OF; MCCARTHYISM.

**Further reading:** Donner, Frank. *The Age of Surveillance: The Aims and Methods of America's Political Intelligence System.* New York: Vintage, 1981; Kessler, Ronald. *The FBI.* New York: Pocket, 1993; Riebling, Mark. *Wedge: The Secret War between the FBI and CIA.* Rev. ed. New York: Knopf, 2002.

## Federalist Papers

The debate over ratification of the proposed CONSTITUTION took many forms. Perhaps the most significant was a series of 85 newspaper articles written by ALEXANDER HAMILTON, James Madison, and John Jay between October 1787 and July 1788. Collectively they are known as the Federalist Papers. Those written by Hamilton often addressed squarely the question of foreign-policy powers.

In Federalist essays 24, 25, and 26, Hamilton spoke to the need to protect the United States from foreign aggression. He called for the creation of a navy to protect and advance America's interests as a "commercial people." He advocated creating a standing army rather than relying upon militias to protect the United States from aggression. In Federalist 28 he sought to reassure Americans that the dangers presented by a standing army in times of peace were not so great as imagined or remembered from past experience. Madison addressed this point in Federalist 41, stating, "How could a readiness for war in time of peace be safely prohibited unless we could prohibit in like manner, the preparation and establishment of every hostile nation?"

Hamilton also sought to assure Americans that the foreign-policy powers to be given to the PRESIDENT did not transform him into an equivalent of the British monarch. In Federalist 69 he writes that "there is no comparison between the intended power of the president and the actual power of the British sovereign. The one can perform alone what the other can do only with the concurrence of a branch of the legislature." In Federalist 75 Hamilton addressed the debate over whether treaty-making powers should be given to Congress or the president. He asserted that "the power of making treaties is, plainly, neither one nor the other. . . . Its objects are CONTRACTS with foreign nation, which have the force of law, but derive it from the obligations of good faith. . . . The power in question seems therefore to form a distinct department, and to belong, properly, neither to the legislative nor to the executive."

See also ARTICLES OF CONFEDERATION.

**Further reading:** Morris, Richard B. *The Forging of the Union, 1781–1789.* New York: Harper and Row, 1987.

## Federalist Party

The Federalist Party grew out of factions that developed within President GEORGE WASHINGTON's administration. The Federalists grouped around the policies of ALEXANDER HAMILTON, who advocated the creation of a strong national government, economic modernization, and a pro-British foreign policy. Aligned against them were allies of THOMAS JEFFERSON who would come to be known collectively as Democratic-Republicans. They called for creating a national government that above all respected states' rights and individual civil liberties. In foreign policy they were pro-French. The evolution of these factions into formal political parties turned heavily on foreign-policy disputes. The political stronghold of the Federalists was with the merchant class and property owners of the North. They also had support among conservative farmers.

A first step in this direction came in 1794 with their disagreement over JAY'S TREATY. The Federalists supported the treaty, while the Democratic-Republicans opposed it. Sent to GREAT BRITAIN to avoid war, John Jay negotiated a treaty that settled few of the new country's economic and security grievances against Britain but did provide for a commercial agreement that was highly valued by the Federalists. Hamilton also succeeded in outmaneuvering the Jeffersonians and their desire to support revolutionary FRANCE in its war with Great Britain when he convinced Washington to include a call for neutrality in Europe affairs in his farewell address. Under JOHN ADAMS the United States adopted a foreign policy fully in line with Federalist thinking as it began preparations for war with France following the XYZ affair. The Federalists also passed the Alien and Sedition Acts in 1798, which had the twin purposes of providing for national security by imprisoning and deporting immigrants suspected of dangerous activity and destroying part of the political base of the Republican Party. President John Adams's decision to seek peace with France rather than go to war caused a rift in the Federalist Party that would help bring the presidency to Thomas Jefferson and mark the effective end of Federalist rule.

Conflict between the parties in the area of foreign affairs continued, although the Federalists did support Jefferson's LOUISIANA PURCHASE, something only a strong central government such as that favored by the Federalists could be expected to do. Voices of Federalist dissent were heard. Some argued that Jefferson had paid too much, and others feared that the Louisiana Territory would give birth to agricultural states whose citizens would be inclined to support Jeffersonian rather than Hamiltonian principles and policies.

The final major rift between the two parties came with the WAR OF 1812. The first signs of partisan conflict came in 1806 during the Jefferson administration when Congress passed the Nonimportation Act that blocked a specific set of goods from being imported from Great Britain. This was followed by the 1807 embargo that forbade all international trade between the United States and Europe. In 1808 it was extended to cover trade with CANADA as well. Federalist supporters were hit particularly hard by these prohibitions. Actual war with Great Britain harmed them even more, and it was opposed by the Federalists in and out of Congress. In 1814–15 Federalists from New England gathered in Hartford, Connecticut, to consider ways of protecting states' rights. A proposal to secede was rejected. The antiwar sentiment given expression at the Hartford Convention was overtaken by the announced signing of the TREATY OF GHENT and ANDREW JACKSON's victory in the Battle of New Orleans.

America's victory in the War of 1812 consigned the Federalists to the margins of American politics, which were now entering the "era of good feelings." By 1820 the Federalists had stopped fielding presidential candidates.

## filibustering

In the 1850s American foreign policy toward Latin America became enmeshed in the issue of slavery. Southerners supported expansion into the region as a way of increasing the potential number of slave states. Abolitionist Northerners opposed it for the same reason. Complicating the situation even further were diplomatic concerns. American officials recognized that pushing too aggressively into the region might create problems with SPAIN. Not supporting the growing tide for independence in Latin America would alienate these forces and perhaps push them toward closer economic ties with GREAT BRITAIN.

With expansionist DIPLOMACY largely held hostage to the domestic political deadlock over slavery and diplomatic concerns, proslavery forces increasingly pinned their hopes on the exploits of private citizens known as filibusters, a term derived from the Dutch that meant pirates or freebooters. At the broadest level filibusters drew their inspiration from the rhetoric and imagery of MANIFEST DESTINY. One step beneath this was a host of other factors that motivated filibusters. The most important factor for American foreign policy was expanding slavery. Others included personal financial

GEN. LOPEZ THE CUBAN PATRIOT GETTING HIS CASH

LOPEZ. We have not Revolutionized Cuba, but then we have Got what we came for, my Comrades came for Glory, I came for Cash, I've Got the Cash, they've Got the Glory, & I suppose we're all satisfied. Im O. P. H. for the United States again. Cant Live under a Military Despotism

A satiric portrait of Venezuelan-born general Narciso López, leader of an 1850 expedition to liberate Cuba from Spanish rule  (*Harper's Weekly*)

gain, glory, and political power. Filibusters frequently enjoyed financial support in the United States and operated out of American ports, primarily New Orleans and Baltimore, with little interference from government officials.

One of the most famous filibusters was General Narciso López, who led an invasion of CUBA in 1849. Earlier in his career he had served in the Spanish military and was a Cuban businessman. Backed by American interests, López put together an army made up of veterans of the MEXICAN WAR and offered them, among other things, a $1,000 bonus and 160 acres of land in Cuba if they succeeded in liberating the island so that it could be annexed by the United States. In 1849 an American naval blockade turned back his invading forces. He tried again in 1850 and succeeded in reaching Cuba, but his forces were soon overwhelmed by the Spanish military, and he found little public support. López managed to escape to FLORIDA, where he mounted another expedition to Cuba in 1851. This time he was captured and executed.

The Cuban cause was picked up by another filibuster, John Quitman. A former governor of Mississippi and general in the Mexican War, Quitman was approached by Cuban exiles living in the United States who offered him a dictatorship on the island. Quitman organized an army of 300 men, but nothing came of his plans, and he gave up in 1855. He ran short of money, and the Pierce administration made clear its opposition to his venture.

Another notable filibuster was William Walker. A lawyer and doctor, Walker sought to "liberate" Lower California from Mexico. In 1853 he succeeded in capturing the capital of Lower California and declared it to be an independent republic, but he was unable to hold his forces together and consolidate power. Walker was tried for violating the Neutrality Act but acquitted. He then turned his attention to NICARAGUA, where he had been invited by the liberals to intervene in the ongoing civil war on their behalf. Walker put together a small force and invaded Nicaragua in 1855, but he soon abandoned the liberals and established himself as president. In an 1856 presidential decree Walker reinstated slavery in Nicaragua. Once again his grip on power was far from secure, and in mid-1857 he was forced to flee. Walker would make four more efforts to take over Nicaragua. In 1860 he was captured by the British, who turned him over to Honduran forces. They executed him.

Walker's exploits in Nicaragua awakened a complicated set of political forces in the United States. Opposing him was Cornelius Vanderbilt, who had obtained the rights to a trans-Nicaraguan canal and who operated a noncanal transport route when that failed. Also opposing him were anxious U.S. government officials who opposed annexation. Walker was supported by Mississippi senator Albert Brown, who wished to see Nicaragua become a slave state, and business opponents of Vanderbilt. One of them was William Cazneau, who would attempt to negotiate a treaty annexing the DOMINICAN REPUBLIC.

Filibustering is an early example of private diplomacy. It illustrates how nonstate actors have the ability to influence foreign policy and the flow of world politics. Filibusters played an important role in American foreign policy at this time due to the political deadlock that existed over slavery. Filibustering faded in importance as the United States became consumed in civil war, which settled the slavery issue and thereby changed the foreign-policy agenda in Latin America.

**Further reading:** Brown, Charles H. *Agents of Manifest Destiny: The Life and Times of the Filibusters.* Chapel Hill: University of North Carolina Press, 1980.

## first ladies and American foreign policy

The position of the first lady is one of the most underresearched topics in American politics, as it relates to both domestic policy and foreign policy. In large part this is because the position of the first lady and any political POWER that derives from it comes from the first lady's marriage to the PRESIDENT. There is no job description, salary, or constitutional statement of power. The first lady's political role is shaped by tradition, personal interest and background, her relationship with her husband and his administration, and public expectations. In combination with these background or conditioning factors, the office of the first lady offers the first lady a platform for advancing domestic and international policies.

Anecdotal and fragmentary evidence points to the frequent involvement of first ladies in American foreign policy. In 1799 Abigail Adams lobbied President JOHN ADAMS on a treaty with the NETHERLANDS. Edith Wilson served as President WOODROW WILSON's communication link with foreign governments and others in the U.S. government while he was incapacitated by a stroke. As a general rule she acted in a neutral fashion, but she did try, but failed, to get Wilson to agree to accept Senator HENRY CABOT LODGE's (R.-Mass.) reservations regarding the LEAGUE OF NATIONS when he made it clear to her that Senate approval of the TREATY OF VERSAILLES hinged on their acceptance.

Eleanor Roosevelt was known to engage in spirited conversations and debates with President FRANKLIN ROOSEVELT over a wide variety of policy issues during his presidency. They often disagreed. She remained a supporter of the League of Nations after Roosevelt abandoned it, and she successfully urged him to drop U.S. neutrality during the Spanish civil war. At YALTA she lamented Roosevelt's willingness to allow Lithuania, Latvia, and Estonia to be absorbed into the Soviet Union (see RUSSIA). Prior to U.S. involvement in WORLD WAR II, Eleanor Roosevelt pushed the STATE DEPARTMENT to admit more Jewish REFUGEES into the United States.

Bess Truman had frequent conversations with President HARRY TRUMAN on the MARSHALL PLAN, although she was not, as a general rule, informed about American foreign-policy initiatives. The most significant of these was the dropping of the atomic bomb on Hiroshima, something she opposed and only learned of through the newspapers. Both Pat Nixon and Jackie Kennedy undertook goodwill tours abroad for their husbands, often improving the overall state of U.S. relations with the visited countries. Robert McFarlane, President RONALD REAGAN's NATIONAL SECURITY ADVISOR, asserts that White House options responding to the IRAN-CONTRA AFFAIR were limited by what Nancy Reagan would allow. In other matters, she counseled Reagan against laying a wreath at Bitburg cemetery in GERMANY, sided with foreign-policy moderates in moving to temper Reagan's harsh anti-Soviet rhetoric, urged him to reduce military spending, and favored a diplomatic solution to the Nicaraguan conflict.

Evidence today points to a more systematic involvement of some first ladies in foreign-policy matters. The two leading cases are Rosalynn Carter and Hillary Rodham Clinton. The most visible foreign-policy initiative undertaken by Mrs. Carter involved traveling abroad. She traveled to Latin America in June 1977. During her trip she emphasized some of the dominant themes of JIMMY CARTER's foreign policy—HUMAN RIGHTS, nuclear ARMS CONTROL, and a reduction in conventional arms sales. She conveyed to Latin American leaders that Carter's definition of human rights embraced promoting economic and social progress as well as furthering political freedoms.

Mrs. Carter's trip was not undertaken in the best of circumstances. A heated conventional arms race was building up in the Western Hemisphere. Shortly before she left, President Carter signed a treaty establishing a nuclear-free zone in Latin America, and while she was in Costa Rica, he signed the American Convention on Human Rights. Both of these documents placed the United States squarely at odds with several of its southern neighbors who saw these documents as unwarranted intrusions into their domestic affairs. Under Presidents Nixon and Ford American foreign policy focused heavily on U.S.-Soviet relations, and little concern was given to these matters. Mrs. Carter was to urge the leaders she met with to sign these two agreements.

Preparation for Mrs. Carter's trip began two months before it took place. Briefings were held by officials from the TREASURY and STATE DEPARTMENTS, the NATIONAL SECURITY COUNCIL, and the ORGANIZATION OF AMERICAN STATES. The countries she visited (Jamaica Costa Rica, Ecuador, Peru, BRAZIL, COLOMBIA, and VENEZUELA) were

Eleanor Roosevelt displays a Spanish translation of the UN Declaration of Human Rights. *(Roosevelt Library)*

chosen by the president and representatives from the State Department and NATIONAL SECURITY AGENCY.

The foreign-policy initiative that stands out as most important during Hillary Clinton's eight-year term as first lady was her promotion of women's and children's rights. The centerpiece of her efforts was her September 1995 participation in the UNITED NATIONS Fourth World Conference on Women held in Beijing. The main issues she addressed included stopping violence against women, empowering women economically and politically, granting sexual rights to women, and ensuring that such programs were funded and implemented.

The Clinton administration announced that first lady Hilary Clinton would attend the conference one day after Harry Wu, a Chinese-American HUMAN-RIGHTS activist, was convicted of spying by CHINA and expelled. The Clinton administration had given serious consideration to not sending Mrs. Clinton to the conference as a sign of its displeasure. Several Republicans, including announced presidential candidates Robert Dole and Richard Lugar, urged the Clinton administration to boycott the conference in protest of China's human-rights record and the fear that the conference would endorse a pro-abortion position. At the conference Mrs. Clinton delivered a strongly worded speech that indirectly criticized China's treatment of women. Her comments were far more stringent than those issued publicly by the administration. An administration official would deny that they signaled a change in U.S. policy.

This was not the only occasion that Mrs. Clinton spoke out on these issues. Earlier that year she spoke at the first UN World Summit on Social Development and called for states to increase their funding for social policies as opposed to weapons procurement. She also spoke at the UN conference on women, where she continued to call for full economic and social opportunities for women. Mrs. Clinton also made trips to Latin America and Asia that highlighted human rights and development issues.

Mrs. Clinton's advocacy of human rights involved collaboration and planning with other executive branch agencies. More than one year's worth of preparation went into the planning for the UN Conference in Beijing. Involved were representatives from her office, the State Department, the National Security Council, the Office of the Ambassador to the UN, and nongovernmental organizations. Similar consultations were held for her other overseas trips.

In both these cases, it is clear that the foreign-policy activities of Mrs. Carter and Mrs. Clinton were not "lone ranger" activities. They were coordinated efforts undertaken with the approval and involvement of key foreign-policy BUREAUCRACIES and the White House. In these activities we can see the potential held by the foreign-policy activity of first ladies for advancing the agendas of presidential administrations, which can highlight issues and steer them onto the policy agenda.

**Further reading:** Watson, Robert, and Anthony Eksterowicz, eds. *The Presidential Companion: Readings on the First Ladies.* Columbia: University of South Carolina Press, 2003.

## Florida, acquisition of

The United States acquired Florida through the Adams-Onís Treaty signed in 1819, which was negotiated by JOHN QUINCY ADAMS. According to its terms SPAIN ceded East Florida to the United States and recognized its earlier annexation of West Florida. The United States also agreed to pay up to $5 million in claims by U.S. citizens against the Spanish government. The Senate unanimously approved the treaty two days after it was signed. Spain, however, delayed for two years, fearing that once in possession of Florida the United States would move quickly to recognize the independence of Spain's rebellious colonies in South America. Because a six-month time limit had accompanied the Senate's ratification vote, a second vote was required. Opposition arose, led by Senator HENRY CLAY, who wished to include the annexation of TEXAS in the agreement. Clay failed, and on February 22, 1821, letters of ratification were exchanged.

Great intrigue accompanied earlier and persistent U.S. efforts to acquire the Floridas. West Florida was occupied by U.S. forces in 1810 following a revolt encouraged by U.S. officials. On October 27, 1810, President James Madison extended U.S. jurisdiction to the Republic of West Florida, asserting that it had actually been part of the LOUISIANA PURCHASE and rightfully belonged to the United States. The Floridas had been identified as territory to be purchased by President THOMAS JEFFERSON in 1803, but they had not been part of the Louisiana Purchase as ultimately concluded. Portions of West Florida were not included in the 1803 cession, but the lands were acquired by the treaty that ended the WAR OF 1812.

With this accomplished U.S. officials turned their attention to East Florida, which they acknowledged would be more difficult to annex. In 1812, prior to the War of 1812, President Madison conspired with George Matthews, a former governor of Georgia, to encourage an insurgency movement in East Florida. The episode proved to be an embarrassing one for Madison, who disavowed Matthews, and captured land was returned to Spain.

Diplomatic talks on acquiring East Florida began in 1816, but they were complicated by Spain's concerns about its other colonial holdings in the New World and pressure from Clay and others, who sought U.S. recognition of their independence. By this time the U.S.-Spanish border had become very porous, and East Florida became home to marauding groups of NATIVE AMERICANS, runaway slaves, and others who used the territory as a base of operations. Late in 1817 President JAMES MONROE commissioned General ANDREW JACKSON to end this threat but to respect the Spanish flag. Jackson pursued hostile Native American forces into East Florida aggressively, but he also ignored his orders and deposed of the Spanish governor, appointed an American in his place, and executed two British subjects.

Jackson's actions set off a political crisis both at home and abroad. In the midst of this uproar SECRETARY OF STATE John Quincy Adams replied to Spanish complaints about Jackson with complaints of his own against the Spanish inability to rule over its property. And he expressed the willingness of the United States to act again if need be. His message was clear: control the territory or cede it to the United States. Shortly thereafter the Adams-Onís negotiations began. They were resumed in 1816, and the agreement was signed on February 22, 1819. In addition to ceding Florida to the United States, Spain also dropped its claim to the OREGON Territory. The United States countered by dropping its claim to Texas as part of the Louisiana Territory.

## Food for Peace

Also known as Public Law (PL) 480, the Food for Peace program was created in 1954 as a means for disposing of large American food surpluses and for helping impoverished states that lacked the financial resources to engage in commercial purchases of food. The expectation was that by doing so the Food for Peace program would protect the domestic price of American agricultural goods and lay the foundations for future agricultural sales abroad by stimulating demand for American agricultural exports. Beginning in the mid-1960s the focus of the Food for Peace program shifted from disposing of surplus food stocks to promoting economic development and combating hunger and malnutrition. It was at this time that the Food for Peace program was phased out in Western Europe and JAPAN.

More recently, as a result of the 1990 Food, Agriculture, Conservation, and Trade (FACT) Act, the Food for Peace program expanded its attention to include the problem of food security. The absence of access to food—food insecurity—is seen as a major contributor to international instability. It is a multidimensional problem that touches upon the success of economic growth strategies, the ability of states to protect the environment, problems of poor health and high rates of infant mortality, migration, the status of women in society, illiteracy, and DEMOCRATIZATION. The FACT Act also redirected Food for Peace dis-

bursement programs away from government-to-government programs to targeted assistance programs addressing human and economic development issues and working more heavily through private voluntary organizations, such as CARE, Lutheran World Relief, Africare, and World Vision Relief and Development, Inc. With the end of the COLD WAR the Food for Peace program is also tasked with helping countries make the transition to democracy.

The existence of multiple missions for the Food for Peace program is built into its legislative funding mechanisms and administrative structure. Title I funds are administered by the AGRICULTURE DEPARTMENT and continue to focus on providing food on concessional terms and developing export markets for American agriculture. In the 1950s and 1960s the Food for Peace program accounted for some 50 percent of U.S. agricultural exports. This has changed dramatically. Today they account for only 4 percent of these exports. In actual amounts, this represents a decline from 18 million metric tons annually in the 1960s to about 4 million metric tons today. The Food for Peace program, however, remains significant for certain products, notably wheat, rice, soybeans, and flour.

The disbursement of Title II funds is coordinated by the UNITED STATES AGENCY FOR INTERNATIONAL DEVELOPMENT (USAID). These funds are directed at disaster relief and support for food programs administered by private voluntary organizations and international organizations. Title III funds are also coordinated by USAID and are targeted for the poorest countries. In fiscal year 1994, private voluntary organizations received access to 770,000 million metric tons of Title II products that were used to help 34 million people. Specific programs they ran included food-for-work projects, maternal- and child-health projects, and school feeding programs. In the Madras state of INDIA, CARE engaged in long-running female education and literacy programs as well as family nutrition programs. Together these programs are credited with reducing the birth rate by 25 percent. A Catholic Relief Services food-for-work program in India is credited with increasing the amount of irrigated land from 26 to 100 percent and agricultural output by more than 90 percent. In Mozambique, World Vision integrates Title II funds into REFUGEE resettlement programs and work-for-food programs that are building roads, schools, and irrigation systems.

The Food for Peace program has not been without controversy. One long-running concern is with administrative efficiency and oversight. A 1993 General Accounting Office produced a report that USAID director Alan Woods described as containing a "stern and appropriate challenge to improve the management" of food assistance programs operating under the Food for Peace framework. A second issue centers on the impact that the Food for Peace program has on economic development in recipient states. Whereas some see it as an important springboard to growth, others see it as retarding the development of indigenous food programs. Finally, a funding debate exists. The Food for Peace program often finds itself competing with economic development programs for assistance funds. The program's supporters seek to portray it as a complementary program that should have access to its own funds.

See also FOREIGN AID; NONGOVERNMENTAL ORGANIZATIONS.

## Ford, Gerald (1913– ) *president of the United States*

Gerald Rudolph Ford was the 38th president of the United States. He is the only person to become president without having been elected to national office. Ford was appointed vice president in 1973 following the resignation of Spiro Agnew, and he became president when RICHARD NIXON resigned in August 1974 as a result of revelations of wrongdoing that resulted from the Watergate investigation. A loyal Republican and supporter of Nixon he granted a full pardon to the former president "for all offenses against the United States" shortly after taking office. This action damaged Ford's credibility with a large segment of the public and placed him in a confrontational position with CONGRESS for the remainder of his presidency. Ford secured the Republican presidential nomination in 1976, overcoming a strong challenge from the right wing of the party in the person of RONALD REAGAN.

Ford inherited Nixon's foreign-policy agenda. The U.S. presence in VIETNAM was winding down but had not yet ended. In 1975 Ford asked Congress for an additional $522 million in military aid for South Vietnam. The truce that Nixon and SECRETARY OF STATE HENRY KISSINGER had negotiated was falling apart, and without this money Ford asserted that South Vietnam would fall. Congress refused, and shortly thereafter Ford announced the end of the U.S. presence in Vietnam and the emergency evacuation of all U.S. personnel as Vietcong troops streamed toward Saigon. Shortly thereafter Ford faced another crisis in Asia when the *Mayaguez* was seized in the Gulf of Thailand by Cambodian naval forces, which claimed that it was on a spy mission. Ford demanded the return of the ship and crew, labeling the Cambodian action piracy. When CAMBODIA did not reply, Ford ordered a military attack on the island where the crew was being held. All of the crew returned safely.

Ford also inherited the STRATEGIC ARMS LIMITATIONS TALKS (SALT) with the Soviet Union (see RUSSIA). An apparent breakthrough occurred in 1974 when Ford and Soviet leader Leonid Brezhnev met at Vladivostok and agreed upon a framework for SALT II. Ford indicated that only minor differences remained to be ironed out, but by 1975 it was clear that the talks had run into serious difficulty. A planned summit in November 1975 was cancelled. In addition to setbacks at the negotiating table, the value of ARMS CONTROL and Nixon's overall policy of DÉTENTE the more general détente were also being called into question in the United States by Reagan in the REPUBLICAN PARTY primary.

The Nixon/Ford policy of détente suffered yet another blow as the Soviet Union continued to expand its influence in Africa. ANGOLA became the central battleground when in 1975 Cuban and Russian forces intervened on the side of the Marxist revolutionary movement. Ford authorized COVERT AID to the pro-U.S. forces, but Congress refused to support the move by passing the Tunney Amendment. Congress also blocked some efforts by the Ford administration to provide pro-U.S. forces in SOMALIA with aid to offset aid being given by the Soviet Union to ETHIOPIA.

**Further reading:** Greene, John. *The Presidency of Gerald R. Ford.* Lawrence: University Press of Kansas, 1994.

## foreign aid

Foreign aid is a tool designed first and foremost to advance U.S. political and security goals. This is a significant point because while the tendency in looking at foreign aid is to evaluate its success or failure in terms of the economic growth it produces, from a policy maker's perspective the real test of foreign aid lies in its political consequences. Often a highly controversial issue with the American public and CONGRESS, the United States actually gives out very little foreign aid. In 1991, for every $100 that the U.S. economy generated, about 20 cents went for foreign aid. In absolute terms, the United States remains the leading donor of foreign aid, but its lead over other states has declined steadily. In the 1960s the United States accounted for some 60 percent of aid given by the leading donor states. More recently this figure has averaged about 20 percent.

Three categories of foreign aid can be distinguished. The first category is humanitarian aid. While some argue that it is a nonpolitical form of foreign aid, the reality is that except in the case of natural disasters that are of such a magnitude that they produce a united global response, most U.S. humanitarian aid ends up in the hands of regimes whose friendship the U.S. values. The most visible ongoing U.S. humanitarian aid program is the FOOD FOR PEACE program (Public Law 480). It makes surplus agricultural goods available to needy developing states for purchase in local currency and at concessional prices. In 1973 only two of the top 20 recipients of PL 480 funds (South VIETNAM and Burundi) were listed as among the poorest states. The situation has changed little since then. During the Reagan administration EGYPT received the most foreign aid. Its fiscal year 1986 budget requested $222.1 million for

Egypt. Under President BILL CLINTON, COLOMBIA moved to the top of the list.

Economic development aid is the second category of foreign aid. The first major economic development aid initiative was the MARSHALL PLAN that sought to foster economic recovery in Europe after WORLD WAR II. Its success led to the POINT FOUR program that was targeted on developing countries. It did not come close to duplicating the success of the Marshall Plan. The inability of the Point Four program to generate economic growth in the Third World would be repeated time and time again by subsequent U.S. foreign-aid programs. In 1989 Alan Woods, head of the Agency for International Development, asserted that with the passage of time U.S. economic development aid had lost its original focus. Instead of being a short-term injection of funds designed to stimulate growth, it had become a permanent part of the economies of developing countries. Dependency and not development was the rule.

Redressing international currency problems have become a major focal point of economically oriented foreign-aid efforts. In the 1980s and 1990s the problem was debt relief. In 1988 BRAZIL's outstanding debt stood at $120.1 billion. MEXICO owed $107.4 billion. First through the BAKER PLAN and then the BRADY PLAN, the Reagan and Bush administrations sought to reduce the level of Third World debt to manageable proportions. In the mid-1990s the Clinton administration was forced to act on short notice to shore up the value of the Mexican peso. It provided Mexico with $12 billion in loans to accomplish this task. The United States felt a great deal of urgency in stabilizing the peso because of the psychological link between the health of the Mexican economy and popular perceptions about the success of the NORTH AMERICAN FREE TRADE AGREEMENT (NAFTA). In the late 1990s the collapse of Asian financial markets required foreign economic aid. Initially the Clinton administration sought to work with the INTERNATIONAL MONETARY FUND to put together ad hoc solutions for individual countries. This proved to be inadequate, and in 1998 the United States met with a group of states known as the Group of 22 to put in place a global aid package.

The third type of foreign aid is security assistance. It is divided into four categories. Foreign military sales make up the largest portion of this category of aid and are used to purchase American military equipment. Security assistance funds are provided to Third World states to finance arms purchases. The military training assistance program provides funds for training foreign military personnel both in the United States and abroad. Economic support funds are grants and loans to states that are not eligible for U.S. foreign aid but are of strategic importance to the United States and in need of aid. Critics of U.S. military assistance assert that rather than being used to protect recipient coun-

tries from foreign threats all too often the aid has been used to fend off domestic challenges. It has allowed regimes to put off needed democratic reforms and limited U.S. options by discrediting the United States in the eyes of reformist elements in local societies. In the end the United States becomes as dependent on the government it is supporting as the government is on U.S. military aid.

Examined over time we find that the relative importance of these three types of foreign aid fluctuated during the COLD WAR. The Truman administration's early foreign-aid program was dominated by economic development aid. Military aid came to dominate with the onset of the KOREAN WAR. By the mid-1960s economic aid was again preeminent, but as the U.S. involvement in Vietnam escalated and weapons transfers to the Middle East accelerated, military aid moved to the forefront again.

Today, three issues dominate the debate over U.S. foreign aid. The first is how much and what type of aid should be provided to RUSSIA. The United States was slow to respond to Russian calls for economic aid. Advocates of aid saw it as a means of moving Russia firmly into democracy. Critics asserted that Russia was still the enemy and that aid would only make it stronger. Russia has requested as much as $50 billion in aid. In fiscal year 1995, the Clinton administration sought $887 million in aid for Russia and the former Soviet republics. One innovative area in which the United States has provided aid to Russia is for the purpose of de-nuclearizing. The Nunn-Lugar bill provides Russia with funds to transport and destroy nuclear and chemical weapons as well as to establish proliferation safeguards.

A second issue involves the continued inability of foreign aid to produce economic growth. A major theme in this debate involves which types of projects should be funded and what sector of the population should be targeted. In broad terms the choice is between funding the poorest sectors of society versus projects that will result in goods that can be readily traded on world markets. Another point of debate is whether to abandon "conditionality," which requires that the recipient country meet certain guidelines in order to receive the aid. Often these guidelines entail implementing painful domestic economic adjustment programs.

A third issue involves the ability of foreign aid to promote post–cold war foreign-policy objectives. Most attention is directed at attempts to promote democracy, protect the environment, or promote HUMAN RIGHTS. Recently antidrug and nuclear proliferation concerns have been added to this list. These concerns often are given political voice through the attachment of "barnacles" to foreign-aid legislation that requires a yearly statement to Congress by the STATE DEPARTMENT attesting to progress in a specific area. Without such certification aid is to be denied unless the PRESIDENT states that it is in the national interest to continue.

In the foreground, U.S. secretary of defense William J. Perry *(right)*, Ukraine minister of defense Valeriy Shmarov *(center)*, and Russian Federation minister of defense General Pavel Grachev *(left)* celebrate the completed dismantlement of Silo 110 by planting sunflowers in the field where the missile silo used to be near Pervomaysk, Ukraine, June 4, 1996. Silo 110 was one of the 160 Ukrainian missile silos being dismantled under the Nunn-Lugar/Cooperative Threat Reduction Program. *(Department of Defense)*

One of the major challenges facing American foreign-aid policy in the coming years will be nation building in places such as AFGHANISTAN and IRAQ. Published accounts in late April 2003 stated that $500 million had already been spent in Afghanistan and that an additional $1.5 billion was expected to be spent by 2005. Estimates of the cost of rebuilding Iraq vary, but many analysts believe it may cost as much as $20 billion per year to station U.S. forces in Iraq and fund Iraqi reconstruction. An estimate in May 2003 by the Cato Institute, a THINK TANK that has a neo-isolationist orientation to United States foreign policy, estimated that already the United States was spending $1 million per day in Iraq.

See also DEMOCRATIZATION; INTERNATIONAL AFFAIRS BUDGET.

**Further reading:** Baldwin, David A. *Economic Development and American Foreign Policy, 1943–1952.* Chicago: University of Chicago Press, 1966; Easterly, William. *The Elusive Quest for Growth.* Cambridge, Mass.: MIT Press, 2001; Lancaster, Carol. *Transforming Foreign Aid: United States Assistance in the 21st Century.* Washington, D.C.: Institute for International Economics, 2001.

## Foreign Service Officer Corps

The STATE DEPARTMENT describes the Foreign Service Officer (FSO) Corps as "the front-line personnel of all U.S. EMBASSIES, consulates, and other diplomatic missions."

They are the professional diplomatic corps of the United States. The Foreign Service was created by the Rogers Act of 1924. This followed a long period in which professionalism generally took a back seat to political patronage. Little training was given to diplomatic personnel, and there was no entrance exam until late in the 19th century. The head of mission often consisted of defeated politicians or long-time political activists. Secretaries and attachés were often related to the head of mission (ambassador) or at least from the same state. Today, FSOs are recruited through a competitive entrance exam that tests their knowledge of international politics, American and world history, economics, and management skills.

Historically, FSOs were seen as generalists who were trained to perform a wide variety of tasks. The principal organizational device for producing such individuals was frequent rotation among functional tasks and geographic areas. Today this has changed, and there is greater emphasis on producing FSOs with specialized skills. This is reflected in the requirement that applicants for the FSO identify an area of specialization or "cone" that they wish to enter. The five cones to choose from are: administrative, consular, political, economic, and public DIPLOMACY. Administrative officers are the resource managers for the Foreign Service and are in charge of the property, financial, and human resources that support U.S. diplomatic missions. Consular officers look after the interests of American citizens abroad, issue visas, and monitor immigration issues. Economic officers specialize in money and banking, trade and commerce, economic development, and transportation and communication matters. They also deal with environmental, scientific, and technology issues, such as oceans, fisheries, space, health, and population problems. Political officers are expected to follow political events within their host country and identify challenges to American NATIONAL INTERESTS. Finally, public diplomacy officers are charged with opening lines of communication between the United States and their host country in order to better promote U.S. national interests.

The heart of the FSO corps is its value system. It has been the subject of repeated studies. Central to the belief system of the FSO is the dual conviction that the only career experience relevant to the work of the State Department is that gained in the foreign service and that the core of this work lies in the area of political reporting, negotiating, and representing U.S. interests abroad. The FSO is empirical, intuitive, and cautious. Risk taking in the preparation of analysis or processing of information is to be avoided. From the perspective of the FSO, the key to survival and promotion is winning the respect of one's colleagues. These qualities are cited by many as contributing factors to the declining influence of the State Department.

Many FSOs feel themselves under siege from a number of different directions. One repeated concern has been charges of elitism, which have made it suspect in many political quarters. During the 1950s FSOs were a prime target of the McCarthy investigations into un-American activities. In 1953, 70 to 80 percent of the highest-ranking FSOs were dismissed, resigned, or were transferred from one post to another. More recently Senator JESSE HELMS (R-N.C.) raised concerns about the political outlooks of many nominees who came before his committee seeking approval.

The representativeness of the FSO corps continues to be a major problem. One reform, "Wristonization," named after its originator Harry Wriston, sought to Americanize the FSO corps by merging it with those civil servants who performed technical jobs in U.S. embassies. Minorities and women are particularly underrepresented today. In late 1993, 56 percent of the FSO corps was white male, 25 percent white female, 7 percent minority male, and 4 percent minority female. This distribution was even more skewed if one concentrated on the senior ranks of the FSO.

The 1954 Wristonization reforms were a mixed success. They did bring new blood into the FSO corps, but they also created overcrowding. More than ever there were now too many FSOs for senior positions. Reductions in U.S. overseas postings have brought about further competition for positions at the top of the FSO career ladder as has the 1980 Foreign Service Officer Act, which reduced the number of senior FSO positions. As a result, between 1986 and 1990, some 350–450 upper-grade FSOs were forced to retire.

Patronage appointments to ambassadorial posts have a long tradition that continues today. Under President JIMMY CARTER 75 percent of all ambassadors were career diplomats. This was up from 40 percent in 1955 and 68 percent in 1962. Approximately 30 percent of President BILL CLINTON's ambassadors were noncareer diplomats. The presence of political ambassadors is often justified on the grounds the political supporters do need to be repaid and that often being an ambassador entails very real financial costs that cannot be met by the U.S. government. Ambassadors see their role as one of being a visible and public representative of the U.S. A frequently cited problem with political ambassadors is their lack of interest in managing the embassy.

Continued challenges face FSOs. "State 2000," a report commissioned by SECRETARY OF STATE James Baker to look to the future needs of the State Department had this to say about the FSOs: "The current Foreign Service work force does not match the State Department's staffing requirements. . . . The Department should establish a requirements-based hiring system recruiting to clearly identified needs. . . . The Department's personnel systems have, in many ways, become self-contained entities, driven by their own dynamics, and often divorced from the institutional priorities they are supposed to serve."

See also MCCARTHYISM.

**Further reading:** Harr, John. *The Professional Diplomat.* Princeton, N.J.: Princeton University Press, 1969.

## Formosa Resolution

The Formosa Resolution of 1955 extended the U.S. COLD WAR security blanket to Asia. Under its terms the United States promised to protect the Nationalist Chinese government on Formosa (TAIWAN) from attack by Chinese Communist forces. The Nationalists led by Jiang Jieshi (Chiang Kai-shek) had fled to Formosa, located 100 miles off the Chinese coast, after their defeat in the Chinese civil war.

Like the SOUTH EAST ASIA TREATY ORGANIZATION (SEATO) that was established in 1954, the focus was not so much on containing Russian aggression as it was on holding in check potential Chinese aggression. The United States and CHINA had become enmeshed in conflict during the KOREAN WAR. In 1953 the Eisenhower administration announced that it would remove the Seventh Fleet from the Formosa Strait. In theory this would permit Jiang Jieshi to make good his promise of returning to mainland China. In truth, Jiang lacked the military resources for such an attack. The move was intended to force China to apply pressure on NORTH KOREA to accept a truce.

As U.S. hostility toward China intensified and fears of COMMUNISM spreading through Southeast Asia grew with the defeat of the French in Indochina, Jiang came to be seen as a valuable Asian ally. During the 1950s Taiwan received an average of $250 million per year in military and economic aid. As a sign of the U.S. commitment to Taiwan in December 1954 the United States signed a mutual defense treaty. This was followed in January 1955 with the Formosa Resolution whereby Congress authorized the PRESIDENT to use military force to defend Taiwan and neighboring islands. The House voted its support 410-3, and the Senate did so by a vote of 85-3.

The United States show of support was not given without case. A few days before the conference establishing SEATO began, the Communist Chinese began shelling the Jinmen (Quemoy) Islands. Along with several other small islands they are located about five miles off the Chinese coast and had served as posts from which the Nationalists could harass coastal shipping and as potential staging areas for an invasion of the mainland. At the time the Chinese action was widely interpreted as a prelude to an invasion of Taiwan, and this prompted the signing of the mutual security pact.

The Communists denounced the agreement and continued shelling the islands, and they actually invaded one,

Yikiang, near the Tachen Islands, where Nationalist forces were stationed. The Nationalists retaliated by bombing the mainland. The Eisenhower administration indicated its willingness to use NUCLEAR WEAPONS if needed to protect Jiang, and the U.S. military readied several Hiroshima-sized bombs for use against coastal cities. With fears of war growing President DWIGHT EISENHOWER indicated that he alone would decide whether or not to use force to protect Taiwan, and his administration prodded Taipei to remove its forces from Tachen and other small islands off the Chinese coast.

Three years of relative calm ended in August 1958 when the Communist Chinese renewed their shelling of Jinmen and Mazu. With Jiang having committed one-third of his forces to the defense of these islands, the Eisenhower administration had little choice but to indicate that the United States would protect these islands and support Jiang should direct military conflict with the Communists take place on the mainland. Soviet leader Nikita Khrushchev warned the administration that the Soviet Union (see RUSSIA) would support Mao Zedong if the Communists were attacked by Jiang's forces. Eisenhower's pledge and Khrushchev's response brought expressions of concern and fear on the part of America's allies that war was imminent. The United States now tried to defuse the situation by announcing that if the Communists would agree to a de facto cease-fire, the United States would recommend a reduction in Nationalist forces on these islands. Moreover, SECRETARY OF STATE JOHN FOSTER DULLES announced that the United States had "no commitment of any kind" to helping Jiang regain control over the mainland. The following month secret meetings between the United States and Chinese ambassadors in POLAND helped bring the second Formosa crisis to an end.

Placed in a larger context, the Formosa Resolution and the accompanying Jinmen crises are representative of the broad grants of authority CONGRESS granted the PRESIDENT during the cold war and the accompanying strategy of BRINKSMANSHIP that was often employed. Eisenhower's handling of the crises also became a point of attack by Democratic presidential candidate JOHN KENNEDY in his televised debate with Vice President RICHARD NIXON, the Republican nominee.

## Fourteen Points

Virtually the sole official war objective of the United States when it entered WORLD WAR I was to defeat GERMANY. President WOODROW WILSON fleshed out the U.S. position in a January 8, 1918, address to CONGRESS. The United States had declared war on Germany in April 1917. In this speech Wilson presented his Fourteen Points. They are summarized in the accompanying table.

In the short run the Fourteen Points were designed to energize the American people, encourage the Russians to

---

| WILSON'S FOURTEEN POINTS |
| --- |
| 1. Abolition of secret diplomacy |
| 2. Freedom to navigate the high seas in peace and war |
| 3. Removal of economic barriers among nations |
| 4. Reduction in armaments |
| 5. Adjustment of colonial claims in the interest of both the inhabitants and the powers concerned |
| 6. Restoration of Russia and a welcome for her in the society of nations |
| 7. The return of Belgium to her people |
| 8. Evacuation and Restoration of French territory, including Alsace-Lorraine |
| 9. Readjustment of Italian frontiers |
| 10. Free opportunity for autonomous development for the people of Austria-Hungary |
| 11. Restoration of the Balkan nations |
| 12. Protection for minorities in Turkey |
| 13. Establishment of an independent Poland |
| 14. Creation of a general association of nations [League of Nations] to secure mutual guarantees of political independence and territorial integrity to great and small states |

---

stay in the war, and weaken the resistance of enemy states by holding out the prospect of a just peace. In the long run they came to serve as the basis for peace negotiations, and they became the center of controversy between America and its allies and between Wilson and the Republican-controlled Senate. The inclusion of the 14th point, a LEAGUE OF NATIONS, in the TREATY OF VERSAILLES would become the principal stumbling block to American ratification of the treaty and full participation in the interwar international order.

In addition to the creation of a League of Nations, the Fourteen Points called for an end to secret diplomacy, freedom of the seas, a reduction in arms, impartial modification of colonial claims, and the removal of economic barriers. It also put forward a series of proposals for boundary adjustments in Europe and the Far East. Wilson's Fourteen Points held great propaganda potential for the Allied and Associated powers (the United States being the only Associated power). The United States set up the American Committee on Public Information to spread Wilson's message. Some 60 million copies were produced. George Creel, its head, had copies dropped from planes behind German and Austro-Hungarian lines. Translations were made into Polish, Italian, and Chinese.

The Fourteen Points clashed with agreements already entered into by the Allies. These "secret treaties" guaranteed them specific territorial rewards that would come about by the seizure of Germany's colonial holdings and the dismemberment of the Ottoman Empire. Wilson was briefed on their content in April 1917 and made no formal challenges to them at the time.

Wilson's Fourteen Points did not stop the German war machine. Germany launched a devastating attack on Russia on March 3, 1918, that led to the signing of the Treaty of Brest-Litovsk. Later that year Germany would launch major offensives along the western front. When these offenses failed it became clear to the German military that victory was no longer possible, and the German government approached Wilson about peace terms, hoping that he would be more moderate in his demands than would the other Allied leaders. Wilson responded to the German overture without consulting the Allies. He insisted that they accept the Fourteen Points before he would consider negotiations. Wilson added to this a demand that the German government step down because he would not negotiate with them. On November 9 Kaiser Wilhelm II abdicated, and a new German government was established. It signed an armistice on November 11.

As it turned out, the armistice was not based on the Fourteen Points. BRITAIN, FRANCE, and ITALY insisted upon two reservations before accepting them as the basis for ending the war. First, the Allies would retain complete freedom of the seas. The original statement on freedom of the seas had been designed to appease the Germans who objected to British naval policies. Second, Germany would have to pay reparations for damages they inflicted upon territory they conquered and occupied during the war.

Further action on the Fourteen Points came during the peace negotiations at the Paris Peace Conference, where the conflict of interests between the United States and its Allies came into the open. Wilson had sought to build a stronger political base in October 1918 when he appealed to voters to return Democratic majorities to both houses of CONGRESS in the upcoming election. Republicans led by Senator HENRY CABOT LODGE (R.-Mass.) had begun to call for "unconditional surrender" while armistice talks with Germany were underway. Voters did not heed Wilson's call. Instead, they gave Republicans control of both the House and Senate, setting up the fateful conflict that was to erupt over ratification of the Treaty of Versailles.

**Further reading:** Knock, Thomas J. *To End All Wars: Woodrow Wilson and the Quest for a New World Order.* New York: Oxford University Press, 1992.

## France

France is the largest West European country, four-fifths the size of Texas. It has a population of 58 million people, largely of Celtic, Latin, and Teutonic (Frankish) descent, blended over the centuries to make up its present population.

From the earliest days of North American colonialism, France has played a part. In the 17th and 18th centuries it held extensive lands from the northern reaches of what is now Labrador, Canada, as far south as Louisiana, and west to the Dakotas. During the reign of Louis XIV (1643–1715), France was Europe's greatest power. Though Louis was at war for more than half his reign he sent few troops to protect his North American assets. Still, colonies would echo patterns of war in Europe, starting with King William's War, or the War of the League of Augsburg in 1689. The English king William declared war on Louis, and across the ocean Canadian troops led by Comte de Frontenac raided the northern frontiers of New York and New England, causing great suffering among the English colonial population.

This marked the beginning of a century of conflict, with four major wars being waged between 1689 and 1763: the War of the League of Augsburg, or King William's War (1689–97); the War of Spanish Succession, or Queen Anne's War (1702–14); the War of Austrian Succession, or King George's War (1743–48), followed by the most important war for the colonies' future, the Seven Years' War (1756–63). Known also as the FRENCH AND INDIAN WAR, this pitted France, its colonies and NATIVE AMERICAN allies, against Britain, its colonies and Native American allies, in a struggle for worldwide control of colonial markets and raw materials. The pivotal battle in the continental theater occurred in 1758, when Major-General James Wolfe was mortally wounded but led his troops to victory over the French forces on the Plains of Abraham. In signing the TREATY OF PARIS, February 1763, France lost all its colonial territories save Guadeloupe and Martinique. Britain obtained title to CANADA, FLORIDA, and all land east of the Mississippi River; even Louisiana was transferred into Spanish hands. It was a time of good feelings and pride for the American colonials, though it would soon give way to unrest and displeasure as GREAT BRITAIN put the screws to the North Americans to try to make up some of the heavy financial losses it suffered in the war. The taxes and legislation subsequently passed by the British government, in fact, contributed directly to the Americans rising in rebellion during the AMERICAN REVOLUTION, 1775 to 1783.

France was arguably the United States's most important ally during its quest for independence, the European country having some very personal reasons for making the ALLIANCE. France sought retribution or, at the very least, to humiliate the English for expelling them from the continent at the end of the Seven Years' War. Early in the American Revolution, the French sent tons of essential military supplies, though no official recognition of American independence could yet be made—international risks were too great for Louis XVI to openly back a cause that had little chance for success. However, the American rout of the British at Saratoga turned the tide of war, and France quickly came on board.

Two treaties, a treaty of amity and commerce and a treaty of alliance, made partners of the European continental nation and the colonies, both in trade and war. The French offers were generous, and when France formally went to war against Britain, thanks largely to masterful DIPLOMACY by BENJAMIN FRANKLIN, it did three monumental things: swore to stand by the rebellious colonies until Great Britain recognized American independence; surrendered claim to all territories east of the Mississippi, those formerly owned by the British; and made no claim to Canada, asking only for the right to take possession of more of the Caribbean. With the Americans in position to offer so little and the French in position to lose even more prestige than it already had, it was a truly poetic arrangement, and one that made a colonial uprising into a world war.

Militarily, France's greatest contribution was in distracting British efforts on the continent—some French ground forces saw action, and the French navy was victorious at Virginia Capes in 1781—but by forcing the English to draw off potential reinforcements to other theaters, it gave the American rebels an advantage. To arrange the peace, the Americans sent Benjamin Franklin, JOHN ADAMS, and John Jay as their delegation to negotiate the Treaty of Paris. Foreshadowing WOODROW WILSON's attempts in Paris almost 140 years later, the Americans arrived as diplomatic juniors into a world where such experience went back centuries. CONGRESS had given the order that the United States merely ask for independence and, on all other matters, defer to the French. Their former allies had made an agreement with SPAIN, putting its needs before those of the Americans. For their part, the American delegation publicly paid respect to France but secretly entered into a bargain with an English agent. The agreement of September 3, 1783, guaranteed American independence, as well as transferred all territory east of the Mississippi (except Spanish Florida) to the United States, provided generous northern and southern boundaries, and gave fishing rights in the North Atlantic.

Just seven years after the American nation earned its sovereignty, the French Revolution erupted, spawned in part, some would argue, from the impressions made on French soldiers in the American War of Independence. Over the last decade of the 17th century, Europe was preoccupied with the revolution, as counterrevolutionary movements sprung up, especially in Britain and Prussia, though Britain and France still had one eye focused on American raw materials, sweeping Washington's neutral country into European affairs. The European war posed a problem for the Americans. If the 1778 treaty was still in effect with France, then they owed support for and involvement in hostilities much as the French aided the Americans in their revolutionary war. However, some argued that the beheading of Louis XVI in 1793 nullified the treaty, as it had been made with the monarchy. Others were repulsed and shocked by the violence and barbarity of the French Revolution, yet many Americans were still supportive, believing republican liberty would emerge.

One of the French Revolution's most supportive associations in the United States were the Democratic-Republican societies, which responded with great fervor to the American visit by Citizen Edmond Genet, minister of the French republic. His time in America would precipitate the first major diplomatic crisis, for Genet's mission was to woo public support and negotiate a commercial treaty with the Washington government, though he soon began enlisting the support of American privateers against British and Spanish shipping, in clear violation of American neutrality. SECRETARY OF STATE THOMAS JEFFERSON gave Genet a warning, yet, in open defiance of diplomatic courtesy, the Frenchman continued his efforts in the same vein, urging Congress to reject GEORGE WASHINGTON's neutrality proclamation and side with revolutionary France. With that, the Americans demanded Genet's recall—he had been uniformly unsuccessful as a diplomat, though he did win the support of many of the people.

During John Adams's presidency, foreign affairs were of paramount concern, for the French, formerly allied with the United States, took affront to a treaty the Americans had signed with the British—JAY'S TREATY. Essentially, in allowing Britain to define the conditions for neutrality, which many felt betrayed not only American national interest but also betrayed France's interests as well, relations between France and the United States deteriorated. Diplomatic blunders and intentional offenses were committed on both sides of the Atlantic, the French refusing to receive the American representative, seizing American shipping, and using French ministers in the United States to try to influence the American presidential election. This time came to be known as the Quasi War, as no official hostilities were declared. In the United States, domestic politics were split between pro- and anti-French politics, the pro side having been deeply embarrassed by actions of late. A delegation was dispatched; some hoped to quiet strained relations, others hoped for all-out war to purge the United States of French influence.

The commission left with the intentions of asking for reparations for the shipping seizures and release from the 1778 treaties, in return for granting the French the equivalent commercial privileges enjoyed by the British under Jay's Treaty. On arrival in France, however, the succession of offenses seemed destined to continue. First, the American delegates were met by obscure diplomatic intermediaries who demanded an enormous bribe. They insisted that the Americans were not permitted to speak with French foreign minister Charles-Maurice de Talleyrand until he was given $250,000. Second, the French government expected a loan of millions of dollars—but the Americans refused. They returned home to cries for war, and they went before Congress to explain what happened, labeling the officials they had met with "X," "Y," and "Z" (and therefore the issue came to be known as the XYZ affair).

No war would result, though, and in 1800 the Treaty of Mortefontaine was signed with France to end the Quasi-War; President John Adams had defused war possibilities a year earlier. Though a provisional army was formed, no formal action was taken before Talleyrand changed his mind, suggesting that an unfortunate misunderstanding had occurred and he would gladly receive another American mission. This also put the Americans in a favorable position for securing the LOUISIANA PURCHASE, and thus it was ultimately a diplomatic coup, although it cost Adams the election of 1800.

The same year as the Convention of Mortefontaine, the Spanish ceded the Louisiana Territory to France, and in January 1803 President Jefferson sent James Madison to Paris with intentions to purchase New Orleans and West Florida, but he found Talleyrand willing to sell all of Louisiana. Napoleon feared French designs on the territory and recognized his weakness abroad rather than fight a costly war and lose the land regardless. Thus, for $15 million the United States doubled the nation's size, purchasing nearly 830,000 square miles.

A critical tenet of Jeffersonianism was "no entangling alliances" with Europe, a carryover from Washington's farewell address, though Jefferson also recognized the importance of the international community for trade, and he knew that the United States could ill-afford to be an island. However, when Europe again became embroiled in war in 1803, the United States again became a pawn in the war, as both France and England seized its shipping. In response to the English-dominated attacks, Congress passed the Nonimportation Act in 1806, prohibiting the importation of English goods that could be acquired elsewhere. The Royal Navy (RN) blockaded Europe's coast completely in retaliation, inciting Napoleon to issue the Berlin Decree, which forbade trade and communication with the British Isles. The United States was independent, but not yet able to defend its decisions internationally—and few great powers were prepared to wholly accept American neutrality.

As the 19th century progressed, so too did American industry and national power. Clearly, this was a nation on the rise, and by the 1820s it began to hunger for the spoils of colonialism that European states had long enjoyed. The United States recognized that the successful revolts by Spain's Latin American colonies in the post-Napoleonic era

was much like its own quest for independence a century earlier, and President James Monroe began looking for a way to safeguard the Americas and look out for U.S. interests in Florida as well. When France's House of Bourbon was restored after the Napoleonic Wars, and it began agitating to reconquer its regime with Spain, it appeared that the United States and Europe had conflicting interests. An agreement by British and American ministers led to the 1823 MONROE DOCTRINE, by which the Unites States agreed to stay out of European affairs and Britain agreed to use the Royal Navy to ensure that Europe would stay out of American affairs.

Emperor Napoleon III toyed with the idea of building an isthmian canal across Latin America, but lacking enthusiasm and resources the notion soon panned out. Coincidentally, the next big push came at the hands of a Frenchman, Ferdinand de Lesseps, who worked toward completion of a French-owned canal across PANAMA, still a part of COLOMBIA. Work began under the Compagnie Universelle du Canal Interoceanique in 1882, but seven years later the company was liquidated, and the Compagnie Nouvelle du Canal de Panama was created to finish the canal. Murmurs of disbelief ran through France, and with the lack of faith came suggestions of selling the canal—maybe to the Americans. The quest for the canal became a scandal in France when realization of the money lost (approximately 1.5 million francs) and the bribery and mismanagement involved led to trials and subsequent fines. The French determined subsequently that they could not possibly finish the canal. The engineering feat passed to the Americans—though it was not a new idea to them either. Earlier they had surveyed land across NICARAGUA for a canal, but ultimately they took over the French route.

When Europe erupted into war in summer 1914, the Germans invaded France as per the Schlieffen Plan's design, and the Americans declared their neutrality, in thought and in action. President Woodrow Wilson was preoccupied with finding a way to negotiate the European peace, and a series of envoys were sent to GERMANY and Britain, the de facto heads of each coalition, each representative of its allies. In this endeavor, he failed, as he did in keeping the United States neutral; the German decision to pursue unrestricted submarine warfare ultimately brought the Americans into the war. While they would fight in France alongside the French—and even loan the French a regiment comprised entirely of African Americans—diplomatic relations were as simple as seeking the common goal: victory in Europe.

Once the armistice was signed in 1918, however, Wilson brought a delegation to Paris for the peace talks, to further his dream of a "concert of power" with the LEAGUE OF NATIONS and to redesign European borders. Wilson met with frenzied accolades in Paris—later a road on the Right Bank was named for him—though his welcome did not foreshadow what he would accomplish. His plan, the FOUR-TEEN POINTS, was as follows: 1. Abolition of secret diplomacy; 2. Absolute freedom of navigation on the seas in peace and war; 3. Removal of all economic barriers to the equality of trade among nations; 4. Reduction of armaments to the level needed only for domestic safety; 5. Impartial adjustments of colonial claims; 6. Evacuation and restoration of all Russian territory; Russia to be welcomed into the society of free nations; 7. Evacuation and restoration of Belgium; 8. Evacuation and restoration of all French lands; return of Alsace-Lorraine to France; 9. Readjustment of Italy's frontiers along lines of Italian nationality; 10. Self-determination for the former subjects of the Austro-Hungarian Empire; 11. Evacuation and restoration of Rumania, Serbia, and Montenegro; free access to the sea for Serbia; 12. Self-determination for the former subjects of the Ottoman Empire; secure sovereignty for Turkish portion; 13. Establishment of an independent Poland, with free and secure access to the sea; 14. Establishment of a League of Nations affording mutual guarantees of independence and territorial integrity.

Twenty-seven nations were represented in Paris, but the "Big Four" dominated the proceedings—France, the United States, Britain, and ITALY. Within this group were several contrasting schools of thought. France, somewhat justifiably, felt that a settlement that punished Germany and ensured that it could never again be the continental aggressor was necessary, whereas Britain saw that without a strong Germany balancing France, there could be no balance of power on the Continent. The United States was more inclined to lean in toward Britain's plan, as this helped create the right climate for the League of Nations, which was intended to ensure that no great wars could ever happen again.

Wilson was forced to compromise his principles for the sake of his greater goals, and of his Fourteen Points, ultimately points 1 through 6, and 14 went unfulfilled, 9 through 12 were compromised, and only numbers 8, 9, and 13 were fulfilled entirely. The Versailles treaty left Germany punished harshly enough to draw resentment from its people, but not harshly enough to please France. The malcontent left in its wake, some argue, led directly to the outbreak of the WORLD WAR II.

As Europe rebuilt and carried on following the war, the cry of "never again" seemed universal. The United States withdrew after its role in the Paris Peace talks in 1919, turning more inward than it had been before the war. However, conscious of security need, in 1928, Secretary of State Frank B. Kellogg accepted the proposal of French foreign minister Aristide Briand to draft a treaty to outlaw war between the two countries, and he went one further by suggesting a general pact against war. The Pact of Paris, or KELLOGG-BRIAND PACT, was signed on August 27, with 15 signatories, including Australia, Belgium, Canada, CZECHOSLOVAKIA, France, Germany, Great Britain, INDIA, the Irish Free State, Italy, JAPAN, New Zealand, POLAND, SOUTH AFRICA, and the United States. Ultimately, 62 countries ratified the treaty, though the fatal flaw of having no measure to enforce its dicta caused widespread disillusionment. It was a high point in U.S.–French diplomatic relations, but in international affairs it failed to have a lasting effect, proving meaningless in the undeclared wars of the 1930s—Japan in Manchuria in 1931, Italy in Abyssinia (ETHIOPIA) in 1935, and the German Anschluss (annexation) of Austria in 1938.

The United States entered WORLD WAR I as a debtor nation but emerged as a creditor, surpassing Britain's banking system. Allied governments owed $10 billion to the United States in war debts, and with each new year in the 1920s, the Americans' economic position became more favorable. As the war-ravaged countries borrowed more and more to rebuild their economies, the balance tipped out of proportion. France and its war allies could not pay back the $10 billion, but the United States would not forgive the debt, either. These financial troubles made the 1921 WASHINGTON CONFERENCE to limit naval building seem almost unnecessary, for while the 5-5-3-1.67 ratio for the United States, Britain, Japan, and France made sense on paper, no country save the United States could afford to build to its allowed quota. Diplomatically, two treaties also emerged from that conference—the Nine Power Treaty, upholding the OPEN DOOR POLICY, and the Four Power Treaty, replacing the Anglo-Japanese alliance with a Pacific security pact signed by the United States, Britain, Japan, and France. Even in conjunction with the Kellogg-Briand Pact, these treaties neither maintained the status quo in Asia nor ensured a lasting peace.

By the late 1930s, Adolf Hitler began to make clear his aggressive intentions in Europe—after the Anschluss with Austria, he made demands for the Sudetenland in Czechoslovakia. Britain and France agreed to meet with Hitler in Munich, with President FRANKLIN D. ROOSEVELT's approval. He even tacitly agreed to accept the outcome, though it soon became clear that appeasement was not the answer to handling Hitler. Next year, Germany invaded Poland, and World War II began.

France declared war on Germany immediately following the Polish invasion, but the United States again opted for neutrality—though Roosevelt acknowledged that he could not ask for it in thought as well as in action. He waged a sort of undeclared war, finding ways around laws to assist the Allies, with whom he sympathized. When France fell a year later, however, there was little more the Americans could do for it.

Postwar France was in ruins, displaced people and leveled northern towns and villages being the most visible signs of destruction. Paris had been occupied, its government fallen, and replaced by a puppet regime in Vichy. The road to repair was long and expensive, and as with World War I, the job of rebuilding Europe fell to the United States. The MARSHALL PLAN constituted a rational effort aimed at reducing the hunger, homelessness, sickness, unemployment, and political restlessness of the European peoples affected by the war, and France was a primary candidate for this aid. The program's official title was the European Recovery Program, aimed at increasing production, expanding European trade, facilitating European economic cooperation and integration, and controlling inflation—the latter of which failed. Designed as a four-year plan, it cost American taxpayers $11,820,700,000,

plus $1,505,100,000 in loans repaid. It was revolutionary because it was not just aid but rather constitutioned a plan requiring a multilateral approach to overcoming the common European economic problems—and in this it was successful. France received a total of $2,713,600,000, second only to Britain in total assistance.

Before it had recovered from the ravages of World War II, France joined the NORTH ATLANTIC TREATY ORGANIZATION (NATO) in 1949, engaged its army in its colony in Indochina (today's VIETNAM) in May 1950, and joined the KOREAN WAR allies fighting COMMUNISM on July 22, 1950. With regard to the latter, France's forces were anemic and badly equipped, though they fought well, placed under command of the 23rd U.S. Infantry Division, where they impressed the commander of the Eighth Army, Lieutenant-General Matthew Ridgway. In spring 1951, the French bat-

American troops parade through the Arc de Triomphe and down the Champs Elysées as crowds throng the sidewalks during the liberation of Paris, France. *(Hulton/Archive)*

talion won an American Presidential Citation for its engineers' bravery, stopping a Chinese offensive in the Hwachon region. After the armistice was signed in July 1953, the French left Korea with accolades, including three American Distinguished Unit Citations.

This was not the only time that French and American forces would fight together in the early 1950s. The French colony of Indochina was embroiled in a situation similar to the one in Korea, and the American aversion to communism was proving strong enough to overcome Washington's reticence to get involved in a colonial issue. This decision was reached formally in February/March 1950, funded by the president just a few months later, and was certainly a precursor to the VIETNAM WAR of the next decades. In Indochina, however, the Americans had no illusion of great expectations. In April 1950, the JOINT CHIEFS OF STAFF would go no further than to say that prompt delivery of the aid would do no more than create the "possibility of success." Indochina and Korea were red herrings—combating the spread of communism in Asia would require a large-scale victory in China. Still, the power of a "red scare" could encourage action by the United States quickly and decisively in the 1950s, even when the situation was far from ideal. Such was Indochina, with the U.S. commitment to force not implying a commitment to victory by the French. On the other side, the French were always loath to take orders or even suggestions from the Americans—it was an uneasy, imperfect alliance, which led to an unprecedented Asian victory over European forces. Before the Americans experienced the stigma of a military loss to a lesser power, the French did; the Geneva Conference of 1954 gave North Vietnam to the Communists, and the Americans supplanted the French in South Vietnam. It was not a good time for the Western alliance.

The COLD WAR was in full swing at this point, though not yet at its peak in terms of East-West tensions. Tensions within the West were also rising, however, in part due to the fallout in France over the Indochina defeat. First, Paris felt that it had not received sufficient aid from Britain or the United States, contributing to its failure. Second, it is possible that the good offices extended by the Soviet Union (see RUSSIA) on France's behalf at the Geneva Conference were repaid by France's rejection of early proposals for a European Defense Community—this alone caused rumblings of uncertainty throughout the West. Finally, it is most certain that American policy regarding South Vietnam in the aftermath of Geneva alienated pro-American factions in France, which would boil over in the SUEZ CRISIS of 1956. The legacy of French involvement in Vietnam was officially over, though President Charles de Gaulle drew on his nation's experience to warn President John F. Kennedy that the Americans would sink deeper and deeper into the quagmire, regardless of money and people thrown into

Vietnam—advice that went unheeded, and the Americans shadowed the French failure in the next decades.

In the Middle East, after EGYPT began soliciting funds from Eastern bloc and Communist countries to build its Aswan High Dam project, the United States withdrew support. Subsequently, Egypt nationalized the project, which compelled the British and French to plan an invasion, as both were stockholders in the Suez Canal Project, and they feared for their investments. At the same time, ISRAEL planned an invasion that was at the time believed to be unilaterally planned but has since been shown to have been a third arm of the British and French plan. They sought to take back the dam and oust the Egyptian president—a plan that was met with disfavor by both the Americans and Soviets. Attempts at diplomacy having failed, the United States took action through the UNITED NATION's Security Council, the Soviet Union following that with diplomatic notes to all three nations, until finally the two joined in an unholy union, threatening sanctions against the British, French, and Israelis. The Americans in particular felt betrayed and dismayed by these nations' decision to invade and seize the canal by force, and French-American relations weakened further.

By the 1960s, the gulf between France and the United States had widened even further. In the years since the end of World War II, Europe had grown stronger and less reliant on the United States, and when the Soviet Union proved with SPUTNIK that its nuclear capabilities had increased, Europeans began doubting the American ability within NATO to provide sufficient deterrence. In light of these developments, the French were the first to voice reservations about policies of the Western alliance, with President de Gaulle singling out American leadership as being primarily problematic. Following its refusal post-Indochina to agree to a European Defense Community, France opted out of NATO in a military context in 1966, announcing that it would no longer assign forces to NATO and that it was withdrawing from the integrated military structure. However, it remains a political member in case of "unprovoked aggression," and military coordination has increased over the last 30 years. Still, in 1967, Allied forces and NATO military headquarters were forced to withdraw from France. The withdrawal of France caused some concern on the international scene, as others began fearing that the alliance was crumbling and that perhaps the United States would be next to withdraw. However, proving its flexibility and resilience, NATO moved headquarters both military and civilian to Belgium the following year, and no other countries succeeded.

France detonated its first NUCLEAR WEAPON in 1966, and it averaged a test once every 63 days between its first and last test, the latter occurring in January 1996. Aside from a tripartite agreement with the United States and

Britain to respect different states' rights in the South Pacific, the United States and France have had few major conflicts of interest or differences of opinion over their shared nuclear capacity. As is typified by its decision to pursue an independent nuclear capability, France's cold war foreign policy combined elements of defiance and accommodation. Both were necessary in a world of diminished French national power, a reinvigorated Germany, and superpower competition. By occasionally challenging the international order and more particularly the United States, France sought to ensure that its voice would be heard in international deliberations.

France has continued down this path in the post–cold war era. The end of the cold war did not alter the geopolitical landscape in the way France had expected. MULTIPOLARITY did not come to pass. Rather a UNIPOLAR INTERNATIONAL SYSTEM was created as the Soviet Union disintegrated and the United States came to hold a virtual monopoly on POWER. Given these developments, France's first post–cold war foreign-policy initiatives were designed to create a balance to American power in Europe. In 1996 France rejoined NATO's military structure to give it a larger voice within that body. But, in addition, France pursued greater military cooperation with Germany so that Europe might possess a military capability independent from the American-dominated NATO system. To this end, the West European Union was revitalized as the defense arm of the EU, and a Eurocorps was established as the potential foundation for a European army. Attempts to turn this vision into reality soon turned sour as Europe's effort to respond to the crisis in the former YUGOSLAVIA without the United States proved ineffective.

France also criticized the pace and direction of NATO expansion, arguing that the United States wished to replace a Europe led by Germany and France by one led by Great Britain and supported by new allies in East Europe. These suspicions took on new meaning when in January 2003 the United States objected to French threats of a UN veto over war with IRAQ, complaining that France and Germany represented the "old Europe" and that the United States was prepared to go ahead with support from the "new Europe," namely, Poland, Hungary, and the Czech Republic.

United States–French relations hit a low point with the IRAQ War. France emerged as the leading opponent at the United Nations to American military action against Saddam Hussein. It was joined in opposition by CHINA, RUSSIA, and GERMANY. Through the summer of 2002 and into the fall, the fundamental issue at stake was whether or not the United States would seek UN approval for military action against Iraq and, if requested, whether it would be given. Some within the GEORGE W. BUSH administration asserted that the United States did not need to have any formal or informal international endorsement of military action.

After Bush's address to the United Nations on the anniversary of the SEPTEMBER 11, 2001, terrorist attacks the Security Council began to consider a new resolution giving the United States the authority to act. France advocated a two-step voting process. One resolution would require Iraq to disarm, and a second vote would be needed to authorize the use of military force. The United States was steadfast in its position that American military action could not be held hostage to a Security Council vote. France argued that only the Security Council could make a decision on going to war. The impasse was broken when a revised U.S. draft resolution was submitted that did not request UN authorization for military action nor did it contain language that made military action automatic. It did hold that Iraq was in "material breach" of its disarmament obligations. Russia and France continued to voice objections, arguing that authorization for U.S. military action was still implicit in the resolution, but on November 8, 2002, the UN Security Council passed a resolution giving Iraq 30 days to produce a "currently accurate, full, and complete declaration of all aspects of its programmes to develop chemical, biological, and nuclear weapons, ballistic missiles. . . ." UN weapons inspectors were to update the Security Council in 60 days.

UN chief weapons inspector Hans Blix gave a series of reports that cited Iraq for noncompliance with inspection procedures but did not identify a clear breach of the United Nations resolution. Because of that, on January 20 France indicated it would block any new Security Council resolution authorizing the use of force against Iraq. On February 24 the United States and Great Britain indicated that they would soon introduce a new resolution that would declare Iraq to be in "further material breach" of UN orders to disarm. This announcement brought forward renewed opposition from Germany and France. They quickly floated a plan to send more weapons inspectors to Iraq, along with UN troops to help the weapons inspectors gain access to all desired sites.

France also moved to block the United States at NATO. On the eve of a NATO summit President Bush invoked the image of Nazi Germany and urged NATO to take a stand against Saddam Hussein. French president Jacques Chirac asserted that "war is not inevitable" and that there should be no rush to a decision. This action prompted Defense Secretary Donald Rumsfeld to label France and Germany as part of the "old Europe."

The diplomatic maneuvering entered into the endgame phase on March 17 when the United States, Great Britain, and Spain announced that they would pull their resolution authorizing military force against Iraq because they had reached the conclusion that "council consensus will not be possible." That night President Bush addressed the nation and gave Saddam Hussein 48 hours to leave Iraq. On Tuesday, March 18, Saddam Hussein rejected Bush's ultimatum. The ground war began on March 20.

France continued to oppose the United States at the United Nations after the war ended. It spoke out against a United States resolution that ended United Nations ECO-NOMIC SANCTIONS against Iraq on the grounds that it gave too much power to the United States. In the end the French capitulated, and the resolution passed unanimously.

**Further reading:** Aldrich, Robert, and John Connell, eds. *France in World Politics.* New York: Routledge, 1989; Cogan, Charles, and Stanley Hoffmann. *France and the United States since World War II: Oldest Allies, Guarded Friends.* New York: Macmillan, 1994; Craig, Gordon A. *The Diplomats: 1939–1970.* Princeton, N.J.: Princeton University Press, 1994; Flynn, Gregory, ed. *Remaking the Hexagon: The New France in the New Europe.* Boulder, Colo.: Westview, 1995.

—Stephanie Cousineau

### Franklin, Benjamin (1706–1790) *diplomat*

One of the founding fathers of the United States, Benjamin Franklin had a full and varied career as a printer, scientist, writer, philosopher, and political leader. He was also among the first American diplomats. As early as 1753 Franklin concluded a treaty with the Iroquois Confederacy for Pennsylvania. It was prompted by growing concerns over French military activity along the Pennsylvania frontier.

Franklin's first foray into transatlantic DIPLOMACY came in February 1757 when the Pennsylvania assembly sent him to London as its agent to meet with British officials regarding a dispute over the ability of the Pennsylvania assembly to tax land owned by the Penn family and other proprietors for the purpose of public projects, such as the defense of the colony. Franklin initially was unsuccessful in his mission, but in 1760 he succeeded in obtaining such powers. During this stay and a later one Franklin authored a series of articles on the colonies that today could be characterized as propaganda or public diplomacy as they were designed to change the view held by the British public of America.

Franklin returned to the colonies for two years, 1762–64, before being sent back to GREAT BRITAIN on another diplomatic mission for the Pennsylvania assembly. This time he was to petition the king to change the form of Pennsylvania's government from proprietary to royal government. He tried unsuccessfully to do so. Moreover, his mission was overtaken by events. The House of Commons passed the Stamp Act in 1765. Franklin opposed the measure but was unable to prevent its passage. Following its repeal in 1766 he was reappointed as agent for the Pennsylvania assembly. In April 1768 Geor-gia also appointed him its agent. New Jersey followed suit in November 1769, as did Massachusetts in October 1770. Franklin was unable to bridge the growing gap between British authorities and colonial leaders, and in 1775 Franklin returned to America. The end of Franklin's stay in Great Britain was also marked by controversy and embarrassment. Franklin admitted that he had played a role in having the confidential correspondence of Thomas Hutchinson, a former governor of Massachusetts, published. The writings suggested the need to limit the rights of the colonists in order to secure public order.

The battles of Lexington and Concord took place while Franklin was on his way home; upon returning to Pennsylvania, he was made one of that colony's delegates to the Second Continental Congress. In November 1775 Franklin was appointed chair of the Committee on Secret Correspondence that had responsibility for the conduct of foreign affairs. In March 1776 an ailing Franklin undertook a mission to CANADA with Charles Carroll, Samuel Chase, and John Carroll to try to convince the Canadian colonies to joint the movement for independence. The mission was a failure. Franklin returned to participate in the writing and signing of the Declaration of Independence.

Almost immediately Franklin entered into diplomatic ventures for the United States. He held talks with Lord Howe on September 11, 1776, on Staten Island and was then appointed to serve as commissioner to FRANCE along with Silas Deane and Arthur Lee. They sailed from Philadelphia on October 27, 1776, and arrived in Paris on December 3. He formally requested aid from the French government for the United States on January 5, 1777. On January 13 he received a verbal promise of 2 million livres in aid. To that figure was added another 6 million livres in January 1778 following the defeat of the British at Saratoga. Franklin was able to obtain recognition of the United States by France. Between December 1777 and February 1778 two treaties were negotiated. One was a treaty of amity and commerce. The second was a treaty of ALLIANCE. In October of that year Franklin was elevated in rank to minister plenipotentiary. This moved reciprocated an earlier French move in the United States but also reflected infighting and dissention within the American delegation.

In 1781 Franklin was chosen along with Henry Laurens and THOMAS JEFFERSON to join John Jay and JOHN ADAMS in negotiating a peace treaty with Great Britain. Franklin began negotiating before Jay and Adams arrived and in contradiction to his negotiating instructions did so without first informing or consulting France. The TREATY OF PARIS was signed by Adams, Jay, and Franklin for the United States on September 3, 1783. Franklin would undertake one more diplomatic task for the United States before leaving Paris in

1785. He worked with Jefferson and Adams to negotiate a treaty with the BARBARY PIRATES in 1784.

**Further reading:** Brands, H. W. *The First American: The Life and Times of Benjamin Franklin.* New York: Doubleday, 2000.

### Frelinghuysen, Frederick (1817–1885) *secretary of state*

Frederick Frelinghuysen was SECRETARY OF STATE from 1881 to 1885 under President Chester Arthur. His tenure in that office is generally placed in contrast with that of his predecessor JAMES BLAINE, who was his opposite in temperament and political outlook. Where Blaine advanced an energetic and interventionist foreign policy, Frelinghuysen preferred a more detached and cautious approach that generally stressed avoiding entanglements.

The most notable about-face in United States foreign policy under Frelinghuysen's leadership came in Latin America. Blaine had backed CHILE in its confrontation with Peru. Frelinghuysen wished to end the U.S. involvement, and Peru was informed that the United States would no longer support its efforts to prevent Chile from acquiring part of its territory. Shortly before leaving office Blaine had called for an international American conference to explore ways of averting war. Frelinghuysen cancelled the conference. Frelinghuysen also did not act on the VENEZUELA BOUNDARY DISPUTE against GREAT BRITAIN. He also instructed a trade mission that was sent to South America not to recommend American involvement in local politics. The commission ignored his charge and recommended that American diplomats be granted broad powers that would allow them to serve as "friendly advisors in any emergency." This rebuff was not totally surprising since many considered Frelinghuysen's caution to be ill-suited for the general temper of the times.

Frelinghuysen was not totally inactive, but his diplomatic effort met with mixed success. He sought and failed, as did Blaine, to renegotiate the 1850 CLAYTON-BULWER TREATY. Frelinghuysen negotiated a treaty with NICARAGUA in December 1884, the Frelinghuysen-Zavala Treaty, which would have made the United States and Nicaragua joint owners of an interoceanic canal through that country. Other provisions in the treaty would have turned Nicaragua into a U.S. protectorate much as the PLATT AMENDMENT did to CUBA years later. The Senate failed to ratify the treaty. Fear of alienating Great Britain and a general lack of interest in taking on such a responsibility on the part of the new GROVER CLEVELAND administration led to its downfall. Other failed initiatives involved commercial agreements with MEXICO, SPAIN, the DOMINICAN REPUBLIC, and HAWAII; the ratification of the Treaty of Berlin; and efforts to curb Great Britain's harsh handling of the Irish home rule movement.

Frelinghuysen's most notable success of sorts was the Treaty of Chemulpo in 1882 that had the effect of recognizing Chinese domination over KOREA and gave the United States MOST-FAVORED-NATION status and extraterritoriality rights there.

### French and Indian War

The French and Indian War took place between 1754 and 1763. It was part of a broader conflict between FRANCE and GREAT BRITAIN for global supremacy. It is significant not only because in defeat France was forced to give up its North American holdings, but also because in the aftermath of the war Great Britain took actions against the colonists that led to the AMERICAN REVOLUTION.

The two countries fought three previous wars in North America in the century prior to the American Revolution: King William's War (1689), Queen Anne's War (1702), and King George's War (1744). Unlike these three, the French and Indian War began in North America and then spread to Europe as the Seven Years' War (1756–63).

The French and Indian War was a three-sided affair. NATIVE AMERICANS tried to keep both the British and French out of the Ohio River valley. The French sought to expand into this region as a means of linking together their colonial holdings in CANADA and Louisiana. The British saw the Ohio River valley as the pathway to the West from their seaboard colonies. The conflict began in 1754 when the American colonists unsuccessfully tried to negotiate a pact against the French with the Iroquois and George Washington unsuccessfully led forces against Fort Duquesne, a French outpost along the Ohio River. In 1755 British regulars also tried but failed to take Fort Duquesne. The two states formally declared war in May 1756.

Early in the French and Indian War, in June 1754, the American colonists met in Albany, New York, in a continental congress. It was called by British authorities in an effort to foster unity in the war effort against France. Seven colonies attended, and they drew up a plan for a federal union. The Albany Congress was a forerunner of future continental congresses, which would take the colonists down the road to independence. Significantly, the Albany Plan of Union that was drawn up by BENJAMIN FRANKLIN gave the colonies the power to make war and peace. Suspicions and distrust among the colonies prevented its adoption.

France successfully continued to resist British advances until 1758 when Louisbourg, a French fortress on Cape Breton Island, fell. That defeat was followed in 1759 by an even more devastating one when General James Wolfe captured Quebec. The TREATY OF PARIS in 1763 gave

Great Britain all French and Spanish holdings in North America east of the Mississippi River except for New Orleans. Shortly after signing the Treaty of Paris, France gave New Orleans and its territory west of the Mississippi, known as Louisiana, to SPAIN in an effort to keep it from falling to the British.

Victory over France had come at a high price to Great Britain. British authorities now sought to recoup their expenses by passing part of the war cost as well as the cost of administering its newly acquired North American holdings onto the American colonists through such measures as the Stamp Act of 1765 and the Tea Act of 1773. Not only did the American colonists resent these measures, they took offense at the inability of the British to take military control over the Ohio River valley from Native American forces. Tensions between the American colonists and Great Britain worsened in 1774 with the passage of the Quebec Act, which made the Ohio River valley part of Canada, and of the Coercive Acts, which would lead to fighting at Concord and Lexington the following year.

**Further reading:** Ferling, John. *Struggle for a Continent: The Wars of Early America.* Wheeling, Ill.: Harlan Davidson, 1993; Jennings, Francis. *Empire of Fortune.* New York: Norton, 1988.

## Fulbright, J. William (1905–1995) *senator*

J. William Fulbright, a Democrat, represented Arkansas in the U.S. Senate from 1945 to 1974. In 1959 he became chair of the Senate Foreign Relations committee, and from that post he became one of the most influential voices in U.S. foreign policy for more than a decade. His committee's six days of televised hearings on the escalating U.S. involvement in VIETNAM in 1966 is widely credited with legitimizing the antiwar movement. Fulbright's own opposition to the war was based on the belief that it was an unconstitutional exercise of presidential power.

Fulbright was first elected to CONGRESS in 1942 and quickly established himself as a liberal internationalist supporting the creation of the UNITED NATIONS and a World Court with the authority to make binding decisions. In the 1950s he publicly challenged Senator Joseph McCarthy's right-wing witch-hunt for communists in the STATE DEPARTMENT, and he voted against continued funding for McCarthy's investigations subcommittee. President LYNDON JOHNSON was a good friend, and Fulbright initially supported his Vietnam policy, including sponsorship of the Gulf of Tonkin Resolution that gave Johnson wide-ranging authority to fight the war as he saw fit.

In the last year of the Vietnam War Fulbright authored a series of congressional resolutions designed to limit the power of the president to commit U.S. forces to combat without the consent of the Senate. This effort culminated in the 1973 WAR POWERS RESOLUTION. He also opposed the antiballistic missile defense system on the grounds that it had little defensive value and was a political gimmick. He had become deeply suspicious of the military and felt that militarism was "undermining democratic procedure and values."

In 1945, in his first year as senator, Fulbright introduced legislation establishing a federally funded exchange scholarship program for faculty and students. This program bears his name, the Fulbright Scholarships, and is considered by many to be one of the most significant contributions to advancing American INTERNATIONALISM in the post–WORLD WAR II period.

See also MCCARTHYISM.

# G

## Gadsden Purchase

Arranged by U.S. minister to MEXICO James Gadsden in 1853 the Gadsden Purchase added 29,640 square miles to the United States. It was the last land acquisition by the United States from the end of the MEXICAN WAR until the AMERICAN CIVIL WAR. The Gadsden Purchase was necessary in order to facilitate the construction of a southern transcontinental railroad route. The Treaty of Guadalupe-Hidalgo that ended the Mexican War had drawn the U.S.–Mexican border in such a way that constructing such a route in this area was all but impossible. The most feasible route lay in territory that remained under Mexican control.

American interest in a transcontinental railroad route had been building for some time and gathered irresistible momentum with the discovery of gold in California. The dominant opinion at the time held that a northern route through the Rockies would be difficult to construct and maintain. Further complicating the construction of a transcontinental railroad was the sectional dispute between the North and the South. Each saw a transcontinental railroad connecting their region with the West as important to their economic growth and political strength within the Union.

Attention thus turned to constructing a transcontinental railroad through MEXICO. Two routes stood out. The first went across the Isthmus of Tehuantepec. The second followed the Gila River. Initial interest focused on the Tehuantepec line, the more southern of the two, and in 1850 a treaty was negotiated giving the United States the right to send troops to protect the railroad. The U.S. Senate agreed to it, but Mexico did not and withdrew the land grant on which the railway was to be built.

President FRANKLIN PIERCE favored the Gila River route and instructed Gadsden to purchase the necessary territory. Gadsden, from South Carolina, was a longtime advocate of a southern rail route. The purchase price was $15 million. The agreement encountered spirited opposi-

tion with the Senate. Many who spoke against it were fearful of slave state expansion. In the end the Senate approved the purchase but reduced the price to $10 million and altered the boundaries to exclude an opening on the Gulf of California. Beyond the purchase of territory the Gadsden Purchase contained a number of other provisions. One freed the United States from damages inflicted by NATIVE AMERICANS raiding into Mexico. The second permitted the United States to send troops across the Tehuantepec to protect the railroad. This right was never exercised, and a 1937 agreement terminated this provision.

## Gaither Committee Report

In the spring of 1957 President DWIGHT EISENHOWER commissioned a committee to study the problem of protecting the American public in the event of a nuclear attack. Composed of prominent private citizens, the committee was chaired by H. Rowan Gaither, head of the Ford Foundation. Its secret report, "DETERRENCE and Survival in the Nuclear Age," was presented to the NATIONAL SECURITY COUNCIL in November 1957, one month after the launching of SPUTNIK into Earth orbit by the Soviet Union. The contents of the report, which exceeded in scope the boundaries set by its original mandate, were leaked to the press almost immediately. Along with the anxious public reaction to Sputnik, the Gaither Committee Report provided a strong stimulus to increased military spending and questioning of the merits of Eisenhower's New Look military posture.

President Eisenhower, who commissioned the report, had hoped that it would calm growing public concerns over the U.S.-Soviet nuclear balance and reaffirm his view that the U.S. bomber fleet provided adequate protection against Soviet nuclear forces. Instead, the Gaither Committee painted a dark picture of the nuclear threat facing the United States. It concluded that by 1959 the Soviet Union would be able to "launch an attack with ICBMs [intercontinental ballistic missiles] carrying megaton warheads against which SAC [the Strategic Air Command] will be almost completely vulnerable under present programs." The report recommended across-the-board increases in defense spending for conventional and NUCLEAR WEAPONS programs as well as for civil defense. All totaled, the Gaither Committee recommended spending an additional $25 billion on defense over what the Eisenhower administration had budgeted.

In exceeding its mandate, the Gaither Committee Report followed in the footsteps of National Security Council Document 68 (NSC-68), which President HARRY TRUMAN had authorized. What was to have been a limited review of America's containment policy emerged as a call to arms. Eisenhower responded much like Truman. Both were leery of the economic consequences of rapid military buildups. The Gaither Report contributed to growing public concern that the Eisenhower administration had allowed a MISSILE GAP to develop, and it served as a prominent theme in the closely contested RICHARD NIXON–JOHN KENNEDY 1960 presidential election.

See also COLD WAR; NUCLEAR STRATEGY; RUSSIA.

## General Agreement on Tariffs and Trade  (GATT)

The General Agreement on Tariffs and Trade (GATT) provided the organizational framework for establishing a post–WORLD WAR II free-trade system. Such a system was instrumental to the growth of the U.S. economy by opening up foreign markets to American goods. In 1995 it was supplanted by the WORLD TRADE ORGANIZATION (WTO) as the key international institution responsible for managing and promoting free trade.

GATT was intended to be an interim measure pending the ratification of the INTERNATIONAL TRADE ORGANIZATION (ITO). The ITO and GATT were both products of the 1947 Havana Charter, which sought to establish an institutional foundation for free trade in the post–World War II international economic order. As was the case with the INTERNATIONAL MONETARY FUND (IMF) and WORLD BANK that were created at BRETTON WOODS in 1947, the ITO represented a reaction to the nationalist economic policies of the interwar period. Although both the Roosevelt and Truman administrations strongly supported the ITO, CONGRESS opposed it. A political ALLIANCE of protectionist Republicans who opposed free trade and liberals who felt that the Havana Charter did not go far enough in promoting free trade blocked consideration of the treaty for three years. In 1950 the Truman administration decided not to submit the Havana Charter to Congress, and the United States withdrew from the agreement.

This left GATT as the lone global instrument for establishing a free-trade system. The central principle driving its decision making was nondiscrimination. It was embodied in the concept of MOST-FAVORED-NATION (MFN) STATUS that held that all goods imported into a country had to receive equal treatment. In essence, this meant that a tax advantage or benefit granted to any state holding MFN status had to be extended to all others holding that status. The only exception allowed was for regional trade groups. This exception was important for the economic development of the European Union, and it was accepted by the United States in the interests of promoting economic growth, something that was believed would hold the potential appeal of communism in check. GATT also insisted upon national treatment of goods, which meant that there could be no legal differentiation between goods made in a country and those imported into it. Finally, GATT established rules for dealing with dumping, subsidies, and most quantitative restrictions on trade. An important omission in GATT's rules was the inability to establish a free-trade system for agricultural goods. Powerful farm groups in the United States and other advanced economies successfully lobbied for international trade in agricultural products that permitted price support, export subsidies, and other protectionist measures.

GATT sought to achieve its objective of creating a free-trade system through a series of negotiating rounds that often took years to complete. Eight rounds were completed between 1947 and 1995. The first round, the Geneva I Round (1947), negotiated approximately 45,000 agreements that reduced global tariffs on manufacturing goods and some agricultural products. The next several rounds, Annecy (1949), Torquay (1951), and Geneva II (1957), were largely for the purpose of admitting new members. The Dillon Round (1960) produced worldwide tariff reductions amounting to about $40 billion. It is the next round, the KENNEDY ROUND (1963), that is generally considered one of the most significant GATT rounds because it cut tariffs by 35 percent on some 80 percent of nonagricultural goods produced by industrialized countries. The TOKYO ROUND (1973) that followed was not as successful in producing tariff reductions, but it did make significant progress on dealing with nontariff barriers to free trade (NTBs). In 1986 the URUGUAY ROUND began, and in 1995 it produced an agreement to establish the WTO as the main vehicle for future trade negotiations.

GATT was a victim of both its own success and its limitations. On the plus side, GATT succeeded admirably in opening up the international economic order to free trade. Only the Communist bloc states were nonparticipants. On the negative side, GATT's coverage was incomplete. Agricultural trade never achieved the level of openness under GATT that manufacturing goods did. This weakness was accentuated by the growing trade in services and intellectual property that also largely took place beyond GATT's reach. The exception granted to regional trading associations grew in significance as the EUROPEAN UNION became a major international economic force and interest in regionalism rivaled that in global free trade. Third World states also came to feel that they had not benefited as greatly from free trade as did advanced states, producing calls in the 1970s for the creation of a new international economic order. The WTO was intended to rectify at least some of these shortcomings by providing a framework in which trade in goods, services, intellectual property, and agriculture could be addressed.

See also INTERNATIONAL TRADE ORGANIZATION.

**Further reading:** Goldstein, Judith. *Ideas, Interests and American Trade Policy.* Ithaca, N.Y.: Cornell University Press, 1993; Isaak, Robert A. *Managing World Economic Change: International Policy Economy.* 2d ed. Englewood Cliffs, N.J.: Prentice Hall, 1995; Spero, Joan, and Jeffrey Hart. *The Politics of International Economic Relations.* 5th ed. New York: St. Martin's, 1997; Stubbs, Richard, and Geoffrey Underhill, eds. *Political Economy and the Changing Global Order.* 2d ed. New York: Oxford University Press, 2000.

## Germany

Approximately the size of Montana, Germany is the second-largest nation in Western Europe, and it is Europe's largest economy. It has 83 million inhabitants; their primarily ethnicity is German, with a Danish minority in the north, a Sorbian (Slavic) minority in the east, and about 7.3 million foreign residents.

The influx of non-English colonists who poured into American ports during the 18th century included Germans, many of whom originated from the upper Rhine Valley, or Palatinate. Many were members of Protestant sects in search of religious toleration, a group of whom settled in Pennsylvania and founded Germantown. By mid-century, the tide had turned, and many more Lutherans came to America in search of a better material world, mistakenly becoming known as the Pennsylvania Dutch because of the similarities between the word *deutsch* (German) and *dutch* (person from Holland). These immigrants arrived speaking a foreign language, and many chose to stay in their own communities, which bred some disputes. Ultimately, the tensions drove some settlers to push farther west to settle in the Shenandoah Valley.

Modern Germany did not unite until 1871 in the Second Reich (empire), making it a young state by European standards, given that even the United States was nearly a century older. However, the German States, as many as 360 of them at one point, had existed in a variety of amalgamations since antiquity. Relations between some of the states and the United States were older than the united Germany; most important was that with Prussia. This northeastern state was renowned throughout Europe for its military system, and Prussians were frequently sent to other states (including the United States during the AMERICAN REVOLUTION) to train armies in the tradition of Frederick the Great. Still, regular diplomatic relations were not established until the Second Reich was in existence.

The first significant interaction between the two nations occurred over a tiny speck of land in the Pacific, pitting American SECRETARY OF STATE JAMES G. BLAINE with the master of European DIPLOMACY, Chancellor Otto von Bismarck. Also involved in this mêlée was GREAT BRITAIN, the three powers fighting over a potential coaling station and naval base: the Samoan islands. The key strategic location of Samoa had garnered substantial international interest since at least the 1870s, when the United States orchestrated a treaty to secure rights for a naval station at Pago Pago, a spectacular natural harbor. Britain and Germany had similar treaties, and problems arose in 1889 when all three countries had naval men-of-war in harbor. In a moment of cosmic chance, however, a sudden typhoon destroyed the fleets, rendering any aggressive action between them impossible. After tensions eased, delegates from each nation met in Berlin to negotiate the problem. The Europeans both wanted to divide the islands, but Blaine held out for authority by the indigenous population, and American control over Pago Pago. The agreement took nearly a decade to conclude and remained tentative even in 1899—Germany took two of the islands, the United States held on to Pago Pago, and both compensated Britain with land elsewhere in the Pacific.

Not long after the Samoan issue was solved, the naval arms race was tipped off when Kaiser Wilhelm II, emperor of Germany, decided to commit to Mahanianism after a timely reading of the didactic *Influence of Sea Power upon History, 1660–1783* (1890). Alfred Thayer Mahan was an American naval captain, brought to the Naval War College by Commodore Stephen B. Luce to teach naval history—a job that allowed him to formulate the most famous policy text of the era. Mahan advocated that for a state to become a great power, it needed to dominate the seas and obtain overseas markets; to do this, it required a capital ship navy—the bigger, the better. The fervor with which industrialized nations converted to Mahan's maxim was not unlike a fever—RUSSIA, JAPAN, FRANCE, Germany, the United States, and, of course, Great Britain, were all swept along. Thus, the naval arms race began, with each nation seeking to outbuild the others. Of greatest concern to Britannia, still ruling the waves, was Germany. The kaiser was a grandson of Queen Victoria, yet he had a pathological need to crush "perfidious Albion" in a naval arms race—neglecting the fact that Mahan gives a list of six necessary factors for a state to even *potentially* dominate the sea, and Germany had but one of them. Across the ocean, the United States had been trying in fits and starts to build a navy suitable for its rising status, though it continued to maintain a quasi-isolationist policy, helped by the insularity of the Atlantic. This put Germany and Great Britain on a crash course during the era of naval building, with the United States watching and building from the wings.

The last major treaty of the 19th century, Secretary of State JOHN HAY's OPEN DOOR into CHINA, brought Germany, Britain, Russia, and the United States together in a diplomatic context. China was an anomaly—too strong a land power, no state could penetrate inland far from the coast to dominate it individually, and with the great age of colonialism on the wane, neither could any state alone afford the attempt. As such, and at American initiation, the four powers mentioned—soon to be joined by France, ITALY, and JAPAN—agreed to section coastal China, keeping the door open to exploit the market but without the necessary military occupation usually required. Diplomatically, it was an American coup, for during a time of rising tensions and shifting power balances, it brought the major powers together and peacefully enticed them to comply with its plan.

Into the 20th century, the strongest powers in the world were still European, which helped impress upon President THEODORE ROOSEVELT that the key to maintaining peace in the world was in stabilizing France, Great Britain, and Germany. Anglo-American rapprochement helped this, but so did Roosevelt's policy of using the Americans' neutral status to prevent the outbreak of a general European war among strong nations. While his commitment to the rapprochement was clear, Kaiser Wilhelm repeatedly underestimated its solidarity, actually believing the president to be pro-German. Roosevelt used this error to his advantage and cultivated a relationship with Wilhelm in the hopes of influencing him. In fact, Wilhelm did seek Roosevelt's support on several diplomatic issues between 1905 and 1909, but the American was the better diplomat in this case, flattering the German emperor and winning his way into a privileged position while never truly giving firm support. When Germany postured aggressively during the Moroccan crisis of 1905 and 1906, Roosevelt was able to draw on his reputation secured during the Russo-Japanese War mediation in Portsmouth, New Hampshire, to arrange conferences in SPAIN between a deeply offended France and a near-belligerent Germany. A treaty was signed preventing war, and Roosevelt continued to be the man to deal with the unstable kaiser. Even when replaced by WILLIAM HOWARD TAFT, the appearance of the Roosevelt-Wilhelm bonds were strong—at least

from the German's perspective. While the ex-president continued to foster relations, he was constantly encouraging Britain to build up its navy, keep Germany from getting too strong, and maintain peace in Europe. Roosevelt was reasonably successful in his diplomacy, but he was also no longer in power.

WOODROW WILSON's 1912 election brought the Democrats back to the White House and ushered in what appeared to be a term of domestic change and inward focus. It could not have been further from the truth. Instead, when the European war erupted in 1914, Wilson immediately began drafting letters to Britain and Germany, the key belligerents, in an effort to convince them to have him mediate the peace. His letters were unsuccessful. Wilson sent an envoy, the unofficially ranked honorary colonel EDWARD M. HOUSE, but he, too, was unsuccessful. Still, Wilson maintained that the United States must remain neutral in spirit and in action, while both Britain and Germany began waging war in ways that made it uncertain—even until 1916—on whose side the Americans would fight, should they be forced into war. Finally, after German U-boats in the Atlantic sank several neutral ships carrying American citizens, most famously the *Lusitania, Arabic,* and *Sussex,* and agreements were made that were subsequently ignored, the neutral Wilson was forced to change his stance. The last straw was the German decision to pursue unrestricted submarine warfare—or to ignore all semblances of international law and to shoot all Atlantic shipping on sight. Somehow, the German high command, the kaiser, and the chancellor—Theobald von Bethmann-Hollweg—all managed to convince themselves that the United States would remain neutral even when its people and trade were being sent to the bottom of the Atlantic indiscriminately. It was the wrong gamble, and on April 4, 1917, Wilson delivered a stirring address to CONGRESS, and the United States was at war. American troops arrived on the European battlefields only in 1918; given the effort already expended by the British and the French with their colonials, the U.S. military contribution in WORLD WAR I was not substantial. However, its resources and the promise of more manpower were critical in the Central Powers' defeat.

When the war ended on November 11, 1918, it did so as an armistice, which is a truce, or mutually agreed laying down of weapons, but not a victory. This distinction is critical in understanding the effects of the VERSAILLES TREATY, the chaos and poverty of the interwar era, and the rise of fascism under Adolf Hitler. Toward the end of 1918, German government officials repeatedly appealed to President Wilson to end the war on the basis of the FOURTEEN POINTS, hanging all their hopes in the first five points that called for open diplomacy, freedom of the seas, removal of trade barriers, reduction in armaments, and impartial settlement of colonial claims based on the interests of the people involved. The Germans sought to pick and choose which of the Fourteen Points they would adhere to, it seemed, failing to recognize points 7, 8, 10, and 13: restoration of an independent Belgium, return of Alsace-Lorraine to France, autonomous development for the nationalities of the Austro-Hungarian Empire, and recognition of an independent POLAND with free access to the sea, respectively. These points were not in line with Germany's interests, but what was most problematic of the postwar settlement was the German war guilt clause. Given the misinformation circulating the German home front and the fact that when the armistice occurred, German forces were still in possession of more territory than they had been prior to the war, to many Germans, the Versailles treaty was unduly harsh, and they called it the Versailles Diktat, implying that Germany had not signed voluntarily. When General von Ludendorff declared that this was the result of Jews, bankers, and the aristocracy selling out the citizens (the Dolchstoss, or "stab in the back," theory) and forcing them to accept defeat, Germans became convinced that they had been done wrong. From Germany's perspective, Wilson's Fourteen Points had graduated into an era of malcontent and rising anti-Semitism.

The Weimar era in Germany, 1919–33, was one of domestic focus as the country essentially crumbled from the rising power it had been prewar into a chaotic state with rampant levels of inflation—in November 1923, there were 400,338,326,350,700,000,000 German marks in circulation! Diplomacy was in absolute shambles, as a series of separatist movements undermined any singular voice working to speak for all Germany. However, prospects for stability improved when Gustav Stresemann was made chancellor in 1923. Instead of inciting resistance to the Diktat, Stresemann encouraged stabilizing the German currency and working with foreign powers because he saw clearly that Germany had no choice. "Foreign powers" in this era implied London and Paris, for when the United States failed to ratify the League of Nations and turned inward, it essentially left Germany to sort itself out on its own. Still, the two nations were financially linked, as the United States was the major Great War creditor nation and Germany was struggling to pay back reparations stipulated at Versailles, affecting the Central Powers' abilities to repay the Americans in turn.

Stresemann's attempts to fulfill the terms of the Versailles treaty stabilized Germany somewhat until the 1929 stock market crash, but it was not uniformly popular among Germans. In whose interests was the KELLOGG-BRIAND TREATY renouncing war signed? Playing on widespread unhappiness, an Austrian veteran of Germany's World War I army began his assent to power, and in 1933 Adolf Hitler had secured sufficient parliamentary power to be appointed chancellor, and, on President von Hindenburg's death the next year, president as well.

Hitler's foreign policy was bold, and he was blatant in his anti-Diktat intentions: He would build an air force (Luftwaffe), introduce male conscription, raise 36 army divisions, expand the navy to 35 percent of the Royal Navy, and remilitarize the Rhineland. A new era was at hand, and with Britain recognizing the Soviet Union as its greatest security threat, the policy of appeasing Hitler began. For his part, U.S. president FRANKLIN D. ROOSEVELT was unconvinced that this was the best way to deal with the fanatic German, but when the European powers' acquiescence in the Austrian Anschluss and the cession of the Sudetenland from CZECHOSLOVAKIA at the Munich Conference in 1938 appeared to keep the peace in Europe, he could not entirely disagree with the status quo. Roosevelt's signing of the NEUTRALITY ACTS of 1935, 1936, and 1937 may well have played directly into Hitler's hands, giving him the extra motivation required to continue with his plans—the American juggernaut had all but said it would not stop him. In the United States, Roosevelt began to find ways to modify the neutrality acts without becoming actively involved in European tensions. Roosevelt's hands were tied; he could not overcome his country's inward focus. Not even war's outbreak in 1939 could shake American resolve, even when hostilities raised the question of their security should Britain be defeated across the Atlantic.

Roosevelt clearly favored the Allies prior to the German declaration of war on the United States in 1941, and diplomacy with Hitler was nearly nonexistent for the first two years of the European war. As the Battle of Britain picked up, it had its effects on American domestic politics, and in 1940 Roosevelt ran for and was elected to an unprecedented third term in office, showing that American sentiments were increasingly with the president as he sought to pull away from neutrality. Anglo-American LEND LEASE flirted with war involvement, yet they remained at peace until Pearl Harbor. Hitler had learned from the biggest German mistake of the previous war and had his submarine commanders avoid American ships. This policy was abruptly reversed when the Japanese, German allies, attacked the United States, and soon diplomacy was a thing of the past.

In the immediate postwar era, diplomacy centered on Germany and involved a few key powers, namely, Britain, the United States, and the Soviet Union. However, after the Potsdam Conference of 1945, when the Soviets said one thing and began clearly to do another, relations between the former allies soured, leading directly to the COLD WAR. Before concerns of Soviet aggression could be contemplated, first the Western world tried to overcome the ravages of war. For this, the MARSHALL PLAN extended American aid to 17

European countries. The Soviet Union was invited to participate, but neither it nor its satellite countries (including East Germany, Finland, Romania, Bulgaria, HUNGARY, Poland, and Czechoslovakia) took part, seeing U.S. aid as an attempt to weaken Soviet control over Eastern Europe—and in fact it was intended at least in part to arrest COMMUNISM's spread. Thus, East Germany went without, but West Germany received 1,390,600,000,000 American dollars.

Two years after the Marshall Plan came into existence, the TRUMAN DOCTRINE's final phase of containment came into effect: the NORTH ATLANTIC TREATY ORGANIZATION (NATO). It exacerbated the growing tensions between East and West in Europe, and the ramifications of it were played out over Germany. The 1948 Berlin blockade (see BERLIN CRISIS, 1948) was Russia's answer to the containment efforts, as Stalin cut all rail and highway traffic from West Germany to West Berlin on June 20, 1948. The United States faced a difficult decision: It could pull out its forces and lose the city—and the confidence of Europe—or it could surmount the Soviet blockade with a massive airlift of food, fuel, and supplies for the 2 million civilians and 10,000 troops in Berlin. Opting for the airlift, Truman also bluffed that U.S. forces was prepared to back up the lift with nuclear power against Soviet intervention, but his bluff was not called, and the airlift continued until 1949, when the Soviets agreed to a summit, and the preblockade status quo was restored.

As Germany struggled through de-Nazification, its new chancellor, Konrad Adenauer, adopted a firm view of the German future. He accepted the political reality of the American superpower status and French fears of a German revival. Above all, he was encouraged by the 1946 statement by SECRETARY OF STATE JAMES F. BYRNES that the United States would remain in Europe, and Germany was a part of Europe—thus, the Americans were committed to helping it get back on its feet. Even with aid and the American superpower on its side, it took until September 1950 for the government at Bonn to establish a foreign office and conduct its own policy. Since then, German-U.S. relations have been the key to American involvement in Europe. Recovery after that point came steadily, and by the end of the 1950s, the Federal Republic of Germany (West Germany) was well on its way to retaking its place as a strong Central European state, having joined NATO (1954) and the European Economic Community (a EUROPEAN UNION precursor, in 1957) and having secured reparations and forgiveness by both the United States and the Soviet Union. Complete fiscal recovery would take decades, but following the U.S. installation of the deutsche mark in 1948, debt forgiveness, and aid, Germany post–World War II was in markedly better shape than Germany post–World War I. Yet this was really a matter of two Germanies, not just one. In July 1955, the victorious Allies

met to discuss the fate of the "German question," or, how to reconcile two states within one nation, and they concluded that no solution existed—reunification involved all of Europe, and it simply was not feasible in the near future.

Following talks between American president John F. Kennedy and Nikita Khruschev, at which Kennedy defended the American presence in Berlin and committed the United States to upholding it, the Berlin Wall was erected in 1961, crushing any possible hopes of a unified East and West Germany. For the cold war's duration, the two states coexisted as members of opposite collective security: East Germany, or the Democratic Republic of Germany, clearly a WARSAW PACT state, and West Germany firmly entrenched in NATO. In 1973, both states were admitted to the United Nations, but rather than suggesting a rapprochement, each side continued to follow the ebb and flow of international relations through their separate alliances.

The great historical challenge of German foreign policy was to avoid "the nightmare of coalitions." This was the prospect that Germany, situated in the center of Europe, would become victim to an encircling coalition of forces. World Wars I and II can be seen as attempts to break out of that encirclement by destroying the coalition. Germany's post–World War II situation was not much different. It lay between two warring coalitions and was vulnerable to a DÉTENTE between them, especially since it was powerless. Adenauer's foreign policy sought to build up Germany's military power without losing the protection of the United States. He did so by integrating Germany into NATO and, in the process, ensuring that no superpower deal would be cut on the future of East and West Germany without West Germany's consent.

By the end of the 1960s signs pointed to a relaxation in U.S.-Soviet tensions that might free each of them from being shackled by the opposition of "their Germanies" to any form of accommodation. Concerns also began to be expressed by the United States about Germany's contributions to NATO. The complaint was not directed solely at Germany, but questions of burden sharing within NATO suggested that the United States wanted to put its participation in NATO on a different financial footing. Against this backdrop, German chancellor Willy Brandt seized the initiative at this time to increase Germany's voice in future decisions over its fate. In 1969, only months after the STRATEGIC ARMS LIMITATION TALKS were launched, Brandt began his foreign policy of Ostpolitik. No longer would Germany's foreign policy only face to the West; Germany would now establish its own relations with the East. Three treaties were signed that had the effect of normalizing German relations with its old enemies. Treaties with the Soviet Union and Poland were signed in 1970 that recognized the "inviolability" of the territorial status quo in East

President John F. Kennedy stands on a platform overlooking the Berlin Wall. *(Kennedy Library)*

Europe and renounced the use of force. In 1972 an agreement was signed with East Germany that had the effect of recognizing it as a separate state. While these foreign-policy initiatives did not openly challenge U.S. foreign policy, they were taken independently of it and altered the geopolitical context in which America's European policy would have to be made.

In October 1989, aided by Gorbachev's glasnost and perestroika, the 40th anniversary of the two Germanies was marked by the opening of the Berlin Wall; soon after reunification, East and West were brought together again. Given the drastic differences in wealth and standardization, this movement has taken many years and is still not yet complete. Bonn ceased to be a capital city, with all facets of government moved back to Berlin. In spite of the uncertainty, Germany remains a major European Union power, and its economy has not been unduly burdened by unification. The introduction of the euro, the EU currency, has been somewhat problematic, however, dropping the deutsche mark's value on the foreign exchange market, then driving up costs by a factor of almost two in the aftermath.

Today, American policy with Germany centers around the preservation of peace and security, and while U.S. troops are no longer in Germany in an occupational context, more than 91,000 U.S. military personnel are still stationed there. This is a symbol of the overlapping common interests these nations share, having emerged from the cold war as very close allies. Further proof of this has been evidenced since SEPTEMBER 11, 2001, with Germany remaining a reliable ally in the war on TERRORISM, although it joined France and Russia in questioning the need for war with IRAQ in 2003.

See also BERLIN CRISIS, 1958; BERLIN CRISIS, 1961.

**Further reading:** Ash, Timothy. *In Europe's Name: Germany and the Divided Continent.* New York: Random House, 1993; Hanrieder, Wolfgang. *Germany, America, and Europe: 40 Years of German Foreign Policy.* New Haven, Conn.: Yale University Press, 1989; Pond, Elizabeth. *After the Wall: American Policy toward Germany.* Washington, D.C.: Brookings, 1990.

—Stephanie Cousineau

## Ghent, Treaty of    See TREATY OF GHENT.

## globalization

Analysts of world politics routinely look to the structure of the INTERNATIONAL SYSTEM to explain state foreign policy behavior and events, such as crises, peace, war, and prosperity. Traditionally it is the distribution of military POWER that has been viewed as the most important aspect of international-system structure. MULTIPOLARITY, BIPOLARITY, and UNIPOLARITY are the most studied distributions of military power. Another school of thought focuses on the economic structure of the international system. Interdependence and IMPERIALISM have been central concepts in their analysis. In the post–COLD WAR period a new characterization of the international economic order has gained prominence and moved into the forefront of the debate over the future shape of world politics. It is globalization.

Globalization is rooted in breakthroughs in technology and government policy. Technological breakthroughs have sped up the pace of international economic transactions. Government policy has encouraged reliance on the market and private sector as a mechanism for promoting economic

development. Combined, they have unleashed economic forces that are global in reach, affecting virtually all sectors of domestic society, including culture, and they operate at a pace that makes government regulation difficult. At the international level globalization has tightened the financial and trade bounds between rich and poor states.

Supporters of globalization view it as a force for global economic growth, peace, and democracy. In particular they assert that in rich states globalization will benefit consumers by providing cheaper goods and workers by providing opportunities for higher-paying jobs in export-oriented sectors. In poor states globalization is seen as producing a level and pace of economic growth that is capable of alleviating poverty and social unrest. Two different sets of opponents of globalization have emerged. The first consists of economic and political analysts who champion the cause of economic and political nationalism. In their view globalization is dangerous because it undermines both of these conditions. States are left attempting to navigate the waters of world politics without being in full control of their assets. They favor adopting a protectionist TRADE POLICY that allows governments to discriminate in favor of domestic producers and workers. A second set of opponents is identified as comprising a global backlash movement. They are made up primarily of citizen activists who reject globalization because it is driven by corporate goals and reject the protectionist alternative because its goal is to protect and develop state power. The global backlash movement is concerned with globalization's impact on the environment, small farmers, indigenous populations, consumers, women, children, and workers and their safety.

While it is the economic and social aspects of globalization that have received the most attention, there are also definite political consequences as well. At the international level concern is expressed about the loss of control by governments and international bodies over monetary and trade relations. Repeats of the ASIAN FINANCIAL CRISIS and earlier Third World DEBT CRISES are feared. At the societal level it has resulted in political protests that challenge the authority and legitimacy of governments and international organizations, such as the INTERNATIONAL MONETARY FUND and WORLD TRADE ORGANIZATION. At the national level the interaction of these two sets of political movements has produced governments that have sought to hold power by evoking nationalist or populist themes as well as calls for strong rulers and curbs on democracy. Defenders of globalization reject the assertion that these political developments are inherent in globalization. Instead they place the dynamics of globalization firmly within the DEMOCRATIC PEACE school of thought. Global economic growth is seen as promoting and sustaining democracy, which in turn is seen as a force for peace.

Globalization thus presents a complex and uncertain setting for the conduct of American foreign policy. Viewed in the most positive light, globalization is to be encouraged not only because it offers prosperity at home but also because it will help bring about a peaceful international system within which American foreign policy will operate. Viewed in a negative light globalization is to be resisted. It will rob American policy makers of control over key economic assets that are needed to accomplish foreign-policy objectives. Furthermore it holds the potential for creating domestic political conditions abroad that will make it difficult for American allies to respond to requests for help and social conditions that may require HUMANITARIAN INTERVENTION. Finally, opposition to globalization within the United States holds the potential for polarizing DOMESTIC POLITICS in debates about the purposes and character of American foreign policy.

**Further reading:** Broad, Robin. *Global Backlash: Citizen Initiatives for a Just World Economy*. Lanham, Md.: Rowman and Littlefield, 2002; Dierks, Rosa G. *Introduction to Globalization: Political and Economic Perspectives for the New Century*. Chicago: Burnham, 2001; Lechner, Frank J., and John Boli, eds. *The Globalization Reader*. Malden, Mass.: Blackwell, 2000.

### Goldwater et al. v. Carter (1979)

This was a lawsuit brought by Senator Barry Goldwater (R-Ariz.) and 20 colleagues against President JIMMY CARTER's decision to terminate the 1955 Mutual Defense Treaty with TAIWAN. The SUPREME COURT turned back the challenge by asserting that, in Justice William Rehnquist's words, "[the] basic issue presented by the petitioners in this case is 'political' and therefore nonjusticiable because it involves the authority of the PRESIDENT in the conduct of our country's foreign affairs."

Carter's action was necessitated by the U.S. decision to recognize the People's Republic of CHINA, Communist China, as the true government of China. Ever since Mao Zedong's (Mao Tse-tung) victory in the Chinese civil war in 1949, the United States has recognized the Nationalist government on Taiwan as the legitimate government of China. President RICHARD NIXON's 1972 trip to China that culminated in the signing of the Shanghai Communiqué signaled the beginning of the end of this policy. According to the Mutual Defense Treaty either side could terminate the treaty with one year's notice. Goldwater argued that presidents must receive a two-thirds supporting vote from the Senate to terminate a treaty just as they require a two-thirds vote to ratify one.

The CONSTITUTION is silent on this point. But Rehnquist noted: "[I]n light of the absence of any constitutional provision governing the termination of a treaty and that different termination procedures may be appropriate for different treaties . . . the instant case in my view . . . must surely be controlled by political standards.'"

As used here, the concept of political questions is a means by which the Supreme Court can remove itself from the battle to control the course of American foreign policy. It is an avenue that the Court used many times during the VIETNAM WAR. The question by whose authority a treaty can be terminated or modified continues to be an important one. For example, it lies at the heart of the tug of war between the president and CONGRESS over whether or not the ANTIBALLISTIC MISSILE TREATY can be modified or terminated in order to construct a national BALLISTIC MISSILE DEFENSE system.

### Goldwater-Nichols Defense Reorganization Act

This act, passed in 1986, is a congressionally inspired attempt to bring greater coherence to the DEFENSE DEPARTMENT. Angered by repeated incidences of waste, abuse, and fraud in the military procurement system, CONGRESS, over the objections of the executive branch, passed the Goldwater-Nichols Defense Reorganization Act, which mandated the creation of a "procurement czar" to oversee the purchase of military equipment and gave increased power to the JOINT CHIEFS OF STAFF in an effort to promote interservice cooperation. The overall impact of the Goldwater-Nichols Act is still in doubt as the military services continue to resist full implementation of its provisions.

The Goldwater-Nichols Act is significant as much for the forces that gave rise to it as it is for the problem it addressed. Lack of true interservice cooperation has been an endemic problem in the history of the Defense Department, as each service has successfully resisted efforts by civilians and the Joint Chiefs of Staff to shape a true national defense policy. Nowhere has interservice competition been as intense as in the area of weapons procurement, with each service insisting on the need for its own inventory of weapons and being largely insensitive to the enormous cost overruns that have accompanied their production. For example, production of the F-22 Raptor was begun in the early 1980s. The U.S. Air Force wanted to purchase 750 of them for a total program cost of $99.1 billion. In 2000 the air force sought only 305 but at a total cost of $68.9 billion, or $266 million per aircraft.

The greater significance of the Goldwater-Nichols Act stems from its congressional roots. This act was passed over the objections of the executive branch. It is an example of a new willingness on the part of Congress not only to set the broad directions of American foreign policy but to shape the institutions which conduct it. Other examples include the congressionally mandated establishment of the OFFICE OF THE SPECIAL TRADE REPRESENTATIVE in the White House and the effort led by Senator JESSE HELMS (R-N.C.) to merge the AGENCY FOR INTERNATIONAL DEVELOPMENT, the ARMS CONTROL AND DISARMAMENT AGENCY, and the UNITED STATES INFORMATION AGENCY into the STATE DEPARTMENT. This assertiveness points to the existence of a much larger area of conflict between the White House and Congress over the control of U.S. foreign policy than typically existed during the COLD WAR.

## Grant, Ulysses S. (1822–1885) *president of the United States*

After serving as the commander in chief of the Union army during the AMERICAN CIVIL WAR, Ulysses Simpson (U.S.) Grant was elected the 18th president of the United States and served from 1869 to 1877. Commentators are divided on his stewardship of American foreign policy. Some portray him as poorly equipped to conduct DIPLOMACY, only saved from committing mistakes by his SECRETARY OF STATE Hamilton Fish. Others see his presidency in more positive terms. He is seen as having moved American territorial expansionism forward and, with Fish, as a president who placed U.S. relations with GREAT BRITAIN on a positive footing with the signing of the TREATY OF WASHINGTON.

One of Grant's most debated failed foreign-policy initiatives was an attempt to annex the DOMINICAN REPUBLIC. In 1869 General Orville Babcock went to the Dominican Republic as Grant's personal representative. There he concluded two treaties. The first called for the annexation of the Dominican Republic by the United States. The second was a fallback agreement that stipulated that should the Dominican Republic not be annexed the United States could purchase Samana Bay for $2 million. Samana Bay was long sought by the U.S. Navy as a coaling station. The annexation bid failed due to the opposition of Senate Foreign Relations Committee chairman CHARLES SUMNER. By a vote of 5-2 the committee rejected the treaty and later the full Senate voted 28-28 to reject it.

This was not the only treaty controversy that Grant was embroiled in. A treaty with Denmark, signed in 1867, that would have transferred control over the Danish West Indies (the Virgin Islands) to the United States for $7.5 million, providing the inhabitants agreed, was before Congress when Grant became president, although it was not receiving active consideration. Grant objected to it, describing it as another of Secretary of State WILLIAM SEWARD's "schemes" and allowed the treaty to die. In Caribbean matters, Fish would also convince Grant not to grant belligerency status to Cuban forces fighting for independence from SPAIN when the popular mood in the United States seemed to support doing so.

On a more positive note the Grant administration successfully negotiated the Treaty of Washington in 1871. The agreement brought to an end lingering controversies with Great Britain concerning the *Alabama* claims and fishing rights with CANADA. It also included a provision for German arbitration of the disputed ownership of the San Juan Islands, which are located between the province of British Columbia and Washington State.

**Further reading:** Campbell, Charles S. *The Transformation of American Foreign Relations, 1865–1900.* New York: Harper and Row, 1976.

## Great Britain

Officially the United Kingdom of Great Britain and NORTHERN IRELAND, Great Britain is slightly smaller than Oregon in size, with an area of 93,000 square miles. It has a population of 59.8 million people. Over three centuries Great Britain used its commercial and naval power to establish a presence on every continent. The territories it ruled collectively fell under the province of the British Empire. The first possessions came to Great Britain through the efforts of private commercial companies that were chartered by the Crown. In North America these colonies plus those set up by religious dissenters formed the basis for the political, economic, and social development of CANADA and the United States.

The diplomatic history of the United States begins on July 4, 1776, when the Continental Congress declared the 13 colonies to be independent of Britain. From that point forward managing relations with Great Britain was the single most pressing foreign-policy problem to confront the United States for more than a century. Great Britain was alternately looked upon as both a great benefactor and model and a primary threat to American security and prosperity. The singular importance of Great Britain in American foreign-policy thinking was not reciprocated. As a global power, Great Britain was on occasion unprepared for American foreign-policy pronouncements and often viewed its relations with the United States, and the colonies before it, in the context of larger struggles with rival great powers for military and economic gain.

A convenient point at which to pick up the first signs that British foreign policy would create the seeds of revolution in the North American colonies is the FRENCH AND INDIAN WAR (1756–63). The war was part of a worldwide struggle between Great Britain and FRANCE for global domination. The war ended with France losing its North American possessions. Lands east of the Mississippi River became the property of Great Britain. Those west of the Mississippi River now fell under Spanish control. With the western frontier now open, American settlers streamed west into the Ohio River valley. There they came into conflict with NATIVE AMERICANS. The resulting wars led to a military conflict and a decision by the British to set the Appalachian Mountains as the western boundary of its colonies. The move was intended to preserve the lucrative fur trade for the British government, but it also angered colonists who saw western lands as a source of wealth for themselves.

Victory in war came with a high price tag, and the British sought to recoup their costs by taxing the colonists to cover the costs of defending and administering the colonies. Numbered among the pieces of tax legislation passed following the French and Indian War was the Sugar Act of 1764, the Stamp Act of 1765, and the Tea Act of 1773. This last measure resulted in the Boston Tea Party and was indicative of the extent to which the colonists resented the British presence and had come to think of themselves as possessing a separate identity. Colonial resistance was met with imperial resistance. The British government of Lord North was determined to reassert its control over the colonies, and in 1774 Great Britain passed the Coercive Acts. It placed the Massachusetts colony under royal control and closed Boston Harbor until restitution was made for the lost tea. Contrary to British hopes this policy did not intimidate the colonists or divide them. Instead, it united them in opposition to Great Britain and led to the calling of the First Continental Congress in September 1774.

Delegates at the meeting voted to boycott British goods if their grievances, which included self-government, were not met. North offered a compromise that was rejected, and he then ordered British forces to put down the rebellion, a decision that led to the famous military encounter between British forces and colonists at Lexington. The Second Continental Congress met in May 1775 and issued a peace proposal known as the Olive Branch Petition. It was presented to King George III, who rejected it in favor of a military solution to his colonial problem. One year later, as political positions in the colonies hardened and became polarized, the colonies declared their independence, and the AMERICAN REVOLUTION began.

The likelihood that the Americans could win their independence would be greatly enhanced if they could secure allies. France, defeated by the British in the French and Indian War, was a logical choice. Not surprisingly the French were slow to respond to the American proposals for an ALLIANCE. This changed in October 1777 when British general John Burgoyne surrendered his forces at the Battle of Saratoga. France recognized the United States by signing a treaty of amity and commerce in 1778. This led Great Britain to retaliate, which in turn led to the signing of a treaty of alliance. Lord North made a late concession, an offer of what amounted to home rule, to the colonists in

March 1778 in an effort to end the rebellion. The proposal reached the United States just after word of the French agreement arrived.

Britain's European opponents used the American Revolution as an opportunity to challenge its naval dominance through the formation of a league of armed neutrality. RUSSIA and the Nordic states of Denmark-Norway and Sweden led the way in 1780. They were later joined by the Holy Roman Empire, Prussia, Portugal, and the Kingdom of the Two Sicilies. The states of the league did not declare war on Great Britain (as had France, SPAIN, and the NETHERLANDS). Their military power was limited, but they did aid the American cause by adopting a hostile posture to Great Britain. The fact that Great Britain was at war with four states was also important in securing the generous terms of the TREATY OF PARIS in 1783. The boundaries of the United States were set at the Mississippi River, Canada, and Spanish FLORIDA. American negotiators pursued the peace treaty independently of the French in violation of their instructions and the terms of the Franco-American alliance. It is also asserted that the British viewed the peace agreement as a way of seeking to disrupt the nascent alliance between the two countries.

Postindependence relations between Great Britain and the United States were slow to develop. The British did not send a diplomatic representative to the United States until 1791. In part this was due to disagreements over the basis on which trade between the two states would be organized, with the United States seeking reciprocity and the British seeking domination. The British inattention to the United States was also due to the outbreak of yet another war between Great Britain and France following the French Revolution. It was to avoid entanglement in this conflict that GEORGE WASHINGTON issued a neutrality proclamation on April 22, 1793.

Declaring one's neutrality is not the same as being treated as a neutral state, and the United States quickly became a target of Great Britain's policy of commercial warfare, which was designed to prevent the French from gaining access to international trade through American merchant vessels. A British Order in Council of June 8, 1793, authorized the confiscation and purchase of all neutral (American) goods headed for ports under French control. A second Order in Council of November 6, 1793, authorized the detention of ships carrying products of a French colony or for use by a French colony. Three hundred American ships were seized, and many of their crew members were impressed into service with the British navy. A second dimension to the growing hostility between Great Britain and the United States involved tensions along the western frontier. The Treaty of Paris called for the speedy evacuation of British forts along the U.S.-Canadian border. This did not happen. Doing so would invite a further expansion of American settlements westward and jeopardize the profitable fur trade and their relations with Native Americans. To justify their actions the British cited America's refusal to pay its debts to Great Britain and its treatment of the Loyalists.

In 1794 George Washington sent John Jay to negotiate an end to these conflicts. Jay's efforts were undercut by ALEXANDER HAMILTON, who greatly valued commercial ties with the British as a means of building the American economy. Armed with the knowledge of the American negotiating position, JAY'S TREATY cost the British little. They merely repeated their earlier pledge to withdraw from their western military forts. No commercial concessions were made, no compensation for seized property was negotiated, and Great Britain's policy of commercial warfare continued. Jay's Treaty averted war, but war would come in 1812.

Incidents at sea and in the West again combined to lead the two countries into the WAR OF 1812. In the West, it had become the accepted wisdom that the British were behind Native American attacks on western settlers. These beliefs were reinforced when, after the Battle of Tippecanoe, new British weapons were found in the possession of the Shawnee Indians. More than 60 Americans were killed in the battle, and more than 100 were wounded. Western war HAWKS eyed Canada as the prize to be won in a war with the British. The problem at sea involved an extension of fighting between France and Great Britain that had stalemated. The British dominated the seas after their victory at Trafalgar in October 1805 over the combined French and Spanish fleets. Napoleon Bonaparte, however, had secured control of the Continent later that year by defeating the Russian and Austrian armies. In 1806 Britain declared a blockade of much of the European coast. Napoleon countered by declaring a blockade of Great Britain. This placed American commercial interests at the mercy of British naval forces and French privateers. American anger with Great Britain was roused to great heights in 1807 when the British attacked and forced the surrender of an American ship, the *Chesapeake,* in actions in search of four escaped British sailors. Presidents THOMAS JEFFERSON and James Madison tried with little effect to force a solution to a policy of economic warfare that included an embargo against both countries and a nonimportation policy directed at Great Britain.

The United States declared war in June 1812. Preoccupied with Napoleon Bonaparte the British were caught off guard by the American action. They moved too slowly to suspend the Orders in Council that had so angered Americans. In theory the success of the American war effort rested on the ability of Napoleon to threaten British security interests and allow the United States to attack Canada. In reality the United States was so unprepared for war that little mattered. Invasions in 1812 and 1813 were easily rebuffed. It helped

matters little that by 1814 Napoleon's forces were in disarray. The American navy fared much better, but naval victories had little impact on the outcome of the war.

The two sides had actually begun peace negotiations the same month that war was declared. RUSSIA offered to mediate the conflict in September 1812 in order to free its ally Great Britain to concentrate on defeating Napoleon. When the offer was officially made in March 1813, it was rejected by the British. Unwilling to completely antagonize Russia, in November the British proposed direct negotiations. When the negotiations that would led to the TREATY OF GHENT began, the British led with terms that amounted to a victor's peace, including the establishment of a large Native American buffer state in the area that today is Indiana, Ohio, Michigan, Illinois, and Wisconsin. After the British sacking of Washington, D.C., the British demanded that any peace agreement recognize territories now occupied, which for them would include parts of Maine. The diplomatic tide turned after the American victory on Lake Champlain, and a compromise was struck that ended the war and restored the prewar status quo. The RUSH-BAGOT AGREEMENT of 1817 marked a positive moment in Anglo-American diplomacy following the War of 1812 as it addressed Canadian and American concerns about the continued presence of armaments along the Great Lakes.

The bulk of British-American diplomatic maneuverings in the years following the War of 1812 were directed southward, to Latin America and the Caribbean. In 1823 Spain sought to reestablish its colonial presence in the Western Hemisphere. This move alarmed the British, who above all sought to maintain the balance of power status quo that existed in Europe. Great Britain proposed a joint Anglo-American declaration to the effect that Latin America was closed to Spanish colonization. The Unites States balked and instead issued a unilateral declaration, the MONROE DOCTRINE. In reality, the Monroe Doctrine required the support of the British navy. Uncoordinated British-American cooperation here was possible because both states shared an interest in keeping Spain out of the Western Hemisphere. Cooperation in the region turned to competition when the subject changed from security to commerce. A key issue would be the construction of and control over an isthmus canal. Not only would this provide additional economic benefits in the region to the owner, it would also be a stimulus to a greater economic presence in the Pacific. Great Britain sought to constrain American economic expansionism with the CLAYTON-BULWER TREATY of 1850 in which both countries agreed to cooperate on the construction of a canal and not to fortify or claim exclusive control over a canal.

Competition rather than cooperation between the United States and Great Britain was also evident along

America's western frontier. An exception to this rule was the Webster-Ashburton Treaty of 1842 that resolved the matter of where the U.S.–Canadian border lay as well as several other outstanding issues. On the broader issue of American expansion, however, Great Britain sought to limit the growing power of the United States. It worked with groups in California and Texas to block American expansion into Mexican territory. It also sought to prevent American expansion into the Pacific Northwest. Neither move was successful as the United States aggressively moved to fill the continent.

Great Britain's major fear, that the United States would become a competing great power, lessened with the outbreak of the AMERICAN CIVIL WAR. The war presented Great Britain with a challenging foreign-policy problem. Economics dictated a Union bias since grain was more important to the British economy than was cotton. Strategic considerations pointed in the opposite direction. Much more would be gained by a Confederate victory since a divided and weakened America posed a much lesser threat to British supremacy than did a united and expanding America. At the same time, given British imperial holdings, support for rebellion in another state set a dangerous precedent. In the end, Great Britain officially adopted a neutral policy, although strong voices were raised in support of intervention on the side of the Confederacy or at least support for a great power mediation of the conflict. One factor complicating any overt British support for the Confederacy was the issue of slavery. ABRAHAM LINCOLN's Emancipation Proclamation had turned British working-class public opinion away from the South. Union resentment over Great Britain's neutrality during the American Civil War as well as British anger over Union attacks on commerce destroyers built in Britain, such as the *Alabama*, soured post–Civil War relations for several years. It was not until the Treaty of Washington in 1871 that many of the outstanding issues from the Civil War were settled.

As a reunified America turned its attention outward, it repeatedly encountered Great Britain. One conflict involved Samoa, where GERMANY, Great Britain, and the United States worked out an agreement. The major area of conflict, however, involved Latin America. Here the United States began to force Great Britain out of NICARAGUA, build an American canal through PANAMA, and involve itself in a VENEZUELAN BOUNDARY DISPUTE between VENEZUELA and British Guiana. The British sought to accommodate the American position in Latin America and began to withdraw from an active role in that region. As in previous foreign-policy disputes between the United States and Great Britain, the United States was aided by British concerns with broader foreign-policy problems. Significant factors in British foreign-policy calculations centered on growing problems with Germany and challenges to its imperial position in AFRICA and Asia. The most significant of these challenges in Africa was the Boer War in SOUTH AFRICA (1899–1902).

In Asia, Great Britain came to fear for its position in CHINA and looked upon the United States as a potential ally. The British had acquired a privileged position in China as a result of the 1839 Opium War that opened five Chinese ports to British trade and made Hong Kong a British colony. It was supportive of the United States in the SPANISH-AMERICAN WAR, although there was no serious consideration given to any form of alliance between the two. Europe's continental powers supported Spain. With the acquisition of the PHILIPPINES in the war along with HAWAII and other islands the United States had firmly established itself as a Pacific power, and Great Britain sought to enlist it in defending the pro-British status quo in China. In a diplomatic exchange reminiscent of the Monroe Doctrine, the British approached the United States twice in 1898–99 about a joint initiative to guarantee equal commercial opportunities for all states in China. The United States refused and acted unilaterally by issuing the OPEN DOOR notes. Unfortunately for the British, once again the United States had proclaimed a policy without providing for its enforcement. Where the Monroe Doctrine was backed up by their naval power, the Open Door notes lacked any form of enforcement. Consequently London entered into treaties with Japan and France as a means of protecting its position in East Asia.

Anglo-American cooperation became more pronounced in the early years of the 20th century, although there were still points of disagreement between the two. Again broader British foreign-policy concerns played a key role in bringing the United States and Great Britain together and pushing them apart. Great Britain's position as the dominant state in the international system was clearly coming to an end. Germany and the United States were poised to pass it as industrial powers. To forestall this decline, Great Britain looked to allies both overseas and in Europe, where it formed the Triple Entente with France and Russia. WORLD WAR I began in the Balkans in 1914 with the assassination of Archduke Francis Ferdinand. Germany's subsequent violation of Belgium's neutrality as it executed the Schlieffen Plan led Great Britain to declare war. It was bound by a 1839 treaty to protect Belgian neutrality in case of war.

WOODROW WILSON adopted a position of neutrality, although his sentiments were pro-British. Problems with the British soon arose. An Order in Council of August 20, 1914, established a policy of intercepting neutral ships carrying contraband to the enemy. The British defined virtually everything but cotton as an illegal good that might help the enemy and was thus subject to seizure. Cotton was exempted for fear of provoking the South into demanding

Prime Minister Winston Churchill *(foreground, right)* addressing the U.S. Congress, December 1941 *(University of Kentucky Libraries)*

that the Wilson administration take steps to protect its interests. The British also imposed a blockade of enemy ports by stationing warships just outside territorial borders to intercept neutral commerce going to Germany. The United States protested these actions, and the British responded with delays, seeking not to provoke the Americans into counteraction while keeping their policy of economic warfare in place. Germany also engaged in economic warfare to prevent supplies from reaching its enemies. Its chosen instrument became the submarine. The death and destruction caused by submarine attacks on ships such as the *Lusitania,* a British passenger ship on which 1,198 lives were lost, turned the American public against Germany. Wilson officially broke relations with Germany on February 1, 1917, when Berlin announced a policy of unrestricted submarine warfare. War followed on April 6, 1917.

Although the United States kept its official distance during World War I, identifying itself as an Associated power rather than an ally and not integrating its forces with those of other states, the United States and Great Britain worked closely together on diplomatic matters. The proposal for a LEAGUE OF NATIONS, while associated with Wilson, was the product of joint discussions. They did not always agree. Great Britain opposed the U.S. position on how to deal with Japanese claims for German territory in Asia and sided with France against the United States on the question of German war reparations. World War I had taken a tremendous toll on British power. An estimated 750,000 soldiers died, and 7 million tons of shipping had been lost. The combina-

tion of victory and declined power framed the foreign-policy problems facing Great Britain in the interwar era.

Militarily it found it necessary to engage in naval disarmament talks, such as the WASHINGTON CONFERENCE in 1921–22 and the LONDON CONFERENCE in 1935. Economically it found it necessary to abandon the gold standard, stop paying its debts to the United States, and move from a policy of free trade to protectionism and preferences for the commonwealth. Diplomatically it became a prime force within the League of Nations, and that body's failures along with British inaction in the Spanish civil war reflected negatively on perceptions of British power. All of these policies were designed to protect the status quo. Great Britain received little help in this regard from the United States because of Washington's embrace of ISOLATIONISM. By the late 1930s the pressure of the revisionist states, Germany, ITALY, and JAPAN, proved too strong. Great Britain's last stand came at Munich in September 1938, where it sought to avoid war by appeasing Germany. The strategy failed miserably. On September 1, 1939, Germany invaded POLAND, and Great Britain and France declared war on Germany. France fell in June 1940, leaving Great Britain alone to fight Germany.

Franklin Roosevelt had become convinced of the need to support Great Britain but was hampered by the NEUTRALITY ACTS of the 1930s from doing so by overt means. Roosevelt worked Congress to loosen these restraints, enabling him to offer Great Britain FOREIGN AID through a program of destroyers for bases and LEND-LEASE arrangements. The signing of the ATLANTIC CHARTER altered the American position from one of neutrality to one of pro-British nonbelligerency. The United States now began to engage in an unofficial naval war with Germany in the Atlantic Ocean. The United States officially became an ally with Great Britain following the Japanese attack on Pearl Harbor on December 7, 1941.

The United States and Great Britain were frequent partners and effective collaborators in wartime summits. Perhaps the major point of disagreement between them arose over U.S. opposition to reestablishing the British colonial empire after the war. Franklin Roosevelt and Winston Churchill met at Casablanca in January 1943. They met again in Washington in May and Quebec City in August. They met again in Cairo in November 1943 with Jiang Jieshi (Chiang Kai-shek) and then at TEHRAN with Soviet leader Joseph Stalin. In February 1945 the Big Three met at YALTA. Their final meeting would take place at POTSDAM in July 1945. Churchill would be replaced by Clement Atlee at this meeting, and Roosevelt was replaced by HARRY TRUMAN. Out of these meetings came key strategic decisions, such as the timing of the opening of the second front against Germany in Europe and the terms of Russian participation in the war against Japan. These meetings also led to the establishment of the key international organization of the postwar era that promoted global cooperation, the UNITED NATIONS, and laid the foundations for the distrust between the Soviet Union and the West that would lead to the COLD WAR.

Post–WORLD WAR II cooperation between the United States and Great Britain in the first decades of the cold war was stronger in some areas than in others. For example, in Asia, Great Britain supported the United States during the KOREAN WAR but also established diplomatic relations with Communist China at the conclusion of the civil war. Cooperation was strongest in Europe where the symmetry of interests in containing COMMUNISM was most pronounced. It was Churchill who spoke of the descending "iron curtain" in Europe in a speech at Fulton, Missouri, on March 5, 1946. Great Britain was the largest recipient of MARSHALL PLAN funds ($3.2 billion) and a founding member of the NORTH ATLANTIC TREATY ORGANIZATION (NATO). The British inability to uphold its traditional defense commitments in the Mediterranean Sea led to the TRUMAN DOCTRINE.

Cooperation was weakest in the Middle East. Great Britain had been the dominant power in the region before World War II, but after the war the United States supplanted it. In 1956 the British in cooperation with France and ISRAEL sought to redraw the geopolitical map of the Middle East through a plan that would return the Suez Canal to British control, remove Egyptian president Gamal Abdel Nasser from power, and solidify the French position in North Africa. The plan was conceived of and executed without American participation. To the surprise of all three states, President DWIGHT EISENHOWER opposed the move. He cut off OIL supplies and financial support in order to make the three nations withdraw their forces. Not only was the SUEZ CRISIS a great failure for the British, but it became a symbol of the decline of British power. No longer were they a great power. Now Great Britain was a weaker ally to a more powerful United States.

The final act in Great Britain's fall from great-power status involved its failed attempt to develop a robust and independent nuclear capability. The British had moved first to develop a NUCLEAR WEAPON but their efforts were overtaken by the American Manhattan Project. Both sides jealously guarded their nuclear secrets, and it was not until 1943 that an agreement on nuclear collaboration was reached. By now, Great Britain was a junior partner and not an equal participant in this collaboration. In fact, the United States had decided that its postwar national security would be best secured through the possession of a nuclear monopoly. The surprise Soviet launching of *SPUTNIK* in 1957 and its demonstration of an intercontinental ballistic missile capability changed American thinking. Once again collaboration took place between the two states, with the

British receiving special access to American nuclear technology. Economically strapped, Great Britain needed access not only to American nuclear technology but also to American missile technology, for without missiles nuclear weapons would be hard to deliver in this new nuclear world. To reduce the costs of developing its own missiles, the United States agreed to provide Great Britain with Skybolt missiles in return for the right to station nuclear forces in Great Britain. In 1962 President JOHN KENNEDY cancelled the Skybolt because of technical problems, effectively leaving Great Britain with no delivery system. To calm the angered British, Kennedy provided them with Polaris missiles but the message was clear. Great Britain had become dependent on the United States for the most important weapons of the cold war. Further documenting this decline was Great Britain's and France's absence at nuclear summit conferences after their presence at the initial one in Geneva in July 1955. The Big Four meeting became the Big Two.

Tensions between the American and British governments would never again reach this intensity. This is not to say that policy differences did not separate the two publics or that the governments did not disagree. Great Britain was reserved in its support for the United States in the VIETNAM WAR and was home to a strong antinuclear movement. More recently Great Britain disagreed with the United States on its policy toward BOSNIA AND HERZEGOVINA in the mid-1990s and opposed lifting the arms embargo to Bosnian Muslims. In large measure policy differences did not create substantial problems in their relationship because of the American penchant for UNILATERALISM. The active cooperation of Great Britain or most other states was not necessarily of great importance. It also reflects what amounts to a role reversal. Where once Great Britain was the great power and tended to view its relations with the United States in terms of a broader agenda, it is now the United States that does so.

There have also been periods of close collaboration between the two. President RONALD REAGAN and Prime Minister Margaret Thatcher developed a close working relationship. The United States was an important ally to Great Britain in the Falkland Islands War with ARGENTINA, supplying it with military intelligence, missiles, and bases. Prime Minister Tony Blair has been President GEORGE W. BUSH's principal ally in the war against TERRORISM following the SEPTEMBER 11, 2001, attacks, in the war against the Taliban in AFGHANISTAN, and in the subsequent conflict with Saddam Hussein and IRAQ.

During the IRAQ WAR, Great Britain was the United States's staunchest ally at the UN. Prime Minister Tony Blair stood steadfast with President Bush in spite of the vocal opposition of many inside and outside of Parliament. Having said this, it should be noted that the British government was not always in full agreement with the American position. It was also concerned with the broad grant of powers sought by the United States in some of the early resolutions and urged Bush to work through the UN when he seemed inclined to embark on a unilateral solution. By the war's end, political commentators across Europe and the Middle East spoke of Blair as a surrogate for the world in his discussions with Bush. Blair's support for the United States reflected both a historical sense of Great Britain possessing a special relationship with the United States and his own personal vision of world politics. In a speech delivered prior to the September 11, 2001, attacks he asserted that the global community must take action against tyrants who oppress their citizens and threaten world peace, but he also called the UN the central pillar of the international community and urged its strengthening.

See also CENTRAL TREATY ORGANIZATION; CONTAINMENT; SOUTHEAST ASIAN TREATY ORGANIZATION.

**Further reading:** Bartlett, C. J. *"The Special Relationship:" A Political History of Anglo-American Relations since 1945.* New York: Addison-Wesley Longman, 1992; Bourne, Kenneth. *Britain and the Balance of Power in North America, 1815–1908.* Berkeley: University of California Press, 1967; Campbell, Charles, S. *From Revolution to Rapprochement: The United States and Great Britain, 1783–1900.* New York: Wiley, 1974; Orde, Anne. *The Eclipse of Great Britain.* New York: St. Martin's, 1996.

—Stephanie Cousineau

## Greece

Modern Greece is about the size of Alabama. It has a population of 10.94 million people and an area of 51,146 square miles. It obtained statehood in 1830 following a war for independence from the Ottoman Empire that began in 1821. GREAT BRITAIN, RUSSIA, and FRANCE all supported Greece against the Turks. The United States recognized Greece in 1833. From independence until WORLD WAR I, Greek foreign policy focused on expanding Greece's boundaries to include all neighboring areas containing a Greek population. Greek leaders were split on what policy to follow during WORLD WAR I. Some favored alignment with the Allies while others, including King Constantine, favored remaining neutral. Pressure from the Allies helped the prowar faction prevail, and Greece entered the war. For its efforts, it received additional territory, and in 1921 it was encouraged to invade Asia Minor. There, Greek forces met defeat at the hands of Kemal Atatürk's forces. A forced exchange of populations followed the establishment of a new border between the two states, and 1.3 million Greek REFUGEES poured into Greece.

Greece was neutral in the initial phase of WORLD WAR II but joined the fighting following ITALY's invasion in October 1939. The Italian invasion was poorly conducted and forced GERMANY to divert its troops to Greece in 1941 for purposes of securing its southern flank. British forces landed in an attempt to block the German advance but failed. During the German occupation that lasted until November 1944, a two-sided resistance movement developed. One faction, the National Greek Democratic League (EDES), supported the monarchy and was pro-West. The second, the EAM-ELAS (National Popular Liberation Army [ELAS] of the Greek National Liberation Front [EAM]), was Communist. They succeeded in controlling much of Greece and engaged in warfare with each other. When British troops landed in September 1944, the EAM-ELAS refused the British order to disarm and fought them.

The monarchy was restored through a plebiscite in 1946, and that same year a full-fledged civil war broke out, prompting Western fears that Greece would follow other states in the Balkans and go communist. The Communist GUERRILLAS were supported by Albania, YUGOSLAVIA, and Bulgaria. Great Britain, exhausted by the war effort, was unable to supply the Greek government with all of the economic and military aid needed to subdue the Communist guerrillas. It fell to the United States to pick up the burden. The instrument for doing so was the TRUMAN DOCTRINE. The civil war ended in 1949 when the army defeated the guerrillas, who had stopped receiving external help. An estimated 100,000 died in the civil war, and 700,000 were displaced by the fighting.

Greece was quickly brought into the Western ALLIANCE, joining the NORTH ATLANTIC TREATY ORGANIZATION (NATO) in 1951. It began receiving considerable amounts of FOREIGN AID from the United States. Between 1946 and 1949, some $1 billion in aid had already been delivered. Between 1946 and 1962, when economic aid was phased out, a total of $11.3 billion in economic and security aid had been given to Greece. In 1953 an agreement was signed allowing the United States to have military facilities in Greece along with extraterritoriality for its military personnel. The one significant problem in U.S.-Greek relations in the early 1950s was Greece's desire to annex Cyprus. The United States saw this dispute as disrupting NATO harmony and threatening to weaken its overall foreign-policy initiatives in the Mediterranean and Middle East.

By the late 1950s American officials had concluded that Greece could not longer be considered a completely trustworthy ally. Relations became more complicated in the early 1960s when the conservatives were voted out of office. In 1964 President LYNDON JOHNSON threatened the termination of American foreign aid to Greece if the Cyprus problem was not settled. This followed an earlier warning to TURKEY about U.S. opposition to a planned invasion of Cyprus. Former SECRETARY OF STATE DEAN ACHESON sought to mediate the dispute and proposed a plan that would allow Greece to annex most of Cyprus. Turkey would receive the remainder. It was rejected by both the Greeks and Cypriot president Archbishop Makarios. In 1967 the Cyprus problem again erupted, and it fell to Cyrus Vance to mediate a solution. He succeeded in convincing Greece to remove most of the troops it had stationed on Cyprus.

Against this backdrop of rising American frustration with Greece, a military coup took place in April 1967. Military officers claimed it was necessary to avert a planned communist coup. While the United States did not plan the military coup, the CENTRAL INTELLIGENCE AGENCY (CIA) was aware of it and did not try to prevent it. Relations between the two states improved significantly. In 1974 the Nixon administration took no action to prevent Greece's overthrow of Makarios in Cyprus. The United States was unable, however, to prevent Turkey from taking military action on its own. It invaded Cyprus and occupied the northern portion of the island, displacing nearly 200,000 Greek Cypriots in the process.

Cyprus is an island in the Mediterranean that was first inhabited by Greeks and later came under the control of the Ottoman Empire. In 1925 it became a British colony. After World War II Cypriot leaders sought to have Cyprus join Greece, but this was rejected by the British. The population of the island is 80 percent Greek. It received its independence in 1960 following an agreement by Great Britain, Turkey, and Greece that Cyprus would never become part of another state. Greece and Turkey were each given military bases on Cyprus, and each was given the right to intervene in Cypriot affairs to guarantee the agreement. For much of its early postwar political history, the key figure on Cyprus was Archbishop Makarios, whom the United States viewed with suspicion because of his neutralist foreign-policy positions. It was feared that he might provide the Soviet Union with a naval base in the Mediterranean Sea.

The restoration of democracy in Greece in July 1974 has sent U.S.-Greek relations down an often tension-filled path. Between 1974 and 1980 Greece withdrew its military personnel from NATO headquarters and abrogated agreements with the U.S. Navy. A particularly ugly incident involved the assassination of CIA station chief Richard Welch in 1975. Welch operated under diplomatic cover, and his identity had been released to the press in the United States as part of revelations of CIA wrongdoing. Many argued that these newspaper stories were directly responsible for his death, while others asserted that everyone in Greece knew of Welch's true identity. Relations were temporarily put on a more sound footing in 1977 when Greece agreed to allow the United States to keep four of seven major naval bases in return for a $700 million military aid package. Relations soon were strained again when President JIMMY CARTER dropped the Turkish arms embargo that had been put into place following its 1974 invasion of Cyprus. In the 1980s a socialist government came into power that regularly feuded with the United States over NATO strategy and relations with communist and radical states. Still, in 1983 it signed an agreement permitting the United States to continue to have access to military bases in Greece.

A number of foreign-policy disputes continue to place Greece at odds with its neighbors. Greece refused to recognize the independence of Yugoslav Macedonia under the name of the Republic of Macedonia following the collapse of Yugoslavia. Greece argued that the name Macedonia held historical significance for Greece and that the country's name and flag had to be changed. The UNITED NATIONS, EUROPEAN UNION, and the United States have been mediating the dispute. Greece and Albania have feuded over illegal Albanian immigration into Greece, the mistreatment of the Greek minority in Albania, and DRUG TRAFFICKING. The Cyprus problem continues and is described as unresolved but manageable. However, President BILL CLINTON was forced to intervene in 1996 to avert an armed clash between Greece and Turkey over the ownership of an uninhabited island. Greece is also active in the Middle East. It has signed a defense cooperation agreement with ISRAEL but is wary about that country's close ties with Turkey. At the same time, Greece traditionally has been supportive of the Palestinians, serving as host for several Israeli-Palestinian meetings.

**Further reading:** Couloumbis, Theodore. *The United States, Greece, and Turkey: Troubled Triangle.* New York: Praeger, 1983; Stearns, Monteagle. *Entangled Alliance: U.S. Policy toward Greece, Turkey, and Cyprus.* New York: Council on Foreign Relations, 1991.

## Grenada, invasion of

Grenada is an island twice the size of Washington, D.C., with a population of about 100,000 people, located 100 miles north of VENEZUELA. The Reagan administration sent U.S. forces to Grenada in 1983 with a threefold mission. They were to rescue American medical students whose safety was said to be endangered by political conditions on the island, restore democracy, and prevent Grenada from being turned into a base from which COMMUNISM could be spread through the region. The object of concern was a new airport being built on Grenada by Cubans that would be large enough to land military aircraft. The Grenadan government maintained that the runways were being built long enough to service large planes carrying tourists.

Maurice Bishop, whose government was overthrown in the 1983 invasion, came to power via a 1979 coup that ousted Eric Gairy. Gairy was a quasi-religious leader who had been the dominant force in Grenadan politics since the

1950s. Over time his rule had become corrupt and repressive, conditions that led to the creation of a leftist opposition movement, the New Jewel Movement (NJM), of which Bishop was a member. Relations between the new government and the United States got off to a rocky start. The NJM was anxious to establish its nationalist credentials and engaged in a campaign of anti-American rhetoric. More ominously from the U.S. perspective, the NJM had asked CUBA for weapons, built up the size of its army, and engaged in a policy of harassing American citizens. The Carter administration adopted a regional approach to dealing with Grenada. It feared that a direct confrontation would push Bishop ever more closely to Cuba and, given Bishop's suspicions of the United States, that other states in the region might have greater influence on him.

The Reagan administration elected to change this policy and adopt a more direct, visible, and confrontational posture. Secretary of Defense Caspar Weinberger referred to Grenada as a "Cuban satellite." The administration sought to isolate Grenada within the region and refused to accredit Grenada's ambassador. In July 1981 the CENTRAL INTELLIGENCE AGENCY (CIA) put together a covert operation, but this plan was dropped due to the opposition of the Senate Intelligence Committee. Large-scale NATO military maneuvers were also held in the Caribbean for the purpose of intimidating Grenada. On March 23, 1983, President RONALD REAGAN illustrated the U.S. concern for growing Cuban influence in Grenada by making public satellite photos of the airport under construction. Earlier that month he had said that "U.S. national security was at stake" in Grenada. Bishop responded to these statements by placing the army on alert and denouncing Reagan's "lies and threats." A June trip by Bishop to Washington did little to relax tensions.

In September a split developed within the NJM as Bernard Coard, one of those who had overthrown Gairy and become minister of finance in the new government, grew disgruntled with Bishop's moderate rule and placed Bishop under house arrest. On October 19, they executed Bishop. On October 25, 1983, 1,900 U.S. Marines and airborne troops invaded Grenada. Three days earlier the Organization of Eastern Caribbean States had requested such an intervention, and President Reagan cited this request as partial justification for his actions. The invasion was a success largely due to the overwhelming military advantage held by U.S. forces and the absence of any serious resistance by Grenadan forces. Only 15 U.S. soldiers were killed. Evidence suggests that little advance planning went into the military action, as invasion forces did not know the location of the medical students nor were they supplied with accurate maps. Significantly, the invasion coincided with the October 23 bombing of the Marine barracks in Beirut, LEBANON, that killed more than 240 U.S.

soldiers and gave the Reagan administration a much needed military success.

The invasion of Grenada set off diplomatic protests around the world. The United Nations General Assembly passed a resolution "deeply deploring" the act by a vote of 108-9. A U.S. veto prevented the Security Council from passing a similarly worded resolution. Even Prime Minister Margaret Thatcher, otherwise RONALD REAGAN's staunchest ally, took public exception to this invasion of a member of the British Commonwealth.

See also ELITE THEORY; MONROE DOCTRINE; REVISIONISM.

**Further reading:** Dunn, Peter, and Bruce Watson, eds., *American Intervention in Grenada.* Boulder, Colo.: Westview, 1985.

## Guatemala

Guatemala is the largest and most heavily populated country in Central America. It has an area of 42,000 square miles, making it about the size of Tennessee, and an approximate population of 12.9 million people. Pedro de Alvarado defeated the Maya in 1523–24, laying the foundation for Spanish colonial rule. Guatemala became independent from SPAIN in 1821, and briefly the country became a part of the Mexican Empire and later joined a federation of the United Provinces of Central America. The United States recognized Guatemala in 1825.

Guatemala did not play a major role in American foreign policy until after WORLD WAR II. This does not mean that the United States was without influence on Guatemala. U.S. firms dominated the Guatemalan economy. No business was more powerful than the United Fruit Company. It became Guatemala's single largest exporter, and many of its key executives and board members had close ties to the U.S. government. For example, both President DWIGHT EISENHOWER'S SECRETARY OF STATE JOHN FOSTER DULLES and his brother, DIRECTOR OF THE CENTRAL INTELLIGENCE AGENCY Alan Dulles, were affiliated with the law firm that represented the United Fruit Company. A subsidiary of the United Fruit Company, the International Railways of Central America, was a towering force in Guatemala's transportation system.

Guatemala moved onto the U.S. foreign-policy agenda in the early 1950s. In 1944 the "October Revolutionaries" overthrew the government of General Jorge Ubico Castaneda, who had ruled since 1931. Colonel Jacobo Arbenz Guzmán was one of the key leaders of the revolt and in 1950 he became president. The October Revolutionaries were social reformers, and Arbenz brought Communists into the government to continue that policy of social and economic reform. One of his goals was to break the monopolies held by the United Fruit Company in agriculture and transportation. Guatemala's economy and political system had long been dominated by the United Fruit Company. It owned hundreds of acres of land, was a principal employer of labor, and controlled the only railroad. A series of dictators maintained political order on terms favorable to the United Fruit Company and other private investors. The holdings of the United Fruit Company were a prime target. In March 1953 elected president Arbenz nationalized approximately 230,000 acres of uncultivated land owned by the United Fruit Company. As compensation he offered a little more than $600,000 in long-term interest bonds. This amount was calculated on the value of the land as reported by the United Fruit Company for tax purposes. The United Fruit Company now corrected itself and stated the true value of the land was in excess of $15 million. His administration built highway systems and a new port, and appropriated land to redistribute to peasants. The United Fruit Company resisted the loss of its land (most of which was lying fallow) and the amount of money Guatalama offered as compensation. His foreign policy also showed a willingness to challenge the United States. When an arms purchase from the United States fell through, Arbenz sought weapons from CZECHOSLOVAKIA.

Spurred by fears of COMMUNISM and American economic losses, the Eisenhower administration tried to isolate Guatemala from other states in the Western Hemisphere. At the Tenth Inter-American Conference in 1954, the United States sought but failed to obtain an ORGANIZATION OF AMERICAN STATES (OAS) statement condemning Guatemala. It had to settle for a resolution labeling communist infiltration "a threat" to the region.

In June 1954 a CENTRAL INTELLIGENCE AGENCY (CIA) COVERT ACTION brought down the leftist-center government of Arbenz Guzmán. His government had undertaken a program of social reform that the Eisenhower administration equated with communist expansion. U.S. ambassador John Peurifoy said of Arbenz: "[He] thought like a Communist and talked like a Communist, and if not actually one, would do until one came along." Evidence suggests that contrary to the claims of the Eisenhower administration, Arbenz's government was not communist-dominated.

The Truman administration's initial response to Arbenz's reform agenda was one of moderate opposition that relied heavily on ECONOMIC SANCTIONS. The Eisenhower administration took a more hard-line approach and equated Arbenz's actions with communist expansion. Even before his March 1953 reforms it had determined that Arbenz was a threat to American security and was determined to remove him from power. Fears were raised about possible threats to the PANAMA CANAL. In March,

1954 Secretary of State John Foster Dulles succeeded in getting the Organization of American States (OAS) to support a resolution asserting that "the domination or control of the political institutions of any American state by the international communist movement . . . would constitute a threat to the entire hemisphere and would require appropriate action." The value of the Caracas Declaration to the United States was lessened somewhat by an amendment that required OAS consultation rather than permitting immediate action.

The covert action operation to remove Arbenz was an operation led and organized by the CIA that was modeled on its recent success in IRAN. The CIA recruited General Carlos Castillo Armas to lead the covert operation. His forces, totaling only some 150 men, received air cover from CIA piloted planes. They encountered little effective resistance, and within one week of the start of the operation Armas took control of the government. The key to the success of the covert action plan lay in its psychological dimension. The bombing of the radio station and army headquarters and other actions created a sense of panic in the capital and convinced Arbenz that he could not defeat Armas's forces and frightened him into surrendering.

After the coup a temporary government led by Armas came into power that proceeded to suspend the Guatemalan congress and all constitutional rights, end land reform, return all of the expropriated land to the United Fruit Company, and abolish all labor rights. A committee was established to identify Communists who could be arrested and killed. Within four months 72,000 people were so identified. The government disenfranchised about 70 percent of the population. Armas then held an election in which he won 99.9 percent of the vote. Where Guatemala had received less than $1 million in U.S. foreign aid between 1944 and 1953, the Armas government received $90 million in the next two years.

The overthrow of Arbenz in Guatemala is significant for the conduct of COLD WAR U.S. foreign policy on several counts. First, it served as a test case for U.S. policy toward social reformers in Latin America. The region had been long dominated by American economic interests but ignored by U.S. policy makers. The growing voices of discontent insured that this would not be the case for much longer. Second, the covert action plan, while a success, also contained a fatal flaw that would surface with the BAY OF PIGS invasion. Although it was planned and carried out successfully, CIA planners failed to take into account the extent to which local political and social conditions were crucial to their success. Arbenz was vulnerable because his reform programs had been ineffective, thus robbing him of important domestic support, a situation that the CIA plan exploited. The same would not be true of Fidel Castro. Finally, revisionist historians and those who employ an ELITE THEORY model in studying how U.S. foreign policy is made cite the Guatemalan case as a textbook example of how economic interests dominate U.S. foreign policy because of the number of high-ranking present and past government officials on the United Fruit Company's Board of Directors.

The end of social reform in Guatemala ushered in a lengthy period of civil war that involved government forces, right-wing death squads, and left-wing guerrillas. JIMMY CARTER criticized Guatemala's HUMAN-RIGHTS record as president, but this criticism ended with the Reagan presidency and its focus on defeating the Sandinistas in NICARAGUA. In the early 1990s a UNITED NATIONS peace process began in Guatemala. Agreements were reached on human rights, resettlement of displaced persons, indigenous rights, and "historical clarification." A peace accord was signed in 1996. The United States, along with COLOM-BIA, MEXICO, VENEZUELA, SPAIN, and Norway, played an important role in supporting the peace agreement. The UNITED STATES AGENCY FOR INTERNATIONAL DEVELOPMENT (USAID) plays a lead role in providing economic assistance to Guatemala to implement the economic and social provisions of the peace agreement.

Most recently the CIA has found itself under fire for its recent covert action programs in Guatemala. In 1995 Jennifer Harbury protested the death of her husband, a Guatemala rebel leader, at the hands of the military. His death plus that of another American, Michael DeVine, led to an internal CIA investigation of its policies in Guatemala. The CIA concluded that while no laws had been broken, the CIA had failed to fully inform CONGRESS of its covert action program in Guatemala. It was revealed that the CIA had paid an army colonel $44,000 in 1992 in spite of his being linked to the murder of DeVine.

Some of the troops of the Guatemalan "liberation army"  (National Archives)

See also EISENHOWER, DWIGHT; IMPERIALISM; MULTI-NATIONAL CORPORATIONS; REVISIONISM; TRUMAN, HARRY.

**Further reading:** Cullather, Nick. *Secret History.* Stanford, Calif.: Stanford University Press, 1999; Immerman, Richard H. *The CIA in Guatemala: The Foreign Policy of Intervention.* Austin: University of Texas Press, 1982.

## guerrilla warfare

Guerrilla warfare is a conflict situation that straddles the line between war and peace and the line between military and political conflict. It is a conflict in which combatants and noncombatants are difficult to distinguish and where victory cannot be won on the battlefield but requires an attention to social, political, and economic reforms. Against a backdrop of nuclear stalemate and terrain that did not lend itself to traditional battles between large armies, guerrilla warfare became a commonly employed strategy by insurgents in developing countries in the 1960s. Both the United States in VIETNAM and the Soviet Union (see RUSSIA) in AFGHANISTAN experienced bloody defeats in guerrilla wars that fundamentally altered their respective foreign policies.

Guerrilla wars are protracted wars. Mao Zedong (Mao Tse-tung) was one of the most successful practitioners of guerrilla warfare. He identified three different military stages. The first stage, that of a strategic defensive, is concerned with establishing a safe zone from which to build up one's military organization and carry out operations against the government. The major challenge facing the guerrillas in this stage is not so much defeating the government as it is in ensuring their continued survival. The principal tactics employed in this stage by guerrilla groups are TERRORISM, covert political activity, and propaganda. Guerrillas are fighting a "war without frontiers" as they attack wherever an opportunity exists in an effort to maximize the chaos that can be produced by a relatively small band of dedicated individuals. This is the longest stage.

The second stage, the strategic stalemate, is characterized by the emergence of clearly identifiable areas that are under the control of either government or guerrilla forces. Hit-and-run attacks and small-scale military encounters now become common, but the guerrilla still avoids direct confrontations and retreats in the face of a stronger enemy. The third stage is the strategic counteroffensive. It resembles conventional warfare and is entered into only when military victory is all but certain. Demoralized, the enemy should put up little resistance.

Mao counseled, however, that victory cannot be achieved on the battlefield alone. It requires separating the people from the government, and military actions must be designed with this in mind. Territory is captured to demonstrate to the people that the government no longer deserves their support. Success ultimately demands that the guerrilla come to be seen as the champion of the people. Thus, once in control of territory guerrillas must demonstrate that they are capable of setting up political, social, and economic programs that address their grievances.

Just as guerrillas cannot triumph solely by achieving victories on the battlefield, they cannot be defeated by military means alone. HENRY KISSINGER, SECRETARY OF STATE and NATIONAL SECURITY ADVISOR under President RICHARD NIXON, stated that "the guerrilla wins if he does not lose. The conventional army loses if it does not win." Social, economic, and political reforms must be undertaken to keep the loyalty of the people. It is by isolating guerrillas from the people that they are defeated. Major obstacles stand in the way of undertaking such reforms. Well-entrenched groups on whom the government depends for support will oppose changing the status quo.

Vietnam and Afghanistan are highly visible cases in which guerrillas defeated governments backed by the greatly superior forces of the United States and the Soviet Union, respectively. In EL SALVADOR and NICARAGUA the United States first opposed left-wing guerrillas and then helped organize the contras, a guerrilla force intended to bring down the socialist government of Daniel Ortega. Since the late 1990s the United States has provided aid to COLOMBIA in its effort to turn back a guerrilla challenge that has become entwined with DRUG TRAFFICKING. Guerrilla warfare presents a particularly difficult challenge for the United States since by definition it violates the clear distinction between war and peace that is central to the AMERICAN NATIONAL STYLE. American policy makers are now reluctant to engage in such conflicts for fear of being dragged into another Vietnam.

For all of its visibility, it needs to be stressed that victory for the guerrilla is far from automatic. Of 19 guerrilla wars taking place in 1988, only the Afghan guerrilla war could be classified as a success at that time. Commentators have identified several preconditions for success. Among the most frequently cited are: (1) an extensive territory within which to maneuver, (2) a sanctuary, (3) external aid, (4) a relatively large rural population, and (5) a government that is unable to launch counterattacks by air or protect its lines of communication.

**Further reading:** Laqueur, Walter. *Guerrilla Warfare: A Historical and Critical Study.* Boston: Little Brown, 1976.

## Gulf War Syndrome

The United States, supported by its allies, fought what was generally hailed at the time as one of the most successful military campaigns in history in 1991 when it defeated Iraqi forces in the PERSIAN GULF WAR. Only 293 Americans died in combat. The war can be broken into two stages. The first was a 39-day air war that began on January 16, 1991. The second was a four-day ground war that began on February 24. From March 4 to 15, after the fighting had concluded, American forces began destroying ammunition facilities that contained chemical weapons. The first signs that the victory may have come at a higher price than at first believed came in fall 1991 when Gulf War veterans began seeking treatment for a variety of illnesses. Symptoms included joint pain, fatigue, headaches, and memory loss. Collectively these illnesses have come to be known as Gulf War Syndrome. In September 1993 soldiers testified before the Senate Banking Committee that they had been exposed to chemicals even though the CENTRAL INTELLI-GENCE AGENCY announced in May 1993 that IRAQ had not used chemical weapons during the war. Ultimately, an estimated 80,000 of the 697,000 Americans who served in OPERATION DESERT SHIELD and OPERATION DESERT STORM claimed they now suffered from Gulf War Syndrome.

The Pentagon's handling of the matter has been roundly criticized. It was only in June 1996 that it acknowledged that some 300 to 400 soldiers might have been exposed to chemicals when Iraq's Kamisiyah facility was destroyed. By October the Pentagon's position changed. It now stated that as many as 20,000 may have been exposed to chemicals but continued to deny that this exposure was the cause of Gulf War Syndrome. In December of that year SECRETARY OF DEFENSE William Perry denied that the Pentagon had engaged in a coverup of evidence linking Gulf War Syndrome to these illnesses.

President BILL CLINTON established an investigative body to study Gulf War Syndrome in May 1995, when a panel of experts was assembled to assess the government's response to these charges. In January 1997 the Presidential Advisory Committee on Gulf War Veterans' Illnesses reported that it could not find a link between chemical or biological weapons and Gulf War Syndrome. It did, however, criticize the Pentagon for its failure to act "in good faith" in responding to the problem.

Some studies have found a link. A Veterans Affairs report released in January 1997 suggested a link between severe joint pain and chemical weapons released at Kamisiyah. A private study also released in January suggested a link between damage to the nervous system and a toxic chemical that was used in flea collars that soldiers wore and in sprays used to protect themselves against insects.

Gulf War Syndrome is significant for American foreign policy in at least three respects. First, it suggests that the cost of military campaigns in which chemical and biological weapons are present is not easily calculated. Second, it demonstrates that these WEAPONS OF MASS DESTRUCTION do not have to be employed in combat for there to be an effect. Third, it points to the limits of science as an instrument for settling policy disputes.

# H

## Haig, Alexander (1924– ) *secretary of state*

Alexander Haig served 18 months as SECRETARY OF STATE under President RONALD REAGAN at the start of his first term in office. He began his career as a military officer who saw combat duty in KOREA and VIETNAM but made his mark as a military adviser to key civilians within the national security establishment. In 1964 he served as military adviser to Secretary of the Army CYRUS VANCE. In 1969 he became the chief military aid of NATIONAL SECURITY ADVISOR HENRY KISSINGER. In 1972 he was promoted two grades and over some 240 more senior officers to four-star general and vice-chief of staff of the army in what was interpreted as an attempt by President RICHARD NIXON to move his people into key positions. In the closing days of the Nixon administration he took over as White House chief of staff. Haig advised Ronald Reagan on foreign-policy issues in the presidential campaign, and over the objection of some of his advisers, Reagan selected Haig to be his first secretary of state.

Haig's tenure as secretary of state was stormy in his relations with both CONGRESS and other members of the Reagan administration. Critics charged that he had neither the temperament nor the intellect to handle such a sensitive post. Staunchly anticommunist in outlook Haig stridently urged the administration and Congress to take a tough stand against communist expansion in Latin America. He went so far as to argue that the Soviet Union (see RUSSIA) had a "hit list" to accomplish its goal of global domination that included EL SALVADOR, HONDURAS, NICARAGUA, and GUATEMALA. He unsuccessfully orchestrated a public relations campaign that included releasing a STATE DEPARTMENT White Paper purporting to show the growing communist threat in the region.

Haig engaged in constant bureaucratic turf battles for control over American foreign policy with SECRETARY OF DEFENSE Caspar Weinberger and Vice President GEORGE H. W. BUSH. The self-proclaimed "vicar" of U.S. foreign policy, he was particularly critical of Reagan's national security team headed by his National Security Advisor, William Clark, whom he depicted as being foreign-policy amateurs who were overly concerned with the domestic consequences of foreign-policy actions. He angered most in the administration and many Americans when, following the attempted assassination of Reagan, he proclaimed himself to be in charge.

## Haiti

Haiti is located on the western one-third of the island of Hispaniola in the Caribbean Sea. The DOMINICAN REPUBLIC occupies the remainder of the island. It is roughly the size of Maryland (10,714 square miles) and has a population of approximately 8.2 million people.

Originally Hispaniola was used by the Spanish as a base from which to explore the Western Hemisphere. French pirates operated out of the western portion of the island, attacking French and English ships. In 1697 SPAIN ceded Haiti to FRANCE. The decline in piracy transformed Haiti into a plantation economy that rested heavily upon African slaves whom the French had brought to work the coffee and sugar plantations. A slave revolt in 1791 led by Toussaint Louverture succeeded in taking the northern portion of Haiti from France. In 1804 the rebelling slaves defeated forces sent by Napoleon Bonaparte and officially established Haiti as an independent state. Haitian forces succeeded in uniting the whole island in 1822. The Dominican Republic broke away again in 1844. The successful slave revolt is credited by many with prompting France to sell the Louisiana Territory to the United States in 1803 in the LOUISIANA PURCHASE. Without Haiti, Louisiana held less economic value for France and was a strategic liability to defend.

Haitian independence was not officially recognized by the United States until 1862, when President Abraham Lincoln recognized the independence of LIBERIA and Haiti. Racism, both overt and subtle, played into the long delay in recognizing Haitian independence. In 1849 President

ZACHARY TAYLOR sent a mission to Haiti to determine its qualifications for recognition. One standard that was to be employed was whether or not the "Spanish race has the ascendancy in that government." An 1826 congressional debate over recognition had raised the issue of whether the recognition of Haiti would "introduce a moral contagion." A member of the Senate preferred only commercial relations and not diplomatic ones, asserting that "the peace of eleven states in this Union will not permit the fruits of a successful Negro insurrection to be exhibited among them."

Between 1853 and 1915 Haiti experienced 22 changes in government. Continuing domestic instability, persistent poverty, and fears of European intervention brought Haiti to the attention of the Taft and Wilson administrations after decades of neglect. The Taft administration sought to address the situation by pressuring Haiti into accepting a major loan in 1910, but this did not correct the situation. WOODROW WILSON moved first to try to secure a naval base at Môle Saint-Nicholas. The United States had been interested in a naval base on Hispaniola since the 1880s, with its primary attention being directed at Samaná Bay in the Dominican Republic. The Wilson administration's overtures were rebuffed as the Haitian government refused to sell the desired land. Interventionist pressure continued to mount as France and GERMANY inquired about a tripartite financial receivership for Haiti. SECRETARY OF STATE WILLIAM JENNINGS BRYAN then proposed a Dominican Republic–type receivership, but before this proposal went very far war broke out in Europe with Germany and France on opposing sides, and another government change took place in Haiti.

In July 1915 Wilson sent U.S. troops to Haiti. Their first task was to organize an election. The United States made it clear that whoever won the election would be expected to sign an agreement giving the United States effective control over Haiti's customs and finances and making it a virtual protectorate of the United States. The American occupation was marked by continued domestic violence and unrest in Haiti, but it provoked little public comment in the United States. Most of this was reserved for U.S. policy toward NICARAGUA and MEXICO. The occupation did not end until 1934.

President HERBERT HOOVER took the first tentative steps in this direction in 1929 when he asked CONGRESS to appropriate funds for a commission to investigate Haiti's future status. C. Cameron Forbes was chosen to chair the commission, and the key question assigned to it was the possibility of American withdrawal. In its report issued in 1930, the Forbes Commission recommended the gradual withdrawal of U.S. Marines. A treaty to bring this about was signed in 1932, but Haiti refused to accept it because some provisions for financial supervision by the United States were to be left in place. President FRANKLIN ROOSEVELT then cleared the way for U.S. forces to leave by signing an executive order to that effect in 1933.

During the COLD WAR Haiti continued to occupy an uneasy place in U.S. foreign-policy thinking. On the one hand concerns were expressed about the political violence, arbitrary rule, and poverty that characterized the regime of François (Papa Doc) Duvalier and his son Jean-Claude (Baby Doc) Duvalier. These concerns led to Haiti's exclusion from the ALLIANCE FOR PROGRESS and the termination of aid by President JOHN KENNEDY. On the other hand, continued concerns over the expansion of COMMUNISM in the Western Hemisphere led several administrations to turn a blind eye to these domestic problems. LYNDON JOHNSON gave Haiti military aid, and President RONALD REAGAN stood by Haitian leaders in his first term. In his second term, Reagan began to distance himself from the Haitian leadership, and Baby Doc Duvalier fled the country on a U.S.-provided aircraft.

One consequence of the political and economic conditions existing in Haiti was a steady stream of REFUGEES to the United States beginning in 1957 when Papa Doc Duvalier took power. The first to leave were members of the upper class. They were followed by members of the urban middle class and semiskilled workers. In the early 1970s many poor and uneducated Haitians began to flee by sea. Between 1972 and 1977 a steady steam of Haitian "boat people" arrived in southern Florida. Almost from the beginning local government officials had applied political pressure on Washington to stop the outflow and to deport those who had already arrived. It became standard practice for the United States to deny Haitian requests for refugee status. It was asserted that they did not meet the key definitional requirement of fleeing communism.

President JIMMY CARTER's signing of the 1980 Refugee Act eliminated this definitional bias and appeared to open the door to classifying Haitians as refugees. This did not happen, and it was not until the Reagan administration that the arrival of boat people was effectively ended. President Ronald Reagan ordered the Coast Guard to intercept Haitian boats and return them to Haiti. As a result in November 1981 only 47 Haitians reached the United States, compared to just over 1,000 in November 1980. In addition to the highly visible act of sending the Haitian boat people back, the Reagan administration also pressured the Haitian government to stop the exodus. It threatened to block international and bilateral economic aid programs designed to help Haiti.

The halt proved to be temporary. In December 1990 Jean-Bertrand Aristide, an ardent opponent of the Duvalier regime and champion of the poor, won election as president with 70 percent of the vote. On September 30, 1991, he was overthrown by a military coup. In the effort to flee the chaos and violence that followed, thousands of Haitians once again took to the sea. Some 40,000 were intercepted by the Coast Guard as President GEORGE H. W. BUSH continued the interdiction policies of the Reagan administration. These numbers was higher than those from the previous 10 years combined. Bush's policy was criticized by BILL CLINTON during the presidential campaign, and he promised to change that policy after his inauguration. After the election Clinton reversed course and made it known he would continue the policy.

Restoring Aristide to power became a goal of U.S. foreign policy that was not easily achieved. The Clinton administration, as had the Bush administration before it, placed ECONOMIC SANCTIONS on Haiti, but they had a limited impact due to lax implementation and poor international cooperation. An apparent end to the crisis appeared at hand in 1993 when the Clinton administration brokered an agreement in a meeting on Governor's Island. This agreement specified a timetable for Aristide's return to power, but it soon collapsed, and stalemate returned. Tightened sanctions had little effect, and in 1993 the Clinton administration sent a ship with troops and military trainers to Haiti. Faced with an unruly crowd at the docks, the USS *Harlan County* returned to the United States.

Pressure for returning Aristide to power continued to build within the United States, yet so did opposition to the use of military force. Senator Robert Dole (R.-Kans.), who would be the REPUBLICAN PARTY presidential nominee in 1996, was one of those who spoke out against using military power. Clinton ultimately accepted the necessity of an invasion and set September 15, 1994, as its date. Earlier that summer the United Nations Security Council passed Resolution 40 that authorized states to use force to restore Haiti's constitutional government. With invasion troops in the air a last-minute delegation led by former president Jimmy Carter convinced General Raoul Cédras to resign. On September 19 an international force landed in Haiti. Aristide returned on October 15. In March 1995 the international force became a PEACEKEEPING force, and its numbers dropped from 21,000 to 6,000 troops. This number steadily declined, and by January 2000 all U.S. forces had departed from Haiti.

**Further reading:** Gayle, Brenda. *Haiti and the United States.* Athens: University of Georgia Press, 1992.

## Hamilton, Alexander (1755–1804) *secretary of the treasury*

Alexander Hamilton was one of the leading American statesmen of the Revolutionary War–era and the first years of the Republic. Hamilton was a critic of the ARTICLES OF CONFEDERATION and argued for a stronger central government. Along with John Jay and James Madison, Hamilton authored the FEDERALIST PAPERS that sought to build public support for the CONSTITUTION. President GEORGE WASHINGTON appointed Hamilton to be the first secretary of the treasury, a position he held until he resigned in January 1795. Among his recommendations were the creation of a national bank, the full payment of debts accumulated by the Continental Congress, and federal assumption of state debts. An ardent nationalist and supporter of the British system of government, he came to clash with THOMAS JEFFERSON, who admired FRANCE and the democratic spirit of the French Revolution. Their disagreements helped lay the foundation for the party system, with Hamilton becoming a leader of the FEDERALIST PARTY and Jefferson a leader of the Democratic-Republicans.

In the realm of foreign policy Hamilton frequently provided counsel to GEORGE WASHINGTON. One early incident followed the French Revolution. France had signed a treaty of ALLIANCE with the United States in 1778. It bound France to the United States, but it did not commit the United States to come to the aid of France. Still, there was concern in the United States that France might go to war with GREAT BRITAIN and request American assistance. Hamilton argued that the agreements were not binding on the United States since they were signed by Louis XVI, who was no longer in power. Jefferson asserted that the agreements had been entered into by the United States and France and not particular governments. Therefore, they were still in force. President Washington agreed with Jefferson, but over his objections he issued a Neutrality Proclamation on April 22, 1793, to keep the United States out of a European war. Jefferson maintained that since only CONGRESS could declare war, only Congress could declare neutrality.

The issue of neutrality had come to a head as a result of the arrival of Citizen Edmond Genet from France. He arrived with little money but sought to obtain American acquiescence in allowing French privateers to enter American ports to seize British merchant ships. He also sought to raise money in the United States for this purpose and appealed directly to the American people for support in this venture rather than working through the Washington administration, where Hamilton opposed these plans.

Jefferson and Hamilton also clashed over trade relations with Great Britain. Jefferson sought to impose discriminatory duties on British goods entering the United States and obtain economic concessions from Great Britain. Hamilton succeeded in blocking any such action. He saw trade with Great Britain as a key component of his plans for national economic growth.

Hamilton was also actively involved in the DIPLOMACY leading to the signing of JAY'S TREATY in November 1794. Relations with Great Britain had been deteriorating due to its policy of seizing American merchant vessels at sea and reports that the British were arming NATIVE AMERICANS along the western borders of the United States. Hamilton was Washington's first choice to lead a negotiating delegation to Great Britain, but due to opposition from the Democratic-Republicans, Washington sent another Federalist, Chief Justice John Jay. Hamilton's strong desire to maintain good economic relations with Britain led him to undermine Jay's negotiating strategy by secretly informing the British that the United States would not join forces with other neutral states to challenge British naval policies.

After leaving Washington's administration, Hamilton was involved in one further foreign-policy issue. President JOHN ADAMS was engaged in the two-year Quasi War with France (1798–1800). There was much talk of war with France at the time, and Adams moved to build up the American military capacity. George Washington agreed to step out of retirement and assume command of the American forces should an invasion occur but only on the condition that Hamilton be named second in command. Hamilton and some Federalists supported war with France as a means to enlarge the United States and further strengthen the federal government. Adams, however, determined to enter into peace negotiations with France. The Treaty of Mortefontaine of 1800 ended the conflict and terminated the agreements signed by the United States and France in 1778 and 1788.

**Further reading:** Rossiter, Clinton. *Alexander Hamilton and the Constitution.* New York: Harcourt, 1964.

## Harding, Warren G. (1865–1923) *president*

Warren Gamaliel Harding was the 29th president, serving from 1921 to 1923. Harding was a REPUBLICAN PARTY stalwart who was loyal to the Ohio party machine. He served one term in the U.S. Senate before becoming president. In the Senate he was a "strong reservationist" in the LEAGUE OF NATIONS debate and largely opposed President WOODROW WILSON's treaty on partisan grounds.

Harding's landslide victory in the 1920 election was viewed at the time as a sort of referendum on—and repudiation of—the League of Nations. Reality was much more complex. Prominent Republicans who supported the League told voters that Harding would bring the United States into the League of Nations. Irreconcilable Republicans asserted that Harding was opposed to League membership. Harding was silent on the matter.

As president, Harding adopted a passive role in policy making, allowing members of his cabinet and strong-willed members of CONGRESS to take the lead. His presidential style is alternatively described as either that of a chairman of the board or facilitator. In the domestic-policy arena this approach to policy making resulted in scandals, such as the

Teapot Dome incident. In foreign policy the results were more benign, as considerable power fell to SECRETARY OF STATE CHARLES EVANS HUGHES.

During his presidency Harding advanced U.S. foreign policy on a number of fronts. One area was disarmament. In his inaugural address Harding announced that he wanted to find "a way to approximate disarmament and relieve the crushing burdens of military and naval establishments." This statement followed a December 1920 proposal by Senator WILLIAM BORAH (R-Idaho) to call a disarmament conference. Harding secretly tried to block Borah's move, but when that failed, he moved to embrace the position. Harding's proposal led to the creation of the WASHINGTON CONFERENCE. Learning from Wilson's mistake, Harding included on the American negotiating team Senator HENRY CABOT LODGE (R-Mass.) and Senator Oscar Underwood (D-Ala.). Borah was not included.

Harding also began to move the United States into a de facto position of cooperation with the League of Nations. At first his administration refused even to open mail from the League of Nations, claiming it did not recognize its existence. By 1923 a noticeable thaw was taking place. The Republican National Committee publicly stated that just because the United States was not a member of the League of Nations did not mean that the United States should not support the good that it was accomplishing. The first cautious steps actually were taken in 1922 when unofficial observers were sent to conferences organized by the League. Harding was not successful, however, in moving the United States into open and direct participation in the League system. Harding sent a treaty of adherence to the World Court to the Senate for its consent in February 1923. Attached to that treaty were four reservations that together guaranteed, according to Harding, that the United States would be "wholly free from a legal relation to the League." Harding died before action was taken. It was not until January 1935 that a vote was finally taken. The Senate defeated the resolution of adherence by a vote of 52-36.

Harding's administration was also active in international economics. In June 1921 he asked Congress for authority to negotiate terms of repayment with countries that owed monies to the United States from WORLD WAR I loans. These loans had been extended on the understanding that repayment arrangements would be worked out after the war. In February 1922 Congress established the World War Foreign Debt Commission. According to its mandate, the commission could not accept repayment at less than 4.25 percent paid out over 25 years and it could not cancel any of the principal. Not one of the debtor states was willing to accept these terms, and the negotiations became lengthy and linked to the broader question of war reparations. This was a link that Washington refused to officially recognize. Harding also signed into law in May 1921 an emergency high tariff that Wilson had vetoed before leaving office. In September 1922 he went further and signed the Fordney-McCumber Tariff, which raised tariff rates even higher.

Harding is given credit for having made the most positive contribution to American foreign policy in improving U.S.-Latin American relations. During the presidential campaign Harding criticized Wilson's policy of interventionism and Secretary of State Hughes worked to terminate existing military interventions in MEXICO and the DOMINICAN REPUBLIC and to indemnify COLOMBIA for the loss of PANAMA.

## Hawaii, annexation of

The annexation of Hawaii marked the first major overseas acquisition of the United States. Growing American interest in Hawaii dated back to 1819 and 1820 when whalers and missionaries came to the Sandwich Islands, as they were then known. The successful imposition of a treaty by FRANCE granting Paris special commercial rights in 1839 led the Hawaiian government to look to the United States as a protector. SECRETARY OF STATE DANIEL WEBSTER was sympathetic to Hawaii's plight but would not enter into a treaty guaranteeing its independence. He did state that "the United States . . . are more interested in the fate of the islands and their Government than any other nation can be." Unsuccessful attempts by a British officer and France to take control of Hawaii further fueled annexation fever.

In 1849 the United States signed a commercial treaty with Hawaii, an act that formally recognized its independence. President FRANKLIN PIERCE's administration negotiated an annexation treaty in 1854. It was rejected by the Senate because it called for immediate statehood. A reciprocity agreement was negotiated the next year, but the Senate rejected it too when Louisiana opposed the measure for fear of the damage that might be done to the price of its sugar crop. Still another reciprocity agreement was signed in 1867. It was rejected by the Senate when some in the Senate feared that this agreement would bring such prosperity to the islands that they would not wish to join the United States. In 1875 a successful reciprocity agreement was signed. The Senate acquiesced out of fear that another rejection might drive Hawaii into an alliance with GREAT BRITAIN. A clause in the agreement stated that Hawaii would not lease or dispose any of its territory to another power. The agreement was renewed in 1884 with a proviso giving the United States the right to a naval station at Pearl Harbor.

By this time a new layer of problems had been added to the U.S.-Hawaii relationship beyond the economic ones centered on sugar production. Hawaiian prosperity brought Chinese and Japanese laborers to offset the labor shortage and created ethnic tensions. Hawaii's political order was now under the control of descendants of the early American missionaries, producing resentment among native Hawaiians.

The McKinley tariff of 1900 inflicted great harm on the economic health of the islands by making foreign sugar coming into the United States more competitive with Hawaiian sugar.

In 1891 Liliuokalani became queen and attempted to impose a new constitution that granted greater political power to native Hawaiians. The American minister to Hawaii, John L. Stevens, responded to pleas of help from American annexationists on Hawaii by sending in U.S. troops from a cruiser in Honolulu. The new government that came to power as a result of Stevens's actions soon sent a committee to the United States to negotiate an annexation agreement. Secretary of State John Foster signed the treaty that would bring Hawaii into the United States as a territory, and President Benjamin Harrison submitted it to the Senate with two weeks left in his term. GROVER CLEVELAND, the next president, withdrew the treaty and appointed James Blount to be his special representative to investigate the events surrounding the overthrow of the Hawaiian monarchy. Contrary to Harrison's claim when he submitted the treaty to the Senate, Blount concluded that Stevens's actions had been instrumental to the success of the revolution. Cleveland sough to restore Liliuokalani to the throne, but the new government led by Samuel Dole resisted, and Cleveland was unwilling to use force to bring this about. On July 4, 1894, Cleveland acquiesced and recognized the new republic of Hawaii.

WILLIAM MCKINLEY replaced Cleveland as PRESIDENT and signed a new annexation treaty soon after taking office, on June 16, 1897. The Hawaiian constitution actually called for union with the United States when it became possible. At this point a new complicating factor emerged. JAPAN now saw Hawaii as a possible possession, and it protested the treaty, saying it would endanger Japanese rights. Japan was also concerned with the passage of discriminatory laws against the Japanese, who made up about one-quarter of the population. Opposition in the Senate to the treaty was strong enough that it remained stalled until Commodore George Dewey's victory in Manila during the SPANISH-AMERICAN WAR whipped up support for annexing Hawaii to "help" Dewey. President McKinley signed the agreement on July 7, 1898.

## hawks

From the late 1960s into the 1980s the most important debates in American COLD WAR foreign policy centered on the use of military force at both the conventional and nuclear levels. The two sides in this highly political and emotional debate were referred to as hawks and DOVES. For all practical purposes, the debate was brought to an end by the fall of COMMUNISM and the end of the cold war.

Hawks believed that COMMUNISM was a hostile, unyielding, and aggressive opponent of the United States.

The center of international communism was the Soviet Union (see RUSSIA). First and foremost, therefore, American foreign policy had to manage the Soviet threat. This required a policy of firm vigilance grounded in military power. The focal point of the debate over the conventional use of force was VIETNAM. Later the debate would extend to cover the value of military aid to the contras and other anti-Soviet forces in the Third World. For hawks the war in Vietnam was one that had to be fought and won. Failure to do so would invite further aggression that would be more difficult to defeat. As such they supported escalating and expanding the war as necessary. At the nuclear level hawks asserted that ARMS CONTROL agreements, such as the ANTIBALLISTIC MISSILE TREATY and the STRATEGIC ARMS LIMITATION talks, were a mistake. Hawks held that American security could not be realized through cooperation with the Soviet Union. In their view DÉTENTE could never replace CONTAINMENT as the foundation for American-Soviet relations.

Looking beyond the immediate threat posed by the Soviet Union, hawks held that the primary cause of war throughout history was military weakness. Weakness invited aggression by challenging states. Their primary reference point was Munich, the pre–WORLD WAR II SUMMIT CONFERENCE in which GREAT BRITAIN and FRANCE unsuccessfully sought to stop aggression by Nazi GERMANY through a policy of appeasement. The recommended policy to deal with aggressors was military superiority. Such superiority would allow states to either deter or defeat a would-be aggressor as the situation demanded.

According to doves the principal danger of the hawk strategy for maintaining international peace and stability was provocation. The challenging state, faced with a situation in which the dominant state is committed to a policy of military superiority, may decide to launch an attack because it feels it has little to loose or because the situation can only get worse.

Viewed in less politicized terms, the debate between hawks and doves is consistent with the conflict between conservative internationalists and idealists or liberal internationalists that has existed for much of the history of American foreign policy.

**Further reading:** Allison, Graham, et al., eds. *Hawks, Doves, and Owls: An Agenda for Avoiding Nuclear War.* New York: Norton, 1985.

## Hay, John (1838–1905) *secretary of state*

John Milton Hay was SECRETARY OF STATE (1898–1905) under two presidents, WILLIAM MCKINLEY and THEODORE ROOSEVELT. He is viewed more as an implementer of presidential policy preferences rather than as an independent initiator of policy. His two major areas of diplomatic activity were Latin America and the Far East.

With regard to Latin America, Hay spent a considerable amount of diplomatic and political energy on laying the foreign-policy foundation for building the PANAMA CANAL. In the mid-1800s both the United States and GREAT BRITAIN showed growing interest in building a canal across the isthmus that would connect the Atlantic and Pacific Oceans. Neither was prepared to allow the other to unilaterally control such a canal. In 1850 the CLAYTON-BULWER TREATY was signed whereby both sides agreed to cooperate in the construction of a canal and not to build fortifications or try to exercise exclusive control over it. Working with British ambassador Julian Pauncefote, Hay signed a treaty in 1900, which permitted the United States to build a canal without prior British approval, but it not lift the ban on fortifications. The year 1900 was an election year, and the Senate refused to accept the treaty, adding amendments that the British found unacceptable. Hay then negotiated a second treaty in 1901 that tacitly permitted the United States to fortify a canal. Hay next proceeded to negotiate with COLOMBIA, which controlled PANAMA. The discussions resulted in the Hay-Herrán Treaty (1903) that gave the United States the right to obtain rights to a canal zone six miles wide for an up-front payment of $10 million and annual payments of $250,000 beginning in nine years. The financial terms were so favorable to the United States that the Colombian senate unanimously rejected the treaty while endorsing continued negotiations. The United States then helped engineer a revolt in Panama and signed a virtually identical agreement with the new government.

In the Far East, Hay is most remembered for his OPEN DOOR notes of 1899 and 1900. European powers had begun to establish spheres of influence in CHINA that threatened American economic interests. In order to protect American trade rights Hay asked those European powers present in China to agree to a formula that would guarantee the equal treatment of all parties. His call met with a cool response, but Hays nonetheless announced that his proposal had been accepted by all concerned. Hay sent a second Open Door note the following year following the outbreak of antiforeign rioting in China. The Open Door notes were hailed as a significant foreign-policy victory in the United States and formed the basis of American foreign policy toward the Far East into the 1930s. However, the United States never put itself in the position of having to take any form of military action to uphold the principles advanced or protect the territorial integrity of China.

See also JAPAN; NICARAGUA.

## Helms, Jesse Alexander (1921– ) *senator*

Jesse Alexander Helms was elected to the Senate from North Carolina in 1972. He served in that body until 2003, choosing not to run for reelection in 2002. He was one of the most controversial political figures of his era through his championing of right-wing causes in both domestic and foreign policy. Helms exerted a significant influence on the direction of American foreign policy as a result of his strongly held views and reluctance to compromise or change his position. His intransigence forced others to accommodate their views to his. Helms's influence was particularly great when he chaired the Senate Foreign Relations Committee from 1995 to 2001. In that position he was able to hold up ambassadorial nominations, treaty votes, and FOREIGN-AID legislation on issues that he opposed. His influence was such that foreign heads of state, such as Vicente Fox of MEXICO, and heads of international organizations, such as Kofi Annan of the UNITED NATIONS, found it necessary to meet with Helms in hopes of securing passage of legislation they favored.

Commentators on the political left and political right in American politics present two widely contrasting views of Helms. Liberals saw him as a backward-looking obstructionist and as a man who advocated an unrealistic foreign policy, one that opposed virtually all multilateral initiatives and placed the United States at odds with the world over such matters as funding for the United Nations, the KYOTO PROTOCOL, the INTERNATIONAL CRIMINAL COURT, the COMPREHENSIVE TEST BAN TREATY, LAND MINES, and most HUMAN-RIGHTS issues. Conservatives saw Helms as a staunch defender of American sovereignty, freedom, and democracy, an opponent of COMMUNISM, and a champion of true American NATIONAL INTERESTS.

Placed in historical context, Helms is the late-20th-century embodiment of the Jacksonian tradition of foreign policy, according to some commentators. Central to this outlook is a reluctance to interfere in the affairs of other states combined with a willingness to strike out at others harshly when American interests are seen as being threatened. This made ISRAEL a natural ally for Helms, since it often found itself as an outcast at the United Nations and other international forums for its policies toward Palestinians. Others see in Helms's support of Israel nothing more than American domestic politics. During his first term the American Israel Public Affairs Committee gave him the lowest rating of any senator and worked to defeat him. After his reelection Helms became a fervent supporter of Israel, working to increase DEFENSE DEPARTMENT funds destined for American Israel Public Affairs Committee and exempt it from cutbacks in foreign aid.

## Helms-Burton Act

Also known as the Cuban Liberty and Democracy Act of 1996, the Helms-Burton Act is a highly controversial piece of TRADE POLICY legislation that has been strongly supported by anti-Castro Cuban nationalists in the United States. Supporters see it as a device for isolating Cuban president Fidel Castro from the Cuban people and the international community, thus hastening his departure from POWER. Critics argue that it only strengthens his hand domestically by allowing him to blame the United States for CUBA's economic problem and isolates the United States from its allies.

The Helms-Burton Act has four parts. Title I seeks to transform what had become a largely unilateral American economic blockade of Cuba into a multilateral one. It also seeks to deny Cuba representation in international financial bodies and threatens sanctions against states that provide Cuba with FOREIGN AID. Title II presents the American list of demands that must be met before normal diplomatic relations can be reestablished. At its core is the demand that neither Fidel Castro nor his brother, Raul, be associated with the government. Also, all properties nationalized in the 1960s must be returned to their American owners or just compensation made, and the government must not jam Radio or TV Martí. Title III allows U.S. nationals to sue foreign companies and the Cuban government for "trafficking" in properties seized during the revolution in Cuba. Included in the group of those who may sue are individuals who were Cuban nationals at the time. Title IV allows the United States to deny entry to executives of foreign firms said to be "trafficking" in such properties. The prohibition extends to family members.

It is Title III that has produced the most intense debate. Never before has the United States taken the position that it will support the claims of individuals who were not its citizens at the time an incident such as expropriation occurred. Also, under international law it is not permissible to bring the citizens of a second country into court over property lost in a third country. U.S. allies reacted angrily to the passage of the Helms-Burton Act. The ORGANIZATION OF AMERICAN STATES strongly opposed it, as did the Inter-American Judicial Committee. CANADA passed legislation that authorized the Canadian attorney general the right to identify foreign laws that impinge on Canadian sovereignty and deny those countries access to Canadian records that might be used in court. MEXICO adopted an "antidote law" to protect firms operating there.

Opposition from American allies in both the Western Hemisphere and Europe was not unexpected. President BILL CLINTON waived the provisions of Title III a total of 10 times. President GEORGE W. BUSH followed suit and waived its provisions in July 2001, the first opportunity he had to do so. On several occasions, however, foreign firms have been told that they "may" be penalized for violating the provisions of Title III. In February 1998 this happened to Premier Oil Plc and British Borneo (both British firms) and GEN Oil (a Canadian firm). Earlier the United States took steps to revoke the visas of executives of a Canadian firm, Sherritt International Corp., and an Israeli firm, EM Group, under terms of Title IV. The logic of the Helms-Burton Act and its passage reflects the importance of the Cuban-American lobby in American electoral politics. Clinton initially expressed reservations about the act and threatened to veto it, but these doubts disappeared when on February 24, 1996 (an election year), Cuban jets shot down two aircraft flown by the Brothers to the Rescue, an anti-Castro organization, over Cuban airspace. Seventeen days later, Clinton signed the bill into law. Bush set the stage for his waiver by a series of harsh anti-Castro comments designed to reassure the Cuban-American community of his continued support for its goal of removing Castro from power.

The Helms-Burton Act is not the first American attempt to isolate Cuba and remove Castro from power through imposing ECONOMIC SANCTIONS. U.S. economic sanctions were put into place soon after Castro took power in 1959 and nationalized property belonging to Americans without compensation. By 1964 all members of the Organization of American States (OAS) except for Mexico had broken diplomatic relations. For its part, the United States was supplementing formal economic sanctions with COVERT ACTION programs designed to topple Castro. In the 1970s allied support for economic sanctions began to weaken. Even the United States entered into quiet talks with Cuba designed to improve U.S. relations. Cuban involvement in ANGOLA, SOMALIA, and ETHIOPIA ultimately blocked movement in this direction, but in 1975 the OAS voted to lift its economic sanctions.

After the end of the COLD WAR and the collapse of the Soviet Union (see RUSSIA), Cuba's main economic benefactor, the United States once again moved to unilaterally impose economic sanctions on Cuba. The instrument was the 1992 Cuban Democracy Act, also known as the Torricelli Act. Congressperson Robert Torricelli (D-N.J.) was the act's primary sponsor. An ardent supporter of anti-Castro efforts, Torricelli was closely allied with and financed by the CUBAN-AMERICAN NATIONAL FOUNDATION. Proposed in an election year it was endorsed by presidential candidate Bill Clinton and President GEORGE H. W. BUSH. Among its provisions were clauses prohibiting trade between Cuba and foreign subsidiaries of U.S. corporations. The UNITED NATIONS repeatedly voted to denounce the act by lopsided votes. In 1997 the vote was 143-3, with only Israel and Uzbekistan voting with the United States.

There is one final feature of the Helms-Burton Act that is of great importance. It codifies into legislation all previous executive orders relating to Cuba. This is significant since it now requires congressional approval to change any of these actions. So long as they remained executive orders, it was the prerogative of the PRESIDENT to keep them in place or lift them.

See also DOMESTIC POLITICS; HELMS, JESSE; INTEREST GROUPS.

## Helsinki accords   See CONFERENCE ON SECURITY AND COOPERATION IN EUROPE.

## Hickenlooper amendments

Bourke Hickenlooper (R-Iowa) sponsored a series of amendments to U.S. FOREIGN-AID legislation in the early 1960s that reflected both the intense anti-COMMUNISM of the period and battles between CONGRESS and the PRESIDENT over the control of foreign policy.

The stimulus behind Hickenlooper's amendments were uncompensated expropriations of U.S. property by nationalist governments. In 1960 Fidel Castro in CUBA nationalized American-owned sugar firms. In 1962 a Brazilian governor nationalized a subsidiary of International Telephone and Telegraph. Hickenlooper's amendments required that the United States terminate foreign aid to any state that expropriated American property without "adequate, effective, and prompt compensation." His amendment to the 1964 Foreign Assistance Act went even further. Angered over the SUPREME COURT's use of the Act of State doctrine in *BANCO NACIONAL DE CUBA V. SABBATINO* (1964), which required U.S. firms to pay the Cuban government for sugar rather than the U.S. citizens whose firms had been seized. Hickenlooper's amendment stipulated that the courts were not to employ the Act of State doctrine unless instructed to by the PRESIDENT based on "the foreign policy interests of the United States."

Hickenlooper's amendments tended to put him at odds with President JOHN KENNEDY, who saw his actions as infringing on presidential foreign-policy prerogatives. In 1962, Kennedy called his amendment requiring the termination of aid "unwise." Its reaction mirrored that of the Eisenhower administration three years before when confronted with a similar measure. SECRETARY OF STATE DEAN RUSK observed that the Kennedy administration and Hickenlooper sought the same ends but that mandatory provisions such as this one "would create very severe complications in our relations with other governments."

## HIV/AIDS

Infectious diseases have emerged as a major global health problem. In 1998, between 25 and 33 percent of the 54 million deaths worldwide were a result of infectious diseases. Deaths due to infectious diseases, such as tuberculosis, malaria, hepatitis, and HIV/AIDS, have surged as a result of changed lifestyles, changed land-use patterns, the inappropriate use of antibiotic drugs, mutations, and pathogens. The HIV/AIDS pandemic is especially great in the developing world, where it is estimated that 95 percent of HIV/AIDS cases are found. Seventy percent of them are in sub-Saharan Africa. In 2000 it was believed that 2.4 million people died from HIV/AIDS and another 25.3 million are infected with the disease. This brought the death toll from HIV/AIDS to 17 million. In SOUTH AFRICA the U.S. census estimates that in 2010, 40 percent of its adult population will be infected with HIV/AIDS and that HIV/AIDS will have been the leading cause of death in 2002. Estimates place the number of HIV/AIDS orphans in Kenya at more than 300,000.

Studies done by the U.S. INTELLIGENCE COMMUNITY expect the number of individuals with HIV/AIDS to grow significantly by 2010. Joining ETHIOPIA and NIGERIA as states where individuals with this disease will show significant increases in numbers are CHINA, RUSSIA, and INDIA. Projections estimate that by 2010 India will have 20 to 25 million people infected with HIV/AIDS and that China will have 10 to 15 million HIV/AIDS cases. Russia will have between 5 and 8 million cases of HIV/AIDS. Ethiopia and Nigeria, where the disease is most advanced today, will show increases off 7–10 million cases and 10–15 million cases, respectively.

The situation in each of these states is somewhat different and highlights the complex nature of the challenge of dealing with the HIV/AIDS pandemic. Ethiopia and Nigeria are expected to be hardest hit because the disease is prevalent throughout the population. In Russia, China, and India, HIV/AIDS is still confined to high-risk groups, such as intravenous drug users, but it is spreading to the larger population. In RUSSIA HIV/AIDS is expected to exacerbate the severe health problems being experienced and the overall decline in population that is occurring. In India and China it is expected to drive up governmental social and health-care costs. None of these states are expected to be able to effectively address the HIV/AIDS pandemic through health or educational programs.

The leading U.S. government agency that deals with the HIV/AIDS pandemic is the UNITED STATES AGENCY FOR INTERNATIONAL DEVELOPMENT (USAID). It works with countries to construct an integrated strategic plan. In Ethiopia USAID's mission focuses on expanding access and use of services for the prevention and control of HIV/AIDS and other sexually transmitted diseases, increasing resources for primary and preventive health care, and increasing access to and demand for contraceptives, with the overall goal of improving family health care. Central to the USAID's strategy for bringing this about are mass-media campaigns, social marketing programs, community-based educational programs, community-based activities targeted on specific populations, such as truck drivers, migrant workers, young adults, and sex workers, using reli-

A young African child carries some of the medicines she takes every day to treat her HIV/AIDS virus, July 2000, Ivory Coast. *(Photo by Ami Vitale/Getty Images)*

gious, labor, and trade groups as well as traditional healers. In addition to this narrow focus on HIV/AIDS, USAID also is involved in programs to address food shortages, vitamin deficiencies, and childhood illnesses. USAID operates in conjunction with a wide variety of NONGOVERNMENTAL ORGANIZATIONS in Ethiopia, including Catholic Relief Services and Save the Children, as well as INTERNATIONAL ORGANIZATIONS, such as the World Health Organization and UNICEF.

Among the program accomplishments cited by USAID is the financing of workshops on mechanisms for financing health service delivery systems, providing health management information systems to 40 district health officials, and training more than 600 frontline workers, providing capacity building support for local nongovernmental organizations that are helping more than 21,000 children affected by HIV/AIDS, and selling almost 49 million condoms and 1.2 million oral contraceptives through its social marketing effort.

Viewed from the broader perspective of American foreign policy, the HIV/AIDS pandemic is more than just a health problem. It is also an economic problem. The WORLD BANK, for example, attributes the low economic growth rate of sub-Saharan economies in part to the spread of HIV/AIDS. It is also a complex security problem. The prevalence of HIV/AIDS among soldiers dramatically reduces the efficiency of the military and creates impediments to joint military activities. The prevalence of large numbers of HIV/AIDS infected people in neighboring states also creates a potential security threat through fears of forced deportations or other mass migrations. Finally, HIV/AIDS can be viewed as a HUMAN-RIGHTS problem. Fears exist that cultural norms and public laws will place women and children who have contracted HIV/AIDS at a disadvantage in receiving help or treatment.

In his 2002 State of the Union address President GEORGE W. BUSH surprised his audience by announcing a new $15 million, five-year initiative to attack the HIV/AIDS problem in Africa. The program does not block funds from going to organizations that promote abortions, but the plan, as approved by the Senate, does earmark one-third of the funds for abstinence programs. It also contains language introduced by Representative Joseph Crowley (D-N.Y.) that provides financial assistance "for the purpose of encouraging men to be responsible for their sexual behavior." The legislation had widespread support from drug manufacturing companies, such as Bristol-Myers Squibb and Abbott Laboratories, that hope to benefit from this FOREIGN-AID undertaking.

**Further reading:** Brown, Lester B., et al. *Vital Signs.* New York: Norton, 1995; Garrett, Laurie. *The Coming Plague.* New York: Farrar, Straus, and Giroux, 1994; Hamilton, Kimberly A. "The HIV and AIDS Pandemic as a Foreign Policy Concern." *Washington Quarterly* 17 (1984).

### *Holmes v. Jennison* (1840)

The case of *Holmes v. Jennison* involved the fate of a Canadian resident, George Holmes, who was indicted for murder in CANADA and fled to Vermont, where Governor Silas H. Jennison signed a warrant for his arrest and extradition back to Canada. Holmes appealed, arguing that Jennison had no right to do so in the absence of an extradition treaty between the United States and GREAT BRITAIN (which was responsible for Canada's foreign affairs).

At issue was the right of a state to make foreign-policy decisions that were at variance with those of the federal government. The Court was evenly split on the matter and

therefore rejected Holmes's appeal. The significance of this case lies in two areas. First, we find in Chief Justice Roger Taney's opinion a continued assertion of supremacy of federal foreign-policy actions over those of states. In his view, "the states by their adoption of the existing CONSTITUTION have become divested of all their national attributes, except as relate purely to their internal concerns." He also asserted, "[T]he framers of the constitution manifestly believed that any intercourse between a state and a foreign nation was dangerous to the Union." The second area of significance of this spilt decision and Chief Justice Taney's opinion lies in the renewed willingness of states to challenge the federal government in foreign policy. A recent celebrated case is *CROSBY V. NATIONAL FOREIGN TRADE COUNCIL,* in which the SUPREME COURT overruled a Massachusetts law as infringing on federal foreign-policy powers.

### Homeland Security, Department of

On November 25, 2002, President GEORGE W. BUSH signed into law the bill creating the Department of Homeland Security. Conceived in the aftermath of the SEPTEMBER 11, 2001, terrorist attacks on the Pentagon and World Trade Center, the legislation had been championed by Bush but encountered considerable opposition in the pre-November 2002 general election. The most significant stumbling block centered on civil-service protections and bargaining rights of those who were slated to work in the new agency. Most Democrats supported a plan that would have required Bush to work closely with unions before changing the personnel system. The PRESIDENT wanted the agency to have the freedom to hire, fire, move, and discipline workers in the Department of Homeland Security. The impasse was broken when the election provided the REPUBLICAN PARTY with a majority in the next CONGRESS.

According to the legislation the Department of Homeland Security is to combine activities from 22 different federal agencies in order to better protect the United States from terrorism. It is envisioned that all agencies will be merged into the Department of Homeland Security by September 20, 2003. The total workforce will bring together 170,000 employees. Agencies targeted for incorporation include the Immigration and Naturalization Service, the Secret Service, the Customs Service, the Federal Emergency Management Agency, the Transportation Security Administration, the Coast Guard, and the Border Patrol.

Originally President Bush had resisted the idea of creating a Department of Homeland Security. He preferred the establishment of an Office of Homeland Security within the White House. He established this office on October 8, 2001, by an executive order. Tom Ridge, who would be nominated by Bush to be the first secretary of the Department of Homeland Security, was selected to serve as the assistant to the president for Homeland Security. Bush's line of action produced a negative response from Congress on two counts. First, as an assistant to the president Ridge's appointment was not subject to confirmation by the Senate nor could he easily be compelled to testify. This angered congressional leaders who sought access to information from the Bush administration about INTELLIGENCE leading up to the 9-11 attacks and steps taken to prevent future terrorist attacks. Second, congressional dissatisfaction with the performance of the CENTRAL INTELLIGENCE AGENCY and the FEDERAL BUREAU OF INVESTIGATION resulted in mounting pressure for organizational reform. Bush changed his position in June 2002, at which time he proposed creating the Department of Homeland Security.

## Hoover, Herbert (1874–1964) *president of the United States*

Herbert Clark Hoover was the 31st president of the United States. Prior to becoming PRESIDENT Hoover had broad exposure to international-affairs problems through his work as head of the American Relief Administration, which provide food for post–WORLD WAR I Europe. He was appointed secretary of commerce by President CALVIN COOLIDGE. He is credited with transforming the COMMERCE DEPARTMENT's small bureau of foreign and domestic commerce into a virtual second STATE DEPARTMENT by increasing the number of overseas offices from 23 to 58 and helping American firms dominate the Latin American market.

As president, Hoover, a Quaker, was an internationalist, but he was staunchly opposed to the use of force to achieve foreign-policy objectives. As a result, his foreign policy often took on strong isolationist overtones. This came through with great clarity in his support for DISARMAMENT and in his response to the Japanese seizure of Manchuria in 1931. In his 1929 inauguration address Hoover stated that the KELLOG-BRIAND PACT that had outlawed war needed to be extended to "pave the way to greater limitation of armament." Consistent with this position he supported the 1930 five-power LONDON NAVAL CONFERENCE that placed additional restrictions on the size of cruisers, submarines, and destroyers as well as extended the moratorium on the construction of capital ships. The agreement was only a limited success. The U.S. Senate ratified the treaty on July 21 by a vote of 58-9. FRANCE and ITALY did not, and Japanese admirals denounced their government for having agreed to it.

Not only did Hoover reject the use of military force either jointly or unilaterally to counter the Japanese occupation of Manchuria, but he also opposed an economic boycott of Japan. The option Hoover selected was diplomatic nonrecognition of Japan's control over Manchuria. Known as the Stimson Doctrine, after Secretary of State

HENRY STIMSON, it informed both JAPAN and CHINA that the United States "does not intend to recognize any situation, treaty, or agreement which may be brought about by means contrary to the covenants and obligations" of the Kellogg-Briand Pact.

Hoover's policy toward Latin America is more positively evaluated. He laid the foundation for the Good Neighbor policy that would be popularized under his successor, FRANKLIN ROOSEVELT. As president-elect Hoover went on a seven-week goodwill tour of the region. In his inaugural address he followed up his trip by announcing that the United States had "no desire for territorial expansion, for economic or other domination of other peoples." Hoover would endorse the Clark Memorandum on the MONROE DOCTRINE that repudiated the ROOSEVELT COROLLARY. It stated that "the right of intervention was not surrendered, only the right to intervene under the Monroe Doctrine." True to its word, in 1932 the U.S. Marines left NICARAGUA and the United States did not intervene in domestic disturbances in MEXICO and BRAZIL. To some extent the onset of the Great Depression aided Hoover's policy shift because it made foreign investment less attractive. The highly restrictive 1930 Hawley-Smoot Tariff proved to be a set back for good relations with Latin America, but it did not undo the more positive foundation that Hoover had established.

**Further reading:** Ferrell, Robert H. *American Diplomacy in the Great Depression: Hoover-Stimson Foreign Policy, 1929–1933.* New Haven, Conn.: Yale University Press, 1957.

## House, Edward Mandell ("Colonel") (1858–1938) *presidential adviser*

"Colonel" Edward House was a key behind-the-scenes foreign-policy adviser of President WOODROW WILSON in the early years of his presidency. His influence was greatest prior to Wilson's remarriage in December 1915. Significant differences arose between Wilson and House during diplomatic negotiations leading up to America's involvement in WORLD WAR I and the PARIS PEACE CONFERENCE that ended the war, although House remained Wilson's key foreign-policy adviser through it all.

Prior to the U.S. entry into World War I, House became an expert on the situation in Europe and what the war meant for the United States. He also undertook several missions to Europe on behalf of Wilson. The first signs of a split in thinking between Wilson and House occurred in 1915 following the sinking of the *Lusitania*. Wilson still believed that U.S. mediation could end the war. House, on the other hand, now saw the conflict as one of democracy versus autocracy and was convinced of the inevitability of

U.S. involvement. His second trip to Europe led to an agreement with British foreign secretary Sir Edward Grey whereby Wilson, on the approval of GREAT BRITAIN and FRANCE, would propose a peace conference. If Germany refused or insisted upon unreasonable terms, the United States would then likely enter the war. The sequence of events outlined in the House-Grey Memorandum never were set in motion, and House agreed to them without consulting Wilson.

Once war began, Wilson put House in charge of studying U.S. war aims and planning for the postwar international order. Negotiations with U.S. European allies did not produce an agreement on war aims, and House proceeded to help draft Wilson's unilateral U.S. statement of war aims, the FOURTEEN POINTS. House then turned his attention to drafting proposals that he shared with Wilson for the LEAGUE OF NATIONS. At the Paris Peace Conference House proved himself to be less committed to the Fourteen Points than Wilson and much more willing to compromise on such key matters as reparations and territorial demands. With Wilson back in Washington for a brief time, House accepted a French proposal to occupy the left bank of the Rhine River and separate an agreement to establish the League of Nations from a German peace treaty. Wilson returned to Paris and pushed House to the side. He rejected his advice that concessions be made in order to ensure the treaty's approval by the Senate. Wilson and House never spoke to one another again after the signing of the TREATY OF VERSAILLES on June 28, 1919.

**Further reading:** George, Alexander, and Juliette L. George. *Woodrow Wilson and Colonel House.* New York: Dover, 1964.

## Hughes, Charles Evans (1862–1948) *secretary of state*

Charles Evans Hughes was SECRETARY OF STATE (1921–25) for Presidents WARREN HARDING and CALVIN COOLIDGE. He would later be named chief justice of the SUPREME COURT. Hughes was a conservative internationalist who opposed WOODROW WILSON on the LEAGUE OF NATIONS, holding that "foreign policies are not built on abstractions. . . . [T]hey are the result of practical conceptions of national interest arising from some immediate exigency or stand out vividly in historical perspective."

Interestingly, one of Hughes's first tasks as secretary of state was to conclude an American peace treaty with GERMANY, since the United States did not join the League of Nations. He did this with the signing of the Treaty of Berlin in 1921. Hughes also was faced with the task of overcoming economic instability in Germany, which had the effect of causing Germany to default on its reparation payments and, in turn, compelling the Allies to suspend their

debt repayment to the United States. Hughes called for a committee of experts to draft a new reparations plan. Known as the Dawes Plan, after Chicago banker Charles Dawes who helped devise it, it called for Germany to receive a loan of $200 million from U.S. and Allied investors and to repay $250 million in reparations in 1925. The plan worked well until 1929, when the stock market crash drastically reduced the amount of investment funds flowing into Germany and global depression set in.

Hughes is best remembered for his championing of the WASHINGTON CONFERENCES in 1921. Convinced that a renewed arms race would unbalance budgets and hurt the economies of all states, he invited representatives from the eight leading naval powers to Washington for a conference designed to find ways of averting such an occurrence. The agreements signed are generally cited as the only major DISARMAMENT agreement prior to the signing of the 1987 treaty to limit the size of U.S. and Soviet intermediate-range ballistic missiles (IRBMs).

## Hughes-Ryan Amendment

The Hughes-Ryan Amendment to the 1974 Foreign Assistance Act requires that the PRESIDENT deliver a presidential finding to CONGRESS that a COVERT ACTION program is in the national interest. The Hughes-Ryan Amendment marked a significant attempt to curb presidential foreign-policy powers.

After decades of compliance with presidential foreign-policy initiatives, in the early 1970s Congress adopted a much more assertive position on the conduct of American foreign policy. VIETNAM was the principal catalyst for this newfound activism, but revelations of questionable covert actions by the CENTRAL INTELLIGENCE AGENCY (CIA) also played a role. Some of these, such as Operation Phoenix, occurred during that war, whereas others took place outside of it. The most notable of these covert action undertakings were the BAY OF PIGS invasion designed to bring down Fidel Castro's regime in CUBA and the Track II plan aimed at removing Salvadore Allende from power in CHILE.

The Hughes-Ryan Amendment is the most significant and enduring congressional effort from this time period to curb presidential powers. Sponsored by Senator Harold Hughes (D-Iowa) and Congressperson Leo Ryan (D-Calif.), the Hughes-Ryan Amendment barred the CIA from spending any funds on operations in other countries (other than those intended solely to obtain information) unless the president "finds" the action to be "important to the national security of the United States" and reports it as such to the appropriate committees of Congress in a timely manner. Eight committees of Congress were designated as recipients of these presidential findings. They were the Armed Services and Appropriations Committees in the

House and Senate, the Senate Foreign Relations Committee, the House Foreign Affairs Committee, and (later because they did not exist at the time) the House and Senate Intelligence Committees. These procedures were streamlined in 1980, reducing the number of committees that needed to be informed to two (the House and Senate Intelligence Committees) and reducing the number of individuals to be informed, in especially sensitive cases to only the chair and ranking minority member of these committees along with the Speaker of the House and the majority and minority leaders of the Senate.

Presidential findings have varied greatly in their degree of specificity. The 1975 presidential finding supporting U.S. activities in ANGOLA was so vague that it referred only to an operation in AFRICA and stated that it would provide "material, support, and advice" to nationalist movements in order to create a "stable climate." The presidential finding on IRAN during the Reagan administration was written after that operation began. DIRECTOR OF CENTRAL INTELLIGENCE William Casey had been directed not to inform Congress. This finding indicated the purpose of these operations to be to (1) establish a more moderate government in Iran, (2) obtain significant intelligence, and (3) further the release of American hostages held in LEBANON.

The presidential findings mandated by the Hughes-Ryan Amendment are significant because they make it impossible for presidents to deny prior knowledge of covert operations. Moreover, the process of presenting presidential findings opens an avenue for congressional participation in the decision-making process. Presidential findings have been modified to take into account congressional views, and operations have been cancelled for the same reason.

## Hull, Cordell (1871–1955) *secretary of state*

Cordell Hull was the longest-serving SECRETARY OF STATE (1933–44). His major area of expertise and interest was free trade and tariff reduction. As a member of CONGRESS he had come to this issue feeling that high tariffs harmed his Tennessee constituents. During WORLD WAR I he adopted a more internationalist perspective and came to believe that free trade was a necessary prerequisite for global prosperity and economic growth. When he was offered the post of secretary of state by President FRANKLIN ROOSEVELT, Hull sought guarantees that he would be permitted to negotiate reciprocal tariff reductions. Hull was also very active in promoting better U.S. relations with Latin America, where he promoted the Good Neighbor policy. At the 1933 Montevideo Conference Hull signed a protocol that made interference in the affairs of other states in the Western Hemisphere illegal. His efforts to promote better rela-

tions with states in the region are credited by many as being responsible for the willingness of most Latin American states to cooperate with the Allies during WORLD WAR II.

Hull's operating style and outlook often placed him at odds with other members of the Roosevelt administration, and he engaged in a constant struggle to keep control over foreign policy in the STATE DEPARTMENT. Hull, as an advocate of free trade, was opposed by those who felt that free trade would disrupt their plans for managing economic recovery in the United States. Hull was a methodical decision maker who wanted to thoroughly examine an issue before acting. This caused Roosevelt to often bypass Hull and rely upon others to carry out his wishes. Undersecretary of State Sumner Wells became a Roosevelt favorite after 1938. Hull had to fight particularly hard to retain control over U.S. foreign policy toward JAPAN and the Far East under pressure from both anti-Japanese HAWKS who demanded ECONOMIC SANCTIONS and other measures against Japan for its war in CHINA and pro-Japanese DOVES who advocated a more conciliatory approach. Hull did not embrace either of these two positions but sought to convince Japan to abandon its concept of a New Order in the Pacific. In late 1941 Hull's efforts came to an end, and in November control over U.S. Far Eastern policy passed to the War and Navy Departments. His influence on U.S. foreign policy continued to decline as the war progressed. Now in failing health, Hull turned his attention to shaping the post–WORLD WAR II order and became an advocate of the UNITED NATIONS. He was awarded the 1945 Nobel Peace Prize for these efforts.

**Further reading:** Dallek, Robert A. *Franklin D. Roosevelt and American Foreign Policy, 1932–1945.* New York: Oxford University Press, 1979.

## human rights

Traditionally the fate of individuals or groups within a country was not seen as a major foreign-policy issue. The Covenant of the LEAGUE OF NATIONS made no reference to human rights. Improving the human condition first became recognized as a legitimate part of world politics following WORLD WAR II, when the organizers of the UNITED NATIONS identified human rights as an area of concern when they wrote its charter. These rights were delineated in the Universal Declaration of Human Rights adopted by the General Assembly in 1948. These rights can be grouped under two headings. The first are civil and political rights. These include the right to life, prohibition of torture, prohibition of slavery, freedom of movement, and right to marry. The second set of rights are social, economic, and cultural. They include the right to work, right to equal pay for equal work, right to education, right to participate in the cultural life of one's community, and protection of mothers and children. The International Human Rights Covenants of 1966 added the rights to self-determination and sovereignty over natural resources to this listing.

At a broad, conceptual level American thinking on human rights coexists uneasily with listing of rights. This comes through quite clearly in the fact that while most Americans profess a deep attachment to human rights, the term *human rights* is virtually absent from the vocabulary of American domestic politics. Three guiding images shape American thinking on human rights and shape American foreign policy in this area. First, Americans feel that human rights essentially are individual political and civil rights. Second, Americans believe that the primary threat to individual political and civil rights comes from the government. Rather than harnessing governmental powers to promote human rights, Americans instinctively think in terms of limiting government power through a system of checks and balances. Third, Americans believe that the proper way to promote human rights is through the legal system or the electoral process. Violence is rejected as a means for securing these rights.

This definition of the human-rights problem places Americans at odds with the experience of many societies. For many in the world violence is an acceptable means of promoting human rights because often all others have failed. For many in the world economic and social rights are issues as equally pressing as political rights due to the amount of poverty and discrimination that exists. And for many in the world social anarchy, economic dislocation, and domestic violence are evils to be avoided and whose solutions may lie in creating a strong government.

Some go further and assert that the American perspective on human rights is not just different but marked by a "profound and troubling arrogance." At its core is the assumption that the United States sets the standard for promoting and protecting human rights. It is other countries and not the United States that have human-rights problems. Assertions that the treatment of NATIVE AMERICANS, the homeless, or Japanese Americans during World War II constitute a human-rights problem are rejected. This arrogance is seen as being displayed in how the United States deals with other countries. CONGRESS requires the STATE DEPARTMENT to submit annual reports on such matters as the human-rights and religious freedom practices of other states. If countries are found wanting, FOREIGN AID is denied unless the PRESIDENT declares it to be in the national interest. Yet, the United States has been extremely reluctant to submit reports on its human-rights practices to international monitoring bodies, and Washington has resisted signing several major international human-rights agreements.

As this example suggests, both Congress and the president have played active roles in defining American human-

rights foreign policy. Congress and the White House both supported the Universal Declaration of Human Rights in 1948. As part of their strategy to defuse support for the BRICKER AMENDMENT that would have severely limited the president's ability to enter into international agreements, the Eisenhower administration promised it would not seek Senate approval of either the Convention on the Prevention and Punishment of the Crime of Genocide or any other human-rights treaty. Congress did not give its consent to the Genocide Treaty until 1987. In the 1960s Congress passed landmark civil-rights legislation as part of President LYNDON JOHNSON's Great Society program but did not take action on the major international human-rights agreements of the decade, such as the 1965 Convention on the Elimination of All Forms of Racial Discrimination and the 1967 Declaration on the Elimination of Discrimination against Women.

Congress began to assume a more activist role on human rights in the 1970s. But because Congress and the president frequently clashed over the content of America's human-rights agenda, the rhetoric and reality of American human-rights foreign policy were often quite different. The defining congressional-presidential human-rights battle of the early 1970s was the JACKSON-VANIK AMENDMENT. A central feature of President RICHARD NIXON's policy of DÉTENTE was to use American trade as a reward for Soviet cooperation on national security matters. Soviet human rights were of little concern to his administration. What mattered was Soviet foreign-policy behavior. The Jackson-Vanik Amendment made the freedom of Soviet Jews to emigrate a prerequisite for the granting of MOST-FAVORED-NATION status. Also controversial was the decision of the Nixon administration to participate in the CONFERENCE ON SECURITY AND COOPERATION IN EUROPE. Out of these negotiations came the 1975 Helsinki accords. Conservatives criticized the agreement as having done little but legitimize the Soviet presence in Eastern Europe because all parties agreed that European borders could not be changed by force. They complained that all that the West achieved was a Soviet pledge to respect human rights. The actual significance of the Helsinki accords proved to be its human-rights provisions. In very little time the follow-up meetings, as stipulated by the Helsinki accords, became regular platforms for monitoring Soviet human rights practices.

The second half of the 1970s saw conservatives in Congress do political battle with President JIMMY CARTER over his human-rights policy. Carter sought to make a commitment to human rights the centerpiece of American foreign policy in the post-Vietnam era. His starting assumption was that oppressive social, political, and economic conditions that led to repression and domestic violence proved most threatening to the enjoyment of human rights. Carter openly criticized many of America's most loyal anticommunist allies in the Third World, such as IRAN, the PHILIPPINES, SOUTH AFRICA, and SOUTH KOREA. As with other aspects of Carter's foreign policy, his commitment to human rights was not always translated into action. The Carter administration defended these lapses as examples of pragmatism and a willingness to take a case-by-case approach. Sympathetic critics saw it as further proof of Carter's inconsistency in foreign policy.

Carter's efforts were most strongly criticized by those who felt that the primary threat to human rights came from COMMUNISM. The case was put most strongly by Jeane Kirkpatrick, who would become the United States ambassador to the United Nations under President RONALD REAGAN. She argued that Carter was wrong in pressuring pro–U.S. authoritarian regimes to reform because they were capable of evolving toward democracy on their own. Communist governments would never turn back to democracy, and therefore they were the greatest threat to human rights. Consistent with this thinking, the administration advanced the Reagan Doctrine, which committed the United States not just to contain communism but also to remove communist governments from power.

With the COLD WAR over the Bush administration faced new grounds in constructing a human-rights policy. The test case proved to be CHINA. Following the death of former Communist Party leader Hu Yaobang in April 1989, student protestors took to the streets demanding democratization and economic reforms. On June 4 Chinese troops attacked the demonstrators on Tiananmen Square, killing hundreds. A crackdown on prodemocracy forces inside and outside of the Chinese government followed. GEORGE H. W. BUSH responded by imposing economic sanctions but by the end of the year his administration was more interested in protecting American strategic and economic interests in China than it was in promoting human rights there. He argued that trade would be a force for promoting human rights in China. Congress was more hawkish on the issue of human rights in China than was Bush. He found it necessary to veto congressional legislation that would have permitted Chinese students to prolong their stay in the United States and lift a congressional ban on loans to companies doing business in China in order to pursue his goals.

Congress continued to try to link trade and human rights in China during the Clinton administration, specifically by means of its yearly vote on extending most-favored-nation status to China. As a candidate for president, BILL CLINTON had promised a more aggressive stance with China on its human-rights violations, but on becoming president he embraced the Bush position. The issue was finally resolved in the final months of Clinton's presidency when he secured permanent normal trade status for China, bringing to an end the yearly vote on its continuance.

One area where post–cold war Congresses and presidents have been of a like mind is in making the expansion of democracy and free-market economies a central feature of American human-rights policy. For Clinton promoting the spread of these two forces was at the core of his administration's strategy of ENLARGEMENT. Congress showed its support for these causes in several pieces of legislation. It passed the Support for East European Democracy Act in 1989 to assist POLAND and HUNGARY and later broadened its terms to cover all of Eastern Europe. In 1992 it passed the Freedom Support Act to help the newly independent states of the former Soviet Union and the Democracy in HAITI Act, and in 1996 it passed the Cuban Liberty and Democracy Act.

The CUBA case and the earlier Jackson-Vanik Amendment illustrate the important role that domestic politics have played in American human-rights foreign policy. Both pieces of legislation were prompted in large measure by heavy lobbying. Other examples include the 1984 requirement that the State Department report annually on such workers' rights as the right to organize and bargain, protection from enforced or compulsory labor, acceptable work conditions, and minimum wage laws for child employment. In 1996 it added religious freedom as an annual reporting requirement.

As the cold war ended the Senate began ratifying international human-rights agreements it had long refused to take action on. In 1987 it gave its consent to the Genocide Convention. In 1992 it consented to the International Covenant on Civil and Political Rights. In 1994 it gave its consent to the Convention against Torture and the Convention on Eliminating All Forms of Racial Discrimination. In giving its consent the Senate has often made use of reservations, understandings, and declarations as a way of limiting the domestic impact of these agreements.

The GEORGE W. BUSH administration suffered an early embarrassment in the area of human rights when in May 2001 the United States was rebuffed in its efforts to obtain a seat on the United Nations Human Rights Committee. The reasons for the rejection are complex but appear to include the United States's repeated condemnations of Cuba's human-rights record and an announced threat to veto any resolution condemning Israeli policy in the occupied territories.

Human rights have played an important role in the post–SEPTEMBER 11, 2001, debate over the proper conduct of American foreign policy. The George W. Bush administration effectively cited human-rights violations by the Taliban and Islamic fundamentalist groups in general in garnering support for the war on TERRORISM. The administration's commitment to human rights was questioned by those who pointed to the scale of the reconstruction and recovery task that awaited the United States in AFGHANISTAN and the relative paucity of funds dedicated to it. Voices of concern were also raised about human-rights violations at home and abroad that were by-products of the war on terrorism. In the United States concern was expressed about violations of the legal and civil rights of those accused of being terrorists or sympathizers. Abroad the concern was that countries would use the war on terrorism as an excuse to crack down on domestic opposition groups.

See also CONFERENCE ON SECURITY AND COOPERATION IN EUROPE; DEMOCRATIZATION; RUSSIA.

**Further reading:** Flood, Patrick J. *The Effectiveness of UN Human Rights Institutions.* New York: Praeger, 1998; Forsythe, David P. *The Internationalization of Human Rights.* New York: Free Press, 1991; Johnasen, Robert C. *The National Interest and the Human Interest: An Analysis of U.S. Foreign Policy.* Princeton, N.J.: Princeton University Press, 1980; Steiner, Henry J., and Philip Alston. *International Human Rights in Context: Law, Politics, Morals.* 2d ed. New York: Oxford University Press, 2000.

## humanitarian intervention

Military interventions were a staple of both American and Soviet COLD WAR foreign policy. The arrival of the post–cold war era has not brought about their passing. What has happened is a transformation in the nature of interventions and the terms of the political debate over their legitimacy. The most prominent cold war interventions were unilateral affairs designed to either support the government of the day or bring about its downfall. For the United States, VIETNAM is an example of the former, and GRENADA is an example of the later. For the SOVIET UNION,

A U.S. Army medic administers medicine to a young Afghan girl during a civil humanitarian mission in central Afghanistan as part of Operation Enduring Freedom, December 2000. *(Photo by Scott Nelson/Getty Images)*

the invasions of CZECHOSLOVAKIA and HUNGARY were designed to prevent reform-minded communist parties from seizing power. Sending troops to EAST GERMANY and AFGHANISTAN constituted efforts at propping up faltering Communist governments. These types of intervention continue to occur in the post–cold war era. The United States sent troops to PANAMA to bring down Manuel Noriega and to HAITI to restore Jean-Bertrand Aristide to power.

Much greater attention, however, is focused on a different type of intervention: humanitarian or peace interventions. Humanitarian interventions come in two forms. Classical PEACEKEEPING operations, which had their start with the UNITED NATIONS in the 1950s, are put into place only after a consensus has formed that it is time to end the fighting. Contemporary peacemaking operations are inserted into ongoing conflict situations in which both sides are prepared to continue fighting. Three post–cold war humanitarian interventions involving the United States have received the most attention: SOMALIA, BOSNIA AND HERZEGOVINA, and KOSOVO. The Bosnian and Kosovan interventions are traced to the collapse of YUGOSLAVIA and the reemergence of ethnic rivalries after more than four decades of Communist rule. The intervention into Somalia began in 1992 as part of an international effort to protect relief workers caught up in an ongoing civil war. It took on an added dimension when U.S. forces sought to disarm the warring factions so that a central government could be reestablished. General Muhammad Farah Aidid resisted this move and attacked U.S. forces, killing more than a dozen. Added to this list can be RWANDA, where the United States and the international community failed to intervene in a civil war that degenerated into genocide.

Humanitarian interventions raise several issues that the United States and the international community have yet to reach consensus on. A fundamental point of debate is timing. When should one intervene? The UN Charter suggests two very different answers. On the one hand it affirms the principle of sovereignty. If strictly adhered to, this would allow humanitarian interventions only when the permission of the host state has been obtained. However, the charter also permits the use of force if a situation represents a threat to international peace and stability. The Security Council used this clause for nonmilitary sanctions against SOUTH AFRICA due to its policy of apartheid and for military aid in support of Kurds in IRAQ.

A second issue is how to intervene. It has two parts. First, should the intervention be seen as a one-shot affair or as part of a longer undertaking? Typically the focus of interventions only has been on the immediate task of stopping the violence. The second part of the question concerns the type of forces that should be sent and the terms they should operate under. Should small contingents of peacekeepers be sent who are to fire upon only when attacked, or should large numbers of fighting forces be sent who are prepared to engage in conventional and unconventional combat with hostile forces? Somalia, Bosnia, and Kosovo typify the first approach, whereas the invasion of Afghanistan to remove the Taliban from power is more consistent with the latter.

A third question centers around the issue of whether humanitarian interventions can be neutral. They are presented as being so, but many argue that neutrality or even-handedness is an illusion. In this view any intervention will tip the domestic balance of power either by protecting a weakened force that is about to be defeated or permitting the stronger side to dominate when both sides are denied access to foreign help. In the Balkans, the United Nations first imposed ECONOMIC SANCTIONS against the Serbs and placed an arms embargo against the Bosnians. Designed to be evenhanded, these steps did not end the fighting but, some argue, permitted the Serbs to engage in their campaign of ethnic cleansing.

Addressing the spoiler problem is the final question confronting those engaged in humanitarian intervention. Spoilers are political-military forces, inside or outside of the country, who feel that they will be disadvantaged by a peace agreement and seek to undermine it. Delay, calculated noncompliance, sabotage, and violence are among the tools that spoilers employ. A successful humanitarian intervention requires that the presence of spoilers be recognized and appropriate strategies taken to neutralize them. In some cases this may involve accommodating their concerns. In others it may require military action.

Humanitarian interventions have been a controversial feature of post–cold war American foreign policy. While President GEORGE H. W. BUSH sent the first U.S. peacekeepers to Somalia in December 1992, the Clinton administration is most associated with humanitarian intervention. Liberal internationalists criticized the Clinton administration for being late to intervene and inconsistent in doing so. Conservative internationalists and neoisolationists criticized the administration for being too eager to engage in humanitarian interventions and for failing to distinguish between true challenges to the national interest that required a military response and cases of "social work" that did not. Upon becoming president GEORGE W. BUSH quickly moved to distance himself from most of BILL CLINTON's humanitarian interventions. Under pressure from the UN and other states, Bush reluctantly agreed to send in a small contingent of U.S. troops to LIBERIA in August 2003, after the IRAQ WAR had ended, to restore order and bring an end to its bloody civil war.

**Further reading:** Daalder, Ivo, H., and Michael E. O'Hanlon. *Winning Ugly: NATO's War to Save Serbia.* Washington, D.C.: Brookings, 2000; Haas, Richard E. *Intervention: The Use of American Military Force in the Post–Cold War World.* Rev. ed. Washington, D.C.: Brookings, 1999; Hoffman, Stanley. *The Ethics and Politics of Humanitarian Intervention.* Notre Dame, Ind.: University of Notre Dame Press, 1996.

## Hungary

Hungary is about the size of Indiana, with an area of 35,910 square miles and a population of 10.1 million people. Modern Hungary came into existence after WORLD WAR I with the downfall of the Austro-Hungarian Empire. Long dominated by Austrian rulers, Hungary had been made an equal partner in this political order by the Ausgleich of 1867. This agreement followed on the heels of a failed bid for independence by Hungary in 1849 and Austria's defeat in the Austro-Prussian War of 1866. The immediate years following World War I were not good to Hungary. After the collapse of the Dual Monarchy in 1918, Hungary declared itself independent, but the government of Michael Károlyi did not last long. Hungary's many minority groups found him suspect, and his government fell. It was replaced in March 1919 by a Communist government led by Béla Kun. A wave of violence followed that led to a Romanian invasion and a wave of reactionary counterviolence. In 1920 the Allies stripped Hungary of considerable territory at the Treaty of Trianon that was part of the overall peace settlement of World War I.

During the interwar period a primary objective of Hungarian diplomacy was regaining these lost territories. Appeals were made to both Presidents HERBERT HOOVER and FRANKLIN ROOSEVELT. In the late 1930s this strategy gave way to one grounded in an ALLIANCE with Nazi GERMANY and Fascist ITALY. Backed by these states Hungary was able to recover much of the land it lost to CZECHOSLOVAKIA, YUGOSLAVIA, and Romania. Hungary declared war on the United States in December 1941. Budapest tried to drop out of WORLD WAR II in October 1944 and was promptly occupied by German forces. Hungary was liberated from German control by the Soviet Union (see RUSSIA), and an armistice was signed in January 1945.

Elections were held later in 1945, and a coalition government was formed. The Communists gained less than one-fifth of the vote. However, supported by the occupying Soviet army, the Hungarian Communist Party used its control over the Ministry of the Interior to eliminate its political opposition. By 1949 the takeover was complete, and the Hungarian People's Republic was established. One of those targeted was Cardinal Mindszenty, who would spend 15 years in "asylum" in the American EMBASSY before being allowed to leave Hungary in 1971. The forced collectivization of agriculture and the imposition of industrial plans that emphasized heavy industry soon followed. In 1949 Hungary joined the Council for Mutual Economic Assistance (CMEA or COMECON), and in 1955 it joined the WARSAW PACT, thus firmly linking it politically, economically, and militarily to the Soviet Union. U.S.-Hungarian relations at this time and for much of the COLD WAR were strained not only because of the cold war competition between the two superpowers but also because of lingering disputes over the failure of Hungary to provide proper compensation for the nationalization of American-owned properties. It was not until 1973 that a bilateral agreement settled this dispute. As a sign of improving relations between the two states, in 1978 the United States returned the historic crown of St. Stephen to Hungary.

Joseph Stalin's death in 1953 led to a relaxation of political repression in Hungary, but economic problems continued. A subsequent attempt to restore Stalinist orthodoxy led to growing unrest that culminated in a student protest on March 23, 1956, during which security forces opened fire. This event set off a popular uprising that brought the reformer Imre Nagy back into power (he had governed briefly from 1953 to 1955). Nagy abolished the one party system under which the Communist Party had enjoyed a monopoly of political power, declared Hungary neutral, and withdrew Hungary from the Warsaw Pact. On November 3, Soviet troops invaded Hungary and restored the Communist Party to power. Nagy was executed in June 1958.

The United States and its allies did nothing to stop the Soviet invasion. The United States, GREAT BRITAIN, and FRANCE were involved in a complex military situation of their own in the Middle East. Great Britain, France, and ISRAEL had conspired to instigate a war with EGYPT under the pretext of keeping the SUEZ Canal open. The United States opposed the operation and demanded that it be stopped. The American nonresponse was seen as a betrayal by the Hungarian freedom fighters. President DWIGHT EISENHOWER's administration had openly talked about "rolling back the iron curtain," and RADIO FREE EUROPE's broadcasts appeared to encourage the belief that American help would be forthcoming. Hungary would realize this goal of independence from the Soviet Union in 1989 as part of the overall collapse of communism. The key moves in Hungary came in May and October 1989. In May Hungary opened its borders with Austria by tearing down barbed wire fences. In October the Hungarian Communist Party met and renamed itself the Hungarian Socialist Party and renounced its past. The final Soviet troops left Hungary in 1991.

The United States has worked closely with Hungary to bring about its military and economic integration into Europe. Hungary joined the PARTNERSHIP FOR PEACE program in 1994 and was admitted to the NORTH ATLANTIC TREATY ORGANIZATION (NATO) in 1999. With the crises unfolding in BOSNIA AND HERZEGOVINA and KOSOVO, Hungary was valued as a "NATO island" of stability in an unstable region. In 2002 Hungary negotiated its entry into the EUROPEAN UNION, a process that is scheduled to be completed in 2004. The United States has also provided Hungary with considerable amounts of FOREIGN AID. Between 1989 and 1993, the Support for East European Democracy Act provided $136 million for economic restructuring and private-sector development.

**Further reading:** Braun, Aurel, and Zoltan Barany. *Dilemmas of Transition: The Hungarian Experience.* Lanham, Md.: Rowman and Littlefield, 1999; Brzezinski, Zbigniew. *The Soviet Bloc: Unity and Conformity.* Cambridge, Mass.: Harvard University Press, 1967.

# I

## idealism

Idealism is the first 20th-century American theoretical perspective on world politics. It represented a dramatic departure from the conventional wisdom of the time. President WOODROW WILSON is closely identified with the development of idealism. The failure of his vision led to its abandonment in the interwar period. After WORLD WAR II, REALISM became the dominant theoretical perspective for studying world politics in the United States. The idealist strand of thought in U.S. foreign policy never vanished entirely. Frustrations with the VIETNAM WAR and the energy crisis of the 1970s helped give rise to renewed interest in liberalism as an alternative to realism. The end of the COLD WAR produced a second wave of interest in neoidealism and Wilsonian thinking about world politics, with many now arguing that Wilson was ahead of his time and that conditions are right for applying his insights to global problems.

Prior to the development of idealism it was assumed that the fundamental characteristics of world politics were unchangeable. The general conditions of peace, prosperity, and stability of the last decades of the 19th century and the first decade of the 20th century reinforced this belief. Writers on world politics largely were content to describe events or explore the writings of political philosophers for insights into the centuries-old dynamics of world politics. WORLD WAR I changed all of this.

Building upon their liberal intellectual traditions many American scholars sought answers in what was essentially a legalistic and moralistic framework. They concluded that war was not inevitable. It was the result of the very international politics designed to prevent it, namely, balance-of-POWER politics. According to its logic all of the major states were engaged in a competitive pursuit of power that required each to take all necessary steps to prevent any other state (or group of states) from becoming so powerful it could dominate the rest.

Led by Wilson this new generation of scholars asserted that war could be prevented by undertaking a number of corrective steps. First, INTERNATIONAL LAW and agreements would be put into place, bringing predictability to world politics and allowing countries to disarm. Second, an INTERNATIONAL ORGANIZATION, the LEAGUE OF NATIONS, would be created. It would give priority to the concept of collective security as the means for realizing national defense. Third, democracies would be established around the world to ensure that leaders would be responsible for their actions and not drag their countries into war. Finally, trade barriers would be reduced as a means of promoting prosperity and mutually beneficial international contacts.

The tone of these writings was optimistic. By the 1930s, however, this optimism seemed misplaced. Two different responses emerged. One argued that these principles were correct and the problem was that policy makers had not been loyal to them. One had to look no further than the United States's refusal to join the League of Nations for proof. A second response argued that the principles were at fault. They described a world that did not exist. Advocates of this second perspective referred to themselves as realists and described the first group as idealists.

The VIETNAM-era resurgence of interest in idealist principles came in the form of an embrace of globalism or liberalism. These perspectives rejected realism's emphasis on states as the dominant actor in world politics and national security as the dominant policy problem. Fostering cooperation rather than winning competitions with other states was the key conceptual issue. Globalists and liberals emphasized the role of international organizations, individuals, and societal groups in world politics. They also placed greater emphasis on economic issues and rejected military power as a means for settling problems. The theoretical debate between these perspectives was never fully resolved before it was overtaken by events, most notably the end of the cold war.

Realism came under heavy attack at the end of the cold war. Not only had it failed to predict the end of the cold war, but its key concepts seemed ill-suited for the evolving post–cold war agenda of promoting democracy, intervening to impose peace, expanding INTERNATIONAL TRADE, curbing the arms race, and recognizing fundamental HUMAN RIGHTS. In sharp contrast to realism, idealism's fundamental concepts and policy prescriptions spoke directly to these very concerns. In the process idealism, now championed as neo-Wilsonianism, was rehabilitated and emerged as the first American perspective on foreign policy in the 21st century.

See also ARMS CONTROL; DEMOCRATIZATION; DISARMAMENT; PEACEKEEPING AND PEACEMAKING.

**Further reading:** Vasquez, John, ed. *Classics of International Relations.* 3d ed. Upper Saddle River, N.J.: Prentice Hall, 1996; Viotti, Paul, and Mark Kauppi. *International Relations Theory.* 3d ed. Boston: Allyn and Bacon, 1999.

## immigration

Immigration policy in the United States has been linked to several different issues in American foreign and domestic policy. One important issue is the racial complexion of the United States. American immigration policy favored Europeans over Asians, Latin Americans, and Africans. A second issue is the composition of the workforce. Much of the nonwhite immigration into the United States was heavily concentrated in agriculture and railroad construction. A third issue is welfare policy. The growing influx of immigrations into the United States has placed a burden on the social welfare system, leading to a backlash in some places. California, for example, passed Proposition 187 in 1994 that denied social service benefits to illegal aliens. Most recently, immigration policy has become linked to national security concerns.

The United States is often described as a nation of immigrants. From 1990 to 1999 about 10 million immigrants legally entered the United States. This number is greater than any decade since the 1940s and almost twice as many as arrived in the 1980s. In terms of point of origin, in 1998 more immigrants came from MEXICO (131,575) than any other foreign country. Collectively AFRICA was second, with more than 40,000 immigrants. CHINA was third, with 36,884, and INDIA was fourth, with 36,482. The only European state in the top 15 was the former Soviet Union (see RUSSIA) that came in sixth, with 30,163. This stands in sharp contrast to earlier periods in American history when immigration laws were written to favor Europeans at the expense of others.

President GEORGE WASHINGTON proposed an open-door admission policy for immigrants, but this was soon reversed with the passage of the Alien and Sedition Acts of 1798 that mandated a 14-year residency requirement before immigrants were eligible for citizenship. This leg-islation also made it illegal for aliens to criticize the government and permitted the PRESIDENT to expel aliens who represented a security threat. The first significant effort at controlling immigration came in 1875 when CONGRESS passed an immigration act that sought to limit the importation of Asian laborers to the United States. It followed this up in 1882 with the Chinese Exclusion Act, also known as the 1882 Immigration Act, which established a 50-cent "head tax" on immigrants. The act was revised in 1884 and 1894 to exclude virtually all individuals of Chinese ancestry.

Around the turn of the 20th century a different concern became the focal point for immigration policy. It was a fear that radicalism, found primarily in Europe, where it found fertile support among lower socioeconomic classes, would infect the United States. In 1917 an immigration act was passed that imposed a literacy test on immigrants and a head tax on individuals from CANADA and Mexico. In 1921 the Emergency Immigration Restriction Act established national quotas. Congress passed the Johnson-Reed Act in 1924 that further elaborated on the quota system and established the U.S. Border Patrol. Controls for Mexican labor were relaxed in 1942 with the passage of legislation that allowed workers to enter the United States temporarily. This legislation was prompted by the manpower shortage in agriculture and some industries as a result of World War II and evolved into the BRACERO PROGRAM. This program was discontinued in 1964. One consequence of the flow of legal short-term Mexican labor into the United States was the development of a parallel illegal immigration flow. In 1954 the United States sought to crack down on the movement of illegal aliens into the United States with Operation Wetback.

After World War II immigration legislation took on an eclectic character. A bill passed in 1952 further strengthened the bias in favor of Europeans. Two years earlier the 1950 National Security Act included political subversives on the list of aliens to be denied entry. In 1965 immigration laws were amended to reduce the prowhite bias in existing statutes, and in place of a quota system, ceilings were established for the Eastern and Western Hemispheres.

By the 1980s immigration legislation began to focus on the problem of illegal immigration. In 1965 fewer than 100,000 illegal aliens were stopped entering the United States. By 1985 this number had grown to more than 1.2 million. The 1986 Immigration and Reform and Control Act imposed civil and criminal penalties on businesses that knowingly employed illegal aliens. It also raised the number of permissible legal aliens to 540,000 per year. The 1990 Immigration Act raised this ceiling even higher, to 700,000 per year, and added preferences to relatives of U.S. citizens and those with high-demand skills. This had the effect of reversing the preference that the 1965 act had given to immigrants from Latin America and Asia. Further reforms were put into place in 1996. The Welfare Reform Act denied federal benefits to legal and illegal immigrants, and the Illegal Immigration Reform and Responsibility Act gave increased funds to the border patrol and expanded the grounds for denying entry.

Most recently, in post–SEPTEMBER 11, 2001, America, immigration policy has become framed largely in terms of stopping the illegal entry of those hostile to the United States. Thirteen of the 19 individuals involved in the September 11, 2001, terrorist attacks had entered the United States illegally, and three of them were in the United States with expired visas. On October 26, 2001, President GEORGE W. BUSH signed the PATRIOT ACT. It gave the Immigration and Naturalization Service and STATE DEPARTMENT access to the FEDERAL BUREAU OF INVESTIGATION's database and allowed the attorney general to detain noncitizens believed to be a national security risk for up to seven days. At that point either charges must be brought or deportation hearings begun. On December 19, 2001, the House passed by a voice vote the Enhanced Border Security and Visa Reform Act that strengthens the system used to track foreign students and banned the issuing of visas from countries that sponsor terrorism.

The cumulative effect of recent immigration into the United States has altered the complexion of the American ethnic landscape. In 1950 the population of the United States was 89 percent white. In 2000, more than 25 percent of the population was nonwhite. It is anticipated that in 2050, the nonwhite percentage of the population will increase to just under 50 percent. Similar changes are evident in the percentage of the U.S. population that is foreign born. In 1970, 5 percent of the population was made up of immigrants, and 12 percent were children of immigrants. It is estimated that in 2040 these numbers will reach 14 percent and 13 percent, respectively. This will approximate the situation in the 1870s after the large-scale arrival of German and Irish immigrants.

In the realm of international affairs, this has led some to speak of the ethnicization of foreign policy. It is argued that the increased prominence of ethnic Americans results in an American foreign policy that is overly sensitive to domestic politics in "home countries" and is easily captured by ethnic lobbying groups.

See also INTEREST GROUPS.

**Further reading:** Brimelow, Peter. *Common Sense about America's Immigration Disaster.* New York: HarperPerennial, 1996; Reimers, David M. *Unwanted Strangers: American Identity and the Turn against Immigration.* New York: Columbia University Press, 1999; Smith, James P., and Barry Edmonstonn, eds. *The Immigration Debate.* Washington, D.C.: National Academy Press, 1998.

## Immigration and Naturalization Service v. Chadha
(1983)

The Supreme Court's ruling in *Immigration and Naturalization Service* (INS) *v. Chadha* struck down the legality of the legislative veto. This is significant because a key provision of the WAR POWERS RESOLUTION, through which CONGRESS has sought to limit the war-making POWER of the PRESIDENT, rested upon the legislative veto. It also was written into legislation covering ARMS TRANSFERS, FOREIGN AID, and providing other states with nuclear material.

Congress invented the legislative veto as a means of dealing with the increasing complexity of public-policy legislation. Congress felt that it could no longer write into legislation detailed administrative procedures and rules to cover all contingencies. It delegated this authority to executive branch agencies with the proviso that either house of Congress could invalidate any action it found objectionable. The SUPREME COURT ruled that the legislative veto was unconstitutional because it violated the system of separation of powers. The Constitution required that all legislation must be passed by both houses and then presented to the president for signature. If the president disapproves of this legislation, he or she may issue a veto that can be overridden by a two-thirds vote of Congress. The legislative veto provides no opportunity for a presidential veto since it is not passed as a law.

In this case, Jagdish Rai Chadha was an alien who had been legally admitted to the United States on a nonimmigrant student visa. He stayed after his visa expired and was ordered by the INS to show cause why he should not be deported. The immigration judge who heard his case permitted him to stay. The Immigration and Naturalization Act requires that all such decisions be reported to Congress. The House passed a resolution vetoing the judge's decision and setting in motion his deportation. Chadha appealed. Chief Justice Warren Burger delivered the Supreme Court's opinion, stating that "convenience and efficiency are not the primary objectives—or hallmarks—of democratic government." Justices White and Rehnquist dissented, asserting that the Supreme Court would have been better served if it had decided the case on narrower grounds and not called into question the constitutionality of congressional review statutes in other pieces of legislation.

Neither Congress nor the president has been willing to openly challenge one another over the constitutionality of the legislative veto following the Chadha decision. Each fears the uncertain consequences of doing so and prefers to operate in a gray area where political losses can be minimized. For Congress the risk is that a direct conflict will permanently rob it of an important political lever used to constrain the president and gather information from the executive branch. The danger for the president is that a successful challenge of the legality of the legislative veto may force Congress into passing legislation that truly limits the president's freedom of maneuver in foreign policy.

## imperialism

Imperialism is significant for the study and conduct of American foreign policy at two levels. First, it is an international economic system that conditions state behavior for both dominant states and subservient states. Second, it is a powerful political slogan that has been employed both in the COLD WAR conflict between the United States and Soviet Union (see RUSSIA) and the conflict between rich, industrialized countries and poor, developing nations.

Most analysts in the United States use the distribution of military power as their starting point for thinking about the structure of the INTERNATIONAL SYSTEM. UNIPOLARITY, BIPOLARITY, TRIPOLARITY, and MULTIPOLARITY are central organizing concepts in these studies. Another intellectual tradition, one more readily found in Europe and the developing world, gives priority to the character of international economic activity. Political, social, and cultural consequences are held to follow from this economic structure.

The most notable starting point for thinking about the structure and operation of imperialist economic systems is Marxism-Leninism. Marxism views capitalism as an inherently exploitative system because while it is the workers who produce a profit through their labors, it is the capitalists who profit. Under capitalism the long-term tendency is for profits to fall. This leads to a series of ever-worsening economic crises that culminates in revolution. The Marxist prediction of revolution proved to be inaccurate, and it fell to Lenin to explain why the Marxist prediction was still valid. He argued that capitalist states had saved themselves by entering into a program of overseas economic expansion that allowed them to obtain huge profits by exploiting colonies. They then used a portion of this profit to buy off segments of the working class at home. For Lenin, the revolution was still inevitable because of the existence of weak links in the international structure of imperialism. Unlike the truly backward states that had been colonized, the "most advanced backward" states would recognize their exploitation and rise up against imperialism, thus denying the capitalist imperialists their exorbitant profits. This would plunge the advanced capitalist states into financial chaos and political revolution.

Contemporary dependency theorists build upon this conceptual foundation but add a political dimension to it that perpetuates and reinforces the economic exploitation of the developing states by the rich. The states of the developing region (the periphery) are prevented from interacting directly with one another. All economic and political interactions flow vertically from the periphery to the rich states (the core) and then back to the other states of the international system. This allows the core to rule the periphery through a divide-and-conquer strategy. The system of linkages that binds the periphery to the core has taken many forms. Originally the periphery was ruled through the presence of military forces from the core state. Later MULTINATIONAL CORPORATIONS and INTERNATIONAL ORGANIZATIONS provided a less visible but equally effective means of control. Today, in an era of GLOBALIZATION, modern mass communication and telecommunication technologies serve as instruments of control by core states over the periphery.

This view of the international system has had many supporters in the developing world. It provided the intellectual foundation for calls for a new international economic order that were heard in the 1970s and critiques of the practices of the WORLD BANK and INTERNATIONAL MONETARY FUND in subsequent decades. It also called into question the motives of U.S. FOREIGN-AID programs and, more generally, cast U.S.-South relations in a conflictual context. The post–cold war global embrace of free-trade capitalism has caused the imperialism dependency paradigm of world politics to recede in importance in the study of world politics. It may become reinvigorated should the antiglobalization critique grow in importance.

For most Americans, imperialism is more familiar as a cold war–era political slogan than it is as a conceptual framework for studying world politics. During the cold war the United States and the Soviet Union each referred to the foreign policies of the other as imperialist. In making this charge they were simultaneously seeking to cast their own foreign policies in a positive, peaceful light and to provide a justification for entering into formal and informal ALLIANCES designed to block the influence of the other. The primary battleground in which this rhetorical contest was played out was the developing world. Third World states were more than just the recipients of competing U.S. and Soviet charges and countercharges of imperialism. They also used imperialism as a political weapon to forge unity among the newly independent colonial states and lay out a role for themselves in world politics as neutral or nonaligned states.

American foreign policy in the 1950s and 1960s often struggled in responding to these charges of imperialism by developing states. A principal problem was the priority given by American policy makers to maintaining good relations with its European allies. This was seen as necessary to ensure the CONTAINMENT of COMMUNISM in Europe. In the Third World it made the United States appear insensitive to the concerns of these states as they sided with their European allies, who were generally reluctant to grant independence. Problems for the United States continued into the 1970s as the focus of world politics shifted to control over natural resources. Highly visible and frequent references to "our OIL" in policy deliberations about the 1973

ORGANIZATION OF PETROLEUM EXPORTING COUNTRIES (OPEC) oil price hikes lent new credibility to Third World charges of imperialism.

The concept of imperialism continues to hold relevance to the study of world politics. The steps leading up to the IRAQ WAR and its aftermath gave rise to speculation that the United States had become an imperial power. Many in Europe referred to its as a hyperpower. It was America's potential imperial position that led many in the United Nations and the world community at large to oppose American military action against IRAQ. The sentiment was that an uncontrollable United States was an even larger danger to world peace than was Iraq.

**Further reading:** Kennedy, Paul. *The Rise and Decline of the Great Powers.* New York: Random House, 1987; Pastor, Robert A., ed. *A Century's Journey: How the Great Powers Shape the World.* New York: Basic, 1999; Williams, William Appleman. *Empire as a Way of Life.* New York: Oxford University Press, 1980.

## India

India is located in South Asia and occupies 1.3 million square miles. This is approximately one-third the size of the United States. It has a population of about 1 billion people. The first significant Western presence in India occurred in the late 1600s when the British East India Company opened trading posts at Madras, Bombay, and Calcutta. A rebellion in northern India resulted in the transfer of political POWER in India from the British East India Company to the British government. By that time they controlled most of modern India, PAKISTAN, and Bangladesh. The key 20th-century figure in India's independence movement was Mohandas Gandhi, who preached nonviolence. GREAT BRITAIN granted independence to India and Pakistan on August 15, 1947. This move was made necessary by the inability of Muslim and Hindu pro-independence forces to agree on a political formula for ruling one South Asian country. The various princely states were free to join either state. The formula worked well in most areas but created conflict in others, such as Kashmir, where the rulers were Hindu (and identified with India) ,but the majority of the population was Muslim (and identified with Pakistan). Kashmir joined India, but this decision has never been accepted by Pakistan.

The 1950s found India and the United States at odds over a number of issues. In 1954 the United States sent military weapons to Pakistan as part of a mutual defense agreement. Pakistan also received American FOREIGN AID for joining two of its alliances, the SOUTHEAST ASIA TREATY ORGANIZATION (SEATO) and the Baghdad Pact, also known as the CENTRAL TREATY ORGANIZATION (CENTO).

The United States saw these as anticommunist alliances, but India perceived that Pakistan was interested in obtaining weapons to counter its power. India preferred to follow a path of nonalignment under its first president, Jawaharlal Nehru. Speaking of SEATO Nehru noted that the United States seemed to view this ALLIANCE in terms of some kind of MONROE DOCTRINE for Southeast Asia. From the American perspective neutrality was impossible in the COLD WAR struggle against COMMUNISM, and by becoming a leader in the nonaligned movement India had become a de facto ally of the Soviet Union (see RUSSIA).

In spite of its deliberate attempts to distance itself from the United States, or perhaps because of them, the United States provided India with large sums of foreign aid. American leaders were determined not to "lose" India. Under President DWIGHT EISENHOWER the United States provided India with $283 million in aid between 1951 and 1956 and $875 million between 1956 and 1961. The Kennedy administration raised this amount to $1.8 billion for the years 1961–65. A Sino-Indian border war in 1962 produced calls of help from India to the United States, which responded with welcomed military assistance.

American aid to India was not welcomed, however, by Pakistan, which was much smaller and viewed India as its primary enemy. By 1965, India and Pakistan were engaged in a border war over Kashmir. The United States responded by placing an arms embargo on both sides. This hurt Pakistan the most because of its inferior military power position vis-à-vis India. For its part, India was angry with the United States for having supplied Pakistan with weapons that made the war possible. The United States again found itself in the middle of an India-Pakistan conflict in 1971. A revolt in East Pakistan against its political and economic domination by West Pakistan produced a large REFUGEE flow into India. President RICHARD NIXON again sought to put the United States in a neutral position by placing an arms embargo on both sides. India then entered into a treaty of friendship with the Soviet Union that, while largely symbolic, angered Nixon. The United States then officially "tilted" toward Pakistan. Foreign aid to India stopped, and military aid was given to Pakistan. Nixon's move angered both sides. It was not sufficient to prevent East Pakistan's independence as Bangladesh, which angered (West) Pakistan and was resented by India as meddling. American relations with India continued to deteriorate throughout the remainder of the 1970s and early 1980s. India particularly objected to the sharp increase in American military aid to Pakistan following the 1979 Soviet invasion of AFGHANISTAN.

After years of relative neglect, U.S.-India relations became a high profile item again in 1998 when India conducted five nuclear explosions on May 11 and 13. Before May ended, Pakistan had followed suit. The United States responded with a series of sanctions that were mandated by earlier congressional actions, such as the Glenn Amendment and Pressler Amendment. ECONOMIC SANCTIONS terminated development assistance worth about $57 billion, ended the sale of military material and dual-use technologies, stopped military financing programs, and blocked India's access to loans and credits from the Export-Import Bank and the Overseas Private Investment Corporation.

The Clinton administration and CONGRESS together pulled back from these restrictions soon after they were put in place. In early July the Senate approved by a 98-0 vote a one-year exemption for India and Pakistan from the terms of the Glenn Amendment. This was followed by passage of the Brownback Amendment (officially known as the India-Pakistan Relief Act of 1998), authorizing the PRESIDENT to waive the provisions of the Glenn Amendment to India and Pakistan, except for those dealing with military assistance and dual-use technologies for one year. In 1999 Congress passed Brownback II, which gave the president the authority to permanently waive all of the provisions of the Glenn Amendment for these states. It also gave the president the right to waive the terms of the Symington and Pressler Amendments as applying to them. The first barred most U.S. assistance to states found trafficking in nuclear enrichment equipment or technology outside of international safeguards. The second prohibited most American aid to nonnuclear states detonating nuclear devices.

An important factor in the American foreign-policy flip-flop was the growing political influence of the Indian-American community in the United States. In 1980 there were only 387,000 Indian Americans in the United States. In 1997 this number had grown to 1,215,000. More important than this growth in numbers was their political organization. In 1993 a congressional Indian Caucus was formed with 115 members. The Indian-American community raised some $4 million for candidates in the 1992 election. A July 1999 conference sponsored by the Indian Friendship Council attracted nearly 40 legislators, including House Minority Leader Richard Gephardt and Benjamin Gilman, chair of the House International Relations Committee.

The Clinton administration also took diplomatic steps to bring strategic stability to South Asia. It established a security dialogue that involved the United States in discussions with both Indian and Pakistan. One concrete goal of these talks was to get the two nations to sign the COMPREHENSIVE NUCLEAR TEST BAN AGREEMENT. This proved to be impossible after the Senate rejected the treaty in 1999 and George W. Bush indicated his opposition to it during his presidential campaign.

Stability in South Asia became even harder to achieve following the SEPTEMBER 11, 2001, terrorist attacks. The United States moved to embrace Pakistan, just as it had fol-

lowing the Soviet invasion of Afghanistan. This in and of itself did not create a stability problem. Indian leaders took a pragmatic and realistic view of the closer ties between the United States and Pakistan. For example, India volunteered to help the American cause by offering military bases and sharing INTELLIGENCE. It also did not point out to the United States that Pakistan had long worked openly with the Taliban. The United States responded by trying to maintain good relations with both states. President GEORGE W. BUSH moved to lift sanctions in place against both Pakistan and India that limited American military sales and cooperation. High-level American officials visited India to discuss the war against TERRORISM and increasing American-Indian military contacts, allowing India to purchase some $1 billion worth of military equipment from the United States in 2002.

As in the past, attempts at maintaining evenhandedness faced serious obstacles. This became evident in December 2001 when militants linked to Islamic extremist groups in Pakistan attacked the Indian parliament, killing nine. India responded with demands that Pakistan take action against the Islamic extremist groups operating there. Pakistan condemned the attack but was hesitant to take any further action. Its government was engaged in a delicate balancing act, simultaneously trying to support the United States in its war against the Taliban and terrorism while not alienating a population that was in many ways sympathetic to that cause. The Bush administration successfully mediated the immediate crisis, convincing India to lower its demands and Pakistan to take corrective action.

See also DOMESTIC INFLUENCES ON U.S. FOREIGN POLICY; INTEREST GROUPS.

**Further reading:** Blackwell, Robert D., and Albert Carnesale, eds. *New Nuclear Nations: Consequences for U.S. Policy.* New York: Council for Foreign Relations, 1993; Brands, H. W. *India and the United States: Cold Peace.* New York: Macmillan, 1990; Khilani, Sunil. *The Idea of India.* New York: Farrar, Straus and Giroux, 1998; McMahon, Robert, J. *The Cold War on the Periphery: The United States, India, and Pakistan, 1947–1965.* New York: Columbia University Press, 1996.

## Indonesia

Indonesia is an archipelago consisting of more than 17,000 islands, 6,000 of which are inhabited. It has an overall land area of 736,000 square miles, making it about three times the size of Texas. Its maritime area is 7,900,000 square miles. The most densely populated island is Java, with more than 107 million people living in an area approximately the size of New York. Indonesia's total population is approximately 210 million people.

Beginning in 1602 the Dutch established themselves as the colonial power in the region and ruled it for three centuries as the NETHERLANDS East Indies. During WORLD WAR II the Netherlands East Indies was occupied by JAPAN. On August 17, 1945, three days after the Japanese surrender here, Indonesia declared its independence. The movement for Indonesian independence predated the Japanese occupation and can be traced back to the early years of the 20th century. The Netherlands was unwilling to grant independence, and like other colonial powers it sought to reestablish its control. Four years of fighting ensued until, in 1949, the Dutch officially recognized Indonesian independence. With its primary focus on building up a united Europe to stop communist expansion, the United States was at first hesitant to oppose the Netherlands in this colonial war but began doing so in 1948.

American relations with Indonesia in the first two decades of independence were volatile. Indonesia declined to joint the SOUTHEAST ASIA TREATY ORGANIZATION (SEATO) that the United States hoped to use as an Asian equivalent of the NORTH ATLANTIC TREATY ORGANIZATION in drawing a global containment ring around the Soviet Union (see RUSSIA). President Sukarno was a leader in the nonaligned movement and hosted its first summit conference in Bandung in 1955. By distancing himself from the United States, Sukarno was able to obtain almost $250 billion in aid from the Soviet Union between 1954 and 1959. Beginning in 1958 a series of rebellions broke out in various parts of Indonesia challenging Sukarno's rule. The most notable of these was in Sumatra. At the time Sukarno charged that the United States was behind the uprisings. Dismissed as untrue at the time, more recent evidence supports Sukarno's charges. In mid-1957 President DWIGHT EISENHOWER, SECRETARY OF STATE JOHN FOSTER DULLES, and DIRECTOR OF CENTRAL INTELLIGENCE Allen Dulles had determined to undertake a covert operation to support rebels on Sumatra and Sulawesi. The operation lasted two years and resulted in Sukarno turning to the Communists and military to suppress the rebellion.

Before it left office, the Eisenhower administration reversed course and decided American interests were best served by supporting Sukarno rather than by overthrowing him. Tensions continued, however, due to Indonesia's repeated efforts to annex West Irian (which had also been a Dutch possession) and its clashes with Malaysia, which had obtained its independence in 1963. In March 1964 American FOREIGN AID to Indonesia all but ended, and that same year Indonesia embarked on a policy of nationalization that harmed American economic interests.

Sukarno was overthrown in a coup that began on October 1, 1965. By then the Indonesian Communist Party was the largest Communist Party outside of the Soviet Union and CHINA. Circumstances surrounding the coup remain unclear, but there is no direct link to the United States. American officials did support his successor, General Suharto, and made little concerted effort to stop the widespread violence that accompanied the coup. Estimates of the number of dead range from 150,000 to 600,000.

Under Suharto relations with the United States improved. In 1966 the United States offered to provide a five-year window of credit for the purchase of large quantities of cotton and rice to help offset severe shortages of these crops in Indonesia. For its part, Indonesia returned many of the properties nationalized by Sukarno's government. In July 1969 President RICHARD NIXON became the first American president to visit Indonesia. In the last decade of his rule (Suharto resigned in 1998) the United States and Indonesia cooperated on naval matters, allowing the United States to send the Seventh Fleet through the Indonesian waters that link the Pacific and Indian Oceans. This was of great strategic importance during the PERSIAN GULF WAR and crises of the Reagan and Bush administrations.

Two points of tension continued beneath the surface, occasionally flaring up in public. The first involved HUMAN-RIGHTS violations. President JIMMY CARTER identified Indonesia as a country where human rights were routinely violated. These charges were documented in the STATE DEPARTMENT's annual report. Although it raised the issue the Carter administration did not forcefully pursue it. His administration continued to supply Indonesia and other states with military aid. Neither the Reagan nor Bush administrations that followed pursued the matter. More recently, Indonesia has come under criticism for its lack of enforcement of international labor standards and violations of workers' rights.

The second issue was East Timor. West Timor is part of Indonesia. East Timor was a Portuguese colony from 1524 to 1975. When Portugal abruptly left, a Marxist group, Fretilin, achieved a position of military and political dominance. Citing domestic unrest in East Timor and security dangers to itself, in 1975 Indonesian forces successfully invaded East Timor and declared it to be part of Indonesia. The UNITED NATIONS never recognized this action. President BILL CLINTON raised this issue in meetings with Suharto in 1993 and 1994. In 1992 CONGRESS cut off grants for military training assistance to Indonesia in protest over an incident in November 1991. This restriction was partially lifted in 1995 but reinstated following violence that broke out after the August 30, 1999, East Timor referendum on independence. In January 1999 Indonesia had agreed to a process that could culminate in independence. This positive vote was a first step in that process, and in May 2002, East Timor became a sovereign state.

Relations between the United States and Indonesia have taken a new and uncertain turn following the SEPTEMBER 11, 2001, terrorist attacks. Indonesia is the world's largest Muslim country, and it has traditionally been concerned with issues of Islamic solidarity in conducting its foreign policy.

**Further reading:** Gardner, Paul F. *Shared Hopes, Separate Fears*. Boulder, Colo.: Westview, 1997; McMahon, Robert J. *Colonialism and Cold War*. Ithaca, N.Y.: Cornell University Press, 1981; Ricklefs, M. C. *A History of Modern Indonesia since 1300*. 2d ed. Palo Alto, Calif.: Stanford University Press, 1993.

## Insular Cases

*Insular Cases* is an overarching term used to group a series of SUPREME COURT cases that took place between 1901 and 1921. Together, they came to define the political and legal status of PUERTO RICO and other territories acquired by the United States around the turn of the 20th century. It defined them as unincorporated territories, a status that placed them in between states and independent countries. Critics assert that it condemned them to exist as colonies in perpetuity.

The key court case in this sequence was *Downs v. Bidwell* (1901). At issue was the existence of a special tariff in 1900 that covered oranges imported from Puerto Rico into the United States. A U.S. firm sued the federal government, arguing that these taxes were illegal since Puerto Rico was a U.S. possession. It had been obtained in 1898 as part of the SPANISH-AMERICAN WAR. Under the Uniformity Clause of the CONSTITUTION, tariffs were to be consistent across the United States. The Supreme Court ruled that while Puerto Rico was not foreign, it was also not a state and there was no evidence that it was a territory that would become a state. It thus existed somewhere in-between a sovereign state and a potential state in the Union. In his plurality opinion Justice Edward Douglas White labeled this gray zone an unincorporated territory. In doing so he was distinguishing it from other territories that the United States had acquired and that from the outset were destined for statehood.

The Insular Cases shed light on two important themes in American foreign policy. The first is expansionism. The Insular Cases brought into the open the fact that this latest round of territorial expansion was going to be different from the western continental expansion of the United States. Even the actions of the FILIBUSTERS, who looked to NICARAGUA and CUBA, envisioned statehood as the ultimate result of their efforts. According to many, with this decision the United States squarely moved into the category of an imperialist state that possessed colonies. The second theme to which the Insular Cases can be tied is racism. Expansion into Central America and the Caribbean had been advocated with one eye toward economic and security concerns and

another to adding slave states that would buttress the South's political power in the Union. With the AMERICAN CIVIL WAR over, the political rationale evaporated, leaving only economic and security concerns. Presumptions of racial superiority and reference to alien races with different religions and customs that might not easily adapt to "the blessings of free government" were commonplace at this time. They link back not only to references made to Mexicans earlier in the 19th century but also before that to NATIVE AMERICANS as the United States turned its eyes westward.

See also IMPERIALISM.

## intelligence

Policy makers rely upon intelligence in making foreign-policy decisions. Intelligence, however, is not raw data or information. It is information that has been analyzed and evaluated in terms of its accuracy and reliability and organized in such a fashion as to be useful to policy makers. Intelligence is not an instrument of foreign policy in the way that DIPLOMACY or economic sanctions are. Instead it is best seen as the foundation on which foreign-policy instruments rest because without quality intelligence policies are unlikely to succeed. Intelligence failures, such as Pearl Harbor and the onset of the Tet offensive in VIETNAM, often are highly politicized and serve as turning points in a country's foreign policy.

Viewed from an organizational perspective, intelligence is the product of institutional efforts. It is principally produced by the CENTRAL INTELLIGENCE AGENCY, the DEFENSE INTELLIGENCE AGENCY, the STATE DEPARTMENT, the NATIONAL SECURITY AGENCY, and the intelligence units of the various armed services. Collectively these and the other intelligence-gathering institutions constitute the INTELLIGENCE COMMUNITY that is headed by the DIRECTOR OF CENTRAL INTELLIGENCE.

To this needs to be added a perspective in which intelligence is also viewed as a process—an intelligence cycle—that both takes place inside of these institutions and that requires their cooperation. The intelligence cycle begins with the identification of a need. This is a problem or area of concern that is of interest to policy makers. It may be tasked, or assigned, to the intelligence community by the president, the NATIONAL SECURITY COUNCIL, or some other official, or it may reflect the professional judgment of members of the intelligence community as to the nature of security threats confronting the United States. This need may be addressed on a routine basis, such as making annual estimates of the Soviet nuclear threat or the state of the Soviet economy, or it may a topic studied on a more limited or onetime basis.

The second step in the intelligence cycle is collection. This involves gathering the raw data on which intelligence reports will be based. The major types of intelligence sources used to collect information are signals intelligence (SIGINT), which is information collected from intercepted communications, radar, and telemetry; imagery measurement and signature intelligence (IMINT), which includes such data as the distinctive radar signature of aircraft and the chemical composition of air and water samples; human-source intelligence (HUMINT), which involves the clandestine and overt collection of intelligence by individuals; and open-source intelligence, which is information gathered from public sources. The National Security Agency is responsible for collecting, processing, and reporting many forms of signals intelligence. The Defense Intelligence Agency is heavily involved in MASINT, measurement and signals intelligence, which provides information on weapons systems, such as ballistic missiles and nuclear warheads. The CIA is a major source of human-source intelligence, along with the State Department and DEFENSE DEPARTMENT. An important collector of open source intelligence is the Foreign Broadcast Information Service (FBIS).

The third step in the intelligence cycle is processing and exploitation. It is at this point that the raw data collected is transformed into a form that permits intelligence professionals to analyze it and make judgments as to its significance given the need being addressed. Two of the major processors of information obtained by technical means are the National Security Agency and the National Photographic Information Center (NPIC), which is located within the CIA's Directorate of Science and Technology.

The fourth step in the intelligence cycle is analysis and production. Often this may be carried out entirely within one institution. Just as likely, however, analyzing and producing an intelligence product will require the participation of professionals from several institutions. An analysis of the Soviet nuclear program, for example, would likely have brought together analysts from the CIA, the State Department, the Defense Intelligence Agency, and the Energy Department. In crises, such as the collapse of YUGOSLAVIA, a special task force would have been created to bring analysts together. Standing task forces address such questions as TERRORISM and nuclear proliferation.

The fifth step in the intelligence cycle is the dissemination of intelligence to the consumer. Five categories of "finished" intelligence are produced. In each case it represents the consensus view of the intelligence community. Current intelligence examines day-to-day events and assesses their significance for U.S. foreign policy. It may take the form of oral briefings or a daily, weekly, or monthly publication. Estimative intelligence helps policy makers focus on evolving or ongoing situations by starting with known facts and then exploring the patterns that emerge from them and their implications for U.S. foreign

Predator unmanned aerial vehicle (UAV) on a reconnaissance flight. The Predator provides near, real-time infrared and color video to intelligence analysts and controllers on the ground. *(Department of Defense)*

policy. The best-known form of this intelligence is the National Intelligence Estimate. A third category of intelligence is warnings intelligence. It informs policy makers that an urgent and threatening situation is developing that may require a policy response. A fourth category of finished intelligence is research intelligence. These in-depth and background studies are conducted by virtually all members of the intelligence community. The two most common forms are basic intelligence, which is encyclopedic in nature, and operational support, which is tailored to the specific needs of operational forces. The final category is scientific and technical intelligence that informs policy makers about foreign technological developments and the performance characteristics of weapons systems. The final stage is feedback, in which the intelligence community seeks out the opinions of consumers regarding their product.

See also COUNTERINTELLIGENCE; COVERT ACTION; ESPIONAGE; RUSSIA.

**Further reading:** Maurer, Alfred C., et al., eds. *Intelligence: Policy and Process.* Boulder, Colo.: Westview, 1985; Lowenthal, Mark. *Intelligence: From Secrets to Policy.* 2d ed. Washington, D.C.: Congressional Quarterly Press, 2003.

## intelligence community

INTELLIGENCE gathering and analysis in the United States is not concentrated in one or two agencies, as is the case in many countries. Rather, responsibility for these tasks is divided among a large number of bureaucratic entities that collectively are referred to as the intelligence community. At its center is the DIRECTOR OF CENTRAL INTELLIGENCE, who simultaneously serves as the head of the CENTRAL INTELLI-

GENCE AGENCY (CIA) and the head of the intelligence community. In this latter role the DCI is supported by an intelligence community staff that works to coordinate efforts in order to minimize duplication and ensure that all important intelligence targets are covered. The staff also monitors the dissemination of intelligence and consumer satisfaction.

The STATE DEPARTMENT's Bureau of Intelligence and Research (INR), the CIA, and the intelligence agencies of the military services can be viewed as charter members of the intelligence community. All of them were given institutional representation on the NATIONAL SECURITY COUNCIL when it was created in 1947. The INR produces political and some economic intelligence to meet the needs of the State Department. Army, navy, and air force intelligence (along with that of the Marine Corps) focus on providing intelligence to support the worldwide activity of these forces. The CIA was created in 1947 and has primary responsibility for the clandestine collection of foreign intelligence, for conducting COUNTERINTELLIGENCE abroad, and for the research and development of technical collection systems.

The first major addition to the intelligence community occurred in 1952 when President HARRY TRUMAN issued an executive directive transforming the recently created Armed Forces Security Agency into the NATIONAL SECURITY AGENCY (NSA). NSA is charged with maintaining the security of U.S. message traffic and intercepting, analyzing, and cryptanalyzing the messages of other states. In 1961 the DEFENSE INTELLIGENCE AGENCY (DIA) joined the intelligence community. It was created as part of a centralization movement within the DEFENSE DEPARTMENT that was intended to shift power from the military services to the SECRETARY OF DEFENSE and the JOINT CHIEFS OF STAFF. It had emerged as the chief rival of the CIA for influence in the preparation of intelligence estimates.

Three other less prominent members of the intelligence community are the FEDERAL BUREAU OF INVESTIGATION (FBI), the Department of the TREASURY, and the Department of Energy. The FBI has primary responsibility for counterintelligence operations within the United States. The Treasury Department openly collects foreign financial and monetary information. The Energy Department openly collects political, technical, and economic information on foreign energy matters. The Energy Department also has inherited the Atomic Energy Commission's mandate to collect and evaluate technical information on the nuclear power programs of other states.

This outline of membership in the intelligence community belies three important points that have influenced its ability to produce intelligence for American foreign-policy makers. First, the concept of a community implies similarity and shared attitudes. Based on this definition the intelligence community is a community in name only. More accurately it is a federation of intelligence agencies that have varying degrees of autonomy in carrying out their intelligence function and analyzing data. The CIA is the only independent agency in the intelligence community. Second, the term *community* is not one found in any statutory regulations, nor is it inherent in the nature of intelligence work. The notion of an intelligence community reflects the continued presence of strong bureaucratic and political pressures to preserve and protect organizational prerogatives. Third, the concept of an intelligence community is not a static one, and we can expect its future composition, as well as the amount of influence wielded by its members, to change as technologies and foreign-policy priorities change. The trend toward GLOBALIZATION and increased importance of economic considerations in American foreign policy may foreshadow such changes.

**Further reading:** Andrew, Christopher. *For the President's Eyes Only: Secret Intelligence and the American Presidency from Washington to Bush.* New York: Harper-Collins, 1995: Ransom, Henry Howe. *The Intelligence Establishment.* Cambridge, Mass.: Harvard University Press, 1970.

## interest groups

Interest-group lobbying represents an important avenue through which the public can express its foreign-policy preferences. Interest groups serve as intermediaries that help organize and channel the public voice and, as such, differ from voting in ELECTIONS and PUBLIC OPINION polls that allow for the direct communication of the public's thinking to policy makers. Commentators are divided on the merits of interest-group activity.

A wide variety of groups are active in trying to influence U.S. foreign policy. Interest-group activity can be conveniently organized into four different categories based on the interest being represented. First, there are economic groups, such as the Chamber of Commerce, the American Farm Bureau Federation, and the American Federation of Labor–Congress of Industrial Organizations (AFL-CIO). Second, there are ethnic groups. Historically, most prominent here are Jewish organizations, such as the American Israel Public Affairs Committee (AIPAC), and groups representing Arab, Greek, Turkish, Chinese, Cuban, and East European Americans. The third type of interest group is composed of foreign governments and businesses. Finally, there are ideological public interest groups that seek to influence U.S. foreign policy in such areas as HUMAN RIGHTS and the environment. Prominent in this category are organizations such as Amnesty International and the Sierra Club.

To its advocates interest groups hold several advantages over the more direct ways through which the public interacts with policy makers. One advantage is that the informational demands on the public are lessened. It is not necessary for the individual citizen to be informed about international events and the policy positions of parties and candidates. The interest group can do this for them. A second advantage is that interest-group lobbying provides citizens with continuous access to policy makers compared to elections and public opinion polls that take place intermittently. Finally, interest groups hold more political clout with policy makers than do elections and public opinion. Their message is more focused, and the political consequences of ignoring them are clearer.

Critics of interest-group lobbying on foreign policy make several counterarguments. First, they assert that internal divisions within interest groups limit their effectiveness in the same way that parties are limited in their ability to represent the views of their members. Unless the interest group has a narrow agenda, internal compromises will mute its voice. Second, rarely is it the case that interest groups are lined up on only one side of a policy problem. It is almost literally the case that for every group that supports increased international environmental controls, for example, another group exists that opposes additional restrictions.

A third objection to interest groups makes quite a different argument. Rather than arguing that interest groups are ineffective, these critics assert that some interest groups are effective—but only for some. These commentators assert that the resources that make groups powerful (leadership, money, access to policy makers, organization, and so on) are unevenly distributed. Instead of competition we find the permanent dominance of some groups over others to the point that we can talk of policy areas being "captured" by some interest groups. Iron triangles come into existence, linking together congressional committees, government agencies, and interest groups. The most powerful statement of this perspective comes from those who see U.S. foreign policy as being driven by the MILITARY-INDUSTRIAL COMPLEX, a coalition of business interests, professional military officers, and government officials. Acting together they give U.S. foreign policy an interventionist and aggressive quality that runs against the preferences of most Americans.

As this debate suggests, establishing the influence of an interest group on a specific policy is difficult. It is not enough to show that an interest group was active in a policy area. We need to show that a direct link exists between its activity and the policy outcome. It also needs to be kept in mind that success is not an all-or-nothing phenomenon. Finally, we need to pay attention to the goals being pursued. Obstructionism, or blocking something from happening, is far easier to achieve in America's system of checks and balances than is getting a new policy initiated.

See also ELITE DECISION-MAKING THEORY; PLURALISM.

**Further reading:** DeConde, Alexander. *Ethnicity, Race, and American Foreign Policy.* Boston: Little Brown, 1992; Destler, I. M. *American Trade Politics: System under Stress.* Washington, D.C.: Institute for International Economics, 1986; Levering, Ralph B. *The Public and American Foreign Policy, 1918–1972.* New York: Morrow, 1978; Lowi, Theodore. *The End of Liberalism: Ideology, Policy, and the Crisis of Authority.* New York: Norton, 1969.

## Intermediate-Range Nuclear Forces Treaty

The Intermediate-Range Nuclear Forces (INF) Treaty between the United States and the Soviet Union (see RUSSIA) was signed by President RONALD REAGAN and General Secretary Mikhail Gorbachev on December 8, 1987. The U.S. Senate ratified the INF Treaty on May 27, 1988, by a vote of 93-5. It entered into force on June 1, 1988. The INF Treaty eliminated all nuclear armed ground-launched ballistic and cruise missiles with ranges between 300 and 3,400 miles. The INF treaty was the first nuclear ARMS CONTROL agreement to actually reduce nuclear arms rather than establish ceilings that could not be exceeded.

The INF Treaty is important not only for what it accomplished—the destruction of 846 U.S. INF missile systems and 1,846 Soviet INF systems by May 1991—but for what it tells us about Western ALLIANCE politics in the waning days of the COLD WAR and the arms control monitoring system it established.

Understanding the full significance of the INF Treaty requires placing it in the context of U.S.–West European relations. One of the enduring issues in this relationship was how to protect West Europe from a Soviet attack. An associated issue was how to ensure that the defense of West Europe did not become separated from the defense of the United States. Placing U.S. troops in Europe through the auspices of the NORTH ATLANTIC TREATY ORGANIZATION (NATO) was one way to couple the defenses of West Europe and the United States. Short- and intermediate-range NUCLEAR WEAPONS was a second mechanism and one that was needed given the advantage in geography and manpower that the Soviet Union would enjoy in a war, especially if it took the form of a blitzkrieg war, such as what occurred in WORLD WAR II when Hitler's forces moved swiftly into FRANCE and the Soviet Union.

In 1977 the Soviet Union began upgrading its deployment of intermediate-range nuclear forces in the European portion of Russia by replacing older SS-4 and SS-5 missiles with new SS-20s, a mobile accurate missile that carried three independently targeted reentry vehicles. Western military analysts saw the SS-20s as a distinct threat to West European security that demanded the deployment of a counterweapon. However, their ability to respond in this fashion was limited by the rejuvenation of peace movements in Europe and the United States by President Reagan's hostile rhetoric toward the Soviet Union and his military buildup. As a way out of this dilemma in 1979 NATO adopted a "dual-track" strategy. It would simultaneously pursue arms control negotiations with the Soviet Union to reduce INF forces to the lowest level possible and prepare to begin installing new ground-launched cruise missiles (GLCMs) and Pershing II ballistic missiles in December 1983 if these talks failed.

The Soviet Union initially refused to enter INF talks due to the existence of a deployment track. In 1980 it relented and began negotiations. Formal talks began in September 1981, and in November President Reagan put forward his "zero option" proposal: The United States would eliminate all of its GLCMs and Pershing II missiles, and the Soviet Union would dismantle all of its SS-20s, SS-4s, and SS-5s. The Soviet Union rejected this formula and repeated efforts to formulate an interim agreement that would permit limit deployments should negotiations fail. One such compromise was the "walk in the woods" agreement reached in Geneva in 1982 that would have prevented the deployment of the Pershing II, limited SS-20 deployment in Asiatic Russia, and established equal levels of INF deployment in Europe. The talks adjourned in a deadlock when in November 1983 the Soviet Union walked out as the first Pershing II deployments began in West GERMANY. Talks did not resume until March 1985, when it was agreed that parallel arms control talks would be held on INF forces, strategic weapons (the STRATEGIC ARMS REDUCTION TALKS, or START), and defense and space issues.

After the presentation of a series of proposals and counterproposals in fall 1985, events began to move at rapid speed as unilateral actions by Gorbachev and Reagan outstripped the progress made by negotiators. In January 1986

General Secretary Mikhail Gorbachev *(left)* and President Ronald Reagan sign the Intermediate-Range Nuclear Forces Treaty. *(Collection of the District of Columbia Library)*

Gorbachev announced a proposal to ban nuclear weapons, including all INF missiles in Europe by 2000. In September 1986 Reagan and Gorbachev met in Helsinki, where they agreed on an equal global INF ceiling of 100 INF missiles, none of which could be in Europe. In April 1987 Gorbachev proposed the elimination of all short-range nuclear missiles, and in June the United States and NATO agreed. In July, Gorbachev agreed to a "double global zero" to eliminate all intermediate- and short-range missile systems. The elimination of INF missiles in Europe moved one more step toward completion when, in August, German chancellor Helmut Kohl announced that Germany would unilaterally dismantle its 72 shorter range Pershing IA missiles and would not replace them if the United States and the Soviet Union eliminated all of their INF missile systems.

Reagan had proposed his zero option in the expectation that it would be rejected. Its purpose was to soothe fears in Europe and the United States about his commitment to arms control. Gorbachev, however, embraced this language when he took the diplomatic offensive in 1985. With little choice but to accept the logic of its own arms control proposal, the Reagan administration now sought to place unacceptable demands on the Soviet Union in the area of inspection and verification. Historically, arms control verification was carried out by national technical means of verification (satellites, and so on) because of unyielding Soviet opposition to on-site inspections. The United States proposed an extensive and intrusive system of on-site inspections as the only way to verify compliance with an INF treaty. Once again Gorbachev surprised the United States and accepted on-site inspections. He also insisted upon "reciprocity"—the United States must also allow onsite inspections. The formal details of the verification regime that was to monitor INF treaty compliance were unveiled in March 1987. In January 1988 President Reagan issued an executive order establishing the On-Site Inspection Agency that was to be responsible for the continuous monitoring of a Soviet missile production facility to confirm that no new missiles were being produced. It also inspected 130 missile sites in East Germany, CZECHOSLOVAKIA, and the Soviet Union. Soviet inspectors engaged in similar actions.

When the Soviet Union collapsed in December 1991, it became necessary to make the bilateral INF treaty a multilateral one. Belarus, Kazakhstan, Russia, Ukraine, Turkmenistan, and Uzbekistan all had INF facilities. All but the last two became active participants in the INF inspection system and in implementing the treaty. These two states have only one INF facility each and do attend meetings of the Special Verification Commission that resolves compliance questions and discusses what additional actions are necessary to improve treaty compliance.

See also DIPLOMACY; DISARMAMENT.

**Further reading:** Krepon Michael, and Dan Caldwell. *The Politics of Arms Control Treaty Ratification.* New York: St. Martin's, 1991.

## international-affairs budget

The international-affairs budget, also known as the Function 150 account of the federal budget, provides the core funding for American foreign policy. Funded out of this account are the activities of the STATE DEPARTMENT and the more than 250 EMBASSIES and posts it maintains around the world. The international-affairs budget also provides funding for activities carried out by the TREASURY DEPARTMENT (debt relief), DEFENSE DEPARTMENT (international military training and education), DEPARTMENT OF AGRICULTURE (food aid), the Export-Import Bank, the UNITED STATES INSTITUTE OF PEACE, the PEACE CORPS, the International Trade Commission, the African Development Foundation, the North-South Center, and the East-West Center, among others.

Funds for the international-affairs budget are included in four different appropriations bills. The first is for Foreign Operations, Export Financing and Related Programs. All of the funds in this appropriation, referred to as Foreign Operations, are part of Function 150. Included here are funds for bilateral assistance programs, such as those for humanitarian assistance, aid programs for East Europe and the former Soviet Union, counter-narcotics and antiterrorism programs, and educational and cultural exchange programs. Second, Function 150 funds are found in the appropriations for the Departments of Commerce, Justice, and State, the Judiciary, and Related Agencies, also known as the C-J-S Appropriation Bill. State Department funds in this account are used to finance U.S. dues to the UNITED NATIONS and other international organizations and smaller international bodies. A third set of funds is found in the Agriculture, Rural Development, Food and Drug Administration, and Related Agencies appropriations bill. Funds for international food-aid programs are contained in this budget. The final appropriations bill is that for the Department of Labor, Health, and Human Services, and Education and Related Agencies. A small portion of these funds are for the U.S. Institute of Peace.

Controversy surrounds the Function 150 account at two levels. First, specific funding programs are controversial. Examples include funding for HIV/AIDS treatment and prevention, family-planning initiatives, and paying United Nations dues. Second, the overall size of the Function 150 account is controversial. For those who see the United State's involvement in PEACEKEEPING operations, humanitarian undertakings, environmental and development programs as social work, the overall budget needs to be kept small. For those who support a foreign-policy agenda built around liberal internationalism or neo-WILSONIANISM principles, the budget is much too small. For most of the 1990s those political forces interested in limiting the size of the Function 150 account were in the ascendancy. Between fiscal years 1991 and 1997, funding dropped almost 30 percent. The trend continued into the 21st century. For the 2001 budget congressional committees cut the Function 150 budget request down to $20 billion, which was $2.3 billion less than it approved for 2000, and increased defense spending to $310.8 billion, which was $4.5 billion more than the Clinton administration had requested.

In terms of the overall share of the federal budget, the decline in the Function 150 account did not begin in the 1990s, however. In the 1960s the Function 150 account made up about 4 percent of the budget. In the 1970s it slipped to an average of 2 percent. In the first half of the 1990s it was down to 1 percent before rebounding in 1998 and 1999. In real-dollar terms, the international affairs budget is now about 20 percent smaller than it was in the late 1970s and 1980s.

## International Criminal Court

On July 17, 1998, the International Criminal Court (ICC) was created at a UNITED NATIONS (UN) conference in Rome, Italy. It was given the power to try individuals on charges of genocide, crimes against humanity, and war crimes. The United States was one of seven states to vote against the agreement. CHINA, IRAQ, ISRAEL, LIBYA, Yemen, and Qatar were the others. On December 31, 2000, the last possible day to do so, President BILL CLINTON directed that the United States sign the treaty even though he had reservations about it. Doing so allowed the United States to participate in implementation discussions. On May 6, 2002, President GEORGE W. BUSH announced that the United States would not submit the treaty for ratification to the Senate and was withdrawing from it. Bush's decision sparked international controversy and raised questions about the United States's role as a leader in world affairs.

The creation of a permanent international criminal court is hailed by HUMAN-RIGHTS advocates and proponents of INTERNATIONAL LAW as one of the most significant developments of the post–COLD WAR era. It is not entirely without historical precedent. Between 1919 and 1994 five ad hoc international commissions, four ad hoc international criminal tribunals, and three bodies to prosecute crimes committed during WORLD WAR I or WORLD WAR II were established. The most famous of these is the Nuremberg Trials of 1946, at which 18 Nazis were convicted of crimes, with 12 being given the death penalty. A similar trial took place in Tokyo. There, 25 Japanese officials were found guilty, and seven were executed.

The ICC is distinguished from these most recent precedents in two ways. First, it is permanent. Second, it is not a tribunal imposed by the victors in a war on the defeated. It is a product of global collaboration. The first step in the creation of the ICC came in 1990 when a group of NONGOVERNMENTAL ORGANIZATIONS submitted a draft of an international agreement to the United Nations. In 1993 the United Nations created a special international tribunal for the former YUGOSLAVIA. The next year it created another special tribunal for RWANDA. Also in 1994 the International Law Commission produced a draft agreement that would create an international criminal court. In December 1995 the United Nations General Assembly took the next step and set up a Preparatory Committee for the Establishment of an International Criminal Court. It was out of the meetings of this body that the ICC was created.

The Clinton administration endorsed the creation of the Yugoslavia and Rwanda special tribunals. In 1997 the STATE DEPARTMENT created the position of ambassador-at-large for war crimes, and David Scheffer was named to it. President Clinton also addressed the UN General Assembly and endorsed the establishment of a permanent international criminal court. Still, in February 1998, with the formal adoption of the ICC treaty only six months away, the United States remained concerned about the relationship between the court and the United Nations. The United States argued that since it played a major role in PEACEKEEPING operations, it wanted to make sure that U.S. personnel would not be subject to unreasonable prosecution, thereby inhibiting the United States from taking necessary risks to save lives and promote peace and security. Key to American thinking was placing the Security Council (where the United States held a veto) in the position of controlling the work of the ICC. This position was opposed by those states that wanted to establish the ICC as an independent prosecutory force.

There was nothing new about the American concern for the ability of an INTERNATIONAL ORGANIZATION or tribunal to limit its freedom of action. In the congressional debate of the creation of the United Nations, similar concerns were expressed. President HARRY TRUMAN assured CONGRESS that joining the UN would not interfere with its authority to declare war, and Matthew J. Connelly, secretary to the president, authored an amendment that specified the World Court would not have jurisdiction over "disputes with regard to matters which are essentially within the domestic jurisdiction of the United States of America as determined by the United States of America." Senator JESSE HELMS, chair of the Senate Foreign Relations Committee, expressed the same sentiment in a March 26, 1998, letter to SECRETARY OF STATE Madeleine Albright. He stated that there could be no compromise that would give the ICC jurisdiction over an American citizen. If that were the case, the treaty would be "dead on arrival."

As passed, the ICC was empowered to prosecute war crimes, acts of genocide, and other crimes against humanity. It can act only if the country where the accused is a citizen is judged unable or unwilling to bring the case to trial in a national court. ICC jurisdiction is also limited to "widespread and systematic" atrocities. In explaining its continued opposition to the Rome treaty, the Clinton administration cited continuing concerns over the relationship of the ICC to national courts, the ambiguity of the crimes over which it had jurisdiction, the extent of Security Council control over the ICC, and the fear that American military personnel could be brought before the ICC. To prevent the latter from happening Helms championed the American Service Members Protection Act in 2001.

In explaining its renunciation of the ICC the Bush administration said it was the only alternative, having failed to repair the treaty. It was described as an unchecked power whose flaws could be exploited by "politically motivated prosecutions." Bush's opposition to the ICC did not end with the decision to renounce American withdrawal. In summer 2002 Washington sparred with the UN Security Council over the continuation of peacekeeping operations in which the United States was involved. Washington went so far as to veto an extension of the United Nations mission in BOSNIA AND HERZEGOVINA. A compromise of sorts was reached when the UN agreed to a resolution denying the ICC jurisdiction over personnel in UN-established or sponsored peacekeeping operations who are from states that do not belong to the ICC for one year. In lieu of the ICC, the Bush administration announced its intent to protect American peacekeeping personnel by negotiating bilateral agreements with countries that include provisions not to extradite Americans for trial. Bilateral agreements were quickly signed with Romania, Bosnia, AFGHANISTAN, and ISRAEL.

Although it did not explicitly reference the International Criminal Court, the Bush administration touched upon its existence tangentially in its public dealings with Saddam Hussein in the period prior to the IRAQ WAR. At one point it suggested that if Saddam Hussein were to flee into exile the United States would not seek to prosecute him as a war criminal. Later the Bush administration reversed itself.

**Further reading:** Scharf, Michael. *Balkan Justice: The Story behind the First International War Crimes Trial since Nuremberg.* Durham, N.C.: Duke University Press, 1997; Sewell, Sarah, and Carl Keysen, eds. *The United States and the International Criminal Court: National Security and International Law.* Lanham, Md.: Rowman and Littlefield, 2000.

## international crises

International crises are one of the most studied forms of international conflict. They represent an acute departure from standard forms of international interaction and stand as a type of no-man's-land between the normal give-and-take of world politics and the existence of a state of war. Once used almost exclusively in a military context, it is now also commonly found in accounts of international monetary policy, as in the global debt crisis and the ASIAN FINANCIAL CRISIS.

International crises are important to the study of U.S. foreign policy because in the nuclear age, crises have become a substitute for war. Historically, wars served as a way of passing POWER and influence from one state to another, and they were an acceptable way in which foreign-policy objectives were realized. With the arrival of NUCLEAR WEAPONS war can no longer play this role, at least not for the superpowers. In short, policy makers must win conflicts that threaten to lead to war without going to war.

Newspaper and television commentaries tend to attach the label *crisis* to a much wider range of events than most analysts of world politics feel is appropriate. From a decision-making perspective, a crisis occurs when policy makers feel that a major threat exists to the core national interests of their state and that they have little time within which to formulate an effective response. From this perspective an international crisis is a type of competitive bargaining relationship in which the purpose is to triumph through a test of wills. The term *crisis management* is often used to describe this bargaining process.

Policy makers tend to be confident of their ability to manage international crises. Commentators have gone so far as to suggest that crises hold a macabre sense of fascination to policy makers because they are the ultimate moment of truth and provide a true test of their leadership qualities. The ever-present danger that an international crisis might escalate into war can be traced to the inherent uncertainty of crisis situations. Crises are confusing, volatile, and explosive situations in which accurate information is in short supply. Signaling intentions and settling disputes under these conditions is a tricky matter.

Not all crises are alike, and successful crisis management begins with a clear understanding of the nature of the crisis one is facing. We can distinguish between three types of international crises. A justification of hostilities crisis involves a situation in which the initiating side has made a decision to go to war and is simply looking for a pretext to do so. It has no interest in reaching a peaceful settlement of the dispute. Rather, it is trying to fix blame. The spin-off crisis involves a situation in which neither side really desires war. Their primary attentions are elsewhere, on another conflict. This type of crisis creeps up on policy makers in an unexpected fashion and takes on a life of its

own. It often begins with the giving of ultimatums whose consequences are not fully appreciated. Spin-off crises may be the most difficult of all crises to manage. The BRINKSMANSHIP crisis is the most common type. It comes about when one state deliberately employs the threat of force against another in hopes of getting the adversary to back down for fear of having to fight a war. The most important factor in tempting policy makers to initiate such a crisis is the expectation that the international balance of power will soon shift in favor of the adversary, leaving it little time to act. Domestic political problems also seem to contribute to the likelihood of policy makers starting a brinksmanship crisis in two very different ways. They may serve to direct the public's attention away from existing problems and unite the country. Alternatively, policy makers may be too weak to resist pressures for an aggressive foreign-policy line.

All three types of international crises are well represented in the history of U.S. foreign policy. The sinking of the USS *Maine* represents a justification of hostilities crisis because American policy makers were determined to go to war against SPAIN and seized the moment. The SUEZ CRISIS of 1957 is also a justification of hostilities crisis, as GREAT BRITAIN, FRANCE, and ISRAEL conspired to create a situation that demanded action against EGYPT. The series of BERLIN CRISES and the CUBAN MISSILE CRISIS can be seen as brinksmanship crises in which the United States and the Soviet Union (see RUSSIA) each deliberately created situations that could quickly escalate to war if the other did not back down. The KOREAN WAR can be seen as a spin-off crisis, as the United States was focused on stopping Communist aggression in Europe and failed to appreciate the potential significance of successful Communist aggression against SOUTH KOREA. The collapse of YUGOSLAVIA and the outbreak of war in the Balkans also contain elements of a spin-off crisis. The United States was preoccupied with the PERSIAN GULF and was not paying enough attention to the deteriorating situation in southern Europe.

**Further reading:** Lebow, Richard Ned. *Between Peace and War: The Nature of International Crises.* Baltimore: Johns Hopkins University Press, 1981; Snyder, Glenn H., and Paul Diesing. *Conflict among Nations: Bargaining, Decision Making and System Structure in International Crises.* Princeton, N.J.: Princeton University Press, 1977; Winham, Gilbert, ed. *New Issues in International Crisis Management.* Boulder, Colo.: Westview, 1988.

## internationalism

Internationalism is a perspective on world affairs that stresses the importance of involvement in happenings beyond one's borders as a means of realizing and protecting goals. Along with isolationism, it is one of two dominant strains in orienting states to world affairs. While internationalism and ISOLATIONISM compete for influence within American policy-making circles and among the public at large, they are not totally at odds with one another. Both build on the same foundations of LEGALISM, MORAL PRAGMATISM, and UNILATERALISM that lie at the heart of the AMERICAN NATIONAL STYLE.

One of the major research questions in studies of American foreign policy is why oscillation occurs between the two. Common explanations given include the arrival of a new generation of policy makers into office, the failure of current or past policies, fluctuations in the business cycle, and domestic problems. Another frequently studied question is the length of an isolationist-internationalist cycle. One study found that on average these cycles lasted 25 to 30 years and that with each completed cycle the depth of internationalism increases. This analysis suggests that the next isolationist phase should begin around 2014.

Whereas isolationism is a relatively coherent perspective on global involvement, internationalism is characterized by deep philosophical and practical differences. Early in the history of the United States the debate that split internationalists was over what state to ally with. Many saw FRANCE as the natural ally of the United States, but for others it was GREAT BRITAIN. In their foreign-policy outlooks THOMAS JEFFERSON and ALEXANDER HAMILTON typified these two perspectives.

Beginning in the 20th century these disputes took on a more philosophical character as internationalist thought split into two branches. One branch is conservative in outlook. It is associated with REALISM. This version of internationalism sees global involvement as necessary because the INTERNATIONAL SYSTEM is dangerous and threatening to American goals. Only by participating can security be realized. For conservative internationalists global involvement is largely a matter of self-centered military involvement, since others cannot be counted upon to keep their promises or abide by international agreements. A second branch is liberal in outlook. It is associated with IDEALISM. Internationalism is championed here not out of sense of fear but out of a sense of common purpose. The problems that divide states and people are not held to lie in the nature of world politics per se but in flawed policies. When these policies are changed so that reason can prevail and problems, such as poverty, discrimination, and exploitation, can be addressed, security will be realized.

In the first decades of the 20th century HENRY CABOT LODGE (R-Wash.) and WOODROW WILSON came to personify the conservative and idealist positions, respectively. Their key battle was over the LEAGUE OF NATIONS. Conservative internationalism was dominant after WORLD WAR II and provided the conceptual foundation for CONTAIN-MENT. The split reemerged with the VIETNAM WAR, during which some internationalists argued for pursuing a strategy of military victory, whereas other internationalists saw the effort as misguided. In some cases this was based on the assertion that American foreign policy had misinterpreted realist principles, but more often it was based on the charge that only a liberal or idealist foreign policy could solve the types of conditions that gave rise to communist movements around the world.

The two branches of internationalism converged in the first decade of the post–COLD WAR era. Most internationalists now championed both DEMOCRATIZATION and free trade (idealist objectives) and a policy of global military activism that was designed to promote international stability and maintain America's dominant position in world affairs (realist objectives). The danger that united them politically was the specter of resurgent isolationism. By the turn of the 21st century signs of discord were again evident. Liberal internationalists supported PEACEKEEPING and humanitarian undertakings as necessary. Many conservative internationalists opposed them as nothing more than international social work. They advocated policies such as constructing an antiballistic missile system and abstaining from international agreements that would limit American freedom of action, such as banning LAND MINES, signing COMPREHENSIVE NUCLEAR TEST BAN agreements, and establishing of an INTERNATIONAL CRIMINAL COURT. All of these were sought by liberal internationalists.

Further dissension surfaced in the debate over whether to go to war with IRAQ. Disagreements occurred within both liberal and conservative branches of internationalism. Predictably many liberal internationalists were opposed to this action, and many conservative internationalists supported it. However, some adherents of each perspective occupied a middle ground in which the use of force was not ruled out but was held to be premature. Reminiscent of the split among conservative internationalists that occurred during the VIETNAM War, some conservative internationalists argued that realist principles were being misapplied. Some liberal internationalists accepted the need to use force but asserted that it was preferable for the United States to act in concert with other states rather than proceed unilaterally.

**Further reading:** Holsti, Ole R., and James Rosenau. *American Leadership in World Affairs: Vietnam and the Breakdown of Consensus.* New York: Routledge, 1984; Kull, Steven, and I. M. Destler. *Misreading the Public: The Myth of Isolationism.* Washington, D.C.: Brookings, 1999; Nye, Joseph, Jr. *The Paradox of American Power: Why the World's Only Superpower Can't Go It Alone.* New York: Oxford University Press, 2002.

# international law

International law is a force for peace in world politics and a vehicle for organizing international activity. The United States has had an uneasy relationship with international law. Traditional American liberal values place a great deal of emphasis on the rule of law and the ability of individuals and states to settle disputes peacefully. Offsetting this natural affinity for international law are those parts of the AMERICAN NATIONAL STYLE that stress UNILATERALISM and exceptionalism. America's status as a global superpower also contributes to this uneasy relationship. As the preeminent state in the international system, the United States benefits from the status quo and the peaceful settlement of disputes, both of which are furthered by respect for international law. On the other hand, because of its overwhelming POWER international law is often viewed as a real or potential obstruction to the pursuit of American NATIONAL INTEREST.

Thinking about the place of international law in world politics generally revolves around two different intellectual traditions. The older of the two is the natural law position that holds that international law grows out of universal and unchanging principles. The chief task facing policy makers is to determine their content. Originally the focus was on the writings of the Catholic Church; later, these principles were found in the secular world through a process of logical and reasoned inquiry. The second intellectual tradition is positivism. It emerged in the 18th century and holds that international law is made by states and is restricted in scope and time to whatever the states agree upon.

Article 38 of the International Court of Justice recognizes three major sources of international law: international conventions or treaties, international customs, and general principles. From a natural law perspective international customs and general principles, such as diplomatic immunity and sovereignty, are of primary importance in determining the nature of international law. Positivists identify treaties as the most importance source of international law because a treaty is only binding for those states that have signed and ratified the agreement. As of 2002 the UNITED NATIONS (UN) listed more than 2,000 treaties in force worldwide. A 1995 listing of U.S. treaties with CANADA comprises more than 60 categories. The American refusal to sign HUMAN-RIGHTS and ARMS CONTROL agreements has been a reoccurring area of controversy in world politics. More recently the GEORGE W. BUSH administration's decision to withdraw from such high-profile treaties as the KYOTO PROTOCOL and the ANTIBALLISTIC MISSILE TREATY have provoked strong negative reactions from other states as well as treaty supporters in the United States. Concern for protecting American decision-making autonomy, the national interest, and economic interests are the most frequently given rationales for refusing to sign or ratify treaties.

International law confronts challenges other than the decision of states not to participate. An equally significant problem is compliance on the part of those who do pledge their allegiance to international law. The most frequently cited reason for complying with international law is self-interest. If a state expects others to honor its treaty commitments and observe international customs and principles in its dealings with them, then they must do likewise. Noncompliance and violations of international law tend to cluster around situations in which states regard each other with distrust and perceive a real conflict between international law and its core values. Under these circumstances international law will be given lip service or interpreted in an arbitrary manner. Alternatively, when international law involves largely routine matters between states that normally maintain good relations, it then will be of considerable importance in settling the dispute.

The institutional embodiment of international law today is the International Court of Justice (ICJ), known as the World Court. It is a branch of the United Nations and serves multiple purposes. It is the constitutional court for the UN, adjudicates grievances brought by states, and can deliver advisory opinions to the General Assembly or Security Council. Fifteen judges sit on the court and serve nine-year terms. Additional judges are added if a case involves a state or states not having a representative on the court.

One of the greatest weaknesses of the court is that while most states have signed the treaty recognizing its existence only about one-third of those have signed that portion of the treaty that gives the court jurisdiction over disputes. The United States has acted both as a supporter and critic of the court. In the mid-1980s the United States withdrew from this portion of the treaty when NICARAGUA brought suit over U.S. mining of its harbors. Earlier, in 1979 the United States sued IRAN over the seizure of the American EMBASSY in Tehran. Iran denied the court's jurisdiction in that case. In 1992 the United States sought to use the court to force LIBYA to turn over two hijackers wanted in regard to the 1988 terrorist bombing of Pan Am flight 103. The court ruled in favor of the United States and rejected Libya's argument. ECONOMIC SANCTIONS were imposed on Libya by the United Nations, but Libya did not turn over the two suspects to the United States.

The World Court is the successor to the Permanent Court of International Justice that was established under the sponsorship of the LEAGUE OF NATIONS. The United States refused to join the League of Nations and also abstained from participation in the Permanent Court's activities, although prominent American jurists, such as CHARLES EVANS HUGHES, would serve on it. The Senate voted to join the court in 1926 but did so with such severe reservations that the court rejected American membership. In 1935 the Senate rejected a treaty that would have permitted the United States to join the Permanent Court. The United States's unwillingness to participate in the League of Nations or the court did not mean that the United States had no interest in international law as a means of promoting peace. It actively participated in and helped organize a series of naval DISARMAMENT conferences held in Washington and London. It also signed a bilateral agreement with FRANCE, the KELLOGG-BRIAND PACT, in 1928 that outlawed war as a means of settling international disputes.

International law faces a number a challenges today. Each also presents challenges to American foreign policy because they push international legal activity into areas of great domestic political controversy and into substantive issues the United States is not supportive of. Feminist scholars assert that international law as it is traditionally construed is gendered, rendering women and children invisible. This problem is compounded by attempts to protect communal rights that may lead to the systematic exploitation of women within these societies. The South argues that international law is biased because it reflects northern values and interests. It became international law only through colonialism and IMPERIALISM. They too demand that its core values be altered to reflect their concerns with economic exploitation and global political inequality. Finally, many are concerned that international law is becoming irrelevant due to its exclusive focus on states. As individuals and nonstate actors grow in importance in world politics, international law must expand to cover their activities also. From the perspective of American policy makers the most controversial manifestation of this line of thought is the creation of the INTERNATIONAL CRIMINAL COURT (ICC). It is a permanent tribunal with the ability to try individuals for war crimes and crimes against humanity. In the face of great international criticism the United States has opted not to participate in the ICC.

**Further reading:** Falk, Richard, et al., eds. *The United Nations and a Just World Order.* Boulder, Colo.: Westview, 1991; vom Glahn, Gerhard, *Law among Nations.* 7th ed. Boston: Allyn and Bacon, 1996; Higgins, Rosalyn. *Problems and Process: International Law and How We Use It.* Oxford: Oxford University Press, 1994; Joyner, Christopher C. *Governing the Frozen Commons: The Antarctic Regime and Environmental Protection.* Columbia: University of South Carolina Press, 1998.

## International Monetary Fund

The International Monetary Fund (IMF) was created in 1944 as part of the BRETTON WOODS system that was established to provide an international management structure for the global monetary system. The rules of the IMF constituted, in part, a reaction to the floating exchange rate sys-

tem of the interwar period, which many saw as contributing to the severity of the Great Depression. Under the terms of the agreement establishing the IMF, countries were to establish a fixed value for their currency relative to an ounce of gold. For the United States this par value was $35 per ounce of gold. Countries pledged to maintain that exchange rate at plus/minus 1 percent. In cases where this would prove to be impossible, the IMF would step in and provide emergency funding to maintain the solvency of the currency. IMF permission would be needed to implement any change in the exchange rate.

The inability of the IMF and WORLD BANK to cope with the severity of the economic challenge facing Europe led to it being eclipsed by the United States as the manager of global monetary relations. The United States acted unilaterally from about 1947 to 1960 as the dollar replaced gold as the standard for international economic transactions. As U.S. deficits mounted, confidence in the dollar declined, and in the 1960s the United States found it necessary to act in concert with other leading states. One of the most significant innovations of this period was the creation of Standard Drawing Rights (SDRs) that were artificial reserve units, or "paper gold" that could be used to settle accounts among central banks. This marked the first time that states had agreed upon an internationally created and managed asset for organizing international monetary transactions.

The Bretton Woods system came to an end in August 1971 when President RICHARD NIXON announced that the United States was leaving the gold standard and would allow the dollar to float. There then followed a period in which the IMF was no longer a central force in international monetary relations, being replaced by a series of ad hoc crisis-oriented national or regional initiatives to manage monetary problems. This changed with the DEBT CRISIS of the early 1980s and subsequent monetary crises in RUSSIA and Asia. The IMF played a leading role in addressing these problems and now serves as a major vehicle through which the United States seeks to manage international monetary relations. The success of these efforts goes a long way to determining whether the trend toward increased GLOBALIZATION will have positive or negative effects for the United States.

When it was founded in 1944, 44 states joined the IMF. In 1998, there were 182 members. Absent during the COLD WAR, all of the formerly planned economies of Eastern Europe and the former Soviet Union are now members. In joining the IMF a country contributes a quota that is equivalent to a deposit they can draw upon in times of need. Quotas serve three purposes. First, they create a pool of money that the IMF can lend to members in financial need. Second, they determine how much a member can borrow. Third, they establish voting powers. The IMF does not operate on the principle of one country-one vote as does the UNITED NATIONS General Assembly; rather, the IMF has weighted voting, with the weight of a vote determined by the size of one's quota, which is adjusted every five years depending upon a state's level of economic performance. In 1998 the United States had 25,000 votes (18.25 percent). GERMANY and JAPAN had the next largest vote totals, with 5.87 percent of the vote.

The IMF is headed by a Board of Governors that has one representative from each member and an Executive Board that consists of 24 members that represent specific states. It meets at least three times per year and operates on the basis of consensus rather than through formal votes. Supporting the Executive Board is a staff of about 2,600. It is headed by a managing director who is also chair of the Executive Board. In addition to providing funds to member states, the IMF also provides technical expertise and supplies extensive statistical summaries of international economic activity that help countries stay informed about the financial conditions and policies of other countries.

With its renewed visibility in international monetary problem solving efforts, the lending practices of the IMF have come in for criticism. A first area of concern is with the weighted voting system, which gives advanced economies a much stronger voice in IMF decision making than less developed states. The United States and the EUROPEAN UNION combine to control almost 50 percent of the votes. Even within these advanced economies concerns are expressed about who really is in charge. At least one step removed from popular control, citizens in these states also feel that their voices are not being heard by the bureaucrats and bankers who hold key positions in the IMF. A second area of concern is with the conditions the IMF attaches to its loans. The IMF does not simply lend money but requires that in accepting the loan the recipient state makes specified changes in its domestic economic policies. Typically this involves privatizing state enterprises, reducing barriers to foreign investments, and reducing spending on domestic programs in order to balance the budget.

At a more general level, critics argue that this is an unwarranted interference in the domestic affairs of states and that wealthy states often escape such requirements when they need financial aid. A more focused criticism of conditionality asserts that often the cure is inappropriate to the problem. This argument was made in the IMF's handling of the ASIAN FINANCIAL CRISIS when it imposed conditions some said were more suited to the problems facing Latin American states. Third, on a philosophical level critics argue that the IMF is insensitive to questions of social justice as IMF conditions generally favor the economic elite in a country at the expense of the workers and poor.

See also GLOBALIZATION.

**Further reading:** Cohen, Benjamin J. *The Color of Money.* Ithaca, N.Y.: Cornell University Press, 1998; Soros, George. *The Crisis of Global Capitalism.* New York: HarperCollins, 1998; Spiro, David E. *The Hidden Hand of American Hegemony: Petrodollar Recycling and International Markets.* Ithaca, N.Y.: Cornell University Press, 1999.

## international organization

International organization can be thought of as operating at two different levels. At the broadest level, international organization refers to the general process of bringing order out of anarchy in world politics. It is a product of the large-scale transformation in social, economic, and political relations brought about by innovations in technology, communication, and transportation. At a more concrete level, international organization refers to a set of actors in world politics whose members are states. Used in this sense, they are often referred to as intergovernmental organizations (IGOs) to distinguish them from NONGOVERNMENTAL ORGANIZATIONS (NGOs), whose members are private groups and citizens.

International organization is important to American foreign policy at both levels. As a condition of world politics, international organization is a key determining factor to the range of problems that confront the United States and the options available for dealing with them. For example, GLOBALIZATION is an aspect of international organization in the broader sense, and dealing with the benefits and costs of globalization are prominent items on the foreign-policy agenda. Viewed in more concrete terms as actors in world politics, international organizations offer the United States a venue and means for realizing foreign-policy objectives. They also represent potential challengers to American interests. We see this in the WORLD TRADE ORGANIZATION (WTO), which offers the United States a vehicle for guaranteeing a free-trade capitalist international economic order but can also threaten its economic interests by its rulings on international trade disputes.

The growth of IGOs has been dramatic. In 1909 there were only 37 IGOs. By 1960 this number had grown to 154, and by 1993 it had risen to 272. The United States is an active participant in IGOs. The traditional American preference for UNILATERALISM has not been forsaken because of its participation in IGOs. It has protected its interests by the establishment of such voting mechanisms as the veto (in the Security Council of the UNITED NATIONS) and weighted voting (in the INTERNATIONAL MONETARY FUND and WORLD BANK.) In other cases, such as the World Trade Organization, it has included language that allows the United States to leave should it become dissatisfied with its rulings. The United States left the United Nations Educational, Scientific and Cultural Organization (UNESCO) in the mid-1980s over the adoption of what the United States considered to be anti-Israeli policies.

Contemporary IGOs vary greatly along a number of dimensions. Some are formal organizations possessing a well-developed bureaucratic infrastructure. The United Nations (UN), International Monetary Fund (IMF), World Bank, and World Trade Organization are examples. Others are relatively informal organizations. Their bureaucratic presence is minimal, and they become active only when heads of state gather in SUMMIT CONFERENCES or their representatives gather in working groups. The Group of 8 (G-8) is an example. Comprised of CANADA, FRANCE, GERMANY, GREAT BRITAIN, ITALY, JAPAN, RUSSIA, and the United States, it meets periodically to discuss common economic concerns.

IGOs may also be distinguished in terms of the amount of power that the organization holds over its members. Traditionally, IGOs have limited power over member states. States do not give up their sovereignty in joining an IGO. In the final analysis compliance is voluntary. In rare cases IGOs do hold significant power over their members. They can compel members to accept their decisions, and members recognize that they have given up at least some of their sovereignty in joining the IGO. When such power exists the IGO is described as a supranational body. The only IGO of significance that approaches a condition of supranationality is the EUROPEAN UNION (EU). One of the long-standing debates in the study of international organization is whether the European experiment in international organization that has culminated in the EU is a model for other regions or an exception to the rule that states remain dominant over the IGOs they belong to.

Most frequently IGOs are distinguished along two dimensions. The first is the nature of its membership. A distinction is drawn between universal IGOs and limited membership IGOS. The UN is a universal IGO, while the African Union and the Association of South East Asian Nations (ASEAN) are limited IGOs. The second dimension is the nature of the tasks undertaken by the organization. Some IGOS are multiple purpose organizations, while others are more highly focused and limited in their charge. The UN is a universal IGO that has a general mandate. The European Union is a regional multipurpose organization. The NORTH ATLANTIC TREATY ORGANIZATION (NATO) and the ORGANIZATION OF PETROLEUM EXPORTING COUNTRIES (OPEC) are examples of limited membership organizations that have a restricted mandate. The Universal Postal Union is a universal membership organization that was established to carry out a specific task, namely, to set up rules for the efficient operation of international mail services.

International-relations scholars are divided over the role that IGOs play in world politics. For realists, IGOs are secondary actors in world politics to states and serve as instruments of state foreign policy. Their actions and policies reflect the balance of POWER among states that make up their membership. Thus, the IGO's leadership must constantly be on the guard against adopting positions that its most powerful states will not support. Should this happen the IGO runs the risk of becoming marginalized in world politics. Idealists believe that IGOs play an autonomous and significant role in world politics. While many neoidealists conceded that at their creation IGOs are instruments of state foreign policy, they contend that over time IGOs come to be important independent forces for peace, cooperation, and global problem solving. In this view, it is not easy for a member state to ignore or go against an IGO's policy, regardless of how powerful it might be.

Regardless of the perspective adopted, commentators agree that a number of significant challenges face IGOs today. A first problem is "mandate congestion." IGOs are called upon to address an ever-increasing number of problems, even within the same policy area. This can be seen in such diverse areas as PEACEKEEPING, debt bailouts, REFUGEE relief, and environmental protection. In the area of peacekeeping alone, recent calls have been heard for IGO interventions in RWANDA, SOMALIA, BOSNIA, KOSOVO, EAST TIMOR, and AFGHANISTAN. A second and related problem is dissatisfaction with IGO performance. Dependent upon member states for the resources and political will to carry out its missions, which is often not forthcoming, IGOs often fail. This leads to recriminations against the organization and a withdrawal of support. Defenders of IGOs argue that often their failure is "willed" by member states who did not really wish to solve a problem and are simply trying to deflect blame or give the appearance of concerns. The third problem is irrelevance. The changing agenda of world politics requires that IGOs adapt if they are to continue to play an important role. NATO faced this challenge after the end of the COLD WAR. Designed as an instrument of containing and defeating the Soviet Union in a European war, it sought to reinvent itself as a peacekeeping force in Europe. Its performance in Kosovo and Bosnia raised as many questions as it answered about its suitability for this new role. The American response to the SEPTEMBER 11, 2001, attacks further threatened to reduce the importance of NATO. The United States largely ignored it in conducting the war in Afghanistan and the planning for the war against IRAQ.

Neither NATO nor the UN was involved in key decisions involving the IRAQ WAR. NATO was at first ignored by the Bush administration, and, when its participation was sought, France and Germany blocked it. The Bush administration engaged in a long diplomatic struggle at the UN to obtain a resolution supporting its use of force and then proceeded without it. The marginalization of international organizations continued after the war, when the United

States obtained a UN Security Council resolution ending 13 years of ECONOMIC SANCTIONS against Iraq, but the resolution gave the United States great freedom of maneuver in deciding how to use Iraqi OIL revenues.

Together these problems have led to questions about the legitimacy and value of IGOs in solving world problems. This has been especially true for economic- and development-oriented IGOs. One response has been to demand greater openness and transparency in IGO decision making as a means of restoring confidence. Doing so, however, often runs counter to the desire of states to use IGOs as instruments of foreign policy. The result has been public demonstrations, such as those that have accompanied IMF, World Bank, and WTO meetings.

See also IDEALISM; NORTH ATLANTIC TREATY ORGANIZATION; REALISM.

**Further reading:** Diehl, Paul F. *The Politics of Global Governance: International Organization in an Interdependent World.* Boulder, Colo.: Lynn Rienner, 1997; Jacobson, Harold K. *Networks of Interdependence: International Organizations and the Global Political System.* New York: Knopf, 1984; Keohane, Robert O. *After Hegemony: Cooperation and Discord in the World Political Economy.* Princeton, N.J.: Princeton University Press, 1984; Lepgold, Joseph, and Thomas G. Weiss, eds. *Collective Conflict Management and Changing World Politics.* Albany: State University of New York Press, 1998.

## international system

The idea that U.S. foreign policy is stimulated by and is a response to events and forces beyond American borders is central to much theorizing about what U.S. foreign policy can and should be. As a motivating and shaping force of U.S. foreign policy, the international system competes with domestic, bureaucratic, and individual factors. The assumed primacy of international factors over those others in the minds of many Americans is evident in the phrase "politics stops at the water's edge." What has never been clear—or politically uncontested—is the proper response to external forces. Conservative INTERNATIONALISM, liberal internationalism, and ISOLATIONISM have each enjoyed periods of dominance.

The idea of an international system is borrowed from the natural sciences. It indicates that the fate of objects is linked together in patterned ways and that the whole is greater than the sum of its parts. What at first glance may appear to be a series of unrelated events takes on a sense of order and meaning because of the way the international system operates. Not everything is part of a system. One of the most important characteristics of systems is that they have boundaries. Those elements inside the system interact with one another with greater frequency and consequence than they interact with elements outside the system. Until comparatively recently we talked of regional international systems, the European system, or the Latin American system, because military, transportation, and communication technologies did not permit the construction of a global international system.

The adoption of a system perspective leaves open the question of what aspect of a system to focus on in charting its influence. In addition to identifying its boundaries and their permeability other possible focal points include the identity and composition of the key actors, the nature of the patterns that exist and the rules that govern them, and the structure of the system. This last focal point directs our attention to the distribution of POWER in the international system. It is the most frequently used starting point in international systems analysis and is the origin of some of the most enduring concepts in the study of U.S. foreign policy. When power is concentrated in one actor we speak of a UNIPOLAR SYSTEM; when it is concentrated in two relatively equal power centers we speak of bipolarity; and when there exist five or more power centers of relatively equal size we characterize the international system as a MULTIPOLAR system.

International systems are not frozen in place for all time. They are dynamic structures that can become unstable or undergo a fundamental transformation as pressures and shocks build up. The COLD WAR was a BIPOLAR system with two relatively equal power centers in the United States and the Soviet Union (see RUSSIA). At the end of the cold war scholars and policy makers debated whether a unipolar or bipolar system was being created. A decade removed from the cold war, the terms of the debate shifted. It was generally acknowledged that a unipolar system was in place, at least militarily, with the United States at the top of the power structure. Two questions now emerged. First, what was the relationship between a unipolar military world and a multipolar economic one? Second, how long could unipolarity last? Some believed it would endure for a long period of time, while others asserted it would quickly pass.

It has been suggested that we can think of the process of system change as being similar to the geological processes that produce earthquakes. Over time a series of pressures build up in the international system just as pressures build along the series of tectonic plates that lie beneath the Earth's crust. Most of the time the effect of these pressures is so slight we do not sense them. However, on occasion the cumulative effect of these pressures is to unleash forces that the international system cannot contain or dissipate. The most momentous system shock is war because it holds the potential to transfer power between rival actors. The close association between war, instability, and system failure is one reason why the peaceful end of the cold war caught so many observers by surprise and is so intensely studied.

Putting the two aspects of the global international system that we have discussed together, structure and system change, allows us to organize those aspects that are of greatest potential consequence for U.S. foreign policy under three headings. First, there are structural constants. The international system is decentralized. There are no central institutions to make or enforce laws. Decentralization does not mean the international system operates in a state of anarchy. Rather, states exist in a competitive atmosphere in which there is an expectation of violence that is tempered by the emergence of a common set of rules that promote predictability and reciprocity. Second, the international system is a self-help system. States must rely on themselves only to accomplish their foreign-policy objectives. To do otherwise runs the risk of manipulation by others or betrayal. The self-help principle challenges policy makers to bring goals and resources into balance. The inability of the United States to do so has been termed the LIPPMAN GAP. Finally, the international system is stratified. By definition it is made up of unequal powers, some of which are better positioned to realize their foreign-policy goals than others. Two key areas of disagreement among post-VIETNAM administrations have been over the degree of inequality that exits in the international system and the identity of the principal challenger to the United States.

Sitting atop these three structural constants are four post–WORLD WAR II trends that have helped transform the international system in an evolutionary rather than revolutionary fashion. The first is a diffusion of power. Power is still distributed unequally, but the shape of the pyramid is changing. Foreign-policy failures are becoming more frequent as the ability of lesser states in the international system to challenge or passively resist great power initiatives has increased. A second trend is issue proliferation. The foreign-policy agenda has become crowded as issues once considered domestic in nature are now partly contested in the international system. These are sometimes referred to as "intermestic issues." A third trend is actor proliferation. States are no longer the only important actors in world politics. INTERNATIONAL ORGANIZATIONS, NONGOVERNMENTAL ORGANIZATIONS, individuals, and groups now play prominent roles in many areas. The result of these two just-mentioned trends is to greatly complicate the patterned interactions states are involved in and the amount of power resources they must direct at problems. The fourth trend is regional diversity. The cold war imposed an overarching logic on U.S.-Soviet interactions. But even before the cold war ended it had become clear that relations in the various regional subsystems could not be managed the same way. A formal and permanent body, the NORTH ATLANTIC TREATY ORGANIZATION (NATO), was an excellent tool for managing relations in Europe, but it did not fit with the realities existing in Asia or the Middle East.

Finally, it is possible to identify some emerging characteristics of the post–cold war era that hold the potential for sparking further transformations in the international system. Numbered among them are the GLOBALIZATION of the international economy, proliferation of WEAPONS OF MASS DESTRUCTION, emergence of forms of power, ethnicization of world politics, advances in communications technologies, spread of democracy, and emergence of new ideas.

See also DEMOCRATIZATION; IMPERIALISM.

**Further reading:** Baldwin, David A., ed. *Neorealism and Neoliberalism: The Contemporary Debate.* New York: Columbia University Press, 1993; Rosecrance, Richard. *Action and Reaction in World Politics.* Boston: Little, Brown, 1963; Russett, Bruce, and John Oneal. *Triangulating Peace: Democracy, Interdependence, and International Organization.* New York: Norton, 2001; Waltz, Kenneth. *Man, the State and War.* New York: Columbia University Press, 1954.

## International Trade Organization

The International Trade Organization (ITO) represented the first post–WORLD WAR II attempt by the United States to organize the international trading system. The Havana Charter agreement establishing the ITO was not ratified by CONGRESS. As a result the GENERAL AGREEMENT ON TARIFFS AND TRADE (GATT) that had been intended to serve as a bridge organization until the ITO was established came to serve as the permanent mechanism for managing post–World War II global trade relations.

During World War II the United States secured an agreement from its allies to construct a more open postwar international trade system. Discussions began in 1943, and in 1945 the United States presented a plan for a multilateral agreement to this end. Final discussions took place in 1947. As it emerged from these deliberations the Havana Charter reflected the belief that a successful postwar trading system required detailed provisions regarding trade practices rather than simply a listing of broad principles and the belief that the charter needed to be part of a broader program designed to promote social stability. The ITO was to have a permanent secretariat, with power residing in a conference of all members. It was to operate within the framework of the United Nations and be open to all its members.

When President HARRY TRUMAN submitted the Havana Charter to Congress for ratification in 1949 he did so by asking for a joint resolution authorizing U.S. participation. Membership in the ITO was opposed by two very different sets of political forces. Protectionists opposed it because they feared the ITO could force the United States to adopt trade policies that would injure American firms. Free traders opposed it because in their view the ITO retained too many trade restrictions. Truman urged Congress to support the ITO in his January 1950 State of the Union address, calling it "an essential step forward in our foreign policy." Opposition continued, and in December his administration announced that the ITO charter would not be resubmitted to Congress for ratification. Instead, the Truman administration indicated that it would shift its attention to GATT as the primary means of organizing international trade. Unlike the Havana Charter, the GATT framework did not include references to economic development goals, commodity agreements, restrictive business practices, or trade in services. All of these would become major items for negotiation in future GATT trade talks.

## Iran

Iran has an area of 636,294 square miles, making it approximately the size of Alaska. It has a population of 66 million people. Known as Persia until 1935, Iran has a long history. The first dynasty ruled Iran from 559 B.C. to 330 B.C.

Modern Iranian history is generally dated to the turn of the 20th century. In 1905 there was a nationalist uprising against the shah, in 1906 a limited constitution was put in place, and in 1908 OIL was discovered. In 1921 Reza Khan, a military officer, seized power, and in 1925 he established himself as shah, thereby founding the Pahlavi dynasty that was to rule Iran almost continuously until 1979.

Iran's strategic location and the discovery of oil there made it the object of competition between GREAT BRITAIN and RUSSIA. A 1907 agreement between these two imperial powers divided Iran into spheres of influence. During WORLD WAR I it was occupied by the armed forces of both states. After the war Iran entered into a trade agreement with Great Britain that the latter hoped to use as a vehicle for domination. Two years later, in 1921, Iran signed a treaty with the Soviet Union in which czarist imperial designs on Iran were formally abandoned.

Iran again became an object of international competition during WORLD WAR II. Two months after GERMANY invaded the Soviet Union, in August 1941, British and Soviet troops entered Iran in order to prevent its oil from falling into Nazi hands. The following month the shah abdicated in favor of his son, Mohammad Reza Pahlavi. After the United States entered World War II, American soldiers were sent to Iran to handle supply operations. By 1944, approximately 30,000 U.S. troops were there. The United States also supplied Iran with $8.5 million in LEND-LEASE aid.

Iran's post–World War II independence and territorial integrity were agreed to by the Allies at the TEHRAN CONFERENCE of 1943. Events soon moved in the opposite direction. Unhappy with Iran's refusal to grant it oil concessions, the Soviet Union organized pro-Soviet independence movements in Iran that led to the establishment of the People's Republic of Azerbaijan and the Kurdish People's Republic in December 1945. Moscow followed this up by refusing to pull its troops out as scheduled in January 1946. With the backing of the British and Americans, Iran took its case to the UNITED NATIONS Security Council. In March 1946 Iran and the Soviet Union reached an agreement resolving their differences. The Soviet Union would withdraw its troops and receive the desired oil concession. Once Soviet troops left in May, the Iranian government sent its forces into the breakaway regions and reestablished its control over them. Soon thereafter the Iranian legislature rejected the agreement, thus denying the Soviet Union access to oil.

The heightened sense of COLD WAR competition with the Soviet Union that came to drive U.S. foreign policy in the late 1940s and early 1950s led American foreign-policy makers to define Iran as key to its strategy of CONTAINMENT. To this end it continued and extended military training missions established during World War II and sought to counter growing domestic unrest with the shah's rule. The key opposition figure was Mohammad Mossadegh, who advocated political democratization and the nationalization of the oil industry controlled by Great Britain. Mossadegh accomplished the latter goal when the shah gave in to rising domestic political pressure and appointed him prime minister in 1951. Great Britain countered this move by instituting a worldwide boycott of Iranian oil. Mossadegh would remain the central figure in Iranian politics until he was overthrown in August 1953.

The coup itself was organized by the CENTRAL INTELLIGENCE AGENCY (CIA) working in cooperation with the British. It quickly became one of the CIA's most heralded success stories and helped build its reputation as an effective instrument of American cold war foreign policy. In truth, Mossadegh fell easily. The CIA precipitated the crisis by having the shah dismiss Mossadegh and flee the country. It then organized anti-Mossadegh street demonstrations and convinced pro-shah military commanders to seize the local radio station and challenge Mossadegh. The shah then returned triumphant, supported by continued CIA operations against opposition forces and an infusion of some $70 million in U.S. emergency aid.

From that point until his overthrow in 1979 the shah maintained close relations with the United States. In 1955 Iran joined the Baghdad Pact that was part of the U.S. circle of ALLIANCES containing Soviet expansion. Working with the CIA the shah established a new intelligence agency, the SAVAK. During the RICHARD NIXON's administration Iran became one of the main regional pillars that the United States hoped to develop into surrogate powers that would be relied upon to perpetuate the regional status quo. To perform this task Iran needed an infusion of modern weapons; over the course of the 1970s, it became a primary recipient of U.S. ARMS TRANSFERS.

The shah's initial request for F-14s and F-15s in 1971–72 was met with resistance in the DEFENSE DEPARTMENT. There was no precedent for providing such sophisticated weapons to a Third World ally. The impasse was broken when President Nixon and his NATIONAL SECURITY ADVISOR HENRY KISSINGER went to Tehran in May 1972 and met with the shah, who was assured in a secret agreement that he was free to order weapons as he wished. Within one month of that meeting the shah ordered 80 F-14s at a total cost of $2 billion. Iranian weapons orders jumped from $500 million in 1972 to $2.2 billion in 1973 and $4.3 billion in 1974. Between 1970 and 1978 a total of $20 billion in arms purchases would be made. In actuality, only about $8 billion worth of American weapons were delivered to Iran. This is because many of the weapons were not to be delivered until the early 1980s, and the post-shah Iranian regime cancelled these purchases.

Beneath the surface, however, not all was well with the U.S.-Iranian relationship. In the late 1950s some in the United States raised voices of concern that the shah's harsh rule threatened to undermine his base of support. After a brief period of liberalization that did bring into the open opposition forces, the shah cracked down, using the SAVAK as an instrument of repression. When JIMMY CARTER

After being forced to flee to Rome, Mohammad Reza Pahlavi, shah of Iran, authorizes a new government for his country. *(Hulton/Archive)*

became PRESIDENT he gave new expression to these old doubts and urged the shah to improve Iran's HUMAN-RIGHTS record. Carter also threatened to reduce American arms sales. The Carter administration's follow-through in both areas was limited and inconsistent, but the net result was to add an element of uncertainty and controversy to the U.S-Iranian relationship.

The beginning of the end of the shah's rule came in 1978 when the exiled Ayatollah Ruhollah Khomeini called for his ouster. Khomeini was at the center of a conservative religion-based protest movement that the shah tried and failed to suppress. The Carter administration responded to the shah's sinking fortunes with expressions of support. Inside the administration a split existed between the Tehran EMBASSY staff, who doubted that the shah could long survive, and analysts in the STATE DEPARTMENT and CIA who were convinced that he could weather the storm. This Washington-based coalition of pro-shah supporters splintered by the end of 1978, with National Security Advisor Zbigniew Brzezinski continuing to take a hard-line pro-shah position and SECRETARY OF STATE CYRUS VANCE seeking an accommodation with moderate opposition forces. By now, however, a workable agreement with these forces was no longer tenable, and the shah fled Iran for EGYPT on January 16, 1979. Khomeini returned to Iran from FRANCE on February 1 and quickly established a new government.

U.S-Iranian relations took a dramatic turn for the worse later that year. Citing the need for medical treatment, supporters of the shah, including Henry Kissinger, urged the Carter administration to allow the shah entry into the United States. In October a reluctant Carter agreed. The response in Iran was intense and swift. Four days later, on November 4, militants seized the U.S. embassy and took 52 Americans hostage. Neither the imposition of ECONOMIC SANCTIONS nor efforts at quiet DIPLOMACY were able to secure their release. The shah's departure from the United States for Panama in December 1979 also had no impact on the hostage situation. On April 24, 1980, shortly after breaking diplomatic relations with Iran, the United States attempted to rescue the hostages through a military operation. The rescue effort ended in failure before it could reach Tehran. In addition to the military failure there was also political fallout. Vance resigned as secretary of state in protest at the mission having been undertaken. The hostages would not be released until January 20, 1981, 30 minutes after RONALD REAGAN was inaugurated president.

By the time the hostages were released Iran was at war with IRAQ. Begun on September 22, 1980, when Iraq invaded Iran, the war continued for eight years, producing an estimated 500,000 to 1,000,000 casualties. The Reagan administration's foreign policy to Iran during this conflict operated on two contradictory levels. Officially the United States was hostile to Iran and adopted policies that demonstrated support for Iraq. It provided Iraq with agricultural credits and permitted the sale of defense-related equipment. The CIA also provided financial support for exiled opposition Iranian forces and made contact with Iranian military officials. In 1987 the United States responded to Iranian and Iraqi attacks on ships in the Persian Gulf by placing Kuwaiti oil tankers under the American flag. Nearly 50 U.S. warships would be stationed in the region to protect these commercial vessels. Because KUWAIT was a financial supporter of Iraq and little was done to prevent Iraq from attacking Iranian tankers, Iran saw this as an unfriendly act. Tensions rose to perhaps their highest levels near the end of the war when in July 1988 the USS *Vincennes* accidentally shot down an Iranian commercial airplane, killing 290 passengers.

Beneath the surface a very different policy had been advanced for part of this time. Officials in the Reagan administration led by NATIONAL SECURITY COUNCIL staffer Lieutenant Colonel Oliver North promoted a plan that would solve two vexing problems: obtaining funding for the contras in NICARAGUA and securing the release of American hostages held in LEBANON. Funding for the contras was blocked by congressional action. Iran was thought to have influence with the hostage takers since Iranian Revolutionary Guards had trained and supplied GUERRILLA groups there. The plan put forward in secret was to sell Iran sophisticated TOW antiaircraft missiles. In return they were to secure the release of the American hostages, and the money derived from the sale would be used to finance the contras. In November 1986 word of the plan was published in a Lebanese newspaper. This news put an end to the initiative and embroiled the Reagan administration in a political controversy that became known as the IRAN-CONTRA affair.

Relations with Iran improved during the GEORGE H. W. BUSH administration. The United States offered to pay damages to the families of the airline passengers who died. It entered into negotiations with Iran that led to an agreement whereby the United States would release $567 million in Iranian assets that had been frozen in U.S. banks by Carter. For its part Iran helped secure the release of the remaining hostages. Iran also adopted a relatively supportive position in the PERSIAN GULF WAR. While it condemned the United States for using force against Iraq, it did nothing to undermine the international economic sanctions against Iraq that the United States helped put in place.

By the end of the Bush administration relations with Iran began to deteriorate. With the COLD WAR over and the Soviet Union falling apart, attention now focused on regional balances of power rather than global ones. From the American perspective the reality in the Middle East was that Iran's military buildup, its attempt to obtain a nuclear capability, and its support for TERRORISM made it as much of a threat as Iraq. In the Clinton administration this outlook

formed the foundation for the policy of DUAL CONTAINMENT in which the United States sought to isolate both states rather than joining with one against the other.

The GEORGE W. BUSH administration has continued this policy of opposition to Iran. In his 2002 State of the Union address Bush identified Iran as part of an axis of evil that threatened international peace and stability. Iraq and NORTH KOREA were the other two members. In particular the Bush administration objected to the following aspects of Iran's foreign policy: (1) its efforts to obtain nuclear weapons, (2) its involvement in international terrorism, (3) its violent opposition to a Middle East peace accord, (4) its subversive regional policies, and (5) its HUMAN-RIGHTS record. American-Iranian relations took a noticeable downward turn during the Iraq War. Iran publicly proclaimed that it had the right to obtain nuclear weapons, and the United States publicly warned it against involvement in the war on the side of Saddam Hussein. Relations continued to deteriorate after the war. The United States first objected to what it saw as Iran's attempt to influence the post-Iraqi political order by manipulating the Shi'ite population. It then accused Iran of aiding the AL-QAEDA terrorists that attacked Western business and residential interests in Saudi Arabia in May 2003 and of having a nuclear weapons program. This led to press reports that the Bush administration was contemplating breaking diplomatic relations with Iran and embarking on plans to destabilize and bring down the Iranian government.

See also ARAB-ISRAELI CONFLICT.

**Further reading:** Amuzegar, Jahangir. *Dynamics of the Iranian Revolution: The Pahlavi's Triumph and Tragedy.* Albany: State University of New York Press, 1991; Bill, James. *The Eagle and the Lion: The Tragedy of American-Iranian Relations.* New Haven, Conn.: Yale University Press, 1988; Cottam, Richard. *Iran and the United States: A Cold War Case Study.* Pittsburgh: University of Pittsburgh Press; Sick, Gary. *All Fall Down: America's Tragic Encounter with Iran.* New York: Penguin, 1985.

## Iran-contra initiative

The Iran-contra initiative by the Reagan administration is significant because it represented the culmination of that administration's efforts to provide funding to the contras in NICARAGUA. It raised serious questions about the control and direction of foreign policy in the Reagan administration and, in the eyes of many, troubling issues involving constitutional questions about the abuse of POWER.

As best determined by the TOWER COMMISSION, which was established to investigate the matter, events unfolded in the following fashion. In early 1984 members of the NATIONAL SECURITY COUNCIL (NSC) staff became concerned about the future of U.S. relations with post-

Khomeini IRAN. Although it was objected to by both SECRE-TARY OF STATE George Shultz and SECRETARY OF DEFENSE Casper Weinberger, ARMS TRANSFERS to Iran as a means of cementing better relations became a permanent agenda item. Soon, however, the focus of these discussions changed to one in which arms transfers to Iran were seen as a vehicle for securing the release of American hostages in LEBANON.

It was the conclusion of the Tower Commission that in August 1984 President RONALD REAGAN authorized the shipment of weapons to ISRAEL, which, in turn, delivered U.S.-made weapons in their possession to Iran. Israeli arms shipments to Iran took place in August and September 1985. On September 15, 1985, the Reverend Benjamin Weir was released by his Lebanese kidnappers.

In the following months NSC staffer Lieutenant Colonel Oliver North and NATIONAL SECURITY ADVISOR John Poindexter began playing a much more active role. In January 1986 a presidential finding was signed allowing the Central Intelligence Agency (CIA) to purchase TOW missiles from the Defense Department and arrange for their transfer to Iran. Arms transfers were conducted in February, May, August, and October 1986. The Iran initiative ended with a failed mission to Iran by National Security Advisor Robert McFarlane. It secured neither the release of the hostages nor improved U.S.-Iranian relations. A total of 1,508 TOW missiles had been sold to Iran.

The amount charged to Iran was in excess of the cost paid by the CIA, with the balance placed in a Swiss bank account under the control of Richard Secord, a retired CIA agent. Evidence gathered by the Tower Commission strongly suggested that this money was used to support the contras in Nicaragua in their struggle against the U.S.–opposed Sandinista government. Such funding, while consistent with the Reagan administration's support for the contras, was in violation of congressional statutes. In October 1984 CONGRESS passed the Boland Amendment that cut off all U.S. funding for the contras unless specifically authorized by Congress. The fiscal year 1985 Defense Department appropriations legislation prohibited the CIA, Defense Department, or any "entity of the U.S. involved in INTELLIGENCE activities" from directly or indirectly supporting paramilitary operations in Nicaragua.

The Reagan administration did not consider the NSC to be covered by this prohibition. As early as September 1984 North began securing support for the contras from private U.S. sources, such as Secord. The Tower Commission concluded that the NSC staff involvement in supporting the contras set the stage for its subsequent link to the Iranian arms sales, but it was unclear whether North sought or received formal authority from his superiors to conduct the diversion of funds. Throughout the Iran-contra initiative NSC personnel failed to inform Congress about the nature or extent of their activities.

The Tower Commission concluded that Reagan's strong personal interest in securing the release of the hostages plus his hands-off management style were major contributing factors to the Iran-contra initiative. It also concluded that the NSC staff and presidential advisers had failed to use the NSC system properly and that excessive secrecy had surrounded the decision-making process.

During the summer of 1987 a joint Senate-House Committee heard 250 hours of testimony from 29 witnesses in an effort to sort out the details of the Iran-contra initiative. Poindexter indicated 184 times that he could not remember an event or conversation. The investigation ended without any formal congressional action being taken against President Reagan.

**Further reading:** Draper, Theodore. *A Very Thin Line: The Iran-Contra Affair.* New York: Hill and Wang, 1991.

## Iranian hostage crisis

The Iranian hostage crisis spanned 444 days between November 4, 1979, and January 20, 1981. Fifty-two American hostages were taken captive by Iranian students. President JIMMY CARTER struggled unsuccessfully to secure their release, and the Iranian hostage crisis became a symbol of the precipitous decline of American global POWER and influence. It became a political albatross around his head and helped ensured his defeat by RONALD REAGAN. Finally, along with the 1979 Soviet invasion of AFGHANISTAN, the Iranian hostage crisis called into question the wisdom and practicality of the HUMAN-RIGHTS agenda advanced by Carter. Reagan's election signaled a return to a more traditionalist foreign-policy agenda, with its emphasis on providing national security through military power.

The origins of the Iranian hostage crisis lay with U.S. COLD WAR support for the government of Shah Mohammad Reza Pahlavi. Forced out of power by a nationalist uprising led by Mohammad Mossadegh in 1953, he was returned to power as a result of a CIA-sponsored COVERT ACTION. The shah became a strong U.S. ally against the Soviet Union (see RUSSIA), but over time his rule came under severe attack from dissident elements in Iran who objected to the westernization of Iranian society. Economic problems, ethnic unrest, and a brutal secret police force further contributed to growing anti-shah sentiment.

Carter visited IRAN in 1977 and publicly supported the shah, referring to Iran as "an island of stability" and congratulating him for earning the "admiration and love" of the Iranian people. One year later riots and demonstrations broke out. The shah responded by declaring martial law. Carter urged the shah to remain firm, but continued unrest forced him to flee to EGYPT on January 16, 1979, after appointing a new government. On October 22 the shah was

An American hostage being paraded before cameras by his Iranian captors *(Hulton/Archive)*

admitted to the United States for medical treatment. The decision to admit the shah was controversial, with former SECRETARY OF STATE HENRY KISSINGER arguing for it. Those opposed cited the potential inflammatory effect it would have in Iran. On November 4, students stormed the EMBASSY and took the Americans hostage.

The Carter administration was undecided on how to respond. NATIONAL SECURITY ADVISOR Zbigniew Brzezinski urged retaliatory military action. SECRETARY OF STATE CYRUS VANCE urged a diplomatic response. Carter responded by freezing Iranian assets in the United States and imposed economic sanctions. He also tried to negotiate through intermediaries to gain the release of the hostages. Stymied by the lack of progress and fearing for the well-being of the hostages, on April 7, 1980, Carter ordered a rescue mission. On April 24, eight helicopters took off from the USS *Nimitz* in the Arabian Sea and six C-130 Hercules transports took off from Egypt to carry out the rescue mission. The mission was cancelled when three of the helicopters were lost in a sand storm. In the course of abandoning the mission a helicopter and C-130 collided, killing eight crew members. Vance, who had not been

involved in the initial decision to conduct a rescue effort, resigned in protest over his exclusion from the decision-making process.

Carter's indecision on how to proceed became an important ingredient in the domestic politics of the Iranian hostage crisis. So too was the media coverage of the crisis. Nightly news telecasts prominently displayed the number of days the hostages were held in captivity and routinely carried pictures of anti-American protests and demonstrations in Iran.

A number of factors came together to resolve the crisis. First, beginning in 1980, Iran became locked in a war with IRAQ. Carter's freezing of Iranian assets in the United States, estimated to be worth about $8 billion, now began to take its toll. Iran needed these funds for its war effort. Second, the shah died in Egypt in July 1980, thereby removing an important political symbol from the conflict. Third, Khomeini's religious clerics had taken control of the Iranian parliament and no longer needed the hostages to promote their political agenda. Finally, Carter had been defeated in his bid for reelection. The hostages were released 30 minutes after Reagan was inaugurated.

## Iran-Iraq War

The Iran-Iraq War lasted almost a decade (1980–88). It is significant for American foreign policy in that the war directly involved the United States in Persian Gulf politics in a manner different from what had ever occurred before. Prior to the war the U.S. involvement was largely restricted to providing military and economic aid to bolster pro-American regimes. Here the United States took on an active military role. In doing so the Reagan administration raised questions about the constitutionality of its actions under the WAR POWERS RESOLUTION.

Saddam Hussein took POWER in IRAQ in 1979 and quickly moved to secure his power domestically through political purges and repression. In September 1980 Saddam directed his energies and ambitions beyond Iraq's borders by launching an attack on IRAN. Several issues came together in this decision. One of the most important was the uncertain status of the balance of power in the Persian Gulf. The United States had promoted both Iran and Iraq as regional powers during the COLD WAR, but Iran's power had been seriously weakened by the fall of the shah and ascent to power of Islamic fundamentalist forces. Perceptions of Iranian weakness made it a tempting target. Religion also played a role. Shi'ite Muslims dominated the political scene in Iran. They believed that there were intermediaries (the ayatollahs) between the people and Allah. Iraq was ruled by Sunni Muslims who believed that each individual had a direct personal relationship with Allah. Finally, some have suggested that personality also played a role. The Ayatollah Khomeini, who would take power in Iran after the downfall of the shah, had been forced out of his 13-year exile in Iraq when Saddam came to power. For his part Saddam sought to establish himself as the political-military leader of the Arab world, a position that fell largely vacant following the death of Egyptian president Anwar Sadat.

Saddam Hussein anticipated a short war. But the war soon took on the characteristics of WORLD WAR I, as neither side could achieve victory, and the war settled down into one of attrition. Eight years of fighting left borders virtually unchanged. Iran mounted human-wave attacks against Iraqi positions and used teenage boys to clear battlefields of LAND MINES. Iraq engaged in chemical-biological warfare.

In 1987 the United States became actively involved in the war when U.S. naval vessels began to patrol the Persian Gulf. Of particular concern to the United States was maintaining the free flow of OIL out of the region and into world markets. As part of this strategy the United States decided to reflag Kuwaiti oil tankers, in essence making them American vessels and giving them the protection of the U.S. Navy. The U.S. Navy became involved in a series of isolated military confrontations. In 1987 an Iraqi aircraft accidentally hit the USS *Stark* with a missile, killing 37 sailors. In July 1988 the USS *Vincennes* shot down an Iranian civilian airliner, killing 290 people.

CONGRESS debated the legality of President RONALD REAGAN's decision to use force in the Persian Gulf in the summer of 1987 but took no action. For its part, the Reagan administration held the War Powers Resolution to be unconstitutional. The House voted down by a 283-186 vote a motion to forbid the reflagging of the Kuwaiti tankers. It then passed a resolution delaying consideration of the measure for three months. A similar move in the Senate failed due to a Republican filibuster. Republicans also successfully filibustered an amendment to a defense authorization act that would have permitted reflagging under the time limits of the War Powers Resolution but did not mention it by name. A joint resolution was then introduced into the Senate to start the 60-day clock of the War Powers Resolution. It too failed. Some members of Congress then unsuccessfully brought suit in the court system against President Reagan for his use of military force in the Iran-Iraq War. The courts refused to act on the case.

The war ended in July 1988 when Ayatollah Khomeini endorsed a proposed cease-fire, and Saddam Hussein followed suit.

**Further reading:** Bakhash, Shaul. *The Reign of the Ayatollahs.* New York: Basic Books, 1984; Jentleson, Bruce W. *With Friends Like These: Reagan, Bush, and Saddam.* New York: Norton, 1994.

## Iraq

Iraq is about the size of California, with an area of 437,000 square miles and a population of 24 million people. Known historically as Mesopotamia, Iraq was conquered in the seventh century by Muslims. In the 16th century the region fell under the control of the Ottoman Empire, and in the 19th century it was formally incorporated into it. British forces invaded Iraq during WORLD WAR I. After the war Iraq became a British mandate under the LEAGUE OF NATIONS. In 1924 over the objection of nationalist political forces, Iraq signed a treaty with GREAT BRITAIN, giving the British military bases and the right to veto Iraqi legislation. In 1930 the British mandate was terminated, and in 1932 Iraq joined the League of Nations as a fully sovereign state.

After WORLD WAR II Iraq became a staunch opponent of ISRAEL. This did not prevent Iraq and the United States from enjoying good relations for most of the 1950s. The United States supplied Iraq with technical and military aid in the mid-1950s, and in 1955 Iraq became a key participant in the American effort to contain communist expansion through its membership in the Baghdad Pact. At this time Iraqi-Soviet relations were strained due to Soviet support of Kurdish nationalists within Iraq. A coup in July 1958 removed Iraq's pro-Western monarchy from power. The new government led by General Abdul Karim Qassim aligned itself with the Soviet Union and in 1959 Iraq withdrew from the Baghdad Pact. The organization's headquarters moved to TURKEY, and it was rechristened the CENTRAL TREATY ORGANIZATION (CENTO). Qassim was overthrown in a 1963 coup that some link to the CENTRAL INTELLIGENCE AGENCY (CIA). With this change in government, relations with the United States improved again, but they would soon turn sour. The crushing Arab defeat in the 1967 Arab-Israeli war caused the Iraqi government to break diplomatic relations with the United States. A 1968 coup would produce another pro-Soviet government, and in 1972 Iraq became the first Arab state to sign a treaty of friendship with the Soviet Union. At that point the United States became an ardent backer of IRAN.

Dramatic changes to American relations with Persian Gulf states occurred in 1979 and 1980. In Iran, the shah fell and was replaced by Islamic nationalists who were hostile to the United States. That same year Saddam Hussein took power in Iraq following yet another coup. In November 1980 Iranian militants seized control of the American EMBASSY in Tehran and took 52 Americans hostage, locking the United States and Iran into a period of confrontation and hostility. Seeking to take advantage of the internal political strife in Iran, establish Iraq as a dominant regional power, and redress long-standing territorial grievances, Saddam Hussein started a war with Iran in 1980. The expected quick victory did not materialize, and the two sides became locked into an eight-year stalemate that inflicted massive casualties on both sides.

During the IRAN-IRAQ WAR the United States tilted toward support for Iraq. In 1982 it dropped Iraq from the list of countries that supported international TERRORISM, opening the way for FOREIGN AID. The United States provided Iraq with previously denied dual-use technologies and shared intelligence on Iran with it. In 1987 the United States reflagged Kuwaiti oil tankers in the Persian Gulf. By placing them under the American flag the United States was guaranteeing their security. This was important to Iraq since Kuwait was a major source of financial aid in Saddam Hussein's war effort. For its part, Iraq dropped its opposition to an Arab-Israeli peace agreement and did not reject a plan proposed by President RONALD REAGAN in September 1982. In 1984 diplomatic relations between the United States and Iraq were resumed after a 17-year hiatus.

The Iran-Iraq War ended in 1988. Iraq emerged from it with its economy in shambles, huge debts, a Kurdish rebellion in the north, and with the region's largest military establishment. The end of the war did not bring a return to peace in regional politics. Iraq began pressing Arab and Western states to forgive its war debts. At an

ORGANIZATION OF PETROLEUM EXPORTING COUNTRIES (OPEC) meeting Hussein called for oil states to reduce their production so that the price of oil would go up, something Iraq desperately needed. KUWAIT was singled out for special criticism. Saddam Hussein also called for the United States to end its military presence in the region and objected to Voice of America broadcasts that implied Iraq was a police state. It was not long before Saddam Hussein's rising rhetoric was matched by action. In July 1990 Iraq's Republican Guard began moving toward the Kuwaiti border. The Bush administration concluded that the purpose of these maneuvers was intimidation rather than a prelude to war. Administration officials in meetings with Saddam Hussein and in testimony before the CONGRESS stated the U.S. position: It would not countenance violence or war in the region, and it would protect its vital interests and those of its allies, but it had no position on Arab-Arab disputes, such as that between Iraq and Kuwait.

On August 2, Iraqi forces invaded Kuwait. The United States responded by freezing all Iraqi and Kuwaiti assets in the United States. Its immediate concern was the security of Saudi Arabia and its vast oil reserves, and the Bush administration pressured the Saudis to allow American troops to be stationed there as a deterrent force. The same day Iraq invaded Kuwait, the UNITED NATIONS condemned the act. On August 6, it passed Resolution 662 that imposed mandatory economic sanctions on Iraq in an effort to compel it to withdraw from Kuwait. Only food and medicine "in humanitarian circumstances" were exempted. On November 29, Resolution 678 established January 15 as the date for this withdrawal and authorized member states to "use all means necessary" to bring this about if Iraq did not voluntarily leave by that date. On January 16, 1991, the United States and a coalition of allies began air strikes against Iraq. After five weeks of aerial bombardment a ground offensive began on February 24 that lasted for 100 hours and succeeded in expelling Iraq from Kuwait. The American goal was not simply to force a retreat from Kuwait but to destroy Iraq's military capability. On February 27, President GEORGE H. W. BUSH announced that Kuwait had been liberated and the military campaign would end. The official end of the war came on March 3 when Iraqi leaders agreed to abide by all UN Security Council resolutions.

Rather than being removed from power by Iraqi domestic forces as the Bush administration expected, Saddam Hussein not only survived, but he also tightened his grip on power. He put down a Kurdish rebellion in the north and a Shi'ite rebellion in the south. In an effort to protect these populations the United States established "no-fly" zones that prevented Iraqi aircraft from attacking them. There was also a "no-drive" zone in southern Iraq intended to prevent Iraq from marshalling troops near the Kuwaiti border.

Internationally, he began to spar with the United Nations over the continued imposition of economic sanctions and weapons inspections. The United Nations had insisted that Saddam Hussein turn over Iraq's WEAPONS OF MASS DESTRUCTION and permit UN inspections of its weapons facilities to ensure that Iraq was in compliance with this UN resolution. Until 1993 Iraq showed little willingness to comply with UN inspection demands. This changed after a series of military actions by U.S. forces. In 1994 the UN reported that all known banned weapons had been destroyed, although it could not verify the state of its weapons development programs. The situation changed for the worse in 1997 when the United Nations reported that Iraq was hiding information on biological weapons and withholding data on chemical and NUCLEAR WEAPONS. Saddam Hussein has refused to permit UN inspections since 1998.

The Clinton administration followed a policy of DUAL CONTAINMENT against Iraq and Iran, seeking to isolate both of them internationally. It also engaged in a series of self-contained military actions against Iraq. In 1993 U.S. bombers struck Iraqi targets in retaliation for violations of the PERSIAN GULF WAR cease-fire agreement, and cruise missiles were launched against the headquarters of the Iranian INTELLIGENCE service in retaliation for an assassination attempt on former president Bush when he was visiting Kuwait. In January 1999 the United States admitted that it had placed American spies on UN inspection teams in order to gather information on Iraqi weapons programs.

In his 2002 State of the Union address President GEORGE W. BUSH identified Iraq as part of an axis of evil, along with Iran and NORTH KOREA. This pronouncement set the Bush administration on a collision course with both Iraq and virtually all members of the international community. With Iraq as defiant as ever, the Bush administration began making the case for taking military action against Iraq. At first the case for military action was loosely tied to Iraq's support of international TERRORISM, but this was dropped in September 2002 as the CIA was unable to produce any substantive evidence linking Iraq to AL-QAEDA or other terrorist groups. U.S. allies were openly skeptical of the need for military action, preferring to press the case for admitting weapons inspectors. RUSSIA and CHINA both promised to veto UN Security Council resolutions calling for the use of force. SAUDI ARABIA announced that it would not permit the United States to use its territory for any military action against Iraq. In the end members of the UN Security Council negotiated acceptable language, and a UN resolution of support was obtained that called for inspectors to return to Iraq and threatened dire consequences if Iraq did not abide by its terms.

Within the United States doubts were also expressed. At one point Bush asserted the right to go to war with Iraq without congressional approval. Both Democrats and Republicans in CONGRESS rejected this position. Bush's own administration was split on the issue, with SECRETARY OF STATE COLIN POWELL being the leading voice for moderation and Vice President Dick Cheney and SECRETARY OF DEFENSE Donald Rumsfeld leading the call for military action. Observers noted several interesting alignments in the White House debate over how to proceed. Those members of the George H. W. Bush administration who were now part of the George W. Bush administration were HAWKS, while others who were not part of the administration but were involved in the Persian Gulf War, such as NATIONAL SECURITY ADVISOR Brent Scowcroft, were less enthused about the prospects of war. The phrase *chicken hawk* also surfaced. It referred to prowar advocates within the administration who had never served in combat and were arguing against those with war experience who urged caution.

The United States went to war with Iraq in 2003. While it was quickly established that OSAMA BIN LADEN and al-Qaeda were responsible for the SEPTEMBER 11, 2001, terrorist attacks, the Bush administration's thoughts almost immediately turned to Iraq. The Bush administration asserted that Iraq was in possession of weapons of mass destruction and represented a threat to world peace. The United States acted unilaterally after lengthy efforts at obtaining a United Nations Security Council resolution failed. The final steps toward war began on March 16 when the United States, GREAT BRITAIN, and SPAIN held a one-hour summit conference on how to proceed. It ended with President Bush issuing an ultimatum to Saddam Hussein to go into exile or face military action. The next day the administration announced that it would pull its resolution authorizing military force against Iraq because it had reached the conclusion that "Council

An Iraqi woman marches while holding a portrait of Iraqi president Saddam Hussein during a parade, February 2003. *(Photo by Oleg Nikishin/Getty Images)*

consensus will not be possible." That night President Bush addressed the nation and gave Saddam Hussein 48 hours to leave Iraq. On Tuesday, March 18, Saddam Hussein rejected Bush's ultimatum.

The ground war began early in the evening on March 20 as United States and British troops crossed into Iraq from Kuwait. The invasion followed a decapitation air strike against the Iraqi leadership. U.S. intelligence sources reported that they believed Saddam Hussein and one or both of his sons were inside one of the bunkers targeted in this attack but were unsure if they were killed. Throughout the war Saddam Hussein would appear in broadcasts urging Iraqis to resist the "aggressors." American intelligence was unable to confirm when the tapes had been made or even if it was Saddam Hussein making the speeches. As coalition ground forces began their movement toward the interior of Iraq, the United States embraced a "shock and awe" bombing campaign designed to destroy Iraq's willingness to resist. Ground forces met uneven resistance, but concerns grew in military circles as the invasion supply line grew to more than 250 miles and coalition forces did not always receive a liberator's welcome. However, by April 7 U.S. forces were in Baghdad, and the city fell. In the process of advancing, the United States made another attempt to kill Saddam Hussein, dropping four 2,000-pound "bunker buster" bombs on one of his fortified underground command centers. As with the earlier decapitation strike, intelligence officials were unable to confirm if Saddam had been killed.

The celebrations of peace were shortlived. Tens of thousands took to the streets to protest the American presence, and American forces killed several civilians.

Republicans criticized President BILL CLINTON's foreign policy for engaging in international social work and ignoring true national security challenges to the United States. Especially objectionable to them were PEACEKEEPING and nation-building operations in places such as SOMALIA, HAITI, and BOSNIA. They had asserted that their foreign policy would be different. In the post 9-11 world the Bush administration found itself engaged in two major nation-building efforts.

While the vision of a democratic and prosperous Iraq defines the long-term purposes of U.S. reconstruction policy, the road map on how to get there is anything but clear. The Bush administration first announced the appointment of retired U.S. Army Lieutenant General Jay M. Garner to oversee reconstruction efforts as head of the Pentagon's Office of Reconstruction and Humanitarian Assistance. On April 28 Garner met with about 300 Iraqis representing groups from across the political spectrum in a preparatory meeting for a larger conference to select an interim government. Not only did that second meeting not take place as scheduled due to continuing political differences among the parties, but in early May career diplomat L. Paul Bremer was named special envoy and civil administrator in Iraq, placing him above Garner in the chain of command. Bremer's appointment reflected the ongoing turf war between the Pentagon and STATE DEPARTMENT for control of the reconstruction effort. Bremer's appointment was an example of a classic bureaucratic compromise. Although he was from the State Department, Bremer was a hard-line conservative who was respected by people in the Pentagon. One of his first tasks was to negotiate an acceptable list of administrators for the reconstruction effort from competing Pentagon and State Department recommendations. Decisions also had to be made as to whom to work with in Iraq. The United States has been inconsistent on this point. Initially it indicated that it would allow Ba'ath Party members to continue to hold government positions in the reconstruction process. Some 2 million Iraqis were members of the Ba'ath Party under Saddam Hussein, and this initial announcement indicated that only the 55 "most wanted" were by definition excluded from holding office. This decision angered many in Iraq, and soon the U.S. reversed itself, banning 15,000–30,000 party members from holding jobs in a new government.

Bureaucratic conflicts in Washington existed alongside real problems in Iraq. Many in the administration expected American forces to be welcomed as liberators. They were unprepared for the speed and intensity with which anti-U.S. sentiment surfaced. Angry Iraqis, for example, blamed the United States for fuel shortages and power outages. American officials were particularly unprepared for the manner in which Shi'ites, who make up 60 percent of Iraq's population, were able to organize themselves for political action. Shi'ite clerics spoke out in fervent tones against the United States. The deputy leader of the Supreme Council for the Islamic Revolution in Iran said, "[T]he American presence is unacceptable and there is no justification for staying in Iran." Shi'ite demonstrators who in some cases numbered in the tens of thousands chanted, "[N]o to imperialism, no to Israel, no to America, and no to Saddam." Such pronouncements led Senator Joseph Lieberman (D-Conn.) to openly express his concern about the establishment of a theocracy in Iraq.

Republican and Democratic senators were also troubled by the looting, violence, and lawlessness that gripped Iraq after the end of the war. Press reports in mid-May noted that Iraqis were tracking down Ba'ath Party members and killing them because they felt the U.S. was being too lenient on them. Their concerns were sufficient to lead Secretary of Defense Donald Rumsfeld to promise that steps would be taken to strengthen the American military presence in Iraq. About 142,000 troops were in Iraq at the time, with about 49,000 of them in and around Baghdad. Rumsfeld promised that 15,000 additional troops would soon arrive.

Senator Richard Lugar (R-Ind.), chairman of the Senate Foreign Relations Committee, has stated that it could take five years for democracy to establish itself in Iraq. Looking beyond the bureaucratic battles in Washington and the very real battles in Iraq, two fundamental nation-building options exist for the United States. The first is an inclusive approach that starts from the premise that if democracy is to be achieved, participants from all political vantage points must be brought into the process. Leaving them on the outside creates opponents to any new government. The second approach is exclusive in nature. It starts from the assumption that some political forces and leaders should not be allowed to participate in a new government given their past actions or what they stand for. Only those committed to a common vision of the future can join the political process. The exclusive approach stresses the need to come to a judgment about past wrongs and punish those responsible as a prerequisite for moving forward. The inclusive approach stresses the need for all to forgive past atrocities and forego the quest for justice in order to move the political process forward.

Further complicating discussions about the governance structure of postwar Iraq was the status of the Kurds in northern Iraq. Backed by U.S. airpower the Kurds, who had been oppressed by Saddam Hussein and lived under U.S. air protection in the northern no-fly zone, were advancing on Mosul and Kirkuk. Control of these cities would give the Kurds control over northern Iraq's largest city and much of its OIL wealth. For the Kurds, who long wished to establish an independent state, these would be significant accomplishments. Yet it was the very possibility of such successes that frightened Turkey and other states in the region that had large Kurdish minorities. Fuel was added to these fears when Kurds returned to Kirkuk and reclaimed land taken away from them 30 years ago and in the process left many Iraqi Arabs homeless.

See also ARAB-ISRAELI CONFLICT.

**Further reading:** Atkinson, Rick. *Crusade.* Boston: Houghton-Mifflin, 1993; al-Khali, Samir. *Republic of Fear.* New York: Pantheon, 1990.

## Iraq War

On SEPTEMBER 11, 2001, AL-QAEDA terrorists struck the World Trade Center and the Pentagon. In its wake President GEORGE W. BUSH proclaimed a global war against terrorists and those who aided and abetted them. While the initial focus of American military action was on the Taliban government of AFGHANISTAN, many within the Bush administration lobbied for expanding the war against TERRORISM to include IRAQ. Numbering among them were Vice President Dick Cheney, SECRETARY OF DEFENSE

Donald Rumsfeld, and Deputy Secretary of Defense Paul Wolfowitz. All served President GEORGE H. W. BUSH during the PERSIAN GULF WAR when the decision was made not to forcibly remove Saddam Hussein from POWER. SECRETARY OF STATE COLIN POWELL was also a member of that administration, but he alone of these individuals opposed war with Iraq.

President George W. Bush did not endorse including military action against Iraq in America's immediate plans for a war against terrorism. However, once the war in Afghanistan was successfully concluded, he signaled that an expansion in the war against terrorism was about to begin. In his January 29, 2002, State of the Union address Bush identified Iraq, IRAN and NORTH KOREA as comprising an axis of evil. Additional evidence that the United States was about to go on the offensive came with the release of a new national security doctrine rejecting DETERRENCE and emphasizing PREEMPTION, the logic being to strike an enemy before it became too powerful.

The key issue argued diplomatically and politically in 2002 was whether or not the United States would seek UNITED NATIONS approval for military action against Iraq and, if requested, whether it would be given. The leading advocates of military action against Iraq asserted that the United States could act unilaterally. Not only did the United States have a right to self-defense, Iraq was still in violation of UN resolutions issued after the Persian Gulf War. President Bush decided to move forward and seek formal international support for military action. In a speech delivered at the UN on the anniversary of the September 11 attacks, Bush challenged the UN to face up to the "grave and gathering danger" of Iraq or stand aside and allow the United States to act. In following this line of action Bush was endorsing Powell's position and overriding the objections of Cheney, Rumsfeld, and Wolfowitz.

Within a week of Bush's address Iraq promised to permit weapons inspectors "without conditions." At the UN, this announcement was hailed as "an indispensable first step." The Bush administration dismissed it as a "tactic that will fail." Iraq's offer led RUSSIA, FRANCE, and others to question whether a new resolution was now needed. Opposition arose in the Security Council to the expansive language of the American draft resolution that gave the United States full and automatic authority to use force if Iraq did not comply and the right to conduct its own inspections. An attempt at a compromise in October failed. The Bush administration was insisting that American military action could not be held hostage to a Security Council vote. France argued that only the Security Council could make a decision on going to war. The revised U.S. draft resolution did not request UN authorization for military action nor did it contain language that made military action automatic. But it did call for intrusive weapons inspections and warned of "severe consequences" should Iraq fail to comply. It also held that Iraq was in "material breach" of its disarmament obligations. A successful compromise was not crafted until November 8, 2002, when the Security Council unanimously approved Resolution 1441, giving Iraq 30 days to give a current, full, and complete report on all aspects of its WEAPONS OF MASS DESTRUCTION program. UN weapons inspectors were to update the Security Council in 60 days. Iraq accepted the UN resolution on November 13. On November 18 UN inspectors began arriving in Baghdad.

Iraq's report to the UN was submitted on December 7, 2002. It was 1,200 pages long. UN chief weapons inspector Hans Blix judged it to contain little new information and that it was "not enough to create confidence" that Iraq was disarming. Blix filed a similar report in early January regarding Iraq's compliance, but he also indicated that inspectors had not yet found any "smoking guns." Subsequent reports referenced Iraq's increased willingness to participate in the inspection process but continued to identify failings in the quality of its participation.

Unhappy with the pace and tenor of the verification process, in December the Bush administration set late January as the decision deadline for Iraq and began moving forces into the region. An estimated 125,000 American troops had already been ordered to the Persian Gulf when on January 20 France indicated that it would block any new Security Council resolution authorizing the use of force against Iraq. The Bush administration then repeated its position that it was willing to go to war without UN support. Intense diplomatic maneuvering returned to the UN in late February when the United States and its principal ally, Great Britain, indicated that they would soon introduce a new resolution that would declare Iraq to be in "further material breach" of UN orders to disarm. This brought forward renewed opposition from Germany and France. They advocated sending more weapons inspectors to Iraq along with UN troops so that they might gain access to all desired sites. On March 5, Germany, France, Russia, and China all announced that they would vote against any resolution authorizing war with Iraq. Once again President Bush indicated that he was prepared to go ahead without UN support.

In preparing to go to war without a supporting UN resolution, Bush moved to put together an ALLIANCE of supportive states. This grouping became known as the "coalition of the willing." Prominent among its members were the former communist states of East Europe that were seeking membership in the NORTH ATLANTIC TREATY ORGANIZATION (NATO). Rumsfeld collectively referred to them as the "new Europe." Shortly after the war began the administration claimed that the coalition of the willing had grown to 46 states, exceeding the number of states that supported the

United States in the Persian Gulf War. The extent of many of these contributions, however, was quite limited. Six states—Palau, Costa Rica, Iceland, the Marshall Islands, Micronesia, and the Solomon Islands—had no army.

Absent in this coalition was NATO. As early as September 2002 Rumsfeld indicated that he did not see NATO as having an important role to play in a war with Iraq. The American position changed in November when on the eve of a NATO summit President Bush invoked the image of Nazi Germany and urged NATO to take a stand against Saddam Hussein. Germany and France, however, remained opposed and blocked NATO action on the American request for support. French president Jacques Chirac asserted that "war is not inevitable" and that there should be no rush to a decision. This action prompted Rumsfeld to label France and Germany as part of the "old Europe." Their opposition continued in February 2003 when they opposed TURKEY's request for NATO help under Article 4 of the NATO Treaty that pledges states to come to the defense of those whose security was threatened. They argued that it was Turkey's actions that would force the crisis into war, thus invalidating Article 4.

Turkey was going to be a key participant in the war against Iraq. It would serve as a transhipment site for war matériel and a staging point for a northern invasion of Iraq. In the end this did not happen, and Turkey largely stayed on the sidelines. Problems in both Turkey and the United States contributed to this result. On the U.S. side, the Bush administration was unable to meet Turkey's demands for economic assistance and postwar security guarantees. On the Turkish side, a newly elected Turkish government was unable to muster the political majority necessary to overcome widespread domestic opposition to the war.

President Bush had also moved to establish a basis for unilateral action by obtaining congressional support for war. Bush turned to CONGRESS for support reluctantly. As late as August 2003 signs from the Bush administration suggested that it did not feel that the formal support of Congress was necessary in order to conduct a war in Iraq. Bush's pubic statements only went so far as to indicate the he would consult with legislators, something that fell short of obtaining their approval. Such support was not guaranteed. In early September, Senator Larry Craig (R-Idaho), chair of the Senate Republican Policy Committee and a strong Bush supporter, indicated that he was not prepared to vote for war at the time. Pressed by leaders in both parties to obtain congressional support, President Bush asked for such authorization on September 19. The White House–drafted resolution authorized the president to "use all means that he determines, including force," in order to enforce the UN Security Council resolutions, defend the national interest of the United States against the threats posed by Iraq, and restore international peace and security in the region.

Congress was supportive of the proposal, but many felt it was far too open-ended an endorsement of presidential war-making powers and was reminiscent of the situation that existed during the VIETNAM WAR. Others continued to call for a multilateral approach to the war. In early October the Bush administration reached a compromise with Congress. The revised resolution was passed on October 10 by a vote of 77-23 in the Senate and 296-139 in the House. The resolution supported efforts by the president to obtain action by the Security Council but then authorized the use of force. Borrowing language from the WAR POWERS RESOLUTION it required the president to notify Congress no later than 48 hours after exercising his authority and required that he report at least once every 60 days to the Congress.

The diplomatic maneuvering leading up to war entered into the endgame phase on March 16 when the United States, Great Britain, and SPAIN held a one-hour SUMMIT CONFERENCE in the Azores. It ended with President Bush issuing an ultimatum to Saddam Hussein to go into exile or face military action. The next evening President Bush addressed the nation and gave Saddam Hussein 48 hours to leave Iraq. On Tuesday, March 18, Saddam Hussein rejected Bush's ultimatum.

The first blow in the war was struck in the early morning hours of March 20 when President Bush ordered a decapitation air strike against the Iraqi leadership. U.S. INTELLIGENCE sources reported that they believed Saddam Hussein and one or both of his sons were inside one of the bunkers targeted in this attack but were unsure if they were killed. Throughout the war Saddam Hussein would appear in broadcasts urging Iraqis to resist the "aggressors." American intelligence was unable to confirm when the tapes had been made or even if it was Saddam Hussein making the speeches. The ground war began early in the evening on March 20 as American and British forces crossed into Iraq from Kuwait. Their progress was uneven. American troops met with little effective resistance, but the British encountered stiffer resistance, especially around Basra. As the invasion supply line grew to more than 250 miles, voices of concern were expressed that U.S. troops were becoming overly vulnerable to attacks by marauding Iraqi forces. A central premise of the war plan was that the United States would be welcomed as a liberator. This was now in doubt. In late March a week-long pause in the ground offensive took place as Pentagon officials reassessed their strategy. When the offensive resumed, American ground forces rapidly advanced on the elite Republican Guard units defending Baghdad. Baghdad fell on April 9.

Along with the ground war, the United States pursued a robust air war. After the initial decapitation strike the air force engaged in "shock and awe" bombing that was designed to destroy Iraq's willingness to resist. As American troops advanced on Baghdad, another attempt was made to kill Saddam Hussein by dropping four 2,000-pound "bunker buster" bombs on one of his fortified underground command centers. As with the earlier decapitation strike, intelligence officials were unable to confirm if he had been killed.

On May 1, aboard the USS *Abraham Lincoln,* President Bush declared victory in the war in Iraq. Celebrations of peace were shortlived, as looting and anarchy soon became the order of the day. American forces found themselves engaged in a series of highly charged encounters with Iraqi civilians in several Iraqi cities. In a very short period of time the United States had gone from liberator to enemy. Tens of thousands took to the streets in Baghdad to protest the U.S. presence; 10 civilians were killed in Mosul, and 13 were killed in Fallujah. Angry Iraqis, for example, blamed the United States for fuel shortages and power outages. Press reports in mid-May 2003 noted that Iraqis were tracking down Ba'ath Party members who were affiliated with Saddam Hussein's regime and killing them because they felt the United States was being too lenient on them. By mid-May congressional concerns had grown to the point where Secretary of Defense Rumsfeld promised that an additional 15,000 troops would be sent to Iraq. At the time, about 142,000 troops were in Iraq, about 49,000 of them in and around Baghdad.

American officials were particularly unprepared for the manner in which Shi'ites, who make up 60 percent of Iraq's population, were able to organize themselves for political action. Shi'ite clerics spoke out in fervent tones against the United States. The deputy leader of the Supreme Council for the Islamic Revolution in Iran said, "[T]he American presence is unacceptable and there is no justification for staying in Iran." Shi'ite demonstrators, who in some cases numbered in the tens of thousands, chanted "[N]o to imperialism, no to Israel, no to America, and no to Saddam." Such pronouncements led some in the Senate to openly worry about the establishment of a theocracy in Iraq.

Before the fighting ended, the Bush administration announced the appointment of retired U.S. Army Lieutenant General Jay M. Garner to oversee reconstruction efforts as head of the Pentagon's Office of Reconstruction and Humanitarian Assistance. The growing violence in Iraq led to a sudden change in plans, and in early May career diplomat L. Paul Bremer was named special envoy and civil administrator in Iraq, placing him above Garner in the chain of command. One of the key decisions American officials faced was which Iraqis to work with in their reconstruction efforts. Initially the United States indicated that it would allow Ba'ath Party members to continue to hold government positions in the reconstruction process. Some 2 million Iraqis were members of the Ba'ath Party under Saddam Hussein, and this initial announcement indicated that only the 55 "most wanted" were by definition excluded from holding office. This decision angered many in Iraq, and soon the United States reversed itself, banning 15,000–30,000 party members from holding jobs in a new government. American authorities also faced a decision regarding how closely to rely upon the Iraqi exile community in the West. Working in favor of giving them an important role in postwar Iraq is the fact that unlike local Iraqi leaders, they are known figures possessing established relationships with U.S. authorities. Working against giving them an important role is their lack of contacts and ties within Iraq that are important for making things happen on the ground.

A final cost analysis of the Iraq War will not be done for some time. The United States has indicated that, unlike in previous conflicts, it will not do a civilian casualty count. The economic costs are also uncertain. In late March the Bush administration submitted a request to Congress for $74.7 billion for the next five months: $63 billion for the war itself, $8 billion in relief funds, and $4 billion for homeland security. In May one THINK TANK estimated that $1 million per day was being spent on reconstruction. The Bush administration, through the AGENCY FOR INTERNATIONAL DEVELOPMENT, was also earmarking money for private firms to engage in reconstruction. Especially controversial was the decision to allow some firms, including Halliburton Co., for which Vice President Dick Cheney once served as chief executive officer, to obtain these contracts without going through a competitive bidding process. Early estimates placed the value of some of these projects at $900 million. Another scenario pegged Hailliburton's potential profit from Iraqi reconstruction at $7 billion.

## Ireland

With an area of around 27,000 square miles, Ireland is slightly larger than West Virginia, and it sits to the west of England and Wales. Its population is approximately 3,800,000, with an annual growth rate of 1.1 percent. Irish history is recorded from as far back as the Roman era, though its earliest inhabitants arrived around 6000 B.C. In modern times, however, much of its history has focused around religion and the country's relationship with GREAT BRITAIN as the Irish sought home rule. When Pope Adrian IV granted Henry II of England overlordship of the island in the 12th century, it marked the beginning of a struggle that continues even today.

During the 18th century, America received waves of Scotch-Irish immigrants, that group forming the largest non-English colonists, though the dominant Protestant English settlers often held them at a disadvantage. Often, the Scotch-Irish would land in Philadelphia and then move inland to stake land claims, farm, and establish themselves wherever they saw fit. They fled their native countries to face tremendous hardship in the New World, though it was often a preferred struggle compared to that waged by their kin who stayed behind, where ethnic tensions between Catholics and Protestants remained strained.

From 1800 to 1921, Ireland formed an integral part of the United Kingdom. There was a gradual lessening of oppression, commencing with restoration of religious freedom to Irish Catholics in 1829. Soon afterward, however, the potato famine of 1846–48 descended, bringing hardship, starvation, and death to Ireland's inhabitants. This created a renewed surge of departures that stretched into the late 1850s, as many of the poorest Irish chose to circumvent the drastic economic depression at home by immigrating across the Atlantic to the United States and CANADA in the holds of "coffin ships." Emerging from discontent with British rule during the famine, the Irish Republican Brotherhood (IRB) formed in Ireland around the same time as a secret society designed to push the British out. Many of its followers were forced to flee from poor economic conditions, but they continued their struggle against Britain from the United States, Canada, South America, and Australia. It was also known as the Irish-American Brotherhood, the Fenian Brotherhood, or simply the Fenians. One of the key organizers and the man who gave the movement its name, John O'Mahony, immigrated to the United States. When habeas corpus was suspended in Ireland in 1866, O'Mahony and other Irish-American Civil War veterans brought the initiative to the western side of the Atlantic Ocean. There, in the same year, under the leadership of General John O'Neill, 800 men attacked Canada across the Niagara River, capturing Fort Erie. This was the first of the "Fenian Raids." Their efforts were ultimately thwarted by U.S. troops, with O'Neill's men forced to withdraw to Buffalo, New York, where approximately 700 men were arrested. Future raids on Campobello Island (off Maine) and from Vermont would also be thwarted. Similarly, with the Fenians' financial support, a series of unsuccessful coups and attempted risings occurred repeatedly in Ireland until the outbreak of WORLD WAR I, though the Fenian movement ultimately splintered, with various offspring rising up to take on the challenge.

The Irish would not enter North America in such substantial numbers again after the island's economy recovered from the famine, but the Irish-American population became an important part of American society into the next century. Adept at politics, by the late 1800s, they had come to dominate big-city government and secured city jobs where previously their religion had held them back. Back in Ireland, however, international relations were dominated by the conflict with Britain over home rule and then independence. The drive to obtain the former officially became an aboveground political movement in 1874, spurred on by a surge of Irish nationalism and the organization of Sinn

Féin ("ourselves alone") especially, created by former Fenian Arthur Griffith.

The "shot heard round the world" drew the focus away from Sinn Féin's struggle, and in protest of the movement's concerns being essentially tabled, James Connolly led the unsuccessful Easter Rising of 1916, which had again looked to the United States for support. In response, Great Britain sought to crush Sinn Féin, which contributed directly to the Anglo-Irish War, 1919–21. The war's outcome led to a partition—temporary, most believed—between Ireland and NORTHERN IRELAND, the latter a Protestant stronghold with powerful ties to Great Britain. Following a civil war in the early 1920s, Ireland was sufficiently independent to declare its neutrality in WORLD WAR II and drop its dominion status in declaring itself a republic in 1949. Occurring 100 years after the famine-induced influx of Irish immigrants to the United States, the Irish republic proceeded to maintain strong ties with the United States for the duration of the 20th century.

U.S.-Irish relations have traditionally been based on common ancestral ties, similar values, and political views. This has broadened to include substantial U.S. corporate involvement in the Irish economy, at the same time the United States maintains the historically good relations between the two nations. Ireland is not a member of the NORTH ATLANTIC TREATY ORGANIZATION, but since 1973 it has been an Organization for Security and Cooperation in Europe member and a EUROPEAN UNION partner. Its participation in security and economic issues has helped it develop an increasingly strong economy since the beginning of the 1990s. With Ireland's stronger economy, IMMIGRATION to the United States has subsided, and this has always been a vital part of the U.S.-Irish relationship. Furthermore, in 1997, the United States initiated a dispute over Ireland's failure to implement copyright legislation in accord with the WORLD TRADE ORGANIZATION (WTO) Agreement on Trade-Relation Aspects of Intellectual Property Rights (TRIPS Agreement), and while hope has been maintained that Ireland will meet its promises to remedy the situation, the United States is prepared to see such issues through to further legislation. Nevertheless, on a fundamental level, Irish-U.S. relations have not been sullied by these differences; Ireland's commitment, financial and political, to support the American war on TERRORISM has drawn gratitude from the U.S. STATE DEPARTMENT in the wake of SEPTEMBER 11, 2001.

**Further reading:** Akenson, Donald H. *The United States and Ireland.* Cambridge, Mass.: Harvard University Press, 1973; Davis, Troy D. *Dublin's American Policy.* Washington, D.C.: Catholic University of America Press, 1987.

—Stephanie Cousineau

## Islam, political

United States foreign policy was slow to focus on Islam as a political force in Middle Eastern politics. Whereas European states had a long history of imperial rule over the region and an even more distant experience with invading armies from the Middle East, the United States did not come into sustained contact with political Islam until after WORLD WAR II.

When the United States began to focus its attention on the Middle East it did so not so much in the context of addressing regional issues but in terms of promoting broader security concerns. Containing the Soviet Union (see RUSSIA) was the cornerstone of American foreign policy, and the Middle East was an area of high concern. In American eyes, the Soviet Union had already demonstrated a desire to expand toward the Persian Gulf when its forces refused to leave IRAN after World War II, and it attempted to establish breakaway pro-Soviet regimes there.

Containing Soviet expansion required the cooperation of conservative Arab states. Starting from this vantage point, the primary threat to American security interests was not Islam but rather secular Arab nationalism that threatened to drive pro-American monarchies from power. EGYPT's Gamal Abdel Nasser embodied this threat, and the United States sought to isolate his political influence. Evidence suggests that President LYNDON JOHNSON explored the possibility of using Islam as a weapon against Nasser. He reportedly sought to get SAUDI ARABIA to sponsor a holy Islamic ALLIANCE against Egypt. Two decades later, President RONALD REAGAN demonstrated a similar willingness to ally with political Islam when he worked with PAKISTAN, Saudi Arabia, and other forces in AFGHANISTAN to force the Soviet Union out of Afghanistan.

Islam replaced Arab nationalism as the primary threat to American security interests in the 1970s. The first signs of this happening came in September 1970 when, one year after a coup that overthrow Libya's conservative government, Colonel Muammar al-Qaddafi came to power in LIBYA. Qaddafi sought to legitimize his rule by employing Islamic symbols and rhetoric. He also used Islam as a foreign-policy symbol as he sought to reach out and support other radical movements in AFRICA.

The perception of danger posed by political Islam to American security interests was reinforced by the 1973 ORGANIZATION OF PETROLEUM EXPORTING COUNTRIES (OPEC) OIL embargo. Put in place after the 1973 Yom Kippur War and in retaliation for American support of Israel, the OPEC oil embargo found traditional allies, such as IRAN and Saudi Arabia, carrying out policies harmful to the United States. Not lost on American officials was the fact that Libya was a member of OPEC and had been a leading force in increasing the price of oil and Arab control over it in the period leading up to the oil embargo.

The key factor in the transformation of Islam from an unknown but relatively benign force into a security threat was the Islamic revolution in Iran that removed the shah from power. Returning from exile Iran's spiritual leader, the Ayatollah Khomeini, called the United States the "Great Satan." Iranian militants seized the U.S. EMBASSY and held 52 Americans hostage for 444 days, leaving the Carter administration humiliated and virtually powerless in its attempts to secure their release. Adjectives such as *extremist, radical,* and *fanatical* that were once used to describe secular Arab nationalist movements were now applied to Islam. Significantly, the steady elevation of political Islam to the status of security threat to the United States since the early 1970s did not translate into the development of a more sophisticated view of its content. Islam as a political force was permanently identified with the policies of the revolutionary government in Iran, which was defined as undemocratic and unrelenting in its hostility toward the United States.

For many Americans the essential correctness of this view of Islam was born out in subsequent years by the repeated willingness of Islamic groups to use TERRORISM to accomplish their goals. If the ARAB-ISRAELI CONFLICT, especially as it was played out in LEBANON and the occupied territories, did not provide enough proof of Americans of the dangers inherent in political Islam, the February 1993 and SEPTEMBER 11, 2001, attacks on the World Trade Center certainly did.

Several explanations have been advanced for this frozen negative image of Islam. One stresses the spillover effect of the negative image of Islam that emerges from the standard European accounts of their interactions with the Muslim world. A second explanation stresses the influence of the long-standing American suspicion of movements that seek to unite religion and politics. Third, some see the explanation in the traditional AMERICAN NATIONAL STYLE of conducting foreign policy, with its tendency to seek absolute security, universalize conflicts, and place the latter in a moral context so that compromise is virtually impossible.

On a policy level, two general approaches have emerged since the early 1970s for dealing with political Islam. The first is a confrontationist perspective. It starts from the assumption that Islam and democracy are fundamentally hostile to one another. The struggle between Islam and the United States is depicted as a clash of civilizations and thus transcends disputes about territory, trade, or natural resources. Confrontationists see linkages between Islamic movements around the world that result in an international network and a global threat. In this sense parallels exist between political Islam in the post–COLD WAR era and COMMUNISM during the cold war.

The second perspective is accomodationist in outlook. It rejects the notions that Islam is a monolithic force and that it is fundamentally hostile to the West. Islam is seen as existing within various political structures, including democracies and monarchies. The key driving forces behind the more radical versions of political Islam are held to lie in the poverty, corruption, and political repression that is so prevalent in many of the states of the South.

One of the consequences of the existence of two different perspectives on how to deal with political Islam is that the United States has not developed a consistent foreign policy toward it. In general, the rhetoric of American foreign policy tends to employ the language and images of the accommodationist perspective. However, when it comes to designing or implementing a line of action, the United States has been reluctant to engage Islamic regimes or movements. For example, the Clinton administration adopted a policy of DUAL CONTAINMENT that sought to isolate both Iran and IRAQ, and GEORGE W. BUSH included both Iran and Iraq in his axis of evil. The Reagan administration perhaps came closest to an accommodationist approach when it secretly sold weapons to Iran in hopes of influencing moderate Iranian authorities to help secure the release of American hostages in Lebanon. The IRAN-CONTRA INITIATIVE floundered when it became public and linked to providing funds for the contras in NICARAGUA.

American dealings with Islamic movements also have been uneven. In the early 1990s the United States engaged in discreet talks with the Egyptian Muslim Brotherhood, a group that was positioning itself as a moderate alternative to President Muhammad Hosni Mubarak but nevertheless engaged in revolutionary rhetoric. By the mid-1990s the United States had broken off talks, and Mubarak suppressed them. In ALGERIA, where the government cancelled an election in 1991 rather than allow the Islamic Salvation Front (FIS) to win, at different times the United States engaged in talks with the FIS and then broke them off. It both supported the government's suppression of the Islamists and pressured the government to proceed with the cancelled election. In TURKEY, when Islamists won an election in 1995, the United States reacted in a pragmatic manner and accepted Prime Minister Necmettin Erbakan's promise that he wanted good relations with the United States.

**Further reading:** Akhtar, Shabbir. *A Faith for All Seasons: Islam and the Challenge of the Modern World.* Chicago: Ivan R. Dee, 1990; Fawaz, A. Gerges. *America and Political Islam: Clash of Cultures or Clash of Interests?* Cambridge, England: Cambridge University 1999; Halliday, Fred. *Islam and the Myth of Confrontation: Religion and Politics in the Middle East.* London: I.B. Tauris, 1995.

## isolationism

Along with INTERNATIONALISM, isolationism is one of two reoccurring general orientations toward the INTERNA-

TIONAL SYSTEM found in American foreign policy. Frequently presented as polar opposites, internationalism and isolation draw their inspiration from similar historical, intellectual, and social forces. They both build on a unilateralist impulse, a sense of MORAL PRAGMATISM, and LEGALISM. Together these traits form the basis for the AMERICAN NATIONAL STYLE of foreign policy.

At different points in time both isolationism and internationalism have been the dominant American perspective in world politics. Frank Klingberg has identified cycles of isolationism (introversion) and internationalism (extroversion) that are 25 to 30 years in duration. The cyclical movement between the pole of isolationism and internationalism is seen as spiral in nature. With every cycle the movement toward internationalism is held to become deeper.

This analysis runs counter to the widespread perception that the American public is becoming increasingly isolationist. It is pictured as turning inward and desiring to avoid international commitments, especially when they raise the possibility of American casualties. Proof for this is held to be the reaction to the American experience in SOMALIA, where 18 U.S. soldiers were killed and the subsequent reluctance to undertake PEACEKEEPING missions in BOSNIA AND HERZEGOVINA and KOSOVO. Also cited as supporting evidence is the decline in the INTERNATIONAL-AFFAIRS BUDGET. Between 1991 and 1998 it declined from $25.4 billion to an estimated $19 billion. This is a drop of some 25 percent. Defense spending, on the whole, is considered to have been relatively immune from isolationist-inspired cutbacks. This is not surprising since isolationists have tended to favor a strong defense as necessary to protect American national interests in a hostile world. What they object to is the perceived tendency for the United States to become involved in nonessential undertakings.

Evidence suggests that the policy maker's image of the American public as increasingly isolationist is not entirely correct. Trend-line PUBLIC OPINION data do not reveal any significant change in public attitudes on this score since the end of the COLD WAR. Similarly there is no evidence of any significant decline in interest in world affairs. What has happened is that the American public no longer gives foreign-policy problems as high a priority as it once did. Several explanations have been advanced for why this gap in perceptions exists on the part of policy makers. Among the most compelling of those put forward are (1) policy makers fail to seek out information on public attitudes, (2) they incorrectly assume that the vocal public that opposes internationalism is representative of the broader public, (3) they incorrectly assume that CONGRESS and the MEDIA are mirrors of the public, and (4) they underestimate the public's ability to understand the need for American involvement in the world.

The most common starting point of discussions of the evolution of isolationism in American foreign policy is

GEORGE WASHINGTON's Farewell Address in which he warned Americans to "steer clear of permanent alliances with any portion of the foreign world" and asserted that "Europe has a set of primary interests which to us have none, or a very remote relation." Its actual roots can be traced back further and find expression in the colonial period. BENJAMIN FRANKLIN put forward isolationist sentiments in the aftermath of the FRENCH AND INDIAN WAR when he complained that the colonies had lived in perfect harmony with the French and Indians and that the war was really a British war. In *Common Sense* (1776) Thomas Paine argued for an isolationist foreign policy, stating that there was not a "single advantage that this continent can reap by being connected with GREAT BRITAIN"and offering the opinion that the United States would never be enemies with SPAIN or FRANCE.

Among the major foreign-policy decisions rooted in isolationist principles are the MONROE DOCTRINE, the refusal to join the LEAGUE OF NATIONS, the NEUTRALITY LEGISLATION of the 1930s, and, more loosely, the fear of future VIETNAMS. As these examples suggest, isolationism has not meant quitting the world. The Monroe Doctrine has served as the basis for a robust and interventionist foreign policy in Latin America. The refusal to join the League of Nations did not stop the United States from organizing the WASHINGTON CONFERENCES or pursuing DISARMAMENT agreements. Support for neutrality in the 1930s went hand-in-hand with the interest of many in the PEACE MOVEMENT in promoting INTERNATIONAL LAW and organization. The end of the VIETNAM WAR did produce an American pullback from the world. It led to a policy of DÉTENTE and the search for surrogate powers, such as IRAN, to take the lead in securing regional stability.

Isolationist sentiment has also not precluded American economic expansion abroad. In fact, isolationists have traditionally sung the praises of overseas commercial ventures as the best means for realizing American security and creating a peaceful international world. Doubting voices have been raised. The NYE COMMISSION in the interwar period investigated charges that banking and commercial interests had steered the United States into WORLD WAR I. More recently some isolationists who opposed U.S. involvement in Balkan PEACEKEEPING efforts charged that these policies were being undertaken solely for the benefit of American corporations that needed stability in the region to ensure a profit for themselves.

**Further reading:** Adler, Selig. *The Isolationist Impulse.* New York: Praeger, 1957; Guinsburg, Thomas N. *The Pursuit of Isolationism in the United States Senate.* Chicago: Garland, 1982; Kull, Steven, and I. M. Destler. *The Myth of the New Isolationism.* Washington, D.C.: Brookings, 1999.

## Israel

Israel is about the size of New Jersey, with an area of 7,850 square miles. It has a population of 6.4 million people, 5.2 million of whom are Jewish. Israel came into existence in 1948. For more than 50 years the Zionist movement had employed both peaceful and violent means to bring about its creation. A landmark step in this direction came in 1918 with the Balfour Declaration, in which GREAT BRITAIN, the major colonial power in the region, along with FRANCE, agreed to the creation of a Jewish state. After WORLD WAR I, Great Britain received the LEAGUE OF NATIONS mandate to govern Palestine, and Jewish immigration reached new heights as the rise of Nazism in GERMANY progressed. Eager to maintain good relations with Arab leaders out of a concern for OIL, Great Britain cut off Jewish immigration to the region.

After WORLD WAR II Great Britain announced its intention to give up its mandate. A UNITED NATIONS (UN) commission recommended the partition of Palestine and the creation of a Jewish and Palestinian state. Arabs rejected this plan and prepared for war. Israel acted first by declaring its independence on May 14, 1948. The United States quickly recognized Israel. The Arab states then attacked. The resulting war left Israel in control of about one-half more land than they were to have under the UN plan. The remaining lands were seized by JORDAN and EGYPT, leaving no freestanding Palestinian homeland.

The United States is Israel's largest trading partner, and the two signed a free-trade agreement in 1985. In 2000, goods valuing $20.8 billion flowed between the two states. Military cooperation is also close. In 1983 the United States and Israel established a consultative body, the Joint Political-cal Military Group. The two states also engage in joint military exercises and collaborate on weapons development programs. The United States supplies Israel with some $2 billion per year in security assistance.

No official treaty or ALLIANCE exists between the United States and Israel, yet the depth of the relationship between the two is normally considered among the strongest that the United States has with any state. The reasons for this are seen as lying both in the nature of Middle Eastern politics that positions Israel as the one constant ally in a region where anti-U.S. sentiment is frequently heard and in the nature of American domestic politics where the Israeli lobby led by the American Israel Public Affairs Committee (AIPAC) has been a potent political force. In reality a more complex relationship exists, one that on occasion has found the two at odds, and where they have not always been close allies.

From the founding of Israel until the 1967 Six-Day War, the United States's relationship with Israel can be described as cool and distant. The initial pro-Israeli position of the Truman administration is commonly ascribed to domestic politics and the desire of President HARRY TRUMAN to court Jewish-American voters. At a deeper level, American support for Israel is linked to five additional factors. The first is a sense of guilt about the Holocaust. Second, there existed a more general humanitarian impulse to support the Jewish REFUGEES arriving from Europe. A third general factor prompting support for Israel was a religious indentification with a common Judeo-Christian biblical heritage. The fourth factor was a strong dose of IDEALISM that supported the idea of creating a new democratic order where none had existed. Finally, there was a strong element of ignorance about the region and Arab culture.

The 1950s and early 1960s frequently found the United States and Israel at odds. President DWIGHT EISENHOWER publicly opposed the joint British, French, and Israeli plan to seize control of the Sinai from Egypt. President JOHN KENNEDY quarreled with Israeli leaders when they refused to allow the United States to inspect Israeli nuclear facilities. Much of American DIPLOMACY to the region was directed at supporting UN efforts to bring about an Arab-Israeli peace agreement. France, not the United States, was then the primary source of weapons for Israel, but the United States had begun to supply Israel with weapons. President Kennedy provided Israel with Hawk antiaircraft missiles, and President LYNDON JOHNSON sold Skyhawk fighter-bombers and tanks. This reluctance to become overly identified with Israel was due in part to the existence of close ties between Washington, European allies, and the newly independent Arab states and a concern for access to oil, which was the traditional concern of European states in the Middle East. However, the more deeply the Soviet Union (see RUSSIA) became committed to Arab states in the region, the more pronounced American cooperation with Israel became.

With the 1967 war the United States became the primary arms supplier to Israel. That war also created tension in the U.S.-Israeli relationship with the Israeli attack on the USS *Liberty,* an INTELLIGENCE ship patrolling the Mediterranean during the Six-Day War. Israel claimed the attack was accidental, but many continue to suspect it was a deliberate move to prevent the United States from discovering the extent of the Israeli war plan. It was in the aftermath of the war that the United Nations passed Resolution 242 that is the benchmark for all American peace proposals. It calls for an exchange of land for peace.

The true beginnings of the American strategic relationship with Israel are dated from the Nixon administration, when NATIONAL SECURITY ADVISOR HENRY KISSINGER engaged in his famous shuttle diplomacy in an effort to bring about a peace agreement after the 1973 Yom Kippur War. It was during these negotiations that the United States began to give Israel written assurances concerning its security. In return the United States hoped to bring about increased flexibility in the Israeli negotiating position regarding the return of lands captured in the 1967 war. One of these promises, a pledge by Kissinger not to negotiate with the PALESTINE LIBERATION ORGANIZATION (PLO), which was contained in a 1975 Memorandum of Understanding, severely restricted American diplomacy for more than a decade. The first negotiations with the PLO did not occur until 1988. The depth of the American-Israeli strategic relationship was limited not only because of its newness but also because of the continued importance of the Soviet Union to American foreign policy. In the Middle East, as elsewhere, all foreign-policy decisions were made with an eye toward their impact on the U.S.-Soviet relationship.

In the 1973 war the United States actively intervened on Israel's behalf. The Arabs had succeeded in launching a surprise attack. Israel conducted a devastating counterattack but required financial help from the United States as well as a major resupply effort. The 1973 war also saw relations between the United States and Soviet Union deteriorate to dangerous levels. Israeli forces continued to occupy territory and attack Arab forces after an armistice was agreed to. Fearing the total destruction of its Arab allies the Soviet Union threatened to send in troops if Israel did not stop. The United States responded by placing its nuclear forces on a state of heightened worldwide alert. In retaliation for its coming to the aid of Israel the ORGANIZATION OF PETROLEUM EXPORTING COUNTRIES (OPEC) placed an oil embargo on the United States that precipitated a major increase in the price of oil.

The Carter administration moved the U.S.-Israeli relationship out of the context of global politics. He approached the ARAB-ISRAELI CONFLICT as a regional problem that was important in its own right and one that the United States had a mission to solve. Under his leadership the United States embarked on a four-year journey of "compulsive peacemaking." His greatest diplomatic success came with the CAMP DAVID ACCORDS in 1978. A side effect of Camp David was to create a much more complex U.S.-Israeli relationship as measured in terms of the amount of military and economic aid given.

Under RONALD REAGAN American foreign policy toward Israel was once again made within a cold war context of U.S.-Soviet competition. Israel was viewed as a key strategic ally in a hostile region. The United States and Israel engaged in joint military exercises and heightened intelligence-sharing activities. The Israeli invasion of LEBANON and the subsequent U.S. PEACEKEEPING mission that resulted in 241 dead marines after a terrorist suicide bomber attacked their headquarters strained this strategic relationship but did not destroy it. At the same time Reagan was building a strategic partnership with Israel, his administration was also reaching out to conservative Arab states, such as SAUDI ARABIA and Egypt, in order to construct a parallel strategic partnership with them.

Two public controversies erupted during the Reagan administration that involved Israel. One was the IRAN-CONTRA affair in which the Reagan administration sought to sell weapons to Iran in hopes of freeing American hostages held in Lebanon and generate funds for the contras in NICARAGUA. The weapons being sold to Iran were intended for Israel, and it was with their agreement that they were being sold to Iran. Not only was this an illegal ARMS TRANSFER, but Congress had forbidden the Reagan administration from providing the contras with money to bring down the Sandinista government in Nicaragua. Second, the Israeli government lobbied for the release of Jonathan Pollard, an American citizen and intelligence analyst captured and convicted of spying for Israel. His release has been steadfastly opposed by the national security BUREAUCRACY.

President GEORGE H. W. BUSH approached Israel in a manner reminiscent of Nixon. Israel was seen as a valuable ally for strategic reasons, but there was little emotional commitment. The relationship between the United States and Israel became particularly turbulent during the PERSIAN GULF WAR when the United States pressed Israel not to retaliate against IRAQ for SCUD missile attacks. Retaliation was standard operating procedure for Israel following attacks on its territory or people. The United States feared that any retaliation would cause Arab states to bolt from the global coalition that it had put together. After the Persian Gulf War Bush would openly quarrel with Israeli leaders and try to mobilize the American-Jewish community against them. The issue was Israel's decision to build additional settlements in the occupied territories at the same time the United States was trying to arrange for the calling of the MADRID ACCORDS that would bring together Israel and its Arab neighbors, including the Palestinians.

American relations with Israel warmed up in the first half of the Clinton administration largely due to the strong personal relationship established between President BILL CLINTON and Prime Minister Yitzhak Rabin. Clinton often deferred to the more experienced Rabin, whose moderate policies, including a de facto ban on further settlements in the occupied territories, created a positive environment in which the Madrid Talks and its secret Oslo counterpart could move forward. Relations changed when Benjamin Netanyahu became prime minister in 1996. His Likud Party took a more hard-line stance in negotiations with the Palestinians, and the United States found itself moving from the role of mediator in this conflict to that of arbitrator. This process culminated in the signing of the WYE RIVER ACCORDS in October 1998. Negotiating over nine days Netanyahu and PLO leader Yasser Arafat agreed that Israel would pull back its troops from 13 percent of the occupied West Bank and from 14 percent of jointly controlled land. In return the PLO agreed to take steps to end attacks on Israel and to bring the PLO Charter into compliance with other PLO documents and statements that recognized Israel's right to exist. A sore point in U.S.-Israeli relations during this period was Netanyahu's efforts to use AIPAC and direct Israeli lobbying to enlist the support of Republicans in Congress to pressure the Clinton administration into being more supportive of Israel.

As Clinton's term ended he attempted another SUMMIT CONFERENCE at Camp David (CAMP DAVID II) in July 2000. In addition to security questions it sought to resolve such issues as the status of Jerusalem and the plight of Palestinian refugees. No agreement was reached, and shortly thereafter renewed violence broke out on the West Bank and Gaza Strip. Former senator George Mitchell (D-Maine) chaired a fact-finding mission that reported in April 2001. It called for an immediate end to the violence followed by confidence-building measures. Little came of this report due to the change of administrations in the United States and escalating violence in the Middle East.

President GEORGE W. BUSH entered office determined to move away from what he perceived to be the liberal international activism of the Clinton administration. Brokering a Middle East peace agreement was high on the list of initiatives that Bush wished to distance his administration from. It was largely content to endorse the idea of a Palestinian state, which Bush announced on October 3, 2001, and leave peace negotiations to the two sides. Events in the Middle East conspired to make this impossible. Israel now publicly opposed creation of a Palestinian state, and escalating tensions brought on by a wave of Palestinian suicide bombers and Israeli reprisals threatened to engulf the region into a full-scale war. The Bush administration changed its position almost completely in May and June 2002. In early May it was still insisting that Israel negotiate with the PLO. For their part Arab officials were calling upon the United States to force Israel to negotiate. By June, this was no longer the case. When Bush outlined his ideas for a Middle East Peace agreement, the administration's tone reflected movement away from neutrality to an acceptance of the Israeli position that Arafat was an obstacle to peace and that the PLO's actions represented acts of TERRORISM that the United States needed to oppose. On June 24, 2002, Bush called for the election of a new leader to replace Arafat along with a series of security and political reforms as preconditions for a new round of talks. The United States would determine when these conditions had been met. No demands were placed on Israel for withdrawing its forces.

With the end of the IRAQ WAR the United States renewed its efforts to obtain a peace agreement in the Middle East between Israel and the Palestinians. The vehicle was a "road map" agreed upon by the United States, RUSSIA, the UNITED NATIONS, and the EUROPEAN UNION. It

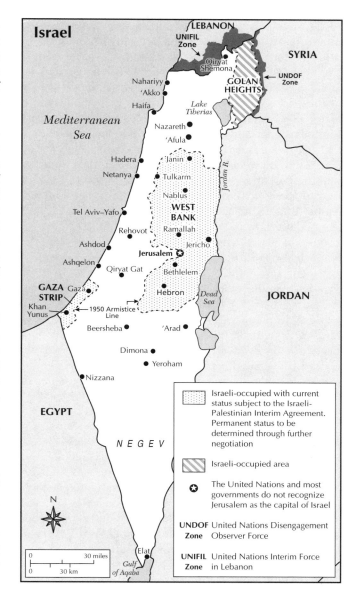

was formulated in 2003 but shelved due to Israel's unwillingness to negotiate with Arafat and the heightened level of terrorism. The road map contained three parts. The first phase called for ending the violence. It called upon Palestinians to end their campaign of terror and Israelis to stop building settlements in Arab territories on the West Bank and in Gaza. The second phase called for establishing a Palestinian state by 2005. In the third phase borders will be determined and the rights of Palestinian REFUGEES to return to their homes now inside Israel will be settled. The road map does not call for negotiations but for simultaneous independent actions by Israel and the Palestinians.

The replacement of Arafat with Mahmoud Abbas, Palestinian Authority prime minister, was a first step in the road map to peace. Abbas was publicly committed to stopping terrorism but failed to do so in his first months in office, as terrorist groups, such as Hamas and the Islamic Jihad, carried out a series of suicide bombings against Israel. This led Israeli prime minister Ariel Sharon to balk at the peace process. For their part, Palestinians were angered at continued Israeli targeting of terrorist leaders for assassination and questioned Sharon's sincerity. On May 25, 2003, the Israeli cabinet revisited the issue and voted by a 12-7 margin to endorse the road map on the condition that the Palestinians give up their right to return to areas currently within Israeli territory. Widespread violence erupted following the end of the IRAQ WAR, and Abbas stepped down from office in September 2003, dealing yet another blow to the peace process.

See also SUEZ CRISIS.

**Further reading:** Bickerton, Ian J., and Carla L. Klausner. *A Concise History of the Arab-Israeli Conflict.* Englewood Cliffs, N.J.: Prentice Hall, 1998; Gilbert, Martin. *Israel: A History.* New York: William Morrow, 1998; Schoenbaum, David. *The United States and the State of Israel.* New York: Oxford University Press, 1993; Yaniv, Avner. *Dilemmas of Security: Politics, Strategy, and the Israeli Experience in Lebanon.* New York: Oxford University Press, 1987.

## Italy

Italy is about the size of Georgia and Florida combined. It has an area of 116,303 square miles and a population of 57.8 million people. Modern Italy emerged as a united country in 1861, with the exception of Rome, which was incorporated into Italy in 1870. Today Italy is an industrial state, but it is a late industrializer, compared to other West European states. Its agricultural and impoverished past contributed greatly to the large influx of Italian immigrants to the United States in the late 19th and early 20th centuries. Before IMMIGRATION laws were tightened in the 1920s an estimated 4.5 million Italians had made the transatlantic journey. Concentrated in the industrial cities of the Northeast United States, these new citizens would form the basis for a powerful ethnic voting bloc in later decades.

Official U.S. foreign relations with Italy in the first half of the 20th century were often strained. A first point of tension surrounded Italy's participation in WORLD WAR I. When the war began Italy was neutral, but offers of territorial prizes by the Allies lured Italy into the war against GERMANY and Austria-Hungary. Italy was rewarded at the Paris Peace Conference but not to the extent that it expected. WOODROW WILSON rejected its claim to portions of the Adriatic coast. These were given to YUGOSLAVIA.

A second point of tension involved Benito Mussolini's foreign policy. Mussolini seized power in 1922, pledging to restore social order and political greatness. He followed through on his promises at home by creating a fascist state. Abroad he embarked on a foreign policy of aggression and aggrandizement, conquering ETHIOPIA over the objections of the LEAGUE OF NATIONS in 1935–36 and seizing Albania in 1939. He also moved Italy closer to Nazi GERMANY, entering into an entente with it in 1936. Initially the United States adopted a tolerant attitude toward Mussolini and only turned against him in the mid-1930s. Italy was at first neutral in WORLD WAR II, but in June 1940 it declared war on FRANCE and GREAT BRITAIN. Militarily it participated in campaigns in North Africa and led an inept invasion of GREECE. It would declare war on the UNITED STATES and the Soviet Union (see RUSSIA) in 1941. Participation in the war on the side of the Axis powers resulted in the loss of its African colonies, including LIBYA and ERITREA. Italy also lost territory to Yugoslavia, France, and Greece. The city of Trieste was established as a free city.

Italy's future role in Europe was highly contested. The Soviet Union sought a voice in the formation of its postwar government, but it was denied. It would cite this when challenged about its role in establishing Communist-dominated governments in East Europe. In each case the key factor centered on whose armies had liberated the country and were physically present. The Communists were a political power to be reckoned with in postwar Italy, and many American policy makers feared that Italian voters would elect a communist government. To prevent that from happening the United States supplied Italy with large amounts of FOREIGN AID and undertook the first COVERT ACTION campaign by the CENTRAL INTELLIGENCE AGENCY to help defeat the communists at the polls.

Italy was viewed as particularly important by American policy makers because of the political instability in Greece and Great Britain's announcement that it could no longer provide for the security of the Mediterranean Sea. This announcement led to the TRUMAN DOCTRINE. Italy moved firmly into the Western ALLIANCE system by 1950. In 1948 it participated in the MARSHALL PLAN for European economic recovery, and in 1949 it joined the NORTH ATLANTIC TREATY ORGANIZATION (NATO). Italy's participation in NATO remains important to U.S. security planning. Some 16,000 American military personnel are currently stationed in Italy at navy, air force, and army bases. Naples serves as the home port for the U.S. Navy Sixth Fleet.

Post–World War II Italy experienced a seemingly endless series of coalition governments. While the political maneuverings that surrounded the formation of successive governments never produced a situation in which Italy became an unreliable COLD WAR ally, it did create periodic conflicts with the United States. In the 1950s and early 1960s the issue was Italy's willingness to trade with the Soviet Union when the United States was still seeking to isolate it. Italy imported large amounts of Soviet OIL, and Italian firms were important investors in the Soviet economy. In the 1960s Italy adopted a pro-Arab position in the ARAB-ISRAELI CONFLICT following the 1967 and 1973 wars. In 1985 the United States and Italy found themselves at odds over the handling of the *Achille Lauro* affair. This cruise ship was hijacked by Arab terrorists, and an American citizen was killed. Italy allowed the organizer of the attack to go free.

In the post–cold war era Italy has emerged as an active supporter of PEACEKEEPING operations. It contributed troops to missions to SOMALIA, BOSNIA AND HERZEGOVINA, and East Timor. It also supported the United States in the PERSIAN GULF WAR.

**Further reading:** Hughes, H. Stuart. *The United States and Italy.* 3d ed. Cambridge, Mass.: Harvard University Press, 1979.

# J

## Jackson, Andrew (1767–1845) president of the United States

Andrew Jackson was the seventh president of the United States and the first "people's president." His major contributions to U.S. foreign policy came as a military leader. In the WAR OF 1812 Jackson served as a major-general of the Tennessee militia and then major-general in the regular army. During that war his forces engineered two significant victories. In 1814 Jackson defeated the Creek Indians who had been allied with the British at the Battle of Horseshoe Bend in Alabama. In the resulting peace treaty the Creeks ceded 23 million acres of territory to the United States. In the final battle of the War of 1812, Jackson's forces inflicted a stunning defeat on the British at the Battle of New Orleans on January 8, 1815. More than 2,000 British troops were killed, and only 20 Americans lost their lives. The battle occurred after the TREATY OF GHENT had been signed on December 24, 1814, ending the war. It nonetheless cemented Jackson's standing as a folk hero with the American public and ended a controversial war on a high note.

In 1818 Jackson led U.S. troops into Spanish FLORIDA during the Monroe administration. Jackson's instructions were broad and gave him great discretion. The intent was to squelch Indian raids into U.S. territory without formally challenging the authority of SPAIN in Florida. Jackson accomplished the first goal, but his actions brought him into direct conflict with Spain and GREAT BRITAIN. He captured Spanish forts and executed two British subjects who he accused of inciting the Indians against the United States Spain demanded an apology. The Monroe administration distanced itself from Jackson and his political nemesis HENRY CLAY, and it orchestrated a Senate probe into Jackson's Florida campaign. After 27 days of debate all four resolutions condemning Jackson were defeated. SECRETARY OF STATE JOHN QUINCY ADAMS defended Jackson in a diplomatic note to Spain. He asserted that unless Spain could keep the peace in Florida more such missions might be needed. The resulting diplomatic maneuvering ended with the signing of the Adams-Onís Treaty of 1819, which transferred Spanish Florida to the United States.

As president, Jackson's foreign policy did not break new ground from its predecessors. He sought to purchase TEXAS but failed. Jackson failed to resolve differences over the Maine-Canada border. A settlement mediated by the king of the NETHERLANDS in 1831 would have given the United States most of what it claimed, but Jackson rejected the award under political pressure from interests in the United States who wanted all of the disputed territory. On a more positive note Jackson succeeded in reopening direct U.S. trade with the British West Indies. This trade had been restricted since the AMERICAN REVOLUTION.

**Further reading:** Belohlavek, John. *Let the Eagle Soar: The Foreign Policy of Andrew Jackson.* Lincoln: University of Nebraska Press, 1985

## Jackson-Vanik Amendment

Named after its sponsors, Senator Henry "Scoop" Jackson (D-Wash.) and Representative Charles Vanik (D-Ohio), the Jackson-Vanik Amendment to the 1974 Trade Reform Act made the extension of MOST-FAVORED-NATION (MFN) STATUS available only to those states that permitted free IMMIGRATION and did not impose more than a nominal tax on citizens wishing to emigrate. The Jackson-Vanik Amendment did not mention the Soviet Union by name but was directed at their restrictive emigration policies concerning Soviet Jews. The Soviet Union asserted that the Jackson-Vanik Amendment constituted an unwarranted intrusion into their domestic affairs and rejected it, thus forfeiting MFN status. It proceeded to further tighten restrictions on Jewish emigration. The number of Soviet Jews leaving in 1973 was 35,000. In 1975 it fell to 13,200.

The 1974 Trade Act was negotiated by the Nixon administration and was a key element in its foreign policy of DÉTENTE with the Soviet Union. President RICHARD

NIXON and SECRETARY OF STATE HENRY KISSINGER sought to use American economic POWER as a lever, as a substitute for military confrontation, and as a means of promoting cooperative behavior on the part of the Soviet Union.

Jackson and Vanik introduced separate amendments in fall 1972 and spring 1973 in response to a comprehensive trade agreement that the Nixon administration had signed with the Soviet Union in October 1972. The core of this agreement was a deal in which the Soviet Union would settle its LEND-LEASE debt to the United States and the United States would grant MFN status, which would allow Soviet goods to enter the United States at the lowest tariff rate enjoyed by any U.S. trading partner.

Congressional debate over the Jackson-Vanik Amendment lasted two and one-half years. With 253 cosponsors, the amendment was approved by the House by a vote of 319-80 on December 11, 1973. It then went to the Senate. While hearings were being held in the Senate on the Jackson-Vanik Amendment and the 1974 Trade Reform Act, discussions were underway among Kissinger, Jackson, and Soviet leaders in search of a compromise. Within the U.S. government, the Nixon administration and congressional leaders crafted a compromise of their own: The PRESIDENT would be allowed to waive the provisions of the Jackson-Vanik Amendment and grant MFN status to the Soviet Union for 18 months. The waiver could be renewed for periods of one year with congressional approval. Despite Soviet president Leonid Brezhnev's displeasure with public references to the Soviet Union as having given assurances on permitting Jewish emigration, it looked like the deadlock had passed. On December 20, 1974, the Senate approved the amended 1974 Trade Reform Act by a vote of 72-4, and the House followed suit by a vote of 323-36. On January 10, 1975, the Soviet Union informed the United States that it would not enter into the trade agreement as amended.

The Jackson-Vanik Amendment is significant because it was an indicator of the degree to which presidential-congressional relations had changed after VIETNAM. No longer was CONGRESS willing to be a compliant partner. It would be an active participant in making foreign policy, and it would be one attuned primarily to domestic considerations and not diplomatic ones. The Jackson-Vanik Amendment also highlighted one of the fundamental flaws of détente. Through détente, Nixon and Kissinger sought to implement a complex policy of carrots and sticks that alternatively rewarded and punished Soviet foreign-policy behavior. This strategy lacked the heavy dose of moralism that is found in the AMERICAN NATIONAL STYLE. The Jackson-Vanik Amendment appealed to this tradition and effectively linked U.S. foreign policy to Soviet domestic policy as well as its foreign policy, thereby taking it out of the hands of the Nixon administration.

See also RUSSIA; TRADE.

## Japan

Japan has an area of 145,902 square miles, making it slightly smaller than California, and a population of 126.8 million people. Located several hundred miles off the Asian mainland, the first Western contact with Japan came in the mid-1500s. During the next century there was sporadic contact with European traders and missionaries. Japan successfully expelled all foreigners and limited commercial contact solely to Dutch and Chinese merchants through the port of Nagasaki for about 200 years.

The opening of Japan to the West dates from the arrival of Commodore Matthew Perry at Tokyo Bay on July 8, 1853. Perry was to open trading relations, acquire coaling stations, and obtain an agreement for protecting American sailors shipwrecked from whaling ships. The mistreatment of sailors by the Japanese was a major point of contention at the time. On July 14, Perry presented the Japanese a letter from PRESIDENT Millard Fillmore outlining the American position. Perry left after 10 days, announcing that he would return the next year for an answer. On March 8, 1854, he reappeared, and on March 31 the Treaty of Kanagawa was signed. It would be approved unanimously by the Senate. Perry accomplished most but not all of his objectives. Two coaling stations were obtained, as was protection for shipwrecked sailors. Perry was less successful in obtaining commercial concessions. The United States received access to two ports, but there were no provisions that guaranteed trade would begin.

The true commercial opening of Japan was accomplished by Townsend Harris in 1858. By terms of a treaty signed on July 29, 1858, the United States obtained access to additional ports as well as more favorable trading and residential rights. The principle of extraterritoriality was established. The United States and Japan also established full diplomatic relations, with the first Japanese delegation arriving in the United States in 1860.

Japanese leaders used the increased economic ties with the West as a spur to reform its feudal political and economic order. The Meiji Restoration of 1866 began a process of industrialization and militarization that transformed Japan into a major world power and set the stage for a series of conflicts with the West. By virtue of its victory in the 1894–95 Sino-Japanese War, it obtained TAIWAN, the Ryukuu Islands, and a presence in Korea. It followed this with a victory in the Russo-Japanese War of 1905. Victory here gave it a dominating position in Manchuria and Korea.

The principal American response to the political and economic disintegration of CHINA was the OPEN DOOR policy. First put forward in September 6, 1899, by SECRETARY OF STATE JOHN HAY, in a diplomatic note sent to Japan, RUSSIA, GREAT BRITAIN, GERMANY, FRANCE, and ITALY, it asked that they adopt a policy of equal treatment for countries trading in their sphere of influence. He followed this up with a second Open Door note on July 3, 1900, when he asked their help in guaranteeing both free trade in China and its "territorial and administrative integrity."

As Japanese power continued to grow President THEODORE ROOSEVELT sought to protect American interests in the Pacific through the Taft-Katsura Agreement of 1905. The two states had already clashed over the American annexation of HAWAII. Japan had protested that action as upsetting the status quo in the region. The purpose of the Taft-Katsura Agreement was to prevent more of this from happening. In essence it recognized Japanese preeminence over Korea in return for a Japanese agreement to respect American control over the PHILIPPINES. That same year Roosevelt received a Nobel Peace Prize for his successful efforts to end the Russo-Japanese War with the TREATY OF PORTSMOUTH.

In 1907 Roosevelt adopted a different strategy for encouraging Japanese cooperation. He directed that the entire American battle fleet of 16 ships be sent on an around-the-world tour as a show of force. Japan was one of the most important ports of call. At the time the United States had the world's second-largest navy and Japan had the fifth largest. This naval visit was followed by the signing of the Root-Takahira Agreement of November 30, 1908, which again pledged both states to respect the status quo in the Pacific and added support for an Open Door policy in China and its political independence and integrity.

Occurring against this backdrop of constructive diplomatic engagement was an American domestic issue that introduced a strong element of tension into American-Japanese relations. Following on the heels of discriminatory and exclusionary policies directed at Chinese immigrants, policy makers now passed laws targeted at Japanese IMMIGRATION. The most notorious of these was a 1906 San Francisco School Board decision that required all Asian schoolchildren to attend racially segregated schools. President Roosevelt first tried to bully the San Francisco School Board into reversing its policy, and when that failed he brokered a compromise agreement. The school board would reverse its policy in return for a promise from Roosevelt to obtain an agreement from Japan ending the influx of Japanese immigrants. Roosevelt did so through a series of diplomatic notes exchanged with Japan in 1907–08 that collectively are referred to as the Gentleman's Agreement. The matter did not end there. The high birth rate among Japanese in California now became the issue. The California legislature passed a law in May 1913 that forbid aliens ineligible for citizenship from owning land. Japanese citizens were not identified specifically, but it was clear to all who was being targeted. President WOODROW WILSON tried to convince California not to enact the legislation but failed.

WORLD WAR I found Japan an ally of the United States, although not immediately. It declared war on GERMANY on August 23, 1914, and captured key German colonial holdings in the Pacific. Having accomplished this Japan then sought to strengthen its position in China by issuing the Twenty-one Demands on January 18, 1915. Unable to effectively resist, China signed a series of agreements with Japan that year that established Japanese preeminence there. The United States was still neutral at this time, and the Wilson administration's response was a refusal to recognize Japan's territorial gains because they violated the Open Door policy. The United States entered the war on April 6, 1917. Later that year in November the United States and Japan signed an agreement, the Lansing-Ishii Agreement, that sought to reconcile two increasingly contradictory positions in the name of allied unity. In it the United States agreed to recognize Japan's special position in China while Japan agreed to recognize the Open Door policy and respect the political integrity of China. At the TREATY OF VERSAILLES peace conference Wilson was forced to abandon his nonrecognition policy. Japan was permitted to hold onto Germany's colonial holdings and its effective control over China's Shantung Peninsula as the price for its joining the LEAGUE OF NATIONS. These concessions did not mean that Japan left the negotiations as a satisfied power. It was deeply resentful over the failure of the league to include a statement of racial equality in its founding document. Wilson had supported such a statement but backed off due to opposition from GREAT BRITAIN.

The American decision not to join the League of Nations did not result in an isolationist foreign policy. Instead, the United States embarked upon an independent policy of INTERNATIONALISM designed to produce global security. The centerpiece of these efforts was the WASHINGTON CONFERENCE of 1921–22. Of great concern to American officials was the prospect of a naval arms race and regional instability in Asia. A series of agreements were designed to address these issues. The Five-Power Treaty put in place a 10-year moratorium on capital ship building and set a tonnage ratio of 5:5:3:1.75:1.75, with the United States and Great Britain at 5 and Japan at 3. A Four-Power Treaty ended an Anglo-Japanese alliance and substituted a multilateral agreement to respect the status quo. A Nine-Power Treaty pledged respect for the Open Door in China. Each of these created some consternation in Japan. It had preferred a 10:10:7 ratio and accepted the smaller one only after an assurance from the United States that it would not fortify the Philippines. Ending the Anglo-Japanese alliance was also controversial since Japan had relied upon it to have a free hand in northern Asia against Russia and China. Japan had come to view China as a special area of influence and supported the Open Door policy only after the United States and Great Britain applied strong pressure. After the conference Japan agreed to evacuate the Shantung Peninsula but secured favorable economic concessions before doing so. Japan improved its naval position relative to the United States and Great Britain somewhat at the London Disarmament Conference in 1930.

These agreements could not hide the fact that tensions were building in the U.S.-Japan relationship. In the United States, the Immigration Act of 1924 prohibited "aliens ineligible for citizenship" from entering the United States. Earlier versions of this legislation would have permitted foreigners to enter the United States under a quota system, but opponents of Japanese immigration succeeded in getting the more restrictive version passed.

In Japan the liberal government of the early 1920s was replaced by a more nationalistic and militaristic one that was determined to establish Japanese supremacy in the Pacific. A first step in this direction came in 1931 when an incident was staged in Manchuria that provided a pretext for Japan to send in troops. The United States took no action to counter the move. It did not support a League of Nations proposal for ECONOMIC SANCTIONS. Instead, the United States adopted a policy of nonrecognition, which it adhered to following Japan's act of aggression with an invasion of China near Shanghai in 1937. Once again the United States remained passive. It did propose invoking the Nine-Power Treaty that guaranteed China's administrative integrity, but the British did not support such a move. Also in 1932 Japan established a puppet state in Manchuria under the name Manchukuo. The United States continued its policy of nonrecognition in the face of this action.

More generally, both sides were also stepping up their military preparations in the 1930s. President FRANKLIN ROOSEVELT targeted funds for the construction of two new aircraft carriers and 30 other naval vessels in 1933. In Japan a 1936 naval study recommended a surprise attack on Pearl Harbor should the American fleet be positioned there.

This aerial photo shows the aftermath of the atomic bomb explosion over Hiroshima. *(National Archives)*

That same year another document, the "Fundamental Principles of National Security," called for northern expansion into both China and Mongolia and southern expansion into territory controlled by European powers. Expansion into China came the following year. On July 7, 1937, Chinese and Japanese troops met at the Marco Polo Bridge. Soon Shanghai and Nanjing fell, and by the end of 1938 Japan controlled most major Chinese ports. President Roosevelt termed the action an "incident" rather than a "war" so that he continued to send supplies to China. Roosevelt imposed a "moral embargo" on the sale of aircraft to Japan. If it came to a war the United States would remain neutral and not send help to either side, something that would hurt China more than Japan.

A complex drama was also being played out between the United States and Japan in the economic arena. In 1938 the United States provided Japan with 44 percent of its total imports. Steel, iron, copper, OIL, machines, and autos figured prominently in the list of items imported. All were vital to a war effort, and the Roosevelt administration moved gingerly not to apply economic pressure on Japan that was so great that it would push Japan into war. In 1939 the United States did inform Japan that it was ending the 1911 commercial treaty between the two states, but this did not end all trade. Further restrictions were put into place in 1940 when aviation fuel and scrap iron were embargoed, but oil was not. In July 1941 Roosevelt froze all Japanese assets in the United States, and the sale of oil ended. Roosevelt took this action based on information that Japan was sending forces toward Indochina (Southeast Asia). In September 1941 Japanese leaders decided to go to war with the United States if the strategic embargo was not lifted by October 15. War came on December 7, 1941, with the Japanese attack on Pearl Harbor.

WORLD WAR II ended on September 2, 1945, with Japan's formal surrender on the USS *Missouri*. Two momentous events preceded that act. On August 6 the world's first atomic bomb fell on Hiroshima. Approximately 130,000 died, and an equal number were injured. On August 9 a second atomic bomb struck Nagasaki, killing some 60,000 people. Great controversy continues to surround the decision to use the atomic bomb against Japan. Traditional accounts stress the importance of military considerations. The atomic bomb was necessary to avert the need for an invasion of Japan that most felt would be needed to end the war. There is no doubt that any such invasion would have brought with it a heavy loss of American lives. Critics of this perspective argue that an invasion was not necessary. Japan was already sending out peace feelers. Momentum—the unquestioned assumption that once built the bomb would be used—may have played a more powerful role than concrete war plans. The revisionist school cites diplomatic concerns as the prime motivating

factor. American policy makers, it is argued, were already looking to the postwar era and the next enemy, the Soviet Union. The atomic bomb was intended to demonstrate American power to the Russians in the most forceful fashion. From the conventional perspective there is no denying the potential diplomatic gains from the use of the atomic bomb, but it is not seen as a key motivating force. It is seen as more of a bonus that was a natural by-product of the military use of the bomb. To these two explanations a third can be added. It is a mixture of revenge for Pearl Harbor and racism. A review of U.S.-Japanese relations reveals the existence of great and persistent antipathy toward the Japanese in some parts of the United States. During World War II large numbers of Japanese and Japanese Americans were interned in detention camps in the United States because their loyalty was suspect. For advocates of this perspective dropping the atomic bomb on Japan was easy because the Japanese were viewed as inferior people. They question whether it would have been used in Europe. The counterargument points to the willingness to destroy both Dresden, Germany, and Tokyo through fire bombings and the lack of any true understanding of how unique the atomic bomb was. Into the first years of the COLD WAR it was simply viewed as the biggest bomb.

The Soviet Union declared war on Japan as agreed to at YALTA on August 8. There would be no joint occupation of Japan, as was the case with Germany. Japan would be governed by American occupation forces commanded by General DOUGLAS MACARTHUR. During the occupation war trials were conducted of leading Japanese officials involved in planning and conducting World War II. A new constitution was written that officially renounced war as an instrument of national policy. It took effect on May 3, 1947. On September 8, 1951, a multilateral peace treaty was signed between Japan and the United States and 50 other countries. The Soviet Union and its allies did not attend the meeting or sign the treaty. Under its terms, Japan's sovereignty was restored and the United States obtained a military base on Okinawa. A separate agreement was signed between the United States and Japan permitting American troops and planes to be stationed on Japanese soil. The United States and Japan also signed a mutual security treaty on February 8, 1952, that allowed the United States to keep military bases in Japan for defense purposes. In it Japan agreed to create a self-defense force that could only be used internally. The Senate ratified the peace treaty in March 1952.

Over time the American military presence and the establishment of a virtual American security protectorate in Japan became a source of friction between the two states. In 1960 a new security treaty was signed that provided for greater consultation between the two sides. Even this was not enough to quell anti-U.S. sentiment. Rioting broke out and President DWIGHT EISENHOWER was forced to cancel a planned visit to Japan. In 1972 Okinawa was returned to Japanese control. American military bases, however, continued to operate there. In 1995 three American servicemen sexually assaulted a Japanese schoolgirl, setting off demands that the American military presence be terminated. A plebiscite the following year in Okinawa produced a 10-1 vote in favor of reducing the number of U.S. soldiers stationed there.

During the cold war and continuing today, economic issues and not military ones have produced the most tension in the U.S.–Japanese relationship. During the occupation MacArthur sought to reform and open Japan's economy and attract American investment. With the outbreak of the KOREAN WAR the emphasis switched from reform to building up Japan as a bulwark against the further spread of COMMUNISM in Asia. A total of $4 billion dollars were spent in Japan during the Korean War on supplies and equipment. Moreover, the United States was willing to accept protectionist policies on the part of Japan in order to spur economic growth. By the early 1960s the Japanese economic miracle was well underway, and the first signs of stress were appearing. For example, in 1961 American textile workers demanded action from the Kennedy administration to save their jobs, which were threatened by cheaper Japanese imports.

The growing trade imbalance with Japan led President RICHARD NIXON to take a series of unprecedented actions. In 1972 he announced that the United States would allow the dollar to float in international currency markets, a move that inflated the value of the yen. The following year Nixon placed an embargo on soybean exports to Japan. These actions followed his 1971 surprise announcement that he would visit China. Cumulatively these Nixon "shocks" marked a watershed in U.S.-Japanese relations. The Japanese economic problem had been formally acknowledged, and future presidents would struggle to devise measures to address it.

In broad terms the American approach has come to stress four themes. First, the United States has been more interested in opening up Japan than protecting the American market from Japanese competition. Second, the United States has cast its position in highly moralistic and ideological tones. Third, protective measures have been put forward with a certain amount of ambivalence limiting their impact. Finally, it also bears noting that the trade relationship has become a thorny domestic issue that has generated pressures that have complicated the search for an agreement.

The initial policy response was to negotiate a series of voluntary export restraints in such wide-ranging areas as autos, steel, and textiles. On the import side of the equation, Japan sought to establish predetermined market shares for American imports, such as beef and citrus prod-

ucts, while avoiding a general opening of the market. The trade imbalance continued to grow despite a realignment in the value of the yen. Between 1985 and 1989 it grew from $39.5 billion to $49.1 billion.

Facing strong congressional pressure for action, President GEORGE H. W. BUSH invoked Section 301 of the Omnibus Trade and Competition Act of 1988. In doing so he identified Japan as having engaged in unfair trade practices and made it subject to retaliatory action by the United States. Bush also sought to move away from sector-by-sector negotiations to one designed to alter Japan's fundamental approach to trade. The vehicle employed was the Structural Impediments Initiative (SII) talks. This marked a departure from the approach of his predecessor, RONALD REAGAN, who had continued to work within the sector approach with his Market-Oriented Sector Specific talks. President BILL CLINTON continued Bush's approach when he met with Prime Minister Kiichi Miyazawa in April 1993, and the two agreed to establish a U.S.-Japan Framework for a New Economic Partnership. Japan was willing to embrace "illustrative criteria" but not numerical targets. A 1994 Clinton initiative ended in failure, and he reinstated the Super 301 clause. President GEORGE W. BUSH met with Japanese leaders at Camp David on June 30, 2002, and they announced the establishment of a U.S.-Japan Economic Partnership for Growth. It too focuses on structural reforms.

The importance of economics in the U.S.-Japanese relationship carries over into the military area. While Japan did not send troops to fight in the PERSIAN GULF WAR, it promised $13 billion in funding for the American war effort—and an additional $3 billion for Middle East states. Most indicative of the intersection of military and economic concerns is the 1987–89 controversy over Japan's new FSX fighter. The United States wanted Japan to purchase one of its existing aircraft while Japan wanted to build it by itself. In 1987 it was decided to coproduce the FSX. CONGRESS reacted angrily, claiming that the United States was "giving away" technology in one of the few areas in which it held an advantage over Japan, and the terms of the agreement had to be renegotiated.

The war against TERRORISM adds a new dimension to the U.S.-Japanese relationship. Japan sent ships, including a destroyer, to the Indian Ocean in support of the U.S. military operation in AFGHANISTAN. This marked the first time since 1945 that Japanese forces had been officially sent overseas as part of a military mission. Japan is also expected to play a key financial role in rebuilding Afghanistan.

**Further reading:** Emmerson, John K., and Harrison M. Holland. *The Eagle and the Rising Son.* New York: Addison-Wesley Longman, 1988; LaFeber, Walter. *The Clash: U.S.–Japanese Relations throughout History.* New York: Norton, 1997; Schoppa, Leonard. *Bargaining with*

*Japan: What American Pressure Can and Cannot Do.* New York: Columbia University Press, 1997.

## Jay's Treaty

After independence foreign relations between the United States and GREAT BRITAIN were anything but smooth. The British not only refused to leave their northwestern posts as they had promised in the TREATY OF PARIS, but they actively worked with NATIVE AMERICANS in an effort to create a buffer blocking further American expansion. Further complicating relations were two 1793 British Orders in Council, which authorized the seizure of all neutral (American) goods headed for French ports and the detention of all ships carrying the products of a French colony or supplies for the use of these colonies. The British seized some 300 American ships and forcibly impressed many crew members into the British navy.

Partisan politics ran through the growing crisis pitting anti-British Jeffersonians against pro-British Federalists. In 1794 ALEXANDER HAMILTON, a Federalist, proposed that a diplomatic mission be sent to London to resolve matters. John Jay, chief justice of the Supreme Court and a Federalist, was selected to negotiate on behalf of the United States. His nomination was opposed by the Jeffersonians (eventually called Democratic-Republicans), and CONGRESS only approved his appointment after three days of acrimonious debate. His instructions precluded signing any agreement that conflicted with any treaties the United States had with FRANCE, which was at war with Great Britain.

Jay had little bargaining power. He knew the British did not want war because it would disrupt trade with North America and complicate their war efforts with France. His one credible ploy was the threat to form an anti-British maritime neutrality pact with Denmark and Sweden. Alexander Hamilton secretly informed the British that the United States had no intention of doing so, thus robbing him of this threat.

On November 19, 1794, Jay signed a treaty with Great Britain that was roundly condemned in the United States Britain once again agreed to abandon the northwestern posts and gave the United States MOST-FAVORED-NATION trade status but restricted its commercial access to the British West Indies. The treaty did not address the British practice of taking slaves when they left U.S. territory, impressing U.S. seamen, interfering with the Native tribes, or seizing U.S. ships. In fact, Jay conceded that the British could seize U.S. goods bound for France if they paid for them and could confiscate without payment French goods on American ships. Jay's Treaty survived a ratification vote in the Senate with the minimum needed, 20-10. An attempt was then made to prevent its implementation by denying funds in the House of Representatives. This too failed, with President Washington refusing requests for diplomatic documents related to the treaty.

Jay's Treaty is significant on several counts. Domestically, it helped shape the American party system, pitting pro-British Federalists against anti-British and pro-French Jeffersonians. On the international level, the treaty did postpone war with Great Britain and cause them to leave their northwestern posts. It also had the indirect effect of causing SPAIN to sign PINCKNEY'S TREATY in 1795. Both of these moves contributed to the rapid pace of continental expansion and westward settlement.

**Further reading:** Bemis, Samuel. *Jay's Treaty: A Study in Commerce and Diplomacy.* Rev. ed. New York: Macmillan, 1960.

## Jefferson, Thomas (1743–1826) *president of the United States, secretary of state*

As one of the founders of the new American republic, Thomas Jefferson left an important legacy in many areas. Foreign policy is no exception. As diplomat, SECRETARY OF STATE (1790–93) under President GEORGE WASHINGTON, and third president of the United States, Jefferson was actively involved in making U.S. foreign policy for a quarter of a century. He started from the premise of American exceptionalism. The United States was the "solitary republic of the world" and "the only monument of HUMAN RIGHTS." Rather than advance the interests of states, U.S. foreign policy would advance individual well-being and societal interests. His foreign policy reflected a dualism or tension that has frequently been present in American foreign policy. Jefferson sought both to stand apart from the traditional Old World practices of international relations and to transform it. Nowhere is this tension more evident than in his thinking about war. Jefferson rejected war, large armies, and the inevitable debts that followed them as factors promoting tyrannical government. Yet he embraced war and the threat of war, "peaceable coercion," when they would advance his interests, such as against the BARBARY PIRATES, NATIVE AMERICANS, or FRANCE and GREAT BRITAIN.

Jefferson's major foreign-policy success occurred in his first term as president. With the LOUISIANA PURCHASE Jefferson was able to double the original size of the United States, provide an avenue for continued westward expansion, and remove the specter of a hostile powerful European state along its western border. Commentators are divided over whether the Louisiana Purchase was the product of skillful DIPLOMACY by Jefferson and American diplomats or the result of luck in that the decision made by Napoleon Bonaparte to sell the Louisiana Territory had little to do with American policy initiatives. What is clear is that in making the Louisiana Purchase Jefferson ran afoul of his own strict interpretation of the CONSTITUTION. Nowhere does the Constitution explicitly grant the PRESIDENT the right to acquire territory. Jefferson believed that a constitutional amendment was necessary for this to happen. Given the time that would be required to do so and the perceived need to act quickly, Jefferson merely submitted the agreement to the Senate, which approved it by a 24-7 vote on October 20, 1803. In doing so he contributed to the principle of implied powers of the federal government.

Jefferson's second term saw him undertake a far less successful foreign-policy initiative. This one involved the principle of peaceful coercion. With France and Britain at war, the United States had emerged as the most important neutral carrier of foodstuffs and other products. Jefferson sought to use this status as leverage to end the conflict as well as to get Great Britain to stop its economic blockade and policy of impressment of seamen. Opposed by the New England states, the hastily drawn up Embargo Act of 1807 prohibited the export of virtually all goods from the United States. In short, the Embargo Act was a self-imposed embargo. Within a year the smuggling of goods out of the United States through CANADA was commonplace, and opposition to the Embargo Act reached the point at which talk of secession in New England was also commonplace. Three days before Jefferson left office, on March 1, 1809, Congress repealed the act and replaced it with the Nonintercourse Act, which permitted commerce with all ports except those under British and French control. Just as with the Louisiana Purchase, the Embargo Act found Jefferson to be anything but a strict constructionist of the Constitution, for he interpreted the power to regulate commerce as including the power to stop all trade.

**Further reading:** Tucker, Robert W., and David C. Hendrickson. *Empire of Liberty: The Statecraft of Thomas Jefferson.* New York: Oxford University Press, 1992.

## Johnson, Lyndon Baines (1908–1973) *president of the United States*

Lyndon Johnson was the 36th president of the United States. He assumed the presidency in 1963 following the assassination of JOHN KENNEDY. Johnson had challenged Kennedy for the 1960 Democratic nomination and was a surprise choice for vice president. Johnson traveled widely as vice president but did not play an important role in the key crises decisions made by the Kennedy administration. Significantly, one place to which Johnson traveled was South VIETNAM, where he came away calling for increased economic and military aid in order to stop the spread of COMMUNISM.

The key foreign-policy problem that consumed Johnson's presidency was Vietnam. Johnson inherited a deterio-

President Lyndon B. Johnson *(left)* meets with his National Security Council, July 1968. *(LBJ Library Collection)*

rating situation in South Vietnam. He was determined to prevent a communist victory there and moved to increase the level of the U.S. commitment. The two central elements in his strategy were the introduction of U.S. ground forces and the massive bombing of North Vietnam. Both became increasingly controversial as the fighting continued and victory proved illusive. Johnson's advisers, most of whom he inherited from the Kennedy administration, began to express doubts about the wisdom of the VIETNAM WAR. Vietnam had become a quagmire from which there appeared no easy exit. The Tet Offensive, in January 1968, was a defining moment for the Johnson administration because it brought home to the extent to which the U.S. military strategy had failed to destroy either the capabilities or the morale of Communist forces. Matters were made worse by the state of politics in South Vietnam. Corrupt and authoritarian rule was the norm, and claims that the purpose of the U.S. involvement was to protect democracy became less and less credible. A third, but subsidiary, element in Johnson's strategy for victory was the periodic use of bombing halts in an effort to entice the North Vietnamese to the bargaining table.

Johnson's conduct of the Vietnam War was a high-profile issue in American politics that drew attention and resources away from his Great Society program. In 1964 Republican presidential candidate Barry Goldwater challenged Johnson for not prosecuting the war with sufficient purpose to bring about victory. In 1968, Johnson faced challenges from within the DEMOCRATIC PARTY in senators Eugene McCarthy and Robert Kennedy, who called for ending the U.S. involvement. In March 1968 Johnson announced that he would not seek reelection. Throughout the war segments of the burgeoning PEACE MOVEMENT and members of CONGRESS led by J. WILLIAM FULBRIGHT questioned the constitutional basis on which the Vietnam

War was being fought. The most frequently cited justification was the Gulf of Tonkin Resolution passed by Congress in 1964 in reaction to North Vietnamese attacks on U.S. PT boats *C. Turner Joy* and *Maddox*, which authorized Johnson to take all steps necessary to protect American lives. Evidence later revealed casts doubt upon the events surrounding the incident and suggests that the information was manipulated to have the desired political effect.

Vietnam was not the only major foreign-policy issue that confronted the Johnson administration. Several events are particularly notable. Fearing that the DOMINICAN REPUBLIC would become another CUBA, in 1965 Johnson sent marines there in order to restore order. Johnson continued the ARMS CONTROL initiatives begun by Kennedy after the CUBAN MISSILE CRISIS. His administration negotiated and a NUCLEAR NONPROLIFERATION TREATY with the Soviet Union (see RUSSIA). It was signed in July 1968 but was not ratified by the Senate due to the Soviet invasion of CZECHOSLOVAKIA in August. During the 1967 Six-Day War between ISRAEL and Arab forces Johnson sent the U.S. Sixth Fleet close to SYRIA in order to forestall a Soviet intervention into the conflict. Particularly frustrating for the Johnson administration was the North Korean seizure of the USS *Pueblo*, an electronics INTELLIGENCE ship. Captured just prior to the Tet Offensive, it led to speculation that NORTH KOREA was about to resume military operations against South Korea. Johnson considered military retaliation but rejected this option, choosing instead to rely upon diplomacy. The crew was returned after 11 months in captivity.

Johnson's handling of foreign policy finds few ardent defenders. He accepted the common COLD WAR wisdom that communism posed a worldwide threat to American security interests, the need to use military force to stop this threat, and the belief that negotiations with communists could easily be interpreted as appeasement. Most commonly cited as contributing to his inability to devise an effective political-military strategy in Vietnam was his tendency to oversimplify and personalize problems and to treat foreign-policy problems as amenable to the same type of arm twisting and personal persuasion that allowed him to succeed on domestic issues.

**Further reading:** Gallucci, Robert. *Neither Peace nor Honor: The Politics of American Military Policy in Viet Nam*. Baltimore: Johns Hopkins University Press, 1975; Geyelin, Philip V. *LBJ and the World*. New York: Macmillan, 1966.

## Joint Chiefs of Staff

The Joint Chiefs of Staff (JCS) was formally brought into existence by the NATIONAL SECURITY ACT OF 1947. It consists of the chairperson, vice chairperson (added in 1986), the chief of staff of the army, the chief of naval operations, the chief of staff of the air force, and the commandant of the Marine Corps. The JCS is supported in its work by a joint staff composed of approximately equal numbers of officers from the army, navy, and air force. The marine contingent is taken out of the navy allocation and comprises about 20 percent of that number.

Cooperation among the armed forces of the United States has had a checkered past. In principle the need for cooperation and joint operations is well recognized. Early examples include navy and army cooperation in the WAR OF 1812 along Lake Champlain and the Battle of Vicksburg during the AMERICAN CIVIL WAR. The first institutionalized attempt at promoting joint planning came after the SPANISH-AMERICAN WAR. In 1903 a Joint Army and Navy Board was established but accomplished little since it was not empowered to enforce its decisions. After WORLD WAR I an effort was made to revitalize the Joint Board. It now had the power to initiate recommendations, but it was still denied powers of enforcement. The Joint Board continued through WORLD WAR II and was officially disbanded in 1947.

The impetus for the current JCS system came during World War II when the United States and GREAT BRITAIN agreed on the need for administrative, tactical, and strategic coordination between their two country's military forces. The British had a military structure in place for this purpose, the Chiefs of Staff Committee. The United States had to invent a counterpart body. Following the advice of Admiral William Leahy, who was President FRANKLIN ROOSEVELT's special military adviser, the United States created a unified high command in 1942. This body operated during World War II without any congressional or presidential mandate.

The chairperson of the JCS is designated as the principal military adviser to the PRESIDENT, SECRETARY OF DEFENSE, and the NATIONAL SECURITY COUNCIL. All members of the JCS, however, have the legal right to offer advice. The 1986 GOLDWATER-NICHOLS ACT, the last major legislative reorganization of the DEFENSE DEPARTMENT also recognizes the chairperson of the JCS as the senior ranking member of the armed forces. The Goldwater-Nichols Act also clarified a lingering point of confusion in the JCS system. During World War II, the Joint Chiefs of Staff exercised command authority over U.S. forces. The 1947 National Security Act defined their role as being planners and advisers. However, a 1948 agreement allowed them to continue functioning in the line of command. The 1986 act stated that the line of command runs from the PRESIDENT to the SECRETARY OF DEFENSE to the commander of the combatant commands.

In addition to the debate over the balance of military power between the JCS and the military commands, two other enduring issues have dominated studies of the JCS.

The first is the relative power and influence of senior military officers vis-à-vis their civilian counterparts in matters of strategy, weapons procurement, and war planning. The second is the ability, or inability, of members of the JCS to rise above their parochial military identifications and provide unbiased national military advice.

See also CIVIL-MILITARY RELATIONS.

**Further reading:** Huntington, Samuel. *The Soldier and the State: The Theory and Practice of Civil-Military Relations.* New York: Vintage, 1957.

## Jordan

Jordan has a population of 5 million people and an area of 34,573 square miles, which is roughly the equivalent of Indiana. It comprises part of a region known as the Fertile Crescent that was under the control of the Ottoman Empire from the early 1500s until WORLD WAR I. In 1920 Transjordan, as it was then known, became a British mandate under the LEAGUE OF NATIONS. The British mandate ended on May 22, 1946, and Transjordan became an independent state.

Transjordan joined other Arab states in opposing Israeli independence in 1948. The armistice agreement of April 3, 1949, that ended that war left Transjordan in control of the West Bank and east Jerusalem. That same month its official name was changed to Jordan, reflecting its acquisition of land west of the Jordan River. In December Jordan and ISRAEL formally concluded an armistice, and in 1950 Jordan annexed the West Bank.

One consequence of this war was an increase in Jordan's population by approximately 450,000 people, most of whom were Palestinians who had been displaced by the war and could not return home. A second large-scale Palestinian refugee flow followed the 1967 war in which Israel captured the West Bank and Jerusalem. This time another 300,000 REFUGEES arrived, bringing the total refugee population to approximately 1 million. These refugees became the foundation for the Palestinian resistance movement, the FEDYAHEEN, which used Jordan as a base to strike against Israeli targets. Jordan and the Palestinians were fundamentally divided over the fate of the West Bank. The Palestinians hoped to create a Palestinian state through which Jordan hoped to reestablish its rule over the area. Fighting between the military forces ensued, and in September 1970 a full-scale civil war broke out that resulted in the Palestinian GUERRILLA forces fleeing to LEBANON and SYRIA.

Jordan's relations with the United States were generally positive at this time in spite of Jordan's opposition to Israel. Jordan participated in discussions regarding the formation of the Baghdad Pact but did not join. Jordan did seek and received U.S. aid in 1958 following the revolution in IRAQ and fears that Egyptian leader Gamal Abdel Nasser would continue his effort to bring down the Jordanian monarchy. British troops were stationed in Jordan from July 17 to November 2, 1958, as a precautionary measure.

Jordan joined with other Arab states in opposing the CAMP DAVID accords signed in 1979 between Israel and EGYPT. All sides had hoped that Jordan would join in the peace process. King Hussein, however, declined, and Jordan remained on the sidelines. Hussein was skeptical that real progress could be made on the Palestinian question and preferred to advocate the Arab rejectionist position. He also objected to the policy emerging in Israel by which Tel Aviv advanced the notion that Jordan was the Palestinian state.

Jordanian relations with the United States became further strained in the 1980s. First, in 1985 CONGRESS blocked the sale of F-16 aircraft, Stinger missiles, and I-Hawk mobile air defense missiles to Jordan. The congressional action was rooted in anger over Hussein's inability to work out an agreement with Palestinian leader Yasser Arafat that would promote Israeli security. Second, on July 31, 1988, Jordan announced that it was renouncing its claims to the West Bank and called upon the PALESTINE LIBERATION ORGANIZATION (PLO) to take authority over it. The United States was unhappy with this move since its policy in the region had long been premised on the idea that any future Palestinian state could somehow be linked to Jordan. The official U.S. position was that the status of this territory can be determined only by negotiations among all parties concerned.

Jordan further angered the United States by siding with Iraq in the PERSIAN GULF WAR, although it did condemn the Iraqi invasion of Kuwait and abide by international ECONOMIC SANCTIONS. This move had severe international economic and political repercussions, but it was hailed within Jordan. Recognizing the continued reality of Jordan's key role in any Arab-Israeli peace progress, the United States moved quickly to restore economic aid after the war ended. By July 1991 the United States had restored $35 million in frozen economic FOREIGN AID. The United States has provided Jordan with more than $2 billion in economic aid since 1952. It continues to reject Jordanian requests for military aid.

Not coincidentally, in 1991 Jordan joined with Syria, Lebanon, and Palestinian representatives to participate in direct peace negotiations with Israel. As a result of these negotiations, sponsored by the United States and RUSSIA, Jordan and Israel signed a nonbelligerency agreement in Washington on July 25, 1994, and a peace treaty on October 26, 1994.

Jordan has acted as a mediator between Israelis and Palestinians in the second intifada that broke out in September 2000.

See also ARAB-ISRAELI CONFLICT.

# K

## Kellogg-Briand Pact

The Kellogg-Briand Pact of 1929 outlawed war as a means of settling disputes. It captivated the attention of American citizens and policy makers who sought some mechanism of creating and maintaining a peaceful INTERNATIONAL SYSTEM in the aftermath of the U.S. refusal to join the LEAGUE OF NATIONS. In fact, the Kellogg-Briand Pact would bring together supporters of the League of Nations and those who had opposed it, such as Senator WILLIAM BORAH (R-Idaho). Although not linked to it in a formal sense, the Kellogg-Briand Pact occurred along side of the DISARMAMENT movement that swept the United States in the 1920s.

Within the United States a key force behind the "outlawry of war" movement was James Shotwell, a professor of history at Columbia University. In 1927 on a visit to FRANCE, Shotwell convinced French foreign minister Aristide Briand to endorse the antiwar position. Briand wrote a letter to the American people, prepared by Shotwell, proposing a treaty between the United States and France outlawing war. The Coolidge administration and SECRETARY OF STATE Frank Kellogg were cool to the idea since they correctly saw it as an attempt by Briand to establish an informal ALLIANCE between the two states. Public pressure, however, was building for an agreement to outlaw war. Senator Borah proposed a compromised that Kellogg seized upon. Rather than a bilateral agreement between the two states, it would be a multilateral agreement outlawing war. Now it was Briand who felt pressured to agree to the proposal.

In August 1928, 15 states met to negotiate the treaty. It was simple and straightforward. The parties to the treaty agreed to renounce war "as an instrument of national policy" and to resolve their disputes "by pacific means." Interpretive notes that stated, "[E]very nation is free at all times and regardless of treaty provisions to defend its territory from attack and it alone is competent to decide whether circumstances require war in self-defense," went largely unnoticed by the American public. In January 1929 the Senate approved the treaty by a vote of 85-1. After all 15

states that attended the conference had ratified the agreement, President HERBERT HOOVER declared it in force on July 24, 1929. It would seem that the Senate had few illusions about the pact's potential to end war: The next item it voted on after approving the treaty was an appropriation of $274 million for 15 heavy cruisers. The Senate also accepted an interpretation put forward by the Foreign Relations Committee that asserted the right of the United States to fight for the MONROE DOCTRINE and the right not to enforce the treaty against violators.

The Kellogg-Briand Pact was soon put to the test in Manchuria when in 1931 Japanese forces pushed Chinese forces out of southern Manchuria. China appealed to the League of Nations and the United States, the latter as a signatory of the Kellogg-Briand Pact, for help. Hoover opposed using economic or military force to compel JAPAN to abandon its newly established position of dominance. Instead, Secretary of State HENRY STIMSON sent identical diplomatic notes to CHINA and Japan saying that the United States would not recognized any territorial gains that came about as a violation of the OPEN DOOR or Kellogg-Briand Pact. The United States, however, took no action to reverse the ongoing establishment of a Japanese puppet state in Manchuria.

**Further reading:** Farrell, Robert. *Peace in Our Time: The Origins of the Kellogg-Briand Pact.* New Haven, Conn.: Yale University Press, 1952.

## Kennan, George Frost (1904– ) *diplomat*

George Kennan is the original architect of CONTAINMENT, the U.S. strategy for engaging the Soviet Union (see RUSSIA) during the COLD WAR. More than any other individual, he provided the intellectual rationale for this policy, basing it on his reading of Russian history and the motives of Soviet leaders. He predicted that in time a firm policy of containment would bring about pressures for domestic reforms and ultimately the mellowing or breakup of Soviet power. Kennan also gained notoriety for his critique of American foreign policy. He was deeply distrustful of the American tendency to pursue legalistic and universalistic solutions to problems and routinely expressed doubts about the capacity of democracies to conduct foreign policy.

Kennan joined the Foreign Service in 1926 and soon established himself as a Russian expert, helping open the first U.S. EMBASSY in Moscow. After several different postings during WORLD WAR II, Kennan returned to Moscow, where in February 1946 he sent his famous "long telegram" to the STATE DEPARTMENT. The telegram was a reply to a request from the TREASURY DEPARTMENT for information on the economic and financial situation in the Soviet Union, but his response went far beyond that. In its 8,000 words Kennan warned of the dangers of communist expansionism and presented his interpretation of the roots of the Soviet worldview. He also argued that war was not inevitable and made the case for a strategy of containment. His position was refined, and in 1947 his remarks appeared in the leading academic foreign-policy journal *Foreign Affairs* as "The Sources of Soviet Conduct" by X. His authorship was hidden so as to allow the piece to serve as a trial balloon by the Truman administration, which was unsure of how to proceed in its dealings with the Soviet Union. The "X" article was well received, and Kennan was catapulted to a leading position within the U.S. foreign-policy establishment and placed in charge of the State Department's new Policy Planning Staff. There he helped SECRETARY OF STATE GEORGE MARSHALL formulate the MARSHALL PLAN for European economic recovery.

Kennan not only made foreign policy in his new position, but he also critiqued it, objecting to the Truman Doctrine, the creation of the NORTH ATLANTIC TREATY ORGANIZATION, and NSC-68. In particular he was concerned with the rush to implement containment strictly in military terms. His vision of containment was based on a combination of economics, politics, and military POWER. Conflicts with DEAN ACHESON, the newly appointed secretary of state, led Kennan to leave the State Department. He would return to government service periodically, serving as ambassador to the Soviet Union and YUGOSLAVIA.

Out of government Kennan was an active and vocal critic of U.S. foreign policy. He opposed President DWIGHT EISENHOWER's aggressive policy of containment and disapproved of the talk of liberating Eastern Europe. In its place he advanced a policy of great power disengagement from Europe. Kennan would later oppose the escalating U.S. presence in VIETNAM but stopped short of calling for an end to the war. He also asserted that the United States had overreacted to the Soviet invasion of AFGHANISTAN, and he opposed its preoccupation with HUMAN RIGHTS during JIMMY CARTER's presidency. RONALD REAGAN was criticized

for his "inexcusably childish" embrace of cold war thinking and his increase in defense spending. More generally, he cautioned against U.S. involvement in trying to solve the domestic and social problems of developing countries.

**Further reading:** Gaddis, John L. *Strategies of Containment: A Critical Appraisal of Postwar National Security Policy.* New York: Oxford University Press, 1993; Kennan, George. *American Diplomacy, 1900–1950.* New York: New American Library, 1951.

**Kennedy, John F.** (1917–1963) *president*
John Fitzgerald Kennedy was the 35th president of the United States, serving from 1961 until his assassination on November 22, 1963. Prior to becoming PRESIDENT, Kennedy served in the Senate, where he sat on the Foreign Relations Committee. Biographers differ on his foreign-policy record as senator. It is alternatively described as lacking in any notable accomplishments and as one in which Kennedy elevated Third World issues, such as nationalism and independence, into the consciousness of U.S. foreign policy.

As a presidential candidate Kennedy charged that the Eisenhower-Nixon administration had been slow to build up American military power and had allowed a MISSILE GAP to develop, giving the Soviet Union (see RUSSIA) a significant lead in this vital area. Evidence later proved this politically effective charge to be false. He criticized massive retaliation as a national security strategy that left the United States unable to respond to limited challenges and was critical of DWIGHT EISENHOWER's "tolerance" of Fidel Castro's rule in CUBA.

Kennedy brought with him to the White House a new generation of foreign-policy experts. Led by ROBERT MCNAMARA as SECRETARY OF DEFENSE, many came out of foreign-policy THINK TANKS and the private sector. Dubbed "the best and the brightest," they approached foreign-policy problems with great confidence and sought to fix them through the application of a managerial and engineering approach to problem solving.

Much of the history of Kennedy's foreign policy is recorded in a rapid-fire series of crises that faced his administration. In some cases they were the result of foreign challenges (the BERLIN CRISIS, 1961, and the CUBAN MISSILE CRISIS). In others they were largely self-inflicted (the BAY OF PIGS). A common theme of Kennedy's crisis management was a tendency to turn the issue into a personal test of wills and a willingness to lead with a military response to the neglect of DIPLOMACY.

The Kennedy administration also proved to have an expansive definition of U.S. NATIONAL INTERESTS that resulted in little distinction being made between core and

President John F. Kennedy is shown signing the Partial Nuclear Test Ban treaty, October 1963.  *(John F. Kennedy Library)*

peripheral interests, as the COLD WAR was global in scope. Diplomatic and military initiatives in Europe and Latin America were joined by a fledgling involvement in Southeast Asia. This breadth of scope was matched by an expansiveness of purpose. The United States became both enforcer and social worker. Containing COMMUNISM through nuclear DETERRENCE was now joined with a flexible response strategy that would allow the United States to counter GUERRILLA insurgencies. Nation-building became the U.S. prescription to fix what ailed developing societies. This effort exhibited a benevolent side with the creation of the Peace Corps, but it also led to a willingness to violate democratic principles through the use of COVERT ACTION against Cuba and the creation of strategic hamlets in VIETNAM as part of Operation Phoenix.

Kennedy's foreign policy is also significant for the strides his administration made in ARMS CONTROL. Little headway had been made here in the Eisenhower administration, and Eisenhower's term in office ended on a low note with the U-2 affair. Where Kennedy's initial inclination had been to build up American nuclear forces, he shifted gears and embraced arms control following the Cuban missile crisis. Opposition within CONGRESS and the military dictated that the Kennedy administration move forward carefully. Rather than a comprehensive nuclear test ban treaty, Kennedy settled for the Partial Nuclear Test Ban Treaty that banned testing in the atmosphere, outer space, and underwater, where inspection would not be an issue. He also moved the United States from a strategy of nuclear superiority that was inherent in the notion of massive retaliation to one of MUTUAL ASSURED DESTRUCTION (MAD) that rested upon nuclear sufficiency.

With Kennedy's death, LYNDON JOHNSON became president and inherited his foreign-policy agenda. Movement on arms control continued until the late 1960s when the deepening U.S. involvement in Vietnam and the Soviet invasion of CZECHOSLOVAKIA produced too much distrust for diplomats and political leaders to overcome. Johnson Americanized the war in Vietnam, a move Kennedy defenders argue he would not have made, with some asserting that had Kennedy been reelected he would have gotten the United States out of Vietnam. Critics of Kennedy argue that U.S. domestic politics in the late 1960s would have made such a move politically difficult to accomplish and that there is little in Kennedy's foreign-policy style that would support such a shift. As the *Wall Street Journal* reflected in 1971, Kennedy's foreign policy was "too much vigor and too little restraint . . . too much eloquence and too little thoughtfulness . . . too much flexibility and too little patience, too much brilliance and too little common sense."

**Further reading:** Beschloss, Michael R. *The Crisis Years: Kennedy and Khrushchev, 1960–1963.* New York: Random House, 1963; Hilsman, Roger. *To Move a Nation.* Garden City, N.Y.: Doubleday, 1967; Schlesinger, Arthur M., Jr. *Thousand Days.* Boston: Houghton-Mifflin, 1965.

## Kennedy Round

The Kennedy Round of trade negotiations held between 1964 and 1967 was the sixth round of multilateral trade negotiations held under the auspices of the GENERAL AGREEMENT ON TARIFFS AND TRADE (GATT). GATT served as the primary instrument for organizing international trade from the end of WORLD WAR II and the creation of the WORLD TRADE ORGANIZATION in 1995. The Kennedy Round is significant because it produced the deepest and most far-reaching set of tariff reductions ever negotiated. The weighted average of tariff reductions on nonagricultural items was 35 percent. The United States reduced tariffs on some 65 percent of total dutiable imports.

The origins of the Kennedy Round negotiations are to be found in both domestic and international political developments. At the international level the newly elected Kennedy administration desired to establish new and better relations with America's West European allies. A major stumbling block to improving relations was the existence of high protective tariffs that the European Common Market had placed around agricultural products. The Kennedy administration determined that a new international trade agreement reducing tariffs would be an important step in improving relations and guaranteeing American products entry into the important European market.

At the domestic level, CONGRESS made the Kennedy Round negotiations possible by passing the Trade Expansion Act of 1962. This piece of legislation replaced the Reciprocal Trade Agreements Act of 1934. The Kennedy administration argued that this act and its many revisions were no longer relevant to an INTERNATIONAL SYSTEM characterized by high levels of international trade and dominated by the United States and the European Common Market. Most significantly it permitted the negotiation of across-the-board tariff reductions instead of working on an item-by-item basis, which had been enshrined in the 1934 act. Under the terms of the 1961 act, the PRESIDENT was permitted to reduce tariffs up to 50 percent of their July 1962 value. An escape clause was also inserted in case the new trade agreement resulted in an unanticipated flood of imports.

The Trade Expansion Act of 1962 contained two other important innovations. First, it offered adjustment assistance to firms and workers that could document that they were injured by foreign competition. Second, it created the OFFICE OF THE SPECIAL TRADE REPRESENTATIVE (OSTR). The person heading this office was designated to be the U.S. chief representative at multilateral trade negotiations and was to hold cabinet-level rank. Creation of the OSTR reflected congressional displeasure over the STATE DEPARTMENT's handling of international trade negotiations. The State Department was widely perceived as being more concerned with maintaining good relations with U.S. allies than it was with protecting American business interests.

The Kennedy Round negotiations began with each of the participating states presenting and then justifying a list of exceptions to the proposed 50 percent across-the-board reduction. As a result of these lobbying efforts two important omissions or failings occurred in the Kennedy Round. First, U.S. negotiators failed to make any significant headway on reducing agricultural tariffs. Second, JAPAN, which benefited greatly from many of the U.S. concessions, failed to reciprocate by opening up its markets to American goods. In Japan and elsewhere, nontariff barriers to trade emerged as an important weapon that countries could use to prevent foreign goods from gaining access to their home markets.

The Kennedy Round is seen by critics as having unfairly opened the American market to global competition and cheap imports and in the process as having contributed to the growing trade imbalance that would eventually help undermine the BRETTON WOODS SYSTEM. It was unfairly opened in their view because of the asymmetries in the concessions reached in those negotiations. In the three years before the Kennedy Round agreement took effect, imports from Japan to the United States exceeded U.S. exports to Japan by 17 percent. One decade later the gap was 50 percent. Unhappiness with the growing trade imbalance became a major force behind U.S. efforts to convene a seventh round of trade negotiations: the TOKYO ROUND negotiations.

**Further reading:** Destler, I. M. *American Trade Politics: System under Stress.* Washington, D.C. Institute for International Economics, 1986; Evans, John W. *The Kennedy Round in American Trade Policy.* Cambridge, Mass.: Harvard University Press, 1971.

### Kissinger, Henry (1923– )  *secretary of state, national security advisor*

Henry Kissinger was SECRETARY OF STATE under Presidents RICHARD NIXON and GERALD FORD (1971–76). He also served as NATIONAL SECURITY ADVISOR to President Nixon (1969–71), holding both posts for a brief time. He is credited with guiding U.S. foreign policy out of the COLD WAR logic that produced the VIETNAM WAR to a foreign policy of DÉTENTE. In the course of doing so the United States signed the STRATEGIC ARMS LIMITATION TALKS (SALT) Treaty I with the Soviet Union and reopened diplomatic relations with CHINA. Kissinger also played a major role through his shuttle DIPLOMACY to bring peace to the Middle East following the ARAB-ISRAELI CONFLICT in 1973. Kissinger and North Vietnamese diplomat Le Duc Tho won the 1973 Nobel Peace Prize for ending the Vietnam War. Critics charge that his secretive decision-making style and aversion to disorder in the developing world led the United States to align itself with right-wing dictators and to condone HUMAN-RIGHTS violations.

Prior to serving in the Nixon administration Kissinger was a leading scholar on the dynamics of world politics and adviser to presidents. Kissinger received his B.A. and Ph.D. from Harvard University and then went on to teach

Secretary of State Henry Kissinger  *(Library of Congress)*

there. In 1957 two of his works were published. *A World Restored* was his doctoral dissertation, and it advanced a theory of world politics that stressed the importance of POWER. Kissinger saw the peace of Europe as having been maintained through a balance of power politics, a policy of bargaining from a position of strength, and the creation of an international order that was seen as legitimate by the major powers. This analysis provided the conceptual framework that would serve as the foundation for the policy of détente. *Nuclear Weapons and Foreign Policy* was written under the auspices of the Council on Foreign Relations. It put forward the argument that NUCLEAR WEAPONS had not fundamentally altered the basic principles of power politics that governed international relations. This led Kissinger to conclude that nuclear weapons remained a viable instrument of foreign policy and that the United States could not advance its national interests by simply relying upon a policy of massive retaliation.

Though he would come to serve as Nixon's key foreign-policy adviser and provide the intellectual foundation for Nixon's policies, Kissinger was not close to Nixon before entering his administration. He was a long-time adviser to Nelson Rockefeller, Republican governor of New York, in his unsuccessful presidential bids. He also advised Democratic presidential candidate JOHN KENNEDY, who defeated Nixon in 1960. Nixon appointed Kissinger to the post of national security advisor at the recommendation of Rockefeller in the hope that it would enhance the standing of his new administration with the East Coast foreign-policy establishment.

Nixon and Kissinger, who also had written on the role of BUREAUCRACY in making foreign policy, concentrated foreign-policy decision-making power in the White House. Kissinger distrusted bureaucracy and saw it as an impediment to his grand design of redirecting U.S. foreign policy. He relied heavily upon "back channel" lines of communication that allowed him to bypass formal lines of communication and interact directly with his contacts in and out of government.

A combination of secrecy and highly visible MEDIA coverage became the hallmarks of his most successful major foreign-policy initiatives: peace negotiations with North VIETNAM, the SALT I negotiations, Nixon's trip to CHINA, and his shuttle diplomacy in the Middle East. These successes did not prove long lasting. Vietnam fell in 1975. Normalization of relations with China failed to progress due to the Nixon administration's preoccupation with the Watergate scandal. SALT I did not lead quickly to SALT II but only to an interim agreement known as the Vladivostock accords. And peace in the Middle East had been purchased at the cost of large sums of FOREIGN AID to ISRAEL and EGYPT. By the time of the 1976 presidential primaries, Kissinger's foreign policy was under attack by both Republican challenger RONALD REAGAN and the Democratic presidential nominee, JIMMY CARTER. Reagan attacked détente as misguided. Where Kissinger sought to make the Soviet Union and China junior partners in managing the post-Vietnam international system in a balance-of-power exercise, Reagan continued to see them as the enemy to be contained, if not defeated. Carter, likewise, opposed Kissinger's emphasis on power politics. He drew attention to the insensitivity within the Nixon-Ford foreign policies to human-rights violations and the failure to pursue real cuts in preceding ARMS CONTROL agreements.

Kissinger left office at the end of the Ford administration. He was appointed by President Reagan to head the Bipartisan Commission on United States Policy toward Central America. Reagan hoped to use the commission to build support for his policies in EL SALVADOR and NICARAGUA. While the commission recommended increased economic aid to the region and military aid to defeat Communist-supported forces, it did not end the political debate over the wisdom of this course of action. The renewed global interest in using international and national courts to try political leaders for decisions they made that inflicted harm on individuals or resulted in denials of human rights has drawn renewed attention to Kissinger's role in ousting Salvador Allende in CHILE and his support for other pro-U.S. dictators.

See also INTERNATIONAL CRIMINAL COURT; RUSSIA.

**Further reading:** Kissinger, Henry A. *Does America Need a Foreign Policy? Toward a New Diplomacy for the 21st Century.* New York: Touchstone, 2002; ———. *The White House Years.* Boston: Houghton-Mifflin, 1979; Staar, Harvey. *Henry Kissinger: Perceptions of a World Leader.* Lexington, Mass.: Lexington Books, 1983.

## Korean War

On June 25, 1950, approximately 75,000 North Korean troops crossed the 38th parallel along a 125-mile front and invaded SOUTH KOREA. The attack caught the United States off guard politically and militarily. The Truman administration responded by calling for an emergency session of the UNITED NATIONS Security Council, but he did not ask CONGRESS for a declaration of war or a resolution of support. HARRY TRUMAN also ordered U.S. military planes and ships into military action below the 38th parallel. The Seventh Fleet was positioned as a barrier between the island of Formosa (TAIWAN), to which Nationalist forces had retreated after losing the Chinese civil war, and the mainland that was now controlled by the Communists, and military aid was sent to the PHILIPPINES and the French in Indochina.

The Korean Peninsula is strategically located in Northeast Asia, and its control was long been contested by CHINA, JAPAN, and RUSSIA. Japanese troops occupied it during WORLD WAR II, and with Japan's defeat Russia and the United States divided Korea into north and south occupation zones at the 38th parallel. Elections were to be held to unify the country, but Russian opposition prevented this from happening, and the temporary dividing line became permanent. Early COLD WAR pronouncements by Truman administration officials did not indicate that the United States held Korea to be of great strategic or diplomatic significance. It was routinely left out of listings of vital American interests in Asia (Japan and the Philippines were typically singled out).

All of this changed with the North Korean attack. In the wake of deteriorating U.S.-Soviet relations in Europe and the recent "fall of China" to Mao Zedong's (Mao Tse-tung) Communist forces, overnight the defense of South Korea became a high priority for Truman and a test of his resolve to stop Communist aggression and avoid a policy of appeasement such as that followed by the European powers in the 1930s against Adolf Hitler. Failure to stand firm was seen as potentially resulting in Japanese and European cold war neutrality.

Truman's initial military response was largely symbolic and proved insufficient. U.S. planes were now authorized to engage in combat above the 38th parallel. Still, the South Korean capital of Seoul fell within days, and on June 30 PRESIDENT Truman agreed to General DOUGLAS MACARTHUR's request to send American combat troops to South Korea. The North Korean advance was so overpowering that it almost pushed U.S. forces off the peninsula. The tide of combat did not turn in favor of the American forces until September 15, 1950, when MacArthur engineered a brilliant landing at Inchon, well behind the line of advance of North Korea's forces.

Emboldened by this sudden turn of events, the Truman administration changed its goals from defending South Korea to uniting the two Koreas. To that end it decided to send U.S. forces across the 38th parallel into NORTH KOREA. With U.S. forces having advanced well into North Korea and approaching the Yalu River, which served as the North Korean–Chinese border, Chinese forces counterattacked. Through diplomatic channels and limited military encounters, the Chinese had indicated their concern with U.S. military action and their determination not to allow U.S. forces to reach the Chinese border. Their warnings were ignored by MacArthur, who greatly discounted the Chinese military's ability to fight. On November 26 some 200,000 Chinese troops push MacArthur's forces back into South Korea. MacArthur asked Truman to permit massive air strikes against China but was turned down. It was March 1951 before Communist forces were

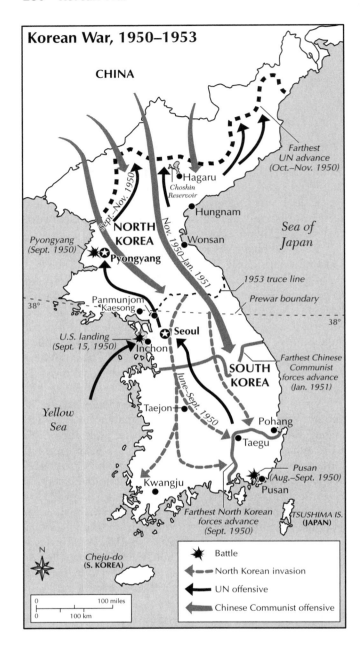

**Korean War, 1950–1953**

CHINA

Farthest UN advance (Oct.–Nov. 1950)

Hagaru
Choshin Reservoir

Hungnam

NORTH KOREA

Sea of Japan

Pyongyang (Sept. 1950)
Wonsan
Pyongyang

1953 truce line

Panmunjom Kaesong
38°
Prewar boundary
38°

U.S. landing (Sept. 15, 1950)
Inchon
Seoul

SOUTH KOREA

Farthest Chinese Communist forces advance (Jan. 1951)

Yellow Sea

Taejon
Pohang
Taegu

Pusan (Aug.–Sept. 1950)
Kwangju
Pusan

Farthest North Korean forces advance (Sept. 1950)

TSUSHIMA IS. (JAPAN)

N

Cheju-do (S. KOREA)

| Battle |
| North Korean invasion |
| UN offensive |
| Chinese Communist offensive |

0 — 100 miles
0 — 100 km

pushed back across the 38th parallel and the military situation stabilized.

Peace talks began in July 1951 at Panmunjom, which was located on the 38th parallel. The talks stalemated and resumed. Republican presidential candidate DWIGHT EISENHOWER promised that if elected he would go to Korea and end the conflict. Eisenhower won the election and went to Korea but could not break the deadlock. A major stumbling block was the inability to arrange for an exchange of prisoners of war (POWs). Truman and Eisenhower were unwilling to send captured Chinese and North Korean soldiers home.

The Eisenhower administration pushed to end the Korean conflict in 1953 by threatening to widen the war. It hinted at the use of atomic weapons against China and the possible resumption of civil war in China through the support of an offensive by Nationalist forces now based on Formosa. Together with Joseph Stalin's death, these actions are credited with bringing about an armistice on July 27, 1953, that established a demilitarized zone between the two states, redrew the existing boundary slightly in South Korea's favor, and established a committee made up of neutral states to address the disposition of POWs.

Total U.S. casualties were placed at 33,000 dead and 105,000 wounded. South Korean dead were numbered at more than 1 million, and combined Chinese and North Korean losses were placed at a similar level. The Korean War cost the United States some $20 billion. With NSC-68 as its conceptual blueprint, the Truman administration's war effort produced a dramatic reordering of American domestic spending priorities. Arms expenditures made up 67 percent of the budget by 1952.

The Korean War represented a major political challenge to the Truman administration both domestically and internationally. At home, Truman found himself under almost continuous political siege. Even before the war began, Truman was the subject of attacks by Senator Joseph McCarthy for being soft on COMMUNISM and for harboring communists within the STATE DEPARTMENT and other government agencies. In April 1951 Truman fired General MacArthur for insubordination. MacArthur had ordered troops to cross the 38th parallel once again, and Truman, supported by the JOINT CHIEFS OF STAFF, saw this move as crippling chances for a cease-fire. MacArthur returned home to a hero's reception and spoke before Congress asserting that the war effort had to be expanded. Korea was the first limited war fought by U.S. forces. As would be the case with Vietnam, large portions of the public found this to run counter to traditional American notions of war and peace, and they came to oppose the war effort or at least those who directed it.

Internationally, Truman turned to the United Nations as the instrument of U.S. foreign policy. The wisdom of doing so has been questioned. Rather than seek a declaration of war from Congress, he sought and received UN support for his actions. Technically, U.S. forces and small numbers of troops from other states fought under a UN command. Truman succeeded only because the Soviet representative boycotted crucial Security Council meetings in protest over the failure to award Mao Zedong's Communist government China's seat. Had the Soviet Union been present, it could have cast a veto over any UN response to the North Korean attack. UN approval for going into North Korea was obtained from the General Assembly under a newly passed "Uniting for Peace Resolution" because the

Soviet Union had by then returned to occupy its Security Council seat.

See also CIVIL-MILITARY RELATIONS; MCCARTHYISM.

**Further reading:** Cumings, Bruce. *The Origins of the Korean War.* 2 vols. Princeton, N.J.: Princeton University Press, 1981 and 1990; Kaufman, Burton. *The Korean War.* Philadelphia: Temple University Press, 1986; Paige, Glenn, D. *The Korean Decision.* New York: Free Press, 1958.

## Kosovo

Kosovo is a province within Serbia, which is one of the two remaining republics of YUGOSLAVIA. Montenegro is the other. Contemporary Yugoslavia came into existence in April 1992 following the secession of BOSNIA AND HERZEGOVINA, CROATIA, Slovenia, and Macedonia. Unlike the rest of Serbia, where they form a majority, Serbs are an ethnic minority in Kosovo, where the dominant ethnic group is Albanian. Kosovo is also a site of great historical significance to Serbs. A 1389 battle between the Serbs and Turks resulted in a crushing defeat for Serb forces and culminated less than a century later in complete Turkish control over Serbian lands. Turkish rule was oppressive for both the Serb nobility and the peasantry. The year 1804 saw the beginnings of a Serb liberation struggle that did not result in Serbian autonomy until 1829, when RUSSIA forced TURKEY to accept the Treaty of Adrianople.

In 1987 Slobodan Milošević became head of the Communist Party, and in 1989 he became president of Serbia. Milošević was a staunch nationalist who put forward a vision of reestablishing Greater Serbia. As a step in this direction, in early 1989 Serbia rescinded Kosovo's autonomy that had been guaranteed by the 1974 constitution. Serbia's action was prompted to some degree by the efforts of the Albanian Kosovars to force non-Albanians to leave the region through acts of TERRORISM. Albanian Kosovars responded to this action by engaging in violent protests that resulted in the destruction of Serbian property as well as the murder and rape of Serbs. In response Milošević sent troops into Kosovo.

For the next several years world attention shifted from Kosovo to Croatia and Bosnia and Herzegovina, where Serb forces were fighting alongside local Serbs to secure as much political power and territory as possible in these new breakaway states. The conflict in Kosovo, however, had not ceased. Milošević encouraged Serbian vigilante groups and financed the return of Serbs who had fled Kosovo. Protests by ethnic Albanians continued over their loss of autonomy. In particular they protested the firing of Albanians from government jobs, the expulsion of Albanian teachers and students from schools, and the closing of hospitals used by Albanians. In May 1992 Albanian Kosovars

went to the polls and elected Ibrahim Rugova as their president and voted for independence.

ECONOMIC SANCTIONS imposed on Serbia by the West and the cost of the war effort in general had seriously weakened the Serb economy and Milošević's grip on power but had not succeeded in forcing him out. He would win the 1997 Yugoslav presidential election. Just prior to this election, in 1996, tension began to escalate in Kosovo. The Albanian Kosovars had engaged in a large-scale public challenge to Serbian direct rule since it was imposed by Milošević in 1989. They strove to set up a parallel and separate society within Kosovo. In 1996 ultranationalist Albanian Kosovars rejected this policy of limited protest and reactivated the Kosovo Liberation Army (KLA). This GUERRILLA group sought the immediate separation of Kosovo from Serbia and soon began to receive funds from outside Yugoslavia that allowed it to purchase modern weapons. The conflict erupted into the open in 1998 when Serbian courts began to impose stiff sentences to Albanians suspected of belonging to the KLA, and the KLA retaliated by attacking Serbian police stations.

Western powers reacted to the impending civil war by demanding that Milošević reinstitute home rule for Kosovo. When Milošević refused the NORTH ATLANTIC TREATY ORGANIZATION (NATO) threatened massive air strikes against Serbia. Milošević temporized in the face of this challenge. In October 1998 he agreed to reduce the number of Serb forces in Kosovo, allow 2,000 foreign monitors to enter Kosovo, permit NATO to enter Yugoslav airspace to verify his actions, and undertake political reforms, including new elections and reform of the constitution. The agreement failed to end the conflict. The KLA rejected it because it did not provide for immediate independence, and Milošević did an aboutface. He proceeded to unleash a massive attack on Kosovo that was designed to eliminate all opposition to Serbian rule. In March 1999 Yugoslav and Albanian leaders met under the auspices of the Contact Group in Rambouillet, France. The Contact Group consisted of GREAT BRITAIN, the United States, FRANCE, and RUSSIA. It had organized in 1994 in an effort to end the fighting in Bosnia. An agreement was reached whereby Kosovo would remain in Yugoslavia for three years. At that time a referendum would be held to determine if the Albanian Kosovars wanted an independent state. In the meantime, there would be political reforms giving them their own political institutions and a NATO-led surveillance force would be sent to Yugoslavia. Yugoslav delegates refused to sign the agreement, and the next day, March 23, 1989, NATO began air strikes against Yugoslav targets.

Initially Milošević defied NATO, but in June he accepted a revised version of the Rambouillet accords. The decisive factor in Milošević's turnabout had less to do with the success of the NATO bombing than the fear that the

KLA would soon be in a position to launch a successful ground war against his weakened Yugoslav forces. Milošević agreed to grant Kosovo autonomy and to permit 50,000 NATO forces to enter Kosovo to monitor the peace. NATO also made an important concession. It dropped any reference in the peace plan to future Kosovo independence. NATO divided Kosovo into five zones for purposes of PEACEKEEPING operations. Great Britain, France, ITALY, the United States, and Germany were each placed in charge of a zone. Their mission was to verify Serbia's withdrawal, maintain law and order until the United Nations could help establish indigenous political and legal structures, prevent further fighting, and foster interethnic reconciliation. This last goal has proved especially difficult to realize. Albanians have attacked and killed Serbs returning home, and Serbs have refused to participate in the new governmental structures being set up. A majority of Albanian Kosovars desire independence, but this position is not supported by Western states, who fear it would lead to still further instability and violence in the region.

**Further reading:** Judah, Tim. *Kosovo: War and Revenge.* New Haven, Conn.: Yale University Press, 2000; Prifti, Peter. *Confrontation in Kosovo: The Albanian-Serb Struggle, 1969–1998.* New York: Columbia University Press, 1999.

## Kuwait

Located on the Arabian Peninsula at the head of the Persian Gulf, Kuwait is slightly smaller than New Jersey, with an area of 6,850 square miles and a population of 2.04 million people. About two-thirds of those living in Kuwait are non-Kuwaiti citizens who were drawn there by the prosperity brought by OIL production. A founding member of the ORGANIZATION OF PETROLEUM EXPORTING COUNTRIES (OPEC), Kuwait contains the world's third-largest oil reserves, following SAUDI ARABIA and IRAQ. More than 80 percent of Kuwait's oil production capacity was destroyed or damaged as a result of the Iraqi invasion and occupation during the PERSIAN GULF WAR. By the end of 1992 Kuwait's oil output had returned to prewar levels.

Modern Kuwait traces its roots back to the founding of Kuwait City in the early 18th century. In the 19th century Kuwaiti leaders sought protection from GREAT BRITAIN to balance the influence of the Ottoman Empire. In 1899 an agreement was signed that effectively made Kuwait a British protectorate. In this agreement Kuwait agreed not to cede territory or receive representatives of foreign governments without British permission. The British agreed to provide the ruling family with an annual subsidy and to protect it. Great Britain became involved in fighting on Kuwait's behalf in 1920 against forces from Saudi Arabia. A 1922 treaty established a neutral zone between these two states, and in 1969 they agreed on a new international boundary. Britain also intervened in 1961 shortly after Kuwait officially became independent. At issue was Kuwait's border with Iraq. It had been set in 1913 under a treaty with Turkey. But in 1932, when Iraq became independent, Baghdad rejected the boundary line and claimed Kuwait, arguing that it was an area under its influence within the Ottoman Empire. In 1961 Iraq threatened to invade. Kuwait received help from Great Britain and then the Arab League. The crisis ended in 1963, with Iraq agreeing to the 1913 boundary.

Kuwait's foreign policy up until the late 1980s was based on the principle of nonalignment in inter-Arab disputes. It violated this rule when it supported Iraq during the IRAN-IRAQ WAR. Iran retaliated by attacking oil refineries, sponsoring TERRORISM within Kuwait, and attacking Kuwait merchant ships. In December 1986 Kuwait requested protection from the United States for its oil tankers. The United States at first resisted but changed its position after the Soviet Union announced that it would do so. In May 1987 11 Kuwaiti tankers were reflagged as American ships and provided with protection by U.S. naval forces.

Relations between Kuwait and Iraq soured after the conclusion of the war in 1988. Intent upon rebuilding its economy, Kuwait tended to ignore OPEC production limits, which drove oil prices down. Iraq needing funds to pay off its war debts and thus promoted high oil prices. At a May 1990 OPEC meeting Iraq's leader, Saddam Hussein, accused Kuwait of stealing $2.4 billion worth of oil reserves from territory along the Kuwait-Iraq border, thereby reopening Iraq's claim to Kuwait. On August 2, 1990, Iraqi forces invaded Kuwait. On August 8 Iraq annexed Kuwait, and on August 28 it declared that Kuwait had become the 19th province of Iraq.

Iraqi forces were expelled from Kuwait seven months later by U.S. forces operating under a UNITED NATIONS mandate. In November 1994 Iraq formally accepted the UN-demarcated boundary line with Kuwait. This border was the same as that in the 1963 agreement.

After the end of the Persian Gulf War Kuwait shed its traditional concern with being overly identified with the United States or other Western powers and signed a 10-year defense agreement with the United States. The agreement allows the United States to stockpile military equipment in Kuwait, calls for joint military exercises, and gives the United States access to Kuwaiti ports and airports. Kuwait has also begun to purchase American military equipment, including the Patriot missile system, 40 F-18 fighters, and M1A2 battle tanks. Between 1991 and 2001 Kuwaiti purchases totaled $5.5 billion. Kuwait followed up its U.S. defense agreement with defense agreements with Great Britain, FRANCE, and, to a more limited extent, RUSSIA.

**Further reading:** Crystal, Jill. *Oil and Politics in the Gulf.* Cambridge, UK: Cambridge University Press, 1995.

## Kyoto Protocol

Negotiated in 1997 the Kyoto Protocol set binding limits and targets on greenhouse gas emissions. The agreement was signed on December 11 by more than 150 countries but not by the United States. On November 1998 President BILL CLINTON determined that the United States would sign the Kyoto Protocol but did not submit it to the Senate as part of the ratification process. In March 2001 President GEORGE W. BUSH announced that the United States was withdrawing from the Kyoto Protocol. The Kyoto Protocol and the Bush decision are significant because they have become joined political symbols in the debate over whether multilateralism or UNILATERALISM should be the primary orientation of American foreign policy in the post–COLD WAR world.

Virtually from the outset the Kyoto Protocol was mired in controversy. Politically it constituted a follow-up accord to the 1992 RIO EARTH SUMMIT. The United States was on the defensive for most of this conference and successfully worked to limit the scope of the agreements that emerged from it. Under pressure from the United States no compliance dates were set for reducing greenhouse emissions in the Rio Treaty. This defensive posture continued at Kyoto. Controversy also surrounded the science of global warming. Global warming is a rise in the Earth's temperature due to an accumulation of greenhouse gases in the Earth's atmosphere. While some of these gases, most notably carbon dioxide, occur naturally, others are the product of human activity. The most important of these are chlorofluorocarbons (CFCs) and hydroflourocarbons (HCHCs). On balance the scientific community has identified CFCs and HCFCs as the primary culprits behind the greenhouse effect and advocated that steps be taken to reduce their presence in the atmosphere. A strongly voiced minority position challenges both the accuracy of the data used to establish a long-term trend toward global warming and the attribution of blame to these substances.

The Senate ratified the Rio Treaty in November 1992, and in 1995 the first formal steps toward Kyoto were taken. At Berlin in spring 1995 an agreement was reached that exempted developing states from having to meet mandatory emissions targets. A second meeting was held in Geneva in July 1996. Here, the United States and other developed countries agreed to move forward on setting legally binding targets, undertake policies and measures toward achieving these goals, and speed up the global transfer of climate friendly technologies.

CONGRESS reacted angrily to the Berlin and Geneva mandates. It objected both to the content of these two agreements and to what it perceived to be the lack of sufficient consultation with Congress over the U.S. bargaining position. In July 1997 it voiced this concern by passing a nonbinding sense of the Senate resolution by a vote of 95-0. The Hagel-Byrd Resolution stated that Congress would oppose any treaty that hurt the U.S. economy and exempted developing countries from having to accept binding emissions targets. Hagel-Byrd also insisted that any Kyoto treaty submitted for ratification should be accompanied by a detailed statement of what legislation would be needed to implement the agreement.

Under the Kyoto Protocol the United States and other advanced industrial states are required to make reductions in six "baskets" of gases within a five-year commitment period, from 2008 to 2012. This time frame reflected the preference of the United States and not its European allies, who preferred 2003 to 2007. There are no specific targets for each basket, and this also was a concession to the United States. No uniform targets were established for reducing emissions. The United States was required to reduce emissions by 7 percent. CANADA's target was 6 percent, and Norway was allowed to increase its level of pollution. Differential targets were agreed to in response to the complaints of developing states and small states that they were not equally responsible for the greenhouse effect. The United States succeeded in including carbon sinks as a means of reducing pollution. These are areas, such as forests, that remove atmospheric carbon dioxide. The United States also succeeded in gaining support for emissions trading between states seeking to meet their targets.

Consistent with U.S. thinking, provisions for market-based controls were included in the Kyoto Protocol. Under this system the traditional command-and-control target reduction system based on technological capabilities is replaced by a results-oriented system that combines an industry's "right to pollute" with incentives to adopt newer, cleaner technologies. Finally, while the commitments of the United States and other developed states considered binding, the commitments to reducing greenhouse gases by developing states was made voluntary.

Opposition to the terms of the Kyoto Protocol was sufficiently strong that the United States did not sign the agreement on December 11. Senator Chuck Hagel (R-Neb.) charged that it contained an anti-American, anti-West bias and objected to the prospect that developing countries could make policy decisions for the United States. Vice President Al Gore quickly declared that the United States would not send the treaty forward for ratification in its present form. Nonetheless in November 1998 the United States signed the Kyoto Protocol. It did so in order to be able to continue to participate in negotiations over its exact terms. A November 2000 meeting in The Hague failed to produce a compromise agreement on how much action the United States would need to take in cutting its greenhouse emissions.

President George W. Bush seemed somewhat favorably disposed to environmental protection in the first months of his administration, and his director of the Environmental Protection Agency lobbied for continued involvement in the Kyoto process. In March 2001 he changed his position on dealing with pollution in both the domestic and the international arenas and announced that the United States was withdrawing from the Kyoto Protocol. His administration joined critics of the agreement in making the following arguments about what were termed the fundamental flaws in the treaty. First, there was faulty science. Second, the targets were unrealistic and would hurt the U.S. economy. Third, the objectives were misguided, and other sources of the greenhouse effect should be targeted.

The Bush administration's decision was roundly criticized on three grounds. First, it overstated the flaws in the treaty. Defenders argued that while problems did exist, the United States had received significant concessions in the drafting of the Kyoto Protocol. Second, the weight of the scientific evidence did support action on man-made greenhouse gases. Third, abandoning Kyoto was politically unacceptable because it signaled movement away from multilateralism and American leadership in international cooperative efforts.

See also CONFERENCE DIPLOMACY; DOMESTIC POLITICS; ENVIRONMENT; INTERNATIONALISM.

**Further reading:** Victor, David. G. *The Collapse of the Kyoto Protocol and the Struggle to Slow Global Warming.* Princeton, N.J.: Princeton University Press, 2001.

# L

## land mines

Land mines have been described as the "Saturday night specials" of the COLD WAR, and they continue to be a weapon of choice today by combatants in the developing world. They are cheap and easy to produce, costing between $3 and $30. It costs an estimated $300 to detect and remove a land mine. In the late 1990s some 200 million land mines were stockpiled. The number of planted land mines grows each year as about 100,000 are removed and 2 million are planted. Land mines have attracted global attention and condemnation in the past decades because it is not just soldiers in war who are killed. The American Red Cross estimates that one person every 20 minutes is killed or injured by a land mine. Most of these people are innocent farmers, children, and women. In December 1997 an international ban on land mines was signed in Ottawa, Canada, without American participation.

The United States has employed land mines in combat since the AMERICAN CIVIL WAR. They were first used on a large scale during WORLD WAR I to slow down and impede the movement of tanks and troops. During WORLD WAR II they played important roles in the North African campaigns and in fighting on the Russian front. The Soviet Union deployed about 222 million mines against German forces, and mines accounted for 2.5 percent of battlefield deaths in Europe. Few mines were employed in the Pacific theater. During the KOREAN WAR land mines accounted for about 4 percent of American casualties. Chinese and North Korean casualties were higher, and today the demilitarized zone separating NORTH and SOUTH KOREA contains a minefield. In VIETNAM the Vietcong used mines against civilian and military targets, and American forces used mines to protect their perimeter. It is estimated that as many as 30 percent of American fatalities in Vietnam were due to land mines.

U.S. foreign policy on the land-mine question has been contradictory. Early American foreign-policy initiatives were supportive of a worldwide ban. Pressure to ban land mines began to build in the late 1980s, and in 1991 the Vietnam Veterans Foundation helped found the International Campaign to Ban Landmines. On October 23, 1992, President GEORGE H. W. BUSH ordered a one-year ban on the export of land mines. In 1993 President BILL CLINTON extended the ban for an additional two years and would later call for the elimination of antipersonnel mines.

At that point momentum within the U.S. government for the elimination of land mines began to waiver. On August 4, 1995, the Senate approved an amendment to the 1996 Defense Authorization Bill sponsored by Patrick Leahy (D-Vt.) that imposed a one-year moratorium on the use of most land mines. The amendment was dropped in committee. There then occurred a remarkable exchange of public letters. On April 3, 1996, 16 four-star generals wrote to protest a ban on land mines and assert their continued military importance to the U.S. military in an era of shrinking forces. Fifteen retired generals wrote a public letter to President Clinton in rebuttal.

The split within the American military and political establishments was reflected in President Clinton's May 16, 1996, announcement that he would pursue a land-mine treaty at a conference in Geneva with two exceptions. First, the United States would continue to deploy dumb mines in Korea and smart mines elsewhere until an agreement was reached. Smart mines self-destruct in a predetermined period of time if they are activated by contact. Dumb mines do not. Critics argue that the distinction on paper is greater than it appears in reality. As proof they argue that in the PERSIAN GULF WAR 1,700 smart mines did not self-destruct. Defenders respond that if all else fails smart mines operate on a battery that is good for only 90 days.

The Clinton position received lukewarm international endorsement. While 61 states met at Geneva, 115 states met in Brussels at a conference convened by Canada to write a treaty banning all land mines. The Clinton administration continued to struggle with its land-mine policy in 1997. In January it announced that the United States would permanently ban the sale of land mines and destroy

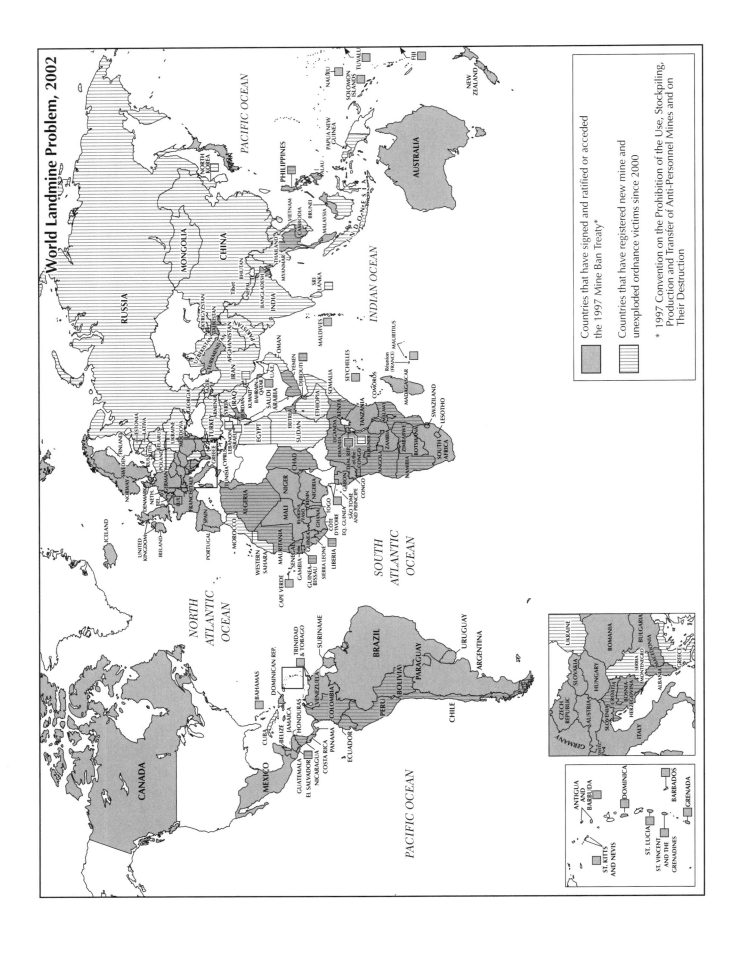

# World Landmine Problem, 2002

Countries that have signed and ratified or acceded the 1997 Mine Ban Treaty*

Countries that have registered new mine and unexploded ordnance victims since 2000

* 1997 Convention on the Prohibition of the Use, Stockpiling, Production and Transfer of Anti-Personnel Mines and on Their Destruction

all U.S. dumb mines. At one point the United States had some 11 million land mines stockpiled. In early June more than 160 members of CONGRESS petitioned Clinton to join the Ottawa process. Still, when formal negotiations began on drafting the Ottawa treaty on June 27, 1997, other states continued to reject the two exceptions proposed by Clinton. The United States remained isolated until the end, when the total ban on land mines was signed in Ottawa on December 2–4, 1997.

The international ban on land mines comprises only part of the land-mine problem. A second dimension is removing land mines. At the current rate of removal, the American Red Cross projects that it would take 1,100 years to destroy all land mines currently in place. Among the most severe cases today are CAMBODIA, where one person in every 236 has lost an eye or limb because of land mines, and ANGOLA, where there are an estimated 15 million deployed land mines in a country of 10 million people.

Between 1993 and 1997 the United States spent more than $137 million on humanitarian de-mining operations. In addition to the DEFENSE DEPARTMENT the lead U.S. agencies involved are the STATE DEPARTMENT and the U.S. AGENCY FOR INTERNATIONAL DEVELOPMENT. Among the successes cited by the United States are a 94 percent drop in deaths due to land mines in Namibia and a 50 percent decline in some areas of Cambodia. The United States has operated humanitarian de-mining programs in AFGHANISTAN, Angola, BOSNIA AND HERZEGOVINA, Cambodia, Costa Rica, ERITREA, ETHIOPIA, Honduras, JORDAN, LAOS, Mozambique, Namibia, NICARAGUA, and RWANDA. American soldiers are not permitted to participate in the de-mining effort itself. They engage in such activities as training local de-miners, educating the local population, improving health care systems that deal with mine injuries, and developing new technologies to remove land mines.

See also MULTINATIONAL CORPORATIONS; NON-GOVERNMENTAL ORGANIZATIONS; RUSSIA.

**Further reading:** Bearsley, Tim. "War without End?" *Scientific American* (June 1967); Burkhalter, Holly. "Phantom Pain: Banning Landmines." *World Policy Journal* (1997).

## Laos

Laos is located in Southeast Asia. It has an area of 91,430 square miles, making it somewhat smaller than Oregon. It has a population of 5.6 million people. Beginning in the 14th century a powerful kingdom emerged in what is today Laos that succeeded in controlling large areas of Southeast Asia. By the early 1700s internal dissention began to weaken this state, and Laos became a target of neighboring states. FRANCE began to exert influence over Laos following its successful colonization of VIETNAM, and in 1893

France formally established a protectorate over it. Subsequently Laos was incorporated with the other French territories of Southeast Asia into the Indochina Union. During WORLD WAR II Laos was occupied by JAPAN, and with Tokyo's support, Laos declared its independence from France. Japan's defeat led to the reoccupation of Laos by France. Along with its other Southeast Asian colonies, Laos was given limited autonomy in a French union.

Proindependence forces found this condition unacceptable and continued to press for full independence from France. A leading force in this struggle was the Pathet Lao, a communist group that was supported by the Viet Minh operating out of Vietnam. Laos achieved its full independence in 1955 as a result of the French defeat in Vietnam the year before. The first government was led by Prince Souvanna Phouma, but it soon collapsed, and civil war ensued. The United States supported the rightist political forces. The neutralists came to align themselves with the Pathet Lao and received support from the Soviet Union (see RUSSIA).

The net result of this political situation was to make Laos an early test case of U.S.-Soviet COLD WAR cooperation. A second Geneva Conference was held in 1961–62 attended by 14 states. The goal was to stabilize the domestic situation in Laos and establish it as a neutral state. This goal required that the two superpowers cooperate. A complicating factor was that while Soviet support for the Pathet Lao was relatively recent, the Viet Minh had been longtime supporters. One of the fears gripping U.S. policy makers was that a Viet Minh triumph in Vietnam would embolden them to create a communist state in Laos.

Neutrality proved to be impossible, and in 1963 open warfare resumed that involved both domestic and foreign forces. The Pathet Lao, with support from North Vietnam, made major gains against a rightist-neutralist government supported by the United States and the Soviet Union. North Vietnam also used Laotian territory as a major transportation route, the Ho Chi Minh Trail. In 1971 South Vietnamese forces invaded Laos in an attempt to cut the Ho Chi Minh Trail. The United States also carried out massive bombing campaigns against North Vietnamese targets in Laos. A 1973 cease-fire brought a coalition government into power. It survived until 1975 when, after the fall of Vietnam, the Pathet Lao triumphed.

Part of the U.S. strategy for defeating the Pathet Lao was to recruit native Hmong tribespeople. With the Communist victory many fled CAMBODIA to THAILAND. Between 1975 and 1996 some 250,000 Laotian REFUGEES, including 130,000 Hmong, made their way to the United States. Relations with Laos were strained until 1982 when Laos's cooperation in searching for Americans missing in Laos during the Vietnam War improved. The two countries have also begun to cooperate on heroin control and eradication efforts. This is a sensitive area since in the 1950s the

CENTRAL INTELLIGENCE AGENCY (CIA) reportedly used profits from DRUG TRAFFICKING to finance COVERT ACTION in Laos. In August 1997 the United States and Laos signed bilateral trade and investment agreements that were submitted to CONGRESS for approval.

## Law of the Sea conferences

Three Law of the Sea conferences held between 1958 and 1982 attempted to establish a universally accepted set of rules for the many different uses to which oceans are put today. The most successful of these was the third UNITED NATIONS Convention on the Law of the Sea (UNCLOS III). It was the longest continuous international negotiation of modern times, running more than 15 years, and it proceeded in a number of forums, including the UN General Assembly, meetings of ad hoc and permanent committees on the seabed, and 11 sessions of the Law of the Sea conference itself. The negotiations are significant because they highlight the complex nature of international negotiations and the cross pressures that surface in formulating national negotiating positions.

A number of different systems have been proposed for governing the seas. In 1493 Pope Alexander VI divided the world's oceans between SPAIN and Portugal, in essence treating them as private property. For most of its history the oceans had been governed by the opposite principle, namely, that the oceans did not belong to any country. This principle underlies the concept of freedom of the seas. According to it, all potential users of an ocean had equal access to it with the exception of a narrow band of water directly off of a state's coast that could be claimed as national property. No one user could claim any part of the ocean as private property or deny its use to others. This principle is associated with the writings of the 17th-century Dutch legal scholar Hugo Grotius.

Implicit in the notion of freedom of the seas are two interconnected assumptions. First, it is assumed that oceans are sufficiently large that all can use them without interfering with one another and that the oceans will not be harmed in the process. Second, it is assumed that the oceans' resources outstrip demand so that scarcity is not a problem. By the mid-20th century the validity of these assumptions was called into question by economic, technological, and political events. Technology now made it profitable to search for and extract petroleum and minerals found on the ocean floor far beyond the coast. These technologies and the economic benefits that followed from the capture of these natural resources were not equally available to all states. It created a first come–first serve logic that developing states argued had the effect of denying them free access under the freedom-of-the-seas principle. Pollution was also becoming a problem. No longer was one state's (or corpo-

ration's) use of the oceans without impact on the ability of others to use it. Finally, states were aligning themselves into competitive blocks that defined their interests in antagonistic terms: East versus West and North versus South. One consequence was to make the oceans an area of competitive rather than a common or shared resource.

It was the United States that took a first important step away from the principle of freedom of the seas when in 1945 President HARRY TRUMAN issued two proclamations. In the first he established "conservation zones" on certain areas of the high seas. No specific boundaries were given, but these were to be areas where only Americans could fish. In the second, Truman extended American control over seabed minerals into the high seas along the continental shelf.

UNCLOS I met from February to April 1958. It was attended by 84 states and produced four conventions. The Continental Shelf Convention codified Truman's second proclamation by recognizing the continental shelf as falling within a state's sovereignty for purposes of resource exploitation. The High Seas Convention spoke the traditional language of freedom of the seas in addressing navigation, fishing, overflight, and the laying of cables and pipelines, but many of its provisions spoke of restraints on these rights. The Convention on the Territorial Sea and the Contiguous Zone defined the interests of coastal and maritime states in the territorial sea but did not establish the boundaries of the territorial sea. The Convention on Fishing and Conservation of the Living Resources of the High Seas required states to cooperate on conservation measures but did not specify a uniform set of rights and duties. UNCLOS II convened in spring 1960 for six weeks in a failed bid to obtain a consensus on the definition of the territorial sea.

Movement for a UNCLOS III had begun to build in the late 1960s. In 1967 the Soviet Union approached the United States about its interest in trying once again to achieve agreement on a 12-mile territorial sea and the size of the contiguous fishing zone. The formal American response came in 1969 when the Nixon administration proposed holding a new conference. Any possibility that the conference would adopt a narrow definition of its task had ended in September 1967. Malta's ambassador to the UN, Arvid Pardo, gave a long and impassioned speech in which he urged the establishment of UN control over the seabed's resources on the grounds that they were the common heritage of humankind. Any movement on Pardo's plan also required a definition of the territorial sea. The United States proposed that a permanent UN Committee be created to study the matter. Its proposal was rejected in favor of an ad hoc committee in which developing states outnumbered developed states and which took as its starting point the language used by Pardo.

The first session of UNCLOS III met in New York from December 3 to 15, 1973. A total of 148 states were in attendance. The first substantive session took place in Caracas from June 20 to August 29, 1974. In addition to representatives of the 148 states, delegates representing 10 UN agencies, 10 intergovernmental organizations, and 33 NON-GOVERNMENTAL ORGANIZATIONS were in attendance. The 11th and final session took place in New York on March 8, 1982. UNCLOS III was adopted on April 30, 1982.

UNCLOS III established the principle of a 12-mile territorial sea accompanied by a 200-mile exclusive economic zone. Given these boundaries the provisions of the treaty can be grouped into four modules. The first deals with the operation of the 200-mile exclusive economic zone. It combined property rights with free transit and communication rights for all states. A second module set out rules governing an intermediate zone that bridges the exclusive economic zone and the high seas. No firm boundary was established for it. The third module established rules for the high seas in the areas of the ocean surface and airspace. The fourth module establishes rules for the deep seabed. It is to be governed by an International Seabed Authority that would be responsible to decision-making bodies whose members were to be democratically elected.

In formulating the initial U.S. position the Nixon administration was buffeted by a politically explosive internal split. On the one hand was the desire of the U.S. Navy to carry out its mission with as few restrictions as possible in terms of where its ships could go and the conditions under which it had to operate. Opposing the navy were mining companies who sought to obtain exclusive control over resources on the seabed. The navy's goal spoke to the creation of a narrow territorial sea. That of the mining companies suggested pursuit of a maximum territorial sea. CONGRESS, along with the Department of the Interior, became allies of the mining firms and advocated unilateral American legislation to protect their interest. The STATE DEPARTMENT lobbied hard against unilateral action. It was not until 1970 that the Nixon administration endorsed the navy position by embracing the concept of a narrow territorial sea and accepting an international authority with jurisdiction over seabed minerals.

The Nixon administration was able to make this decision in large measure because of the relatively small role that control over natural resources played in world politics. Beginning in the mid-1970s this changed, and American foreign policy on the law of the sea began to focus on the economic, especially free and unfettered access to these resources. The OIL crisis spawned by the actions of the ORGANIZATION OF PETROLEUM EXPORTING COUNTRIES (OPEC) had brought this change about as it spurred fears of further embargoes and policies of denial involving other minerals and natural resources. In June 1980 Congress acted on these concerns by passing the Deep Seabed Hard Mineral Resources Act. It authorized American commercial mining operations under a system of reciprocity with other like-minded states.

RONALD REAGAN campaigned on a platform of opposition to the deep seabed authority, and on March 2, 1981, in the first months of his presidency, the State Department announced that it was conducting a review of the American position and the treaty. A few days later the top U.S. negotiators were replaced. On January 29, 1982, a few months before the beginning of the 11th and final negotiating session, the Reagan administration announced that while most provisions of the draft convention were acceptable, some of those involving the deep seabed regime were not. It listed a series of specific objections. They involved technology transfer and revenue-sharing provisions, production controls that might be imposed by the international authority, the internal decision-making procedures of the international authority and its ability to make binding decisions on the United States, continued national access to these resources, and the undesirable precedent it might set for other international organizations in the area of establishing collective ownership of resources.

Later the United States would produce a "Green Book" of draft amendments to the UNCLOS III Treaty. All were rejected. Finally, on April 30, the United States called for a vote on deep seabed mining provisions. Up until this point all agreements had been adopted by consensus with no formal votes being taken. The United States was one of four states, along with ISRAEL, TURKEY, and VENEZUELA, to vote against the deep seabed mining convention. It passed by a vote of 130-4 with 17 abstentions. On July 9, 1982, President Reagan announced that the United States would not sign UNCLOS III.

The concerns identified by the Reagan administration continued to guide U.S. policy on UNCLOS III even after its term in office ended. The United States ratified UNCLOS III in 1994 only after amendments were added, giving Washington a virtual veto over the mining and allocations of deep ocean resources.

See also CONFERENCE DIPLOMACY; DIPLOMACY; RUSSIA.

**Further reading:** Friedheim, Robert L. *Negotiating the New Ocean Regime.* Columbia: University of South Carolina Press, 1993; Hollick, Ann L. *United States Foreign Policy and the Law of the Sea.* Princeton, N.J.: Princeton University Press, 1981.

## League of Nations

The League of Nations emerged from WORLD WAR I as the characteristic international organization of what was to be a new era of world politics. It was based on the principles of IDEALISM as expressed in WOODROW WILSON'S FOURTEEN POINTS and a rejection of the balance-of-POWER politics that had dominated European thinking about the conduct of international relations. The League of Nations never lived up to this billing. It was all but crippled from the outset by the refusal of the United States to become a member. Wilson, a Democrat, failed to convince the Republican-controlled U.S. Senate of the merits of the League of Nations. HENRY CABOT LODGE led the opposition. A nationalist internationalist, Lodge demanded that Wilson accept reservations to the TREATY OF VERSAILLES. His refusal to do so precipitated one of the great political battles of American diplomatic history. Also opposed to the League of Nations were a group of "irreconcilables" whose isolationist outlook prevented reaching any type of political accommodations with Wilson.

The founding document of the League of Nations was the Covenant. It contained 26 articles that laid out its operating procedures and philosophy. Structurally, the league had three parts: an assembly, a council, and a secretariat. Both the assembly, made up of all members, and the council, made up of the great powers (originally, GREAT BRITAIN, FRANCE, ITALY, JAPAN, and later GERMANY and the Soviet Union) and other states whose membership rotated, could take up any matter "affecting the peace of the world." All decisions in these bodies were made on the principle of unanimity. The importance of DISARMAMENT was recognized in the Covenant, and guarantees were made regarding acts of aggression. A system for governing colonial territories was established. Provisions were also made for a Permanent Court of International Justice, also known as the World Court. The league was headquartered in Geneva, Switzerland, and had as founding members all of the victors of World War I, save the United States and most neutral statem. Among those who joined later were Germany (1926), MEXICO (1931), and the Soviet Union (1934).

The League of Nations enjoyed some initial successes in settling international disputes involving small powers, such as a conflict between Sweden and Finland in 1921, and it helped to avert war in the Balkans between GREECE and Bulgaria in 1925. These successes were quickly overshadowed by its persistent failure to affect the behavior of the more powerful states in the interwar INTERNATIONAL SYSTEM. France defied the league by occupying the Ruhr in 1923, Italy was not swayed by league ECONOMIC SANCTIONS from attacking ETHIOPIA in 1935, Germany rearmed the Rhineland in 1936 and seized Austria in 1938, and Japan invaded Manchuria in 1937. Worse, it lost key members. Germany withdrew in 1933, and the Soviet Union was expelled for invading Finland in 1939. By 1940, the League of Nations had virtually ceased to exist. It dissolved itself in 1946. Its place in world politics was taken by the UNITED NATIONS, which was created out of the political debris of WORLD WAR II.

While the United States did not join the League of Nations, it did not totally ignore it either. For example,

because it was not a member of the league, it did not join the World Court, yet an American always sat as a judge in its deliberations. The United States also attended a 1932 disarmament conference that was sponsored by the league and met in Geneva. Rising tensions between France and Germany prevented any agreement from being reached, in spite of the work done by a preparatory commission that had been set up in 1925. The conference adjourned deadlocked in June 1933.

In spite of the American refusal to join, the establishment of the League of Nations is seen as a significant event in American foreign policy because it gave concrete expression to a uniquely American vision of international politics. It is a vision that remains at odds with the power-politics thinking of most states. However, within United States the popularity of this view has fluctuated. During the COLD WAR, for example, REALISM was the dominant paradigm for studying world politics. Wilson's vision of world politics has been rediscovered and rehabilitated in the post–cold war era.

See also COLLECTIVE SECURITY; LONDON NAVAL CONFERENCE; RUSSIA; WASHINGTON CONFERENCES; WILSONIANISM.

**Further reading:** Knock, Thomas T. *To End All Wars: The League of Nations and the Quest for a New World Order.* New York: Oxford University Press, 1992; Kuehl, Warren F. *Keeping the Covenant: American Internationalism and the League of Nations, 1920–1939.* Kent, Ohio: Kent University Press, 1997; Northedge, F. S. *The League of Nations: Its Life and Times, 1920–1946.* New York: Holmes and Meier, 1986.

## Lebanon

Lebanon sits on the eastern edge of the Mediterranean, with a population of approximately 3.6 million people and an area of 4,105 square miles, making it smaller than Connecticut. No official census has been taken since 1932 because of the extreme sensitivity to the religious balance within the country between Christians and Muslims. On its borders are two historical rivals, ISRAEL and SYRIA. These internal and external realities have determined the course of much of Lebanon's post–WORLD WAR II history.

From 1516 to 1918 modern Lebanon and the region around it were under the control of the Ottoman Empire. FRANCE received the LEAGUE OF NATIONS mandate for Lebanon and Syria following WORLD WAR I. A 1936 treaty with France set up a three-year transition period that was to lead to Lebanese independence, but the agreement was not ratified by the French legislature. During World War II Lebanon was ruled by representatives of the French Vichy regime until a joint British and Free French military force liberated Lebanon in 1941. Spurred by the British, a new independence movement gained strength, and Lebanon became an independent state on January 1, 1944. All French troops did not withdraw, however, until 1946.

The United States first became involved in Lebanese affairs in 1958. That year EGYPT and Syria formed the United Arab League, and many Muslims in Lebanon hoped Lebanon would join. The government of President Camille Chamoun was pro-West and had no intention of doing so. Open rioting broke out in Lebanon, and the army refused to intervene. At the same time an Egyptian-inspired anti-Western military coup took place in IRAQ. In the face of this deteriorating situation Chamoun asked for American troops. President DWIGHT EISENHOWER laid the foundation for such a move in 1957 when he announced the EISENHOWER DOCTRINE. Under the doctrine Eisenhower pledged U.S. military support to any government requesting assistance against communist-inspired aggression. On July 15, 1958, U.S. Marines arrived in Lebanon. They left in October and numbered approximately 1,500 at their height.

U.S. troops would next go to Lebanon in 1983. They arrived in the aftermath of a devastating civil war that began in 1975–76 and after two Israeli interventions. The civil war pitted the militias of the dominant Christian Maronite community against militias aligned with the Lebanese National Movement (LNM), which drew its strength from political groups disillusioned with the established Muslim leadership. Syria was a traditional supporter of the LNM and its ally, the PALESTINE LIBERATION ORGANIZATION (PLO). Now, however, it intervened to support the Maronite leaders out of fear that a radical Muslim victory would prompt an Israeli invasion of Lebanon.

An uneasy truce took hold in 1976. The PLO continued to use southern Lebanon as a base to launch attacks against Israel, and Israel provided arms to the Maronite Christians, who used this backing to challenge the Syrians, now exerting a dominant influence over Lebanese affairs. In March 1978 Israeli forces invaded southern Lebanon to create a security zone there that was placed under the jurisdiction of its ally, the Free Lebanon Movement. In June 1982 Israel attacked again. This time it succeeded in forcing the Palestine Liberation Organization (PLO) out of Lebanon. In September the United States, France, ITALY, and GREAT BRITAIN sent a 5,000-person PEACEKEEPING force to Lebanon to try to stabilize the political situation.

Events proceeded at a dizzying pace and worked against the accomplishment of this mission. On April 18, 1983, a suicide attack on the U.S. EMBASSY killed 63. On May 17 Lebanon, Israel, and the United States agreed on a conditional Israeli withdrawal from Lebanon. The agreement collapsed due to Syrian opposition. In September 1983 a partial unilateral Israeli withdrawal sparked heavy fighting in central Lebanon. On October 23, 1983, a suicide bombing killed 241 American soldiers. These incidents

U.S. Marines in Beirut, Lebanon *(Hulton/Archives)*

fostered doubt in the United States about the wisdom of sending U.S. forces to Lebanon and President RONALD REAGAN's constitutional authority to do so. It also created political pressure on the Reagan administration to withdraw them. On March 5, 1984, the Lebanese government withdrew from the May 17 agreement, and the marines began their departure. Coupled with the Israeli withdrawal, this left Syria as the dominant power in Lebanon. Closure of sorts did not come until September 30, 1989, when with support from the United States and Soviet Union, SAUDI ARABIA sponsored a peace conference. The Ta'if Agreement of October 22 reestablished the domestic political balance between Christians and Muslims in Lebanon and the legitimacy of Syrian domination. The latter was reaffirmed in a May 1991 treaty of mutual cooperation.

Lebanon's relations with Israel, and thus indirectly with the United States, remain complex. Lebanon was party to the 1991 peace talks sponsored by the United States and RUSSIA in Madrid, SPAIN, and continued to participate in those negotiations when they moved to Oslo, Norway. Unlike JORDAN and the Palestinians, Lebanon has not signed an agreement with Israel. Israel also renewed its military activities in southern Lebanon in April 1996. The target this time was the Hezbollah, who were targeting Israeli villages and troops. On May 23, 2000, Israeli troops unilaterally left Lebanon, ending the 22-year occupation.

See also ARAB-ISRAELI CONFLICT.

**Further reading:** Deeb, Marius. *The Lebanese Civil War.* New York: Praeger, 1980; Rabinovich, Itamar. *The War for Lebanon, 1970–1985.* Ithaca, N.Y.: Cornell University Press, 1986.

## legalism

Legalism is one of the foundational building blocks on which the AMERICAN NATIONAL STYLE of foreign policy is built. The other two are UNILATERALISM and MORAL PRAGMATISM. Together they support both an isolationist and internationalist perspective, thereby allowing both to coexist.

Legalism grows out of a rejection of POWER politics as a means for preserving national security and the liberal view that people are rational beings who favor the peaceful settlements of disputes. A central task of U.S. foreign policy is to create a global system of international institutions and rules that will allow states to settle disputes without recourse to war. U.S. sponsorship of the LEAGUE OF NATIONS, UNITED NATIONS, GENERAL AGREEMENT ON TARIFFS AND TRADE, and the WORLD TRADE ORGANIZATION all are consistent with the legalist thrust to foreign-policy making.

The rule-making component of legalism is found in the repeated use of the "pledge system" in trying to solve foreign-policy problems. In creating a pledge system the United States puts forward a statement of principle and then asks other states to pledge their support for it. Seldom present is any meaningful enforcement mechanism. The OPEN DOOR POLICY exemplifies this strategy. The United States unilaterally proclaimed its opposition to spheres of influence in CHINA and then asked other powers to do likewise, but it did not specify any sanctions against a state that reneged on its pledge. The WASHINGTON NAVAL CONFERENCE and the KELLOGG-BRIAND PACT are pre–WORLD WAR II examples of the pledge system. ARMS CONTROL agreements with the Soviet Union (see RUSSIA) during the COLD WAR followed in the tradition of the pledge system. These treaties specified the nuclear inventories that each side was permitted to possess without including any effective enforcement mechanisms.

On occasion legalism has placed a heavy burden on U.S. policy makers. Not able to make use of the traditional "reason of state" rationale for their actions, they have had to cloth their actions in terms of legal principles. The United States fought the KOREAN WAR under the United Nations flag to underscore the illegality of NORTH KOREA's invasion of SOUTH KOREA. Global support was similarly sought for military action against IRAQ in the PERSIAN GULF WAR and international TERRORISM. A request by the Organization of Eastern Caribbean States was cited by President RONALD REAGAN in justifying the U.S. invasion of GRENADA. President GEORGE W. BUSH unsuccessfully challenged the legalist bent in the American national style when at first he resisted going to CONGRESS or the United Nations for support in a war against IRAQ. However, Bush acted in accordance with the principle of legalism when he asserted that the IRAQ WAR could be justified by reference to Iraq's many violations of UN resolutions that it disarm and permit weapons inspectors onto its territory.

## Lend-Lease

The Lend-Lease Act of 1941 provided a vehicle for the administration of FRANKLIN ROOSEVELT to provide FOREIGN AID to the Allies and circumvent the restrictions of the NEUTRALITY LEGISLATION of the 1930s that isolationists hoped would keep the United States out of war.

Beginning in 1935 CONGRESS had passed a series of neutrality acts that prohibited the United States from providing arms to countries at war. The 1937 Neutrality Act contained a cash-and-carry provision that allowed belligerents to purchase supplies other than weapons from the United States provided they paid in cash and transported it in their own vessels. As Europe moved closer and closer to war, Roosevelt tried to get Congress to revise the 1937 Neutrality Act and drop the prohibition on arm sales. He argued that rather than keeping the United States out of war this strict version of neutrality actually ran the risk of dragging the United States into war because it was uneven in its impact. Only with added military resources could GREAT BRITAIN and FRANCE successfully resist GERMANY. Isolationists continued to resist Roosevelt's call for greater flexibility in the neutrality legislation, but after Adolf Hitler invaded POLAND he was able to get Congress to pass a revised act.

The 1939 Neutrality Act dropped the ban on selling arms to belligerents and permitted their purchase on a cash-and-carry basis. The fundamental problem now confronting Roosevelt was the absence of British funds with which to purchase weapons. Asking the American people to become the "arsenal of democracy," Roosevelt proposed that the United States lend Great Britain the war matériel it needed. Great Britain would return these goods at the conclusion of the war. He made the analogy of a neighbor whose house was burning and was in need of your garden hose. You do not demand payment up front before lending the hose. Republican isolationists countered that the more accurate analogy was one of lending chewing gum—you did not want it back after it was used.

In January 1941 Roosevelt introduced his legislation. Debate in Congress was intense, with Senator Robert Taft (R-Ohio) asserting that the proposed Lend-Lease legislation would give the PRESIDENT unprecedented powers to carry on undeclared wars all over the world. The measure, calling for an expenditure of up to $50 billion, passed along an almost straight party-line vote. The House approved it by a vote of 260-165, and the Senate did likewise by a vote of 60-31. Roosevelt signed the measure on March 11, 1941.

Continued German submarine warfare presented the next problem that Roosevelt had to overcome in getting aid to Great Britain. The neutrality legislation still prohibited having these goods carried on American ships or having American ships enter into combat zones. Opponents of Lend-Lease had argued that the inevitable consequence of providing military aid to the Allies was delivering that aid on U.S. convoys and that this would lead to war. Roosevelt took that next first step in October 1941 when he called for repeal of the 1939 Neutrality Act.

To the surprise of America's allies, President HARRY TRUMAN abruptly terminated Lend-Lease aid one week after Japan's surrender. Great Britain and the other Allies had hoped for a continuation of the Lend-Lease program in order to help start their postwar recovery. About $11 billion of Lend-Lease aid had gone to the Soviet Union, and some $31 billion went to Great Britain. The total amount owed to the United States was reduced by about $10 billion through a reverse Lend-Lease program in which foreign goods were sent to the United States. By 1953 a series of repayment agreements had reduced the total Allied debt to be paid to the United States to about $1 billion.

## Liberia

Located in western Africa and fronting the Atlantic Ocean, Liberia is slightly larger than Ohio, with an area of 43,000 square miles, and it has a population of 3,239,000 people. The first Europeans to establish contacts in Liberia were Portuguese explorers in 1461. British traders arrived in 1663, but they were forced out by the Dutch.

In the 1820s freed slaves from the United States began arriving in Liberia. The first group of 86 arrived in 1820 and established a settlement at Christopolis. The main force in promoting black IMMIGRATION to Liberia was the American Colonization Society. It had been established in December 1816–January 1817 for the purpose of helping freed slaves return to Africa. CONGRESS provided some funding for their cause in 1819 when it appropriated

$100,000 to help return blacks that had been illegally brought into the United States. The establishment of Liberia became possible when in 1821 agents for the American Colonization Society purchased Cape Mesurado from local De chiefs. Approximately 11,000 freed African-American slaves immigrated to Liberia before the start of the AMERICAN CIVIL WAR. Immigration from the United States virtually came to an end at that time. Today, their descendants, who are often referred to as Americo-Liberians, make up 5 percent of the population.

The American Colonization Society governed the region until July 26, 1847, when Liberia declared its independence. The freed American black slaves ran into opposition on two fronts in seeking to govern their new country. First, they were opposed by indigenous African tribes. Second, they encountered predatory opposition from French and British colonial expansionists who seized much of the land the American Colonization Society had originally obtained. Newly established Liberia also experienced severe international debt problems. The situation became so extreme that after a LEAGUE OF NATIONS inquiry implicated the government in slave trading, international control over Liberia was contemplated.

Violence has rocked Liberia since 1980, when Master Sergeant Samuel K. Doe took power in a coup. Doe was the first native-born Liberian to lead the country, and his seizure of power marked the end of Americo-Liberian political domination. His government was corrupt and oppressive, and in 1989 rebel forces based in Côte d'Ivoire and led by Charles Taylor invaded Liberia. The United States contemplated sending troops to Liberia when Taylor's forces threatened to take foreign hostages. Doe was assassinated in 1990, but the civil war continued until 1996. By then some 200,000 people had died. Taylor was elected president in 1997. The United States worked with the UNITED NATIONS, the Organization of African Unity, and the Economic Community of West African States to disarm and demobilize the warring factions. Cease-fires never held, and fighting continued. Liberia also involved itself in Sierra Leone's civil war by supplying rebels there with arms in exchange for diamonds. In 2000 the United Nations placed an 18-month ban on international diamond sales from Liberia in an attempt to weaken the Revolutionary United Front's forces in Sierra Leone.

The civil war never really ended, and on August 14, 2003, some 200 U.S. Marines joined Nigerian forces that were part of a West African peacekeeping effort. It was the first time U.S. troops had been deployed to Africa since their 1992 mission to SOMALIA. U.S. forces received a warm welcome. President George W. Bush was reluctant to send in U.S. forces and set Taylor's exile as a precondition for doing so. Taylor fled to NIGERIA and was under indictment by a UN-backed tribunal for international war crimes.

## Libya

Located in northern Africa and bordering the Mediterranean Sea, Libya has a population of 5,240,000 people and is larger than Alaska, with an area of 679,358 square miles. The region was conquered by the Arabs in the seventh century, at which time ISLAM became the dominant religion. In the mid-16th century Libya was conquered by the Ottoman Empire. It remained under loose Turkish control until 1911 when ITALY invaded and made it a colony. In 1934 Italy officially defined this region as Libya and in 1939 made it an administrative part of Italy. Libya was liberated from Italian rule in WORLD WAR II as part of the fighting in North Africa and placed under joint British-French administrative rule. The Allies were unable to decide on Libya's future, although by terms of the 1947 peace treaty with Italy, Libya was to be given its independence. The issue was turned over to the UNITED NATIONS. The UN affirmed the 1947 decision, and on December 24, 1951, Libya became independent.

Libya's initial independence foreign policy was pro-Western in orientation. Libya was extremely poor and provided the United States and GREAT BRITAIN with military bases in return for economic aid. Seeds of change were planted in 1958 when OIL was discovered. As oil revenues increased Libya moved to reduce this foreign military presence. Most British troops left by 1966. In 1970 British bases were closed, and the United States was forced to leave Wheelus Air Base when its lease expired. It had played a central role in U.S. nuclear strike plans against the Soviet Union. The major development changing Libya's foreign policy was a September 1, 1969, military coup. A central figure in the takeover was Colonel Muammar al-Qaddafi. An ardent admirer of EGYPT's Gamal Abdel Nasser, Qaddafi moved Libya into the forefront of Arab opposition to ISRAEL and the West. One of his first targets were Western oil companies. Qaddafi successfully pressured independent oil companies into making concessions. Other ORGANIZATION OF PETROLEUM EXPORT-ING COUNTRIES (OPEC) followed suit. The price of oil began to rise, and control began to shift from the oil companies to the oil-producing states. Libya joined with other OPEC states in placing an embargo on oil sales to the United States and raising the price in response to U.S. support for Israel in the 1973 Arab-Israeli War. Much of its newfound wealth was used to purchase weapons from the Soviet Union and support TERRORISM, further angering the United States.

Relations with the United States deteriorated significantly in the 1980s. In August 1981 two Libyan jets fired on American aircraft participating in a routine naval exercise in international waters. The American planes shot down one of the Libyan planes. Qaddafi's support for terrorism became a major issue. An April 5, 1986, terrorist attack on a discothèque in Berlin killed two U.S. soldiers and injured 229 people. The Reagan administration cited this attack as justification for punitive bombings of Libya and the imposition of ECONOMIC SANCTIONS. Already in place were bans on Libyan oil exports to the United States and Export-Import Bank financing of development projects in Libya. Two years later Libya was implicated in the December 21, 1988, terrorist attack against Pan Am Flight 103 that crashed over Lockerbie, Scotland, killing 259 people on the plane and 11 more on the ground. Libya rejected an American and British request for the extradition of two Libyan nationals in connection with the bombing. In retaliation the United Nations imposed an arms embargo and placed limits on air travel to and from Libya in 1992. Also in the late 1980s Libya was found to be in the process of building a chemical weapons plant at Rabta.

Libya changed its position on terrorism in the 1990s. In 1999 it surrendered the two Libyan suspects, who were then tried in a Scottish court. One was found guilty, while the other was acquitted. The UN then suspended its sanctions. In August 2003 Libya formally accepted responsibility for the bombing and made arrangements to compensate the victims' families. This cleared the way for removing all of the remaining ECONOMIC SANCTIONS.

See also ARAB-ISRAELI CONFLICT; RUSSIA.

**Further reading:** Bills, Scott L. *The Libyan Arena.* Kent, Ohio: Kent State University Press, 1995; St. John, Ronald. *Qaddafi's World Design: Libyan Foreign Policy, 1969–1987.* London: Saqi Books, 1987.

## Lincoln, Abraham (1809–1865) *president of the United States*

Abraham Lincoln was the 16th president of the United States (1861–65). Since he was president during the AMER-ICAN CIVIL WAR, standard accounts of his presidency do not dwell heavily on matters of foreign policy. Not surprisingly, the emphasis is on Lincoln's relationship with his generals, the military conduct of the civil war, and his policy on slavery. Some accounts suggest that the timing of Lincoln's Emancipation Proclamation can be linked to foreign-policy concerns. It is argued that American diplomats stationed in Europe urged such action in order to build support in European capitals for the U.S. cause and dissuade them from recognizing the Confederacy.

Lincoln rose to prominence as a WHIG in Illinois. He served one term in the House of Representatives (1847–49), where he spoke out against continental expansionism and the war with MEXICO. On December 22, 1847, Lincoln introduced "spot resolutions," in which he called upon President JAMES POLK to identify the spot of soil where American blood was spilled that started the war. Lincoln's assertion, along with others who opposed the war, was that the spot was actually in Mexican territory. Lincoln next gained notoriety for his opposition to the Kansas-Nebraska Act of 1854 that opened up the Kansas Territory to slavery in violation of the Missouri Compromise of 1820. He was defeated in 1855 as the Whig candidate for the Senate and the following year helped found the REPUBLICAN PARTY in Illinois and soon became its leader. In 1858 he was the Republican nominee for the Senate and entered into a series of debates with the Democratic nominee, Senator Stephen A. Douglas.

The war began when Confederate forces fired on Fort Sumter in Charleston, South Carolina, on April 12, 1861. By the time Lincoln was inaugurated, seven Southern states had seceded. Lincoln relied heavily on his SECRETARY OF STATE, WILLIAM SEWARD, in foreign affairs. Lincoln had defeated the better-known Seward for the Republican presidential nomination of 1860. Lincoln was informed just after his inauguration that Fort Sumter had only enough supplies to last a week. At first his cabinet, led by Seward, recommended that Lincoln abandon the outpost. Seward, acting as the "premier" of Lincoln's administration, informed Confederate officials to this effect. Lincoln changed his mind and overruled Seward. He chose to resupply Fort Sumter with food but not ammunition or men. This was unacceptable to the Confederacy, and the war began.

It was Lincoln's custom, however, to support Seward and accept his counsel. He rejected arguments put forward by CHARLES SUMNER, chair of the Senate Foreign Relations Committee, and others that Seward was too powerful. Lincoln also allowed Seward to take the lead in handling the Trent affair and the Alabama claims cases with GREAT BRITAIN. In the former, the American seizure of four Confederate diplomats off of a neutral British ship, the *Trent*, raised the prospect of war between the United States and GREAT BRITAIN. In the latter, British shipyards were providing the Confederacy with blockade-running warships.

**Further reading:** Paludan, Phillip S. *The Presidency of Abraham Lincoln.* Lawrence: University Press of Kansas, 1994.

## Lippmann gap

The *Lippmann gap* is a phrase used to denote the constant struggle that the United States (or any state) faces in balancing resources and commitments. It takes its name from political columnist Walter Lippmann (1889–1974), who often wrote on foreign-policy matters. In the 1930s Lippmann held an isolationist perspective on world affairs, but as Nazi GERMANY amassed greater amounts of POWER he became an internationalist and embraced the fundamental tenets of REALISM.

Lippmann was a columnist for the *New York Herald Tribune* whose work was syndicated in more than 200 newspapers. He also wrote several influential books on U.S. foreign policy. Best known is his *United States Foreign Policy: Shield of the Republic.* In this piece he argued that foreign policy "consists in bringing into balance with a comfortable surplus of POWER in reserve, the nation's commitments and the nation's power." Samuel Huntington would take this argument, dub it the Lippmann gap, and extend this analysis forward.

Writing in 1943, Lippmann characterized different periods in U.S. foreign policy as solvent or insolvent, depending upon whether power resources and commitments were in balance. The period from 1789 to 1823 was insolvent. From 1824 to 1898 it was solvent, only to return to insolvency, which led to WORLD WAR II. Huntington goes on to characterize the postwar period up until the late 1960s as solvent. Since then, he argues, it has once again become insolvent. Writing in the late 1980s, Huntington noted that the typical response of American presidents in the post-VIETNAM era to the Lippmann gap has been to reject the option of cutting America's commitments. Instead, they have focused on diplomatic and military means of acquiring sufficient power to meet them. For the Nixon, Ford, and Carter administrations this involved getting U.S. allies to carry a larger share of the burden of dealing with the Soviet Union (see RUSSIA) and getting the Soviet Union to agree to ARMS CONTROL agreements that limited its power and thereby limited the power the United States needed to counter it. President RONALD REAGAN altered this strategy by pursuing a military buildup.

Post–COLD WAR PRESIDENTS have continued to struggle with the Lippmann gap. The United States placed itself in a leadership position in efforts to force IRAQ out of KUWAIT. Yet President GEORGE H. W. BUSH found it necessary to create a global coalition against Iraq in the PERSIAN GULF WAR, and neither he nor his successors have been able to punish Iraq enough to bring about Saddam Hussein's removal from power. Although reluctantly and often without clarity of purpose, President BILL CLINTON repeatedly placed the U.S. in leadership roles in the Balkan conflicts. He too found it necessary to engage in coalition-building in order to bring the necessary political, economic, and military resources to bear against the Serbs.

**Further reading:** Steel, Ronald. *Walter Lippmann and the American Century.* Boston: Little Brown, 1980.

## Lodge, Henry Cabot (1850–1924) *senator*

Henry Cabot Lodge served as a Republican U.S. senator from Massachusetts from 1893 to 1924. For more than 20 years he sat on the Senate Foreign Relations Committee.

Early in his career he was a protégé of TEDDY ROOSEVELT and advocated a nationalistic and aggressive version of INTERNATIONALISM. He supported the construction of a strong navy, the construction of the PANAMA CANAL, and the acquisition of the PHILIPPINES.

Lodge is best remembered for his political conflicts with President WOODROW WILSON. Lodge opposed Wilson's policy toward MEXICO, characterizing it as weak and ineffective. Initially he supported Wilson's position of neutrality but became strongly pro-British as WORLD WAR I progressed and sought the unconditional surrender of GERMANY. Lodge's most famous clash with Wilson came over ratification of the TREATY OF VERSAILLES and the establishment of the LEAGUE OF NATIONS. Chairing the Senate Foreign Relations Committee in 1919 and 1920, Lodge led the Senate's opposition to the treaty. He believed that the "weak" peace advocated by Wilson would allow Germany to rearm and once again threaten European peace and stability. He also rejected the concept of collective security that was embodied in the League of Nations, preferring a foreign-policy posture that preserved U.S. freedom of action. Lodge sponsored a series of "reservations" that were designed to address what he saw as defects in the treaty. Senator WILLIAM BORAH (R-Idaho) and other

Henry Cabot Lodge  *(Library of Congress)*

"irreconcilables" supported his amendments but promised to oppose the treaty no matter how it was revised. Wilson proved unable to bring himself to accept Lodge's amendments and sought to go over the head of the Senate to the American people to gain support for his treaty. Not only did this strategy fail as the Senate refused to ratify the Treaty of Versailles and join the League of Nations, but Wilson suffered a crippling stroke during this campaign that limited his effectiveness for the remainder of his presidency.

See also CONGRESS; CONSTITUTION, U.S.

**Further reading:** Widenor, William C. *Henry Cabot Lodge and the Search for American Foreign Policy.* Berkeley: University of California Press, 1980.

## Logan Act (1799)

The Logan Act of 1799 is seen as providing early congressional approval for a presidential monopoly in the conduct of American foreign policy. The stimulus for congressional action involved an exercise in personal diplomacy by a private American citizen. George Logan, a Quaker, went to FRANCE in an effort to negotiate an agreement that would avert war between the United States and France. Congress responded by passing "An Act to Prevent Usurpation of Executive Functions." It stated that "if any person being a citizen of the United States . . . shall, without the permission or authority of the government of the United States directly or indirectly commence or carry on any . . . intercourse with any foreign government . . . with an intent to influence the measures or conduct of any foreign governments . . . or defeat the measures of the government of the United States . . . they shall be deemed guilty of a high misdemeanor."

This law continues to be in place but has been ignored more than it has been enforced. President RICHARD NIXON cited the Logan Act in 1972 when, during the presidential campaign, Pierre Salinger tried to enter into discussions with North VIETNAM on behalf of Democratic presidential candidate George McGovern. In 1984 President RONALD REAGAN, however, did not use the Logan Act to stop the Reverend Jesse Jackson from going to SYRIA in an attempt to obtain the release of a downed navy flier.

## London Naval Conference

The London Naval Conference was the concluding act in the series of DISARMAMENT conferences conceived of in the 1920s. The United States played a leading role in all three. The first was the WASHINGTON CONFERENCE OF 1921 that produced a treaty placing limits on the size and composition of the world's major navies. The treaty did not cover all classes of naval vessels but only aircraft carriers, battle ships, and battle cruisers. The naval arms race now shifted to submarines, cruisers, and destroyers. The United States sought to curb this new arms race at a hastily called meeting in Geneva in 1927. That meeting failed to produce an agreement. President HERBERT HOOVER had established a good relationship with British prime minister Ramsey MacDonald, and during his visit to the United States in the fall of 1929, the British government issued an invitation to FRANCE, ITALY, JAPAN, and the United States to attend a disarmament conference in London in 1930.

The United States and GREAT BRITAIN had already accepted the concept of parity in all categories of ships. The chief task at London in this area was devising a formula that would take into account such factors as the age of ships, their speed and armor, and the quality of their weapons. Much more problematic were the security demands of France. It refused to accept any new limitations on its navy, arguing that it faced the prospect of a two-front naval war—in the Mediterranean Sea against Italy and in the Atlantic against GERMANY. Italy insisted upon parity with France. Japan also wished to change the ratios established at Washington, creating a 10:10:7 formula for all classes of ships. It achieved this ratio only for smaller ships.

The London Naval Treaty succeeded in establishing the first set of limitations on all classes of naval weapons. The "holiday" on constructing battleships and heavy cruisers was extended for another five years. Limits were also placed on submarines, cruisers, and destroyers. Rules were established prohibiting unrestricted submarine warfare. A less positive development was the introduction of an "escalator clause" that allowed each state to exceed its limits if it felt threatened by the naval power of a state not bound by the treaty. Moreover, France and Italy did not sign all parts of the treaty. They abstained from the section putting forward the ratios that would be permitted.

The Senate ratified the London Naval Treaty in July 1930 by a vote of 58-9. By 1933, however, the United States was engaged in a naval rearmament effort. President FRANKLIN ROOSEVELT diverted $250 million from the National Recovery Act for a new ship-building program to catch up to the other powers who were already at their treaty quota levels. Preparations began in 1934 for a second London Naval Conference, as had been agreed to in 1930. Japan made it clear it would no longer accept an inferior position, and on December 29, 1934, it gave the required two years notice of its intent to withdraw from the Washington Naval Treaty of 1922. The Three-Power Treaty (United States, Great Britain, and France) that emerged in 1936 called for qualitative rather than quantitative naval limits and contained an escape clause. The 1936 London Naval Treaty was quickly overtaken by events. In January 1938 Roosevelt asked CONGRESS for a billion-dollar naval appropriations outlay. The legislation was passed in May. In March 1938 the United States, Great Britain, and France all invoked the escape clause in the 1936 treaty. The naval arms race that preceded WORLD WAR II was now fully underway.

See also ARMS CONTROL; CONFERENCE DIPLOMACY.

**Further reading:** Kaufman, Robert G. *Arms Control during the Pre-Nuclear Era.* New York: Columbia University Press, 1990.

## Louisiana Purchase

The acquisition of the Louisiana Territory in 1803 by President THOMAS JEFFERSON opened up the West to American expansion by removing the presence of a powerful foreign power from the continent. Determining the exact boundaries of the Louisiana Territory would be a major preoccupation of U.S. foreign policy for the next several decades. The Louisiana Purchase also helped establish the principle that territory could be added to the United States by treaty as an implied federal POWER in the CONSTITUTION.

The Louisiana Territory consisted of some 828,000 square miles, which today comprises all or part of 15 states. Control over it was a question that brought together the interests of SPAIN, FRANCE, GREAT BRITAIN, and the United States. For the United States, control over the Louisiana Territory was a question of national defense and domestic politics. The presence of a strong state on America's western border presented a continuous threat to its national security by virtue of both geography and the link it provided to the seemingly endless wars among European states fought to perpetuate or upset the continental balance of power. In terms of domestic politics, the right to westward expansion, as well as the economic necessity of access to New Orleans, was taken as a given by most Americans. Rumors of French acquisition of the Louisiana Territory produced talk of secession and direct military action.

Spain had obtained control over the Louisiana Territory in 1762 from France as compensation for its losses to Great Britain in the Seven Years' War. It proved to be problematic compensation, costing Spain more to control than it was worth. Moreover, it appeared to be virtually indefensible against attack and was proving to be an ineffective check to American expansion that might someday threaten Spain's southern holdings in MEXICO. PINCKNEY'S TREATY of 1795 had reduced tensions between the United States and Spain by giving the Americans the right to navigate the Mississippi River and the right of deposit at the port of New Orleans (the right to transfer their goods to oceangoing vessels).

For its part, France wished to reacquire the Louisiana Purchase as part of Napoleon Bonaparte's plans to reestablish a French presence in the New World. The centerpiece

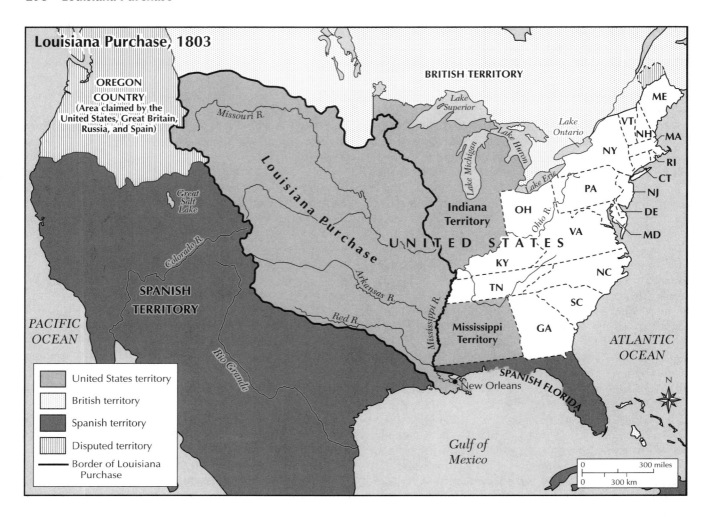

**Louisiana Purchase, 1803**

OREGON COUNTRY (Area claimed by the United States, Great Britain, Russia, and Spain)

BRITISH TERRITORY

SPANISH TERRITORY

UNITED STATES

Indiana Territory

Mississippi Territory

SPANISH FLORIDA

New Orleans

PACIFIC OCEAN

ATLANTIC OCEAN

Gulf of Mexico

Great Salt Lake

Missouri R.

Louisiana Purchase

Colorado R.

Arkansas R.

Red R.

Rio Grande

Mississippi R.

Ohio R.

Lake Superior

Lake Michigan

Lake Huron

Lake Erie

Lake Ontario

ME, VT, NH, MA, NY, RI, CT, NJ, PA, DE, OH, VA, MD, KY, TN, NC, SC, GA

United States territory
British territory
Spanish territory
Disputed territory
Border of Louisiana Purchase

0    300 miles
0    300 km

of that effort was to regain control over the sugar-rich Caribbean island of Saint-Domingue, which had broken lose from foreign control through a slave rebellion in 1795. The Louisiana Territory would provide the French empire with needed foodstuffs and a port to support its commercial operations in Saint-Domingue. To this end, Napoleon arranged to acquire the Louisiana Territory from Spain in 1800 in exchange for part of northern ITALY. France took possession in 1802.

Jefferson responded with alarm to news that a transfer of control was taking place. He observed in an open letter to the U.S. minister in Paris: "[T]here is on the globe one single spot, the possessor of which is our natural and habitual enemy. It is New Orleans." The natural solution to the dilemma presented by French control over the Louisiana Territory was an ALLIANCE with Great Britain, and Jefferson hinted as much in his letter. Such a strategy was not without its dangers. First, an alliance with Great Britain might provoke war with France rather than deter it. Second, it raised the prospect of Great Britain reestablishing

itself on America's western frontier. Matters became more urgent when Spain suspended the right to deposit at New Orleans. Americans incorrectly interpreted this as a move inspired by France.

Responding to the suggestion of Pierre Samuel du Pont de Nemours, Jefferson dispatched James Monroe to Paris to join Robert Livingston with instructions to offer to buy New Orleans and FLORIDA for $10 million. If talks went badly and France appeared ready to close the Mississippi River to U.S. commerce or begin hostilities, Monroe and Livingston were to go to Great Britain and discuss an alliance. Unexpectedly, Napoleon was not in a defiant mood. His military campaign against Saint-Domingue had gone poorly, and the prospect of renewed war between France and Great Britain seemed very real. Defending the Louisiana Territory against the British would be costly and difficult. Rather than face this prospect Napoleon offered the whole of the Louisiana Territory to the United States for about $15 million. Within one week, France and Great Britain went to war.

Napoleon's offer created a series of dilemmas for American officials. Monroe and Livingston had not been authorized to make such a purchase, but the opportunity proved too great to pass up. Once agreed to, Jefferson now faced a dilemma. He was a strict constructionist of the CONSTITUTION, which did not contain any provision allowing him to purchase territory. A constitutional amendment would be necessary for this. But there was no time. Instead, Jefferson chose simply to submit the purchase to CONGRESS for its approval, which it did by a vote of 24-7. France had controlled the Louisiana Territory for 20 days.

**Further reading:** Kaplan, Lawrence. *Entangling Alliances with None: American Foreign Policy in the Age of Jefferson.* Kent, Ohio: Kent State University Press, 1987; Tucker, Robert W., and David C. Hendrickson. *Empire of Liberty: The Statecraft of Thomas Jefferson.* New York: Oxford University Press, 1992.

# M

## MacArthur, Douglas (1880–1964) *general of the army*

Douglas MacArthur served as commander in chief of U.S. forces in the Pacific during WORLD WAR II and was placed in charge of the occupation of JAPAN, where he imposed a constitution that forbade Japan from possessing an army. His broader importance to the conduct of American foreign policy lies in his test of wills with President HARRY TRUMAN during the KOREAN WAR. The clash between MacArthur and Truman involved more than just a personality conflict between two men. It involved differing opinions about the importance of Asia versus Europe to America's national security, the manner in which wars should be conducted, and America's place in the world.

MacArthur was educated at West Point and served as an aide to President THEODORE ROOSEVELT early in his career. He rose to the rank of brigadier general in WORLD WAR I. In the interwar period MacArthur held a number of prominent posts in the PHILIPPINES. During World War II MacArthur rose to the newly created rank of general of the army. It was MacArthur who accepted the Japanese surrender on September 2, 1945. MacArthur was named commander of the UNITED NATIONS (UN) military forces in SOUTH KOREA after the North Korean attack. He continued to hold his position as commander of Allied forces in Japan.

During the Korean War MacArthur orchestrated a controversial but successful landing at Inchon that, along with a breakout of U.S. troops from the southern tip of the peninsula, turned the tide of battle against North Korean forces. U.S. war aims now changed. No longer interested in just forcing NORTH KOREA back over the 38th parallel that divided North and South Korea, the United States now sought to unite the country, a goal endorsed by MacArthur. A quick and stunning victory appeared to be within his grasp, and optimism ran high. Chinese troops had been engaged in combat in early November, but they had broken off the fighting. Then, to the surprise of MacArthur, who had discounted CHINA's military capability, Chinese forces unleashed a devastating counteroffensive that drove U.S. forces back deep into South Korea.

MacArthur responded to this unexpected turn of events by demanding that China be attacked both in Manchuria, which he argued served as a sanctuary north of the Yalu River, and from TAIWAN, where the Nationalist forces had retreated after being defeated by Mao Zedong (Mao Tsetung) in the recently concluded Chinese civil war. He sought permission from Washington for the use of "20–30 atomic bombs against China, the laying down of a radioactive belt across North Korea to seal it off from China and the use of a half a million Chinese nationalist troops."

The implication left by MacArthur's requests and the public outcry was that this stunning military defeat occurred because the Truman administration had placed unwarranted restraints on his actions. For MacArthur war and peace were two very different things, and wars were to be fought on terms set by military leaders. For Truman and his advisers in Washington an essential aim of the Korean War was to keep it limited. Old rules did not apply, and military and political considerations now went hand-in-hand.

MacArthur continued his public attacks on Truman's policies in the following months. In February he called Truman's strategy wholly unrealistic. In March, when U.S. troops under the direction of General Matthew Ridgeway returned to the 38th parallel, Truman planned on a diplomatic initiative designed to settle both the Korean conflict and perhaps address questions about legitimate government of China. MacArthur was informed of this and instructed not to initiate any major actions north of the 38th parallel. MacArthur agreed but then preempted Truman by issuing his own public ultimatum to China in which he threatened to expand the war into China unless it settled the Korean conflict on his terms, terms that explicitly excluded any linkage to Taiwan or the status of China's seat in the United Nations.

This outburst was followed by a letter to Republican minority leader Joseph Martin. Martin had sent MacArthur a copy of a speech in which he said the only reason to be in Korea was to win and that the Truman administration should be "indicted for the murder of thousands of American boys." MacArthur congratulated Martin on his speech, agreeing that "we must win" and that "if we lose this war to COMMUNISM in Asia the fall of Europe is inevitable." This was the last straw for Truman, who fired MacArthur on April 11, 1951.

MacArthur returned to the United States and received a hero's welcome. He addressed a session of CONGRESS, during which he continued his attacks on Truman's handling of the Korean War. The Truman administration countered by presenting its case at the joint Senate Foreign Relations Committee and House Armed Services Committee hearings on MacArthur's dismissal. At the hearings, they successfully shifted the focus away from MacArthur's attacks on military strategy to his insubordination. Supported by the JOINT CHIEFS OF STAFF, the Truman administration made the case that the U.S. CONSTITUTION demanded civilian control of the military and that MacArthur's actions violated this principle.

See also CIVIL-MILITARY RELATIONS.

## Madison, James (1751–1836) president of the United States, secretary of state

James Madison was the fourth president of the United States (1809–17). He also served as SECRETARY OF STATE under THOMAS JEFFERSON (1801–09). Madison is widely recognized to be a key architect of the CONSTITUTION and the father of the Bill of Rights. Along with ALEXANDER HAMILTON and John Jay, he authored the FEDERALIST PAPERS. Madison achieved notoriety in foreign affairs both as secretary of state and PRESIDENT.

As secretary of state he was responsible for Jefferson's response to British and French attacks on neutral American ships: the Embargo of 1807. It placed a complete embargo on American trade with other states. The logic to this move was based on the presumption that Europe needed American goods more than America needed European goods. For Europe, American goods were necessities. For America, European goods were luxuries. The Embargo of 1807 had the unintended affect of producing a sharp depression in the United States. American export to GREAT BRITAIN declined by an estimated 80 percent in 1808, and imports from Great Britain declined by some 56 percent that same year. Talk of secession was common in New England in the winter of 1808–09. CONGRESS replaced the embargo three days before Jefferson's term as president ended. On March 1, 1809, it passed legislation limiting nonintercourse to belligerent states. In 1810 the Nonintercourse Act expired and was replaced by one that promised to restrict American trade with one of the two warring European states provided that it would recognize America's

neutrality and end its naval blockades and forced seizures of American ships. Devised by now-president James Madison this new legislation was known as Macon's Bill Number 2.

Shortly thereafter Napoleon Bonaparte made an ambiguous offer that suggested FRANCE would accept the U.S. plan. Madison treated Napoleon's response as an official acceptance of it and asked Great Britain to endorse it as well. When the British refused, Madison reimposed nonintercourse with Great Britain. Combined with the anti-British sentiments of the congressional war HAWKS led by HENRY CLAY and JOHN C. CALHOUN, this action made war virtually inevitable. On June 18, 1812 Congress declared war. After 30 months of fighting the WAR OF 1812 concluded with the signing of the TREATY OF GHENT. Its terms left largely unresolved the disputes that had caused the conflict, notably the impressment of American sailors, restrictions on trade, and perceived attacks on American sovereignty and independence.

Madison's handling of the war is the subject of debate. Many are critical of the path that led to war, the lack of preparations for war, the political disunity among the regions that was evident during the war, and the conduct of the war itself. Others are more positive in their evaluation. They point to Madison's success in working with congressional Republican leaders to forge a consensus for the war and his policy initiatives after the war, such as calling for a protective tariff for American industries and a new national bank that helped stimulate the growth of a national economy.

**Further reading:** Stagg, J. C. A. *Mr. Madison's War: Politics, Diplomacy, and Warfare in the Early American Republic, 1783–1830.* Princeton, N.J.: Princeton University Press, 1983.

## Madrid accords

Hoping to capitalize on its victory in the PERSIAN GULF WAR, the GEORGE H. W. BUSH administration began to plan for an Israeli-Arab SUMMIT CONFERENCE. In March and April SECRETARY OF STATE James Baker made trips to the Middle East to gauge support for such a meeting. He found the climate lukewarm. This changed in July when Syrian president Hafez al-Assad announced his willingness to attend an Arab-Israeli summit conference. JORDAN and LEBANON soon agreed. Israel was last to agree, balking at the format suggested by SYRIA and opposing Soviet participation. In early August it gave its consent after procedural compromises were worked out. In early October Israel and the Soviet Union (see RUSSIA) resumed full diplomatic relations. On October 31, 1991, the jointly U.S.- and Soviet-sponsored Madrid Conference opened.

The plan called for a three-day meeting followed later by multilateral talks on such key regional issues as ARMS

President Bill Clinton *(center)* watches as Israeli prime minister Yitzhak Rabin *(left)* shakes hands with Palestinian leader Yasser Arafat in the garden of the White House after the signing of a deal that transferred much of the West Bank to Palestinian control, September 13, 1993. *(Hulton/Archive)*

CONTROL, water rights, and the ENVIRONMENT. These talks began on December 10 but quickly adjourned on December 18. A key stumbling block was the Palestinian desire to break away from the Jordanian delegation and meet separately with Israel, something Israel had been unwilling to do from the very outset of negotiations over setting up the conference. Talks resumed in January, February, April, and May in various locations, but little progress was made.

The United States was not a formal party to any of the talks so as not to impose its solution on the situation. This did not prevent deep strains from developing between the United States and ISRAEL. During the talks Prime Minister Yitzhak Shamir was at the same time politically weak at home and faced hostility from the United States. More than 300,000 Russian immigrants had arrived in Israel since 1989, and Shamir's solution to the need for additional housing was to build new homes in the occupied territories. To carry this out in June 1991 Israel sought a $10 billion loan guarantee from the United States. The Bush administration wanted the loan request deferred until after the conference because of long-standing Arab anger over the building of new settlements, but Israel persisted. In September 1991, when the United States was trying to convince Israel to attend the Madrid Conference, it formally made the request. The Bush administration reacted angrily. It asked CONGRESS to delay acting on the request and threatened to veto any congressional action in support of the loan. It demanded that Israel stop construction of new settlements. The Bush administration approved the request only after the Shamir government lost a June 1992 election. A new round of talks began in

August and made progress in the area of Palestinian autonomy, but the upcoming U.S. presidential election prevented any agreements from being reached.

The Madrid talks continued under the Clinton administration but soon deadlocked as violence again erupted in the Middle East. The Clinton administration tried and failed to move the talks forward by putting its own peace proposal on the table, thus abandoning its neutral posture. The true breakthrough came in Oslo, Norway, where Israeli foreign minister Shimon Peres and PALESTINE LIBERATION ORGANIZATION (PLO) leader Mahmoud Abbas had been meeting secretly. On August 29, 1993, they announced agreement on a broad framework that would provide mutual recognition of Palestinian autonomy in Gaza and Jericho. The final status of the territories would be determined after five years.

Parallel talks then began in Oslo and in Washington (as part of the Madrid process). Agreements were reached in both settings. All totaled, 11 rounds of negotiations were held between the Madrid Summit and the Israel–PLO Declaration of Principles of September 13, 1993, in which these two parties agreed to recognize each other and set out the principles for a plan to establish peaceful relations. This agreement was made possible by the one agreed a few days earlier. On September 10 the PLO recognized Israel's right to exist in peace and security, and Israel recognized the PLO as the legitimate representative of the Palestinian people.

## Manifest Destiny

*Manifest Destiny* is the summary phrase used to capture the logic and emotion behind America's policy of continental expansion that gripped the United States from 1815 to 1845. During this time period the United States acquired FLORIDA, TEXAS, OREGON, and territory from MEXICO totaling about 1,263,301 square miles and tripling America's population from 8,419,000 in 1815 to 22,018,000 in 1848.

A variety of factors contributed to this expansion. Strategic and economic forces played major roles as the United States sought to protect itself from real and imagined threats, an outlet for a growing population, and continued economic opportunities for its farmers, industrialists, and businesspeople. As significant as these factors were, equally important were the language and imagery that accompanied and in many respects drove this expansionism. Writing in 1845 newspaper editor John L. O'Sullivan stated that the United States had a "manifest destiny to overspread the continent allotted by Providence to the free development of our yearly multiplying millions." This phrase soon found its way into a congressional speech in which it was argued that America's right to

Oregon was founded on "the right of manifest destiny to spread over the whole continent."

Manifest Destiny neither implied nor contained a formal military strategy for expansion. In fact, to advocates none was needed because the process of expansion envisioned in Manifest Destiny was seen as natural and inevitable. As Americans spread out across the continent, they would bring with them their way of life and the principles of democratic government. The inherent superiority of American values was sure to be recognized by those with whom they came into contact and would gladly be adopted.

Conceived of in these terms, America's westward expansion offered little to those whose lands were to become incorporated into the United States. The failure to assimilate and prosper was the fault of those receiving America's goodness. It was not due to any shortcomings in the message being delivered. It was not unexpected, therefore, that they should resist. This sense of racial superiority was reflected in U.S. foreign policy toward NATIVE AMERICANS and Mexicans. Unlike its foreign policy toward the stronger Anglo-Saxon GREAT BRITAIN, which was marked by a combination of aggressive language and an acceptance of the need to negotiate, its foreign policy toward these groups was more consistently aggressive.

Advocates of Manifest Destiny generally thought in continental terms, although some also saw CUBA as falling within its boundaries. With continental expansion largely completed with the acquisition of Oregon and California, the strains of Manifest Destiny became muted. They resurfaced only in moderate form in SECRETARY OF STATE WILLIAM SEWARD's purchase of ALASKA from RUSSIA. They emerged with far more energy in the last two decades of the 19th century as the United States debated whether or not to become an imperial power with holdings in the Pacific. Referred to by some as the "new manifest destiny," this debate revealed the ongoing American conviction of racial superiority. Its new intellectual and strategic foundations were based on the writings of Charles Darwin, who advanced the notion of "survival of the fittest," and Alfred Thayer Mahan, who asserted that history favored "island nations" and that sea power was the defining characteristic of a great power. HAWAII and Samoa would be the first focal points of the new Manifest Destiny, followed by the PHILIPPINES, at the turn of the century.

See also AMERICAN NATIONAL STYLE.

**Further reading:** Horsman, Reginold. *Race and Manifest Destiny.* Cambridge, Mass.: Harvard University Press, 1981; Weinberg, Albert K. *Manifest Destiny: A Study of National Expansion in American History.* Chicago: Peter Smith, 1958.

## Mariel boatlift

The Mariel boatlift was a massive exodus of Cubans to the United States. Its beginnings can be dated to May 13, 1979, when 12 Cubans sought asylum on the grounds of the Venezuelan EMBASSY in Havana by crashing a bus through a gate. On January 16, 1980, 12 Cubans tried but failed to gain entry to the grounds of the Peruvian embassy. On April 4, amid increasing tension and further attempts to obtain asylum at the Peruvian embassy, Cuban president Fidel Castro announced that anyone wishing to leave CUBA should go to the embassy. Over the next two days more than 10,000 appeared.

This onslaught created an international crisis over how to resettle the Cubans. President JIMMY CARTER stated that the United States would admit 3,500 Cubans but expected that there would be international cooperation and prescreening in Costa Rica, where the REFUGEES were being flown. As the number of refugees rose to more than 7,000 in mid-April, Castro announced that he was terminating the "air bridge" between Cuba and Costa Rica. At this point matters took an unexpected turn. On April 19, 1980, two privately owned U.S. boats sailed into Mariel Harbor to bring 49 Cubans to the United States. The next day Castro announced that anyone wishing to leave for the United States was free to depart from Mariel Harbor.

This announcement set in motion the "Freedom Flotilla." Between April 21 and 30 an estimated 6,300 Cubans arrived in the United States. The numbers of refugees rose so quickly that on May 6, President Carter declared a state of emergency for South Florida. A week later Carter stated that those Cubans who lacked relatives in the United States, an estimated 35 percent, would not be allowed to remain. He would also call for a halt to the Freedom Flotilla and instruct the Coast Guard to stop boats going to Cuba. Castro ended the Mariel boatlift on September 26, 1980. By then an estimated 125,200 Cubans had fled to the United States. Official estimates place the number of Mariel refugees residing in the Dade County area at more than 90,000.

The domestic root causes of the Mariel boatlift were economic and political. In 1979 the Cuban economy began to falter badly due to a slump in world sugar prices and an infestation of sugar rust. In January 1980 the CENTRAL INTELLIGENCE AGENCY warned that social and political pressures were reaching a point at which a repeat of the 1965 Camarioca boatlift was possible. The political element was provided by Castro's miscalculation of the Cuban response to his offer of free exit for those wanting to leave.

The Mariel boatlift was not the first Cuban refugee flow to the United States during the Castro regime, but it changed how the United States defined Cuban refugees. Earlier arrivals had been welcomed. They were seen either as having made an important political statement in leaving

Cuba or as potential contributors to the American economy. This was not the case with the Mariel boatlift. These refugees were not seen as contributing to American political or economic power. Instead, they were viewed as drains on social services and police departments and as a threat to American workers. Public opinion turned against the Cubans. At one point 91 percent of those responding to a Gallup poll favored a halt to the Cuban influx until unemployment rates in the United States fell to 5 percent.

The Mariel boatlift is significant for several reasons. First, it demonstrated that U.S.-Cuban relations were far more complex that in the earlier COLD WAR years. Second, it demonstrated the extent to which the United States was losing control over the INTERNATIONAL SYSTEM. Carter could not end the Mariel boatlift on his own. He required Castro's cooperation to bring this about. Third, the Mariel boatlift occurred during an election year. Domestic political considerations complicated the American response to it, as well as the response to the large refugee flow from HAITI that paralleled the Mariel boatlift. Although not directly related to the Mariel boatlift, the following year the CUBAN-AMERICAN NATIONAL FOUNDATION was established. It would become the leading Cuban-American lobbying group in the United States. Since its founding, it has been vehemently anti-Castro in its outlook.

## Marshall, George C. (1880–1959) *general, secretary of defense, secretary of state*

George Catlett Marshall, Jr., was SECRETARY OF STATE and SECRETARY OF DEFENSE in the Truman administration. He played key roles in many of the early COLD WAR foreign-policy initiatives of the United States. Prior to becoming secretary of state Marshall had a distinguished career as a military officer. He served as principal aide to General John Pershing and army chief of staff. One week after retiring from the army at the mandatory age of 65, Marshall was named special emissary to CHINA, where he was charged with negotiating a peace in the Chinese civil war between the Nationalist forces of Jiang Jieshi (Chiang Kai-shek) and the Communist forces of Mao Zedong (Mao Tse-tung). These efforts failed, and in January 1947 President HARRY TRUMAN ended the mission. Marshall reported on the rise of COMMUNISM and on the corruption of the Nationalists and concluded that preventing a Communist victory would require a military and political effort on the part of the United States from which it would "practically be impossible to withdraw." Truman heeded this advice and provided the Nationalists with only limited aid after that.

It was while seeking to find a peaceful solution to the Chinese civil war that Marshall was offered the position of secretary of state. Marshall's appointment was hailed as a sign of BIPARTISANSHIP. Upon assuming that position, Marshall set out to reorganize the STATE DEPARTMENT. He assumed a policy-making role and delegated the day-to-day running of the State Department to undersecretaries. Among the highly skilled people whom Marshall appointed to key positions were GEORGE KENNAN and DEAN ACHESON.

As secretary of state Marshall helped oversee several key foreign-policy decisions that laid the foundation for U.S. CONTAINMENT policy. One was the decision to provide economic recovery aid to Europe. He proposed the MARSHALL PLAN in a commencement address at Harvard University in 1947. In 1948, Marshall urged Harry Truman to reject the recommendation of General Lucius Clay, the commanding officer of U.S. occupation troops in GERMANY, to use military force to break the Russian blockade of Berlin. Marshall urged an airlift of supplies, which was the policy Truman adopted. He would play a leading role in establishing America's ring of ALLIANCES that came to encircle the Soviet Union and its allies through discussions that led to the founding of the NORTH ATLANTIC TREATY ORGANIZATION (NATO) and the ORGANIZATION OF AMERICAN STATES (OAS). Marshall was less successful in trying to convince Truman not to recognize the state of ISRAEL in 1947 after it declared independence. Marshall feared that doing so would damage American relations with the Arab world and U.S. access to OIL. He also saw the decision as representing an unwarranted intrusion of domestic politics into foreign-policy decision making.

Marshall resigned in 1949 due to ill health and was replaced by Dean Acheson. He returned to the Truman administration as secretary of defense in 1950 following the outbreak of the KOREAN WAR. Recognized for his great organizational skills in putting together the U.S. military machine that defeated the Axis powers in WORLD WAR II, Marshall's task as secretary of defense was to rebuild the U.S. military apparatus into a force capable of winning in KOREA. Marshall supported Truman in his decision to relieve General DOUGLAS MACARTHUR of his command in Korea for publicly criticizing and refusing to accept Truman's decision to fight a limited war in Korea and continue the U.S. policy of a Europe-first national security strategy. Marshall came under heavy attack from Senator Joseph McCarthy for this decision, as well as for his earlier reluctance to come to the aid of Jiang Jieshi (Chiang Kai-shek) in allowing China to fall to the Communists. He was accused by them of allowing communists to infiltrate the State Department and for being soft on communism. Marshall retired in 1951 and won the Nobel Peace Prize in 1953 for his work on the European economic recovery.

See also MCCARTHYISM; RUSSIA.

**Further reading:** Stoler, Mark. *George C. Marshall: Soldier-Statesman of the American Century.* New York: Macmillan, 1989.

## Marshall Plan

The Marshall Plan, or the European Recovery Program, as it was more formally known, was a blueprint for European economic recovery presented by SECRETARY OF STATE GEORGE MARSHALL at a Harvard University address in June 1947. Marshall asserted, "[I]t is logical that the United States should do whatever it is able to do to assist in the return of normal economic health in the world, without which there can be no political stability and no assured peace." Focusing his comments on Europe, DEAN ACHESON, who would succeed Marshall as secretary of state in 1949, noted that action was necessary "even without full Four-Power [Soviet Union (see RUSSIA), GREAT BRITAIN, FRANCE, and the United States] agreement to effect a larger measure of European, including German, recovery."

By 1947 the United States had already provided Europe with approximately $9 billion in loans and grants, but European economic recovery after WORLD WAR II was

Nations in the Marshall Plan, 1948

proceeding slowly. In February 1947 German production fell to 29 percent of its 1936 level. At the end of 1946 Great Britain had just managed to reach prewar level of production. Concerns in the United States about the political stability of Europe mounted. In particular it was feared that communists might come to power in France and Italy. One-fourth of the French electorate had voted communist. Concerns were also expressed about the danger posed to the health of the U.S. economy by the large European deficit.

A precondition for the aid package Marshall proposed was European agreement on a plan of action. Europe was to take the initiative, identifying common needs and a common recovery plan. In mid-June the British and French foreign ministers met in Paris to begin formulating a European proposal. The Soviet Union was invited to join them. Evidence suggests that the United States did not want Soviet participation in the Marshall Plan but for political reasons felt obliged to extend the offer to all European states. A precondition for Soviet participation was that Moscow agree to abide by the decisions of the planning group and that it contribute raw materials to the recovery effort.

Fresh on the heals of the TRUMAN DOCTRINE, Soviet leaders were suspicious of Western motives and labeled it "a plan for interference in the domestic affairs of other countries." The Paris Conference reached a deadlock, and the Soviet Union pulled out of further negotiations. It also pressured CZECHOSLOVAKIA to do the same. As a countermove it put forward its own Molotov Plan and resurrected the Cominform.

Discussions continued throughout 1947. The Truman administration submitted a $17 billion aid package to Congress, and in March 1948 Congress approved $4 billion in aid for the first year. The vote occurred against a backdrop of a recent Communist coup in Czechoslovakia, pending elections in Italy, and a growing crisis in GERMANY. The Marshall Plan ended in 1952, having directed over $13 billion toward European economic recovery. In 1951 the Economic Cooperation Administration that oversaw this effort was absorbed by the Mutual Security Administration, and military aid began to replace economic aid as the centerpiece of U.S. aid to Europe. By 1952, 80 percent of American aid to Europe was military.

The Marshall Plan was an economic success. By 1950, European production exceeded prewar levels by 25 percent. The Marshall Plan also had larger political consequences. It represented a small but important step forward in European economic cooperation and integration that would culminate decades later in the creation of the European Union. Politically as well as economically, the Marshall Plan was an important contributor to the dividing of Germany and all of Europe into "East" and "West." This division would take on a military dimension in 1949 with the establishment of the NORTH ATLANTIC TREATY ORGANIZATION (NATO).

**Further reading:** Gimbell, John. *The Origins of the Marshall Plan.* Stanford, Calif.: Stanford University Press, 1976.

## massive retaliation

The phrase *massive retaliation* was the centerpiece to the Eisenhower administration's nuclear DETERRENCE policy. The doctrine of massive retaliation also was the first attempt by U.S. strategists to systematically lay out a policy for using NUCLEAR WEAPONS that recognized their unique character. An important feature of massive retaliation as a nuclear doctrine is that its purpose was deterrence, namely, preventing Soviet aggression. Rejected was the notion that nuclear weapons could be used to force change or "roll back the iron curtain."

In his speech outlining the doctrine, SECRETARY OF STATE JOHN FOSTER DULLES called for moving away from what he described as the reactive approach to containing communist expansion embraced by the Truman administration. Local conventional defenses, Dulles asserted, were inadequate to the task of containing the "mighty landpower of the Communist world." Emergency measures to deal with communist aggression were costly, and they seldom provided permanent solutions. The way to deter aggression was to reinforce local defenses with the "further deterrent of massive retaliatory power." From now on, the United States would "retaliate instantly, by means and at places of [its] own choosing" to acts of Soviet aggression. The Eisenhower administration's defense plans left little doubt that this meant nuclear weapons. NATIONAL SECURITY COUNCIL (NSC) Paper No. 162/2 directed the JOINT CHIEFS OF STAFF to "plan to use nuclear armaments of all shapes and sizes in the future whenever this would work to the advantage of the United States."

As early as 1948 Dulles has been convinced that the use of nuclear weapons in war was almost inevitable. President DWIGHT EISENHOWER was of a like mind on this point. He believed that any conflict on the level of the KOREAN WAR or greater would go nuclear. Dulles did not specify in his speech or elsewhere what acts of aggression would lead to their use, although the implication always given was that the number of possible triggers was not small. The vagueness was calculated and deliberate. It was intended to induce caution on the part of the Soviet Union (see RUSSIA) since Moscow could not be sure what actions might provoke the United States to use its nuclear weapons.

Dulles's belief that nuclear weapons could be used to fight a war and that wars occurred because aggressor's misread the POWER held by their opponents combined in his eyes to make massive retaliation a credible (believable) deterrent. It was not long before the credibility of deterrence was challenged, however. Almost immediately some questioned whether such a vague and all-encompassing threat would deter a wide range of aggressive acts. In concrete terms, the question was, short of a Pearl Harbor or direct attack on the continental United States, would the United States respond to aggression with nuclear weapons? If the answer was no, then the Soviet Union would not be deterred.

Soon a second critique would be added. When first articulated massive retaliation was a one-way threat. The United States had the ability to deliver nuclear weapons against the Soviet Union, but Moscow lacked the ability to retaliate against U.S. targets. This changed when the Soviet Union successfully tested an intercontinental ballistic missile (ICBM) and sent *SPUTNIK* into Earth orbit. Now the mere possession of a nuclear capability was not enough to deter the enemy. Attention had to be given to plans to protect one's nuclear forces and population centers. Moreover, the possibility also existed that the Soviet Union could deter the use of American nuclear weapons.

By the end of the Eisenhower administration the wisdom of massive retaliation and the New Look defense policy of which it was part were widely questioned. In the Kennedy administration bold assertions about the use of nuclear weapons, such as that contained by the phrase *massive retaliation*, were replaced by efforts to produce more calculated and measured answers that addressed specific questions concerning survivability and composition of U.S. nuclear forces and the requirements for fighting different types of nuclear wars, a requirement that would become institutionalized through the refinement of the Single Integrated Operational Plan (SIOP).

Massive retaliation is significant to the development of American nuclear deterrence policy not only for what it tried to do (lay out a doctrine for the use of nuclear weapons) but also because it established a point of reference and language for future deterrence debates. Its development was part of a truly innovative period of strategic thought that helped bring into focus the key questions that all future strategists would have a deal with.

**Further reading:** Kahan, Jerome. *Security in the Nuclear Age: Developing U.S. Strategic Arms Policy.* Washington, D.C.: Brookings, 1975.

## McCarthyism

McCarthyism burst onto the U.S. political scene on February 9, 1950. On that date in Wheeling, West Virginia, Senator Joseph McCarthy gave a speech in which he claimed to have a list of 205 names "that were known to the SECRETARY OF STATE as being members of the communist party and who nevertheless [were] still working and shaping policy in the STATE DEPARTMENT." McCarthy's charges were never documented, but his speech set off a nationwide search for Communists and communist sympathizers within the government and in positions of influence throughout American society. McCarthy's charges had a particularly demoralizing impact on those who worked in the STATE DEPARTMENT. Many individuals had their careers ruined, creating major gaps in the department's expertise. This would come back to haunt the United States as it turned its attention to Southeast Asia and VIETNAM in the early 1960s.

Joseph McCarthy was the junior Republican senator from Wisconsin. He was first elected to the Senate in 1947 and reelected in 1952. Up until his Wheeling speech McCarthy had not been prominently involved in the anticommunist investigations of the late 1940s. The most politically charged of these was the investigation into the activities of former State Department employee Alger Hiss. Two weeks before this speech Hiss was convicted of perjury for having denied that he passed secret material to Whitaker Chambers, a Communist agent.

McCarthy's charges had an immediate impact at the State Department, where 91 employees, many of whom were homosexuals, were fired as security risks. A special subcommittee of the Foreign Relations Committee investigated McCarthy's charges. In July 1950 it denounced them as false and accused McCarthy of having engaged in unethical behavior. Republicans labeled the Democratic-controlled committee's report a whitewash. Emboldened by the positive response he received from the public, McCarthy continued his attacks. In 1951 he accused SECRETARY OF DEFENSE and former Secretary of State GEORGE C. MARSHALL of being an accomplice in a communist conspiracy that led to Mao Zedong's (Mao Tse-tung) victory in the Chinese civil war. McCarthy characterized the conspiracy as being "so immense and an infamy so black as to dwarf any previous such venture in the history of man."

In 1953 with the Republicans now in the majority, McCarthy became chair of the permanent Subcommittee on Investigations of Government Operations. His first target was Charles Bohlen, whom President DWIGHT EISENHOWER had nominated to be ambassador to the Soviet Union. Bohlen was confirmed but only after a bruising battle in which Eisenhower did not directly confront McCarthy, who now turned his attention back to the State Department. In 1953 he and his closest advisers, Roy Cohen and C. David Shine, began touring U.S. EMBASSY libraries searching in an effort to uncover communist and other subversive materials. Secretary of State JOHN FOSTER DULLES sought to preempt McCarthy and ordered questionable books to be banned from these libraries. Books were pulled off the shelves and burned. Dulles did not stop there. He demanded positive loyalty oaths from State Department personnel and ran background checks on them that involved the use of lie detectors and phone taps. Almost 200 individuals identified as security risks were fired as a result of these investigations. Before 1953 ended, McCarthy would charge that President Eisenhower had not acted with sufficient purpose to rid the U.S. government of communist subversives.

In 1954 McCarthy turned his attention to the U.S. Army. The immediate target was an army dentist, Major Irving Peress, who was a member of the left-wing American Labor Party. Called before McCarthy's committee he invoked the Fifth Amendment in explaining why he had refused to answer questions on the loyalty certification. McCarthy demanded that he should be court-martialed, but the army had already begun processing his honorable discharge papers. This infuriated McCarthy even more. He now demanded to know who had approved the honorable discharge. Peress's commanding officer, General Ralph Zwicker, was forced to testify over the objections of Secretary of the Army Robert Stevens.

McCarthy's attack on the army proved to be his undoing, as a coalition of political forces mobilized against him. Respected television commentator Edward R. Murrow denounced McCarthy. So too did leading members of the REPUBLICAN PARTY, who now feared that McCarthy's attacks could cripple the Eisenhower administration's ability to conduct foreign policy. Vice President RICHARD NIXON accused McCarthy of using "reckless talk and questionable methods." The army also stood up to McCarthy. It charged that McCarthy and Cohen had sought special treatment for Schine when he was drafted into the army in 1953. The war of words between the army and McCarthy escalated to the point that McCarthy's own subcommittee voted to investigate the matter, with McCarthy temporarily resigning as chair. Republican Karl Mundt replaced him.

The televised hearings ran from April 22 to June 17, 1954, and exposed McCarthy's bullying tactics, abrasive style, and the way he manipulated unsubstantiated charges. Cohen was forced to resign as the committee issued a report in August criticizing him for using his position to obtain preferential treatment for Schine. Republicans on the committee blocked the Democratic effort to implicate McCarthy as well. Nevertheless the Senate soon moved to censure McCarthy. A motion to censure had been introduced by Republican senator Ralph Flanders on July 30. A select committee under the chair of Senator Arthur Watkins conducted hearings. The Watkins report was issued on November 8 and recommended censure. McCarthy responded by accusing the Select Committee of having fallen under the influence of the Communist Party and identified himself as a "symbol of the resistance to communist subversions." On December 2, 1954, the Senate voted to censure McCarthy by a vote of 67–22. McCarthy remained in the Senate for the next two and a half years before dying in 1957 of what most believe to have been alcoholism.

The roots of McCarthyism run deep in American political culture and are not simply explained by any excesses of partisan politics. McCarthyism was but one strand of what historian Richard Hofstadter once referred to as the "paranoid style in American politics." Periodically there explodes on the American political landscape a wave of antiradicalism. In 1798 it resulted in the Alien and Sedition Acts. In the mid-1800s it helped form and support the Know-Nothing Party. In the 1920s it produced the Red Scare. In the 1960s it led the FEDERAL BUREAU OF INVESTIGATION to investigate the PEACE MOVEMENT to see if it was controlled from abroad. Because their occurrence is so closely tied with America's involvement in international conflicts, this antiradicalism can also be seen as a reflection of America's frustrations with realizing its quest for absolute security.

The State Department was particularly hard hit by McCarthy's attacks and the actions taken by Secretary of State John Foster Dulles to cleanse it of subversives. Among those forced out of the State Department were FOREIGN SERVICE OFFICERS John Paton Davies, Jr., John Carter Vincent, and John Service. Their principal crime was to have served in CHINA and correctly concluded that Jiang Jieshi's (Chiang Kai-shek) government was too corrupt to survive. Believing that Mao Zedong (Mao Tse-tung) would emerge triumphant, they recommended that assistance be directed to him. Service was dismissed in 1951 after the Civil Service Commission's Loyalty Review Board concluded that there was "reasonable doubt as to his loyalty." Vincent was accused of associating and collaborating with Communists. The Loyalty Board recommended his dismissal for his "studied praise of Chinese Communists." Vincent retired under pressure in 1952. The Loyalty Board did not find reasonable doubt in the case of Davies, but nevertheless Dulles forced him out of the State Department in 1954. Under prodding from McCarthy, Dulles appointed a special panel to review the case. It found Davies guilty of "a definite lack of judgment." Their departure and that of other "China hands" created a gaping hole in the State Department's knowledge of China and South east Asia when, less than a decade later, the United States began its involvement in Vietnam.

See also CONGRESS; DOMESTIC INFLUENCES ON U.S. FOREIGN POLICY; ESPIONAGE.

**Further reading:** Griffith, Robert K. *The Politics of Fear.* Amherst: University of Massachusetts Press, 1987.

## McNamara, Robert S. (1916– ) *secretary of defense*

Robert S. McNamara played major roles in shaping world politics during his tenure as SECRETARY OF DEFENSE in the

Kennedy and Johnson administrations (1961–67) and as president of the WORLD BANK (1968–81).

McNamara joined the Kennedy administration after briefly serving as president of Ford Motor Company. He joined the company when it was experiencing economic difficulties and rose through the ranks from general manager to president. He was the first person from outside the Ford family to hold this position. At the DEFENSE DEPARTMENT McNamara brought with him a conviction that the Pentagon's traditional method of resource allocation that centered on the prerogatives of the three military services was inefficient and had to give way to a more centralized budgetary process that emphasized roles and missions. This brought him and the "whiz kids" he brought with him from Ford into direct and open conflict with the service chiefs. The most bitterly contested battles were with General Curtis LeMay, who was the air force chief of staff and a proponent of the manned bomber, having served as head of the Strategic Air Command. He resisted McNamara's efforts to redirect spending to intercontinental and submarine-launched ballistic missiles and to develop a fighter that could be used by both the air force and the navy.

McNamara is most remembered for his role in the policy deliberations over the VIETNAM WAR. During President JOHN KENNEDY's administration McNamara advocated sending U.S. military advisers to VIETNAM and was confident that they would be able to leave by 1965. By 1964, however, he had altered his view of what it would take to defeat the North Vietnamese and argued for a massive increase in Vietnam-related defense spending, and in 1965 he supported General William Westmoreland's requests for an additional 585,000 troops. By 1966 McNamara was beginning to have doubts about the morality and effectiveness of the bombing attacks against North VIETNAM. In August 1967 he drafted a peace proposal that was rejected by North Vietnam. It would have suspended bombing in return for productive peace discussions. In November 1967 he called upon President LYNDON JOHNSON to end the bombing, freeze U.S. troop levels in South Vietnam, and turn the primary responsibility for fighting the war over to the South Vietnamese forces.

Johnson refused to accept McNamara's advice, and McNamara soon left the administration to join the World Bank as president. During his tenure at the World Bank McNamara redirected its spending priorities away from large industrial projects to ones that emphasized agriculture and education. McNamara asserted that widespread poverty was the most fundamental problem facing the global community. During his tenure he succeeded in raising World Bank spending from $1 billion to $12 billion and made it a major force in international development projects in developing countries.

Defense Secretary Robert McNamara using a pointer on a map of Vietnam *(National Archives)*

After leaving the World Bank McNamara became a strong advocate of ARMS CONTROL. Along with McGeorge Bundy and Gerald Smith, he authored an influential article in *Foreign Affairs* in 1982 that called for a no-first-use policy of NUCLEAR WEAPONS in Europe. Highly controversial at the time, this was the policy that the NORTH ATLANTIC TREATY ORGANIZATION (NATO) adopted under a different name in 1990. In 1995 McNamara authored a controversial account of the role he played in Vietnam decision making. While admitting that he lied to the American public and made mistakes, critics asserted that his confessions did not go far enough and labeled *In Retrospect: The Tragedy and Lessons of Vietnam* "shallow and deeply disingenuous."

**Further reading:** Art, Robert. *The TFX Decision: McNamara and the Military.* Pittsburgh, Pa.: University of Pittsburgh Press, 1988; McNamara, Robert. *Argument without End: In Search of Answers to the Vietnam Tragedy.* New York: Public Affairs Press, 1999.

## media

Today the media is one of the most pervasive influences on American foreign policy. This has not always been the case, and it is easy to forget how recent a phenomenon the media is. Consider a comparison between the CUBAN MISSILE CRISIS and the PERSIAN GULF WAR: SECRETARY OF DEFENSE ROBERT MCNAMARA observed that he did not turn on the TV once during the Cuban missile crisis, whereas DIRECTOR OF CENTRAL INTELLIGENCE William Webster watched CNN to find out where Iraqi missiles were landing. The Kennedy administration knew about missiles in Cuba for six days before the information was broadcast to the American public, but President GEORGE H. W. BUSH was expected to respond instantly to the Iraqi invasion of KUWAIT. It is not unreasonable to expect that had the Cuban missile crisis occurred in the 1990s, American television might have discovered the presence of Soviet missiles in CUBA about the same time that the INTELLIGENCE COMMUNITY did in 1962.

In concrete terms the media has affected the conduct of American foreign policy along several different dimensions. First, it has accelerated the decision-making process. No longer is there a lag between events and the need for a public response. The perceived need for quick action often results in missteps. Administrations find it necessary to correct and alter policies they have just announced as a clearer picture of events emerge. In the process they run the risk of appearing to be incompetent or to have deliberately mislead the public with earlier statements. Second, the media has altered the relationship between policy makers and the intelligence community. No longer do the CENTRAL INTELLIGENCE AGENCY or other INTELLIGENCE units have a monopoly of information. The media is a competing source of both critical facts and instant analysis. This has forced the intelligence community to reassess its role in the policy process and the value that it provides policy makers.

Third, the media has altered the relationship between policy makers in Washington and those in the field, be they ambassadors or generals. The media provides an opportunity for those in Washington to micromanage events. Live broadcasts during the Persian Gulf War of SCUD missiles and the Patriot antimissile defense system, tanks on the street in Moscow during the attempted coup against Mikhail Gorbachev, or Chinese students protesting on Tiananmen Square lessen their dependence on these officials for information or policy recommendations. In seizing this opportunity policy makers in Washington run the risk of making poor decisions because of the incomplete and often biased picture of events they are seeing.

Fourth, the media has created a new policy area. It is no longer sufficient to have a Persian Gulf policy or a DRUG-TRAFFICKING policy. Administrations now need to have a media policy that accompanies and reinforces this policy. The inability of the Clinton administration to frame its policy in HAITI or BOSNIA AND HERZEGOVINA in a coherent fashion allowed the media to impose its own definition of the situation on news stories. Doing so reinforced the image that Clinton's foreign policy had lost its sense of vision and competence.

Several elements go into making a successful media story. One is the ability to personalize the issue. The war against TERRORISM is defined in terms of OSAMA BIN LADEN. The conflict with IRAQ is defined in terms of Saddam Hussein. The Israeli-Palestinian conflict is depicted as a personal struggle between two opposing leaders. The inability to personalize a story is also held responsible for the difficulty in reporting on environmental issues, trade policy, and international financial matters. A second important element is held to be the continuing development of a story line. The administration's media policy must pick a theme and continue to expound on it rather than go in multiple directions. The use of official sources and late-breaking news are the final elements to a successful media policy.

Finally, media coverage has an impact on PUBLIC OPINION and the domestic context within which policy is carried out. One example of this impact is the spiral of silence. It asserts that people will refuse to give voice to their concerns or opinions if they do not hear others voicing them. The result is to produce a misleading sense of what the public thinks on an issue due to self-censorship. The media by the nature of its coverage of an event can create conditions ripe for a spiral of silence. For example, during the Persian Gulf War, the networks devoted 2,855 minutes to the war between August 8 and January 3. Only 29 minutes out of this total showed popular opposition to the war.

While general agreement exists on these points, considerable disagreement exists on the overall impact of the media on foreign policy or its motives. The "CNN effect" school of thought holds that the media now drives American foreign policy by its coverage of events. Policy makers are now placed in the position of responding to media coverage. They are reduced to crisis managers who no longer determine foreign-policy priorities or engage in long-term planning. A normative split exists among those who hold this view. Some see it as good, returning foreign policy to the public and taking it out of the hands of elites who are divorced from the concerns of American society. Others fear that the CNN effect will result only in ruin as professionalism is trumped by populism in the foreign-policy decision-making process.

At the other end of the continuum are those who see the media and policy makers as engaged in collusion. In this view the issue of media ability is overstated. The media is seen as dependent upon policy makers for guidance on what to cover and when. News stories on drug trafficking do not just appear. They happen because someone in the policy-making process (a congressperson about to hold a hearing on the subject or DEFENSE DEPARTMENT official about to release a report) has convinced representatives of the media that there is a story here. When the media drives policy, it is only because policy makers have failed to construct a good media policy. This perspective is widely held by isolationists who argue that media coverage of foreign affairs has a strong internationalist bias regardless of its specific details.

In between these two extremes can be found a third school of thought that sees the media's coverage of foreign affairs as being biased but not for the reasons given above.

Rather, the bias is found in the internal dynamics of media news coverage. Cost considerations are paramount. A uniform global presence is prohibitive. Decisions have to be made on where to station reporters. Rating points are important and so is the need is to find stories people want to see. This has several consequences. It causes the media to "follow the flag." People are more interested in foreign events at which the United States is present at a SUMMIT CONFERENCE or war then when it is not. People are also interested in events from regions they can relate to. This is used to explain why there is so little coverage of AFRICA compared to Europe. People want to see events that have "sizzle." Coups and civil war provide highly visual footage. Economic development problems do not.

A final issue of debate is whether or not the media's impact on foreign policy today is a new phenomenon. The dispute pits those who see its all-encompassing presence and ability to bring the world into our homes on virtually a real-time basis as unprecedented against those who view it as the latest manifestation of struggle for control over American foreign policy that goes back to the publication of the FEDERALIST PAPERS and runs through the yellow journalism of the turn of the 20th century.

Before and during the IRAQ WAR, media coverage played a major role in American foreign policy. The Bush administration recognized that in order to succeed, a policy must be communicated to the American public effectively through the media. Prior to his address to the UNITED NATIONS in September 2002, all five members of Bush's "war cabinet" appeared on television talks shows. On October 8, SECRETARY OF DEFENSE Donald Rumsfeld appeared on five different morning talks shows. As war with Iraq approached General Tommy Franks, who would command U.S. forces in Iraq, hired James Wilkinson to serve as his chief spokesperson. Wilkinson was recommended by Secretary of Defense Donald Rumsfeld and had served as deputy communications director for President Bush. The purpose, according to unnamed sources, was to have someone with Franks whom Rumsfeld and the White House trusted at press briefings.

Once the war began, the major media news outlets commenced live round-the-clock reporting from Iraq using 600 embedded reporters. The White House was prepared for this stepped-up coverage and devised a plan for getting its message across. The plan, conceived in March, went as follows: Prior to the beginning of the morning news shows the White House would provide a briefing. An afternoon briefing would be held at Central Command Headquarters in Qatar. Prior to that a conference call among key participants would establish talking points, and a list of senior officials available for interviews would be put together. Every evening the Office of Global Communications would put out a "Global Messenger" e-mail with key quotes and talking points to U.S. government agencies, EMBASSIES, and other facilities.

It is still too early to make final evaluations about the role of the media in covering the war, but two themes have emerged. The first is that the media was slow to discover and give voice to those opposed to the war. It was only in February 2003 that leading opponents of the war replaced administration spokespeople on the talk-show circuit. This was seen as significant by media observers because where once the media was in the forefront of public debates over war and peace, it now seemed to be "bringing up the rear." The second is that the massive amount of media coverage was not able to overcome "the fog of war." Embedded reporters noted that theirs was a microscopic view of the war and that they were not able to see big picture. Moreover, collectively their reporting suffered from mood swings. Alternatively acting as a cheerleader for war and as an impatient critic of the war effort, embedded reporters were also not able to show the Arab side of the war.

**Further reading:** Cohen, Bernard. *The Press and Foreign Policy.* Princeton, N.J.: Princeton University Press, 1963; Friedland, Lawrence L. *Covering the World: International Television.* New York: Twentieth Century Fund, 1992; Johnson, Douglas V., II. *The Impact of the Media on National Security Decision Making.* Carlisle, Pa.: U.S. Army War College, 1994; Sigal, Leon V. *Reporters and Officials: The Organization and Politics of Newsmaking.* Lexington, Mass.: D.C. Heath, 1973.

## Mexican War

The origins of the Mexican War are found in the steadily intensifying conflict between the United States and MEXICO over TEXAS and California. Mexico had viewed each of these territories as a buffer zone protecting its core territory from foreign encroachment. In time, the constant westward movement of American settlers into these two territories generated repeated conflicts. The initial U.S. response was to try to acquire these territories through purchase. In neither case was Washington successful.

Texas was acquired following a successful revolt against Mexico in 1836. There followed a period of nine years in which Texas was an independent country. Twice it applied for annexation by the United States, and each time the treaty bringing this about was defeated largely because the question of Texas statehood was inexorably linked to the future of slavery in the United States. In 1845, President JOHN TYLER adopted a different strategy. He sought annexation via a joint resolution of CONGRESS. The resolution passed in spring 1845, and in July Texas voted to accept annexation over an offer of guaranteed independence by

Mexico, which up until this time had refused to recognize Texas as an independent country.

Following Texas's vote to join the United States, Mexico broke diplomatic relations with the United States. Almost immediately President JAMES POLK dispatched U.S. troops led by General Zachary Taylor to occupy a position south of the Nueces River. Rumors of a possible Mexican invasion of Texas prompted this move, although Polk's true purpose may have been less to defend Texas than to coerce Mexico into accepting the loss of Texas and settling other outstanding claims. The stationing of these forces was significant since Texas's borders with Mexico were in dispute. In its treaty of independence, Texas claimed all territory up to the Rio Grande. Mexican authorities continued to hold to the more traditional Texas boundary of the Nueces River.

Polk then dispatched John Slidell to Mexico, which had agree to receive a U.S. emissary in order to settle the Texas boundary dispute. Slidell, however, arrived empowered not only to discuss Texas but also the issue of out-

**U.S. Annexation of Mexican Land, 1845–1853**

Legend:
- Ceded by Mexico, 1848
- Annexed by United States, 1845
- Gadsden Purchase, 1853
- ■ Fort

CANADA

Oregon Territory

Minnesota Territory

Wisconsin

Unorganized Territory

Iowa

U N I T E D   S T A T E S

Missouri

Salt Lake City

Denver

Bent's Fort

Arkansas

San Francisco

Las Vegas

Santa Fe

Albuquerque

Fort Smith

PACIFIC OCEAN

Los Angeles

Tucson

El Paso

*Purchased by United States from Texas, 1850*

*Disputed by Mexico and Texas from 1836*

*Assigned to Texas by U.S., 1850*

**Texas**
*Independent of Mexico, 1835*
*Republic, 1836*
*Admitted as state, 1845*

Louisiana

Red R.

San Antonio

Chihuahua

MEXICO

Rio Grande

Gulf of Mexico

Monterrey

standing money owed by Mexico to the United States for destruction of U.S. property and lives arising out of clashes in the 1830s, as well as the future of California. Slidell was to offer Mexico $40 million and the cancellation of all U.S. claims against Mexico in return for a U.S.-Mexican boundary along the Río Grande running to the 32nd parallel and then west to the Pacific Ocean, thus giving the United States control over California. Slidell's terms were rejected. Three days after hearing about the rejection, Polk ordered Taylor's forces to move to the Rio Grande. The Mexican general opposite Taylor warned him to retreat to the Nueces River.

Polk's cabinet was split over the wisdom of going to war with Mexico solely on the basis of its rejection of Slidell's offer and outstanding debts. War seemed likely to all concerned, and on April 23 Mexico declared a "defensive war" against the United States. The next day its forces opened fire on Taylor's troops, killing or injuring 16 soldiers. With news of American casualties in hand, Polk asked for a declaration of war, stating that Mexico had invaded U.S. territory and "shed American blood on American soil."

Polk's war plan was relatively simple. He would seize the territory he had tried to purchase from Mexico and force Mexico to accept this loss through the peace treaty. The military aspect of this strategy did not prove difficult. Problems lay elsewhere. First, Polk could not publicly admit to his war aims since they were controversial. In their opposition to the war Whigs argued that Polk had deliberately provoked a war in order to acquire California. Polk limited his public statements to saying he sought "an honorable peace and thereby secure ample indemnity for the expenses of war." Second, the success of Polk's strategy required that Mexico sign a peace treaty agreeing to the loss of California. No defeat in battle or series of military setbacks produced such a willingness on the part of the Mexican government. Polk had no one with whom to negotiate.

In order to force the issue, in April 1847, Polk sent Nicholas Trist, the chief clerk in the STATE DEPARTMENT, to accompany General Winfield Scott's army, which was on the offensive in Mexico, so that he might negotiate with Mexican officials. Trist was instructed to insist upon territorial indemnity that would give the United States much of California, including San Diego. As compensation for Upper California and New Mexico, Trist was to offer Mexico $25 million. Contact was finally made in August when a truce was established between the U.S. and Mexican forces. Trist's terms were rejected. The Mexican counterproposal limited the California land transfer to include the ports of San Francisco and Monterey.

Trist forwarded these terms to Washington, where Polk reacted angrily. Mexican forces had since broken the truce, and fighting resumed. Polk recalled Trist in October, and in his December annual message to Congress Polk asked for additional troops. Trist did not return to Washington. Instead in November he responded to a peace overture by moderate Mexican leaders and entered into a new round of negotiations. On February 2, 1848, he signed the Treaty of Guadalupe-Hidalgo that ceded California and New Mexico to the United States and confirmed the Río Grande as Texas's border. In return the United States agreed to pay Mexico $15 million and assume responsibility for $3.25 million in war claims by U.S. citizens against Mexico.

The agreement left Polk in a difficult situation. He had rejected Trist but wanted his treaty. Moreover, the WHIG PARTY now controlled the House and in January 1848 passed a resolution condemning the war as "unnecessarily and unconstitutionally begun by the President of the United States." If he delayed or sought to have someone negotiate a similar treaty he might not receive enough funds from Congress to continue fighting the war. At the same time unorganized pressure was building to seize all of Mexico, something Polk had no desire to attempt. Faced with this situation, Polk submitted the treaty for approval, and the Senate did so by a vote of 38-14 on March 10, 1848.

Continental expansion was virtually completed with the conclusion of the Mexican War. The final piece of the puzzle was acquired in 1853 with the GADSDEN PURCHASE. The discovery of gold in California had fueled the need to construct a transcontinental railroad. One of the most desirable routes was through an area south of the Gila River, which was in Mexico. James Gadsden, a southern railroad man, was sent to Mexico to purchase the right of way. He not only acquired this land but also a large tract of land in what is now southern Arizona and New Mexico.

See also MANIFEST DESTINY.

## Mexico

Mexico is about three times the size of Texas and has a territory of 761,600 square miles. It has a population of 97.5 million people. Mexico was conquered by Spanish forces during the period 1519–21. It remained a Spanish colony for nearly 300 years. Independence was declared in 1810, but a treaty with SPAIN recognizing Mexican independence was not signed until 1821. The Mexican Empire that came into existence at that time contained within its boundaries what today comprises GUATEMALA, Belize, Honduras, NICARAGUA, Costa Rica, California, Arizona, New Mexico, and TEXAS. The United States recognized Mexican independence on January 27, 1823.

Texas became the immediate point of controversy between the two neighbors. The U.S.-Mexican border at independence was set by the Adams-Onís Treaty of 1819 between the United States and Spain. SECRETARY OF STATE JOHN QUINCY ADAMS had never completely reconciled himself to placing Texas outside of the western boundary agreed to in this treaty. As PRESIDENT he twice sought to purchase this region, but Mexico was not interested in selling. President ANDREW JACKSON made a similarly unsuccessful effort in 1829.

While these direct overtures were rebuffed, a much more complex dynamic was also at work. Texas was relatively unpopulated territory, and prior to independence Spanish authorities had offered attractive land grants to prospective settlers. The new Mexican government continued this policy of encouraging American immigration to Texas. Fourteen years after the first land grant was made in 1821 to Moses Austin, there were about 30,000 non-Mexican settlers in Texas. The Mexican government had put procedures and restrictions in place that were designed to encourage assimilation, but they failed, and pressures for annexation both within Texas and the United States steadily gathered momentum.

Texas declared its independence in 1835. General Antonio López de Santa Anna's forces scored a decisive victory over the Texans at the Alamo and soon thereafter crushed opposition forces at Goliad, where more than 300 volunteers were executed. Santa Anna's fortunes changed unexpectedly, and he was forced by Sam Houston to sign a treaty recognizing Texas's independence. Texas desired immediate annexation by the United States but failed to secure it. The growing domestic battle over slavery would postpone Texas statehood until 1845.

Statehood did not end the dispute between Mexico and the United States. American officials now turned their attention to Mexico's remaining northern territories. President JAMES POLK offered Mexico $40 million. It refused. Polk then sent American military forces into territory traditionally claimed by Mexico hoping to provoke Mexico into a military confrontation that would allow him to obtain through war what he could not purchase. When that too failed, Polk turned to DIPLOMACY. John Slidell was instructed to offer as much as $40 million for New Mexico and California. His efforts were rejected, and, once again, American military maneuvers took place.

This time Mexico reciprocated, and war was declared. Hostilities ended with the signing of a peace treaty on February 2, 1848. Negotiated by Nicholas Trist, the treaty gave California and New Mexico to the United States and affirmed that the Rio Grande was Texas's southern border. Mexico received $15 million, and the United States assumed $3.25 million of claims against it by American citizens. Ratification in the United States was complicated by problems internal to the Polk administration (Polk had recalled Trist, who disobeyed these order to negotiate the treaty) and American politics (an all-Mexico movement had gained strength, which sought to annex the entire country). One more piece remained to complete the Mexican-American

diplomatic story concerning Texas. The boundary drawn was inconsistent with the territory needed to build a southern railroad across the United States. To rectify this, James Gadsden, in the GADSDEN PURCHASE, obtained the necessary territory from Mexico for $10 million in May 1853.

American attention was drawn away from Mexico by the AMERICAN CIVIL WAR. This event created an opportunity for European powers to reestablish their presence in the Western Hemisphere. FRANCE sought to establish a foothold by placing Ferdinand Maximilian of Austria on the Mexican throne. The opportunity to do so occurred in October 1861. After Mexico suspended payments on foreign loans, France, Spain, and GREAT BRITAIN agreed to send a joint military expedition to Mexico to recover money owed them. Spain and Great Britain withdrew their forces, but France proceeded to conquer Mexico. Once the Civil War ended, the United States sided with the Mexican government of Benito Juárez and demanded that Maximilian and his forces withdraw. Juárez returned to power in 1867, and Maximilian was killed by a firing squad.

Border incidents were a constant feature of U.S.-Mexican relations before and after the Civil War. Pressures rose during both the Grant and the Hayes's administrations for military action, but none was forthcoming. It would not be until the Mexican Revolution that U.S. troops would again enter Mexico. In May 1911 Francisco Madero succeeded in forcing General Porfirio Díaz from power. Madero was then replaced by General Victoriano Huerta in a second coup in February 1913. President WILLIAM HOWARD TAFT had taken a hands-off attitude toward the Mexican Revolution, but his successor, WOODROW WILSON, refused to recognize Huerta's government. In November 1913 Wilson demanded Huerta's resignation, and in February 1914 he lifted an arms embargo to Huerta's leading opponents. It is with regard to Huerta that Wilson reportedly announced, "I am going to teach the South American republics to elect good men."

April 1914 brought the opportunity to take even more forceful action. U.S. sailors were arrested at the port of Tampico for entering a restricted area. Wilson demanded more than the apology that was offered. He wanted the American flag raised and a 21-gun salute. Mexico refused. Wilson then seized on the fact that a German ship carrying arms to Huerta was about to dock at Veracruz. To prevent this from happening Wilson ordered U.S. forces to occupy Veracruz. CONGRESS approved this action on April 20. The next day armed warfare began that resulted in nearly 100 dead and wounded Mexicans. This outcome produced an anti-American outcry in Mexico and Latin America. Wilson was able to extract himself from this embarrassing situation with the help of ARGENTINA, BRAZIL, and CHILE—the ABC Powers—who offered to mediate a settlement. The negotiations failed to produce an agreement, but they did buy Wilson diplomatic time. Huerta resigned in July, and in 1915 the United States recognized the government of General Venustiano Carranza. The fighting did not end, however. General Francisco Villa conducted cross-border raids into the United States. One such raid into Columbus, New Mexico, prompted Wilson to order General John Pershing and his forces into Mexico to capture Villa. After 10 months Pershing was withdrawn on February 5, 1917.

One of the early constant concerns that American officials had with regard to Mexico was the possibility that it might become a base from which European powers could exert an influence in the hemisphere or halt American westward expansion. The encounter with Maximilian fit this mold. So too did the ZIMMERMANN TELEGRAM incident in 1917. On the eve of unrestricted submarine warfare against the United States, GERMANY instructed its minister to Mexico to offer Mexico an ALLIANCE. At war's end Mexico was to gain back territory lost to the United States between 1848 and 1853. Mexico rejected the offer. The British intercepted the telegram and made it public as part of London's strategy to get the United States to abandon its neutrality and enter the war. Mexico remained neutral in WORLD WAR I.

Territorial and security concerns were gradually replaced by economic ones in Mexican-American foreign relations. The American economic stake in Mexico was considerable. By the early 1890s the United States was buying 75 percent of Mexico's exports and accounted for some 50 percent of its imports. Ports, railroads, and copper mines were financed with American capital. By 1911 American firms accounted for about 40 percent of all foreign investment in Mexico. This American economic presence had long been a contributing factor to the growth of anti-American Mexican nationalism, but it had not generated direct conflict. This scenario changed following the Mexican Revolution. In 1918 Carranza declared that Article 27 of the 1917 constitution gave Mexico ownership rights of all subsoil properties. The most economically significant of these were minerals and OIL. Carranza asserted that Article 27 was retroactive in its coverage so that all existing oil fields and mines were the property of the Mexican government. U.S. firms were heavily invested in these areas and stood to lose large sums of money. They controlled about 60 percent of the Mexican oil industry. A temporary agreement was reached in 1923 whereby Mexico agreed not to apply Article 27 retroactively. A 1927 agreement went one step further, and Mexico agreed to recognize pre-1917 ownership rights. The oil issue continued to fester through the 1930s. In 1938 Mexico nationalized all foreign oil holdings following a strike by Mexican oil workers. American oil companies demanded $260 million in compensation. After much negotiation an agreement was reached in November 1941, one month before Pearl Harbor, that would pay U.S. companies $42 million.

During the COLD WAR American foreign policy tended to look beyond Mexico. There were tense moments, such as when Mexico refused to honor the economic blockade against CUBA and criticized the 1965 invasion of the DOMINICAN REPUBLIC. In the early 1980s it parted ways with the United States again. Mexico was among the first to offer economic aid to the Sandinistas and in 1981 declared that it would seek to tighten "the links of friendship that bind us with the revolutions of Cuba and NICARAGUA." It has been economics more than geopolitics that continues to sit atop the foreign policy agenda in U.S.-Mexican relations.

Perhaps the most enduring issue has been Mexican IMMIGRATION into the United States. Up until the Great Depression an informal open border had existed between the two countries. Mexican labor, most of it unskilled, was an important source of labor in seasonal industries, such as mining, agriculture, and construction. The depression brought this to a halt and even set in motion a reverse migration back to Mexico. A new wave of immigration began in 1942. A shortage of labor due to WORLD WAR II produced Public Law 45, which provided for Mexicans to enter the United States as emergency labor to replace soldiers serving in the armed forces. Better known as the BRACERO PROGRAM, it remained in effect until 1964, when the United States allowed it to lapse. Mexican immigration continued unabated, and in the 1970s at least 2 million Mexicans crossed illegally into the United States to look for work. By the 1990s it was estimated that illegal immigration from Mexico accounted for 55–60 percent of all nonlegal residents in the United States. Illegal rather than legal immigration was the norm because the Walter-McCarran Immigration Act of 1952 created a quota system for legal immigrants that gave preference to skilled workers. Later legislation sought to alter this condition but did not succeed completely in removing the barriers put in the way of creating a true open border. It is estimated that nearly 340 million legal border crossings from Mexico to the United States occur each year.

Rather than being seen as an economic asset Mexican illegal immigration came increasingly to be seen as a threat to American workers, taking jobs away from them and driving down wages. It was also seen as a drain on state and federal social service systems. President JIMMY CARTER sought new immigration legislation to address the problem, but it was not until 1986 that Congress passed the Immigration Reform and Control Act. It provided amnesty for those residing in the United States since 1982, partial amnesty for others, and penalties for employers who knowingly employed illegal workers. Early in his administration President GEORGE W. BUSH floated the idea of granting amnesty to as many as 3 million Mexicans living illegally in the United

Suspected illegal immigrants are searched by a U.S. Border Patrol agent. *(McNew/Getty Images)*

since the crisis occurred barely two years after the signing of the NORTH AMERICAN FREE TRADE AGREEMENT (NAFTA), of which Mexico is a key part. The international community constructed a $52.8 billion credit facility to help Mexico, with the United States providing $20 billion of this total. Mexico paid back the $13.5 billion actually provided by the U.S. TREASURY with interest.

A final set of economic issues surrounded the creation of NAFTA. President Carlos Salinas of Mexico proposed the creation of a free-trade area encompassing the United States and Mexico in 1990. It was soon expanded to include CANADA. Both the negotiations that led to creation of NAFTA and the ratification process by which it was approved were filled with controversy. Two of the most complex issues centered on protecting workers' rights and setting environmental standards. Both were the subjects of side agreements negotiated with Mexico by President Clinton that were considered to be politically necessary in order to ensure congressional approval. On an economic level NAFTA has produced significant successes. Bilateral trade between the United States and Mexico grew by $17 billion between 1993 and 1996, with a net surplus for the United States of $7 billion. Estimates placed U.S. job losses due to NAFTA at 100,000, but overall unemployment levels remained low. The major points of friction involve trucking, sugar, corn syrup, high fructose, and agricultural products.

**Further reading:** Bethell, Leslie. *Mexico since Independence.* Cambridge, UK: Cambridge University Press, 1991; Langley, Lester D. *Mexico and the United States.* New York: Macmillan, 1991; Pastor, Robert A., and Jorge Castaneda. *Limits to Friendship.* New York: Knopf, 1988.

States. Bush was criticized for harboring secret political purposes in raising this issue. It was portrayed by many as part of a Republican effort to improve the party's standing among Hispanic voters. Little came of the initiative to the dismay of Mexican leaders who had hoped it signaled a greater American willingness to address the immigration issue.

A second and recurring issue has been Mexican debt. Pinning its hopes on rising oil and natural gas prices, Mexico borrowed heavily to finance economic development projects. In August 1982 falling oil prices and a general slowdown in the international economy forced Mexico to announce that it could not service—that is, pay the interest on—its foreign debts. Through the BAKER PLAN and the BRADY PLAN, the United States took a leading role in managing its DEBT CRISIS. A second debt crisis hit Mexico in December 1994. The peso collapsed on international financial markets as foreign investors pulled their funds out of Mexico. The United States led an international financial rescue effort. It had little choice

## military-industrial complex

The concept of a military industrial complex was introduced into the vocabulary of American foreign policy by C. Wright Mills in the 1950s. Consistent with the principles of ELITE THEORY Mills argued that American foreign-policy decision making cannot be explained by the activities of INTEREST GROUPS, as is asserted by PLURALISM. Instead it is best explained by the domination by of the policy-making process by a relatively small group of like-minded individuals who come from similar socioeconomic backgrounds. In his formulation, the key components of the POWER elite that determined national security policy were found in the higher ranks of the American military establishment and in the defense industry. These groups had a vested interest in belligerent foreign policies. War and the preparation for war were not necessarily in the American NATIONAL INTEREST, but they did serve the economic and professional interests of these groups. Moreover, the groups were not distinct.

Retired military officers held important positions in defense industries, and both defense industrialists and military officers were found in CONGRESS. In the early 1960s, for example, General Dynamics Corporation, which produced the Polaris submarine among other weapons systems, employed 200 retired military officers. Its president was a former secretary of the army.

Mills's argument gained notoriety in 1961 when, in his farewell address to the nation President DWIGHT DAVID EISENHOWER, himself a retired general, asserted, that "[I]n the councils of government we must guard against the acquisition of unwarranted influence, whether sought or unsought, by the military-industrial complex." Given credence by Eisenhower's comments, the notion that elites rather than the public made American foreign policy and did so to advance their own ends was a powerful idea in the debate over how to explain American foreign policy in the 1960s. It drove analyses of the VIETNAM WAR, COVERT ACTION operations in Third World states, and the ARMS RACE.

By the late 1960s elite-theory analysis was losing much of its influence on the study of American foreign-policy making. Attention began to shift from societal influences on decision making to the dynamics of the decision-making process itself. The BUREAUCRATIC POLITICS model and the SMALL GROUP DECISION-MAKING model emerged as powerful new competitors as to the notion that policy making could be explained in terms of a RATIONAL ACTOR model, in which little attention at all was given to the policy-making process. Instead, foreign policy was viewed as a logical response to external challenges.

Still, its influence has remained strong. Two contemporary problem areas illustrate this point. The first is the search for a "peace dividend" with the end of the COLD WAR. Expectations ran high that defense spending could be cut and money saved or transferred to social programs. Proponents of the military-industrial complex would argue that this will not happen, due to the vested interests of the military industry and associated groups to keep these programs in place. An excellent example is the difficulty experienced in trying to close military bases in the United States or cut funding for military weapons systems. The second problem area is reconstruction in IRAQ, where several large American firms have received no bid contracts for large projects.

**Further reading:** Koistinen, Paul. *The Military-Industrial Complex: A Historical Perspective.* New York: Praeger, 1980; Leslie, Stuart. *The Cold War and American Science: The Military-Industrial-Academic Complex at MIT.* New York: Columbia University Press, 1993; Mills, C. Wright. *The Power Elite.* New York: Oxford University Press, 1959; ———, and Proxmire, William. *Report from the Wasteland: America's Military-Industrial Complex.* New York: Praeger, 1970.

## missile gap

The phrase *missile gap* refers to a charge leveled in the late 1950s and early 1960s that the Eisenhower administration had allowed the Soviet Union to gain a dangerous advantage over the United States in the number of intercontinental ballistic missiles (ICBMs) it possessed. Ultimately evidence surfaced that the missile gap did not exist. The missile gap episode in American politics is significant for the light it sheds on the operation of the national security BUREAUCRACY. It also marks an important point of transition from a period in which nuclear strategy was addressed only by experts to one in which it become a topic of general public concern. Like the BOMBER GAP that preceded it, the missile gap typifies a general pattern of overreaction to the Soviet threat that characterized U.S. foreign policy for much of the COLD WAR period.

On the political front, the missile gap gained prominence after the Soviet Union launched *SPUTNIK* into Earth orbit and successfully tested an ICBM. The Eisenhower administration unsuccessfully tried to downplay these achievements, but the American public responded with great concern. While some in the REPUBLICAN PARTY charged that the Eisenhower administration had allowed the Russians to gain a dangerous military advantage, it was the Democrats who pressed the issue the hardest. JOHN F. KENNEDY had been doing so since 1956. In 1958 he asserted on the Senate floor that "we are rapidly approaching that dangerous period . . . [which has been called] the 'gap' or missile-lag period. . . . [where] the deterrent ratio might well shift to the Soviets so heavily . . . as to open them a new shortcut to world domination." Kennedy identified this time period as 1960–64. Kennedy made the missile gap a major issue in his successful and tightly contested 1960 presidential campaign against RICHARD NIXON, who had served as DWIGHT EISENHOWER's vice president.

The existence of a missile gap became a hotly contested question within the national security bureaucracy, pitting the CENTRAL INTELLIGENCE AGENCY (CIA) against the military. NATIONAL INTELLIGENCE ESTIMATES (NIEs) are secret documents that represent the consensus view of the INTELLIGENCE COMMUNITY on a foreign-policy problem. In November 1957 an NIE stated that the Soviet Union could have 500 operational ICBMs by the end of 1962 or as early as 1961. No hard evidence supported this claim. Rather it reflected an estimate of Soviet production capabilities and an assumption about what the Soviet Union needed to do in order to carry out its stated nuclear strategy. By 1958 the CIA had evidence that called this estimate into question. CIA monitoring of Soviet missile tests showed that very few ICBMs had been tested, certainly not at the level that would precede a large-scale deployment. U-2 photographs also called into question fears of a large-scale deployment of ICBMs. It was not until the February 1960

NIE, however, that doubts officially emerged. Those doubts were not shared by the military services, who saw their budgets as dependent upon the existence of a Soviet threat. The Strategic Air Command (SAC) was particularly eager to use INTELLIGENCE estimates to advance its case for additional resources. The 1960 NIE contained numerous dissents and pushed back the date by which the Soviets would deploy 500 ICBMs until at least mid-1963. In August 1960 the United States launched its first successful intelligence gathering satellite, *Discoverer*. It covered Soviet territory not covered by U-2 overflights and found no additional supporting evidence for the missile-gap argument.

In September 1961, the CIA issued a special NIE that put an end to the missile gap. It now concluded that the Soviet Union did not possess 50 to 100 operational ICBMs in mid-1961 and constituted only a "limited threat during the months immediately ahead to our nuclear striking force." The CIA stated that the Soviet Union possessed six ICBMs.

See also DETERRENCE; NUCLEAR STRATEGY; NUCLEAR WEAPONS; RUSSIA.

**Further reading:** Kahan, Jerome. *Security in the Nuclear Age: Developing U.S. Strategic Arms Policy*. Washington, D.C.: Brookings, 1975.

## Missouri v. Holland (1920)

*Missouri v. Holland* is the leading constitutional case dealing with the conflict between states' rights and the treaty power of the federal government. The case involved a treaty between the United States and GREAT BRITAIN that protected migratory birds flying between the United States and CANADA. Canada was not a party to the agreement because at the time of the treaty its foreign relations were legally controlled by Great Britain. In order to implement the provisions of the treaty, Congress enacted legislation that authorized the DEPARTMENT OF AGRICULTURE to established regulations for the hunting of these birds. The state of Missouri challenged both the legality of the treaty and the laws designed to implement it as an invasion of states' rights as reserved under the Tenth Amendment.

This was not the first effort made to protect the migratory birds. In 1913 CONGRESS passed legislation doing so. A district court overturned the law, declaring that it went beyond the limits of congressional power. This decision led the PRESIDENT to sign a treaty with Great Britain in 1916.

Chief Justice Oliver Wendell Holmes, delivering the majority opinion for the SUPREME COURT, dismissed Missouri's argument. He held that acts of Congress "are the supreme law of the land only when made in pursuance of the CONSTITUTION while treaties are declared so when made under the authority of the United States." As such,

the legality of the legislation to enact the treaty does not depend on the subject of the legislation (as Missouri argued, claiming states' rights). It only depends on whether the treaty falls within the treaty-making power of the United States. The only acknowledged limit placed on treaty-making power is that the United States cannot do anything that is explicitly forbidden by the Constitution.

*Missouri v. Holland* would be expanded upon 14 years later in UNITED STATES V. BELMONT, in which executive agreements were treated as equivalent to treaties. It would also serve as a reference point for those who sought to curb the U.S. treaty-making power through the BRICKER AMENDMENT.

## Monroe Doctrine

The Monroe Doctrine of 1823 constitutes one of the major turning points of American foreign policy. Generations of American PRESIDENTS from THEODORE ROOSEVELT to JOHN KENNEDY to RONALD REAGAN have invoked it in putting forward foreign policies designed to keep "foreign" influences out of the Western Hemisphere. Yet, at the time, it was not recognized as such. It put forward no new foreign-policy principles, nor was it even referred to as the "Monroe Doctrine" until the 1850s.

Having defeated Napoleon, in 1815 the conservative states of Europe formed a Holy ALLIANCE to maintain order. In 1820 and 1821 a series of revolutions broke out in SPAIN, Portugal, GREECE, and Naples. Greece eventually secured its independence, but other rebellions were put down. Concerns were raised that European continental powers would next turn to crushing the newly independent states of the Americas. GREAT BRITAIN had joined the Holy Alliance but now feared that a resurgent Franco-Spanish alliance could threaten access by British merchants to these markets. In August 1823 British foreign secretary George Canning raised the possibility with U.S. minister to Great Britain Richard Rush of a joint American-British declaration intended to prevent FRANCE from interfering into the affairs of these new democracies or gaining territory in the Americas through conquest or cession. This was welcome news to Rush since the United States had been trying for some time to enlist British participation in such a policy, but he lacked instructions from Washington to accept such a proposal. Rush forwarded the matter to Washington but informed Canning that the proposal would be improved if it contained a British promise to recognize these states, something it was unwilling to do.

President James Monroe was inclined to accept Canning's offer. He consulted with former presidents James Madison and THOMAS JEFFERSON, both of whom also urged its acceptance. SECRETARY OF STATE JOHN QUINCY ADAMS opposed the idea. He felt that the possibility of a

European intervention into Latin America was remote and was confident that should such a move be made the British would be forced to counter it with or without an agreement with the United States. Adams was also concerned that Canning's proposed language could be read to mean that the United States had to abandon hope of acquiring TEXAS, California, and CUBA. Finally, ever the nationalist, Adams resisted the idea of playing a secondary role to Great Britain in a matter involving the defense of the Western Hemisphere.

Adams's position carried the day, and the question now became how to proceed with a unilateral American statement. Adams preferred a series of diplomatic notes. Monroe preferred including a statement in his regular message to CONGRESS. The first draft presented to the cabinet in November 1823 was defiant in tone and contained supportive references to the cause of the Greek revolutionaries and angry remarks about French activity in Spain. Adams objected and succeeded in having these references toned down substantially.

As presented to Congress on December 2, 1823, the Monroe Doctrine was made up of three parts. The first part dealt with noncolonization and was primarily directed at RUSSIA. In 1821 Moscow had issued a warning to other states not to come within 100 miles of Russian America (ALASKA). This edict was interpreted as evidence of renewed Russian interest in pushing the southern boundary of Alaska deep into the OREGON country, thus establishing a Russian colonial presence in North America. The next section dealt with the possibility of European interference in the Americas. Monroe warned the European monarchies that the United States would view "any attempt on their part to extend their system to any portion of this hemisphere as dangerous to [its] peace and safety." He continued, "[W]e could not view any interposition for the purpose of oppressing them, or controlling in any other manner their destiny . . . in any other light as the manifestation of an unfriendly disposition toward the United States." Monroe concluded that the policy of the United States continued to be one of not interfering in the internal concerns of any European power.

Monroe's pronouncement met with widespread approval within the United States, although some questioned his positioning of the United States as protector of newly established democracies, and some feared it would involve the country in foreign conflicts. European powers reacted with displeasure, terming the statement arrogant and blustering. Great Britain reacted with a mixture of support and muted anger. Canning had been working on his own to ensure that France would take no action against the former Spanish colonies in the Americas. He had accomplished this goal through the Polignac Memorandum. Canning published this document in 1824 in an effort to make clear that it was the British navy and not the United States that was guaranteeing the continued independence of the former Spanish colonies. For their part the newly independent states of Latin America responded with caution. They too recognized the importance of the British navy. Moreover, when COLOMBIA, BRAZIL, and MEXICO proposed an alliance with the United States based on Monroe's address, they were rebuffed.

**Further reading:** May, Ernest. *The Making of the Monroe Doctrine.* Cambridge, Mass.: Harvard University Press, 1975; Smith, Gaddis. *The Last Years of the Monroe Doctrine, 1945–1994.* New York: Hill and Wang, 1994.

## Montreal Protocol

On September 16, 1987, the Montreal Protocol on Substances That Deplete the Ozone Layer was signed. The protocol established target dates for replacing chloroflourocarbons (CFCs) and other harmful chemicals that were held to be responsible for destroying the ozone layer. Its supporters cite the agreement as pathbreaking in two respects. First, it was a preventive action. It was not a response to an environmental disaster that had already occurred but was motivated by fears of future problems. Second, the agreement had an open-ended quality to it. Revisions and adjustments were expected to be made in future meetings. This stood in contrast to earlier treaties, such as the LAW OF THE SEA III agreement, which, regardless of how long the negotiations lasted, were seen as "one-shot affairs" that established a new status quo. From a procedural perspective the Montreal Protocol is also significant for two other reasons, namely, because of the interaction of domestic and international interests in formulating the American position and because of the role played by science and technology in raising the issue and identifying solutions.

The ozone layer is a thin layer of molecules surrounding the Earth. It is significant because of its ability to absorb certain wavelengths of ultraviolet radiation that are dangerous to humans. The distribution of ozone also holds the potential for altering climate patterns around the world. CFCs were invented in the 1930s and were considered safe. They became an important coolant in refrigerators and air conditioners, a propellant in spray containers, and an insulator in plastic foam materials. This benign view changed in the 1970s when evidence began to accumulate that the presence of increasingly large quantities of CFCs in the air was reducing the ozone layer and redistributing ozone in the stratosphere.

The first international conference to address the depletion of the ozone layer was held in March 1977 in Washington and was sponsored by the UNITED NATIONS ENVIRONMENT

Programme (UNEP). It concluded by recommending further research and monitoring of the problem. In April 1980 the UNEP's governing council passed a nonbinding resolution calling for the reduced use of CFCs, but no targets were set. It followed this up by organizing the Ad Hoc Working Group of Legal and Technical Experts for the Preparation of a Global Framework Convention for the Protection of the Ozone Layer in Stockholm in January 1982. The negotiations stretched over three years and made little progress. In late 1983 the United States joined the Toronto Group, made up of CANADA, Finland, Norway, Sweden, and Switzerland. The Toronto Group advocated the idea of CFC emission reductions. The Toronto Group was opposed by a coalition of European states within the European Community (EC). The United States and the EC were the world's major producers of CFCs. The major difference between Europe and the United States was that EC CFC production was heavily export oriented, and American firms had already begun to invest in new technology that would make them less dependent on CFCs.

The next step on the road to Montreal took place in March 1985 when 43 states met in Vienna and signed the Vienna Convention. It contained both a statement of obligation on the part of those signing it to take appropriate measures to protect the ozone layer and a mechanism for gathering data. Because of the continuing lack of agreement on how to proceed, no specific chemicals were identified as ozone-depleting. In a separate agreement sponsored by the United States and its allies, it was agreed that negotiations would be reopened in 1987 to set legally binding controls within the context of the framework agreed to at Vienna.

Following a series of preparatory meetings in Geneva and Vienna, the Montreal meetings began on September 8, 1987, and were attended by 60 states. At Montreal an agreement was reached regarding what specific chemicals would be controlled, the base year to be used in making calculations, and how those restrictions would be applied in relation to production and consumption of CFCs. Agreement was also reached on a plan to restrict international trade in restricted chemicals. Finally, the special needs of developing states were addressed by promising financial and technological aid and permitting these states to increase domestic consumption of CFCs for 10 years in order to meet domestic needs.

Pressure for revising the timetables and targets set in the Montreal Protocol quickly built as new scientific evidence emerged and the cost of action was found to be less onerous than first thought. The first meeting of the parties to the Montreal Protocol took place in Helsinki, Finland, on May 2, 1989. More than 80 states sent delegates. Widespread agreement existed for eliminating all ozone-depleting substances by the end of the century. Less agreement existed on helping developing states generate and obtain new technologies for this purpose. At Helsinki, then at London in March, developing states began to raise their voices in opposition to the plans of the developed states, arguing that the ozone-depletion problem was not of their doing and that their development plans should not be held hostage to efforts to address it. The most that rich states would agree to was the creation of working groups to assess the issue. In June 1990 delegates convened again in London to formally amend the Montreal Protocol by expanding the list of chemicals covered and speeding up the time frame for phase out, along with advancing an innovative formula for funding the needs of developing states.

The Senate approved the Montreal Protocol in March 1988 by a vote of 83-0. That vote along with the leadership position often taken by the United States in the negotiations does not accurately reflect the depth of the dispute within the U.S. government on how to proceed. On at least four different occasions Washington either reversed or came close to reversing its position. These incidents were reflective of the opposition by key domestic political and economic forces within the Reagan administration to the agreement. From the outset an uneasy combination of bureaucratic forces lay behind the U.S. position. SECRETARY OF STATE George Shultz became the primary advocate of the treaty, and Secretary of the Interior Donald Hodel was its primary opponent. The STATE DEPARTMENT was designated as the lead negotiating agency and chaired the interagency task force that studied the question. It reported its progress to the White House Domestic Policy Council. It took a personal decision by President RONALD REAGAN to break the bureaucratic stalemate in favor of the treaty late in his term of office. In doing so he surprised his conservative supporters, just as he did in advocating nuclear DISARMAMENT.

See also CONFERENCE DIPLOMACY; ENVIRONMENT; KYOTO PROTOCOL; RIO EARTH SUMMIT.

**Further reading:** Benedick, Richard E. *Ozone Diplomacy: New Directions in Safeguarding the Planet.* Cambridge, Mass.: Harvard University Press, 1991.

## moral pragmatism

Moral pragmatism is one of the foundational building blocks on which the AMERICAN NATIONAL STYLE of foreign policy is built. The other two are UNILATERALISM and LEGALISM. Together they support both an isolationist and internationalist perspective, thereby allowing both to coexist.

The moral pragmatist tendency in American foreign policy can be broken down into two parts. First, Americans assume that foreign policy can be judged by moral standards and that American morality provides that standard. By definition American actions are defined as morally correct and justifiable. Flawed policy initiatives are attributed to leadership deficiencies or breakdowns in organizational routines and not the values that gave rise to these policies. Typical of this logic were the Nye investigations that charged U.S. involvement in WORLD WAR I had come at the behest of banking interests and the McCarthy investigations following the "loss of CHINA."

Second, American foreign policy tends to be pragmatic in spirit because it typically takes the form of an engineering approach to foreign-policy problem solving. Significantly, it is assumed that a solution exists. The preferred American method for uncovering a solution to a problem is to break it down into smaller ones, the way an engineer would take a blueprint and break a project down into smaller tasks. In the process of addressing these smaller tasks the bigger political picture is often lost. When this happens the result can be a substitution of means for ends or the overreliance on canned solutions for newly emerging problems.

The NEUTRALITY LEGISLATION of the 1930s provides an example of the influence of moral pragmatism on American foreign policy. As first put forward the legislation was easy to implement but paid little attention to the realities of world politics. Weapons were not to be sold to either side, but such a policy all but guaranteed that the stronger side would prevail and invited aggression. Its influence was equally present during the COLD WAR. Right-wing dictators were supported, governments overthrown, states invaded, and INTERNATIONAL LAW violated in the name of defeating COMMUNISM. Some commentators suggest that the ultimate expression of America's pragmatic approach to foreign-policy problems is its reliance upon air power in the post–COLD WAR world to deal with problems such as ethnic cleansing, aggression, and TERRORISM.

Evidence of moral pragmatism was evident in the manner in which the IRAQ WAR was conducted. The correctness of America's mission was taken as a given by the GEORGE W. BUSH administration. American strategic planning approached the conduct of the war as an engineering challenge directed at the problem of removing Saddam Hussein from power with minimum loss of life. It was divorced from the subsequent and larger problem of nation building.

See also MCCARTHYISM.

## Morgenthau Plan

Named after Secretary of the TREASURY Henry Morgenthau, Jr., the Morgenthau Plan was a proposal embraced for a short period of time by President FRANKLIN ROOSEVELT for turning post–WORLD WAR II GERMANY into an essentially agrarian state. It reflects the traditional moralistic, legalistic, and engineering approach to solving foreign-policy problems that is part of the AMERICAN NATIONAL STYLE. The Morgenthau Plan is also significant when viewed in the context of the evolving American view on the shape of post–World War II Europe.

Planning for the future of postwar Germany took place over several SUMMIT CONFERENCEs held during World War II. At a 1943 summit meeting at Casablanca, Roosevelt and British prime minister Winston Churchill agreed on a policy of "unconditional surrender" in dealing with Germany. For Roosevelt such a policy was desirable on two counts. First, he believed that one of the reasons for the failure of the TREATY OF VERSAILLES to produce a lasting peace was due to confusion over peace terms. Germany surrendered on the basis of the FOURTEEN POINTS, but these terms were later modified by the British and French, who sought to impose a victor's peace. Roosevelt also felt that the German people as a whole bore responsibility for World War II, and he sought to punish them: "Every person in Germany should realize that this time Germany is a defeated nation, collectively and individually. . . . [Understanding this] they will hesitate to start any new war."

The success of the Normandy invasion that opened up a second front led to another Roosevelt-Churchill summit conference in Quebec in 1944. At Quebec, the two leaders agreed upon a plan for dividing Germany into occupation zones. They also agreed to Morgenthau's plan for turning Germany into a "potato patch." His plan would divide Germany, with parts going to POLAND, the Soviet Union (see RUSSIA), Denmark, and FRANCE. Two remaining independent German states would remain, but they would be stripped of heavy industry. Roosevelt endorsed the plan over the objections of his SECRETARY OF STATE CORDELL HULL and Secretary of War HENRY STIMSON and persuaded Churchill to agree to it. They stated that their intent was to create a Germany that was "primarily agricultural and pastoral in its character."

Roosevelt soon abandoned the plan but, damage had been done. Nazi Germany put the Morgenthau Plan to use as a propaganda tool. German newspapers reported that the plan would mean starvation for 50 percent of the German population and urged "unconditional resistance." Even after Germany's surrender, echoes of the Morgenthau Plan continued to color American thinking about how to deal with postwar Germany.

## Morocco

Slightly smaller than California at 172,413 square miles, Morocco is located on the northern coast of AFRICA and has a population of 28.5 million people. Morocco also claims sovereignty over the Western Sahara, which consists of another 102,703 square miles. The United States recognized Morocco in 1777, and formal relations date from 1787, when a treaty of peace and friendship was signed. Morocco has been the site of frequent struggles between foreign powers for dominance and influence. An attempt was made to preserve Moroccan independence at the 1880 Madrid Conference that was attended by the United States. In 1904 FRANCE entered into a secret agreement with SPAIN to partition Morocco and with GREAT BRITAIN not to oppose British rule in EGYPT in return for a similar agreement on London's part to give France a free hand in Morocco. GERMANY opposed these maneuverings in 1905 but agreed to French domination in 1911 in return for French acquiescence to German claims in equatorial Africa. France granted independence to Morocco on March 2, 1956, after struggling for most of the 20th century with nationalist movements.

Since gaining independence Morocco has followed a moderate line in its foreign policy. Morocco became the second Arab state to host an Israeli leader when, in 1986, Israeli prime minister Shimon Peres visited King Hassan II. This was followed by the opening of liaison offices in each country in 1994. These offices were closed following the outbreak of the intifada in 2000. Morocco condemned IRAQ's invasion of KUWAIT and sent troops to help defend SAUDI ARABIA. It has also voiced public support for the United States in the war against TERRORISM following the SEPTEMBER 11, 2001, terrorist attacks. Total American assistance to Morocco between 1999 and 2001 was $88.1 million. In fiscal year 2001 the U.S. AGENCY FOR INTERNATIONAL DEVELOPMENT provided Morocco with $14.1 million in assistance.

The most contentious issue in Morocco's foreign policy involves its claim to the Western Sahara. Morocco's claim is based on the argument that local tribal leaders were loyal to the Moroccan sultan. This claim is challenged by the Polisario (Popular Front for the Liberation of Seguía el-Hamra and Río de Oro), an independence movement headquartered in ALGERIA. It was organized in 1969 to oppose Spanish occupation of the region. Spain ruled over the Western Sahara from 1904 to 1975. In that year Spain, Morocco, and Mauritania announced a tripartite agreement that set up an administrative structure for the Western Sahara but sidestepped the question of sovereignty. Spain's governance role ended almost immediately, and in 1979 Mauritania signed a peace treaty with the Polisario. Moroccan troops then moved into the portion of the Western Sahara vacated by Mauritania. In 1988 Morocco and Polisario agreed on a UNITED NATIONS peace plan that was to lead to a resolution of the matter through a popular referendum. It has yet to take place. The United States supports the cease-fire and recognizes Morocco's administrative control over the Western Sahara, but it has not endorsed its claim to sovereignty over it.

## most-favored-nation status

Most-favored-nation (MFN) status is a principle for organizing international TRADE relations that emphasizes nondiscrimination—that is, states automatically extend the same trade terms on a commodity being imported regardless of the country of origin. They can show no preference for goods coming from one country as compared to others.

Virtually from the founding, the value and merits of a trading policy based on MFN principles has played a major role in American tariff policy debates. BENJAMIN FRANKLIN, THOMAS JEFFERSON, and JOHN ADAMS were all advocates of free trade and sought to gain nondiscriminatory access to European markets. The United States's first trade treaty, the Franco-American Treaty of Amity and Commerce of 1778, came close but did not realize this goal. MFN treatment was conditional rather than unconditional. ALEXANDER HAMILTON argued the opposite position, favoring a system of tariff barriers that would protect American businesses from foreign competition. After the WAR OF 1812 HENRY CLAY echoed his position by promoting an American system that raised import duties in order to protect American industries.

From the AMERICAN CIVIL WAR through the Great Depression protectionism was the dominant theme in American trade policy, and from 1860 to WORLD WAR II every Republican presidential candidate ran on a protectionist platform that emphasized protective tariffs. An emphasis on MFN principles was not totally absent, however. In 1922 the Fordney-McCumber Act raised tariffs from an average of 9.1 percent to 14 percent and permitted the PRESIDENT to retaliate against foreign tariff discrimination. But in implementing the tariff the WARREN HARDING administration decided to adopt unconditionally the MFN principle. No longer would a third party have to provide equivalent concessions to the United States in order to gain MFN status. It would be granted automatically, thereby avoiding the need for time-consuming negotiations on a country-by-country basis.

The MFN principle was central to the 1934 Reciprocal Trade Agreement Act. Designed to reverse the use of high tariffs to protect American products, it authorized the president to enter into trade negotiations that would lead to as much as a 50 percent reduction in tariffs. Again, in order to speed up the negotiating process and energize world trade, the act stipulated that any bilateral agreements would be extended unconditionally on the basis of the MFN principle.

After World War II the MFN principle became a centerpiece of the GENERAL AGREEMENT ON TARIFFS AND TRADE (GATT) process of tariff reduction. Because the Soviet Union (see RUSSIA) and its allies did not join GATT, the United States came to use MFN status as a political and economic weapon against them during the COLD WAR. This was especially true during the Nixon administration, when the United States sought to tie the granting of MFN status to modifications in Soviet foreign policy as part of its foreign policy of DÉTENTE. RICHARD NIXON hoped that obtaining MFN status would be enough of an inducement to get the Soviet Union to sign nuclear ARMS CONTROL agreements and stop supporting anti-Western movements in the developing world. His strategy was frustrated when CONGRESS, through the 1974 JACKSON-VANIK AMENDMENT, tied MFN status to modifications in Soviet domestic policy, most notably the treatment of Soviet Jews.

In 1989, following the Tiananmen Square incident in CHINA, Congress sought to link MFN status for China to improvements in its HUMAN-RIGHTS policy. China was not granted MFN status until 1999. By then, the Clinton administration had redefined MFN status to mean "normal trading status" in an effort to defuse the domestic politics surrounding the vote.

**Further reading:** Mendoza, Miguel, R., et al., eds. *Trade Rules in the Making: Challenges in Regional and Multilateral Negotiations.* Washington, D.C.: Brookings, 1999; Moon, Bruce E. *Dilemmas of International Trade.* Boulder, Colo.: Westview, 1996.

## multinational corporations

Multinational corporations (MNCs) are not new actors in world politics. Their roots can be traced back to such firms as the British East India Company and Hudson Bay Company. As with their predecessors, modern MNCs are viewed as both economic and political actors. The 1602 charter of the Dutch East India Company gave it the right to make war and peace, seize foreign ships, establish colonies, and coin money. As economic actors some MNC's today dwarf many states. In 1996 General Motor's revenues of $164 billion exceeded the gross national products of CHINA, ISRAEL, POLAND, and VENEZUELA. Taken together, the revenues of the top 10 MNCs exceeded that of all of AFRICA. Politically, MNCs are alternatively viewed as aggressive predators or significant components of private authority networks that promote international economic cooperation.

The debate over the role of MNCs in world politics was increased during the 1960s and 1970s. One strand of thought was heavily influenced by the historical record of American foreign policy in Latin America. There, the United States had repeatedly come to the aid of American corporations whose profits were threatened by hostile governments. The United Fruit Company was a major beneficiary of U.S. support. During the COLD WAR, for example, the United States repeatedly backed American business authoritarian rulers in NICARAGUA, the DOMINICAN REPUBLIC, CHILE, and GUATEMALA. Those who challenged the political order were labeled communists. From this perspective MNCs were lit-

tle more than appendages of the U.S. government and instruments of IMPERIALISM. Advanced economies were not immune from this threat. French political commentator Jean-Jacques Servan-Schreiber characterized American MNCs as part of the American cultural challenge to Europe.

A second line of analysis drew its inspiration from revelations that came to light during the 1973 ORGANIZATION OF PETROLEUM EXPORTING COUNTRIES (OPEC) crisis regarding the economic POWER and behavior of the multinational oil companies that were collectively known as the seven sisters. What this data revealed were great profits, the ability to dominate developing states, and significant political clout within the government of the home state. From this perspective MNCs had emerged as independent international actors that could threaten the sovereignty of most states. Still another interpretation held that MNCs were a force for global peace because they promoted economic interdependence and that states that traded with one another could not afford to engage in military conflict. Finally, some asserted that while MNCs made great profit from their international activities and were often able to leverage home and host state governments, their expansion was rooted in defensive motives. Only by exporting and then engaging in overseas production could MNCs hope to retain their economic competitiveness as technologies matured and new firms entered the market.

The debate over the role that MNCs played in world politics gradually dissipated in the face of declining prices for oil and other natural resources, global economic recession, the international DEBT CRISIS, and the renewed emphasis on the cold war in American foreign policy under President RONALD REAGAN. In this new international economic and political environment, the economic potential and power of MNCs were still recognized, but their political significance was given less attention.

The debate was rejoined with the end of the cold war, and many of the earlier themes resurfaced. American foreign policy again provided one anchor for the debate. In the contemporary debate the view that MNCs could be a force for peace and cooperation emerged as the establishment view within the United States and the international development community. Earlier it had been a fringe perspective voiced largely by the MNCs themselves. Promoting democracy and promoting free-trade capitalism were inseparable themes in the foreign policies of Presidents GEORGE H. W. BUSH, BILL CLINTON, and GEORGE W. BUSH. Consistent with this perspective, at the Conference on Sustainable Development held in Johannesburg, South Africa, in 2002, MNCs played a prominent role as discussions focused on creating public-private partnerships in the South.

The second line of inquiry rooted in American foreign policy returns to the matter of the relationship between MNCs and the U.S. government. No longer is the issue couched in terms of a conspiratorial relationship. It is now studied as a bargaining relationship, and the question of concern is the ability of the United States to get MNCs to comply with American economic sanctions. These are referred to as secondary sanctions. As of May 1998, CONGRESS had passed legislation imposing sanctions against more than 335 companies. One example is the HELMS-BURTON ACT that placed sanctions on firms doing business in CUBA. The IRAN and LIBYA Sanctions Act also imposes sanctions on firms doing certain types of business with these states. One study found that these sanctions were effective only about 50 percent of the time, but this success rate is greater than that for sanctions against states.

GLOBALIZATION provides the second anchor for the contemporary debate on MNCs. One perspective sees MNCs as the potential source of rules for international economic relations. At the URUGUAY ROUND of international trade negotiations MNCs, such as Johnson and Johnson, IBM, Hewlet-Packard, General Electric, and General Motors, identified the absence of international standards and protection for property rights as a major trade problem. Working together they devised a solution to the problem, and it was adopted as part of the Uruguay Round agreements.

The second perspective marks a return to the view that MNCS are predators. This perspective comes through most clearly in the positions held by antiglobalization forces. They fear that international trade agreements and development policies favor MNC interests and neglect the needs of labor, the ENVIRONMENT, and local cultures. These concerns were also voiced by opponents of the NORTH AMERICAN FREE TRADE AGREEMENT (NAFTA). The political pressure they generated led the Clinton

Antiglobalization protestors demonstrate against a transatlantic dialogue meeting in Chicago, Illinois, November 2002. *(Photo by John R. Whitney/Getty Images)*

administration to negotiate understandings with MEXICO that added protections to the NAFTA agreement.

**Further reading:** Barnet, Richard J., and Ronald Muller. *Global Reach: The Power of Multinational Corporations.* New York: Touchstone, 1974; Cox, Ronald, ed. *Business and the State in International Relations.* New York: Harper-Collins, 1996; Friedman, Thomas L. *The Lexus and the Olive Tree.* New York: Farrar, Straus & Giroux, 1999; Vernon, Raymond. *Sovereignty at Bay.* New York: Basic, 1971.

## multipolarity

A multipolar system is one in which there are at least five relatively equal states. Often referred to as a balance-of-power system, multipolarity formed the backdrop for most early U.S. foreign-policy initiatives as GREAT BRITAIN, FRANCE, SPAIN, and RUSSIA were key actors in a succession of European multipolar systems. The United States itself became an important player in a multipolar system during the interwar period. Notwithstanding its refusal to participate in the LEAGUE OF NATIONS, the United States was one of the major powers between WORLD WAR I and WORLD WAR II.

Mobility and flexibility are the key words in a multipolar system. The large number of poles, or POWER centers, and the even distribution of power means that identifying friends and foes is not determined in advance by the structure of the system. Any state is as much a potential friend as it is a potential enemy. The particular alignment of forces in existence at any one point in time will depend upon the specific issue being contested. ALLIANCES are formed to deal with issues as they arise, and they dissolve when the security threat has passed. Ideological differences between poles are held to be of secondary importance to the need to maintain flexibility. Imbalances in power are to be avoided but are not seen as irreversible. Neither neutral states nor international organizations play significant roles in a multipolar system.

The essential rules of a multipolar system can be summarized as follows. First, states should increase their power capabilities but negotiate rather than fight. Second, states should stop fighting before they eliminate one of the major states in the system. Third, defeated states should be allowed to reenter the INTERNATIONAL SYSTEM as an acceptable alliance partner. Fourth, states should oppose any state or coalition of states that seeks to realize a position of dominance. Fifth, states should oppose any actor whose foreign policy is based on an unlimited or utopian vision of world order instead of narrowly defined national interests.

The collapse of the interwar multipolar system can be traced to the failure of the major powers to follow the rules of multipolarity. Rather than move forthrightly to oppose

Adolf Hitler's plans for creating an expansive Third Reich, the other powers temporized. Great Britain and France engaged in appeasement, while the United States clung to a policy of official neutrality. Analysts have noted that the AMERICAN NATIONAL STYLE, with its emphasis on moral purpose and LEGALISM, makes for a poor fit with the multipolar system's demand for a balance-of-power policy and its deemphasis on ideology. American foreign policy thus can be expected to have difficulty following the rules.

A contemporary example that illustrates this point is U.S. foreign policy in the Persian Gulf. U.S. aims have vacillated between defeating IRAQ and eliminating Saddam Hussein from power. The rules of multipolarity point toward restoring Iraq as a full player in the Persian Gulf, not crippling it or marginalizing it through sanctions and covert operations. A similar tension is evident in the U.S. foreign policy toward IRAN in which the United States has hesitated to normalize relations. The Clinton administration followed a policy of DUAL CONTAINMENT by which it sought to isolate both states. Rather than pursue flexibility, the United States has treated the region as bipolar and sought to build a permanent alliance with SAUDI ARABIA. Pointing to the fall of the shah of Iran and the consequences that followed from it analysts caution that there is nothing permanent about Saudi loyalty.

A major challenge facing U.S. foreign policy today is the need to operate in an international system in which economic power has taken on increased importance compared to military power. Historically, international systems were defined as bipolar or multipolar in terms of the distribution of military power. In the post–COLD WAR era the world is not multipolar in a military sense, but it is rapidly moving in that direction economically. It is unclear which set of rules should be followed if a crisis erupts that brings the military and economic international systems into conflict with one another. Conflicts over OIL and other natural resources hold the clearest potential for creating such a scenario.

See also BIPOLARITY; UNIPOLARITY.

**Further reading:** Gilpin, Robert. *War and Change in World Politics.* New York: Cambridge University Press, 1981; Gulick, Edward V. *Europe's Classical Balance of Power.* Ithaca, N.Y.: Cornell University Press, 1955; Walt, Stephen W. *The Origins of Alliances.* Ithaca, N.Y.: Cornell University Press, 1987.

## MX missile

The MX (missile experimental) was intended to be a centerpiece of the U.S. nuclear rearmament program in the late 1970s and early 1980s. In the end the MX was redefined to be a temporary instrument. Originally it had been proposed that 200 MX missiles were to be deployed. Only 50 were actually deployed. The MX is significant to the study of American defense strategy for what it reveals about the weapons procurement process and the problems involved in constructing a credible deterrent.

The term *MX* first appeared in 1973, and it was described in an air force magazine as an air-launched missile. In 1974 the air force requested funding for research into and development of a new generation of mobile intercontinental ballistic missiles (ICBMs). The Minuteman ICBM was the backbone of the American land-based nuclear deterrent force. Through the 1960s doubts had begun to surface regarding their vulnerability to Soviet missiles since they could easily be targeted. A mobile missile would be more difficult to target with certainty and therefore more survivable. Bureaucratic competition with the navy over who would control the bulk of the next generation of ballistic missiles led the air force to concentrate most of its attention on the performance characteristics of the MX rather than its basing mode. By requiring that the MX possess a hard-target kill capability, something that submarine-launched ballistic missiles did not possess due to their smaller payloads and greater inaccuracy, the air force hoped to maintain control over future missile programs.

The desire of nuclear strategists and policy makers to move the United States in the direction of a nuclear war fighting capability added a sense of urgency to the development of the MX. The United States lacked a NUCLEAR WEAPON capable of destroying Soviet missile silos. Consequently, in 1975 the air force redefined the MX from a mobile ICBM into one that could be launched from refitted Minuteman silos. The MX now increasingly became the subject of public controversy. Placing the MX in a silo did nothing to improve its invulnerability. But mobility implied concealment and deception, and this ran counter to the spirit of the STRATEGIC ARMS LIMITATION (SALT) process that the Nixon and Ford administrations had entered in hopes of curbing the nuclear arms race.

Had GERALD FORD won the 1976 presidential election, he was prepared to authorize a full-scale deployment of a mobile MX system. The air force plan called for moving the MX back and forth on railroad tracks in shallow underground tunnels. They would be launched by breaking through the earth cover protecting them. JIMMY CARTER opposed the plan and ordered the DEFENSE DEPARTMENT, air force, and White House to review the concept. All three rejected it.

Carter came to view the MX as a bargaining chip in the SALT II negotiations. It sought to obtain reductions in the Soviet land-based ICBM inventory in return for not proceeding with the MX. When this failed the MX took on the characteristics of the largest Soviet missile: It was to have 10 warheads like the Soviet SS-18 and be the approximate size of the SS-19. With U.S.-Soviet relations worsening, in June 1979 Carter approved the full-scale deployment of the MX but did not select a basing mode. In August 1979 the administration selected a "race track" basing mode in which each MX would be housed in one of 200 separate oval race tracks, each of which would have 23 shelters. A transport would shuttle the MX from shelter to shelter. Widespread opposition from the western United States, where this multiple aim point system would be constructed, led Carter to withdraw the proposal in 1980. Republican presidential candidate RONALD REAGAN criticized Carter's handling and pace of the MX. He proposed placing the MX in hardened Minuteman silos as an interim measure until a permanent basing mode could be identified.

The Reagan administration struggled with trying to find an acceptable mobile basing mode. Congress instructed the administration to select a permanent solution by July 1983, one year earlier than its own proposed deadline. After several proposals failed to gain acceptance, including one referred to as "densepack" that would put 100 MX missiles into hardened silos in a tightly constructed column 14 miles long, the Reagan administration established a bipartisan committee led by Brent Scowcroft to study MX basing. Scowcroft had been Ford's NATIONAL SECURITY ADVISOR, and his commission contained two former SECRETARIES OF DEFENSE and two former SECRETARIES OF STATE as members. The Scowcroft Commission recommended developing a new smaller, single warhead missile to replace the MX. It again called for placing the MX in hardened Minuteman silos as an interim step. In general their report treated the MX more as a bargaining chip in ARMS CONTROL talks with the Soviet Union than as a permanent addition to the U.S. nuclear arsenal.

Reagan endorsed the commission's recommendations and sent them to Congress for action. The Senate would vote on MX funding more than 12 times. Finally, in May 1985, after much bargaining, a compromise was reached between the White House, Senate, and House that established a 50-MX limit for 1986. In 2001, the U.S. nuclear inventory remained at 50 MX missiles.

See also DETERRENCE; RUSSIA.

**Further reading:** Holland, Lauren, and Robert Hoover. *The MX Decision: A New Dimension in U.S. Weapons Procurement Policy.* Boulder, Colo.: Westview, 1985.

# N

## Namibia

With an area of 320,827 square miles, Namibia is the size of Texas and Louisiana combined. It has a population of 1.8 million people. Located in southern AFRICA, its first European contacts began in the early 15th century with the arrival of Portuguese, Dutch, and British expeditions. In the 18th century British and German missionaries arrived, and these two governments would contest for control of the region until 1884, when GERMANY formally established a protectorate over the region, and it became known as South West Africa. German colonial rule was met with resistance by the indigenous population. By 1908 Germany had killed nearly 54,000 of the 70,000 native Herero people. During WORLD WAR I, South West Africa fell under the control of SOUTH AFRICA, which was given a mandate to rule over it by the LEAGUE OF NATIONS in 1920. After WORLD WAR II South Africa refused to surrender its mandate to the UNITED NATIONS, and in 1966 the United Nations revoked that mandate. In 1968 it announced that South West Africa would become known as Namibia upon receiving independence. South Africa rejected the UN's position, asserting it had no jurisdiction over South West Africa.

The year 1966 also saw the creation of the South West Africa People's Organization (SWAPO). Operating from Zambia and then ANGOLA, it undertook a campaign of GUERRILLA WARFARE against South African forces in Namibia. It was not long before the independence struggle became intertwined with COLD WAR international politics. SWAPO turned to the Soviet Union (see RUSSIA) for aid. This allowed South Africa to depict its attempt to hold onto Namibia as anticommunist. By the mid-1970s SWAPO and other pro-independence groups had gained control over the northern half of Namibia. In 1978 the United Nations called for a cease-fire and UN-monitored elections. South Africa refused, and fighting continued.

The United States became involved in two important initiatives in the 1970s and 1980s. First, in 1977 the United States joined with West Germany, FRANCE, CANADA, and GREAT BRITAIN to form the Contact Group. It undertook a series of diplomatic initiatives that were designed to bring about independence. Their efforts culminated in Security Council Resolution 435 of April 1978, which called for UN-supervised elections. South Africa resisted this plan and unilaterally held elections in December 1978. Second, the incoming Reagan administration put forward the policy of constructive engagement. According to its primary author, assistant SECRETARY OF STATE for Africa Chester Crocker, any progress on Namibia was linked to a broader settlement of fighting in southern Africa. Specifically, it linked the removal of Cuban forces from Angola with the exit of South African forces from Namibia. Seven months of intense negotiations in 1988 culminated in a complex agreement that achieved Crocker's basic aims. As a result, on April 1, 1989, Namibia began the process of moving toward independence. On March 21, 1990, Namibia became independent. During the transition period a United Nations Transition Assistance Group (UNTAG) helped to maintain law and order and monitor the electoral process. The United States contributed more than $100 million to UNTAG.

## national intelligence estimates

National intelligence estimates (NIEs) have long been considered the best-known and most controversial product of the INTELLIGENCE COMMUNITY. Their history, detailed through the declassified CENTRAL INTELLIGENCE AGENCY (CIA) volumes that deal with the CUBAN MISSILE CRISIS, the Soviet military estimates, and the final years of the COLD WAR, provide a unique insight into the thinking that guided American national security policy for almost 50 years.

NIEs comprise the collective judgment of the INTELLIGENCE community on future developments with regard to a specific problem or topic. The process for producing an NIE is roughly as follows. Primary responsibility for producing the NIE is given to a single individual. Originally this would be a member of the Board of National Estimates. Today, it falls to a national intelligence officer. The terms of reference for the estimate are collectively determined and circulated to the intelligence committee for comment. A draft version is then written and serves as the basis for discussion and negotiation among analysts and those representatives of the intelligence community tasked with participating in writing the NIE. Once the estimate is agreed upon, it is presented to the DIRECTOR OF CENTRAL INTELLIGENCE for approval. NIEs on Soviet military power took approximately one year to move through this cycle. Many take months to produce, but urgent estimates, special NIEs (SNIEs), can be produced in days or even faster. Two SNIEs were produced during the CUBAN MISSILE CRISIS, and six were written during the 1961 BERLIN CRISIS.

The high point of NIE influence was in the 1950s and early 1960s. Perhaps the most significant of these compromised the 11 Series that dealt with the Soviet Union. Between 1960 and 1962 at least 14 NIEs were issued on such topics as the Soviet space program, Soviet policy toward AFRICA, Soviet capabilities for long-range attack, and trends in the Soviet economy. Their influence declined as the United States became entangled in VIETNAM and continued to lessen in the Nixon administration. HENRY KISSINGER relied heavily upon his own expertise and that of the NATIONAL SECURITY COUNCIL staff in formulating policy options and assessing future trends. In the 1970s their influence continued to remain limited due to the changing foreign-policy agenda introduced by President JIMMY CARTER, internal dissention within the intelligence community and disagreement among political leaders over the extent of the Soviet threat, and the emergence of competing intelligence products. In the last years of the Carter administration only about a dozen NIEs were written. NIEs became more important in RONALD REAGAN's administration as a means for expressing the collective judgment of the intelligence community, but they have not regained their original position of prominence. Thirty-eight NIEs were written in 1981 and sixty in 1982.

Evaluating the impact of NIEs on policy makers is difficult. Former participants in the process describe it as a no-win situation for the intelligence community. If an NIE supports a policy maker's preconception about the nature of a problem, it is dismissed as unnecessary or redundant. If it presents a perspective policy makers disagree with, it is dismissed as flawed. If the estimate proves to be incorrect, then the intelligence community is blamed for an intelligence failure.

The record for accuracy is mixed. In the 1950s and 1960s NIEs both overestimated and underestimated Soviet ICBM deployments. The failure of the intelligence community to predict the end of COMMUNISM and fall of the Soviet Union was subject to much congressional and public second-guessing. The root causes of these shortcomings are many. Part of the problem lies with the inherent difficulty of predicting international futures. A second set of problems is found in the area of management and coordination. In most cases, for example, at least one intelligence agency correctly anticipated how the situation would unfold but could not convince other members to agree. Such resistance may reflect an attempt to protect bureaucratic turf, but it may also reflect a belief that the evidence simply did not support that conclusion at the time. In an attempt to address this possibility, new emphasis has been placed on allowing dissenting footnotes to appear more prominently in the main text of NIEs. Third, inaccuracies may reflect conceptual biases held by the members of the intelligence community. This issue surfaced in the mid-1970s when conservative critics of U.S. foreign policy complained that the intelligence community was systematically underestimating the Soviet threat. Their charges led to the famous B Team exercise in which competing sets of analysts with different conceptual starting points addressed the same issue and then tried to reconcile their differences. Members of the B Team held a more conservative view of Soviet intentions than did their A Team counterparts, who came from the intelligence community.

See also RUSSIA.

**Further reading:** Adams, Sam. *War of Numbers: An Intelligence Memoir.* South Royalton, Vt.: Steerforth Press, 1994; Steury, Donald P., ed. *Intentions and Capabilities: Estimates on Soviet Strategic Forces: 1950–1983.* Washington, D.C.: Center for the Study of Intelligence, 1996.

## national interest

The national interest is one of the most fundamental concepts used in the study of international politics. It is also one of the most difficult to define and to give concrete meaning. This has often made it the subject of intense political competition and led scholars to question its utility as a guide to foreign policy.

U.S. foreign policy, as with the foreign policies of all other states, is justified with references to the "national interest." It is a concept that suggests great importance, the presence of a threat, and urgency. Yet invoking the national interest in defense of a policy has seldom ended disagreement over the course of action the United States should take. ISOLATIONISM and INTERNATIONALISM have been justified as in the national interest, as has acquiring territory and refusing to do so, and the merits of entering into HUMAN-RIGHTS agreements, and whether to engage in COVERT ACTION. At different points in time, MANIFEST DESTINY, neutrality, and the CONTAINMENT OF COMMU-

NISM became virtually synonymous with the American national interest.

While the ambiguity of the national interest limits its utility as a guide to action, it makes it a powerful political tool. Competition to define the national interest is often intense because whereas the goals and values that a state may pursue are virtually endless the same is not true for the resources needed to realize them. Decisions must constantly be made about which goals to emphasize and which to neglect. The recurring gap between ends and means is a prevalent theme in U.S. foreign policy and is captured in the phrase *the LIPPMANN GAP*, named after journalist Walter Lippmann, who frequently wrote on problems in U.S. foreign policy.

Capturing the language or terms of reference within which the debate over the national interest is important because not all foreign-policy goals are compatible with a given definition of the national interest. This was one of the major problems facing President FRANKLIN ROOSEVELT in the 1930s when the debate over the national interest was anchored in the idea of neutrality and memories of foreign entanglement in WORLD WAR I. It required a large expenditure of political resources to move the debate away from this point of reference so that policies he favored could be implemented freely. Similar problems faced those advocating the advancement of human rights in Third World countries so long as the dominant frame of reference for the debate over the U.S. national interest was containing communism. From an analytic perspective, attention to the language in which a debate over the national interest is cast can reveal much about the distribution of political power in the United States at a given point in time.

For all of its vagueness, the national interest is not a concept without meaning. Scholars note that it directs our attention to a specific category of goals: national goals. They stand apart from societal interests and global interests. According to this formulation it is not enough that farmers desire a tariff to protect their goods from foreign competition, that firms wish to gain entry into the CHINA market, or that labor is worried about losing jobs due to a free-trade agreement. What is important is whether or not the policy serves the national interest. A common theme in writings on U.S. foreign policy is the ability of ethnic and business groups to gain control over U.S. foreign policy. The most famous expression of this concern is found in President DWIGHT EISENHOWER's warning to be wary of the influence of the MILITARY-INDUSTRIAL COMPLEX. Similar concerns exist about confusing the global interest with the national interest. President GEORGE W. BUSH's 2001 rejection of the KYOTO PROTOCOL, an international agreement for protecting the ENVIRONMENT, reflects the view that what may be good for the global community may not be compatible with American national interest.

The conflict between global interests and national interests is frequently found in realist writings on U.S. foreign policy and world politics more generally. Self-help, self-interest, and the pursuit of POWER are central to their view of how the national interest should be constructed. This position is not shared by a group of scholars identified as idealists, globalists, liberals, or neo-Wilsonians. In their view there is no fundamental incompatibility between the national interest and the global interest. One of the principal shortcomings of U.S. foreign policy has been the failure to recognize this and enter into cooperative undertakings with other states. Arnold Wolfers, an early COLD WAR realist, sought to bridge the gap between these two positions in making a distinction between possession goals and milieu goals. The realization of both sets of goals were in the national interest. Gaining access to OIL or creating a larger market for one's exports (possession goals) would matter little unless there existed a stable and prosperous international economic order (a milieu goal).

**Further reading:** Goldstein, Judith. *Ideas, Interests and American Trade Policy.* Ithaca, N.Y.: Cornell University Press, 1993; Isaak, Robert A. *American Democracy and World Power.* New York: St. Martin's, 1977; Krasner, Stephen D. *Defending the National Interest: Raw Materials Investments and U.S. Foreign Policy.* Princeton, N.J.: Princeton University Press, 1978; Trubowitz, Peter. *Defining the National Interest: Conflict and Change in American Foreign Policy.* Chicago: University of Chicago Press, 1998; Tucker, Robert W. *The Purposes of American Power: An Essay on National Security.* New York: Praeger, 1981.

## National Reconnaissance Office

The National Reconnaissance Office (NRO) was established by executive order in August 1960 following months of debate within the executive branch. It is a DEPARTMENT OF DEFENSE agency that is staffed by Department of Defense and CENTRAL INTELLIGENCE AGENCY (CIA) personnel. Its mission today is to oversee the development and operation of "space reconnaissance systems and related INTELLIGENCE activities needed to support global information superiority."

In creating the NRO the Eisenhower administration was responding to ongoing problems in the U.S. satellite and missile programs as well as the embarrassment of having a U-2 spy plane shot down over the Soviet Union on the eve of a summit CONFERENCE with Soviet leader NIKITA KHRUSHCHEV in Paris. A key point of debate in establishing the NRO was whether such a program should remain under the control of the air force or should be made national in scope.

This latter perspective won out, and the NRO was charged with managing the government's entire satellite reconnaissance program. Satellites are considered to be the most productive system for gathering image and photo intelligence. The KH-11 satellite, first launched in December 1976, for example, was used to try to find where in the U.S. EMBASSY in Tehran the American hostages were being held in 1980. It also revealed the existence of Soviet programs to construct new super submarines and mini aircraft carriers and disproved reports of a new Soviet chemical-biological warfare center. Early satellites sent back their information via capsules. This meant that the information received was often several weeks old. This system was replaced by one using digital imagery to return pictures to Earth in near real time. Satellite reconnaissance does, however, have its limitations. It is very expensive and satellites cannot be launched on short notice to address newly developing intelligence needs. For these reasons, satellite systems operate in tandem with aircraft reconnaissance systems to provide the INTELLIGENCE COMMUNITY with image and photo intelligence.

Throughout its history the NRO has been the subject of controversy and conflict. The National Foreign Intelligence Board was given responsibility for determining collection priorities and their implementation. Within the intelligence community DIRECTORS OF CENTRAL INTELLIGENCE repeatedly sought to exercise greater control over its actions as a means of buttressing their leadership position within the intelligence community. Matters came to a head in the Carter administration when DCI Stansfield Turner argued for greater CIA control on the basis of the increased importance of economic and other nonmilitary information to national security. SECRETARY OF DEFENSE Harold Brown countered, arguing that without the tactical intelligence provided by satellites the military would be unable to accomplish its assigned missions.

It was not until 1973 that the existence of the NRO became public knowledge and then only because of an oversight when a Senate report inadvertently failed to remove its name from a list of intelligence agencies whose budgets were to be made public. Even then it retained a quasi-secret character with few if any references to it being found in Defense Department documents. In 1996 part of its imagery functions were hived off and combined with elements from other organizations, including the Defense Mapping Agency and National Photographic Interpretation Center in a newly created National Imagery and Mapping Agency.

In February 1995 more than 800,000 images of CORONA, a photoreconnaissance program were made public, revealing for the first time the scope of its past work and technological accomplishments.

See also ESPIONAGE; INTELLIGENCE; NATIONAL INTELLIGENCE ESTIMATES; RUSSIA.

## National Security Act, 1947

The National Security Act of 1947 is the key piece of organizational reform in the post–WORLD WAR II history of American foreign policy. At the time of its passage most attention was directed to its provisions for unifying the armed forces. Less controversial was the creation of the CENTRAL INTELLIGENCE AGENCY (CIA). The Japanese surprise attack at Pearl Harbor had convinced most policy makers of the need for reform in this area. The major point of controversy was whether the DIRECTOR OF CENTRAL INTELLIGENCE (DCI) should be a military officer. The 1947 National Security Act permitted the DCI to be either a civilian or a military officer, but the CIA was not placed under military control.

At the time the National Security Act of 1947 was passed, the key component parts of the U.S. INTELLIGENCE consisted of a National Intelligence Authority and a Central Intelligence Group that was headed by the director of central intelligence. They came into existence on January 22, 1946, by virtue of an executive order signed by President HARRY TRUMAN. The 1947 National Security Act replaced the Central Intelligence Group with the CIA and gave it five specific tasks: (1) to advise the NATIONAL SECURITY COUNCIL on intelligence matters, (2) to make recommendations to the National Security Council for coordinating the intelligence activities of departments and agencies, (3) to coordinate and evaluate intelligence and provide for its dissemination within the government, (4) to perform for the benefit of existing intelligence agencies additional services as the National Security Council may direct, and (5) to perform other functions and duties relating to national security intelligence as the National Security Council may direct.

It is this last task, "to perform other duties," that serves as the basis for CIA COVERT ACTION and ESPIONAGE. The first presidential authorization to engage in covert action came very quickly. In late 1947 the CIA began a covert-action program to counter communist political gains in West Europe. ITALY, FRANCE, and GERMANY were the primary points of concern.

The National Security Act of 1947 also listed a number of provisions that placed limits on the CIA. It was not permitted to have a police force, subpoena and law enforcement powers, or internal security functions. The CIA was also not to supersede most departmental intelligence functions. A particularly sensitive area were relations with the FEDERAL BUREAU OF INVESTIGATION, which jealously guarded its prerogatives and access to the PRESIDENT.

The National Security Act of 1947 was formally amended in 1949 in an effort to strengthen the administrative powers of the director of the CIA, who also functions as the head of the INTELLIGENCE COMMUNITY. These amendments also freed the CIA from most civil-service regulations governing the hiring of personnel and the need to disclose its budget or the "organizations, names, official titles, salaries, or numbers of personnel employed." CONGRESS has failed to pass a legislative charter that builds upon the 1947 National Security Act or its 1949 amendments. Instead, changes have taken place via the issuance of a series of executive orders by presidents and other officials. It was National Security Council Directive 10, for example, that authorized the CIA to establish an Office of Special Projects that became the institutional home for covert-action programs.

The United States had fought World War II with two distinct military departments, the War Department and the Department of the Navy. The air force had achieved quasi-independent status within the army. No political or military authority existed above these two bureaucracies other than the president. The internal inefficiencies of this system and the need to cooperate with the British, who possessed a more centralized military BUREAUCRACY, produced informal arrangements during World War II that served to promote coordination among the military services. Included among them was a JOINT CHIEFS OF STAFF system. Ever concerned with protecting their independence and status, the unification of the military services was the most politically charged aspect of the 1947 National Security Act.

In the end, a compromise was reached. The air force was established as a separate institution, and a National Military Establishment and the position of the SECRETARY OF DEFENSE were created to coordinate the activities of the three military services. The services, however, kept their cabinet-level status. The 1947 National Security Act also gave legal foundation to the Joint Chiefs of Staff. The 1949 amendments to the National Security Act transformed the National Military Establishment into the DEPARTMENT OF DEFENSE and dropped the three services from the cabinet. It also created the position of chair of the Joint Chiefs of Staff as well as an Office of the Secretary of Defense. These changes were intended to place the military more fully under civilian control and provide for greater coordination of the military's activities. Unlike the case with the CIA, further changes in the operating rules and structure of the military have tended to come through legislation, such as the GOLDWATER-NICHOLS ACT.

## national security advisor

The national security advisor directs and oversees the work of the NATIONAL SECURITY COUNCIL (NSC) staff. The NSC was created by the 1947 NATIONAL SECURITY ACT for the purposes of bringing greater coherence and coordination to U.S. foreign policy. Under President HARRY TRUMAN, the work of the NSC was directed by Sidney Souers, who held the position of executive secretary. It was President DWIGHT DAVID EISENHOWER who transformed this position into that of the national security advisor.

The national security advisor plays an important role in the formation of U.S. foreign policy because he or she is uniquely positioned to serve as a communication link between the PRESIDENT and the key foreign-policy BUREAUCRACIES. Moreover, because they do not bring a bureaucratic perspective to foreign deliberations they are often seen as protectors of the president's interests. The actual influence of the national security advisor has varied considerably over time but the net impact has been to establish this individual and the NSC staff as a formidable political force in making foreign policy.

A key turning point in this transformation occurred in the Kennedy administration. Up until then the national security advisor had not been a prominent figure. But now, the NSC became less important than the staff, and it was the national security advisor who managed the staff and ensured that it was responsive to presidential interests and perspectives. A second change came when President LYNDON JOHNSON replaced McGeorge Bundy with Walt Rostow as national security advisor. Appointed by President JOHN KENNEDY, Bundy saw himself as a facilitator. Rostow was more concerned with policy advocacy than policy management and actively promoted his own ideas.

President RICHARD NIXON created an elaborate system of NSC committees but positioned National Security Advisor HENRY KISSINGER at the center of the system. Combined with the selection of a passive SECRETARY OF STATE, William Rogers, the result was a White House–centered foreign-policy apparatus that operated independently from either the STATE DEPARTMENT or NSC bureaucracy.

The importance of the personality and stylistic fit between the president, secretary of state, and national security advisor became fully evident in the Carter and Reagan administrations. President JIMMY CARTER picked a strong National Security Advisor in Zbigniew Brzezinski, who clashed frequently with CYRUS VANCE, a veteran foreign-policy specialist whom Carter appointed as secretary of state. Carter sought to manage the IRANIAN HOSTAGE CRISIS through the NSC, but decisions made there were not always effectively communicated to the rest of the foreign-policy establishment. Vance resigned in protest over not being informed about the hostage rescue effort. RONALD REAGAN selected a series of weak national security advisors who were unable to mediate between the perennially warring Secretary of State George Shultz and SECRETARY OF DEFENSE Caspar Weinberger, or control the opinionated DIRECTOR OF CENTRAL INTELLIGENCE William Casey. Only with the selection of General Colin Powell as national security advisor did the NSC system operate smoothly.

The trend since the Reagan administration has been to select knowledgeable and low-key individuals who can provide the president with expert advice but not invite running conflicts with the other foreign-policy bureaucracies. This trend continued both under President BILL CLINTON and President GEORGE W. BUSH, who selected Sandy Burger and Condoleezza Rice for the post of national security advisor, respectively. In one sense this returns the NSC system to its earlier operating style. Offsetting this change is the reality of an increased size and more bureaucratic nature of the NSC operation. When it began the NSC had a staff of about 10 people, and it now employs about 225. Of necessity this means that in the future the national security advisor will have to be as much a bureaucratic manager as a policy adviser or facilitator.

## National Security Agency

The National Security Agency (NSA) was established by a secret executive order, National Security Council Intelligence Directive (NSCID) No. 6 entitled, "Communications Intelligence and Electronics Intelligence," on September 15, 1952. That directive remains secret. A version of NSCID No. 6 dated February 17, 1972, states that the director of the NSA "shall exercise full control over all SIGINT collection and processing activities of the United States and to produce SIGINT in accordance with the objectives, requirements, and priorities established by the DIRECTOR OF CENTRAL INTELLIGENCE Board." So secret was the NSA that its existence was not even mentioned indirectly by U.S. government organizational manuals until 1957 when a reference appeared to a organization performing "highly specialized technical and coordinating functions relating to national security."

SIGINT is signals INTELLIGENCE. It is gathered by Earth-based collectors, such as ships, planes, or ground sites, as well as by satellites. *SIGINT* is typically used as an overarching term referring to three different types of efforts to gather intelligence. First, it refers to intelligence obtained by intercepting communications. Second, it refers to intelligence gathered by monitoring data relayed during weapons testing. Third, it can refer to electronic emissions of weapons and tracking systems. Protecting and securing NSA Earth-based collection platforms has often presented significant challenges to U.S. foreign policy. In 1967 the U.S. *Liberty*, a signals collection ship, was bombed inadvertently by Israeli forces during the June 1967 Arab-Israeli War. TURKEY has repeatedly threatened to evict the United States from listening posts in retaliation either for U.S. support of GREECE in conflicts over Cyprus or for American support of Armenian claims of Turkish genocide. NSA listening posts in IRAN were a reason that the United States continued to support the shah in Iran in the face of rising opposition.

One of the major challenges faced by the NSA is deciphering the raw information it obtains. Much of SIGINT is encrypted. The information is encased in a code that must be broken. Decoding information thus is a major component of

NSA's work. Given the volume of information that must be studied and the time-sensitive nature of intelligence work, computers are an important tool for finding patterns within the flow of information and determining what it means. The high cost of its computer systems makes the NSA budget the largest of all members of the INTELLIGENCE COMMUNITY.

NSA is not to engage in analysis. It is a collector of raw information. The job of translating that information into intelligence falls upon the analytic agencies, such as the CENTRAL INTELLIGENCE AGENCY and the DEFENSE INTELLIGENCE AGENCY. The line between collecting SIGINT and interpreting it is a fine one, and in reality analysis does take place. Often this creates tension in the intelligence community when the results of NSA information gathering/analysis can be presented directly to policy makers and not filtered through other agencies. This occurred during the Carter administration when Admiral B. R. Inman, head of NSA, reported that it had found evidence of a previously unreported Russian "combat brigade" in CUBA. Director of Central Intelligence Admiral Stansfield Turner was angered by Inman's conclusion, feeling it crossed the line from collection to analysis. The report subsequently became public and created a serious problem for the administration. SECRETARY OF STATE CYRUS VANCE had denied the allegations in private. Now, satellite photos confirmed the presence of between 2,000 and 3,000 Russian troops in Cuba. For its part the CIA and other elements of the intelligence community believed that those troops had been in Cuba for at least three years.

Beyond breaking foreign codes, the NSA is charged with the task of making and protecting U.S. codes. The highly sensitive nature of this work has made the NSA a target for penetration by foreign intelligence services. One of the more publicized cases of foreign penetration was the arrest of Richard Pelton in 1985. Pelton had worked for NSA from 1965 to 1979, and he worked for the Soviet Union from 1980 until his arrest. Among the operations compromised was a project to tap Soviet underwater cables in the Sea of Okhotsk, off the coast of Siberia.

The NSA also become embroiled in domestic controversy because of its involvement in plans designed to "disrupt" and "neutralize" American citizens considered to be dangerous because of their opposition to VIETNAM. The existence of a secret charter governing its behavior became a major argument for writing legislative charters for the members of the intelligence community. These efforts stalemated, and no legislative charter for the NSA has been written.

See also ARAB-ISRAELI CONFLICT; ESPIONAGE; PEACE MOVEMENTS; RUSSIA.

**Further reading:** Bamford, James. *The Puzzle Palace.* Boston: Houghton Mifflin, 1982.

## National Security Council

The National Security Council (NSC) was created in 1947 by the NATIONAL SECURITY ACT. This act also created the CENTRAL INTELLIGENCE AGENCY (CIA) and the position of SECRETARY OF DEFENSE, along with a National Military Establishment, which is the forerunner of the DEFENSE DEPARTMENT. These changes were motivated by the U.S. experience in WORLD WAR II that pointed to the need for greater coordination among government agencies in the war effort. To that end, the NSC was to advise the PRESIDENT "with respect to the integration of domestic, foreign and military policies relating to national security." By law it has four members: the president, vice president, secretary of defense, and SECRETARY OF STATE. Others attend at the invitation of the president. It is headed by a NATIONAL SECURITY ADVISOR, who has emerged as a powerful voice in U.S. foreign-policy making.

Since its inception, the NSC has grown from a small presidential staff of some 10 people to a bureaucratic body with 225 people, including 100 professional national security analysts. In getting to this point, the NSC has gone through four distinct phases, each of which had its own characteristics. The first phase runs from 1947 to 1960. During this period the NSC moved from a purely advisory body into an overly institutionalized one. President HARRY TRUMAN was cautious in using the NSC to the point of not attending its early meetings. He wanted to avoid setting any precedent that would give it the power to supervise executive-branch agencies or establish a norm of group responsibility for foreign policy. The outbreak of the KOREAN WAR changed Truman's approach to the NSC. He began using it more systematically. All national security issues were now brought to his attention through the NSC system, and a reliance upon outside consultants was replaced by a system of senior staff backed by assistants.

The transformation of the NSC into a more formal institution continued under President DWIGHT EISENHOWER, who created a two-part structure. A Planning Board was created to help make policy, and an Operations Coordinating Board was established to oversee the implementation of NSC decisions. Where Truman's NSC was chaired by an executive director, Eisenhower created the position of national security assistant, commonly referred to as the national security advisor. Eisenhower's NSC was criticized for becoming overly bureaucratic. Rather than increasing presidential foreign-policy options, it restricted them out of a concern for preserving bureaucratic turf and prerogatives. This negative image is now being challenged by some presidential and national security scholars who see its relatively small size and straightforward division of labor as a model for future presidents to emulate.

The second phase of the NSC's history began with the Kennedy administration and continued until 1980. Under JOHN KENNEDY, the formal and hierarchically structured system established by Eisenhower gave way to a system that emphasized informal operating procedures. Stress was placed on multiple lines of communication, direct presidential contacts with lower-level officials, the creation of ad hoc working groups, and the acquisition of outside expertise. In the process the NSC was eclipsed by the NSC staff and the national security advisor as the primary force in presidential level foreign policy making.

In spite of bureaucratic reorganizations undertaken by Presidents LYNDON JOHNSON, RICHARD NIXON, and JIMMY CARTER, the focus of the NSC during these administrations continued to be on the national security advisor and the staff. Each of these presidents selected strong-willed advisors and actively intervened into the policy-making process. One consequence was not only the decreased importance of the NSC but also that of the STATE DEPARTMENT. The NSC met only three times in 1973, compared to 37 times in 1969. Key decisions were made outside of the formal NSC process, in Tuesday lunch group meetings during the Johnson administration and Friday breakfast meetings in the Carter administration. Under Nixon such important decisions as the invasion of CAMBODIA, HENRY KISSINGER's trip to CHINA, the Paris Peace negotiations, and placing U.S. troops on worldwide alert during the Yom Kippur War in 1973 were all made outside of the NSC system.

During the Reagan administration the NSC entered a third phase in which it fell into disuse. The national security advisor became a spectator with little foreign-policy influence or stature, and as a consequence the NSC staff ceased to function either as a policy-making or as a policy-coordinating body. With no bureaucratic force or individual able to coordinate foreign policy, an unprecedented degree of bureaucratic infighting and fragmentation paralyzed Reagan's foreign policy. Even more damaging, when the NSC staff did become involved in policy matters, it either became engulfed in bureaucratic trivia through its 100 task forces and 75 committees or actually conducted foreign policy in secret. This was the case with the IRAN-CONTRA AFFAIR, in which National Security Council staffer Lieutenant Colonel Oliver North engineered a plan that would finance the contras with arms sales to Iran. Through the Boland Amendment CONGRESS had made it illegal for the U.S. government to finance the Nicaraguan contras.

After the Reagan administration, the NSC was transformed once again into a more collegial body in which the more extreme turf battles of the past were avoided and the national security advisor assumed a more active role in policy making.

The evolution of the NSC traced above has been shaped by the interaction of three forces. First, there has been an increase in presidential involvement in foreign-policy matters. The NSC has become the primary instrument of this involvement. Second, foreign policy has become increasing complex, which brings more and more bureaucratic forces into play and heightens the need for policy coordination. The third factor is the politicalization of foreign policy. This has led to an increased attention to legislative relations, presidential speech-making, and public communications within the NSC system.

The significance of the NSC is found in the problem it was intended to address: the need for greater coherence and coordination in American national security policy. The problem is as pressing today as it was in 1947. Many analysts today call for recasting the NSC, making it less of an operating body or consensus builder and returning it to its original roots as a relatively small group of professionals who can (1) manage the president's daily foreign-policy activity, (2) coordinate the foreign-policy process, (3) ensure that the foreign-policy system makes timely choices, and (4) monitor the implementation of decisions.

See also ARAB-ISRAELI CONFLICT; NICARAGUA.

**Further reading:** Destler, I. M., et al. *Our Own Worst Enemies: The Unmaking of American Foreign Policy.* New York: Simon and Schuster, 1984.

## Native Americans

With its emphasis on western expansion, neutrality in the affairs of Europe, and the promotion of commercial trade, much of America's early foreign-policy activity was directed at securing control of the continent. This brought it into direct and repeated contact with not only European powers but also Native Americans.

European colonizers did not find an empty continent when they journeyed to the New World. Between seven and 12 million Native Americans lived north of MEXICO. GREAT BRITAIN, FRANCE, and SPAIN would come to control these lands that would later be incorporated into the United States as it expanded territorially. Foreign relations between the Native Americans and the colonial powers varied. Native Americans became allies of the French in the fur trade but competitors of the English, who sought to take their land and use it for their own agricultural and commercial purposes.

The British pattern of conflictual relations with Native Americans emerged as the dominant one for the new American Republic. The Ohio country was an early destination for Americans heading west. While Great Britain ceded this land to the United States as part of the TREATY OF PARIS of 1783, Native Americans continued to assert that it and other land west of the Appalachian Mountains belonged to them. The resistance of Native Americans to the westward expansion of Americans produced extended periods of violence. Three military expeditions were sent to this region in the 1790s. The third, led by General Anthony Wayne, resulted in a peace treaty.

By the early 1830s there were still 125,000 Native Americans living east of the Mississippi River. Two very different answers dominated the debate over what to do about the ongoing "Indian question." Assimilationists held that the answer was to convert Native American societies from those based on hunting and gathering into one based on agriculture. The Cherokee, who were concentrated largely in the Southeast, successfully adopted this strategy in the 1820s and 1830s, only to be forced from their lands by the state of Georgia after gold was found. The Cherokee sued in federal court and won twice, with Chief Justice John Marshall ruling that they could keep their land. The Court, however, could not enforce its decisions, and the Jackson administration chose not to stop Georgia's forced expulsion of the Cherokee to land west of the Mississippi, an episode immortalized as the "trail of tears," in which 4,000 of the approximately 16,000 Cherokee died.

The Cherokee had become victims of the second solution to the Indian question: removal. In 1830 Congress passed the Indian Removal Act, which appropriated $500,000 to remove Native Americans west of the Mississippi. President ANDREW JACKSON negotiated 94 removal treaties, and by 1840 virtually all Native Americans had been removed east of the Mississippi River. Where the Cherokee turned to the courts to stop their forced removal, the Seminoles fled into the Florida swamps and fought a GUERRILLA war against the U.S. Army from 1835 to 1842. The Black Hawks put up brief resistance in the north, returning across the Mississippi River into Illinois in 1831 in an attempt to reclaim their lands. They were defeated the next year in the Black Hawk War and forced to return west of the Mississippi River.

It was not long before the removalist solution of pushing the Native Americans west of the Mississippi River for their own good and the good of American settlers began to unravel. Westward expansion did not stop at the Mississippi River, and land that was once seen as a sanctuary for Native Americans now became an obstacle to the creation of a truly continental state. In 1851 CONGRESS passed the Indian Appropriation Act, which called for the compulsory relocation of Native Americans onto federal reservations. While most tribes did not try to resist this new policy of concentration, some did. Most notable among them were the Sioux, Cheyenne, Comanche, Arapahoe, and Apache. Their resistance would form the core of the Plains Wars that erupted during the 1860s and 1870s and that ended with the Grand Sioux War. Fighting on a lesser scale continued into the 1880s and ended with the battle at Wounded Knee in 1890, which was the last battle between Native Americans and the U.S. Army.

See also MANIFEST DESTINY.

**Further reading:** McConnell, Michael. *A Country Betrayed*. Lincoln: University of Nebraska Press, 1984; Wooster, Robert. *The Military and the United States Indian Policy, 1865–1903*. New Haven, Conn.: Yale University Press, 1968.

## Netherlands

At 16,485 square miles in area, some of which was reclaimed from the North Sea, the Netherlands is just smaller than Vermont and New Hampshire together. The population of 15.7 million is predominantly Dutch (Germanic with some Gallo-Celtic mixed in). A strong right-wing movement has emerged recently in reaction to the large minority communities of Moroccans, Turks, and Surinamese, most of whom have a common Muslim background.

Dutch history is rife with invasions and splintering prior to the Union of Utrecht in 1579, which brought the seven northern provinces together as the Republic of the United Netherlands. The harsh rule of the Spanish Habsburgs in the earlier half of the 16th century stood in stark contrast to the United Netherlands's "golden era" of the 17th century. The Dutch settled New York in 1614 but lost their American colony to Britain in 1664. In seeking to eliminate Dutch competition to British trade, in 1660, the English Parliament passed legislation known as the "Navigation Acts," the most important commercial legislation prior to the signing of American independence in the latter half of the next century. Three Anglo-Dutch wars were fought in this era, as Britain strove to protect its commerce and customs income from being stolen by Dutch and French smugglers. By the 18th century the colonists accepted the legislation, and smuggling had all but dried up between Europe and the colonies. However, illegal Dutch tea importation to the colonies and Britain's attempt to inflict seemingly more punishing legislation with the Tea Act of 1773 would later lead the 13 colonies into war.

As a great sea and colonial POWER, the Dutch projected their might into the South Pacific, Caribbean, and AFRICA. However, wars with SPAIN, FRANCE, and GREAT BRITAIN in the 18th century, along with a decline in technical superiority, led to the empire's weakening. Still, the Netherlands stood against Great Britain in an ALLIANCE with the Americans in the AMERICAN REVOLUTION, playing a small role, but one that was nonetheless appreciated by the colonists. In 1782, the Netherlands was the second country to recognize American independence, and between 1782 and 1794 the Dutch loaned the Americans more than 30 million Dutch guilders—the entire U.S. foreign debt—strengthening already close ties.

A defeat by Napoleon Bonaparte's force in 1795 ousted the House of Orange from power and all but severed ties between the Netherlands and the United States. William of Orange was reinstated as king following Napoleon's defeat at Waterloo in 1815. However, the harshness of the Dutch Reformed Church and economic hardships led to the final mass influx of Dutch people to the United States. Together with Belgium, the Netherlands stood as the Kingdom of the United Netherlands until 1830, when the former rebelled to form its own kingdom, and, in 1848 the Netherlands became a constitutional monarchy. However, peace would not remain long in the region, though it would last the duration of the 19th century.

The German Schlieffen plan, the war plan undertaken by the Second Reich upon the outbreak of WORLD WAR I, projected Dutch, Belgian, and Luxembourger territorial invasions. The plan was modified in 1906 because it was thought that the Dutch would not give the German army permission to cross the Netherlands, and thus Holland was bypassed, with the northern Germany army sweeping to the south through Belgium. The Netherlands maintained its neutrality for the war's duration but was involved in the TREATY OF VERSAILLES of 1919, especially Article 227, Part VII, the Penalties Clause. After charging former German emperor William II of Hohenzollern with committing a supreme offense against international morality and the sanctity of treaties, the treaty postulated, "[A] special tribunal will be constituted to try the accused, thereby assuring him the guarantees essential to the right of defense. It will be composed of five judges, one appointed by each of the following Powers: namely, the United States of America, Great Britain, France, ITALY and JAPAN." As such, the Dutch were requested to surrender the emperor to the court, William having fled GERMANY for the Netherlands prior to the armistice of 1918. Holland refused his extradition, though, finding the charges to be comprised of retroactive criminal law.

The Netherlands had been neutral prior to both world wars, a status they maintained only through the first. Adolf Hitler invaded the Netherlands on May 10, 1940. The nation capitulated five days later, and the royal family fled to London, with some members proceeding to CANADA. On September 17, 1944, Operation Market Garden involved two British paratroop units and two American paratroop units, who jumped into the Netherlands to secure bridges over the Rhine, but the operation was unsuccessful. Still, it brought the Allies into western Holland, though the Netherlands would not be fully liberated until 1945.

At the war's end the new government's first task was to supply the population with food, fuel, clothing, and appropriate housing. Following the devastation wrought by the war, another wave of mass IMMIGRATION, largely to North America, occurred again. However, to ease the Dutch and other European countries in rebuilding, the MARSHALL PLAN was developed to help the nearly 270 million people affected by the war in Western Europe. Between 1948 and 1954, the Netherlands received a total of $1.1 billion in Marshall Plan aid, which was $109 per capita—a rate second only to Iceland. During this time, parts of the Dutch empire were also granted either independence or near complete autonomy, as the Dutch pulled out of INDONESIA (Dutch East Indies) in 1949 after a failed military operation designed to hold the colony. Subsequently, Suriname was given its autonomy in 1975, but the Dutch retained the Netherland Antilles (Dutch West Indies—Curaçao, Bonaire, Saba, St. Eustatius, St. Maarten) and Aruba.

WORLD WAR II shattered early 20th-century Dutch neutrality, and in the more than 50 years since then, the Dutch have become active participants in the world. In 1947 it developed a customs union with Belgium and Luxembourg (BENELUX); the Netherlands was also among the first signatories to the UNITED NATIONS Charter, and within the organization, it has sought to develop the international legal order, improve compliance with HUMAN-RIGHTS instruments, protect the ENVIRONMENT, and promote sustainable development. These goals are in line with U.S. goals, which keep the ties between the countries strong. The Dutch-U.S. relationship comprises one of the world's longest, dating back to the Revolution.

With the establishment of the International Court of Justice, the Permanent Court of Arbitration, the International Criminal Tribunal for the former YUGOSLAVIA (responsible for trying war criminals from former Yugoslavia), and the INTERNATIONAL CRIMINAL COURT (ICC), the Netherlands has grown in importance as a center of INTERNATIONAL LAW. However, with regards to the ICC, there has been a disaccord between the United States and the court's statutes, though this does not have bearing specifically or solely on the Netherlands. CHINA, INDIA, and ISRAEL have also voiced objections, with the Americans' primary goal to ensure that only UN Security Council members be given the ability to refer cases to the court. This would rule out the possibility of an independent prosecutor, an option that has met with disapproval from many countries, including the Netherlands.

While legal matters may be the Netherlands's greatest single contribution to the international community, it is far from its only area of participation. The Netherlands shares membership with the United States in the NORTH ATLANTIC TREATY ORGANIZATION (NATO), and this ALLIANCE forms the cornerstone of Dutch security policy. The Netherlands is also a member of the Organization for Security and Cooperation in Europe. The Dutch are active in the EUROPEAN UNION as well. The EU-U.S. partnership exists along a broad range of activities, not the least of which are peace and security in the Balkans and Middle East and distribution of FOREIGN AID. One of the greatest liaisons, however, is in the area of international DRUG-TRAFFICKING control.

The Dutch-U.S. cooperation in controlling drug running in the Caribbean is excellent, though the efforts are not limited to that region. As a member of the UN Commission on Narcotic Drugs and the UN International Drug Control Program, the Netherlands is serious about investing in efforts to counter international narcotics.

—Stephanie Cousineau

## neutrality legislation, 1930s

CONGRESS passed a series of four neutrality acts in the 1930s that were designed to keep the United States out of WORLD WAR II. They reflected the isolationist mood of the country and the general conclusions of the NYE COMMITTEE that it was the self-interest of bankers and arms merchants that had propelled the United States into WORLD WAR I. The neutrality legislation became a constant source of political tension between Congress and President FRANKLIN ROOSEVELT, who opposed many of its features and, on occasion, actively worked to circumvent them. Critics of the neutrality legislation argued that it would not accomplish its goal of keeping the United States out of World War II. It was backward-looking (fixating on the forces and events that led to U.S. involvement in World War I) and not attuned to the political-military realities of Europe.

Congressional debate over a neutrality act began in 1935 against the backdrop of the Chaco War between Bolivia and Paraguay and the widely anticipated Italian offensive against ETHIOPIA. Roosevelt endorsed the concept of an arms embargo but favored legislation that would grant him the freedom to prohibit weapons sales only to the aggressor. Congress refused and passed the first Neutrality Act, which barred weapons sales to all participants. Opponents of Roosevelt's plan asserted that the act of selling weapons to the "victim" of aggression would involve the United States in the conflict and would be a violation of the principle of neutrality. The act also warned Americans that they traveled on belligerent vessels at their own risk. This warning was a reprise of the lengthy debate that occurred on the eve of World War I when the Wilson administration debated how to respond to German submarine warfare against British vessels carrying American passengers. The death of Americans in these attacks became one of the justifications given by WOODROW WILSON for declaring war on GERMANY.

Roosevelt publicly objected to the act's "inflexible provisions" and warned that the Neutrality Act might drag the United States into war. Nonetheless, he signed it into law on August 31, 1935. In October 1935 ITALY invaded Ethiopia. Roosevelt acted quickly to invoke the Neutrality Act and stop arms shipments to either side. Consistent with its isolationist impulse, the United States refused to join with the LEAGUE OF NATIONS in imposing an embargo on Italy for being the aggressor. Instead, Roosevelt and SEC-

RETARY OF STATE CORDELL HULL called for Americans to undertake a "moral embargo" against Italy and suspend trade in OIL, steel, and other vital goods.

In 1936 Congress passed the second Neutrality Act. The first act was set to expire, and the 1936 act extended its provisions for an additional year. The 1936 Neutrality Act also added new provisions. Under the terms of the first act, the president could at his direction extend the arms embargo to any state entering the conflict. The 1936 legislation required him to do so. Second, the administration was not barred from making loans to belligerents. This new clause incorporated the logic of the Nye Committee's report.

The intent of the 1936 Neutrality Act faced a difficult test in the 1936 Spanish civil war that pitted General Francisco Franco against the Spanish Republican government. Germany and Italy supported Franco. FRANCE, GREAT BRITAIN, and the Soviet Union (see RUSSIA) supported the Republicans. Roosevelt sought to follow the lead of France and Great Britain and deny weapons to either side. The problem was that the neutrality legislation did not authorize him to act in cases of civil wars. Moreover, traditional U.S. policy toward Latin America had been to sell weapons to governments involved in a civil war while denying them to the insurgents. With voluntary controls not working, Roosevelt asked Congress to amend the 1936 act to include civil wars. It did so through a joint resolution passed in January 1937.

Congress took up the matter of neutrality legislation again that spring. The 1936 act was set to expire in May. The third Neutrality Act passed by a joint resolution on April 30, 1937. The 1937 Neutrality Act was of indefinite duration, and its content represented a compromise among competing factions that disagreed over the wisdom of the neutrality legislation as it had evolved but were united in their desire to keep the United States out of war. The amount of discretionary power to be given to the PRESIDENT again was a major point of debate as Roosevelt increasingly sought ways to involve the United States in collective security undertakings. The new legislation made travel on belligerent ships through "danger zones" unlawful. It permitted belligerents to buy other supplies from the United States provided they paid in cash and transported these goods in their own vessels. The cash-and-carry provisions of the 1937 act were limited to two years. The ban on loans was continued, and U.S. merchant ships trading with belligerents were not allowed to arm themselves.

The continued march of events toward war in Europe led Roosevelt to call for repeal of the neutrality legislation in his January 1939 address to Congress. He argued that attempts to deliberately legislate neutrality had failed to protect U.S. security interests: "Our neutrality laws may operate unevenly and unfairly . . . the instinct of self-preservation should warn us that we ought not to let that happen anymore." He followed this address for large increases in defense expenditures. On May 1, the cash-and-carry provisions of the 1937 act expired, and Roosevelt asked Senate leaders to secure the approval of Congress to repeal the arms embargo so that weapons could be shipped to Great Britain and France. Isolationist sentiment remained strong, and in August Congress adjourned without taking action.

Adolf Hitler's troops poured into POLAND on September 1, 1939. Two days later Great Britain and France declared war on Germany. Two weeks after the invasion Roosevelt called Congress into special session and asked for the revision of the neutrality legislation. Six weeks of heated debate led to the passage of the fourth Neutrality Act on a near perfect party-line vote, with only a handful of Republicans voting for the new act. The 1939 act permitted the president to provide short-term credits of 90 days to belligerents. It also repealed the arms embargo and allowed the Allies to purchase weapons on a cash-and-carry basis. In a concession to isolationists it forbade any U.S. ship from entering into areas designated as combat zones by the president. Roosevelt signed the act into law on November 4, 1939.

Commentators have referred to these neutrality acts as representing an attempt at "storm cellar" neutrality. From this point forward, Roosevelt led the United States on a path away from traditional neutrality to one of nonbelligerency. The United States was actively aiding Britain and France, but its participation stopped short of declared war. With Great Britain strapped for cash, Roosevelt first agreed to swap 50 American destroyers for the right to establish navy and air bases on British territory in the Western Hemisphere. This was followed by the LEND-LEASE ACT of 1941, which circumvented the cash portion of the cash-and-carry section of the Neutrality Act. Finally, in November 1941 Roosevelt asked Congress to repeal the Neutrality Act so as to allow the arming of U.S. merchant vessels and the abolition of combat areas so that U.S. ships could carry Lend-Lease goods directly to the Allies. It did so by a vote of 50-37 in the Senate and 212-194 in the House.

**Further reading:** Divine, Robert. *The Illusion of Neutrality.* Chapel Hill: University of North Carolina Press, 1968.

## New York Times v. United States (1971)

Popularly known as the Pentagon Papers case, it involved an attempt by the Nixon administration to block the *New York Times* and *Washington Post* from publishing additional portions of a classified DEFENSE DEPARTMENT history of U.S. involvement in VIETNAM on the grounds that to do so would threaten U.S. national security. This 7,000 page, 47-volume compendium had been given to the *New York Times* by Daniel Ellsberg, a Pentagon employee who had been involved in its writing. After one court of appeals refused to stop the continued publication of the Pentagon

Papers and a second court of appeals agreed to, the case went to the SUPREME COURT.

By a 6-3 vote and with the justices writing nine different opinions, the Supreme Court refused to support President RICHARD NIXON. In a brief statement the Court said: "[A]ny system of prior restraint of expression comes to this court bearing a heavy presumption against its constitutional validity" and that the Nixon administration had not succeeded in "showing justification for . . . such restraint." Justices Hugo Black and William O. Douglas adopted the most adamant position, commenting that "the word 'security' is a broad, vague generality whose contours should not be invoked to abrogate the fundamental law embodied in the First Amendment. The guarding of military and diplomatic secrets at the expense of informed representative government provides no real security for our Republic." Justice Thurgood Marshall took the least expansive view in joining the majority. Noting the absence of any congressional legislation in this area, he asserted. "[T]he CONSTITUTION provides that Congress shall make laws, the PRESIDENT execute laws, and courts interpret laws. . . . It did not provide for government by injunction in which the courts and the Executive Branch can 'make law' without regard to the actions of Congress."

The Pentagon Papers case is significant because it shows that while the Court has been generally supportive of claims of presidential power versus CONGRESS, it recognizes limits to presidential foreign-policy power when the president interacts with the public.

## Nicaragua

Nicaragua is located in Central America. It is slightly larger than New York State, with an area of 50,446 square miles. The first permanent Spanish settlement in the area was established in 1524. Nicaragua gained its independence from SPAIN in 1821 and then for a brief time became part of the Mexican Empire and then a member of a federation of independent Central American provinces. It became an independent republic in 1838 and was recognized by the United States in 1851.

Virtually from the outset, Nicaragua was an object of American expansionist interests. The deepening domestic crisis over slavery in the United States prevented the administrations of FRANKLIN PIERCE and James Buchanan from acting on these impulses, but it did open the door for American adventurers (also known as FILIBUSTERS) to press forward. The most notable was William Walker, who sought to reintroduce slavery and actually succeeded in becoming president of Nicaragua from 1855 to 1857. Walker was overthrown after he opposed Cornelius Vanderbilt's plans to build an interoceanic canal through Nicaragua.

Of most concern to the United States at this time was the strong position held by the British in the region. They held a commanding presence along the Mesquito Coast (along the Atlantic Ocean), and this complicated any direct or indirect American expansionist plans. SECRETARY OF STATE JAMES BLAINE tried unsuccessfully to renegotiate the 1850 CLAYTON-BULWER TREATY. The treaty recognized the British position of influence and prevented either GREAT BRITAIN or the United States from unilaterally building a canal. His successor, FREDERICK FRELINGHUYSEN, took a more direct route. Ignoring the British, he negotiated an agreement with Nicaragua in 1884 that provided for joint ownership of an Isthmian canal and U.S. protection for it. The agreement was never voted on in the Senate, and it lacked sufficient votes for passage when it was tabled by the new GROVER CLEVELAND administration. The diplomatic room needed to build an American canal was finally cleared in 1901 when Secretary of State JOHN HAY negotiated two treaties with the British, ambassador to the United States, Sir Julian Paunceforte. The first treaty recognized the United States's right to build a canal, and the second treaty recognized its right to control and fortify a canal.

Nicaragua was the long time front-runner in the race to locate an interoceanic canal. The United States had already negotiated two treaties with Nicaragua in 1849 that laid the foundations for such a canal. One provided for U.S. control over a canal route in return for supporting Nicaraguan claims along the Mesquito Coast. The second confirmed an agreement giving Vanderbilt the right to build a canal. Rather than submit these agreements to CONGRESS, President Zachary Taylor negotiated an agreement with the British for joint control over a canal, the Clayton-Bulwer Treaty. In the end, however, Nicaragua lost out to COLOMBIA. Intense bargaining had shifted the political balance of power within the U.S. Senate at the very end, and it passed a Nicaraguan bill calling for the construction of a PANAMA CANAL.

Nicaragua did not slip completely out of view. Seemingly overnight Nicaraguan president José Zelaya was transformed from loyal ally to dangerous opponent as his desire for regional hegemony collided with the American interest in promoting regional stability in order to safeguard the Panama Canal. A 1907 peace conference had failed to stabilize the region, and in 1909 President WILLIAM HOWARD TAFT sent a naval squadron to the Mesquito Coast to block a Nicaraguan invasion of EL SALVADOR. With his position weakened, Zelaya was forced from power in December 1909. His successor sought to hold onto power but did not fare any better. In 1910 U.S. Marines were put ashore in order to protect American lives and property, but they also had the effect of ensuring the victory of the anti-Zelaya forces.

Adolfo Díaz won the presidential election in 1911. Central to Secretary of State Philander Knox's thinking about how to ensure stability was the reorganization of Nicaraguan finances. The United States insisted upon a new loan from Washington to cover Managua's existing European debt, and when the government resisted, a warship was sent to show the flag. An American was then positioned as collector general of customs. The next year, faced with a rebellion inspired by liberal opponents, Díaz called for and received U.S. forces to help him stay in power. Two months of fighting led to a 14-year U.S. occupation.

In 1913 the outgoing Taft administration further sought to cement the American position in Nicaragua by signing a treaty giving the United States a renewable 99-year lease on two islands in the Caribbean, the right to a naval base on the Pacific Ocean, and the right to build a canal. In return Nicaragua was to receive $3 million. The WOODROW WILSON administration inherited the treaty and added to it a provision authorizing American intervention, making it similar to the PLATT AMENDMENT for CUBA. The Senate refused to endorse this revision, and in 1916 the Bryan-Chamorro Treaty was accepted.

U.S. forces left Nicaragua in 1925 following U.S.-sponsored elections. They returned the next year as domestic unrest continued. Until 1933 when they withdrew again, U.S. forces engaged rebel leader Augusto César Sandino's forces in often bloody conflict. A key contributing factor to President HERBERT HOOVER's decision to remove American forces was the economic depression that gripped the United States. In place of American troops, the United States now placed responsibility for maintaining order on the Nicaraguan National Guard under the leadership of Anastasio Somoza García.

Anastasio Somoza seized power in 1936 and ruled until he was assassinated in 1956. He was a COLD WAR ally of the DWIGHT EISENHOWER administration and played a key support role in the CENTRAL INTELLIGENCE AGENCY (CIA)–organized overthrow of Jacobo Arbenz Guzmán in GUATEMALA in 1954. His sons would succeed him, and they continued his policy of support for the United States. Nicaragua was the launching point for the BAY OF PIGS invasion of Cuba in 1961, and Nicaraguan troops participated in the occupation of the DOMINICAN REPUBLIC in 1965. By the mid-1970s the Ford administration began to try to distance itself from the government of Anastasio Somoza due to its widespread corruption and repression. The Carter administration continued this trend and went so far as to seek out opposition political forces.

The Somoza period ended in 1978 when Anastasio Somoza Debayle fled to Paraguay in July 1978. However, the beginning of the end began as early as 1961 when leftist opposition forces formed the Sandinista National Liberation Front (FSLN). Centrist forces united around

A band of contra right-wing guerrillas training in the jungle of northern Nicaragua, 1980 *(Hulton/Archive)*

newspaper editor Pedro Joaquín Chamorro in 1974. In 1978 he was assassinated under orders of Somoza, and the FSLN now emerged as the opposition force behind which all anti-Somoza forces united.

JIMMY CARTER's administration was skeptical of the new Sandinista government led by Daniel Ortega Saavedra. The Carter administration looked upon the Sandinista's with suspicion, considering them Marxists who valued Cuba and the Soviet Union as allies and saw the United States as the enemy. Trying to avoid a total break in U.S.-Nicaraguan relations along the lines of that which occurred between the United States and Cuba following Fidel Castro's takeover, the Carter administration advanced a $15 million reconstruction package and asked Congress for $75 million in foreign aid for Nicaragua. After much debate, Congress approve funds with the proviso that the president terminate funding if he concluded that Nicaragua was aiding a foreign insurgency. Convinced that Nicaragua had, in fact, aided the January 1981 FLMN offensive in El Salvador, Carter suspended aid to the Sandinistas. He also authorized the CIA to support anti-Sandinista forces in Nicaragua.

El Salvador—not Nicaragua—was the first place in Central America that RONALD REAGAN's administration sought to demonstrate a new American toughness against COMMUNISM. It identified the left-wing revolutionary opposition movement known as the Farabundo Martí National Liberation Front (FMLN) as receiving aid from Cuba, the Soviet Union, and other Communist states. And the Sandinista government of Nicaragua had, in fact, helped the FMLN mount an ill-fated January 1981 offensive against the El Salvadoran government. Along with modernizing the El Salvadoran military, stopping the flow of weapons from Nicaragua into El Salvador became an early foreign-policy objective of the Reagan administration.

This connection between the two states led President Ronald Reagan to intensify American opposition to the Sandinistas. The new Reagan administration terminated the aid package in April 1981. In November President Reagan signed Presidential Directive 17, which called for the creation and funding of a secret anti-Sandinista guerrilla force that would become the contras. DIRECTOR OF CENTRAL INTELLIGENCE William Casey told the Senate INTELLIGENCE Committee that what was intended was a $19 million program that would lead to the establishment of a 500-person force targeted on the Cuban infrastructure in Nicaragua that was responsible for training and aiding the FLMN in El Salvador. The Carter administration had also explored this option tentatively. After Somoza and his forces fled Nicaragua, Carter had signed an intelligence finding authorizing funds to keep domestic opposition to the Sandinistas alive.

In early 1982, buoyed by some early successes, the Reagan administration expanded the goals of the contras to include bringing down the Sandinista government. By 1985, the contras had grown in number from 12,000 to 15,000. The Sandinistas responded by increasing the size of the Nicaraguan military from 5,000 in 1979 to 119,000 in 1985. The CIA stepped up its covert-action program. Its contacts bombed an airport in Nicaragua in 1983 (just as two U.S. senators were landing), mined harbors in 1984, and distributed psychological warfare pamphlets that could be read as advocating assassination.

From the outset Congress was skeptical of the Reagan administration's contra policy. In December 1982 the House approved the Boland Amendment (I) that prohibited the use of U.S. funds to overthrow the Sandinista government. The Senate reacted angrily to having been kept in the dark about the mining of harbors. Widespread HUMAN-RIGHTS violations attributed to the contras also sparked congressional opposition. After information about the CIA's psychological warfare manuals became public, it passed another Boland Amendment (II) that terminated all aid to the contras effective October 1, 1984.

In an effort to counter its congressional opposition and build public support for its policies, the Reagan administration created a bipartisan commission to study the situation in Central America. The Kissinger Commission issued a report in January 1984 that called for economic aid for the region, continued but qualified support for the military in El Salvador, and invoked the DOMINO THEORY in giving its support to the contras.

Following its reelection and convinced of the need to remove the Sandinistas from power, the Reagan administration decided to expand the war in Nicaragua under the direction of the NATIONAL SECURITY COUNCIL and Lieutenant Colonel Oliver North. Since it could not use American funds for this purpose, it turned to allies. SAUDI ARABIA

($32 million), the sultan of Brunei ($10 million), and TAIWAN ($2 million) are known to have contributed funds. The administration also secretly sold weapons to moderates in IRAN in the dual hope of bringing about the release of Americans held hostage in LEBANON (see IRANIAN HOSTAGE CRISIS) and using the money from the weapons sales to fund the contras. When it became public the IRAN-CONTRA affair created a political crisis for the Reagan administration. Not only had the Reagan administration apparently violated one of its own fundamental foreign-policy principles of never dealing with terrorists, but by secretly selling weapons and using the monies to bring down the Sandinistas, it had violated terms of the Boland Amendment, thus defying Congress and breaking the law.

One of GEORGE H. W. BUSH's first acts as president was to try to defuse this political powder keg. A truce was reached with Congress in which funds would continue to be provided to the contras and elections would be held in Nicaragua. To the surprise of virtually everyone, the Sandinistas were defeated. Violeta Barrios de Chamorro, wife of the slain newspaper editor and leader of the United Nicaraguan Opposition, was elected president in 1990. U.S. FOREIGN AID was restored in the mid-1990s, and today the United States is Nicaragua's main trading partner, accounting for 25 percent of its imports and 60 percent of its exports.

**Further reading:** Kornbluh, Peter. *Nicaragua.* Washington, D.C.: International Policy Studies Institute, 1987; Pastor, Robert. *Condemned to Repetition: The United States and Nicaragua.* Princeton, N.J.: Princeton University Press, 1987; Walker, Thomas, ed. *Revolution and Counterrevolution in Nicaragua.* Boulder, Colo.: Westview, 1991.

## Nigeria

About the size of California, Arizona, and New Mexico combined, with an area of 336,700 square miles, Nigeria is AFRICA's most populous state, with 120 million people. There are about 250 different ethnic groups in Nigeria, the largest being the Hausa and Fulani in the north, the Yoruba in the southwest, and the Igbo in the southeast. These ethnic and regional divisions have been politically significant since they bring together different cultural traditions. The Hausa and Falani are Muslim, the Yoruba are split evenly between Christian and Muslim, and the Igbo are predominantly Catholic.

European traders, primarily the Portuguese, British, French, and Dutch began establishing outposts in Nigeria in the 17th century as part of their slave trade. GREAT BRITAIN gradually established itself as the dominant power in the region following the Napoleonic Wars, first through trade and then by conquest. In 1914 it formally established the colony and protectorate of Nigeria. Nigeria became independent on October 1, 1960. Seven years later, on May 30, 1967, the eastern part of Nigeria, where the Igbo were dominant, declared its independence as the Republic of Biafra. This action followed a series of political upheavals that divided Nigeria along regional and ethnic lines. Nigerian forces prevailed, and Biafra surrendered on January 15, 1970. More than 1 million Biafrans are estimated to have died of malnutrition during the struggle. The civil war strained relations between the United States and Nigeria. The United States did not provide military aid to Nigeria to prosecute the war, and private American relief agencies came to the aid of the Biafrans.

OIL production had begun in Nigeria in the 1950s, and the oil crisis of the 1970s dramatically increased its overall national wealth. Today its proven oil reserves are estimated to be 25 billion barrels, and its average daily production in 2001 was 2.2 million barrels per day. Natural gas reserves are placed at more than 100 trillion cubic feet. The United States is Nigeria's largest customer for crude oil, accounting for 40 percent of total oil exports. Nigeria first became an important source of oil for the United States in 1973 when it did not participate in the Arab-led embargo on oil sales to the United States.

On May 29, 1999, an elected civilian government took power in Nigerian after 15 years of military rule. The HUMAN-RIGHTS violations that characterized this period, along with the absence of movement toward democracy, complicated U.S.-Nigerian relations. In 1993, after a presidential election was annulled, the United States imposed sanctions on Nigeria, including a ban on military aid and a prohibition on senior Nigerian government officials entering the United States. Human-rights abuses also led to an interruption in plans for committing $150 million annually in assistance between 1993 and 2000. Closer ties were reestablished in 1999 following a Vital National Interest Certification by President BILL CLINTON that lifted restrictions on U.S. government programs in Nigeria.

The United States has a long record of giving aid to Nigeria. Between 1954 and 1974 the United States had provided Nigeria with about $360 million in FOREIGN AID. These programs were phased out due to the large surge in revenues produced by its oil sales. The United States again began providing assistance in the 1980s as oil prices plummeted and governmental corruption took its toll on the Nigerian economy. The U.S. AGENCY FOR INTERNATIONAL DEVELOPMENT committed $135 million between 1986 and 1996. In 1992 funding was added for an HIV/AIDS prevention and control program.

**Further reading:** Ate, Bassey. *Decolonialization and Dependence*. Bloomington: Indiana University Press, 1987; Thompson, Joseph E. *American Policy and African Famine*. Westport, Conn.: Greenwood, 1990.

## Nixon, Richard (1913–1994) *president of the United States*

Richard Milhous Nixon served as 37th president of the United States. Nixon's initial foray into foreign policy came in 1948 when he joined the House Un-American Activities Committee. His chief target was Alger Hiss, a former STATE DEPARTMENT official who Nixon maintained had communist connections. In 1950 he ran for the Senate and defeated the incumbent, Helen Gahagan Douglas, whom he branded as being "soft on COMMUNISM." In 1952 he was elected vice president. Nixon continued his hard anticommunist line in the Eisenhower administration and traveled extensively, including trips to the Soviet Union (see RUSSIA), POLAND, and VIETNAM, which was then under French control. Nixon lost the 1960 presidential election in a close vote to JOHN KENNEDY. Eight years later he staged a remarkable political comeback to defeat Hubert Humphrey for the presidency. Reelected in 1972, Nixon resigned as PRESIDENT before the House could vote on articles of impeachment for his role in the Watergate scandal.

Upon becoming president Nixon did a major about-face in his approach to dealing with communists. Working closely with his NATIONAL SECURITY ADVISOR and later SECRETARY OF STATE HENRY KISSINGER, Nixon changed the fundamental direction of U.S. foreign policy from one of confrontation to one based on accommodation and recognition of limited common interests. In Nixon and Kissinger's view the switch from CONTAINMENT to DÉTENTE was necessary for two reasons. First, the American people would no longer support the type of military policy needed to stop the spread of communism. Second, international stability was only possible if all major states felt they had a vested interest in maintaining the system. This meant establishing working relations with the Soviet Union and CHINA and not condemning their every action.

The immediate obstacle to implementing Nixon's grand strategy was Vietnam. A way had to be found to end the U.S. involvement in the war. The answer chosen was the Vietnamization of the war effort. The primary danger to the strategy was that North Vietnam would not hold off its attacks on the South long enough to allow the United States to build up South Vietnamese fighting capabilities. Nixon and Kissinger sought to solve this problem through a two-prong approach of massive bombing of the North and an invasion of CAMBODIA to destroy Communist sanctuaries. The policy produced a public outcry against the war in the United States and did not succeed in buying South Vietnam the time needed to take over control of its defense. Peace negotiations began in 1969 and a peace treaty was signed in 1973 that allowed North Vietnamese forces to remain in the South. Two years later, in 1975, the government of South Vietnam fell in the face of an unexpected Communist offensive when CONGRESS refused to sanction additional U.S. forces.

Against the backdrop of Vietnam, Nixon broke new ground in U.S. relations with the Soviet Union and China. He entered into ARMS CONTROL negotiations that produced the STRATEGIC ARMS LIMITATION TALKS (SALT) Treaty I. More generally, Nixon and Kissinger sought to engage the Soviet Union in a relationship that rewarded cooperative behavior and punished actions considered to be destabilizing. The provision and denial of economic and technological benefits lay at the heart of this linkage strategy. Nixon shocked the world in 1972 with his visit to the People's Republic of China. The Shanghai Communiqué issued by the United States and China at the end of his visit emphasized that strong differences still separated the two states, but the process of communication had begun, and China's isolation from the mainstream of world politics was over.

Nixon's willingness to work with Communists did not extend to the developing world. In the Middle East he authorized large arms transfers to IRAQ and IRAN in an effort to establish them as pro-U.S. bulwarks against the expansion of communism into the region. In CHILE, where the pro-Marxist Salvador Allende won the presidency, Nixon authorized a covert operation to try to stop this from happening and then to bring his government down.

While it is generally recognized that Nixon redirected American foreign policy in important ways after Vietnam and broke that policy free of its COLD WAR moorings, his foreign policy was not without its critics. Conservative commentators question the fundamental logic of détente. They assert that there was no evidence to support the view that the Soviet Union could be treated as a partner rather than an enemy. They cite as proof of their argument the continued Soviet adventurism in the Third World and cheating in arms control agreements that led to a renewed cold war under President RONALD REAGAN. Liberal critics asserted that Nixon had not gone far enough. To them, Vietnam was a symbolic of the emptiness of POWER-politics thinking. The need was to embrace a different form of INTERNATIONALISM and not seek to recast U.S. foreign policy simply on a different set of power relations such as was implied by détente. It was the internationalist agenda that JIMMY CARTER appealed to in his presidential campaign against President GERALD FORD, who assumed the presidency when Nixon resigned and continued his policies.

**Further reading:** Ambrose, Stephen. *Nixon: Triumph of a Politician.* New York: Simon and Schuster, 1989; Hoff, Joan. *Nixon Reconsidered.* New York: Basic, 1994; Litwak, Robert. *Détente and the Nixon Doctrine: Foreign Policy and the Pursuit of Stability.* Cambridge, U.K.: Cambridge University Press, 1984.

## Nixon Doctrine

The Nixon Doctrine involved part of an attempt by President RICHARD NIXON to formulate a policy that would allow the United States to remain the dominant power in the INTERNATIONAL SYSTEM after VIETNAM but not require that it send troops abroad to contain the spread of COMMUNISM. First announced in 1969 and then elaborated upon in Nixon's 1971 foreign-policy report to CONGRESS, the Nixon Doctrine stated that while the United States would help free countries to defend themselves they must provide for their own military defense, with the U.S. providing military and economic assistance. In short, there would be no more VIETNAM WARS.

Along with the Nixon Doctrine, the Nixon administration pursued two other initiatives as part of its strategy to redirect American foreign policy. The most narrowly constructed was Vietnamization, which sought to turn over responsibility for defending South Vietnam to the South Vietnamese. This policy was fully in accord with the Nixon Doctrine, and Southeast Asia was the original region targeted by Nixon in 1969. The second and more broadly conceived policy initiative was DÉTENTE. It sought to engage the Soviet union (see RUSSIA) and CHINA into a dialogue that would transform their relationship with the United States from one of competition and open distrust into one of limited cooperation and muted conflict.

One of the major consequences of the Nixon Doctrine was a massive increase in the level of ARMS TRANSFERS to regional powers that Nixon hoped would serve as surrogate powers to contain the spread of communism. INDONESIA, the PHILIPPINES, SAUDI ARABIA, IRAN, PAKISTAN, and SOUTH KOREA became prime recipients of this aid. A particularly troubling situation developed in the Middle East. The rapid increase in OIL prices brought on by the ORGANIZATION OF PETROLEUM EXPORTING COUNTRIES (OPEC) allowed these states to purchase weapons rather than receive them as FOREIGN AID. This resulted in ever more sophisticated weapons flowing into the region. The close political identification between these regimes and the United States that accompanied these arms transfers became an important factor in the downfall of the shah of Iran and the development of anti-American sentiment elsewhere.

The Nixon administration did not remain totally faithful to the spirit of the Nixon Doctrine. In an effort to buy sufficient time for Vietnamization to work, Nixon ordered the invasion of CAMBODIA and LAOS. Faced with the prospect that Salvador Allende would rule CHILE with Communist support, Nixon and his NATIONAL SECURITY ADVISOR, HENRY KISSINGER, orchestrated a CENTRAL INTELLIGENCE AGENCY (CIA) COVERT-ACTION operation that led to his removal from power through a military coup.

**Further reading:** Litwak, Robert. *Détente and the Nixon Doctrine: Foreign Policy and the Pursuit of Stability.* Cambridge, UK: Cambridge University Press, 1984.

## nongovernmental organizations

Nongovernmental organizations, also referred to as NGOs, are a category of international actors whose members are private citizens and groups, although they may accept funding from states. They are contrasted with intergovernmental organizations (IGOs) and INTERNATIONAL ORGANIZATIONS whose members are states. Numerically NGOs often have been more prevalent than IGOs, while IGOs consistently have been considered the more important international actors. In 1909 there were 37 IGOs and 176 NGOs. In 1960 the number of IGOs grew to 154 while the number of NGOs exploded to 1,255. This dramatic growth spurt continued into the 1990s. In 1993 the number of IGOs had grown to 272, and the number of IGOs now stood at 4,830. As with IGOs, NGOs range in form from those with well-developed bureaucratic structures to those that are better seen as loose ALLIANCES that exist with a minimal amount of day-to-day coordination.

The growth of NGOs is a result of the same basic set of factors that supports the creation and operation of IGOs, plus some additional ones. Like IGOs, NGOs are a product of an increasingly open INTERNATIONAL SYSTEM, global interdependence, and the expansion of the foreign-policy agenda to include nonnational security problems. The surge in NGOs also reflects the growing involvement of groups and individuals in foreign-policy issues, the ease of cross-national contact among like-minded political forces, and disenchantment with existing political organizations.

NGOs play a number of different roles in world politics. Each one of them places them into potential conflict with states. One of the most visible roles is agenda setting. NGOs draw attention to issues and problems that states have neglected. Environmental, ARMS CONTROL, and HUMAN-RIGHTS problems are representative examples. Greenpeace has been an active and aggressive NGO in the areas of environmental and nuclear issues. Amnesty International and Human Rights Watch are active human rights–focused NGOs. A second role of NGOs is to provide information on policy problems. In 2000, more than 1,550 NGOS were registered with the UNITED NATIONS, and more than 580 had consultative status that allows them to participate in key decision-making forums. Third, and most recently, NGOs have begun to play an active role in implementing solutions to global problems. NGOs such as CARE and the International Committee of the Red Cross have always been very visible in dealing with disaster relief problems. We now see them active in other settings, such as REFUGEE aid, PEACEKEEPING, and LAND MINE removal.

Oxfam and Doctors Without Borders are two prominent NGOs active in implementing policies in these issue areas. NGOs are able to play this role because they do not bring the "political baggage" with them that states do and are therefore seen as less threatening to national sovereignty and less judgmental in their actions.

The increasingly visible role that NGOs play in world politics has led many to challenge one of the fundamental tenets of early NGO activity, namely, that NGOs were above politics. Commentators note that by their very involvement in intrasocietal conflicts they are altering the domestic political balance of power. At the most basic level, by providing aid to the oppressed or vanquished, they are helping those forces survive. On occasion NGO resources, such as food or equipment, become the object of conflict and get expropriated by combatants. NGOs also find themselves competing for scarce resources from donors. One commentator has gone so far as to refer to this competition as a humanitarian circus, noting that NGOs were competing with each other for contracts in KOSOVO while ignoring the situation in AFRICA.

The United States has often found itself to be the target of NGO criticism and scorn. It has frequently been criticized by NGOs for not doing enough in promoting human rights, protecting the ENVIRONMENT, pursuing nonproliferation agreements, or protecting religious freedoms, among other policy areas. For example, both the STATE DEPARTMENT and Amnesty International produce annual report cards on human-rights abuses around the world, and the two often diverge in their judgments. When it comes to implementing policies, a more supportive relationship tends to prevail. The United States funds and works closely with NGOs in carrying out programs to remove land mines and fight against HIV/AIDS.

**Further reading:** Anderson, Mary B. *Do No Harm: How Aid Supports Peace or War.* Boulder, Colo.: Lynne Rienner, 1999; Weiss, Thomas, G., and Leon Gordenker, eds. *NGOs, the UN, and Global Governance.* Boulder, Colo.: Lynne Rienner, 1996.

## North American Free Trade Agreement (NAFTA)

The North American Free Trade Agreement (NAFTA) is an ambitious attempt to promote free trade within the Western Hemisphere. It was proposed by Mexican president Carlos Salinas de Gortari in August 1990 and signed with great fanfare by the PRESIDENTS of MEXICO and the United States and the prime minister of CANADA in October 1992. After ratification by their respective legislatures, NAFTA took effect on January 1, 1994.

Second only to the EUROPEAN UNION in size, NAFTA created a regional trading zone of 370 million people with an economic base of $6 trillion. It promoted the free flow of goods among Mexico, Canada, and the United States by eliminating trade barriers for most goods over a 15-year period. In many respects NAFTA was more concerned with "free investment" than it was with "free trade." TRADE barriers between the three states were already low, and the primary areas in which economic gains could be achieved lay in promoting investments and creating export platforms.

Mexican leaders were attracted to the idea of creating a regional free-trade area due to the poor economic performance brought about by an import-substitution strategy that sought to protect weaker Mexican firms from foreign competition in the hope that over time they would become stronger and lessen Mexican dependence on foreign states. Canada and the United States had recently created a free-trade zone between them, the 1989 U.S.-Canada Free Trade Agreement, and incorporating Mexico into the agreement was vital if new foreign funds were to be attracted to Mexico. The concept of a continental free-trade zone had surfaced in U.S. politics in the early 1980s. President RONALD REAGAN endorsed the idea in his 1980 presidential campaign, as did President GEORGE H. W. BUSH in his 1988 campaign.

Bush's administration was split over the wisdom of proceeding with NAFTA negotiations. The NATIONAL SECURITY COUNCIL, the COMMERCE DEPARTMENT, and the STATE DEPARTMENT supported the idea. The DEPARTMENT OF AGRICULTURE and the OFFICE OF THE SPECIAL TRADE REPRESENTATIVE opposed it. In spring 1981 President Bush indicated he would go ahead with NAFTA negotiations and informed CONGRESS that he would ask for FAST-TRACK authority to conclude the negotiations. If granted by Congress, such authority dictated a simple "yes or no" vote by Congress on the NAFTA treaty. Amendments would not be permitted. Only after entering into a series of agreements with business, labor, and environmental interests on what the treaty would include was the Bush administration able to secure fast-track authority; in May, however, both houses of Congress defeated motions to deny the Bush administration this power.

NAFTA talks began in Toronto on June 12, 1991, and ended in San Antonio on October 7, 1992, with the signing of a 2,000-page agreement. Each side entered the negotiations with a set of nonnegotiables, and progress was slow. Seven senators from energy states, for example, took exception to Mexico's unwillingness to loosen its control over the exploration, development, and refinement of petrochemicals. At one point there were some 1,200 contested provisions that had to be worked out before an agreement could be signed.

NAFTA negotiations were concluded during the 1992 presidential campaign, and the Bush administration had hoped to reap considerable electoral benefits from its signing, especially in Texas and California, two states that were major exporters to Mexico. Instead of cementing Bush's standing as a global leader, NAFTA became the centerpiece of political controversy. Third-party candidate Ross Perot asserted that NAFTA was the product of a conspiracy among Washington insiders and that it would cost many American workers their jobs. Democratic presidential candidate BILL CLINTON straddled the fence on NAFTA, finally giving conditional support to it, depending on whether certain "serious" omissions could be dealt with in the final text. By November, polls indicated that only 21 percent of the American public supported NAFTA.

It fell to President Clinton to negotiate the final details of the NAFTA treaty. He insisted that three side deals be added to the treaty as EXECUTIVE AGREEMENTS and thus not part of the treaty voted on by Congress. They covered the issues of how to deal with surges in the flow of foreign goods into the United States, environmental problems, and organized labor's concerns about controlling the influx of undocumented workers from Mexico into the United States. As Congress readied to vote, it was clear that these side deals were not enough to guarantee that it would not be defeated. The Clinton administration entered into another series of political side deals with key legislators. On November 17, 1993, the Senate approved NAFTA by a vote of 61-38, and the House gave its approval by a vote of 234-200.

NAFTA has experienced a mixed record of success. Two-way trade between the United States and Mexico jumped from $83 billion in 1993 to $157 billion in 1997, and Mexico had moved ahead of JAPAN as the United States's second leading trade partner. A major threat to NAFTA's future was the onset of the Mexican currency crisis of 1994, which threatened to destroy the investment climate in Mexico and by extension NAFTA's credibility. Confronted with this prospect the Clinton administration had little choice but to put together a multilateral aid package to protect the peso. Uncertain still is the direction NAFTA is moving in. President Bush in 1990 put forward an Enterprise for the Americas plan that envisioned a hemispheric free-trade area. Vice President Al Gore put forward a similar vision in 1993. Both Presidents Bush and Clinton identified CHILE as the next member of NAFTA.

See also DOMESTIC INFLUENCES ON U.S. FOREIGN POLICY; ELECTIONS; SECTIONALISM.

**Further reading:** Mendoza, Miguel R., et al., eds. *Trade Rules in the Making: Challenges in Regional and Multilateral Negotiations.* Washington, D.C.: Brookings, 1999; Vernon, Raymond, et al. *Iron Triangles and Revolving Doors: Cases in U.S. Foreign Economic Policy Making.* New York: Praeger, 1991.

## North Atlantic Treaty Organization

The North Atlantic Treaty Organization (NATO) was established in 1949. It was the first peacetime ALLIANCE entered into by the United States since 1778, when it made an alliance with FRANCE. NATO became a pillar of U.S. COLD WAR CONTAINMENT and DETERRENCE policy against the Soviet Union. With the passing of the cold war NATO has begun a twofold process of transformation. First, it is trying to evolve from a collective defense organization to one dedicated more to PEACEKEEPING activities. Second, it faces the prospect of no longer holding an effective monopoly over the use of force by the United States's European allies as they seek ways of constructing an independent European military capability.

NATO has struggled to define an independent role for itself in dealing with the crisis in the Balkans and establishing a forum for promoting East-Central European security. NATO agreed to send a 6,000-person implementation force to BOSNIA AND HERZOGOVINA as part of the DAYTON ACCORDS. This followed a period of open disagreement between the United States and its European allies over the wisdom of a NATO bombing campaign when NATO peacekeeping forces were on the ground. It also adopted a belligerent role in the KOSOVO crisis when it began a bombing campaign after Serbian president Slobodan Milošević rejected NATO demands to stop its policy of ethnic cleansing. Following the air campaign NATO forces led the Multilateral Implementation Force in Kosovo (KFOR), whose goal was to permit Kosovar Albanians to return to their homes. NATO also supplied logistical support to the UNITED NATIONS High Commissioner on REFUGEES in its efforts to end the suffering in Kosovo.

NATO was built upon three overlapping foundations. The first was the need to rebuild the states of Western Europe and secure them as allies against the Soviet Union and communist expansion. The MARSHALL PLAN addressed the first objective. It provided European states with $10.25 billion over three years to help revive their economies. East European states had been invited to participate but did not because of pressure from the Soviet Union. Their nonparticipation was not unexpected, and it marked the beginnings of a clear division of Europe into two cold war camps. NATO would address the second objective and build upon small steps that had already been taken to draw West European states closer together militarily. In 1947 GREAT BRITAIN and FRANCE signed the Dunkirk Treaty. In 1948 these two states along with Belgium, the NETHERLANDS, and Luxembourg signed the Brussels Treaty. It linked the six states together in a mutual defense pact for five years.

A second foundation was Article 51 of the UNITED NATIONS Charter. A major subject of debate at the conference establishing the United Nations (UN) was the relationship between regional security organizations and the UN. The Soviet Union saw the two as incompatible, but the United States was unwilling to terminate agreements already in place with Latin American states. In the end it was agreed that regional defense alliances could operate within the United Nations system.

The third foundation was the conviction on the part of American leaders that the United States could not be permitted to slip back into the isolationist mood that had gripped the country between the two world wars. NATO and other regional defense organizations would provide such a mechanism. In 1948, longtime isolationist senator Arthur Vandenberg (R-Mich.), who had become a convert to INTERNATIONALISM after Pearl Harbor, sponsored a resolution supporting "regional and other collective self-defense" efforts consistent with the UN Charter. The Senate approved it in June.

On April 9, 1949, the United States and 10 allies met in Washington, D.C., to establish NATO. The key provision of the North Atlantic Treaty was Article 5. It states that an attack on one or more of NATO's members in Europe or North America would be considered an attack against all of them. Article 5 did not mandate a specific response. Rather it stated that countries would respond in accordance with Article 51 of the UN Charter and take "such action as it deems necessary, including the use of force." This wording was necessary so as not to infringe on the constitutional power of CONGRESS to make war. NATO was to remain in force indefinitely, but after 10 years any member could request a review of the treaty, and members could withdraw after 20 years. To manage its affairs NATO established a governing council, the North Atlantic Council, and a defense committee that would recommend what military action should be taken if the need arose. This defense committee is joined by a committee of senior military officers that is in charge of operational planning and is headed by the supreme allied commander for Europe.

President HARRY TRUMAN submitted the NATO Treaty to the Senate for its consent on April 12. The treaty came under close scrutiny, with some senators complaining that it was an "old-fashioned military alliance." Some introduced reservations prohibiting the stationing of U.S. troops in Europe and the transfer of weapons to Europe. In his testimony against the treaty HENRY WALLACE argued that it would inflame the Soviet Union, turning it into "a wild and cornered beast," and should thus be rejected. On July 21, 1949, the Senate gave its approval by a vote of 82-13. Truman ratified it shortly thereafter, and on August 2, 1949, the treaty officially went into effect.

Throughout its history NATO has had to confront and overcome a series of obstacles to internal unity that often intersected with one another. Five have been particularly important. The first involves membership. The founding members of NATO were the United States, France, Great

Britain, Belgium, the Netherlands, Luxembourg, Denmark, Iceland, ITALY, Norway, Portugal, and CANADA. GREECE and TURKEY joined in 1952 with little controversy. West Germany's bid for membership was fraught with controversy. The outbreak of the KOREAN WAR, growing fears of Soviet conventional military forces in Europe, plus West Germany's rapid economic recovery and the prospect of German rearmament, led many to support West German membership in NATO. France was not, however, prepared to have GERMANY become an ally or allow German troops to be stationed on French soil. Its National Assembly refused to ratify a plan originally proposed by French premier René Pleven in October 1950 to integrate Germany into the western alliance through the European Defense Community (EDC). German troops were to have been merged with those of the other six members of the EDC, and thus there would be no German army per se. They were even to wear EDC uniforms. NATO endorsed the

NATO and Warsaw Pact Countries, 1955

concept at a February 1952 Lisbon summit meeting, and later that year a protocol was agreed to link the EDC to NATO and committing NATO to the defense of EDC states. Following the French rejection of the EDC the British proposed an alternative route to NATO membership for Germany. Along with Italy it would join with the six states that signed the Brussels Treaty and create the West European Union. That organization came into being in 1955, and with it Germany became a member of NATO.

The issue of membership next arose with the end of the cold war. (SPAIN was admitted in 1982 with relatively little controversy.) That issue became mixed with the question of purpose. If NATO was to remain a collective defense alliance, then membership should remain selective and limited. If NATO was to become a collective security organization, then the former members of the WARSAW PACT and those states that emerged out of the collapse of the Soviet Union should be encouraged to join. Key issues for either option were the pace of expansion and whether to permit RUSSIA to join. For its part, Russia strongly opposed NATO expansion to its borders. In 1991 NATO created the North Atlantic Cooperation Council to provide a forum for NATO and the former Warsaw Pact states to discuss these issues. A gesture halfway toward expansion was created in 1994 with the PARTNERSHIP FOR PEACE. States joining the Partnership for Peace could "consult" with NATO but were not members nor were they covered by any defense agreements. At its Madrid Summit in July 1997, the Czech Republic, HUNGARY, and POLAND were invited to begin talks leading to membership. They formally joined on March 12, 1999.

The second major issue is burden sharing. The great disparity in economic and military strength between the United States and its European allies in NATO's early years made it inevitable that the United States would assume the lion's share of NATO's costs. By the 1960s, with European economic recovery appearing to be complete and American global military commitments, especially VIETNAM, rising in cost, it was no longer clear to Americans why they should bear the primary cost. Concerns were expressed about "free riders." These were European states that enjoyed the benefits of NATO's protective shield but paid little to maintain it. European states countered that they were paying a high political price for NATO. Soldiers were stationed on their soil, and it would be in their countries that NATO and Warsaw Pact armies would clash and nuclear warheads fall. In the 1960s Senator Mike Mansfield (D-Mont.) introduced a series of resolutions calling for reducing U.S. forces in Europe as a means of forcing Europe to pay more for its own defense. In 1974 Senators Henry Jackson (D-Wash.) and Sam Nunn (D-Ga.) succeeded in getting legislation passed that required NATO countries to help offset part of the U.S. balance-of-

payments deficit that was linked to stationing U.S. troops in Europe. More recently, concerns with burden sharing have led to renewed interest in the often-debated concepts of jointly produced and standardized NATO weapons.

A third issue has been the scope of NATO operations. The central issue here is the desirability of NATO undertaking out-of-area operations. From the American perspective the principal rationale for creating NATO was as a counter to Soviet influence and possible military aggression against West Europe. For some West European states, notably France and Great Britain, NATO provided them with the ability to more forcefully pursue military action designed to hold onto their colonial holdings. At a minimum it freed up their military forces for this purpose, and it held the possibility of bringing NATO's might to bear in these struggles. The United States resisted any notion that NATO should engage in these out-of-area operations. Matters came to a head when the United States did not support the British and French attempt to wrestle control of the Suez Canal from EGYPT. As the U.S. involvement in Vietnam deepened, there were occasional calls that NATO should help or at a minimum pick up a greater share of the burden of defending Europe. The issue of out-of-area operations has risen again with the end of the cold war. To some, peacekeeping in the Balkans represented this type of operation because it placed NATO troops outside of the core military area that they had been prepared to operate in. Some have questioned the wisdom of creating an independent European military force for fear that the only type of operations it might be capable of taking will be out-of-area peacekeeping operations in Africa, the Middle East, and around Russia's rim.

The fourth area of controversy surrounded NATO's nuclear deterrent posture. From the outset NATO defense planners had assumed the need to rely on NUCLEAR WEAPONS as a means of deterring a Soviet attack on NATO states. The Eisenhower administration's doctrine of MASSIVE RETALIATION provided the initial framework for thinking about NATO's nuclear deterrent posture. In the United States, massive retaliation gave way to flexible response when the Kennedy administration took office. Flexible response required the ability to stop Soviet aggression at all levels of violence. In the nuclear realm this meant increased attention to tactical nuclear weapons. NATO would not formally accept this change in thinking until 1967. Meanwhile, President JOHN KENNEDY made an additional proposal that created controversy within NATO. He called for the creation of a Multilateral Nuclear Force (MLF) wherein ships manned by troops from different NATO members would jointly share command responsibility for nuclear forces. Only Germany supported the concept, and it quietly disappeared in 1964. The nuclear question arose anew in the mid-1970s with a debate over how to respond to the Soviet Union's installation of a new generation of medium-range missiles, the SS-20. NATO lacked an equivalent nuclear weapon. In 1979 NATO agreed to modernize its nuclear forces by developing the Pershing II in 1983 if the Soviet Union did not agree to negotiate the withdrawal of their SS-20s before that date. This two-track policy reflected the extent of the disagreement in NATO over the place of nuclear weapons in NATO's deterrent strategy, the extent of the Soviet threat, and European suspicions of President RONALD REAGAN's intentions and leadership. Deployment went ahead, and the issue was not resolved until December 1987 when Reagan and new Soviet leader Mikhail Gorbachev signed the Intermediate Nuclear Forces Treaty, which called for the removal of all Eurostrategic weapons.

The fifth and final perennial point of controversy within NATO has been the definition of its mission. From the very outset there had been disagreement about its purpose. One view held that NATO was to be a fully integrated transatlantic military alliance. The other held that NATO was primarily to be an instrument for providing political and psychological support to West Europe. At most, advocates of this perspective saw NATO as providing a modest military shield. Typical of this more political perspective on NATO's role was the assertion that the major contribution NATO could make to the stability of Europe was bringing the United States in, keeping the Soviet Union out, and holding the West Germans down. This debate, never fully addressed, has resurfaced with the end of the cold war. It centers on asking which goal NATO is better suited to accomplish: serving as the political basis for a new Concert of Europe where not only the great powers but also secondary powers could meet and map out the future, or being a military alliance dedicated to providing collective security on the Continent.

On March 23, 2003, NATO members signed a protocol that will permit seven new states to join: Bulgaria, Estonia, Latvia, Lithuania, Romania, Slovakia, and Slovenia. Serbia and Montenegro has announced its intention to join NATO's partnership program.

NATO was largely left out of American planning for the IRAQ WAR. As early as September 2002 SECRETARY OF DEFENSE Donald Rumsfeld indicated that he did not see NATO as having an important role to play in a war with IRAQ. This possibility "hadn't crossed [his] mind." The American position changed in November when on the eve of a NATO summit President GEORGE W. BUSH invoked the image of Nazi Germany and urged NATO to take a stand against Saddam Hussein. This call for action was for naught, as in January 2003 France and Germany helped block NATO action on the American request for support. French president Jacques Chirac asserted that "war [was] not inevitable" and that there should be no rush to a decision. This action

prompted Rumsfeld to label France and Germany as part of the "old Europe." German and French opposition continued in February when they were joined by Belgium in opposing plans to come to Turkey's aid in case of war. Article 4 of the treaty pledges states to come to the defense of those whose security was threatened. These three states argued that it was Turkey's actions that would force the crisis into war, thus invalidating Article 4. As tension mounted between NATO and the United States, the DEFENSE DEPARTMENT made public the possibility of removing American troops from Germany and stationing them in Eastern Europe. These states, many of whom were seeking admittance to NATO, were supporters of the Iraq War and were referred to by Rumsfeld as the "new Europe."

See also ARAB-ISRAELI CONFLICT; IMPERIALISM; NUCLEAR DETERRENCE STRATEGY: UNITED STATES; NUCLEAR DETERRENCE STRATEGY: PEACEKEEPING; RUSSIA; SUEZ CANAL.

**Further reading:** Goldgeier, James M. *Not Whether but When: The Decision to Enlarge NATO.* Washington, D.C.: Brookings, 1999; Joffe, Joseph. *The Limited Partnership.* New York: Harper, 1987; Yost, David. *NATO Transformed: The Alliance's New Roles in International Security.* Washington, D.C.: United States Institute of Peace, 1999.

## North Korea

North Korea has an area of 47,000 square miles, making it approximately the size of Mississippi. It has a population of 21.2 million people. The United States does not maintain diplomatic relations with North Korea. It is engaged in talks pursuant to the 1994 Agreed Framework, which would provide for an exchange of diplomatic missions at the liaison office level.

North Korea came into existence as a result of JAPAN's surrender in WORLD WAR II. At Cairo and then YALTA, the Allied powers had promised independence for Korea after the war but did not specify a timetable. They also agreed upon an occupation involving the United States, CHINA, the Soviet Union, and GREAT BRITAIN. Japan surrendered before the details of this policy could be worked out, and instead it was agreed that the Soviet Union would accept the surrender of Japanese troops north of the 38th parallel and American forces would accept their surrender south of it. Efforts at establishing a single Korean government faltered, and on September 9, 1948, the North established the pro-Soviet Democratic People's Republic of Korea. Border clashes with the American-backed government of the South followed, and on June 25, 1950, North Korea forces launched a surprise invasion of the South.

The initial North Korean attack was a stunning success and almost pushed U.S. forces off of the Korea

Peninsula. General DOUGLAS MACARTHUR's equally unexpected counterattack from Inchon allowed South Korean and American forces to cross into North Korea. Unification now became the goal, but it was thwarted when Chinese forces counterattacked and pushed the Americans back down below the 38th parallel. Armistice negotiations began in July 1951 and lasted for two years before an agreement between the UNITED NATIONS, Chinese forces, and North Korean forces was signed on July 5, 1953.

From that point forward the United States had virtually no contact with North Korea for some 40 years. The United States followed a policy of diplomatic, economic, and military isolation. A notable exception to the absence of contact between the United States and North Korea occurred during the VIETNAM WAR when in January 1968 North Korea captured an American spy ship, the USS *Pueblo,* and held its crew captive, to the embarrassment of the Johnson administration. For its part, North Korea focused its diplomatic energies on navigating between its often-feuding benefactors, China and RUSSIA. In 1961, during the COLD WAR, North Korea signed mutual security treaties with both the Soviet Union and China. While both are still in place, the end of the cold war and the death of longtime ruler Kim Il Sung contributed to a growing sense of international isolation.

Systematic American engagement with North Korea did not come until the Clinton administration. It was a result of developments that began in the early 1980s when North Korea began building a small nuclear reactor at Yongbyon. This reactor would be capable of producing seven kilograms of plutonium annually, which is enough to produce one bomb per year. In 1984 construction began at two additional sites, which, when operational, would together provide North Korea with the ability to produce up to 30 bombs per year. International concern over North Korea's intentions lessened the following year when it agreed to sign the Nuclear Non-Proliferation Treaty (NPT). International pressure was next applied to North Korea when evidence mounted that it was once again pursuing nuclear capability by constructing a plutonium reprocessing plant and a high-explosive testing facility. This time, North Korea responded by signing an agreement in 1992 with the International Atomic Energy Agency (IAEA), which put its nuclear facilities under IAEA safeguards.

Events took a turn for the worse in February 1993 when the IAEA presented North Korea with a one-month deadline to allow inspection of two undisclosed nuclear waste sites. North Korea responded in March by announcing its intention to withdraw from the NPT in three months. This announcement set off a series of negotiations between North Korea, the United States, and the IAEA over the conditions under which international inspections would take place. A meeting in June between U.S. and North Korean representatives led to a decision by North Korea to "suspend" its decision to withdraw from the NPT. The next month an agreement was reached in Geneva whereby the United States agreed to support North Korea's request for light-water nuclear reactors in return for its compliance with IAEA safeguards. Rather than resolving the crisis, these agreements only set the stage for a still more serious confrontation.

In March 1994 North Korea reversed course and refused to permit IAEA inspectors to visit all of its nuclear facilities. Early the next month, North Korea shut down one of its smaller reactors in order to begin unloading the core, prompting a warning by SECRETARY OF DEFENSE William Perry that the spent fuel would be sufficient to produce four or five nuclear bombs. It began unloading the fuel rods on May 14. American policy makers were not of one mind regarding developments in North Korea. One problem was conflicting INTELLIGENCE. In 1993, the CENTRAL INTELLIGENCE AGENCY believed that there was a 50-50 chance that North Korea had a bomb. The DEFENSE INTELLIGENCE AGENCY declared it already had a working NUCLEAR WEAPON. The STATE DEPARTMENT concluded that there was little hard evidence to support the view that North Korea had gone nuclear. Meetings with North Korea were described as a "disaster" and proposals labeled "insincere."

To show its resolve, the United States moved forward on two fronts. It asked the UN to impose sanctions on North Korea, and it sent Patriot missiles to SOUTH KOREA as part of a general military buildup in the region. With a military confrontation perhaps only days away, events again took an unexpected turn. Where North Korea had earlier refused to receive a high-ranking U.S. delegation, it welcomed former president JIMMY CARTER as an unofficial envoy. Carter telephoned the White House from North Korea, indicating that he had arrived at an agreement in principle with North Korean leaders that would place a freeze on its nuclear program.

New U.S.-North Korean talks began in July, and an agreement, the Agreed Framework, was reached, calling for the creation of a nuclear-free zone on the Korean Peninsula. In addition, North Korea was to receive international financial and technological assistance in the construction of two light-water reactors. North Korea and the United States also agreed to move toward the full normalization of trade and diplomatic relations. Clinton's agreement was very controversial, with many arguing that he had paid too high a price to obtain North Korea's agreement to a deal that was fatally flawed since it only required North Korea to freeze its nuclear program. Tensions rose in 1998 when the United States identified an underground site it suspected of being involved in nuclear activities. The crisis was defused somewhat when in March 1999 North Korea agreed to permit access to the site. Tensions continue, how-

North Korean leader Kim Jong Il, August 2002  *(Getty Images)*

ever, because the CIA reported to CONGRESS that North Korea was continuing to seek technology that could be used in its nuclear program.

The year 1998 also saw North Korea launch a Taepodong-1 ballistic missile on August 31. As part of the American response, President BILL CLINTON called upon former secretary of defense William Perry to lead a comprehensive review of U.S. policy toward North Korea. His report was issued on October 12, 1999. It called for a two-step process of moving forward by which North Korea would address areas of American concern and the United States would reduce pressures on North Korea. If North Korea did not act to reduce its long-range and nuclear missile threats, the United States would have to take other steps to meet its security concerns. Supervision of North Korea's actions is carried out by a Trilateral Commission composed of representatives from the United States, SOUTH KOREA, and Japan.

In its first two years in office the GEORGE W. BUSH administration had two distinct policies toward North Korea. Initially its rhetoric suggested a willingness to continue with Clinton's policy of engagement and support the sunshine policy of South Korean president Kim Dae-Jung. This changed with the SEPTEMBER 11, 2001, terrorist attacks. Bush now saw North Korea as a source of international conflict and included it as one of the three members of the axis of evil, along with IRAN and IRAQ. North Korea complained about this designation but generally kept a low profile and avoided provoking the United States. It officially supported the global condemnation of TERRORISM and indicated a willingness to sign United Nations–sponsored treaties against terrorism.

Tensions between the United States and North Korea increased substantially during the IRAQ WAR as North Korea engaged in a form BRINKSMANSHIP with the United States. In October 2002 it publicly announced that it possessed nuclear weapons. The Bush administration quickly asserted that this was a violation of the 1994 agreement reached with the Clinton administration. North Korea complained that it was the Unites States that violated the agreement by failing to end hostile relations and normalize diplomatic and economic ties. The North Korean announcement caught the Bush administration by surprise and placed it in a difficult position. Its national security policy of PREEMPTION suggested military action, but the administration was not yet prepared to act accordingly. Its first response was to try and isolate North Korea by cutting off all diplomatic ties until the nuclear program was stopped. Asian allies fearful of the consequences of political and economic unrest in North Korea refused to go along with this plan. In November the Bush administration raised the stakes by cutting off OIL shipments to North Korea. In retaliation, North Korean authorities announced they were restarting work on three abandoned nuclear power plants.

By January 2003 behind-the-scenes diplomatic maneuverings and pressure from its Asian allies led President Bush to offer North Korea agricultural and energy aid if it dismantled its nuclear weapons program. SECRETARY OF STATE COLIN POWELL indicated that it was possible that the United States might provide North Korea with security guarantees. The Unites States also moved to involve regional powers such as Russia, Japan, and South Korea in resolving the crisis. Still, the crisis continued, as on January 10 North Korea announced that it was leaving the Nuclear Non-Proliferation Treaty. It followed this up by rejecting aid talks with the United States that were conditioned on its giving up its nuclear weapons program. In mid-April North Korea took an additional step, announcing that it had successfully began reprocessing spent nuclear fuel rods. In doing so, it announced that one of the lessons of the just concluded Iraq War was that North Korea must possess a "powerful physical deterrent" to protect itself from the United States. This announcement also came on the eve of diplomatic meetings with the United States that were being brokered by China. An overall settlement of the dispute was further hampered by the often-repeated comment made by President Bush: "I loathe [North Korean leader] Kim Jong Il."

See also ESPIONAGE; WEAPONS OF MASS DESTRUCTION.

## Northern Ireland

Northern Ireland is part of the United Kingdom of Great Britain and Northern Ireland. It consists of 26 districts that total 5,462 square miles, making it somewhat larger than Connecticut. In 1989 its population was estimated to be 1.58 million people, 40 percent of whom were Catholics. While it has rarely been a top of the agenda foreign-policy issue, Northern Ireland constitutes a complex foreign-policy problem for the United States. Four factors come together to make it so.

The first factor is the internal dynamics of the problem. Historically Northern Ireland has been part of the province of Ulster. In the early 17th century the British put down an Irish rebellion and confiscated a great deal of land from its Catholic owners. These properties were given to English and Scottish settlers, who were Protestants. Demands for political separation of this increasingly Protestant part of IRELAND from the rest of Catholic Ireland emerged in the late 19th century as calls for home rule for Ireland began to be heard. The split finally came in 1920 with the passage of the Government of Ireland Act, which divided Ireland in two and created Northern Ireland. The Irish Free State, which later became the Republic of Ireland, was established in 1922 and refused to recognize the division of Ireland into two parts as final.

While violence became a constant presence in Northern Ireland's political history, the conflict escalated in the 1960s as the Catholic population grew in size. Nonviolent civil-rights protests by middle-class Catholics in 1968 led to a brutal crackdown by the Protestant government and engendered widespread violence, forcing the British to send in troops in August 1969. Both the Protestants and Catholics became radicalized. The Ulster Defense Group was a principal Protestant terrorist organization, and the Irish Republican Army (IRA) was the military arm of the illegal Sinn Féin Party. In 1969 the IRA split into two factions, with a new "provisional wing" emerging that unleashed a campaign of TERRORISM that extended into Britain in 1974. In response to these attacks GREAT BRITAIN passed the Prevention of Terrorism Act that outlawed the IRA in Britain. Also in 1974 hard-line Protestants won 11 of 12 seats in the British House of Commons and sponsored a crippling general strike. In the wake of this escalating tension, Great Britain passed the Northern Ireland Act of 1974 by which it took direct control of Northern Ireland. This action did not, however, put an end to the violence.

Tentative steps toward addressing the situation in Northern Ireland began to take shape in the early 1990s. In 1993 an Anglo-Irish declaration held out the prospect of peace talks that would be open to all parties that renounced violence. In 1994 the IRA declared a cease-fire as did Protestant paramilitary forces. The following year formal talks began that were attended by Sinn Féin. A new wave of terrorism by the IRA in 1996 that included bombings in London temporarily put an end to the peace process, but movement began again in 1997 as a new cease-fire was announced in July. These talks produced an agreement that led to the formation of a new Northern Ireland Assembly. The refusal of the IRA to disarm, a condition insisted upon by moderate Protestant leaders, led the British to suspend the new government in 2000 and 2001. In October 2001 the IRA agreed to disarm, but Protestant paramilitary forces refused.

The second factor that makes Northern Ireland such a complex foreign-policy problem for the United States is that it involves the internal affairs of a key ally, Great Britain. Traditionally in foreign policy the domestic affairs of other states are not a matter for DIPLOMACY. All that is of concern is their foreign policy. American pressure on Great Britain to change its policy or publicly criticize its handling of the matter could only be expected to alienate it. Moreover, the 1960s were also a decade of racial and political unrest in the United States, making leaders hesitant to criticize an ally facing similar problems. President JIMMY CARTER was the first to officially treat Northern Ireland as a foreign-policy matter. His administration went so far as to cite Northern Ireland as a factor for including Great Britain on the STATE DEPARTMENT's list of states that violated HUMAN RIGHTS. RONALD REAGAN brought the question of Northern Ireland up in talks with British prime minister Margaret Thatcher in the early 1980s and urged her to adopt a flexible position. The Reagan administration also sought to show its support for Great Britain by tightening the language of an existing extradition treaty that had allowed IRA members fleeing to the United States to escape the grasp of British authorities. CONGRESS responded to the news of a 1985 Anglo-Irish agreement that sought to lay the foundation for peace talks by passing a FOREIGN-AID bill for Northern Ireland that totaled $120 million over three years. President BILL CLINTON would personally involve himself in the peace process by making the first presidential trip ever to Northern Ireland in November 1995. He also championed the creation of an international commission to solve the problem. It was chaired by former senator John Mitchell. In January 1996 his commission recommended that peace talks proceed without DISARMAMENT, but this position was rejected by Protestants and British prime minister John Major.

A third factor that influences the U.S. position on Northern Ireland is the manner in which the issue has become involved in American domestic politics. As the violence escalated in Northern Ireland, Catholics looked to the descendants of the Irish immigrant community for help. The Northern Aid Committee (NORAID) was set up in 1970. A supporter of the IRA, it came under investigation by the FEDERAL BUREAU OF INVESTIGATION because of its fund-raising practices and because it was smuggling weapons to the IRA. A second group was established in 1974, the Irish National Caucus. Its mission was to lobby Congress and American PUBLIC OPINION to support Sinn Féin and the IRA. In 1977 these efforts led to the creation of the Ad Hoc Congressional Committee for Irish Affairs that counted 100 members and sought congressional hearings on Northern Ireland. Supporters of the IRA were blocked by the political power of the Speaker of the House of Representatives Thomas P. "Tip" O'Neill (D-Mass.), who opposed the use of violence to settle the dispute. He would be joined in public statements opposing political violence and terrorism in Northern Ireland by Senator Edward Kennedy (D-Mass.), Senator Daniel Patrick Moynihan (D-N.Y.), and others. In 1981 supporters of the nonviolent position organized as the Friends of Ireland. It should be noted that at the same time that these officials criticized Catholic groups for engaging in violence, they also criticized the British for their failure to take positive steps to solve the problem.

The final factor contributing to the policy dilemma facing the United States in formulating a Northern Ireland policy is the presence of terrorism. On the one hand this has been a recurring element of the problem, and the United States has not always taken a consistent position on how to deal with terrorism. In 1975, for example, the State Department refused to issue visas to Sinn Féin members on the grounds that they were terrorists. However, in 1994 Bill Clinton reversed this ban and allowed Sinn Féin leader Gerry Adams to enter the United States on the ground that his presence would contribute to peace. The terrorist dimension is also a new aspect of the problem. Following the tragic events of SEPTEMBER 11, 2001, opposition to terrorism has become a high-profile component of American foreign policy. In the United States the GEORGE W. BUSH administration instituted a series of controversial domestic policies designed to lessen the terrorist threat. Abroad, leaders such as Vladimir Putin of RUSSIA have used terrorism as a rationale for dealing aggressively and violently with internal ethnic conflicts.

Progress to peace in Northern Ireland ended once again on May 1, 2003, when British prime minister Tony Blair suspended the May 29 local elections in Northern Ireland. Blair blamed the IRA for failing to make a clear statement that it would end its 30-year effort to force the British out of Northern Ireland. Neither Blair nor Irish prime minister Bertie Ahern said they would make their blueprint for peace public without assurances that the IRA would disarm and end its war against Great Britain. The peace process had become sidetracked some six months earlier when the 1998 Good Friday Peace Accord was suspended due to allegations that the IRA was running a spy ring inside the Belfast government.

**Further reading:** Mitchell, George. *Making Peace.* New York: Knopf, 1999; Taylor, P. *Behind the Mask: The IRA and Sinn Fein.* New York: HarperCollins, 1997.

## NSC-68

NATIONAL SECURITY COUNCIL Paper No. 68 (NSC-68) was commissioned by President HARRY TRUMAN on January 30, 1950. Entitled "United States Objectives and Programs for National Security," NSC-68 came to establish the blueprint for implementing U.S. CONTAINMENT policy in the wake of the KOREAN WAR.

NSC-68 was produced by a team drawn from the STATE DEPARTMENT and DEFENSE DEPARTMENT that worked under the direction of Paul Nitze and the Policy Planning Staff of the State Department. Its purpose, according to SECRETARY OF STATE DEAN ACHESON, was to "bludgeon the mass mind of 'top government' that not only could the PRESIDENT make a decision that the decision could be carried out." Painting a dark picture of Soviet intentions NSC-68 asserted that "a permanent and fundamental alteration in the shape of international relations" had occurred and that if the goals and purposes of "American life" were to be advanced and preserved, American foreign policy must be fundamentally changed. Foremost among those changes were a significant increase in defense spending (up to 50 percent of U.S. gross national product, if need be) and a willingness to challenge the Soviet Union (see RUSSIA) wherever it might strike and not just at a limited number of key points.

Nitze had just replaced GEORGE KENNAN as head of the State Department's Policy Planning Staff. Kennan was the author of the "X" article on which U.S. containment policy was originally built. His reading of the Soviet threat emphasized traditional Russian national interests, the absence of a timetable for aggression, the need to distinguish between areas that were vital to U.S. national security and those that were not, and the necessity of giving primary attention to economic and diplomatic threats rather than military ones.

NSC-68 concluded the opposite. It painted a world of good versus evil, one that lacked nuance and subtlety. The source of Soviet power lay in a large military establishment and an ideology that was fundamentally hostile to the West. The defeat of free institutions anywhere was now equated with the defeat of freedom everywhere. And because Soviet hostility was unrelenting and scripted according to Marxist-Leninist principles, explained the paper, negotiation and accommodation were rejected in favor of achieving an offensive military superiority. Even the first use of atomic weapons was not ruled out.

The BERLIN CRISIS, 1948, the fall of CHINA, and the detonation of a Soviet atomic device all served to shift the political balance of power within the Truman administration away from Kennan's position. Still, the economic implications of NSC-68 gave Truman pause, and he did not endorse its recommendations. That changed with the North Korean attack on SOUTH KOREA in June 1950. A rapid buildup of American military power was now seen as necessary, and NSC-68 provided both the blueprint and the justification for it. Recoiling at the economic costs of containing COMMUNISM prescribed by NSC-68, DWIGHT EISENHOWER sought to find a new and less expensive strategic framework for U.S. foreign policy. He found it in the New Look.

**Further reading:** Gaddis, John L. *Strategies of Containment.* New York: Oxford University Press, 1982.

## nuclear compellence strategy: United States

In a strategy of nuclear compellence, a state uses NUCLEAR WEAPONS to realize political objectives by getting the enemy to stop what it is doing or force it to do something that it would otherwise not do. Nuclear compellence has not received as much attention as NUCLEAR DETERRENCE or even NUCLEAR WAR, but it has been a recurring tactic in U.S.–Soviet relations. It is also a strategic posture that may become important in the post–COLD WAR era as the United States finds itself confronting rogue states that possess nuclear weapons or other WEAPONS OF MASS DESTRUCTION.

Since the 1950s both the United States and Soviet Union unsuccessfully engaged in nuclear compellence. Some have argued that President DWIGHT EISENHOWER's strategy of MASSIVE RETALIATION contained a compellence threat: Stop engaging in aggression, or we will use nuclear weapons against the Soviet Union. Likewise, the pubic announcement of a new deterrent strategy of limited strategic options by the Carter administration also contained a compellence threat. The goal was to get the Soviet Union to stop its program of outfitting its large intercontinental ballistic missiles (ICBMs) with multiple independently targeted reentry vehicles (MIRVs). More recently, President RONALD REAGAN's announcement of the STRATEGIC DEFENSE INITIATIVE (SDI) is seen as having a compellent role. The purpose was to neutralize the blackmail potential inherent in the Soviet Union's large missiles.

These examples speak to a compellence strategy that is designed to counter a general threat that grows out of the overall nuclear relationship between two states. A second type of compellence strategy seeks to counter threats that are specific and immediate. Richard Betts has identified 10 cases in which the United States suggested that nuclear weapons might be used if the dispute was not settled. They range from low-risk crisis situations, such as the BERLIN CRISIS 1948, the KOREAN WAR, and the TAIWAN straits crises of 1954 and 1958, to such high-risk crises as the 1958 and 1961 Berlin Crises, the CUBAN MISSILE CRISIS, and the 1973 Yom Kippur War.

Evidence drawn from an examination of these cases points to the conclusion that the willingness of U.S. policy makers to threaten nuclear coercion was not strongly influenced by assessments of the nuclear balance of power. The primary motivating factor was a "balance of interests" perspective that suggested the United States had more at stake in the crisis than did the Soviet Union, so it would back down. Interestingly, evidence drawn from the two cases of Soviet nuclear compellence (the 1956 SUEZ CRISIS and 1959 Sino-Soviet border clashes) suggests that it was motivated by balance of power considerations.

The differences in motivation are important. In many instances both the balance of interests and the balance of power in a situation are subject to conflicting interpretations. Making correct calculations about the opponent's willingness to take risks or compromise is made even more difficult if one is not operating within the same strategic calculus. Many commentators make this very point about the strategies of rogue states and those who have only recently acquired nuclear weapons. They may not be operating within the same set of overall strategic principles that guided U.S.-Soviet nuclear competition, so their behavior in a crisis may not conform to cold war experiences.

Finally, it should be noted that compellence can also be a strategy for the use of conventional weapons. In the PERSIAN GULF WAR, the United States unsuccessfully tried to compel IRAQ to withdraw from KUWAIT through its buildup of military force in the region. When this failed it was forced to go to war to accomplish this goal. The United States was similarly unsuccessful in its efforts to compel Haitain leaders to change their policy and allow Jean-Bertrand Aristide to return to power in HAITI until an invasion force was virtually underway.

See also ARAB-ISRAELI CONFLICT; NUCLEAR DETERRENCE STRATEGY: UNITED STATES; NUCLEAR DETERRENCE STRATEGY: RUSSIA.

**Further reading:** Betts, Richard. *Nuclear Blackmail and Nuclear Balance.* Washington, D.C.: Brookings, 1987; Lynn-Jones, Sean M., et al., eds. *Nuclear Diplomacy and Crisis Management.* Cambridge, Mass.: MIT Press, 1990.

# nuclear deterrence strategy: Soviet Union

U.S. and Soviet DETERRENCE strategies during the COLD WAR were not identical. This created a communication barrier that had to be overcome in seeking to avoid war and pursue ARMS CONTROL. American strategists long refused to accept Soviet statements of nuclear doctrine and strategy at face value since they did not fit with the language U.S. strategists employed. Over time, U.S. and Soviet strategists came to understand each other, allowing a nuclear arms control regime to come into existence with agreed upon standards of behavior. The emergence of new nuclear powers in the post–cold war era once again highlights the role that communication and perception play in nuclear strategy and the construction of a successful deterrence policy.

Unlike Western writings on deterrence that tended to use the terms *strategy* and *doctrine* interchangeably, Soviet commentators assigned them very precise and different meanings. Military doctrine is the official view of the nature of the wars the Soviet military must be prepared to fight and the political purposes to be achieved. Its content was set by the Communist Party leadership and tended to be quite stable over time. When change came about it was largely the result of the death or replacement of a leader or a shift in the nuclear balance. The purpose of military strategy was to ensure that the Soviet military was prepared to fight these wars. Strategy was subordinate to doctrine, but it was a force, along with economic and political factors, that shaped doctrine.

Early Soviet writings on nuclear strategy showed great concern with the possibility of a surprise nuclear attack and with the nature of the next European war. The surprise attack scenario dominated Soviet writings throughout the 1950s and for much of 1960s. In 1955 a Soviet military journal contained an article stating that "surprise attack with the massive employment of new weapons can cause the rapid collapse of a government. . . . [T]he duty of the Soviet Armed Forces is not to permit an enemy a surprise attack on our country." With the advent of nuclear parity between the two nuclear arsenals, the fear of surprise attack became a less prominent theme in Soviet writings because it raised the cost of the U.S. of using NUCLEAR WEAPONS.

Soviet writings on the next war in Europe long stressed that escalation from conventional war to nuclear war was "inevitable." Over time this language softened to use phases such as *most likely* and then *probable*. By the mid-1970s a NUCLEAR WAR in Europe was reduced to merely a "possibility." The most frequently discussed scenario involved a conventional war escalating into a full-scale nuclear confrontation in 10 to 15 days due to significant territorial losses suffered by NORTH ATLANTIC TREATY ORGANIZATION (NATO) countries.

Prior to the ascendancy of Mikhail Gorbachev to the position of leader of the Communist Party, Soviet strategic thinking had come to center on five key themes. First, the best deterrent was an effective war-fighting capability. Second, theoretically, victory was possible. Third, it pays to strike first. Fourth, restraint was foolhardy. Fifth, numbers of weapons matter. Whereas the United States sought to deter a nuclear attack by threatening a damaging retaliatory strike, Soviet strategy appeared to do the same objective by threatening the United States with defeat and massive damage.

Gorbachev's New Thinking laid the foundation for one final shift in Soviet nuclear strategy before the end of the cold war. Among the points he stressed was the danger of accidental war. This path to nuclear war had all but been ignored in Soviet writings for a long time. Second, Gorbachev's New Thinking emphasized the point that Soviet security should not be viewed in a zero-sum context. Its security did not necessarily come at expense of the United States. Instead, U.S. and Soviet security were mutually dependent upon one another. Third, Gorbachev introduced the notion of "defensive defense." Soviet military power needed to be able to deny an enemy the ability to take Soviet territory, but it would be unable to conduct a strategy of offensive denial in which it would go deep into enemy territory as part of its defensive posture.

As can readily be imagined, far less is known about Soviet deployment decisions than about U.S. deployment decisions. Stephen Meyer concluded that based on Soviet military planning literature, military histories, and force structure and deployment data, there was no single Soviet strategy for using nuclear weapons. Just as in the United States, the Soviet military offered policy makers a series of graduated options from which to choose depending upon the circumstances. These options appeared to include preemption, launch on tactical warning, launch under attack, and second strike.

There is evidence of a less than perfect fit between Soviet declaratory and deployment policy. Again, this duplicates the situation in the United States. For example, American policy makers long feared a Soviet surprise attack, and given the emphasis on surprise attack in Soviet thinking, this was logical. Given their alert status it appears that Soviet intercontinental ballistic missiles (ICBMs) were incapable of instigating this type of attack. No Soviet strategic bombers were kept on alert status, and only a small fraction of its submarine-launched ballistic missiles (SLBMs) were available for use. The Soviet civil-defense system required at least one week start-up time if it was to protect Soviet citizens and industrial targets from retaliatory strikes. U.S. INTELLIGENCE GATHERING and early warning systems would have been able to detect changes in the readiness levels in all of these areas, making surprise highly unlikely.

See also ESPIONAGE; INTELLIGENCE; NUCLEAR COMPELLENCE: UNITED STATES; NUCLEAR DETERRENCE STRATEGY: UNITED STATES.

**Further reading:** Allison, Graham, et al., eds. *Hawks, Doves, and Owls.* New York: Norton, 1985; Holloway, David. *The Soviet Union and the Arms Race.* New Haven, Conn.: Yale University Press, 1983; Kolkowicz, Roman, and Ellen Mickiewicz, eds. *The Soviet Calculus of Nuclear War.* Lexington, Mass.: Lexington, 1986. Murray, Douglas, and Paul Viotti. *The Defense Policies of Nations.* Baltimore: Johns Hopkins University Press, 1982.

## nuclear deterrence strategy: United States

Recognition that NUCLEAR WEAPONS were unique and could not be used to fight a war in the manner of traditional weapons came slowly. It was only in the 1950s that nuclear strategy per se came into its own as a field of study, largely due to the efforts of civilian strategists, many of whom worked for the Rand Corporation, an air force THINK TANK. Up until then it was assumed that World War III would follow the pattern of WORLD WAR II: Bombers would deliver their (nuclear) payloads against the enemy's civilian and industrial centers. Since then, U.S. DETERRENCE strategy has not been static but has evolved over time. These changes can best be traced if a distinction is drawn between how U.S. nuclear weapons have been deployed and the rhetoric that has been used to present it to the world. The fit between the two, deployment and declaratory deterrence policy, has often been loose.

The Eisenhower administration was the first to put forward a fully articulated strategy for using nuclear weapons that acknowledged their unique nature. It emphasized deterrence through a declaratory policy of MASSIVE RETALIATION directed at the Soviet Union for acts of Soviet aggression anywhere in the world. The United States had the capability to execute such a threat because of its significant advantage in nuclear weapons. The weakness of this strategy was its lack of credibility. The dual 1957 Soviet successes in launching *SPUTNIK* and an intercontinental ballistic missile called into doubt the merits of massive retaliation since it was now only a matter of time until the United States became vulnerable to a Soviet nuclear threat.

The Kennedy administration replaced massive retaliation with that of flexible response. It was now held that the Soviet Union would be deterred by the knowledge that the United States possessed a wide range of nuclear and non-nuclear options that would allow it to respond effectively to any act of aggression. Nuclear options were envisioned as growing out of a strategy of controlled response, wherein the selection of nuclear targets would be tailored to the political objectives at stake in the conflict. The Johnson administration jettisoned President JOHN KENNEDY's policy, which was based on the idea of limited strategic

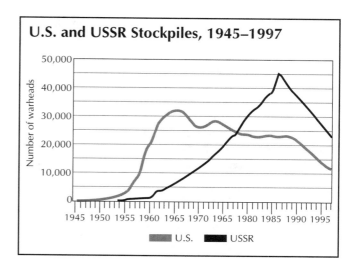

options, with a policy of assured destruction. Once again the United States sought to deter the Soviet Union by threatening to destroy its population and industrial centers. The CUBAN MISSILE CRISIS was largely responsible for this change. It suggested that instead of gradations of nuclear war, there really did exist a firebreak between conventional and nuclear war.

Subsequent changes in U.S. COLD WAR declaratory deterrence policy were largely variations on these themes. President RICHARD NIXON replaced assured destruction with that of flexible targeting, marking a return to an emphasis on controlled nuclear responses. President JIMMY CARTER's countervailing strategy essentially continued Nixon's policy, though it added a very visible reference to the possession of a nuclear war-fighting capacity as part of its set of options. President RONALD REAGAN added to this a damage-limiting dimension and the stated need to be prepared to "endure" and "prevail" in a long nuclear confrontation with the Soviet Union.

The changes chronicled above in U.S. declaratory policy have not always been matched by corresponding changes in U.S. deployment policy. During the cold war the classification of targets remained consistent, as did the inclination to plan for the use of all available nuclear weapons. What changed most was the number of pre-planned options from which policy makers could choose.

During the 1950s, each military command developed plans for using those weapons under its control. In 1956 the Strategic Air Command had selected 2,997 targets. In 1960 the Eisenhower administration approved the creation of a National Strategy Target List (NSTL) and a Single Integrated Operations Plan (SIOP) after war games indicated that more than 300 duplicate targets existed. The first NSTL identified 2,600 separate targets from on overall list of 4,100 targets. Only 151 were urban-industrial targets, with the remainder being classified as military or nuclear capable. Plans called for using all 3,500 warheads if time permitted.

President Kennedy and SECRETARY OF DEFENSE ROBERT MCNAMARA oversaw the construction of SIOP-63. In spite of the switch to flexible response, this SIOP contained a preemptive strike option and had provisions for using all U.S. nuclear weapons. There is no indication that this SIOP was altered when flexible response was replaced by assured destruction. SIOP-6, put forward by Reagan, contained 50,000 potential targets, up from the 25,000 in SIOP-5. The number of targets far outstripped the capacity of the U.S. nuclear arsenal. One official study estimated that if U.S. forces were on alert they could destroy 8,500 targets. If not, the number fell to 5,400.

Post–cold war nuclear deterrence thinking has not yet reached the stage where a new strategic vision has emerged concerning the nature or purpose of U.S. nuclear forces. A largely symbolic change occurred in 1994 when President BILL CLINTON and Soviet president Boris Yeltsin agreed to "detarget" their strategic missiles. In September 1994 the Clinton administration released the results of its "nuclear posture" review that was intended to guide U.S. nuclear thinking until 2003. Its conclusions involved an endorsement of the status quo. Two missions were identified for U.S. strategic forces: counter the Russian strategic threat and serve as a retaliatory force against "hostile and irresponsible" states. The review accepted the STRATEGIC ARMS REDUCTION TREATY (START) II ceiling of 3,500 warheads as a long-term goal but called for pre-

serving the capacity to reconstitute the U.S. nuclear arsenal should Russia emerge as a threat by holding large numbers of nuclear weapons in reserve.

In general terms, a debate now exists in the United States between maximalists, who see a continued need for large and extensive nuclear forces, and minimalists, who hold that large numbers of nuclear weapons are not needed. Maximalists base their position on what they see as the continued existence of threats to U.S. national security. They call for a strategic that is roughly consistent with the logic of limited strategic options, including the possession of a war-fighting capability. Few maximalists want a nuclear force of less than 3,000 warheads, and some argue for as many as 5,000 warheads. Minimalists see the only legitimate purpose of nuclear weapons as one of deterring an attack on the United States itself. An arsenal of less than 3,000 warheads is seen as being sufficient. Some minimalists argue for as few as 100 warheads.

In September 2002 President GEORGE W. BUSH announced a shift away from relying on deterrence to provide for American national security. Arguing that the world had changed since the SEPTEMBER 11, 2001, terrorist attacks on the United States, he advanced a strategy of PREEMPTION in its place.

See also NUCLEAR COMPELLENCE: UNITED STATES; NUCLEAR DETERRENCE STRATEGY: SOVIET UNION; NUCLEAR WAR; RUSSIA.

**Further reading:** Krepon, Michael. *Rethinking the Unthinkable.* New York: Macmillan, 2002; Mandlebaum,

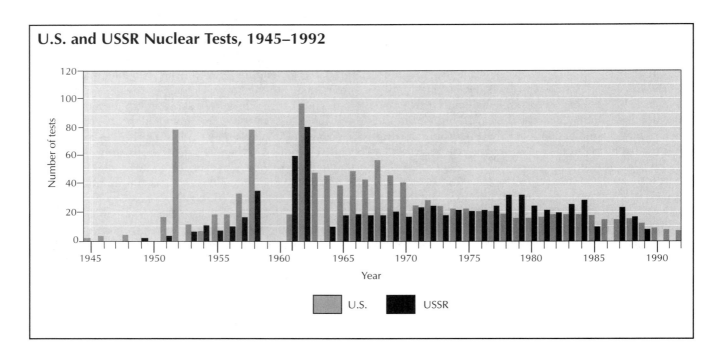

**U.S. and USSR Nuclear Tests, 1945–1992**

Michael. *The Nuclear Question: The United States and Nuclear Weapons, 1946–1976.* Cambridge, Mass.: Cambridge University Press, 1979; Miller, Steven E. *Strategy and Nuclear Deterrence.* Princeton, N.J.: Princeton University Press, 1984; Smoke, Richard. *National Security and the Nuclear Dilemma: An Introduction to the American Experience.* Reading, Mass.: Addison-Wesley, 1984.

## nuclear war

The question of whether or not one can fight and win a nuclear war is one of the most controversial issues of the nuclear age. By all accounts the closest that the United States and the Soviet Union came to nuclear war was the CUBAN MISSILE CRISIS. The Soviet placement of missiles in Cuba was unacceptable to the Kennedy administration, which demanded their removal. One of the options given serious consideration to by Kennedy was an air strike against these missile sites. Participants in these discussions acknowledged that doing so could have set in motion a chain reaction of moves and countermoves that would have quickly escalated to involve nuclear attacks.

U.S. COLD WAR nuclear strategy never embraced officially the pursuit of a first-strike capability, but it has, on occasion, grounded its second-strike strategy on the concept of limited strategic options. According to this deterrence strategy, credibility is best maintained through the possession of an ability to use nuclear weapons in a variety of combat scenarios rather than through the threat of a massive counterstrike. Both the Carter and Reagan administrations spoke of the need to endure and prevail in extended nuclear confrontations with the Soviet Union. General fear of a nuclear war and President RONALD REAGAN's confrontational language toward the Soviet Union energized the PEACE MOVEMENT in the United States and Europe in the 1980s.

Soviet writings on nuclear strategy during the early cold war period were very concerned with a surprise attack as the most probable path to nuclear war. They also seemed convinced that a conventional war in Europe would of necessity escalate into a nuclear confrontation. By the 1970s, with the advent of a rough parity in the two nuclear arsenals, Soviet writings softened on this point, with escalation into a nuclear confrontation now termed probable rather than inevitable. These writings continued to maintain that the best deterrent was a war-fighting capability and that, regardless of the amount of destruction that a nuclear war would unleash, there would be a winner. It was only with Mikhail Gorbachev's New Thinking that Soviet nuclear policy moved away from its emphasis on the achievement of superior numbers and aggressiveness to a position of arms control and restraint.

The destructive potential of a nuclear war is not easily imagined. The uranium bomb dropped on Hiroshima killed 64,000 civilians. During the cold war the combined strategic arsenals of the United States and the Soviet Union contained the destructive potential of approximately 1 million Hiroshimas. To capture more clearly the nature of a nuclear attack, in 1980 the Office of Technology Assessment (OTA) estimated the damage that would be done by dropping a 1-megaton bomb (equivalent to 75 Hiroshimas) on Detroit.

If dropped without warning at the intersection of I-75 and I-90, second- and third-degree burns would occur over an area seven to eight miles from the blast site and ignite clothing up to 13 miles away. If the bombs were detonated at 6,000 feet, the shock wave resulting from the explosion would destroy every structure within a 2.7-mile radius, and from 2.7 to four miles individual residences would be destroyed. Almost no one in the inner 2.7-mile radius who was not in a fallout shelter could survive such a blast. About one-half the population 2.7 to four miles from the blast would be killed, largely as a result of falling buildings and flying debris. The greatest danger for people four to seven miles from the blast site would be the fires that would probably burn for 24 hours and consume one-half of all buildings. Nuclear radiation would also claim large numbers of lives. Severe illness sets in at 200 rems, and an exposure to 600 rems over a six- to seven-day period is fatal to 90 percent of those exposed. A 1-megaton surface blast would expose 1,000 square miles to a total dosage of 900 rems.

The OTA also estimated the casualties that would follow from an attack on key U.S. military-industrial targets, such as command and control facilities; a limited attack on U.S. strategic and nuclear targets; and a full-scale attack on these targets. In the first scenario it was estimated the Soviet Union would use 100 1-megaton bombs. In the last scenario an estimated 2,839 warheads would be used against 1,215 targets, involving a total of 1,342 megatons. The attack on key military-industrial targets was projected as resulting in 3 million to 11 million dead and 23 million to 35 million casualties. The full-scale attack was projected as producing 13 million to 24 million dead and 25 million to 64 million casualties. The wide range of potential outcomes reflect the important role that assumptions make in determining casualties.

General atmospheric effects are also assumed to follow from a nuclear explosion, and they became captured in the phrase NUCLEAR WINTER. These would result from the sunlight-blocking action of the dust particles raised into the atmosphere by a nuclear explosion along with the smoke from the fires that would break out.

With the end of the cold war, fear of calculated actions leading to a nuclear war involving the United States have receded. The dominant concerns now focus on an accidental war involving the Soviet Union that is brought on by a corrosion of its nuclear command and control system and a nuclear war involving second-tier states, such as INDIA

During the atom bomb tests, this house is lit up and then completely destroyed by the nuclear blast, Yucca Flat, Nevada, 1952. *(Hulton/Archive)*

and PAKISTAN. One measure designed to lessen the first possibility is the Nunn-Lugar Bill that provides aid to the Soviet Union to retire its missiles. Global ARMS CONTROL and DISARMAMENT efforts are currently directed at the second possibility.

Since the SEPTEMBER 11, 2001, terrorist attacks, the United States has increasingly become concerned with the possibility that terrorist organizations will obtain access to NUCLEAR WEAPONS. Such organizations could do this in a number of ways. One possibility is by allying themselves with governments pursuing a nuclear capability. NORTH KOREA and IRAN are frequently mentioned in this regard. Another possibility is that terrorists might gain access to nuclear weapons or production facilities thought to be secure. Should they succeed in these efforts, they would possess an independent nuclear capability.

See also NUCLEAR COMPELLENCE: UNITED STATES; NUCLEAR DETERRENCE STRATEGY: UNITED STATES; NUCLEAR DETERRENCE STRATEGY: SOVIET UNION.

**Further reading:** Harvard Study Group. *Living with Nuclear Weapons.* New York: Bantam, 1983; Office of Technology Assessment. *The Effects of Nuclear War.* Montclair, N.J.: Allanheld, Osmun, 1980; Schroeer, Dietrich. *Science, Technology and the Nuclear Arms Race.* New York: Wiley & Sons, 1981.

## nuclear weapons arsenals

Nuclear weapons are not interchangeable. Differences in such areas as accuracy, payload, speed, vulnerability, and control make them suitable for some military purposes and disqualify them for others. Traditionally, nuclear weapons have been grouped into three categories: strategic, theater, and battlefield. Strategic nuclear weapons have been most

crucial to the development of U.S. DETERRENCE policy and the COLD WAR competition between the United States and SOVIET UNION. They have also been the primary concern of those seeking to control the global proliferation of nuclear weapons.

The table on the opposite page presents an overview of the world's nuclear arsenal. It shows that there are eight acknowledged nuclear powers today. All but ISRAEL admit to possessing nuclear weapons. The U.S. and Soviet Union have the largest arsenals, while INDIA and PAKISTAN possess the smallest. More than 30,000 warheads were believed to exist in 2000. This is down from the peak year of 1986, when nearly 70,000 warheads were in the combined inventories of the five nuclear powers. All totaled, an estimated 128,000 nuclear warheads were built between 1945 and 2000.

A close look at the U.S. and Soviet strategic arsenals during the cold war shows that they were not identical in makeup. Strategic nuclear weapons are most readily distinguished from one another by their delivery systems. Manned bombers are the original delivery system of the nuclear age. They have been joined by land-based intercontinental ballistic missiles (ICBMs) and submarine-launched ballistic missiles (SLBMs). Throughout the cold war the United States and Soviet Union had different mixes of these nuclear weapons systems, with the United States having a relatively equal reliance on all three legs of the "nuclear triad" and the Soviet Union relying most heavily upon ICBMs.

Each of these three strategic nuclear weapons systems has their own advantages and disadvantages. Foremost among the advantages of the manned bomber is its ability to carry large payloads and deliver them with great accuracy. It can also be recalled or have its destination altered after it has been dispatched to its target. On the negative side, bombers have a long flight time, which gives the enemy ample warning, and they are highly vulnerable to prelaunch attack, although steps can easily be taken to improve their survivability through dispersal, stealth technology, and other measures.

ICBMs have the advantage of being highly accurate and the fastest reacting leg of the triad. Early generations of ICBMs were powered by liquid fuel that was stored separately from the missile and contained one warhead. Today, they are propelled by solid or storable liquid fuel, giving them launch times of one to two minutes. It takes an ICBM approximately 30 minutes to fly 7,000 miles, dramatically reducing the warning time available to an enemy. ICBMs are now fitted with multiple independently targeted reentry warheads or vehicles (MIRVs) that permit one missile to launch warheads against different targets. The U.S. MX and Soviet SS-18 are capable of carrying 10 warheads. The accuracy of ICBMs is now so great that no amount of hardening missile silos can effectively guarantee their survival in case of an attack. Circular error probability (CEP) is the measure of missile accuracy. It represents the radius of a circle within which 50 percent of the warheads fired at a target will fall. The MX has a CEP of 300 to 400 feet. Recognizing the practical difficulties of defending a fixed missile site from attack, both the United States and the Soviet Union began to deploy mobile ICBMs.

Early SLBMs were greatly limited in range and were fairly inaccurate. The newest generation of SLBMs have overcome both of these limitations. The Trident II has a CEP of 400 feet and a range of 4,000 to 6,000 miles. U.S. Poseidon submarines carry 16 missiles that are equipped with 10 to 14 warheads. SLBMs are valued for their invulnerability. This very invulnerability also creates command and control problems. The tight control that can be exercised over manned bombers is not possible with submarines due to the need for secrecy and the difficulty that radio waves have in penetrating the ocean.

One of the great controversies of the nuclear age is the cost of the cold war nuclear arsenal. At issue are not only the total cost of these weapons and their support systems but also what other societal goals went unfunded in the name of national security. The U.S. Nuclear Weapons Cost Study Project has put the U.S. price tag at $4 trillion. It estimated that the cost of building the bomb, including uranium enrichment plants, reactors, and laboratories, was $375 billion. The cost of delivering the bomb was estimated to be $2 trillion. Building the command and control systems for nuclear operations, including spy satellites and warning systems, was estimated to have cost $368 billion. Initiatives designed to provide defense against the bomb such as President RONALD REAGAN's STRATEGIC DEFENSE INITIATIVE (SDI), cost $368 billion. Finally, the project esti-

| Country | Suspected Strategic Nuclear Weapons | Suspected Nonstrategic Nuclear Weapons | Suspected Nuclear Weapons |
|---|---|---|---|
| China | 250 | 150 | **400** |
| France | 350 | 0 | **350** |
| India | 60 | ? | **60+?** |
| Israel | 100–200 | ? | **200+?** |
| Pakistan | 24–48 | ? | **48+?** |
| Russia | ~6,000 | ~4,000 | **~10,000** |
| United Kingdom | 180 | 5 | **185** |
| United States | 8,646 | 2,010 | **10,656** |

### WORLD'S NUCLEAR ARSENALS

*Center for Defense Information, 2003*

mated that $15 billion has been spent on dismantling warheads and storing surplus fissionable material.

The size of the U.S. and Soviet nuclear arsenals has declined markedly since the end of the cold war. With the ratification of the STRATEGIC ARMS REDUCTION TREATY (START) II by the Russian Duma in 2000, the active strategic arsenals of the two states is reduced to between 3,000 and 3,500 warheads. This is down from the 6,000 agreed to under START I. President GEORGE W. BUSH and Russian president Vladimir Putin negotiated another substantial reduction in the size of the two nuclear arsenals in 2002. They agreed to a nuclear force no larger than 2,200 deployed warheads by December 31, 2012. The inability of the Russian economy to support a nuclear arsenal any larger than this was a prime factor in prompting the agreement.

The nuclear inventories of the other nuclear powers were left unaffected by the START process. Still, the Chinese, British, and French nuclear forces all declined in size during the 1990s. To their numbers must now be added Pakistani and Indian nuclear weapons.

In May 2003 President GEORGE W. BUSH announced that the United States would pursue the development of a new generation of battlefield nuclear weapons. Movement forward in this direction would reverse a 1993 ban on the development of low-yield nuclear weapons. In addition to building low-yield bombs whose explosive power was 5 kilotons or less, the administration planned to build a high-yield "bunker buster" bomb.

**Further reading:** Sagan, Scott, and Kenneth Waltz. *The Spread of Nuclear Weapons: A Debate Renewed.* New York: Norton, 2003; Trachenberg, Marc. *History and Strategy.* Princeton, N.J.: Princeton University Press, 1991.

## nuclear winter

First advanced in 1983 by a team of scientists, the concept of a nuclear winter added a new dimension to the destructive potential of NUCLEAR WEAPONS and the need for ARMS CONTROL. Up until this, studies of NUCLEAR WAR had focused on the immediate and short-term consequences of nuclear explosions. Emerging from the TTAPS study, so named after the initials of the last names of its authors, the concept pointed to the long-term atmospheric and climatic consequences of even the limited use of NUCLEAR WEAPONS. In doing so it helped move the nuclear debate out of the closed circle of military and strategic professionals, often referred to as the "nuclear priesthood," who spoke in the neutral language of DETERRENCE, and involved large portions of the American public who found the concept of nuclear war frightening.

The concept of nuclear winter was politically charged because in the early 1980s the COLD WAR between the United States and the Soviet Union heated up. A central theme of President RONALD REAGAN's foreign policy was the need to beef up U.S. nuclear forces. This was necessary, he argued, in order to close the "window of opportunity" that had risen. His concern was that continued Soviet nuclear expansion coupled with American restraint had created a situation in which the Soviet Union might engage in nuclear blackmail against the United States. Reagan also spoke openly of the need to possess a nuclear war fighting ability. Arms control was placed on hold until a more equal military footing had been established.

The TTAPS study identified four effects that would follow after the conclusion of a nuclear war that would produce long-term negative global environmental consequences: (1) obscuring smoke in the atmosphere, (2) obscuring dust in the stratosphere, (3) the fallout of radioactive debris, and (4) the partial destruction of the ozone layer. Together these four effects would produce severe and prolonged low temperatures—a nuclear winter.

The potential for even small temperature changes to have significant environmental impacts has long been suspected. It is speculated that the 1815 explosion of the Tambora volcano in Indonesia produced a global temperature drop of less than 1 degree centigrade. The following year brought hard freezes in Europe and North America that led 1816 to be referred to as "the year without a summer" in Europe and "eighteen-hundred and froze to death" in the United States. A 1-degree centigrade drop in temperature is sufficient to eliminate wheat growing in Canada. In March 1982 the El Chacon volcano erupted in Mexico. As a result the intensity of sunlight in Hawaii was reduced by 21 percent and the intensity of the solar noon was reduced by 15 to 20 percent in Boulder, Colorado, in November.

The TTAPS study examined several dozen different nuclear war scenarios in order to better understand the climatic impact of nuclear weapons ranging in magnitude from a small low-yield attack carried out only against cities to a massive nuclear confrontation involving 75 percent of the world's nuclear arsenal. In cases where more than 10,000 nuclear warheads were used, the full recovery time to ordinary daylight was more than one year. Under conditions of an attack in which 1,000 nuclear explosions took place, normal temperatures are regained after 100 days. A severe counterforce attack was projected as involving the detonation of 700 nuclear explosions and an unleashing of a total of 5,000 megatons of explosives. For the latter case, it is estimated that land temperature would not return to the freezing point for at least one year.

Carl Sagan was the primary spokesperson for the TTAPS report. In 1983 Paul Ehrlich and another group of scientists examined the biological consequences of nuclear war. They focused their study on one scenario, a 10,000-megaton attack. Ehrlich noted that both cold and dark, two of the principal consequences identified in the TTAPS report, are inimical to green plants and photosynthesis. His study concluded that virtually all land plants in the Northern Hemisphere would be killed or destroyed if the war occurred just before or during growing season. If the attack occurred in fall or winter the consequences would be felt in the next growing season.

Destruction of the ozone layer would permit more ultraviolet light to penetrate into the atmosphere. One response that plants have to additional amounts of ultraviolet light is to reduce photosynthesis. Many animals would die of cold, starvation, or thirst due to the freezing of surface water. Plants in the tropics would not be totally spared. Large-scale injury could result due to reduced temperatures and daylight. Aquatic life would also be threatened due to decreases in oxygen and the absence of daylight for photosynthesis. Erhlich's group concluded pessimistically, "[U]nder these conditions, we could not exclude the possibility that the scattered survivors would not be able to rebuild their populations."

See also NUCLEAR COMPELLENCE: UNITED STATES; NUCLEAR DETERRENCE STRATEGY: UNITED STATES; NUCLEAR DETERRENCE STRATEGY: SOVIET UNION.

**Further reading:** Ehrlich, Paul, et al. *The Cold and the Dark: The World after Nuclear War.* New York: Norton, 1984.

## Nye Committee

The Nye Committee is famous for popularizing the notion that the American entry into WORLD WAR I was the result of conspiratorial efforts by the business community and arms manufacturers. Its public hearings and report played a major role in stimulating support for the NEUTRALITY LEG-

ISLATION of the 1930s. In broader perspective, the Nye Committee's perspective on world politics reflects a reoccurring theme in U.S. foreign-policy making that elites are working behind the scenes to steer U.S. foreign policy in directions that are inconsistent with the broader American NATIONAL INTEREST.

Gerald Nye served as a Republican senator from North Dakota from 1925 to 1944. He served as chair of the Senate committee investigating the munitions industry from 1934 to 1936. Nye was a strong supporter of agrarian interests and was convinced that business interests were directing U.S. foreign policy at the expense of farmers. The springboard for Nye's investigation was an article published in the March 1934 issue of *Fortune*. It asserted that large profits in the trade in weapons had incited war. That same year arms manufacturers were characterized as "merchants of death" in a widely read book.

Months of investigations produced evidence of huge profits by arms manufacturers and bankers. Carried out in the midst of the Great Depression, the Nye Committee's findings resonated well with the American public who, according to PUBLIC OPINION polls, now considered intervention into World War I to be a mistake.

Two general conclusions seemed to follow from the Nye Committee's work. First, ISOLATIONISM and not INTERNATIONALISM was the proper foreign-policy orientation for the United States. Second, to stay on an isolationist course required limiting the foreign-policy powers of the PRESIDENT. To that end Nye worked with other isolationist senators, including Arthur Vandenburg, to pass neutrality legislation in the mid-1930s. Vandenburg would abandon his isolationism with the Japanese attack on Pearl Harbor and become a leading proponent of post–WORLD WAR II internationalism. Nye supported going to war against JAPAN but remained isolationist in outlook and was defeated in his 1944 reelection bid.

Viewed in a more general context, the Nye Committee's conclusion that behind-the-scenes manipulation by business interests was the primary moving force behind U.S. foreign policy is a recurrent theme in academic and popular studies of U.S. foreign policy. In the 1960s the radical-revisionist school of U.S. foreign policy placed U.S. business interests at the heart of U.S. foreign policy toward Latin America and the South more generally. During JIMMY CARTER's administration opponents, invoking an ELITE-THEORY perspective, cited the presence of many members of the Trilateral Commission. In RONALD REAGAN's administration it was the presence of members of the Committee on the Present Danger that drew concern.

See also MILITARY-INDUSTRIAL COMPLEX.

## Office of Strategic Services (OSS)

The Office of Strategic Services (OSS) was the forerunner of the CENTRAL INTELLIGENCE AGENCY (CIA). Prior to its creation, a U.S. INTELLIGENCE service as such barely existed. No separate intelligence agency existed within the STATE DEPARTMENT. In 1922 it had only five employees classified as having intelligence responsibilities. In 1943 still only 18 FOREIGN-SERVICE OFFICERS were its main source of intelligence. The army and navy were only marginally better. In the 1930s naval intelligence employed only 20 permanent civilian employees. The army was limited by congressional mandate to having no more than 32 military attachés. The focus of intelligence work was on preventing subversive acts rather than on anticipating enemy actions. The only active nonmilitary force in U.S. intelligence in the interwar years was the FEDERAL BUREAU OF INVESTIGATION (FBI) under J. Edgar Hoover.

The driving force behind the OSS was William J. "Wild Bill" Donovan. His thinking about the purposes of an intelligence organization and how it should be organized was heavily influenced by the British. Keenly aware of the need to coordinate defense efforts with United States in anticipation of WORLD WAR II, the British government and British intelligence made a concentrated effort to forge links with the United States. As noted above, the problem they encountered was the absence of any type of centralized intelligence service with which to partner. Initially the FBI was seen as the most logical partner, but Hoover's personal ambitions and penchant for publicity led GREAT BRITAIN to explore an alternative channel.

Donovan became that channel. He toured Europe in 1940 at the invitation of Prime Minister Winston Churchill as President FRANKLIN ROOSEVELT's personal representative and was coached on intelligence matters by William Stephenson, who was a key British intelligence officer operating out New York City. Donovan came to embrace the British notion of a centralized intelligence service responsible for ESPIONAGE, INTELLIGENCE GATHERING analysis, and subversive operations. Hoover opposed the creation of such an agency out of fear that it would lead to a diminished role for the FBI in intelligence matters. Adolf Hitler's June 22, 1941, invasion of the Soviet Union put an end to this bureaucratic turf struggle as President Roosevelt endorsed Donovan's vision of a centralized intelligence agency and by executive order established the Office of Coordinator of Information. Donovan was named coordinator. A year later this office was renamed the OSS and placed under the jurisdiction of the JOINT CHIEFS OF STAFF.

The OSS was divided into several different functional branches. The Research and Analysis branch carried out economic, political, and social analyses. The Secret Intelligence branch carried out clandestine collection activities. The Special Operations branch carried out sabotage and worked with resistance forces. The Counterespionage branch was charged with protecting American intelligence operations from enemy penetrations. The Morale Operations branch engaged in propaganda activities. The Operational group conducted GUERRILLA WARFARE and COVERT-ACTION operations in enemy territory, and the Maritime Unit conducted maritime sabotage operations.

The OSS was a high-energy organization that was able to recruit an impressive array of talent. It also encountered fierce bureaucratic opposition. The FBI was able to largely keep the OSS out of Latin America, and General DOUGLAS MACARTHUR excluded the OSS from CHINA. The military did not cooperate fully in sharing intelligence sources and material for analytic purposes.

At the end of World War II Donovan proposed to President HARRY TRUMAN that the OSS be maintained and serve as a peacetime intelligence organization. Truman disagreed, and in 1945 he disbanded the OSS. Its various functions were distributed among existing intelligence organizations. For example, the Research and Analysis branch went to the State Department, and the Secret Intelligence branch and Counterespionage branch were transferred to the War Department. A centralized intelligence service would be reborn in 1947 with the passage of the NATIONAL SECURITY ACT that created the CIA.

See also COUNTERINTELLIGENCE; RUSSIA.

**Further reading:** Troy, Thomas F. *Wild Bill and Intrepid: Donovan, Stephenson, and the Origins of the CIA.* New Haven, Conn.: Yale University Press, 1996.

## oil

In his National Energy Policy released on May 17, 2001, President GEORGE W. BUSH identified dependency on foreign oil as threat to American national security. Domestic oil production peaked in the United States in 1971. By 1966 the United States had moved from being a leading exporter of oil to an importer of one-half of its oil. In 2000 CANADA was the leading source of imported oil for the United States, providing 1,648,000 barrels of oil per day. It was followed, in order, by VENEZUELA (1,480,000), SAUDI ARABIA (1,452,000), MEXICO (1,329,000), and NIGERIA (777,000). Studies suggest that the American demand for oil will increase by 20 percent by 2015.

The link between oil and national security is not new, but it has taken on new urgency in the minds of many by the SEPTEMBER 11, 2001, terrorist attacks in the United States. A closer examination shows that protecting access to foreign deposits of oil and maintaining stable prices has been a recurring objective of American foreign policy. It was an important concern for the United States and its enemies in both world wars. During the COLD WAR international oil politics were typically overshadowed by the global geostrategic military conflict between the United States and the Soviet Union. Only occasionally, such as with the 1973 oil crisis, did the international politics of oil command top billing. By the time the crisis had passed, the price of oil had quadrupled.

This may be changing. Many commentators on world politics believe that the struggle to control natural resources will become the central battleground of post–cold war international relations. Concerns over the amount and price of oil were cited by President GEORGE H. W. BUSH as a rationale for the PERSIAN GULF WAR, which some commentators refer to as the First Oil War. During that war the price of oil surged to $40 per barrel. These same concerns have also been cited as a reason why the GEORGE W. BUSH administration appeared so determined to go to war with IRAQ in 2002. Iraq has an estimated 112 billion barrels of proven oil reserves that place it second only to Saudi Arabia, with 262 billion barrels of proven reserves the richest of oil states. Even though the U.S. dependence on oil from the Middle East is falling, from 34 percent in 1977 to 26 percent in 2000, Middle Eastern oil is still vitally important to the United States because of Europe and JAPAN's dependence

on it. The continued American vulnerability to foreign oils shocks was also evident in late 2002–early 2003 when a political crisis in Venezuela led to strikes and a drastic curtailment in the flow of oil out of that country. A price hike was quickly felt in the United States. It should also be noted that while a far cry from the dependence level of the 1970s, the 2002 level of Middle East oil dependence is more than double what it was in the mid-1980s.

Controlling natural resources has both political and economic dimensions. Politically it entails creating domestic governmental and regional stability so that access to these natural resources can be secured. But access is not all that is required. Secure and affordable transportation systems must be developed, and in some cases processing or refining operations must be created. This dramatically increases the number of states that importing countries must be concerned with. For example, oil from the Caspian Sea is identified by many as the next great source of oil. Obtaining oil from the Caspian Sea will require at a minimum paying attention to the political situation in Armenia, Azerbaijan, Georgia, IRAN, Kazakhstan, Kyrgyzstan, RUSSIA, Tajikistan, Turkmenistan, and Uzbekistan. A similarly long list of states can be drawn up in AFRICA, where the Bush administration identified NIGERIA and ANGOLA as important sources of additional oil for the United States.

A second political dimension involves a triangular relationship between the host state where the natural resource is located, the MULTINATIONAL CORPORATIONS (MNCs) that are engaged in exploration, production, and distribution, and the home state of those MNCs. The distribution of political POWER in this relationship changes over time. Initially it is the MNC that is most powerful. They possess the skills and financial resources to find and extract the natural resource. The host government needs them and can offer little except future and potential profits. Historically the major oil companies, known as the seven sisters (Mobil, Texaco, Gulf, Chevron, Exxon, Royal Dutch Shell, and British Petroleum) organized themselves as vertically integrated corporations to ensure the smooth transfer of oil from drilling to marketing. This not only provided for economies of scale, but it also boosted their leverage with host states. The seven sisters also entered into agreements among themselves to protect their interests at the expense of others. The 1928 Red Line agreement established the principle of joint production of Middle East oil and the exclusion of independent oil firms from the region. The Achnacarry agreement provided worldwide production limits along with marketing and price formulas that were intended to keep their profits high.

Once in place, however, the host government now has the advantage since the MNC cannot simply pick up and go somewhere else as would be the case with a manufacturing firm. It must remain where the natural resource is and accept lower profits. And, in the case of oil production, it must accept the entry of independent oil firms into these states. This transition in bargaining power was slow to come in the oil industry because of the domineering diplomatic and military position that GREAT BRITAIN and then the United States played in Middle Eastern politics. Bringing in and pressuring less economically powerful and nonvertically integrated oil companies was a key move made by radical Arab leaders, such as LIBYA's Muammar al-Qaddafi plan in 1969 to break the power of the seven sisters.

As ELITE THEORY and the revisionist interpretation of American foreign policy argue, the home governments of the MNC have often intervened into the affairs of the host state in order to protect these firms. The CENTRAL INTELLIGENCE AGENCY's COVERT ACTION to bring down the government of Mohammad Mossadegh in Iran and restore the shah to power is a case in point. The American involvement in the Mexican Revolution was also heavily influenced by the discovery of oil and threats of nationalization by the Mexican government. Often, client governments have been established in these states to ensure the needed stability. However, in the process these governments have tended

to become corrupt and brutal, laying the foundation for revolution. In this changing political environment, MNCs have demonstrated strong survival instincts. In 1973, for example, the oil companies became compliant partners with the oil-producing states to restrict the flow of oil to the United States and raise prices.

A third political dimension to the international politics of oil centers on the relations between the oil-producing countries. Historically, the core group of oil production is found in the ORGANIZATION OF PETROLEUM EXPORTING COUNTRIES (OPEC). This body was founded in 1960 by Iran, Iraq, KUWAIT, Saudi Arabia, and Venezuela. It was OPEC that succeeded in redirecting profits from the MNCs to the national economies of the producing states. It was OPEC that succeeded in bringing about the dramatic increase in the price of oil following the 1973 Arab-Israeli War. Its success sparked fears of a world of OPECs in which resource cartels would dictate terms to the industrialized states of the North. Oil proved to be the exception rather than the rule, and cartels in other materials could not match their success. In fact, since the late 1970s when the revolution in Iran produced another spike in the price of oil,

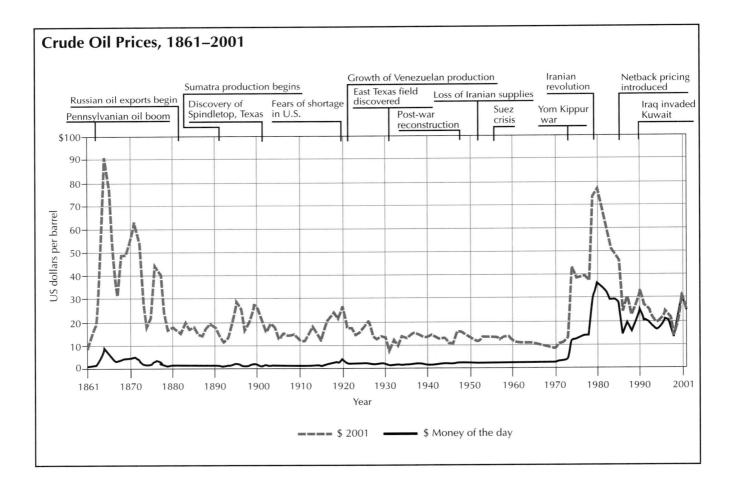

**Crude Oil Prices, 1861–2001**

OPEC has struggled to keep prices high. At that time the price of oil climbed to $34 per barrel. In 1985–86 the price of oil fell from $31 per barrel to $10 per barrel. It has been beset by internal problems, such as that between Iraq and other OPEC states following the IRAN-IRAQ WAR that led to its invasion of Kuwait, and the inability to convince non-OPEC states, such as Russia, to curtail their production. In terms of production, in 2000 the Arab members of OPEC produced 2,209,00 barrels of oil per day. The other members of OPEC produced 2,501,000 barrels per day, and non-OPEC members produced 5,799,000 barrels of oil daily.

From an economic perspective the situation is also complex. Popular fears center on running out of natural resources. This is a theoretical and practical concern for nonrenewable natural resources, such as oil, but not for renewable natural resources, such as grains. The more pressing concern, however, is not running out of oil but the rising price of oil when production peaks and scarcity becomes more pronounced. As we have seen with earlier rapid upswings in the price of oil, the impact is slowed economic growth, increased national indebtedness, global financial turbulence, and political instability. When, and if, this point is reached is a matter of debate. The center of the controversy concerns the ability of technological breakthroughs to alter the economics of oil and other natural resources through the development of substitutes and improving efficiency. The warring sides can be described as technological optimists and technological pessimists.

In looking to the future a number of strategies have been suggested for dealing with America's oil dependency. First, the United States can increase its strategic reserve. In 2002 it held a 60-day supply of oil, or 544 million barrels. Second, the United States can try to diversify imports. Such a policy potentially brings the U.S. government and MNCs into conflict. MNCs will be driven by cost and profit considerations. The United States will be interested in stability of supply. Third, the United States can increase domestic drilling. Energy demands increased by 17 percent in the 1990s, but domestic production increased by only 2 percent. At issue here is the environmental impact of this policy. A fourth option is to increase energy efficiency. In 2002 sports utility vehicles (SUVs) had the lowest gas mileage since 1980. One estimate suggests that changing SUVs to meet the current mileage standard for cars would save a million barrels of oil per day.

Considerations about the supply and price of oil played prominent roles in the debate over the IRAQ WAR. Many commentators held that it was access to Iraqi oil that motivated President GEORGE W. BUSH to invade Iraq and not its possession of WEAPONS OF MASS DESTRUCTION. During the war great fears were expressed that Saddam Hussein might order the destruction of Iraqi oil fields, thus throwing international oil markets into chaos and creating dangerous conditions on the battlefield. This did not happen to any large extent. After the war control over Iraq's oil became a topic of international controversy. The UNITED NATIONS had permitted the limited sale of Iraqi oil on international markets while its ECONOMIC SANCTIONS were in place. The purpose of these sales was to allow Iraq to purchase foodstuffs. After the war the United States sought and obtained control over Iraqi oil to help finance the country's reconstruction. RUSSIA and FRANCE opposed the high degree of control the United States obtained, preferring international control. Russia also sought to ensure that Iraqi oil revenues would be used to pay off existing contracts. The American plan approved by the United Nations provided Iraqi oil with protection from claims by foreign governments until 2007. Russia and France reluctantly supported the UN resolution.

A further complicating factor in the oil situation is the status of the Kurds in northern Iraq. As a result of the war the Kurds gained access to important Iraqi oil and mineral resources in northern Iraq. For the Kurds, who long wished to establish an independent state, this was a significant accomplishment. It also frightened TURKEY and other states in the region that had large Kurdish minorities.

**Further reading:** Adekman, M. A. *The Genie Out of the Bottle, World Oil since 1970.* Cambridge, Mass.: MIT Press, 1995; Klare, Michael. *Resource Wars: The New Landscape of Global Conflict.* New York: Henry Holt, 2001; Yergin, Daniel. *The Prize: The Epic Quest for Oil, Money and Power.* New York: Simon and Schuster, 1991.

## Olney, Richard (1835–1917) *secretary of state*

Richard Olney served as attorney general from 1893 to 1895 and SECRETARY OF STATE from 1895 to 1897. During this period of time he entered into important diplomatic discussions involving CUBA, HAWAII, and VENEZUELA's BOUNDARY DISPUTE with Great Britain. Olney is best remembered for his blunt statement, known as the Olney Corollary to the MONROE DOCTRINE, which was directed to GREAT BRITAIN and claimed American hegemony in Latin America.

As secretary of state Olney inherited a long-standing conflict between Venezuela and Great Britain over Venezuela's boundary with British Guiana. Venezuela had long sought but failed to enlist American support for its cause. This changed with the GROVER CLEVELAND administration. President Grover Cleveland decided to support Venezuela and instructed Olney to implement that policy. Olney did so with characteristic bluntness. In a memorandum approved by Cleveland and sent to London on July 20, 1895, Olney stated that Great Britain had violated the Monroe Doctrine in its border dispute with Venezuela. He claimed that the United States possessed virtually hegemonic or unlimited power in Latin America because "its infinite resources combined with its isolated position render it [the United States] master of the situation and practically invulnerable as against any powers." He continued, "[T]he United States is practically sovereign on this continent and its fiat is law upon the subjects to which it confines its interpretation."

The British response was four months in coming and just as hostile in tone. In it, the British government rejected the legitimacy of the Monroe Doctrine: "The United States is not entitled to affirm as a universal proposition . . . that its interests are necessarily concerned in whatever may befall those states simply because they are situation in the Western Hemisphere." Tensions rose and then fell as the United States and Great Britain worked out an agreement to end the boundary crisis. A key step in this process was Britain's recognition of the legitimacy of the Monroe Doctrine by accepting the legitimacy of America's interest in the boundary dispute. In November 1896 Olney and British minister to the United States Julian Pauncefote agreed on a procedure for settling the matter based on arbitration. Interestingly, Venezuela was not a party to these deliberations.

Venezuela was not the only Latin American problem Olney would confront. He and the Cleveland administration also faced important decisions over Cuba. Revolution broke out in Cuba in 1895. By 1896 rebel forces controlled almost two-thirds of the island. SPAIN then sent General Valeriano Weyler y Nicolau to Cuba. His brutal methods prevented a rebel victory but in the process destroyed much of Cuba's society and economy. The Cleveland administration sought to navigate its way through the revolution in Cuba by neither recognizing Cuban independence nor granting Cuban belligerency status. Olney urged that Spain continue to exercise it sovereignty over Cuba but grant it the rights and powers of local self-government. Spain rejected Olney's effort at mediation, and the problem of how to deal with Cuba continued to fester for the remainder of Cleveland's presidency.

Earlier, as attorney general, Olney had been equally blunt in his handling of a crisis in Hawaii. Pressures for annexation had been building, and when the Cleveland administration came into office a treaty of annexation was before CONGRESS. Cleveland withdrew the treaty and sent James Blount to Hawaii to examine the events leading to the uprising that deposed Queen Liliuokalani. Cleveland was inclined to return the queen to power. Olney vehemently opposed sending U.S. military forces to Hawaii for this purpose, asserting that "the United States had no right to redeem the original wrong." Cleveland came to agree with Olney and turned the matter over to Congress.

**Further reading:** Eggert, Gerald G. *Richard Olney*. University Park: Pennsylvania State University Press, 1974.

## Open Door policy

The Open Door policy defined the U.S. relationship with CHINA at the turn of the 20th century. It represented an attempt on the part of the United States to involve itself in world affairs without becoming entangled in ALLIANCES. The roots of the Open Door policy can be traced to colonial America and the nascent belief in the virtues of free trade and noninvolvement in the affairs of other states. These principles were applied to China in the mid-1840s as U.S. economic interests expanded into Asia. In 1842, at the conclusion of the Opium War, U.S. warships visited China and requested that the United States be granted treatment equal to that of European states with regard to commerce. The following year China opened an additional five treaty ports to Western states under the principle of equal, or MOST-FAVORED-NATION, treatment. That same year Caleb Cushing arrived in China as the first American commissioner. He was supported by a fleet of four warships. His mission was to obtain trading privileges equal to those enjoyed by the British. He succeeded in 1844 with the signing of the Treaty of Wanghia (Wangxia).

In the period following the signing of Cushing's treaty, American trade with China grew considerably. Internal violence within China also grew. One particularly bloody episode was the Taiping Rebellion, which lasted from 1850 to 1864 and claimed 20 million lives. The United States was inclined to support the Chinese government against its challengers because it was primarily interested in commerce and feared that a weakened China would be carved up by European powers. Concerns about Chinese weakness became especially pronounced following China's poor performance in the Sino-Japanese War of 1894. GREAT BRITAIN was also alarmed, and in 1898 and 1899 approached the United States about a joint declaration to ensure free and open trade in China. Both times the United States demurred because of its concern for involvement with foreign states.

Consistent with its preference for UNILATERALISM, SECRETARY OF STATE JOHN HAY issued a statement on his own, dated September 6, 1899, that was directed to GERMANY, RUSSIA, ITALY, JAPAN, FRANCE, and Great Britain. Known as the first Open Door note, it requested that each of these states pledge that they would not interfere with "vested interests" within their spheres of influence. While not all of the replies were fully supportive, Hay declared that they were, and on March 20, 1900, declared that their assent was "final and definitive." The first Open Door note was not legally binding on other states and required little of them. Even its limited objectives were soon threatened, however, by the outbreak of the Boxer Rebellion, which endangered Western economic holdings in China.

Hay now put forward a corollary to his first Open Door. He announced that it was the policy of the United States to "preserve Chinese territorial and administrative integrity" as well as safeguard the principle of free trade. Hay did not request that other states respond to this pronouncement. It was simply put forward as American policy in China. While Hay's position was widely supported in the press, it could not be enforced. No state openly challenged Hay's policy, but political dynamics in the region worked against it. If unchecked, the growing strength of Russia and Japan threatened to replace free trade with imperial dominance. The two states went to war in 1905, and President THEODORE ROOSEVELT mediated an agreement between the two.

One side product of Roosevelt's diplomatic efforts was an agreement with Japan in which the United States recognized Japan's domination of Korea in return for a Japanese pledge of noninterference in the PHILIPPINES. In effect this put a closed door in place in Korea and strengthened American domination of the Philippines. In 1905 Japan and the United States reaffirmed the open door in China with the Root-Takahira Executive Agreement of November 30, 1908. The agreement was negotiated without consulting China, and many feared that rather than fortifying Chinese sovereignty it only weakened it by de facto recognizing the growing domination of Chinese affairs by Japan. And, in fact, it was Japan's growing influence in China that led to the collapse of the Open Door policy with the issuance of the Twenty-one Demands in 1915.

## Open Skies

DISARMAMENT proposals dominated U.S.-Soviet nuclear weapons negotiations in the first decade after the end of WORLD WAR I. Typically, they involved plans to do away with NUCLEAR WEAPONS or, as with the BARUCH PLAN, place them under international control. President DWIGHT EISENHOWER's Open Skies proposal reflects a change in thinking that is much more consistent with the spirit of ARMS CONTROLs that would guide U.S.-Soviet nuclear negotiations in the 1960s and early 1970s. Whereas disarmament focuses on reducing or eliminating the number of weapons in existence, arms control is concerned with placing restraints on the use of force.

Eisenhower made his Open Skies proposal at the Four Power Geneva Summit Conference in July 1955. The development of intercontinental ballistic missiles (ICBMs) introduced a new element into the strategic equation. First-generation ICBMs were highly vulnerable and slow-reacting weapons that were incapable of being recalled. They created a "reciprocal fear of surprise attack." The Open Skies attempted to reduce the risk of a surprise attack by (1) exchanging blueprints on all military forces and installations, (2) permitting verification through aerial reconnaissance, and (3) reinforcing aerial reconnaissance with a system of onsite inspection.

Analysts are uncertain over the true purposes behind the Open Skies proposal. Some see it largely as an exercise in COLD WAR propaganda because there was little doubt that the Soviet Union (see RUSSIA) would reject the proposal. As recently as May 1955 the Soviet Union had made clear that in their view American disarmament had to precede any verification system. A second interpretation asserts that Eisenhower was personally committed to reducing the dangers of NUCLEAR WAR and furthering U.S.-Soviet cooperation. They note that Eisenhower made his Open Skies proposal over the objections of his staunchly anticommunist SECRETARY OF STATE JOHN FOSTER DULLES. Finally, a third interpretation maintains that Eisenhower's true motives in putting forward the Open Skies proposal was to legalize aerial reconnaissance. While not an immediate concern to the United States, this was important because of the U-2 spy plane that the United States relied upon for information about Soviet missile developments. At the time the Open Skies proposal was put forward, the Soviet Union did not have the capability of shooting down a U-2. This would change, and the United States wanted to have overflight rights established so as not to be charged with ESPIONAGE and violating Soviet airspace.

The Soviet Union rejected the Open Skies proposal. General Secretary Nikita Khrushchev called it "nothing more than a bald espionage plot." The Soviets also objected to the plan because it did not include provisions for aerial reconnaissance over other countries, it did not provide for arms reductions, and it would not prevent the concealment of military forces.

Over the next few years events overtook the Open Skies proposal. In 1957 the Soviet Union launched *SPUTNIK* into orbit around the Earth. This added a whole new dimension to the question of national control over air space. In 1960 the Soviet Union shot down a U-2 spy plane over its territory. The U-2 INCIDENT and the revelations of U.S. overflights changed the debate from a theoretical question of the limits of sovereignty to one that had a real politicomilitary dimension.

**Further reading:** Krepon, Michael, and Amy Smithson, eds. *Open Skies, Arms Control, and Cooperative Security.* New York: St. Martin's, 1992.

## Operation Desert Shield

Operation Desert Shield was launched by President GEORGE H. W. BUSH in the wake of IRAQ's August 2, 1990, invasion and occupation of KUWAIT. Caught off guard by the Iraqi attack, the Bush administration's first priority was to protect SAUDI ARABIA and its vast OIL reserves from the Iraqi forces that were massing along the Iraq-Saudi border. To accomplish this objective, the Bush administration sought and obtained permission from Saudi Arabia to station U.S. soldiers on its soil. This move was unprecedented. Even though it was a major player in ARMS TRANSFERS with the United States, the conservative Saudi government had never allowed U.S. soldiers into the country for fear of alienating more radical Islamic states, which would object to their presence anywhere near Mecca or other Islamic holy places located in Saudi Arabia.

It was the third week of August before the international coalition of forces assembled under U.S. leadership could confidently ensure that an Iraqi attack against Saudi Arabia could not succeed. The United States was the major contributor with 430,000 troops. GREAT BRITAIN (35,000), EGYPT (30,000), and FRANCE (17,000) were significant contributors of military personnel. Saudi Arabia provided 66,000 front-line troops. In addition to organizing army troops, Operation Desert Shield also put in place a naval force to protect Saudi Arabia. The core of the naval force was provided by the United States. It sent more than 100 ships, including six aircraft carriers. Great Britain and France sent 18 and 14 ships, respectively. This coalition of forces would come to provide the foundation for Operation Desert Storm in January 1991. JAPAN and GERMANY provided funding rather than troops. The largest financial contributors were Saudi Arabia and Kuwait. Each gave more than $16 billion. Foreign states gave a total of some $54 billion to the effort.

On November 8, 1990, just after the midterm elections, the Bush administration announced that it was sending reinforcements to the region. This move signaled a shift in U.S. thinking. ECONOMIC SANCTIONS were no longer viewed in a favorable light as a means of forcing Iraq out of Kuwait. Instead, a large military force would be assembled that would try to intimidate Saddam Hussein into withdrawing from Kuwait and, failing that, could undertake an offensive military operation. When the compliance deadline established by UNITED NATIONS Resolution 678 went unmet, the PERSIAN GULF WAR entered its offensive phase with the launching of OPERATION DESERT STORM.

## Operation Desert Storm

Following IRAQ's August 2, 1990, invasion of KUWAIT, the United States organized an international military coalition to defend SAUDI ARABIA from attack. Known as OPERATION DESERT SHIELD, these military forces became the nucleus for an offensive military campaign, Operation Desert Storm, under the command of General H. Norman Schwarzkopf to evict Iraqi forces from Kuwait.

The first move in Operation Desert Storm came on the morning of January 15, 1991, the day that the UNITED NATIONS resolution requiring Iraq to evacuate Kuwait had set as a deadline, when President GEORGE H. W. BUSH

authorized an air offensive for the following day. American, British, Saudi, and Kuwaiti warplanes took part in the first wave of attacks that began at 12:50 A.M. Saudi time on January 17. Coalition aircraft averaged 2,000 sorties per day (the equivalent of one round-trip mission per plane). On January 23, General Colin Powell, chairman of the JOINT CHIEFS OF STAFF, declared that the United States and its allies had achieved air superiority and control of Iraqi air space. The major Iraqi counterblow was the launching of SCUD missiles against Israeli and Saudi targets. The attacks proved ineffective because of their small payload and lack of accuracy. The United States scored a major diplomatic success at this point in the conflict by convincing the Israelis not to retaliate, a move the Bush administration feared would draw the Arab members away from the coalition.

The ground phase of Operation Desert Storm began on February 24. It lasted exactly 100 hours. Approximately 700,000 troops were assembled in and around Saudi Arabia for the attack, but fewer than 400,000 actually participated in it. Great uncertainty surrounded the beginning of the campaign due to lack of knowledge about the abilities of Iraq's army and Saddam Hussein's strategy. American, British, and French forces led a blitzkrieg operation deep into Iraq when the fighting began. With his forces defeated and surrounded, Saddam Hussein announced that Iraq had withdrawn from Kuwait on February 26. Fighting continued until February 28, when President Bush announced that the coalition's military objectives had been met. American war casualties were listed as 125 combat deaths. Approximately 63,000 Iraqi soldiers were taken as prisoners of war, and between 25,000 and 100,000 were killed. As many as 30 percent of Iraqi forces in Kuwait deserted. British estimates place the number of Iraqi tanks destroyed at 3,500, out of 4,200.

Operation Desert Storm was hailed as a stunning military success. Two points of controversy have since arisen. Both surround the conduct of the war. While American battle casualties were minimal, in the years following the war large numbers of war veterans came down with a series of crippling illnesses that collectively are referred to as GULF WAR SYNDROME. Veterans' groups claim the illnesses are linked to their exposure to the destruction of chemical weapons stocks. The Pentagon has steadfastly denied that any such link exists and has been criticized for its handling of the matter. The second issue involves the decision to terminate the war without removing Saddam Hussein from power. Several different considerations led the Bush administration to this decision. First, it expected that he would be toppled by dissident Iraqis. Second, there was concern that if events moved too quickly Iraq might disintegrate along the lines of LEBANON.

With Saddam Hussein in power, Iraq systematically moved to resist United Nations sanctions and frustrate

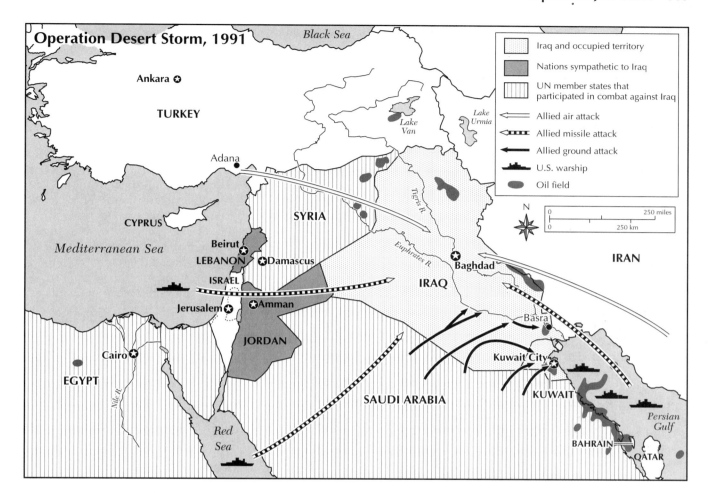

Operation Desert Storm, 1991

the UN Special Commission on Iraq, which was set up to supervise the destruction of its WEAPONS OF MASS DESTRUCTION. In 2002 President GEORGE W. BUSH used Iraq's noncompliance as a central theme in moving the United States toward war with Iraq, a war which commenced in March 2003.

## Operation Just Cause

On December 20, 1989, 13,000 U.S. troops invaded PANAMA, joining with the 13,000 U.S. forces already stationed there. Air support dropped 422 bombs. Resistance by the Panamanian Defense Forces (PDF) was minimal, and U.S. forces achieved control over Panama in five days. Pentagon estimates placed U.S. casualties at 23 soldiers dead and more than 100 wounded. Revised estimates of Panamanian losses were 50 soldiers dead. The goal of Operation Just Cause was to capture Panamanian leader Manuel Antonio Noriega, install the democratically elected government of Guillermo Endara, and protect American citizens. Noriega was able to elude

American forces for a short period of time before surrendering on January 4, 1990.

Noriega's involvement in DRUG TRAFFICKING had become a major embarrassment to the Bush administration. In September 1989 President GEORGE H. W. BUSH gave a major speech in which he cited drugs as the United States's gravest domestic threat. Anxious to take action, one Bush administration official described policy deliberation on Panama as "a decision in search of an excuse." That excuse came on December 15. The Noriega-controlled General Assembly declared a "state of war" with the United States. The next day the PDF killed an American soldier and injured two others at a roadblock. In a second incident the same day a U.S. soldier was beaten and his wife sexually harassed.

Noriega emerged as the dominant political force in Panama in 1983 when he took control of the National Guard, later renamed the PDF. He was a protégé of Omar Trujillo, who had ruled Panama from 1968 until his death in a plane crash in 1981. Noriega quickly became a valuable ally of the Reagan administration, supporting its policies in

EL SALVADOR and NICARAGUA. At the same time he set Panama up as a center for money laundering of drug profits and allowed the Colombian Medellín cartel to use Panama as a transit route and sanctuary. The Reagan administration knew of this but turned a blind eye toward it so long as he continued to support Washington's anticommunist policies in the Western Hemisphere.

Relations between the United States and Noriega changed dramatically in February 1988 when federal prosecutors in Miami secured a 12-count indictment against Noriega under the Racketeer Influenced and Corrupt Organizations Act (RICO) for shipping drugs, laundering money, and taking bribes to protect drug traffickers. If convicted on all counts, Noriega faced up to 145 years in prison and $1.145 million in fines. These revelations came on top of charges made in June 1987 by the second-ranking PDF officers that Noriega had engaged in electoral fraud and was behind assassinations. The STATE DEPARTMENT asked the Justice Department to drop the charges if Noriega went into exile, but he refused.

As evidence of the scale of Noriega's involved in drug trafficking mounted, the Reagan administration turned on him. In May 1988 President RONALD REAGAN declared the one goal of U.S. foreign policy was "the removal of Noriega from power." Vice President Bush, who was running for president, stated that the United States must be prepared "to do whatever is necessary including military force" to protect "sacred" U.S. interests in Panama. On the economic front the United States announced that Panama Canal Commission payments of about $7 million per month would be placed in an escrow account, and Noriega's access to Panamanian bank accounts in the United States was blocked. The total cost of ECONOMIC SANCTIONS against Panama was placed at $450 million. Finally, the CENTRAL INTELLIGENCE AGENCY engaged in between one and five COVERT-ACTION operations designed to remove Noriega from power.

In Panama an election was scheduled for May 1989. An election observation team led by former president JIMMY CARTER denounced the results as fraudulent. The ORGANIZATION OF AMERICAN STATES (OAS) spoke out against Noriega, criticizing him for the way in which the election was conducted. It also tried to facilitate a peaceful transfer of POWER from Noriega's hand-picked candidate to that of opposition leader Endara. Noriega refused to cooperate with the OAS and denounced U.S. interference in Panamanian politics. In spite of OAS criticism of Noriega, Latin American states did not impose sanctions on Panama.

While popular in the United States, the invasion of Panama was met with protests in the Western Hemisphere. Bush had not consulted with U.S. allies, and the OAS expressed its deep regret over the military intervention. The UNITED NATIONS General Assembly also passed a resolution condemning the invasion. Operation Just Cause

had little impact on Panama's role in international drug trafficking. At his trial Noriega tried unsuccessfully to have evidence of his ties to the CIA made public. He was convicted on eight counts and sentenced to 40 years in prison without parole.

## Operation Uphold Democracy

On September 18, 1994, President BILL CLINTON gave the order to launch an invasion of HAITI at one minute past midnight. At 6:45 A.M. the next morning, 61 planes with troops aboard were on their way to Haiti. While this was happening former president JIMMY CARTER was in Haiti and deeply involved in negotiations with ruling general Raoul Cédras. The draft agreement on the table called for amnesty for the military rulers and the return to power of deposed president Jean-Bertrand Aristide by October 15. With news in hand that U.S. troops had been mobilized, an agreement was reached. The planes were recalled, and the invasion canceled. The following day U.S. troops, whose numbers would reach 20,000, occupied Haiti without encountering any organized resistance.

Aristide, a Catholic priest who embraced liberation theology, which encouraged political activism in the name of achieving social justice, was elected president in December 1990. In September 1991 Aristide was overthrown by a military coup and forced into exile. General Cédras assumed power with the support of the military and business leaders. The ORGANIZATION OF AMERICAN STATES (OAS) condemned the coup and called for Aristide's return to POWER. It also imposed a trade embargo on Haiti. Negotiations between the OAS, Cédras, Aristide, and others produced no tangible progress on a compromise solution.

Worsening conditions in Haiti led to the onset of a sharp increase in the number of Haitians taking to the seas and seeking refuge in the United States. This directed U.S. attention away from a focus on returning Aristide to power. By January 1992, the U.S. Coast Guard had intercepted approximately 12,600 Haitians at sea. By May, 34,000 requests for asylum had been processed. In an effort to stop the outflow President GEORGE H. W. BUSH now ordered the Coast Guard to intercept the Haitians and return them to Haiti without processing their requests for REFUGEE status. Democratic presidential candidate Bill Clinton condemned this decision as immoral and promised to reverse it if elected. Shortly before taking office, President-elect Bill Clinton was informed by the Bush administration that INTELLIGENCE pointed to a massive exodus of as many as 200,000 Haitians, who would leave for the United States upon his inauguration. Clinton then announced that Bush's policy would stay in place, a move denounced by Aristide as imposing a "floating Berlin Wall" around Haiti.

In June 1993 the UNITED NATIONS became involved in trying to bring about a political compromise by placing a worldwide embargo on OIL shipments to Haiti. In July an agreement was reached. The Governors Island accord permitted Aristide to return as president by October 30, allow Cédras to step down as head of the army, and provide a general amnesty for all of those involved in the September 1991 coup. However, as the October deadline approached, Cédras calculated correctly that President Clinton had been sufficiently weakened by the SOMALIA peacekeeping mission that he would not risk U.S. lives to return Aristide to power. On October 11, rather than confront a crowd of heavily armed civilians, the USS *Harlan County* and its 200 lightly armed troops withdrew from Port-au-Prince Harbor.

After briefly abandoning Aristide's cause in favor of a centrist solution, which did not exist, the Clinton administration once again turned its attention to forcing Cédras from power. Domestic politics in the form of a hunger strike by Randall Robinson, head of TransAfrica, and pressure from the Black Caucus in CONGRESS, in addition to continued concerns about uncontrollable refugee flows, pushed Clinton in this direction. In late July a UN Security Council resolution was obtained authorizing the United States to "use all necessary means to facilitate the departure from Haiti of the military leadership." In September naval ships moved closer to Haiti, and warplanes conducted overflights. Clinton's determination to act did produce domestic resistance in the United States. A PUBLIC OPINION poll showed that 73 percent of the public opposed sending troops. Senator Robert Dole (R-Kans.) questioned if U.S. NATIONAL INTERESTS were at stake.

The Haitian case and Operation Uphold Democracy are significant early examples of the challenges facing the United States in the post–COLD WAR uses of military power. Carried out in the name of restoring a democratically elected government, it was concern for stopping the influx of Haitian boat people into the United States and domestic political considerations that drove U.S. policy. It also highlights the difficulties that the UN and OAS have had in trying to play leading roles in promoting democracy. Neither organizations provided a suitable substitute for U.S. military power, nor were they in a position to control its use. Finally, the decisions leading up to Operation Uphold Democracy are consistent with the prevailing wisdom that Americans are not willing to support uses of military force that result in high numbers of casualties.

## Oregon Territory

The Oregon Territory comprised a stretch of lands reaching from the 42nd parallel, which marked its southern border with Spanish California, to the line of 54°40' in the north, beyond which lay Russian ALASKA. GREAT BRITAIN and the United States each claimed the Oregon Territory, citing different precedents and justifications. The Treaty of 1818 produced a 10-year agreement between the two states that gave each free access to the entire region. The joint occupation agreement was extended indefinitely in 1827. For the next decade the Oregon Territory remained at most a secondary concern for U.S. and British policy makers. The Webster-Ashburton Treaty of 1842, which fixed the U.S.-Canadian border in the Northeast and Midwest, purposefully did not address the Oregon dispute. DANIEL WEBSTER's own preference, expressed in 1841, was for a policy of "wise and masterly inactivity." He was convinced that over time American settlements in the region would determine the outcome in America's favor.

It was only in the mid-1840s that real pressure for a solution began to build. The American population in the Oregon Territory had grown from about 300 in 1841 to 5,000 in 1845. By this time, however, the scope of the dispute had narrowed to involve a relatively small area as each side had come to acknowledge the legitimacy of each other's claim to large portions of the Oregon Territory. The British repeatedly offered to use the Columbia River as the territorial divide, and the United States offered to use the 49th parallel.

In his successful presidential campaign of 1844, JAMES POLK made clear his interest in "reoccupying" Oregon and "reannexing" TEXAS. The two were linked by American domestic politics. Southerners looked to Texas as an area where slavery could expand, and Northerners saw Oregon as a free-soil area. Expressing much bravado and employing the MONROE DOCTRINE as partial justification, President JAMES POLK lay claim to the whole of the Oregon Territory in his annual message to CONGRESS in December 1845.

In April 1846 Congress passed a resolution giving the required one-year notice to terminate the joint occupation agreement. The British used this opportunity in June to suggest that the 49th parallel serve as the dividing line between American and British Oregon. In effect, the British were abandoning their claim to all of the disputed area. Polk wished to reject the offer but was convinced by his cabinet to take the highly unusual step of referring the agreement to the Senate for its advice prior to taking any action. The Senate acted quickly and, after only two days of discussion, recommended that it be accepted by a vote of 38-12. Three days later, on June 15, 1848, the treaty was signed, and three days after that it was approved by the Senate by a vote of 41-14.

## Organization of American States (OAS)

The Organization of American States (OAS) was created at the Ninth International Conference of American States meeting in Bogotá, Colombia, in 1948. Along with the signing of the American Treaty of Pacific Settlement, these two documents completed the work begun with the signing of the 1945 Act of Chapultepec. They created a constitutional foundation for inter-American relations. The OAS formally replaced the inter-American system that consisted of a series of ministerial meetings to address common concerns.

The OAS is a multipurpose regional INTERNATIONAL ORGANIZATION. Its aims include (1) strengthening peace and security in the region; (2) preventing conflicts and encouraging the peaceful settlement of disputes; (3) providing common action in the face of aggression; (4) seeking solutions to political, judicial, and economic problems among members; and (5) promoting cooperative action in economic, social, and cultural undertakings.

As originally established, the OAS had a secretariat based in Washington, a permanent executive body, called the Council; a "supreme organ" called the Inter-American Conference; and the Meeting of Consultation of the Ministers of Foreign Affairs designed to take up urgent matters as needed. In 1967 a series of charter amendments were adopted that significantly altered this structure and took effect in 1970. The General Assembly now serves as the supreme organ. There is a Permanent Council, consisting of one representative from each state that has duties in dispute resolution and carrying out General Assembly directives. An inter-American Juridical Committee acts as an advisory body, promoting INTERNATIONAL LAW in the region. Specialized councils and agencies supervise extensive programs, draft treaties, and organize conferences in such areas as education, science, culture, HUMAN RIGHTS, women's affairs, child welfare, health, and NATIVE AMERICAN affairs. In crisis situations member states can request a Meeting of Consultation of the ministers of foreign affairs. The OAS headquarters and staff remain stationed in Washington.

The most frequent assessment made regarding the overall performance of the OAS is that it has been wounded repeatedly by U.S. manipulation and neglect, but it is far from dead. In the area of collective security, the United States has either made the OAS a reluctant partner in operations against the DOMINICAN REPUBLIC, GUATEMALA, and CUBA or ignored it, as it did in GRENADA and PANAMA. Economically, the role of the OAS as a force for regional economic and social cooperation has repeatedly been upstaged by periodic U.S. initiatives, such as the ALLIANCE FOR PROGRESS, the CARIBBEAN BASIN INITIATIVE, the ENTERPRISE FOR THE AMERICAS INITIATIVE, and the NORTH AMERICAN FREE TRADE ASSOCIATION (NAFTA). In the area of international law, the United States has cited the principle of regionalism and OAS jurisdiction to deflect cases of aggression brought against it or one of its regional allies at the UNITED NATIONS by Guatemala, Cuba, and HAITI.

The OAS, however, has not been without successes. It served as a peacemaker in the soccer war between EL SALVADOR and HONDURAS in 1969–70 and carried out a number of fact-finding and conciliatory missions during the COLD WAR. Since the end of the cold war, the OAS has become an important force in certifying elections as free and fair and played an active role in restoring President Jean-Bertrand Aristide to power in Haiti. That doing so ultimately required the threat of military action by U.S. forces highlight the continuing dilemma faced by the OAS in its relations with the United States. When the United States feels its national security interests are at stake, there is little that the OAS can do to influence events. It is only when the United States is relatively unconcerned with a situation or values OAS neutrality in solving a problem that the OAS can exert an independent influence.

**Further reading:** Martz, John D., and Lars Schoultz. *Latin America, the United States, and the Inter-American System.* Boulder, Colo.: Westview, 1980; Smith, Peter. *Talons of the Eagle: Dynamics of U.S.–Latin American Relations.* New York: Oxford University Press, 1996.

## Organization of Petroleum Producing Countries

The Organization of Petroleum Exporting Countries (OPEC) was formed by IRAQ, IRAN, SAUDI ARABIA, KUWAIT, and VENEZUELA in 1960 in response to a decision by Standard Oil and other OIL companies to cut their prices. Its goal was to return oil prices to their previous levels and force the oil companies to consult with them in making pricing decisions. In the 1960s Qatar, LIBYA, INDONESIA, ALGERIA, NIGERIA, Ecuador, the United Arab Emirates, and Gabon would join.

OPEC's founding did not bring about an immediate change in the nature of international oil production or politics. Oil had long been dominated by a cartel. However, it was a cartel of oil companies rather than states. Known as the seven sisters these oil companies (Exxon, Gulf, Chevron, Mobil, Texaco, Royal Dutch Shell, and British Petroleum) conspired to set production levels and establish a global pricing system. Oil-producing states were compliant junior partners in this system. Early agreements provided these states with as little as 21 cents per barrel of oil produced. Prior to WORLD WAR II Middle East oil, coming primarily from Iran and Iraq, accounted for less than 5 percent of global production.

The global economic recovery that followed World War II began to change this situation in a number of important respects. First, the Middle East became a more prominent source of oil. By the end of the 1950s, 25 percent of the world's oil came from this region. By the 1970s it had reached 50 percent. Second, the grip on oil production by the seven sisters was being challenged by independent oil producers, such as Amoco, Occidental, and Getty, that were willing to sell oil below the agreed upon price levels. Third, the oil-producing governments were becoming more aggressive as their development needs—and need for oil revenues—grew. Venezuela led the way obtaining a 50-50 split on oil profits.

The founding of OPEC in 1960 did not stabilize the price of oil in and of itself. Rather this was achieved by the Eisenhower administration through a change in the tax system. The extra taxes oil companies paid to OPEC states would be equaled in the reduced tax they owed the United States. The stability this produced in international oil markets did not outlast the decade. In June 1968 OPEC declared that member states had the right to set oil production levels and oil prices. They also raised the tax rate to 55 percent of profits. The following year Muammar al-Qaddafi came to power in Libya and pressured independents into accepting higher prices and taxes. Following his example, OPEC states achieved similar agreements from the seven sisters in February 1971.

These gains proved to be fleeting as in December the United States devalued the dollar, thereby reducing the buying power of the money received by OPEC. The OPEC states responded by negotiating new pricing and production agreements with oil companies in 1972 and 1973. They also began to nationalize foreign oil companies, thereby gaining more direct operational control over them. Libya moved first in 1971, nationalizing British Petroleum's holdings there. Saudi Arabia, Kuwait, Qatar, and the United Arab Emirates followed Libya's lead in 1972 by negotiating participation agreements with their oil companies. In 1972 oil companies controlled 92 percent of the oil leaving the Middle East. By 1982 they controlled less than 7 percent.

OPEC had a summit meeting scheduled for Vienna on October 8, 1973, with the major oil companies. Its objective was to negotiate a substantial price increase. Two days before it began, on October 6, EGYPT and Syria attacked ISRAEL, setting off the 1973 Yom Kippur War. Against this backdrop OPEC sought to double the price of oil from $3 to $6. The meeting ended with no agreement. The OPEC states reconvened on October 16 in Kuwait. They agreed to a 5 percent cut in oil production per month until Israel left the occupied territories and to impose the $5.12 per barrel price increase that they had left Vienna proposing. Saudi Arabia announced it would reduce production 10 percent.

Matters escalated quickly in the following days and months. On October 19 President RICHARD NIXON asked CONGRESS for $2.2 billion in emergency aid for ISRAEL.

Libya immediately announced an oil embargo. The next day Saudi Arabia announced it would cut production 25 percent. By October 22, most OPEC states had adopted similar price hikes and denial policies. With oil prices skyrocketing on international markets, OPEC met in December and announced the new price of a barrel of oil was $11.65. The oil embargo was not leak-proof, and Middle East oil did reach the United States. U.S. government estimates in 1974 placed the cost of the embargo at half a million jobs and a loss of between $10 and $20 billion in the size of the overall gross national product.

The OPEC embargo against the United States was officially lifted on March 18, 1974. Indirectly this decision reflected a positive response to American efforts to bring about a settlement of the Arab-Israeli dispute following the war. NATIONAL SECURITY ADVISOR HENRY KISSINGER shuttled between Arab and Israeli capitals in an effort to bring about a disengagement of their forces. In January 1974 Egyptian president Anwar Sadat urged OPEC states to recognize the "evolution" in the U.S. position toward a more evenhanded stance in the ARAB-ISRAELI CONFLICT.

The 1973 oil embargo and price hike represented the height of OPEC's success. It became the standard against which other cartel's were judged and stood at the center of a debate over whether "oil was the exception" or if other commodity cartels could match its performance. The historical record made clear that on balance 1973 was an exception. In the years that followed, OPEC's strength was undermined by the appearance of significant non-OPEC oil producing states, such as GREAT BRITAIN, MEXICO, and the Soviet Union, and by internal conflicts among its members, the most notable being the IRAN-IRAQ WAR and then the Iraqi invasion of KUWAIT, which resulted in the PERSIAN GULF WAR. Western states also reduced their dependence on OPEC oil through conservation and diversification programs.

There were spikes in the price of oil. One occurred in the late 1970s and early 1980s. The global recession that was produced by the 1973 oil embargo brought about an 18-month OPEC price freeze. In December 1978 OPEC agreed on a four-phase price hike totaling 14.5 percent. Turmoil in Iran, however, drove market prices much higher. President JIMMY CARTER responded by proposing a comprehensive energy plan that included conservation programs, tax credits, phased-in price hikes, and programs to compel consumers to switch to alternate energy sources. Congress opposed the plan, and only parts of it became law. Following the Iranian Revolution in 1979, Carter lifted price controls on domestic oil and announced that the United States would limit future oil imports to 8.5 million barrels per day. President RONALD REAGAN speeded up the price decontrol timetable set by Carter and abandoned most of his conservation and alternative fuel programs.

A second spike occurred during the Persian Gulf War. The decision by the United States and the UNITED NATIONS to place an economic embargo on Iraq had the effect of removing Iraqi oil from world markets. Added to this was the removal of Kuwaiti oil. Saudi Arabia moved quickly to announce an increase of 2 million barrels per day in its oil production (Iraq produced about 3 million barrels per day, and Kuwait produced 2 million barrels per day). The United States further calmed international markets by announcing it would protect Saudi Arabia. Still, prices rose before they fell.

The more enduring problem for OPEC since 1973 has been overproduction and low prices. In March 1983 OPEC set production quotas for the first time. Cooperation held for about 15 months. Cheating had become so commonplace that by in January 1986 the price of a barrel of oil fell to $20, down from a 1981 high of $35 per barrel. This was a 10-year low. The price of oil, however, would go lower. In late March 1990 it fell to below $18 per barrel. By June the price was about $14 per barrel. The Persian Gulf War failed to bring about any fundamental realignment in this picture. In September 1992, OPEC oil production reached an 11-year high. One year later, the price of oil remained low, between $14 and $16 per barrel.

OPEC played an important role in maintaining stability in international oil markets in the period surrounding the IRAQ WAR. Before the war began, OPEC states increased their production of oil in order to prevent a spike in global oil prices that might follow from the destruction of Iraqi oil fields. While such price hikes would bring them great profits, they would also cripple the economies of the rich countries in the world where they invested much of this money. With the war over and fears of an oil shortage a memory, OPEC moved to cut oil supplies in order to prop up the price of oil and keep it within a target range of $22–$28 per barrel. The resumption of extensive Iraqi oil production holds the potential for seriously disrupting international oil markets. While only producing at a small capacity in the immediate postwar period, there were more than 8 million barrels of oil stored in TURKEY ready for export. The ability to do so came in May 2003 when the United Nations lifted its ECONOMIC SANCTIONS on Iraq. The UN resolution lifting these sanctions placed the United States in charge of disbursing oil revenues.

See also CENTRAL ASIAN REPUBLICS.

**Further reading:** Ahrari, Mohammed E. *OPEC: The Failing Giant.* Lexington: University of Kentucky Press, 1986; Amuzegar, Jahanagir. *Managing the Oil Wealth: OPEC's Windfalls and Pitfalls.* London: I.B. Tauris, 2000; Blair, John. *The Control of Oil.* New York: Pantheon, 1976.

## Ostend Manifesto

Issued in October 1854 the Ostend Manifesto has been described as the "quintessential statement of ardent expansionism of Young America." It asserted that the acquisition of CUBA was vital because "Cuba [was] as necessary to the North American republics as any of its present members." It urged the United States to undertake an "immediate and earnest effort" to purchase Cuba from SPAIN.

The Ostend Manifesto resulted from the efforts of the FRANKLIN PIERCE administration to buy Cuba. In April 1854 SECRETARY OF STATE W. L. Marcy wrote to the American minister in Spain, Pierre Soule, directing him to offer a maximum sum of $130 million to "detach" Cuba from Spain. After Spain rejected the offer, Pierce directed Marcy to have Soule meet with the American ministers to FRANCE and GREAT BRITAIN, John Mason and James Buchanan, respectively, to compare opinions as to what course of action the United States should follow with regard to Cuba. The ministers met in Ostend, Belgium. The Ostend Manifesto concluded that if Spain was unwilling to sell Cuba, as they all knew it was, it was time for the United States to answer the question "[D]oes Cuba, in the possession of Spain, seriously endanger our internal peace?" If the answer was yes, the Ostend Manifesto stated, "by every law, human and divine, we shall be justified in wresting it from Spain if we possess the power."

The political impact of the Ostend Manifesto was completely opposite from what was intended. Written as a secret report it was leaked to the American and European press, who publicized it widely. News of it arrived in Washington on November 4, 1854, an election day that saw the DEMOCRATIC PARTY take heavy losses in the North. Abolitionist forces had deserted them over the recently passed Kansas-Nebraska Act that had opened the possibility of another slave state entering the Union. Political support for annexing Cuba, which would also be a slave state, now vanished. Rather than embrace the Ostend Manifesto, the Pierce administration sought to distance itself from it. Marcy wrote to Soule instructing him not to press the matter with Spain but only engage in "free and friendly intercourse." Soule, who was the principal author of the manifesto, also became its principal scapegoat and resigned his post.

# P

## Pakistan

Located in South Asia, Pakistan has an area of 310,527 square miles, approximately twice the size of California. It has an estimated population of 135 million people. Pakistan achieved its independence on August 14, 1947. British traders arrived in South Asia in 1601 but did not fully establish a colonial presence until the second part of the 18th century. A pro-independence movement began in the early 20th century, but unity was difficult to maintain in the face of Muslim-Hindu conflict, and in the 1930s support crystallized for creating a separate Muslim state within the British Commonwealth. In granting independence to this region after WORLD WAR II, the British endorsed this approached by creating a Hindu INDIA and a Muslim Pakistan. The princely states of the subcontinent were free to join either. Initially, Pakistan comprised two parts, East and West Pakistan, which were separated by more than 1,000 square miles of Indian territory. East Pakistan obtained its independence from West Pakistan in a complex civil war in 1971 and became Bangladesh. The British formula created a crisis in Kashmir, where the rulers were Hindu but the majority of the population was Muslim. Facing hostile military activity from forces located in Pakistan, the ruler called upon India for protection. Armed forces were sent in, and in October 1947 Kashmir formally joined India. Pakistan did not recognize the decision, and its status has proven to be a repeated point of tension between the two sides that has produced several wars and near wars.

Virtually from the outset Pakistan's relations with the United States have been carried out with one eye on India. The first formal bonds between the United States and Pakistan were established through the latter's participation in two of the United States's COLD WAR regional ALLIANCE systems, which were designed to contain Soviet expansion. It joined both the Baghdad Pact, also referred to as the CENTRAL TREATY ORGANIZATION (1955), and the SOUTHEAST ASIA TREATY ORGANIZATION (1954). Along with the United States and Pakistan, other members of CENTO were GREAT BRITAIN, TURKEY, IRAQ, and IRAN. SEATO members included the United States, Great Britain, FRANCE, the PHILIPPINES, New Zealand, Australia, and THAILAND. In each case Pakistan's primary goal was not to deter communist expansion but to acquire weapons to balance the power of India.

Relations deteriorated in the early 1960s. In 1962 a long-standing border dispute between CHINA and India erupted into violence as Chinese troops stormed into India. Much to the dismay of Pakistan, the United States provided India with military hardware. Growing doubts about the value of the American alliance were reinforced in 1965 when fighting broke out between India and Pakistan over Kashmir. Rather than support its ally Pakistan, the United States placed an arms embargo on both sides. The net effect, however, was to hurt the smaller Pakistan.

In 1971 the United States "tilted" toward Pakistan in the India-Pakistan conflict that resulted in Bangladesh's independence, although once again it suspended military aid. U.S. support did not help East Pakistan hold onto West Pakistan or alter the reality that India emerged from the war stronger than ever in its conflict with a now truncated Pakistan. ARMS TRANSFERS to Pakistan were resumed in 1975, but economic aid, except for food, was cut off in 1979 as required by the Symington Amendment to the Foreign Assistance Act of 1961 that prohibited such aid from states believed to be trying to acquire NUCLEAR WEAPONS.

The Soviet invasion of AFGHANISTAN altered the U.S.–Pakistan relationship again. Pakistan now became a valuable ally, providing training sites, refuge zones, and weapons for the Mujahideen GUERRILLAS that the United States was supporting in an effort to force the Soviet Union (see RUSSIA) out of Afghanistan. CONGRESS waived the Symington Amendment, and in 1981 the United States agreed to provide Pakistan with $3.2 billion in military and economic FOREIGN AID. In 1986 a $4 billion economic and military assistance package to run from 1988 and 1993 was approved. By 1990 Pakistan was the third-largest recipient of U.S. military assistance, behind EGYPT and ISRAEL.

After the Soviet withdrawal U.S.-Pakistan relations deteriorated yet again, largely due to congressional restrictions imposed on aid bound for states attempting to acquire a nuclear capability. In October 1990 all U.S. aid was frozen under the provisions of the Pressler Amendment, which suspended all new military and economic aid to states unless the PRESIDENT certifies that the state does not "possess a nuclear explosive device." In 1998 the Glenn Amendment imposed sanctions on credits, military sales, economic assistance, and loans. Following the 1999 military coup that placed General Pervez Musharraf in power, Section 508 of the Foreign Appropriations Act was invoked, which restricted military and economic aid. As a result of these restrictions, prior to the SEPTEMBER 11, 2001, terrorist attacks American aid to Pakistan was limited to funding REFUGEE and counternarcotics programs. In 1999 the United States provided approximately $70 billion for humanitarian assistance to Afghanistan and Afghan refugees located in Pakistan.

The Indian and Pakistani nuclear explosions of May 1998 set off yet another round of U.S. sanctions against Pakistan (and India), as mandated by the Glenn Amendment. This time, however, the United States moved quickly to lessen their impact. An important motivating factor was the fact that Pakistan had become the leading buyer of U.S. white wheat and the third-largest buyer of wheat in general. Without export financing, these purchases would not take place as scheduled in mid July. In early July the Senate approved by a 98-0 vote a one-year exemption for India and Pakistan from the terms of the Glenn Amendment. This was followed by passage of the Brownback Amendment (officially known as the India-Pakistan Relief Act of 1998) that authorized the president to waive for one year the provisions of the Glenn Amendment for India and Pakistan except for those dealing with military assistance and dual-use technologies. President Clinton embraced the Brownback Amendment and resumed funding for military training programs and economic assistance programs to these states. In 1999 Congress passed Brownback II, which gave the president the authority to permanently waive all of the provisions of the Glenn Amendment for India and Pakistan. It also gave the president the right to waive the terms of the Symington and Pressler Amendments for them. In addition to economic concerns these votes were influenced by a desire to retain some form of strategic leverage over India and Pakistan now that they had officially gone nuclear as well as to acknowledge the growing political influence of the Indian-American community (and to a lesser extent the Pakistani-American community) in the United States.

The Clinton administration also responded to the Indian nuclear explosions by beginning a series of stability talks. Deputy Secretary of State Strobe Talbott led the U.S.

delegation that hoped to avoid a Pakistani nuclear test by offering foreign aid and other inducements. After the Pakistani test the talks continued and focused on bringing strategic stability to South Asia. One concrete goal was to get the two sides to sign the COMPREHENSIVE TEST BAN TREATY. This proved to be impossible after the Senate rejected the treaty in 1999 and GEORGE W. BUSH indicated his opposition to it during his presidential campaign.

In its 2000 annual volume, *Patterns of Global Terrorism,* the STATE DEPARTMENT identified Pakistan as a major supporter of international TERRORISM. Yet, for reasons consistent with those noted above, neither President GEORGE H. W. BUSH nor BILL CLINTON had labeled Pakistan as a terrorist state. With the September 11, 2001, terrorist attacks in the United States the possibility that this might happen disappeared. Once again Pakistan was a valuable ally against an enemy located in Afghanistan. Defeating the Taliban and capturing OSAMA BIN LADEN would require its help. To induce Musharraf to support the American effort by way of providing intelligence and military staging areas as well as clamping down on pro-Taliban and fundamentalist Islamic forces in Pakistan, he was promised that Pakistan's diplomatic isolation would end and that significant American support would be forthcoming. It was. After the September 11th attacks, Bush received authority to waive all restrictions on arms sales and weapons exports for five years as part of the war against terrorism.

Musharraf did not have a free hand in joining the global war against terrorism. He walked a political tightrope. Pakistan had been the only government to maintain formal diplomatic relations with the Taliban, and most of the Taliban's members are Pashtuns, the dominant ethnic group in Pakistan. The ability of militant groups within Pakistan to create regional problems for Pakistan and the United States burst into the open on December 15, 2001, when five members of two different extremist groups stormed the Indian parliament, killing nine people. While Pakistan quickly condemned the act tensions between India and Pakistan rose to the brink of war. The United States helped avert war by privately urging India to backdown on its demands and encouraging Pakistan to crack down on these groups. Continued tensions with Pakistan exist over its relationship with NORTH KOREA. In late 2002 Pakistan was identified as the likely source of material for NORTH KOREA's ongoing attempts to develop a nuclear capability.

**Further reading:** Blackwell, Robert D., and Albert Carnesale, eds. *New Nuclear Nations: Consequences for U.S. Policy.* New York: Council for Foreign Relations, 1993; McMahon, Robert J. *The Cold War on the Periphery: The United States, India, and Pakistan, 1947–1965.* New York: Columbia University Press, 1996; Shahid, Javed. *Pakistan: The Continuing Search for Nationhood.* Boulder, Colo.: Westview, 1991.

## Palestine Liberation Organization

The Palestine Liberation Organization (PLO) came into existence as a result of a decision made at an Arab SUMMIT CONFERENCE called by Egyptian president Gamal Abdel Nasser in January 1964. The Arab-Israeli War of 1948 had created thousands of homeless Palestinian REFUGEES. In the aftermath of the 1956 war, many had begun to organize. Two of the most significant were the Arab National Movement led by George Habash and Fatah led by Yasser Arafat. Nasser hoped to combine these smaller groups into the larger PLO and to use the PLO as a vehicle for channeling Palestinian support for his leadership of the Arab world. The founding document of the PLO called for the liberation of Palestine and made no reference to UNITED NATIONS (UN) resolutions that spoke to the need for both Arabs and Israelis to work their differences out through diplomatic channels. Ahmed Shukairy was chosen to head the PLO.

Nasser, who controlled the Arab League that officially sponsored the 1964 summit, proved unable to control the various Palestinian resistance groups that sprang up in the region. Their military raids and terrorist activities were carried out without regard for the PLO. Especially after the 1967 Six-Day War, in which Arab states had suffered a crushing military defeat at the hands of the Israeli military, these groups came to be seen by Palestinians as the true defenders of their interests. Arafat's Fatah emerged as the largest of these groups, conducting operations against ISRAEL from SYRIA and JORDAN, and in 1969 he became chairman of the PLO. From the outset, it had been Arafat's position that the Palestinians needed to establish a political force independent of the Arab states if they were to recapture the lands lost in 1948, and he set the PLO in this direction.

Jordan's King Hussein had made it clear as early as 1964 that the PLO was to have no authority to operate in Jordan. After the 1967 war, however, the PLO began using Jordan as a base for attacks on Israel. This brought Israeli reprisals and threatened Jordan's political stability. In September 1970 Habash's Popular Front for the Liberation of Palestine hijacked three Western airliners in Jordan and set off a political crisis that led to expulsion of the PLO from Jordan by the Jordanian military. Out of this conflict emerged the Black September movement that would be responsible for many of the most violent terrorist attacks in the ARAB-ISRAELI CONFLICT, including the murder of nine Israeli athletes at the 1972 Munich Olympic Games.

Although it was not involved heavily in military action during the 1973 Arab-Israeli War, the PLO was central to three political development, that followed in its wake. In October 1974 the Arab states recognized the "right of the Palestinian people to establish an independent national authority under the command of the Palestine Liberation Organization, the sole legitimate representative of the Palestinian people." In November Arafat would address the General Assembly of the United Nations, which granted the PLO observer status. Third, as part of his shuttle diplomacy, NATIONAL SECURITY ADVISOR HENRY KISSINGER engineered a Sinai II agreement between Israel and EGYPT in September 1975. It produced a new cease-fire line and established a new UN buffer zone. Part of the price Kissinger paid was an agreement with Israel that the United States would neither recognize nor negotiate with the PLO so long as it did not recognize Israel's right to exist. This position was adopted in the face of evidence that the PLO under Arafat was now focusing on creating a mini-Palestinian state.

The PLO's terrorist attacks against Israel from LEBANON, where it fled after being forced out of Jordan, led to two Israeli military invasions. The first occurred in 1978, the second in 1982. This latter one was intended to drive the PLO out of Lebanon. To an extent it succeeded. The PLO was forced to retreat to Beirut. U.S. special envoy Philip Habib then negotiated an agreement allowing the PLO to leave Lebanon. Arafat now set up headquarters in Tunis, Tunisia. Contrary to the expectations held by Israeli leaders, the PLO did not fade away as a political or military force. It would reemerge as a major player.

An Arab summit held at the same time as the PLO evacuation from Lebanon reaffirmed its role as the sole legitimate representative of the Palestinian people. This pronouncement undercut the ongoing efforts of the United States to bring Jordan into the stalled CAMP DAVID peace process as the spokesperson for the Palestinians. Arafat also moved the PLO forward as a potential participant in the peace process. As part of a joint Jordanian-PLO initiative he made public statements that implied a willingness to work within the framework of UN Resolution 242 that sought a settlement through an exchange of peace for land and a recognition of Israel's right to exist. Arafat was prevented from moving to a more forthright position as sought by the United States due to the strength of rejectionist elements within the PLO. The final factor reenergizing the PLO was the intifada, the general uprising among the Arab people in the West Bank and Gaza in December 1987. The PLO did not instigate or orchestrate its origins, but the intifada strengthened the PLO because it was the PLO that the people looked to for leadership—not the Arab states.

In July 1988 King Hussein of Jordan formally relinquished Jordan's claim to the West Bank and recognized the PLO's right to rule over it. Jordan had incorporated what was left of the UN–proposed Palestinian state following the 1948 war. Arafat followed this up on November 15, 1988, with the announcement that the PLO recognized the legitimacy of UN Resolution 242. A declaration rejecting TERRORISM was also announced. The Reagan administration continued to demand a more explicit statement of the PLO's recognition of Israel's right to exist before beginning talks. This statement came on December 14, and four hours after it was made the

Reagan administration announced its willingness to enter into talks with the PLO. Little progress was made in these talks, and they were broken off by the United States following an attempted terrorist attack by a PLO splinter group.

U.S.-PLO diplomatic ties took on new life after the PER-SIAN GULF WAR when the Bush administration put forward a peace initiative designed to bring all parties together at an international conference. Israel was the last to agree and did so only on the condition that it could veto which Palestinians attended as part of a Jordanian-Palestinian delegation and that it would not be asked to negotiate directly with the Palestinians. The MADRID negotiations made little headway, but parallel talks were being held in secret in Oslo, Norway, between Israel and representatives of the PLO. The heart of the agreement they reached provided for mutual recognition and the establishment of Palestinian autonomy in Jericho and Gaza, with other territory to be added.

On September 13, 1993, with President BILL CLINTON present, Israel prime minister Yitzhak Rabin and Arafat signed a document recognizing each other and pledging to end their conflict. The Clinton administration followed up this White House ceremony by promising $500 million in economic aid to the new Palestinian entity. Not unexpectedly, given the long-standing hostilities in the Middle East, this peace initiative stalled. Clinton sought to restart it near the end of his term by inviting Israeli prime minister Ehud Barak and Palestinian Authority chairman Yasser Arafat to a meeting at Camp David (CAMP DAVID II) in July 2000. Its failure contributed to the beginning of a second intifada in the occupied territories.

President GEORGE W. BUSH was not inclined to play the role of peacemaker. He was, however, prepared to recognize the existence of a full-fledged Palestinian state under PLO rule. His interest in doing so faded as the violence rose. In 2002 Bush endorsed the hard-line position of the Israeli government that Arafat was an obstacle to peace and must be removed before peace talks could begin. In September Arafat's compound came under heavy Israeli attack in retaliation for suicide bombings. The Bush administration, which at that very time was seeking congressional and UN support of an attack on IRAQ, labeled the Israeli move counterproductive and abstained on a UN Security Council vote calling for Israel to stop.

Arafat's presence and his inability to control terrorist attacks against Israel was used by Israeli prime minister Ariel Sharon as a rationale for abandoning the peace process in 2002. President George W. Bush supported him in this and declared that there could be no further movement toward peace until Arafat's power was curbed. An important step in this direction occurred on April 29, 2003, when the Palestinian parliament confirmed Mahmoud Abbas and his cabinet. Arafat had sought to prevent Abbas from taking power but failed. Abbas publicly opposed terrorism but was unable to prevent or stop a new wave of suicide bombings that took place after he assumed office. As the violence increased, Palestinian confidence in the leader decreased, and he was removed from office. Ahmed Qureia became the new prime minister.

**Further reading:** Said, Edward W. *The War for Palestine: Rewriting the History of 1948.* Cambridge, UK: Cambridge University Press, 2001; ———. *The End of the Peace Process: Oslo and After.* New York: Pantheon, 2000; Walker, Tony. *Behind the Myth: Yasser Arafat and the Palestinian Revolution.* New York: Random House, 1995.

## Panama

Panama occupies a strategically important position in the Western Hemisphere, forming a land bridge between North and South America. Slightly smaller than South Carolina, it has an area of 29,762 square miles and a population of 2.9 million people. The first Europeans explored the isthmus in 1501 searching for gold. In 1717 what is today Panama, along with Ecuador, COLOMBIA, and VENEZUELA, became part of the Viceroyalty of New Granada. In 1819 this area became the Republic of Greater Colombia. In 1830 Ecuador and Venezuela withdrew, but Panama remained part of Colombia.

Panamanian independence was achieved in 1903 and was intimately linked to the decision to build an interoceanic canal through Panama instead of NICARAGUA, which had been the preferred site. A lobbying campaign led by Philippe Bunau-Varilla, who had served as an engineer on an earlier PANAMA CANAL project and held a financial interest in a newly formed Panama Canal Company, and Mark Hanna, REPUBLICAN PARTY boss, turned the political tide in the United States for a Panama Canal in 1902.

SECRETARY OF STATE JOHN HAY was then instructed by President TEDDY ROOSEVELT to arrange for a treaty with Colombia that would permit the United States to build, operate, and protect a Panama Canal. The Hay-Herrán treaty of 1903 accomplished this, but its terms were so favorable to the United States that the Colombian congress unanimously rejected the treaty. Under its terms the United States received a six-mile wide canal zone for $10 million plus an annual payment of $250,000. Impatient with this turn of events, the administration discretely threw its support to a coup being organized by Bunau-Varilla in New York City. The three keys to the plan were bribery, the creation of a 500-person "army," and the arrival of the USS *Nashville*. The day after the *Nashville* arrived the revolt began, and the revolutionaries were able to prevail as the *Nashville* prevented Colombian reinforcements from arriving. The revolt began on November 3, 1903. The next day independence was declared. U.S. recognition followed in three days. Fifteen days later the Hay–Bunau-Varilla Treaty was signed that provided Panama with the same amount of money offered to Colombia by the earlier treaty. This time, however, the treaty provided for a 10-mile wide canal zone over which the United States would be able to "act as if it were sovereign." By the treaty the United States also guaranteed Panama's independence. The new Panamanian government approved the treaty virtually sight unseen, and the U.S. Senate gave its approval in February 1904 by a vote of 66-14.

By the 1950s terminating U.S. control over the Panama Canal had become a rallying point for Panamanian nationalists. In 1959, for example, students and others rioted in the Canal Zone and sought to raise a Panamanian flag. President DWIGHT EISENHOWER ultimately relented and allowed the Panamanian flag to fly in the Canal Zone for the first time in the 20th century. Rioting also broke out in 1964, but this time President LYNDON JOHNSON was not interested in making concessions and made it clear he would not tolerate attacks on the American flag. Against this backdrop negotiations on the future of the canal made little progress.

True progress on addressing the status of the Panama Canal was not made until President JIMMY CARTER took office. He quickly moved to negotiate two treaties that were signed in 1977. One treaty abrogated the 1903 treaty and provided for the political reintegration of the Canal Zone back into Panama as well as provided for additional revenues for Panama from the canal's operation. The second treaty gave the United States the right to defend the "neutrality" of the Panama Canal in perpetuity. Panamanians approved the two treaties by a 2-1 vote in a national plebiscite. The treaties encountered rough passage in the U.S. Senate. In March 1978, the Senate approved the neutrality treaty by a 68-32 vote. The treaty voiding the 1903 treaty was approved in April by a similar vote. In each case this represented a one-vote margin. Crucial to the passage of these treaties was a memo of understanding signed by Panamanian president Omar Torrijos that permitted the United States to intervene until 2000 to prevent aggression directed at the Panama Canal or transit through it. Another condition gave the United States the right to intervene in Panamanian affairs, with military force if necessary, if the canal were ever shut down.

Controversy returned to U.S.-Panamanian relations in the 1980s. At the heart of the problem was General Manuel Noriega, who assumed power in 1983. Noriega, who had long been on the CENTRAL INTELLIGENCE AGENCY's (CIA) payroll, was a strong ally of the United States in its anticommunist Central American policies. In particular he proved valuable in training and aiding the contras in their battles with the Sandinistas in Nicaragua. The problem was that Noriega had also enmeshed himself in DRUG TRAFFICKING. As early as 1985 the Reagan administration had begun to warn Noriega about the dangers inherent in this activity but did little to stop him. That changed in February 1988 when two Florida grand juries indicted Noriega on charges of transporting Colombian drugs into the United States. The United States froze Panamanian assets in the United States and tried to induce Noriega to voluntarily leave Panama. Nothing came of these efforts, and talks were broken off in May 1988. The Reagan administration then explored the possibility of a COVERT-ACTION plan to remove Noriega from POWER, but it was never implemented. Not only did the ECONOMIC SANCTIONS fail to have the desired effect of removing Noriega from power, but they also alienated many middle-class Panamanians who had been supporters of the United States. Unemployment reached almost 80 percent. Faced with Noriega's refusal to leave and mounting economic woes, the United States relented and lifted the financial embargo.

Upon taking office President GEORGE H. W. BUSH imposed economic sanctions on Panama in hopes of forcing Noriega out. Not only did this fail, but Noriega continued to lash out at the United States verbally. Harassing incidents against U.S. military personnel in the Canal Zone became more common and violent. Using one such incident as a pretext, Bush ordered 22,500 troops to invade Panama. OPERATION JUST CAUSE was a domestic political success in the United States and a military success in Panama, although popular resistance was greater than expected. Noriega was captured fleeing the Vatican EMBASSY. Brought to trial in Miami in January 1990, he was convicted of cocaine smuggling charges in April 1992 and sent to prison.

See also CONGRESS.

**Further reading:** Conniff, Michael L. *Panama and the United States.* Athens: University of Georgia Press, 1992; Hogan, J. Michael. *The Panama Canal in American Politics.* Carbondale: Southern Illinois University Press, 1986.

## Panama Canal, acquisition of

The acquisition and construction of the PANAMA Canal marked a major turning point in American foreign policy. It propelled the United States into a position of prominence in Latin America, with GREAT BRITAIN receding into a secondary role. It also reflected the emergence of a new sense of MANIFEST DESTINY that was rooted in a combination of social darwinism, racism, and a sense of obligation to maintain order in world affairs.

Interest in an interoceanic canal had long existed in the United States. It received a noticeable boost during the SPANISH-AMERICAN WAR when the battleship *Oregon* was ordered to move from the Puget Sound to the Caribbean Sea near CUBA. Had a canal existed, the *Oregon* could have made the trip in one-third less time.

The main diplomatic obstacle to building a canal was the CLAYTON-BULWER TREATY of 1850 that called for the

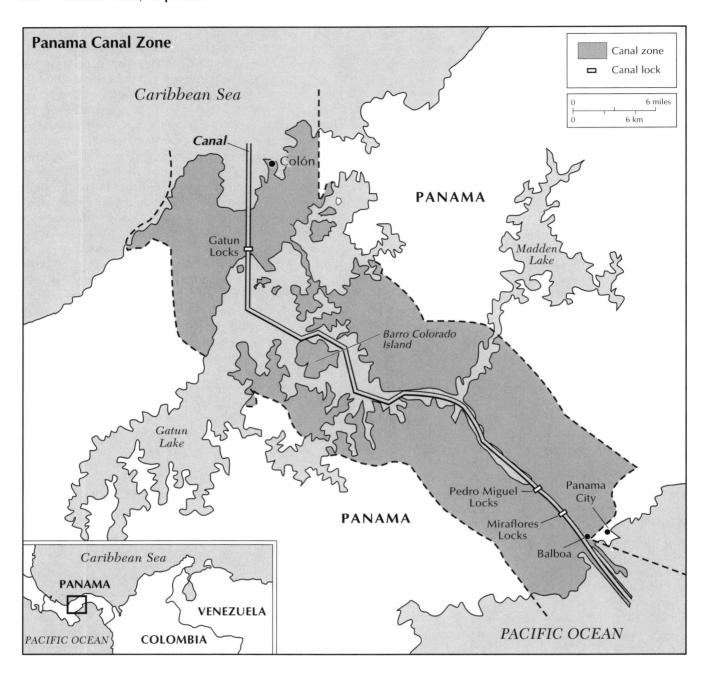

**Panama Canal Zone**

Caribbean Sea

Canal

● Colón

PANAMA

Gatun
Locks

Madden
Lake

Barro Colorado
Island

Gatun
Lake

Pedro Miguel
Locks

Panama
City

Miraflores
Locks

PANAMA

Balboa

PACIFIC OCEAN

Canal zone
Canal lock

0    6 miles
0    6 km

Caribbean Sea

PANAMA

VENEZUELA

PACIFIC OCEAN

COLOMBIA

joint Anglo-American construction and operation of a canal. In January 1900 CONGRESS began considering a bill that would have violated the terms of the Clayton-Bulwer Treaty by authorizing the construction of an American canal. Alarmed at what this would do to U.S.-British relations, SECRETARY OF STATE JOHN HAY urged the British ambassador to the United States, Sir Julian Pauncefote, to have his government renegotiate the agreement. Involved in the Boer War and not wanting to antagonize the United States, the British agreed, and in

February 1900 the Hay-Pauncefote Treaty was signed. It permitted the United States to build, own, and maintain an Isthmian canal but forbade the United States to fortify it. The treaty became embroiled in the politics of the 1900 presidential election, with most of the attention being drawn to the prohibition on fortifying the canal. When the Senate approved the treaty in 1901, it added three amendments that the British refused to accept. A second Hay-Pauncefote Treaty was signed in November 1901 that was silent on this point and thus gave the

United States the right to fortify a canal. It was approved by the Senate in December. The British found it necessary to accept the U.S. position for two reasons. First, Great Britain was becoming preoccupied with GERMANY and wished to retain the good will of the United States. Second, it was no longer in a position to afford to station military and naval forces in the Caribbean. It would be up to the United States to defend the region, so it had no real objections to defenses along a new canal.

With the diplomatic obstacles to building a canal removed, the issue now became where to build it. Two options existed. One route went through NICARAGUA. The second route went through Panama. Most legislators supported the Nicaraguan route. Two commissions (1895 and 1899) had also endorsed the Nicaraguan route, and in January 1902 the House passed the Hepburn Bill by a vote of 308-2 authorizing the PRESIDENT to proceed with the construction of a Nicaraguan canal. Supporters of the Panama route enlisted the aid of Republican political boss Mark Hanna, who had become a senator from Ohio. Their efforts were also aided by the fact that THEODORE ROOSEVELT was now president, and he strongly preferred the Panamanian route. Roosevelt ordered the second commission to reconsider its recommendation. It did so and now supported the Panama route. The Senate endorsed this revised recommendation, and the House accepted this verdict. A bill was signed on June 28, 1902, authorizing the PRESIDENT to obtain the right of way for such a canal from COLOMBIA. Should he fail to accomplish this within a reasonable amount of time and on reasonable terms, he was to begin negotiations with Nicaragua.

Secretary of State Hay now set out to negotiate a treaty with Colombia of which Panama was part. Hay threatened Colombia with a Nicaraguan canal if it did not agree to U.S. terms. On January 22, 1903, Hay and the Colombian representative in Washington, Dr. Thomas Herrán, signed a treaty giving the United States a 100-year lease on a strip of land six miles across the isthmus for $10 million and an annual rent of $250,000 to begin in nine years. The lease was renewable at the "sole and absolute option" of the United States. The U.S. Senate approved the treaty in March, but senators in Bogotá balked. It ignored a threat of retaliation from Hay and unanimously rejected the Hay-Herrán Treaty on August 12, 1903. At issue was money. Colombia's Senate wanted the cost of the lease raised to $15 million. It also sought to obtain $10 million from the New Panama Canal Company that would build the canal. The United States was to pay it $40 million for its assets. The United States, bowing to the pressure of the lobbyists for the New Panama Canal Company, asserted that Colombia had no right to any of this $40 million. Colombia countered that the New Panama Canal Company's franchise expired in one year, and at that point

Colombia could seize its assets and sell them to the United States, thus reaping all of the profits.

A small group of Panamanian leaders, worried about the prospects of losing the canal to Nicaragua, began to plot a revolt against Colombia. They joined forces with representatives of the New Panama Canal Company, most notably Philippe Bunau-Varilla, who had been chief engineer for the French-owned Panama Canal Company. In October 1903 he met with Hay and Roosevelt. He came away from that meeting convinced that if a revolution were to take place the United States would not let it fail. Later that month the United States ordered warships to the region. On November 2 they received instructions to prevent Colombia from seizing the railroad or landing troops near the isthmus should revolution break out. This decision represented a departure from long-standing U.S. practice and a novel interpretation of the Bidlack Treaty of 1850. This treaty had pledged the United States to defend the neutrality of the isthmus. The target had always been Great Britain, and the United States had never acted without the consent of Colombia.

The Panamanian revolt began on November 3, and on November 4 Panama declared itself to be an independent state. Colombia asked the U.S. for help to put down the rebellion on November 6, promising to sign the Hay-Herrán Treaty. The United States rejected the request and instructed the U.S. consul-general in Panama to recognize Panamanian independence. Bunau-Varilla became Panama's first ambassador to the United States. On November 18 the Hay–Bunau-Varilla Treaty was signed granting the United States title in perpetuity to a 10-mile strip of land. Panama was named a protectorate of the United States, thus guaranteeing its independence. The Senate approved the treaty on February 23, 1904, by a vote of 66-14. Liberals and Democrats referred to the events in Panama and U.S. participation in them as scandalous. Teddy Roosevelt defended his action as being "justified by the interests of collective civilization."

Construction of the Panama Canal began in May 1904, and it was opened 10 years later, on August 15, 1914. More than 1,000 merchant ships passed through the Panama Canal in its first year of operation. Both the WILLIAM HOWARD TAFT and WOODROW WILSON administrations sought to patch up relations with Colombia. Wilson negotiated a treaty in 1914 that expressed regret for the U.S. involvement in the Panamanian revolution and offered $25 million in compensation. Republicans opposed the move, but in 1921, after Roosevelt's death, they supported a similar measure that did not contain an expression of regret. The Senate approved this treaty on April 21, 1921.

**Further reading:** Hogan, J. Michael. *The Panama Canal in American Politics.* Carbondale: Southern Illinois University Press, 1986.

## Panama Canal Treaties

The Panama Canal Treaties were signed by President JIMMY CARTER and Panamanian president Omar Trujillo on September 7, 1977. The treaties transferred control of the canal to PANAMA and guaranteed its permanent neutrality. They were the subject of a bitter domestic political battle in the United States that pitched conservatives led by RONALD REAGAN, who saw the canal as a keystone to America's hemispheric defense, and liberals, who saw the need to establish a new partnership with Latin America. On March 16, 1978, the Senate approved the neutrality treaty by a vote of 68-32. On April 18, it approved the Panama Canal Treaty by the same vote. The U.S. CONSTITUTION requires a two-thirds majority vote to ratify treaties.

President Carter was not the first president to seek a new Panama Canal treaty. Three major attempts were made to change the 1903 Hay–Bunau-Varilla Treaty between 1903 and 1955. President LYNDON JOHNSON tried and failed to do so. Three treaties were signed in 1967 but never sub-

Former president Jimmy Carter shakes hands with Panamanian president Mireya Moscoso on December 14, 1999, at the Miraflores Locks of the Panama Canal during a ceremony signifying the turnover of the Panama Canal. Carter was the architect of the 1977 treaty that handed the canal over to Panama. *(John Davenport/Getty Images)*

mitted to the Senate for ratification. RICHARD NIXON and GERALD FORD had spoken of doing so, and negotiations began in 1973 when Ellsworth Bunker was confirmed by the senate as ambassador-at-large for this purpose. In 1974 SECRETARY OF STATE HENRY KISSINGER and Panama's foreign minister got so far as to sign a statement of principle regarding the future of the Panama Canal.

On January 27, 1977, the Carter administration's Policy Review Committee of the NATIONAL SECURITY COUNCIL held its first meeting and recommended that the United States move quickly to negotiate a new treaty. Where opponents of a new treaty saw the increasing prevalence of anti-U.S. violence in Panama as blackmail intended to force the United States out of the canal, Carter viewed the nationalist grievances as legitimate and saw a new treaty as a way of providing better protection for the canal than could the continued and indefinite presence of U.S. military personnel.

After six months of negotiations the United States and Panama had agreed upon two treaties. The Panama Canal Treaty required the United States to eliminate the Canal Zone and transfer the property and the responsibility for running the canal back to Panama in 2000. Up until that time Panama would gradually assume an increased role in running the canal under the auspices of a new Panama Canal Commission. The Treaty on the Permanent Neutrality of the Canal declared that the canal would be permanently neutral and gave the United States and Panama the right to defend the canal after 2000. Only Panamanian forces, however, were to be stationed on Panamanian territory.

The treaties were signed on September 7, 1977. On September 16 they were submitted as one document to the Senate for its consent. There ensued the second-longest treaty ratification debate in history. A total of 192 changes were offered during the course of these debates, and 88 were voted upon. Three major changes in the two treaties were made, each of which required the approval of Panama. All involved the neutrality treaty.

In his testimony, Secretary of State CYRUS VANCE stated that nothing in the treaty prevented the United States from intervening in order to protect the neutrality of the canal. General Trujillo objected to this interpretation of the treaty as well as to the meaning of the statement that allowed U.S. military ships to move "expeditiously" through the canal. Hastily arranged meetings between Carter, Trujillo, and Senate Majority Leader Howard Baker (R-Tenn.) produced the necessary compromise, whereby the U.S. wording would go into the treaty as a statement of understanding. The second and more difficult change involved an amendment that allowed the United States to use military force in Panama after 2000 to keep the canal open. Carter endorsed this change, and it was attached to the neutrality treaty as a condition. Panama objected since this gave the United

States the right to intervene into its internal affairs. The issue was resolved by inserting language into the condition that omitted any reference to the use of force and affirmed that the U.S. right to keep the canal open was not a right to intervene in Panama. The third and least controversial change was the insertion of a condition stating that nothing in the treaty precluded the United States and Panama from entering into an agreement permitting the stationing of U.S. forces in Panama after 2000.

The political struggle over the Panama Canal Treaties now shifted to the House of Representatives. While it has no constitutional role in ratifying treaties, the House does have a constitutional role in appropriating funds. Implementing the Panama Canal Treaties required passing implementing legislation by both houses. Primary jurisdiction to the implementing legislation was given to the House Merchant Marine and Fishing Committee, whose chair opposed the treaties. In lieu of the Carter administration's bill, he proposed his own, which among other things changed the new Panama Canal Commission from a government corporation to a government agency whose funds would have to be approved each year and required that all land transfers to Panama be voted on rather than occur automatically. His bill was approved by the House but objected to by Panamanian officials who cited some 30 provisions that violated the treaty as approved by the Senate and agreed to by Panama. The Senate passed implanting legislation more consistent with the language of the treaty. A conference committee produced a bill with language that reflected the Senate's bill. After first being defeated in the House, the conference committee version was finally accepted by the House by a vote of 232-188, only four days before the treaty was scheduled to take effect.

The Panama Canal Treaties are significant for the light they shed on the politics of treaty ratification. They show the degree to which the Senate has become a major player in the treaty process. The insertion of reservations, conditions, and new interpretations can cripple treaties, and this is one reason why presidents have sought FAST-TRACK authority in trade negotiations. The Panama Canal Treaties also serve to illustrate the role that the House of Representatives can play in formulating treaty through its budgetary powers.

See also CONGRESS; DOMESTIC INFLUENCES ON U.S. FOREIGN POLICY.

## Paris, Treaty of   See TREATY OF PARIS.

## Partnership for Peace

The Partnership for Peace (PfP) is an institution created by the NORTH ATLANTIC TREATY ORGANIZATION (NATO) in 1994. It serves as a formal vehicle for bilateral interaction between NATO members and nonmembers. According to the PfP invitation document, NATO will consult with any PfP member that perceives a direct threat to its territorial integrity, political independence, or security. Individual partnership plans are drawn up according to the needs of the partner. The basic aims are to create more transparency in defense matters, ensure the democratic control of the military, and enhance the prospects for joint military action with NATO.

The need for such an institution grew out of the collapse of the Soviet Union and the dissolution of the WARSAW PACT alliance along with NATO's uncertainty over how to respond to the altered geopolitical landscape of Europe. Originally viewed as a type of halfway house to full membership in NATO by mid-1994 22 former Warsaw Pact states had joined the PfP. RUSSIA joined in June 1994. The PfP receded in importance once NATO made the decision in 1997 to expand by inviting the Czech Republic (see CZECHOSLOVAKIA), POLAND, and Ireland to join, bringing its membership to 25.

Membership in the PfP brought advantages to nonNATO members beyond those available through the North Atlantic Council, which was created in 1991 to serve as a forum for NATO and former Warsaw Pact states to discuss their future relations. PfP members are granted the right to consult with NATO should they feel threatened. PfP membership also provides a mechanism for these states to participate in PEACEKEEPING operations and military planning exercises with NATO. The practical effect of this was to lay the foundation for integrating the militaries of PfP states into NATO's military structure. It also had the effect of accomplishing two short-term NATO goals. The first was facilitating transparency in military planning. The second was ensuring the democratic control of military forces. Both were seen as important interim steps toward reducing the possibilities of accidental or premeditated military conflict in Europe at a time when few rules governing military relations were in place. PfP members are not, however, covered by Article 5 of the North Atlantic Treaty, which pledges members to come to the defense of one another.

While the need for an institution like the PfP was widely recognized in the absence of a NATO decision to expand, the PfP as been subject to extensive criticism. Some voiced concern that the creation of the PfP raised more questions about the future of NATO than it solved: Would it remain a collective defense organization? Would it become a collective security body? Would it simply become a faceless amalgam of NATO and the Warsaw Pact? These concerns over NATO's uncertain future grew the longer it took NATO authorities to decide how to proceed with expansion. Others feared that by inviting PfP members to consult with NATO if they felt threatened but not guaranteeing protection a situation in which

NATO's credibility could easily be called into question was created. Finally, others were critical that the PfP solution to NATO's membership dilemma did not directly address the key question: What was the place of Russia in post–COLD WAR Europe? Russia viewed NATO expansion into Eastern Europe and the BALTIC STATES as a hostile action and a continuation of cold war encirclement. NATO remained the enemy. Inviting Russia to join NATO signaled that this was not the case, but extending an invitation required a thoroughgoing rethinking of NATO's mission and structure.

## peacekeeping and peacemaking

Peacekeeping operations became a staple of UNITED NATIONS (UN) activity in the 1960s. This was a product of two sets of forces. First, there occurred a rapid expansion in the membership of the UN due to the end of colonialism. The presence of newly independent developing countries transformed the General Assembly from a grouping of states largely aligned with the United States to one in which expressions of nonalignment and neutrality were common, especially among the larger states, such as INDIA, INDONESIA, and EGYPT. Second, the COLD WAR conflict between the United States and the Soviet Union had now shifted to the Third World. True neutrality was not possible according to the rules of a bipolar INTERNATIONAL SYSTEM. Accordingly the unstable domestic political situation in many of the newly independent states created inviting opportunities for each side in the cold war to seek out allies.

Because the outbreak of the cold war made collective security impossible, the UN searched for alternative methods of promoting international peace. The answer arrived at was preventive DIPLOMACY. It called for the UN to undertake a twofold role. Prior to the outbreak of violence the UN needed to be actively involved in diplomatic efforts to find a peaceful solution. If this failed and conflict erupted, the UN was to organize peacekeeping missions. These were military forces inserted into a conflict situation by the invitation of the host state. The purpose of peacekeeping missions was straightforward. In the short run they were to stop violence and prevent its reoccurrence. In the long run they were to create a stable political environment in which peace negotiations could be carried out.

The success of peacekeeping efforts depended on several factors. First, the military forces had to be seen as neutral. This requirement meant that they could not be composed of U.S. or Soviet troops (or those of closely allied states). It also meant that they had to be lightly armed and obey strict rules of engagement that placed them in a reactive posture. Second, the peacekeeping operation had to have the support of the United States and the Soviet Union. Peacekeeping operations were not funded out of the regular UN budget. Without adequate financial sup-

port they would wither away. Peacekeeping operations also required that both the United States and the Soviet Union were willing to accept a "second best" solution to the problem. Each victory by an ally was viewed as the best outcome, and defeat was the solution to be avoided, but successful peacekeeping required that both sides accept some version of a neutral outcome. Third, each of the domestic sides to the dispute had to be willing to accept a similar outcome. Their goals did not necessarily coincide with the goals of their external superpower supporters.

The UN had a mixed record as a peacekeeper in the broadest sense of the term. One study found that of some 160 INTERNATIONAL CRISES between 1945 and 1975 the UN became involved in 95 cases and helped resolve 28 of them. The best known UN peacekeeping operations in this period include the United Nations peacekeeping operation in the Sinai following the SUEZ CRISIS (UNEF I), the United Nations Operation in the CONGO (ONUC), and the United Nations Emergency Peacekeeping Force in Cyprus (UNFICYP). Each produced different results. UNEF I managed to keep the Egyptian and Israeli armies at bay until Egypt requested they leave in 1967, but it did not create conditions favorable to a lasting peace. In fact, their exit set the stage for the 1967 Arab-Israeli War. ONUC is held to be the most problem-plagued UN peacekeeping mission, and most consider it to have been a failure. UNFICYP stabilized the situation in Cyprus but only succeeded in freezing the conflict rather than resolving it.

In the last decades of the cold war, the international community's interest in peacekeeping was minimal. With the fall of Soviet COMMUNISM, there was renewed hope that the UN's peacekeeping mission could be reinvigorated. These hopes were temporarily dashed by the failed 1994 mission in SOMALIA. In its aftermath President BILL CLINTON issued a presidential directive that laid down strict conditions governing American support for such UN operations. What the Somalia case had made clear was that this second generation of peacekeeping missions would be different from earlier ones. These would now be peacemaking missions.

Peacemaking operations differ from peacekeeping operations in several important respects. First, the legitimacy of peacekeeping operations derived from two sources. They were approved by the Security Council and invited in by the host state. No invitation is necessary in peacemaking operations. Second, the peacekeepers' military mission was minimalist and defined in reactive terms. Under peacemaking UN forces have far greater latitude of action. They are, in fact, potentially combat forces. This change in mission has led to a change in the complexion of these forces. Peacekeeping forces were largely comprised of nationals from many different small states. Peacemaking forces tend to come from a single command authority.

In the Balkans the UN turned over important peacemaking responsibilities to the NORTH ATLANTIC TREATY ORGANIZATION. In East Timor, the UN supported an Australian-led peacemaking mission. As a consequence of these changes, although neutrality is still an important principle governing these operations, it is not the paramount one.

Finally, it should be noted that two problems that plagued the conduct of peacekeeping operations continue to exist. The first is the financial cost of peacemaking operations. In 1994, with UN peacemaking forces operating in BOSNIA AND HERZEGOVINA, CAMBODIA, and Somalia, the cost was $3.547 billion. The second reoccurring problem is that of political will. Just as not every crisis in the cold war resulted in the establishment of a peacekeeping operation, not every post–cold war crisis has brought about a peacemaking operation. The most notable case of a nonpeacemaking operation was in RWANDA, where widespread genocide was taking place. In the cold war the underlying reason for inaction was that the United States and the Soviet Union cared too much about a country to accept the second-best solution provided by peacekeeping. In the post–cold war era the reason for inaction appears to be that no one cares enough about a country to create a peacemaking force. The delay in sending forces to LIBERIA is consistent with this view.

**Further reading:** Boutros-Ghali, Boutros. *An Agenda for Peace.* 2d ed. New York: United Nations Press, 1992; Cahill, Kevin. *Preventive Diplomacy.* New York: Basic, 1996; Crocker, Chester, et al., eds. *Managing Global Chaos.* Washington, D.C.: United States Institute of Peace Press, 1996; Durch, William J. *UN Peacekeeping, American Policy, and the Uncivil Wars of the 1990s.* New York: St. Martin's, 1996.

## peace movements

There exists a number of ways by which the public voice can enter into the foreign-policy decision-making process. PUBLIC OPINION, ELECTIONS, and INTEREST-GROUP activity are the most conventional means for doing so. Less conventionally, political protest in both its violent and nonviolent forms has also been an avenue for expressing the public voice. It has been used by those who feel alienated or disenfranchised by the more established mechanisms of influencing decision making. Peace movements operate in a boundary zone between the conventional and unconventional avenues of influence. Their exact location is dependent upon the political tenor of the times, the message they convey, and the mechanisms used to convey that message.

It is after the WAR OF 1812 that the peace movement emerges as an organized social and political force independent from churches. The first two important organizations established were the New York Peace Society in August 1815 and the Massachusetts Peace Society in December 1815. Their creation led to the establishment of others, and in 1828 a federation of peace societies was established, the American Peace Society. It would become a fixture on the political landscape, although its influence and level of activism would vary greatly. This pre–AMERICAN CIVIL WAR peace movement was relatively small and geographically compact. Most peace societies were to be found in New England, and they held about 300 members. The peace movement was also internally divided. One faction was made up of those who opposed all wars regardless of their purpose or the provocation that brought them into being. A second group believed that some wars could be justified. This philosophical division led to an organizational division as well. While both groups of peace supporters coexisted within the American Peace Society, some formed a more radical organization, the American Anti-Slavery Society. Further organizational splintering came about due to the Civil War. The American Peace Society supported the North. It felt able to do so on the grounds that there was a distinction between civil and international wars. Many of the more absolutist pacifists left to help establish the Universal Peace Society that was founded in 1866. It would soon expand its set of concerns to include more than the abolition and prevention of war. The plight of immigrants, NATIVE AMERICANS, and women were also on its agenda.

The peace movement languished after the end of the Civil War until the turn of the 20th century. It was reinvigorated by the growth of peace movements in Europe and new leadership in the United States. At the same time it faced important challenges. The SPANISH-AMERICAN WAR was very popular, and imperialist sentiment ran high. A common theme voiced by the peace movement was that the war was a mistake and would in the end lead to an upsurge of support for abolishing war. Veteran peace activists in New England organized the Anti–IMPERIALISM League to oppose military action in the PHILIPPINES and colonialism, but the new organization never matured or became a central force in the peace movement. An important boost in the fortunes of the peace movement came in 1910 when Andrew Carnegie gave $10 million to establish the Carnegie Endowment for International Peace. It permitted the peace movement to produce literature, hold conferences, and otherwise circulate ideas regarding INTERNATIONAL ORGANIZATION and INTERNATIONAL LAW as guarantors of peace.

This theme had emerged very early in the history of the peace movement. The initial point of interest centered on arbitration treaties, which required both parties to seek international arbitration of disputes when they arose. This internationalist and legalist line of thinking within the peace movement would resonate well with American foreign-policy makers in the last years of the 19th century and the first decades of the 20th century. President THEODORE ROOSEVELT would win a Nobel Prize for his mediation efforts in the Russo-Japanese War. SECRETARIES OF STATE JOHN HAY, ELIHU ROOT, and WILLIAM JENNINGS BRYAN all supported such treaties. The KELLOGG-BRIAND PACT sought to outlaw war. WOODROW WILSON would propose the LEAGUE OF NATIONS, and even after its rejection by the Senate, the United States participated in the WASHINGTON and LONDON DISARMAMENT CONFERENCES.

In many ways the Carnegie Endowment for International Peace came to symbolize one strand of the peace movement. It was professional in membership, internationalist in outlook, and establishment in orientation. It constituted a lobbying campaign from the inside of the political system directed at policy-making elites, many of whom were sympathetic to its members' ideas. It did not have an organizational or philosophical monopoly over those who belonged to this strand of the peace movement. A competing body was formed in June 1915. The Peace Enforcement League held that not only were international law and organization fundamental to peace but also that to be effective there needed to exist an international enforcement mechanism. Embedded in this proposal was the concept of PEACEKEEPING.

With the onset of WORLD WAR I a second strand took shape. It was progressive in outlook, focusing on people in the street rather than policy elites. Its concern was with social and domestic problems as they related to peace and not the practice of international relations. War was not a stand alone issue for these peace advocates but one linked to a broader agenda. This strand of the peace movement embraced two themes: international mediation of disputes and reductions in military spending. The Women's Peace Party, which became the Women's International League for Peace and Freedom, was a leading force in pursuit of the first goal. The Anti-Preparedness Committee and its successor the American Union against Militarism were central players in pursuit of the second goal. Still a third and overlapping strand of the peace movement was symbolized by the efforts of the Fellowship of Reconciliation. Founded in 1915 its members were absolute pacifists who rejected war. It worked extensively with churches and conscientious objectors, who often faced prison and persecution for their beliefs.

In the 1930s two important developments occurred in the life of the peace movement. One was the 1936 creation of the Emergency Peace Campaign, which sought to bring together the pacifist and internationalist strands of the peace movement. Rather than being an organization to which people belonged, the Emergency Peace Campaign sought to work through existing peace organizations, churches, and other venues to spread its message. Because it was a loose coalition it often spoke with a mixed voice,

and it soon collapsed under the weight of philosophical disagreements. An important factor in its dissolution was the Ludlow Amendment. Representative Louis Ludlow (D-Ind.) proposed a constitutional amendment that mandated a national referendum before Congress could declare war. It had been supported by the National Coalition for the Prevention of War, but not all peace groups were behind it. The League of Nations Association, for example, lobbied against it, and those groups that supported it found themselves in an awkward political alliance that included socialists and conservative isolationists.

In the first years after WORLD WAR II the focus of the peace movement returned to themes close to the heart of its establishment internationalist strand. Liberal internationalists worked tirelessly for the creation of the UNITED NATIONS. They were not opposed in this effort by the pacifist strand, but it was uneasy with the apparent big, POWER domination of the United Nations. A more radical proposal emerged from scientists who had helped build the atomic bomb. The Federation of American Scientists endorsed the idea of world federalism as a means of providing for international control over atomic energy. Rapidly growing COLD WAR tensions and spy scandals involving work on the atomic bomb made world federalism suspect and robbed it of its political power.

The progressive and pacifist strand of the peace movement stepped to the forefront as NUCLEAR WEAPONS testing and the arms race became a permanent feature of world politics in the 1950s. Two groups emerged in 1957 that attacked the problem through different methods. The Committee for a Sane Nuclear Policy relied on the type of education campaign for which the peace movement had become known since the founding of the Carnegie Endowment. The second group, drawing inspiration from Mohandas Gandhi, preached civil disobedience and direct action. It was the Committee for Non-Violent Action. Among its protest targets were the Nevada office of the Atomic Energy Commission, the Strategic Air Command's headquarters outside Omaha, and the Polaris submarine base in New London, Connecticut. The two organizations also differed in their goals. The Committee for a Sane Nuclear Policy sought a comprehensive nuclear test ban treaty. The Committee for Non-Violent Action had a more extensive agenda that included civil-rights issues.

America's participation in the VIETNAM WAR would be the next issue to energize the peace movement. Muted voices of protest were present early in the war. Among those groups active were the Friends Committee on National Legislation, the Women Strike for Peace, and the Student Non-Violent Coordinating Committee. VIETNAM protest became highly visible in 1965 when the Students for a Democratic Society organized the first major antiwar protest demonstration. It would be the first of many mass protests that became identified with the antiwar movement. These protests successfully demonstrated the depth of antiwar feeling among the American public. A total of 200,000 would march in San Francisco in spring 1967, and 100,000 would march that fall in Washington, D.C. As many as 500,000 would protest in November 1969. What these protests were not able to do was to unite the multitude of antiwar movements into a coherent political force. Questions of protest tactics and strategy along with disagreements over the proper policy to pursue in Vietnam constantly tore at the movement's unity. An important symbolic force in the anti-Vietnam peace movement was Vietnam Veterans Against the War. They lent a credibility to the peace movement that pacifists could not generate on their own. Central to their argument was that war crimes and atrocities, such as those that First Lieutenant William Calley had been charged with, were really the responsibility of those who planned and organized the war effort.

The cold war would provide two final rallying points for the peace movement. In the 1980s concern over President RONALD REAGAN's loose rhetoric about NUCLEAR WAR and the buildup in military spending energized a campaign to halt the nuclear arms race. The Nuclear Freeze Campaign emerged in 1981 as a device to link activist groups and provide information. In June 1982 it organized a march in New York City that was estimated to have attracted 1 million people. Their cause was quickly taken up by members of Congress, notably Senator Ted Kennedy (D-Mass.), as a way of challenging Reagan's foreign policy. The House Foreign Affairs Committee reported on a nonbinding nuclear freeze resolution in 1983 that passed by a vote of 286-149. Its significance was soon overtaken, however, when that same body voted approval for funding the MX MISSILE. The second rallying point was Reagan's NICARAGUA policy. The HUMAN-RIGHTS violations associated with groups supported by the United States brought forward a wave of protests.

The end of the cold war has not meant the end of the peace movement. As we have noted, forces within the peace movement have long embraced causes that extend beyond the immediate problem of war to include social and political issues. In the post–cold war era GLOBALIZATION has provided a focal point for protest groups that have been active in the peace movement. Demonstrations in Seattle and Washington, D.C., have sought to highlight what are perceived to be the antidemocratic operating style and pro-business agendas of the WORLD BANK, INTERNATIONAL MONETARY FUND, and WORLD TRADE ORGANIZATION. The 2003 war against IRAQ sparked considerable protest directed against the administration of GEORGE W. BUSH.

**Further reading:** Chatfield, Charles. *The American Peace Movement: Ideals and Activism.* New York: Twayne Publishers, 1992; DeBenedetti, Charles. *The Peace Reform in American History.* Bloomington: Indiana University Press, 1980.

## Pentagon Papers

The Pentagon Papers was a secret DEPARTMENT OF DEFENSE study of U.S. decision making on VIETNAM that covered the period from America's involvement in Indochina during WORLD WAR II through May 1968, when the Paris peace talks began. Its publication by the *New York Times* led to a major SUPREME COURT case regarding the extent of presidential national security POWERS. The Pentagon Papers are also significant for the light they shed on national security decision making.

SECRETARY OF DEFENSE ROBERT MCNAMARA commissioned the Pentagon Papers study, officially known as "History of U.S. Decision Making Process on Vietnam Policy," on June 17, 1967. McNamara and some of his colleagues in the Pentagon were becoming increasingly disillusioned with the VIETNAM WAR and saw the study as a means of shedding light on the path that had led them to the current debacle. Thirty-six people worked on the project. They produced a 47-volume document that contained more than 3,000 pages of narrative and 4,000 pages of documentation. Only 15 copies of the final report were produced. Reportedly, attempts by McNamara to have the Johnson administration release the report failed.

In spite of its length, the Pentagon Papers do not constitute a definitive history of the U.S. involvement in Vietnam. Principal participants could not be interviewed, and researchers did not have access to complete files of the STATE DEPARTMENT, CENTRAL INTELLIGENCE AGENCY, or the White House. Moreover, researchers did not try to integrate the material into an integrated narrative account. They instead chose to compartmentalize their discussion. For example, the Kennedy administration's decision making on Vietnam is divided into five sections. The Johnson administration's conduct of the war is divided into sections dealing with the land war, the air war, political relations with South Vietnam, and secret diplomacy. All occur simultaneously, but no single section draws them together.

The *New York Times* obtained a copy of the Pentagon Papers minus the four volumes on the secret diplomacy of the Johnson administration. It began running them as a series on June 13, 1971. Citing national security threats, the Nixon administration tried to stop their publication after the first three installments appeared. The *Washington Post* and other newspapers soon joined with the *New York Times* in publishing the Pentagon Papers. On June 30 the Supreme Court ruled by a 6-3 vote to reject the Nixon administration's argument and permit the newspapers to continue to publish them.

As a footnote to the history of Pentagon Papers, it was Daniel Ellsberg who gave them to the *New York Times*, and it was Ellsberg's psychiatrist whose office was broken into by the "plumbers" unit established by President RICHARD NIXON to stop leaks whose existence became known during the Watergate investigation.

**Further reading:** Shapiro, Martin, ed. *The Pentagon Papers and the Courts: A Study in Foreign Policy Making and the Freedom of the Press.* San Francisco: Freeman, 1972.

## Persian Gulf War

The Persian Gulf War was the first major international conflict of the post–COLD WAR era. The immediate reaction was to view it as both a major diplomatic and a military success for the United States. The Bush administration succeeded in putting together a global coalition to oppose IRAQ's occupation of KUWAIT and then a military operation that brought about his withdrawal with minimal American loss of lives. Its long-term significance for American foreign policy and world politics, however, is not as clear.

The first stage of the conflict begins in early 1990 and ends with Iraq's August 2 invasion of Kuwait. It is dominated by rising tensions between the United States and Iraq and Iraq and its Arab neighbors. On February 15, 1990, Iraq protested a Voice of America broadcast on global DEMOCRATIZATION that characterized Iraq as a state in which "secret police were widely present." U.S. ambassador April Glaspie wrote a letter of apology stating that the United States did not question the "legitimacy" of the government of Iraq nor was it seeking to interfere in its domestic affairs. Iraqi president Saddam Hussein repeated his attacks on the United States in a late February meeting of the Arab Cooperation Council, in which he also stated that Arab states needed to provide Iraq with $30 billion in aid for its military effort against IRAN in the 1980–88 IRAN-IRAQ WAR. Failure to do so, he threatened, would cause Iraq to "take steps to retaliate." That war had cost Iraq more than $500 billion. OIL sales were the key to Iraq's recovery, but the price of oil was steadily dropping.

A flurry of diplomatic activity followed. King Hussein of JORDAN tried and failed to broker an agreement between Iraq and the other Middle East oil-producing states. Saddam Hussein continued his verbal attacks on the United States, and the Bush administration responded by labeling them as "inflammatory" and "irresponsible." It also considered imposing ECONOMIC SANCTIONS. In May, Saddam Hussein stepped up his verbal offensive. At a summit meeting of Arab states he charged that Kuwait and other quota-busting oil-producing states were "virtually waging an economic war" against Iraq. The May summit did produce an agreement to limit the production of oil, but Kuwait

indicated that it would reevaluate its position in the near future. Hussein would soon charge Kuwait with being part of a "Zionist plot aided by imperialists." Low oil prices were termed a "dagger" pointed at Iraq. These outbursts set off a new round of diplomatic activity to defuse the growing crisis. This included meetings with Ambassador Glaspie, who insisted that the United States wanted better relations with states in the region but would "defend [its] vital interests" and the sovereignty of their "friends" in the Persian Gulf. The exact meaning of this last comment was unclear since on July 31 a high-ranking STATE DEPARTMENT spokesperson told CONGRESS the United States had "no defense treaty relationship with any Gulf country."

Accompanying this hostile rhetoric were troop movements by key units of Iraq's Republican Guard toward the Kuwaiti border. The United States was disturbed by this action but concluded that their purpose was to intimidate rather than invade. The United States continued to hold to this interpretation right up until the invasion, although on July 31 elements of the INTELLIGENCE COMMUNITY concluded that war was now imminent given the scale and direction of recent Iraqi troop movements. Within 11 days Saddam Hussein had moved eight divisions to within 300 to 400 miles of the Kuwait border. Given that the United States only had 10,000 military personnel in the region and that most of them were naval forces there was little that the United States could do to prevent the invasion.

The second period of the Persian Gulf War encompasses the time span between the invasion of Kuwait and the beginning of the bombing campaign in January 1991. On August 2, 1990, Kuwait was invaded by Iraqi troops, who took control of most of the country within a matter of hours. That same day President GEORGE H. W. BUSH froze all Iraqi and Kuwaiti assets and moved to stop all trade and financial dealings with Iraq. On August 4, he stated that the invasion "could not stand," and the UNITED NATIONS voted to impose economic sanctions. On August 24, it authorized the use of force to impose those sanctions. Iraq rejected UN calls for withdrawal and promised the "mother of all battles" should force be used against it.

U.S. diplomatic efforts were directed at creating and holding together an anti-Iraq coalition that would support the use of force. Diplomatic initiatives by FRANCE and RUSSIA called into doubt allied unity in September and October, but by November unity was achieved. Most significant were an agreement by CHINA not to veto a UN resolution authorizing the use of force and the willingness of SAUDI ARABIA to actively participate in the war effort by allowing the United States to place bases there. On November 29, the Security Council voted 12-2, with China abstaining, to set January 15, 1991, as the deadline for Iraq's peaceful exit from Kuwait. It authorized member states to "use all

U.S. Air Force F-15C fighters fly over a Kuwaiti oilfield that has been torched by retreating Iraqi troops during the Gulf War, 1991. *(Hulton/Archive)*

means necessary" to bring about Iraq's complete and unconditional withdrawal.

Within the United States a vigorous debate was taking place over the wisdom of going to war with Iraq over Kuwait. Zbigniew Brzezinski and HENRY KISSINGER, NATIONAL SECURITY ADVISORS to PRESIDENTS Carter and Nixon, respectively, were on different sides, with Brzezinski counseling against war and Kissinger for it. Admiral William Crowe, chairman of the JOINT CHIEFS OF STAFF under Reagan, argued for giving economic sanctions more time. The CENTRAL INTELLIGENCE AGENCY estimated that Iraq already had lost more than 90 percent of its imports and 97 percent of its exports. In January 1991 CONGRESS took up the question of whether to support the use of military force as requested by Bush or continue to rely upon sanctions. On January 12, the House of Representatives voted 250-183 to support the president. The Senate did so by a 52-47 margin.

On January 16, 1991, OPERATION DESERT STORM began. Coalition aircraft took off from Saudi Arabia to begin the air campaign against Iraq. Coalition air forces would fly more than 109,000 sorties, drop 88,500 tons of bombs, and shoot down 35 Iraqi planes. On January 17, Iraq responded by launching Scud missile attacks on Saudi Arabia and ISRAEL. One of the major concerns U.S. war planners had was Israel's response to these attacks. The fear being that if Israel retaliated, then Arab members of the coalition would defect. Israel did not retaliate, and the coalition held together.

On January 23, after a failed Soviet-Iraq peace initiative and the refusal of Iraq to begin a large-scale withdrawal of its forces from Kuwait, coalition forces launched a ground assault into Iraq. On February 28, Iraq announced a cease-fire and agreed to a meeting of military commanders to discuss terms for ending the war. The UN Security Council approved Resolution 686, setting out the terms for ending hostilities on March 2. The following day Iraq agreed to these terms. On April 3 the UN Security Council approved Resolution 687, which established a permanent cease-fire in the Persian Gulf War and ended international sanctions against Iraq. Iraq accepted these terms on April 6, formally ending the war.

Several debates exist over the lasting significance of the Persian Gulf War for American foreign policy. At the strategic level commentators note that, although a military success, the Persian Gulf War was also a DETERRENCE FAILURE (Kuwait was invaded) and a compellence failure (Iraq was not persuaded to leave Kuwait). Many also believe that the Persian Gulf War will prove to be the exception rather than the rule for post–cold war conflicts. More typical, they assert, are the type of conflicts in BOSNIA AND HERZEGOVINA and SOMALIA, in which aggression is not as clear cut and fighting is more constrained by population centers and geography. At the tactical level debate centers on the value of air power and technology, such as the Patriot missile defense system, versus ground troops, and the role of the MEDIA. Finally, the very wisdom of fighting the war or at least its war aims had been called into question by Saddam Hussein's ability to stay in power and defy UN weapons inspectors, prompting a second conflict, the Iraq War, in March 2003.

See also DETERRENCE; GULF WAR SYNDROME; NUCLEAR COMPELLENCE; OPERATION DESERT SHIELD.

**Further reading:** Mazarr, Michael, et al. *Desert Storm: The Gulf War and What We Learned.* Boulder, Colo.: Westview, 1993; Woodward, Bob. *The Commanders.* New York: Simon and Schuster, 1991.

## personality

Personality is one of several influences at work in determining the direction of U.S. foreign policy. Most Americans take it as an article of faith that it matters deeply who is elected to office because it is individuals who make policy. The historical record of U.S. foreign policy, however, provides no easy answers as to the relative importance of personality over other factors. The central questions that must be answered in assessing the influence of personality on U.S. foreign-policy making are: Under what conditions does personality matter, how should we think about personality, and whose personality is most likely to matter?

The individual whose personality is studied most frequently in U.S. foreign policy today is the PRESIDENT. This reflects the growing concentration of foreign-policy POWER in the executive branch and the tendency of presidents to want to be at the center of foreign-policy decision making. If we were to look at U.S. foreign policy prior to WORLD WAR II, our focus must expand to include the personalities of SECRETARIES OF STATE or other cabinet-level officials and key members of CONGRESS. Prominent examples include WILLIAM BORAH, DANIEL WEBSTER, HENRY CLAY, and WILLIAM SEWARD. Today we cast an eye to these individuals under two sets of circumstances. First, cases are examined in which the president has delegated a great deal of power to his aides. This was the case with RONALD REAGAN and was long thought to be the case with DWIGHT EISENHOWER. Studies of their presidencies invariably turn to the personalities of key figures such as William Casey, Oliver North, and JOHN FOSTER DULLES. Second, cases are studied in which the American public is split over competing visions of U.S. foreign policy. This was the case after World War II and after VIETNAM. Foreign-policy accounts here place great emphasis on the personalities of Arthur Vandenberg, Joseph McCarthy, HENRY KISSINGER, and J. WILLIAM FULBRIGHT.

Not all situations permit the force of an individual's personality to come through. Some situations are so highly structured and the options available so limited that it is hard to imagine personality making a difference in the selection of a policy. Other situations are so fluid and chaotic that it is equally hard to single out personality as an important factor in the choice of a policy. The most favorable situation for individuals to exert an influence on foreign policy is one that lies in between. It is organized enough to permit meaningful action, and credible choices exist. From a presidential personality perspective this tends to translate into issues that are new on the foreign-policy agenda, occur early in an administration, and attract a president's ongoing personal attention. Under the first two conditions there are few bureaucratic, INTERNATIONAL SYSTEM engendered, or domestic political constraints on the president, so personality can play a big role in the decision. In the last case, the force of a president's personality may be sufficient to overcome these constraints.

There exists no single way to classify presidential personalities. This is an important point because different classification schemes will result in different groupings of presidents. Presidents who are said to be alike in one formulation of presidential personality may be separated into two or more groups in another. The choice of a classification system depends primarily upon two considerations. First, what traits are most important in understanding an individual's personality? Is it their degree of optimism or pessimism, a need to dominate others, or their sense of self-esteem? Second, what type of data is going to be used? The most frequent sources of information used in these accounts as memoirs, public statements, and biographies. They do not always produce a coherent or accurate picture. Not all of the statements attributed to him may actually have been spoken by the president. They may reflect the need to have a statement ready for the evening news.

The best-known framework for classifying presidential personality has been offered by James David Barber. His scheme is based on the degree of involvement a president exhibits in using the powers of the presidency (active-passive) and the degree satisfaction a president feels (positive-negative). Each of the resulting types of presidential personality can be seen as having different consequences for U.S. foreign policy.

The active-positive put a great deal of energy into being president and derive a great deal of satisfaction from the effort. They are seen as achievement-oriented, and they view politics as a game to be mastered. They are capable of changing direction as needed but also tend to overreach and not appreciate how irrational politics can be. HARRY TRUMAN, FRANKLIN ROOSEVELT, JIMMY CARTER, JOHN KENNEDY, BILL CLINTON, and GEORGE H. W. BUSH are examples. The active-negative also expends a great deal of energy but rarely feels satisfied. Victory is never achieved. This president has a great deal of difficulty changing directions and gets locked into losing positions. LYNDON JOHNSON, RICHARD NIXON, and WOODROW WILSON are examples. The passive-positive exerts relatively little effort into being president but gains satisfaction from it. Politics holds appeal, but the role is seen as limited, as authority is delegated to others. Ronald Reagan is one of the most difficult presidents to classify, but he has been put into this category. The passive-negative does not like politics. The president participates out of a sense of duty and with a restricted sense of role. Eisenhower was long classified as a passive-negative. Recent evidence suggests that he took a much more active role behind-the-scenes in setting the tone and direction of American foreign policy than was commonly realized.

The IRAQ WAR brought into focus President GEORGE W. BUSH's personality. While not characterized as a deep thinker in terms of the complexity of policy issues, Bush is seen as self-confident and possessing a clearly defined political style that allows him to achieve his goals. He describes himself as a "gut player." Others around him define him as an impatient policy maker who wants solutions to problems. In going public with a policy position President Bush typically begins by asserting a maximalist policy position in bold, highly partisan, and noncompromising tones. If resistance is encountered, he shifts the premises on which his policy is based in order to garner support for it. All the while the message is kept simple and repeated again and again. One issue at a time is focused on to the exclusion of others so that the message is not diluted or linked to other issues. Finally, if need be, compromises may be made, but all the while a public aura is maintained that any compromises were made on the administration's terms.

**Further reading:** Barber, Janes David. *The Presidential Character: Predicting Performance in the White House.* Englewood Cliffs, N.J.: Prentice Hall, 1985; Greenstein, Fred I. *Personality and Politics.* Chicago: Markham, 1969.

## Philippines

The Philippines is an archipelago of more than 7,000 islands totaling 117,187 square miles, making it slightly smaller in land area than New Mexico. It is located in the Southwest Pacific and has a population of 76.5 million people. The first economic contact between the United States and the Philippines occurred in the 1790s. The Philippines was a Spanish colony for 377 years, from its conquest by Ferdinand Magellan in 1521 until its takeover by the United States in 1898.

The United States acquired the Philippines as a result of the SPANISH-AMERICAN WAR. Although fought primarily over CUBA, U.S. contingency plans had called for taking the Philippines should fighting break out. Commodore George Dewey destroyed the Spanish fleet in Manila Harbor on May 1, 1898. Manila surrendered in August. The Treaty of Paris, signed on December 10, 1898, formally ended the war and made the Philippines a U.S. possession. The Senate ratified the treaty on February 6, 1899, by a vote of 57-27, slightly more than the two-thirds vote necessary to approve treaties.

The acquisition of the Philippines proved a controversial issue both in the United States and the Philippines. Within the United States it set off a heated political debate between pro- and antiimperialist forces. Unlike the case of Cuba, there was no equivalent of the Teller Amendment for the Philippines, in which in the United States pledged not to acquire it. Arguments in favor spoke of MANIFEST DESTINY, economic gain, and national security. Opponents, some of whom supported continental expansion and the annexation of HAWAII, challenged President WILLIAM MCKINLEY's decision to acquire the Philippines on racial and moral grounds and with the argument that domestic problems took precedence over foreign policy.

In the Philippines the American takeover occurred in the midst of an ongoing war for independence led by Emilio Aguinaldo. On June 12, 1898, he declared Philippine independence from SPAIN and was unwilling to replace Spanish domination with American domination. Fighting between his forces and American troops began on February 4, 1899, and lasted until 1902. Initially the Philippine-American War took the form of conventional warfare, but in its later stages it involved a GUERRILLA WARFARE. One estimate places the number of casualties in this war at 4,165 Americans dead and 200,000 Filipinos dead. The cost of the war was determined to be about $160 million.

With the acquisition of the Philippines, the American period began. It continued until the Philippines were conquered by Japan in WORLD WAR II. WILLIAM HOWARD TAFT was the first American colonial governor of the Philippines, serving from 1900 to 1913. Other notable governors included Leonard Wood and HENRY STIMSON. Although their terms in office differed in style and temperament, they shared a general focus on working with elites and treating Filipinos as if they were backward people who would benefit from American tutelage.

Pressures for Philippine independence built during the American period. WOODROW WILSON made Philippine independence a part of his platform in 1913, but CONGRESS would not support such legislation. The Jones Act that emerged in 1916 made only a vague promise that the Philippines would be granted independence after a stable government existed. It continued to give the American appointed governor general the right to veto decisions made by the Philippine legislature. The next major move toward independence came with the 1934 Tydings-McDuffie Act, which set up a 10-year transition period for independence. It terminated the position of governor general and designated the Philippines as a commonwealth. Economic self-interest was an important factor in this move. The Great Depression in the United States had created conditions that made agricultural interests and labor hostile to Filipino competition.

During the first half of the 20th century a number of important American foreign-policy initiatives were undertaken at least partially with the Philippines in mind. The

1908 Root-Takahira Agreement between the United States and JAPAN pledged each side to respect each other's territorial possessions in the Pacific and the general status quo in the region. In practical terms, this helped protect the Philippines and Hawaii and allowed Korea to fall under Japanese domination. At the WASHINGTON NAVAL CONFERENCE of 1920–21, the Five-Power Treaty established a tonnage ratio for capital ships that was intended to stabilize the Pacific and prevent an arms race. As part of that agreement the United States pledged not to fortify the Philippines.

Filipino independence was granted after World War II, on July 4, 1946. The Philippines' official independence date would later be changed to July 12 to commemorate the day that Aguinaldo declared Philippine independence from Spain. The first years of Philippine independence were marked by an extreme dependence on the part of the Philippines for American economic FOREIGN AID and national security. This was manifested in a series of highly inequitable agreements signed between the two states. The Bell Trade Act of 1946 gave the United States a one-sided free-trade agreement with the Philippines. The United States had open access to the Philippine market, but key Philippine goods such as sugar came into the United States under a quota system. The next year the United States and the Philippines signed a military bases agreement that allowed the United States to maintain and operate a series of military installations there. It was under this agreement that the United States obtained 99-year leases on 23 bases, including Subic Bay and Clark Air Base, two of the major COLD WAR American military bases in the Pacific.

Philippine and American authorities also fought a peasant-based and Communist-inspired guerrilla movement from 1945 to 1953, the Hukbong Mapagpalaya ng Bayan (HUK or HMB). This insurgency fed American early cold war fears that the Philippines was one of the nations under the DOMINO THEORY that might fall to COMMUNISM. President Ferdinand Marcos used the ongoing threat from Communist guerrillas as part of his 1972 rationale for declaring martial law. With the passage of time Marcos's regime became increasingly corrupt and HUMAN-RIGHTS violations more prevalent. Economic growth suffered. President JIMMY CARTER singled out the Philippines for criticism of human-rights violations during his presidency.

The beginning of the end for Marcos came in 1983 when opposition leader Benigno Aquino was assassinated. Marcos had long since established his credentials as a loyal American ally who had been supported by the CENTRAL INTELLIGENCE AGENCY, and President RONALD REAGAN continued to support him as opposition mounted. Political forces inside the REPUBLICAN PARTY, however, began to urge Reagan to abandon him for fear of creating another situation such as that in IRAN, where prolonged support for the shah helped propel anti-American forces into power. Among them was Senator Richard Lugar (R-Ind.), chair of the Senate Foreign Relations Committee, who judged a 1986 election that Marcos won to be fraudulent. Reagan confidant Senator Orin Hatch (R-Idaho) also urged the president to distance himself from Marcos. The end came for Marcos on February 25, 1986, when two of his key military leaders deserted him and joined forces with the civilian opposition led by Corazon Aquino, widow of Benigno Aquino. Marcos went into exile in Hawaii.

The most significant development in the decade following Marcos's removal from power was the adjustment of American military presence in the Philippines. In 1991, a draft treaty was agreed upon that gave the United States use of Subic Bay Naval Base for 10 years. Clark Air Base was abandoned by the United States because of damage done by the eruption of Mt. Pinatubo. The Philippine senate rejected the treaty, and when no agreement was reached, the Philippines informed the United States on December 6 that it would have one year to withdraw from its facilities. The withdrawal was completed ahead of schedule, and American forces left on November 24, 1992. In February 1998 the two states negotiated the Visiting Forces Agreement, which facilitated the arrival of American warships in the Philippines and joint military exercises.

U.S.-Philippine relations took a new turn after the SEPTEMBER 11, 2001, terrorist attacks on the World Trade Center and the Pentagon. President GEORGE W. BUSH spoke of unleashing a global war against TERRORISM, and the Philippines became a early point of expansion in that war outside of AFGHANISTAN. In January 2002, U.S. Special Forces began arriving in the Philippines to help fight Muslim guerrillas linked to OSAMA BIN LADEN. A total of nearly 1,300 U.S. military troops were dispatched to the southern Philippines to provide counterterrorism training for dealing with the Abu Sayyaf guerrillas. In June the Bush administration approved an expansion in their role that allowed them to move beyond serving as advisers to joining Philippine forces on patrols. The military operations succeeded in significantly weakening the Abu Sayyaf movement, but they did little to counter more significant insurgent threats elsewhere. In August the United States and the Philippines agreed in principle to establish a joint senior civilian group to coordinate military policy.

See also ALLIANCES; IMPERIALISM.

**Further reading:** Brands, H. W. *Bound to Empire.* New York: Oxford University Press, 1992; Cullather, Nick. *Illusions of Influence.* Stanford, Calif.: Stanford University Press, 1994.

## Pierce, Franklin (1804–1869) *president of the United States*

Franklin Pierce served as the 14th president of the United States from 1853 to 1857. In his one term in office, Pierce supported expansionist efforts to enlarge the commercial and political reach of the United States. His administration concluded the GADSDEN PURCHASE in 1854 that completed the process of land acquisition from MEXICO. He was president at the height of the FILIBUSTERING by private Americans who sought to expand the territory of the United States by annexing NICARAGUA, CUBA, the DOMINICAN REPUBLIC, and parts of Mexico. His support for William Walker, who seized Nicaragua and was made its president, placed his administration in direct conflict with GREAT BRITAIN, whose interests in Central America were most directly affected by the filibusters. Pierce recognized Walker as Nicaragua's president in May 1856 as part of election-year politics within the United States.

He sought and failed to acquire rights to Samana Bay in the Dominican Republic. It was to have been a coaling station and would have provided the navy with a strategically placed port to use in the Caribbean Sea. Pierce also positioned his administration to annex Cuba. The triggering event was the Cuban seizure of the American vessel *Black Warrior*. This ship was engaged in coastal trade along the American coast and frequently used Havana as a port of call between New York and Mobile. On February 28, 1854, Cuban officials seized the ship, saying it lacked proper papers to dock in Havana. Pierce sought to use the *Black Warrior* incident to incite the American public and pressure SPAIN to abandon Cuba. He failed, largely due to domestic political problems. The recently passed Kansas-Nebraska Act had torn apart the DEMOCRATIC PARTY and left the country deeply divided on the future of slavery. Acquiring Cuba, a probable slave state, was politically impossible.

Looking to the Pacific, Pierce also had designs on HAWAII. In 1854 the Pierce administration negotiated an annexation agreement with Hawaii. The treaty was not approved by the Senate because it contained a provision calling for immediate statehood. As in Latin America Pierce supported and encouraged private individuals in their efforts to expand U.S. influence. In the Pacific it was primarily commercial interests that he supported in laying claim to largely uninhabited islands that held potential economic value.

**Further reading:** Gara, Larry. *The Presidency of Franklin Pierce.* Lawrence: University Press of Kansas, 1991.

## Pike Committee

The Pike Committee, also known as the House Select Committee on INTELLIGENCE, is the less well known of two committees established in 1975 to examine charges of illegal activities by the CENTRAL INTELLIGENCE AGENCY (CIA). The other committee was the CHURCH COMMITTEE. Together their hearings helped usher in a new era of intelligence oversight marked by greater congressional participation.

The House and Senate each set up special committees to investigate the CIA in the wake of revelations by the *New York Times* that the CIA had systematically engaged in illegal activity virtually since its creation. Included in these acts were cases of wiretapping, mail openings, and spying on Americans.

The Pike Committee was the second committee established by the House for this purpose. The first committee was headed by Lucien Nedzi (D-Mich.). He was head of the House armed services subcommittee on the CIA. Controversy surrounded the committee's efforts from the start. It became known that Nedzi had been briefed about improper CIA actions in his previous position. Another committee member, Michael Harrington (D-Calif.), was a strong critic of the CIA who leaked information to the press and had been a key force in bringing to light CIA involvement in efforts to bring down Salvador Allende in CHILE. In July the House abolished the Nedzi Committee and formed a new one headed by Otis Pike (D-N.Y.). It was tasked with the same purpose but contained neither Nedzi nor Harrington.

Whereas the Church Committee focused on illegal activities, the Pike Committee directed its attention to managerial and organizational issues. It sought to determine the usability and accuracy of the information provided by the CIA to policy makers. Though seemingly less sensitive than the agenda pursued by the Church Committee, the Pike Committee operated under the great handicap of not being trusted by the executive branch. It repeatedly engaged in battles over access to secret information and what information it would be allowed to make public. So contentious were its deliberations that the House refused to publish its final report because it contained information still classified as secret.

See also CONGRESS; COVERT ACTION; INTELLIGENCE COMMUNITY.

## Pinckney's Treaty

Negotiated in 1795, Pinckney's Treaty (also known as the Treaty of San Lorenzo) was immensely popular in the United States because it spurred economic development in the American Northwest by providing an outlet for transporting goods down the Mississippi River to New Orleans.

SPAIN had been an ally of GREAT BRITAIN against FRANCE but withdrew from that ALLIANCE in 1795 because of the threat posed by the French army to Spain. While this action made Spain more secure, it left its North American holdings vulnerable to a possible Anglo-American alliance. To Spanish officials, JAY'S TREATY in 1794 signaled that an improvement in U.S.-British relations had occurred and made this threat more credible. Therefore, in 1794 Spain requested that the United States send a representative to Madrid. Spain sought to engage the United States in a triple alliance with Spain and France against Great Britain, but Pinckney refused, as his negotiating instructions focused on obtaining free navigation rights on the Mississippi River.

Pinckney's Treaty gave the United States unrestricted navigation rights on the Mississippi and the right of deposit in New Orleans. It settled the disputed southwestern boundary with Spain at the 31st parallel. Finally, each side agreed not to incite NATIVE AMERICANS to engage in attacks against the other.

**Further reading:** Bemis, Samuel F. *Pinckney's Treaty: America's Advantage from Europe's Distress, 1783–1800.* New Haven, Conn.: Yale University Press, 1960.

## Platt Amendment

The Platt Amendment was named after Orville Platt, Republican senator from Connecticut, and it constituted an amendment to the 1901 U.S. Army Appropriations Bill. The Platt Amendment specified the terms under which the U.S. military occupation of CUBA would end and effectively relegated Cuba to the status of a U.S. protectorate. It provided the legal justification for three U.S. military interventions in Cuba in 1906–09, 1912, and 1917–22.

The end of the SPANISH-AMERICAN WAR left the United States in an ambiguous position with regard to Cuba's future. U.S. forces occupied the island, and by terms of the treaty ending the war, SPAIN had been forced to relinquish its control over Cuba. Yet, in the years leading up to the outbreak of war, the United States had come to distrust the Cubans, who freely destroyed U.S. property and engaged in a scorched-earth policy intended to force Spain leave. Cuban self-government was thus not looked upon favorably. The Teller Amendment, appended to the declaration of war, clearly stated that the United States had no intention of annexing Cuba. Some expansionists wished to disregard this pledge, but popular support for annexing Cuba suffered as a result of an insurrection in the PHILIPPINES that had been acquired by the United States in the Spanish-American War.

The Platt Amendment was the WILLIAM MCKINLEY administration's solution to navigating through this maze of conflicting pressures. It contained five principal clauses. First, Cuba was not to enter into any treaty impairing its independence or permitting a foreign power to gain control over the island. The main fear was that GERMANY would use Cuba to establish a beachhead in the Western Hemisphere. Second, Cuba would not incur an excessive amount of international indebtedness. If Cuba did so, it risked the possibility of intervention. Third, the United States had the right to intervene into Cuban affairs for the purpose of maintaining order and Cuban independence. Fourth, Cuba agreed to a U.S.-sponsored sanitation program. Fifth, Cuba agreed to sell or lease to the U.S. sites for naval and coaling stations. The United States subsequently acquired Guantánamo Bay. In 1901, under pressure from U.S. military governor Leonard Wood, the Cuban legislature added the provisions of the Platt Amendment to the constitution. The measure led to mass demonstrations and was passed by a one-vote margin. In 1903 it was incorporated into a treaty between the two states.

European states reacted negatively to the Platt Amendment. The one-sided nature of its provisions led newspapers to observe that it represented "the beginning of absolute control by the Americans." And, in fact, pressures for annexation continued within the United States with several resolutions to that effect introduced into CONGRESS. President THEODORE ROOSEVELT surprised most observers when he ended the U.S. occupation in 1902. Domestic unrest continued, however, and in 1906 U.S. occupation forces returned at the request of the Cuban president.

It was not until 1934 that the Platt Amendment was terminated. By this time it had become clear that the Platt Amendment had become counterproductive. Rather than serving to legitimize U.S. intervention into Cuba, it had become a lightning rod for those political forces in the Western Hemisphere who opposed U.S. domination. The setting for announcing this decision was the 1934 Montevideo Conference that launched FRANKLIN ROOSEVELT's Good Neighbor policy.

**Further reading:** Perez, Louis, Jr. *Cuba under the Platt Amendment, 1902–1934.* Pittsburgh: University of Pittsburgh Press, 1986.

## pluralism

Pluralism is regarded as the orthodox interpretation of how the American policy-making system works. It asserts that POWER is fragmented and diffused throughout American society. Political power takes many forms. It can involve actors who adhere to a position, money, status, or organizational abilities. Many groups have the power to participate in policy making, and no one group is powerful enough to dictate policy. The natural state of affairs is held to constitute an equilibrium or balance among competing groups. Because of this, policy is a product of bargaining between groups, and the adopted policy reflects the interests of those groups who are in the majority at the time. Government acts as an umpire in supervising the competition and sometimes compelling a settlement should a stalemate arise.

The traditional focal point of INTEREST-GROUP activity is CONGRESS, and as Congress has assumed a more active and visible role in foreign-policy making, the role of interest groups appears to many as playing a more prominent role in U.S. foreign-policy formulation. Congress is not, however, the only place in the U.S. political system where lobbying occurs. The president is lobbied directly by interest groups. The BUREAUCRACY is also a major target of interest-group activity. Recently we have seen a great deal of foreign lobbying at the state level as states compete with one another for foreign investment and have imposed economic sanctions on governments for their HUMAN-RIGHTS policies.

Business groups, ethnic groups, labor, and farmers are among the interest groups whose foreign-policy activity has received the most frequent study. Lobbying by foreign interests is on the rise in the United States and has produced an often intense debate. Critics assert that foreign lobbying is dangerous because the more American policy makers listen to foreign interests the less they are listening to American interest groups. Supporters assert that it is only natural that foreign governments and firms would lobby the U.S. government given the global importance of U.S. foreign policy and that it is incorrect to assume that there is a natural division of opinion among interests groups that pit American interest groups against foreign lobbyists. More often than not, American and foreign interests will be on both sides of an issue. Grassroots groups that mobilize to lobby on specific issues, such as ending apartheid in SOUTH AFRICA, promoting a nuclear freeze, or denouncing the WORLD TRADE ORGANIZATION, have also succeeded in influencing the direction of U.S. foreign policy and are cited by pluralists as proof of the competitive nature of the American political system.

Pluralism stands in sharp contrast to ELITE THEORY in how it interprets the interaction between society and the government in making U.S. foreign policy. Where elite theory sees government as a tool of a permanent dominant class in society, pluralists stress the existence of a fluid balance of power among sectors of society with government serving as a neutral arbitrator. In between these two positions stands a view that acknowledges the importance of interest groups to making foreign policy but rejects the assertions that they are engaged in competitive behavior or that the government is neutral.

Sometimes referred to as interest-group liberalism or iron triangles, the picture drawn here is one of a fragmented government in which interest groups enter into permanent and exclusive alliances with different portions of the government so as to shape policy to meet their needs. New groups or poorly organized groups find themselves shut out of the decision-making process. Just as important, these relationships reduce the ability of the U.S. government to plan because it is unable to speak with one voice or examine problems from a national perspective.

**Further reading:** Lowi, Theodore J. *The End of Liberalism: Ideology, Policy, and the Crisis of Authority.* New York: Norton, 1969; Spanier, John, and Eric Uslaner. *American Foreign Policy and the Democratic Dilemmas.* New York: Holt, Rinehart and Winston, 1985.

## Point Four Program

The Point Four Program was an early COLD WAR initiative by the Truman administration to redirect U.S. foreign policy in an internationalist direction after WORLD WAR II. It called for worldwide technical assistance to developing states for the purpose of promoting economic development and dampening the appeal of COMMUNISM.

In his 1949 inaugural address to CONGRESS, President HARRY TRUMAN proposed four foreign-policy initiatives: first, the creation of a NORTH ATLANTIC TREATY ORGANIZATION to unite the states of this region in a mutual defense pact; second, support for the UNITED NATIONS; third, support for the MARSHALL PLAN, an economic recovery plan for Europe; fourth, a technical assistance plan for the developing world. The goal was to make "the benefits of . . . scientific advances and industrial progress available for the improvement and growth of underdeveloped areas." Conceptually, the Point Four Program filled a void in the emerging U.S. foreign-policy agenda by providing a vehicle for establishing a U.S. presence in many of the states just emerging from colonial status or that existed outside the scope of the Marshall Plan.

Quickly known as the Point Four Program, Truman's plan met with a mixed reception in Congress. Senator Robert Taft (R-Ohio) opposed the measure because it aimed to spread taxpayer's money "around the world in places where there is no particular demand for it." Part of Taft's concern was that while the sum requested was not particularly large it could lead to large FOREIGN-AID expenditures. In June 1950 Congress passed a $35.4 million Point Four Program. In 1953 Congress expanded Point Four funding to $155.6 million.

The goals of the Point Four Program were long range in nature, and its logic reflected that element of the AMERICAN NATIONAL STYLE that placed great faith in technological and engineering solutions to policy problems. Throughout its existence the Point Four Program operated largely on the fringes of U.S. foreign policy. Notable successes included fighting malaria in PERU and typhus in IRAN, building a hydroelectric plant in MEXICO, and constructing irrigation systems in JORDAN. In time other basic needs, low-cost, people-intensive foreign-aid initiatives, such as the Peace Corps, would supplant it. The Point Four Program was also condemned to operating in the shadows of the much larger U.S. military assistance programs to developing states and the growing use of COVERT ACTION that sought to achieve short-term foreign-policy objectives.

See also INTERNATIONALISM.

# Poland

Located in central Europe, Poland is about the size of New Mexico. It has an area of 120,725 square miles and a population of 39 million people. Today Poland is an ethnically homogeneous state, with 98 percent of the population being Polish and 90 percent Roman Catholic. This has not always been the case. Homogeneity has come about through shifting borders, mass population movements, and the targeting of Jews for annihilation by Nazi GERMANY during WORLD WAR II.

Poland's political history has been marked by periods of greatness, extinction, independence, subjugation, and domination. Poland's age of greatness came early in its history. The Jagiello dynasty was founded in 1386 and continued until 1572. Under it, political POWER was consolidated, arts and sciences flourished, the economy grew, and Poland's borders were successfully defended from foreign attack. Two centuries later, Poland had disappeared from the map of Europe as an independent state. Internal economic and political weakness plus the diplomatic maneuverings of neighboring great powers, each of whom feared that another would gain control over Poland, led to a series of partitions in 1772, 1793, and 1795 between Austria, Prussia, and RUSSIA that ultimately resulted in the disappearance of Poland. Russia emerged from these negotiations with the largest piece of Polish territory. It would be another century before Poland would effectively be resurrected to its former size. This happened at the Paris Peace Conference that ended WORLD WAR I. The reestablishment of Poland was one of WOODROW WILSON'S FOURTEEN POINTS. The United States recognized Poland in 1919. Controversy surrounded its resurrection. Negotiators established a Polish-Soviet border that awarded Russia much of what had been eastern Poland. Polish officials objected to the proposed boundary, known as the Curzon Line, and instead demanded the 1772 boundary. War broke out between the Soviet Union and Poland, and the exact boundary was not settled until the Treaty of Riga in 1921.

The interwar years found Poland caught between two great powers, Germany and the Soviet Union, each of which harbored territorial ambitions at Poland's expense. Poland sought safety in a series of ALLIANCES. The most notable was with FRANCE and Romania, the Treaty of Locarno, in October 1925. August 1939 proved to be a fateful month for Poland. First, negotiations with GREAT BRITAIN, France, and the Soviet Union for a military pact collapsed. Next, the Soviet Union and Germany negotiated a nonaggression agreement, the Molotov-Ribbentrop Pact, which contained a secret protocol for dividing Poland between them. Two days later, on August 25, Poland signed a treaty of alliance with Great Britain and France. On September 1, Germany invaded Poland, starting World War II. Soviet troops entered Poland on September 17, and all but a small part of Poland was divided between the two invaders. In June 1941, Germany attacked the Soviet Union, and all of Poland came under German control.

A complex political-military scene developed within Poland during World War II. A government in exile was established in London, and within Poland the Polish Home Army was created to engage in GUERRILLA WARFARE against the Nazis. The United States recognized this government as the legitimate government in 1939. A rival government, however, would be created under the protection of the Soviet Union when its troops reentered Poland in 1944. It was known as the Lublin government or, more formally, the Polish Committee of National Liberation. Relations between the two governments were strained from the outset. In August 1944, with Russian troops poised outside Warsaw, an uprising against the Nazis occurred within the city. Soviet troops did not advance, and some 200,000 Poles were killed, most of whom were affiliated with the London government. Just as damaging to the relations between the London and Lublin governments was the 1943 German announcement that it had discovered a mass grave in the Katyn Forest where the Russians had killed 10,000 Polish officers. The Soviet Union denied the charge but admitted its truth in 1990. All totaled, about 6 million Poles were killed, 2.5 million were deported to Germany as forced labor, and more than 3 million Jews were killed in concentration camps.

The fate of Poland was one of the most hotly debated items at the agenda of the wartime SUMMIT CONFERENCES between the United States, Great Britain, and the Soviet Union. While American and British sympathies lay with the London government, military realities and the desire to establish a postwar working relationship with the Soviet Union led to the decision at TEHRAN and YALTA to recognize the Lublin government as the basis for the postwar Polish government. Stanisław Mikołajczyk, the leader of the London government, was instructed to work with the Lublin government in fashioning a coalition government. These negotiations also established Poland's postwar boundaries. It lost territory in the east to Russia and gained territory in the west from Germany. The integration of Poland into the Soviet sphere of influence and satellite status proceeded quickly. Government-controlled elections in January 1947 gave political power to the Communists, and in October Mikołajczyk fled into exile. In 1949 Poland joined the Council for Mutual Economic Assistance (CEMA or COMECON), and in 1955 it became a founding member of the WARSAW PACT.

Two significant challenges to Communist rule took place in Poland that brought with it a liberalization of the political and economic order. The first occurred in June 1956 when workers and students rioted in Poznań over deteriorating economic conditions. Władysław Gomułka, who had been purged from the party in 1949 and then imprisoned for his noncomformist views, was elected head of the Communist Party. Under his leadership Poland was able to pursue a policy of political and economic liberalization and accommodation with the Catholic Church without provoking a Soviet military response, as had occurred in Hungary in 1956. Over the following decades economic conditions worsened, and political freedoms once again were restricted. Attempts by the government to raise food prices in 1976 led to another round of worker riots and strikes. In 1980 strikes at the Gdańsk shipyards led to the creation of the independent trade union, Solidarity, under the leadership of Lech Wałesa. Alarmed at the possibility that a truly independent political force might be forming, Polish authorities, with the support and urging of the Soviet Union, began a crackdown. In December 1981 martial law was declared. Solidarity was outlawed, and its leaders arrested or detained. The United States and other Western states responded to these events by imposing ECONOMIC SANCTIONS on Poland. They included a ban on high-technology sales and no new credits for food purchases. Martial law was formally lifted in July 1983, but it would be 1986 before nearly all of the political prisoners would be released. The United States began lifting its sanctions against Poland in 1984. Poland elected its first noncommunist government in 40 years in September 1989. In December, the constitution was amended to replace any reference to the Communist Party as having a "leading role" in Poland, and in January 1990 the Communist Party dissolved itself. In October of that year Wałesa was elected president.

Since the end of the COLD WAR, Poland's primary foreign-policy goal has been to integrate itself into the political, military, and economic fabric of Europe. It joined the NORTH ATLANTIC TREATY ORGANIZATION (NATO) as a full member in 1999, after joining the PARTNERSHIP FOR PEACE in 1994. Poland completed negotiations to join the EUROPEAN UNION in 2002 and is expected to become a full member in 2004.

Historically, American relations with Poland had been among the most friendly and cordial that it had with any of the Soviet Union's East European satellites. This is a reflection of both the political influence held by the large number of Polish-American citizens in the United States and American sympathy for the Polish reform movement that was begun by Gomułka in 1956. MOST-FAVORED-NATION STATUS was restored in 1957, and in 1971 it was arranged for the Export-Import Bank to make loans to Poland. More recently, Poland has received the most significant allocation of funds from the Support for East European Democracy Act (SEED). As of April 1994, $123.7 million in investments and loans have gone to Poland. The United States has also provided Poland with more than $36 million for environmental protection projects.

**Further reading:** Brzezinski, Zbigniew. *The Soviet Bloc: Unity and Conformity.* Cambridge, Mass.: Harvard University Press, 1967; Starr, Richard, ed. *Transition to Democracy in Poland.* New York: St. Martin's, 1998.

**Polk, James** (1795–1849) *president of the United States*
James Knox Polk was the 11th president of the United States. He served one term in office (1845–49), choosing not to run for reelection. A strong supporter of ANDREW JACKSON's political agenda, Polk was the first "dark horse" presidential candidate to be elected, running on a platform that advocated westward expansion to OREGON and TEXAS. Both WHIG presidential candidate HENRY CLAY and his DEMOCRATIC PARTY challenger MARTIN VAN BUREN opposed Texas annexation because it risked war with MEXICO. As president, Polk succeeded against Whig opposition to enlarge the United States by not only acquiring Texas and Oregon but also California.

The process of Texas "reannexation," as Polk referred to it, had gone through a troubled process. Two treaties of annexation had been rejected by the Senate. President JAMES TYLER, a supporter of annexation, took Polk's victory as a sign of popular support for the move and in his last days in office supported a joint resolution annexing Texas. This did not end the matter, however, since the borders of Texas were not uniformly accepted, and MEXICO broke off diplomatic relations with the United States following the annexation vote. Relations with Mexico were also strained by Polk's interest in acquiring California. A failed diplomatic mission to Mexico by James Slidell was followed by a U.S. military move into disputed territory. Mexico responded by declaring a defensive war against the United States. Several soldiers were killed and injured in a military encounter that Polk used as a justification for war.

Polk's strategy was to seize the land he wished to annex in Texas and California and then sign a peace treaty. The first part of his strategy was easily accomplished. The second presented great difficulties since the Mexican government would not discuss peace terms. In some desperation he sent Nicholas Trist to Mexico to negotiate. Trist was recalled by an angry Polk when he sent a draft treaty back to Washington that went against Polk's instructions. Trist, however, did not return to Washington. He went on to agree to a different treaty, the Treaty of Guadalupe Hidalgo, that accomplished Polk's objectives. Combative with CONGRESS and secretive in his handling of the war (his goal of acquiring California was not made explicit), Polk encountered intensifying opposition from the Whigs to the war. Uncertain over his ability to obtain continued funding for the war from a Whig-controlled Congress, Polk submitted Trist's treaty to the Senate, which ratified it by a vote of 38-14.

Polk was able to obtain the disputed Oregon Territory from Great Britain without resorting to war through the Oregon Treaty of 1846. Here, too, Polk proved himself to be a combative negotiator, calling for an end to the existing joint occupation agreement with GREAT BRITAIN that had been used to finesse the issue of ownership of Oregon since 1818. Not seeking war, the British offered to accept the long-standing U.S. position that the border separating British and American Oregon be drawn at the 49th parallel. Polk wished to reject this offer but was convinced by his cabinet to accept it.

**Further reading:** Bergeron, Paul. *The Presidency of James K. Polk.* Lawrence: University of Kansas Press, 1987.

## population policy

World population growth reflects the changing balance between births and deaths. The rate of growth is not evenly spread around the world. In some countries it is rising more sharply in others, and in some cases national populations are declining. Almost all of the future population growth is expected to occur in regions of the world that traditionally occupied marginal areas in world politics. RUSSIA and Europe's portion of the world population will shrink from 22 percent in 1950 to a projected 13 percent in 2050. It is estimated that by 2050 GERMANY will lose 21 percent of its current population. Japan's population may decrease by one-third over this same time span. Most of the additional 1.5 billion people that are expected to be added to the world's population will live in AFRICA and Asia.

A standard measure used to chart and predict population changes is the fertility rate. It refers to the average number of children that women in a country have. Over time, small differences in childbearing levels translate into large differences in populations. For example, if women around the world averaged 2.5 children, the world's population would be greater than 27 billion in 2050. If they averaged 1.6 children, it would only reach 7.7 billion in 2050 and decline to 3.6 billion in 2150. In 2003 the world's highest fertility rates were found in SOMALIA (7.0), Niger (6.9), Yemen (6.8), and Uganda and the Democratic Republic of the Congo (both 6.7). In 2003 the lowest fertility rates were in Bulgaria (1.1) and the Czech Republic, Latvia, HUNGARY, Slovakia, and Singapore (all 1.2). The world average is 2.7. This is down from 5.0 in the 1970s. The United States's fertility rate is 2.1.

Population policies are strategies for realizing a particular level of population growth or change. About one-third of all states have population policies designed to reduce their national level of population growth. Some, such as FRANCE, GREECE, and Hungary, have policies intended to increase their population. While the United States does not have an explicit overall population goal it is trying to achieve, it does manage population growth to a limited extent by managing the number of immigrants and REFUGEES allowed to enter the United States each year.

The most controversial method for managing population growth is to affect the fertility rate through family-planning programs. INDIA has had family-planning programs in place since 1952. CHINA put a one-child policy in place in 1971. It combines contraception policies with economic incentives. Although it has produced a 40 percent decline in population growth, the Chinese policy has also encouraged abortions and infanticide of girls. MEXICO set up a family-planning program in 1973 that combines family-planning services, health programs, sex education, and population information programs.

In the late 1960s the United States played a leading role in providing developing states with these programs. The key international actor in this policy area is the UNITED NATIONS Population Fund. Today, support for family-planning programs has become an emotionally charged foreign-policy problem in the United States. Antiabortion activists assert that population-control policies are coercive and immoral. CONGRESS adopted this position when it passed legislation prohibiting the use of U.S. funds to pay for abortions carried out as part of international family-planning campaigns. In 1984 President RONALD REAGAN went even further when he issued an executive order prohibiting U.S. funds from going to NONGOVERNMENTAL ORGANIZATIONS conducting abortions. President BILL CLINTON reversed this ban in January 1993. President George W. Bush quickly moved to reinstate the ban upon taking office in 2001.

See also DEMOGRAPHICS, GLOBAL; INTEREST GROUPS; RELIGION.

**Further reading:** Moffet, George D. *Critical Masses: The Global Population Challenge.* New York: Penguin, 1994; Myers, Norman, and Julias Simon. *Scarcity or Abundance: A Debate on the Environment.* New York: Norton, 1992.

## Portsmouth, Treaty of　See TREATY OF PORTSMOUTH.

## Potsdam Conference

The Potsdam Conference, April 16–August 2, 1945, was the last of the major WORLD WAR II SUMMIT CONFERENCES. GERMANY had surrendered on May 8, 1945, and JAPAN would surrender on September 2. Joseph Stalin continued to represent the Soviet Union (see RUSSIA) as he had throughout the war. Following FRANKLIN ROOSEVELT's death, HARRY TRUMAN became president, and this was his first meeting with Stalin. Winston Churchill came to Pots-

*(From left to right)* Clement Atlee, Harry Truman, and Joseph Stalin at Potsdam, 1945  *(National Archives)*

dam representing GREAT BRITAIN but was replaced by Clement Atlee when Churchill's Conservative Party was defeated in an election and lost its majority in Parliament. Many of the key issues discussed at Potsdam were carry-overs from the YALTA CONFERENCE.

Germany was a central point of contention at Potsdam. By the time of the Potsdam Conference American thinking about Germany's future had undergone a significant change. The emphasis on punishment found in the MOR-GENTHAU PLAN was replaced by a concern for reconstruction and continental economic recovery. Thus, when the topic of reparation arose, Truman refused to agree upon any specific figure. He stated that for all practical purposes any reparations extracted from Germany by one of the victors must be taken from their occupation zone alone. Russia unsuccessfully opposed these points. Eastern Germany, their occupation zone, was largely agricultural and would be unable to provide the funds or material needed to rebuild the Soviet economy.

Truman's plan also held major political ramifications. The thinking at Yalta had been that Germany would be divided politically into occupation zones but treated as a single economic unit. The Soviet Union correctly realized that Truman's plan meant that Germany would be divided politically and economically. Events in the three Western zones, those administered by the United States, FRANCE, and Great Britain, would now effectively be beyond their reach. And, in fact, these occupation zones later merged to become West Germany.

POLAND also resurfaced as an issue at Potsdam. Its new western boundary temporarily was set at the Oder-Neisse line. Western complaints about the absence of free elections in Poland were met with Soviet complaints about the exclusion of Communist Parties from the political process in

GREECE. The defining feature in each case was determined by whose army had defeated German forces and served as the occupying power. In Eastern Europe, where Soviet forces ruled, Western parties were finding themselves systematically excluded from governing. The reverse held true in Greece and ITALY, where Western forces were the "liberators." Looking to Asia, Moscow again agreed to enter the war against Japan while Great Britain and the United States issued calls for unconditional Japanese surrender.

The Big Three at Potsdam also agreed to establish a Council of Foreign Ministers that would meet to take care of unfinished business. Topics still to be settled included peace treaties with German satellites, the fate of Italian colonies, the withdrawal of Allied troops from IRAN, and the future of the Dardanelles Straits. The last two would prove to be early COLD WAR battlegrounds.

In addition to the decisions reached, the Potsdam Conference is significant because it represents the first case of atomic diplomacy. It was during the Potsdam Conference that the United States successfully detonated a nuclear device at Alamogordo, New Mexico. Armed with the knowledge that the atomic bomb was a reality, Truman's negotiating posture changed. No longer was securing Soviet involvement in the war with Japan a top priority. Instead, Truman became more rigid and confident in dealing with Stalin. Negotiations appeared to give way to a pointed exchange of views. The Potsdam Declaration also contained a veiled reference to Truman's newfound military power. The alternative to unconditional surrender was defined as "prompt and utter destruction."

**Further reading:** Alperovicz, Gar. *Atomic Diplomacy: Hiroshima and Potsdam.* Rev. ed. Boulder, Colo.: Westview, 1985.

## power

In traditional international-relations thinking, power is the central concept in world politics. It forms the basis of such political relationships as IMPERIALISM and hegemony. It also provides us with a yardstick against which to compare states by letting us refer to them as great powers, regional powers, or small powers. From a policy-making perspective power is a resource that must be acquired and managed carefully if NATIONAL INTERESTS are to be realized. The central thrust of the LIPPMANN GAP is that American foreign-policy makers have rarely done this well, as goals and objectives have routinely outpaced the resources necessary to accomplish them. Today, the pursuit of power is complicated by disagreements over what makes a state powerful in the contemporary INTERNATIONAL SYSTEM.

Historically the most sought after power resources have been those that contribute to the military power of a state. Six ingredients of power stand out in this regard. The first is geography. Involved here is both the location of a state compared to others and its size and defensibility. The second ingredient is population. A large population offers leaders the ability to have both a large army and a large workforce at the same time. Education and skill levels are also important in judging the impact of population on national power, as is the age distribution of the population and its ethnic mix. The third key ingredient is the nature of its military establishment. Here we are concerned with the characteristics of its weapons, strategy, and personnel. Natural resources are a fourth key ingredient of power. The ultimate goal is self-sufficiency, but, failing that, a state must possess secure access to key natural resources. The fifth ingredient is economic wealth, for without it states will lack an industrial infrastructure capable of producing the weapons of war or the financial means to acquire them from other states. Finally, states need national will. Lacking a sense of collective unity, pride, or morale, states will be unable to maximize the potential of the other ingredients of power. Small states possessing a strong sense of national will are held to be capable of defeating more powerful states. The United States experienced this reality in VIETNAM, and it is a problem that plagues PEACEKEEPING and humanitarian military operations in the post–COLD WAR era.

Beginning in the 1970s, with the successful embargo led by the ORGANIZATION OF PETROLEUM EXPORTING COUNTRIES (OPEC) and continuing into the 21st century with talk of the significance of GLOBALIZATION, many commentators have argued that military-centered power thinking is no longer relevant. What is needed is power thinking that focuses on economic power. In this view, possession of large land masses or large armies is irrelevant to the definition of a powerful state. GERMANY and JAPAN are cited as prime examples of the new wave of powerful states whose power is rooted in the ability to TRADE rather than dominate. One key ingredient of power for trading states is competitiveness. A second and interrelated ingredient is the possession of modern technology. The third ingredient is the political capacity to shape society and formulate policies that allow one's economy to respond to changing domestic and global economic conditions.

Most recently a third vision of power resources has emerged. In this view the key to foreign-policy success today lies with the ability of a state to shape the values and ideals that guide global policy-making efforts. Unlike the "hard" forms of military and economic power, this type of power is "soft." It is not easily manipulated by policy makers but provides an all encompassing context and reference point within which decisions are made. Supporters of this view cite the global appeal of democracy as evidence of America's possession of soft power. Cynics point to the global reach of American consumer culture as evidence that soft power is little more than an instrument of economic imperialism spread by globalization.

Ever since the VIETNAM WAR a debate has raged within U.S. policy-making and academic circles over how much power the United States possesses. It was common wisdom that after Vietnam American power had receded. This was the impetus to the policy of DÉTENTE. President RONALD REAGAN rejected this declinist thesis and asserted that American military power was, or could be, as robust as ever. His critics argued that the policies his administration followed to demonstrate American military power had an adverse effect on the health of the American economy and that because of this the United States was falling further and further behind Japan, Germany, and other economic powers.

The end of the cold war produced yet another debate over power. It was acknowledged that the United States was now the only remaining superpower and that the world was militarily unipolar. From an economic point of view, however, the world appeared to be multipolar. As the ASIAN FINANCIAL CRISIS gripped that part of the world in the late 1990s, America's economic strength appeared to be on the rise, only to be called into question again by globalization, which seemed to rob all states of economic power in the traditional sense. Global markets rather than states seemed to be the new centers of power.

The SEPTEMBER 11, 2001, terrorist attacks on the World Trade Center and the Pentagon have set off a new power debate. At issue is what combination of power resources are needed to win a global and unprecedented war against TERRORISM. Military power was used to defeat the Taliban in AFGHANISTAN but failed to capture OSAMA BIN LADEN, and terrorist attacks attributed to his organization continue. Military force has been unleashed to depose Saddam Hussein in IRAQ as a first demonstration of preemptive action. Economic power is held by some to be necessary to rebuild Afghanistan so that terrorist groups will not reemerge and to develop other societies so that the appeal of terrorists will be lessened. Others argue that now more than ever soft power is important. What is needed is the ability to attract people around the world to American values and culture rather than repel them from it. Democracy, the rule of law, respect for civil rights and liberties, and tolerance are held to have universal appeal and give the United States a strong natural advantage in defeating terrorism.

**Further reading:** Kennedy, Paul. *The Rise and Decline of the Great Powers.* New York: Random House, 1987; Morgenthau, Hans, and Kenneth Thomson. *Politics among Nations.* 6th ed. New York: Knopf, 1985; Nye, Joseph S., Jr. *Bound to Lead: The Challenging Nature of American Power.* New York: Basic, 1990; Rothgeb, John, Jr. *Defining Power.* New York: St. Martin's, 1992.

## preemption

On September 20, 2002, President GEORGE W. BUSH put forward a new national security strategy for the United States. He argued that while the United States enjoys a position of unparalleled military strength and great economic and political influence, it still faces enemies. He continued that this challenge is different from the past because the enemies are no longer great states with large armies but shadowy networks of individuals. Because of this Bush asserted that the long-standing American policy of basing its security on a policy of DETERRENCE can no longer work. In its place he announced that the United States would adopt a policy of preemption. It will take anticipatory action and strike first in self-defense.

His announcement brought forward concern by strategists that the Bush administration was embarking upon a dangerous policy. Their critique focused on three issues. The first asserts that the administration's policy was blurring the distinction between preemptive military action and preventive military action. Both involve striking first in self-defense but differ in their time frame, as do the precipitating threats. Prevention involves striking first when the danger to one's national security appears great and war is inevitable but not imminent. Preemption involves striking first when war appears unavoidable and imminent. In the former case, war may be years or months away. In the latter it may be only a matter of hours. World politics recognizes the legitimacy of preemption but is less supportive of prevention. A second concern with the Bush doctrine of preemption focuses on the danger that other states may also adopt this policy. This will create an INTERNATIONAL SYSTEM that is perpetually on the brink of war or beset by INTERNATIONAL CRISES as states engage in a dialogue of competitive preemptions since only one state can preempt successfully. A third concern is that historically the strategy of preemption/prevention has not been successful. JAPAN's attack on Pearl Harbor can be seen as a preventive attack. It succeeded, but Japan lost the war. ISRAEL has practiced preemption and prevention, but security remains elusive and terrorist attacks continue. Together these concerns lead some strategists to question the ability of preemption to serve as the basis for a national security policy as opposed to being one option in a more broadly defined national security strategy.

These general concerns quickly found concrete expression. The first test case for preemption was IRAQ, and the Bush administration began laying the political and military foundation for a preemptive strike. Iraq's possession of WEAPONS OF MASS DESTRUCTION lay at the heart of the administration's case for preemption. In the midst of building this case anther crisis emerged that also seemed to qualify for a preemptive strike. NORTH KOREA admitted that it had resumed its efforts to obtain nuclear weapons. North Korea was identified by Bush as a member of the axis of evil, along with Iraq and IRAN. The Bush administration, however, argued that preemption was not necessary in this situation and that a peaceful resolution of the conflict was possible, although it would not engage in talks with North Korea.

## president

The CONSTITUTION designates the president as the commander in chief of the armed forces. This seemingly clear-cut statement hides a complex political reality, for it is CONGRESS that declares war and Congress that appropriates the funds necessary to fight a war. In the 1930s, Congress passed legislation intended to limit presidential war powers. The NEUTRALITY LEGISLATION was designed to prevent the president from moving the United States toward war through his or her own actions. It is also not clear to all whether this statement was to be taken literally or if it was a symbolic statement of sovereign power.

The ultimate degree to which a president can carry out this commander in chief power is determined as much by political considerations as it is by a strict reading of the Constitution. Several examples exist where presidents found the political resources to propel the United States to war: JAMES POLK sent troops into territory claimed by MEXICO; HARRY TRUMAN ordered U.S. forces to fight the KOREAN WAR; JOHN KENNEDY, LYNDON JOHNSON, and RICHARD NIXON committed U.S. forces to the VIETNAM WAR; RONALD REAGAN sent troops to GRENADA; GEORGE H. W. BUSH oversaw the PERSIAN GULF WAR; and GEORGE W. BUSH sent troops into IRAQ. The Constitution, it has been observed, is an invitation to struggle.

The struggle is evident in the area of DIPLOMACY as well. No reference can be found in the Constitution to the president as "the director in chief" of foreign affairs. The president is empowered to make treaties "by and with the consent of the Senate." The president is also able to enter into EXECUTIVE AGREEMENTS that are binding on her or his administration but not on those that follow. FRANKLIN ROOSEVELT's LEND-LEASE agreement with GREAT BRITAIN on the eve of WORLD WAR II is such an agreement. So too were the numerical limits placed on U.S. and Soviet NUCLEAR WEAPONS as part of the STRATEGIC ARMS LIMITATION TALKS I (SALT I) ARMS CONTROL treaty. The political reaction to the SALT I formula was such that the number of weapons permitted was placed in the text of the STRATEGIC ARMS LIMITATION TALKS II (SALT II) Treaty. In the 1950s concerns by political conservatives and isolationists was such that the BRICKER AMENDMENT, which would have required senatorial consent to executive agreements, almost passed.

The president is empowered to appoint ambassadors but again does so with the consent of the Senate. The president can avoid the political battle over these appointments by sending her or his personal representatives abroad. While the political controversies over ambassadorial appointments has escalated since the 1970s, the practice of sending personal representatives abroad is long established. WOODROW WILSON relied heavily for a time on Colonel EDWARD HOUSE. Franklin Roosevelt sent William Donovan to Great Britain as his personal representative in a move that led to the creation of the OFFICE OF STRATEGIC SERVICES, the forerunner to the CENTRAL INTELLIGENCE AGENCY. Richard Nixon made great use of HENRY KISSINGER as his personal diplomatic representative when Kissinger was NATIONAL SECURITY ADVISOR.

Presidents may sever diplomatic relations with other states. Historically this move has been a harbinger of war. Wilson did so in 1917 when he broke diplomatic relations with GERMANY. A similarly inspired move was made by Franklin Roosevelt in 1939 when he terminated the Japanese treaty of 1911. This act allowed his administration to impose an economic embargo on JAPAN. A more complex case came when JIMMY CARTER broke diplomatic relations with the government on TAIWAN in order to recognize the government on mainland CHINA. Conservative senators led by Barry Goldwater (R-Ariz.) took the case to the SUPREME COURT (GOLDWATER ET AL. V. CARTER) to reverse the decision. The Court, however, ruled against the plaintiffs, asserting that breaking diplomatic relations and the treaty that established those relations was a political question.

Presidents engage in a wide range of TRADE POLICY initiatives, ranging from imposing ECONOMIC SANCTIONS to offering FOREIGN AID to setting tariffs. Yet the president does not have a free hand in this. Congress is given the power to regulate commerce. Historically this has meant high tariffs. Moving the United States toward a free-trade policy on both a global and a regional level has required that the president obtain FAST-TRACK authority from Congress. Guaranteeing a single "yes-no" vote on a proposed trade agreement, the fast-track procedure prevents the insertion of crippling amendments. Obtaining fast-track authority is not guaranteed and requires close cooperation between the two branches. Congress has also begun to attach reporting requirements to grants of foreign aid in which by the president, through the STATE DEPARTMENT, certifies the country in question is making process in such areas as HUMAN RIGHTS and DRUG TRAFFICKING.

Finally, the president serves as the spokesperson for the United States in addressing the world. This role is more than symbolic, since policy declarations influence perceptions as to what direction American foreign policy will take. These announcements can have the political effect of severely limiting the ability of Congress, INTEREST GROUPS, or other political forces to block the policy. Among the most significant examples of presidents using this

spokesperson role to steer American foreign policy are GEORGE WASHINGTON's farewell address, the MONROE DOCTRINE, the TRUMAN DOCTRINE, and George W. Bush's address to the nation following the SEPTEMBER 11, 2001, terrorist attacks on the United States.

In assessing the extent to which modern presidents are able to win the political battle for controlling the direction of American foreign policy, analysts and commentators direct their attention to two dimensions of the presidency. The first is presidential PERSONALITY. The second is the presidential BUREAUCRACY. Presidents struggle to comprehend what is going on and struggle to obtain the support from those who, in theory, work for them. Presidents rule not by giving commands but by persuading. Personality and bureaucracy are two major tools presidents rely upon to succeed.

Personality is important in several respects. First, it determines whether a president takes an active or passive approach to the presidency. At issue here is how much energy the president puts into exercising the powers of the presidency. Passive presidents have included DWIGHT EISENHOWER, WILLIAM HOWARD TAFT, and RONALD REAGAN. Personality also determines whether the president takes a positive view or a negative view of the political tasks being faced. Positive personality presidents are held to be more likely to be flexible in the policy positions they adopt and better at compromising than negative personalities. Notable active presidents have included Truman, Carter, Clinton, Bush, JOHN KENNEDY, Franklin Roosevelt, and THEODORE ROOSEVELT. Among the negative presidents have been Wilson, Lyndon Johnson, JOHN ADAMS, and Nixon.

Another element held to be important in examining presidential personality is the extent to which presidents have open- or closed-belief systems. Open-belief systems allow individuals to change their minds as new information is obtained. Closed-belief systems are resistant to change. The most thoroughgoing study of belief systems has not involved a president but a close adviser to a president, SECRETARY OF STATE JOHN FOSTER DULLES, who was found to have had a closed-belief system regarding the nature of the Soviet threat.

Presidential bureaucracy is studied at two levels. The first is the operation of the key presidential foreign-policy bureaucracy, the NATIONAL SECURITY COUNCIL (NSC). Special attention has been paid to the changing role played by the national security advisor and the extent to which the NSC has operated as a collegial body versus a highly institutionalized one that is organized in a hierarchical fashion around committees and subcommittees. The second level at which the presidential bureaucracy has been studied is that of a president's general strategy for controlling the bureaucracy. Franklin Roosevelt employed a competitive model in which overlapping areas of jurisdiction existed and departments competed with one another for his attention. A second model establishes a formalistic system in which rules and procedures for processing information and vetting opinions are established. Truman, Nixon, Reagan, and Eisenhower operated this way. More recently, a third managerial style has come to be favored. It seeks to establish a collegial system in which advisers are brought together in problem-solving teams. Kennedy, Clinton, Carter, George H. W. Bush, and George W. Bush have all opted for this type of managerial strategy but with different results. In the final analysis what matters most about how an individual handles the office and powers of the presidency is the quality of the decisions that are made. Thus, it is not surprising that presidential decision making has been a frequently studied subject. These studies can be broken down along several different dimensions that often overlap in any one study. One set of studies is concerned with the process by which decisions are made. SMALL-GROUP DECISION MAKING, BUREAUCRATIC POLITICS, ELITE THEORY, and a RATIONAL-ACTOR perspective are among the most frequently employed. They each take a different conceptual cut at how participants in the policy process interact. The nature of these interactions is then used to explain how the decision was arrived at and often the quality of the decision as well. A second set of studies is concerned with the content of the decisions. Here one sees distinctions being made between trade policy, HUMAN-RIGHTS policy, environmental policy, and nuclear strategy. The assumption behind these studies is that no one single type of foreign-policy problem exists and that different dynamics operate in different substantive areas. The third set of studies is concerned with the manner in which issues appear on the policy agenda and flow through it. Historically of most concern have been INTERNATIONAL CRISES that burst suddenly and surprisingly onto the scene, demand immediate attention, and carry grave consequences. Interest is now also being focused on issues that arise during the beginning of a president's term and those that arise at the very end. The former are heavily influenced by the nature of the presidential transition. The latter appear to be heavily influenced by a president's desire to secure a place in history or leave a positive legacy. They also appear to point to individual's whose decisions are no longer held captive by the political forces that operated in the earlier part of the presidency, such as PUBLIC OPINION, ELECTIONS, and relations with Congress.

**Further reading:** Barber, James David. *The Presidential Character: Predicting Performance in the White House.* Englewood Cliffs, N.J.: Prentice Hall, 1985; Heclo, Hugh, and Lester M. Salamon, eds. *The Illusion of Presidential Government.* Boulder, Colo.: Westview, 1981; Hess, Gary, R. *Presidential Decisions for War: Korea, Vietnam and the Persian Gulf.* Baltimore: Johns Hopkins University Press, 2001; Neustadt, Richard. *Presidential Power: The Politics of Leadership.* New York: John Wiley and Sons, 1960.

## Prize Cases (1863)

It is on the basis of a deeply divided SUPREME COURT's ruling in the Prize Cases that modern PRESIDENTS lay claim to much of their war-making power. Speaking for the majority, Justice Robert Grier stated that it is up to the president to "determine the degree of force the crisis demands."

The case involved the decision of South Carolina and other Southern states to leave the Union in 1861. With CONGRESS in recess, President ABRAHAM LINCOLN issued a proclamation stating that federal laws were being obstructed and calling out the militia to suppress the rebellion. He also ordered a blockade of Southern ports. When Congress returned to session it passed legislation recognizing that a state of rebellion existed and legislation approving Lincoln's earlier proclamations.

Prior to congressional endorsement of his actions, a number of ships and their cargo were seized by the U.S. Navy in the course of implementing its blockade. The seized goods were condemned as prizes in federal court. The owners of the cargo appealed this decision, arguing that Lincoln acted illegally in setting up the embargo since no state of war had been declared by Congress. The majority of the Court rejected this argument. Grier asserted that "if a war be made by invasion of a foreign nation, the President is not only authorized but bound to resist by force. He does not initiate the war, but is forced to accept the challenge without waiting for any special legislative authority. And whether the hostile party be a foreign invader, or State organized in rebellion, it is none the less a war, although the declaration be unilateral."

See also CONSTITUTION, U.S.

## public diplomacy

Public diplomacy is a form a modern DIPLOMACY. It consists of the statements and actions of leaders that are intended to influence PUBLIC OPINION. Public diplomacy is alien to classic diplomacy that emphasized secrecy and confidential bargaining among like-minded elites. Public diplomacy has been described as the "theater of POWER." It is conducted through such varied means as public statements, press briefings, and state visits. The messages conveyed in public may or may not correspond to what is actually said in private.

Public diplomacy is important because of the increased role that public opinion and legislatures play in modern diplomacy. Leaders no longer can be confident that agreements they negotiate automatically will be supported by their government or those of the other participants. For that reason they cannot afford to wait until an agreement has been reached to build public support for it at home or abroad. And they have come to realize that direct communication to foreign and domestic audiences during the negotiations can influence its ultimate outcome.

President BILL CLINTON is widely recognized as one of the most skilled practitioners of public diplomacy. He brought an American-style political-campaign atmosphere to his trips abroad that sought to win foreign publics over to his cause. This stands in sharp contrast to President RONALD REAGAN's forays into public diplomacy. His reference to the Soviet Union as the "evil empire" played well at home but scared the public abroad. President GEORGE W. BUSH faced a delicate balancing act in his efforts to influence global public opinion to support a war against TERRORISM. He tried to both enlist support for a global campaign and convince the world that the United States was not targeting the entire Muslim population.

Public diplomacy has become big business. Many foreign governments contract with consulting firms to help promote their interests in the United States. KUWAIT was represented by Hill and Knowlton, a large public relations firm, during the PERSIAN GULF WAR. At one time President Samuel Doe of LIBERIA paid a Washington lobbyist $800,000 to improve his image. CANADA has employed more than 60 firms to promote its interests and image, while GREAT BRITAIN has used more than 40. The emphasis on obtaining public support means that public diplomacy often takes on the character of propaganda in which half-truths and falsehoods are used to manipulate the responses of an audience. One of the great dangers of public diplomacy is that it creates images and expectations in the public's mind that cannot be sustained. The resulting gap between words and deeds can lead to disillusionment and a withdrawal of support from foreign-policy initiatives.

**Further reading:** Manheim, Jarol B. *Strategic Public Diplomacy and American Foreign Policy.* New York: Oxford University Press, 1994; Newson, David D. *The Public Dimension of Foreign Policy.* Bloomington: Indiana University Press, 1996.

## public opinion

Public opinion polls are one of the major barometers that policy makers and analysts use to gauge the level of public support for a policy or policy maker. They are also studied for their impact on foreign-policy decisions. Evidence points to the conclusion that while public opinion constrains policy makers it does not determine U.S. intervention policy. More generally it appears that public opinion rarely serves as a stimulus to foreign-policy innovation. It

does appear capable, however, of placing foreign-policy issues on the agenda. The nuclear freeze during the Reagan administration is an example.

While public opinion polls have become commonplace, for several reasons interpreting them is not always easy. One problem is that the wording used can skew the results. For example, in November 1990 Americans were polled about their support for a war against IRAQ. One question asked, "[D]o you agree or disagree that the United States should take all action necessary, including the use of military force, to make sure that Iraq withdraws from KUWAIT. A total of 65 percent said yes. Only 28 percent of respondents agreed, however, to the statement "The United States should initiate war against IRAQ in order to drive Iraq out of Kuwait and bring the situation to a close." Second, there is a problem with crises that are of only a short duration or result in a notable success. The invasion of GRENADA under RONALD REAGAN and GEORGE H. W. BUSH's invasion of PANAMA are examples. In both cases a "halo effect" sets in as considerable numbers of respondents no longer voice concerns that were known to exist prior to the event. Finally, there is a problem with voter knowledge. In 1964 only 38 percent of Americans knew that the Soviet Union was not a member of the NORTH ATLANTIC TREATY ORGANIZATION (NATO) and only 58 percent knew that the United States was a member. In 1983 only 8 percent knew that the United States supported the government in EL SALVADOR and opposed the government in NICARAGUA. In 1993 only 43 percent knew which continent SOMALIA was on.

Studies of public opinion have addressed a series of issues that relate to the conduct of American foreign policy. A research question focused on the consistency of the public's outlook. Initial findings suggested that the public was moody. This was seen as dangerous because a moody public would be unreliable in times of crisis. Presidents would not be able to count on their support. This position gave way to one that emphasized stability in the public's outlook. It could be expected to "rally around the flag" in times of crisis. Heavily debated here was the impact of the public's lack of awareness and knowledge of world affairs on their outlook on events. Several recent studies suggest that even though the public may not be informed about the details of world affairs, it does hold well-developed views as to its general preferences. It appears that the more serious the domestic problems relative to the external challenges facing the United States, the greater its isolationist tendencies.

A second research question focused on the content of the public's outlook on foreign policy matters. Prior to Pearl Harbor it was clear to all that on the whole the American public was isolationist. After that it became internationalist. Between 1949 and 1969, 60 to 80 percent of the public favored an active role in world affairs. This internationalist consensus came apart with the American participation in the VIETNAM WAR. Three different outlooks competed for dominance coming out of the Vietnam experience. One was COLD WAR internationalism. It was an extension of the conservative INTERNATIONALISM rooted in REALISM that supported CONTAINMENT. The world was viewed as a dangerous place that required American's involvement, vigilance, and the pursuit of military power. Liberal internationalism drew its inspiration from WILSONIANISM and IDEALISM. It also saw the INTERNATIONAL SYSTEM as threatening but saw those threats as growing out of poverty, discrimination, and oppression. These were conditions that could not be solved through military power but required economic assistance. The third outlook to emerge from the Vietnam War was neo-ISOLATIONISM. Adherents of this perspective recognized the need for military power and saw the international system as threatening but questioned the wisdom of an activist or interventionist foreign policy.

A great deal of speculation has centered on what type of event(s) would be necessary to unify the American public's outlook on world affairs. Neither the PERSIAN GULF WAR nor the initial phases of the war against TERRORISM have succeeded in doing so.

A third direction of public opinion research has focused on American's attitudes toward specific features of foreign policy. The one that has received the most attention is its attitude toward the use of military force. The conventional wisdom coming out of Vietnam was that the American public would not support military action if it resulted in American casualties. For that reason, any military involvement would have to be short and involve the overwhelming application of force. The Persian Gulf War was fought with the Vietnam syndrome in mind. President BILL CLINTON's removal of U.S. forces from Somalia was also consistent with this outlook. Recent research suggests that the American public's unwillingness to tolerate casualties is overstated. An alternative line of analysis has focused on the purposes to which military power is put. Case study analysis indicates that the American public is most supportive of the use of military force when it seeks to impose foreign-policy restraints on other countries. It is less supportive of the use of military force when the objective is internal regime change.

Finally, studies of public opinion have sought to identify what it is about the international system that Americans perceive as threatening. An important source of information on this topic is a poll conducted periodically by the Council of Foreign Relations. In their 1998 poll Americans identified stopping the spread of NUCLEAR WEAPONS, stopping the flow of illegal drugs, protecting American jobs, and combating international terrorism as the top-four goals in order of importance for the United States. A significant point that emerged from this study was that the public ranked economic issues higher than did policy elites in their responses.

This gap between public opinion and elite opinion is one of the major impediments to public opinion playing a greater role in foreign-policy decision making. ELITE THEORY holds that policy makers do not recognize or accept the legitimacy of public views that differ from their own. A second impediment is bureaucratic inertia. BUREAUCRACY operates according to standard operating procedures and is not responsive to changes in public opinion. A final factor clouding the relationship between public opinion and policy making is the role of the MEDIA. Much controversy exists over whether the media's coverage of foreign policy is capable of manipulating public opinion and whether it provides it with a clear and direct channel to policy makers.

Throughout the period leading up to the IRAQ WAR and during the war itself, the GEORGE W. BUSH administration took great pains to ensure that the public supported the war. Looking to the period before the war, public opinion was generally supportive. Between November 2001 and January 2003, the percentage of Americans supporting war with Iraq vacillated between the low 60 percent range and the high 70 percent range. Beneath this high level of overall support, however, doubts existed about the wisdom of war and anxiety over its outcome. A December 2002 poll found that 58 percent of Americans wanted more evidence for why war was necessary and that a similar number favored acting only with the support of the UNITED NATIONS. By early February 2003 the Bush administration had managed to change these numbers. Now a full 60 percent of the American public supported war, even over the objections of the UN. Interestingly, this same poll found that 56 percent of Americans opposed participating in postwar recovery efforts in Iraq if the United States would have to keep troops there for more than a year and spend $15 billion.

These results are consistent with most studies of public opinion, which find that the American public is inclined to support the president in times of an INTERNATIONAL CRISIS. This is known as the "rally around the flag" effect. It was vividly evident in March following President Bush's nationwide address giving Saddam Hussein an ultimatum. Support for Bush jumped from 59 percent the week before to 71 percent.

The public remained behind the war once it began. In April, 77 percent supported the decision to go to war. Both women (72 percent) and men (82 percent) supported the war. The biggest difference in level of support was race. Eighty-one percent of white respondents supported the war, while only 49 percent of African Americans supported it. Polls showed that support for the war continued to remain high even when threats of casualties rose. In late March and early April, 80 percent expected a hard and bloody battle for Baghdad. Nevertheless, a *Newsweek* poll taken in August 2003 showed Bush's approval rating had fallen to 53 percent, down 18 points since April, as violence in postwar Iraq continued to mount.

**Further reading:** Almond, Gabriel. *The American People and Foreign Policy.* New York: Harcourt, 1950; Cohen, Bernard. *The Public's Impact on Foreign Policy.* Boston: Little, Brown, 1973; Mueller, John, *War, Presidents, and Public Opinion.* New York: Wiley and Sons, 1973; Wittkopf, Eugene. *Faces of Internationalism: Public Opinion and American Foreign Policy.* Durham, N.C.: Duke University Press, 1990.

## Puerto Rico

The island of Puerto Rico lies in the northern Caribbean Sea. It has a population of some 3.5 million people. With an area of 3,435 square miles, it is less than one-half the size of New Jersey. Puerto Rico came under the control of the United States in 1898 as a result of the SPANISH-AMERICAN WAR. By virtue of the Teller Amendment the United States pledged not to acquire CUBA as a result of the war. No such promise was made for other territories that might be conquered. U.S. military forces successfully occupied Puerto Rico on July 25, 1898, after encountering limited resistance from Spanish forces.

Virtually from the outset Puerto Rico came to inhabit a kind of no-man's-land in its relations with the United States. The Foraker Act of 1900 ended the U.S. military occupation of Puerto Rico but did not settle its ultimate fate. The three options debated today were also present then: independence, statehood, or some type of special status. The prospect of statehood raises images of an American Quebec—that is, a state that does not share the dominant culture or language of the others. Beyond political equality statehood raises the issue of the desirability of further assimilation into the American culture. If the answer is either statehood or enhanced commonwealth status, there is no doubt that Puerto Rico will figure heavily in many political decisions. President BILL CLINTON was widely criticized for his 1999 pardon of 11 Puerto Rican terrorists. The move was labeled politically inspired and designed to help Hilary Clinton's chances of winning a New York State seat in the Senate. As senator, Hilary Clinton has strongly supported the Vieques protestors. Independence raises security concerns. During WORLD WAR II Puerto Rico was described as the Gibraltar of the Caribbean, and it continues to figure prominently in the thinking of conventional warfare specialists because of its training facilities. Advocates of independence assert that Puerto Rico could become a catalyst for a Caribbean common market.

In the INSULAR CASES (1901–22) the SUPREME COURT ruled that the United States could acquire territory and govern them as colonies without having to commit itself either to making them states or granting them independence. They were to be unincorporated territories of the United States, "foreign to the United States in a domestic sense." Puerto Rico and Guam fell into this category. The awkwardness of this status is illustrated by the 1917 Jones Act, which granted Puerto Ricans U.S. citizenship and provided for the popular election of its legislature but continued the practice of having the president select Puerto Rico's governor and gave the U.S. CONGRESS the final authority concerning local legislation.

Regardless of the debate over its political status, by the 1930s the Puerto Rican economy had become linked to that of the United States through the establishment of large sugar plantations and absentee ownership. Widespread poverty among the peasants resulted and helped fuel a strong nationalist movement led by Albizus Campos that produced frequent clashes with U.S. authorities. Campos was arrested in 1936 under the Sedition Act of 1918 on what are described as trumped-up charges that grew out of the murder of the chief of police by nationalist sympathizers. He spent almost 10 years in jail. In 1937, the U.S.-appointed governor, General Blanton Winship, ordered the police to fire upon members of Campos's Nationalist Party. Twenty-two were killed and 97 wounded.

The onset of the post–World War II era brought political reforms and continued violence. In 1948 the Elective Governor Act was passed by Congress, permitting Puerto Ricans to elect their own governor for the first time. In 1952 Congress recognized the Constitution adopted by Puerto Rico's legislature that proclaimed Puerto Rico to be a commonwealth. A yes-no referendum that year on the issue supported commonwealth status by a vote of 81-19 percent. Largely unmoved by these actions, pro-independence forces continued their efforts. In the early 1950s pronationalist forces led armed attacks on Blair House, President HARRY TRUMAN's temporary residence, and the U.S. Congress. The Puerto Rican government responded with widespread arrests and began compiling a blacklist of pro-independence supporters that grew to more than 100,000 files.

Periodically either the Puerto Rican government or the United States Congress has organized, or considered organizing, referendums designed to settle the question of Puerto Rico's future. One proposed in 1936 would have given Puerto Ricans the option of independence. It was not held, and, given the larger context of the Great Depression, few would have voted for this option since Puerto Rico had become heavily dependent on U.S. government programs to save its economy. Between 1934 and 1937 a federal agency, the Puerto Rican Reconstruction Administration, built hydroelectric projects and ran public health programs, much as was happening in the continental United States.

In 1967 Congress sanctioned a binding referendum. The July 23 vote showed 60 percent in favor of continued commonwealth status, 39 percent in favor of statehood, and the remaining votes going for independence. For a little more than 20 years the 1967 referendum was the final word on Puerto Rico's status. In 1989 Governor Rafael Hernández Colón revived the question and called for a referendum. Congress considered supporting the measure, but it in the end took no action. Key issues debated included whether Puerto Ricans living in the United States could vote on the question and whether the federal government should be responsible for the costs of implementing the decision. Puerto Ricans voted on December 8, 1991. The vote resulted in a solid defeat for an enhanced commonwealth status, although the wording of the proposal was vague and confusing. The new governor, Pedro Rosello, supported statehood. In 1993 he organized a referendum that produced still a different result. The November 14 vote showed 48.4 percent supported commonwealth status to 46.2 percent who supported statehood. A total of 4.4 percent supported independence. Shortly after that vote Senator Don Young (R-Ala.) introduced a bill in Congress in November 1994 calling for yet another binding referendum. The question this time was "incorporation" into the United States. Both Speaker of the House Newt Gingrich (R-Ga.) and President Bill Clinton supported the measure. It passed the House of Representatives by a vote of 209-208 but died in the Senate. Rosello responded to the decision not to proceed with a binding referendum by calling for one more plebiscite on statehood. A December 1998 vote had voters choosing between five options. "None of the above" received 50.2 percent of the vote, compared to 46.5 for statehood.

The most recent point of controversy in U.S.–Puerto Rican relations has also involved the possibility of a referendum. Since World War II the U.S. Navy has used part of the island of Vieques as a bombing range and training area for landing exercises. The 9,300 residents of the island have long complained and sought to put an end to these exercises. Matters reached a boiling point in April 1999 when a Puerto Rican civilian guard was accidentally killed during a bombing exercise. Negotiations between Rosello and the White House produced a compromise. The residents of Vieques would decide on whether or not to permit continued bombing past May 2003 in a referendum scheduled for November 2001. Up until then the navy would continue to use the island as a target range but would not use live ammunition. President Clinton also promised $40 million in money for job-training purposes. An additional $50 million would be forthcoming if the residents voted to permit the navy to continue using it.

This compromise did not last. The fiscal year 2002 Defense Budget passed in December 2000 removed the provision for a referendum and permitted the navy to continue using Vieques as a training area and to use live ammunition. The bill states only that "the Secretary of the Navy may close the Vieques training range if the Secretary certifies that alternative equivalent or superior facilities exist." Senator John Warner (R-Va.) said this cancellation gives Puerto Ricans time to rethink their position following the events of SEPTEMBER 11, 2001. In spring 2002 the USS *George Washington* used the Vieques training site but employed nonexplosive ordnance consistent with Clinton's 1999 presidential directive. Puerto Rican nationalists responded by protesting the action and attacking U.S. troops.

President GEORGE W. BUSH ordered an end to these bombing exercises in May 2003. On January 13, 2003, the U.S. Navy began what it described as the last live firing exercise on Vieques. Instead of using Vieques, the navy announced that it would switch these operations to several mainland bases.

See also IMPERIALISM.

**Further reading:** Carr, Raymond. *Puerto Rico.* New York: New York University Press, 1984; Fernande, Ronald. *Puerto Rico: Past and Present.* New York: Praeger, 1998.

# Q

## al-Qaeda

Al-Qaeda is a terrorist organization responsible for planning and conducting a series of deadly attacks against the United States. In early 1995 it plotted to kill President BILL CLINTON on a visit to the PHILIPPINES. It was also responsible for plotting a dozen bombings of American trans-Pacific flights that year. In August 1998 it bombed American EMBASSIES in Nairobi, Kenya, and Dar es Salaam, Tanzania. These attacks killed at least 301 individuals and injured more than 5,000. In 1999 it was responsible for planning to set off a bomb at Los Angeles International Airport. On October 12, 2000, al-Qaeda organized the attack on the USS *Cole* that was in Aden, Yemen. This attack killed 17 naval personnel and injured 39. On SEPTEMBER 11, 2001, terrorists affiliated with al-Qaeda hijacked airliners and crashed them into the World Trade Center and the Pentagon. An estimated 3,000 people died or are missing as a result of these attacks. Al-Qaeda has not restricted itself to targeting Americans. In 1994 it plotted to kill Pope John Paul II during a visit to the Philippines.

Al-Qaeda was founded by OSAMA BIN LADEN in 1988 as an instrument for organizing Arabs against the Soviet occupation of AFGHANISTAN. Its goal is to create a fundamentalist transnational Islamic state. As a means to this end, al-Qaeda seeks to expel Americans and other non-Muslim Westerners from Muslim countries. To accomplish this objective al-Qaeda works with other Islamic and non-Islamic extremist groups. The Taliban, which ruled Afghanistan, was a key ally of al-Qaeda, offering them a secure base from which to conduct their global operations. It was for this reason that the GEORGE W. BUSH administration made removing the Taliban from POWER its first major objective in the global war against TERRORISM following the September 11, 2001, terrorist attacks. The Taliban were defeated in January 2002, but it appears that Osama bin Laden was neither killed nor captured. However, it is believed that the military operation in Afghanistan severely crippled al-Qaeda's organizational base and infrastructure. In a further attempt to weaken al-Qaeda, President Bush signed Executive Order 13224, which froze the U.S.-based assets of individuals and organizations believed to be involved in funding terrorism. As of March 2002, 189 groups and individuals were covered by this order. Between September and December 2001, the United States blocked an estimated $34 million. Another $33 million in assets were blocked by U.S. allies. These efforts at depleting al-Qaeda's financial strength have been hindered to some extent by the personal fortune of Osama bin Laden, who is believed to have inherited millions of dollars. Additionally, much of the money used by al-Qaeda and other terrorist groups circulates outside of the conventional international financial system in the form of cash, precious gems, and other commodities.

In the months following the September 11, 2001, terrorist attacks, thousands of al-Qaeda members were arrested in more than 60 countries. Still, al-Qaeda has functioning cells operating around the world and consisting of several thousand members. Periodically Osama bin Laden has appeared on video clips or in voice recordings. Some experts believe he is sending signals to his forces through these appearances. Al-Qaeda burst back into prominence shortly after the end of the IRAQ WAR. It was identified as responsible for attacks on Western residences and businesses in Riyadh, SAUDI ARABIA, that killed at least 34 people including eight Americans. The United States announced that it expected more attacks from al-Qaeda as it sought to reestablish itself as a terrorist organization.

**Further reading:** Bodansky, Yossef. *Bin Laden: The Man Who Declared War on America.* New York: Forum, 1999; Reeve, Simon. *The New Jackels: Ramzi, Yousef, Osama bin Laden and the Future of Terrorism.* Boston: Northeastern University Press, 1999.

# R

## Radio Free Europe

Radio Free Europe (RFE) was set up in 1949. Along with Radio Liberty (RL), which began operations in 1951, these two "radios" broadcast into Eastern Europe and the Soviet Union, respectively. They broadcast the "truth" into these regions in the hopes of producing domestic unrest and creating instability. Each was established under boards of directors made up of prominent Americans to give the appearance that they were privately funded and operated institutions. In the case of RFE it was the Committee for a Free Europe. For RL it was the American Committee for Liberation. In reality RFE and RL were CENTRAL INTELLIGENCE AGENCY (CIA) "proprietaries," or secretly owned properties and companies that were funded by the U.S. government and operated out of the CIA's Directorate of Plans. Less interested in broadcasting the truth, they were instruments of U.S. propaganda.

The highlight of RFE and RL covert propaganda operations came when they broadcast Soviet leader Nikita Khrushchev's secret speech condemning the excesses of Joseph Stalin. Since all the East European leaders except for Marshal Tito in YUGOSLAVIA had been put into power by Stalin, Khrushchev's denunciation also called into question their right to rule. This speech helped set in motion a reform movement in Eastern Europe that would lead to revolts in POLAND and HUNGARY in 1956. The most controversial chapter in their history came during the Hungarian uprising against the Soviet Union. RFE transmitted back into Hungary without comment local broadcasts from Hungary carrying appeals for help from the United States, rumors that such help would be forthcoming, and anti-Soviet stories. Taken together these stories gave encouragement to the Hungarians to continue in their efforts to overthrow COMMUNISM. When WARSAW PACT troops

Poster advertising Radio Free Europe *(Library of Congress)*

**409**

invaded, however, no U.S. support was forthcoming. In fact, the Eisenhower administration had concluded that it would make no effort to "roll back the iron curtain." The RFE's behavior in Hungary stood in sharp contrast to its response to unrest in Poland. In the latter case, their broadcasts warned rioting Poles against further rebellion.

In 1967 their connections to the CIA were revealed. Congressional hearings followed, and in 1976 RFE and RL were merged into RFE/RL and openly funded by CONGRESS. They operate under the guidance of the Board for International Broadcasting. Today, RFE/RL's activities extend beyond the traditional European COLD WAR boundaries. In 1979 RL began operating Radio AFGHANISTAN as part of the U.S. response to the Soviet invasion of that country. It also operates Radio Free IRAQ and the RFE/RL Persian Service.

On October 1, 1999, following the incorporation of the United States Information Agency into the STATE DEPARTMENT, formal oversight of RFE/RL was given to the Broadcasting Board of Governors. Also included under their jurisdiction are the Voice of America and Radio Martí.

See also COVERT ACTION; CUBA; RUSSIA.

## RAND Corporation

The RAND Corporation was established in 1948 as a private nonprofit research organization that engaged scientists, mathematicians, and civilian strategists in explorations of military planning with a special concern for the impact that technological breakthroughs, such as those associated with the atomic bomb, radar, and rocketry, held for the use of force. It evolved out of Project RAND, which was set up under a special contract between the U.S. Air Force and the Douglas Aircraft Corporation in October 1945. The very first RAND report was released in 1946: Preliminary Design of an Experimental World-Circling Spaceship. It was concerned with the design, performance capabilities, and uses of satellites. Today it conducts research on such diverse topics as defense policy, education policy, labor policy, and the role of government in social and economic problem solving in the United States.

Within RAND two important national security research arms are Project Air Force and the National Security Research Division. Project Air Force supports the long-range planning of the air force, the original contractor of RAND studies. It examines potential strategies that might be employed in the changing security environment, aerospace developments, personnel and training issues, and resource-management strategies. Its National Security Research Division conducts research for RAND's non–air force and army clients. Numbered among them are other parts of the DEFENSE DEPARTMENT, the U.S. INTELLIGENCE COMMUNITY, and the ministries of defense of U.S.

allies. Recent topics studied include domestic responses to terrorist threats involving WEAPONS OF MASS DESTRUCTION, the possible benefits of Defense Department outsourcing, and GULF WAR SYNDROME illness. RAND is most famous for the studies it did during the 1950s and early 1960s on nuclear strategy. It is no exaggeration to state that many of the key terms in our nuclear vocabulary (*counterforce, first strike, second strike,* and *limited nuclear options*) had their origins in RAND.

One of these early studies conducted by Albert Wohlstetter examined the question of selecting and using overseas bases for use by the air force. At the time, the technology needed to perfect intercontinental ballistic missiles (ICBMs) was not yet in place, and the air force relied heavily upon bases in Europe as staging grounds for delivering nuclear weapons against the Soviet Union. Contrary to the position held by the air force, Wohlstetter concluded that the Strategic Air Command (SAC) was vulnerable to a surprise Soviet attack. His report urged the creation of an early warning radar system and that overseas bases be used only for refueling. This report provided part of the intellectual underpinning for one of the most famous articles published on NUCLEAR DETERRENCE policy. "The Delicate Balance of Terror," published in *Foreign Affairs,* made the case to the wider defense community that deterrence did not rest simply on the possession of U.S. nuclear forces but required a coherent strategy for development and use of weapons that could survive a Soviet first strike.

Another important RAND study was led by William Kaufmann, who was concerned that the U.S. nuclear policy of MASSIVE RETALIATION did not really deter the Soviet Union. Instead, it encouraged them to engage in acts of limited or controlled aggression. What was needed, Kaufmann concluded, was a deterrence policy in which the threat matched the level of aggression. His arguments were central to the development of the concept of limited war that was embraced by the Kennedy administration. They also laid the foundation for thinking in terms of NUCLEAR WAR as something other than a spasmodic exchange of missiles. In turn, this led to the development of such nuclear concepts as controlled escalation, counterforce targeting, and a "no-cities" targeting policy that were incorporated into the Single Integrated Operational Plan (SIOP) then being revised by the Kennedy administration.

See also RUSSIA; THINK TANK.

## Rapacki Plan

The Rapacki Plan was 1957 Polish proposal to create a nuclear-free zone in Central Europe. The United States rejected the plan. The immediate context of the Rapacki Plan was ongoing East-West conflict over the fate of GERMANY. Soviet leader Nikita Khrushchev was concerned that

West Germany would be integrated in the NORTH ATLANTIC TREATY ORGANIZATION (NATO) and gain access to NUCLEAR WEAPONS. To forestall this in 1958 he embraced the 1957 plan put forward by Polish foreign minister Adam Rapacki. The proposed nuclear-free zone would have included POLAND, CZECHOSLOVAKIA, East Germany, and West Germany. It would have prohibited the manufacture, stockpiling, or installation of nuclear weapons in this area.

The United States rejected the proposal on the grounds that it would contribute to, rather than lessen, the ongoing tensions in Europe by perpetuating the division of Germany into two parts and that, given the large size of the Russian military establishment, this relatively small nuclear-free zone would add little to the security of Europe. The American rejection of the Rapacki Plan presented the Soviet Union (see RUSSIA) with a propaganda coup by placing the Soviet Union on the side of DISARMAMENT and the United States as its opponent. The Rapacki Plan was not unique in this regard. Many of the ARMS CONTROL and disarmament proposals of the era were put forward more with an eye toward their propaganda value than their substantive merits.

There were some in the United States who urged its acceptance. The most notable was GEORGE KENNAN, who in a series of lectures in 1957 called for restrictions on nuclear weapons in Central Europe, a unified and neutral Germany, and disengagement of conventional forces from the region. The Rapacki Plan would also reappear in modified versions in other Polish plans, namely, the Gomullka Plan for a nuclear freeze (1963–64) and the Jaruzelski Plan for confidence and security building measures (1967).

## rational-actor decision-making model

The rational-actor model is the most frequently employed model for studying foreign policy. At its core is an action-reaction process in which foreign-policy decisions are viewed as calculated responses to the actions of another. In carrying out these calculations the United States is viewed as a unitary actor. It can be treated as a single entity. There is no need for the analyst to delve into the intricacies of governmental structure, domestic politics, or personality in trying to understand why policies are selected. The United States can be treated as a "black box," responding with one voice to the challenges and opportunities that are presented by the INTERNATIONAL SYSTEM and the actions of other states. We implicitly employ this model when we speak of U.S. goals, U.S. fears, the U.S. NATIONAL INTEREST, and U.S. prestige.

The calculations by which U.S. foreign policy is selected are assumed to be rational. There are four basic elements of a rational decision-making process: (1) goals are clearly stated and ranked in order of preference, (2) all options are considered, (3) the consequences of each option for one's goals are assessed, and (4) a value-maximizing choice is made. This last point means that the policy option that is chosen allows states to realize their most important goals at the least cost or risk.

Rational-actor decision-making analysis is carried out in two different ways. The first approach is inductive and is frequently employed by diplomatic historians. The analyst tries to understand the foreign-policy decision by placing himself or herself in the position of the government so that the logic of the situation as it existed can be understood. The second approach is deductive. It is exemplified by game theory and is frequently employed by military strategists and DETERRENCE theorists. Rather than rely upon actual events to support its analysis, the deductive approach relies upon logic and mathematical formulations of how states should (rationally) respond under a given set of conditions.

The rational-actor model is attractive because it places relatively few informational demands on the observer. Thus, it is often relied upon in crisis situations in which circumstances are subject to rapid changes and in situations in which accurate and timely information is hard to obtain. Such was the case during the COLD WAR when the United States confronted the Soviet Union (see RUSSIA) over BERLIN and CUBA. More generally, it was also true of Soviet nuclear policy in which the number of weapons and their deployment patterns but little else were discernible. Critics contend that the logic of the rational-actor analysis downgrades the importance of chance, accidents, and coincidence in foreign affairs. They also assert that U.S. foreign policy may not be nearly as purposeful as the rational-actor model implies. Foreign policy also may be motivated as much by internal factors as external ones. Incorporating internal factors requires moving away from the notion that the state is a unitary actor. Finally, the rational-actor model has been criticized for its inattention to implementation problems. The analysis stops when the policy is chosen. Implementation is assumed to be automatic rather than problematic.

The major competitors to the rational-actor decision-making model build on these critiques. PLURALISM emphasizes INTEREST-GROUP competition. ELITE THEORY focuses on the values of a narrow sector of American society as setting the overall foreign-policy agenda. BUREAUCRATIC POLITICS sees governmental bargaining and BUREAUCRACY as the prime force in policy making. SMALL-GROUP DECISION MAKING focuses on how the dynamics of group interaction can determine policy. Along with the rational-actor model, this last approach is also frequently employed to study crisis decision making. The other models are employed most often to analyze long-running policy issues, such as TRADE, FOREIGN AID, weapons policies, and military interventions.

**Further reading:** Allison, Graham, and Philip Zelikow. *Essence of Decision: Explaining the Cuban Missile Crisis.* 2d ed. Boston: Addison Wesley Longman, 1999. Lake, David, and Robert Powell, eds. *Strategic Choice and International Relations.* Princeton, N.J.: Princeton University Press, 1999.

**Reagan, Ronald** (1911–  ) *president of the United States*
Ronald Wilson Reagan served two terms as the 40th president of the United States. Elected in 1980, he had made an unsuccessful bid for the Republican presidential nomination in 1976, losing to the incumbent president, GERALD FORD. In that campaign Reagan clearly established himself as a spokesperson for conservative internationalists. He roundly attacked DÉTENTE and ARMS CONTROL, calling for a stronger U.S. stance against COMMUNISM.

An attention to administrative detail and factual knowledge about world events were not Reagan's strong points as president. He did, however, possess a clear worldview that guided the broad outlines of his foreign policy. At its center was the conviction that world politics could be understood as a struggle between good and evil. The Soviet Union (see RUSSIA) was an aggressive and hostile state, an "evil empire," that systematically sought to exploit all situations to its advantage. It was its direct or indirect presence rather than local conditions that was the root cause of instability throughout the world.

He followed this belief with two general guidelines for action. First, one should remain loyal to one's allies. He agreed with Jeane J. Kirkpatrick's argument that there was a fundamental difference between authoritarian regimes and communist or totalitarian ones. Kirkpatrick had made this argument in a critique of President JIMMY CARTER's HUMAN-RIGHTS policy and willingness to abandon longtime authoritarian allies, and she went on to become Rea-

President Ronald Reagan *(center)* and Senator Edmund Muskie *(right)* listen as Senator John Tower *(left)* reports on his commission's investigation into the Iran-contra initiative. *(Reagan Library)*

gan's first ambassador at the UNITED NATIONS. Second, Reagan embraced the realist argument that the only way to discipline and thwart the designs of aggressive states was through the buildup and application of military power. Reagan also possessed a faith in the ability of technology to solve problems. This outlook is deeply engrained in the AMERICAN NATIONAL STYLE and found expression in his calls for both new weapons systems. such as the MX MISSILE, the B-1 bomber, and Trident II submarine, and his advocacy of the STRATEGIC DEFENSE INITIATIVE (SDI), which became popularly known as "Star Wars."

There was one aspect of Reagan's worldview that did not always fit comfortably with the others. This was a conviction that NUCLEAR WEAPONS should be done away with. It surfaced early in his administration in the form of calls for meaningful weapons reductions as part of the STRATEGIC ARMS REDUCTIONS TALKS (START) process and his willingness to trade away U.S. nuclear deterrent forces in a summit meeting with Soviet leader Mikhail Gorbachev.

Reagan was particularly sensitive to what he saw as Soviet-inspired unrest in Latin America. Leftist unrest in EL SALVADOR and NICARAGUA were singled out as textbook cases of aggression by the "Havana-Moscow axis." In opposing communism in Nicaragua through the creation of the contras and in GRENADA through an invasion, Reagan went beyond the COLD WAR doctrine of CONTAINMENT. The REAGAN DOCTRINE called for containing communism from spreading and working to remove it from POWER should it seize control of the government. The Reagan Doctrine also supplied the rationale for helping the Mujaheddin in AFGHANISTAN and for engineering a settlement that linked removal of South African forces from NAMIBIA with the removal of Cuban forces from ANGOLA.

U.S.-Soviet relations mellowed over time. Initially, Reagan's rhetoric was so hostile that it produced a backlash in the United States and Europe that pushed a reluctant Reagan into arms control talks. By the end of his administration, however, several important arms control agreements were in place, such as the INTERMEDIATE-RANGE NUCLEAR FORCES TREATY and START I. Reasons for this change can be found in many places. The most hawkish of Reagan's advisors (Kirkpatrick, William Casey, and Caspar Weinberger) had left the administration. On the Soviet side, Gorbachev came to power and redirected Soviet foreign policy with his New Thinking.

Reagan's tendency to see world politics in simple terms, in which good fought against evil and loyalty mattered, contributed to several of his foreign-policy failures. He sent U.S. Marines to serve as peacekeepers in LEBANON following the Israeli invasion of 1982. Four months later 241 marines were killed in a terrorist attack. Reagan later admitted that he "didn't appreciate fully enough the depth of hatred and complexity of the problems that make the Middle East such a jungle." His single-minded determination to help the contras and bring home Americans being held hostage by terrorists led to the IRAN-CONTRA INITIATIVE. Reagan's unwillingness to abandon the leader of the PHILIPPINES Ferdinand Marcos contributed greatly to the political crisis that gripped that country in the early 1980s and threatened American military bases.

Viewed from a policy-making perspective, Reagan's presidency was marked by near constant turmoil. Within his administration there was a rapid turnover in NATIONAL SECURITY ADVISORS and an ongoing power struggle between SECRETARY OF DEFENSE Weinberger and SECRETARY OF STATE George Shultz that Reagan refused to stop. Controversy continues to surround the question of how much Reagan knew about the Iran-contra affair. CONGRESS and Reagan battled frequently over his disinterest in arms control, providing aid to the contras (which was prohibited by the Boland Amendments), and his administration's unwillingness to take forceful steps to end apartheid in SOUTH AFRICA.

Evaluations of Reagan's foreign policy are perhaps as diverse as for any president. Defenders assert that Reagan's combination of military buildup, hostile rhetoric, and measured military action brought about an end to the cold war. Some critics portray him as a lucky president who succeeded in spite of himself due to the internal economic and leadership problems being experienced by the Soviet Union and the absence of any serious military or economic crisis in the world. Still others criticize Reagan of softening his stance against communism as his administration progressed. In their eyes, the last years of his administration looked like "Carterism without Carter."

**Further reading:** Oye, Kenneth, et al., ed. *Eagle Resurgent.* Boston: Addison Wesley, 1987; Scott, James M. *Deciding to Intervene: The Reagan Doctrine and American Foreign Policy.* Durham, N.C.: Duke University Press, 1996.

## Reagan Doctrine

The Reagan Doctrine was the policy position adopted by the Reagan administration in 1985 that the purpose of U.S. foreign policy was to nourish and defend freedom and democracy and that to accomplish this goal the United States would "defy Soviet sponsored aggression and secure rights which have been ours since birth." The Reagan Doctrine is significant because it went beyond previous statements of CONTAINMENT, such as those embodied in the TRUMAN, NIXON, or CARTER DOCTRINES, by adding an offensive component.

Traditionally the United States had pledged itself to defend free states from communist aggression. Under the Reagan Doctrine the United States would also actively work to remove communist regimes from POWER. Before Reagan, the closest that the United States had come to such a policy position was the "rollback" philosophy of the Eisenhower administration. President DWIGHT EISENHOWER and SECRETARY OF STATE JOHN FOSTER DULLES, however, did not follow through on this pledge when given the opportunity as a result of the Hungarian revolution of 1956.

The Reagan administration's record of accomplishment in reversing communist gains was mixed. In AFGHANISTAN, its help for the Islamic GUERRILLA forces, the Mujaheddin, played a significant role in increasing the cost of the Soviet occupation and bringing about their withdrawal. On the negative side, this policy resulted in a large amount of U.S. arms flowing into the hands of the guerrillas, which they continued to use after the war was over, often against U.S.-supported interests. In ANGOLA, the Reagan Doctrine led to U.S. support for the Union for the Total Independence of Angola (UNITA) led by Jonas Savimbi. Here, the United States succeeded in forcing the withdrawal of Cuban forces but was unable to control Savimbi, who continued to fight even after UNITED NATIONS PEACEKEEPING forces arrived. Perhaps the clearest success was in CAMBODIA, where U.S. support for anticommunist forces led to the withdrawal of Vietnamese troops.

In terms of rhetoric, no country was more central to judgments about the success or failure of the Reagan Doctrine than was NICARAGUA. Removing the Sandinistas from power was a high-priority goal of the administration virtually from the outset. Yet congressional opposition and a hesitant public forced the Reagan administration to move cautiously and then covertly through the IRAN-CONTRA INITIATIVE in trying to remove them from power. The Sandinistas remained in power at the end of the Reagan administration. In succeeding Reagan, President GEORGE H. W. BUSH sought to extract the United States from the Nicaraguan conflict by endorsing free ELECTIONS. To the surprise of many, the Sandinistas were voted out of office in these elections.

**Further reading:** Scott, James M. *Deciding to Intervene: The Reagan Doctrine and American Foreign Policy* Durham, N.C.: Duke University Press, 1996.

## realism

Realism was the dominant intellectual perspective used in studying world politics in the 20th century. It began to emerge as a powerful perspective in the United States after WORLD WAR I as the euphoria of victory gave way to distress over Adolf Hitler's rise to power and the increasingly conflictual tone of world politics. In its ascendancy to a position as the conceptual foundation on which post–WORLD WAR II U.S. foreign policy came to be based, realism surpassed IDEALISM (later to reemerge as liberalism or neo-WILSONIANISM) and ISOLATIONISM. For realists world politics was not something that could be avoided nor was it an arena in which laws or international institutions and agreements could safeguard American NATIONAL INTEREST. World politics was a constant struggle for POWER that was carried out under conditions that bordered on anarchy. There was little room for embracing universal principles or for taking on moral crusades.

Realism's intellectual roots can be traced back to the writings of Thucydides (400 B.C.), Machiavelli (1469–1557), and Thomas Hobbes (1588-1679). Thucydides wrote a history of the Peloponnesian War in which he detailed the struggle for international dominance between Athens and Sparta. Central to his thesis was the argument that war was inevitable due to Athen's rising power and the fear it produced in Sparta. Machiavelli presented a pessimistic view of human nature and stressed the centrality of power as a force shaping human behavior. Hobbes wrote of the necessity for having strong governments to maintain order in an anarchic world.

The acknowledged founding voice of post–World War II American realism was Hans Morgenthau, who captured the essence of realism in stating that leaders "think and act in terms of interests defined as power." Morgenthau and other realists who emphasize human nature and the drive for power are often referred to as classical realists. They view individuals as inherently selfish and bent on acquiring power. Peace is possible only when states (leaders) follow their own narrowly defined national interests. Over time a split developed within realism, with a new group of scholars identifying themselves as neorealists. They shifted their attention from the controlling influence of human nature to the central role played by the structure of the INTERNATIONAL SYSTEM. International systems emerge spontaneously out of the efforts of states to secure their own survival through the acquisition of power. Once created, international systems become a force that states cannot control but that controls states instead.

Regardless of their point of emphasis, realists agreed that objective laws governed the struggle for power and the quest for survival. This made it possible both to predict the consequences of different courses of action and to prescribe a correct policy. In the early COLD WAR period this policy line was CONTAINMENT. The realist policy consensus began to unravel with VIETNAM, with some realists arguing that U.S. involvement was necessary and others that it was a mistake. The ability of realism to produce policy recommendations that were fundamentally at odds with each other greatly weakened its hold on the scholarly community and allowed for a new voices to enter the policy arena in the 1970s. The failure of realism to anticipate the end of the cold war brought forward another wave of theoretical challengers in the 1990s. Realism has responded by incorporating new ideas and extending its area of concern to include such aspects of world politics as cooperation and the development and operation of INTERNATIONAL ORGANIZATIONS and regimes.

One early challenger to realism was liberalism. It was also internationalist in outlook but rejected realism's emphasis on power and the struggle for survival. Like Wilsonianism before it, liberalism put great faith in the ability of people to act rationally and cooperate in creating meaningful INTERNATIONAL LAWS and organizations. A second early challenger to realism was dependency theory. It rejected realism's tendency to downplay the significance of economic power and to separate foreign and domestic policy into two mutually exclusive spheres of activity. After the end of the cold war constructivism and feminism emerged as challenging theoretical perspectives. Each points to the need to explore the mental maps policy makers employ in trying to understand world politics and the ways in which these maps are created and distort our view of the world. Within the policy-making community the greatest post–cold war challenge to realism has come from neoliberalism, with its emphasis on promoting democracy and HUMAN RIGHTS and carrying out PEACEKEEPING operations.

In spite of its predictive shortcomings, the elastic nature of its fundamental concepts and explanatory reach allows realism to continue to cast a huge shadow over U.S. foreign-policy making. Other theoretical perspectives continue to occupy a secondary position. It is the rare successful policy maker who does not claim that he or she is a foreign-policy realist. The pull of realism is so strong because, on the one hand, policy makers look to the past and are fearful that the alternative to realism is isolationism, not liberal INTERNATIONALISM. And, on the other hand, they look at the contemporary international system and see evidence all around them of the continued struggle for power.

**Further reading:** Baldwin, David A., ed. *Neorealism and Neoliberalism: The Contemporary Debate.* New York: Columbia University Press, 1993; Brown, Michael E., et al., eds. *The Perils of Anarchy: Contemporary Realism and International Security.* Cambridge, Mass.: MIT Press, 1995; Viotti, Paul R., and Mark Kauppi. *International Relations Theory: Realism, Pluralism, and Globalism.* New York: Macmillan, 1987.

## Reciprocal Trade Agreement Acts

The Reciprocal Trade Agreement Act of 1934 was passed as an amendment to the Tariff Act of 1930, better known as the SMOOT-HAWLEY TARIFF. The Smoot-Hawley Tariff raised the duties on many goods imported into the United States to near record levels and is generally criticized for producing an international economic and political backlash against the United States. The Reciprocal Trade Agreement Act reversed the trend of highly protectionist tariffs passed by Republican administrations. It provided the legislative basis for U.S. trade policy from 1934–62. At that point it time it was supplanted by the GENERAL AGREEMENT ON TARIFFS AND TRADE (GATT) process.

President FRANKLIN ROOSEVELT was not a keen supporter of lowered tariffs when he entered office in the midst of the Great Depression. However, his SECRETARY OF STATE, CORDELL HULL, was a firm believer that free trade provided one of the keys to American economic recovery. Roosevelt asked CONGRESS for the authority to enter into trade negotiations because "of the startling decline in world trade entailing far-reaching unemployment at home and because of the need for speedy action on the part of the U.S. government." Opponents worried that certain domestic economic interests would be sacrificed so that others might profit. This would destabilize the American economy. Others argued that trade protectionism was an integral aspect of domestic economic recovery and should not be abandoned.

Roosevelt signed the measure into law in 1934. It permitted the PRESIDENT to raise or lower tariffs on a reciprocal basis by as much as 50 percent of the 1930 level if doing so would result in increased export opportunities for U.S. products. The Reciprocal Trade Agreement Act also stipulated that the negotiations had to proceed on an item-by-item basis as opposed to across-the-board cuts. Some had opposed the act because it transferred the power to make tariffs from Congress to the president. In an effort to retain some ownership over the tariff-setting process, Congress limited the president's right to enter into tariff agreements to three years. At the end of three years the president would have to come back to Congress and request a renewal of this authority.

From 1934 to 1947 the United States entered into 32 reciprocal trade agreements. All but that with IRAN were negotiated with West European or Latin American states. Many of the agreements were of little real economic value, since they involved duplicative or inconsequential concessions. Still, they provided psychological reassurance that international trading relations had entered a new era. When the Roosevelt administration sought to renew its trade negotiating authority in 1937 the STATE DEPARTMENT called it "a powerful instrument . . . to strengthen the foundations of world peace."

In 1962 President JOHN KENNEDY asked CONGRESS to pass the Trade Expansion Act. He argued that new legislation was necessary because the Reciprocal Trade Agreement Act had become obsolete due to the many amendments added over the years and the emergence of the European Economic Community as a powerful regional trading body. The 1962 act became the basis for the KENNEDY ROUND negotiations in the GATT process.

**Further reading:** Rothgeb, John. *U.S. Trade Policy: Balancing Economic Dreams and Political Reality.* Washington, D.C.: Congressional Quarterly Press, 2001.

## refugees

The modern refugee movement dates from WORLD WAR II. Though a constant feature of international politics since then, the prominence of refugees as an issue has fluctuated greatly. Since the 1990s addressing the international refugee flow has been a highly controversial problem for American foreign policy and the larger international community. In part this is due to the scope of the problem. All totaled, approximately 10.7 million refugees were receiving assistance from the UNITED NATIONS High Commissioner for Refugees in 1985, and 27.6 million were receiving assistance in 1995. In 1998 AFGHANISTAN had produced 2,736,000 refugees. RWANDA had produced 2,257,000 refugees, and LIBERIA was responsible for 794,000 refugees. The United States ranked as the seventh most-hospitable state for refugees, taking in 591,000. IRAN had the most refugees, with 2,236,000.

Controversy over refugee policy is also due to the special nature of refugee status. Under INTERNATIONAL LAW individuals identified as refugees have special rights that are not accorded to migrant workers or other individuals who cross international boundaries. The most important of these is the principle of nonrefoulment, which states that refugees cannot be sent back to their homeland without their permission. By legal convention a refugee is an individual fleeing persecution by a government. Typically this is interpreted to refer to the loss of political rights. Excluded from this definition are people fleeing generalized conditions of insecurity and oppression. Economic and environmental factors are excluded as grounds for claiming persecution. One of the major issues in international refugee policy is the legalistic and European-oriented nature of this definition. Many hold that it is largely irrelevant to the contemporary refugee problem. In 1969 the Organization of African Unity (now the African Union) adopted a more expansive definition of who was a refugee. It defined a refugee as one who was fleeing generalized conditions of insecurity and oppression due to colonial rule or other reasons.

President HARRY TRUMAN drafted the first post–World War II U.S. refugee policy when he issued an executive order on December 22, 1945, permitting 40,000 refugees to come into the United States outside of the procedures set by U.S. IMMIGRATION laws. In 1948 the Displaced Persons Act was passed that allowed those displaced by war to come to the United States as refugees. More than 390,000 did so by 1952. During most of the COLD WAR the United States worked from a modified reading of the narrow definition of a refugee. Conceptually it treated individuals fleeing their homeland due to a well-founded fear of persecution due to race, RELIGION, nationality, PUBLIC OPINION, or membership in a particular group. In concrete terms the United States treated individuals fleeing communist countries as refugees while refusing to grant refugee status to individuals fleeing right-wing governments that were American allies or to individuals fleeing poverty. In 1956 the United States admitted 32,000 Hungarians following the uprising there. The duality in U.S. refugee policy came through quite clearly in the differential treatment afforded Cubans fleeing their homeland in the first years after Fidel Castro seized power and the Haitian exodus of the 1970s, as well as later Cuban outflows.

Some 100,000 Cubans arrived in the United States between January 1959 and December 1960. Both the Eisenhower and Kennedy administrations welcomed these Cubans as a symbolic indictment of the newly established Communist government in Cuba, but it was also expected that they would soon return home. Another outflow occurred in 1980 when 130,000 Cubans arrived as part of the MARIEL BOATLIFT. At first President JIMMY CARTER welcomed them with "open arms," but this policy was soon altered as the numbers increased. Carter now sought to stop the boatlift and deny entry to Cubans, arguing that Castro was "dumping" unwanted individuals on the United States.

Also in 1980, 11,000 Haitian boat people came to the United States. Since 1972 it had been U.S. policy to deny refugee status to all people fleeing HAITI. One reason has been because Haitians lacked the domestic lobbying apparatus that the Cubans possessed. A second was fear of casting doubt on the legitimacy of the Duvalier regime, a U.S. ally, and perhaps encouraging dissidents to challenge it. In 1980 Carter signed the 1980 Refugee Act that eliminated the definitional bias in favor of those fleeing communism. This opened the way to treat Haitians as refugees, but instead the Carter administration defined them as entrants. On September 29, 1981, President RONALD REAGAN instructed the U.S. Coast Guard to intercept Haitian boats at sea and send nonpolitical refugees back to Haiti. Once again, a narrow definition of refugee was being employed.

According to the 1980 Refugee Act the PRESIDENT and CONGRESS agree each year on the number of refugees to be admitted to the United States and their country of origin. In 1999, 78,000 refugees were permitted, with 12,000 coming from Africa, 9,000 from East Asia, 48,000 from Europe, 3,000 from Latin America, and 4,000 from the Near East/South Asia. An additional 2,000 could come from any region. In 1996 Congress expanded the list of persecutions that could be cited by a potential refugee to include coercive population-control policies. Thousands of individuals per year can be admitted to the United States on these grounds. Between 1985 and 1998 the three largest refugee groups admitted to the United States came from the former Soviet Union (see RUSSIA) (432,540), VIETNAM (397,746), and LAOS (106,227).

The 1990s brought a new and controversial dimension to U.S. refugee policy when U.S. troops began to play active roles in PEACEKEEPING operations where refugees were present. They have sought to ensure the safety of refugees as well as provide food and other forms of aid. The two most notable cases have been in KOSOVO, where the United States contributed 7,000 of the 50,000 peacekeeping force, and SOMALIA, where 18 American soldiers were killed as part of the United Nations Humanitarian Intervention. In Kosovo the issue was not only the presence of American peacekeepers but also the overall nature of the American participation. Republicans in Congress argued that the U.S.-led bombing campaign actually worsened conditions on the ground for the Kosovar Albanians and the general refugee situation. As of June 29, 1999, 90,298 Kosovars had been evacuated. Slight more than 8,800 came to the United States.

Beyond criticisms of specific deployments, the major critique leveled at the use of U.S. forces to help in refugee crises is that it is not in the national interest. This line of analysis is advanced by those who continue to see the threats to American interests as being military in nature. From their perspective involvement in refugee problems amounts to "social work." It serves only to involve the United States in the domestic politics of other states and divert American attention from real threats. Supporters of using American forces to deal with refugee situations reject this charge. They assert that the primary threats to American security stem from such domestic problems as poverty, exploitation, and discrimination—the very factors that often produce refugee flows. If anything, they are critical of the lack of anticipatory and preventive action taken by the United States and the international community in dealing with refugee problems and the unwillingness to commit U.S. forces to crisis situations, such as those in Rwanda and Liberia.

**Further reading:** Kritz, Mary M., ed. *United States Immigration and Refugee Policy.* Lexington, Mass.: Lexington Books, 1983; Loescher, Gil. *Refugee Movements and International Security.* Adelphi Paper 268. London: Brassey's, 1992; Weiner, Myron, ed. *International Migration and Security.* Boulder, Colo.: Westview, 1993.

# religion

United States foreign policy has often underestimated the role that religion plays in determining the actions of other states. Rather than being viewed as fundamental driving forces of foreign policy, religious influences are treated as aberrant factors that exist outside the mainstream of political life. The same holds true for the influence of religion on the content and conduct of American foreign policy. When present it tends to be dismissed as a deviation from the norm rather than as an enduring influence that is on occasion capable of determining specific U.S. foreign-policy decisions. The influence of religion on U.S. foreign policy can be assessed by examining its influence over time and by examining the lobbying efforts of contemporary religious groups. The differing stories they tell point to the complex interaction between religion and American foreign policy.

A long-term perspective yields the conclusion that the influence of religion on American foreign policy has been moderate and that it has often been mixed with other forces pushing in the same direction or overwhelmed by those pushing in opposite ones. Four major findings emerge. First, while concepts such as MANIFEST DESTINY and the belief that the United States was destined to be a "city upon a hill" rested heavily upon Reformation-era Protestant thought and notions of Protestant superiority to Catholicism, the American sense of mission was built upon broader roots. Racism, concerns for economic advantage, and perceptions of national security threats also contributed to the U.S. sense of mission. Second, no major diplomatic initiative turned on religious issues alone. Third, serious religious ideas have had only an indirect impact on policy makers. President JIMMY CARTER once commented that, unlike some of his religious critics, he could find no Scripture saying that the United States should possess a B-1 bomber or air-launched cruise missile. Finally, foreign policy has had significant effects on the American domestic religious scene. In the 1800s Protestant nativist fears were raised that the West would be conquered by Catholics and Mormons. During the VIETNAM WAR churches and congregations often were bitterly divided over the legitimacy and morality of that war. The loyalty of American Jews and Catholics has often been called into question when the interests of U.S. foreign policy seemed to be at odds with that of ISRAEL or the pope. The SEPTEMBER 11, 2001, terrorist attacks on the World Trade Center and the Pentagon led both to attacks on mosques and attempts to disentangle the terrorist acts of Islamic extremists from the central tenets of Islam.

A shift in focus to the contemporary lobbying activities of religious groups in the United States points to a greater degree of influence. It reveals that religion holds the potential to mobilize citizens in the same manner as economic interests and ethnicity. This is particularly true with regard to the activities of the Christian Right over the past few decades. Primarily identifying with the REPUBLICAN PARTY, members of the Christian Right were staunch supporters of RONALD REAGAN. His administration did little to advance their key domestic goals, such as banning abortion and permitting prayer in schools. They did, however, find in his hard-line anticommunist foreign policy a powerful vehicle for projecting their values onto the political scene. Pat Robertson's Christian Broadcasting Network gave $3 to $7 billion to U.S.-backed anticommunist forces in NICARAGUA, GUATEMALA, and HONDURAS. Jerry Falwell emerged as a strong defender of apartheid in SOUTH AFRICA. Pat Robertson supported Zaire's corrupt leader Mobutu Sese Seko, an ALLIANCE that allowed Robertson's African Development Corporation to gain access to Zaire's diamond mines. More generally, the Christian Right has supported Israel to the point of creating visions of a new crusade in Palestinian minds. In founding the Moral Majority in 1979, for example, Falwell declared it to be pro-Israel and declared that "whoever stands against Israel stands against God."

The UNITED NATIONS and the INTERNATIONAL MONETARY FUND have also been lobbying targets for the Christian Right because of their family-planning and population-control programs. A UN Convention on the Rights of the Child has been opposed by the Family Research Council, a body headed by Gary Bauer that is dedicated to defending the Judeo-Christian value system. One of their position papers declares that the convention interferes with the parent-child relationship and has "the potential to destroy all that is best in Christian civilization, replacing it with a profoundly chaotic, harmful, and ultimately evil empire."

Finally, an important mobilizing issue for the Christian Right has been the persecution of Christians, particularly in RUSSIA, CHINA, and the SUDAN. Largely because of their lobbying efforts in October 1998, CONGRESS created a White House office for reporting on religious persecution worldwide and permits the PRESIDENT to employ ECONOMIC SANCTIONS and other measures to punish offending countries.

The Christian Right does not hold a monopoly on foreign policy–oriented interest group activity by religious organizations in the United States. The United States Catholic Conference supports FOREIGN-AID programs, describing them as a "moral obligation." It supports legislation to promote religious freedom abroad but opposes economic sanctions. Catholic bishops criticized U.S. nuclear strategy. The American Jewish Congress helped draft legislation that penalized companies abiding by the Arab boycott of Israel. The American Muslim Council spoke out against U.S. air strikes against IRAQ in 1998. It called upon the Clinton administration to address the religious persecution of Chinese Muslims and wanted Serbian leader Slobodan Milošević tried as a war criminal for acts of genocide carried out in KOSOVO. The Friends Committee on National Legislation is the lobbying arm of the Society of Friends (Quakers) and has urged Congress to support the international ban on LAND MINES, the COMPREHENSIVE TEST BAN TREATY, and the United Nations by paying all U.S. back dues.

Religious groups were outspoken in their support and opposition to the IRAQ WAR. Mainline Protestants and Catholics tended to oppose the war. Evangelical groups tended to support it. They contested the issue in the pulpit, on the Internet, on television talk shows, and in the halls of government. The Conference of Catholic Bishops sent a letter to President Bush questioning his decision to expand the war against TERRORISM to include Iraq. The World Council of Churches sent a representative to lobby Congress. In televised addresses evangelical Christian ministers asserted that Jesus did not condone war but did not oppose it either. One stated, "I can't say whether war is right or wrong. . . . All I can say is, God instituted government to carry the sword to protect innocent people and to punish evildoers."

See also DOMESTIC INFLUENCES ON U.S. FOREIGN POLICY; ISLAM, POLITICAL.

**Further reading:** Johnston, Douglas, and Cynthia Sampson. *Religion: The Missing Dimension of Statecraft*. New York: Oxford University Press, 1994; O'Brien, Conor Cruise. *God Land: Reflections on Religion and Nationalism*. Cambridge, Mass.: Harvard University Press, 1988.

## Republican Party

Born in the years prior to the AMERICAN CIVIL WAR, the Republican Party ran its first presidential candidate, John Fremont, in 1856. Its second presidential candidate, ABRAHAM LINCOLN, won the 1860 election, sparking the secession of the Southern states. Opposed to the extension of slavery to territories seeking admission to the Union, the Republican Party platform of that year also addressed foreign-policy issues of the day, calling for high tariffs. Like its competitor the DEMOCRATIC PARTY, the Republican Party is less of an ideological party than it is an electoral party whose objective is to win elections. Thus, while foreign-policy issues may at times unify the Republican Party against the Democrats, they may also divide it internally.

After the Civil War the Republicans and Democrats shared many positions. They both favored a high tariff but for different reasons. The Republicans did so in order to protect domestic manufacturers from foreign competition; the Democrats favored a high tariff in order to raise revenue. In the late 1800s and early 1900s the electoral fate of the Republicans became increasingly tied to manufacturing and commercial interests. The result was a foreign policy that supported expansionism under WILLIAM MCKINLEY and THEODORE ROOSEVELT. The emphasis on military

power as a means of expansion gave way to DOLLAR DIPLOMACY under WILLIAM HOWARD TAFT. Not all Republicans endorsed expansionism when it extended beyond Latin America. The Republican Speaker of the House, for example, opposed the acquisition of the PHILIPPINES.

The electoral success of the Republican Party masked a growing disagreement that would burst into the open in 1912 when Teddy Roosevelt bolted the party and ran for president on the Progressive Party ticket. Progressives were more oriented to social reform than were the "old guard" members of the party. The Progressives were divided on foreign policy. Some favored an internationalist policy, while others gravitated toward ISOLATIONISM, fearing that an internationalist foreign policy would drain resources and attention from social issues. Both groups attacked WOODROW WILSON's foreign policy on the eve of WORLD WAR I. Internationalists criticized his neutrality as being weak, while isolationists decried it as biased toward GREAT BRITAIN. These two wings of the party would coalesce again to oppose the LEAGUE OF NATIONS after the war. HENRY CABOT LODGE was the principal spokesman for the internationalist wing, whose support Wilson needed to overcome the opposition of the unreconcilable isolationist Republicans led by Robert La Follette. Wilson was unwilling to meet the conditions attached by Lodge, and the League of Nations went down to defeat.

During the interwar period the Republican Party championed high tariffs and isolationism. In favoring the latter they were joined by a number of prominent Democrats and opposed by liberal Republicans, such as Wendell Willkie and Thomas Dewey. Willkie would oppose Roosevelt in 1940, and Dewey would be the party's nominee in 1944 and 1948. As powerful as it was during this period, the isolationist wing was politically neutralized by the Japanese attack on Pearl Harbor. Some of its leaders, such as Arthur Vandenberg, would become strong internationalists in the early COLD WAR years and lend their support to a bipartisan foreign policy. Others, such as Robert Taft, would continue to advance isolationist themes.

During the COLD WAR the Republican Party enjoyed a reputation as being the defenders of American national security, whereas the Democrats suffered under the image of being weak on COMMUNISM. President HARRY TRUMAN's battles with DOUGLAS MACARTHUR and the McCarthyite investigations into allegations of ESPIONAGE during WORLD WAR II in Truman's STATE DEPARTMENT helped set this image, as did President DWIGHT EISENHOWER's two terms in office. A foreign-policy rift was again developing within the Republican Party. Conservatives led by Barry Goldwater favored an anticommunist policy more aggressive than CONTAINMENT. He was soundly defeated in 1964, but his critique reemerged in the early 1970s as conservatives within the party grew restless with RICHARD NIXON's policy of DÉTENTE. RONALD REAGAN unsuccessfully challenged GERALD FORD in 1976 for the party's presidential nomination but would be elected twice in the 1980s.

The influence of Reagan's strong sense of nationalism, moralistic outlook on world affairs, and unilateralist orientation extended beyond his presidency. They became the defining features of a Republican perspective on foreign policy for a generation of leaders who would serve under GEORGE H. W. BUSH and GEORGE W. BUSH. Again, not all Republicans shared this outlook. In the aftermath of the cold war some became "deficit HAWKS," favoring budget reductions and retrenchment from world affairs over a foreign policy of power projection. Both wings of the party did agree that most HUMANITARIAN INTERVENTIONS were not in America's NATIONAL INTEREST.

One of the frustrations of the Republican Party has been an inability to turn the positive public perceptions of its handling of foreign policy into broader electoral support or a mandate for its domestic agenda. George H. W. Bush was unable to win reelection in spite of his popularity over the PERSIAN GULF WAR because of the economic malaise that gripped the country and the political truism that "all politics is local." The influence of SECTIONALISM is just as strong on foreign policy as it is on domestic policy. This was evident in the way in which both parties courted the Cuban vote in recent elections and through the HELMS-BURTON ACT. It can also be seen in the effort of the George W. Bush administration to use possible changes in IMMIGRATION policy to attract Mexican Americans to the Republican Party in the first months of his presidency.

See also CONGRESS; DOMESTIC INFLUENCES ON U.S. FOREIGN POLICY; ELECTIONS; INTEREST GROUPS; PUBLIC OPINION.

## revisionism

Revisionism was an important theoretical perspective for studying American foreign policy in the 1960s and early 1970s. Chronologically, it was the third perspective to emerge in American writings in the 20th century. The first perspective is associated with the writings of WOODROW WILSON and is identified as IDEALISM or WILSONIANISM. It rejected the emphasis on POWER and competition in European writings on world politics and replaced them with an emphasis on INTERNATIONAL LAW and INTERNATIONAL ORGANIZATION and a faith in the ability of people to work together and foster cooperation among states. Idealism gave way to REALISM after WORLD WAR II. Realism returned the study of world politics to a focus on power and competition. In its initial form it held that the struggle for power and limits to cooperation were rooted in human nature. Realism became the basis for America's COLD WAR

foreign policy of CONTAINMENT. However, American policy makers added a political dimension to realism's theoretical argument about the nature of world politics. It became the accepted wisdom that the cold war had been the fault of the Soviet Union. The United States had been provoked into it, and that in the absence of Soviet aggression a peaceful world order would prevail.

Revisionists took issue both with the realists emphasis on the pursuit of power and with the political argument advanced by American policy makers. Revisionists saw the driving force of world politics as economic in nature. For them, discussions about the balance of power missed the central dynamic of world politics. Foreign policy was not made in response to objective external threats to national security but out of the drive for profit. To understand foreign policy one did not look outward to the actions of other states but inward to the values and social identities of those in positions of power, namely, the elite. The end result of foreign policy was not security but wealth and exploitation. In place of an aggressive Soviet Union, revisionists saw an aggressive United States that had provoked a counterresponse from the Soviet Union.

Revisionist accounts of American foreign policy flourished in the late 1950s and early 1960s. They sought to document how the threat of COMMUNISM was used as a cover or excuse for aggressive policies designed to advance economic interests. Pathbreaking studies examined the pattern of military spending in the United States and introduced such ideas as the MILITARY-INDUSTRIAL COMPLEX and Pentagon welfare capitalism. The argument introduced was that a high level of military spending had little to do with security threats and everything to do with profits for firms that had become totally dependent on military contracts for their survival. Studies of U.S. foreign policy toward Latin America and, more generally, the Third World focused on uncovering the relationship between American firms and American policy-making institutions. The argument here was that the threat of communism was invoked to protect American business interests from social reformers who threatened their profits but hardly represented a threat to U.S. national security. Revisionists raised questions about why the atomic bomb was used against JAPAN at the end of World War II. The conventional account held that it was necessary to defeat Japan without an invasion of the home islands. Revisionists charged it was dropped for political purposes. It was an attempt to intimidate the Soviet Union and gain the upper hand in the post–World War II INTERNATIONAL SYSTEM.

Revisionism began to lose its influence in the late 1960s. Several factors contributed to its demise. First, the emphasis on elites in American foreign policy became overshadowed by a growing interest in the role that BUREAUCRACY played in decision making. Second, the substantive focus of studies on American foreign policy came to rest on questions of NUCLEAR STRATEGY, DETERRENCE, and ARMS CONTROL. These were issues approached most readily from a military-power perspective that assumed a RATIONAL-ACTOR approach to policy making. Third, in some sense revisionism became a victim of the VIETNAM WAR. While commentators debated the wisdom of the war and the extent to which a Communist victory represented a security threat to the United States, few could find a convincing economic rationale for the war.

Revisionism did not fade from the scene without leaving a legacy upon which subsequent studies of American foreign policy have built. Its spirit is present in virtually all studies that question power-based interpretations of American foreign policy. Most notably it is present in studies that ask why concerns for advancing HUMAN RIGHTS and environmental protection and eradicating global poverty are so seldom present on the American foreign-policy agenda.

See also DOMINICAN REPUBLIC; ELITE DECISION-MAKING THEORY; GUATEMALA; RUSSIA.

**Further reading:** Kolko, Gabriel. *The Roots of American Foreign Policy.* Boston: Beacon Press, 1969; Parenti, Michael, ed. *Trends and Tragedies in American Foreign Policy.* Boston: Little, Brown, 1971.

## Rio Pact

The Rio Pact, more formally known as the Inter-American Treaty of Reciprocal Assistance, was signed by the United States and 19 Latin American states at the Inter-American Conference for the Maintenance of Continental Peace and Security held just outside Rio de Janeiro, Brazil, August 15–September 2, 1947. It is a collective security agreement that stipulates that an attack on any one member is an attack against all. The provisions came into effect when two-thirds of the signatories approved. The agreement states that no member would be required to contribute armed forces without its consent.

The Rio Pact formalized U.S. attempts to create a COLLECTIVE SECURITY system in the Western Hemisphere. The most immediate precursor to the Rio meeting was a February 1945 meeting at Chapultepec, in Mexico City. The Inter-American Conference on Problems of War and Peace had been called in part to discuss the problem of ARGENTINA, where Juan Perón had come to power and created a fascist state. It was decided that if Argentina declared war on the Axis powers and adhered to an agreement just negotiated, it could join the UNITED NATIONS. The ACT OF CHAPULTEPEC was not formally a treaty but was seen an instrument that folded the MONROE DOCTRINE into a defensive system based on collective security principles. The Act of Chapultepec was termed a temporary agreement

with a true defense treaty to be negotiated after the war. The Rio Pact was that treaty. The meeting to negotiate it had been postponed due to continued Argentine-U.S. conflicts over Argentina's domestic and foreign policies.

The Rio Treaty was significant at the time because it represented the first case in which a regional defense organization was created within the context of the UNITED NATIONS (UN) system. The Soviet Union had argued that such arrangements were antithetical to the UN. The U.S. and its allies saw no inconsistency, and a compromise formula (Article 51) was reached that permitted their formation. As the first case it served as a model for later regional security arrangements involving the United States, most notably the NORTH ATLANTIC TREATY ORGANIZATION (NATO).

The significance of the Rio Pact declined as U.S. power increased and became global in scope. This fact effectively reduced the Rio Pact to playing a symbolic and supportive role for U.S. military initiatives. No state or combination of states in the region could oppose the United States. As it declined in influence, other regional organizations gained in stature in the eyes of American policy makers. The ORGANIZATION OF AMERICAN STATES (OAS) emerged as a favorite instrument of U.S. foreign policy during the COLD WAR. More recently the NORTH AMERICAN FREE TRADE AGREEMENT (NAFTA) has moved into the forefront of U.S. hemispheric international relations as economic issues have gained in importance.

See also INTERNATIONAL ORGANIZATION; RUSSIA.

## rogue states

Rogue states are a category of developing states identified as particularly threatening to American security interests in the first decade after the end of the COLD WAR. The concept of rogue states is significant because it provided a rationale for continued high levels of military spending and war planning.

The concept of rogue states was developed by then-chairman of the JOINT CHIEFS OF STAFF General Colin Powell after the fall of the Berlin Wall in 1989. This event symbolized the end of the cold war, and with the wall went the significance of the Soviet Union to U.S. national security planning. Powell called for redirecting American military planning from global war to "regional and contingency responses to non-Soviet threats." Powell argued that the United States needed a base military force of 1.6 million active-duty personnel to be able to fight and win two regional wars simultaneously.

Powell did not use the term *rogue state* in developing his proposal. It entered the vocabulary of U.S. foreign policy during the PERSIAN GULF WAR with the revelations that Iraq was pursuing nuclear, biological, and chemical weapons. These were weapons against whose possession and use a widespread global consensus had long since developed, thus IRAQ was placed in the category of a rogue, or outlaw, state. In the following decade IRAN, LIBYA, and NORTH KOREA would also be placed in this category.

Throughout the 1990s, the belief that rogue states constituted the major threat to American national security interests guided American military planning and much of its diplomacy. The bottom-up review conducted by SECRETARY OF DEFENSE Les Aspin early in the Clinton administration's first term endorsed the idea of possessing a military capable of fighting two regional wars at the same time. A 1997 Quadrennial Defense Review also endorsed this position. Diplomatically, the Clinton administration sought to isolate Iran and Iraq through a strategy of DUAL CONTAINMENT and applied ECONOMIC SANCTIONS against those states, along with Libya.

U.S. foreign policy began to move away from the rogue-state doctrine in the latter part of the Clinton administration. A number of factors prompted this move. First, U.S. allies never fully embraced it. Their support for economic sanctions and military action against Iraq and Iran, in particular, was often lukewarm. Second, there were not many rogue states, and this number did not increase over time. This made constructing a military strategy around their existence difficult. Third, the term became counterproductive politically within the United States. This became evident when the Clinton administration entered into negotiations with North Korea to curb its pursuit of nuclear power. Conservatives questioned whether one could or should negotiate with a rogue state. INDIA and PAKISTAN's detonation of nuclear weapons had a similar effect. They were not labeled rogue states, making it unclear what the defining characteristic of a rogue state was.

In 2000, the Clinton administration formally abandoned the concept of rogue states. It reappeared in an altered form in President GEORGE W. BUSH's State of the Union address when he labeled Iran, Iraq, and North Korea as members of an axis of evil.

See also NUCLEAR WEAPONS; RUSSIA; WEAPONS OF MASS DESTRUCTION.

## Roosevelt, Franklin D. (1882–1945) *president of the United States*

Franklin Delano Roosevelt was the 32nd president of the United States, serving from 1933 to 1945. His foreign-policy initiatives can be divided into two categories: interwar DIPLOMACY and wartime diplomacy through SUMMIT CONFERENCES.

Prior to the outbreak of WORLD WAR II, Roosevelt conducted his foreign policy within the consensus of American ISOLATIONISM. Although not an isolationist, Roosevelt was not completely opposed to a passive American presence on the international scene. He feared that too activist a role in world affairs would detract from his efforts to rebuild the American economy and society through his New Deal legislation. In his inaugural address he stated, "[I]n the field of foreign policy, I would dedicate this nation to the policy of the good neighbor." In the coming years he was true to his word. Roosevelt declined to participate in a 1933 London economic conference that was intended to stabilize the international monetary system. He took no action to counter Italy's war against ETHIOPIA, Nazi GERMANY's remilitarization, Francisco Franco's victory in the Spanish civil war, or Japanese advances in CHINA (other than not to recognize the legality of its conquests). Even his more positive foreign-policy pronouncements, such as the Good Neighbor policy in Latin America, were designed to reduce pressures for U.S. intervention and involvement in world affairs.

Roosevelt's outlook had changed somewhat by the late 1930s, but he still did not directly challenge the isolationist consensus that existed in the country. In 1935, 1936, and 1937 CONGRESS passed NEUTRALITY LEGISLATION that prohibited Americans from lending money or selling weapons to belligerents. A major force behind this legislation were hearings held by NYE COMMISSION, whose major theme was that bankers and commercial interests had lobbied President WOODROW WILSON into war and profited handsomely from the war. One consequence of the neutrality legislation was that it favored the more powerful state, which was least in need of external sources of military and financial aid. In his 1939 annual message to CONGRESS he called for revision of the Neutrality Act so that the United States could give aid to any country whose security was important to the United States. Roosevelt argued that such aid rather than neutrality would best keep the United States out of war. Suspicious of Roosevelt's true motives, Congress refused to do so, and the neutrality legislation was not amended to allow GREAT BRITAIN and FRANCE to buy weapons from the United States until later in 1939 after Germany invaded POLAND. They did so under the LEND-LEASE plan. Instead of paying in cash (which they lacked) they were permitted to receive U.S. goods in turn for leases on their overseas possessions. British vessels carrying these goods were sunk in large numbers by German submarines. More than 500,000 tons of shipping were being lost each month. Roosevelt then invoked the MONROE DOCTRINE, stating that the North Atlantic fell within the Western Hemisphere and authorized U.S. ships to patrol these sea lanes.

Roosevelt held a Europe-first outlook on the coming global conflict and did not address as much energy to managing U.S. relations with JAPAN. The Roosevelt administration signaled its displeasure with Japan's aggressive policies in July 1939 when the STATE DEPARTMENT informed Japan that the United States would terminate a commercial treaty that had been in place since 1911. The

President Franklin D. Roosevelt asking Congress to declare war on Japan on December 8, 1941, the day after the attack on Pearl Harbor *(Library of Congress)*

United States followed this up 1940 when it put into place an embargo on aviation fuel and top-grade scrap iron. The first half of 1941 saw a flurry of disorganized diplomatic initiatives between the two sides in an effort to avoid the coming confrontation. The bottom line, however, placed the two sides in a stalemate. Japan was determined to obtain OIL from British and Dutch oil fields in Asia unless the United States dropped its embargo. The United States, however, would only do so in return for Japanese promises to respect China's sovereignty and territorial integrity. This was something Japan was not prepared to do.

Roosevelt also began his "wartime" summitry during the interwar period. His first conference with British prime minister Winston Churchill was arranged in secret off the coast of Placentia Bay, Newfoundland, in August 1941. Discussions included how to deal with Japan (Great Britain actively sought to engage the United States, and the United States resisted) and Germany (the British sought military aid and protection for their vessels in the North Atlantic, and U.S. Army chief of staff GEORGE MARSHALL preferred to build up U.S. ground forces). The ATLANTIC CHARTER was the signature document that emerged from their meeting. This eight-point statement brought back memories of Woodrow Wilson's FOURTEEN POINTS and in time came to be treated as a statement of U.S. war aims.

Roosevelt's main war aim was to achieve victory with the least possible loss of American lives. To this end he endorsed plans for an invasion of North Africa rather than the cross-English Channel invasion the British desired. It also made it imperative that he involve the Soviet Union in the war against Japan. This had the secondary effect of making it imperative that Soviet leader Joseph Stalin remain a willing partner in the war against Germany. Disagreements over issues that might split the United States, Great Britain, and the Soviet Union, such as the division of Europe and the shape of the UNITED NATIONS, could not be allowed to disrupt Big Three wartime summit conferences at TEHRAN (1943) and YALTA (1945). Roosevelt died less than two months after returning from the Yalta Conference.

Roosevelt did formulate clear ideas about the future world he wanted to create. While not disavowing the notion of a successor to the LEAGUE OF NATIONS, his vision of the postwar peace rested upon the existence of "Four Policeman," each of which would be responsible for keeping peace and stability in their region. Roosevelt favored a harsh peace against Germany, including permanent partition, since he held that the German people were as responsible for the war as was Adolf Hitler. He opposed the reestablishment of colonial empires by Great Britain and France. Roosevelt did not establish the type of cordial relationship with French leader Charles de Gaulle that he did with Churchill and had little sympathy for France's hopes of reemerging as a major power after the war.

Historians comment on Roosevelt's decision-making style almost as much as on his foreign-policy record. Roosevelt was his own SECRETARY OF STATE and often did not inform Secretary of State CORDELL HULL of key decisions, preferring to rely on a core group of personal advisers led by Harry Hopkins. Caring little for bureaucratic structure, Roosevelt preferred multiple lines of communication that often placed agencies at cross purposes. He was also supremely confident of his ability to establish working relationships with other leaders (such as Stalin) to the neglect of finding more enduring grounds on which to establish relations. Finally, Roosevelt was also noted for stretching the truth and manipulating information. For example, at the Newfoundland meeting that produced the Atlantic Charter, Roosevelt secretly agreed to a request from Churchill to allow the U.S. Navy to convoy British merchant ships as far as Iceland. This placed Germany and the United States on a collision course. In September German U-boats attacked the USS *Greer.* Roosevelt used this as a pretext for announcing that from now on U.S. ships would shoot at German submarines, starting what amounted to an undeclared naval war.

**Further reading:** Burns, James MacGregor. *Roosevelt: The Lion and the Fox.* New York: Harcourt, 1963; Dallek, Robert. *Franklin D. Roosevelt and American Foreign Policy, 1932–1945.* New York: Oxford University Press,

1979; Feis, Herbert. *Churchill, Roosevelt, and Stalin: The War They Waged and the Peace They Sought.* Princeton, N.J.: Princeton University Press, 1957.

## Roosevelt, Theodore (1858–1919) *president of the United States*

Theodore Roosevelt was the 26th president, serving from 1901 to 1909. He assumed the presidency on WILLIAM MCKINLEY's death at the hands of an assassin on September 14, 1901. Roosevelt had been McKinley's vice president, a position he reportedly obtained through the efforts of New York's REPUBLICAN PARTY political boss Thomas Platt, who had grown disillusioned with Roosevelt's reformist policies as governor of that state. Prior to holding that position Roosevelt had served briefly as assistant secretary of the navy in McKinley's first administration and established himself as an ardent supporter of a strong navy and American IMPERIALISM. Roosevelt gained prominence during the SPANISH-AMERICAN WAR for his service as a Rough Rider in CUBA.

As president Roosevelt pursued a forceful and aggressive foreign policy that was predicated on the goal of establishing the United States as a major player in world politics and the preeminent state in the Western Hemisphere. Not surprisingly, a central focus of his foreign policy became the construction of an American canal across Central America. Such a canal would dramatically shorten the time necessary for American military and commercial vessels to move from the Atlantic to the Pacific Oceans. For Roosevelt it was important not only that the United States build a canal but also that it should be allowed to defend it. The CLAYTON-BULWER TREATY of 1850 with GREAT BRITAIN stipulated that both states jointly defend any canal. One of Roosevelt's first foreign-policy objectives as president was to arrange for a modification of this agreement. He accomplished this with the signing of the HAY-Paunceforte Treaty on November 18, 1901.

Still uncertain, however, was where to build the canal. NICARAGUA was the choice of a study done by the Walker Isthmian Canal Commission. Roosevelt, however, had come to favor a route through PANAMA and prodded first the commission and then CONGRESS to reverse course and endorse the Panama route. At this time Panama was part of COLOMBIA; accordingly, the STATE DEPARTMENT opened negotiations with it for obtaining the right of way. These talks led to the successful negotiation of a treaty, the Hay-Herrán Treaty, on March 17, 1903. The agreement collapsed shortly thereafter when the Colombian government sought to obtain additional payments beyond what was agreed to. Roosevelt then switched his strategy and conspired to help Panama break away from Colombia as a prelude to purchasing the land necessary to build a canal. A treaty to this effect was signed on November 18, 1903,

less than two weeks after the United States recognized Panama's independence.

Roosevelt's vision of America's role in the Western Hemisphere extended far beyond the construction and operation of the PANAMA CANAL. In an address to Congress on December 6, 1904, in what came to be known as the ROOSEVELT COROLLARY to the MONROE DOCTRINE, Roosevelt argued that it was necessary for the United States to act as a hemispheric police officer. It would have to punish wrongdoing and establish order when governments were incapable of doing so. This position marked a change from one he advanced in a December 1901 address to Congress in which he stated that the United States would not prevent European states from punishing hemispheric governments for misbehaving. A financial dispute among VENEZUELA, Great Britain, and GERMANY changed Roosevelt's mind. The two European states were angry with Venezuela for failure to pay debts owed to them and began to use force to obtain payment. Roosevelt at first approved of their plans but then became concerned with the precedent it set. Of particular concern was the situation in the DOMINICAN REPUBLIC, which was also deeply in debt and faced the threat of hostile European military action. Armed with the newly minted Roosevelt Corollary, Roosevelt forced the Dominican Republic to accept American control over its customshouse as a means of putting its finances back in order.

As befit someone who espoused a strong navy, Roosevelt's interests extended beyond the Western Hemisphere. The political and military balance of POWER was of special concern to Roosevelt due to the American acquisition of the PHILIPPINES during the Spanish-American War. In a July 1905 agreement between Secretary of War WILLIAM HOWARD TAFT and Japanese prime minister Taro Katsura, the United States agreed to recognize JAPAN's special relationship with KOREA. In return Japan agreed to a policy of neutrality with respect to the Philippines, thus ensuring America's domination over the archipelago. A month later, in August, Roosevelt would bring together Japanese and Russian diplomats in a meeting in Portsmouth, New Hampshire, where he would help engineer a resolution of the Russo-Japanese War. He earned the Nobel Peace Prize for his efforts.

Roosevelt also played mediator in a European conflict over the fate of North Africa. In 1904 FRANCE had agreed to British domination over EGYPT in return for control over MOROCCO. Germany moved quickly to challenge this arrangement by staking its own claim to Morocco. Neither Great Britain nor France accepted the German position. Unwilling to simply back down and admit defeat, Kaiser Wilhelm asked Roosevelt to mediate the dispute. He agreed, and discussions were held in 1906 at Algeciras, SPAIN. Roosevelt resolved the conflict by getting Germany to agree to pro-French compromise on the matter. While this ended the crisis, Roosevelt did not escape criticism at home for his efforts. He was castigated for violating the traditional American principles of ISOLATIONISM and nonintervention into European affairs.

Roosevelt handpicked Taft to be his successor as the Republican presidential candidate in 1908. After Taft's election, however, they parted company over what Roosevelt perceived to be his probusiness policies. Roosevelt challenged Taft for the 1912 Republican Party nomination. After he failed, Roosevelt ran as a third-party candidate. This ensured the victory of WOODROW WILSON. In retirement Roosevelt often spoken out against Wilson's foreign policy. He opposed Wilson's efforts to compensate Colombia for the loss of Panama and argued against American neutrality in the opening years of WORLD WAR I.

**Further reading:** Burton, David H. *The Learned Presidency: Theodore Roosevelt, William Howard Taft, and Woodrow Wilson.* Madison, N.J.: Fairleigh Dickinson University Press, 1988; Collin, Richard H. *Theodore Roosevelt's Caribbean: The Panama Canal, the Monroe Doctrine, and the Latin American Context.* Baton Rouge: Louisiana State University Press, 1990.

## Roosevelt Corollary

The MONROE DOCTRINE was issued in 1823. It warmed foreign powers to stay out of the Western Hemisphere, while reserving for the United States the right to expand its own influence in the region. President THEODORE ROOSEVELT modified the Monroe Doctrine in 1904 in an address to Congress. Roosevelt announced that "chronic wrongdoing . . . may . . . ultimately require intervention by some civilized nation, and in the Western Hemisphere the adherence of the United States to the Monroe Doctrine may force the United States, however reluctantly, . . . to the exercise of an international police power."

Roosevelt's corollary to the Monroe Doctrine was sparked by the growing indebtedness of Latin American states to Europe and their inability to repay those loans. This situation led some European states to contemplate military action to obtain repayment by seizing an indebted state's customshouses. Under the Roosevelt Corollary it would be the United States that acted as police officer of the hemisphere and took such action. In 1905 it entered into an agreement with the DOMINICAN REPUBLIC to take over Dominican customshouses. The United States would retain 45 percent of the receipts to cover its expenses and use the remainder to pay off outstanding Dominican debts. Political unrest in the Dominican Republic led WOODROW WILSON to take the Roosevelt Corollary to its logical conclusion when in 1916 U.S. Marines were dispatched to that country, and a military government established. Similarly

inspired American interventions were occurring in NICARAGUA and HAITI during this time period.

FRANKLIN ROOSEVELT sought to depart from the Roosevelt Corollary and lay a new framework for hemispheric relations in advocating the Good Neighbor policy in 1933. Franklin Roosevelt's policy represented more of a shift in tactics than in goals. The United States continued to view the Western Hemisphere as an area of special influence. This continuity in policy became evident when the COLD WAR began to intensify in the 1950s. American presidents used the Monroe Doctrine and, less vocally, the Roosevelt Corollary, as the basis for interventionist policies designed to keep the Soviet Union (see RUSSIA) out of the region.

## Root, Elihu (1845–1937) *secretary of state, secretary of war*

Elihu Root served as SECRETARY OF WAR (1899–1904) and SECRETARY OF STATE (1904–09) under Presidents WILLIAM MCKINLEY and THEODORE ROOSEVELT. He won the Nobel Peace Prize in 1912 for his contributions to peace and his establishment of an "enlightened" colonial system. Root made particularly noteworthy contributions to U.S. foreign policy in several different areas.

In Latin America, Root formulated U.S. colonial policy in PUERTO RICO (he would do the same for the PHILIPPINES) and as secretary of war authored the PLATT AMENDMENT to the U.S. army appropriations bill of 1901, which put forward the conditions under which the Unites States ended its ongoing military occupation of CUBA. The Platt Amendment denied the Cuban government the right to enter into any agreement that would impair its independence as determined by the United States and gave the United States the right to intervene for the purpose of maintaining good government. Later, Root would work with Roosevelt on the ROOSEVELT COROLLARY to the MONROE DOCTRINE, which gave the United States the self-proclaimed power for preserving stability in the hemisphere.

As secretary of state, Root moved to settle an ongoing fisheries dispute in the North Atlantic through international arbitration. American anglers claimed the right to fish off the coast of Newfoundland by virtue of an 1818 treaty. Angered over their presence, the Newfoundland legislature began passing laws that hampered their efforts. In 1909 GREAT BRITAIN, which conducted foreign relations for CANADA, and the United States agreed to submit the dispute to the International Court of Justice at The Hague. In a compromise decision handed down in 1910, U.S. anglers were to be protected against unreasonable local regulations, but the right of Newfoundland to make laws covering fishing in these waters was confirmed. An Anglo-American commission signed a convention in 1912 modifying this agreement somewhat and established a permanent body of deal with any future disputes as they arose. This agreement effectively removed fisheries as an area of major tension in U.S.–Canadian/British relations.

Finally, Root also made contributions to U.S. foreign policy in the Far East with the signing of the Root-Takahira EXECUTIVE AGREEMENT in 1908. It provided that the United States and JAPAN would (1) work to maintain the status quo in the Pacific, (2) respect each other's territorial possessions, (3) uphold the OPEN DOOR in CHINA, and (4) support by pacific means the independence and integrity of China. The agreement was welcomed in the U.S. press as a victory and affirmation of the Open Door policy and offered protection for the Philippines and HAWAII. Instead, it had the opposite effect because it recognized Japan's economic domination of and military interest in Manchuria and what is now NORTH and SOUTH KOREA. Roosevelt recognized this agreement as a partial retreat from the Open Door but felt that U.S. economic interests in these regions were too small to risk the possibility of military conflict in order to maintain a principle.

**Further reading:** Leopold, Richard W. *Elihu Root and the Conservative Tradition.* Boston: Scott Foresman, 1954.

## Rush-Bagot Treaty

The Rush-Bagot Treaty of 1817 established limits to the permissible levels of U.S. and British naval armaments on the Great Lakes. The treaty was one of a series of Anglo-American agreements signed following the WAR OF 1812. One such agreement was a four-year commercial treaty concluded in 1815 that was to replace JAY'S TREATY. It freed American and British trade from discriminatory duties and for the most part reestablished postwar commercial relations. Other treaties dealt with pressing matters that had not been addressed by the TREATY OF GHENT that ended the War of 1812. The Rush-Bagot Treaty fell into this category.

During the War of 1812 both sides had come to see control over the Great Lakes and Lake Champlain as critically important to winning the war. At the time the war ended, the United States and GREAT BRITAIN had embarked on the beginnings of what was potentially a costly naval arms race to fortify their positions there. In 1815 the Madison administration proposed a mutual disarmament agreement. It was confident that the United States could move quickly in a time of crisis and build enough naval ships to gain the upper hand in any future conflict. The British were not interested in a naval arms race, recognizing that ships built to defend the Great Lakes would be of little value to the British navy on the open seas. British foreign secretary Lord Castlereagh was receptive to the proposal, wishing to limit the size of the two navies

to that which only was necessary only to guard against smuggling. The actual signing of the agreement was delayed until April 1817, when acting SECRETARY OF STATE Richard Rush and British minister to the United States Charles Bagot agreed to limit each side to a police and customs naval force of light vessels.

Bagot wanted the agreements to be permanent and urged the newly elected president JAMES MONROE to submit the agreement to the Senate as a treaty. Monroe hesitated but finally did so, and the Senate gave its approval in April 1818. It is important to note that the Rush-Bagot Treaty did not, as is often suggested, provide for the complete disarmament of the Great Lakes. Both sides retained some naval vessels. It was, however, the first agreement that led to the reciprocal reduction of naval forces. The agreement also did not extend to the land frontier between the United States and CANADA. It was not until the Treaty of Washington in 1872 that border fortifications were truly abandoned.

## Russia

Russia has an area of 17,075,000 square miles, making it about 1.8 times the size of the United States. It has a population of 145,471,000 people, of which 82 percent are ethnic Russians. As a country, Russia exists before and after the Soviet Union. The czars came into power in 1614 and ruled until 1917, when the monarchy was overthrown by the Bolshevik Revolution and a Communist system was established. The Soviet Union came into existence in 1922 as a federation of republics. The Soviet Union collapsed in December 1991. On December 8 the presidents of the Russian, Ukrainian, and Belarus Republics met to create the Commonwealth of Independent States (CIS) and declared the Soviet Union no longer existent. By December 22, 11 of the republics of the Soviet Union had become members of the CIS. Two days before, the Russian Republic announced that it was assuming control over the Soviet Foreign Ministry, the KGB, and the Supreme Soviet. Politically isolated by these events, Soviet president Mikhail Gorbachev resigned. On December 26, the Supreme Soviet passed a resolution acknowledging that the Soviet Union no longer existed. The Russian Republic assumed control of the former regime's EMBASSIES and took its seat at the UNITED NATIONS.

During the COLD WAR U.S.-Soviet relations were at the center of world politics and characterized by conflict and competition. Only during the RICHARD NIXON administration, with its policy of DÉTENTE, and the JIMMY CARTER administration, with its emphasis on HUMAN RIGHTS, was this not the case. Détente was predicated on the assumption that some measure of cooperation was possible between the United States and the Soviet Union, and

Carter's human-rights policy sought to deemphasize the centrality of the Soviet Union to U.S. foreign policy. The importance of Russia/the Soviet Union to American foreign policy and the high degree of conflict involved had not always been the norm. In the first years of U.S. history, both of these two 20th-century superpowers existed on the fringes of world politics, which was European centered. Their interactions were thus intermittent, not necessarily hostile, and often framed with an eye toward dealings with GREAT BRITAIN, FRANCE, Prussia, or SPAIN. After the cold war the United States's relationship with Russia took on a new complexity. For the United States, Russia remained an important player in world politics because of its size, location, and NUCLEAR WEAPONS. The success of Russia's domestic struggle to embrace of democracy and capitalism was also seen as important to the creation of a peaceful post–cold war era. For the Soviet Union, relations with the United States similarly present a mixed agenda. Russia's economic and political weaknesses have in many respects reduced it to the status of a regional power and made it dependent on the West for aid. But this is a condition that

Russian leaders have difficulty accepting. They continue to expect to be treated as a superpower by the United States and are leery of its hegemonic economic and military position in the contemporary INTERNATIONAL SYSTEM.

### Imperial Russia

As noted above, early interactions between the United States and Russia were limited. They did not exchange diplomatic representatives until 1809, and a commercial treaty was not signed until 1832. Russia unsuccessfully sought to mediate a resolution of the WAR OF 1812. The offer was made in September 1812 and accepted by the United States in March 1813, but it was rejected by the British. Russia's interest was not in helping the American as much as it was in ending the war in order to obtain additional British help in stopping Napoleon Bonaparte. Also at this time, the United States and Russia began to come into conflict with one another in the Pacific Northwest. Russian settlements had reached into what is today California, and in 1812 the czar issued a proclamation (*ukase*) warning states to keep their navies away from Russian America

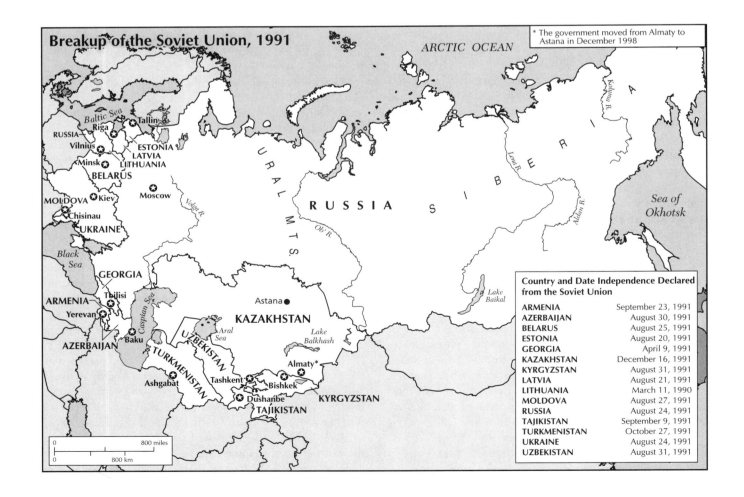

**Breakup of the Soviet Union, 1991**

\* The government moved from Almaty to Astana in December 1998

| Country and Date Independence Declared from the Soviet Union | |
|---|---|
| ARMENIA | September 23, 1991 |
| AZERBAIJAN | August 30, 1991 |
| BELARUS | August 25, 1991 |
| ESTONIA | August 20, 1991 |
| GEORGIA | April 9, 1991 |
| KAZAKHSTAN | December 16, 1991 |
| KYRGYZSTAN | August 31, 1991 |
| LATVIA | August 21, 1991 |
| LITHUANIA | March 11, 1990 |
| MOLDOVA | August 27, 1991 |
| RUSSIA | August 24, 1991 |
| TAJIKISTAN | September 9, 1991 |
| TURKMENISTAN | October 27, 1991 |
| UKRAINE | August 24, 1991 |
| UZBEKISTAN | August 31, 1991 |

(ALASKA). With the MONROE DOCTRINE as a backdrop, SECRETARY OF STATE JOHN ADAMS negotiated an agreement with Russia in 1824 limiting the southern edge of its presence in North America. As with the later decision to sell Alaska to the United States, this agreement was motivated more by internal Russian politics than external considerations related to the United States.

During the AMERICAN CIVIL WAR Russia was an ally of the Union, but this was of little consequence to the outcome of the war. A similar situation had prevailed during the AMERICAN REVOLUTION, when Catherine II issued a proclamation of armed neutrality that on paper worked to the benefit of the rebelling colonists but was of limited value. In both cases the target of Russia's actions was Great Britain, whose power and influence it hoped to weaken. The most significant diplomatic interaction between them occurred in 1867 when Secretary of State WILLIAM SEWARD arranged for the purchase of Alaska for $7 million. The agreement grew out of the conviction on Russia's part that the United States was determined to expand into Alaska and that Russia would be unable to prevent this from happening. Rather than lose it piecemeal through ever-expanding American settlements, the decision was made to sell the territory. Also motivating the Russian decision was the fact that the Russian American Company that controlled Alaska clashed increasingly with Americans, and Russia wished to avoid bad relations with the United States, given more pressing problems in Europe and Asia.

In the later part of the 19th century, relations between the United States and Russia began to take on a more overtly conflictual flavor. In Asia, Russia was one of the recipients of OPEN DOOR notes from Secretary of State JOHN HAY on September 6, 1899. Even though Hay would declare that he had received "final and definitive" assent to his plan for ensuring equal commercial opportunities in CHINA, the Russian response had been evasive and unsupportive. Russian foreign policy in Asia soon created an additional challenge for American foreign policy. In 1900 Russia moved troops into Manchuria following the Boxer Rebellion. Of special interest to all parties was the soon to be completed Trans-Siberian railroad. On February 4, 1904, JAPAN, which was Russia's principal competitor for domination of northern Asia, broke diplomatic relations and two days later attacked the Russian fleet at Port Arthur. President THEODORE ROOSEVELT would win a Nobel Prize for his mediation of this dispute at Portsmouth, New Hampshire, the following year.

American sympathies during the Russo-Japanese War had been with Japan. In part this was due to their underdog status against the much larger Russia, but it also reflected growing American displeasure with Russian domestic policies that spilled over into foreign-policy conflicts. Central to the worsening Russian image in America was its treat-

ment of Jews. In 1903, at Kishinev, some 50 Russian Jews were murdered and between 100 and 500 injured in a pogrom before police stepped in. Similar events would follow in other parts of Russia over the next years. Protestors in the United States demanded that action be taken, but because they involved the domestic affairs of a state and not its foreign policy little was done. One consequence of these pogroms that had begun in 1881 following the assassination of Czar Alexander II was a dramatic increase in the Jewish population in the United States. It grew tenfold between 1880 and 1914, reaching 3 million. Lobbying by the American Jewish Committee became intense, and in 1911 President WILLIAM HOWARD TAFT terminated the 1832 commercial treaty that had granted Russia MOST-FAVORED-NATION status. He did so on the grounds that Russia was discriminating against American citizens on the basis of their religious beliefs. The technical issue here was Russia's treatment of naturalized Americans who had fled Russia and now returned to engage in business ventures. Since emigration from Russia was generally illegal, when these individuals returned, they were arrested or harassed. For their part, Russia, leaders reacted angrily to the American moralistic criticism of their domestic affairs.

### Soviet Union

WORLD WAR I found the United States and Russia as allies and strange partners in a war that President WOODROW WILSON claimed was being fought to make the world safe for democracy. It was not surprising then that most Americans responded favorably to news of the Russian Revolution. Support soon gave way to concern, and concern led to military intervention. The Bolsheviks rejected the American definition of war aims. In spring 1918 Russia's new government struck out on its own and negotiated the Treaty of Brest-Litovsk with GERMANY that effectively ceded much of western czarist Russia to Germany in return for peace. In support of the Allied powers the United States sent 14,000 troops into Russia in the fall of 1918 to try to defeat the Bolsheviks. The intervention was not enough to turn the tide in Russia's civil war or reopen an eastern front in the war against Germany. It was enough to further alienate the Communists from the United States. The intervention has been used by some as the starting point for the COLD WAR.

For more than a decade official American and Soviet foreign relations were frozen. Recognition did not come until 1933 when WILLIAM C. BULLITT arrived in Moscow as the first U.S. ambassador to the Soviet Union. A number of factors stood in the way of normalizing relations. The Soviet government had nationalized American industries without compensation, and it refused to pay czarist debts. Religious groups lobbied against recognition, as did organized labor and business. Finally, the Red Scare of the 1920s, along with Communist propaganda of world revolution, had helped to create an anticommunist hysteria in the United States. As part of the agreement that led to diplomatic recognition, the Soviet Union agreed to stop directing Communist propaganda against the United States. Discussions regarding debt repayment were postponed. Russia had expected to receive a significant loan from the United States following recognition, but this did not happen because of the Johnson Act of 1934, which forbid loans to states owing money to the United States. Russia then dropped consideration of debt repayment. It should be noted that beneath this official separation, trade between the two countries flourished. In 1930, 25 percent of all imports into Russia came from the United States.

It was President FRANKLIN ROOSEVELT who normalized diplomatic relations with the Soviet Union. He saw nonrecognition as another of the failed and flawed policies he had inherited from Republican administrations. He also saw Germany and Japan as greater threats to American security and viewed the Soviet Union as a potential partner against them. While Roosevelt did not fully trust Joseph Stalin, he did not demonize him either. To Roosevelt, Stalin was a political boss, "Uncle Joe," who, like all political bosses, wished to remain in power and who was thus someone who could be worked with. This did not mean that cooperation between the Soviet Union and the United States (and Great Britain and France) was seamless in the period leading up to WORLD WAR II or during the war. The Soviet Union's invasion of Finland in 1939–40 alienated many Americans. During the war the Soviet Union constantly pressured the British to open up a second front against Adolf Hitler, but to no avail. Stalin was convinced that Winston Churchill's refusal to do so was born of a desire to cripple the Soviet Union in the postwar world. The United States refused to recognize the Soviet Union's annexation of the BALTIC STATES of Lithuania, Estonia, and Latvia following France's collapse in 1940. The shape of the postwar world also divided the allies. Conferences at TEHRAN in November 1943, YALTA in February 1945, and POTSDAM in August 1945 were marked by repeated disagreements over the fate of POLAND and other states in Eastern Europe, the creation of the UNITED NATIONS, and the war against Japan.

If the cold war conflict between the United States and Soviet Union was not yet in existence by the end of World War II, it was by 1947. Sounds of discord were audible in 1946. In February Stalin spoke of the incompatibility of communism and capitalism. GEORGE KENNAN then sent his "long" telegram from the American embassy in Moscow to Washington, D.C., in which he outlined the conceptual basis of containment. In March Churchill gave his fabled "iron curtain" speech.

Deeds followed words. Each side saw its own actions as defensive and saw the other as operating according to a tightly scripted aggressive plan. Russian pressure on

TURKEY for control over the Dardanelles Straits and Communist GUERRILLA WARFARE in GREECE combined with the British declaration that it could not longer provide for the defense of these states led to the TRUMAN DOCTRINE. Announced in March 1947, it pledged the United States to come to the defense of free democracies. This was followed in June by the announcement of the MARSHALL PLAN for economic recovery of Europe and the creation of the NORTH ATLANTIC TREATY ORGANIZATION (NATO) in April 1949. In between, the United States, Great Britain, and France had unified their German occupation zones into one, and the CENTRAL INTELLIGENCE AGENCY engaged in its first COVERT ACTION to prevent a victory by the Italian Communist Party in 1948 elections. Back on the Soviet side of the ledger, the Communists had engineered a coup in CZECHOSLOVAKIA, removing pro-Western parties from the government. More generally, Communist Parties loyal to Stalin were consolidating their power in Eastern Europe everywhere but in YUGOSLAVIA, and in 1955 the WARSAW PACT was created as a counter to NATO. This pattern of building conflict soon spread beyond the confines of Europe. Under the guidance of Mao Zedong (Mao Tsetung), the Communists won the Chinese civil war in 1949, and one year later NORTH KOREA invaded SOUTH KOREA.

Stalin died in 1953, and after a power struggle within the Kremlin he was succeeded by Nikita Khrushchev. In 1956, in a secret speech to Communist Party leaders, Khrushchev condemned the excesses of Stalin's rule. He replaced Stalin's dictum that war between capitalism and communism was inevitable with the concept of peaceful coexistence. This formulation of the cold ward asserted the ultimate triumph of communism but held out the prospect that conflict could be managed and made safer. One means for making it safer was for both parties to work through surrogates, or local allies, rather than confront each other directly. This became the rule as the cold war battlefield shifted from Europe and Korea to the developing world. The prize to be captured here was the loyalty of states emerging from independence in Africa and Asia and the allegiance of Arab nationalists in the Middle East.

Almost immediately Khushchev's speech created problems for the Soviet Union in East Europe. In attacking Stalin, Khrushchev had also attacked his puppets there, and a reform movement soon began that sought to put more nationalistic and reformist leaders in power. Khrushchev was not prepared to allow this to happen. In Soviet eyes East Europe remained an invaluable buffer zone between it and the West. Soviet and Warsaw Pact troops would put down these movements in Poland and HUNGARY in 1957 and a decade later in Czechoslovakia. Conflict would also grow between the Soviet Union and China. Long-standing boundary disputes, questions about ideological purity, and personal competition between Mao and Khrushchev all contributed to this split. Such was the depth of cold war competition that the United States was slow to recognize that the split was occurring and to adjust its policies accordingly.

Khrushchev would be removed from power in 1964 and ultimately be succeeded by Leonid Brezhnev. Foreign-policy setbacks contributed heavily to his ouster. No incident was more damaging than the CUBAN MISSILE CRISIS. The reckless and ill-conceived decision to place offensive missiles in Cuba had been based in part on a desire to offset American nuclear superiority. All it did was reveal Soviet weakness. Brezhnev embarked upon a twofold strategy. First, the Soviet Union undertook a large-scale buildup of its nuclear forces. Second, it entered into a series of ARMS CONTROL agreements with the United States through the aegis of the STRATEGIC ARMS LIMITATION TALKS (SALT). The first major agreement, a Test Ban Treaty, was reached under Khrushchev in 1963.

In pursuing these arms control agreements, Brezhnev was a partner in PRESIDENT Richard Nixon's policy of détente. It was designed to provide less conflictual foundation for U.S.-Soviet relations following VIETNAM. At its core was a strategy of linkage in which good Soviet behavior in military matters was to be rewarded with economic advantages, the most important of which was to be most-favored-nation status. Détente did not work as promised. The Nixon administration was unable to deliver on its promise of economic gain. Led by Senator Henry "Scoop" Jackson (D-Wash.), Congress held most-favored-nation status hostage to improved treatment of Soviet Jews. And while it cooperated on nuclear matters, the Soviet Union continued to press for an advantage in AFRICA. The two superpowers also nearly came to blows in the Middle East, where in 1973 the Soviet Union threatened to send troops to protect EGYPT if Israeli forces did not stop fighting.

Brezhnev's major foreign-policy success outside of arms control came in 1975 with the signing of the Helsinki accords. More than anything, Soviet leaders desired a solution to the "German problem." No World War II peace treaty existed, and the threat of changing Europe's political borders, including the very existence of East Germany, was both real and frightening. The Helsinki accords established that the borders of Europe could not be changed by force. The Soviet Union appeared to give up very little to achieve this concession from the West. Their concessions were located in Basket Three of the agreement and consisted of accepting a series of human-rights guarantees for its citizens. President GERALD FORD was heavily criticized in the United States by conservatives for accepting this agreement. Few on either side of the iron curtain realized at the time that Basket Three would become the principal tool of the West to open up the Soviet Union in the coming years.

Brezhnev died in November 1982. He was succeeded as head of the Communist Party by Yuri Andropov (1982–84),

Soviet leader Nikita Khrushchev *(right)* and President John F. Kennedy shake hands at the U.S. embassy in Vienna, Austria, 1961. *(Hulton/Archive)*

Konstantin Chernenko (1984–85), and Mikhail Gorbachev (1985–91). The last years of the Brezhnev era were marked by social, economic, and political stagnation at home and by foreign-policy crises abroad. In 1979 Soviet forces invaded AFGHANISTAN to help the pro-Moscow Communist Party gain and consolidate its power. Afghanistan proved to be the Soviet Union's VIETNAM, sapping its military strength and provoking domestic opposition. Under the guise of the REAGAN DOCTRINE, the United States would send arms to the Mujaheddin, the anticommunist guerrillas. It would be 1988 before the Soviet Union could extricate itself from this quagmire. Brezhnev-era stagnation also left a dangerous political and security situation in East Europe. Under terms of the Brezhnev Doctrine announced in 1968 to justify the invasion of Czechoslovakia, it was up to the Soviet Union to determine what type of political reform was permissible in East Europe. By 1983 in Poland the Solidarity trade union led by Lech Wałesa had demonstrated significant political strength and was working toward a national referendum on Poland's foreign policy and governmental system. After months of warnings, in December 1983 the Polish government cracked down on Solidarity and imposed martial law. Weaknesses at home also created foreign-policy problems. RONALD REAGAN set in motion a major increase in defense spending that the Soviet Union could not match.

Gorbachev would try, but he failed to save the Soviet Union. Domestically he instituted economic and political reforms under the banners of perestroika (restructuring)

and glasnost (openness). In foreign policy his ascendancy to the head of the Communist Party brought about a change in U.S.-Soviet relations. Along with pulling Soviet troops out of Afghanistan, he allowed greater freedom for the Soviet Union's East European satellites by renouncing the Brezhnev Doctrine, reducing Soviet support for Communist insurgent forces in NICARAGUA, and engineering the removal of Cuban troops from ANGOLA. These actions brought about a lessening of tensions between Washington and Moscow. Gorbachev and Reagan also engaged in a series of summit conferences. They first met in November 1985. They met again in November 1986 in Reykjavík, Iceland, where Gorbachev proposed eliminating intercontinental ballistic missiles. It was an offer Reagan apparently accepted and then rejected because Gorbachev had insisted on terminating the STRATEGIC DEFENSE INITIATIVE as the price for the agreement. Another summit was held in Washington in December 1987 at which time the INTERMEDIATE-RANGE NUCLEAR FORCES (INF) TREATY was signed.

The conceptual foundation of Gorbachev's foreign-policy initiatives was known as New Thinking. It rejected the idea that the security of the Soviet Union could be attained through military means alone. Moreover, security was no longer seen in zero-sum terms. Instead, Soviet security could be achieved only in cooperation with others. DIPLOMACY and interdependence played key roles in the New Thinking, pushing concepts associated with the idea of class struggle to the margins of Soviet foreign policy.

### Democratic Russia

Russian foreign policy after the fall of the Soviet Union has been under the direction of Boris Yeltsin, who ruled from 1991 to 1999, and Vladimir Putin, who assumed the presidency after Yeltsin. Russia has yet to put its relations with the United States on a firm footing. In the words of one commentator, they are "uneven, unpredictable, and unreliable."

A number of factors contribute to this. Russia's weak domestic situation limits Russia's ability to acquire and display power on the international stage. The privatization of industry, agriculture, and commercial enterprises has created a kind of economic anarchy in which great disparities in wealth have appeared along with an explosion in crime and corruption that makes economic growth difficult to generate or sustain. The Russian military is also beset by problems involving the quality of its weapons, most of which are more than a decade old, and the morale of both enlisted personnel and the officer corps. Conditions within the military are poor, and its status within society is greatly diminished as is its size. In 1988 there were 5 million people in uniform. The Russian army today has about 1.5 million. Ethnic tensions continue to sap its political strength.

The war in Chechnya drags on, and attempts to bring it to an end by escalating the conflict have failed. A total 40,000 Russian troops entered this breakaway province in December 1994. A cease-fire was negotiated in August 1996, but it proved unsatisfactory to the Russian leadership when Chechnya began to act as if it were an independent state. A treaty of normalization was signed in May 1997 that kept Chechnya in Russia, but it has accomplished little. By 1999 relations between Russia and Chechnya had deteriorated sharply as Chechen terrorist attacks against Russia were becoming common and a situation bordering on lawlessness prevailed in Chechnya. Once again Russia went to war with Chechnya. In 2000 Russian forces had made significant military advances but could not sustain their successes due to the financial cost of the venture and the rising tide of Chechen TERRORISM against Russians.

Just as important as the weak domestic base on which Russia is seeking to build a foreign policy, Russian-American relations are in flux because of the nature of the foreign policy goals Russia is trying to realize in a post–cold war era characterized by American dominance. Above all, Russian leaders wish to reestablish Russia's place as a great power. The first step in this direction is solidifying its influence and control over the countries along its border, an area often referred to as the Near Abroad. This has put it into conflict with the United States on several occasions. A continuing sore point is NATO expansion. The United States maintains that NATO expansion is not directed at containing Russia, but Russian leaders feel otherwise. Moscow opposed the admission of Poland, Hungary, and the Czech Republic in 1997. With NATO's latest round of expansion bringing it to Russia's doorstep, these suspicions run even higher. For historical reasons Russia opposed a strong NATO presence in the former Yugoslavia. It claimed a historical affinity with the Bosnian Serbs. Russia was mollified when in 1994 it was made a member of the Contact Group (composed of the United States, France, and Great Britain) that was working to bring peace to BOSNIA AND HERZEGOVINA. In 1999 Russia denounced NATO's bombing of Serbia targets during the KOSOVO crisis for similar reasons. In each case Russia was unable to press its position to the fullest for fear of alienating the United States, a concession to its continuing weakness. Russia's Chechen war has also brought it criticism from the West for human-rights violations associated with the fighting. The Russians hope that in the post–SEPTEMBER 11, 2001, international environment U.S. sensitivities to policies it describes as antiterrorism will be altered. Increased U.S. acceptance of its Chechen policies is offset by fears of increased U.S. interest in and influence over the CENTRAL ASIAN REPUBLICS.

A second element of reasserting its position as a great power is to engage the United States in arms control talks. Russia remains the second most powerful nuclear state and believes it should be treated accordingly. Economic weakness, however, dictates reducing the size of its nuclear arsenal. For symbolic reasons, rather than have these reductions come about by default, Russia wishes to partner with the United States. President GEORGE W. BUSH and Putin signed an agreement in 2002 to implement deep cuts in their respective nuclear inventories. The treaty calls for reducing the number of deployed nuclear warheads to 2,200 by December 21, 2012. The uneasy nature of this arms control partnership was revealed in Putin's insistence that the agreement be formalized in a binding document and not simply exist as an understanding between he and Bush and Putin's continued opposition to Bush's plans for constructing a BALLISTIC MISSILE DEFENSE system.

Finally, reasserting its position as a great power requires that Russia pursue an independent foreign policy. It cannot simply follow the American lead. Its support must be sought and given. The Russian foreign-policy initiative that has brought it into most conflict with the United States is its support for countries the United States considers to be global pariahs. At the top of that list are IRAN and IRAQ. Russia has sold conventional weapons to Iran and has helped Iran construct a civilian nuclear power reactor. It voiced opposition at the United Nations to U.S. military action against Iraq in 2002 and favors lifting UN sanctions against Iraqi oil exports in the hopes that increased Iraqi oil sales will allow Baghdad to pay off its debt to Russia.

Along with France, Russia emerged as one of the main opponents to the IRAQ WAR at the UN Security Council. A main point of contention was the extent to which any UN resolution would automatically provide the United States with the authority to go to war. Russia voiced its opposition to any resolution that even provided implicit authorization. After much negotiation, Russia joined with other Security Council members on November 8, 2002, to unanimously approve Resolution 1441, giving Iraq 30 days to produce a "currently accurate, full, and complete declaration of all aspects of its programmes to develop chemical, biological, and nuclear weapons, ballistic missiles." UN weapons inspectors were to update the Security Council in 60 days. Russia continued to oppose the United States in the coming months. When on February 24 the United States and Great Britain indicated that they would introduce a new resolution that would declare Iraq to be in "further material breach" of UN orders to disarm, Russia joined with France, Germany, and China in announcing that they would not allow passage of a resolution authorizing war with Iraq. In the end, the United States went forward without a supporting UN resolution.

Compared to its anger with France, United States relations with Russia remained relatively cordial. President Bush had worked hard to establish personal relationship with President Putin prior to the conflict, and the two sides worked to maintain it. After the Iraq War ended, Russia ratified the STRATEGIC OFFENSIVE REDUCTION TREATY (also known as the Moscow Treaty). Ratification had been delayed due to Russian opposition to the IRAQ WAR. Relations with the United States did not improve immediately. Russian leaders were angered by Bush administration accusations that Russian firms were illegally doing business with Iranian firms and helping Iran acquire a WEAPONS OF MASS DESTRUCTION capability.

**Further reading:** George, Alexander L., et al., eds. *U.S.-Soviet Security Cooperation: Achievements, Failures, Lessons.* New York: Oxford University Press, 1988; Hoffmann, Erik P., and Frederick Fleron, Jr., eds. *The Conduct of Soviet Foreign Policy.* New York: Aldine, 1980; Mandelbaum, Michael, ed. *The New Russian Foreign Policy.* New York: Council on Foreign Relations, 1998; Service, Robert. *A History of Twentieth-Century Russia.* Cambridge, Mass.: Harvard University Press, 1998; Ulam, Adam. *Expansion and Coexistence, Soviet Foreign Policy, 1917–1973.* New York: Praeger, 1974.

## Rwanda

Rwanda is about the size of Maryland, with an area of 10,169 square miles. It has a population of 7.6 million people and is one of the most densely populated states in AFRICA. Three ethnic groups are found in Rwanda: the Hutu (85 percent), the Tutsi (14 percent), and the Twa (1 percent). The Tutsi are believed to have migrated to the region in the 14th or 15th centuries and established dominance over the more numerous Hutu, whom they reduced to virtual serfdom. GERMANY was the first European state to establish a presence in Rwanda, and in 1890 the region formally became the German colony of German East Africa. Belgium conquered the territory in WORLD WAR I, and it became part of the Belgian mandate of Ruanda-Urundi under the LEAGUE OF NATIONS. After WORLD WAR II the UNITED NATIONS assigned Belgium trusteeship responsibilities for this territory. Throughout, the traditional social hierarchy of Tutsi domination over the Hutu was left in place. It was only in the late 1950s that demands for change from the Hutu began to be heard, and encouraged by the Belgian military, a Hutu revolt broke out in November 1959 and overthrew the Tutsi monarchy. An estimated 100,000 Tutsi fled into exile.

On July 1, 1962, Rwanda and Burundi became independent states. Continued ethnic-centered violence within Rwanda and with its neighbors resulted in a steady stream of REFUGEES coming into Rwanda and leaving it. By 1990 an estimated 500,000 Tutsi lived outside Rwanda. On July 5, 1973, the civilian government of Rwanda was overthrown by the military, and General Juvenal Habyarimana assumed power. In 1990 the Rwandan Patriotic Front (RPF), a group composed largely of Tutsi refugees, invaded Rwanda from Uganda. President Idi Amin of Uganda had long charged Rwanda with supporting groups trying to overthrow him. After some two years of fighting, the RPF was repelled, and a cease-fire went into effect on July 31, 1992. As part of the agreement Habyarimana acceded to a new power-sharing compromise.

Along with the president of Burundi, Habyarimana was killed when their plane was shot down on April 6, 1994, as it was landing at Rwanda's capital city. This incident set off a period of unprecedented violence that lasted until the beginning of July. As many as 800,000 Tutsi and moderate Hutu were killed by organized militias. At the same time as this genocide was being carried out, the RPF resumed its invasion of Rwanda, and on July 16 they took control of the government. An estimated 2 million Rwandans had fled the country due to the fighting. This refugee flow reversed itself in October 1996 following an uprising by ethnic Tutsi in Zaire. The last two weeks of November saw 600,000 Rwandans return from Zaire. In December some 500,000 returned from Tanzania.

The combination of genocide and civil war produced one of the world's largest HUMANITARIAN relief efforts in history. More than 200 NONGOVERNMENTAL ORGANIZATIONS were conducting humanitarian programs. Between mid-1994 and the end of 1995, more than $307.4 million in relief funds were targeted on Rwanda and refugee camps outside of the country. The United States was a major financial contributor in these efforts. Still, the United States and the West were heavily criticized for their failure to intervene soon enough in the crisis to bring an end to the genocide. Rwanda is seen as a classic example of the failure of PEACEKEEPING operations and the selective attention of the dominant powers in world politics. The United Nations had authorized a 5,500-person peacekeeping force but delays prevented it from arriving until July. The international community was seen as being similarly negligent in its slow response to the return flow of refugees into Rwanda. Scores died due to starvation and the outbreak of cholera. Critics hold that only those domestic crises that appear to directly threaten their interests such as BOSNIA AND HERZEGOVINA and HAITI produce meaningful action.

Violence returned to Rwanda in 1997 as fighting broke out between the military and Hutu guerrillas. In 1998 Rwanda along with Uganda invaded the CONGO (formerly Zaire) to aid antigovernment rebels in bringing down the government. Although a cease-fire was established in this conflict in May 2000, fighting broke out between Rwandan and Ugandan forces in the Congo. In July 2002 Rwanda and the Congo leaders signed a peace agreement, and by October Rwanda had pulled the last of its troops out of the Congo. In May 2003 Rwandan voters supported a constitution designed to prevent another genocide.

# S

## Saudi Arabia

Saudi Arabia is one of the dominant states in the Persian Gulf. Located on the Arabian Peninsula, it is about one-quarter the size of the United States, with an area of 784,233 square miles. It has a population of 22.7 million people. Ruled by an absolute monarchy it is one of the most conservative states in the region. The Saudi state began to emerge in 1750 through an ALLIANCE of a local ruler, Muhammad bin Saud, and an Islamic reformer, Muhammad Abd al-Wahhab. The modern Saudi state came into existence in 1932, following a series of military victories under King Abd al-Aziz ibn Saud. The United States established diplomatic relations with Saudi Arabia in 1933, but an EMBASSY was not opened there until 1944.

The first significant official contacts between the United States and Saudi Arabia came during WORLD WAR II, when President FRANKLIN ROOSEVELT grew concerned about the flow of OIL during the war and set up a military training program there. After the war concerns about the spread of COMMUNISM led President HARRY TRUMAN to enter into a secret agreement with Saudi Arabia promising its support for Saudi territorial and political independence. In 1951 the United States and Saudi Arabia entered into a mutual defense assistance agreement. In 1953 a military training mission was established. Between 1952 and 1962 the United States maintained an air base at Dharan. The United States was forced to leave when Saudi Arabia refused to renew the agreement in part due to anger with U.S. support for ISRAEL. That did not end U.S.-Saudi defense relations. President JOHN KENNEDY entered into still another secret agreement to defend Saudi Arabia. He gave the Saudi government visible support after an Egyptian-inspired coup failed. He sent a squadron of fighters to train in Saudi Arabia.

Saudi oil reserves are the largest in the world, with 95 percent of all Saudi oil being produced on behalf of the Saudi government by state-owned ARAMCO, the Arabian-American Oil Company, now renamed the Saudi Arabian Oil Company. Oil was discovered in 1936, and production began in 1938, although it was not until after World War II that oil production became significant. Before World War II, Saudi Arabia earned slightly less than one-half million dollars from petroleum. By 1950 this amount had grown to $56 million, and in 1956 it reached $200 million. Oil, its price and availability, became major issues following the 1973 Arab-Israeli War. As a sign of solidarity with Arab states, the ORGANIZATION OF PETROLEUM EXPORTING COUNTRIES (OPEC), of which Saudi Arabia was a member, placed an embargo on oil to the United States that had the effect of producing a dramatic rise in its price. Saudi revenue from oil sales rose from $2.7 billion in 1972 to nearly $25 billion in 1975. Tensions between the United States and Saudi Arabia during the OPEC–oil crisis were somewhat muted by the fact that within OPEC Saudi Arabia acted as a force for moderation. In 1974 it opposed additional price hikes and urged the resumption of oil sales to the United States.

The sudden flow of petro dollars into Saudi Arabia coincided with changes in U.S. foreign policy. The Nixon administration had begun to look for ways to shore up the American international presence after VIETNAM. In the Middle East it identified IRAN and Saudi Arabia as surrogate powers whose military capabilities could be enhanced through arms sales and grants and who would act to advance American interests in the region. Flush with their newfound wealth, Saudi Arabia was able to demand sophisticated "top shelf" military hardware rather than surplus weapons, which had been the mainstay of earlier arms agreements. By 1980, the value of U.S. arms sales to Saudi Arabia had reached $34.9 billion. A total of 97 percent of this amount was transferred between 1973 and 1980.

The single most controversial U.S. ARMS TRANSFER to Saudi Arabia occurred in the first year of the Reagan administration. In 1978 the Carter administration agreed to sell Saudi Arabia 60 F-15 fighters as part of a broader package of arms sales. In order to lessen congressional and

Israeli objections, the Carter administration placed operational restrictions on these aircraft that would limit their potential as offensive weapons that could threaten Israel. Shortly after this agreement was reached and before the planes were delivered, the political landscape of the Middle East changed dramatically with the fall of the shah of Iran, the main pillar that the United States had built its Middle East policy around. Saudi Arabia now requested that some of these restrictions be lifted. The Carter administration rejected the request but softened the rejection with a promise to speedily consider other Saudi requests. In its first major foreign-policy act, the Reagan administration decided to approve the revised sale in February 1981. Under its terms Saudi Arabia would receive F-15s equipped with fuel pods and bomb racks plus late model Sidewinder missiles.

As was the case with JIMMY CARTER's proposed arms sale to Saudi Arabia, congressional opposition was fierce. RONALD REAGAN bowed to this pressure and temporarily halted the arms sale. To the surprise of everyone he announced an even more expansive arms sale in April. In addition to the F-15s, Saudi Arabia was to receive five AWACS patrol planes. These Airborne Warning and Control Systems, Reagan argued, were necessary to offset the deteriorating situation in the Middle East and the prospect of a Soviet push into the region. To supporters of Israel they gave Saudi Arabia a significant offensive capability by extending the military effectiveness of the F-15. After intense lobbying by the Reagan administration, CONGRESS approved the arms sale to Saudi Arabia by a vote of 50-48 on October 28, 1981. This would not be the last major arms sale to Saudi Arabia by the Reagan administration. In 1984, worried about the destabilizing effect of the IRAN-IRAQ

U.S. and Saudi military personnel survey the damage to Khobar Towers in Dhahran, Saudi Arabia. A fuel truck carrying a bomb exploded outside the U.S. military facility, killing 19 U.S. soldiers, June 25, 1996. *(Department of Defense)*

WAR on the region, it approved the sale of 400 Stinger anti-aircraft missiles to Saudi Arabia.

Saudi Arabia was an important ally of the United States during the PERSIAN GULF WAR. Early in the conflict President GEORGE H. W. BUSH indicated that the United States was prepared to use military power to defend Saudi Arabia from Iraqi forces if necessary. In fact, Iraq did attack Saudi Arabia with air and ground forces during the war but with little effect. During the war U.S. and coalition troops were stationed in Saudi Arabia, and thousands of Saudi troops participated in the war effort. Coalition forces left in 1991, but some 6,000 U.S. troops remained behind. In 1995 and 1996 they became targets of terrorist attacks. Saudi Arabia was reluctant to formalize any defense agreement with the United States after the Persian Gulf War due to criticism from Arab states that it was becoming overly identified with the United States.

U.S.–Saudi relations became strained following the SEPTEMBER 11, 2001, terrorist attacks. Fifteen of the 19 hijackers were Saudi nationals, and OSAMA BIN LADEN is a Saudi who has been banned from Saudi Arabia since 1991. While cordial in its official dealings with Saudi Arabia, the GEORGE W. BUSH administration has complained privately that the Saudis were not doing enough to stop TERRORISM. In August and September 2002 these concerns took on a public air when conservative Republicans began to complain about human-rights violations in Saudi Arabia and a briefing to the Defense Policy Board by a representative of the RAND CORPORATION that called Saudi Arabia a "kernel of evil" was leaked to the press. This was followed by a lawsuit by families of those who died in the September 11th attacks that names members of the Saudi royal family and Saudi Arabian banks as codefendants. President Bush moved to mend the growing split in meetings with key Saudi leaders at his Texas ranch. These meetings ended with the Saudis reaffirming their opposition to a war against Saddam Hussein and announcing that the United States could not use Saudi soil in any way for an attack on IRAQ.

American-Saudi relations were extremely complex and tension-filled in the period surrounding the IRAQ WAR. Prior to the war, the United States unsuccessfully pressured Saudi Arabia to permit U.S. troops to use Saudi territory to launch attacks on Iraq. Unofficial sources in Washington also continued to complain about Saudi Arabia's failure to cooperate fully in antiterrorism efforts following the September 11, 2001, attacks. One RAND analyst created additional controversy in spring 2003 by describing Saudi Arabia as an enemy of the United States. After the war the United States reacted with frustration and anger to the AL-QAEDA–inspired terrorist attack in May that was targeted on Western business and residential properties in Riyadh and killed eight Americans. On May 1 the STATE DEPARTMENT issued a warning that based on INTELLIGENCE reports, an attack on American interests in Saudi Arabia was a real possibility. Only a week before, Saudi officials had fought a gun battle with al-Qaeda members and raided a terrorist safehouse, uncovering more than 800 pounds of explosives. Because of security concerns, the United States briefly closed its embassy in Saudi Arabia after the attack.

See also ARAB-ISRAELI CONFLICT.

**Further reading:** Anderson, Irvine H. *Aramco, the United States and Saudi Arabia.* Princeton, N.J.: Princeton University Press, 1987; Long, David, E. *The United States and Saudi Arabia: Ambivalent Allies.* Boulder, Colo.: Westview, 1989; Safran, Nadav. *Saudi Arabia: The Ceaseless Quest for Security.* Cambridge, Mass.: Harvard University Press, 1985.

## secretary of defense

The position of a civilian secretary of defense was created by the 1947 NATIONAL SECURITY ACT. The secretary was to preside over a newly create National Military Establishment that would place the army, navy, and the just-created air force under her or his control. The 1949 amendments to the 1947 National Security Act transformed the National Military Establishment into the DEPARTMENT OF DEFENSE and took away cabinet-level status for the three military service secretaries.

Secretaries of defense generally have adopted one of two role orientations. The first is that of a generalist who recognizes and defers to military expertise. He or she is concerned with coordinating and integrating the judgments received from the military professionals under his or her command. The generalist sees the position as the Defense Department's representative in the policy process. In contrast, the functionalist rejects the notion that there is a unique area of military expertise and sees himself or herself as first among equals in making defense policy. Above all else, the functionalist seeks to efficiently manage the Defense Department in accordance with presidential policy objectives. The point of departure is moving the Defense Department in the direction the president wants and not one of respecting military prerogatives above all else. Each role orientation presents different problems for CIVIL-MILITARY RELATIONS. In the first case, military policy may become detached from the overriding political objectives it is intended to serve. In the second, the military may feel its professionalism threatened and take steps to reassert its independence from what it sees as unjust political interference.

Among the early secretaries of defense, James Forrestal adopted the generalist orientation, while ROBERT MCNAMARA was a functionalist. McNamara's tenure was significant because of his efforts to expand the range of issues that the secretary of defense had control over and the methodology used in making decisions. Until McNamara, even functionalist secretaries largely restricted themselves to managing the budgetary process and mediating between interservice rivalries. McNamara sought and acquired a strong voice in setting defense policy by instituting a cost-benefit budget system that was organized around missions rather than services. McNamara used this system to approve the Poseidon submarine, the F-111 fighter, and the Minuteman III intercontinental BALLISTIC DEFENSE MISSILE. He rejected the Skybolt missile and the B-70 manned bomber.

McNamara did not set a pattern that all who followed him embraced. Melvin Laird, secretary of defense under President RICHARD NIXON, adopted a generalist orientation, as did Dick Cheney under GEORGE H. W. BUSH. Les Aspin, who served under President BILL CLINTON, was very much the functionalist and often came into sharp conflict with the military during his brief tenure. This was most notable in his advocacy of changing the policy with regard to gays in the military and his attempts to implement thoroughgoing defense program reviews. As these three examples show, prior service in government is no predictor of the role orientation that will be adopted, as Laird, Cheney, and Aspin had all served with distinction in the House of Representatives. Donald Rumsfeld adopted a functionalist orientation under GEORGE W. BUSH. He struggled in this role prior to the SEPTEMBER 11, 2001, terrorist attacks but became a powerful figure afterward, notably in decision making on the war with IRAQ.

## secretary of state

THOMAS JEFFERSON was the first secretary of state, but he was proceeded as chief diplomat of the United States by Robert Livingston and John Jay. Both served as secretaries of foreign affairs, heading up the STATE DEPARTMENT's predecessor agency, the Department of Foreign Affairs. Early secretaries of state were important political figures, many of whom went on to serve as PRESIDENT. Numbered among them were Jefferson, James Madison, JAMES MONROE, JOHN QUINCY ADAMS, MARTIN VAN BUREN, and JAMES BUCHANAN. With the passage of time, fewer political notables held this position, and many secretaries of state in the late 1800s were relatively anonymous figures. Secretaries of state began to reemerge as important political figures after WORLD WAR I, as the United States became more involved in world affairs. After WORLD WAR II secretaries of state as often as not have been nonpoliticians. Regardless of their background they have often struggled to exert influence on foreign policy. Their principal challengers have been SECRETARIES OF DEFENSE and NATIONAL SECURITY ADVISORS.

In practice, post–World War II secretaries of state have had to make a choice and become either advocates of the State Department's perspective or serve as the loyal ally of the president. Adopting the first perspective makes the secretary of state suspect in the White House. His or her advice is suspect because it does not start with the president's best interests at heart. Adopting the second requires disassociating oneself from the STATE DEPARTMENT. The result may be a sense of drift and alienation on the part of professional diplomats. Neither perspective is dominant. ALEXANDER HAIG adopted the first role orientation. Dean Rusk, JOHN FOSTER DULLES, and George Shultz adopted the second. CYRUS VANCE and Warren Christopher tried, and failed, to combine them.

The position of secretary of state is one of contradictions. For the world outside the United States, the secretary of state is in Haig's famous phrase, "the vicar of foreign policy." He or she is the representative of the United States and only the president's voice carries more weight. Looked at from a domestic perspective, however, a very different image emerges. The challenges of balancing the interests of the president and the professional FOREIGN SERVICE OFFICER CORPS within the State Department is not an easy one. On more than one occasion, secretaries of state have had to admit that they had not been informed of key decisions. Vance resigned in protest over his exclusion from the Carter administration's decision making on the IRANIAN HOSTAGE rescue effort. Shultz claimed he was only marginally informed about the plan to sell weapons to IRAN in hopes of securing the release of American hostages in LEBANON.

Many secretaries of state have left office subject to great criticism. Dean Rusk and James Byrnes had their leadership skills questioned. DEAN ACHESON was criticized for his aloofness and arrogance. Warren Christopher and James Baker were criticized for being overly sensitive to domestic political considerations. Haig, Dulles, and HENRY KISSINGER were criticized for their overly zealous attempts to dominate the foreign policy–making process.

The domestic weaknesses of the secretary of state can be traced to three factors, none of which are under his or her control. The first is the predisposition of the president to deal with foreign-policy matters. William Rodgers suffered as secretary of state because President RICHARD NIXON wanted to centralize foreign policy in the White House. Christopher encountered problems because President BILL CLINTON was at first not interested in foreign affairs and changed his positions frequently. Shultz's effectiveness was limited by President RONALD REAGAN's unwillingness to settle the ongoing dispute between himself and secretary of defense Casper Weinberger. COLIN POWELL, GEORGE W. BUSH's secretary of state, engaged in a long-running political battle with Secretary of Defense Donald Rumsfeld over the conduct of the war against TERRORISM and the dispute with IRAQ.

The second factor is the broadened agenda of U.S. foreign policy that has allowed experts in other departments to become important bureaucratic and political forces in decision making. This was first evident in the military arena and is now also true in international economics. Finally, the State Department and Foreign Service have become vulnerable pawns in the battle between CONGRESS and the president to control foreign policy. Lacking the support of domestic pressure groups enjoyed by the Defense Department or COMMERCE DEPARTMENT, the State Department has no political allies to lobby Congress on its behalf other than foreign governments, whose motives are easily suspect. Ambassadorial appointments are regularly challenged, budgets are held hostage to politically inspired amendments, and administrative reorganizations are forced upon it.

See also EMBASSIES.

## sectionalism

Standard accounts of American foreign policy speak of the importance of the NATIONAL INTEREST in selecting goals and objectives that are to be pursued or defended. More recently it has come to be recognized that the various geographic sections of the United States have distinctive and different stakes in how the United States conducts its foreign policy. Viewed from this perspective American foreign policy is not a matter of constructing a strategically proper response to overseas challenges and opportunities. It is a political question of identifying how the different regions of the United States are affected by these events and how to create winning political coalitions between competing regions.

Adherents of this sectionalist/geographic perspective on American foreign policy have identified three periods of intense regional competition for control of the decision-making system in Washington that makes foreign policy. The first period of contestation occurred in the 1890s. At the strategic level, the debate over American foreign policy during this period pitted imperialists against antiimperialists. The second struggle took place in the 1930s when supporters of ISOLATIONISM faced off against advocates of INTERNATIONALISM. The third period of debate occurred in the 1980s when internationalists were opposed by those who objected to the rising costs of an activist foreign policy.

In each case sectional conflict drove these debates and was grounded in regional economic differentiation. This is evident in two ways. First, regions that specialize in export-oriented economic activity favor policies that support free trade and promote international stability, because without stability international trade and investment does not flourish. Those regions whose products are not competitive or are threatened by foreign goods will be more protectionist-oriented and unwilling to shoulder the burdens of international leadership. Second, those regions that gain the most from defense spending in terms of jobs created and increases in income will be more supportive of high levels of military outlays and foreign policies that build on them. An analogous regional struggle exists over the benefits of a peace dividend that might accompany an American withdrawal from world affairs.

In the 1890s the industrial Northeast supported the activist and expansionist foreign policy of IMPERIALISM, because it brought with it access to foreign markets and raw materials. The agrarian South preferred to continue relying upon the British navy to keep export markets open for its agricultural products. The South sold its goods primarily to Europe and therefore would benefit little from opening up markets in Latin America or Asia. The West sided with the Northeast. Key for this region was the promise of military (naval) contracts for Washington, Oregon, and California. In the 1930s bankers and industrialists in the North joined forces with the agricultural South to press for an end to global protectionism and an increased role in world affairs for the United States. For political and economic forces in the Northeast, profit was a sufficient motive for advocating internationalism. For the South internationalism also had a domestic dimension. Profits from trade held the potential for warding off further federal government involvement in their affairs because economic recovery would make it unnecessary. The West remained staunchly isolationist. Its markets were domestic. As such, continued protectionism rather than a switch to internationalism offered Westerners the greatest hope for prosperity. Finally, in the 1980s the declining "rustbelt" Northeast favored protectionism and limited international involvement. No longer benefiting from an open international trade system, the Northeast was no longer interested in supporting high levels of taxation or government spending that allowed the United States to maintain a global American military presence. It was opposed by the expanding sunbelt economies of the West and South, which supported a more robust and visible international presence.

In many respects the sectionalist approach to American foreign policy reverses the central thrust of REALISM without denying its fundamental argument. Realism sees American foreign policy as a response to struggles for POWER, wealth, and hegemony among countries. Sectionalism sees American foreign policy as a response to struggles for power, wealth, and hegemony among regions within the United States.

**Further reading:** Trubowitz, Peter. *Defining the National Interest: Conflict and Change in American Foreign Policy.* Chicago: University of Chicago Press, 1998.

## September 11, 2001

Four separate terrorist incidents took place in the United States on September 11, 2001. Together they constituted

Smoke billows from the World Trade Center's twin towers after they are struck by commercial airliners that had been hijacked by terrorists. *(Shaw/Getty Images)*

the worst international terrorist attack ever on American soil. More than 3,000 individuals died in these attacks carried out by 19 members of the AL-QAEDA terrorist group. President GEORGE W. BUSH characterized the attacks as an act of war against the United States.

The first attack occurred when American Airlines flight 11 departed from Boston at 7:45 A.M. It was going to Los Angeles, but shortly after takeoff it was hijacked by five terrorists and was deliberately piloted into the North Tower of the World Trade Center at 8:46. The second attack occurred when five terrorists hijacked United Airlines flight 175. It departed Boston for Los Angeles at 7:58. At 9:03 it crashed into the South Tower of the World Trade Center. Soon thereafter the two towers collapsed (10:05, South Tower; 10:28, North Tower). Next, four hijackers took control of United Airlines flight 93 going from Newark to San Francisco. It left Newark at 8:10 A.M. and at 10:10 A.M. the plane crashed into a field in Stony Creek Township, Pennsylvania, when the hijackers were overpowered by people on the plane. All 45 persons on board died. The intended target of this hijacked airliner is not known. The final hijacking occurred on American Airlines flight 77. It left Washington Dulles Airport for Los Angeles at 8:10 A.M. At 9:39 it crashed into the Pentagon, killing a total of 189 individuals.

The United States undertook a multidimensional response to the terrorist attacks. On the diplomatic front the United States sought and obtained the support of virtually every country in condemning these attacks. Important bilateral negotiations took place with PAKISTAN and CHINA to ensure their support for planned military action. Negotiations with China centered on overcoming its sensitivities to the global exercise of American power; those with Pakistan were designed to secure its support for war along its border with AFGHANISTAN. On the multilateral level, support was sought from the UNITED NATIONS, the NORTH ATLANTIC TREATY ORGANIZATION, the EUROPEAN UNION, and other bodies. PUBLIC DIPLOMACY also played an important role in the United States's strategy. It was necessary to emphasize that it was embarking on a war against TERRORISM and not a war against Islam.

ECONOMIC SANCTIONS were also put into place. With Executive Order 13224, President Bush froze U.S. financial assets of organizations and individuals believed to be supporting international TERRORISM as well as prohibiting transactions with these organizations. COVERT ACTION also played a role as contacts with resistance groups in Afghanistan were intensified and funds made available to bribe and induce regional warlords to abandon the Taliban and to seek out and destroy al-Qaeda strongholds. Through executive orders the Bush administration also removed some of the prohibitions against engaging in

The west-facing wall of the Pentagon sags where a hijacked American Airlines flight with 64 passengers aboard was purposely crashed into this spot in an act of terrorism. (R. D. Ward/Department of Defense)

assassination as part of covert action. The military operation against al-Qaeda and its key ally, the Taliban government of Afghanistan, was known as Operation Enduring Freedom. It began on October 7, 2001. With the support of forces from 55 different countries, U.S. forces succeeded in removing the Taliban from power by January 2002 and seriously weakening al-Qaeda's infrastructure. Evidence suggests that it did not succeed in killing or capturing OSAMA BIN LADEN, al-Qaeda's founder and mastermind.

A final dimension of the Bush administration's response occurred in the area of law enforcement. On October 26, 2001, Congress passed the USA PATRIOT ACT that significantly broadened the powers of U.S. law enforcement agencies to investigate and prosecute persons suspected of engaging in terrorist acts or supporting those acts. Following the November 2002 midterm elections, CONGRESS passed legislation establishing the DEPARTMENT OF HOMELAND SECURITY as part of a broad strategy to prevent future terrorist attacks against the United States.

The Bush administration's response to the terrorist attacks of September 11 already has been subject to great scrutiny. One area of concern has been the preparedness and performance of the INTELLIGENCE COMMUNITY. In particular, the CENTRAL INTELLIGENCE AGENCY (CIA) and the FEDERAL BUREAU OF INVESTIGATION (FBI) have been heavily criticized for their work, and calls were heard for establishing new INTELLIGENCE agencies. It was only with great reluctance and under heavy political pressure that the Bush administration agreed in November 2002 to establish a bipartisan and independent commission to investigate the performance of the intelligence community. Such was the emotional fervor attached to this question that both of its original cochairs, HENRY KISSINGER and George Mitchell, felt compelled to resign.

Concerns were also voiced over the extent to which the Bush administration was willing to go to obtain information on terrorism from domestic sources. Civil libertarians and others feared that constitutional rights to free speech, a speedy trial, and access to counsel were being undermined by the war against terrorism.

The military conduct of the war itself also came under criticism. Two of the most common themes voiced were (1) that the military effort was conducted at the expense of the nation-building and economic-development challenges in Afghanistan and elsewhere that needed to be undertaken to attack the root causes of terrorism and (2) that in the war the United States had relied too heavily on local allies to defeat the Taliban and al-Qaeda, thereby apparently allowing Osama bin Laden to escape. A less frequently heard, yet politically powerful, criticism came from conservative commentators. They asserted that the Bush administration had failed to live up to its responsibilities by not putting together a large enough military force to conduct the war against terrorism in Afghanistan and elsewhere unilaterally.

Controversy also followed the Bush administration's efforts to move American foreign policy and the war on terrorism to the next stage after Afghanistan. Bush's announcement of a new security policy based on PREEMPTION was met with skepticism by military and civilian analysts. So too was his identification of IRAQ as the next target of American military power. The war waged against Iraq that began in March 2003 engendered opposition both domestic and foreign.

**Further reading:** Talbott, Strobe, and Nayan Chanda, eds. *The Age of Terror: America and the World after September 11.* New York: Basic Books, 2002.

## Seward, William (1801–1872) *secretary of state*

William H. Seward was SECRETARY OF STATE from 1861 to 1869. He had led on the first two rounds in the Republican presidential convention of 1860 before losing to ABRAHAM LINCOLN. He became Lincoln's secretary of state and also served in that capacity under Andrew Johnson. During the AMERICAN CIVIL WAR the main focus of Seward's diplomacy was to ensure the neutrality of European powers. Seward was handicapped in his efforts to negotiate with GREAT BRITAIN and FRANCE by the actions of Senator CHARLES SUMNER, who chaired the Senate Foreign Relations Committee. Sumner and other abolitionists sought to undermine Seward's standing in the cabinet and abroad in hopes of forcing him from office so that Sumner might become secretary of state.

Seward was a committed expansionist whose desires to add to the territory of the United States had been stymied by the Civil War. Once the war ended, Seward sought to obtain naval and coaling stations in the Caribbean. He had become convinced of the need for such bases because of the success of Confederate blockade runners. Land controlled by SPAIN, Denmark, HAITI, and the DOMINICAN REPUBLIC were his targets. CONGRESS turned down a plan to obtain a harbor in the Dominican Republic and then to annex the entire island. In 1867 he signed a treaty with Denmark that transferred the Virgin Islands to the United States for $7.5 million, subject to a vote of approval of the island's residents. The Danish government approved the treaty, and the residents of the Virgin Islands did likewise. However, CONGRESS did not endorse the plan. The House of Representatives by a vote of 93-43 stated that it was "under no obligation to vote money to pay for such purchase unless there is a greater present necessity." The Senate had not yet acted on the treaty when PRESIDENT Andrew Johnson left office. His successor, ULYSSES S. GRANT, opposed the treaty and removed it from the Senate's consideration.

Other unsuccessful expansionist targets included CUBA, HAWAII, PUERTO RICO, CANADA, Greenland, and Iceland.

Sewards's greatest success was the purchase of ALASKA. He accomplished this in great haste and secrecy. The actual agreement was negotiated late at night and announced to a surprised Senate the next day. In his haste to make the purchase Seward increased his offer from $5 million to $7.2 million when the Russian minister, Edourd de Stoeckl, refused to lower his asking price. De Stoeckl had, in fact, been instructed to accept an offer of $5 million. The purchase ran into opposition in both the Senate and the House. Sumner became an important ally of Seward in the battle for Senate approval. He did not share Seward's enthusiasm for obtaining Alaska but was concerned with maintaining good relations with RUSSIA.

**Further reading:** Ferris, Norman B. *Desperate Diplomacy: William H. Seward's Foreign Policy, 1861.* Knoxville: University of Tennessee Press, 1976.

## single integrated operational plan (SIOP)

The single integrated operational plan (SIOP) is the U.S. strategic blueprint for using NUCLEAR WEAPONS. The first SIOP was produced in the last year of the Eisenhower administration and was the product of two very different forces. For President DWIGHT EISENHOWER and his SECRETARY OF DEFENSE Thomas Gates, the SIOP was intended to bring MASSIVE RETALIATION that threatened the Soviet Union (see RUSSIA) with a swift and overwhelming nuclear blow should it engage in aggression against the United States or its allies. Beneath this unifying vision, the practical reality was that in the 1950s each military command developed its own plans for using the nuclear weapons under its control. Gates saw this situation as economically wasteful and questioned the military value of having some targets scheduled to be attacked again and again. For the military services the move to embrace the SIOP was about controlling nuclear options, weapons, and budgets. The Strategic Air Command (SAC) had established dominance in the area of nuclear targeting, and it wished to use the SIOP as a way of holding the navy and its new Polaris submarine–launched BALLISTIC DEFENSE MISSILE in check and guaranteeing SAC a lengthy list of targets to strike.

Officially designated as SIOP-62 (it was to take effect in 1962) the plan produced by this review broke targets down into three categories: nuclear capable, other military, and urban-industrial. A total of 2,600 installations for attack from approximately 1,050 designated ground zeros (DGZs) were identified. Plans called for launching all 3,500 nuclear warheads if sufficient warning time existed. If not, an alert force of 800 bombers and missiles would attack approximately 650 DGZs with more than 1,400 weapons.

The SIOP underwent several revisions during the COLD WAR. Each was the product of bargaining within the national security BUREAUCRACY and was guided by presidential instructions on the nature of U.S. nuclear strategy. SIOP-63 sought to broaden the range of nuclear options by incorporating a "no-cities" version of a nuclear response. SIOP-5 took effect in 1976, and it added the concept of "escalation control" to the SIOP and organized the U.S. response into four options (major, selective, limited, and regional) and four target categories (nuclear forces, other military, leadership, and economic-industrial). SIOP 5F, which took effect in October 1981, contained 50,000 targets, including 5,000 leadership targets. The concept of "protracted NUCLEAR WAR" was introduced into SIOP-6 that went into effect in 1983. The number of targets in SIOP-6 was reduced to 14,000, but there was added emphasis on leadership targeting. SIOP-6F took effect in October 1989 and incorporated the concept of "adaptive target planning."

Two aspects in the development of the SIOP stand out as particularly significant in the history of American NUCLEAR DETERRENCE POLICY. First, from the very outset, the SIOP was a capabilities-driven plan rather than an objectives-driven plan. It took as its starting point the number of weapons available and sought to find uses for them rather than starting from the question of what was wanted and then assigning weapons to it. Second, while changes were made in successive SIOPs, the magnitude of these changes did not fully correspond to changes in official policy. That is, movement from massive retaliation to flexible response to assured destruction to strategic sufficiency did not produce corresponding changes in the SIOP. The SIOPs' resistance to change calls into question how successful presidents were in controlling and directing America's nuclear forces and is cited by advocates of DISARMAMENT and ARMS CONTROL as reasons for eliminating all nuclear weapons.

**Further reading:** Pringle, Peter, and William Arkin. *SIOP: The Secret U.S. Plan for Nuclear War.* New York: Norton, 1983; Rosenberg, David. "The Origins of Overkill." *International Security* 7 (1983).

## small-group decision-making model

This policy-making model focuses on the dynamics of small-group decision making. Advocates of this perspective hold that many critical foreign-policy decisions are made neither by an individual policy maker nor by large bureaucratic forces. This model is often employed to understand INTERNATIONAL CRISIS decision making. Unlike the RATIONAL-ACTOR MODEL that is also often used to analyze crisis decision making, the small-group model does not treat the United States as a unitary actor responding to external stimuli but rather emphasizes the psychological dimension of policy deliberations.

Three types of small groups are prominent in U.S. foreign-policy decision making. First, there is the informal small group that meets regularly but lacks an formal institutional base. The Tuesday lunch group of the Johnson administration and Friday breakfast group of the Carter administration are examples. Second, there is the ad hoc group that is created to deal with a specific problem and then ceases to function after it is resolved. The Executive Committee (ExCom) of the NATIONAL SECURITY COUNCIL that President JOHN KENNEDY created to deal with the CUBAN MISSILE CRISIS is an example. The third type is the permanent small group that possesses an institutional base and is created to perform certain tasks. These may be interagency working groups or subcommittees of the National Security Council.

From a policy maker's perspective small-group decision making offers a number of advantages over relying upon either a single individual or bureaucratic forces to settle an issue. Compared to bureaucratic decision making, secrecy can be more readily maintained; innovation is more likely; swift and decisive actions will be considered; and a free and open exchange of views can be expected, because there will be no organizational interests to protect. Small groups also bring more expertise and judgment to bear on important issues than any individual decision maker could likely possess.

In spite of the apparent advantages small groups have over bureaucratic or individual decision making, history records numerous examples of highly questionable decisions emerging from small groups. Numbered among them are key decisions in VIETNAM and KOREA, the BAY OF PIGS, and the IRAN-CONTRA INITIATIVE. In retrospect, it seems clear that these policy failures are due to the presence of strong in-group pressures on members to concur in the group's decision. This pressure produces a "deterioration of mental efficiency, reality testing, and moral judgment." The term *groupthink* has been coined to capture this phenomenon. Groupthink manifests itself in predictable ways. For example, policy makers stereotype the enemy, they come to believe in the group's inherent morality, an illusion of invulnerability comes to characterize their decisions, and they begin to engage in self-censorship.

Groupthink is a tendency and not a permanent condition of small-group decision making. The more tight-knit the group is or the greater the pressures for concurrence-seeking behavior, the more likely it is to occur. Its occurrence can be minimized by the adoption of leadership styles that emphasize debate and open discussion, the creation of multiple groups, and encouraging the deliberate challenging of key assumptions.

Groupthink has been criticized for establishing an unrealistic benchmark, namely, perfect decision making, as the criteria against which to judge the performance of small groups. That small groups sometimes fail to produce good decisions is no more an indictment of small groups than is the fact that individuals sometimes make bad decisions. Another indictment of the small group decision-making model is the great information demands it places on researchers. Very seldom will we find small-group decision making documented to the point at which we can conclusively establish that groupthink and not personality or some other factor was the key ingredient in a decision.

**Further reading:** Janis, Irving, *Groupthink: Psychological Studies of Policy Decisions and Fiascoes.* 2d ed. Boston: Houghton Mifflin, 1982; Janis, Irving, and Leon Mann. *Decision Making: A Psychological Analysis of Conflict, Choice, and Commitment.* New York: Free Press, 1977.

## Smithsonian Agreement

The 1971 Smithsonian Agreement was a first attempt to manage international monetary relations after the end of the BRETTON WOODS SYSTEM. Its significance lies in both the forces that made the agreement necessary and the content of the agreement, intended to serve as a temporary measure that would give states time to negotiate a long-term solution.

In the 1960s the growing pace of monetary interdependence grew faster than the international community's ability to manage these relations. Large-scale capital flows created exchange rate and balance of payments problems, as well as interfered with the ability of national leaders to set interest rates and control inflation. The dominant role played by the U.S. economy in the international monetary system largely made the United States immune to many of these negative effects. However, by the late 1960s this began to change. Inflation induced by the VIETNAM WAR and the growing unwillingness of Europe and JAPAN to realign the value of their currencies with the U.S. dollar placed the United States in a defensive position as the strength of the dollar declined and the U.S. economy weakened.

The American response to this situation has been described as one of benign neglect. U.S. officials did little to counter the pace at which U.S. dollars were being held abroad. With little interest being shown by the United States from 1968 to 1971, a state of paralysis came to grip international monetary management practices. All of this changed in 1971 when the United States experienced a trade deficit for the first time in the 20th century, and there was a run on the dollar. U.S. gold reserves declined to about $10 billion, compared to foreign holdings of dollars that were valued at about $80 billion.

On August 15, 1971, President RICHARD NIXON stunned the world when he announced without consulting U.S. allies that U.S. dollars would no longer be convertible to gold and that the United States would impose a 10 percent surcharge on imports. His actions marked the end of the Bretton Woods system. There followed an intense period of discussions between the United States and its allies over how to proceed. The United States insisted that (1) it would not devalue the dollar, (2) there must be currency realignment regarding the value of surplus currencies, (3) there must be a modification in the unfair trading practices of other states, and (4) there must be greater burden sharing regarding military expenditures.

In December 1971 the United States led a meeting at the Smithsonian Institution to establish new rules for international monetary relations. It was agreed that the value of the U.S. dollar would be reduced by 10 percent in relation to gold, the value of foreign currencies relative to the dollar would be adjusted, and exchange rates could fluctuate plus or minus 2.25 percent of their newly established values. This was twice the range permitted by the Bretton Woods system.

President Nixon championed the Smithsonian Agreement as "the greatest monetary agreement in the history of the world." In fact, it amounted to little more than an exercise in crisis management that sought to reestablish elements of the Bretton Woods system until a more permanent solution could be found. The international community failed in its attempt to do so, and, in 1973, at Paris, the international monetary system moved from a managed fixed exchange rate system to a floating exchange rate system.

See also DEBT CRISIS; INTERNATIONAL MONETARY FUND.

## Smoot-Hawley Tariff

The Smoot-Hawley Tariff, or the Tariff Act of 1930, is one of the most controversial tariffs in American diplomatic history. It was enacted after 18 months of congressional debate, spanning the period from January 1929 to June 1930. The average duty on dutiable goods under the Smoot-Hawley Tariff was placed at 44.9 percent. By way of comparison, this contrasts sharply with the 1922 Tariff Act, which raised tariffs from 9.1 percent to 14 percent.

Much of the controversy surrounding it stems from the mythology that has grown up around it. The Smoot-Hawley Tariff was not the highest tariff in American history, as it is often portrayed, but it did represent a return to the high tariffs sponsored by the Republicans in the post–Civil War era. The highest tariff was the Tariff of

Abominations of 1828 at 61.7 percent. An important difference between the Smoot-Hawley Tariff and these earlier tariffs was the range of goods exempted from tariffs. Under the Smoot-Hawley Tariff, two-thirds of imports entered the United States duty-free. In the late 19th century an average of 50 percent of imports did so. The cause-effect connection between the Smoot-Hawley Tariff and the Great Depression is also tenuous. The measure passed eight months after the stock market collapsed. More so than the Smoot-Hawley Tariff itself, some commentators assert that the bitter partisan debate within CONGRESS created an atmosphere of political uncertainty that contributed to the psychological pressures leading to the stock market's collapse. Another point of contention centers on the impact that the Smoot-Hawley Tariff had on U.S. TRADE POLICY. The traditional position holds that it substantially hurt U.S. exports due to foreign retaliation. They cite as evidence the fact that U.S. exports fell in value from an average of $5 billion per year between 1925 and 1929 to about one-third that level in 1933–34. The opposing position holds that this was not the case. Official data shows that dutiable and nondutiable imports fell by the same percentage level between 1929 and 1932. Finally, it is argued that the American public turned on those who supported the Smoot-Hawley Tariff. Both Senator Reed Smoot (R-Utah) and Representative Willis Hawley (R-Oreg.) were defeated in 1932, but the tariff seems to have played little if any role in their defeats.

FRANKLIN ROOSEVELT's victory in 1932 and his appointment of staunch free-trade advocate CORDELL HULL as SECRETARY OF STATE signaled that change would soon come to U.S. international economic policy. In 1934 Congress passed the RECIPROCAL TRADE AGREEMENTS ACT. This act formally left the Smoot-Hawley Tariff in place but authorized the PRESIDENT over the next three years to raise or lower tariffs by as much as 50 percent from their 1930 levels.

## Somalia

Located on the Horn of AFRICA, Somalia is slightly smaller than Texas, with an area of 246,200 square miles. Somalia has been without a government since 1991, and no reliable census exists. Estimates place the population at 7.4 million people. Somalia's modern history begins in the 19th century when GREAT BRITAIN, FRANCE, and ITALY all established a colonial presence in the region. Italian and British forces fought for control of the area during WORLD WAR II. After the war Great Britain ruled over both British Somaliland and Italian Somaliland until 1950, when Italian Somaliland became a UNITED NATIONS trust territory and was put back under Italian control for 10 years, after which it was expected to become independent. Italy had formally given up claim to Italian Somaliland in 1947. In a key 1948 decision, Great Britain turned the Ogaden and adjacent Somali territories over to ETHIOPIA, a territory it controlled. Italian influence had expanded into this region in the late 1920s. Italian Somaliland received its independence on July 1, 1960. Days before Great Britain had granted independence to British Somaliland, and on July 1 the two new states merged to form the United Republic of Somalia.

The early years of independence witnessed the emergence of a number of divisive conflicts. One pitted the north (formerly British Somaliland) against the south (formerly Italian Somaliland). A second dispute centered on priorities. Modernists sought to undertake a program of economic and social development. Others wanted to create a Greater Somalia that would unite Somalia with Somali-dominated areas of Kenya and Ethiopia and with French Somaliland (now Djibouti).

Early Somali foreign policy stressed nonalignment, and it received aid from both sides during the COLD WAR. In 1969 the Somali president was assassinated, and Major General Mohammed Siad Barre took power. Somalia became increasingly aligned with the Soviet Union (see RUSSIA), and in 1974 the two states signed a treaty of friendship and cooperation. Somalia's foreign policy also became more aggressive in its pursuit of bring outlying Somali areas into the country. Conflicts began along the Somali-Ethiopian border, and the Western Somali Liberation Front began operating in the Ogaden region of Ethiopia. In July 1977 the Somali army moved into the Ogaden to aid these forces. Ethiopia succeeded in repelling the Somali invasion with the help of Soviet arms and Cuban forces in March 1978. This marked a major reversal in the geopolitics of the region since the Soviet Union had been Somalia's primary benefactor. In retaliation Barre expelled all Soviet advisers in November 1977 and abrogated the friendship treaty.

Barre now tuned to the United States for help. In 1980 an agreement was reached, giving U.S. forces access to military bases in Somalia. Two years later the United States provided Somalia with military assistance to repel an Ethiopian invasion. While Barre helped make Somalia a strategic asset to the United States during the 1980s, his rule provoked a rebellion in the northwest, where in 1991 the former British Somaliland declared its independence as Somaliland. Barre also fled into exile in NIGERIA that year. Leaders of two rival factions, Mohammed Ali Mahdi and Mohammed Farah Aidid, each claimed the presidency. Civil war and a severe drought resulted in more than 300,000 deaths and prompted a United Nations HUMANITARIAN intervention in 1992.

Neither a UN sponsored cease-fire or the UN PEACE-KEEPING intervention succeeded in restoring order. In

A Somali gunman speaks to a child during the famine of 1992 that was caused by drought and civil war between opposing clans in Baidoa, Somalia. *(Greg Marinovich/Getty Images)*

December 1992, after he was defeated in his reelection bid, President GEORGE H. W. BUSH announced OPERATION RESTORE HOPE. He sent 27,000 U.S. soldiers to Somalia to join with UN peacekeepers. The purpose of their mission was defined in humanitarian terms. They were to provide enough security that food could be distributed and a minimum amount of civil order restored. By June 1993 failure was evident as fighting between the warring factions resumed.

Aidid also began to attack UN forces. One ambush led to the deaths of 23 Pakistani peacekeepers. This incident led to an expansion in the scope of the UN and U.S. operation. Capturing Aidid now became a primary objective. On October 3–4 clashes between Aidid's forces and U.S. troops resulted in 18 U.S. soldiers being killed. With the media broadcasting images of U.S. soldiers being dragged through the streets of Mogadishu, an intense debate broke out in the United States over participation in peacekeeping operations, and demands were heard for the withdrawal of U.S. forces from Somalia. President BILL CLINTON subsequently gave this order, and U.S. troops were gone by the end of March 1994.

Since 1991 more than 12 attempts have been made at national reconciliation. A legitimate and effective central government still does not exist, and the country continues to splinter. Somaliland continues to exist as a breakaway republic. It has been joined by Puntland (northeast) and Jubaland (south), which declared their independence in 1998, and Southwestern Somaliland, which declared its independence in 2002. The domestic political chaos that has gripped Somalia since 1991 has also allowed a number of radical Islamic groups to establish bases of operations there. In the aftermath of the SEPTEMBER 11, 2001, terror-ist attacks on the World Trade Center and Pentagon, the activities of these groups has received close attention by U.S. policy makers. Many are seen as practitioners of international TERRORISM or conduits for money transfers to terrorist groups.

**Further reading:** Hirsch, John L., and Whert B. Oakley. *Somalia and Operation Restore Hope.* Washington, D.C.: United States Institute of Peace, 1995; Lefebvre, Jeffrey. *Arms for the Horn: U.S. Security Policy in Ethiopia and Somalia, 1953–1991.* Pittsburgh: University of Pittsburgh Press, 1991.

## South Africa

Located on the southern tip of AFRICA and about twice the size of Texas, with an area of 470,462 square miles, South Africa has a population of 45 million people. Seventy-five percent of these are black, 13 percent are white, 9 percent are of mixed ancestry, and the remaining 3 percent are Asian. The first European settlement in contemporary South Africa was established in 1652 by the Dutch East India Company. These settlers, along with French Huguenot REFUGEES and German immigrants, constitute the foundation of the Afrikaner, or white, population who put in place the system of apartheid.

GREAT BRITAIN took control of the region around the Cape of Good Hope as a result of the Congress of Vienna. In order to escape British rule, many Afrikaners (also known as Boers) undertook the "Great Trek" that took them deeper into the interior, where they established the Boer republics of the Orange Free State and the Transvaal. The discovery of diamonds and gold in the area led to growing conflict between the British and Boers. In 1899 Transvaal and the Orange Free State declared war on Great Britain. The Boer War ended in 1902, with the British victorious, and the two republics became part of the British Empire. On May 31, 1910, the Union of South Africa was created by merging the Boer republics with the British colonies of the Cape and Natal.

Several significant developments occurred in the first years of independence. Political power in South Africa was placed in the hands of the white population. In 1912 the pro-Afrikaner Nationalist Party and the pro-black South Africa Native National Congress were founded. The latter would later become known as the African National Congress (ANC). These two political groups would be in the forefront of the post–WORLD WAR II struggle over apartheid. Also around this time South Africa took control over NAMIBIA. It was a German colony (then known as South-West Africa) that South African troops had captured during WORLD WAR I. It was then given to South Africa as a mandate territory by the LEAGUE OF NATIONS.

After the end of World War II, the Afrikaner Nationalist Party firmly established itself in power, and in 1948 it put into place the system of apartheid, which mandated separateness among races. This policy extended into virtually all areas of life and was supported by a series of laws restricting freedom of movement through passbooks that blacks were required to carry and the establishment of a series of independent black homelands inside of South Africa.

Concerned above all else with stopping the spread of COMMUNISM, the Truman administration defined apartheid as a domestic issue outside of the jurisdiction of bodies such as the UNITED NATIONS. Subsequent COLD WAR administrations varied in their embrace of this position, but the fear of communist expansion into Africa inhibited most from taking any firm action to end apartheid. Under President DWIGHT EISENHOWER the United States entered into a series of cooperative security-oriented agreements with South Africa. President JOHN KENNEDY, responding to the deaths of 69 unarmed apartheid protestors at Sharpeville, recalled the American ambassador and joined with the other members of the UN Security Council in condemning South Africa's policies, but relations soon returned to normal. Under President RICHARD NIXON, bringing about domestic reform in South Africa was second in importance to protecting American strategic and commercial interests.

A temporary sea change occurred in U.S. policy toward South Africa in the Carter administration when, in May 1977, it made it clear to the South African leadership that it supported majority rule in South Africa, Rhodesia (today ZIMBABWE), and Namibia. This pronouncement followed the 1976 rebellion in Soweto that led to more than 600 deaths. The death of black activist Stephen Biko in 1977 further isolated South Africa in its dealings with the United States and the world. Biko died while in police custody. American foreign policy returned to more familiar ground when the Reagan administration took office. Its policy of constructive engagement called for giving primary importance to security concerns and seeking to bring about domestic reform in South Africa through a policy of quiet persuasion. Constructive engagement also linked progress on achieving black rule in Namibia with a favorable settlement of the political and security situation in ANGOLA, where Cuban troops supported an anti-American regime.

Reagan was unable to sustain political support for his policy within CONGRESS after a general uprising began in South Africa in September 1984. With Congress ready to impose sanctions, RONALD REAGAN issued an executive order that was less sweeping in range. It banned nuclear cooperation, prohibited new loans, and forbade the sale of computers and other technology used to support apartheid. Conditions in South Africa continued to deteriorate, and in 1986 Congress passed the Comprehensive Anti-Apartheid Act (CAAA). Its provisions included a ban on new U.S. investments and loans and a trade embargo. Moreover, it specified a series of areas in which South Africa had to make "substantial progress" before the sanctions could be lifted. These included freeing political prisoners, ending the state of emergency, legalizing banned political parties, giving black South Africans political freedoms, repealing discriminatory laws, and ending apartheid. Reagan vetoed the bill. His veto was overridden by a vote of 313-83 in the House and 78-21 in the Senate.

As is suggested by the imposition of ECONOMIC SANCTIONS, U.S. firms had a significant presence in South Africa. Their operations became a principal target of antiapartheid activists in the United States. The most notable attempt to influence their decision making were the 1977 Sullivan Principles. Named after their author, Reverend Leon Sullivan, the Sullivan Principles established a code of conduct for American firms doing business in South Africa. They included ending segregation in the workplace and imposing equal pay and equal employment opportunities. In the 1990s antiapartheid activists extended their focus to include pressuring large investors, such as universities and pension funds, to divest themselves of stock in companies operating in South Africa. As a result, between 1982 and 1989, the value of American investments in South Africa declined from $2.3 billion to $700 million. Similarly, the number of American firms operating there dropped from more than 300 in 1985 to less than 130 in 1990. Finally, many states and local governments passed legislation against firms doing business in South Africa. Often they were barred from entering into contracts with state agencies.

The beginning of the end for apartheid came in September 1989 when F. W. de Klerk became president. In February 1990 he lifted the ban on the ANC and other antiapartheid parties, then released ANC leader Nelson Mandela from prison, where he had been held for 23 years due to his opposition to apartheid. In 1991 President GEORGE H. W. BUSH lifted the ban on new investments imposed by the CAAA. The remaining prohibitions were repealed by Congress in 1993, following agreement between the ANC and the South African government on a new constitution that ended apartheid. The United States also began providing increased amounts of development assistance to South Africa. In 1992 approximately $80 million annually was going to such programs. Following Mandela's election as president in 1994, the Clinton administration announced a three-year, $600 million economic package. The U.S. AGENCY FOR INTERNATIONAL DEVELOPMENT spends $50 million annually. One point of emphasis in these programs has been promoting DEMOCRATIZATION. A second concern is with promoting health. South Africa is one of the countries most infected by HIV/AIDS. The United States provides additional funding for anticrime and antiterrorism programs and for military training education.

**Further reading:** Barber, James, and John Barratt. *South Africa's Foreign Policy.* New York: Cambridge University Press, 1990; Borstelmann, Thomas. *Apartheid's Reluctant Uncle.* New York: Oxford University Press, 1993; Crocker, Chester. *A High Noon in Southern Africa: Making Peace in a Rough Neighborhood.* New York: Norton, 1992.

## Southeast Asia Treaty Organization (SEATO)

The Southeast Asia Treaty Organization (SEATO) was formed in 1954 by the United States as part of its strategy of containing the Soviet Union during the COLD WAR. It became the formal instrument through which the United States first extended military assistance to South VIETNAM.

The 1954 Geneva agreement that ended the French occupation of Indochina had separated Vietnam into two units, North and South, with the 17th parallel as a dividing line. It was understood that the line was temporary and that elections would be held to determine who would rule over the single unified country of Vietnam. All sides expected the Communists to win this election; because of this, they agreed to remove their forces to a position north of the 17th parallel.

President DWIGHT EISENHOWER and SECRETARY OF STATE JOHN FOSTER DULLES moved quickly to shore up the Western position in the region. Within six weeks after the Geneva meeting ended, the United States, GREAT BRITAIN, FRANCE, Australia, New Zealand, PAKISTAN, THAILAND, and the PHILIPPINES met in Manila in September 1954 to create SEATO. Dulles wanted to include CAMBODIA, LAOS, and "the free state of Vietnam" in SEATO but met with resistance from France. Paris pointed out that this would violate the Geneva accords that barred these newly independent states from joining ALLIANCES. Dulles circumvented this prohibition and overrode French opposition by inserting a protocol into the treaty designating these states as having their security guaranteed by SEATO even though they were not members.

Before 1954 ended the United States had become firmly identified with the regime of Ngo Dinh Diem, whose government had replaced that of Emperor Bao Dai in the south. In 1955, with the support of the United States, Diem announced that since he had not personally signed the Geneva accords, he was not bound by them and would not hold elections. He declared South Vietnam to be an independent country.

SEATO's operative language mirrored that found in NORTH ATLANTIC TREATY ORGANIZATION (NATO) documents. An attack on one was deemed to be an attack on all. Each would respond in accordance with their constitutional practices, and in case of subversion all parties would consult for purposes of common action. Unlike NATO, however, SEATO had no unified command or combined military forces. American air and sea power were expected to provide its core deterrent force with member states contributing ground forces as needed. Even more significantly, SEATO did not include as members most of the regional countries. INDIA, Burma, and INDONESIA, for example, all preferred to follow a neutral path. Only Thailand could be considered a Southeast Asian state.

These weaknesses limited SEATO's ability to serve as a true regional defense organization. President RICHARD NIXON's trip to CHINA in 1971, which led to normalization of relations between these two states, further undercut SEATO's standing in the region since the fear of Chinese aggression had been a key factor in its creation. The fall of South Vietnam in 1975 foreshadowed its demise, and SEATO was officially dissolved in 1977.

See also CONTAINMENT.

## South Korea

South Korea has a population of 47.5 million and is about the size of Indiana, with an area of 38,000 square miles. Serious American interest in Korea first appeared in the latter half of the 1800s. In 1866 the merchant ship *General Sherman* made an uninvited visit to Korea in hopes of fostering trade. Korea was commonly referred to at the time as the "Hermit Kingdom" for its distrust of foreigners and desire to remain isolated. The ship was destroyed, and the crew killed in a dispute with Koreans. In 1871 a party of five American warships arrived in Korea to address the *General Sherman* incident and open trade relations. Korean forces opened fire on the naval force, and the resulting conflict left at least 300 Koreans dead. JAPAN was the first outside power to succeed in opening Korea in 1876. The United States became the first Western country to establish relations with Korea with the signing of the Treaty of Chemulpo in 1882. It guaranteed MOST-FAVORED-NATION status for the United States and granted other trade and residence rights to Americans.

American interest in Korea was secondary to its principal concerns elsewhere in the Pacific, involving Japan, CHINA, and the PHILIPPINES. This was clearly evident in the aftermath of the Russo-Japanese War of 1904–05. According to the terms of the Taft-Katsura Agreement signed in Tokyo in July 1905, the United States recognized Japan's special position in Korea in return for a Japanese pledge to forgo any aggressive actions toward the Philippines. Later that year, in November, Japan informed the United States that it would conduct foreign relations for Korea. The United States complied with the Japanese position by closing its diplomatic office in Korea.

Korea continued to play a minor, and in its view neglected, role in great power politics through the first half of the twentieth century. At the Versailles Conference that drew up the peace treaty ending WORLD WAR I, Korea was excluded from the list of countries to which the principle of self-determination would apply. At the December 1942 Cairo Conference, the United States, GREAT BRITAIN, and the Soviet Union promised Korea its independence "in due course." At the YALTA CONFERENCE in April 1945, it was agreed that a trusteeship would be established for Korea under the auspices of the United States, China, the Soviet Union, and Great Britain. Japan's quicker-than-expected surrender changed those plans, and instead two occupation zones were created dividing Korea at the 38th parallel. This line had been agreed upon as the demarcation point establishing which forces Soviet or American would accept the surrender of Japanese forces. Movement toward creating a provisional government floundered, and the 38th parallel became a de facto political boundary separating Korea into NORTH KOREA (under Soviet control) and South Korea (under American control).

The marginalization of South Korea in American thinking continued in the immediate post–WORLD WAR II period. In an interview in March 1949 General DOUGLAS MACARTHUR told Japanese reporters that the American defense line in Asia runs from the Philippines through the Ryukyu Islands and through Japan. This placed the Korean Peninsula outside the American defense perimeter. SECRETARY OF STATE DEAN ACHESON made a virtually identical statement in January 1950 to reporters in Washington. Some observers point out that in doing so the United States was not necessarily abandoning South Korea. The Truman administration was confident that South Korea could defend itself and at times had feared that South Korea would seek to invade North Korea.

It thus came as a major surprise that the United States responded so forcefully to the unexpected June 25, 1950,

A South Korean soldier *(left)* and a U.S. soldier stand guard at the truce village of Panmunjom in the demilitarized zone (DMZ) between North and South Korea, 2003. *(Chung Sung-Jun/Getty Images)*

North Korean invasion of South Korea. The KOREAN WAR was marked by major pendulum swings in the relative fortunes of the two sides. The initial North Korean attack all but pushed U.S. forces off of the peninsula. MacArthur's brilliant landing at Inchon behind the North Korean line of attack crippled Pyongyang's forces and set the stage for an American and South Korean invasion of North Korea. The enormity of MacArthur's victory caused policy makers in Washington to change their objective from reestablishing the status quo to unification. In their haste and exuberance American officials failed to heed Chinese warnings that they would not accept American forces in North Korea. As U.S. troops approached the Yalu River, the border between North Korea and China, the Chinese counterattacked and drove them back down across the 38th parallel.

Truce negotiations began on July 10, 1951. They soon bogged down, and an armistice was not reached until July 27, 1953. Neither the United States nor South Korea officially signed the document, and no formal peace treaty has yet been signed. By now DWIGHT EISENHOWER was president. During his campaign he promised to go to Korea to end the war. He did so for three days in December 1952. Movement in these talks was only forthcoming, however, when Eisenhower reportedly threatened China with military action—including the use of NUCLEAR WEAPONS—if a truce was not signed. The historical record is unclear as to whether the threat of military action on the part of the United States contributed to breaking the deadlock. Evidence also points to the economic hardship created by the war on North Korea and China as important factors.

In the aftermath of the Korean War, South Korea became a loyal anticommunist ally of the United States. A 1954 United States–South Korea Mutual Defense Treaty was approved by the Senate by a vote of 81-6 and pledged the two states to consult with one another and meet any common danger in accordance with their constitutional processes. The United States currently maintains some 37,000 military personnel in South Korea to aid its security efforts. During the 1950s and 1960s it was ruled by a succession of autocratic rulers who often showed little regard for HUMAN RIGHTS. But as was commonplace during the COLD WAR, these shortcomings were overlooked if the country was a firm ally. When JIMMY CARTER became PRESIDENT, South Korea was one of those American allies whom he singled out for criticism for human-rights violations. Tensions between the two allies also grew over an unsuccessful attempt by the United States to reduce its military presence in South Korea. A reevaluation of the North Korean threat ended this initiative. It followed on an earlier successful move by the Nixon administration to reduce the American presence in South Korea as part of his effort to move the burden of defending allies from the United States to those states. Relations between the two soured briefly in the 1970s amid charges of influence peddling in Washington by South Korea, known as Koreagate.

In addition to questions about its human-rights policy, the United States and South Korea have clashed over Seoul's economic policies. In its early years of statehood South Korea relied heavily on U.S. FOREIGN AID as its economy struggled. At one point its per capita gross domestic product was actually lower than that in North Korea. By the early 1960s this had begun to change, and by the 1970s, South Korea had moved from being viewed as a developing state to a newly industrializing one. Along with Singapore, Taiwan, and Hong Kong, it became known as one of the four "Asian Tigers" whose economies had taken off due to a strategy of export-led production. An indicator of this growth is its automobile exports, which grew from about $30 million per year to almost $1 billion.

Much like it did with Japan, this economic success also transformed Korea from a country viewed solely as a military ally into one that had also become an economic competitor. By 1985 officials in the United States had come to view trade with Korea as a crucial test case for trade with other developing economies. Of particular concern involved the U.S. view that South Korea pursued an unreasonable policy with regard to international property rights protection. Its copyright laws offered little protection for publishers, musicians, motion picture companies, or computer software companies. American firms estimated that about $150 million was being lost annually. South Korea argued that it was doing nothing that other developing countries, including the United States, had done before. It regarded intellectual property as a common inheritance of all people and saw the United States's position on intellectual property rights as interventionist.

The year 2000 brought renewed attention to the U.S.–South Korea–North Korea triangular relationship. On June 13, 2000, South Korean president Kim Dae-Jung made the first ever visit by a South Korean head of state to North Korea, where he met with Kim Jong Il. Lower-level bilateral meetings and conferences between the two governments followed. South Korea's Sunshine policy brought forward expressions of hope that a reconciliation between the two Koreas was in the offing. By 2002 those hopes had been largely dashed. The GEORGE W. BUSH administration did not share Kim Dae-Jung's enthusiasm for improving relations. Bush went so far as to identify North Korea as part of an axis of evil in his 2002 State of the Union address. Kim's political standing in South Korea became shaky amid charges of corruption and opposition from conservative political forces. American intransigence and Kim's political problems once again froze North Korean–South Korean relations.

In 2003 the United States and South Korea found themselves at odds over two important issues. First, South Korea was not a supporter of the IRAQ WAR. Second, South Korea opposed any form of military action against North Korea due to its open pursuit of nuclear weapons. It described military action as "unthinkable." South Korea was placed in a difficult position in the United States–North Korea conflict because of North Korea's insistence that the United States deal with it directly. Many in South Korea also resented President George W. Bush's comment that "I loathe [North Korean leader] Kim Jong Il." This comment is seen by them as having scuttled any chance of success that South Korea's Sunshine policy may have had. Only after the Iraq War ended was there significant movement along regional diplomatic lines involving RUSSIA, Japan, and South Korea in negotiations with North Korea.

See also ALLIANCES; ECONOMIC INSTRUMENTS; TRADE POLICY.

## Soviet Union   See RUSSIA.

## Spain

The Kingdom of Spain occupies 194,884 square miles, including the Balearic and Canary Islands, which is approximately the size of Arizona and Utah combined. Its population of 40 million gives it a lower population density than most European countries, making it roughly equivalent to New England. The Spanish people are comprised of several distinct ethnic groups, including the Basques, Catalans, and Galicians. These groups have been united since the Reconquista, lasting until 1492, and leading to the unification of present-day Spain in 1512. This was Spain's golden age. During the 16th century, it became the most powerful country in Europe. Since the late 1400s, it had been deriving immense wealth and gold from the Americas, but much of this was squandered through long, costly wars and an ill-devised economy—it had to declare bankruptcy twice. Regardless, the earliest ties between Spain and what would become the United States were made during this era, and their relationship, although it would chart a bumpy path, would lead to close ties in the 21st century.

From the American perspective, it is hard to imagine a history without Spain. From Christopher Columbus discovering Florida in 1492 to Spanish-American colonies coexisting with the newly independent United States of America in 1776 to the SPANISH-AMERICAN WAR of 1898, major defining episodes in U.S. history have been closely intertwined with Spain. On the eve of the AMERICAN REVOLUTION, Spain's North American empire consisted of parts of today's FLORIDA north to today's South Carolina and west to today's California. It was a substantial area of territory that would grow and shrink over the next century and a half, as land changed hands between Spain, FRANCE, and the independent United States.

When the War of Independence began in 1776, it was a colonial uprising, pitting the rebellious thirteen colonies against GREAT BRITAIN. The surrender of British general John Burgoyne at Saratoga the next year gave significant reason for European powers watching from the wings to get involved—suddenly it seemed as if the Americans might have a chance at winning. Spain, like France, was eager to take retribution against Great Britain for the outcome of the Seven Years' War (1756–63), in which Britain power took possession of Spanish Florida by the terms of the Paris Peace Treaty. On June 16, 1778, Spain declared war on Britain, yet it did not ally with the Americans. All in all, its participation was fairly minimal; Spain joined the battle for a strategic gain, namely, Florida. At the war's end, Spain became the first to recognize the United States as an independent state, and by the TREATY OF PARIS of 1783, Madrid reincorporated Florida into its empire.

Postwar diplomacy did not go well for the new American republic, however; it suffered humiliation at the hands of both Britain and Spain regarding the terms of the Paris Peace Treaty. Seeing the Americans powerless to enforce their rights, Britain refused to evacuate troops from the Northwest Territory. While this was regrettable, far more problematic was Spain's decision to ignore the southern boundary. Spain still claimed sovereignty over lands from Georgia to the Mississippi River, and its continental agents conspired with hostile bands of NATIVE AMERICANS to resist U.S. expansion, finally closing the Lower Mississippi region to American citizens. This caused great consternation among western farmers, for use of that main waterway was critical to sustaining the Ohio River valley's economic growth. Congress appointed a New Yorker, John Jay, to undertake discussions with the Spanish to regain navigational rights, but Jay's attempts angered those in the South, who felt they had been sacrificed for the North's interests. The American position called for direct trade with Spain from New England, agreeing that if that concession was granted, they would forgo navigation on the Mississippi for 25 years—terms for which the South called foul. Recognizing how dangerously divisive the disagreement could be, CONGRESS called off negotiations, and the issue remained unsolved for a time.

By the mid-1790s, greater organization had come to the new republic, and the Americans managed to deal with the embarrassing diplomatic issues left in the wake of the Paris Peace Treaty. First, the British withdrew from the Great Lakes and Northwest Territories, after instigating a few battles between Native Americans and settlers, with the last of their troops moving into CANADA in 1796. Settlement of the British dispute left the southern boundary one of the major diplomatic concerns, and in that regard Americans found themselves in a position of good luck and good negotiating. As the situation in Europe became increasingly hostile, volatile, and complex, Spain found itself in a position to encourage the Americans to reopen the Mississippi navigation question. In the time since the river had been closed to U.S. passage, the Spanish had resorted to tactics similar to those employed by the British in the North—they incited Native Americans to attack and harass settlers. The situation seemed poised to disintegrate further when the United States signed JAY'S TREATY with Britain. The Spanish incorrectly assumed this was an ALLIANCE designed to strip them of their North American colonies, and they frantically began offering concessions to the America envoy in Madrid to avoid this disaster.

Thomas Pinckney secured the opening of the Mississippi, the right to deposit goods in New Orleans without paying duties, a defined southern barrier along the 31st parallel, and a promise to stay out of Native American affairs. The Treaty of San Lorenzo (or PINCKNEY'S TREATY) was signed in 1795, ratified unanimously in 1796, and left both states content with the North American territorial arrangement—for the time being. At the turn of the 19th century, Europe was embroiled in wars that led incumbent President THOMAS JEFFERSON to believe that he could spirit away European colonial lands—especially from a notoriously weak Spain. In that regard, Jefferson had his eye on the Louisiana Territory and Florida, with the intent to follow up DIPLOMACY with forceful occupation, should it be required. The 1801 conquest of Spain by France gave the PRESIDENT a moment's pause, however, for French leader Napoleon Bonaparte appeared interested in rekindling France's North American ties. When French forces were dispatched to the Caribbean to put down a rebellion, it suddenly seemed that the United States could be on the brink of war, causing the Spanish-held New Orleans to close the port to American traffic.

A diplomatic unit comprised of Robert Livingston and JAMES MONROE was sent to try to buy New Orleans, with the American president under the impression that should their diplomatic efforts fail, the United States would be forced to go to war and depend on British support to take the key southern ports so vital to its economic existence. Fortunately, by the time Monroe made the Atlantic passage to meet Livingston in Paris, Napoleon had lost interest in North America—his troops had been decimated by tropical disease in the Caribbean. To the complete surprise of the American delegation, they were able to secure the LOUISIANA PURCHASE for a mere $15 million—doubling the size of the continental United States. The end result of these transactions saw the United States in possession of the land south of the Great Lakes as far west as the Rocky Mountains and as far south as Spanish Florida, which then comprised parts of the coastal lands of today's Alabama, Mississippi, and Louisiana.

In the early years of the 1800s, Spanish-American boundaries continued to be debated and argued. Between 1810 and 1812, the United States moved in to claim the stretch of the Gulf Coast between the Mississippi and Perdido Rivers, leaving Spain in possession of East Florida. As this region became an object of great interest for President James Monroe and his secretary of state, JOHN QUINCY ADAMS, the question on many peoples' minds was, how long? In 1816, General ANDREW JACKSON invaded East Florida under the auspices of pursuing hostile Seminole. Jackson went beyond his orders and, in 1818, occupied the territory; soon the United States demanded that Spain yield it for the sake of American security. The Spanish Empire was growing increasingly weak, hurt by Latin American revolutions, which left it in a poor position to evict U.S. forces. Under the Adams-Onís Treaty of 1819, Spain ceded to pressure and relinquished East Florida, in exchange for some forgiveness of debt owed to Americans. Adams pushed to fulfill still more of his perceptions of U.S. continental destiny, and under the same treaty, still using the confrontation in Florida as an excuse, enticed Spain to give up its claim to the Pacific Coast north of California. Spain was insistent on retaining TEXAS, but Adams also managed to renegotiate the boundary between Spanish and American property, creating the potential for a second American ocean front.

When James Monroe secured his second term in the executive mansion in 1820, the diplomatic focus remained on securing more of Spain's North American holdings. Continued revolts in Latin America led to U.S. recognition of the revolutionary governments, seeing in their efforts a spirit paralleling that which had led to the American Revolution in 1776. Although prior to 1822 the United States had maintained a neutral course, Monroe and Adams believed such diplomatic actions could patronize Spain and threaten ongoing negotiations for East Florida. This touched off a spiral of events in Europe. By recognizing the Latin American nations diplomatically, the United States had put itself on a course of direct opposition with most major European powers. Austria, RUSSIA, and Prussia were deeply committed to halting the progress of the revolutionary society, and following Napoleon's defeat and the restoration of monarchies in France and Spain, the other monarchical powers of Europe stood behind France and encouraged a French incursion to quell a rebellion in Spain. A renewed House of Bourbon could lead to a drive to restore the old empire, striking fear in the hearts of the United States and Great Britain. The emergence of this European Concert pushed the traditionally hostile Americans and British to draft joint policies to prevent the return of an aggressive French kingdom, facilitated by a weakening Spain. To ensure American neutrality and keep the European powers from exacting their antirevolutionary wrath on the new Latin American nations, the United States enacted the MONROE DOCTRINE in 1823. This guaranteed that the United States would stay out of European affairs, and with the Royal Navy providing the force to ensure it, that the European powers would stay out of the Americas.

In 1821, Spain granted independence to MEXICO, which then encompassed today's Texas, New Mexico, Arizona, California, Nevada, Utah, and most of Colorado. Trade flourished between this new state and the United States, but the end result was driven by American expansionary interests rather than a new respect for the status quo. However, the Spanish Empire now much reduced, this was no longer the weary Madrid's problem. Spain's saga of boundary disputes and territorial exchanges with the United States had come to a close with the transfer of West Florida in 1845. Spain's problems at home and with the colonies it still held drew the bulk of Madrid's attention until the dying years of the 19th century, when conflict over the governing of some far-flung islands brought Spain and the United States back on a collision course.

No single event helped affirm American great POWER status as much as the Spanish-American War of 1898. There are a variety of schools of thought to explain what drove the United States to confront Spain. One suggests that the American people could not abide the blatant abuse of colonized people at the hands of European brutes "on our doorstep," referring to CUBA. Another suggests that for economic purposes, the United States was interested in Cuban sugar cane and intervened to help its own needs. Finally, another suggestion—and one that links to the path charted by the United States in the 20th century—is that the United States intervened for foreign policy's sake, because if another power controlled Cuba, it could make American Caribbean designs nearly impossible to follow through with. Regardless of the reasons why, President WILLIAM MCKINLEY on his election in 1897 urged neutrality. He dispatched envoys and emissaries to Madrid and kept a close eye on the situation, finally moved to do more when rioting broke out in Cuba, and Spain's efforts to put it down were considered "inhumane." McKinley ordered the battleship *Maine* to Havana's harbor in early 1898 as a show of American strength and to protect American citizens. Days later, a diplomatic gaffe occurred when the Spanish ambassador to Washington, Enrique Dupuy de Lome, had a private letter stolen from his possession, which was reprinted in the yellow presses. The letter accused McKinley of being "weak" and a "bidder for the admiration of the crowd," causing a deep rift in already cool U.S.-Spanish relations. De Lome resigned and returned to Madrid, but in his wake uncertainty remained over the state of negotiations.

Days after the ambassador returned home, the *Maine* exploded in Havana's harbor, apparently the victim of a mine. More than 250 lives went down with the ship, and in the fury that followed, an inquiry was launched that confirmed Spanish responsibility for the carnage. In fact, recent examinations prove that it was an internally sparked explosion, resulting perhaps from a faulty boiler. At the time, however, cries of "Remember the *Maine*, to Hell with Spain!" rose up to illustrate the clear view in the United States. Within the American cabinet were both HAWKS and DOVES, with men like THEODORE ROOSEVELT and WILLIAM JENNINGS BRYAN calling for war, yet McKinley remained neutral, remembering the carnage of the AMERICAN CIVIL WAR and not wanting to subject Americans to a similar fate. The president did, however, ask for and receive unanimous approval from CONGRESS for a $50 million emergency defense appropriation, causing some alarm across the Atlantic. However, alarm did not encourage the Spanish to defer to McKinley's demands, and on March 27, 1898, he cabled his final terms in the negotiations. He asked for an armistice, an end to the reconcentration policy, and a move toward Cuban independence. While Madrid was willing to concede some points, the American president felt that it was not enough. Reluctantly, McKinley began to prepare the nation for war.

On April 19, Congress passed a joint resolution calling for Cuban independence and authorizing the president to use the army and navy to expel Spain from the island. A subsequent amendment by Senator Henry M. Teller (R-Colo.) ensured some benevolence in the American position, pledging that the United States would not subsequently annex the island to merely uproot one occupation force for another. Six days later, after Spain severed diplomatic relations, McKinley blockaded Cuba and raised 125,000 volunteers. Congress officially passed a declaration of war.

Though the Americans were ill-prepared, ill-equipped, and simply ill, after consuming bad food and contaminated water in training camps in the South, the "splendid little war" was mercifully brief. The Spanish fleet was destroyed in Manila Bay half a world away, and U.S. land forces defeated Spain in every engagement. The war was over merely two months after it began. As per the TELLER AMENDMENT, Cuba was not annexed but occupied to assist it in rebuilding after many years of Spanish misrule. The PHILIPPINES, however, were another matter. This archipelago lying between the South China Sea and Pacific Ocean was distinctly *not* on America's doorstep. McKinley had struggled over what to do with the Philippines—the Spanish Empire had all but collapsed, it could not take control over the islands again. What else could be done? Leaving them for another expanding nation would simply return the Philippines to its previous fate. However, making it an American protectorate would draw on U.S. resources and add a responsibility without yielding full American control. Also, in expressing an attitude much prevalent at the time, Americans felt that the Filipinos were not ready for their independence. Feeling that his hands were tied, the president ordered annexation. When U.S. and Spanish officials met in Paris to discuss a peace treaty, it was made official: Cuba was granted independence, Spain assumed its debt, PUERTO RICO and Guam were transferred to American hands, and, in exchange for $20 million, so too were the Philippines.

Spain and the United States engaged in few diplomatic confrontations through the first half of the 20th century, the former turning inward to deal with emerging republicanism and eschewing participation in WORLD WAR I. Declaring its neutrality allowed Spain, like the United States, to benefit from trade and export, but as a whole the era was far less profitable than it was to the United States, a great financial stratification being its true legacy. Following a period of dictatorial rule between 1923 and 1931, the Second Republic was established, soon dominated by political polarization and resulting in the leftist Popular Front victory in 1936, which sparked civil war. When General Francisco Franco's Nationalist forces proclaimed victory in 1939, the state was exhausted financially and politically, leading to its neutrality in the WORLD WAR II. However, Spain exhibited a pro-Axis bent, which was repaid with Allied isolation after their victory in 1945.

The postwar era was difficult for Spain. Mired in ISOLATIONISM and domestic problems, Madrid did not join the UNITED NATIONS until 1955, having suffered a diplomatic boycott in 1945. This concession was only granted on the heels of a concordat signed between the Vatican, the United States, and Spain, wherein the United States was eager to expand its COLD WAR defenses. By this pact, the United States was allowed to create military bases in Spain in exchange for financial aid amounting to more than $625 million over six years. This was its first step back onto the international scene, yet financially Spain was still unable to participate fully in the industrialized world's trade, and it was not yet wholly accepted politically. The INTERNATIONAL MONETARY FUND stabilized its currency in 1959, after which a move toward liberalization and increased attempts to secure direct foreign investments began in earnest. Still, foreign trade remained a small part of its economy, and Spain remained the most closed state in Western Europe. By the 1960s and 1970s, the situation was reversed. Economic expansion continued, bringing it into greater contact with the United States, and following Franco's death in 1975 and the first elections in 1977, Spain had gone from a completely isolated state to a full participant in European and world affairs. The first order of business following Franco's death and the return to democracy was to break out of isolation and join the European Community, which it did in 1985. Today, Spain's EUROPEAN UNION membership is the cornerstone of its international policy.

Spain joined the NORTH ATLANTIC TREATY ORGANIZATION (NATO) in 1982, though it remained an alliance member only, not having its own military officers as participants NATO commands until 1996. Since then, however, it has participated with the United States and other NATO allies in military operations in the former YUGOSLAVIA, including the air war against Serbia in 1999, and Spanish armed forces and police personnel make up part of the international PEACEKEEPING forces still in BOSNIA AND HERZEGOVINA and KOSOVO. A Spanish general currently commands NATO forces in Kosovo.

Spanish-American relations have warmed considerably in the last quarter of a century, though one source of potential friction between the two remains their Middle Eastern policies. The United States has been largely pro-Israeli, whereas Spain gives the Arab countries a priority of interest due to their interrelated economies—specifically, Spain's OIL and gas imports—and several Arab countries have substantial investments in Spain. However, this fact has not been a major cause of friction between the two. Relations are regulated by the 1989 Agreement on Defense Cooperation, currently under review, which moderates cooperation in NATO and American use of facilities at Spanish military installations.

With a long history of waging war on domestic TERRORISM, Spain was quick to offer support to the United States in the wake of the SEPTEMBER 11, 2001, terrorist attacks. However, Spain has also refused to extradite the terrorists allegedly within its borders if the United States seeks the death penalty. Spain proved a staunch ally of the United States in the March 2003 war on IRAQ, although Spanish citizens registered considerable opposition.

**Further reading:** Cortada, James W. *Two Nations over Time: Spain and the United States, 1776–1977.* Westport, Conn.: Greenwood, 1978.

—Stephanie Cousineau

## Spanish-American War

Although only some 10 weeks in duration, the Spanish-American War of 1898 is considered to be a turning point in U.S. foreign policy. The United States had not fought a foreign war since 1848, but it had established itself as a hemispheric power. The Spanish-American War transformed the United States into a global POWER through the acquisition of the PHILIPPINES. The conflict brought forward and highlighted a complex array of domestic factors that continue to shape decisions regarding the use of force by the United States.

A rebellion by Cuban nationalists in 1895 set in motion events leading to the Spanish-American War. The struggle quickly took on a callous character. The insurgents adopted a scorched-earth policy in the hope that SPAIN would give CUBA up once the island no longer offered them economic benefits. The Spanish army under the direction of General Valeriano Weyler y Nicolau determined that the only way to defeat the Cubans was to force people out of their vil-

lages and reconcentrate them in fortified towns. The lack of adequate sanitation and food resulted in more than 20,000 deaths, many of which were women and children.

President GROVER CLEVELAND maintained a position of neutrality over the opposition of many in CONGRESS who urged that he side with the Cubans. A congressional resolution to this effect was passed in 1896. The resolution also called upon Cleveland to offer goods and services to end the war. Cleveland resisted these pressures both because he believed the Cubans were deliberately destroying American property and because he saw their actions as politically motivated. WILLIAM MCKINLEY was elected president in 1896 and continued Cleveland's policy of neutrality but did offer to act as an intermediary in ending the conflict. A new Spanish government offered concessions, but they proved insufficient to stop the fighting. In his first message to Congress, in December 1897, McKinley spoke of the need to give Spain a "reasonable chance" to effect positive changes in Cuba. A few months earlier the U.S. minister to Spain had announced that the United States had "no intention of annexing Cuba, nor did it aspire to the responsibilities of a protectorate."

In January 1898, Spanish loyalists in Cuba rioted in opposition to Spain's willingness to grant Cubans political rights equal to those given Spaniards and to accept the principle of eventual home rule for Cuba. The *Maine*, a second-class battleship, was sent to Havana as a "friendly courtesy" but was really designed as a show of U.S. resolve in the face of possible threats to American property growing out of the rioting. At this time, the *New York Journal* published a letter it secretly obtained in which the Spanish minister to the United States described McKinley as a "would-be politician," among other insults. Against this backdrop of rising tensions, the *Maine* blew up, killing more than 250 people on February 15.

The sinking of the *Maine* was seized upon by the American press. Already, Joseph Pulitzer's *New York World* and William Randolph Hearst's *New York Journal* had become embroiled in a circulation war that fed off of sensationalistic headlines. Their inflammatory headlines now reached new heights as "war extras" were produced. Offsetting the prowar pressure from newspapers was the concern of the business community for the costs and destruction that would accompany war. They urged a lesser form of intervention that would bring an end to the fighting. McKinley urged patience until a naval investigation could determine the cause of the explosion that sank the *Maine*. On March 28, it ruled that a submarine had blown up the Maine. A 1976 naval study concluded that the probable cause was spontaneous combustion in a coal boiler next to munitions.

The same day that the naval board announced its finding, the United States issued an ultimatum to Spain demanding, an immediate armistice, an end to the recon-

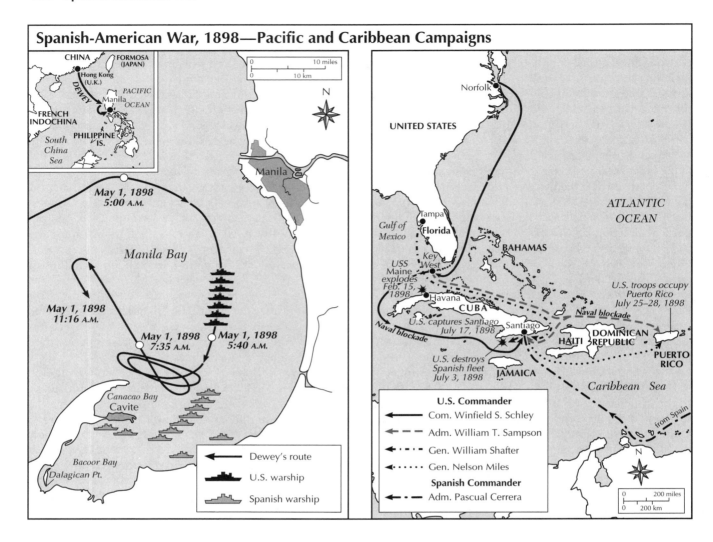

## Spanish-American War, 1898—Pacific and Caribbean Campaigns

centration policy, and Cuban independence. Spain quickly met most of these conditions. It offered to end the reconcentration policy and implement an armistice if one was requested by the Cubans. Hoping for American intervention, the Cubans did not want to request an armistice. Unable to gain the backing of other European powers for a war with the United States, Spain agreed to end all hostilities in Cuba, in effect giving in to all U.S. demands.

Pressure, however, continued to mount, and McKinley now feared that he might loose his reelection bid in 1900. WILLIAM JENNINGS BRYAN, his likely DEMOCRATIC PARTY opponent, was on record as favoring a "free Cuba." Two days after Spain capitulated, on April 11, McKinley asked Congress for authority to use force to end the conflict. In his address he lay blame on both Cuba and Spain for the violence. On April 19, Congress passed a joint resolution authorizing intervention. It declared Cuba to be free, demanded the withdrawal of Spain, directed the

president to use force if necessary to achieve these ends, and stated that the United States had no intention of annexing Cuba. This last stipulation is known as the TELLER AMENDMENT and is named after Senator Henry Teller (R-Colo.). It was adopted without dissent and reflected two competing sets of concerns. The first was a humanitarian impulse not to become a colonial power but rather to fight for higher moral purposes. The second was a concern by U.S. sugar producers that Cuban sugar not be allowed to escape taxation by U.S. tariffs. McKinley signed the joint resolution on April 25.

The war ended quickly. The first U.S. move came in the Philippines, where on May 1 Admiral George Dewey sailed into Manila Bay and destroyed the Spanish fleet. An American Expeditionary Force would not reach the Philippines until June 30, having first stopped to take control of Guam. Spanish forces fared no better in Cuba, where the Spanish fleet was destroyed in Santiago Harbor, caught between American naval and ground forces. U.S. troops also occupied PUERTO RICO.

On August 12, 1898, Spain signed a protocol ending the war on U.S. terms. McKinley had indicated his conditions for ending the war on July 30: surrender of Cuba, cession of Puerto Rico and Guam to the United States, and the American occupation of Manila, pending a final determination of the Philippines future. Formal peace negotiations began on October 1. Fearing that the Senate might reject the treaty, McKinley appointed four avowed expansionists to the five-person American peace commission. Three of its members were senators with seats on the Foreign Relations Committee.

The Philippines became the major stumbling block in the negotiations. At first, McKinley did not seem particularly interested in acquiring more than rights to a coaling station. By the end of the negotiations he sought total control over it for the United States. His policy shift followed rather than led public thinking. The American business community now eyed CHINA as a market, and the Philippines would serve to protect American interests in the region. Church groups and others argued that the United States had a moral obligation to help the backward Filipinos and could not allow them to fall back under Spanish (or German rule), and they were not ready for independence, they continued. McKinley claimed to have found the answer to what to do about the Philippines in prayer. On December 12, Spain signed a treaty giving up its sovereignty over Cuba and ceding Guam, Puerto Rico, and the Philippines to the United States.

The Treaty of Paris faced tough going in the Senate, where members faced lobbying by Anti-Imperialist Leagues mobilized to prevent its ratification. Senator HENRY CABOT LODGE, (R-Mass.) led the fight for ratification. William Jennings Bryan was an unexpected supporter. An opponent of IMPERIALISM, he urged accepting the treaty and then giving the Philippines its independence. The treaty passed 57-27, one vote over the number needed.

See also RELIGION.

**Further reading:** Musicant, Ivan. *The Banana Wars: A History of United States Military Interventions in Latin America from the Spanish-American War to the Invasion of Panama.* New York: Macmillan, 1990; Perez, Louis, Jr. *The War of 1898: The United States and Cuba in History and Historiography.* Chapel Hill: University of North Carolina Press, 1998; Wayne, Morgan H. *America's Road to Empire: The War with Spain and Overseas Expansion.* New York: Wiley, 1965.

## Sputnik

*Sputnik* was launched on October 4, 1957. It was a satellite 22 inches in diameter and weighing 184 pounds. *Sput-*

*nik* dwarfed in size the six-inch and three-and-one-half pound satellite that was set to be launched in December by an American Vanguard missile. *Sputnik* was put into Earth orbit as part of the celebration of the International Geophysical Year (IGY). Organizers of this event had called upon the international community to work together to launch a satellite into Earth orbit that year. After the IGY began in July 1957, Soviet announcements of an impending satellite launch became routine occurrences, but it was not until August that a successful missile launch took place. In the United States, proposals to launch a scientific satellite to commemorate the IGY competed with ongoing proposals for launching a military satellite. The United States knew that the Soviet Union (see RUSSIA) was working on a satellite program of its own, and a staff report to Assistant SECRETARY OF DEFENSE Donald Quarles recommended going ahead with the scientific satellite as a means of testing the principle of "freedom of space."

*Sputnik* was a major technological accomplishment and one whose propaganda value the Soviet Union sought to exploit to its fullest potential. The greater significance of *Sputnik,* however, lies in the areas of domestic and international politics. The Eisenhower administration sought to downplay the significance of *Sputnik* in stating that the United States had never seen itself in a race with the Soviets to launch an Earth-orbiting satellite. Public reaction, however, was quite different. Frequent comparisons were made to the surprise at Pearl Harbor. A spirited debate began over science, education, space exploration, national security, and fiscal policy that continued into the 1960s. *Sputnik* became a political symbol that was used to counter and discredit such hallowed ideas as balanced budgets, local initiative, and limited government. An important ingredient in this growing public debate was the GAITHER COMMITTEE REPORT, which painted a grim picture of the Soviet threat and the American ability to respond to it. Of immediate concern to the Eisenhower administration was a precipitous drop in Eisenhower's public standing. In January 1957 his approval rating stood at 79 percent. By November, it had fallen to 57 percent.

The consequences for international politics and American national security were even greater. Up until the launching of *Sputnik,* the United States held a military and psychological advantage over the Soviet Union through the possession of what amounted to a "one-way" threat. The United States could strike at the Soviet Union using bombers stationed at military bases in West Europe, but the Soviet Union could not strike back. The ability to launch a large satellite into space along with the successful testing of an intercontinental ballistic missile (ICBM) served notice that this advantage would soon disappear. The United States would now also be vulnerable to NUCLEAR WEAPONS. Where a decade before, Americans had feared the existence of a BOMBER GAP, they now heard defense experts warn of the growing dangers inherent in the MISSILE GAP developing between the United States and the Soviet Union.

**Further reading:** Divine, Robert. *Eisenhower and Sputnik.* New York: Oxford University Press, 1993; Launius, Roger, et al., eds., *Reconsidering Sputnik.* Amsterdam, Netherlands: Harwood Academic Publishers, 2000.

**State Department** **(United States Department of State)**
With roots reaching back to the Department of Foreign Affairs established by the Continental Congress on January 10, 1781, the State Department is the oldest cabinet-level department. President GEORGE WASHINGTON renamed it the State Department in 1789, and THOMAS JEFFERSON became the first SECRETARY OF STATE in March 1790.

The Department of State is the lead U.S. foreign-affairs agency, and the SECRETARY OF STATE is the president's principal foreign-policy adviser. The State Department serves as a transmission belt for information between the United States, foreign governments, and INTERNATIONAL ORGANIZATIONS and as a resource for senior policy makers to draw upon when needed. Both of these tasks have become increasingly difficult to accomplish with the large and diverse American foreign-policy agenda. The United States maintains diplomatic relations with some 182 countries and some 70 international organizations. In the late 1960s an average of more than 4,000 messages were processed by the State Department each day. By the mid-1980s this number had grown to approximately 100,000 messages, reports, and instructions per day. In 1997 the State Department processed some 3 million cables.

Several key offices attached to the office of the secretary of state bear commenting upon. The Policy Planning Staff serves as a source of advice for the secretary of state and has primary responsibility for formulating and coordinating long-term policies. The office was created in 1947 by GEORGE KENNAN. The Office of Resources, Plans and Policy is responsible for advising the secretary of state on the foreign-affairs budget. The Office of the Coordinator of Counterterrorism coordinates an interagency Working Group on Counterterrorism and has primary responsibility for developing, coordinating, and implementing American counterterrorism policy.

Reporting directly to the secretary of state are six undersecretaries of state. The undersecretary for political affairs is the State Department's chief crisis manager and is responsible for integrating U.S. bilateral foreign policy. Beneath the undersecretary are six assistant secretaries

responsible for different groupings of countries and one responsible for multilateral relations involving international organizations. The undersecretary for economic, business, and agricultural affairs is the primary adviser on international economic policy. The undersecretary for ARMS CONTROL and international security affairs manages U.S. nonproliferation, arms control, ARMS TRANSFERS, and security assistance policy. The undersecretary for global affairs coordinates U.S. foreign policy on such diverse topics as HUMAN RIGHTS, the ENVIRONMENT, narcotics control, labor, democracy, oceans, REFUGEES, and science. The under secretary for PUBLIC DIPLOMACY and public affairs has jurisdiction over public information programs as well as cultural and economic exchanges. Lastly, the undersecretary for management is tasked with coordinating the personnel, infrastructure, and support services needed by the State Department.

The Department of State has primary responsibility for (1) leading interagency coordination in developing and implementing foreign policy, (2) managing the foreign-affairs budget and foreign-affairs resources, (3) leading and coordinating U.S. representation abroad, (4) conducting negotiations with foreign countries, and (5) coordinating and supporting the international activities of other U.S. agencies.

Its role as a lead agency in the development and execution of foreign policy is challenged both in the United States and abroad. Within the United States, the NATIONAL SECURITY ADVISOR and the NATIONAL SECURITY COUNCIL have often eclipsed the secretary of state and the State Department as the principal sources of policy ideas. The DEFENSE DEPARTMENT has long been a competitor in military policy, and the U.S. OFFICE OF TRADE REPRESENTATIVE provides an alternative source of economic advice for the PRESIDENT. Abroad, the ambassador is nominally the head of the "country team" in U.S. EMBASSIES, but his or her authority is often resisted by personnel assigned to it by other agencies. This has been a long-standing sore point with regard to representatives from the CENTRAL INTELLIGENCE AGENCY (CIA) working undercover and conducting surveillance or COVERT-ACTION operations. Also contributing to its overseas problems are budgetary cutbacks. Between 1993 and 1996 the State Department cut more than 2,000 employees and closed five embassies and 26 consulates, as well as branch offices.

Its overall budget authority, while intact, has been heavily compromised by congressional reluctance to pass foreign-affairs appropriations or attach restrictions on how it can be spent and congressional willingness to micromanage the foreign-affairs budget. Examples of the former include reporting requirements that stipulate that the State Department annually must certify that aid recipients meet human-rights, DRUG TRAFFICKING, arms control, or environmental targets. The most prominent example of the latter was the effort spearheaded by Senator JESSE HELMS (R-N.C.) to integrate two formerly independent agencies, the U.S. INFORMATION AGENCY (USIA) and the ARMS CONTROL AND DISARMAMENT AGENCY (ACDA) into the State Department. A third, the U.S. AGENCY FOR INTERNATIONAL DEVELOPMENT (USAID), retains its independent status but now reports to the secretary of state rather than the president.

The State Department's role as chief negotiator has been compromised by three trends. The first is presidential SUMMIT DIPLOMACY. Of necessity this relegates the State Department to a support role and one that is even further diminished, depending upon the degree to which the National Security Advisor has the president's ear. The second is the highly technical nature of many negotiations that privilege more specialized agencies. The third is the greater visibility given to negotiations by the MEDIA and the accompanying increased involvement of special INTEREST GROUPS and congresspeople in these negotiations.

Controversy surrounds the reasons for this progressive decline in the State Department's influence. Some cite the changing nature of foreign-policy problems. Others lay blame at the door of the president for not fully utilizing the skills and expertise housed in the State Department. Still others are critical of the role played by FOREIGN SERVICE OFFICERS. They comprise the backbone of the State Department but have been criticized for being too generalist in the skills they possess and far too cautious in how they approach foreign-policy problems.

**Further reading:** Campbell, John. *The Foreign Affairs Fudge Factory.* New York: Basic Books, 1971; Destler, I. M., Leslie Gelb, and Anthony Lake. *The Unmaking of American Foreign Policy.* New York: Simon and Schuster, 1984; Warwick, Donald. *A Theory of Public Bureaucracy: Politics, Personality, and Organization in the State Department.* Cambridge, Mass.: Harvard University Press, 1975.

## Stimson, Henry (1867–1950) *secretary of state, secretary of war*

Henry Lewis Stimson had a long career in public service. He served as SECRETARY OF STATE under President HERBERT HOOVER (1929–33) and as SECRETARY OF WAR under Presidents WILLIAM HOWARD TAFT (1911–13) and FRANKLIN ROOSEVELT and HARRY TRUMAN (1940–45). In between stints as secretary of war and prior to serving as secretary of state, Stimson held the position of governor general of the PHILIPPINES (1927–29). He also undertook a mission to NICARAGUA for President CALVIN COOLIDGE in 1927 in an effort to bring political stability to that country. U.S. Marines had been stationed there since 1912, except

for a brief withdrawal in 1925. He succeeded in negotiating the Treaty of Tipitapa.

Stimson's most significant contribution to U.S. foreign policy as secretary of state was his proclamation of the Stimson Doctrine in response to the Japanese occupation of Manchuria. Unable to convince Hoover to impose ECONOMIC SANCTIONS on JAPAN for its occupation of Manchuria Stimson announced that the United States would not recognize any territorial changes that occurred in violation of the LEAGUE OF NATIONS Covenant or the KELLOGG-BRIAND PACT. The action had little impact on Japan. It soon established a puppet government in Manchuria and continued its policy of expansionism in Asia that led to WORLD WAR II.

As secretary of war under Roosevelt and Truman, Stimson held conflicting views on relations with the Soviet Union (see RUSSIA) and the shape of the postwar international order. He generally shared Roosevelt's view that Soviet leader Joseph Stalin could be worked with and was sympathetic to his desire to create a buffer zone around the Soviet Union. He urged that the United States abandon its monopoly on NUCLEAR WEAPONS and establish an international body for this purpose in order to head off an arms race with the Soviet Union. However, after the Soviet Union rejected the BARUCH PLAN, he became an advocate for creating a strong U.S. nuclear force. Stimson's ambivalence about the shape of the future is also evident in the role he played in the decision to drop the atomic bomb on Hiroshima. Though he was reluctant to recommend this course of action, as Truman's chief adviser on the military use of the bomb, Stimson made the key recommendation that led to its use.

**Further reading:** Current, Richard H. *Secretary Stimson: A Study in Statecraft.* New Brunswick, N.J.: Shoestring Press, 1954; Ferrell, Robert H. *American Diplomacy in the Great Depression: Hoover-Stimson Foreign Policy, 1929–1933.* New Haven, Conn.: Yale University Press, 1957.

## Strategic Arms Limitation Talks

The Strategic Arms Limitation Talks (SALT) constituted a series of nuclear ARMS CONTROL negotiations between the United States and the Soviet Union (see RUSSIA). These talks resulted in the SALT I Treaty in 1972 agreed to by President RICHARD NIXON and Soviet president Leonid Brezhnev; the VLADIVOSTOK ACCORDS agreed to by Brezhnev, and President GERALD FORD, and the SALT II Treaty signed by Brezhnev and President JIMMY CARTER in 1979. SALT I was ratified by the Senate, but SALT II was not. RONALD REAGAN campaigned against ratification of SALT II in his successful bid for the presidency; upon becoming

PRESIDENT, he replaced SALT with the STRATEGIC ARMS REDUCTION TALKS (START).

For President RICHARD NIXON, the SALT talks were an important ingredient in his post–VIETNAM WAR policy of DÉTENTE, the goal of which was to demobilize the Soviet threat to the United States. Diplomatically this meant treating the Soviet Union as an equal partner in world affairs. It also meant reducing the size of the Soviet military. In this regard a SALT agreement had three objectives. First, it was to make the U.S.-Soviet nuclear arms race more predictable by documenting the number of weapons possessed by each side. Second, it would bring about parity by establishing numerical limits. Third, it would prevent the development of certain weapons systems, most specifically the ANTIBALLISTIC MISSILE (ABM) system.

SALT negotiations were carried out against a complex set of background factors. One was the emergence of a more aggressive CONGRESS. No longer willing to serve as a compliant tool of the president, the post–Vietnam War Congress saw itself as having an important role to play in setting the direction of American foreign policy. A second factor was changing PUBLIC OPINION. Over the life of the SALT talks, the American public became increasingly disenchanted with détente in general and skeptical of the benefits of entering into agreements with the Soviet Union. Third, this was also a period of tremendous technological change in the development of NUCLEAR WEAPONS. Two examples illustrate this point. The United States developed multiple independently targeted reentry vehicles (MIRVS). This allowed the United States to put multiple warheads on a missile and direct them at different targets, greatly complicating any defense system. Also, accuracy improved such that error was now measured in distances of 0.1 miles rather than in miles.

The SALT talks constituted a significant milestone in U.S.-Soviet relations because they marked a period of successful nuclear cooperation between rivals. Earlier periods of arms control had produced few tangible products and degenerated into exercises in propaganda. Critics of SALT assert that the agreements produced did not result in true reductions in the number of weapons. They merely provided justifications for larger U.S. and Soviet nuclear inventories. This was the position taken by the Reagan administration. Other critics make the same point, but they point to the continued development of new weapons systems even while SALT was being negotiated. For example, the political cost of securing the approval of the JOINT CHIEFS OF STAFF for SALT I was developing the Trident submarine. The cost of obtaining their endorsement of SALT II was the MX MISSILE system.

**Further reading:** Newhouse, John. *Cold Dawn: The Story of SALT.* New York: Henry Holt, 1973.

## Strategic Arms Limitation Talks I

The agreement resulting from the first Strategic Arms Limitation Talks I (SALT I) was signed by President RICHARD NIXON and Soviet president Leonid Brezhnev in May 1972 after two and one-half years of negotiations. The pact existed in two parts. The first was a treaty. The ANTIBALLISTIC MISSILE (ABM) TREATY limited the United States and the Soviet Union (see RUSSIA) to two ABM sites within their territory. One could be around their respective capitals and the other around a BALLISTIC MISSILE DEFENSE site. Limits were also placed on the number of ABM launchers for each site. The second part of the pact involved an EXECUTIVE AGREEMENT. The Interim Agreement on Strategic Offensive Weapons limited the number of land-based and sea-based intercontinental missile launchers for a five-year period. The Senate ratified the ABM Treaty on August 3, 1972.

President Nixon embraced the concept of ARMS CONTROL talks with the Soviet Union in early 1969 as part of his DÉTENTE strategy. The goal was to set limits on Soviet power so as to make the U.S.–Soviet superpower relationship more manageable. An important consideration in this strategy was the widespread belief that the American public would not support high levels of defense spending or aggressive foreign policies after VIETNAM. Support for this view could be found in the one-vote margin of victory in an August 1969 Senate vote to support the deployment of an ABM system around missile sites in the Midwest.

The Nixon administration also faced a growing strategic problem. The United States had successfully tested a multiple independently targeted reentry vehicle (MIRV) in 1968 that gave it the capacity to place multiple warheads on missile launchers and direct them at different targets. The Soviet Union had not yet perfected MIRV technology but could be expected to do so and therein lay the problem. The size of the U.S. intercontinental ballistic missile force (ICBMs) was relatively stable. That of the Soviet Union was undergoing dramatic growth. It had increased from 292 ICBMs in 1966 to 858 in 1968 and was projected to continue growing. These numbers with MIRVs in place would give the Soviet Union a decided military advantage.

The solution arrived at by the Nixon administration was to offer to limit ABM construction in return for a five-year freeze on nuclear weapons expansion. The treaty was valuable to the United States because it stopped Russian missile expansion, whose numbers exceeded those possessed of the United States, but did not require the United States to abandon any of its programs. For the Soviet Union, SALT I was valuable because Moscow retained a long-term right to deploy MIRV warheads. Moscow also saw the treaty as recognition of their politicostrategic parity with the United States.

The SALT I Treaty enjoyed broad support among the American public. Opposition came primarily from political conservatives, but even their opposition was limited out of the loyalty that conservative Republicans showed to President Nixon. Within the Senate, Senator Henry "Scoop" Jackson (D-Wash.) emerged as the key spokesperson for the conservative position. Jackson focused on the inequality in numbers that the executive agreement permitted. He rejected the argument made by SALT I supporters that the U.S. qualitative superiority more than compensated for the Soviet Union's quantitative superiority. Jackson was at a disadvantage in making his case because the numbers were contained in the executive agreement and not the treaty. As part of the political deal to gain the Senate's approval of SALT I, it was agreed that in future agreements the numbers would be part of a treaty and thus subject to senatorial ratification. This agreement was contained in the Jackson Amendment that the Senate endorsed by a 56-35 vote.

SALT I is significant because it comprises part of a series of arms control agreements negotiated between the United States and the Soviet Union during détente. It was followed by the VLADIVOSTOK ACCORDS and SALT II. This last treaty was not ratified and became a symbol of declining U.S.-Soviet relations. The SALT process was replaced by the STRATEGIC ARMS REDUCTION TALKS (START) in the Reagan administration. The influence of the ABM Treaty continues to be felt. The limitations it placed on the construction and development of ABM systems and ABM technologies serves as a central point in the debate between those who wish to construct a ballistic missile defense system and their opponents. This policy debate ended, at least for the moment, when in December 2001 President GEORGE W. BUSH announced that the U.S. was withdrawing from the ABM Treaty and that the U.S. would build a national ballistic missile defense system. This action effectively terminated the treaty in June 2002.

**Further reading:** Smith, Gerald C. *Doubletalk: The Story of the First Strategic Arms Limitation Talks.* New York: Doubleday, 1980.

## Strategic Arms Limitation Talks II

The second Strategic Arms Limitation Talks (SALT II) formally began in November 1972. The apparent outlines of an agreement were reached in November 1974, with the signing of the VLADIVOSTOK ACCORDS. The political vulnerability of the Ford administration to conservative attacks on its ARMS CONTROL policy in particular and DÉTENTE more generally led the Ford administration to pull back from a possible signing of SALT II in mid-1975. Technological breakthroughs also complicated the negotia-

tion process. The U.S. cruise missile and the Soviet backfire bomber presented new challenges. Both had strategic potential given their range but were not easily accommodated into the framework of the Vladivostok accords. In January 1976 SECRETARY OF STATE HENRY KISSINGER succeeded in negotiating a compromise agreement on how to count the cruise missile and the backfire bomber. GERALD FORD's administration was divided over the value of the agreement, and JIMMY CARTER apparently rejected it during the presidential campaign.

President Jimmy Carter wanted to move quickly on arms control. His second NATIONAL SECURITY COUNCIL paper consisted of a review of SALT II options. Speed was important because in October 1977 SALT I's five-year interim agreement would expire. Carter also shared the belief held by liberal proponents of arms control that the Vladivostok accords did not go far enough in placing limits on the size of the U.S. and Soviet nuclear arsenals. Thus, when negotiations resumed in March 1977, his administration proposed far- and deep-reaching cuts. The Soviet negotiators reacted angrily, for they had expected the Vladivostok accords to serve as the basis for the agreement. They saw the Carter proposal as an effort to undermine arms control and as a threat to Brezhnev's political standing in Moscow.

It would take two years of talks to work out a negotiating framework that would bring together elements of the Vladivostok accords and Carter's deep-cut position. It was agreed in September 1977 that SALT II would contain: a treaty lasting until 1985 organized around a three-tiered agreement on weapons systems, such as that proposed under the Vladivostok accords with some reduction in numbers; a three-year protocol on controversial issues; and a statement of principles based on the idea of deep cuts that would serve as the basis for future negotiations. The next 21 months were spent filling in the details of the agreement. Both sides had agreed to abide by the terms of the lapsed interim agreement while negotiations were completed. The SALT II Treaty was signed on June 18, 1979.

Salt II encountered significant and immediate problems when presented to the Senate for ratification. Senator Henry "Scoop" Jackson (D-Wash.) led the conservative opposition in the Senate, as he had with SALT I. Outside of the Senate, the American public had become less supportive of arms control. Revelations about the presence of a Soviet brigade in CUBA, Soviet support for a Marxist regime in ETHIOPIA, and charges of Soviet violations of SALT I created an atmosphere hostile to arms control. The Committee on the Present Danger, led by former SALT negotiator Paul Nitze, provided a powerful and organized voice against SALT II. In fact, some commentators assert that by late 1979 details of SALT II were not the focal point of the debate. One important exception was a growing concern for the ability of the American INTELLIGENCE COMMUNITY to verify the agreement.

SALT II was never voted on by the Senate. The Soviet invasion of AFGHANISTAN led President Carter to withdraw the treaty from consideration. At best, its prospects had been slender. Few supporters numbered the necessary 67 votes for its ratification. The Senate Foreign Relations Committee defeated a number of killer amendments before sending the treaty to the full Senate, but even then it did so with 23 amendments, any of which could have provoked the Soviet Union to abandon the treaty.

The SALT II Treaty is significant because it marks the end of a period of U.S.-Soviet collaboration. It shows how fragile agreements can be due to changing domestic and international conditions. Within the study of American foreign policy, the SALT II Treaty is studied for what it reveals about the underlying dynamics of congressional-executive relations. Finally, the SALT II Treaty is instructive for the impact of presidential transitions on foreign policy. An agreement based on the Vladivostok accords that was negotiated by a Republican administration was easily within the reach of the incoming Democratic Carter administration but rejected in favor its own treaty.

**Further reading:** Caldwell, Dan. *The Dynamics of Domestic Politics and Arms Control: The SALT II Treaty Refusal.* Columbia: University of South Carolina Press, 1991; Talbot, Strobe T. *Endgame: The Inside Story of SALT II.* New York: HarperCollins, 1980.

## Strategic Arms Reduction Talks

The Strategic Arms Reduction Talks (START) replaced the STRATEGIC ARMS LIMITATION TALKS (SALT) as the principal vehicle for conducting ARMS CONTROL talks with the Soviet Union. It has produced two treaties, START I and START II plus a commitment to pursue START III.

In his campaign for the presidency against JIMMY CARTER, RONALD REAGAN had characterized the SALT II treaty as fatally flawed because it placed the Soviet Union in a position of military superiority. He stated that only after restoring the military balance between the two sides could a meaningful arms control agreement be negotiated. Reagan's first concrete proposal was his "zero option" that was presented in November 1981. It dealt with intermediate-range nuclear forces stationed in Europe. In the same speech in which he unveiled his zero option, Reagan indicated that his administration was readying for a new round of strategic arms talks, to be known as START.

Little visible movement was forthcoming, and public concern began to mount over the administration's commitment to arms control and its loose language about NUCLEAR WAR. The nuclear freeze movement became the focal point of efforts to push the Reagan administration back to the arms control negotiating table. In June 1982, more than 500,000 people gathered in New York to protest the arms race, and calls for a nuclear freeze were approved in eight states.

To blunt this criticism and regain the political initiative on arms control, the Reagan administration unveiled a two-step START proposal in May 1982. In the first step a reduction in the number of intercontinental ballistic missiles and submarine-launched ballistic missile warheads and launchers would be set. In the second step equal limits on throw weights would be set. The Soviet Union rejected the proposal, but negotiations continued. In May 1983 Reagan put forward a revised START proposal built around the concept of a nuclear "build down," which called for each side to reduce the overall size of its nuclear forces as it proceeded with weapons modernization. The Soviet Union also rejected this proposal as "old poison in new bottles" but continued to negotiate. A breakthrough came at the 1986 Reykjavík Summit when the two sides agreed to reduce all strategic nuclear weapons by 50 percent over a five-year period.

This breakthrough proved to be somewhat illusory, since it was July 1991 before President GEORGE H. W. BUSH and Soviet president Mikhail Gorbachev signed the START I Treaty. START I was submitted to the Senate for ratification in November 1991. It was ratified in October 1992. Deeper cuts were agreed to shortly thereafter when Bush and Boris Yeltsin agreed to a START II Treaty in January 1993. Rather than the product of a new round of protracted negotiations, this agreement was more the result of a series of unilateral actions. In September 1991 Bush announced a series of moves that included taking all strategic bombers off of high alert and stopping the development and deployment of mobile intercontinental ballistic missiles (ICBMs). Gorbachev responded by calling for the elimination of all land-based tactical nuclear weapons as well as other measures. In his January 1992 State of the Union address, Bush called for reducing by one-third the number of submarine-launched ballistic missiles in return for RUSSIA, Ukraine, and Kazakhstan eliminating all of their heavy warheads ICBMs. Yeltsin proposed even deeper cuts, leaving each side with 2,500 warheads.

START negotiations were hampered by a rapidly changing international landscape that included the breakup of the Soviet Union and the dispersal of its nuclear inventory among four states: Russia, Belarus, Ukraine, and Kazakhstan. After several months of negotiations a protocol was signed whereby the last three of these new nuclear states agreed to destroy their nuclear weapons by 1999. After this, START I was ratified in October 1992. Progress, however, was slow, and these deadlines were not met. START II was ratified by the Senate in 1997, but now Russian concern with NORTH ATLANTIC TREATY ORGANIZATION (NATO) expansion and the war in YUGOSLAVIA created impediments to the agreement. The United States's continued interest in a BALLISTIC MISSILE DEFENSE system and Russia's objections to such a system further complicated matters. It was only in April 2000, after Vladimir Putin was elected president, that the Russian Duma gave its approval to START II. Even though START II had not yet been ratified by the Duma, in 1997 President BILL CLINTON and Yeltsin signed a set of principles establishing the outlines of a START III Treaty. Progress on SALT III has been limited due to continued political and economic difficulties in Russia.

**Further reading:** Beschloss, Michael R., and Strobe Talbot. *At the Highest Levels: The Inside Story of the End of the Cold War.* Boston: Little, Brown, 1993.

## Strategic Arms Reduction Treaty I

The Strategic Arms Reduction Treaty I (START I) is the first treaty signed as a result of the STRATEGIC ARMS REDUCTION TALKS begun by President RONALD REAGAN. START I is the most complicated and comprehensive ARMS CONTROL ever negotiated. The treaty, when combined with its various statements of understanding, data exchanges, definitions, protocols, declarations, letters of correspondence, and related agreements, runs to 280 pages. START I sets central limits of 1,600 strategic offensive delivery systems and 600 warheads. Sublimits are established for various categories of delivery systems. The net effect of START I was to bring about a 46 percent reduction in Soviet throw weight. The treaty also contained significant provisions dealing with a system of notifications and inspections to monitor compliance.

President GEORGE H. W. BUSH submitted START I to the Senate for ratification on November 25, 1991. One condition attached by the Senate Foreign Relations Committee was that the four Soviet successor states (RUSSIA, Kazakhstan, Belarus, and Ukraine) that had come into possession of the Soviet Union's nuclear arsenal would agree to be legally bound by the treaty. A May 23, 1992, protocol signed by these states pledged their adherence to START I. The Foreign Relations Committee also called for a compliance report by the PRESIDENT and the rapid conclusion of a START II Treaty based on a June 17, 1992, agreement signed by Bush and Russian president Boris Yeltsin on June 17, 1992, in Lisbon. The Senate Armed Services Committee and the Senate Select Committee on INTELLIGENCE expressed strong reservations about compliance, verification, and monitoring issues. The Senate gave its approval by a vote of 93-6 on October 1, 1992.

START I entered into force in December 1994. An extensive system of on-site inspections was established. Between March 1995 and July 1995, U.S. inspectors visited 65 locations in the former Soviet Union. Thirty-six sites in the United States were visited. Both the United States and Russia reduced their nuclear forces ahead of the timetable set by the treaty. Kazakhstan, Belarus, and Ukraine have returned all of the nuclear weapons on their territory to Russia. Deteriorating economic conditions in Russia and the three former Soviet republics have made the cost of complying with START I (and START II) a major concern. Rather than eliminate or alter agreed upon practices for reducing force levels, the United States established the Nunn-Lugar Cooperative Threat Reduction program to provide needed financial resources.

START I is significant because it marked the beginning of a new era in U.S.-Soviet arms control agreements. Where the STRATEGIC ARMS LIMITATION TALKS (SALT) carried out by the Nixon, Ford, and Carter administrations produced treaties that largely ratified existing nuclear inventories, START I successfully brought about cuts in the number of nuclear weapons. It was rapidly overtaken by START II, whose main features were agreed upon even before Senate approval was given to START I.

## Strategic Arms Reduction Treaty II

The Strategic Arms Reduction Treaty II (START II) is the second product of the STRATEGIC ARMS REDUCTION TALKS (START) process begun by President RONALD REAGAN. The principles underlying the agreement were set at a June 1992 meeting between U.S. president GEORGE H. W. BUSH and Russian president Boris Yeltsin. The final details were worked out in December 1992, and START II was signed on January 3, 1993. The Senate Foreign Relations Committee began its hearings on the START II Treaty in March 1993 but suspended hearings until START I had entered into force (December 1994) and there was evidence that the Russian Duma was going to take action on START II. Hearings resumed in January 1995, with the committee giving its approval in December, and the full Senate following suit by a vote of 87-4 on January 26, 1996.

The treaty sets in motion a two-phase reduction in the number of strategic NUCLEAR WEAPONS that each side can possess. By the end of Phase I, the United States and Russia are to reduce their inventory of strategic nuclear warheads to 3,800–4,250. Sublimits are established for the numbers that can be deployed on heavy bombers, on submarine-launched ballistic missiles (SLBMs), and as multiple independently targeted reentry vehicles (MIRVs) on intercontinental ballistic missiles (ICBMs). Phase I is to be completed seven years after the START I treaty enters into force. Phase II requires that each side reduce its total number of deployed strategic nuclear warheads to between 3,000 and 3,500. None may be on MIRVed ICBMs, and limits are placed on the number of warheads that may be placed on SLMS, although these may be MIRVed. Phase II was to be completed by 2003.

The Russian Duma took up the START II Treaty in July 1995, with members expressing reservations about the costs of dismantling weapons and "downloading" multiple warhead missiles into single warhead missiles in order to meet START II weapons limits as well as about the strategic implications of a reduced nuclear force for Russian national security concerns. Continued domestic political conflict within Russia as well as social and economic upheavals sidetracked Russian ratification of START II. Russian resentment over NORTH ATLANTIC TREATY ORGANIZATION (NATO) expansion into Eastern Europe and involvement in BOSNIA AND HERZEGOVINA and KOSOVO further contributed to a political atmosphere in which ratification of START II was impossible. Ratification came only in April 2000 after Vladimir Putin was elected president.

The lengthy delay in gaining Russian approval of the START II created significant problems for the deadlines established by the treaty. In March 1997 a summit conference took place in Helsinki between President BILL CLINTON and Yeltsin, at which time a protocol to the treaty was signed extending the dates for Phase I and Phase II reductions. Phase I reductions were completed in December 2001, and Phase II reductions are moved back from January 1, 2003, to December 31, 2007.

## Strategic Arms Reduction Treaty III

In an attempt to overcome Russian opposition to the STRATEGIC ARMS REDUCTION TREATY II (START II), President BILL CLINTON and President Boris Yeltsin met in Helsinki in March 1997 and agreed to extend the time period specified by START II for the reduction of U.S. and Russian nuclear arsenals and to lay the foundation for a START III Treaty. The target figure set for START III reductions was 1,500 warheads for each side. Proposed START III reductions were seen as necessary in order to calm Russian fears that due to economic constraints they would not be able to keep Russian nuclear forces at the START II levels, leaving the United States with a strategic advantage.

The negotiations promised to be complex and challenging. In fall 2000 Russian officials were calling for START III negotiations to begin but warning that they would not move forward on START III if the United States sought to amend the SALT I ANTIBALLISTIC MISSILE (ABM) TREATY. Earlier in May 2000, in congressional testimony, the JOINT CHIEFS OF STAFF endorsed further cuts but only down to 2,000–2,500 deployed NUCLEAR WEAPONS. They said deep cuts could have an "unpredictable impact on DETERRENCE" and might scrap some bombers and submarines needed for conventional war.

Events overtook the START III agreement when in 2002 President GEORGE W. BUSH and Russian president Vladimir Putin agreed to cut back the number of deployed warheads in their nuclear arsenals to 2,200 by 2012. The approach was tentatively titled the STRATEGIC OFFENSIVE REDUCTIONS TALKS (SORT).

## Strategic Defense Initiative

Also known as "Star Wars," the Strategic Defense Initiative (SDI) was a long-term research and development program designed to identify viable policy options for creating a nuclear defense system. It was introduced by President RONALD REAGAN in a March 1983 speech that called upon the scientific community to find a way to escape a situation in which the security of free people "did not rest upon the threat of instant U.S. retaliation to deter a Soviet attack. . . . [I]s it not worth every investment necessary to free the world from the threat of NUCLEAR WAR?"

Originally, the decision as to which system to pursue was scheduled to be made in the 1990s. However, in early 1987, the Reagan administration began examining the possibility of an early deployment of SDI. As envisioned by most observers, Reagan's SDI system involved a series of four layers that when combined formed a protective shield. Each layer performed the same tasks: search out and detect targets, track them, distinguish between real and dummy targets, and intercept and destroy the real targets.

The four layers correspond to the four phases in an intercontinental missile's (ICBM) trajectory. The boost phase occurs immediately following launch and lasts several hundred seconds. The major advantage in attacking incoming missiles in this phase is that there are relatively few targets, and these are vulnerable and easily detected. The major difficulty is the short length of time available and the exotic nature of the technologies needed to counterattack. The second phase is the post-boost phase. It also lasts only a few hundred seconds. In this stage the "bus" deploys its warheads and penetration aids. Defense is complicated by the added number of targets and the need to discriminate between real and dummy warheads. The third phase lasts approximately 1,000 seconds. It is the mid-course phase. Warheads and dummies are easily targeted here but still need to be distinguished. The final phase is the reentry phase that lasts 30 to 100 seconds. The atmosphere acts as a filter, separating real and dummy targets. The problem is the shortness of time available to act. Targets have "keep out" distances beyond which warheads must be intercepted and destroyed if they are to be protected.

The Reagan administration gradually cut back on the scope and funding level of the SDI program without ever formally abandoning its goal of creating a workable defensive nuclear shield. This changed in 1989 when SECRETARY OF DEFENSE Dick Cheney stated that the SDI program had been "oversold" as a leak-proof system. He indicated that it was "extremely remote" that such an umbrella could be built. Still, the Bush administration moved ahead with a revised version of SDI, known as "brilliant pebbles." In this plan missiles would be sent into space and orbit the Earth in layers. They would possess the ability to detect the launch of enemy missiles and then ram into them at high speed, thus destroying them.

SDI officials came to an end in May 1993 when President BILL CLINTON's Secretary of Defense Les Aspin announced that the SDI Office was being closed and replaced by a BALLISTIC MISSILE DEFENSE Office. It had the mission of developing follow-on programs to the Patriot missile system used in the PERSIAN GULF WAR. The focus of research thus shifted from space-based missiles to short-range ground-launched missiles.

SDI was neither the first nor the last missile defense system investigated by American policy makers. Its most famous predecessor was the antiballistic missile (ABM) system advanced by Secretary of Defense ROBERT MCNAMARA. More recently both the Clinton and GEORGE W. BUSH administrations have pursued BALLISTIC MISSILE DEFENSE systems of one type or another.

SDI is significant to the conduct of American defense policy on several dimensions. First, it involves a case study of the difficulty of moving from an abstract idea to a concrete piece of technology. Second, it highlights the problems involved in integrating many individual technologies into complicated systems. Third, SDI was very controversial with regard to both cost and desirability. The logic of COLD WAR nuclear DETERRENCE rests upon the principle of mutual assured destruction (MAD). Under this condition neither side can escape retaliation and destruction should it go first. A defensive shield would negate this condition by giving one side an advantage. Its existence therefore is held to be destabilizing.

**Further reading:** Miller, Steven E., and Stephen Van Evera, eds. *The Star Wars Controversy.* Princeton, N.J.: Princeton University Press, 1986; Thompson, E. P., ed. *Star Wars.* New York: Pantheon, 1985; Trucker, Robert W., et al. *SDI and U.S. Foreign Policy.* Boulder, Colo.: Westview, 1987.

## Strategic Offense Reductions Treaty (Moscow Treaty)

Signed by President GEORGE W. BUSH and Russian president Vladimir Putin, the Strategic Offensive Reductions Treaty (SORT) was concluded in Moscow on May 24, 2002. The treaty overtakes the never negotiated STRATEGIC ARMS REDUCTIONS TREATY (START) III and was negotiated against the backdrop of the announced withdrawal by the United States from the 1972 ANTIBALLISTIC MISSILE (ABM) TREATY.

SORT breaks new ground in treaty language. It starts from the premise that RUSSIA is a friend of the United States and not an enemy. The body of the treaty contains only 10 sentences. It lacks the appendices, caveats, statements of understanding, and covenants found in earlier ARMS CONTROL agreements. In essence, the treaty permits each side to do as it pleases so long as their nuclear arsenal is reduced to 2,200 deployed warheads by December 31, 2012. As one senator observed, unlike in previous cases in which verification was a major concern, in this treaty "there are no mileposts for performance. There is nothing really to verify except good faith." Bush would have preferred no treaty at all in his minimalist approach to arms control. A simple verbal agreement would have sufficed. The Russians were not interested in such a loose construction. SECRETARY OF STATE COLIN POWELL overcame Bush's reluctance to negotiate a treaty and opposition from Vice President Dick Cheney and SECRETARY OF DEFENSE Donald Rumsfeld in clearing the way for SORT.

The agreement was negotiated in six months. The Russians wanted a treaty that would eliminate the number of missiles, long-range bombers, and submarines. Bush wanted to restrict deployed warheads. Bush had promised to cut the size of the U.S. NUCLEAR WEAPONS ARSENAL in his presidential campaign and sought the agreement as a means of fulfilling this promise. Putin sought an agreement because Russia could not afford to maintain its nuclear arsenal at its current size. Putin also sought to insert language that promised an American missile defense system would not be directed at Russia. Information sharing proved to be another roadblock to the agreement, as the two sides could not agree on what information to provide the other with. In the end it was agreed that the START I inspection and notification system would be used until a new system would be agreed upon. A third problem centered on how much time needed to be given if one side wanted to withdraw from the treaty. The United States wanted only a six-month warning or 45 days if the 2,200 warhead limit was going to be exceeded. Russia felt this was too little warning.

Three weeks prior to the Bush-Putin meeting, both sides informed their negotiators that they wanted to sign an agreement at the May summit. Agreement was reached through compromise and brevity. Weapon systems were not addressed, and warheads were not to be destroyed, so no inspection system was needed. No mention was made of missile defense systems. A three-month warning period for withdrawal from the treaty was set.

The Senate took up consideration of the treaty in July 2002. The Senate gave its approval to the treaty in March

2003, but Russian ratification was not forthcoming until May 2003, due to Russian opposition to the IRAQ WAR.

## Sudan

Sudan is the largest country in Africa. It has an area of 967,500 square miles, making it almost as large as the continental United States. It has a population of 30 million people. Modern Sudan existed as a collection of small independent political units until 1820, when EGYPT conquered and unified much of the region. In 1855 a Nationalist revolt led to the establishment of an independent kingdom that was brought under joint British-Egyptian control in the 1890s. GREAT BRITAIN, which exercised the dominant influence over Sudan, divided Sudan into northern and southern administrative zones in 1924. Northern Sudan is heavily Muslim, whereas the South is predominantly Christian and animist. In 1948 the Independence Front based in the North sought political union with Egypt. This did not transpire, and instead Egypt and Great Britain determined in 1953 to give Sudan its independence, effective January 1, 1956. Fearing they would be discriminated against, the southern Sudanese rebelled in 1955, setting off a 17-year civil war that ended in 1972. The civil war resumed in the early 1980s, sparked in large measure by the government's September 1983 decision to embark upon an Islamicization campaign. More than 4 million southerners have been displaced in the fighting.

Sudanese foreign policy has been defined largely in terms of solidarity with Arab causes. In June 1967 Sudan declared war on ISRAEL and broke diplomatic relations with the United States. Relations improved in the early 1970s when a Communist coup was thwarted, and Soviet influence reduced. By the mid-1980s Sudan was the largest recipient of American development and military aid in sub-Saharan Africa. A 1989 coup brought a military government into power that has instituted a harsh penal code based on Islamic law that includes amputations and stonings. U.S. aid was suspended at this point. Sudan opposed IRAQ's invasion of KUWAIT but also opposed U.S. military action against it.

In the early 1990s Sudan's support for terrorist causes became a major source of concern for the United States. Noted terrorists, including OSAMA BIN LADEN, Abu Nidal, and Carlos the Jackal, operated out of Sudan. In 1993 President Clinton put Sudan on the list of states that sponsored international TERRORISM. His administration followed this up in 1997 with comprehensive economic and financial sanctions. In August 1998 the United States launched retaliatory missile strikes against a suspected chemical weapons manufacturing plant in Sudan for its support of the terrorists who bombed American embassies in East Africa. After the SEPTEMBER 11, 2001, terrorist attacks in the United States,

Sudan publicly supported U.S. efforts against the AL-QAEDA terrorist network, but it also criticized U.S. air attacks on the Taliban and opposed widening the war against terrorism.

On the economic front, the United States has worked with Sudan since 1986 to provide emergency humanitarian aid for those displaced in the civil war. One of the recurring points of controversy is the government's diversion of aid intended for the South to the North. More generally, the combination of drought, inflation, civil war, and the imposition of Islamic law led to an economic collapse. Sudan became the world's largest debtor to the WORLD BANK and INTERNATIONAL MONETARY FUND in the early 1990s. Sudan began exporting OIL in October 2000, which has resulted in some improvement in its economic outlook. However, serious problems remain.

See also ARAB-ISRAELI CONFLICT; ISLAM, POLITICAL.

**Further reading:** Woodward, Peter. *Sudan, 1899–1989: The Untold Story.* Boulder, Colo.: Westview, 1989.

## Suez crisis

The Suez crisis of 1956 effectively marked the end of British and French efforts to play the role of superpower independent from the United States in world affairs. Acting without U.S. approval but expecting that it would come, BRITAIN, FRANCE, and ISRAEL planned a military operation against EGYPT that was designed to reestablish British control over the Suez Canal. The Eisenhower administration, however, publicly rebuked the British and French for their actions and sponsored a UNITED NATIONS resolution that demanded their withdrawal.

U.S. attention had been drawn to the Middle East in the early 1950s as the Eisenhower administration sought to create an ALLIANCE network that would further encircle the Soviet Union. It was to be patterned on the SOUTHEAST EAST ASIA TREATY ORGANIZATION (SEATO). To that end, in 1955 the Baghdad Pact was formed, linking TURKEY, IRAQ, IRAN, PAKISTAN, and Great Britain. The United States did not formally join due to Israeli objections.

Egypt had been a British colony. In 1952 Colonel Gamal Abdel Nasser led a successful revolt against the pro-British monarch, King Farouk. Once in power Nasser promised to take control of the Suez Canal from Great Britain. He also promised land reform, and in 1955 the United States offered to fund the construction of the Aswan Dam that would provide electric power and water. The offer was withdrawn abruptly in 1956 as U.S. officials reacted negatively to Egypt's involvement in an anti-Israel alliance, proclamations of COLD WAR neutrality, and purchase of arms from Soviet ally CZECHOSLOVAKIA. This last move posed a direct challenge to the ability of the Baghdad Pact to stop communist influence in the Middle East.

Nasser responded by seizing the Suez Canal. This act provided the spark for the British, French, and Israelis. Their plan called for Israel to attack Egyptian positions in the Sinai Desert and push toward the Suez Canal. Great Britain and France would use this as a pretext for their own military intervention. The Israeli attack occurred on October 29, 1956. After a French and British veto of a UN Security Council resolution condemning Israel, British, and French forces joined the conflict on October 31. A cease-fire was called on November 6, and in December UN peacekeepers took up positions in the Suez and returned the canal to Egypt. CONGRESS had held up approval of DWIGHT EISENHOWER's Middle East resolution, also known as the EISENHOWER DOCTRINE, until Israeli forces had left the Sinai and assurances had been given that Israel would not face a cut off in aid because of its participation in the crisis.

The United States was somewhat ambivalent at the outset of this drama. Washington sympathized with its allies' desire to bring stability to the area, and it distrusted Nasser, but it did not want war. In the end the United States reacted negatively for several reasons. First, the Suez crisis diverted attention from the Soviet Union's invasion of HUNGARY that was going on at the same time. Second, the United States feared that this action would open up the Middle East to Soviet influence. Many commentators note that it was the U.S. decision not to fund the Aswan Dam project that actually opened the door to Soviet influence in the region. Third, the conflict occurred on the eve of a presidential ELECTION. A war in the Middle East would have complicated the Eisenhower administration's reelection efforts, and U.S. diplomats worked through September and October to forestall military action by Washington's allies.

See also ARAB-ISRAELI CONFLICT; RUSSIA.

## summit conferences/diplomacy

Summit DIPLOMACY, the face-to-face meetings of leaders, is an important element of modern diplomacy that has been made possible by breakthroughs in transportation and communication technologies. Given the United States's military and economic dominance since WORLD WAR II, American PRESIDENTs have been among the most active practitioners of summit diplomacy.

Three different eras of American summitry can be identified. The first consisted of WORLD WAR II summit conferences designed to hold together the wartime coalition and establish the outlines of the postwar world. The second consisted of East-West COLD WAR superpower summits. The earliest summits pitted the United States against the Soviet Union as cold war rivals. Later ones were designed to institutionalize DÉTENTE and then to manage the transition to the post–cold war era. The era of summitry

overlaps the second chronologically somewhat but has a different focus and set of players. Beginning in 1975 these involved summit meetings of Western leaders that were designed to manage their international economic relations. Over time noneconomic issues such as TERRORISM and nuclear proliferation worked their way on to the agenda.

Summit diplomacy is popular for a number of reasons. First, it allows policy makers to establish personal relationships with their counterparts that can dispel stereotypes and provide a foundation of trust on which future agreements can be based. President FRANKLIN ROOSEVELT valued his summit meetings with British prime minister Winston Churchill and Soviet leader Joseph Stalin for this very reason. Second, summit diplomacy permits leaders to circumvent the conservatism, indecision, and blocking action that often emerges from decision-making processes dominated by bureaucratic forces, thus permitting dramatic breakthroughs to be achieved. This was most dramatically evident at the CAMP DAVID Summit held by President JIMMY CARTER that brought Egyptian president Anwar Sadat and Israeli prime minister Menachen Begin together.

Offsetting these positive traits are a number of negative ones. First, because leaders are freed from constraints they may enter into ill-conceived agreements. The Reykjavík Summit between President RONALD REAGAN and Soviet leader Mikhail Gorbachev is frequently cited as an example, with Reagan temporarily accepting Gorbachev's proposal to do away with strategic NUCLEAR WEAPONS. A second potential disadvantage of summit diplomacy is that leaders will give too much credence to their personal evaluations of the opponent. Soviet leader Nikita Khrushchev reportedly came away from his 1961 Vienna summit conference with President JOHN KENNEDY convinced that he could intimidate him. Finally, there is the danger that the very act of holding a summit conference or ending one with a broad statement of agreed upon principles will be mistaken for an actual solution of a problem. U.S.-Japanese conferences designed to deal with trade imbalances often had this quality. In these cases the failure to solve the policy problems was compounded by raised public expectations that something has been done. Public disillusionment can greatly complicate future diplomatic ventures.

The United States engaged in a brief, highly symbolic summit conference as the official launching point for the IRAQ WAR. On March 16 the United States, GREAT BRITAIN, and SPAIN held a one-hour summit conference in the Azores. It ended with President GEORGE W. BUSH issuing an ultimatum to Saddam Hussein to go into exile or face military action. The next day they announced that they would pull their resolution authorizing military force against IRAQ from the UNITED NATIONS because they had reached the conclusion that "council consensus will not be possible."

That night President Bush addressed the nation and gave Saddam Hussein 48 hours to leave Iraq. On Tuesday, March 18, Saddam Hussein rejected Bush's ultimatum.

See also CONFERENCE DIPLOMACY; RUSSIA.

**Further reading:** Eubank, Keith. *Summit Conferences, 1919–1960.* Norman: University of Oklahoma Press, 1966; de Menil, George, and Anthony Solomon. *Economic Summitry.* New York: Council on Foreign Relations, 1983; Weihmiller, Gordon R., and Dusko Doder. *U.S.-Soviet Summits: An Account of East-West Diplomacy at the Top, 1955–1985.* Washington, D.C.: Georgetown University, Institute for the Study of Diplomacy, 1986.

## Sumner, Charles (1811–1874) *senator*

Charles Sumner, senator from Massachusetts, chaired the Senate Foreign Relations Committee from 1861 to 1871. Strong willed, politically ambitious, and an outspoken abolitionist, Sumner was a commanding figure in American foreign policy during this period. Sumner worked tirelessly to force SECRETARY OF STATE WILLIAM SEWARD out of President ABRAHAM LINCOLN's AMERICAN CIVIL WAR cabinet. Surprisingly, then, it was Sumner who played a crucial role in supporting Seward's purchase of ALASKA in 1867. On the day in which the Senate voted on the measure, Sumner gave a lengthy and impassioned speech supporting it. On April 9, 1867, the Senate gave its approval by a vote of 37-2. Significantly, Sumner included in his supportive speech a warning against "indiscriminant and costly annexation."

These words would prove to be prophetic when President ULYSSES GRANT sent a treaty to the Senate that provided for the annexation of the DOMINICAN REPUBLIC and the assumption of its international debts. Grant and Sumner were political rivals who belonged to different wings of the REPUBLICAN PARTY. Grant, however, recognized the importance of Sumner's backing for the annexation and thought that he had obtained a pledge of support. In fact, Sumner would vigorously oppose the treaty. For his part Sumner favored establishing a protectorate in which the Dominican Republic and other states in the West Indies would form an independent confederacy under U.S. protection. Without Sumner's support the Senate Foreign Relations Committee rejected the treaty by a vote of 5-2 in March 1870, and the full Senate likewise rejected it with a 28-28 tie vote in June. Grant and his allies were now determined to force Sumner out as chair of the Senate Foreign Relations Committee. They succeeded in March 1871, when the Republican caucus voted 26-21 in favor of his ouster.

Sumner played an important role in still another Grant foreign-policy undertaking. This centered on resolving the *Alabama* claims. During the Civil War the Con-

federacy had arranged for the purchase of warships from Great Britain. Collectively these ships inflicted considerable damage upon Northern merchant ships. The United States protested this action and threatened to modify the 1818 Neutrality Act so that the United States could sell warships to belligerents in future conflicts that Great Britain might be involved in. In 1869 Sumner raised the stakes even higher.

With the dispute not yet settled, he proclaimed that Great Britain owed the United States $15 million in direct damages and that when combined with other indirect losses the total escalated to $110 million. Sumner then added on the costs of a prolonged Civil War because he asserted that British support allowed the Confederacy to fight for two more years. This brought the grand total owed to $2.125 billion. While not directly saying so, Sumner made it clear that he did not expect Great Britain to be able to pay such a price and that he would accept CANADA as payment. Sumner's speech produced an impasse in talks to settle the *Alabama* claims, and it would not be until 1871 when the Treaty of Washington was signed that this was accomplished.

**Further reading:** David, Donald. *Charles Sumner and the Rights of Man.* New York: Random House, 1970.

## Supreme Court

The Supreme Court is the branch of the federal government that is least continuously involved in foreign affairs. Supreme Court decisions have, however, played significant roles in determining the shape of U.S. foreign policy over time and in several areas. The justices have arbitrated disputes between the legislative and executive branches, the national government and states, and the national government and citizens.

The Supreme Court sits atop the federal judiciary. In FEDERALIST PAPERS 78 ALEXANDER HAMILTON described the judiciary as the "least dangerous" of the branches of government. And initially it enjoyed relatively little prestige. This began to change when John Marshall became chief justice. He broke new ground when, in 1803, in *Marbury v. Madison*, Marshall advanced the notion of judicial review by declaring part of the Judiciary Act of 1789 unconstitutional. The idea of judicial review is not found in the wording of the CONSTITUTION, but it is implied in the belief that the courts were best qualified to interpret the Constitution. Hamilton had alluded to this role in Federalist 78 when he argued that since the Constitution was the clearest expression of the public's will, by allowing the Constitution to check the other branches, judicial review would serve as a surrogate voice for the people. It is the power of judicial review and the grant of original Supreme

Court jurisdiction over matters involving the United States and foreign governments that provides the Supreme Court with its point of entry into influencing U.S. foreign policy.

The popular perception is that the Supreme Court exists above politics in rendering its decisions. The reality is just the opposite. Politics pervades the Court's activities from the selection of its members to the cases it decides to hear to its verdicts. Justices have lifetime appointments. Appointed by the PRESIDENT and approved by the Senate, justices are selected on a combination of merit, geography, race, gender, and political ideology. In legislative and executive branch politics, ideology is generally defined on a liberal-conservative continuum. In judicial politics it is also relevant to discuss ideology in terms of how open justices perceive the Constitution to be to reinterpretation. At one end of the continuum we find strict constructionists who hold that the only way to change the meaning of the Constitution is through a constitutional amendment. It cannot be done via judicial interpretation. At the other we find those who believe in a position referred to as judicial interpretivism that holds that the Constitution is a living document and that the founders could not have foreseen all of the circumstances in which decisions would be needed.

The Supreme Court receives some 7,000 petitions per year to hear cases. That number is ultimately reduced to between 90 and 120 cases. Political ideology, public opinion, INTEREST-GROUP activity, and the actions of the legislative and executive branches all go into deciding which of these cases will be heard. The most common path to the Supreme Court is through an appeal, or writ of certiorari, of a decision by a lower federal court. The remaining cases are brought to the Supreme Court through the right of appeal from state supreme court decisions. Less than 1 percent of the cases reach the Supreme Court as the court of original jurisdiction. One requirement for a case to be heard is that it involves real injury. The Court cannot give an advisory opinion. The case must also involve a legal principle and not a "political question." The doctrine of political questions has been frequently employed by the Supreme Court to sidestep foreign-policy disputes. In 1987, for example, 110 members of CONGRESS brought suit in *Lawry v. Reagan*, asserting that President RONALD REAGAN had violated the Constitution by failing to comply with the WAR POWERS RESOLUTION during the IRAN-IRAQ WAR when he sent U.S. naval vessels into a combat zone. The Supreme Court refused to hear the case on the grounds that it was a political question involving the two other branches of the federal government.

Supreme Court decisions are eminently political. They not only hold the potential for shaping the outcome of a specific issue but also for altering (or reaffirming) the distribution of political power within the United States for long periods of time. In the case of its foreign-policy decisions, the Supreme Court has left a decided impact in three areas. First, its rulings have consistently supported the POWER of the federal government over states. It did so with its ruling in *WARE V. HYLTON* and in 2000 with its ruling in *CROSBY V. NATIONAL TRADE BOARD*. Second, the Supreme Court has consistently upheld the power of the presidency over the other two branches. It has done so through rulings supporting the PRESIDENT over Congress such as in *U.S. V. CURTISS-WRIGHT EXPORT CORPORATION*. It also has frequently declined to hear cases that might involve the courts in a battle with the president by invoking the doctrine of political questions and the states' rights doctrine. Finally, the Supreme Court has sought to draw lines separating the acceptable and unacceptable exercise of government foreign-policy powers when the rights of American citizens are involved. In its rulings in *YOUNGSTOWN SHEET AND TUBE COMPANY V. SAWYER* and *Nixon v. New York Times*, also known as the PENTAGON PAPERS case, the Court found that the executive branch had overstepped these limits.

In writing on the distribution of power between Congress and the president Justice Robert Jackson observed that a "twilight zone" exists in which both the president and Congress have concurrent power and where the distribution of power is uncertain. Foreign-policy issues are frequently found in this twilight zone. There is little likelihood that this situation will change in the future. Debates over the president's power to make war have, if anything, become more complex in an era of HUMANITARIAN INTERVENTIONS, ethnic civil wars, and TERRORISM. The spread of GLOBALIZATION ensures that it is only a matter of time until international TRADE POLICY, labor, and environmental issues involving some combination of the federal government, state governments, and individuals comes before the Supreme Court. Perhaps most challenging to the Supreme Court's ability to make authoritative decisions will be the development of international courts of justice claiming to have jurisdiction that extends to activities within states and is not restricted to their "foreign affairs."

**Further reading:** Congressional Research Service. *Foreign Policy Effects of the Supreme Court's Legislative Veto Decision*. Washington, D.C.: Congressional Research Service, February 23, 1984; Henkin, Louis. *Constitutionalism, Democracy, and Foreign Affairs*. New York: Columbia University Press, 1990.

## Syria

Syria has an area of 71,504 square miles and a population of 17 million people. Counting territory occupied by ISRAEL, it is about the size of North Dakota. Syria has historically been referred to as the Levant, a region that included the contemporary states of Syria, LEBANON, most of Israel and JORDAN, western IRAQ, and northern SAUDI ARABIA. The modern Syrian state came into existence following WORLD WAR I and the defeat of the Ottoman Empire, when FRANCE received a LEAGUE OF NATIONS mandate over the area comprising Syria and Lebanon. In 1926 Lebanon was made a separate state, and in 1936 a treaty was signed that gave Syria a high degree of autonomy but not independence from French rule. After WORLD WAR II, in early 1946, France granted independence to both Syria and Lebanon, but French troops continued to be stationed there. They did not leave until April 1946.

After independence Syria became one of the Arab states most opposed to Israel and hostile to Western influence in the region. It took part in the 1948–49 war, and it entered into economic and military agreements with the Soviet Union in response to the formation of the Baghdad Pact in 1955. Syria briefing joined with EGYPT to form the United Arab Republic from 1958 to 1961. Its territory, the Golan Heights, was invaded by Israel during the 1967 Six-Day War, and the land continues to be occupied by Israeli forces. Syria again fought with Egypt against Israel in the 1973 Yom Kippur War. In 1982 its troops fought against Israeli forces in Lebanon after Israeli prime minister Menachem Begin announced that Israel was annexing the Golan Heights. Syrian forces had entered Lebanon in 1976 as part of a PEACEKEEPING operation intended to end that country's civil war. They continue to remain in Lebanon as Syria now exerts a dominant influence over that country's political affairs.

U.S.-Syrian relations were long strained by Damascus's anti-Israeli and anti-Western stance. Beginning in the 1990s cooperation between the two has improved somewhat. Syria participated in the U.S.-led coalition of states that fought against Iraq in the PERSIAN GULF WAR. Syria also participated in the multilateral Madrid Middle East peace conference in October 1991. In March 2000 President Hafez al-Assad met with President BILL CLINTON in Geneva. Offsetting these positive developments has been continuing American concern over Syrian links to international TERRORISM. Syria has been on the STATE DEPARTMENT's list of states that sponsor international terrorism since the first edition in 1979. This designation places export sanctions on Syria and prevents it from receiving most forms of American FOREIGN AID and American military equipment.

Syria and the United States came into conflict during the IRAQ WAR. The United States warned Syria against supporting IRAQ and Saddam Hussein. In Washington voices were raised suggesting that military action against Syria might be forthcoming if that country did not change its policies.

See also ARAB-ISRAELI CONFLICT; PALESTINE LIBERATION ORGANIZATION; RUSSIA.

**Further reading:** Pipes, Daniel. *Syria beyond the Peace Process.* Washington, D.C.: Washington Institute for Near East Policy, 1996.

# T

## Taft, William (1857–1930) *president of the United States, secretary of war*

William Howard Taft was the 27th president. Before being elected to that position he served as governor of the PHILIPPINES under President WILLIAM MCKINLEY and as secretary of war under President THEODORE ROOSEVELT. Roosevelt involved Taft deeply in implementing his foreign policy. Taft was sent to CUBA in 1906 to try to mediate the conflict between warring political factions. The crisis was resolved when Taft assumed the position of governor. Taft also went to Asia, where he negotiated an agreement with Japanese prime minister Taro Katsura. The Taft-Katsura Agreement recognized JAPAN's primacy in Manchuria, and in return Japan adopted a policy of noninterference in the Philippines. The Taft-Katsura accord became the basis for the Root-Takihara Agreement of 1908.

Taft was Roosevelt's choice to succeed him as president, and he defeated WILLIAM JENNINGS BRYAN for the presidency in 1908. Roosevelt would soon break with Taft over Taft's currying of favor with conservatives and business interests within the REPUBLICAN PARTY. Roosevelt challenged Taft for the party's presidential nomination in 1912, and, failing to get it, he formed the Progressive Party. In the three-way race for the presidency that year, Democrat WOODROW WILSON was victorious. Taft was appointed Chief Justice of the SUPREME COURT by WARREN HARDING in 1921, and he held that position until one month before his death in 1930.

As Roosevelt's designated successor, the expectation was that Taft's foreign policy would be in line with that of his predecessor. In some respects this was true, because Taft was interested in promoting a visible and robust American presence abroad. His emphasis on economic development in the Caribbean was also a logical extension of the ROOSEVELT COROLLARY to the MONROE DOCTRINE. Under it, the United States rejected the right of European states to intervene in the Western Hemisphere to protect their investments. Taft's administration now took up the challenge of creating and preserving economic order itself. Taft's approach, however, gave his foreign policy a character that was quite different from that of Roosevelt's foreign policy. Taft dispatched dollars instead of troops to achieve stability and influence in the Caribbean. The reserved Taft also relied heavily on his SECRETARIES OF STATE to take the lead in foreign policy, whereas the energetic Roosevelt had largely acted as his own secretary of state.

Known as DOLLAR DIPLOMACY, Taft's foreign policy was predicated on increasing American investments in key countries as a way of acquiring political and strategic influence. In Cuba, for example, American sugar investments jumped from $50 million in 1896 to $220 million in 1913. More was involved than simply increasing investments. Dollar DIPLOMACY also led to the direct control over a country's finances. Such was the case in NICARAGUA. Taft also continued to endorse the use of military power when American commercial interests were threatened. In 1912 he sent troops to both Cuba and Nicaragua to protect American economic interests.

Taft also applied dollar diplomacy to Asia but with less strategic success for the United States or financial gain for American business interests. His strategic goal was to limit the growing Japanese influence in Manchuria and CHINA. The economic wedge to realize this goal was American business participation in railroad consortia. He achieved this initial objective by forcing the British, French, and Germans to accept American participation in the Hukuang Rail project. However, little came of the project, and his administration was unable to parlay participation into a broader and deeper American economic presence in China. A second effort at involving the United States in railroad construction was even less successful. Secretary of State PHILANDER KNOX proposed American involvement in financing a Manchurian railroad that would allow China to more effectively control the region. This attempt to block Japanese economic penetration and domination over Manchuria produced a negative reaction from Tokyo and

RUSSIA, which also had economic designs on the region. In the case of JAPAN, the Taft administration's policy of pushing an OPEN DOOR was at variance with the Root-Takahira Agreement of 1908, which recognized Japan's special position in Manchuria.

Taft did enjoy moderate success in dealing with less visible problems. Through his personal intervention he was able to obtain an agreement in 1911 from Japan, Russia, and GREAT BRITAIN (for CANADA) to protect pelagic seals from extinction due to excessive hunting on the open seas. Once estimated at 4 million, the number of these seals had been reduced to some 100,000 by 1910. The agreement provided compensation from the United States to both states and brought the pelagic seal population to approach earlier levels by 1938. The Taft administration also presided over agreements with Great Britain, peacefully settling fishing disputes along the New England coast and border disputes with Canada. Less successful was the Taft administration's effort to negotiate a reciprocity agreement with Canada. The measure was passed in 1911 but only after Taft called CONGRESS into a special session and applied a great deal of political pressure on Republicans to endorse the agreement. Opponents within the United States portrayed the agreement as part of a plan to take over Canada. This led to a political crisis in Canada that culminated in the election of an antireciprocity government, and the deal fell through.

After leaving the presidency, Taft supported American participation in WORLD WAR I and membership in the LEAGUE OF NATIONS.

**Further reading:** Scholes, Walter V., and Marie V. Scholes. *The Foreign Policies of the Taft Administration.* Columbia: University of Missouri Press, 1973.

## Taiwan

Taiwan is located off the southeastern coast of CHINA. It is about the size of West Virginia, with an area of 14,000 square miles, and has a population of 22.2 million people. On January 1, 1979, the United States ended its formal diplomatic relations with Taiwan by recognizing the People's Republic of China as the sole legal government of China. On April 10, 1979, President JIMMY CARTER signed the Taiwan Relations Act that established a mechanism for conducing unofficial relations with Taiwan. It empowered a private, nonprofit organization, the American Institute in Taiwan, to issue visas and provide assistance to American citizens in Taiwan. The government on Taiwan created an equivalent organization to conduct its relations in the United States.

The first Westerners to reach Taiwan were Dutch traders in 1624, who ruled over the island until 1661. The first major influx of migrants from the Chinese mainland came during this period. In 1664 a Chinese force expelled the Dutch, occupied Taiwan, and used it as a base to try to reestablish the Ming dynasty that had just fallen on the mainland. In 1683 Manchu forces from the mainland conquered Taiwan and ruled it until 1895 when, under the Treaty of Shimonoseki, China ceded Taiwan to JAPAN following the Sino-Japanese War. Japan ruled Taiwan for 50 years, from 1895 to 1945, after which it was returned to China.

In 1949 Jiang Jieshi's (Chiang Kai-shek) Nationalist forces retreated to Taiwan having lost out to Mao Zedong's (Mao Tse-tung) Communist forces in the Chinese civil war. Opinion in the United States was divided over how to proceed with regard to supporting Jiang. The Truman administration had become increasingly frustrated with Jiang Jieshi's government during the civil war. It permitted foreign aid but denied him military assistance. A number of leading Republicans, including Senator Robert Taft of Ohio and former president HERBERT HOOVER, opposed abandoning Jiang. Uncertainty over how to proceed vanished once the KOREAN WAR began. Taiwan was now seen as a valuable and strategic ally. When fighting broke out HARRY TRUMAN positioned the U.S. Seventh Fleet between Taiwan and the mainland to prevent any expansion of the war in that direction.

In the 1950s repeated clashes between Taiwan and China made the United States and Taiwan close allies and produced a series of Formosa Strait Resolutions. In 1953 President DWIGHT EISENHOWER announced that he was removing the Seventh Fleet from the Formosa Straits. This was accompanied by loose talk from Taiwan about military action against China. The reality was that Eisenhower did not want any such military action, and he made that clear to Jiang. He also extracted a promise that Jiang would not take any military action without consultations with the United States.

In 1954, with tensions rising between Taiwan and China, Eisenhower asked for and received congressional support to take whatever action he felt necessary to defend Taiwan. Congress passed the FORMOSA RESOLUTION on January 24, 1955, after four days of debate. A crisis atmosphere again gripped the region in 1958. China shelled two small and relatively insignificant islands off the coast that were occupied by Taiwanese forces. Jiang promised to defend these islands and dedicated about one-third of his army for that purpose. This move drew U.S. opposition, and SECRETARY OF STATE JOHN FOSTER DULLES went to Taiwan to meet with Jiang. On October 28, 1958, after three days of talks, Jiang announced that the Nationalist government on Taiwan would not use force to regain control over the mainland. The Eisenhower administration would cite the Formosa crises as evidence of its skill in handling foreign policy. It has become associated with the policy of BRINKSMANSHIP, wherein tensions are deliberately raised in order to bring about a settlement of the dispute.

With the passing of the Formosa Straits crises of the 1950s, U.S.-Taiwanese relations entered a period of stability. All of this changed with President RICHARD NIXON's 1972 trip to Beijing. It marked a symbolic turning point in U.S.-Taiwan relations. No longer was containing Communist China the United States's primary foreign-policy objective in the Pacific. Nixon's policy of DÉTENTE required improved American relations with Communist China as a means of balancing the power of the Soviet Union (see RUSSIA). The United States maintained official relations with both Chinas until January 1, 1979, when President JIMMY CARTER officially recognized the People's Republic of China (PRC) as the legitimate government of China. Historically both the PRC and Taiwan have maintained that they were the sole government of China and rejected any formulations that would support a two-China logic. Taiwan moved only slightly away from this position in 1991 when it acknowledged that the PRC controls the mainland.

The decision to recognize the PRC as the government of China required that the United States terminate its 1954 Mutual Defense Treaty with Taiwan. This did not, however, mean an end to U.S. arms sales to Taiwan. The weapons were defined as defensive and were held to be consistent with the Taiwan Relations Act, which stated that peace and stability in the area were of interest to the United States. ARMS TRANSFERS were also consistent with a 1982 joint communiqué between the United States and the PRC that pledged the United States not to conduct a policy of long-term arms sales to Taiwan. The United States promised to "gradually reduce its sale of arms to Taiwan" and seek a peaceful resolution to the Taiwan-PRC dispute. Notwithstanding these statements, American arms sales to Taiwan have proven to be a recurring sore point in U.S.-PRC relations. Whenever tensions flare, such as in 2001, following the forced landing of an American spy plane by the Chinese air force, increased arms sales are a standard American response. At that time President GEORGE W. BUSH promised to protect Taiwan and approved new, limited weapons sales.

In addition to military ties, the United States maintains strong economic ties with Taiwan. It is Taiwan's leading trading partner. It accounts for 25 percent of its exports and provides 17 percent of its imports. Overall, Taiwan is the United States's seventh-largest trading partner. U.S. commercial ties with Taiwan increased after derecognition, but they are expected to lessen as Taiwan improves relations with the PRC. Taiwan lifted its travel ban to the mainland in 1987, and between 1987 and 2001 more than 10 million trips were made. Direct cross strait shipping began in 1997, and Taiwan's annual trade with the PRC in 1998 was valued at $22.5 billion.

Until 1986 politics on Taiwan were dominated by the Nationalist Party (KMT), whose chairman also served as president. On March 18, 2000, an opposition candidate was elected president for the first time. Dating back to Jiang's term in office, the statements and actions of Taiwan's presidents have often served as a catalyst for friction between the United States, Taiwan, and the PRC. In 1995 Taiwan's president Lee Teng-hui made a high-profile "unofficial" trip to the United States, where Congress treated him as if he were a head of state. The PRC countered by recalling its ambassador to the United States and refusing to accept the credentials of the new U.S. ambassador. In August 2002, President Chen Shui-bian stated that Taiwan was "not part of another country, a local government, or province of another country." He made these remarks to a pro-Taiwanese independence group. China quickly countered with a promise to "deal a heavy blow to the separatist forces and foreign forces that attempt to intervene in China's reunification." Chen then moved to defuse the situation stating that his remarks were oversimplified and canceled an upcoming antisubmarine exercise.

**Further reading:** Ross, Robert S., ed. *After the Cold War: Domestic Factors and U.S.-China Relations.* Armonk, N.Y.: M. E. Sharpe, 1998.

## Tehran Conference

The Tehran Conference is significant because it was the first face-to-face meeting between President FRANKLIN ROOSEVELT and Soviet leader Joseph Stalin. British prime minister Winston Churchill was also present.

Through a series of WORLD WAR II SUMMIT CONFERENCES, Roosevelt and Churchill had managed to establish a

*(From left to right)* Soviet leader Joseph Stalin, President Franklin D. Roosevelt, and British prime minister Sir Winston Churchill at the Tehran Conference, Persia, 1943 *(Hulton/Archive)*

strong personal relationship that facilitated wartime planning. No equivalent relationship had been established between Stalin and Roosevelt. Relations between the Soviet Union and its Western allies had deteriorated to the point where SECRETARY OF STATE CORDELL HULL, then 72, undertook a trip to Moscow in October 1943 to reassure Stalin that plans were underway for a second-front offensive in FRANCE.

In late November Roosevelt and Churchill traveled from Cairo, where they had participated in a summit conference with Jiang Jieshi (Chiang Kai-shek), to Tehran, where they met with Stalin for the first time. The Tehran Conference lasted from November 28 to December 1. In addition to providing an opportunity for the three leaders to meet, several important issues were addressed at the meeting. Perhaps most significant was the fate of POLAND. The Soviet Union wanted Poland's eastern border moved to coincide with the boundaries established by the Molotov-Ribbentrop Pact. At Tehran Churchill agreed and suggested that Poland be compensated for lost territory, moving its western frontier to the Oder River. This would encompass about 200 miles of German territory and displace at least 6 million Germans. Citing the upcoming ELECTION and the importance of the Polish-American vote, Roosevelt stated that he could not publicly be associated with any such agreement. Stalin also insisted that any future government of Poland had to be composed of leaders acceptable to the Soviet Union. This point was crucial because during the war the Polish government in exile had been located in London. Conflict between the pro-Western London Poles and the procommunist Lublin Poles would be a major source of tension for the remainder of the war and into the early post–World War II years. Even prior to the Tehran Conference, there was ill will between these two groups. The Red Cross was investigating charges, later proven true, that the Soviet Union had murdered more than 10,000 Polish prisoners, many of whom were army officers, in the Katyn Forest in 1941.

Also at Tehran, Roosevelt proposed a new postwar INTERNATIONAL ORGANIZATION, the UNITED NATIONS, that would be dominated by "four policeman" who would have responsibility for dealing with threats to world peace. Stalin agreed but was skeptical. For his part Stalin confirmed that once GERMANY was defeated, the Soviet Union would enter the war against JAPAN. Roosevelt suggested that, as compensation, the Soviet Union should receive a free port in CHINA. The next meeting of the Big Three would take place at Yalta, where many of these points reappeared on the agenda.

See also POTSDAM CONFERENCE; RUSSIA; YALTA CONFERENCE.

**Further reading:** Mayle, Paul. *Eureaka Summit: Agreement in Principle and the Big Three at Tehran, 1943.* Newark: University of Delaware Press, 1987.

## Teller Amendment

The Teller Amendment was one of four passed by CONGRESS in a joint resolution of April 19, 1898, that served as a prelude to the declaration of war against SPAIN that was issued on April 25, 1898. The Teller Amendment stated that the United States had no intention of annexing CUBA. The other three amendments were (1) Cuba was declared to be an independent country, (2) Spain was told to withdraw, and (3) the PRESIDENT was directed to use military force to bring about these two previously stated goals.

Senator Henry Teller (R-Colo.) sponsored the amendment. He was a political outsider who switched parties three times and advanced causes, such as women's suffrage, ahead of his time. At face value the Teller Amendment put a humanitarian stamp on the soon-to-be war with Spain. A far more complex picture lay behind the scenes. Teller's main motive in putting forward his amendment was to protect Western sugar beet farmers from the possibility of added domestic competition should Cuba be annexed. Teller's amendment was introduced before a Senate that was divided on how to proceed. Advocates and opponents of expansion could be found. Rationales also varied. Some opposed annexation of Cuba on racial grounds. Others did so on economic grounds different from those that guided Teller's amendment. They feared that with annexation the United States would become responsible for Cuba's considerable external debt. President WILLIAM MCKINLEY was lukewarm in his support for Cuban annexation and had no objections to the amendment.

**Further reading:** Healy, David F. *The United States in Cuba, 1989–1902.* Madison: University of Wisconsin Press, 1963.

## terrorism

Terrorism is violence undertaken for purposes of intimidation. The study of terrorism is characterized by a fundamental duality that complicates analysis and policy making. Acts of terrorism can be committed by many different political actors. Governments engage in terrorism, as do practitioners of GUERRILLA WARFARE. Yet we do not label all of those who engage in political terrorism as terrorists. Terrorists are the enemy. They are fanatics with whom we disagree. They tend to be identified with lost causes and unsuccessful struggles. Those whose goals we support are freedom fighters or loyal allies.

Terrorism is not a new phenomenon. Studies have detailed its existence as far back as the campaign of Jewish zealots against the Romans in Palestine over a period from A.D. 6 to 135. Terrorism is evolving, however. This is most clearly seen in the motives of terrorists. Old terrorism was motivated primarily by political concerns. Attention was divided between revolutionary terrorist groups such as the Irish Republican Army and the PALESTINE LIBERATION ORGANIZATION, state-sponsored terrorists, such as the Libyan terrorists whose bomb destroyed Pan Am Flight 103, and state terrorism, in which the government terrorizes its own population, such as that carried out by Augusto Pinochet in CHILE. To label these forms of terrorism as "old" does not signify that they are disappearing. Amnesty International estimates that in 1995 some 100,000 individuals were tortured, raped, or subjected to other forms of mistreatment at the hands of government authorities in 114 countries. The SEPTEMBER 11, 2001, terrorist attacks against the World Trade Center and the Pentagon are very much in the spirit of the old terrorism.

Alongside the old terrorism are new forms of terrorism. One of these narcoterrorism, in which financial gain is the primary motivating factor. A second is superterrorism. This is defined as terrorist acts that involve the use of nuclear devices or chemical-biological agents. The Japanese cult Aum Shinriyko's 1995 nerve gas attack on the Tokyo subway system is an example of superterrorism. Fears of superterrorism against the United States led President GEORGE W. BUSH in late 2002 to make smallpox vaccine available to the American public. The third new form of terrorism is cyberterrorism. Here, terrorists attack their enemies through the Internet and cripple their communication systems, destroy or corrupt information sources, and compromise computer capabilities.

The pace and intensity of terrorist attacks has varied over time. The STATE DEPARTMENT has done yearly studies of terrorism that are recorded in its volume *Patterns of Global Terrorism.* Examining the years 1981–2001 reveals that terrorist incidents were lowest in 1998, when 274 attacks occurred. In 1996 there with 296 terrorist incidents, the only other year in this time period where less than 300 attacks occurred. Terrorism was at its highest in 1987, when 666 attacks took place. In the four-year period 1986–88, more than 600 terrorist attacks occurred each year. These are the only years in which more than 600 attacks took place.

A more focused examination of the period 1996–2001 reveals great year-to-year variation along a number of dimensions. Because of the terrorist attacks on the World Trade Center and the Pentagon on September 11, 2001, North American casualties due to terrorism soared to an estimated 3,315 persons. This is not the most in any one year. In 1998 casualties due to terrorism reached 5,379 in Africa. The next highest one-year total came in 1997, when there were 1,507 casualties. At the other extreme, in four of these years, there were no casualties in North America. The greatest number of casualties in any one year in Latin America was 195 in 1998. As can be imagined by the immense number of casualties produced by the World

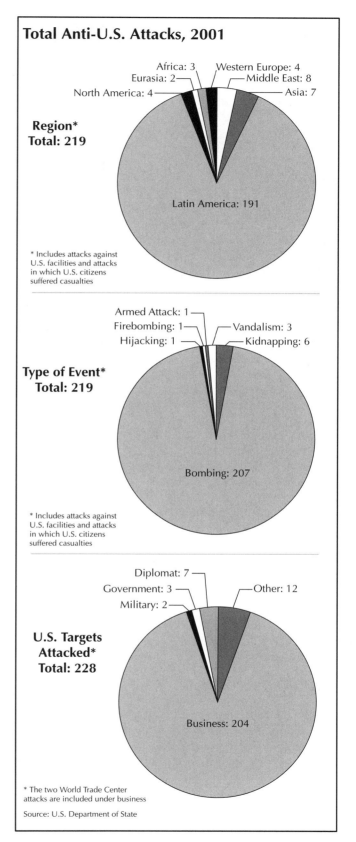

**Total Anti-U.S. Attacks, 2001**

**Region\***
**Total: 219**

Africa: 3   Western Europe: 4
Eurasia: 2   Middle East: 8
North America: 4   Asia: 7
Latin America: 191

\* Includes attacks against U.S. facilities and attacks in which U.S. citizens suffered casualties

**Type of Event\***
**Total: 219**

Armed Attack: 1
Firebombing: 1   Vandalism: 3
Hijacking: 1   Kidnapping: 6
Bombing: 207

\* Includes attacks against U.S. facilities and attacks in which U.S. citizens suffered casualties

**U.S. Targets Attacked\***
**Total: 228**

Diplomat: 7
Government: 3   Other: 12
Military: 2
Business: 204

\* The two World Trade Center attacks are included under business

Source: U.S. Department of State

Trade Center and Pentagon attacks, the overall number of casualties is not related to the overall number of terrorist attacks. In 2001, for example, there were only 4 terrorist attacks in North America. The 5,379 casualties in Africa in 1998 were produced by 21 attacks. During this period the largest number of attacks occurred in Latin America in 2000 and 2001, when 192 and 194 attacks occurred, respectively. They resulted in only 20 and 6 casualties, respectively. In order of preference, terrorists strike most frequently against business facilities. Such attacks ran from a low of 235 in 1996 to a high of 397 in 2001. Diplomatic targets are next in frequency. The most attacks against this target occurred in 1999, when there were 59 attacks. The least amount of attacks took place in 2001, with 18. Government targets are third in frequency. Terrorists struck a high of 27 times in 2000 and a low of 10 in 1999. Last in frequency among identifiable targets were military targets. Terrorist attacks against them ranged from 17 in 1999 to 4 in three different years.

Because of the overall significance of the September 11, 2001, terrorist attacks on redirecting the focus of American foreign policy, it is worth taking a closer look at terrorism in 2001. Overall, there were 219 anti-American terrorist attacks in 2001. The most, 191, occurred in Latin America. The fewest occurred in Eurasia and Africa, with two and three, respectively. Looked at in terms of type of event, 207 of these attacks involved bombings. The next most frequent type of event was kidnappings, with 6. Businesses were the most frequent target, accounting for 204 attacks. Terrorists attacked military targets least often in 2001. They attacked them twice. This pattern was consistent with the overall form that global terrorism took in 2001. Businesses were the most frequent targets by far, accounting for 397 terrorist strikes, compared to 18 for the next most-frequent target, diplomatic facilities. Overall, there were 253 terrorist bombings recorded. Kidnappings were the next most-favored terrorist event, with 36.

Once again great variation appears when one looks beyond the statistics to regional factors that are at work in fostering or encouraging terrorism. In AFRICA, most terrorism is the result of domestic or civil unrest and regional tensions. The CONGO, Liberia, and Sierra Leone are among the states where insurgent groups have regularly and indiscriminately used terrorism to try to achieve their goals. International terrorist groups, including AL-QAEDA and Hezbollah, have ties to African states. Al-Qaeda cells were also found in Singapore and Malaysia. Domestic conditions again figure prominently in East Asian terrorism. DRUG TRAFFICKING, trafficking in persons, organized crime, and government corruption create public resentment and frustrations that terrorist groups are able to exploit. In Peru and COLOMBIA terrorism is closely associated with drug trafficking and narcotics. More broadly, Latin America is seen as a region where terrorists raise millions of dollars through criminal enterprises.

Following the September 11, 2001, terrorist attacks, President Bush identified four policy principles that would guide his administration's terrorism policy. First, the United States will make no concessions or strike any deals with terrorists. Second, the United States will bring terrorists to justice for their crimes. Third, the United States will isolate and bring pressure to bear on states that sponsor terrorism to force them to change their behavior. Fourth, the United States will bolster the counterterrorist capabilities of allies.

In strategic terms three broad strategies have been identified for dealing with terrorism. They may be employed singularly or in combination. The first line of action addresses the underlying causes of terrorism. The roots of terrorism are perceived to lie in social, political, and economic injustices. Terrorist attacks are designed to draw attention to these conditions (as well as bring notoriety to the terrorists). The logic of this strategy for defeating terrorism is that if the inequities that terrorist seek to highlight can be ameliorated, then the terrorists will have less popular support, and it will be easier for governments to treat them as criminals. The second line of action is retaliation. Military action is a prominent form of retaliation, but it is not the only option. Economic and diplomatic retaliation are also possible. COVERT ACTION is still another retaliatory option. The final option stresses enhancing security efforts. The goal is to make terrorist attacks more difficult. Success here is seen as relying on both unilateral and multilateral action.

Of particular concern to the United States in constructing a strategy to deal with terrorism has been the problem of state-sponsored terrorism. Seven states are designated as sponsors of terrorism by the United States: CUBA, IRAN, IRAQ, LIBYA, NORTH KOREA, SYRIA, and SUDAN. Designating a country as a sponsoring of international terrorism imposes four sets of sanctions. First, a ban on arms-related exports and sales is imposed. Second, controls are put into place governing the export of dual-use technologies, which are technologies that have both military and nonmilitary value to the receiving state. Third, economic FOREIGN AID is prohibited. Fourth, a series of miscellaneous restrictions are put into place. These include implementing mandatory American opposition to loans by the WORLD BANK and other financial organizations, denying companies and individuals tax credits earned for investments in those states, revoking diplomatic immunity to allow families of terrorist victims to engage in civil law suits, prohibiting the DEFENSE DEPARTMENT from signing contracts for more than $100,000 with companies controlled by states on terrorist list, and requiring individuals having financial dealings with these states to obtain a TREASURY DEPARTMENT license.

Following the September 11, 2001, terrorist attacks and the successful American-led operation against al-Qaeda and the Taliban government of Afghanistan, the pace of global terrorism diminished. Thoughts that the war against terrorism had been won vanished as the IRAQ WAR ended. There was renewed terrorism in the Middle East as ISRAEL and the Palestinians sought to resume the path to peace. Al-Qaeda launched a successful terrorist attack against Westerners in Saudi Arabia in May 2003 that killed 34. This was followed shortly thereafter by a terrorist attack in MOROCCO. The State Department briefly closed its embassy in Saudi Arabia and issued advisories warning against travel by Americans to Kenya, Malaysia, INDONESIA, and the PHILIPPINES. At home, the Bush administration raised the terrorism alert level.

**Further reading:** Alexander, Yonah, and Michael Swetman. *Cyber Terrorism and Information Warfare: Threats and Responses.* Dobbs Ferry, N.Y.: Oceana Publishers, 2001; Campbell, Kurt M., and Michelle Fournoy. *To Prevail: An American Strategy for the Campaign against Terrorism.* Washington, D.C.: Center for Strategic and Security Studies, 2001; Kegley, Charles, Jr., ed. *International Terrorism: Characteristics, Causes, Controls.* Rev. ed. New York: St. Martin's, 2002; Talbott, Strobe, and Nayan Chanda, eds. *The Age of Terror: America and the World after September 11.* New York: Basic, 2002.

## Texas, annexation of

The annexation of Texas is significant because in conjunction with the MEXICAN WAR that soon followed, it virtually completed the continental expansion of the United States. Historians note that the Texas revolt that led to independence from MEXICO came about naturally. However, the same was not true for Texas annexation.

The story of Texas independence from Mexico involves both steadily increasing settlement by Americans, who never came to see themselves as Mexicans, and short-sighted policies of the Mexican government in dealing with this situation. Mexico had come to view Texas as a buffer between the United States and itself. In 1821 it started the process of encouraging settlement by granting a large tract of land to Moses Austin. By 1835 there were about 30,000 Americans in Texas, compared to about 3,000 Mexicans. Not unexpectedly, conflicts arose over RELIGION and the status of slavery in Texas. Most settlers were Protestants and not Catholics, and many came with slaves, who had been freed by a decree of the Mexican president in 1829.

Against a backdrop of armed clashes between settlers and the Mexican government, the United States tried to purchase Texas from Mexico. In the eyes of many Americans, this constituted the reacquisition of Texas. The United States had abandoned its dubious claim to ownership of Texas as part of the Louisiana Territory in the Adams-Onís Treaty of 1819, by which the United States had acquired FLORIDA. Neither the administrations of JOHN QUINCY ADAMS nor ANDREW JACKSON succeeded in these efforts.

The actual beginnings of the Texas revolt can be dated to the 1834 effort by General Santa Anna to impose tight centralized control over Mexico. On March 2, 1836, the Texan government adopted a declaration of independence. A few days later Santa Anna defeated independence forces at the Alamo in San Antonio. Later in March, Mexican forces massacred captured Texan forces at Goliad. Victory seemed all but assured for Santa Anna when, on April 21, his forces were defeated in a battle at the San Jacinto River. On May 14, Sam Houston, the leader of the Texan troops, forced Santa Anna to sign two treaties. The first declared an end to hostilities and stipulated evacuation of all Mexican forces from Texas. The second specified the Rio Grande as Texas's boundary with Mexico. Santa Anna would quickly disavow both agreements.

Both houses of CONGRESS passed resolutions favoring the recognition of Texas. President Jackson, however, withheld recognition of the Republic of Texas until his last days in office, nearly a year after the Battle of San Jacinto, largely in order to prevent a fissure in the DEMOCRATIC PARTY and to ensure the election of MARTIN VAN BUREN as president. Once recognized by the United States, Texas asked to be annexed. The South backed annexation, with some hoping to create as many as five new slave states. The North rejected it, the proposal for annexation was defeated, and Texas formally withdrew its application in October 1838.

Texas remained an independent state for the next nine years. It was routinely threatened with invasion by Mexico, which refused to accept its independence. GREAT BRITAIN and FRANCE signed treaties of amity and commerce with Texas. Great Britain in particular was anxious to establish good relations with Texas, viewing it as a potential ally and counterweight to the United States in the Americas. It would also be an alternative source of cotton and a market for British manufactured goods.

Concern with British intentions and a change in U.S. administrations brought about another attempt at annexation in 1844. President JAMES TYLER supported annexation of Texas, and Texans were assured that this time they would be admitted to the Union. Unfortunately, the political tide turned against Texas when, in arguing for annexation, SECRETARY OF STATE JOHN CALHOUN also entered into a defense of slavery. On the eve of the Polk-Clay presidential ELECTION, the Senate voted down the treaty by a vote of 35-16.

JAMES POLK won the election on a platform that included Texas annexation. President Tyler then moved to acquire Texas not through treaty but through a joint resolution that did not require a two-thirds majority vote. The resolution passed the House by a vote of 120-98 in February 1845 and the Senate by a vote of 27-25 in March. In the summer of 1845 Texans called a convention to decide between joining the United States and a Mexican offer of guaranteed independence. They chose to join the United States, and on December 29 President Polk signed the final resolution bringing Texas into the United States.

## Thailand

Known as Siam until 1938, Thailand is about the size of Texas, with an area of 198,114 square miles. Thailand has a population of 62 million people. Thailand is the only state in Southeast Asia that did not fall under the power of a colonial ruler. It did so by playing off competing imperial powers and ceding land when necessary to neighboring states. Its beginnings as a state are dated from 13th century. Contact with Europe began in 1511, when Portuguese traders and missionaries arrived. A failed coup in 1688 that was supported by FRANCE led to the closing of Siam to all foreigners for more than a century. GREAT BRITAIN was the first European power to officially recognized Siam with a Treaty of Amity and Commerce in 1826. The United States entered into formal relations with Siam in 1833.

Japanese forces took control of Thailand in December 1941 and pressured the Thai government to declare war on the United States and GREAT BRITAIN. In 1943 the United States supported an anti-Japanese GUERRILLA movement. Thailand regained its independence after the Japanese defeat, and after a period of domestic strife it emerged in the early 1950s as a strong ally of the United States, receiving military equipment, supplies, training, and infrastructure assistance. Thailand was a founding member of the SOUTHEAST ASIA TREATY ORGANIZATIONS (SEATO), and from 1954 until the group's dissolution in 1977 Bangkok was the location of its headquarters.

While not a source of major conflict, Thailand suffered from the decades of fighting in Indochina. During the VIETNAM WAR it provided the United States with valuable military bases and airfields from which bombing campaigns against North VIETNAM were conducted. Communist forces based in North Vietnam and Malaysia operated in Thailand and conducted raids against U.S. and government facilities. By 1972 more American military personnel were stationed in Thailand than in South Vietnam. After the Vietnam War ended Thailand, became a resettlement site for hundreds of Thousands of Cambodian and Laotian REFUGEES fleeing the atrocities of the Communist governments that seized power in those states.

Thailand remains a key American ally today, with military cooperation between the two taking place within the framework of a joint U.S. Military Advisory Group. About 20 joint military exercises take place each year. The United States is also Thailand's largest trading partner. In 1999 imports from the United States were valued at $14.3 billion and exports to the United States totaled $5 billion.

## think tanks

Think tanks are private research organizations that seek to influence public policy. They have been referred to as "idea brokers" and are now an important part of the landscape of American politics. They help define the issues on the policy agenda and options for addressing them. Foreign policy is an area in which think tanks have become especially active. One study identified 30 leading tanks. Seventeen dealt exclusively or in part with international issues.

Think tanks have become a significant force in American politics and, more important, in Washington, D.C., politics for several reasons. First, foreign policy has become much more complex. The foreign-policy agenda is no longer restricted to national security issues but encompasses TRADE, finance, HUMAN RIGHTS, the ENVIRONMENT, and cultural issues. Moreover, it is no longer sufficient to pay attention to the words or actions of a limited number of major powers. Small states, subnational actors, and INTERNATIONAL ORGANIZATIONS must now also be studied and understood.

Second, the information abilities of the government have been overwhelmed by this expanded foreign-policy agenda. Traditional sources of information, such as the STATE DEPARTMENT, the Congressional Research Service, and congressional staffers, have been unable to meet the demand at either end of the time spectrum, and think tanks have stepped into the breach. Long-range planning and strategic speculation are now commonly produced by think tanks, as is current information on breaking stories.

Third, CONGRESS has become more involved in the foreign policy–making process. It has sought out information about foreign policy independent of that provided to it by the executive branch. Think tanks have emerged as a prime source of that information. Finally, think tanks have become important because neither the public nor elites are united in their thinking on foreign policy. Multiple and competing perspectives on foreign policy require multiple and competing policy recommendations backed up with supporting information. Think tanks provide these options and the information to support them.

A brief survey of four think tanks illustrates the range of perspectives that are represented by these organizations. The Institute for Policy Studies (IPS) was founded in 1963 by Richard Barnett and Marcus Raskin. Disillusioned with policy making centering on VIETNAM, they founded IPS to provide "progressive politicians, policy makers, and activists with practical recommendations for reform." IPS calls for international DISARMAMENT, dismantling the CENTRAL INTELLIGENCE AGENCY (CIA), the nonviolent promotion of democracy, and a 50 percent cut in the military budget. The Brookings Institution is often referred to as the democratic government in exile. Established in 1927 as part of the good government movement of that era, it gained a reputation in the 1960s as being politically left of center in its approach to nuclear issues and other foreign-policy problems. Today it is very much a centrist organization, recruiting Republicans and Democrats. The Heritage Foundation was established in 1973, drew its support from the conservative wing of the REPUBLICAN PARTY, and became a major force in Washington during the Reagan administration. It advocates a policy of strong defense, support for the NORTH ATLANTIC TREATY ORGANIZATION (NATO), and support for free-trade agreements such as NORTH AMERICAN FREE TRADE AGREEMENT (NAFTA) and trade with the former Soviet Union. The Cato Institute is a libertarian organization founded in 1976. It advocates a policy of minimal foreign-policy involvement. Its papers cite SOMALIA and BOSNIA AND HERZEGOVINA as mistakes, call for an armistice in the international drug war, and argued against a military response to the North Korean nuclear program.

Think tanks exert their influence in many ways. First and foremost they are a source of personnel for administrations and congressional offices. The American Enterprise Institute contributed 20 members to the Reagan administration. The Center for Strategic and International Studies (CSIS) has been a regular contributor to presidential administrations. Included in that number is James Woolsey, who served as DIRECTOR OF CENTRAL INTELLIGENCE under President BILL CLINTON. Morton Halpern of IPS was a member of Clinton's national security team in charge of democratic enlargement.

A second means by which think tanks exert influence is through the organization of conferences. In 1993 the Heritage Foundation held 120 lectures, seminars, and debates. CSIS, a centrist organization created in 1962 to study the then-new field of national security, listed almost 50 ongoing round tables in its 1993 report. Some suggest that this is the most important service rendered by think tanks. These conferences provide a unique opportunity for like-minded individuals throughout Washington, D.C., to get together and exchange ideas. Discussions in a CSIS working group, for example, led to the GOLDWATER-NICHOLS ACT that reorganized the DEFENSE DEPARTMENT.

A third means by which think tanks exert influence is through the public statements of their staff. This can take the form of congressional testimony, op-ed pieces in newspapers, and appearances on television news and talk shows. These public appearances help draw attention to the increasingly partisan views of think tanks and help build support for them.

In the final analysis the influence of think tanks is difficult to determine with precision. As much depends on the recipients of their information as on their ability to promote policy ideas and analysis. President Clinton was known to be indifferent to foreign-policy issues and frequently to shift positions. He was thus a difficult target for think tanks. GEORGE H. W. BUSH, who preceded him in office, had a great deal of foreign-policy experience and surrounded himself with personal confidants rather than think-tank scholars. President RONALD REAGAN was an ideologue who focused on the big picture. This provided fertile ground for think tanks to influence policy.

See also INTEREST GROUPS; RAND CORPORATION; RUSSIA.

**Further reading:** Abelson, Donald E. *American Think Tanks and Their Role in U.S. Foreign Policy.* New York: St. Martin's, 1996; Smith, James A. *The Idea Brokers: Think Tanks and the Rise of the New Policy Elite.* New York: Free Press, 1990.

## Tibet

Tibet is a landlocked autonomous region within CHINA. It has a population of approximately 2.3 million people and is 471,700 square miles in size, making it somewhat larger than the combined area of Kansas and Nebraska. Under the leadership of the Dalai Lama, who is in exile, and the support of NONGOVERNMENTAL ORGANIZATIONS around the world, Tibet is seeking its independence. Both the government of the People's Republic of CHINA on the mainland and the Republic of China on TAIWAN claim Tibet as an integral part of China, and neither supports its bid for independence. Official U.S. policy also defines Tibet as part of China.

Tibet became an independent political unit in the seventh century. In the 12th century Tibet, along with China, fell under the domination of the Mongols. In 1720 the Manchu Qing dynasty replaced the Mongols as rulers of China, and from that time forward China has claimed suzerainty or jurisdiction over Tibet. Their rule was often loose, and interference in Tibetan affairs was nominal. In 1912 with the fall of the Qing dynasty in China, the Dalai Lama declared Tibet independent. GREAT BRITAIN organized a tripartite conference in 1913 held at Simla, INDIA, that brought together Tibet, China, and Great Britain in an attempt to clarify the political status of Tibet. The British were spurred to act due to Tibet's critical geographical position, placing it near India and in proximity to RUSSIA, one of its main imperial rivals for influence in Central Asia. At the conference the Dalai Lama agreed to a plan where by Tibet would be broken into two parts. Outer Tibet would be placed under Chinese sovereignty. Inner Tibet would return to Chinese suzerainty. This made Inner Tibet not fully inde-

President George W. Bush meets with the Dalai Lama at the White House, 2001. *(Courtesy of the White House)*

pendent but implied a high degree of domestic autonomy. China rejected the treaty, claiming all of Tibet as its territory. In 1965 the Tibet Autonomous Region (TAR) was created by the Chinese authorities. The TAR roughly corresponds to Inner Tibet as defined in 1913.

The chaotic state of domestic affairs that existed in China following the end of the Qing dynasty in 1911 and through the Japanese occupation in WORLD WAR II created a situation in which Tibet and other parts of China became de facto independent states. With the triumph of the Communists in the civil war in 1949, China sought to reestablish its control over these territories. Full reintegration occurred in 1951 through a treaty between China and Tibet that designated it as a national autonomous region.

In March 1959 a full-scale revolt against Chinese rule broke out in Tibet. Chinese forces put down the rebellion, and the Dalai Lama fled to India, accompanied by CENTRAL INTELLIGENCE AGENCY (CIA) personnel. The CIA was a key player in Tibetan-Chinese relations in the 1950s. A COVERT ACTION to support these resistance forces was the last major CIA attempt to support such forces in Communist-ruled states. Tibetans were trained in the United States beginning around 1951. Once trained they were flown to India and Nepal, where they would make the journey back to Tibet. While the Tibetans believed the CIA sincerely supported their efforts, most within the CIA viewed the operation as having more propaganda than strategic value. Little chance was given to their success. Raids did occur. They were planned by CIA officers and often led by CIA contract mercenaries.

During the 1950s and 1960s the United States sought to keep public attention focused on Tibet through a series of UNITED NATIONS resolutions condemning the Chinese Communist government. It did so in 1959, 1961, and 1965. In exile the Dalai Lama received an annual stipend of $180,000, plus an additional $1.5 million to aid his efforts to return to Tibet. American assistance ended with the Nixon administration's 1971 decision to normalize relations with China as part of its strategy of DÉTENTE. Without its American support the pro-Tibetan independence movement made little headway for the remainder of the decade inside or outside of Tibet.

Renewed movement began in the mid-1980s. Activist groups began a concerted effort to promote Tibet independence by arranging for the Dalai Lama to go on extensive speaking trips, enlisting college students, and recruiting high-profile Hollywood entertainers to the cause. Two organizations—the International Campaign for Tibet and the Free Tibet Campaign—came to form the core of the Tibet lobby. Their efforts received a major boost in 1989 with the Tiananmen Square incident, in which the Chinese government turned on prodemocracy protestors. That same year the Dalai Lama won the Nobel Peace Prize.

Even prior to Tiananmen Square CONGRESS had responded to the growing public support for a free Tibet with hearings and, in 1987, invited the Dalai Lama to speak. Congressional pressure on PRESIDENTS has led to three notable developments in the 1990s. First, since 1995 the STATE DEPARTMENT's Annual Country Reports on HUMAN-RIGHTS practices has included a separate section on Tibet within the China chapter. Second, since 1998 the State Department has issued an annual report on international religious freedom. Again, the China chapter contains a discussion of Tibet. Third, in 1997 the Clinton administration agreed to establish the position of special coordinator for Tibetan issues. For several years Congress had pressed for the creation of such a position with ambassador rank. Clinton's action created the post but did not accord it ambassador rank.

Congressional support for Tibet in the face of continued administration support for a one-China policy that includes Tibet has created a complex policy environment. Many supporters in Tibet and outside fail to make a distinction between congressional support and U.S. public support. This has led to feelings of disappointment and anger by supporters who see little progress. It has also strengthened the hand of hard-line elements in China who wish to crack down on Tibet. They cite congressional action as proof of the true intentions of the American government. Against the backdrop of these crosscurrents, Chinese and Tibetan authorities have held periodic discussions on the future of Tibet since 1978.

See also DOMESTIC INFLUENCES ON U.S. FOREIGN POLICY; INTEREST GROUPS.

## Tokyo Round

The Tokyo Round of trade negotiations held between 1973 and 1979 was the seventh round of multilateral trade negotiations held under the auspices of the GENERAL AGREE-MENT ON TARIFFS AND TRADE (GATT). GATT served as the primary instrument for organizing international trade from the end of WORLD WAR II to the creation of the WORLD TRADE ORGANIZATION in 1995. The Tokyo Round is significant because it extended the GATT system of free-trade agreements to cover nontariff barriers (NTB) to trade. NTBs emerged as a favored device of states seeking to prevent foreign goods from entering home markets following the KENNEDY ROUND negotiations that dramatically reduced the tariffs on manufacturing and commercial goods traded in the international markets.

Movement toward the Tokyo Round began within five months of the conclusion of the Kennedy Round negotiations in 1967 when an agreement was reached within GATT to prepare for a new round of negotiations. The Trade Act of 1974 provided the framework for U.S. participation. It permitted the U.S. to negotiate a 50 percent reduction in post–Kennedy Round tariffs and the elimination of tariffs of less than 5 percent. The act also allowed the president to negotiate on nontariff barriers to trade. These were defined as policies of national governments intended to protect domestic markets, such as quotas and onerous customs procedures, as well as domestic policies that had the same effect, such as export subsidies, government procurement policies, environmental standards, and packaging or labeling requirements.

The 1974 act insisted that in these negotiations the United States needed to seek reciprocal outcomes and not simply reciprocal tariff reductions. The goal was to improve the global competitiveness of United States firms by assuring them greater access to foreign markets. The United States was not to offer concessions to states that were not willing to offer substantial and equivalent opportunities to American firms.

In still another major innovation, CONGRESS established a FAST-TRACK procedure for considering trade legislation. It guaranteed a vote within 90 days on implementing legislation and prohibited any legislative amendments from being attached to the trade bill as presented by the PRESIDENT. In return, Congress was to maintain regular and close consultation with the executive branch in the negotiation of any trade agreement.

The Tokyo Round reduced tariffs on manufactured goods by industrialized states by an average of 26.4 percent. The United States reduced tariffs on dutiable manufacturing imports on average from 8.1 to 5.6 percent. These figure represented a compromise between the EUROPEAN UNION and the United States over how to reduce tariffs. The U.S. sought an across-the-board percentage reduction on all existing tariffs, while the European Union sought to have high tariffs reduced by more than lower tariffs.

The primary focal point of the Tokyo Round negotiations were on NTBs. The agreements reached here were binding only on those states that signed the agreement. A series of codes were approved that established a framework that would lead to the equal treatment of foreign and domestic goods. They centered on promoting transparency, accountability, and a mechanism for resolving disputes. The most important and controversial code permitted states to impose countervailing duties equal to the amount of any subsidy being given if it could prove that the subsidy caused "material injury" to a domestic industry. Exceptions were also negotiated and permitted. In the code on government procurement the United States excluded defense procurement contracts as well as procurement by the Energy and Transportation Departments and other selected agencies. In addition the code covered purchases only in excess of $190,000.

Using the fast-track procedures, Congress approved the Tokyo agreements with little debate. The House voted for them by a 395-7 margin, and the Senate followed suit by a vote of 90-4.

The impact of the Tokyo Round agreements was limited by three factors. First, relatively few states signed the agreement that established the code. Ten years after they went into effect, only 40 out of 100 states had signed the NTB agreements. Second, implementation rested on the political will of the various states. To combat this problem, in 1979, Congress amended section 301 of the trade act to allow the president to take retaliatory action against states that unjustly discriminate against U.S. goods. Third, the overall health of the international economy declined sharply at this time due to the ORGANIZATION OF PETROLEUM EXPORTING COUNTRIES (OPEC) OIL price hikes stemming from the 1973 Arab-Israeli War. The international standing of the U.S. economy also showed serious signs of weakening. In 1975 it had a $8.9 billion trade surplus. In 1978 the United States was running a trade deficit of $34 billion. The inability of the Tokyo Round to fully address the NTB problem was one of the factors that led to the next round of GATT negotiations, the URUGUAY ROUND.

**Further reading:** Baldwin, Robert. *Trade Policy in a Changing World Economy.* Chicago: University of Chicago Press, 1988; Low, Robert. *Trading Free.* New York: Twentieth Century Fund, 1993.

## Tower Commission

The Tower Commission, officially the PRESIDENT's Special Review Board on the Future Role of the NATIONAL SECURITY COUNCIL staff, was established by President RONALD REAGAN by Executive Order 12575 on December 1, 1986. The three-person commission was charged with conducting a comprehensive review of the National Security Council (NSC) staff's future with regard to the development, coordination, oversight, and conduct of foreign and national security policy as well as its proper role in operational activities. Its members were former Republican senator of Texas John Tower who Reagan selected as its chair, former Democratic senator of Maine and SECRETARY OF STATE Edmund Muskie, and retired air force general Brent Scowcroft, who had established himself as a trusted adviser of President Reagan. They were to submit their report within 60 days.

The Tower Commission was created to investigate two recently disclosed policy initiatives that were conducted by Reagan's NSC staff. In November 1986 it was revealed that since 1985 the United States had been participating in secret dealings with IRAN over the sale of military weapons. As part of this deal there was the expectation that Iran would use its influence to secure the release of American hostages being held in LEBANON by terrorists with ties to Iran. This secret policy was being pursued at a time when the United States was publicly working to isolate Iran because of its support for TERRORISM and when Washington had an arms embargo against Iran in place. Furthermore, the Reagan administration had been adamant that it would not negotiate with terrorists. It was then revealed that a second secret policy initiative was in place linked to the Iranian weapons deal. Money from the sale of weapons to Iran was to be diverted to a private bank account for use in support of the U.S.-backed contras who were fighting against the Sandinista regime in NICARAGUA. This secret policy was being developed at a time when CONGRESS, through the Boland Amendments, had prohibited the use of U.S. funds by the CENTRAL INTELLIGENCE AGENCY to overthrow the Sandinistas.

One important contribution the Tower Commission made to the historical record of the Reagan administration's foreign policy was to construct a narrative history of the arms sales. The report notes that its narrative of the IRAN-CONTRA INITIATIVE was "necessarily incomplete." Not only did the tight time frame mitigate against a thoroughgoing investigation, but some key witnesses refused to testify, and important documents from other countries were not available. Still, the Tower Commission notes in its report that it was able to "set out in considerable detail mistakes of omission, commission, judgement, and perspective" of people at the senior levels of the NSC system.

This narrative showed that the Iran-contra affair was not a Watergate-type conspiracy actively directed by the president from the White House. Rather it painted a picture of a president involved in the policy process but inattentive to the implementation of the policy and its full consequences for American foreign policy. As Senator Muskie observed, "[T]he policy was a wrong policy, and it was the President's policy." The lack of presidential attention and his failure to insist upon accountability created a situation in which American foreign policy was inconsistent and worked against itself and in which a parallel government came into being that existed beyond the reach of oversight of any kind.

In looking at the operation of the NSC staff, the Tower Commission concluded that the issues raised by the Iran-contra affair were not new. Every administration had faced similar problems. The commission did not endorse sweeping changes in the NSC system, arguing that "not all major problems—and Iran/Contra has been a major problem—can be solved simply by rearranging organizational blocks or passing new laws." They noted that the NSC system will not work unless the president makes it work. The commissioners recommended that no substantive changes be made in the 1947 NATIONAL SECURITY ACT and that the Senate should not confirm the president's choice of a NATIONAL SECURITY ADVISOR. It did recommend that the position of legal adviser in the NSC system be enhanced. On the congressional side it recommended replacing the INTELLIGENCE committees of the House and Senate with a single joint committee modeled after the Joint Committee on Atomic Energy that had once existed.

**Further reading:** *The Tower Commission Report.* New York: New York Times Books, 1987.


## trade policy

Two broad strategic outlooks compete for dominance in contemporary American trade policy. The first is free trade. There is nothing inevitable about free trade. International free-trade systems exist because they serve the NATIONAL INTERESTS of the dominant state. From about 1944 to 1962, access to American markets was used as an inducement to get other states to adopt policies favored by the United States. Goals included speeding European economic recovery, gaining access to raw materials, and strengthening military alliances. Even though the economic POWER of the United States is not as dominant as it was in the early COLD WAR era, the United States continues to use free trade to advance its interests at the bilateral, regional, and global levels.

At the bilateral level this has taken the form of establishing normal trade relations with key states. This was long referred to as MOST-FAVORED-NATION STATUS. The most significant trade negotiation of late was the 13-year effort of CHINA to obtain this status. For China obtaining normal trade status was crucial not only for gaining entry into the American market on competitive terms with other states but also because it laid the groundwork for membership in the WORLD TRADE ORGANIZATION (WTO). The United States has also used free trade on a regional level to advance its interests. This is most evident in the creation of the NORTH AMERICAN FREE TRADE AGREEMENT (NAFTA). At the global level it is the WTO that the United States relies on to maintain and expand a free trade system. The first round to WTO talks began in Qatar in 2002.

Competing with free trade as the strategic foundation for American international trade policy is the idea of strategic trade. Its advocates maintain that a free-trade international economic order no longer works to the advantage of American firms due to government-created market imperfections around the world. The proper response, in their view, is for the United States to actively intervene in the global marketplace in order to create comparative advantages for selected industries. Only in this way can the United States remain a global economic leader.

A strategic trade policy requires two things of the U.S. government. The first is that it must identify key sectors of the economy to support. Second, it must ensure that these firms are not shut out of foreign markets. One danger in this approach is that an overly aggressive strategic trade policy might spawn a trade war as other governments move to protect their firms. Another problem cited by many is the difficulty of identifying what is and is not an American firm. The principal impetus behind strategic trade policy was the failure of American firms to penetrate the Japanese market in the 1970s. A key piece of legislation supporting presidential efforts at strategic trade policy is the Omnibus Trade and Competitiveness Act of 1988. Section 301 gives the PRESIDENT the right to impose retaliatory sanctions against states that unfairly treat American firms. JAPAN, INDIA, and BRAZIL are among the states that have been identified as unfair traders.

A third outlook on how to organize American trade policy also exists. It is protectionism. Once dominant, protectionism now has relatively few adherents, but it remains important because of the political clout its advocates carry. At the most basic level, protectionism is based on the belief that self-sufficiency is preferable to involvement in international transactions. ALEXANDER HAMILTON and HENRY CLAY were early proponents of an economic system focused nationally as opposed to internationally.

Protectionism in trade fit well with a foreign policy of diplomatic and military ISOLATIONISM as is evidenced by the the high tariff legislation passed by CONGRESS in the 1920s and 1930s. Protectionism was also furthered by the log-rolling that characterizes much of its legislative activity. An industry hurt by high tariffs (taxes) on material it needed would be compensated by tariffs or quotas in another area of concern. Carried to its extreme, this process of horse trading creates impressive congressional majorities for protectionist legislation. Congress recognized this danger and in the post–WORLD WAR II era began to place limits on its ability to manipulate trade legislation for domestic political purposes. One key measure was granting presidents FAST-TRACK AUTHORITY that forces Congress into a "yes-no" vote on trade legislation and prevented it from attaching protectionist amendments to treaties. For a while fast-track authority was granted routinely, but recently it has become highly politicized.

Protectionism is also advanced as a policy that helps endangered economic sectors of society. When these sectors are politically powerful, as farmers once were and steel is today, protectionist policies often triumph. However, such legislation is typically treated as an exception to the rule rather than as a statement of overall U.S. trade policy. This situation promises to become even more politically explosive as the WTO rules against such practices and forces the United States and other countries to find other ways of protecting these domestic economic interests.

**Further reading:** Cohen, Stephen. *Fundamentals of U.S. Trade Policy.* Boulder, Colo.: Westview, 2002; Grieco, Joseph, and G. John Ikenberry. *State Power and World Markets: The International Political Economy.* New York: Norton: 2002; Ratner, Sidney E. *The Evolution of the American Economy.* New York: Macmillan, 1993; Winha, Gilbert. *The Evolution of International Trade Agreements.* Toronto: University of Toronto Press, 1992.

## Treasury Department (United States Department of the Treasury)

With the increased prominence of international financial issues on the global agenda, the Treasury Department has become a highly visible new bureaucratic force in foreign-policy making. One of its central missions is to "promote prosperous and stable American and world economies." To accomplish this goal as well as its other missions, such as managing the government's finances, the Treasury Department is organized into a series of offices and bureaus. Offices are headed by assistant secretaries, who report to undersecretaries. They are charged with policy formulation and the overall management of the department. Bureaus, which comprise 98 percent of the Treasury Department's workforce, are responsible for carrying out specific tasks assigned to the Treasury Department. The key foreign-policy office is the Office of International Affairs, which advises and assists in the formation and execution of U.S. international economic policy.

The undersecretary of the treasury for international affairs is the chief adviser to the secretary of the treasury on international issues and represents the Treasury Department on these topics within the administration, with CONGRESS, and in international meetings. Beneath the under secretary and assistant secretary for international affairs are a series of deputy assistant secretaries, who are responsible for specific areas. They include trade and investment policy; technical assistance policy; international monetary and financial policy; international development, debt, and environmental policy; and geographically organized offices.

Three activities illustrate the range of involvement of the Treasury Department in international economic matters and point to its significance as a foreign-policy actor. First, it is involved in the creation and development of the International Trade Data System (ITDS). The goal of the ITDS is the development of a system for collecting all of the important information about U.S. exports and imports in order to improve U.S. trade policy and procedures. An important force in the development of the ITDS was the signing of the NORTH AMERICAN FREE TRADE AGREEMENT and its requirements for standardizing data-reporting methods.

Second, the Treasury Department is active in screening foreign direct investment coming into the United States. The major piece of legislation to which the Treasury Department is responding is the Exon-Florio Provision of the 1988 Omnibus Trade and Competitiveness Act that establishes a mechanism by which the U.S. government can review foreign direct investment and determine if it threatens national security. The Exon-Florio Amendment requires that the PRESIDENT receive notification of any merger or takeover of a U.S. firm by a foreign entity. The Committee on Foreign Investment in the United States (CFIUS), chaired by the secretary of the treasury, investigates the matter and makes a report to the president. The president may then block the foreign acquisition.

Third, the Treasury Department has played a major role in addressing international DEBT CRISIS and currency problems. It first assumed this role in the 1980s when developing states began to experience severe debt repayment problems. Through the BAKER PLAN (named for Secretary of the Treasury James Baker) and then the BRADY PLAN (named for Secretary of the Treasury Nicholas Brady), the United States sought to fashion a plan that simultaneously would provide for debt repayment as well as political and economic stability in the Third World. Next, the Treasury Department took a lead role in trying to stabilize the peso in MEXICO when that currency came under intense pressure. More recently, it was active in seeking solutions to the ASIAN FINANCIAL CRISIS that crippled many East Asian economies in the late 1990s.

**Further reading:** Cohen, Stephen. *The Making of U.S. International Economic Policy*. Westport, Conn.: Greenwood, 2000.

## Treaty of Ghent

The Treaty of Ghent (1814) ended the WAR OF 1812 between the United States and GREAT BRITAIN. This was a war for which the United States was not prepared to fight. Neither its army nor its navy was up to the task, and popular sentiment was divided between pro- and anti-British opinion. The war itself did not go well, with failed campaigns against CANADA. Negotiations began in June 1812 but soon stalemated, as neither side was willing to concede. In September, Czar Alexander I of RUSSIA offered to mediate the dispute. He hoped to bring an end to the conflict in order to redirect British energies to stopping Napoleon Bonaparte. The United States accepted his offer, but the British rejected it. Not willing to see the conflict become part of a European peace settlement or to totally anger the czar, the British proposed direct talks with the United States.

President James Madison appointed a five-person delegation: JOHN QUINCY ADAMS, HENRY CLAY, Albert Gallatin, James Bayard, and Jonathan Russell. The British responded more slowly and sent to Ghent, Belgium, an inexperienced team of negotiators, which led the Americans to assume that they were not really interested in achieving a peace agreement. It needs to be noted that at this time the British were preparing for the Congress of Vienna, a landmark conference in European diplomatic history that rewrote the political map of Europe.

The British presented what was in essence a victor's peace terms. They asserted that the United States must never maintain war ships or fortifications on the Great Lakes, and they demanded the creation of a large buffer state for NATIVE AMERICANS south of the Great Lakes that would be equal in size to today's Ohio, Indiana, Michigan, Illinois, and Wisconsin. The American delegation prepared to return to the United States when confronted with these terms. President Madison also made the British terms public in a successful attempt to unite the country behind the war effort. The British then softened their terms. The War of 1812 was expensive, and they did not wish to see it continue. Their hopes now rested on a series of military victories that would force the United States to accept London's terms. This victory came when British forces captured Washington, D.C. British negotiators now demanded that the peace treaty be signed on the basis of territory occupied by each side, which would give it much of Maine. Quickly, however, news came of a stunning British defeat on Lake Champlain. Now faced with the prospect of not being able to invade the United States successfully, the British agreed to compromise terms.

Signed on December 24, 1814, the Treaty of Ghent made no reference to the issues that had led the United States to go to war or to any of the British territorial demands or terms made earlier in the negotiations. It simply reaffirmed the situation as it existed prior to the outbreak of hostilities. Both sides agreed to return territory, establish peace with the Native Americans, and move to end the slave trade (something both sides had already outlawed). A permanent commission was also established to deal with U.S.-Canadian border disputes. The Senate unanimously approved the treaty in 1815. The Treaty of Ghent thus is significant not so much for what it accomplished as for what it symbolized. The treaty legitimized the United States as an international actor. As such, the War of 1812 has been referred to by some as the "second war for American independence."

**Further reading:** Updyke, Frank. *The Diplomacy of the War of 1812*. Gloucester, Mass.: P. Smith, 1965; ———, and White, Patrick. *The Critical Years: American Foreign Policy, 1793–1823*. New York: Wiley, 1970.

### Treaty of Paris (1783)

The Treaty of Paris (1783) brought the AMERICAN REVOLUTION to an end. The first article of the treaty established American independence from GREAT BRITAIN. The second article established its boundaries. They ran from the Atlantic Ocean to the Mississippi River in the west and from Spanish East and West FLORIDA in the south to a line relatively consistent with today's U.S.-CANADA border. The third article dealt with fishing rights in and around Newfoundland. The British had sought to exclude U.S. anglers from these waters, but the objections of JOHN ADAMS held the day, and Americans were given the "liberty" to fish here. Along with the exact location of the northern border, the question of fishing rights remained a sore spot in British-American relations and would be a subject of the Webster-Ashburton Treaty (1842).

Article Four provided that debts owed British merchants at the time of the American Revolution would have to be repaid. This was a point on which the British insisted and American negotiators accepted after much wrangling. Articles Five and Six represented attempts by the British to protect the economic interests of those who had remained loyal during the war. These articles "earnestly recommended" that states restore property seized from them. Article Seven forbid the British to carry away slaves. Article Eight provided that both states should have navigation rights to the Mississippi River.

The Paris Peace Treaty gave generous terms to the United States. The British generosity is best understood in the context of calculations of future self-interest (the British hoped to avert future friction over western expansion, establish profitable commercial relations with the United States, and prevent the United States from becoming overly dependent on and aligned with FRANCE) and a need to address ongoing international disputes (Great Britain was at war with three other states: France, SPAIN, and the NETHERLANDS). The treaty did not go into effect until a British-French treaty was agreed to, thus fulfilling the terms of the Franco-American ALLIANCE of 1778 by which neither agreed to sign a separate peace. This occurred in January 1783. All treaties were signed on September 3, 1783. CONGRESS approved the treaty on January 14, 1784.

**Further reading:** Bemis, Samuel F. *The Diplomacy of the American Revolution*. Bloomington: Indiana University Press, 1957; Morris, Richard B. *The Peacemakers: The Great Powers and American Independence*. New York: Harper and Row, 1965.

### Treaty of Portsmouth

The Treaty of Portsmouth in 1905 ended the Russo-Japanese War and earned President THEODORE ROOSEVELT the Nobel Peace Prize in 1906. Fighting began between these two states in 1904 with the surprise Japanese attack at Port Author that destroyed RUSSIA's Asian fleet. Tensions between Russia and JAPAN had been building for some time as each sought to establish regional supremacy in East Asia.

Japan's success initially produced a warm response in Washington. A Japanese victory was seen as less threatening than a Russian victory to the U.S. OPEN DOOR policy in CHINA. It was not long, however, before the extent of the Japanese victory produced concerns about whether or not a victorious Japan might not also threaten the viability of the Open Door policy along with the U.S. ability to protect its position in the PHILIPPINES. A July 1905 memorandum signed by Secretary of War WILLIAM HOWARD TAFT and Japanese prime minister Taro Katsura in Tokyo sought to resolve the second issue. In it Japan renounced any aggressive tendencies toward the Philippines, and the United States approved Japanese suzerainty over Korea.

Roosevelt sought to secure the first objective by brokering a peace between the two combatants that would leave a rough balance of POWER in place. In spite of its impressive military accomplishments, Japan needed peace. The war effort had drained its treasury. Japanese leaders accepted Roosevelt's offer to arrange a mediated settlement. In early August 1905 talks began in Portsmouth, New Hampshire. Roosevelt monitored the negotiations but did not personally play the role of mediator. The treaty was agreed to in late August, when both sides accepted a compromise formula put forward by Roosevelt. Talks had deadlocked over the future of the island of Sakhalin. Under the terms of Roosevelt's compromise, Russia accepted the division of Sakhalin, and Japan dropped its demand for indemnity. Russia also gave up its holdings in Manchuria and Korea.

Viewed from the perspective of global politics, the Treaty of Portsmouth is significant because it established Japan's role as a major regional power. It marked the first time an Asian power had defeated a major European power. The Treaty of Portsmouth did not accomplish Roosevelt's goal of engineering a stable balance of power in the region. The treaty was not well received in Japan, where people blamed the United States for denying Japan its indemnity payments from Russia. Japanese resentment of the United States grew even more pronounced when, in 1906, the San Francisco School Board created special "Oriental Schools" to segregate Koreans, Japanese, and Chinese children from white children. Japan's foreign policy also violated the spirit of the Open Door. While it reopened Manchuria to foreign trade, it discouraged foreign investment, and in 1910 Japan formally annexed Korea.

See also IMMIGRATION.

## Treaty of Versailles

The Treaty of Versaillies was the peace agreement that ended WORLD WAR I. The United States played a leading role in the negotiations as President WOODROW WILSON sought to construct a peace built around his FOURTEEN POINTS. A key element of his vision for the future was the establishment of a LEAGUE OF NATIONS to guarantee world peace and the political and territorial integrity of states. The U.S. Senate refused to ratify the treaty as negotiated or with amendments ("reservations"). The absence of the United States from the League of Nations proved to be a major impediment in its PEACEKEEPING efforts. The United States's refusal to join the League of Nations also became symbolic of the isolationist and unilateral approach to world politics that the United States adopted in the interwar era.

GERMANY surrendered on November 11, 1918. The Fourteen Points, modified in two important respects by the Allies, had served as the basis for the armistice talks. On November 18, Wilson shocked the American public and angered his Republican opponents when he announced that he personally would go to Paris as a member of the American peace commission. He delivered a second shock later that month when he announced the membership of the U.S. delegation. Only Henry White, a career diplomat, was a Republican, and no members of the Senate were included. The other members were Colonel EDWARD HOUSE, SECRETARY OF STATE Robert Lansing, and General Tasker Bliss, who was a member of the Supreme War Council in Paris. The partisan nature of this delegation foreshadowed the partisan reception the Treaty of Versailles would receive in the Republican-controlled Senate. Led by Senator HENRY CABOT LODGE (R-Mass.), chair of the Senate Foreign Relations Committee, Republicans served notice of their intent to challenge Wilson when, on March 4, 1919, 39 senators—one more than was needed to defeat any treaty—signed a "Round Robin" that declared that the concept of a League of Nations should be considered only after a peace treaty was signed and that they would not vote for a peace treaty in its current form.

With Wilson in attendance, the peace conference held its first meeting on January 12, 1919. He brought with him an advisory staff numbering almost 1,300. It quickly became apparent that America's European allies had no intention of allowing free-press coverage of the deliberations as was implied by the phrase OPEN COVENANTS of peace contained in the Fourteen Points. It also became clear that if work were to progress quickly, it had to take place in smaller settings. A Council of Ten was created, but in March it too gave way to the Council of War, namely, Wilson, French premier Georges Clemenceau, British prime minister David Lloyd George, and Italian premier Vittorio Orlando. Neither Germany nor RUSSIA was invited to the conference.

Wilson pressed for action on the League of Nations. He got the conference to agree on January 25 to make the League an integral part of the peace treaty, and on February 11 he presented the League of Nations Covenant to the conference. Wilson had chaired a committee composed of representatives from 14 states who wrote the document. At the center of the League Covenant was a clause (Article 10) that built on the concept of collective security. It required all members to respect and preserve the independence of all members against external aggression. Having accomplished this, Wilson returned to the United States, where he sought to sell the League Covenant and the emerging peace treaty to skeptical Senate Republicans, who, as noted above, had produced a resolution indicating their opposition to it.

The League of Nations Covenant was put together in such haste that even defenders of the concept saw the need for immediate changes. For example, there was a need to exempt domestic issues, such as IMMIGRATION and tariffs from the League's jurisdiction, provide a mechanism for leaving the League, and permit the United States to act under the terms of the MONROE DOCTRINE. When Wilson returned to Paris on March 14, he succeeded in modifying the original covenant. Obtaining Allied acquiescence in these revisions, however, left him vulnerable to demands by others.

GREAT BRITAIN opposed Wilson's idea of making German colonies the common property of the league. Wilson found it necessary to settle for the concept of league mandates and accept the division of Germany's holding among the Allies along the lines laid out in the secret treaties. FRANCE demanded additional territorial guarantees against any future German attack. Wilson refused to permit France to gain control over land west of the Rhine River because it violated the principle of self-determination. He did agree to the permanent demilitarization of the Rhine region and Allied occupation for 15 years. As part of this agreement,

Germany's coal-rich Saar region was to be administered by the league for 15 years, at which time a plebiscite would be held to determine its future. France and Great Britain also insisted upon reparations for damages done by German forces. Wilson resisted but gave in on this point. He also failed in an attempt to fix the amount that Germany owed. This was to be determined by a Reparations Commission. Japan sought to acquire Germany's colonial holdings in Asia, its economic rights in the Shantung province in CHINA, and the inclusion of a statement of racial equality. While its territorial demands were largely met, JAPAN was rebuffed on the last point with Wilson voting against Tokyo.

German delegates came to Versailles on May 7, 1919, to receive the newly minted 200-page treaty. With many of its protests over the new terms rejected, Germany signed the Treaty of Versailles on June 28, 1919. Treaties with the other defeated powers soon followed. The battle over the treaty now shifted to the U.S. Senate, where Republican opposition would lead to its defeat.

PUBLIC OPINION strongly supported the Treaty of Versailles when it reached the U.S. Senate for ratification in July 1919. Thirty-two state legislatures had endorsed it, and two others did so with only minor reservations. Senator Lodge described the opposition position as "hopeless." Lodge, however, pressed on, packing the Senate Committee on Foreign Relations with six "irreconcilable" Republican senators, and he set upon a strategy of delay. That strategy began to pay off as, by early September 1919, public support for the treaty began to wane. In an effort to regain public support for the treaty, Wilson undertook a cross-country tour of the United States. He often met with enthusiastic crowds but collapsed in exhaustion in September 25, 1919, in Pueblo, Colorado. Wilson returned to Washington, where he suffered a massive stroke on October 2. Without Wilson's leadership, public opinion for the treaty began to slip.

Before Wilson set out on his trip, the Senate Foreign Relations Committee voted out the treaty with 45 amendments and four reservations. All of the amendments were defeated. Lodge next introduced a resolution of approval accompanied by 14 reservations. Wilson was willing to accept some of the "minor" reservations but balked at accepting any reservation that threatened the principle of COLLECTIVE SECURITY (Article 10). On November 19, the Treaty of Versailles with the Lodge reservations was defeated by a vote of 39-53. The no votes came from a coalition of irreconcilable Republicans and Wilsonian Democrats who wished to see the treaty pass without any reservations attached.

The Senate came under heavy pressure to reconsider its position. Lodge went so far as to negotiate a compromise package with Democrats before irreconcilable Republicans forced him to stop. On May 15, 1920, a final vote was taken on the treaty with 15 reservations attached. It failed by a vote of 35-49. Once again the majority was composed of irreconcilable Republicans ("the Battalion of Death") and Democrats loyal to Wilson's vision of the treaty. CONGRESS would officially declare World War I over by passing a joint resolution on July 2, 1921. In August President WARREN HARDING negotiated separate peace treaties with Germany, Austria, and HUNGARY.

**Further reading:** Bailey, Thomas A. *Woodrow Wilson and the Great Betrayal.* New York: Crown, 1945; Sharp, Alan. *The Versailles Settlement: Peacekeeping in Paris, 1919.* New York: St. Martin's, 1991.

## Trilateral Commission

The Trilateral Commission was established in 1973 by David Rockefeller, chairman of the board of directors of Chase Manhattan Bank. Its stated purpose was to bring together private citizens from the United States, CANADA, Europe, and JAPAN to promote cooperation among their countries and foster a willingness on the part of these states to undertake shared leadership responsibilities in an increasingly interdependent world.

This benign image was soon replaced by another one, stressing the conspiratorial nature of the Trilateral Commission. This image was rooted in the ELITE THEORY interpretation of American foreign-policy making that stresses the close personal ties and shared backgrounds of key policy makers. Elite theory posits that leaders pursue goals that are at odds with those held by the rest of American society and tend to manipulate the public voice rather than listen to it. Members of the Trilateral Commission who came to occupy positions in the Carter administration included the PRESIDENT, NATIONAL SECURITY ADVISOR Zbigniew Brzezinski, SECRETARY OF STATE CYRUS VANCE, SECRETARY OF DEFENSE Harold Brown, Secretary of the TREASURY Michael Blumenthal, and Deputy Secretary of State Warren Christopher. This same line of analysis was applied to the Reagan administration that replaced it. Here, it was the Committee on the Present Danger that was placed at the center of the analysis.

The Trilateral Commission originally was to operate only for three years. Its life has been extended for successive three-year intervals since then. In 2001, the Trilateral Commission was made up of about 350 leaders from business, MEDIA, academia, public service, labor unions, and NONGOVERNMENTAL ORGANIZATIONS. Its annual meeting rotates among the three regions from which its membership is drawn. Each regional group is led by a notable figure. For example, the Japan Group, which has now been expanded to an Asia Pacific Group, was originally led by Takeshi Watanabe, who had served as president of the

Asian Development Bank. He was succeeded by Isamu Yamashita, founder of Sony.

Usually the Trilateral Commission publishes one or two reports each year. They are not intended to reflect a consensus view of commission members. They are the product of collaborative work by a team of authors. Recent reports include *Engaging Russia* (1995), *Maintaining Energy Security* (1996), *Advancing Common Purposes in the Broad Middle East* (1998), and *The New Central Asia* (2000).

## tripolarity

A tripolar system has three relatively equal poles or POWER centers. Compared to other distributions of power in the international system, tripolarity has not received a great deal of attention. In large part this is because they are presumed to be unstable and will easily transform into a bipolar structure. Two interrelated factors make tripolarity relevant to discussions of the future of U.S. foreign policy. The first is the emergence of economic power as particularly important in the post–COLD WAR era. The second is the emergence of three large regional trading blocks located in Europe, Asia, and North America. Debate exists among commentators as to the ideal number of trading blocks for global prosperity and the number which is most likely to result in economic wars.

The defining characteristics of a tripolar system are respect for spheres of influence and limited foreign-policy goals. The primary danger to be avoided is isolation. The best way to ensure that this does not come about is to avoid undertakings that would drive the other two powers into a counteralliance. The presumed rules of a tripolar system are the following: First, each power should aim to reduce collusion between the other powers to a minimum. Second, it is in the interests of each state to bluff or blackmail its chief adversary by threatening collusion with the third power. Third, the surest way to provoke the other two into collusion is to display undue aggressiveness.

DÉTENTE, as put into practice by the Nixon, Ford, and Carter administrations, essentially was a tripolar system in which the United States, the Soviet Union (see RUSSIA), and CHINA were the three poles. Viewed from the perspective of tripolarity, détente failed for three reasons. First, just as with MULTIPOLARITY, tripolarity's demand for flexibility and the need to change sides runs against the AMERICAN NATIONAL STYLE, with its emphasis on morality and LEGALISM. Second, the Soviet Union continued to engage in aggressive behavior that violated tripolarity's emphasis on restraint. This was especially the case with the invasion of AFGHANISTAN, which for all practical purposes ended détente. Third, China was not nearly equal to the United States or the Soviet Union in power and thus did not provide a stable third pole around which to practice the rules of tripolarity.

## Truman, Harry (1884–1972) *president of the United States*

Harry S. Truman was the 33rd president of the United States. He became president in 1945 when President FRANKLIN D. ROOSEVELT died. Truman had served as vice president for only 82 days. The consummate organization politician, he had been a compromise choice for vice president in 1944 when the DEMOCRATIC PARTY was unable to agree on either SECRETARY OF STATE JAMES BYRNES or Secretary of Commerce HENRY WALLACE. Truman had little input into domestic- or foreign-policy matters as vice president. In the Senate his only exposure to foreign policy had been as chair of a committee to investigate the National Defense Program for corruption.

This isolation from important policy-making responsibilities changed with dramatic suddenness. Only three months into his presidency, Truman attended the POTSDAM CONFERENCE in July 1945 where he, Soviet leader Joseph Stalin, and British prime minister Clement Atlee, who took over for the just-defeated Winston Churchill, met for the last of the great WORLD WAR II SUMMIT CONFERENCES. The meeting is significant because many date this as the point at which Truman began his conversion to an anti-Soviet perspective. Commentators note that his willingness to compromise with the Soviet Union lessened considerably after receiving news of the successful testing of the atomic bomb. Truman rejected advice from Secretary of State Byrnes that a demonstration explosion be held for the Japanese and

President Harry Truman *(left)* and Assistant Secretary of State Adlai Stevenson *(Courtesy of the White House)*

accepted the recommendation from an advisory committee that the atomic bomb should be used in combat.

A second turning point in Truman's foreign policy thinking came in 1946–47. Though not an isolationist, many of Truman's initial foreign-policy actions gave little indication that he expected the United States to be actively involved in settling international disputes. After JAPAN surrendered he canceled the LEND-LEASE program that Roosevelt had used to funnel aid to Europe. He terminated the OFFICE OF STRATEGIC SERVICES (the forerunner of the CENTRAL INTELLIGENCE AGENCY) and parceled its tasks out to other agencies or ended them. He sought to limit the number of U.S. occupation forces in GERMANY and Japan to a low level. In 1946 and 1947 he came to embrace the arguments of his more internationalist advisers that the United States must take the lead in meeting Soviet challenges in IRAN and Germany. His conversion is epitomized by his announcement of support for GREECE and TURKEY (the TRUMAN DOCTRINE) and his administration's decision to provide Europe with badly needed economic recovery aid (the MARSHALL PLAN).

The onset of the KOREAN WAR marks a third turning point in Truman's evolving worldview. According to his domestic critics, the Truman administration had "lost" CHINA when the Nationalist forces led by Jiang Jieshi (Chiang Kai-shek) fled to TAIWAN and Mao Zedong (Mao Tsetung) and the Communists seized power. Truman's reluctance to intervene in China's civil war reflected the selective and Eurocentric view of CONTAINMENT that GEORGE KENNAN had advocated. Truman became an instant and energetic convert to the global view of containment contained in NSC-68 when NORTH KOREA invaded SOUTH KOREA on June 25, 1950.

Truman's handling of foreign policy generated considerable controversy. His anti-Soviet stance angered many of those, such as Byrnes and Wallace, who had worked with Roosevelt and shared his view that Stalin was a leader with whom one could establish a working relationship. Truman forced both of them out of his administration. His anticommunism was not enough to save Truman from right-wing McCarthyite attacks that he allowed communists to hold important positions within the government and sabotage U.S. foreign policy. Disagreements with General DOUGLAS MACARTHUR over how to prosecute the Korean War and who was in charge led Truman to dismiss the general. MacArthur received a hero's welcome on his return to the United States.

Both positive and negative evaluations of Truman's foreign policy begin by acknowledging that he laid the foundation for America's cold war foreign policy. Supportive evaluations stress his strong leadership in the face of domestic opposition and low opinion ratings, his willingness to commit U.S. power to stop Soviet aggression, and his selection of highly qualified individuals, such as GEORGE MARSHALL, DEAN ACHESON, and GEORGE KEN-

NAN, to lead the STATE DEPARTMENT. Critical assessments stress that Truman had a limited sense of history and a low degree of tolerance for those who disagreed with him. The result was a parochial INTERNATIONALISM that lent itself to simplistic interpretations of events and the selection of policy options that often lacked nuance and were presented in universalistic and moralistic terms.

See also CIVIL MILITARY RELATIONS; COMMUNISM, SOVIET; MCCARTHYISM; RUSSIA.

**Further reading:** Ferrell. Robert H. *Harry S. Truman: A Life*. Columbia: University of Missouri Press, 1994; McCullough, David. *Truman*. New York: Simon and Schuster, 1992.

## Truman Doctrine

On March 12, 1947, President HARRY TRUMAN delivered a dramatic speech to a special joint session of Congress. He asked CONGRESS to provide $400 million for economic assistance to GREECE and TURKEY to help them resist Soviet-inspired aggression. But he did not stop there. Truman asserted that "it must be the policy of the United States to support free peoples who are resisting attempted subjugation by armed minorities or outside pressures. . . . [W]e must assist free peoples to work out their own destinies in their own ways."

Prior to WORLD WAR II, Greek security had been guaranteed by the British. This situation was expected to resume after the war, but heavy war losses prevented GREAT BRITAIN from coming to their defense, being unable to doing so in the face of mounting Soviet-inspired pressures. In Greece the problem was an unrelenting civil war between a pro-British government in Athens and leftist rebels who took control of the countryside when German forces withdrew from Greece in 1944. A truce signed in 1945 unraveled in 1946, when the Greek government attempted to eliminate its political opposition. Corruption, inefficiency, and brutality were hallmarks of this regime, and the Communist-controlled National Liberation Front had many supporters. Evidence also suggests that Joseph Stalin was not particularly supportive of the Greek Communist Party because he perceived it as too nationalist to be controlled. Yet Truman presented it as a straightforward case of Soviet-supported aggression.

Turkey was involved in an ongoing dispute with the Soviet Union (see RUSSIA) over control of the Dardanelles Straits. These straits controlled access to the Black Sea. From Moscow's point of view unfettered transit through the Dardanelles to the Mediterranean was crucial to its ability to act as a great power. At the same time, the Dardanelles served as an entry point for hostile naval forces to enter the Black Sea. During the war, Turkey had permitted German naval forces to do so, and Moscow felt its security threatened. After World War II Stalin insisted upon international control over the straits, making the comparison with Britain's concern that EGYPT might close the Suez Canal (an analogy that proved to be quite prescient given the 1956 SUEZ CRISIS). Turkey interpreted this as a threat to its national sovereignty, and this is how Truman presented it to CONGRESS.

In February 1947 London informed the United States that it would no longer be able to meet its defense commitments to Greece. SECRETARY OF STATE DEAN ACHESON met with congressional leaders and outlined the need for action, citing "a highly likely Soviet breakthrough" in Greece and the danger of "infection" elsewhere by this "eager and ruthless opponent." Congressional leaders agreed to support the request, provided Truman made his case to the full Congress and the American people.

Many commentators see Truman's speech as the equivalent to a U.S. declaration of COLD WAR against the Soviet Union. It provided a rationale for U.S. activism in world affairs by declaring that the world "was divided between two antithetical ways of life: one based on freedom, another on coercion" and that "we shall not realize our objectives . . . unless we are willing to help free peoples to maintain their free institutions and their national integrity." U.S. security was seen as inseparable from the security of other states. ISOLATIONISM or a retreat back to a hemispheric orientation to world affairs was impossible. Moreover, the domestic politics of states, whether they were democratic or totalitarian, was now important. The Truman Doctrine, as the contents of this speech came to be known, also identified an enemy at least indirectly with its references to aggression by "totalitarian regimes." This phrase was applied almost exclusively to the Soviet Union and its allies.

Truman's speech was tremendously effective. The Truman Doctrine is widely credited with helping transform the American public's view of the United States's place in the world. It moved COMMUNISM to the center stage of American foreign policy and cemented the notion that U.S. security was tied to the fate of others. Critics took exception to two aspects of his presentation. First, in the case of both Greece and Turkey, it oversimplified a complex reality. Second, it spoke in universal tones: Communism everywhere had to be stopped. GEORGE KENNAN, the author of the CONTAINMENT policy that the Truman Doctrine advanced, wrote in 1947 of the need for the United States to abandon legalistic and universal responses to international problems and focus on the particulars of the situation.

The Greek crisis ended in October 1949 when the rebels stopped fighting. More than 350 American military officers served as advisers to the Greek military in its successful campaign. The Dardanelles crisis continued to fester for several years into the cold war.

**Further reading:** Kuniholm, Bruce R. *The Origins of the Cold War in the Near East: Great Power Conflict and Diplomacy in Iran, Turkey, and Greece.* Princeton, N.J.: Princeton University Press, 1979.

## Tunisia

Found on the north coast of Africa, Tunisia has a population of 9.6 million people and an area of 63,378 square miles, making it slightly smaller than Missouri. Virtually all Tunisians are Muslim. This is a result of the Muslim conquest of the region in the seventh century. Tunisia became assimilated into the Ottoman Empire in the 16th century. Late in that century the region became a stronghold for the BARBARY PIRATES. The Barbary pirates operated out of northern Africa and preyed on ships sailing the Mediterranean Sea. After independence American shipping was no longer protected by British money and consequently ceased in the region. After a series of ineffective treaties were signed, the U.S. Navy defeated the pirates in 1815.

Mounting debts to European states in the 19th century led to their intervention into Tunisian affairs and the establishment of a French protectorate in 1881. Tunisia remained a French colony until 1956 when it was granted full independence. Tunisia generally has adopted a moderate position in the ARAB-ISRAELI CONFLICT. In 1965 it became the first Arab state to call for the recognition of ISRAEL. It also allowed Tunis to become the headquarters of the PALESTINE LIBERATION ORGANIZATION (PLO) from 1982 to 1993. This is the period running from when it was forced out of LEBANON until the Palestinian Authority received recognition via the Oslo accords.

While no formal security treaty links the United States with Tunisia, relations have been positive. From 1957 to 1994 the UNITED STATES AGENCY FOR INTERNATIONAL DEVELOPMENT ran technical and economic assistance programs in Tunisia. The program ended that year because Tunisia's economic progress removed it from the list of countries eligible for such aid. Between 2001 and 2002 the United States–North African Economic Partnership, which is designed to promote economic development in the Maghreb, steered $1.3 billion annually into the region. Relations were strained in the late 1980s when Israel carried out a series of attacks on the PLO's headquarters and assassinated a PLO terrorist. Tunisia also objected to U.S. intervention in IRAQ in the PERSIAN GULF WAR.

## Turkey

Slightly larger than Texas, Turkey has an area of 296,000 square miles and a population of 65.5 million people. Bridging two continents, Asian Turkey comprises 97 percent of the country and is separated from European Turkey by the Bosphorus, the Sea of Marmara, and the Dardanelles. The modern Turkish state emerged out of the ashes of the Ottoman Empire with the Treaty of Sèvres in 1920. Its current borders were more or less established by the 1923 Treaty of Lausanne. Turkey became a secular state in 1924, although 98 percent of its population is Muslim.

Along with its neighbor and rival, GREECE, Turkey was an early COLD WAR battleground. After WORLD WAR II the Soviet Union sought to extent its political influence into the Mediterranean Sea. It supported Communist GUERRILLAS in Greece in that country's civil war and pressured Turkey for military bases in the Turkish Straits that linked the Black Sea to the Mediterranean. GREAT BRITAIN was the longtime protector of Mediterranean states, but the expenses of World War II and the damage inflicted on its economy by the war effort precluded continuing this role. Fearing the consequences of Soviet expansion into this region, President HARRY TRUMAN announced on March 12, 1947, that the United States would provide aid to Greece and Turkey. Known as the TRUMAN DOCTRINE, this announcement, with its expansive language concerning the need to protect free states against communist pressure, was one of the first major cold war policy pronouncements by the United States. Since that time the United States has provided Turkey with more than $4 billion in economic FOREIGN AID and $14 billion in military aid.

In an attempt to win acceptance as a member of the NORTH ATLANTIC TREATY ORGANIZATION (NATO), Turkey sent almost 30,000 troops to Korea. It became a NATO member in 1952 along with Greece. In the following years Turkey became a close and active ally of the United States. In 1955 it joined the Baghdad Pact that sought to contain Soviet expansion into the Middle East. After IRAQ left the ALLIANCE in 1959, the pact's headquarters moved to Turkey, and the organization was renamed the CENTRAL TREATY ORGANIZATION (CENTO). Military installations in Turkey would come to be vital to American efforts to collect electronic and photographic INTELLIGENCE about the state of the Soviet missile program. The United States used bases in Turkey for its involvement in LEBANON in 1958.

American weapons in Turkey were also central to one of the most dramatic conflicts in the cold war: the CUBAN MISSILE CRISIS. In order to bolster European confidence in the American nuclear shield following the Soviet's launching of *SPUTNIK* in 1957, the United States moved to place Jupiter missiles in Turkey. They became operational in July 1962. In October 1962 Soviet missiles were discovered in CUBA. In the course of the negotiations to end the crisis, the Soviet Union demanded the removal of American missiles in Turkey as a condition for removing their missiles in Cuba. A shocked President JOHN KENNEDY did not even realize the missiles were there and felt unable to make such a public swap. In the end American missiles were removed from Turkey as part of a secret understanding.

In the aftermath of the Cuban missile crisis, U.S.-Soviet relations moved gradually from conflict to DÉTENTE, and the American concern with communist expansion shifted from Europe to Asia. These shifts lessened the importance of Turkey in American security thinking and opened the way for other issues to emerge that complicated their relationship. The first to appear was competition with Greece over Cyprus. Turkish Cypriots constituted a minority there, and in late 1963 Greek Cypriot terrorists began a campaign to bring about a union of Greece and Cyprus. Part of President LYNDON JOHNSON's strategy to defuse the crisis involved denying Turkey the use of any U.S. weapons to invade Cyprus and defend the Turkish Cypriots. Turkey resented this move as well as Johnson's raising doubts about U.S. commitments to Turkey as a member of NATO should it take military action. Not quite a decade later, in 1974, Turkey and Greece again clashed over Cyprus, following the assassination of Cypriot president Archbishop Makarios, an assassination orchestrated by the military government in Greece. Turkish troops invaded Cyprus to protect Turkish Cypriots. Congress responded by placing an arms embargo on Turkey. Turkey retaliated by suspending U.S. operations at key military installations in Turkey. The arms embargo was lifted in 1978. Basing rights were restored in 1985 after an agreement was reached that provided for an increase in the level of Turkish exports to the United States.

The second issue involved allegations of genocide against Turkey's Armenian minority. Responding to political pressure from Armenian Americans in 2000, 141 members of the House cosponsored a nonbinding resolution that condemned Turkey for past genocide against Armenians. Turkey protested the issue vigorously to the Clinton administration, threatening to cut off base rights for use in flights over Iraq. Along with intense lobbying, Turkey's pressure on the Clinton administration was enough to have the vote canceled.

The end of the cold war and the rise of Islamic fundamentalism altered American perceptions of Turkey. Its secular political order was now advanced by some as an alternative model for Muslim states in contrast to the theocratic political order found in IRAN. Turkey later came to be viewed as a pivotal ally against IRAQ in the PERSIAN GULF WAR. Between 1991 and 1993 nearly $8 billion worth of NATO military equipment made its way to Turkey. It became the third-largest recipient of American foreign aid, behind ISRAEL and EGYPT, and the fifth-largest ARMS TRANSFER client. Between 1984 and 1994 it purchased $7.8 billion worth of arms from the United States.

However, the Persian Gulf War did bring to life a new problem for Turkish-U.S. relations. Turkey is home to an estimated 12 million Kurds, many of whom desire to establish a homeland of their own, Kurdistan, and break away from Turkey. By the late 1990s some 30,000 had died in fighting surrounding the Kurdish rebellion that began in 1984. The Kurds had also been the target of domestic policies roundly criticized by HUMAN-RIGHTS advocates. Because Kurds within Iraq were a major source of opposition to Saddam Hussein, the United States moved to protect them and tried to work with them as a force capable of removing him from power. Turkey feared that the U.S. policy of support for the Kurds could spill over and disrupt its political system.

Turkey expressed its concerns in the summer of 2002 as talk of war with Iraq heated up. As in the Persian Gulf War, it sought guarantees that it would be compensated for its support. In that war Turkey was promised $1 billion per year to offset the loss of its largest trading partner in Iraq. That money never materialized, and the loss of trade with Iraq is estimated to have reached $12–$50 billion by 2002. This time Turkey was reportedly interested in arranging for reductions in their military debt and obtaining special consideration for arms and technology transfers. It also wanted assurances of U.S. support for continued financial assistance from the INTERNATIONAL MONETARY FUND (IMF). Its economy nearly collapsed in 2001, and Turkey received $16 billion from the IMF to prop it up.

Turkey emerged as a focal point of U.S. military and diplomatic policy in the months leading up to the IRAQ WAR. Turkey was central to American war plans for opening a northern front and moving supplies to U.S. forces in the region. A great deal of American frustration was evident as Turkey's newly elected leaders struggled with the decision over whether or not to actively participate in the war. A key problem was that Turkey's concerns were different from those of the United States. Turkish leaders worried about the consequences that might follow from either an influx of Kurdish refugees into Turkey or the establishment of an autonomous Kurdish region in northern Iraq. Turkey also sought economic compensation from the United States because war with Iraq would hurt its economy. Turkey suffered through a recession following the 1991 Persian Gulf War as its trade with Iraq fell from $2.5 billion to $122 million. U.S. plans in place in February 2003 called for making $6 billion in grants available to Turkey. Turkish leaders demanded $10 billion in aid. Later than month the U.S. sought to sweeten the offer by offering Turkey a limited exception from textile-protection legislation by allowing the Pentagon to buy Turkish textiles for U.S. troops. In 1991 this exception was also granted, and it was valued at $100 million. In March Turkish leaders added conditions that called for stronger guarantees from the United States that ethnic Turkomans in Iraq would be treated fairly in postwar Iraq and that Turkey would be given a voice in determining the fate of the Kurds in northern Iraq. In the end Turkey limited its involvement to permitting overflights of its territory, and much of the war material that was scheduled to be shipped through Turkey was redirected to Persian Gulf bases.

See also DOMESTIC INFLUENCES ON U.S. FOREIGN POLICY; ECONOMIC SANCTIONS; RUSSIA.

**Further reading:** Kuniholm, Bruce R. *The Origins of the Cold War in the Near East: Great Power Conflict and Diplomacy in Iran, Turkey, and Greece.* Princeton, N.J.: Princeton University Press, 1979.

**Tyler, John** (1790–1862) *president of the United States*
John Tyler was the 10th president of the United States (1841–45) and the first to reach that office through the death of the president. He was elected as William Henry Harrison's vice president; both were Whig candidates. Harrison died within one month of the inauguration on April 4, 1841. Prior to becoming vice president, Tyler had served as governor of Virginia and as a congressperson and senator from Virginia.

Tyler and WHIG PARTY leaders clashed frequently. After Tyler vetoed the creation of a national bank for the second time, all of the members of his cabinet, except for SECRETARY OF STATE DANIEL WEBSTER, resigned. Webster stayed on until he was able to complete the negotiation of the Webster-Ashburton Treaty with GREAT BRITAIN that settled a boundary dispute along the Canadian border and set up a joint policy to deal with the African slave trade.

Tyler was a strong advocate of continental expansion and saw TEXAS as a natural addition to the Union. His second secretary of state, A. P. Upshur, negotiated a treaty with Texas, but it was rejected by the Senate because of the debate over slavery. Tyler failed to get the Whig nomination in 1844. JAMES POLK won the general election on a platform that favored expansionism. In the last days of his administration Tyler invited Texas to become a state after Congress passed a joint resolution making it possible.

# U

## U-2 incident

On May 1, 1960, two weeks before a scheduled U.S.-Soviet SUMMIT CONFERENCE meeting in Paris intended to deal with Berlin, a high-altitude American spy plane was shot down 1,200 miles inside Soviet territory. At the summit meeting, Soviet leader Nikita Khrushchev demanded an apology for the U-2 overflight. When none was forthcoming he left the meeting, returning an element of tension and distrust into U.S.-Soviet relations that both Eisenhower and Khrushchev had hope to overcome through earlier summit meetings and as symbolized by the "spirit" of Camp David.

U-2 overflights had begun in 1956. They supplied the CENTRAL INTELLIGENCE AGENCY (CIA) and U.S. government with information about Soviet military capabilities, most significantly those surrounding its nuclear missile program. U-2 overflights had also produced information about the situation in the Suez in 1957 when FRANCE and GREAT BRITAIN stopped providing the United States with information about their activities.

It appears that in this instance the plane had engine trouble. Pilot Gary Francis Powers parachuted to Earth and was captured. The initial story put forward by the Eisenhower administration on June 3 was that a NASA research plane studying weather patterns had crashed over TURKEY. On June 5, Khrushchev announced that an American plane had been shot down after violating Russian air space. The STATE DEPARTMENT now stated that a civilian weather plane had probably strayed over Soviet airspace accidentally. Khrushchev then produced pictures of Gary Francis Powers, photo reconnaissance equipment, and pictures of Soviet military installations. The State Department then acknowledged that the plane "probably" was on an INTELLIGENCE operation. Eisenhower then took responsibility for the mission, asserting that the U-2 flight was necessary to avert another Pearl Harbor. Eisenhower's statement appears to have undercut Khrushchev's standing within the Soviet Politburo, giving hard-liners who

U-2 "Dragon Lady" *(National Archives)*

opposed the ongoing thaw in U.S.-Soviet relations an opening to undermine the Paris summit.

The U-2 incident also needs to be read in the context of a debate within the Eisenhower administration over spy planes and satellites in general. The Eisenhower administration was concerned with two different aspects of aerial ESPIONAGE at the time of the U-2 incident. First, it was beginning to focus on moving beyond manned spy planes as a source of intelligence. A 1950 RAND report had identified spy satellites as an important factor in the emerging cold war balance of POWER between the United States and Soviet Union (see RUSSIA). The primary problem that they identified was the potential of countries to the loss of sovereignty that would result from overflights. Consequently the Eisenhower administration became particularly concerned with establishing legality of overflights in INTERNATIONAL LAW. Second, in the short run the administration was concerned with the development of an intercontinental ballistic missile (ICBM) capability on the part of the Soviet Union. Acquisition of these weapons was identified in the 1954 Killian Commission report as the single largest threat to American air dominance. The U-2 was an important source of intelligence on Soviet ICBM construction.

**Further reading:** Redlow, Gregory, and Donald Welzenbach. *The CIA and the U-2 Program 1954–1974.* Washington, D.C.: The Center for the Study of Intelligence, 1974.

### *Underhill v. Hernandez* (1897)

This case involved the use of the Act of States doctrine by the SUPREME COURT to remove itself from a foreign-policy dispute and in the process strengthen the hand of the PRESIDENT. The case involved an American citizen, Underhill, who was working in Bolívar, VENEZUELA. The city was captured by revolutionary forces led by General Hernandez. Underhill applied for a visa to leave the city. His request was denied by General Hernandez. Underhill filed suit for damages, alleging assaults and affronts by Hernandez's soldiers. The revolutionary movement for which Hernandez fought would be recognized by the United States as the legitimate government of Venezuela.

The Supreme Court dismissed the suit, asserting that the Act of States doctrine, by which states are obliged to respect each other's independence and "not sit in judgment on the acts of governments of another," cannot be confined "to lawful or recognized government or to cases where redress can manifestly be had through public channels." Furthermore, it argued, "The acts complained of were the acts of a military commander representing the authority of the revolutionary party as a government which afterwards succeeded and was recognized by the United States."

The use of the Act of States doctrine in this manner is significant because it prevents individuals from bringing suit in U.S. courts that could force presidents to take military or political action to correct a situation or provoke an international controversy between the United States and another state.

### unilateralism

Unilateralism is one of the foundational building blocks on which the AMERICAN NATIONAL STYLE of foreign policy is built. The other two are MORAL PRAGMATISM and LEGALISM. Together they support both an isolationist and internationalist perspective, thereby allowing both to coexist.

Unilateralism is a predisposition to act alone in addressing foreign-policy problems. It does not dictate a specific course of action. ISOLATIONISM, INTERNATIONALISM, and NEUTRALITY are all consistent with its basic orientation to world affairs. The unilateralist thrust of U.S. foreign policy represents a rejection of the balance-of-

POWER approach for providing national security. The American historical experience was such that except for brief periods security largely could be taken for granted and collaborative efforts were not needed.

The best-known statement of the unilateralist approach is the MONROE DOCTRINE. The United States rejected a British proposal for a joint declaration to prevent European powers from reestablishing their position in Latin America following the end of the Napoleonic Wars, only to turn around and issue a unilateral declaration to the same end. In 1904 the ROOSEVELT COROLLARY was added that made the United States the self-proclaimed police officer of the Western Hemisphere. Unilateralist thinking was evident in the refusal of the United States to join the LEAGUE OF NATIONS.

It is present just beneath the surface when one examines the pattern of U.S. participation in post–WORLD WAR II INTERNATIONAL ORGANIZATIONS. U.S. interests in the UNITED NATIONS are protected through its veto in the Security Council and by a system of weighted voting in international financial organizations, such as the INTERNATIONAL MONETARY FUND. When these safeguards are absent, the United States has demonstrated a willingness to act unilaterally and, if need be, in defiance of the global consensus, as it did in refusing to participate in the KYOTO PROTOCOL and in constructing a missile defense system.

Unilateralism has also characterized the American use of force in the post–COLD WAR world. President GEORGE H. W. BUSH assembled a global coalition against IRAQ, but it was the United States that decided when to begin the ground war and when to end it. It was the United States that declared the coalition's objectives to have been met. The pattern repeated itself in the war against TERRORISM. President GEORGE W. BUSH also put together a global coalition to wage war against Iraq in March 2003, but there was no doubt that the military operations were essentially a unilateralist effort with token participation by allies.

### unipolarity

A unipolar INTERNATIONAL SYSTEM is one in which there is one dominant power. The principal forms of interaction and communication run vertically from the dominant state, the hegemon, downward to the weaker states. One of the first major foreign-policy debates in the United States was over whether or not a unipolar system had come into existence with the end of the COLD WAR. The principal alternative argued for was a multipolar system. Once a consensus developed that the international system was unipolar, the debate shifted to one over whether such a system could endure for a long period of time or if it was merely transitional. In practical terms this turned into debates over the responsibility of the United States for keeping world order and to what extent the United States should base its defense strategy on the continued existence of unipolarity.

In its pure form significant contacts among the weaker states in the system are few in number, due to the overwhelming control exercised by the hegemon. By definition, true defensive ALLIANCES do not exist, since the dominant state has no need for them. There appear to be three rules for the hegemonic state in a unipolar system: First, maintain or increase one's power. Second, insist on maintaining the status quo. Third, respond to challenges with restraint.

The closest cold war approximations to unipolarity occurred at the regional level in Latin America and Eastern Europe from the late 1940s into the early 1970s. The United States and the Soviet Union, the two dominant states, were able to impose their will upon the weaker states in each system. The Soviet Union sent troops into HUNGARY (1956), East Germany (1953), and CZECHOSLOVAKIA (1968) to bring wayward governments back into line or to put down domestic unrest. The United States helped engineer the overthrow of the Arbenz government in GUATEMALA (1956) and that of Salvador Allende in CHILE (1972), and it sent troops into the DOMINICAN REPUBLIC (1965). In neither case was control total. Perfect unipolar systems did not exist. CUBA successfully defied the United States, and YUGOSLAVIA did the same toward the Soviet Union.

In regard to the contemporary debate over unipolarity, the argument against developing a defense strategy based on the permanence of unipolarity stems from the assertion that unipolar systems contain within themselves the seeds of their own destruction. Weaker states have two choices. They can bandwagon and join with the dominant state in a supporting role, or they can seek to balance its power by joining with others in opposition to it. The logical choice is to balance, since bandwagoning leaves the weaker state totally at the mercy of the hegemon. The balancing strategy holds the possibility of success because as lesser states acquire more power the costs of leadership increase for the hegemon, and it will be forced to make concessions. The opposing position maintains that unipolarity is stable and not easily challenged by the actions of other states. The chief threat to continued unipolarity comes from DOMESTIC INFLUENCES ON U.S. FOREIGN POLICY. It is the danger of not doing enough due to the opposition of INTEREST GROUPS and PUBLIC OPINION, divided government, or fears of electoral defeat. If the hegemon does not act, then other states have no choice but to acquire more power.

See also BIPOLARITY; MULTIPOLARITY; RUSSIA; TRIPOLARITY.

**Further reading:** Kapstein, Ethan, and Michael Mastanudo, eds. *Unipolar Politics: Realism and State Strategies after the Cold War.* New York: Columbia University Press, 1999.

## United Nations

The United Nations (UN) is the successor INTERNATIONAL ORGANIZATION to the LEAGUE OF NATIONS. Its more immediate origins can be traced back to FRANKLIN ROOSEVELT'S WORLD WAR II DIPLOMACY, in which he advocated creating an organization that would continue the wartime cooperation among the "Four Policemen" (the United States, CHINA, GREAT BRITAIN, and the Soviet Union [see RUSSIA]) and allow them to protect international peace. Representatives from these four states came together at Dumbarton Oaks in Washington, D.C., in August 1944 to negotiate the foundations for the United Nations. The UN Charter was adopted in San Francisco in a follow-up conference that ran from April 25 to June 26, 1945, which was attended by 282 delegates from 46 states.

Activity and political power in the United Nations is organized around six different institutions. In the General Assembly, all members have one vote. It serves as a type of global parliament in which issues are debated and resolutions or declarations are passed. The General Assembly can also pass a convention, which is a multilateral treaty. A recent example is the COMPREHENSIVE TEST BAN TREATY of 1996. The Security Council is a smaller body, composed of permanent and nonpermanent members. The five permanent members (the Four Policeman plus FRANCE) possess a veto over its decisions. It is the Security Council that is empowered to adopt economic and military sanctions against states. The third key organ of the United Nations is the Economic and Social Council. With varying degrees of authority, it coordinates the activities of many specialized UN agencies, such as the Commission on HUMAN RIGHTS, the World Health Organization, and the United Nations High Commissioner on REFUGEES, that work to promote higher standards of living and improve overall economic conditions. The fourth organizational component of the UN system is the Secretariat. It serves as the bureaucratic core of the UN and is headed by the secretary general. The fifth component is the Trusteeship Council. Its role of helping colonial territories transition to sovereign statehood and administering UN trust territories has declined in importance over time. The final component is the International Court of Justice, or World Court. It serves both as the constitutional court of the UN and a court in which states voluntarily can bring cases and settle their grievances.

The United States's relationship with the UN has varied over time. As noted above, at first the United States saw the UN as a means of preserving the great-POWER wartime ALLIANCE that had been created to defeat GERMANY and JAPAN. This vision did not last long, as the COLD WAR began to unfold and U.S.-Soviet rivalry became the dominant feature of international politics. Cracks in this vision began to appear almost from the beginning. The Soviet Union and many smaller states saw the United States as overbearing at

San Francisco. Particularly contentious was the United States's refusal to seat POLAND, where great controversy surrounded the establishment of a postwar communist government, and its insistence on allowing Argentina to join, even though it had only declared war on Germany in March.

With the demise of this vision, the UN now came to be seen as an instrument of American foreign policy. The overwhelming majority that the United States enjoyed in the General Assembly coupled with its veto in the Security Council made this possible. The high point of U.S. domination of the UN came with the KOREAN WAR, which was fought under the UN flag. This was made possible because the Soviet Union was boycotting meetings of the Security Council over the UN's refusal to award China's seat in the UN to Communist China. Realizing that this would not happen again, the United States used its majority in the

General Assembly to pass the Uniting for Peace Resolution that gave the General Assembly jurisdiction over military matters if the Security Council was deadlocked.

With the end of colonialism the composition of the General Assembly changed dramatically. The UN now became a tool of the newly independent states in their struggle to stay outside of the cold war competition between the United States and the Soviet Union. The principal innovation to this end was the establishment of PEACEKEEPING forces that might restore order and prevent either superpower from intervening. In general the United States and the Soviet Union both supported peacekeeping forces as a second-best solution to having the other take control of a Third World state. A notable exception was the CONGO, where the UN peacekeeping effort became highly politicized and failed. When the interests of these states shifted

First Security Council Session, London 1946  (UN Photo/Marcel Bolomey)

from cold war nonalignment to economic growth, the relationship between the UN and the United States became more conflictual. The United States found itself on the defensive as the UN called for creating a New International Economic Order that was less hospitable to capitalism and more responsive to the needs of developing states.

With the end of the cold war the relationship between the United States and UN has changed again. The exact nature of this relationship is not yet clear. Officials within the UN saw the end of the cold war as an opportunity to assert an independent role for the UN in world affairs. Secretary General Boutros Boutros-Ghali spoke of a mission that included preventive diplomacy, peacemaking, peacekeeping, and peace building. There was even talk of creating a standing UN military capability. This vision has proven to be too expansive, and the UN continues to struggle with the age-old dilemma faced by international organizations. On the one hand, they seek to advance the cause of common action and the establishment of a global consciousness, yet they are also instruments of the states that created them and cannot get too far ahead of them in any vision of the future.

At the same time that the UN was seeking to extend its role in world politics, American policy makers turned to the United Nations to accomplish some of its foreign-policy objectives. This has been especially true in the Persian Gulf, where President GEORGE H. W. BUSH and President GEORGE W. BUSH went to the UN to garner support for their wars with IRAQ. George Bush did so more willingly. He had hoped to use UN authorization as the sole basis for conducting the war, but opposition to this move within CONGRESS forced him to obtain a resolution of support from it as well.

The United States obtained several Security Council Resolutions against Iraq, beginning with one on August 2, 1990, that condemned the invasion of KUWAIT and culminating with Resolution 678 on November 29. It authorized the use of "all necessary means" to uphold the UN's previous resolutions should Iraq fail to comply by them by January 15, 1991. In the UN debate over how to proceed, the United States argued that Resolution 661 of August 6 that imposed a mandatory embargo on Iraq gave the United States the right to use force if the embargo was circumvented by Iraq. France, China, and Russia insisted that a new UN resolution was necessary for the United States to use force.

This debate in the Persian Gulf War on the terms by which a UN resolution might authorize the United States to use military force against Iraq was replayed in 2002 when George W. Bush was pressured by allies to go to the UN for approval of any military action. France, China, and Russia again were the primary roadblocks to obtaining such a resolution. Here again the United States claimed that Iraq's violation of previous UN resolutions gave the United States the authority to sue military force, while other states asserted a new resolution was necessary. It required weeks of bargaining and negotiation to find language for a new resolution that was acceptable to the United States and those states that felt military action, especially unilateral action, was premature.

The UN was the center of international DIPLOMACY in the period leading up to the IRAQ WAR. The fundamental issue at stake was whether or not the United States would seek UN approval for military action against Iraq and, if requested, whether it would be given. Some in the Bush administration asserted that the United States did not need UN approval because Iraq was still in breach of UN resolutions passed following the Persian Gulf War. President Bush addressed the United Nations on the one-year anniversary of the SEPTEMBER 11, 2001, terrorist attacks and challenged it to face up to the "grave and gathering danger" of Iraq or stand aside and allow the United States to act.

In his speech Bush indicated that he would work for a new resolution. Just before his speech, Secretary-General Kofi Annan had warned against taking unilateral action. Within a week Iraq promised to permit weapons inspectors "without conditions." Annan hailed the move as "an indispensable first step." The Bush administration called it a "tactic that will fail," asserting that the issue was not inspections but disarmament. But the Bush administration pressed ahead, and in-mid October it undertook what it described as a final attempt to bridge the gap with opponents over the wording of a compromise resolution. The gap between the opposing positions was still large. The United States was steadfast in its position that American military action could not be held hostage to a Security Council vote, while France argued that only the Security Council could make a decision on going to war. The revised U.S. draft resolution did not request UN authorization for military action nor did it contain language that made military action automatic. It did call for intrusive weapons inspections and warned of "severe consequences" should Iraq fail to comply. It also held that Iraq was in "material breach" of its DISARMAMENT obligations. Russia and France continued to object, and on November 8, 2002, a compromise was crafted that allowed the Security Council to act unanimously. Resolution 1441 gave Iraq 30 days to produce a "currently accurate, full, and complete declaration of all aspects of its programmes to develop chemical, biological, and NUCLEAR WEAPONS [and] ballistic missiles."

The lengthy debate revealed two very different sets of concerns. The first was over Iraq's violations and the threat that country presented to international security. The second was over the American position of unchallenged military dominance in the international system. The United States had become a "hyperpower" that threatened world peace with its recklessness.

Iraq accepted the UN resolution on November 13. On November 18 UN inspectors began arriving in Baghdad. Debate then continued in the United Nations over the findings of the inspector's VERIFICATION reports. On December 7, Iraq submitted a 12,000-page report. Two weeks later chief UN weapons inspector Hans Blix stated that the report contained little new information from that provided in 1997 and that it is "not enough to create confidence" that Iraq is disarming. Later reports continued to present these themes but added that the inspectors had not found any "smoking guns."

Just prior to a report of December 19, 2002, the Bush administration set late January as the decision deadline for Iraq. France indicated that it would block any new Security Council resolution authorizing the use of force against Iraq as intense diplomatic discussions began at the United Nations. The United States and Great Britain introduced a new resolution that would declare Iraq to be in "further material breach" of UN orders to disarm. France, Russia, Germany, and China opposed the resolution. After a brief SUMMIT CONFERENCE in the Azores with Spanish and British leaders, President Bush let it be known that the allies would remove their resolution authorizing military force against Iraq from discussion because they had reached the conclusion that "Council consensus will not be possible."

**Further reading:** Claude, Inis, L., Jr. *Swords into Plowshares: The Problems and Progress of International Organization.* 3d ed. New York: Random House, 1964; Durch, William J. *UN Peacekeeping, American Policy, and the Uncivil Wars of the 1990s.* New York: St. Martin's, 1996; Laurd, Evan, *A History of the United Nations.* New York: St. Martin's, 1982; Mingst, Karen, and Margaret Karns. *The United Nations in the Post–Cold War Era.* Boulder, Colo.: Westview, 1995.

## United States Agency for International Development (USAID)

The United States Agency for International Development (USAID) was established through an executive order by President JOHN KENNEDY in 1961. This followed the passage of the 1961 Foreign Assistance Act by CONGRESS. It reorganized U.S. FOREIGN-AID programs by dividing them into military and nonmilitary foreign aid. The hope was that freed from political and military objectives that drove existing foreign aid programs, it would be truly possible to address Third World development needs. This reorganization was undertaken against a backdrop of declining public and leadership support for foreign aid.

USAID has both regional and functional bureaus. Regional bureaus address development needs in sub-Saharan Africa, Asia and the Near East, Latin America and the Caribbean, and Europe and Eurasia. Functional bureaus focus on global programs and humanitarian responses. USAID has provided more than $4.3 billion in aid to Bangladesh since its independence in 1971. It has been actively involved in BOSNIA AND HERZEGOVINA as part of the DAYTON PEACE ACCORDS. It has provided more than $650 million to the five newly independent CENTRAL ASIAN STATES that became independent with the collapse of the Soviet Union (see RUSSIA).

The 1961 Foreign Assistance Act necessitated that an organization be established to advance U.S. long-term economic and social-assistance programs. USAID was the first U.S. organization with this mission, but it did not start totally from scratch. In 1953 the Foreign Operations Administration was set up as an independent agency outside of the STATE DEPARTMENT to coordinate economic and technical assistance. Within a year it was merged with the International Cooperation Agency that was part of the State Department and therefore was more limited in terms of what actions it could take as compared to an independent agency. As part of its start-up USAID unified existing aid programs housed in the International Cooperation Agency, the Development Loan Fund, the Export-Import Bank, and the FOOD FOR PEACE program.

USAID set up operations with few guidelines or restrictions on what type of factors to take into account in developing foreign-assistance programs. Its early efforts were heavily influenced by a theory of economic development put forward by Walt Rostow. He argued that countries passed through stages of economic growth. Particularly crucial from the perspective of USAID was the "takeoff" stage. To guide countries through these stages, USAID planners developed country specific long-term development planning schemes.

USAID has experienced a checkered history. The first major program undertaken by USAID was the ALLIANCE FOR PROGRESS that sought to promote economic development in the Western Hemisphere. This was a highly visible program for the Kennedy administration, and it brought instant status to USAID. By the 1970s USAID's fortunes had changed as policy makers once again had become disillusioned with foreign aid's ability to contribute to U.S. national security objectives or deliver economic development in its recipients. Repeated efforts have been made since then to reform foreign assistance, and the future role of USAID has been a frequent point of discussion. For example, in 1979 an International Development Cooperation Agency was set up through an executive order of President JIMMY CARTER to coordinate the various multilateral and bilateral foreign-assistance efforts engaged in by U.S. government agencies. It had little success and quietly disappeared from the scene during the Reagan administration. Accompanying these organizational woes has been a general decline in the importance of bilateral aid compared to multilateral aid, a decline that translates into loss of bureaucratic influence.

With the end of the COLD WAR, USAID has refocused its diminishing resources away from countries considered to be politically important to the United States in the cold war struggle against the Soviet Union to promoting democracy in key states and providing humanitarian assistance. Its organizational existence continued to come under attack. Senator JESSE HELMS (R-N.C.), chair of the Senate Foreign Relations Committee, combined his dislike for foreign-aid programs with his dislike for government inefficiency into a proposal to fold the UNITED STATES INFORMATION AGENCY and the ARMS CONTROL AND DISARMAMENT AGENCY back into the State Department. The Clinton administration accepted his proposal as the political price for allowing the Chemical Weapons Convention to come up for a vote. Under the new system, USAID retains its independent status but its director reports to the SECRETARY OF STATE rather than the PRESIDENT.

## United States Information Agency

The United States Information Agency (USIA) was created in 1953. It was incorporated in the STATE DEPARTMENT on April 1, 1999, as part of a reorganization that also brought the ARMS CONTROL AND DISARMAMENT AGENCY into the State Department. A two-year phase-in period was put into place by President BILL CLINTON's executive order. During the transition period, the director of USIA will also serve as the new undersecretary of state for public DIPLOMACY. This integration grew out of a plan put forward in 1997 by Vice President Al Gore to streamline and reinvent government and by the political need to address the concerns of Senator JESSE HELMS (R-N.C.), chair of the Senate Foreign Relations Committee. He opposed most Clinton foreign-policy initiatives and favored reorganizing the State Department to incorporate the quasi-independent agencies for USIA, the Arms Control and Disarmament Agency, and the UNITED STATES AGENCY FOR INTERNATIONAL DEVELOPMENT (USAID).

USIA was founded in 1953 in order to consolidate the public-diplomacy activities begun by the United States during WORLD WAR II. It had a twofold mission. First, USIA was to distribute information about American political and social developments to people in other countries. In these efforts it was to be objective and nonpolitical. The goal was to correct misperceptions of the United States abroad and to correct distortions in Soviet propaganda. The Truman administration, for example, had called for a "campaign of truth" in which there would be no concerted effort by U.S. information agencies to conceal problems or shortcomings in American society. The second mission tasked to USIA was to serve as a policy instrument in what the Eisenhower

administration saw as a "war of cultures" between the United States and the Soviet Union (see RUSSIA). Objectivity was not valued here. The need was to portray American society in the most positive light in order to dampen the appeal of COMMUNISM around the world. The tension between these objectives presented constant problems for the USIA as it conducted its business.

By law, USIA could not distribute its material in the United States. Its focus was to be overseas. An inventory of the activities it carried out includes coordinating cultural and educational exchanges, publishing periodicals for foreign distribution, operating libraries, sponsoring touring lectures and exhibits, and managing radio broadcasting networks and a television service. To carry out its mission, the United States Information Service was created. Some 9,000 individuals were employed in it. They were stationed in more than 140 countries and more than 160 cultural centers.

During the COLD WAR USIA libraries and exhibits frequently were targets for anti-American protests in the developing world. One of the most famous cold war photographs captures an impromptu debate over the merits of capitalism between Vice President RICHARD NIXON and Soviet leader Nikita Khrushchev at a 1959 USIA exhibit in Moscow touting the "Miracle Kitchen of Today." Russian visitors to the exhibit were told that it was capable of serving "17,500 dishes ranging from ready-to-bake biscuits and oven-ready vegetable pies to instant coffee and Jello."

The most famous cultural and educational exchange sponsored by USIA was the Fulbright program, which seeks to foster greater cross-cultural understanding through the exchange of students, scholars, and practitioners between the United States and other societies. Created in 1946, the Fulbright program continues to operate and encompasses a variety of exchange programs. More than 250,000 individuals have had the opportunity to visit and study in other countries because of it. Specific programs target scholars, mid-career professionals, elementary and secondary teachers, and graduate students. In its early years the Fulbright program was a particularly important vehicle for presenting a positive and visible image of the United States in developing states.

USIA is perhaps best known for its sponsorship of Voice of America (VOA). Established in 1942 during WORLD WAR II, VOA was the official voice of the U.S. government overseas. It provides a mixture of news, music, entertainment, and public-affairs broadcasting in more than 50 languages reaching an estimated 91 people worldwide each week. The tension between providing information and serving as a propaganda arm of U.S. foreign policy has frequently been acute in VOA's operations. During the Reagan administration the pendulum swung heavily in the direction of propaganda. This is most clearly seen in the creation of Radio Martí in 1983.

Named after Jose Martí, an important figure in the Cuban independence movement, and staffed by members of FLORIDA's Cuban exile community, Radio Martí broadcasts a hostile, anti-Castro message back to CUBA. In 1990 TV Martí began operation. The end of the cold war has seen a continued expansion in VOA activities. In 1994 its Chinese branch began a TV and radio simulcast of "China Forum." In 1996 VOA began a weekly radio–TV simulcast in Farsi to IRAN and broadcasts in Afan Oromo and Tigrigna to ETHIOPIA and ERITRIA.

As part of restructuring in 1999, VOA now falls under the jurisdiction of the Broadcasting Board of Governors. It oversees all U.S. government and government-sponsored nonmilitary international broadcasting: VOA, RADIO FREE EUROPE/Radio Liberty, Radio and TV Martí, Worldnet Television, and Radio Free Asia. Broadly stated the purpose of the Broadcasting Board of Governor is twofold. First, it is to "serve as a firewall between the international broadcasters and the policy making institutions." Second, it is to evaluate effectiveness. These two goals reflect the continued importance of and tension in the original missions of USIA.

**Further reading:** Bogart, Leo. *Cool Words, Cold War: A New Look at the USIA's Premises of Propaganda.* Washington, D.C.: American University Press, 1995.

## United States Institute of Peace

The United States Institute of Peace (USIP) was established in 1984 with the mission of strengthening "the nation's capabilities to promote the peaceful resolution of international conflicts." USIP has come to play a leading role in both government and academic circles as a source for ideas about how to create and preserve international peace. Its origins need to be understood in both conceptual and political terms.

Conceptually, the USIP typifies the American approach to thinking about world politics. Americans adopt an engineering approach to problem solving. It is one that emphasizes constructing formulas (be they legal, political, or military) and applying them to problems the way an engineer would go about working from a blueprint in constructing a bridge. It was hoped that by studying conflict, the USIP could develop a series of formulas and problem-solving techniques that would promote peace. In some respects the USIP was able to make use of the relatively new field of peace studies for guidance in searching for these techniques. Much work had been done on conflict resolution in the domestic arena, and both scholars and practitioners hoped to apply these findings to international conflicts. The creation of the USIP also reflects a sense of American exceptionalism. The 1984 legislation creating it states that the USIP was to be a "living institution embodying the heritage, ideals, and concerns of the American people for peace."

Politically, the creation of the USIP involved a test of strength between the liberal and conservative wings of the American political system. From 1935 to 1976 more than 140 bills were introduced into CONGRESS to establish peace-related bureaucratic departments and committees of Congress. At least twice, during the VIETNAM WAR and during the Reagan administration's military buildup, significant portions of the American public came together to launch peace movements. These groups argued for the creation of a government-sponsored peace academy to offset the influence of the military academies and military graduate institutions, such as the National War College and National Defense University.

In 1981 a commission charged by Congress to look into the matter called for the creation of a national peace academy. Legislation to create it was introduced in 1983 and became the subject of sharp debate. In the end Congress approved the measure in large part as a tribute to one of the bill's sponsors, retiring senator Jennings Randolph (D-W.V.). Its passage and subsequent startup reflect the typical bargaining and compromise that occurs in Washington. The USIP was funded as an amendment to the DEPARTMENT OF DEFENSE appropriations bill. It was defined as an institute rather than an academy, and it was not permitted to grant degrees. The Reagan administration appointed a conservative board to oversee its operations, and early USIP studies tended to define peace in terms of defeating COMMUNISM. They focused heavily on such military subjects as intermediate-range nuclear forces and low-intensity conflict.

Its agenda has broadened with the end of the cold war and the surge in PEACEKEEPING activities. USIP projects underway in 2001 included a cross-cultural negotiation study that examined how cultural differences influence negotiations, a coercive diplomacy study that sought to shed light on how positive inducements can be combined with punitive sanctions to achieve foreign-policy goals, and a HUMAN-RIGHTS implementation project that sought to distill lessons from the successes and failures of past U.S. human-rights policies.

The USIP is located in Washington, D.C., and is governed by a 15-member bipartisan board of directors appointed by the PRESIDENT. Eleven of its members are from outside of government. By terms of its original charter the USI was prohibited from securing private funding. This prohibition was dropped in 1992. Congress appropriated $10.9 million to the USIP for 1994. Approximately one-fourth of its budget is directed to funding individual scholars and educational institutions engaged in peace research. Also included is funding for secondary education and college teachers to attend USIP workshops and prepare curriculum material.

## United States Trade Representative, Office of the

The U.S. Trade Representative (USTR) is the title given both to an agency located within the Executive Office of the President and to the individual who heads this agency. The Office of the U.S. Trade Representative was created by CONGRESS as part of the 1962 Trade Expansion Act. It was originally known as the Office of the Special Trade Representative and received its current name in 1980. The individual heading the USTR holds ambassador rank and cabinet-level status.

The USTR is responsible for developing and coordinating U.S. international trade, commodity, and direct investment policy. The office leads or directs international negotiations with other countries on these matters. This includes all matters that fall within the jurisdiction of the WORLD TRADE ORGANIZATION. To accomplish these tasks the USTR is divided into five areas: bilateral negotiations; multilateral negotiations; sectoral activities; analysis, legal affairs, and policy coordination; and public outreach. Each year in accordance with the provisions of the 1974 Trade Act, the USTR produces a National Trade Estimate Report on Foreign Trade Barriers. In it, the USTR inventories the most important foreign trade barriers affecting U.S. exports of goods, services, foreign direct investment, and protection of intellectual property rights. It also identifies what actions are being taken to eliminate or reduce these trade barriers.

An important facet of the work of the USTR is the interagency coordination of trade policy. To that end it has set up a Trade Policy Review Group, which operates at the senior civil-service level, and a Trade Policy Staff Committee. The deliberations of these two bodies are chaired by USTR and are composed of representatives from 17 different federal agencies and offices. The Trade Policy Staff Committee is supported by more than 60 subcommittees responsible for special policy areas plus task forces that address specific issues.

The 1974 Trade Act also mandated the establishment of a private sector advisory committee system in order to make sure that U.S. trade policy accurately reflected U.S. economic and commercial interests. After approximately 25 years of operation, there existed 33 advisory committees, with a membership of almost 1,000 nominated by members of CONGRESS, trade associations, organization, publications, or individuals who have an interest in U.S. trade policy. At the top of this hierarchy of advisory groups is the 45-person President's Advisory Committee for Trade Policy and Negotiations. Some policy trade advisory councils are administered solely by USTR, while others are jointly administered by USTR and the Environmental Protection Agency, the Department of Labor, the DEPARTMENT OF COMMERCE, and the DEPARTMENT OF DEFENSE.

The establishment, location, and operation of the USTR highlight the extent to which international trade policy is pulled both by domestic and foreign pressures. Congress created the USTR largely out of frustration with the STATE DEPARTMENT's handling of international trade. It felt that the State Department was too concerned with the policy positions of foreign states and was not sufficiently responsive to American business interests. Placing the USTR within the White House and not establishing it as a traditional executive agency marked a further sign of congressional displeasure with international trade policy. The 1974 Trade Act's requirement that policy advisory councils be established, including one at the presidential level, points to continued congressional concern that neither State nor Commerce, Treasury, or Agriculture is fully meeting the needs of American business interests. More recent public and congressional reactions to the World Trade Organization and the NORTH AMERICAN FREE TRADE ACT indicate that these concerns have not subsided, thus ensuring that the USTR will remain at the center of a volatile policy area.

See also TRADE POLICY.

**Further reading:** Dryden, Steve. *Trade Warriors: The USTR and the American Crusade for Free Trade.* New York: Oxford University Press, 1995.

## *United States v. Belmont* (1934)

The case of the *United States v. Belmont* grew out of the 1933 diplomatic recognition of the Soviet Union (see RUSSIA) by the Roosevelt administration. Relations between the two states had been broken following the 1917 Russian Revolution and the coming to POWER of the Bolshevik (Communist) Party. A sticking point in reestablishing relations was the settlement of claims against the Soviet Union made by Americans who lost property without compensation when the Communists nationalized foreign-owned companies. Through an EXECUTIVE AGREEMENT, the Litvinov Agreement, it was determined that compensation would be made and that the U.S. government would act as agent for the Soviet Union in collecting and dispersing funds. To this end, the United States brought suit to collect money deposited in the New York bank of August Belmont by the Petrograd Metal Works prior to 1918. A U.S. Court of Appeals rejected the U.S. claim. The case went to the SUPREME COURT, which ruled in favor of the U.S. government.

Justice George Sutherland delivered the Supreme Court's opinion, stating that "no state policy can prevail against the international compact involved here." He also noted that the Court did not "pause to inquire . . . whether in fact there was any policy of the State of New York to be infringed." He concluded that "plainly the external powers of the United States are to be exercised without regard to state laws or policies."

In making this ruling the Supreme Court further delineated issues broached in the decision given in *MISSOURI V. HOLLAND* (1920), which concluded that treaties took precedence over state laws. The case here involved not a treaty but an executive agreement. The CONSTITUTION recognizes a difference between the treaties and agreements or compacts but does not indicate how they differ legally. They clearly differ in how the Senate responds to them. It must ratify treaties but has no say in executive agreements. In the *U.S. v. Belmont*, the Supreme Court was asserting that they were equal in its eyes, and both superceded state law. As with *Missouri v. Holland, U.S. v. Belmont* served as an important impetus to the BRICKER AMENDMENT, a constitutional amendment that, had it passed, would have required Senate ratification of executive agreements and stipulated that if treaties were to have the effect of domestic law they would have to be made pursuant to powers granted to the federal government.

## United States v. Curtiss-Wright Export Corp.
### (1936)

*United States v. Curtiss Wright Export Corp.* (1936) presents a bold statement by the SUPREME COURT of presidential dominance in foreign policy. The case centers on the constitutionality of a presidential embargo on arms sales to Bolivia and Peru in an attempt to end the Chaco War. In 1934 CONGRESS passed a joint resolution delegating to President FRANKLIN ROOSEVELT the authority to stop the flow of arms to these states if he thought it would help bring about a cease-fire. Roosevelt soon announced an arms embargo for this purpose. Curtiss-Wright Export Corp. was charged with violating the embargo.

Curtiss-Wright Export Corp. challenged the constitutionality of Roosevelt's action. It asserted that according to the CONSTITUTION, Congress possessed the power to regulate commerce. This was not a POWER that Congress could give away to the PRESIDENT. It was power for Congress to use or not use and nothing more. If Congress wanted to prevent arms sales to Bolivia and Peru, the proper course of action was to pass a law.

Justice George Sutherland, speaking for the SUPREME COURT, rejected this argument and put forward a broad interpretation of presidential power in the realm of foreign policy. He drew a sharp distinction between foreign and domestic policy: "The two classes of power are different, both in respect of their origins and their nature. The broad statement that the federal government can exercise no powers except those specifically enumerated in the Constitution . . . is categorically true only in respect of our internal affairs."

Sutherland and the Court held that foreign policy was different. Sutherland asserted: "Sovereignty is never held in suspense. When, therefore, the external sovereignty of GREAT BRITAIN in respect of the colonies ceased, it almost immediately passed to the Union. . . . The Union existed before the Constitution. . . . The powers to declare and wage war, to conclude peace, to make treaties, to maintain diplomatic relations with other sovereignties if they had never been mentioned in the Constitution would have vested in the federal government as necessary concomitants of nationality. . . . [T]he President alone has the power to speak or listen as a representative of the nation. . . . Congressional legislation . . . must often accord to the President a degree of discretion and freedom from statutory restriction which would not be advisable were domestic affairs alone involved."

## Uruguay Round

The Uruguay Round was the eighth round of GENERAL AGREEMENT ON TARIFFS AND TRADE (GATT) talks. These negotiating rounds have been the principal instrument by which the post–WORLD WAR II international economic system of free trade has been managed. The Uruguay Round is significant because these negotiations led to the creation of the WORLD TRADE ORGANIZATION (WTO). GATT became the organizing device for free trade largely by default and out of necessity. Together with the INTERNATIONAL TRADE ORGANIZATION (ITO), GATT was created in 1947 as part of the Havana Charter. The ITO, however, never came into existence. Opposition within the U.S. Congress led the Truman administration to abandon it.

Prior to the beginning of the Uruguay Round, the last GATT round was the TOKYO ROUND that began in 1973 and concluded in 1979. While the Tokyo Round made progress on reducing nontariff barriers to free trade, by the early 1980s there had emerged a general feeling that the international trade system was in danger of collapse. Departures from GATT rules had become common, and bilateral agreements rather than global ones were increasingly employed as a means of settling trade disputes. This was especially true in U.S.-Japanese economic relations, in which the United States was now routinely protesting the treatment given to U.S.-made goods by JAPAN. This deteriorating situation led the Reagan administration to call for a new round of GATT talks in 1983. Initially the EUROPEAN UNION opposed such a conference, but it relented, and in 1986 the Uruguay Round was officially begun at a special meeting of GATT held in Punta del Este, Uruguay. The actual negotiations began in 1987.

Trade negotiations in the Uruguay Round were organized into 15 groups that involved four broad sets of concerns. One set of concerns involved carry-over items from previous rounds, such as tariffs and safeguards. A second set of concerns involved issues of importance to the developing economies. Important here was trade in natural resource–based products. The third set of concerns centered on strengthening GATT as an institution and reforming its rules for dispute settlement. No effective enforcement mechanism existed, and protection of third parties to a trade dispute was weak and ineffective. Finally, some negotiations were directed at expanding the reach of GATT to cover new areas of trade, such as services, investment, and intellectual property.

When the Uruguay Round began, most expected that the major battle lines would be drawn between the rich countries of the North seeking added markets and the poor countries of the South seeking to protect their fragile economies from external domination. This proved not to be the case, as during the 1980s most developing states had embraced an export-oriented development strategy that required free trade. Instead, the major line of cleavage was between the United States on the one hand and Europe and Japan on the other. The most divisive issue was agriculture, with the United States called for phasing out all direct farm subsidies. Talks came to at a virtual deadlock in 1988, and they were suspended until April 1989. Progress was forthcoming again in 1991 and 1992, and an agreement seemed near. President BILL CLINTON took office in 1993 and received FAST-TRACK negotiating authority from CONGRESS to conclude a new GATT agreement. This authority expired on December 15, 1993, and officials secured an effective deadline for an agreement. A flurry of negotiations between the United States and Europe then followed, most of which dealt with reducing barriers to free trade in agriculture. On December 15 it was announced that an agreement had been reached. The 400-page treaty covering some 10,000 products and containing 22,000 additional pages of tariff schedules was signed by 144 countries in Marrakesh, MOROCCO, on April 15, 1994, and its provisions took effect on January 1, 1995. The most significant of those provisions was the establishment of the WTO.

President Clinton hailed the new agreement as a "vision of economic renewal." Criticism, however, could be found all across the political spectrum. On the conservative right, Pat Buchanan labeled the treaty "a wholesale surrender of American sovereignty" for the powers it gave the WTO. On the political left, Ralph Nader voiced a similar concern. He condemned the treaty as making governments around the world "increasingly hostage to an unaccountable system of transnational governance designed to increase corporate profit." These concerns have remained at the forefront of public evaluations of WTO decision making and led to large-scale public protests at a variety of international trade meetings.

**Further reading:** Kenen, Peter, ed. *Managing the World Economy: Fifty Years after Bretton Woods*. Washington, D.C.: Institute for International Economics, 1994; Preeg, Ernest. *Traders in a Brave New World: The Uruguay Round and the Future of the International Trading System*. Chicago: University of Chicago Press, 1997.

## USA PATRIOT Act

Officially known as the Uniting and Strengthening America by Providing Appropriate Tools Required to Intercept and Obstruct Terrorism Act, the USA PATRIOT Act was adopted by CONGRESS on October 25, 2001, and signed into law the following day by President GEORGE W. BUSH.

The USA PATRIOT Act, a 324-page document, emerged as the Bush administration's immediate legislative response to the SEPTEMBER 11, 2001, terrorist attacks on the World Trade Center and the Pentagon. Its intent was to provide law enforcement officials with an enhanced ability to investigate and prosecute TERRORISM. One of its provisions expanded the definition of engaged in terrorist activity to include providing support for groups that an individual "knew or should have known were terrorist organization." Among its primary targets were the monetary transactions and electronic communications employed by terrorists. Financial institutions and agents now had to provide additional verifiable information about their customers. The government also had easier access to electronic information. Rather than obtain a wiretap order, authorities were able to use search warrants to read opened voicemail messages and electronic mail from Internet providers. The USA PATRIOT Act also expanded the list of toxins that are classified as dangerous and required background checks of scientists who work with them. As further evidence of the act's scope, companies transporting wastes must now provide background checks for drivers transporting hazardous material.

One of the most important set of provisions in the USA PATRIOT Act affected the conduct of INTELLIGENCE activities in the United States. Intelligence surveillance was not permitted when foreign intelligence was a "significant purpose" rather than "the purpose" of the undertaking. The act broadened the authority of the government to contract for terrorist information with individuals once placed off limits because of HUMAN-RIGHTS violations or other transgressions. It also contained a number of directives intended to promote intelligence sharing and cooperation among intelligence agencies. Included here was the prompt disclosure of information obtained in a criminal investigation and the establishment of a virtual translation center within the INTELLIGENCE COMMUNITY.

Many of the provisions of the USA PATRIOT Act (some of which contain sunset provisions that take effect on December 31, 2005) and the speed with which it was passed have raised concerns among many onlookers. The legislation was passed so quickly that there were no committee reports or votes taken, thus denying law-enforcement officials and outside experts the opportunity to comment on its provisions. Furthermore, the absence of typical committee hearings deprived implementers and legal officials of insight into the congressional intent in passing the USA PATRIOT Act. Its key provisions were worked out in negotiations between Attorney General John Ashcroft, Senator Patrick Leahy (D-Vt.) and Senator Orrin Hatch (R-Utah). A particularly controversial provision calls for increasing the national DNA database to include not only samples from convicted terrorists but also "any crime of violence." The crimes to be included in this database have been debated since its controversial initial creation in October 1998. Also controversial is the extended time that aliens suspected of being involved in acts of terrorism may be detained.

Immediately following the passage of the USA PATRIOT Act, many felt that it marked only the first step of a lengthy legislative process on how to deal with terrorism rather than the end point of these efforts. The lack of consensus of the meaning of particular provisions established the foundation for a second round of legislative activity. Congress also had yet to establish oversight procedures for measuring the effectiveness of these provisions and for judging the actions of those who were carrying them out. The sunset provisions written into many portions of the USA PATRIOT Act guarantee that Congress will have return to these issues in the future.

# V

**Vance, Cyrus Roberts** (1917–2002) *secretary of state, diplomat*

Although born in West Virginia, Cyrus Vance embodied the values and traditions of the East Coast establishment that once dominated the American diplomatic corps. Educated at Yale, Vance served Democratic presidents from JOHN KENNEDY to JIMMY CARTER and earned a reputation for honesty. He was eulogized as a principled statesman. During his career, which included service as secretary of the army (1961–62), deputy secretary of defense (1964–67), chief negotiator to the Paris Peace Talks on VIETNAM (1968–69), special envoy to Cyprus (1967), SECRETARY OF STATE (1976–80), and head of UNITED NATIONS efforts to bring peace to YUGOSLAVIA (1991–92), Vance's preferred method for dealing with foreign-policy problems was to eschew grand designs in favor of patient negotiation and pragmatism.

Vance is best remembered for his 1980 resignation as secretary of state in the Carter administration. Early in the administration Vance was instrumental in helping Carter develop his HUMAN-RIGHTS policy. Over time he became embroiled in a political tug of war with NATIONAL SECURITY ADVISOR Zbigniew Brzezinski for dominance in foreign-policy making. One critical policy in which the two clashed was over how to respond to the IRANIAN HOSTAGE CRISIS. Vance favored a negotiated solution and feared that rash action would make the situation worse. Brzezinski favored bold action. With Vance absent, Brzezinski and Carter agreed upon a rescue effort, Eagle Claw. When Vance found out about the plan, he tried to get Carter to change his mind. When this did not happen, Vance informed Carter that he would resign as secretary of state regardless of how the rescue mission turned out. It failed, never reaching the hostages and killing eight American soldiers in the attempt. The last secretary of state to resign in protest had been WILLIAM JENNINGS BRYAN, who left office in opposition to America's entrance into WORLD WAR I.

Secretary of State Cyrus Vance *(left)* confers with President Jimmy Carter. *(Carter Library)*

Vance would have one more significant foreign-policy assignment. In 1991–92, along with former British foreign minister David, Lord Owen, he led a United Nations effort to end the fighting in the former Yugoslavia. Together they authored a controversial peace plan for BOSNIA AND HERZEGOVINA and CROATIA. Some characterized it as a sham while others saw it as the best last hope for peace. It would have created a single Bosnian state, organized around 12 ethnic subregions.

**Further reading:** Vance, Cyrus. *Hard Choices: Critical Years in American Foreign Policy.* New York: Simon and Schuster, 1983.

**Vandenberg, Arthur** (1884–1951) *senator*

Arthur Hendrick Vandenberg was a Republican senator from Michigan who played a decisive role in moving the United States from interwar ISOLATIONISM to post–WORLD WAR II INTERNATIONALISM. Vandenberg served in the

Senate from 1928 until his death in 1951. He became chair of the Senate Foreign Relations Committee in 1946.

Early in his political life, Vandenberg was a disciple of THEODORE ROOSEVELT and supported his internationalist policies. However, he opposed President WOODROW WILSON's interventions into Latin American, calling them a product of "missionary DIPLOMACY." He initially was a supporter of Wilson's FOURTEEN POINTS but opposed U.S. membership in the LEAGUE OF NATIONS, because he believed doing so would conflict with the freedom to intervene into Latin American affairs contained in the MONROE DOCTRINE. In the Senate he became a protégé of Senator WILLIAM BORAH (R-Idaho) and moved to an isolationist outlook on foreign-policy issues. The ultimate statement of this view was his co-authoring of the 1937 NEUTRALITY ACT. Vandenberg also joined with Senator Gerald Nye (R-N.D.) in his investigations into the influence of arms manufacturers and bankers on the U.S. decision to enter WORLD WAR I.

The Japanese attack on Pearl Harbor was instrumental in converting Vandenberg to an internationalist position. He stated that the attack "ended isolation for any realist." From that point forward Vandenberg entered into a series of uneasy political ALLIANCES with DEMOCRATIC PARTY presidents. He served on a committee to create a bipartisan foreign policy. FRANKLIN ROOSEVELT appointed him a delegate to the 1945 San Francisco Conference that established the UNITED NATIONS (UN). In return, Vandenberg played a leading role in securing Senate approval for the UN Charter and making sure that the charter did not prohibit regional security agreements. The right to do so, contained in Article 51 of the Charter, became the legal basis on which the United States grounded its participation in the NORTH ATLANTIC TREATY ORGANIZATION (NATO) and the RIO PACT.

Vandenberg was a valuable congressional ally of President HARRY TRUMAN in building Republican support for his early foreign-policy initiatives such as the TRUMAN DOCTRINE and the MARSHALL PLAN. Though he conferred regularly with the Truman administration, he was not a close confident of Truman, nor were his opinions held in particularly high regard. Vandenberg remained committed to bipartisanship after the outbreak of the KOREAN WAR, and he did not join Senator Joseph McCarthy and other Republicans in their attacks on Truman for losing CHINA and being soft on COMMUNISM.

See also INTERNATIONALISM; MCCARTHYISM; NYE COMMISSION.

## Venezuela

Located in northern South America, with an area of 352,143 square miles, Venezuela is more than twice the size of California. The first permanent Spanish settlement was established in Venezuela in 1522. Movement toward independence began in the late 18th century, and independence was declared in 1811. Complete independence was realized in 1821. Along with the current countries of COLOMBIA, PANAMA, and Ecuador, Venezuela formed the Republic of Gran Colombia. In 1830 Venezuela left this union to become a sovereign state. The United States recognized Venezuela in 1835.

Early U.S. relations with Venezuela were not very extensive. Two major diplomatic encounters occurred around the turn of the 20th century. Both were rooted more in American hemispheric foreign-policy designs than they were in a concern for Venezuela per se. The first took place in 1895 and centered on a boundary dispute between Venezuela and GREAT BRITAIN over British Guiana. Framing the matter of its ill-defined boundary with British Guiana in the context of the MONROE DOCTRINE, Venezuelan authorities had lobbied every SECRETARY OF STATE since the mid-1870s for support. It was not until the administration of President GROVER CLEVELAND that true support was forthcoming. Domestic politics appears to be the primary reason for this sudden interest in Venezuela's cause. Cleveland sought a foreign-policy triumph against the British to improve his standing with the American voters. His secretary of state, RICHARD OLNEY, sent the British a note invoking the Monroe Doctrine and accusing them of violating it. The British responded harshly and rejected the legitimacy of the Monroe Doctrine. Tensions eased as the two sides finally agreed to arbitration, after the British had changed their position and recognized the legitimacy of the Monroe Doctrine. The Olney-Pauncefote Treaty settled the boundary line, excluding Venezuela from these discussions.

The second major involvement was an Anglo-German-Italian blockade of Venezuela in 1902. At issue was Venezuela's failure to pay claims owed to citizens and corporations of these states. The THEODORE ROOSEVELT administration did not object, the Monroe Doctrine not withstanding, because these states indicated that their military action would not result in the acquisition or permanent occupation of Venezuelan territory. Once the blockade was in place, however, the Roosevelt administration began to reconsider its position. It began a round of diplomatic activity that led to an agreement whereby claims would be submitted to either the Permanent Court of Arbitration in The Hague or a mixed-claims commissions. American frustration with the financial situation in Venezuela and government policies that included the seizure of U.S. property led it to support the overthrow of President Cipriano Castro.

COLD WAR relations between the United States and Venezuela were largely noncontroversial, save for a 1959 visit by Vice President RICHARD NIXON to Caracas. He was met at the airport by protestors, and, leaving the airport, his motorcade was stopped and the windows in his car broken. Nixon had traveled to South America quite successfully earlier in the 1950s. His hostile reception in Caracas reflected two points of grievance with the United States. The first was a general anger at American support for right-wing dictators and the poverty that characterized many of their regimes. Second, in the months preceding Nixon's visit, the United States had given asylum to the ousted Venezuelan dictator, Marcos Pérez Jiménez, and his head of the secret police. In its analysis of the situation, American officials alternately stressed the problem of poverty and blamed it on Communists.

More recently economic issues have been the focal point of U.S.-Venezuelan relations, and their positive or negative character has generally reflected the overall state of the international economy and the nationalist economic policies of Venezuelan leaders. American economic interest in Venezuela began to grow after WORLD WAR I. The object of American attention was OIL, and by 1929 Venezuela had become one of the world's leading petroleum exporters. Today some 60 foreign oil companies from 14 countries operate in Venezuela, and oil accounts for almost 80 percent of its export earnings and one-third of its gross domestic product. On the opposite side of the ledger, the United State supplies Venezuela with one-third of its food imports. Overall, the United States is Venezuela's leading trade partner, and it is the United State's third-largest export market in Latin America. Venezuela's economic position weakened in the 1980s, and it found itself unable to repay its international debts and in need of American assistance.

Venezuela's rich natural resources have also placed it in the position of serving as an advocate for the developing world, often opposing the United States. It is a founding member of the ORGANIZATION OF PETROLEUM EXPORTING COUNTRIES (OPEC), and in 1973 Caracas advocated policies that led to a quadrupling of world oil prices. In the 1970s Venezuela was a strong supporter of calls for a New International Economic Order. More recently it has been cautious in its support for regional free-trade arrangements in the Western Hemisphere.

In this century two issues have brought Venezuela and the United States into conflict. The first involves the international DRUG-TRAFFICKING problem. Venezuela is not a major producer of opium, but it is a major transportation route for opium and cocaine, and it serves as a site for money laundering. Bordering on Colombia, the major drug center in the hemisphere, Venezuela plays a key role in any regional U.S. strategy for addressing this problem. The second issue has surrounded position taken by Washington in a failed 2002 coup attempt. The GEORGE W. BUSH administration moved quickly, and many in Venezuela

argued that it was too quickly, to back the new government. Ultimately the coup failed, and President Hugo Chávez remained in POWER. Bush's actions strained U.S.-Venezuelan relations and called into question the administration's support for democracy in the hemisphere.

See also DEMOCRATIZATION; VENEZUELAN BOUNDARY DISPUTE.

**Further reading:** McCoy, Jennifer, et al., eds. *Venezuelan Democracy under Stress* Piscataway, N.J.: Transaction Publishers, 1995.

## Venezuelan boundary dispute

The Venezuelan boundary dispute between VENEZUELA and GREAT BRITAIN was over ownership of some 50,000 square miles of sparsely populated jungle that, nonetheless, was of strategic value because it guarded the mouth of Venezuela's most important river. No firm border between Venezuela and British Guiana had been established in this region, although a British survey team had set a boundary, known as the Schomburgk line, in 1841. Venezuela rejected this line because it favored British Guiana and repeatedly called upon Great Britain to enter into arbitration. Great Britain resisted because it considered Venezuela's claims excessive and feared that an arbitration panel might award it too much land.

As the second Cleveland administration began, Venezuela turned to the United States for help by hiring William Scruggs, who later became a minister to Venezuela under President WARREN HARDING, to lobby CONGRESS. Scruggs produced an inflammatory and one-sided pamphlet that made it appear that Great Britain was the aggressor. Congress responded in 1895 by unanimously passing a resolution calling for arbitration. Public opinion had further turned against Great Britain, because in April 1895 it had sent troops to Nicaragua in order to collect funds owed it.

In June 1895 SECRETARY OF STATE RICHARD OLNEY sent a diplomatic note to London asserting that Great Britain was violating the MONROE DOCTRINE, which he defined as a "doctrine of American public law," and insisted that Great Britain submit the boundary dispute to arbitration. The British delayed in responding, but when they did, they rejected the Monroe Doctrine as having any validity under INTERNATIONAL LAW. Neither Olney's note nor the British response was cast in tempered language, and upon receipt of the response GROVER CLEVELAND was left with little room to maneuver. He responded by delivering a speech to Congress requesting funds for an investigating commission to determine where the boundary line should be properly drawn. He continued by saying that the United States "must resist be every means in its power" any British attempt to exercise jurisdiction over territory the United States determines to be Venezuelan. His rhetoric fueled a wave of anti-British sentiment that made war appear quite possible.

The British had little desire to go to war. Venezuela was relatively unimportant to them, and they faced challenges from GERMANY and mounting troubles in SOUTH AFRICA. Within the United States business interests and many clergy also opposed war. In 1897 they agreed to a treaty of arbitration with Venezuela, and at this point the American boundary commission disbanded. The decision of the arbitrators was not handed down until 1899. Their decision largely followed the Schomburgk line and did not give significantly more territory to Venezuela than the British had offered on previous occasions.

Curiously, the incident marked the beginning of a new period of Anglo-American cooperation, as it demonstrated a capacity for both sides to engage in mutually beneficial cooperation. The Venezuelan boundary dispute also revealed a willingness to challenge foreign powers in the Western Hemisphere and gave evidence of the sense of belligerent nationalism that soon would burst into the open with the SPANISH-AMERICAN WAR.

**Further reading:** Eggert, Gerald G. *Richard Olney.* University Park: Pennsylvania State University Press, 1974.

## verification

Our tendency is to assume that an ARMS CONTROL or DISARMAMENT agreement is complete when it is signed and ratified. This is not the case. Some of the most difficult problems come in creating a system for its implementation. The key management issues center on establishing agreed upon procedures for monitoring behavior, getting agreement on what constitutes acceptable behavior, and devising procedures for resolving disputes. Collectively, these constitute the verification problem.

Verification techniques—those that can be used to monitor an agreement—can be broken down into three categories. Throughout the 1950s, the UNITED STATES insisted upon, and the Soviet Union rejected, on-site inspection as the only way of effectively monitoring treaty behavior. In the 1960s advances in missile, satellite, radar, and airplane technology led both the United States and the Soviet Union to embrace national technical means of verification (NTM) as the primary means by which treaty behavior would be verified. NTMs were specified in the STRATEGIC ARMS LIMITATIONS TALKS (SALT I & II) Treaties as the means for verification. In the SALT I Treaty, each side pledged not to take steps to interfere with the other's ability to conduct NTM verification. SALT II extended this pledge by prohibiting each side from deliberately denying the other telemetry necessary for verifica-

tion. *Telemetry* refers to the electronic signals given off by a missile during testing. Scientists use telemetry to evaluate a missile's performance and capabilities.

Impressive as NTM capabilities are, they are not without limits. For example, at distances of greater than 625 miles, seismic detectors have great difficulty distinguishing between a small underground nuclear explosion and an earthquake. Because of such limitations, on-site inspection continues to have its supporters. The INTERMEDIATE-RANGE NUCLEAR FORCES (INF) TREATY contained extensive on-site verification provisions concerning the number of missiles to be destroyed and procedures for observing their destruction as well as the facilities that produced them and that housed them when they were operational. A controlled system of short-notice inspections was put in place. There were also provisions for the continuous observation of some missile factories.

Because on-site inspection also has its limitations, the United States and the Soviet Union have developed a series of cooperative verification measures such as data exchanges on the production and transportation schedules of missiles, so as to make NTM and on-site inspections more effective. An important type of cooperative measure is the development of agreed upon counting rules. The issue arises from the fact that while one can count missiles, it is all but impossible to count the number of warheads on each missile. To that end the United States and the Soviet Union set up a system of artificial counting rules. One governed the capabilities of intercontinental ballistic missiles: Once a deployed missile is tested with a given number of warheads, then every missile of that type will be assumed to carry the number of warheads. Such counting rules have also constituted a major negotiating point with regard to the capabilities of submarine-launched ballistic missiles and manned bombers.

In making judgments about what constitutes acceptable behavior, the broad concern in arms control agreements is with preventing the opponent from achieving a "break-out" capability—that is, the ability to gain a short-term military advantage that cannot be countered. In the nuclear area, typically this has led to a focus on deployed missiles. Another possibility is to focus on research and development. SALT I permitted continued research and development of antiballistic missile system (ABM) technologies so long as they did not lead to system or component testing. Dating back to President RONALD REAGAN's STRATEGIC DEFENSE INITIATIVE (SDI), or Star Wars, this prohibition has been a major stumbling block in constructing a BALLISTIC MISSILE DEFENSE SYSTEM.

In seeking to prevent the Soviet Union from gaining a break-out capability, the United States has employed two different verification standards. Between 1963 and 1979 the standard was one of adequate verification, which President RICHARD NIXON defined as "whether we can identify attempted evasion if it occurs on a large enough scale to pose a significant risk and whether we can do so in time to mount a sufficient response." President Reagan set a standard of effective verification. This proved to be a more demanding standard, as many of the activities considered acceptable or unverifiable by the Nixon and Carter administrations were now labeled as violations of existing agreements. A point of contention was the Krasnoyarsk radar station that the United States claimed was in violation of the ANTIBALLISTIC MISSILE TREATY because it tracked missiles. For a long time the Soviet Union denied these charges, only to admit to them in 1989.

The final element of a verification system is creating means for resolving differences of interpretation. SALT I created the Standing Consultative Commission (SCC) to arbitrate misunderstandings in a quiet and confidential manner. The Reagan administration viewed the SCC as a body that simply papered over Soviet arms control violations by redefining them as acceptable practices. It preferred to engage in a public debate with the Soviet Union. An underlying point of dispute in these two approaches is whether to treat accusations of unacceptable behavior as a normal part of DIPLOMACY, due as much to vague language and changed circumstances—the SCC approach—or as deliberate and manipulative violations—the Reagan administration approach.

Verification promises to become an even more challenging aspect of American foreign policy as the scope of arms control agreements expands to include conventional military technologies and dual-use technologies (those with uses in both military and nonmilitary sectors) and becomes global rather than bilateral in scope. Efforts by the United States to construct a national ballistic missile defense system inject an unknown element into the future of verification diplomacy. Should arms control and disarmament become completely replaced by such systems, verification would become an anachronism. However, should arms control and disarmament become a necessary component of these systems through their ability to limit the threat being defended against, then verification diplomacy will continue to be vital.

The issue of verification was at the center of UNITED NATIONS deliberations over whether or not to pass a resolution authorizing the United States to go to war against IRAQ. The immediate issue in the summer and fall of 2003 was Iraq's willingness to admit weapons inspectors. Inspectors had last been in Iraq in 1998, and Resolution 1284 passed in 1999 had called for 60 days of active inspections to determine the current state of weapons production in Iraq. The Bush administration considered these discussions to be little more than a delaying tactic on the part of Iraq. In his address to the United Nations on the one-year anniversary of the SEPTEMBER 11, 2001, terrorist attacks on the World Trade Center and the Pentagon, President GEORGE W. BUSH challenged the United Nations to address the Iraqi threat. Within a week Iraq promised to permit weapons inspectors "without conditions." United Nations Secretary-General Kofi Annan hailed the move as "an indispensable first step," but the United States continued to regard it as a delaying move that held little substance or merit. Bush was also concerned that the lengthy timetable of new inspections, perhaps up to one year, would make international action impossible. As feared by Bush, Iraq's offer led Russia, France, and others to question whether a new resolution was now needed. A compromise was not reached until November, when the Security Council unanimously passed a resolution giving Iraq 30 days to produce a "currently accurate, full, and complete declaration" of all facets of its WEAPONS OF MASS DESTRUCTION programs.

Iraq accepted the UN resolution on November 13, and five days later United Nations inspectors began arriving in Baghdad. Iraq's report to the UN was 12,000 pages long but contained no new information from that which it provided in 1997 according to chief United Nations weapons inspector Hans Blix. He delivered two reports in January, one in February, and one in early March. Each of them contained a similar theme. Iraq was not yet fully in compliance with the spirit of the United Nations resolution, but no definitive evidence of weapons of mass destruction had been found. The United Nations's chief nuclear weapons inspector, Mohamed El Baradei, echoed these comments and stated that several additional months would be needed to complete the inspection. Iraq agreed "in principle" to destroy Al Samoud 2 missiles because the UN inspectors found that their range exceeded the 150 kilometer limit established in 1991.

These verification reports formed the backdrop against which the Security Council debated issuing a second resolution authorizing force. In the end no agreement was reached. France, Russia, Germany, and China all made known their opposition to such resolution. Great Britain supported the United States, and in March after a SUMMIT CONFERENCE meeting with SPAIN in the Azores, the three allies decided not to press for a vote and went to war. One of the early puzzles of the IRAQ WAR was the inability of the United States to document the existence of Iraqi weapons of mass destruction after the war ended, thus calling into question both the quality of American INTELLIGENCE and Bush's motives.

See also NUCLEAR DETERRENCE STRATEGY: NUCLEAR WAR; NUCLEAR WEAPONS; RUSSIA.

**Further reading:** Gottfried, Kurt, and Bruce Blair, eds. *Crisis Stability and Nuclear War.* New York: Oxford

University Press, 1988; Tsipis, Kosta, et al., eds. *Arms Control Verification: The Technologies That Make It Possible.* Washington, D.C.: Pergamon, 1986.

## Versailles, Treaty of    See TREATY OF VERSAILLES.

## Vietnam

Located in Southeast Asia, Vietnam comprises 127,243 square miles, about the combined size of Ohio, Kentucky, and Tennessee, and it has a population of 77.3 million people. CHINA's Han dynasty conquered the northern part of the area that today is Vietnam in 111 B.C. and ruled for 1,000 years. Vietnam achieved independence in 939 and gradually extended its political grip southward. The first Europeans arrived in 1535. In 1858 the French began their colonization of Indochina, and in 1867 they established the colony of Cochin China. In 1887 they merged their colonial possessions in Southeast Asia into a union of Indochina. Three of these territories (Tonkin, Cochin China, and Annam) were later merged by JAPAN to form Vietnam.

Japan had become the de facto ruler of Indochina during WORLD WAR II, although it allowed the French Vichy regime to formally continue in power until March 1945. At that time they established the Vietnamese state under the leadership of Emperor Bao Dai. The primary opposition to Bao Dai came from Ho Chi Minh and the Viet Minh. This was an ALLIANCE of opposition forces that included Communists and Nationalists. Bao Dai's government proved ineffective, and at the end of World War II Ho Chin Minh claimed power and set up a government in Hanoi.

FRANCE had already made known its intention of reestablishing control over Indochina. The French Union was to be the mechanism for accomplishing this goal. It would grant some limited autonomy to local governments but keep key economic, political, and foreign-policy decisions in the hands of the French. Ho Chi Minh's government refused to accept the proposed arrangement, plunging the region into a colonial war. The French Indochina War lasted from 1946 to 1954. It ended with the French defeat at Dien Bien Phu. In order to gain support for its cause, in 1950 France granted Vietnam independence within the French Union. Bao Dai was named as ruler. The United States and its allies recognized his government. Ho Chi Minh's government was recognized by the Soviet Union (see RUSSIA) and China. The United States had maintained a largely neutral role in this struggle. During World War II, President FRANKLIN ROOSEVELT had spoken of placing Indochina under the trusteeship of the UNITED NATIONS. The fall of China to Communist forces led by Mao Zedong (Mao Tse-tung), however, had changed the political landscape and pushed President HARRY TRUMAN's administration to recognize Bao Dai's regime.

By 1954 the United States was paying 80 percent of the French war cost, but it refused to send military forces to help Paris. As a result the French were forced to admit defeat. The Geneva Conference of that year created a temporary truce line along the 17th parallel in Vietnam. Ho Chi Minh ruled north of it, Bao Dai ruled south of it. A 300-day grace period was established to allow the free movement of people, but the agreement called for reunification of the two Vietnams through a July 1956 election. Ho Chi Minh was expected to win.

The Geneva accords of July 29, 1954, were agreed to verbally by representatives of the French Union and the Viet Minh. The United States attended the meeting but did not sign. It promised to abide by the pact. South Vietnamese prime minister Ngo Dinh Diem refused to permit the 1956 elections on the grounds that South Vietnam had not signed the Geneva agreement. Earlier, in 1954, he withdrew South Vietnam from the French Union and on October 25, 1955, he declared South Vietnam to be an independent state. The United States quickly recognized it. It then placed South Vietnam under the protection of the SOUTH EAST ASIA TREATY ORGANIZATION (SEATO), further solidifying the division of North and South Vietnam into two separate states.

The United States began to actively support South Vietnam but resisted sending it military personnel until 1961, when President JOHN KENNEDY sent advisers to assist the government's efforts to defeat the Vietcong. By late 1961 the Vietcong, a GUERRILLA force associated with North Vietnam, controlled almost one-half of South Vietnam. For the next decade American military forces joined with the South Vietnamese government in a futile effort to defeat the Communists who sought reunification. At its peak, the American military involvement reached almost 550,000 troops in 1969. The United States also became involved in the domestic politics of South Vietnam. For example, its withdrawal of support for Diem was a critical factor in his overthrow in 1963.

Peace talks to end the war began in January 1969 and culminated in an agreement in January 1973. The withdrawal of U.S. forces left South Vietnam in a precarious position. Beset by political corruption, economic difficulties, and a weak military, the South Vietnamese government began abandoning the defense of outlying areas. The end came in January 1975, when North Vietnamese regular military forces began a major offensive. On July 2, 1976, North and South Vietnam were officially reunited as the Socialist Republic of Vietnam.

U.S.-Vietnamese relations were limited for almost 20 years. This changed dramatically on July 11, 1995, when President BILL CLINTON announced the resumption of formal diplomatic ties. A key factor prompting this decision was Vietnamese cooperation on the highly sensitive and important issue of Americans missing during the VIETNAM WAR. The United States estimated in 2001 that 1,363 Americans remain unaccounted for. Between 1973 and 2001, 578 Americans were accounted for and the remains of 258 were identified. In recognition of Vietnamese cooperation on this issue, in 1994 the United States removed a trade embargo with Vietnam. In 1998 President Clinton granted Vietnam a waiver from the JACKSON-VANIK AMENDMENT that limits trading privileges with the United States due to HUMAN-RIGHTS concerns. In the case of Vietnam it involves emigration policy. This waiver must be renewed each year. On July 13, 2000, the two countries signed a bilateral trading agreement that made permanent Hanoi's normal trade status with the United States when it was approved by Congress. By 2001, the United States had become the seventh-largest foreign investor in Vietnam's economy. President Clinton made the first ever presidential visit to the unified Vietnam in October 2000.

**Further reading:** Fitzgerald, Francis. *Fire in the Lake.* Boston: Little, Brown, 1972; Hess, Gary. *The United States and Vietnam.* New York: Macmillan, 1998; Karnow, Stanley. *Vietnam: A History.* 2d ed. New York: Viking, 1991.

## Vietnam War

The United States's involvement in Vietnam spanned the terms of six presidents. The cost of the war and the level of destruction was staggering: 55,000 Americans died; 7 million tons of bombs were dropped; at its high point, 541,000 U.S. troops were in Vietnam; a total cost of $150 billion; and untold numbers of North and South Vietnamese died.

The Vietnam War marked a turning point in American foreign policy. CONTAINMENT of communist expansion was accepted by virtually all segments of opinion at the outset of the conflict. By its end the consensus on containment was shattered, and deep disagreements split elites and the public on the purposes and conduct of American foreign policy. DÉTENTE emerged temporarily as the new guiding framework, but it never enjoyed the support that containment did. More enduring has been the existence of a "Vietnam syndrome" that cautions policy makers against committing American troops to combat due to the negative public reaction to battlefield deaths.

The lasting influence of the Vietnam War can also be found in debates over the proper role of the MEDIA in reporting on American foreign policy and the standards against which the performance of American personnel should be judged. Operation Phoenix and the Mai Lai massacre have become symbols of misguided and immoral

U.S. helicopters airlift soldiers into battle against Vietcong guerrillas, Quang Tri, 1965. *(United States Army)*

CENTRAL INTELLIGENCE AGENCY (CIA) and military behavior. Even the Pentagon's own internal study of Vietnam, the PENTAGON PAPERS, became the focal point of a constitutional struggle over the limits of a free press.

HARRY TRUMAN was the first president who had to make a decision on Vietnam. In 1947 he rejected French efforts to enlist American support for reestablishing its pre–WORLD WAR II position of colonial dominance in Indochina. Instead, he urged FRANCE to end its war against Ho Chi Minh, who, although one of the founders of the French Communist Party, had been a loyal World War II ally against JAPAN. By 1952, however, the Truman administration was underwriting one-third of the French war effort, and Ho Chi Minh was redefined as a national security threat. The transformation was keyed by French reluctance to participate in a European Defense System, something the United States saw as key to containing the Soviet Union (see RUSSIA) in Europe. Support for the French in Indochina was the price for French participation.

President DWIGHT D. EISENHOWER continued this commitment, and by the end of 1953 the United States was paying approximately one-half of the French war costs. Money was not enough to save the French, and in 1954 with its forces under siege at Dien Bien Phu, France informed the United States that, unless it sent troops, Indochina would fall to the Communists. Eisenhower refused to send troops, and the French withdrawal began and officially ended with the 1954 Geneva peace accords. It established a "provisional demarcation line" at the 17th parallel. Pro-French troops regrouped south of this line, and pro-Communist forces, which controlled three-quarters of Vietnam at the time, moved north of it.

Elections were scheduled for 1956 to determine who would rule over all of Vietnam.

The United States did not sign the Geneva peace accords but pledged not to use force or the threat of force to disrupt them. But shortly after the accords were signed, the United States worked with other states in the region to create the SOUTH EAST ASIA TREATY ORGANIZATION (SEATO). Part of a global system of ALLIANCES designed to stop the spread of communism, it extended its protection to "the free people under the jurisdiction of Vietnam." Ho Chi Minh and the Viet Minh (North Vietnamese Communist forces) saw this as a violation of the Geneva accords because it treated the 17th parallel as a permanent international border. In

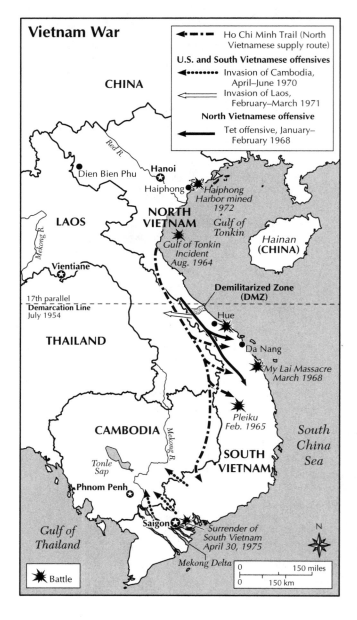

Vietnam War

Ho Chi Minh Trail (North Vietnamese supply route)

**U.S. and South Vietnamese offensives**
Invasion of Cambodia, April–June 1970
Invasion of Laos, February–March 1971

**North Vietnamese offensive**
Tet offensive, January–February 1968

1955, Ngo Dinh Diem declared himself president of the Republic of Vietnam (South Vietnam) and asserted that since South Vietnam had not signed the Geneva accords it was not obligated to abide by them and hold elections.

By the end of the Eisenhower administration, 1,000 U.S. military advisers were stationed in Vietnam. Under President JOHN KENNEDY this commitment continued and expanded. The key turning point was the Taylor-Rostow Report, which asserted that South Vietnam could only be saved by the introduction of 8,000 combat U.S. troops. Kennedy rejected this conclusion but did send in an additional 15,000 advisers. The Taylor-Rostow Report is significant for several reasons, one of which is that it helped redefine the Vietnam issue from that of a political struggle embedded in a GUERRILLA war into a more conventional military conflict in which victory was to be found on the battlefield.

Under President LYNDON JOHNSON the U.S. involvement expanded to include combat troops and bombing raids on North Vietnam, as the JOINT CHIEFS OF STAFF pressured Johnson to put aside self-imposed restraints so that the war might be won more quickly. The August 1964 Gulf of Tonkin Resolution provided the rationale for bombing the North. The resolution authorized Johnson to take whatever steps he felt necessary to repel further attacks on U.S. forces and prevent further aggression. It was passed in response to a North Vietnamese attack on two U.S. ships in the Gulf of Tonkin. The details of this event are still clouded in controversy.

Continued advances made by the Vietcong on the ground prompted General William Westmoreland to request an additional 50,000 combat troops in April 1965. This number was increased in June to 200,000. Even this proved to be insufficient, as in January 1968 Communist forces unleashed a countrywide offensive that succeeded in penetrating the U.S. EMBASSY compound in Saigon. The Tet Offensive proved to be militarily premature. The United States successfully regrouped and, with the benefit of a massive bombing attack on the North, defeated the Communist forces. Politically, however, it was a great success, delivering a crippling psychological blow to the United States by showing just how difficult it would be to achieve a military victory in Vietnam. In March 1968 Johnson announced a bombing halt; he also declared that he would not be a candidate for reelection.

President RICHARD NIXON sought to extricate the United States from Vietnam through a process dubbed as "Vietnamization" whereby South Vietnam gradually would assume the primary military burden of defeating the Communists. The inherent weakness of Vietnamization was that a peaceful transition period was needed within which to build up South Vietnamese forces. Nixon tried to create this breathing room though a massive bombing of the

North and an invasion of CAMBODIA, which was intended to eliminate military sanctuaries. Nixon's strategy failed when in spring 1972 North Vietnam forces attacked across the 17th parallel and forced a re-Americanization of the war.

The Paris peace talks had begun in earnest in 1969 but made little progress. Now Nixon offered a new peace plan that included a promise to withdraw all U.S. forces after an Indochina-wide cease-fire was established together with an exchange of prisoners of war. With its Chinese and Russian benefactors now more interested in DÉTENTE with the United States than victory in Vietnam, the North Vietnamese indicated a willingness to end the conflict. The South Vietnamese, fearing for their future, now balked. On December 18, 1972, the Paris peace talks broke off in a stalemate. On December 18 the United States began a massive bombing campaign against the North as a demonstration of resolve to both North and South Vietnamese leaders. On December 30 the talks resumed, and a peace treaty was signed on January 23, 1973.

President GERALD FORD was in office when Vietnam fell in 1975. On March 12 what began as a normal military engagement turned into a rout. In rapid succession key South Vietnamese cities fell. On April 29 the United States evacuated Vietnam, and on April 30 South Vietnam surrendered unconditionally.

**Further reading:** Gallucci, Robert. *Neither Peace Nor Honor.* Baltimore: Johns Hopkins University Press, 1975; Gelb, Leslie, with Richard Betts. *The Irony of Vietnam: The System Worked.* Washington, D.C.: Brookings, 1979; Sheehan, Neil. *A Bright Shining Lie: John Paul Vann and America in Vietnam.* New York: Random House, 1988; Wirtz, James J. *The Tet Offensive: Intelligence Failure in War.* Ithaca, N.Y.: Cornell University Press, 1991.

## Vladivostok accords

The Vladivostok accords was a strategic ARMS CONTROL agreement signed by President GERALD FORD and Soviet president Leonid Brezhnev in November 1974. It followed on the STRATEGIC ARMS LIMITATION TALKS Treaty (SALT I) and was intended to lay the foundation for a SALT II treaty that would be ironed out at a mid-1995 SUMMIT CONFERENCE.

The agreement consisted of a formula for a 10-year-long SALT II treaty. The treaty would impose overall ceilings for strategic delivery systems as well as limitations on the number of intercontinental ballistic missiles (ICBMs) that could be fitted with multiple independently targeted reentry vehicles (MIRVs) and the number of bombers that could be armed with long-range missile.

Unlike SALT I, the Vladivostok accords were based on the principle of equal numbers. This was not enough, however, to overcome conservative opposition. REPUBLICAN PARTY presidential candidate RONALD REAGAN was particularly outspoken against the agreement, as was Senator Henry "Scoop" Jackson (D-Wash.), who was a leading critic of SALT I. Of particular concern to these opponents were possible restrictions that would be placed on the numbers of cruise missiles and disagreements over how to count the new Soviet Backfire bomber. They also felt that the Vladivostok accords did not adequately restrict the throw weight of Soviet ICBMs. Under pressure from these challengers, and with his administration having come into office under the cloud of the Watergate scandal that forced RICHARD NIXON to resign, President Ford did not push for a full SALT II agreement that would be presented to the Senate prior to the 1976 election. Liberal supporters of arms control were also less than enthused with the Vladivostok accords because of the continued high levels of NUCLEAR WEAPONS each side was permitted to retain.

The Vladivostok accords are significant for what they reveal about the influence of domestic politics on arms control agreements. They show that they are much more than technological exercises in counting and placing limits on weapons. The agreement also shows the difficulty and danger of setting precise limits to weapons systems and of developing formulas for counting weapons in a period of rapid technological change. It is not only difficult to agree upon what these numbers are, but it also makes VERIFICATION of treaty compliance a difficult and highly politicized endeavor.

## Wallace, Henry (1888–1965) *secretary of commerce*

Henry Agard Wallace served in several different capacities in the FRANKLIN ROOSEVELT administration. He was appointed secretary of agriculture in 1933 and was elected vice president in 1940. His outspoken views caused Roosevelt to drop him from the ticket in 1944, but as a reward for his continued loyalty Wallace was appointed secretary of commerce in 1945.

President HARRY TRUMAN fired Wallace as secretary of commerce in September 1946 for publicly advocating a policy of accommodation with the Soviet Union (see RUSSIA) at a time when the administration was moving to embrace a get-tough policy. Wallace's thinking on foreign-policy matters was widely characterized as either being visionary or idealist for his opposition to war. He joined with Secretary of War HENRY STIMSON in voicing opposition to dropping the atomic bomb on Hiroshima. The same month he was fired, he told a large gathering, "[G]etting tough never brought anything real and lasting—whether for schoolyard bullies, businessmen, or world powers." He spoke out against the MARSHALL PLAN, referring to it as the "Martial Plan," and opposed the creation of the NORTH ATLANTIC TREATY ORGANIZATION (NATO) because he felt it backed the Soviet Union into a corner.

In 1948 Wallace ran for president as the candidate of the Progressive Party. He was roundly attacked by Truman for his sympathetic, pro-Soviet outlook. Truman characterized him as a "national danger" and "a sabotage front for Uncle Joe Stalin." For his part, Wallace asserted that Truman had become an unwitting tool of American fascists. Wallace only received about 2 percent of the popular vote.

## Ware v. Hylton (1796)

*Ware v. Hylton* is the first SUPREME COURT case involving a conflict between a state law and a treaty. At issue was a Virginia law of 1777, which nullified the debts Virginians owed to GREAT BRITAIN, and the TREATY OF PARIS, which ended

the AMERICAN REVOLUTION and expressly required that all debts be repaid. Virginia refused to accept these provisions of the Treaty of Paris, and under the ARTICLES OF CONFEDERATION there was little the federal government could do to enforce them. This situation changed with the signing of the CONSTITUTION; Article VI made treaties the supreme law of the land. This included the Treaty of Paris, even though it predated the Constitution.

Citing the supremacy clause of the Constitution, the Supreme Court in *Ware v. Hylton* ruled that the Treaty of Paris nullified the earlier Virginia law. Justice Samuel Chase stated: "[A] treaty cannot be the supreme law of the land, that is of all the United States, if any act of a State Legislature can stand in its way." In a subsequent ruling, *AMERICAN INSURANCE CO. V. CANTER* (1828) the Supreme Court would extend this logic to a case in which the Constitution had not been so explicit as to the relationship of the powers of states versus those of the federal government.

## War of 1812

The War of 1812 pitted the United States against GREAT BRITAIN. Though the United States suffered significant defeats, such as the British capture of Washington, D.C., and had few noteworthy military victories, especially early in the war, the War of 1812 is seen as having legitimized the United States as a state that had to be taken seriously by the powers of Europe. In North America it had the effect of breaking the ALLIANCE between the British and NATIVE AMERICANS in the Northwest that helped speed American expansion.

Just as the consequences of the War of 1812 were felt at both the international and the continental level, so too were the factors that contributed to the onset of war. At the international level FRANCE and Great Britain had been locked in almost continuous conflict since 1793. The United States sought to remain neutral in the conflict, a stance that

This cartoon gloats over the naval losses suffered by Britain early in the War of 1812. King George III stands at left, his nose bleeding and eye blackened by his opponent President James Madison. *(Harper's Weekly)*

offered it great commercial advantages. Great Britain, possessing a far stronger navy than did France, had repeatedly angered the United States with its violations of United States maritime rights as a neutral. Foremost among these were the issuance of Orders in Council that limited where in Europe the United States could sell its goods and the impressment of U.S. sailors into the British navy. Closer to home, the United States objected to the British refusal to abandon its northwestern posts as promised in the TREATY OF PARIS and the continued aid it was giving to Native Americans who were resisting the United States's westward expansion into the Northwest Territory.

A series of failed diplomatic initiatives preceded the war. It had been THOMAS JEFFERSON's hope that the Monroe-Pinckney Treaty of 1806 would bring an end to the impressment of U.S. sailors by the British. The two American negotiators were not able to get Great Britain to accept these terms and agreed to a less restrictive treaty in violation

of their instructions. Jefferson refused to submit the treaty to the Senate for ratification and asked that they reopen negotiations. Jefferson next moved to implement a self-imposed embargo on U.S. trade in hopes of forcing an end to the conflict between Britain and France. The Embargo Act of 1807 prohibited all U.S. merchant ships and goods from leaving U.S. ports. The resulting economic distress caused within the United States, especially in New England, led to talk of secessions and the measure was lifted in 1809 and replaced by a Nonintercourse Act that only limited trade with Great Britain and France. In 1810 even this prohibition was lifted with the threat to reimpose the ban. Angered at Great Britain's continued refusal to lift the Orders in Council, the United States moved in 1811 to outlaw the importation of any goods from Great Britain into the United States.

With U.S. grievances still unresolved, HENRY CLAY and his fellow "war HAWKS" succeeded in getting a declaration of war approved by both houses. The vote was 79-49 in the House of Representatives and 19-13 in the Senate. Voting fell clearly along both party and sectional lines. Representatives from the North and the East voted against the war, while those from the South and West voted for it. All FEDERALIST PARTY members voted against the declaration, while 93 of 116 Democratic-Republicans supported it. Federalists, whose stronghold was in the Northeast, argued that the United States had no quarrel with Britain over CANADA, a favorite target of the Democratic-Republicans, who assumed that it could be captured easily and then used as political barter to either achieve other objectives or be annexed. War hawks argued that to continue to accept such mistreatment at the hands of the British amounted to recolonization.

As suggested by the closeness of these votes, the United States was not united behind the prospect of war. Nor was its army or navy prepared for war. In fact, it appeared that the war hawks expected Great Britain to make concessions rather than fight. Five days after the declaration of war, President James Madison began to explore the possibility of a peace, stating that the United States wished to avoid "any serious collision" but that Great Britain would have to terminate the Orders in Council and end impressment. By the time Madison's terms reached British leaders, they had already repealed the Orders in Council but refused to end impressment. Convinced that they had given enough, the British proposed a cease-fire that Madison rejected because America's war aims were not totally met.

In 1813 RUSSIA offered to mediate a settlement of the war. It wished to redirect British attention to stopping Napoleon Bonaparte and restore American trade to its prewar level. Madison accepted the invitation. Attempts to conquer Canada had gone poorly, and with Napoleon's invasion of Russia having produced disastrous results, he now feared that Great Britain might try to prosecute the war with the United States more vigorously. On a more positive note from the American perspective, military campaigns in 1813 and 1814 seriously crippled the power of Native American forces east of the Mississippi River. The British rejected Russia's offer but, not wishing to alienate the Czar Alexander I, proposed direct talks with the United States as an alternative. Madison accepted this offer and sent a strong negotiating team led by JOHN QUINCY ADAMS. The British team was not nearly as strong, as their most experienced diplomats were at the Congress of Vienna.

Conducted in Ghent, Belgium, the talks lasted from August 8, 1814, until December 24, 1815. The United States quickly dropped its insistence that a British commitment to end their policy of impressment be incorporated into the peace treaty. The British, however, did not adopt an equally conciliatory position. Instead, they put forward terms that reflected their position of military superiority in North America and a desire to find ways to better provide for Canada's security in the future. Numbered among them was the demand for an Indian buffer state as a permanent barrier to westward expansion in the Northwest. In receipt of the British terms for peace and recognizing them to be unacceptable, Madison made them public in a successful effort to shore up American resolve. The British now began to move away from their opening position. Military setbacks in 1814 forced the British to conclude that a military victory was not yet within reach. The cost of another military campaign was also seen as prohibitively high. It then agreed to a treaty, the TREATY OF GHENT, which made little mention of the issues that brought the two sides to war and merely restored the prewar status quo.

**Further reading:** Horsman, Reginald. *The War of 1812.* New York: Knopf, 1969; Updyke, Frank. *The Diplomacy of the War of 1812.* Gloucester, Mass.: P. Smith, 1965.

## War Powers Resolution

The War Powers Resolution was passed in 1973 over President RICHARD NIXON's veto. It represents the most far-reaching effort by CONGRESS to reassert its POWER in the area of war making. No PRESIDENT has recognized its constitutionality.

The war powers of the constitution are split into three parts. Congress possesses the power to declare war and to raise and maintain the armed forces. The president is designated as commander in chief. In the abstract these powers fit together nicely, but in practice this has not been the case. The realities of world politics, especially for the dominant powers, demand that states possess a standing military establishment capable of going into combat without further mobilization. Once having created such a military force, it has little control over how it is used. Congress has declared war only five times: the WAR OF 1812, the MEXICAN WAR, the SPANISH-AMERICAN WAR, WORLD WAR I, and WORLD WAR II. Yet the United States has fought more than 125 "wars." There was no declaration of war in Korea, the CUBAN MISSILE CRISIS, VIETNAM, the PERSIAN GULF, KOSOVO, the war against TERRORISM following the SEPTEMBER 11, 2001, terrorist attacks on the Pentagon and World Trade Center, or the attack on IRAQ in March 2003.

The immediate impetus for the War Powers Resolution was the VIETNAM WAR. During the 1950s and 1960s Congress had been quite willing to provide the president with sweeping grants of authority to use force. Typical of these was the 1955 Formosa Resolution that authorized President DWIGHT EISENHOWER to use military force to defend TAIWAN and neighboring islands. The House voted its support 410-3, and the Senate did so by a vote of 85-3. The key resolution in Vietnam was the Gulf of Tonkin Resolution that authorized Present LYNDON JOHNSON to use military force to protect American soldiers in Vietnam. It passed by a vote of 88-2 in the Senate and unanimously in the House.

With the War Powers Resolution, Congress sought to reclaim its constitutional war-making powers. It required the president to (1) "in every possible instance" consult with Congress before committing U.S. troops into "hostilities or into situations where imminent involvement in hostilities" are likely, (2) inform Congress within 48 hours after the introduction of troops if there is no declaration of war, and (3) remove U.S. troops within 60 days (90 days in special circumstances) if Congress does not either declare war or adopt a joint resolution supporting the action. Congress can terminate military action before the 60-day window is closed by passing a concurrent resolution.

The debates were emotionally charged, and the House and Senate each passed their own version of the War Powers Resolution. The House version specified certain conditions under which the president could commit U.S. troops into combat situations. The Senate version that prevailed contained no such list because senators thought it was an unwarranted infringement on the president's commander in chief powers. Senator Thomas Eagleton (R-Mo.), an original sponsor of the bill, voted against it because he felt it gave the president too much authority by recognizing her or his right to commit troops without prior congressional consultation.

The most controversial aspect of the War Powers Resolution is its use of a legislative veto to control the president's use of military force. As we noted above, Congress can force presidents to remove troops from combat situations by passing a concurrent resolution. Because resolutions are not laws, they cannot be vetoed by the president. This, presidents have argued, is unconstitutional. Only by passing legislation that is subject to a presidential veto and then a congressional override can Congress bind the president's hands. The SUPREME COURT agrees. In the 1983 *IMMIGRATION AND NATURALIZATION SERVICES V. CHADHA* case, it ruled the legislative veto to be unconstitutional.

In spite of this ruling the War Powers Resolution's constitutionality has yet to be formally challenged. It still is the fundamental document governing the distribution of power between Congress and the president in making war. This does not mean that changes have not been proposed. One line of thought is that the War Powers Resolution should be repealed and that Congress and the president should return to use of the traditional tools of political bargaining and persuasion. A second suggestion is that the notification provisions should be repealed and replaced by provisions that would allow Congress to move quickly to pass legisla-

tion terminating military activities if it sees fit. The creation of a permanent consultative group has also been proposed. In the wake of PEACEKEEPING OPERATIONS in HAITI and SOMALIA, Senate Majority Leader Robert Dole (R-Kans.) introduced a "peace powers act" to place restraints on a president's ability to send U.S. troops on these types of missions. Dole also sought to repeal that part of the War Powers Resolution requiring the president to withdraw troops in 60 days if Congress does not give its approval. In 1995 the House rejected this move by a vote of 217-201.

**Further reading:** Koh, Harold. *The National Security Constitution: Sharing Power after the Iran-Contra Affair.* New Haven, Conn.: Yale University Press, 1990; Sheffer, Martin S. *The Judicial Development of Presidential War Powers.* Westport, Conn.: Greenwood. 1999; Turner, Robert F. *The War Powers Resolution: Its Implementation in Theory and Practice.* Philadelphia: Foreign Policy Research Institute, 1983.

## Warsaw Pact

The Warsaw Pact was the most important COLD WAR multilateral organization linking together the Soviet Union (see RUSSIA) and its East European allies. It was founded on May 14, 1955, with the signing of a Treaty of Friendship, Cooperation, and Mutual Assistance. Its original members were Albania, Bulgaria, CZECHOSLOVAKIA, East GERMANY, HUNGARY, POLAND, and Romania. Albania withdrew in 1961 when it backed CHINA in the Sino-Soviet dispute. Romania stopped participating in Warsaw Pact exercises beginning in 1958. The Warsaw Pact was dissolved in 1991, following the 1990 decisions of Czechoslovakia, Poland, and Hungary to no longer participate in military exercises.

Steps toward creating the Warsaw Pact were first taken in 1952 with a military conference in Prague, Czechoslovakia, that was attended by Czechoslovakia, Poland, Hungary, the Soviet Union, and China. Another step forward was taken in 1954 with an international conference of Communist Parties held in Moscow. The meeting voiced its concern over West German remilitarization and warned that communist states were prepared to take countermeasures. Nine days after West Germany was admitted to the NORTH ATLANTIC TREATY ORGANIZATION (NATO), the Warsaw Pact was announced. NATO had now been in existence for six years.

Like NATO, the Warsaw Pact was both a military ALLIANCE and a political alliance. A united military command was created in January 1956. A formal agreement regarding the stationing of Soviet troops on East European soil did not come about until 1956, after the Polish and Hungarian uprisings had taken place. Politically, the Warsaw Pact provided an opportunity for ritualistic shows of unity on the part of the Communist world and a mechanism for distancing East European states from West Europe. Perhaps the Warsaw Pact's most important action, the invasion of Czechoslovakia (1968), was taken in Moscow and was not made by its Political Consultative Committee.

Before its demise, the Warsaw Pact indirectly became an important player in conventional ARMS CONTROL efforts. Much of the early work on VERIFICATION and confidence-building measures that has become standard in ARMS CONTROL and DISARMAMENT proposals was first focused on the problem of conventional arms control in Europe. It thus became a vehicle for fostering East-West cooperation, instead of a symbol of cold war confrontation.

**Further reading:** Blackwell, Robert, and F. Stephen Larrabee. *Conventional Arms Control and East-West Security.* Durham, N.C.: Duke University Press, 1989.

## Washington, George (1732–1799) *president of the United States*

George Washington was the first president of the United States. Prior to assuming the presidency he played key roles in the political development of the United States as commander in chief of the Continental army during the AMERICAN REVOLUTION and chair of the Constitutional Convention in 1787.

The first foreign-policy challenge facing President Washington came from unexpected quarters. It was a minor incident that held potentially significant consequences. In summer 1789 Spanish officials seized British commercial ships that had entered the Nootka Sound on the coast of Vancouver Island, which was under British jurisdiction. British leaders saw this as an opportunity to extend their control over North America. It was assumed that British forces would strike at Spanish holdings in FLORIDA and the Louisiana Territory and that they would ask for U.S. permission to send troops across U.S. territory. Agreeing to this request might mean war with SPAIN; denial could lead to war with GREAT BRITAIN. Fortunately for President Washington, Spain was forced to capitulate to the British demands and war did not take place. Spain's main ally against Great Britain was FRANCE, which was consumed by the French Revolution and unable to provide additional military aid.

The principal foreign-policy problems facing President Washington for the remainder of his term in office were maintenance of neutrality in European wars and avoidance of war with France. Within a few months of Washington's inauguration, the French Revolution erupted. In February 1793 the new French republic declared war on Great Britain. Washington's cabinet was split as to whether the United States would be best served allying with Great Britain (as ALEXANDER HAMILTON and the FEDERALIST PARTY wanted) or with France (as THOMAS JEFFERSON and the Democratic-Republican Party wanted). Anger with Great Britain for its refusal to leave its forts along the American frontier as promised by the TREATY OF PARIS, its incitement of the NATIVE AMERICANS against American settlers, and its policy of impressment made war with Great Britain appear likely. War was averted with JAY'S TREATY. The treaty did not really address the root causes of American unhappiness with Great Britain, but it did provide Americans with MOST-FAVORED-NATION STATUS to trade, which opened up trading opportunities for American merchants. The treaty also led to the signing of PINCKNEY'S TREATY with Spain, by which the United States obtained navigation rights on the Mississippi River and the right of deposit at New Orleans.

Under the terms of the ALLIANCE of 1778, the United States was pledged to come to the aid of France "forever" in defense of the French West Indies. France's declaration of war against Great Britain raised the possibility that such aid would be requested. A debate took place within the Washington administration over whether the United States should honor this alliance. Hamilton argued no. He asserted that the treaty had been signed with the French monarchy and it no longer existed. Jefferson asserted that the alliance was still in force, since it was an agreement between two nations and not two governments. Once again, Washington escaped the need to make a decision because U.S. help was not requested. This allowed him to issue his Neutrality Proclamation on April 22, 1793. He declared that the United States would be "friendly and impartial toward the belligerent powers."

It was not long before the Neutrality Proclamation would be put to a test. In 1793 Citizen Edmond Genet arrived as the first French minister to the United States from the new republic. Rather than adopt the role of diplomat, Genet actively lobbied the American people to reject the Neutrality Proclamation and come to the aid of France. He also hired 14 privateers, or pirates, who attacked American merchant vessels. Genet's actions enraged Washington, and even pro-French supporters in the cabinet now abandoned him.

Washington is perhaps best remembered for his farewell address. Written largely by James Madison and then revised by Hamilton, Washington warned against the growing dangers of parties and political factions in American politics. Speaking about foreign affairs, Washington called for a policy that would "steer clear of permanent alliances with any portion of the foreign world." Future generations of isolationists repeatedly have cited his farewell address in support of their position. At the time, Washington's address was praised by Federalists who had called for ending the alliance of 1778 with France. Democratic-Republicans were displeased with it as was France.

**Further reading:** Gilbert, Felix. *To the Farewell Address.* Princeton, N.J.: Princeton University Press, 1961; Mac-Donald, Forrest. *The Presidency of George Washington.* Lawrence: University of Kansas Press, 1974.

## Washington Conference

The end of WORLD WAR I found two contradictory trends at work in the United States. First, the United States, along with GREAT BRITAIN and JAPAN, had begun to expand their navies. U.S. expansion began with the Naval Appropriations Act of 1916. The goal was to establish a navy second to none, and the United States came close to realizing that goal. At the end of the war only Great Britain had a larger navy. In 1919 President WOODROW WILSON established a separate Pacific Ocean battle fleet. The Harding administration decided to station most of the U.S. fleet permanently in the Pacific Ocean. The second trend was a desire to cut government spending and reduce expenditures on weapons.

The first significant move to acting on these second concerns came from isolationist senator WILLIAM BORAH (R-Idaho), who in 1920 offered a resolution inviting Great Britain and Japan to an arms limitation conference. President WARREN HARDING favored expanding the navy, but under mounting pressure from the American public he endorsed the idea of a DISARMAMENT conference in his inaugural address. At the suggestion of the British, Harding widened the focus of the conference to include Far Eastern security affairs, to include ITALY and FRANCE for purposes of the disarmament talks, and to include Belgium, CHINA, PORTUGAL, and the NETHERLANDS to discuss Far Eastern security matters. The Soviet Union was not invited because the major powers had not yet recognized the new Communist government. Harding broke with Wilson's strategy of excluding CONGRESS from the negotiations by including ELIHU ROOT, a former Republican senator, and current senators HENRY CABOT LODGE (R-Mass.) and Oscar Underwood (D-Ala.).

SECRETARY OF STATE CHARLES EVANS HUGHES opened the conference on November 12, 1921, with a dramatic call for arms limitation. He proposed a 10-year "holiday" on constructing capital ships (battle ships and battle cruisers), plus scrapping existing ships so that a ratio of 5:5:3 would exist between the U.S., British, and Japanese navies. In less than 15 minutes Hughes had "destroyed" 66 ships. The deal proposed by Hughes involved an agreement by the United States to forego achieving potential naval dominance and for Great Britain and Japan to accept cutbacks in their existing fleets. With its finances drained from World War I, Great Britain did not object. Japan balked initially but agreed when the United States promised not to further fortify its Pacific bases other than HAWAII. Great Britain made a similar promise. This gave Japan added

security, even if its navy was smaller. At this point France unexpectedly objected to a restriction to 1.7 ships in the overall equation. France finally agreed but maintained the right to unrestricted growth in other categories of naval vessels. The Five-Power Naval Treaty was signed on February 6, 1922, and was to remain in effect until 1936 when any of the five states might give two years notice of their intention to no longer abide by the treaty. In addition to establishing a ratio of 5:5:3:1.67:1.67 on the number of capital ships, aircraft carriers, and cruisers, the agreement also set limits on the size of their guns and overall weight.

One roadblock to signing the Five-Power Naval Treaty had been overcome in December 1921 with the signing of a Four-Power Treaty on security in the Pacific. A major point of contention in Pacific security politics was the Anglo-Japanese alliance that Great Britain had renewed in 1911 for an additional 10 years. Despite efforts to make it clear that the alliance was not directed at the United States, demands arose in the United States for a navy equal in size to the combined British and Japanese navies. The Four-Power Treaty provided a way for Great Britain to end the treaty and remain on good terms with Japan. All four states (United States, Japan, Great Britain, and France) promised to respect each other's rights in the Pacific and refer disputes to a joint conference.

A second agreement was also signed at the Washington Conference on February 6, 1922. The Nine-Power Treaty promised to respect the sovereignty, independence, and territorial and administrative integrity of China. The signatory's also agreed to uphold the principles of the OPEN DOOR and help China form a stable government. The idea for the agreement came from Great Britain, and Japan only agreed to the treaty after both Great Britain and the United States applied pressure. The agreement stopped short of binding the nine powers to defend the Open Door, and it did not address existing violations of the Open Door policy. Thus, it was largely symbolic in nature, although many Americans championed the agreement as making the Open Door a reality.

The three treaties negotiated at the Washington Conference produced strong opposition within the United States. Hughes was accused of giving away too much in agreeing to the Five-Power Naval Treaty. However, with Congress unlikely to appropriate funds for fortifications beyond Hawaii, Hughes had in reality given away nothing. Isolationists led by Borah claimed that the Four-Power agreement was an alliance in disguise and opposed it. In March 1922 the Senate gave its unanimous approval to the Nine-Power Treaty, approved the Five-Power Treaty with one negative vote, and approved the Four-Power Treaty by only four votes, while attaching a reservation stating that it was not an alliance.

The Washington Conference itself left a mixed legacy. With two of the Big Three powers represented from outside Europe (United States and Japan), the conference signaled a shift in the global balance of power. On the positive side, it was the first general international agreement on reducing naval armaments. On the negative side, it interfered with efforts by the LEAGUE OF NATIONS to organize global disarmament talks in Geneva. The agreements reached in Washington also did not end the naval arms race. Rather nations switched to submarines, destroyers, and cruisers. President CALVIN COOLIDGE called upon states meeting at a 1927 League of Nations disarmament conference in Geneva to meet with the United States in a separate meeting to address the new naval arms race. After six weeks of talks, the meetings adjourned without any agreement having been reached. The next attempt at curbing naval buildups would come at the LONDON NAVAL CONFERENCES in 1930.

## weapons of mass destruction  (WMD)

*Weapons of mass destruction* is an umbrella term used to describe three categories of weapons: chemical, biological, and nuclear. It is a term that came into prominence as the COLD WAR was winding down and attention began to shift from an almost exclusive focus on NUCLEAR WEAPONS as a means of delivering widespread destruction to other methods. In 1980 the Soviet Union was the only state believed to possess a biological arsenal. By 2000 an estimated 17 states possessed these weapons. The number of states having chemical weapons went up from 12 to 20 in the same time span. In addition to a concern for states using weapons of mass destruction as part of a military strategy, fear also exists that terrorist groups now possess such weapons. Documents captured from Afghan residences linked to the AL-QAEDA terrorist group suggest that it may be seeking such weapons.

There is nothing new about chemical and biological warfare. Its history predates the nuclear era. Poisoning water wells, for example, is an age-old military strategy for weakening cities under siege. Biochemical warfare was a prominent feature of WORLD WAR I. German troops released deadly chlorine gas against French forces at Ypres, Belgium, on April 15, 1915. In 1917 they used mustard gas. Almost 100,000 people were killed by biochemical agents during the war, and more than 1 million were injured. Prior to WORLD WAR II, ITALY used chemical weapons in ETHIOPIA. During World War II, JAPAN dropped bacteria-laced bombs in CHINA.

Periodic cases of chemical and biological contamination surfaced during the cold war. The United States used Agent Orange as a defoliant during VIETNAM. It has been linked to cancer and other diseases among Vietnam veterans. In April 1979 an outbreak of anthrax occurred in Sverdlovsk, RUSSIA, that resulted from a leak at a Soviet biological weapons facility. In 1984 an accident at a Union Carbide chemical plant in Bhopal, INDIA, killed almost 4,000 people and injured 200,000. IRAQ used chemical weapons against IRAN and dissident Kurdish communities within Iraq during the 1980–88 IRAN-IRAQ WAR.

After the cold war ended in 1989, the use of chemical and biological agents came to be associated with terrorists and individuals as well as states. Reports suggest that BOSNIA AND HERZEGOVINA and CROATIA may have used chlorine-filled shells in the early 1990s. On March 20, 1995, members of the Japanese terrorist group Aum Shinrikyo released sarin nerve gas into the Tokyo subway system, killing 12 people and injuring more than 5,000. In October 2001, just a month after the SEPTEMBER 11, 2001, terrorist attacks on the World Trade Center and Pentagon, the United States was rocked by the discovery that anthrax-laced letters had been mailed through the postal system. By the time the threat ended, five people had died from inhaling anthrax, and 17 had been injured. More than 30,000 people were given prescriptions for antibiotics. Cleaning up the Hart office building in Washington took 96 days and cost $10 million.

One of the most hotly debated post–cold war incidents involving weapons of mass destruction centers on the PERSIAN GULF WAR. After the war scores of American soldiers became ill, and they asserted that it was the result of their exposure to chemical and biological agents during that war. The Pentagon rejected their arguments, but as cases of GULF WAR SYNDROME continued to mount commissions were established to investigate the matter. On January 7, 1997, a presidential advisory committee ruled that no conclusive link exists between their illnesses and chemical weapons or biological weapons but criticized the

U.S. soldiers race to put on protective gas masks during a training exercise near the Iraqi border, 2003.
*(Scott Nelson/Getty Images)*

Pentagon for not acting in good faith in carrying out earlier investigations.

ARMS CONTROL agreements are the traditional means for addressing the threat posed by weapons of mass destruction. The first agreement was reached in Geneva in 1925. It prohibited the use of chemical and biological weapons in war. The United States signed the treaty but did not ratify it until January 22, 1975. Prior to that, on November 25, 1969, President RICHARD NIXON unilaterally renounced the use of biological weapons. One year later he extended his policy to include toxins. In 1972 a Biological and Toxin Weapons Convention came into force that prohibited the production and stockpiling of these weapons. The United States ratified the treaty on December 16, 1974. In January 1993 President GEORGE H. W. BUSH signed the Chemical Weapons Convention that barred the production and use of chemical weapons.

GEORGE W. BUSH's opposition to the Chemical Weapons Convention is both philosophical and empirical. Philosophically, he is not supportive of international multilateral agreements that bind the United States. On a practical level, his administration argues that it is difficult, if not impossible, to guarantee that the conditions of the treaty are being met because chemical weapons can be made from substances commonly used in many forms of commercial manufacturing. In the United States alone, more than 800,000 plants are capable of producing lethal chemical agents. Concern has also been expressed about the cost to American firms. Many fear that valuable secret proprietary information would be lost under the treaty's inspection procedures.

In place of international agreements, the Bush administration has advanced a strategy of defense centered around the OFFICE OF HOMELAND SECURITY that was proposed after the September 11 terrorist attacks. It would coordinate the efforts of about 45 different federal agencies. In his 2003 budget Bush sought to increase the level of spending to counter bioterrorism from $1.4 billion to $6 billion. The Bush administration has also targeted hundreds of millions of dollars for expanding the national pharmaceutical stockpile so that 20 million people could be treated for exposure to such biological diseases as anthrax and smallpox. Several dimensions of this initiative are hotly debated. One issue surrounds the question of who should be vaccinated and whether vaccination can be made mandatory. A second concern relates to the safety of the vaccines. Potentially life threatening side effects exist, especially for those with HIV/AIDS, leukemia, or lymphoma and for those who use immunosuppressive drugs.

Partly lost in the attention that chemical and biological weapons have received is the continuing problem of nuclear weapons. Eight states are now believed to possess deliverable nuclear weapons: the United States, GREAT BRITAIN, FRANCE, Russia, CHINA, INDIA, PAKISTAN, and ISRAEL. NORTH KOREA admitted it was seeking a nuclear capability in October 2002. Iraq and Iran are assumed to be pursuing such a capability. One major area of concern left unaddressed by traditional arms control agreements is an accidental launch of nuclear weapons and the illegal trade in nuclear weapons. Both fears are most heavily focused on Russia, due to the collapse of the economy and concerns for the integrity of the command and control system. The United States had provided funds to Russia through the Nunn-Lugar program to destroy and deactivate warheads. Bush reduced funding for this program by 75 percent prior to the September 11 terrorist attacks. He has since asked for increased funding.

Iraq's possession of weapons of mass destruction was the principal rationale presented by President Bush as he made the case for the IRAQ WAR at the UNITED NATIONS and in the United States. Fears had also been expressed that Iraq might use such weapons against coalition forces during the war. These fears proved unfounded. One of the perplexing features of the war was the inability of U.S. forces to find a "smoking gun" that established the credibility of Bush's position. Such was the concern that in May 2003 the CENTRAL INTELLIGENCE AGENCY announced that it would review its intelligence on the subject. PUBLIC OPINION polls showed that Americans were not alarmed at the inability to find these weapons but that Bush's credibility abroad was further shaken.

**Further reading:** Cole, Leonard. *The Eleventh Plague: The Politics of Biological and Chemical Warfare.* San Francisco: Freeman, 1997; Miller, Judith, et al. *Germs: Biological Weapons and America's Secret War.* New York: Simon and Schuster, 2001; Roberts, Brad. *Biological Weapons; Weapons of the Future?* Washington, D.C.: Center for Strategic and International Studies, 1993.

## Webster, Daniel (1782–1852) *secretary of state, House member, senator*

Daniel Webster was a two-term SECRETARY OF STATE (1841–43 and 1850–52) who served under three presidents, William Henry Harrison, JOHN TYLER, and Millard Fillmore. As a member of CONGRESS he opposed the WAR OF 1812, the annexation of TEXAS, and the MEXICAN WAR. As the economy of New England changed from shipping to manufacturing, Webster also became a strong supporter of high tariffs and protectionism.

Webster's most notable achievements as secretary of state came in his first term in that office. In 1842 he negotiated the Webster-Ashburton Treaty that possibly averted a third U.S. war with GREAT BRITAIN. The treaty settled a long-festering boundary dispute between the United States and CANADA. It also contained a number of innovative elements. First, the United States and Great Britain agreed to maintain independent navies off the west coast of Africa that would cooperate in suppressing the African slave trade. The slavery issue had almost undermined the negotiations. The United States was hypersensitive to any infringement on its maritime rights and routinely refused to allow Great Britain to board its ships in search of slave traders. Knowing this, slave traders often flew the American flag. Cooperation was to bring this practice to an end. In practice, it did not, but it did defuse tensions. Second, the treaty also contained extradition provisions that would be repeated in later treaties signed by the United States. It called for the extradition of individuals charged with such nonpolitical crimes as forgery and murder. The issue was a sensitive one because several participants had fled to the United States and continued fighting after the suppression of the Canadian rebellion of 1837. They seized a U.S. ship, killing a crew member. Later one member of this band was arrested in New York after bragging that he had participated in the affair. A controversy followed over who should have jurisdiction in trying the case, the United States or Great Britain.

Virtually the only major issue now left in dispute between the United States and Great Britain was the boundary of the OREGON Territory. Lord Ashburton's negotiating instructions did not allow him to enter into an agreement on this point. The treaty was not without its critics. It is the only treaty in which the United States conceded territory, about 5,000 square miles along the Maine–New Brunswick border, and it was attacked by expansionists who overlooked the fact that in return for this American concession the British conceded some 6,500 square miles in what is today Minnesota. Observers consider the Webster-Asburton Treaty significant because it represented a true compromise by both sides and helped put U.S.-British relations on a more amicable and secure footing, which facilitated solving later problems in the 1840s and 1850s.

**Further reading:** Current, Richard. *Daniel Webster and the Rise of National Conservatism.* Prospect Heights, Ill.: Waveland Press, 1992.

## Whig Party

The Whig Party (1834–56) was part of the "second American party system," along with the DEMOCRATIC PARTY. The Whigs' strongest supporters were Eastern merchants and those with ties to commerce. Evangelical Protestants made up another group of strong Whig supporters. Whigs believed in a strong government that funded internal improvements and regulated banks. In the area of foreign policy, the Whig Party favored high protective tariffs and

generally opposed territorial expansion. Whigs felt that commerce and markets would create a secure international environment for the United States. Their emphasis was on national development through the construction of roads, canals, and railroads. They felt that priority should first be given to improve the territory the United States already possessed before acquiring additional territory. Some Whigs also opposed expansion because it would bring NATIVE AMERICANS and Mexicans into the United States and create additional proslavery states.

Two principal nemeses for the Whig Party were Presidents ANDREW JACKSON and JAMES POLK. Jackson's dealing with the French over compensation for the seizure of American merchant ships following the Napoleonic Wars frightened and angered the Whigs. Both states severed diplomatic relations, and war loomed on the horizon. They feared serious financial losses from a war and labeled Jackson's actions "course and offensive," in "bad taste," and "legalized piracy." James Polk's uncompromising attitude toward GREAT BRITAIN and extensive American claims on OREGON also drew their ire. DANIEL WEBSTER, a leading Whig, noted that "in seeking acquisitions to be governed as Territories & lying at a great distance from the United States . . . we ought to be governed by our prudence and caution." Whigs also opposed the MEXICAN WAR. They accused Polk of having lied and of not having tried to avoid war as he claimed. The Whigs, who now controlled the House of Representatives, passed a resolution calling the war "unnecessarily and unconstitutionally begun by the President." Nevertheless, the Senate ratified the treaty ending the war a few months later. Earlier, in the administration of JAMES TYLER, the Whigs had opposed admitting TEXAS into the Union and had sufficient votes to defeat the annexation treaty by a vote of 35-16. Texas was then admitted via a congressional resolution that only required a simple majority in each house. All but two Whigs opposed the resolution.

## Wilmot Proviso

The Wilmot Proviso (1846) is an amendment added by Representative David Wilmot (R-Penn.) to a funding bill sought by President JAMES POLK during the MEXICAN WAR. Polk sought $2 million to end the war. The funds were earmarked to pay MEXICO for the territory it would lose. The Wilmot Proviso stipulated that as a condition of obtaining this money, neither slavery nor involuntary servitude would be permitted in any of the territory obtained from Mexico. The House passed the Wilmot Proviso by a vote of 83-64, but CONGRESS adjourned before final action was taken. Polk requested $3 million when the next session of Congress convened in 1847. The House again attached the Wilmot Proviso. This provision was objected to by the Senate, and the compromise bill that was finally approved did not contain it.

The Wilmot Proviso is significant because even in defeat it placed the issue of slavery at the center of the debate on American foreign policy. Wilmot was an ardent abolitionist. TEXAS had just been admitted to the Union as a slave state, and his proviso was intended to prevent other slave states from being carved out of the soon-to-be acquired Mexican territory. The consequence of failing to add additional slave states was recognized by all. It would make the South a permanent minority in the Union and create the possibility that slavery might be outlawed.

The Wilmot Proviso played a key role in the formation of the Free Soil Party, which emerged as an ALLIANCE uniting radical Democrats, antislavery Whigs, and the antislavery Liberty Party. David Wilmot was one of its founders. Neither the WHIG PARTY nor DEMOCRATIC PARTY addressed the Wilmot Proviso in the 1848 election, but the Free Soil Party endorsed it. Its strong showing in New York gave that state's electoral votes to the Whig presidential candidate ZACHARY TAYLOR and helped him to gain the presidency.

## Wilson, Woodrow (1856–1924) *president of the United States*

Thomas Woodrow Wilson was the 28th president and served two terms. He was first elected in 1912. Illness prevented him from becoming the DEMOCRATIC PARTY's nominee for a third term in 1920. Wilson was elected on the 46th ballot of the Democratic convention in 1912 and won a three-way battle for the presidency against Republican president WILLIAM HOWARD TAFT and Progressive Party candidate and former Republican president THEODORE ROOSEVELT. He was narrowly reelected in 1916 on a plank of having kept the United States out of WORLD WAR I. Prior to being elected president, Wilson's only elected public office was the governorship of New Jersey, to which he was elected in 1910. He had served as president of Princeton University from 1902 until he resigned and ran for governor.

Wilson possessed a strong sense of purpose and self-confidence. In foreign policy it led him to reject Taft's DOLLAR DIPLOMACY, with its emphasis on the compatibility between private business and American national interests, and replace it with DIPLOMACY that emphasized morality and the promotion of democracy. The change in outlook did have some immediate positive consequences, although they tended to be largely symbolic in nature. Secretary of State WILLIAM JENNINGS BRYAN secured a series of bilateral treaties in which both parties agreed to submit disputes to international dispute-resolution mechanisms before going to war. Wilson raised the possibility of independence for the PHILIPPINES and sought to smooth relations with COLOMBIA, which had been strained since the building of the PANAMA CANAL and the American role in supporting PANAMA's breakaway from Colombia that helped make the canal possible.

Wilson was less successful when seeking to put U.S. foreign policy on a new footing in cases in which the stakes were higher. In Asia, Wilson abandoned Taft's policy of seeking to involve American firms in railroad projects in CHINA only to reverse field and endorse the policy in hopes of restraining the actions of other foreign powers. Wilson's sympathy and support for the fledgling democratic government of China angered JAPAN, which continued to harbor imperialist ambitions on the Asian mainland.

MEXICO presented a seemingly intractable problem for Wilson's new diplomacy. In 1913 Mexico's democratic government was overthrown by Victoriano Huerta. The Wilson administration refused to recognize Huerta's rule because, Wilson argued, it lacked the support of the Mexican people. Wilson then began a campaign to force Huerta from power. He used an April 21, 1914, incident in which some American sailors were arrested by Huerta's forces to seize the port of Veracruz. This limited intervention failed. ARGENTINA, BRAZIL, and CHILE—the ABC powers—then unsuccessfully mediated the dispute. The issue became mute when Huerta was forced into exile by Mexican revolutionary forces. U.S. forces withdrew from Veracruz on November 23. Huerta's defeat did not bring Wilson's Mexico problem to an end. His administration backed Venustiano Carranza as Mexico's new leader. This act angered Francisco "Pancho" Villa, who also sought to replace Huerta. Villa's forces now undertook a series of border raids in which more than 30 Americans were killed. Over Carranza's objections, Wilson sent General John Pershing and 6,000 soldiers into Mexico on March 16, 1916, in search of Villa. In the course of his mission, U.S. troops fought Mexican government troops, killing some 14 Americans and 40 Mexicans. Pershing's forces were withdrawn in February 1917. Wilson's decision was motivated in large part by the growing prospect of war with GERMANY. Mexico's rejection of the ZIMMERMAN TELEGRAM and its offer of ALLIANCE with Germany had cemented Mexico as an American ally in the upcoming struggle. Wilson now rejected demands by those who advocated continued intervention in Mexico to establish democracy and protect American economic interests, citing the Mexican people's right to self-determination.

Wilson's penchant for using force to promote American interests and his vision of promoting democracy led to a series of military interventions in the Caribbean during his administration. He sent troops to HAITI in 1915, the DOMINICAN REPUBLIC in 1916, CUBA in 1917, and NICARAGUA in 1921.

Wilson's presidency is best remembered for his stewardship of American foreign policy during World War I and his efforts to bring the United States into the LEAGUE OF

NATIONS. World War I began in Europe in August 1914, and Wilson's immediate foreign-policy objective was to keep the United States out of the war. This entailed both a policy of neutrality in the face of German submarine warfare against American vessels bound for GREAT BRITAIN and a search for a means of bringing the war to an end. Against the advice of Bryan, Wilson refused to order American ships out of the Atlantic war zone, arguing that the United States had to take a more activist stance in order to protect its right as a neutral state to engage in free trade. Wilson's policies ultimately provoked Bryan to resign because he was convinced they would lead to war with Germany. As part of his strategy of promoting peace in Europe, Wilson communicated directly with European leaders, sent his personal confidant Colonel EDWARD HOUSE on a series of missions to meet with them, and publicly presented his own vision of peace, which he defined as "peace without victory."

Ongoing German submarine warfare had resulted in several notable sinkings, including the *Lusitania* on May 7, 1915, the *Arabic* on August 19, 1915, and the *Sussex* on March 24, 1916. The cumulative effect of these actions plus a German decision announced on February 1, 1917, to begin a policy of unrestricted submarine warfare overwhelmed Wilson's policy, and on April 2, 1917, he asked CONGRESS for a declaration of war against Germany. The issue, he asserted, was not only one of protecting America's right to freedom of the seas but also one to make the world "safe for democracy."

On January 8, 1918, Wilson again addressed Congress. He now formally stated his war aims and vision of a new world order. His FOURTEEN POINTS would serve as the basis for the U.S. negotiating position at the upcoming Paris peace conference. In a move that had great political significance for the ratification debate over the TREATY OF VERSAILLES, Wilson elected not to take any Republicans or senators to the negotiating team. This angered his opponents and set the stage for a struggle of wills between Wilson and Senator HENRY CABOT LODGE (R-Mass.). A Republican who opposed the League of Nations, Lodge became chair of the Senate Foreign Relations Committee, which would have jurisdiction over treaty ratification, when the Republicans took control of Congress after the 1918 midterm elections.

Wilson returned to the United States on July 8, 1919. Two days later the Senate was presented with the Treaty of Versailles. Wilson's stubbornness and sense of mission refused to allow him to enter into compromises that were needed to obtain consent from the Senate. Failing to change the minds of senators, Wilson embarked on a three-week cross-country trip, visiting 29 cities and giving 35 speeches in hopes of arousing public support for his peace plan. His journey ended in Pueblo, Colorado, on September 25, 1919, when he collapsed. Now back in Washing-ton, Wilson suffered a stroke on October 2. This brought an effective end to not only his lobbying efforts on behalf of the League of Nations but also his control over foreign policy. The treaty was rejected by the Senate in votes on November 19, 1919, and March 19, 1920.

Wilson left a complex legacy to future American foreign-policy makers and commentators. Many of those who followed would disparage his vision of international politics and brand it IDEALISM. They would advance a contrary approach rooted in REALISM. With its emphasis on POWER politics, realism served as the dominant paradigm for studying and practicing foreign policy through the COLD WAR years. The end of the cold war, however, brought forward a revival of WILSONIANISM, and in many ways its vision of a peaceful world of democratic states now lies at the center of contemporary thinking about American foreign policy.

**Further reading:** Burton, David H. *Taft, Wilson and World Order.* Madison, N.J.: Fairleigh Dickinson University Press, 2003; Healy, David. *Gunboat Diplomacy in the Wilson Era.* Madison: University of Wisconsin Press, 1976; Macmillan, Margaret. *Paris 1919: Six Months That Changed the World.* New York: Random House, 2003.

## Wilsonianism

Wilsonianism is an outlook on world politics associated with President WOODROW WILSON and his FOURTEEN POINTS. It was discredited in the 1930s by a newer generation of students of world politics who labeled it IDEALISM and who identified themselves as realists. Identifying Wilsonianism as idealist implied that it was a fundamentally flawed vision of world politics that offered little guidance to future generations of American foreign-policy makers. With the end of the COLD WAR, an event that REALISM failed to predict, Wilsonianism has received renewed attention and respect as a theoretical perspective for organizing thinking about world politics.

Wilsonianism has its roots in 19th-century liberalism. It contains four main points: (1) a COLLECTIVE-SECURITY organization, (2) restraints on weapons, (3) democracy, and (4) the free flow of goods across national borders. None of these were considered to be natural occurrences in world politics by Wilson's European contemporaries. In their world, peace—more accurately, the absence of war—rested on a foundation of national power supplemented by exclusionary ALLIANCES. Wilson advanced a competing vision of world politics in which war and the preparation for war were not the normal condition. Peace would be the norm.

Advocates of Wilsonianism draw a distinction between Wilson the scholar and Wilson the politician. They assert that the failure of the Wilsonian vision after WORLD WAR I had much more to do with the latter than it did the former.

Critics of Wilsonianism raise two issues about its content. First, much as is the case with realism, they argue that the term is now so elastic and in vogue that virtually everyone claims to be a disciple of Wilson. One respected scholar has gone so far as to argue that RONALD REAGAN was the "most Wilsonian of presidents since Wilson's time," given his commitment to expanding democracy and reforming the INTERNATIONAL SYSTEM to safeguard American NATIONAL INTERESTS. A second line of criticism asserts that Wilsonian principles served to rationalize policy rather than guide it. Wilson is seen as freely changing sides and using or applying his standards unevenly. At the heart of this criticism is the belief that one cannot separate Wilson the scholar and Wilson the politician into two mutually exclusive categories. Inconsistency in action must ultimately reflect upon the impracticality of the body of ideas being espoused.

Still, even a cursory inspection of the political landscape after the end of the cold war shows that three of Wilson's four key principles for the construction of a peaceful international order enjoy wide followings. ARMS CONTROL initiatives are advanced for small weapons as well as nuclear ones. Democracy is seen as more than a lofty goal for states to aspire to or a temporary condition. GLOBALIZATION and regional free-trade areas, the two dominant international economic trends of the post–cold war era, both rest upon a foundation of free trade. Only the existence of a collective-security organization is lacking, as the UNITED NATIONS has yet to succeed in claiming sufficient support from its members to acquire such status. But even here, Wilson's vision is not totally absent. Wilsonians would argue that the presence of the first three elements of Wilson's vision makes the fourth less crucial. With the threat of global war receding, regional INTERNATIONAL ORGANIZATIONS and ad hoc coalitions of states are able to assume the role of peacekeeper in its stead.

See also DEMOCRATIZATION; INTERNATIONAL LAW.

## women and American foreign policy

Women have long been invisible in the study of American foreign policy. The role they play and have played can be highlighted by using three different frameworks employed in feminist writings on international relations. The first seeks to highlight the role and activities of women in foreign policy. The goal is to bring into the open significant behavior that has gone unnoticed. The second framework seeks to redirect and reformulate scientific inquiry into international relations by bringing gender to the forefront of these studies. Postmodern feminist studies seek to problematize women in the study of international relations. They are unconvinced that simply focusing more directly on women will produce a full understanding of the role that women and gender play in world politics.

A number of different foci have been adopted for studying women and American foreign policy that are consistent with the first perspective, and it is the most commonly employed of the three frameworks. One approach is to highlight the role that women have played in the PEACE MOVEMENT. Women were among the first to organize in response to the mobilization for war in Europe that led to WORLD WAR I, and they worked to prevent its reoccurrence. Members of the Women's Peace Union renounced individual participation in war and had 40,000 members in 1920. In 1915 the Woman's Peace Party was organized. Its platform called for a "convention of neutral nations in the interest of an early peace." Members argued that war would divert attention from pressing problems in the United States and threaten individual civil liberties. An outgrowth of this meeting, held in The Hague, was the formation of the radical and pacifist Women's International League for Peace and Freedom. Not only did this organization work for the LEAGUE OF NATIONS, but it was also instrumental in securing the NYE COMMISSION, set up to investigate charges that munitions makers and bankers had been responsible for World War I. During WORLD WAR II, a Women's Action Network for Victory and Lasting Peace was formed to coordinate the activities of women's peace organizations. The antiwar movement of the 1960s and 1970s saw women peace activists organized along a number of different fronts. The politically oriented Women Strike for Peace and the Women's International League for Peace and Freedom coexisted with the less politically focused Another Mother for Peace. During the nuclear-freeze movement, some 1,300 women from the Women's Pentagon Action employed civil disobedience at a demonstration in Washington.

In addition to focusing on political action by groups of women that influenced the debate over the conduct and practice of American foreign policy, a second focus within this first approach has been to highlight the role of individual women. Traditionally this has involved documenting the heroic action of women in combat situations and the actions of highly respected national figures, such as Eleanor Roosevelt. More recently the focus has been extended to cover the foreign policy–related activities of FIRST LADIES, such as Rosalynn Carter and Hillary Rodham Clinton, and the activities of key women officeholders. Three women that stand out in this regard are Jeane J. Kirkpatrick, Madeleine Albright, and Condoleezza Rice. Kirkpatrick was appointed by President RONALD REAGAN to be ambassador to the UNITED NATIONS. Often highly critical of that INTERNATIONAL ORGANIZATION, she gained a national reputation by arguing that President JIMMY CARTER's HUMAN-RIGHTS policy was flawed because it failed to distinguish between communist regimes that could not be reformed and pro-American authoritarian regimes that held the potential for becoming democratic. Albright was the first woman to serve as SECRETARY OF

STATE. She held that position in President BILL CLINTON's second term. Prior to that she had served on the NATIONAL SECURITY COUNCIL staff under Carter and was Clinton's ambassador to the UN. Rice was appointed by President GEORGE W. BUSH to be his NATIONAL SECURITY ADVISOR. An expert on Soviet foreign policy, she had taught and served as provost of Stanford University before the appointment.

The second framework for studying women and American foreign policy seeks to highlight the influence of gender on political activity. This has become a prominent topic in public opinion studies that deal with national security issues, as women have repeatedly been less willing than have men to support high levels of defense spending or use force to solve problems. For example, Gallup polls in the early to mid-1990s showed that where 44 percent of men favored sending troops to BOSNIA AND HERZEGOVINA, only 38 percent of women did so; where only 34 percent of men favored ending the ban on homosexuals in the military, 51 percent of women did favor ending the ban; and where 78 percent of men favored sending U.S. troops to SAUDI ARABIA after IRAQ invaded KUWAIT, only 54 percent of women supported this action.

The relationship between gender and political activity in the foreign-affairs area has also been highlighted by lawsuits brought by women FOREIGN SERVICE OFFICERS and women who work in the CENTRAL INTELLIGENCE AGENCY (CIA), claiming hiring and promotion discrimination by these organizations. In 1976 the STATE DEPARTMENT formally admitted discrimination did exist. More recently both the CIA and the UNITED STATES INFORMATION AGENCY settled discrimination suits. Within the military an added dimension to the problem of discrimination surrounds the debate over placing women in combat positions.

The third framework seeks to place gender at the center of theoretical inquiry so that its influence on American foreign policy can be better understood. This is not a new concern. In the early 1900s suffragists argued that many of the fundamental problems of world politics were due to gender injustice and the masculine tendency to resort to force to solve problems. A central tenet of feminist theorizing on world politics today is that the distinction between the private sector and the public sector reflects a masculine view of the world. Furthermore, POWER is conceived of in terms of domination and control, due to its masculine roots. A feminist interpretation of power is oriented around concepts and activities related to nurturing and collaboration. A feminist conception of NATIONAL INTEREST is multidimensional and contextually contingent, whereas masculine definitions are almost totally power centered.

**Further reading:** Carpol, Edward, ed. *Women and American Foreign Policy.* New York: Greenwood Press, 1987; Jeffreys-Jones, Rhodri. *Changing Differences: Women and the Shaping of American Foreign Policy, 1917–1994.* New Brunswick, N.J.: Rutgers University Press, 1995; Sylvester, Christine. *Feminist Theory and International Relations.* Cambridge, England: Cambridge University Press, 1994.

## World Bank

The World Bank, officially established as the International Bank for Reconstruction and Development (IBRD), was established in 1944 as part of the BRETTON WOODS SYSTEM. It was created out of a conviction that a speedy post–WORLD WAR II European economic recovery was crucial to global economic growth and that one major impediment in the way of this recovery was insufficient investment funds. Neither the World Bank nor the INTERNATIONAL MONETARY FUND (IMF), also created at Bretton Woods, was able to cope with the magnitude of the European economic recovery problem. Beginning in 1947, through the economic assistance provided through the MARSHALL PLAN and military assistance provided to members of the NORTH ATLANTIC TREATY ORGANIZATION (NATO), the United States successfully assumed unilateral management responsibilities for the international economic system.

By the 1960s with the success of European recovery now assured and COLD WAR competition with the Soviet Union (see RUSSIA) heating up, the efforts of the World Bank were redirected to Third World states. It is in this role that the World Bank has become a major force in international economic-policy making. It is the world's largest source of development funds. In fiscal year 2000, it provided more than $15 billion in loans. The World Bank has also become a target along with the IMF and WORLD TRADE ORGANIZATION, for those who are concerned with the negative effects of GLOBALIZATION. Many citizens in both rich and poor countries fear a loss of control over economic matters within their borders and see these international economic institutions as the key decision makers who must be controlled or stopped. Of particular concern is the perceived lack of attention given by these bodies to environmental, labor, and social justice issues. At its April 2000 meeting in Washington, D.C., some 20,000 protestors demanded that Third World debts be forgiven and added steps be taken to fight poverty.

Technically, the World Bank is owned by its members, who receive "shares" in it based on the level of their contributions. In 2000 more than 180 countries belonged to the World Bank. The United States is the single largest shareholder. In 1995 it accounted for 17.5 percent of the World Bank's total deposits. This is down from 29.3 percent in 1965. The World Bank also raises funds by selling bonds and other debt securities to pension funds, insurance companies, banks, and individual investors. States receiving loans are charged interest, and maturity runs generally from 15 to 20 years.

The World Bank is governed by the Board of Governors, who represent each of the member states, and the 25-person Board of Executive Directors, five of whom come from the largest five donors. The executive directors appoint a president, who typically is an American. The president oversees the World Bank Group, a collection of institutions, each of which has a distinct mission. The IBRD provides market-based loans and development assistance to middle-income countries and credit-worthy poor countries. The International Development Administration provides loans to the poorest states, who pay a fee of less than 1 percent of the loan to cover administration costs. These loans amount to about one-quarter of all World Bank Group lending. The International Finance Corporation promotes growth in the developing world by promoting private sector investment. The Multilateral Investment Guarantee Agency helps encourage private investment in developing countries by providing loan guarantees to foreign investors against losses due to noncommercial risks. Finally, the International Centre for Settlement of Investment Disputes helps to reconcile disputes between foreign investors and host countries.

Because of the vast sums of money it controls, the World Bank's economic development philosophy is crucial to the type of development efforts that take place in the Third World. Once the supporter of large-scale infrastructure projects, it now officially endorses lending policies that stress sustainable social and human development, strengthened economic management, and governance and institution building. Still, to many critics, the World Bank remains an extension of U.S. foreign policy and the drive to promote free-market capitalism. The result is that the interests of the foreign investor take precedence over the needs of the poor people in the host state. Criticism is also voiced over the level of spending. Adjusted for inflation, spending in 1999 was down from the level of World Bank spending in the early 1990s. Finally, some critics assert that, as with the IMF, the World Bank exhibits a strong Western bias that is visible in its selection of leaders and its "businesslike" approach to lending money, which involves charging interest and attaching conditions to granting loans.

**Further reading:** Danaher, Kevin, ed. *50 Years Is Enough: The Case against the World Bank and the International Monetary Fund.* Boston: South End Press, 1994; Gwin, Catherine. *U.S. Relations with the World Bank, 1945–1992.* Washington, D.C.: Brookings Institution, 1994.

## World Summit on Sustainable Development

Held in Johannesburg, SOUTH AFRICA, from August 26 to September 6, 2002, the World Summit on Sustainable Development (WSSD) was attended by some 65,000 delegates. Mandated by a 1999 UNITED NATIONS General Assembly resolution, the WSSD sought to enact an action plan to move forward the agreements reached 10 years earlier at the EARTH SUMMIT, RIO DE JANEIRO. The WSSD was also tasked to address new issues that had risen to prominence since Rio, such as clean water and globalization. The progress reached was moderate at best, and the American position on issues was widely criticized.

The concept sustainable development dates back to the 1972 UN Conference on Human ENVIRONMENT in Stockholm. It became popularized by the 1987 Brundtland Report (also known as the Report of the World Commission on Environment). It defined sustainable development as development that was "consistent with future as well as present needs." It is also commonly defined as improvements in social well-being, such as education and health care, that are consistent with a clean environment. Procedurally the concept of sustainable development includes a presumption that those affected by development decisions, especially the poor, should have a voice in making them. In 1992 the Rio Declaration outlined key policies for achieving sustainable development.

In preparation for the WSSD, a lengthy series of preparatory meetings were held to review progress made since Rio and identify steps that needed to be taken. The process began by having regional meetings that were broken down to include "eminent persons" roundtables and subregional preparatory meetings in different countries. Once these were completed a series of global preparatory committee meetings were held. The Johannesburg meeting itself was divided into two phases. In the first phase delegates and civil society were to address organizational and partnership issues. In the second phase heads of state addressed the summit.

The WSSD summit produced a 70-page nonbinding plan. Areas addressed included increasing the size of depleted fisheries and promoting cooperation between businesses and governments to deliver electricity, health care, and clean water to the poor in developing states. The agreement stressed methods of implementation and avoided specifying binding reduction schedules. For example, in the area of renewable energy, the WSSD agreement called upon states to act "with a sense of urgency" to increase the global share of renewable energy sources. The United States opposed targets in the area of renewable energy technologies as "unrealistic." In advancing this approach and working against setting specific targets, the GEORGE W. BUSH administration was accused of watering down the agreement. Bush was one of the few foreign leaders not to attend the conference, and he was also criticized for his failure to attend. SECRETARY OF STATE COLIN POWELL was the highest-ranking U.S. official at the WSSD, and he was heckled during his speech.

The use of public-private partnerships to advance sustainable development was one of the most controversial aspects of the summit. Business interests were all but absent at Rio. In Johannesburg approximately 700 companies were represented, and by one count 230 agreements between companies, countries, and NONGOVERNMENTAL ORGANIZATIONS were reached. In advocating this implementation strategy the Bush administration was accused of pursuing a probusiness agenda. These charges were most vocally raised by the two antisummits being held alongside the WSSD. One was the Global People's Forum, made up of representatives from trade unions, relief agencies, and antiglobalization groups. The second, and more radical, was organized by the Landless People's Movement and the Anti-Privatization Forum. This antisummit was dominated by South Africans who held the Global People's Forum to be too conservative and too ready to work with the businesses and governments represented at the WSSD. One of the most important issues for these protestors was land. Almost 80 percent of the arable farmland in South Africa remains in the hands of white farmers.

At the end of the summit supporters of the WSSD raised doubts as to the value of future summits. Some remarked that the time for such large "jamboree" summits is past. Critics asserted that what is needed now are smaller summits that are focused on solving problems rather than making public statements leading to minimal action.

See also CONFERENCE DIPLOMACY; ENVIRONMENT; GLOBALIZATION; MULTINATIONAL CORPORATIONS.

## World Trade Organization

The World Trade Organization (WTO) was founded in 1995 and succeeded the GENERAL AGREEMENT ON TARIFFS AND TRADE (GATT) as the centerpiece of the international trading system. GATT managed international trade negotiations through a series of negotiating rounds. The last GATT round was the URUGUAY ROUND. It lasted from 1986 to 1994 and approved the establishment of the WTO. Important earlier trade negotiating rounds included the KENNEDY ROUND and the TOKYO ROUND.

WTO agreements cover three basic areas. The first is goods. GATT agreements serve as the basis for trade rules concerning goods. The second area involves services, such as banking, insurance, telecommunications, and the travel industry. These sectors are covered by a new General Agreement on Trade in Services (GATS). The third area involves trade in intellectual property such as copyrights, patents, and trademarks now covered by the TRIPS Agreement.

The WTO has more than 140 members that account for 97 percent of the world's trade. Decisions are made through a variety of mechanisms. The foremost decision-making body is the Ministerial Conference, which meets at least once every other year. Below it is the General Council. It meets several times per year in Geneva, Switzerland, where the WTO is headquartered. One level below the General Council are a series of councils that deal with specific areas of international trade: Goods Council, Services Council, and Intellectual Property Council. There also exist specialized committees, working groups, and working parties to deal with individual agreements. These decision-making groups are serviced by a secretariat that is headed by a director general. The secretariat lacks any formal decision-making power.

A key feature of the WTO system is its dispute resolution process. Judgments are made by a panel of specially appointed independent experts who make their ruling based on the agreement in question and the individual countries' commitments under the agreement. The WTO dispute resolution system produces binding agreements, unlike the GATT system in which decisions lacked the power of enforcement. This has resulted in a dramatic increase in the number of disputes brought forward. From 1947 to 1994 only about 300 disputes were raised under GATT procedures. In the first seven years of the WTO's existence almost 250 cases have been brought.

The United States has been both a winner and a loser in this process. In January 2003, for example, the WTO rejected a U.S. law, the Byrd Amendment, that is designed to help the struggling American steel industry. Six months earlier, in July 2002, it upheld American restrictions on importing shrimp into the United States caught by countries that did not use devices to protect sea turtles. Given the traditional American penchant for UNILATERALISM, the presence of a binding dispute-resolution system has been a point of controversy within the United States. American membership in the WTO was qualified with an exit provision if the dispute-resolution system was found to work against American interests. In January 2003 the United States acted unilaterally to block a WTO agreement that would have given other countries access to cheaper drugs by letting poor states override patent protections and import generic drugs to tackle epidemics. A total of 143 states accepted the draft plan. The United States argued that the proposed wording could be construed to cover drugs for noninfectious diseases, such as asthma and diabetes, and that doing so would undermine research and development.

In November 2001 the WTO's fourth Ministerial Conference met in Doha, Qatar. The outcome of the negotiations provided a mandate for a new round of international trade talks. In the view of some, the Doha Round rescued the WTO process from the "stain" of Seattle, where protestors took to the streets and the momentum for further liberalization of international trade was stopped. Twenty-one different subjects were noted in the Doha Declaration, including implementation problems faced by the South in meeting current WTO obligations. Critics asserted that although it was included in the Doha Declaration, this problem did not receive serious attention at the meeting. Also included were issues that had been under discussion in other WTO forums, including trade in agriculture, services, and intellectual property rights, especially as they relate to pharmaceuticals. This has emerged as a major concern for the developing world as it tries to address the HIV/AIDS problem. Some argue that the most important additions to the Doha Declaration are the "Singapore issues." These are nontrade issues that were addressed by working groups set up by the 1996 Singapore Ministerial Conference. They include investment, competition policy, government procurement, and trade facilitation. The Doha Declaration does not initiate negotiations on any of these but continues to move them forward in international discussions.

The WTO has become the subject of intense controversy in its brief existence. In some cases the issues are specific to its operation. Concerns have been raised about its values and priorities. The assertion is that commercial interests dominate concerns for the ENVIRONMENT, worker health and safety, and development. The end result is seen as increased global poverty and not global growth. A second set of concerns center on its decision-making system, which has been described as medieval. The WTO defends itself by pointing to provisions for transparency in important decision forums. Critics assert that key decisions are made out of sight and off the record. At Doha, for example, complaints were raised about the United States threatening HAITI and the DOMINICAN REPUBLIC with loss of preferential trade arrangements if they opposed the U.S. position. NIGERIA, which at one point led the opposition to a draft of the Doha agreement, suddenly came out for it at the same time that it received a promise of economic and military FOREIGN AID from the United States. PAKISTAN did a similar flip-flop, after receiving an aid and debt reduction package.

Beyond specific complaints, the WTO had emerged as one of the lightening rods for those who oppose GLOBALIZATION. Along with the INTERNATIONAL MONETARY FUND and the WORLD BANK, it has become a symbol of capitalism run amok and the inability of governments to protect their citizens or the environment. The economic processes these institutions foster are seen as destroying local cultures and further removing important decisions from the control of the individuals who are affected by them.

**Further reading:** Aaronson, Susan. *Taking Trade to the Streets.* Ann Arbor: University of Michigan Press, 2001; Hormats, Robert, and Kevin Nealer. *Beginning the Journey.* New York: Council of Foreign Relations Press, 2002; Sampson, Gary. *The Role of the World Trade Organization in Global Governance.* New York: United Nations University Press, 2001.

## World War I

The outbreak of war in Europe caught the United States by surprise. From June 28, 1914, when Archduke Francis Ferdinand was assassinated until April 6, 1917, when the United States declared war on GERMANY, the two principal focal points of U.S. DIPLOMACY were on maintaining its neutrality and seeking a diplomatic solution to the conflict. More effort was put into the former than the latter.

President WOODROW WILSON issued a formal declaration of neutrality in August 1914. Maintaining American neutrality was complicated by several factors. First, many Americans had only recently emigrated to the United States and still had strong ties with their homelands. While most of these "hyphenated Americans" wished to keep the United States out of World War I, they did not necessarily hide their sympathies for either the Allied or the Central powers, leading Wilson to urge Americans to be "impartial in thought as well as action." Second, within Wilson's cabinet, only SECRETARY OF STATE WILLIAM JENNINGS BRYAN was not pro-Ally. Third, the principles of neutrality, especially as they related to maritime trade, had grown obsolete. Both the British and the German navies adopted policies based on expediency and military advantage rather than INTERNATIONAL LAW in dealing with U.S. merchant vessels. Soon after fighting began, Bryan asked both sides to abide by the principles of the 1909 Declaration of London on the laws of the sea. The British had objected to the terms of this declaration because they felt it nullified the military advantage they held by virtue of possessing a large navy. Attempts to get both sides to agree to its terms in 1914 also failed, and the United States withdrew its proposal.

Even if it was desired, implementing a policy of true neutrality was not easily done because any action or inaction was bound to advantage one side over the other. For example, in the eyes of Germany, the United States quickly became the arsenal of the Allies. Technically both Germany and GREAT BRITAIN could buy weapons from the United States, but the British blockade had the effect of denying Germany American-made weapons. At first the Allies paid for these weapons in cash. FRANCE sought a loan from J. P. Morgan & Company. Upon the advice of Secretary of State Bryan it turned down the request. Bryan had said such a loan was "inconsistent with the true spirit of neutrality." Within two months, in October 1914, this position was reversed. As the war progressed the Allies obtained larger and larger loans to allow them to purchase American goods. Secretary of State Robert Lansing argued that this was necessary to prevent a depression.

The earliest challenges to American neutrality came from Great Britain. It moved to impose a near total blockade on trade with Germany. In the course of doing so London violated or enlarged upon basic interpretations of

INTERNATIONAL LAW to the point were they were nonrecognizable. For example, under existing international law, merchant ships could be stopped and searched for contraband. Now the British forced these ships into port where they were detained and underwent lengthy searches. The United States routinely protested British actions but never pressed the matter. For their part, the British were careful not to totally alienate the Wilson administration. On occasion it agreed to pay for cargo it seized.

In time it would be German violations of American neutrality that would push the United States into war. International law required that belligerents provide for the safety of the crew and passengers of any ship it searched for contraband and sank. Submarines were ill suited for this purpose. Germany began its submarine attacks on February 5, 1915, by declaring the seas around Great Britain a war zone. On March 28 it sank the British liner *Falaba,* killing one American and setting off a heated debate in the STATE DEPARTMENT. Bryan argued that if Americans traveled on belligerent vessels, they did so at their own risk. True neutrality demanded inaction on the part of the United States. Robert Lansing, who would soon replaced Bryan as secretary of state, argued that the United States must defend the rights of Americans to travel on Allied ships. Bryan won the day, and Wilson did not protest the German action.

On May 7, a German U-boat attacked and sunk the British passenger liner *Lusitania.* A total 128 Americans were among the 1,198 who died. Germany defended its actions by asserting that the *Lusitania* also carried rifle cartridges. Wilson now sent a diplomatic note to Germany demanding that it disavow the sinking. He drafted a follow-up diplomatic note that Bryan objected to for fear that it would lead to war. In the second note, Wilson added a demand that Germany pay damages and stop its attacks on passenger ships. Bryan resigned rather than send the second note and was replaced by Lansing, who did so. Only in 1916 did Germany agree to assume some liability for its actions. With Wilson considering breaking diplomatic relations, Germany sought to reduce tensions by secretly ordering its submarines not to attack unarmed passenger ships. This policy was followed until August 1915 when, in violation of these orders, the *Arabic* was sunk. In yet another attempt to defuse the growing conflict, Germany now announced that it would not attack unarmed passenger ships without warning unless they tried to escape. In spite of this *Arabic* pledge, German attacks did not stop, and on March 16, 1916, Berlin announced a policy of attacking unarmed merchant ships without warning.

On March 24, several Americans were injured when German submarines attacked the French passenger liner *Sussex* in the English Channel. This was a direct violation of the *Arabic* pledge, and Lansing counseled Wilson to break diplomatic relations with Germany. On May 4, Germany issued the *Sussex* pledge in an effort to head off war. In it, Berlin promised not to attack merchant ships without warning. Germany unsuccessfully sought to add a condition to this pledge, namely, that the United States would work to end the British food blockade of Germany.

DOMESTIC INFLUENCES were never far from the forefront in Wilson's efforts to maintain American neutrality. Just prior to the *Sussex* crisis, Congress was poised to pass a resolution warning Americans against traveling on belligerent ships. Only Wilson's personal intervention prevented this from happening. Wilson also faced pressure from pro-Allied interventionists who advocated increased defense preparedness. THEODORE ROOSEVELT, ELIHU ROOT, and HENRY CABOT LODGE were leading spokespeople for this cause. At first Wilson opposed added defense spending, but he changed his position after the sinking of the *Lusitania.* In July 1915 he instructed the secretaries of navy and war to draw up plans for an expanded military establishment. Wilson took his argument for defense preparedness directly to the American public in January 1916 when pacifists and peace groups pressured CONGRESS to resist these added expenditures. Wilson campaigned in 1916 as the candidate of peace and won reelection by a narrow margin over CHARLES EVANS HUGHES, who also promised to keep the United States out of war.

Prior to the election, in January 1916, Wilson sent one of his closest advisers, Colonel EDWARD HOUSE to Europe to bring an end to the war. House reached an agreement with British foreign minister Sir Edward Grey on a memorandum stating that whenever Great Britain and France felt the conditions were right, the United States would call a peace conference. Under its terms, the United States would "probably" intervene on the side of the Allies, if Germany either refused to attend the conference or refused reasonable terms at the conference. Nothing came of the House-Grey Memorandum. The Allied military situation improved in the following months, and Grey came to have serious doubts about Wilson's ability to secure a declaration of war from Congress.

After the election Wilson again sought to play peacemaker. He prepared identical notes to the two sides proposing a peace conference. However, prior to sending these notes, Germany notified Wilson on December 12, 1916, that it wished to discuss peace terms. This placed him in the awkward position of siding with Germany against the Allies in ending the war. Wilson temporized, and on January 22, 1917, he addressed the Senate and called for a "peace without victory" and for the creation of a LEAGUE OF NATIONS. Wilson's vision satisfied neither the Allied nor the Central powers. Germany responded by declaring a policy of unrestricted submarine warfare on

American soldiers manning a firing position behind barbed wire in a trench at Dieffmatten, in Alsace, France *(National Archives)*

January 31. German military leaders recognized that this would force the United States into the war but, as one strategist stated, "[T]hings cannot be worse than they are now." Initially Wilson resisted the advice to arm American merchant ships. His reluctance evaporated with the release of the ZIMMERMANN TELEGRAM. Intercepted and decoded by the British, it was a communication from German foreign minister Arthur Zimmermann to the German minister in MEXICO instructing him to inquire about Mexico's willingness to go to war against the United States. In return Mexico would receive its lost territories of Arizona, New Mexico, and TEXAS.

When the Zimmermann Telegram was made public, Congress was considering Wilson's request for authority to arm U.S. merchant ships as part of a policy of "armed neutrality." The House now quickly approved this request, but a dozen senators led by Robert La Follette (R-Wisc.) and George Norris (R-Neb.) successfully filibustered against the measure. On April 2, 1917, Wilson took the next step and delivered his war message to a joint session of Congress.

Four days later Congress passed a formal declaration of war by a vote of 373-50 in the House and 82-6 in the Senate.

The United States entered the war as an Associated, rather than an Allied power to stress its continued tradition of independence in world politics. The American contribution to the Allies victory was significant along a number of dimensions. At first the Allied Powers were most interested in securing additional funds from the United States for the war effort and the protection of the U.S. Navy for its shipping. Later, U.S. ground forces would play a key role in repelling Germany's last great offensive in March 1918.

The United States put forward its own statement of war aims in Wilson's FOURTEEN POINTS. In many respects they clashed with the secret treaties that the Allied powers had already made among themselves. The Fourteen Points became the center of diplomatic maneuvering that took place at the peace conference that convened on January 12, 1919. Five months later a peace treaty, the TREATY OF VERSAILLES, was signed, only to be rejected by the U.S. Senate after a long and acrimonious debate.

**Further reading:** Ferrell, Robert. *Woodrow Wilson and World War I, 1917–1921.* New York: Harper and Row, 1985; May, Ernest R. *The World War and American Isolation, 1914–1917.* Cambridge, Mass.: Harvard University Press, 1959.

## World War II

World War II was a watershed in U.S. foreign policy. Prior to the war, isolationist sentiment dominated American thinking on world politics. After, it INTERNATIONALISM emerged triumphant. Whereas the United States had rejected membership in the LEAGUE OF NATIONS, it enthusiastically joined the UNITED NATIONS. Both world wars altered the landscape of the INTERNATIONAL SYSTEM. Whereas after World War I, the United States was one of several major powers, after World War II, it was but one of two.

The road to World War II was a tortuous one for President FRANKLIN ROOSEVELT, who had determined that neutrality in the steadily escalating conflict between GREAT BRITAIN and GERMANY did not serve American interests. From 1935 forward he worked to amend—if not circumvent—the NEUTRALITY LEGISLATION of 1935, 1936, 1937, and 1939. Imposed on him by an isolationist CONGRESS and supported by an American public who wanted to avoid war, these neutrality acts limited the ability of the United States to provide weapons or other supplies to Great Britain. It was only by means of the last of these neutrality acts that Roosevelt was able to openly tilt U.S. FOREIGN AID toward Great Britain, first through LEND-LEASE aid and then by having U.S. ships help convoy this aid safely through war zones. With these acts the United States had moved from a position of neutrality to one of nonbelligerency.

U.S. relations with JAPAN in the period leading up to World War II combined elements of hostility with a desire to avoid direct confrontation. In July 1937 Japanese forces invaded CHINA, and war in the Pacific began. The United States joined the League of Nations in condemning the Japanese action but took no concrete steps to reverse it. In a move that had little practical significance, President Roosevelt did not invoke the provisions of the neutrality act in this conflict, as he had when ITALY invaded ETHIOPIA in 1935. In hopes of avoiding an incident that might lead to direct conflict, the United States began to evacuate American citizens from China. In December Japanese aircraft sank a U.S. gunboat, the *Panay*, which was helping in the evacuation.

Japan quickly apologized two days after the attack. Alarmed at the surge in prowar sentiment in the United States, Representative Louis Ludlow (D-Ind.) introduced a constitutional amendment that would have required a national referendum before a declaration of war unless it stemmed from an attack on U.S. soil. A total 218 Congress-people signed a petition supporting the measure, and 80 percent of those questioned in PUBLIC OPINION polls agreed with it. Heavy lobbying by the Roosevelt administration prevented the bill from being forced out of committee by a margin of 21 votes.

In November 1938 Japan declared the establishment of a new order in Asia, the Greater East Asia Co-Prosperity Sphere. Continued Japanese aggression led for calls in the United States for an economic embargo, and in July 1939 the STATE DEPARTMENT notified Japan that it was giving the required six months notice of termination of the Treaty of Commerce and Navigation of 1911, a move that would free the way for imposing an economic embargo. Congress followed this up in July 1940 by passing legislation that placed selected strategic materials under a strict licensing system. Aviation fuel, gasoline, and high-grade iron and steel scrap metal were included under this law.

Hoping to end U.S. sanctions, Japan's ambassador to the United States, Admiral Kichiasburo Nomura, began a series of informal talks with SECRETARY OF STATE CORDELL HULL in March 1941. Six different proposals, three by each side, grew out of these talks, which covered various aspects of Japan's foreign policy, including its signing of the Tripartite Agreement with Germany and Italy and its expansion into China and the Pacific. The talks stalemated. In July Roosevelt imposed additional ECONOMIC SANCTIONS on Japan, including freezing all funds in the United States and closing the PANAMA CANAL to Japanese vessels.

A Japanese government divided over the pursuit of war sought to renew negotiations with the United States. There ensued a series of proposals and counterproposals over the terms of such a meeting with the United States insisting—and Japan agreeing—that it would not use force against its neighbors. Having broken the Japanese code, the United States had no faith in such promises. U.S. and Japanese negotiators now worked at cross-purposes more clearly than ever. Japan sought a quick agreement recognizing its conquests, while the United States sought to prolong the negotiations. The end came when on November 26, 1941, Hull rejected the last Japanese proposal and countered with his Ten-Point Plan. It called for Japan to withdraw from China, withdraw its support from the puppet government it had established there, and pull out of the Tripartite Pact. Japan rejected it. On December 1 the Japanese Imperial Council approved a war plan, and on December 7 its forces struck Pearl Harbor.

U.S. war aims had been established a few months earlier at a meeting between Roosevelt and British prime minister Winston Churchill in Newfoundland with the signing of the ATLANTIC CHARTER. In some respects a restatement of President WOODROW WILSON's FOURTEEN POINTS, the Atlantic Charter presented a vision of a DEMOCRATIC PEACE. Its principles were reaffirmed at the

Moscow Summit Conference of August 1943, at which time the Soviet Union also gave a vague promise to support a postwar international security organization.

Roosevelt took an activist role in World War II DIPLOMACY, relegating Secretary of State Hull to a secondary position. The instrument of choice for resolving conflicts among the Allies and putting in place the postwar institutional architecture was the SUMMIT CONFERENCE. Beginning with the Roosevelt-Churchill meeting in Newfoundland and ending with the POTSDAM CONFERENCE in July–August 1945, some 18 major conferences were held. Significant topics taken up at these meetings included the question of opening a second front. This was

desperately sought by the Soviet Union and opposed with equal intensity by Great Britain. Both sides recognized that at stake were not only questions of war losses but also the future political shape of Europe. The establishment of a United Nations and the Soviet Union's entry into the war against Japan became linked items in discussions at the YALTA CONFERENCE. The "unconditional surrender" of Germany was advanced as a goal by Roosevelt and Churchill at the Casablanca summit. In making this pronouncement they hoped to reassure the Soviet Union of their loyalty and avoid a repeat of World War I, when the Germans surrendered on the basis of the Fourteen Points only to have the British and French impose harsher conditions. The fate of

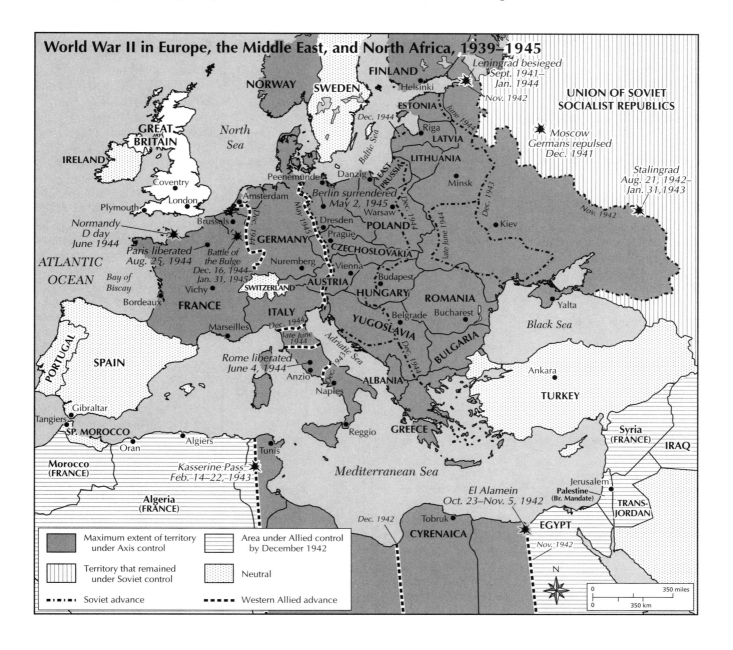

World War II in Europe, the Middle East, and North Africa, 1939–1945

**World War II in the Pacific, 1942–1945**

First atomic bomb dropped on Hiroshima Aug. 6, 1945

Okinawa I. U.S. landing April 1, 1945

Guadalcanal I. U.S. landing Aug. 7, 1942

Extent of Japanese conquests
Pockets of Japanese resistance
Western Allied advance
Other Allied advance

POLAND was settled at Yalta. And the WORLD BANK and INTERNATIONAL MONETARY FUND were established at BRETTON WOODS in 1944.

Other issues also divided the Allies. Relations between the United States and FRANCE were rocky, as French leader General Charles de Gaulle sought to reestablish

France's position as a major power. The United States found itself at odds with France and Great Britain over the postwar status of their colonial holdings. The United States experienced continued frustrations in dealing with China. Accorded "great power" status by Roosevelt, the Nationalist forces of Jiang Jieshi (Chiang Kai-shek) focused far less on defeating Japan than they did on the inevitable renewal of their civil war with Mao Zedong (Mao Tse-tung), so they were ineffective in fighting Japan.

One of the most momentous and controversial foreign-policy decisions made during World War II was the decision to drop the atomic bomb on Hiroshima. Working under the code name "Manhattan Project," British, American, and Canadian scientists carried out work on the atomic bomb in secret. In 1945 a committee under the chair of Secretary of War HENRY STIMSON recommended against a demonstration explosion of the atomic bomb and for its use against war production facilities in Japan. When news of the successful testing of the atomic bomb on July 16, 1945, at Alamogordo, New Mexico, reached President HARRY TRUMAN at the POTSDAM CONFERENCE, his attitude toward cooperation with the Soviet Union hardened. Up until this point U.S. officials had eagerly sought Soviet participation in the war against Japan. On August 6 the first atomic bomb was dropped on Hiroshima. On August 8 the Soviet Union declared war on Japan and sent troops into Manchuria. On August 9 the second atomic bomb was dropped on Nagasaki. The following day the Japanese government offered to surrender. The formal surrender took place on September 2.

See also CONFERENCE DIPLOMACY; RUSSIA.

**Further reading:** Dallek, Robert, *Franklin D. Roosevelt and American Foreign Policy, 1932–1945.* New York: Oxford University Press, 1979; Feis, Herbert. *Churchill, Roosevelt, and Stalin: The War They Waged and the Peace They Sought.* Princeton, N.J.: Princeton University Press, 1957; ———. *Japan Subdued: The Atomic Bomb and the End of the War in the Pacific.* Princeton, N.J.: Princeton University Press, 1961; Smith, Gaddis. *American Diplomacy during World War II.* New York: McGraw Hill, 1985.

## Wye River accords

Wye River, Maryland, was the site of an October 1998 summit meeting between Israeli prime minister Benjamin Netanyahu and PALESTINE LIBERATION ORGANIZATION (PLO) leader Yasser Arafat that was arranged by President BILL CLINTON. The goal was to reenergize the peace process that had begun with the talks that had produced the

MADRID ACCORDS in 1991 and had since become stalled. Clinton played an active role in these deliberations. Neither side seemed particularly interested in making concessions without his presence. The Wye River Memorandum is significant as an example of summit and personal DIPLOMACY. It is best viewed not as a self-contained exercise but as part of a larger ongoing stream of negotiations to deal with a complex problem.

After nine days of often intense negotiations, an agreement was reached on October 23. The memorandum established a procedure and three-stage timetable for the transfer of lands in the occupied territories from Israeli control to the Palestinians. It also formally committed the Palestinians "to take all measures necessary to prevent acts of TERRORISM, crime, and hostilities directed against ISRAEL." To accomplish this task a bilateral Israeli-Palestinian security cooperation program was set up along with a U.S.-Palestinian Committee, and a U.S.-Palestinian-Israeli committee. The Palestinians agreed to modify those provisions of the Palestinian National Charter that advocated destroying Israel.

Put into perspective commentators suggested that the terms of the Wye River Memorandum were quite modest in that they focused primarily on shoring up the implementation of agreements already discussed. The land being exchanged was sparsely populated. Left unanswered was the status of Jerusalem and the fate of Palestinian REFUGEES and prisoners in Israeli jails. The memorandum established May 4, 1999, as the deadline for achieving an agreement on all outstanding issues.

Israel also used the occasion to try to arrange the release of Jonathan Pollard, an American INTELLIGENCE analyst who had been caught spying for Israel. Charges of betrayal dogged Israeli politicians, who as a group turned their backs on Pollard's plea for help and who sought to depict his espionage activities as part of a single-man operation for which the Israeli government bore no responsibility. Obtaining his release and return would be a major coup for Netanyahu. The Clinton administration refused to release Pollard. Offsetting the pressure brought to bear by Israeli and Jewish-American lobbying groups was the attitude of the national security BUREAUCRACY that releasing Pollard would make it easier to others to engage in ESPIONAGE against the United States by reducing the penalty for spying.

The momentum engendered by the Wye River Memorandum proved to be short lived. Less than two years later Clinton would again bring Israeli and Palestinian leaders together at Camp David to resolve outstanding differences. This time no agreement would be reached.

# Y

## Yalta Conference

Held from February 4 to 11, 1945, near the end of WORLD WAR II, the Yalta Conference is perhaps the best known of the World War II SUMMIT CONFERENCES. It brought together President FRANKLIN ROOSEVELT, British prime minister Winston Churchill, and Soviet leader Joseph Stalin. The agenda was lengthy and complex, dealing with issues pertaining to both the conduct of World War II and the shape of the postwar international order.

POLAND was a principal topic of concern. Its boundaries were pushed westward, giving it part of GERMANY and ceding part of its territory to the Soviet Union (see RUSSIA). Stalin demanded as much in order to deny any future invader a clear path into his country's heartland. In return Churchill and Roosevelt elicited a vaguely worded promise that the Communist-led government now in place in Warsaw would be expanded to include democratic forces and that free ELECTIONS would be held. Similar promises were secured for governments elsewhere in Eastern Europe.

GERMANY's future was also decided. It was agreed that a French occupation zone would be carved out of the British and American zones. Russian demands for reparations from Germany for war-related losses and expenses produced only a promise to consider the issue in the future once Germany's financial ability was established. A total $20 billion was established as a target figure for future talks. Western powers objected to reparations, citing the heavy economic and political blows it dealt to Germany after WORLD WAR I, a factor many consider to have been instrumental in creating conditions that allowed Adolf Hitler to rise to power. Stalin agreed to enter the war against JAPAN two months after Hitler was defeated. He also agreed to recognize the government of Jiang Jieshi (Chiang Kai-shek) and not that of Mao Zedong (Mao Tse-tung). In return he received promises that territory lost to Japan in 1905 would be returned and that Russia would receive control over the Kurile Islands.

A final major agreement centered on the structure of the UNITED NATIONS. Stalin sought membership for all 16 Soviet republics in the General Assembly and Security Council and veto power over both substantive and procedural matters. A compromise was reached whereby the Soviet Union received three seats in the General Assembly, and Security Council vetoes were to be limited to substantive issues. The three leaders also agreed on April 25 as the date for the organizational meeting of the United Nations in San Francisco later that year.

Bargaining at Yalta was carried out against a backdrop of conflicting foreign-policy goals, mutual suspicion, and an unbalanced military situation. The United States, for example, cared most about a deal on the United Nations and getting Soviet help against Japan. It distrusted Great Britain because of its continued imperial ambitions. Militarily, the West was at a disadvantage vis-à-vis Russia. Its forces were just recovering from a slowdown during the Battle of the Bulge and Russian forces were moving rapidly through Eastern Europe.

The agreements themselves were controversial. Many were cast in vague terms. Permitting democracy in Poland meant something quite different to Stalin than it did to Churchill and Roosevelt. Some would reappear on the agenda as unfinished business at the POTSDAM CONFERENCE that summer. Defenders of the Yalta Declaration saw the document as a valiant effort by Roosevelt, operating from a position of weakness, to extract as much as possible from Stalin. Critics saw it as a sellout comparable to the prewar Munich agreement because it effectively placed postwar Eastern Europe under Soviet control.

**Further reading:** Theoraris, Athan. *The Yalta Myths: An Issue in U.S. Politics, 1945–1955.* Columbia: University of Missouri Press, 1970.

*(From left to right)* Winston Churchill, Franklin D. Roosevelt, and Joseph Stalin at Yalta  *(Library of Congress)*

***Youngstown Sheet and Tube Co. v. Sawyer*** (1952)
This historic case involved the exercise of presidential foreign-policy POWER against private actors rather than another branch of government. The SUPREME COURT ruled 6-3 against the constitutionality of President HARRY TRU-MAN's order to nationalized the country's steel mills. Justices wrote six different majority opinions. They thus failed to establish clear guidelines limiting such powers, although the collective weight of their opinions was to urge caution on the PRESIDENT. A more recent ruling in *DAMES & MOORE V. REGAN* (1981) suggests that the Court has become more sympathetic to Truman's assertion of presidential power.

The setting for this case was the KOREAN WAR and an impending nationwide shutdown of the steel industry. President Truman judged this action to be dangerous to the war effort and issued an executive order directing Secretary of Commerce Charles Sawyer to seize and operate the steel mills. Truman informed CONGRESS of his action and lawmakers declined to take any action. This was in spite of the case that the 1947 Taft-Hartley Act denied the government the right to seize private property in order to settle a labor dispute. The steel companies brought suit to block Truman's action. Truman defended his actions as consistent with his constitutional powers as commander in chief of the armed forces.

Justice Hugo Black stated, "[T]he President's power, if any, to issue the order must stem from either an act of Congress or from the CONSTITUTION itself. . . . The order cannot properly be sustained as an exercise of the President's military power as Commander in Chief of the Armed

Forces." Justice William Douglas observed, "[I]f we sanction the present exercise of power by the President, we would be expanding Article II of the Constitution and rewriting it to suit the political conveniences of the present emergency."

## Yugoslavia

At present, Yugoslavia is composed of two constituent republics: Serbia and Montenegro. Together they are about the size of Kentucky and have a total population of 8 million people, of whom 62.6 percent are Serbs. This truncated Yugoslavia came into existence in April 1992, following a series of political tremors that resulted in the creation of three new states: CROATIA, Slovenia, and BOSNIA AND HERZEGOVINA. The birth of these new states and the emergence of a Serbian-dominated Yugoslavia was accompanied by much violence and hatred. The shock waves this produced reverberated throughout Europe and the international community. In Europe it recalled earlier periods in which continent-wide conflicts, such as WORLD WAR I, were born in the Balkans. It called into question the ability of INTERNATIONAL ORGANIZATIONS such as the UNITED NATIONS, regional ones such as the NORTH ATLANTIC TREATY ORGANIZATION (NATO), and European states to carry out PEACEKEEPING activities and HUMANITARIAN INTERVENTIONS. Finally, it sparked a debate over the dynamics of ethnic conflict, with some pointing to primordial differences between the peoples of the region and others pointing to elite manipulation of nationalistic feelings and grievances.

Yugoslavia came into existence in 1918, following World War I when the independent states of Serbia and Montenegro were joined with Croatia, Slovenia, and Bosnia-Herzegovina to form the Kingdom of Serbs, Croats, and Slovenes. These latter three territories had been part of the Austrian-Hungarian Empire that was defeated in that war and dismembered. Serbian king Peter I was proclaimed the ruler of this new state. Foreign and domestic problems soon faced Yugoslavia. Externally, it had territorial disputes with ITALY. Internally, violent political challenges came from Croat Nationalists who demanded more autonomy.

Instability gripped the region in 1941. Yugoslavia gravitated toward the Axis powers only to have a military coup in March 1941 lead to a declaration of neutrality. Almost immediately GERMANY invaded and dismembered Yugoslavia. Puppet Croatian and Serbian states loyal to Nazi Germany were created; Montenegro and Slovenia were divided among Italy, HUNGARY, and Germany; and Macedonia was given to Bulgaria. While King Peter II set up a government in exile in London, GUERRILLA groups fought against the Axis forces in Yugoslavia. The most important were a loyalist group led by Dragoljub Mihajlović known as the Chetniks and a communist group led by

Josip Broz, Mashal Tito. By 1943 the two groups were fighting each other in anticipation of the post–WORLD WAR II era when all sides expected that Yugoslavia would emerge again as an independent state. Tito and his Communist forces emerged as the stronger of the two and the more effective anti-Nazi fighting force. German forces fled Yugoslavia in October 1944, and the Soviet army entered as the liberating force. Tito became premier of the unity government and took full control following the November 1945 elections, elections that his noncommunist opponents had abstained from participating in.

From his post as head of the Yugoslav Communist Party, Tito provided the glue that held Yugoslavia together. An observation often made was that he was the only true Yugoslav. As did the other newly installed Communist leaders in East Europe, Tito set out to eliminate his political opposition and gain control over the economy. He aligned himself with Soviet leader Joseph Stalin, but he soon broke away from Moscow. In 1948 Yugoslavia was expelled from the Cominform, the international organization that Stalin had formed in 1947 to help gain control over Communist Parties outside the Soviet Union (see RUSSIA) and ensure their loyalty to him. Tito resisted Stalin's efforts at domination. He was able to do so largely because of his standing within Yugoslavia as a resistance fighter. Unlike many Communist leaders in Eastern Europe, Tito had a power base independent of Stalin.

The United States and Western Europe welcomed this sign of independence and sought to nurture it and provide protection for it. In less than 10 years the United States provided Yugoslavia with some $2 billion in FOREIGN AID. In 1954 Yugoslavia signed a military defense agreement with GREECE and TURKEY. Tito's relations with the Soviet Union improved after Stalin's death and Nikita Khrushchev's de-Stalinization program. An agreement was signed in 1956 acknowledging that there existed "differing roads to socialism." However, relations quickly soured when the Soviet Union used force to put down national communist movements in Hungary in 1956 and POLAND in 1957. As a sign of his independence from Moscow, Tito would go on to establish an important role for himself in the nonaligned movement. He would also loosen economic and political controls, including ending the collectivization of agriculture, decentralizing administrative power, establishing workers councils, and relaxing restrictions on the Catholic Church.

Tito died in 1980, and he was replaced by a collective leadership. The formula proved unworkable as economic and political tensions increased, pulling the six republics further and further apart. The key figure in the post-Tito political order was Slobodan Milošević, who became head of the Serbian Communist Party in 1987 and president of Serbia in 1989. His goal was to reestablish Greater Serbia, a feat that could only be accomplished by mobilizing and unifying the Serb populations in Croatia, Macedonia, and Bosnia and Herzegovina. Signs of impending trouble came in 1989 when Serbia sent troops into KOSOVO and rescinded its autonomy. Kosovo is a province in Serbia where ethnic Albanians outnumbered Serbs by nine to one.

In 1990 the end game for Yugoslavia was near. Slovenia and Croatia elected noncommunist governments and threatened secession if they were not granted greater autonomy. In May 1991 Serbia prevented a Croat from assuming the leadership position of the collective presidency. Both republics declared their independence on June 5. In September Macedonia declared its independence, and in October Bosnia-Herzegovina voted for independence. The Serbs who now controlled the Yugoslav government and army did not accept these decisions. The army moved into Slovenia in an attempt to block its secession. The move failed, as the Slovenians provided a unified and effective opposition. The European Community negotiated a peace agreement that failed to hold, but by the end of July 1991 all Yugoslav troops had left Slovenia, and in January 1992 Slovenia was recognized as an independent state by the European Community.

Fighting continued longer in Croatia, where a sizable Serb minority existed. The new Croatian government's unwillingness to consider Serb demands for cultural and political autonomy helped lead to the formation of Serb paramilitary groups that received their arms from the Yugoslav army. Foreshadowing the atrocities that would become increasingly commonplace, the Serbs engaged in a policy of ethnic cleansing as they drove Croats from Serb-held lands. Fighting began to dissipate in early 1992, when the European Community negotiated a series of tenuous cease-fires and the United Nations sent in a 14,000-person peacekeeping force. This was in February 1992 and by now the Serbs controlled 30 percent of Croatia. In 1993 Croatian forces attacked Serb strongholds throughout the country, and in 1995 they recaptured much of the territory they had lost. In the process some 300,000 Serbs fled to Bosnia and Yugoslavia.

The most gruesome fighting was yet to come. The United States and the European Community recognized Bosnia and Herzegovina's independence in April 1992. Bosnians Serbs, who were a minority in this new country, opposed the move and with the help of the Serbian (Yugoslav) army began to detach Serb-populated regions. They announced the creation of the Serbian Republic of Bosnia and Herzegovina. Croats in Bosnia and Herzegovina, who were also worried about the prospect of domination by the Muslim majority, also established their own independent political unit, the Croation Community of Herzeg-Bosnia. The result left little of the original country of Bosnia and Herzegovina. With about 30 percent of the population,

the Serbian Bosnians took control of about 65 percent of the country. Half of the remainder was claimed by the Croatian Bosnians, who made up 20 percent of the population.

The international community through the UNITED NATIONS sought to end the fighting by placing ECONOMIC SANCTIONS and an arms embargo on all parties in May 1992. The result was disastrous for the Muslim population. Compared to the Serbs, they were poorly armed, and the embargo condemned them to a position of military inferiority. Worse, it permitted the Serbs to carry out their policy of ethnic cleansing in which thousands of Muslims were killed, deported, and raped. Rather than intervene militarily to end the fighting, Western states backed the creation of a series of safe zones in Bosnia and Herzegovina to which the Muslim population could flee.

The war in Bosnia and Herzegovina became a complicated affair, involving local forces as well as the armies of Serbia and Croatia. A cease-fire between the Croats and Bosnians was not arranged until 1994. It led to the establishment of a Federation of Bosnia and Herzegovina. Serb forces continued fighting, and in 1995 they began attacking UN "safe zones." Finally, in 1995 negotiations between the Bosnians, Croats, and Serbs began in Dayton, Ohio. Negotiations ensued after Serbia announced that it was suspending assistance to the Bosnian Serbs. The UN's economic sanctions were starting to hurt Serbia's economy. and Milošević had become concerned that the alliance with the Bosnian Serbs was no longer serving Serbia's interests. Economic sanctions were taking their toll on its economy, and he wished to settle the conflict. The agreement reached in Dayton called for the establishment of a central government and two autonomous regional governments, one controlled by the Serbs and the other by the Bosnians and Croats. The DAYTON ACCORDS also called for sending in PEACEKEEPING troops under the auspices of NATO. These troops were to leave in June 1998 but remained there beyond that date.

The tenuous peace achieved in Bosnia and Herzegovina did not end the fighting in the Balkans. The conflict now shifted to Kosovo. Relations between the Serbs and Kosovars had remained tense, and by 1998 GUERRILLA WARFARE was common. Late that year Milošević began a major military campaign against the separatists. Failed negotiations and continued oppression of the Albanian Kosovars led to a decision by NATO to begin bombing Serbian targets in March 1999. In response, Serbs forcefully expelled hundreds of thousands of ethnic Albanians from Kosovo. In June, NATO peacekeepers (KFOR) entered Kosovo and placed it under a UN protectorate (UNMIK).

For his part, Milošević was elected president of Yugoslavia in 1997. He ran for reelection in September 2000 after the constitution was amended in July to permit presidents to serve a second term. Milošević was defeated by Vojislav Kostunica, who ran with the support of 18 opposition parties under the collective banner of the Democratic Opposition of Serbia. Milošević only conceded defeat on October 5 after a general strike was called. By this time Milošević had become the target of an international war crimes tribunal for his ethnic-cleansing campaigns. Kostunica had first refused to turn Milošević over to this body, but in June 2001 Milošević was surrendered. In 2002 the government took the additional step of setting up a commission to coordinate cooperation with the international war crimes tribunal to help arrest indicted war criminals hiding in Yugoslavia.

Just before the 1999 NATO bombing campaign, the United States and its European allies broke diplomatic relations with Yugoslavia. On October 5, 2000, the U.S. EMBASSY reopened. Since that time the flow of American FOREIGN AID to Yugoslavia has gradually resumed. In May 2002, SECRE-TARY OF STATE Colin Powell certified that Yugoslavia had made significant progress in implementing the Dayton Accords, that it had released political prisoners, and that it was cooperating with the international criminal tribunal. This certification cleared the way for the resumption of FOREIGN AID and funding by the WORLD BANK and INTERNATIONAL MONETARY FUND. In 2002 the total amount of U.S. foreign aid to Yugoslavia exceeded $180 million. In February 2003, Yugoslavia became a loose federation of two republics and is now known as Serbia and Montenegro. In 2002 Serbia and Montenegro entered into negotiations to recast Yugoslavia into a looser political federation; in 2003 it was agreed that this would be done and that a referendum would be held in three years on the question of full independence.

**Further reading:** Cohen, Leonard. *Broken Bonds.* New York: HarperCollins, 1993; Thomas, Robert. *The Politics of Serbia in the 1990s.* New York: Columbia University Press, 1999; Woodward, Susan. *Balkan Tragedy: Chaos and Dissolution after the Civil War.* Washington, D.C.: Brookings, 1995.

# Z

## Zimbabwe

Formerly known as Rhodesia, Zimbabwe is about the size of Montana, with an area of 150,760 square miles, and is located in southern AFRICA. It has a population of 11.9 million people. The Portuguese were the first Europeans to explore the region in the 16th century, but a significant European presence did not begin until 1888, when GREAT BRITAIN declared the region a British sphere of influence. The next year the British South Africa Company was established to administer the region, and in 1895 the region became officially known as Rhodesia. In 1923 the white settlers of Southern Rhodesia were given the choice of becoming a separate colony or joining SOUTH AFRICA. They rejected union, and Southern Rhodesia became a self-governing colony. Its status changed again in 1953 when Southern Rhodesia was joined with Northern Rhodesia and Nyasaland to form the Federation of Rhodesia and Nyasaland. This union dissolved in 1963 when black governments took power in Northern Rhodesia and Nyasaland. These two states became Zambia and Malawi, respectively, in 1964. Led by Prime Minister Ian Smith, Southern Rhodesia (now known as Rhodesia) declared its independence on November 11, 1965.

The announcement amounted to an act of defiance against Great Britain, which was prepared to grant Rhodesia independence but wanted to do so in the context of majority rule. The Smith government was committed to a policy of white supremacy. Deciding against using military power to regain control over Rhodesia, Great Britain turned to the UNITED NATIONS. For the first time ever, on December 16, 1966, the Security Council voted to impose mandatory ECONOMIC SANCTIONS on a state. On May 29, 1968, it expanded the sanctions to cover virtually all aspects of economic interaction between Rhodesia and the rest of the world.

The United States was not in full solidarity with these sanctions. Within the United States the question of Rhodesian independence became intertwined with domestic politics. Civil rights groups opposed it, while Southern conservatives supported it. In 1971 CONGRESS weighed into the issue by passing the Byrd Amendment. Sponsored by Democratic senator Harry F. Byrd of Virginia, it prevented the United States from banning the import of any material that was also being imported from a communist state. Chromium fell into this category. Before the Byrd Amendment was repealed in 1975, the value of American imports of chromium from Rhodesia jumped from $13.3 million in 1972 to $45 million.

Within Rhodesia two large pro–majority rule independence movements challenged white minority rule. The first was the Zimbabwe African National Union (ZANU) led by Robert Mugabe. The second was the Zimbabwe African People's Union (ZAPU) led by Joshua Nkomo. In 1976 British and American diplomatic initiatives led to a meeting between the Smith government and black leaders, including Mugabe and Nkomo, in Geneva. Little progress was made, and it was not until March 3, 1978, that the Smith government signed an "internal settlement" agreement that provided for qualified majority rule. A white-only referendum approved the agreement, and in 1979 Bishop Abel Muzorewa became the first black prime minister of Zimbabwe-Rhodesia.

Fighting and peace negotiations continued, and an agreement was later reached on September 10, 1979, at Lancaster House that Zimbabwe-Rhodesia would revert to British colonial status until a transition was completed to majority self-rule. On April 18, 1980, Zimbabwe became independent, and Mugabe became prime minister. Estimates place the number of lives lost in the independence struggle at between 20,000 and 25,000. Even then fighting continued, as ZAPU and ZANU were unable to coexist within the new government. Political repression and mass murders were common. Another peace agreement was reached in 1987, but HUMAN-RIGHTS violations continued. Between 1980 and 1984 the United States provided more than $200 million in FOREIGN AID to Zimbabwe. It also pledged $380 million in aid in 1986 but then suspended aid due to ongoing violence within the country. Aid was resumed in 1988.

At the turn of the 21st century one of the most controversial policy lines being pursued by Mugabe was the confiscation without compensation of land owned by white farmers. Western countries had offered to help finance a land-distribution program but withdrew their support when Mugabe made it clear he would act unilaterally.

**Further reading:** Omer-Cooper, J. D. *A New History of Southern Africa.* New York: Holmes and Meier, 1993.

## Zimmermann Telegram

The Zimmermann Telegram was a secret message sent in 1917 by German foreign secretary Arthur Zimmermann to the German ambassador in MEXICO instructing him to offer Mexico an ALLIANCE should the United States declare war on GERMANY. In return for Mexico's support, it would receive territories previously lost to the United States: TEXAS, New Mexico, and Arizona. Mexico was also to invite JAPAN to join in this anti-U.S. alliance. The Mexican government never acted on this offer. The Zimmermann telegram is significant because it helped move American opinion further against GERMANY in the period leading up to the declaration of war.

The Zimmermann telegram was sent on January 17, 1917, against a backdrop of rising international tensions and the near certainty of war. President WOODROW WILSON was reelected in 1916. During the campaign Germany made it known that it was willing to accept a mediated solution to the conflict, but, failing this, it might resume unre-stricted submarine warfare. Wilson was slow to act after winning reelection. It was not until January 1917 that Wilson outlined his thoughts on peace to the Senate. His vision of "peace without victory" was not shared by either GREAT BRITAIN or Germany.

On January 31, the German ambassador informed the Wilson administration that effective February 1, Germany would resume unrestricted submarine warfare. On February 3, the United States broke diplomatic relations with Germany. Still hoping to keep the United States out of war, Wilson told CONGRESS that only "actual overt acts" would convince him that Germany was serious about its threat. In mid-March Germany made good on its threat by sinking four American merchant ships.

The British had intercepted and decoded the Zimmermann telegram, but they did not reveal its existence. It was only on February 24 that they gave American authorities a slightly modified version of the telegram that had just been sent to the German ambassador to the United States. Wilson made the telegram public on March 1 in an effort to break an isolationist Republican filibuster of his request for permission to arm American merchant ships. Senators Robert La Follette (R-Wisc.) and George Norris (R-Neb.) prevailed, and the measure was defeated. Wilson then acted upon his own authority and ordered these ships to be armed. With submarine warfare underway, in early April Wilson asked Congress for a declaration of war. The Senate voted to declare war by a vote of 82-6, and the House gave its support by a vote of 373-50.

**Further reading:** Tuchman, Barbara. *The Zimmerman Telegram.* New York: Viking Press, 1958.

# Bibliography

Acheson, Dean. *Present at the Creation: My Years in the State Department.* New York: Norton, 1969.

Allison, Graham. *The Essence of Decision: Explaining the Cuban Missile Crisis.* Boston: Little Brown, 1971.

Alperovitz, Gar. *Atomic Diplomacy.* New York: Vintage, 1967.

Ambrose, Stephen. E. *Rise to Globalism: American Foreign Policy 1938–1976.* Baltimore: Johns Hopkins University Press, 1976.

Aron, Raymond. *The Imperial Republic.* Cambridge, Mass.: Winthrop, 1974.

Bailey, Thomas. *A Diplomatic History of the American People.* 10th ed. Englewood Cliffs, N.J.: Prentice Hall, 1980.

Baldwin, David A. *Economic Statecraft.* Princeton, N.J.: Princeton University Press, 1985.

Bamford, James. *The Puzzle Palace.* Boston: Houghton-Mifflin, 1982.

Barber, James David. *Presidential Character: Predicting Performance in the White House.* Englewood Cliffs, N.J.: Prentice Hall, 1985.

Barnet, Richard J. *Roots of War.* New York: Atheneum, 1972.

Barnett, A Doak. *China Policy.* Washington, D.C.: Brookings, 1977.

Beckman, Peter R., et al. *The Nuclear Predicament: Nuclear Weapons in the Cold War and Beyond.* 2d ed. Englewood Cliffs, N.J.: Prentice Hall, 1991.

Beisner, Robert. *From the Old Diplomacy to the New: 1865–1900.* Arlington Heights, Ill.: Harlan Davidson, 1975.

Bell, Coral. *The Diplomacy of Détente.* New York: St. Martin's, 1977.

Bemis, Samuel. *A Diplomatic History of the United States.* 4th ed. New York: Holt, 1955.

Berle, Adolf A., Jr. *Latin America: Diplomacy and Reality.* New York: Harper and Row, 1962.

Beschloss, Michael R. *Mayday: Eisenhower, Khrushchev and the U-2 Affair.* New York: Harper and Row, 1986.

Bialer, Seweryn, and Michael Mandelbaum. *The Global Rivals: The Soviet-American Contest for Supremacy.* New York: Knopf, 1989.

Bill, James A. *The Eagle and the Lion.* New Haven, Conn.: Yale University Press, 1988.

Blechmann, Barry M., and Stephen S. Kaplan. *Force without War.* Washington, D.C.: Brookings, 1978.

———. *The Politics of National Security.* New York: Oxford University Press, 1990.

Brennan, Donald G., et al., eds. *Arms Control, Disarmament and the National Security.* New York: Productivity Press, 1961.

Brzezinski, Zbigniew. *The Soviet Bloc: Unity and Conflict.* Cambridge, Mass.: Harvard University Press, 1960.

———. *Power and Principle: Memoirs of the National Security Adviser, 1977–1981.* New York: Farrar, Straus and Giroux, 1985.

Caldwell, Daniel. *The Dynamics of Domestic Politics and Arms Control.* Columbia: University of South Carolina Press, 1991.

Campbell, Charles. *The Transformation of American Foreign Relations, 1865–1900.* New York: Harper and Row, 1976.

Caridi, Ronald, J. *The Korean War and American Politics.* Philadelphia: University of Pennsylvania Press, 1969.

Carpenter, Ted Galen. *Peace and Freedom: Foreign Policy for a Constitutional Republic.* Washington, D.C.: Cato Press, 2002.

Carter, Jimmy. *Keeping Faith.* New York: Bantam, 1982.

Chace, James. *The Consequences of Peace: The New Internationalism and American Foreign Policy.* New York: Oxford University Press, 1992.

Chatfield, Charles. *The American Peace Movement: Ideals and Activism.* New York: Twayne, 1992.

Cingranelli, David. *Ethics, American Foreign Policy and the Third World.* New York: St. Martin's, 1993.

Clemens, Walter C. *The Superpowers and Arms Control: From Cold War to Interdependence.* Lexington: University of Kentucky Press, 1973.

Cline, Ray S. *The CIA: Reality vs. Myth.* Washington, D.C.: Acropolis Press, 1982.

Cohen, Benjamin J. *In Whose Interest?* New Haven, Conn.: Yale University Press, 1986.

Cohen, Bernard. *The Press and Foreign Policy.* Princeton, N.J.: Princeton University Press, 1963.

Cohen, Roger, and Claudio Gati. *In the Eyes of the Storm.* New York: Farrar, Straus and Giroux, 1991.

Cohen, Warren. *America's Response to China.* New York: Columbia University Press, 1990.

Colby, William, and Peter Forbath. *Honorable Men: My Life in the CIA.* New York: Simon and Schuster, 1978.

Combs, Jerald A. *The History of American Foreign Policy.* New York: Macmillan, 1975.

Cook, Franklin. *The Diplomacy of the Civil War.* New York: Random House, 1975.

Cottam, Richard W. *Iran and the United States.* Pittsburgh, Penn.: University of Pittsburgh Press, 1988.

Council on Foreign Relations. *The War on Terror.* New York: Council on Foreign Relations, 2002.

Crabb, Cecil V., Jr., and Pat M. Holt. *Invitation to Struggle.* 4th ed. Washington, D.C.: Congressional Quarterly, 1992.

Cummings, Bruce. *The Origins of the Korean War.* Princeton, N.J.: Princeton University Press, 1981.

Dallek, Robert. *The American Style of Foreign Policy.* New York: Knopf, 1983.

———. *Franklin Roosevelt and American Foreign Policy, 1932–1945.* New York: Oxford University Press, 1979.

Dallin, Alexander. *Black Box: KAL 007 and the Super Powers.* Berkeley: University of California Press, 1985.

Davis, Lynn Etheridge. *The Cold War Begins: Soviet-American Conflict over Eastern Europe.* Princeton, N.J.: Princeton University Press, 1974.

DeCeonde, Alexander. *A History of American Foreign Policy.* 3d ed. 2 vols. New York: Scribner's, 1978.

DePorte, A. W. *Europe between the Superpowers.* New Haven, Conn.: Yale University Press, 1985.

Destler, I. M. *American Trade Politics.* 2d ed. Washington, D.C.: Twentieth Century Fund, 1992.

———. *Making Foreign Economic Policy.* Washington, D.C.: Brookings, 1980.

Dinerstein, Herbert. *The Making of a Missile Crisis.* Baltimore: Johns Hopkins University Press, 1976.

Divine, Robert. *The Illusion of Neutrality.* Chapel Hill: University of North Carolina Press, 1968.

Donnelly, Jack. *International Human Rights.* Boulder, Colo.: Westview, 1993.

Donovan, John C. *The Cold Warriors: A Policy-Making Elite.* Lexington, Mass.: Lexington Books, 1974.

Doran, Charles. *Myth, Oil and Politics.* New York: Free Press, 1977.

Dull, Jonathan. *A Diplomatic History of the American Revolution.* New Haven, Conn.: Yale University Press, 1985.

Dulles, Allen W. *The Craft of Intelligence.* New York: Harper and Row, 1963.

Durch, William. *UN Peacekeeping, American Policy, and the Uncivil Wars of the 1990s.* New York: St. Martin's, 1996.

Fairbank, John King. *The United States and China.* Cambridge, Mass.: Harvard University Press, 1971.

Feinberg, Richard E. *Intemperate Zone: The Third World Challenges to U.S. Foreign Policy.* New York: Norton, 1983.

Feis, Herbert. *The China Tangle.* Princeton, N.J.: Princeton University Press, 1953.

———. *Between War and Peace: The Potsdam Conference.* Princeton, N.J.: Princeton University Press, 1960.

Ferrell, Robert H. *American Diplomacy.* 4th ed. New York: Norton, 1988.

———. *American Diplomacy in the Great Depression: Hoover-Stimson Foreign Policy, 1929–1933.* New Haven, Conn.: Yale University Press, 1957.

Fleming, D. F. The *Cold War and Its Origins, 1917–1960.* Garden City, N.Y.: Doubleday, 1961.

Franck, Thomas M., and Edward Weisband. *Foreign Policy by Congress.* New York: Oxford University Press, 1979.

Freedman, Lawrence. *The Evolution of Nuclear Strategy.* 2d ed. New York: St. Martin's, 1989.

Friedberg, Aaron. *The Weary Titan.* Princeton, N.J.: Princeton University Press, 1988.

Fullbright, J. William. *The Arrogance of Power.* New York: Vintage, 1967.

Gaddis, John L. *The United States and the End of the Cold War.* New York: Columbia University Press, 1992.

———. *The Strategies of Containment.* New York: Oxford University Press, 1982.

Galloway, John. *The Gulf of Tonkin Resolution.* Rutherford, N.J.: Fairleigh Dickinson University Press, 1970.

Garten, Jeffrey. *A Cold Peace.* New York: Times Books, 1992.

Gelb, Leslie, and Richard K. Betts. *The Irony of Vietnam.* Washington, D.C.: Brookings, 1979.

Gelb Leslie, et al. *The Pentagon Papers.* New York: Bantam, 1971.

George, Alexander L., and Richard Smoke. *Deterrence in American Foreign Policy.* New York: Columbia University Press, 1974.

———, et al., eds. *U.S.-Soviet Security Cooperation.* New York: Oxford University Press, 1988.

Gilbert, Felix. *To the Farewell Address: Ideas of Early American Foreign Policy.* Princeton, N.J.: Princeton University Press, 1961.

Gilpin, Robert. *The Political Economy of International Relations.* Princeton, N.J.: Princeton University Press, 1987.

———. *American Scientists and Nuclear Weapons Policy.* Princeton, N.J.: Princeton University Press, 1962.

Golan, Galia. *Yom Kippur and After.* New York: Cambridge University Press, 1977.

Goldstein, Judith. *Ideas, Interests, and American Trade Policy.* Ithaca, N.Y.: Cornell University Press, 1993.

Goldston, Robert. *The American Nightmare: Senator Joseph R. McCarthy and the Politics of Hate.* Indianapolis: Bobs-Merrill, 1973.

Graebner, Norman. *Cold War Diplomacy: American Foreign Policy, 1945–1960.* Princeton, N.J.: Princeton University Press, 1962.

Grieco, Joseph C., and G. John Ikenberry. *State Power and World Markets: The International Political Economy.* New York: Norton, 2003.

Haas, Richard. *Intervention: The Use of American Military Force in the Post Cold War World.* New York: Carnegie Endowment for Peace, 1994.

Halberstam, David. *The Best and the Brightest.* New York: Random House, 1972.

———. *War in a Time of Peace.* New York: Simon and Schuster, 2002.

Halle, Louis J. *Cold War as History.* New York: Harper and Row, 1991.

Halliday, Fred. *The Making of the Second Cold War.* New York: Norton, 1986.

Halperin, Morton H. *Bureaucratic Politics and Foreign Policy.* Washington, D.C.: Brookings, 1974.

Harding, Harry. *A Fragile Relationship: The United States and China since 1972.* Washington, D.C.: Brookings, 1992.

Harr, John. *The Professional Diplomat.* Princeton, N.J.: Princeton University Press, 1969.

Henkin, Louis. *Foreign Affairs and the Constitution.* New York: Norton, 1972.

Herken, Gregg. *Counsels of War.* New York: Oxford University Press, 1987.

Hersman, Rebecca C. *Friends and Foes: How Congress and the President Really Make Foreign Policy.* Washington, D.C.: Brookings, 2000.

Hess, Gary. *Presidential Decisions for War: Korea, Vietnam, and the Persian Gulf.* Baltimore: Johns Hopkins University Press, 2001.

Hilsman, Roger. *To Move a Nation: The Politics of Foreign Policy in the Administration of John F. Kennedy.* Garden City, N.Y.: Doubleday, 1967.

Hoffman, Staley. *Gulliver's Troubles, or the Setting of American Foreign Policy.* New York: McGraw Hill, 1968.

Hook, Steven W. *National Interest and Foreign Aid.* Boulder, Colo.: Lynn Rienner, 1995.

Hoopes, Townsend. *The Limits of Intervention.* New York: Norton, 1969.

Hosmer, Stephen, and Thomas Wolfe. *Soviet Policy and Practice towards the Third World Conflicts.* Lexington, Mass.: Lexington Books, 1983.

Hufbauer, Gary, et al. *Economics Sanctions Reconsidered.* Washington, D.C.: Brookings, 1990.

Hughes, Barry B. *The Domestic Context of American Foreign Policy.* San Francisco: W. H. Freeman, 1978.

Hunt, Michael H. *Ideology and U.S. Foreign Policy.* New Haven, Conn.: Yale University Press, 1987.

Huntington, Samuel. *The Soldier and the State: The Theory and Practice of Civil-Military Relations.* New York: Vintage, 1957.

Ikenberry, G. John. *American Foreign Policy: Theoretical Essays.* 4th ed. New York: Longman, 2002.

Immerman, Richard H., ed. *John Foster Dulles and the Diplomacy of the Cold War.* Princeton, N.J.: Princeton University Press, 1979.

Janowitz, Morris. *The Professional Soldier: A Social and Political Portrait.* New York: Free Press, 1960.

Jeffrey-Jones, Rhodri. *Changing Differences: Women and the Shaping of American Foreign Policy, 1917–1964.* New Brunswick, N.J.: Rutgers University Press, 1995.

Jervis, Robert. *The Illogic of American National Strategy.* Ithaca, N.Y.: Cornell University Press, 1984.

Johansen, Robert. *The National Interest and the Human Interest: An Analysis of U.S. Foreign Policy.* Princeton, N.J.: Princeton University Press, 1980.

Johnson, Chalmers. *Blowback: The Costs and Consequences of American Empire.* New York: Owl, 2000.

Johnson, Loch K. *America's Secret Power.* New York: Oxford University, 1989.

Joffe, Joseph. The *Limited Partnership.* Cambridge, Mass.: Ballinger, 1987.

Jones, Howard. *The Course of American Diplomacy.* 2d ed. Chicago: Dorsey, 1988.

Jordan, Amos, et al. *American National Security: Policy and Process.* Baltimore: Johns Hopkins University Press, 1989.

Kanet, Roger, ed. *The Soviet Union and the Developing Nations.* Baltimore: Johns Hopkins University Press, 1974.

Kaplan, Lawrence. *Entangling Alliances with None: American Foreign Policy in the Age of Jefferson.* Kent, Ohio: Kent State University Press, 1987.

Kapstein, Ethan, and Michael Mastanduno, eds. *Unipolar Politics: Realism and State Strategies after the Cold War.* New York: Columbia University Press, 1999.

Karnow, Stanley. *Vietnam: A History.* New York: Viking, 1983.

Katznelson, Ira, and Martin Shefter, eds. *Shaped by War and Trade: International Influences on American Political Development.* Princeton, N.J.: Princeton University Press, 2002.

Kennan, George F. *Memoirs, 1925–1959.* Boston: Little, Brown, 1968.

Kennedy, Robert F. *Thirteen Days: A Memoir of the Cuban Missile Crisis.* New York: Norton, 1969.

Kissinger, Henry. *The White House Years.* Boston: Little, Brown, 1979.

———. *Nuclear Weapons and Foreign Policy.* New York: Harper and Brothers, 1969.

Klare, Michael. *Resource Wars: The New Landscape of Global Conflict.* New York: Owl, 2001.

Knorr, Klaus, and Frank Trager, eds. *Economic Issues and National Security*. Lawrence: University Press of Kansas, 1977.

Koch, Stuart. *Selected Estimates on the Soviet Union, 1950–1959*. Washington, D.C.: Central Intelligence Agency, 1993.

Kolko, Gabriel. *The Roots of American Foreign Policy*. Boston: Beacon, 1969.

Kritz, Mary, ed. *United States Immigration and Refugee Policy*. Lexington, Mass.: Lexington Books, 1983.

Kuehl, Warren. *Keeping the Covenant: American Internationalism and the League of Nations, 1920–1939*. Kent, Ohio: Kent State University Press, 1997.

Kull, Stephen, and I. M. Destler. *Misreading the Public: The Myth of a New Isolationism*. Washington, D.C.: Brookings, 1999.

Kuniholm, Bruce. *The Origins of the Cold War in the Near East: Great Power Conflict in Iran, Turkey, and Greece*. Princeton, N.J.: Princeton University Press, 1979.

La Feber, Walter. *America, Russia and the Cold War*. New York: Wiley, 1976.

———. *The Clash: U.S.-Japanese Relations throughout History*. New York: Norton, 1997.

Lake, Anthony. *Entangling Relations: American Foreign Policy in Its Century*. Princeton, N.J.: Princeton University Press, 1999.

Larson, Deborah Welch. *Origins of Containment*. Princeton, N.J.: Princeton University Press, 1985.

Lebow, Richard Ned, and Janice Gross Stein. *We All Lost the Cold War*. Princeton, N.J.: Princeton University Press, 1994.

Lippmann, Walter. *U.S. Foreign Policy: Shield of the Republic*. Boston: Little Brown, 1943.

Lukas, John. *A New History of the Cold War*. Garden City, N.Y.: Doubleday, 1966.

Lundestad, Geir. *The American Empire*. New York: Oxford University Press, 1990.

Luttwak, Edward N. *The Pentagon and the Art of War*. New York: Simon and Schuster, 1985.

Macmillan, Margaret. *Paris 1919: Six Months That Changed the World*. New York: Random House, 2003.

Maddox, Robert, J. *The New Left and the Origins of the Cold War*. Princeton, N.J.: Princeton University Press, 1973.

Mandlebaum, Michael. *The Nuclear Question: The United States and Nuclear Weapons, 1946–1976*. Cambridge, Mass.: Cambridge University Press, 1979.

———, and Strobe Talbot. *Reagan and Gorbachev*. New York: Viking, 1989.

May Ernest. *The Making of the Monroe Doctrine*. Cambridge, Mass.: Harvard University Press, 1975.

———. *The World War and American Isolationism, 1914–1917*. Cambridge, Mass.: Harvard University Press, 1959.

McElroy, Robert W. *Morality and American Foreign Policy*. Princeton, N.J.: Princeton University Press, 1992.

Miller, Steven, ed. *Conventional Forces and American Defense Policy*. Princeton, N.J.: Princeton University Press, 1986.

Morris, Richard. *The Forging of the Union, 1781–1789*. New York: Harper, 1987.

Mueller, John. *War, Presidents and Public Opinion*. New York: Wiley, 1973.

Munro, Daniel. *Intervention and Dollar Diplomacy in the Caribbean, 1900–1921*. Princeton, N.J.: Princeton University Press, 1964.

Nathan, James A., and James K. Oliver. *Foreign Policy Making and the American Political System*. 4th ed. Glenview, Ill.: Scott Foresman, 1989.

Newhouse, John. *Cold Dawn: The Story of SALT*. New York: Henry Holt, 1973.

Newson, David. *The Public Dimension of Foreign Policy*. Bloomington: Indiana University Press, 1996.

Nogee, Joseph L., and Robert Donaldson. *Soviet Foreign Policy since World War Two*. New York: Pergamon, 1988.

Nye, Joseph S., Jr. *Bound to Lead*. New York: Basic Books, 1990.

———. *The Paradox of American Power: Why the World's Only Superpower Can't Go It Alone*. New York: Oxford University Press, 2002.

Osgood, Robert. *Ideals and Self-Interest in America's Foreign Relations*. Chicago: University of Chicago Press, 1953.

———. *Retreat from Empire?* Baltimore: Johns Hopkins University Press, 1973.

O'Toole, G. J. A. *The Encyclopedia of American Intelligence and Espionage*. New York: Facts On File, 1988.

Paster, Robert A. *Whirlpool*. Princeton, N.J.: Princeton University Press, 1993

———. *Congress and the Politics of U.S. Foreign Economic Policy*. Berkeley: University of California Press, 1980.

———, ed. *A Century's Journey: How the Great Powers Shape World Politics*. New York: Basic Books, 1999.

Patterson, Thomas G., et al. *American Foreign Relations*. 5th ed. 2 vol. Boston: Houghton Mifflin, 2000.

Payne, Keith. *Strategic Defense*. Lanham, Md.: Hamilton Press, 1986.

Payne, Richard J. *The Western European Allies, the Third World, and U.S. Foreign Policy*. New York: Greenwood, 1991.

Prados, John. *The Soviet Estimate: U.S. Intelligence Analysis and Soviet Strategic Forces*. Princeton, N.J.: Princeton University Press, 1986.

Pierre, Andrew. *The Global Politics of Arms Sales*. Princeton, N.J.: Princeton University Press, 1985.

Pratt, Julius W. *A History of United States Foreign Policy*. New York: Prentice Hall, 1955.

Prestowitz, Clyde. *Trading Places*. New York: Basic Books, 1988.

Quandt, William B. *Decade of Decisions: American Policy toward the Arab-Israeli Conflict, 1967–1976*. Berkeley: University of California Press, 1977.

Rappaport, Armin. *American Diplomacy in the Twentieth Century.* 3d ed. New York: Macmillan, 1994.

Richelson, Jeffrey T. *The U.S. Intelligence Community.* Cambridge, Mass.: Ballinger, 1985.

Ripley, Randall B., and James Lindsay. *Congress Resurgent.* Ann Arbor: University of Michigan Press, 1993.

Rosen, Steven J. ed. *Testing the Theory of the Military Industrial Complex.* Lexington, Mass.: Heath, 1973.

Rosenau, James N., and Ole R. Holsti. *American Leadership in World Affairs.* Boston: Allen and Unwin, 1984.

Rothgeb, John. M., Jr. *U.S. Trade Policy: Balancing Economic Dreams and Political Realities.* Washington, D.C.: Congressional Quarterly Press, 2001.

Russet, Bruce M. *Grasping the Democratic Peace.* Princeton, N.J.: Princeton University Press, 1993.

Schelling, Thomas, and Morton Halperin. *Strategy and Arms Control.* New York: Pergamon Brassey, 1985.

Schoultz, Lars. *Beneath the United States: A History of U.S. Policy toward Latin America.* Cambridge, Mass.: Harvard University Press, 1998.

Schraeder, Peter. *United States Foreign Policy toward Africa.* New York: Cambridge University Press, 1994.

Shawcross, William. *Sideshow: Kissinger, Nixon and the Destruction of Cambodia.* New York: Pocket, 1979.

Sheehan, Neil. *A Bright Shining Lie.* New York: Random House, 1988.

Sick, Gary. *All Fall Down.* New York: Penguin, 1986.

Smith, Gaddis. *American Diplomacy during World War II.* New York: McGraw Hill, 1985.

Smith, Jean. *The Constitution and American Foreign Policy.* St. Paul, Minn.: West, 1989.

Smith, Peter. *The Talons of Eagles: Dynamics of U.S.–Latin American Relations.* New York: Oxford University Press, 1996.

Smoke, Richard. *National Security and the Nuclear Dilemma.* 3d ed. New York: Random House, 1992.

Snow, Edgar. *Red Star over China.* New York: Random House, 1937.

Sokolovski, V. D., ed. *Soviet Military Strategy.* Englewood Cliffs, N.J.: Prentice Hall, 1963.

Spanier, John W., and Steven Hook. *American Foreign Policy since World War II.* Washington, D.C.: Congressional Quarterly Press, 1995.

———, and Eric M. Uslaner. *How American Foreign Policy Is Made.* 4th ed. New York: Holt, Rinehart and Winston, 1985.

Spero, Joan, and Jeffrey Hart. *The Politics of International Economic Relations.* 5th ed. New York: St. Martin's, 1996.

Steel, Ronald. *Pax Americana.* New York: Viking, 1967.

Steinbrenner, D. *The Cybernetic Theory of Decision.* Princeton, N.J.: Princeton University Press, 1974.

Stoessinger, John G. *Crusaders and Pragmatics.* 2d ed. New York: Norton, 1985.

Szulc, Tad. *The Illusion of Peace: Foreign Policy in the Nixon Years.* New York: Viking, 1976.

Talbott, Strobe. *Endgame: The Inside Story of SALT II.* New York: Harper and Row, 1979.

Tow, William. *The Limits of Alliance.* Baltimore: Johns Hopkins University Press, 1990.

Treverton, G. F. *Making the Alliance Work: The United States and Europe.* Ithaca, N.Y.: Cornell University Press, 1985.

Trubowitz, Peter. *Defining the National Interest: Conflict and Change in American Foreign Policy.* Chicago: University of Chicago Press, 1998.

Tucker, Robert H., Charles B. Keely, and Linda Wrigley, eds. *Immigration and U.S. Foreign Policy.* Boulder, Colo.: Westview, 1990.

Tucker, Robert W. *The Purposes of American Power.* New York: Praeger, 1981.

———. *The Radical Left and American Foreign Policy.* Baltimore: Johns Hopkins University Press, 1971.

Ulam, Adam B. *Expansion and Coexistence: The History of Soviet and Foreign Policy, 1917–1967.* New York: Praeger, 1968.

Ullman, Richard H. *Securing Europe.* Princeton, N.J.: Princeton University Press, 1991.

Victor, David. *The Collapse of Kyoto and the Struggle to Slow Global Warming.* Princeton, N.J.: Princeton University Press, 2001.

Warwick, Donald. *A Theory of Public Bureaucracy: Politics and the Organization of the State Department.* Cambridge, Mass.: Harvard University Press, 1975.

Whitaker, Jennifer Seymour. *Africa and the United States: Vital Interests.* New York: New York University Press, 1978.

White, Patrick. *The Critical Years: American Foreign Policy, 1793–1823.* New York: Wiley, 1970.

Williams, William Appleman. *The Tragedy of American Diplomacy.* New York: Norton, 1988.

Wittkopf, Eugene R. *Faces of Internationalism.* Durham, N.C.: Duke University Press, 1990.

Woodward, Bob. *Bush at War.* New York: Simon and Schuster, 2002.

———. *The Commanders.* New York: Simon and Schuster, 1991.

Wolfe, Thomas. *Soviet Power and Europe, 1945–1970.* Baltimore: Johns Hopkins University Press, 1970.

Yankelovich, Daniel, and I. M. Destler, eds. *Beyond the Beltway.* New York: Norton, 1994.

Yergin, Daniel. *The Prize: The Epic Quest for Oil, Money, and Power.* New York: Simon and Schuster, 1991.

———. *Shattered Peace.* Boston: Houghton-Mifflin, 1997.

Zagoria, Donald. *The Sino-Soviet Conflict, 1956–1961.* Princeton, N.J.: Princeton University Press, 1962.

# Index

Page numbers in **boldface** indicate main entries; *italic* indicates illustrations; *m* following a page number indicates a map.

**A**

Abbas, Mahmoud 261–262, 302, 378
ABMs *See* antiballistic missiles
abortions 398
Acheson, Dean *1,* **1–2,** 36, 196–197, 305, 352, 486
*Achille Lauro* affair 263
Achnacarry agreement 363
Act of Chapultepec (1945) 2, 25, 372, **420**
Act of State doctrine 35–36, 210, 490
Adams, Abigail 163
Adams, Charles Francis 15
Adams, Gerry 352
Adams, John **2–3,** *3,* 18, 161, 206
Adams, John Quincy **3–4**
  Clay, Henry 80
  Cuba 108
  Florida 164, 165, 449
  Monroe Doctrine 318–319
  Texas 313–314
  War of 1812 480, 512
Adams-Onís Treaty (1819) 3–4, 164, 264, 313, 449, 473
Adenauer, Konrad 186
Afghan Interim Authority 7
Afghanistan **4–7,** 5*m*
  bin Laden, Osama 40–41
  drug trafficking 136
  foreign aid to 168
  humanitarian intervention in 218
  population youth bulge 124, 125
  Reagan Doctrine 413
  refugees 415
  Soviet Union invasion of 4–6, 65, 89, 375, 408
Afghanistan War 6–7, 55, 63, 66, 68, 106, 269, 376, 438
Africa **7–9,** 87, 211, 212, 222 *See also* specific countries
African Development Foundation 233
African National Congress (ANC) 443, 444
African Union 415
Afrikaner National Party 443, 444

Agenda 21 139
Agent Orange 516
aging population trend 124–125
Agreement on Defense Cooperation (1989) 451
Agreement on Trade-Relation Aspects of Intellectual Property Rights (TRIPS Agreement) 256
agriculture 155–156, 165, 182
Agriculture, U.S. Department of (USDA) **9–10,** 11, 51, 165, 233, 318
Ahern, Bertie 352
Aidid, Mohammed Farah 82, 218, 442, 443
AIDS *See* HIV/AIDS
Airborne Warning and Control Systems (AWACS) patrol planes 434
Air Force, U.S.
  aircraft *6, 39, 389,* 433
  civilian-military relations 78
  cooperation among armed forces 272
  counterintelligence 104–105
  intelligence 230
  MX missiles 325
  National Security Act and 331
  RAND Corporation 410
Air Pollution Control Act (1955) 150
*Alabama* Claims 16, 464
Alaska **10,** 62, 427, 439, 464
Albanian Kosovars 281–282
Albany Congress 179
Albright, Madeleine 521–522
Algeria **10–11**
Algiers 36
Alien and Sedition Acts (1798) 161, 222
Allende, Salvador 70, 105
Alliance for Progress **11–12,** 494
alliances, overview **12–13**
al-Qaeda *See under* Q
ambassadors 101, 147, 148, 169, 454
America First Committee **13–14**
American Anti-Slavery Society 385

American Civil War **14–16**
  Democratic Party and 120
  Great Britain 16, 464
  Lincoln, Abraham 294–295
  peace movement 385
  Prize Cases (1863) 403
  Seward, William 439
American Colonization Society 293
American Committee for Liberation 409
American Committee on Public Information 170
American Enterprise Institute 475
*American Insurance Co. v. Canter* (1828) **16**
American Israel Public Affairs Committee (AIPAC) 259
American Jewish Committee 427
American Muslim Council 417–418
American national style **16–17**
  exceptionalism x, 16, 270, 496
  faith in technology 395, 412, 496
  internationalism 16, 17, 236
  isolationism *See* isolationism
  legalism 16–17, **292**
  moral pragmatism 16–17, **320–321**
  unilateralism 16–17, **490**
American Peace Society 385
American Protective League (APL) 159
American Revolution **17–19,** *18*
  Adams, John, and 3
  Articles of Confederation 29
  Canada 61
  espionage 152
  France 17–19, *18,* 171–172, 178
  Germany 183
  Great Britain 191
  Loyalists 61
  Netherlands 335
  Spain 448
  Treaty of Paris 3, 19, 172, 178, 179–180, 191, 448, **481,** 510

American Service Members Protection Act (2001) 234
American System 80
American Treaty of Pacific Settlement (1948) 372
American Union against Militarism 386
Ames, Aldrich 68, 153
Amin, Idi 432
Amnesty International 343
Angell Treaty (1881) 72
Angkor, Kingdom of 58
Angola 8, **19–20,** 110–111, 166, 413
Annan, Kofi 209, 493
Antarctic Treaty (1959) 130
antiballistic missiles (ABMs) 20–21, 33, 455
Antiballistic Missile (ABM) Treaty **20–21,** 33, 34, 456
antiglobalization 324, *324*
Anti-Imperialism League 385
Anti-Privatization Forum 524
antiradicalism 308
ANZUS Pact (1951) **21–22**
apartheid 444
*Arabic* 526
Arab-Israeli conflict **22–25,** 259–262
  Camp David accords **59–61,** 64, 142, 273
  Camp David II 61, 261
  Gaza 61, 260, 261, 273, 377, 378
  Golan Heights 466
  Jerusalem 61, 273
  Jordan and 273
  Kissinger, Henry 23, 259–260, 278, 377
  Libya 294
  Madrid accords 260, **301–302,** 378
  Organization of Petroleum Exporting Countries 373
  Palestine Liberation Organization (PLO) 23, 24, 273, 302, **377–378,** 486, 531
  Six-Day War 142, 377, 466
  Sudan 462

Suez crisis 141, 143, 176, 195, 384, **462–463**
Syria 466
Tunisia 486
West Bank 61, 260, 261, 273, 377
Wye River accords 260–261, **531**
Yom Kippur War 23, 142, 373
Arab League 377
Arab National Movement 377
Arafat, Yasser 24, 61, *302*, 377, 378, 531
Arbenz Guzmán, Jacobo 198–199
Argentina 2, **25–26**, 117, 118, 136
Aristide, Jean-Bertrand 82, 204, 205, 370, 371, 372
Armas, Carlos Castillo 199
arms control **26–27** *See also* disarmament
    antiballistic Missile Treaty **20–21**, 33, 34, 456
    Arms Control and Disarmament Agency **27**
    clandestine collection of information and 80
    cold war 87
    Comprehensive Test Ban Treaty 26, 82, 94, 226
    doves and 135–136
    Intermediate Nuclear Forces Treaty 231–232
    Kennedy, John F., and 276–277
    McNamara, Robert, and 309
    MX missiles 326
    Partial Nuclear Test Ban Treaty 276, *276*
    Reykjavík Summit 93, 130, 458
    Russia 430–431
    Strategic Arms Limitation Talks I (SALT I) 126, 278, 325, **456–457**, 505, 509
    Strategic Arms Limitation Talks II (SALT II) 166, 325, **457–458**, 504
    Strategic Arms Reduction Talks (START) 26, 130, **458–459**
    Strategic Arms Reduction Treaty I (START I) 53, **459**
    Strategic Arms Reduction Treaty II (START II) 53, 458–459, **459–460**
    Strategic Arms Reduction Treaty III (START III) 359, **460**
    Strategic Offense Reductions Treaty (Moscow Treaty, SORT, 2003) 26, 431, **461–462**
    verification **504–506**
    Vladivostok accords 509
    Warsaw Pact and 514
    weapons of mass destruction 517
Arms Control and Disarmament Agency (ACDA) **27**

Arms Export Control Act (1974) 27
arms transfers **27–29**, 244, 246, 259, 260, 342, 433–434, 469
Army, U.S. 78, 104–105, 230, 272, 308, 331
Arnold, Benedict 152
Arthur, Chester 72
Articles of Confederation **29**, 36
Ashcroft, John 500
Asian financial crisis **29–30**, 239
Aspin, Les 421, 435, 461
Aspin Group 146
al Assad, Hafez 301, 466
assured destruction *See* mutual assured destruction
Aswan Dam 141, 176, 463
Atlantic Charter (1941) **30–31**, 422, 528–529
Atlee, Clement 398–399, *399*
atmospheric pollution 150
atomic bomb, Hiroshima and Nagasaki 57, *267*, 268, 531
Austin, Moses 314, 473
Australia 21–22

**B**
Ba'ath Party 251, 254–255
Baghdad Pact 68–69, 85, 375, 462, 487
Bagot, Charles 425
Baker, Howard 382
Baker, James 117, 301
Baker Plan (1985) **32**, 117, 316
balance-of-power system *See* multipolarity
Balfour Declaration (1918) 22, 259
ballistic missile defense (BMD) 21, **32–34**, *33*, 82, 459, 461
Baltic states **34–35**
*Baltimore*, USS 69–70
bananas 156
*Banco Nacional de Cuba v. Sabbatino* (1964) **35–36**
Bangladesh 375
Bao Dai 506
Barak, Ehud 61
Barbados 64
Barbary pirates 7–8, **36**, 486
Barber, James David 390
Barnett, Richard 474
Barre, Mohammed Siad 442
Baruch Plan 1, **36–37**
Batista, Fulgencio 38, 109
Battle Act (1950) 104
Bauer, Gary 417
Bay of Pigs 37*m*, **37–38**, 86, 110
beef hormones 156
Begin, Menachem 23, 59–60
Belarus 458, 459
Belgium 96, 154, 335, 336, 431
Belgrade conference (1977–78) 96
belief systems 402
Belmont, August 497
BENELUX 336
Beneš, Edvard 115
Berlin crisis (1948) **38–39**, *39*, 85, 186
Berlin crisis (1958) **39**, 86
Berlin crisis (1961) **39–40**, 86
Berlin Wall 39–40, 89, 155, 186, 187, *187*
Betts, Richard 353

Biafra 341
Bicesse accord (1991) 20
Bidlack Treaty (1850) 381
Biko, Stephen 444
Bildt, Carl 117
bin Laden, Osama 6–7, **40–41**, *41*, 106, 408, 438
biochemical warfare *See* weapons of mass destruction (WMDs)
Biodiversity Treaty 139, 140
Biological and Toxin Weapons Convention (1972) 517
Bipartisan Commission on United States Policy toward Central America 279
bipolarity x, **41–42**, 241
Bishop, Maurice 197–198
Bismarck, Otto von 183
Black, Hugo 338, 533–534
Black Hawk War (1832) 334
Black September movement 377
*Black Warrior* 108, 393
Blaine, James 25, **42**, 69, 179, 183
Blair, Tony 195–196, 352
Blix, Hans 494, 505
Blount, James 207, 366
Blumenthal, Michael 483
Bohlen, Charles 307–308
Boland Amendment (1982) 246, 340
Bolivia 69
bomber gap **42–43**
Bonaparte, Charles 159
Borah, William E. **43**, 206, 274, 296, 515
Bosch, Juan 134
Bosnia and Herzegovina *44*, **44–45**, 534–535
    Clinton, Bill 81–82, 82
    Croatia 107
    Dayton Accords 44–45, **116–117**, 535
    humanitarian intervention in 218, 219
    North Atlantic Treaty Organization 345
    Russia and 430
    Vance-Owen Plan 44, 116, 501
Boutros-Ghali, Boutros 493
Boxer Rebellion (1900) 72
boycotts 140
bracero program **45–46**, 315
Brady, Nicholas 47, 117
Brady Plan **46–47**, 316
Brandt, Willy 95, 186
Bratislava Manifesto (1968) 48–49
Brazil **47**, 117
break-out capability 504–505
Bremer, L. Paul 251, 254
Bretton Woods system **48**, 238, 441, 522
Brezhnev, Leonid 48, 166, 265, 429, 455, 456–457, 509
Brezhnev Doctrine 48–49
Briand, Aristide 174, 274
Bricker, John 49
Bricker Amendment **49**, 157, 498
brilliant pebbles 461
brinksmanship **49–50**, 235, 350
British East India Company 225, 323

British Petroleum 372
Broadcasting Board of Governors 410, 496
Brock, William 155
Brookings Institution 475
Brothers to the Rescue 111, 210
Brown, Albert 162
Brown, Harold 127, 129, 330, 483
Brownback Amendment 376
Brownback Amendment II 376
Brundtland Commission 139, 523
Bryan, William Jennings **50**, 120, 525, 526
Bryan-Chamorro Treaty (1916) 132, 339
Brzezinski, Zbigniew 64, 244, 247, 331, 389, 483, 501
Buchanan, James 108, 374
Buchanan, Pat 499
Bullitt, William C. **50–51**, 427
Bulwer, Henry 80
Bunau-Varilla, Philippe 91, 378
Bundy, McGeorge 309, 331
Bunker, Ellsworth 382
bureaucracies **51**, 331–332, 402–403
bureaucratic-politics decision-making models xiv, **51–52**
Bureau of Export Administration 92
Bureau of Intelligence and Research 230
Burger, Sandy 332
Burger, Warren 223
Burlingame, Anson 72
Burlingame Treaty (1868) 72
Burma 136
Burton, Dan 112
Bush, George H. W. **52–54**, *53*, 89
    ambassadorial appointments 148
    Arms Control and Disarmament Agency 27
    arms transfer policy 28
    ballistic missile defense 33
    Bosnia and Herzegovina 44
    Central Intelligence Agency 68
    China 53–54, 76, 217
    Cuban Democracy Act 210
    debt crisis 117
    democratization 122
    Earth Summit 139, 151
    Enterprise for the Americas Initiative 149–150
    Ethiopia 154
    Haitian refugees 205, 370
    International Emergency Economic Powers Act 116
    Iran 245
    Israel 260
    Japan 269
    Lippman gap 295
    Madrid accords 24, 301–302
    multinational corporations 323
    Nicaragua 340
    North American Free Trade Agreement 344
    oil 363
    Palestine Liberation Organization 378

Bush, George H. W. *(continued)*
Panama 369, 370, 379
Persian Gulf War 54, 249,
260, 367–369, 388, 434,
490, 493
reelection 419
Somalia 443
Strategic Arms Reduction
Treaty I 459
Strategic Arms Reduction
Treaty II 459–460
Bush, George W. **54–56,** *55, 476*
Afghanistan 6–7, 438
Arab-Israeli conflict 24,
261–262, 378
arms transfers 29
ballistic missile defense 21,
34
Bosnia and Herzegovina 117
Chemical Weapons
Convention 517
China 55, 76–77
democratization 122
fast track authority 158–159
global pact on tobacco use
95
Helms-Burton Act 209
HIV/AIDS 211
Homeland Security,
Department of 212–213
humanitarian intervention
219
human rights 217–218
India 226
International Criminal Court
233, 234
Iraq War 17, 56, 100,
250–251, 252–255, 311,
405–406, 490, 505
Kyoto Protocol 151, 283,
284
Liberia 293
Mexican immigration 46,
315–316
multinational corporations
323
Northern Ireland 352
North Korea 50, 350–351,
447
nuclear weapons reduction
26, 359, 431, 461–462
Pakistan 226
Patriot Act 223, 499–500
personality of 391
preemption strategy 56,
252, 356, **401**
public diplomacy 404
al-Qaeda 408
Strategic Offense
Reductions Treaty
(Moscow Treaty) 26,
**461–462**
Taiwan 76–77
terrorism 55, 438–439, 472
Venezuela 503
World Summit on
Sustainable Development
523
World Trade Organization
158
Byrd, Robert 156
Byrd Amendment 156, 537
Byrnes, James 1, **56–57**

**C**
C-54 aircraft *39*
Cairo Conference (1942) 446
Calhoun, John C. **58**
California 162, 266, 311–313
Calley, William 387
Cambodia **58–59,** 166, 341
Camp David accords **59–61,** 64,
142, 273
Camp David II **61,** 261
Campos, Albizus 406
Canada **61–63**
Cleveland, Grover 81
drug trafficking 137
fishing and seal hunting
rights 42, 81, 424–425,
468
Franklin, Benjamin 178
Free Trade Agreement
(FTA) 63
grain quotas 141
Helms-Burton Act 209
*Missouri v. Holland* (1920)
318
North American Free Trade
Agreement (NAFTA)
343–344
oil 363
public diplomacy 404
Rush-Bagot Treaty 192, 425
War of 1812 480–481, 512
Webster-Ashburton Treaty
(1842) 193, 488, 517–518
Canada–United States Free Trade
Agreement (FTA) 63
canals *See* interoceanic canals;
Panama Canal
Canning, George 318, 319
Caracas Declaration 199
CARE 165, 343
Caribbean Basin Initiative (CBI)
**63–64**
Carnegie, Andrew 385
Carnegie Endowment for
International Peace 385, 386
Carranza, Venustiano 315, 519
Carroll, Charles 178
Carroll, John 178
cartels, commodity 373
Carter, Jimmy 60, **64–65**
Africa 8
ambassadorial appointments
169
arms transfer policy 28,
433–434
Camp David accords 23–24,
59–60, 64, 142
China 76, 189
Cuban refugees 416
elite decision-making theory
146
El Salvador 146
energy plan 373
Haiti 205, 370
human rights policy 71,
216–217, 227, 244, 446
International Emergency
Economic Powers Act
116
Iranian hostage crisis
246–247, 501
and Israel 260
Mariel boatlift 303–304

Mexican immigration 315
MX missiles 325–326
national intelligence
estimates, use of 328
national security advisor 331
National Security Agency
332
National Security Council
333
Nicaragua 339
Northern Ireland 351
North Korea 349
nuclear deterrence strategy
355
Panama 370, 379, *382,*
382–383
on religion and foreign
policy 417
Saudi Arabia 433–434
South Africa 444
Soviet invasion of
Afghanistan 8, 64, **65**
Strategic Arms Limitation
Talks II 457–458
Taiwan 189, 468
Trilateral Commission 483
Carter, Rosalynn 163–164
Carter Doctrine 8, 64, **65**
Case, Clifford 157
Casey, William 130, 215, 331, 340
Case-Zablocki Act (1972) 49, 157
Caspian Sea 363
Castlereagh, Lord 425
Castro, Fidel 109–111, *110*
Alliance for Progress 11
assassination plots against
110
*Banco Nacional de Cuba v.
Sabbatino* 35–36
Bay of Pigs 38
Helms-Burton Act 209–210
Mariel boatlift 303–304
Catholicism 417
Catholic Relief Services 165
Cato Institute 131, 475
Cazneau, William 162
Cédras, Raoul 370, 371
CENTO *See* Central Treaty
Organization
Central and South American
Telegraph Company 69
Central Asian republics (CARS)
**65–67**
Central Intelligence Agency (CIA)
**67–68,** 229–230 *See also*
intelligence
Afghanistan 7, 55, 106
Angola 19
assassination plots 77, 97,
106, 110
and bomber gap 43
as bureaucracy 51
Cambodia 59
Chile 70, 71
Church Committee and 70,
77–78, 96–97, 106
counterintelligence
104–105
covert action 77–78,
105–106
Cuba 38, 110
Defense Intelligence Agency
and 119–120

Democratic Republic of the
Congo 97
democratization and 123
directorates of 67–68
director of central
intelligence 129–130
discrimination and 522
embassies and 149
espionage 152–153
FBI and 159
Greece 197
Guatemala 199, 200
Hughes-Ryan Amendment
214–215
intelligence cycle and
228–229
Iran 243, 246
Iraq 106
Laos 288
missile gap 317–318
National Intelligence
Estimate 67
National Reconnaissance
Office (NRO) 329–330
National Security Act and
330–331
North Korea 349, 350
Operation CHAOS 105
Pike Committee and 393
Radio Free Europe
409–410
September 11, 2001 438
Tibet 476
Vietnam War 507
Central Intelligence Group 67
Central Treaty Organization
(CENTO) **68–69,** 85, 375, 487
CFCs *See* chlorofluorocarbon
(CFC) emissions
Chadha, Jagdish Rai 223
Chambers, Whitaker 307
Chamorro, Pedro Joaquín 339
Chamorro, Violeta Barrios de 340
Chamoun, Camille 291
Chase, Samuel 178, 510
Chechnya 430
chemical and biological warfare
*See* weapons of mass
destruction (WMDs)
Chemical Weapons Convention
(1993) 517
Cheney, Dick 56, 250, 252, 461
Chen Shui-bian 469
Cherokee 334
*Chesapeake* 192
Chevron 372
Chiang Kai-shek *See* Jiang Jieshi
chicken hawks 250
Chile **69–71,** 105, 117
China **71–77**
aging population 124, 125
antiballistic missile system
against 21
arms sales by 76–77
Boxer Rebellion 72
Burlingame Treaty 72
Bush, George H. W. 53–54,
76, 217
Bush, George W. 55, 76–77
civil war 73–74, 468
Clinton, Bill 76, 82, 217
Coolidge, Calvin 103
détente 125–126, 342, 484

dollar diplomacy 72
family-planning programs 398
Four Power Treaty (1921) 73
*Goldwater et al. v. Carter* 189
Great Britain 71, 72, 193
HIV/AIDS in 211
immigration 72, 222
Iraq War 56, 77, 253
Japan 72, 265, 266, 267, 268, 274
Korean War 74, 279–280, 446
MacArthur, Douglas 74, 300
Marshall, George C. 73–74, 304
missionaries in 71
most-favored-nation status of 76, 82, 323, 478
Nine Power Treaty (1922) 73
Nixon, Richard 75, 75–76, 342, 469
nuclear testing 94
Open Door policy 72, 132, 184, 193, 208, 265, 266, **366–367,** 425, 427, 481–482, 515
Soviet Union 74–75, 76, 87–88, 428–429
Stimson Doctrine and 213
Taft, William 467–468
Taiping Rebellion 366
Taiwan (Formosa) 73, 74, 76–77, 86, 169–170, 468–469
Tiananmen Square 53–54, 76, 217
Tibet and 475–476
Treaty of Wangxia (Wanghia) 72, 366
Truman, Harry S. 73–74
United Nations and 491
U.S. official diplomatic relations 76
U.S. trade relations 71–72, 76
Wilson, Woodrow 519
World War II 73
Chinese Exclusion Act (1882) 222
Chirac, Jaques 177, 348
chlorofluorocarbon (CFC) emissions 151, 283, 319–320
Chrétien, Jean 63
Christian Maronites 291
Christian Right 417
Christopher, Warren 483
Church, Frank 71, 77
Church Committee 70, 71, **77–78,** 96–97, 106
Churchill, Winston 194, *194*
   Atlantic Charter 30, 422, 528–529
   Casablanca Conference 321
   Potsdam Conference 398–399
   Tehran Conference *469,* 469–470
   Yalta Conference 49, 533, *534*

CIA *See* Central Intelligence Agency
cipher machines 152–153
circular error probability (CEP) 359
civil-military relations **78–79,** 435
Civil Service Commission Loyalty Review Board 308
clandestine collection **79–80** *See also* espionage
clandestine support 105
Clark, William 203
Clark Amendment 19, 20
Clark Memorandum 213
classical diplomacy 128–129
Clay, Henry **80,** 164, 165, 480, 511–512
Clay, Lucius 304
Clayton, John 80
Clayton-Bulwer Treaty (1850) 42, **80–81,** 90–91, 338, 379–380
Clean Air Act (1970) 150
Cleveland, Grover 42, **81,** 207, 365–366, 451, 502, 503
Clinton, Bill **81–83,** *82*
   ambassadorial appointments 148, 169
   Angola 20
   arms transfer policy 29
   ballistic missile defense 33, 461
   Bosnia and Herzegovina 81, 82
   Camp David II 24, 61
   Canada 141
   Central Asian republics 67
   China 76, 82, 217
   Comprehensive Test Ban Treaty 82, 94
   Croatia 107
   Cuba 111, 112, 210
   democratization 122
   dual containment 137–138, 250, 325, 421
   elite decision-making theory 146
   enlargement policy 149, 217
   European Union 155–156
   foreign aid policy 167
   Greece 197
   Gulf War Syndrome 202
   Haiti 82, 205, 370–371
   Helms-Burton Act 209, 210
   humanitarian intervention 219
   human rights policy 217
   India 226
   International Criminal Court 233, 234
   Iran and Iraq 137–138, 250, 325, 421
   Israel 24, 61, 260–261, 531
   Japan 269
   Kyoto Protocol 151, 283
   land mines 285, 287
   Lippman gap 295
   Madrid accords 302, *302*
   Mexico 316
   multinational corporations 323
   North American Free Trade Agreement 158, 344
   Northern Ireland 351, 352

North Korea 82
Pakistan 376
Palestine Liberation Organization 378
public diplomacy 404
Puerto Rico 406, 407
Strategic Arms Reduction Treaty II 356, 460
Strategic Arms Reduction Treaty III 460
Sudan 462
Tibet 476
Turkey 197
United Nations 384
Uruguay Round (GATT) 499
Vietnam 506–507
Wye River accords 260–261, 531
Clinton, Hillary Rodham 164, 406
closed-belief system 402
CNN effect 310
coalition of the willing 13, 17, 253
Coard, Bernard 198
code making and breaking 332
Coercive Acts (1774) 191
Cohen, Roy 307, 308
Cohen-Nunn Act (1986) 119
Colby, William 77
cold war **83–89,** *84m See also* communism
   Acheson, Dean, and 1–2
   Afghanistan 4–6, 65, 89, 375, 408
   Angola 110–111
   ballistic missile defense and 32–34
   Bay of Pigs *37m,* **37–38,** 86, 110
   beginning of 83, 85, 485, 486
   Berlin crises **38–40,** 85, 86, 186
   Berlin Wall 39–40, 89, 155, 186, 187, *187*
   bipolarity 41
   bomber gap 42–43
   Brezhnev Doctrine 48–49
   brinksmanship 49–50
   Bush, George H. W. 53
   Byrnes, James 57
   Canada 62
   Carter, Jimmy 64
   Chile 70
   China 74–76, 87–88
   containment *See* containment
   Cuban missile crisis 87, 110, **112–114,** *113, 133,* 153, 309–310, 429, 487
   Czechoslovakia 87
   Democratic Party and 121
   democratization and 123
   détente *See* détente
   Dominican Republic 134
   domino theory **135,** 143, 146
   doves and 135–136
   Dulles, John Foster 138
   Eisenhower, Dwight D. 143–144
   El Salvador 146
   espionage during 152, 489–490

foreign aid and 167
France 176
Germany 185–187
Great Britain 195
Guatemala 199
hawks and 207–208
imperialism during 224
Iran 85, 243
Johnson, Lyndon 272
Korean War *See* Korean War
Marshall, George C. 304
Mexico 315
missile gap 317–318
moral pragmatism and 321
Nicaragua 88–89
North Atlantic Treaty Organization 345–103–104
nuclear weapons *See* nuclear weapons
peace movement 386–387
Point Four Program **395**
Reagan Doctrine and 88
realism and 414
refugee policy 416
Taiwan (Formosa) 169–170
United Nations and 384
Vietnam War *See* Vietnam War
Warsaw Pact 85, 383, **513–514**
*Cole,* USS 41, 408
collective security **89–90**
Colombia **90–91,** 136, *137,* 201, 208, 378–379, 381
Cominform 534
Comintern 83
Commerce Department, U.S. 51, **91–92,** 104, 213
Committee for a Free Europe 409
Committee for a Sane Nuclear Policy 386–387
Committee for Non-Violent Action 386
Committee of the Red Cross 343
Committee on Foreign Investment in the United States (CFIUS) 480
Committee on the Present Danger 146
Committee to Defend America by Aiding the Allies 14
commodity cartels 373
Commodity Control List 104
Common Agricultural Policy (CAP) 155–156
Common Market *See* European Economic Community
*Common Sense* (Paine) 258
communications intelligence (COMINT) 79
communism *See also* cold war
   Acheson, Dean 1–2
   Africa 8
   ANZUS Pact 21
   Bullitt, William C. 50–51
   Central Treaty Organization 68–69
   Chile 70
   China 73–76
   Cominform 534

communism *(continued)*
Comintern 83
containment *See*
containment
Czechoslovakia 115
Democratic Party and 121
democratization and 123
détente 341, 342
domino theory **135,** 143,
146
doves and 135
Dulles, John Foster 138
Eisenhower, Dwight D.
141–142, 144
El Salvador 146
FBI 159–160
Greece 487
Grenada 197–198
Guatemala 199
hawks 207–208
Hickenlooper amendments
210
human rights 217
Hungary 219
Indochina 227
Italy 262
Korean War 279, 280
Marshall, George C. 304
McCarthyism 307–308
Point Four Program 395
Reagan, Ronald 412, 413
Red Scare (1919–20) 159
Republican Party and
418–419
Soviet Union 83, **92–94**
Truman Doctrine 485–486
Vietnam 506, 507–508
Yugoslavia 534
compellence strategy, U.S. **353**
Comprehensive Anti-Apartheid
Act (CAAA) 444
Comprehensive Test Ban Treaty
(1996) 26, 82, 94, 226
conference diplomacy **94–95,**
129, 463–464
Conference on Confidence and
Security Building Measures
(1984) 26
Conference on Disarmament
(1993) 94
Conference on Security and
Cooperation in Europe
(Helsinki accords, 1973–75)
**95–96,** 126, 216, 429
Congo, Democratic Republic of
the (Zaire) 8, **96–98,** 384
Congress, U.S. **98–101**
American Revolution and
17–19
budgetary powers 99
Central Intelligence Agency
77–78
confirmation power 101,
401–402
Defense Department 119,
189–190
drug trafficking 136
elections 144–145
executive agreements 49,
157
fast-track authority
158–159, 477, 479
gadflies 99

*Goldwater et al. v. Carter*
189
House Foreign Affairs
Committee 99
human rights 216
implementation oversight
98–99
Iraq War 100, 253–254
Kyoto Protocol 283
legislative veto 98, 223, 513
Logan Act (1799) 296
Massachusetts Burma Act
107–108
party loyalty 99–100
policy entrepreneurs 99
resolutions 98
Senate Foreign Relations
Committee 99
staff aids and 99
think tanks and 99
Tibet 476
Trade Representative, Office
of the 497
*United States v. Curtiss-
Wright Export Corp.* **498**
war, declaration of 100,
101–102, 180, 223, 248,
465, 512–513
Congressionalists (Chile) 69
Connelly, Matthew J. 234
Connolly, James 256
conservative internationalism
236, 405, 412
Constantine, King of Greece 196
Constitution, U.S. xiii, **101–102**
acquisition of new territories
16
Articles of Confederation
29
civil-military relations 78
Federalist Papers 160–161
Madison, James 301
Supreme Court 464–465
war 101–102
Contact Group 281, 327
containment **102–103**
Iran 243
Kennan, George 85, 102,
274–275, 352, 411
Marshall, George C. 304
North Atlantic Treaty
Organization 345–346
NSC-68 352–353
Southeast Asia Treaty
Organization 445
symmetrical *vs.*
asymmetrical strategies
102, 103
Truman, Harry 485
Vietnam War 507
Continental Shelf Convention
288
contract labor 45–46
contras 88, 245–246, 260, 340,
478
Convention of 1800 3
Convention on Fishing and
Conservation of the Living
Resources of the High Seas
288
Convention on the Territorial Sea
and the Contiguous Zone 288
Coolidge, Calvin **103,** 274, 516

Coordinating Committee for
Multilateral Export Controls
(COCOM) **103–104**
Corwin, Edwin 98, 101
Costa Rica 64, 136
Council on Foreign Relations 146
counterespionage 104
counter-force targeting 127
counterintelligence 67, 68,
**104–105,** 160
Counter Intelligence Program
(COINTELPRO) 160
countervalue targeting 127
covert action 67–68, 77–78,
**105–106,** 123, 143, 214–215
Craig, Larry 100, 253
Creel, George 170
crisis management 235
Croatia 44, **106–107,** 116, 501,
534–536
Crocker, Chester 20, 327
crony capitalism 30
*Crosby v. National Foreign Trade
Council* (2000) **107–108,** 212
Crowe, William 389
Crowley, Joseph 212
cryptanalysis 152
*C. Turner Joy* 272
Cuba **108–111** *See also* Cuban
missile crisis
Alliance for Progress 11
Angola 110–111
*Banco Nacional de Cuba v.
Sabbatino* 35–36
Bay of Pigs **37–38,** 86, 110
Castro, Fidel *See* Castro,
Fidel
economic sabotage
105–106, 110
espionage and 153
Ethiopia 154
filibustering 162
Grenada 197, 198
Helms-Burton Act 209–210
independence 109
López, Narciso 108, 162, *162*
Mariel boatlift **303–304**
Olney, Richard 365, 366
Operation Mongoose
105–106, 110
Ostend Manifesto 108, 374
Pierce, Franklin 393
Platt Amendment **394,** 424
Quitman, John 108, 162
refugees 111, 416
Spain 366
Spanish-American War
449–450, 451–453, 452*m*
Taft, William 467
Teller Amendment 109,
394, 470
terrorism and 472
U.S. annexation of 108–109,
374
Cuban-American National
Foundation **111–112,** 210,
303
Cuban Council for Liberty 112
Cuban Democracy Act (Torricelli
Act, 1992) 112, 210
Cuban missile crisis 87, 110,
**112–114,** *113,* 153, 309–310,
429, 487

Culper Net 152
Curtiss-Wright Export Corp.
498
Cushing, Caleb 71, 366
cyberterrorism 471
Cyprus 196–197, 384, 487
Czechoslovakia 48–49, 87,
**114–115**
Czech Republic 114–115

**D**

Dalai Lama 475–476, *476*
*Dames & Moore v. Regan* (1981)
**116**
Dardanelles 85, 485–486
Darwin, Charles 303
Dasch, George John 159
D'Aubuisson, Roberto 147
Davies, John Paton, Jr. 308
Dawes, Charles 214
Dawes Plan 214
Dawson-Sanchez Treaty 133
Dayton Accords 44–45,
**116–117,** 535
Deane, Silas 18, 129, 178
debt crisis (1980s) **117–118,** 167
Baker Plan **32,** 117, 316
Brady Plan **46–47,** 316
Enterprise for the Americas
Initiative 149–150
Treasury Department and
480
Decatur Stephen 36
decision-making models xiii–xiv
bureaucratic-politics xiv,
**51–52**
elite **145–146,** 316–317,
395, 405, 419, 483
pluralistic 394–395
rational-actor model xiii–xiv,
**411–412**
small-group xiv, 37–38,
**440–441**
Deep Seabed Hard Mineral
Resources Act (1980) 289
Defense Authorization Bill (1996)
285
Defense Department, U.S.
**118–119**
as bureaucracy 51
Defense Intelligence Agency
**119–120**
de-mining operations 287
director of central
intelligence 129
Goldwater-Nichols Defense
Reorganization Act 119,
189–190, 272
international-affairs budget
233
McNamara, Robert 309
National Reconnaissance
Office **329–330**
nine unified commands of
118
Pentagon Papers 337–338,
**387–388**
RAND Corporation 410
secretary of **435**
Defense Intelligence Agency
(DIA) **119–120,** 153, 228–229,
230, 349
deforestation 150

"The Delicate Balance of Terror" (RAND Corporation) 410
Delors, Jacques 155
democracy 122–123, 257
Democratic Party 99, **120–121**
democratic peace **121–122,** 149, 188
Democratic-Republicans 120, 161, 270
Democratic Republic of Germany 186
democratization 121, **122–124,** 149, 217, 252
demographics, global **124–125**
Denmark 190, 439
Derg 154
détente **125–126**
    Angola 19
    China 75, 126
    Conference on Security and Cooperation in rope (Helsinki accords) **95–96,** 126, 216, 429
    as containment strategy 102–103
    Ford, Gerald 166
    Jackson-Vanik Amendment 126, 264–265
    Kissinger, Henry 125–126, 265, 278
    Nixon, Richard 75, 88, 125–126, 341, 342
    Shanghai Communiqué 75, 126, 189
    Strategic Arms Limitation Talks I 126, 278, 325, 455–456, **456–457,** 505, 509
    tripolarity and 484
"Deterrence and Survival in the Nuclear Age" (Gaither Committee) 181
deterrence failures **126–127**
deterrence strategies **127–128, 354–357**
    massive retaliation **306–307,** 355, 410
    mutual assured destruction 32, 127, 128, 355
    single integrated operational plan 307, 355–356, **439–440**
    Soviet **354–355**
DeVine, Michael 200
Dewey, George 452
Díaz, Adolfo 131, 132, 339
Díaz, Porfirio 45
Diem, Premier *See* Ngo Dinh Diem
diplomacy **128–129**
    American national style of 17
    American Revolution 17–19
    classical 128–129
    conference 94–95, 129
    modern 129
    multilateral 94–95
    public opinion and 129, 403–404
    summit 129
Directorate for Operations (CIA) 67–68
Directorate of Intelligence (CIA) 67

director of central intelligence (DCI) 67, **129–130,** 229–230
disarmament **130–131**
    Arms Control and Disarmament Agency **27**
    Baruch Plan 36–37
    Borah, William E., and 43
    Intermediate Nuclear Forces Treaty 130, 231–232
    London Naval Conference 296–297
    Strategic Arms Reduction Talks 26, 130, **458–459**
    Strategic Arms Reduction Treaty I 53, **459**
    Strategic Arms Reduction Treaty II 53, 458–459, **459–460**
    Strategic Arms Reduction Treaty III 359, **460**
    verification **504–506**
    *vs.* arms control 26, 130
    Washington Conference 43, 73, 130, 174, 214, **515–516**
Disengagement of Forces Agreement (1974) 23
Distant Early Warning (DEW) 127
Doctors Without Borders 343
Doe, Samuel K. 293, 404
Doha Declaration 524–525
Dole, Robert 164, 205, 513
dollar diplomacy 72, **131–132,** 467
domestic influences on U.S. foreign policy xii–xiv, **132–133**
    elections 132, **144–145**
    gender 522
    interest groups 132, **230–231,** 394–395, 417–418
    media xiii, 132, 146, **309–311**
    peace movements **385–387**
    public opinion 129, 132, 310, 403–404, **404–406**
    think tanks 99, 132, **474–475**
Dominican Republic **133–135**
    drug trafficking 136
    Grant, Ulysses S. 190
    Johnson, Lyndon 272
    Pierce, Franklin 393
    Roosevelt Corollary 423, **424**
    Sumner, Charles 464
domino theory **135,** 143, 146
Donovan, William J. "Wild Bill" 67, 362
Douglas, William O. 338, 534
Douglas Aircraft Corporation 410
doves **135–136**
*Downs v. Bidwell* (1901) 228
Drug Enforcement Agency, U.S. *137*
drug trafficking 91, **136–137,** 336, 369, 370, 379, 503
dual containment 122, **137–138,** 250, 325, 421
dual-use technologies 472
Duarte, José Napoleon 146–147

Dubček, Alexander 87, 115
Dulles, Alan 129, 152, 198, 227
Dulles, John Foster **138**
    brinksmanship 49
    Eisenhower, Dwight D. 138, 144
    Guatemala 198, 199
    Indonesia 227
    massive retaliation strategy 306
    McCarthyism and 307–308
    Southeast Treaty Organization 445
    Taiwan (Formosa) 170, 468
Duquesne, Frederick Joubert 159
Dutch East India Company 323, 443
Duvalier, François (Papa Doc) 204
Duvalier, Jean-Claude (Baby Doc) 204

**E**
Eagleton, Thomas 513
EAM-ELAS National Popular Liberation Army of the Greek National Liberation Front 196
Earth Summit, Rio de Janeiro **139–140,** 151, 417, 523
East Timor 227
East-West Center 233
economic development aid 167
economic interest groups 230–231
economic power 399–400
economic sabotage 105–106, 110
economic sanctions **140–141,** 324
Ecuador 136
Egypt **141–143**
    Arab-Israeli conflict 22–23
    Camp David accords 59–60
    Eisenhower, Dwight D. 143
    France 176
    Great Britain 176
    Operation Desert Shield 368
    political Islam 256, 257
    Sudan 462
    Suez crisis 141, 143, 176, 195, 384, **462–463**
Egyptian Muslim Brotherhood 257
Ehrlich, Paul 360
Eighth International Conference of American States (1938) 25
Eisenhower, Dwight D. *143,* **143–144**
    *Banco Nacional de Cuba v. Sabbatino* 35–36
    Bay of Pigs 38
    Berlin crisis (1958) 39
    brinksmanship 49–50
    Central Treaty Organization 68–69
    China 74, 169, 170
    democratization 123
    Dominican Republic 134–135
    domino theory 135, 143
    Dulles, John Foster 138
    Egypt 141–142, 143, 462–463

Gaither Committee Report 181–182, 453
    Guatemala 199
    India 225
    Indonesia 227
    Israel 259
    Japan 269
    Khrushchev, Nikita, and 86
    Korean War 280, 446
    Lebanon 291
    massive retaliation 143, 306–307, 355, 439–440
    McCarthyism and 307, 308
    military-industrial complex 317
    military intelligence units 119
    missile gap 317–318
    National Security Council 333
    New Look defense policy 102, 143
    Open Skies proposal **367**
    Panama 379
    Southeast Asia Treaty Organization 445
    *Sputnik* and 453
    Suez crisis 141, 143, 195, 462–463
    Taiwan (Formosa) 169–170, 468
    U-2 incident 489–490
    Vietnam 87, 445, 507
Eisenhower Doctrine 141–142, **144,** 291
El Baradei, Mohamed 505
elections 132, **144–145**
electronic intelligence (ELINT) 79
elite decision-making theory **145–146,** 316–317, 395, 405, 419, 483
Ellsberg, Daniel 337, 388
El Salvador 64, **146–147,** 201, 339
embargo 140
Embargo Act (1807) 271, 301, 511
embassies **147–149,** *148,* 454
    ambassadors 101, 147, 148, 169
    coordination problems 148–149
    Foreign Service Officer Corps 148, **168–169,** 436, 522
    international-affairs budget 233
    Iranian hostage crisis 244
    McCarthyism and 307–308
    organization 147
    responsibilities 147–148
    safety of 149, 408
Emergency Immigration Restriction Act (1921) 222
Emergency Peace Campaign 386
*Empress of China* 71
Endara, Guillermo 369, 370
Energy Department, U.S. 230
Enhanced Border Security and Visa Reform Act (2001) 223
enlargement **149,** 217

Enterprise for the Americas
    Initiative (EAI) **149–150**
environment **150–151**
    Earth Summit, Rio de Janeiro
        **139–140**, 151, 523
    Kyoto Protocol 140, 151,
        **283–284**, 329
    Law of the Sea conferences
        288–289
    Montreal Protocol 151,
        **319–320**
    nongovernmental
        organizations 343
    nuclear winter **360**
    World Summit on
        Sustainable Development
        523–524
Erbakan, Necmettin 257
Eritrea **151–152**, 154
Eritrean Liberation Front 151
Eritrean Popular Liberation Front
    151
espionage 79–80, **152–153**, 159,
    329–330, 332, 367, 489–490
Estonia 34–35
Ethiopia 151, 152, **153–154**, 211,
    442
ethnic cleansing 44, 107, 116, 535
ethnic interest groups 230–231
EU *See* European Union
Euro bills and coins 155
European Coal and Steel
    Community 154
European Community (EC) 155
European Economic Community
    (EEC, Common Market) 86,
    154, 277, 346–347
European Free Trade Association
    154
European Monetary System 154
European Recovery Program *See*
    Marshall Plan
European Union (EU) **154–157**
    agriculture 155–156
    evolution of 154–155
    General Agreement on
        Tariffs and Trade 183
    Germany 188
    military integration 156
    monetary system 154, 155
    Netherlands 336
    U.S. steel industry 156
    West European Union
        156–157
Evian accords 10
exceptionalism x, 16, 270, 496
executive agreements 49, 101,
    **157**, 344, 401, 497–498
Export Control Act (1949) 104
Export-Import Bank 11, 233
Exxon 372
Exxon-Florio Amendment 480

**F**
F-15 fighters *389*, 433
F/A-18 Hornet *6*
Faget, Mariano 153
Falkland Islands 25, 195
Falwell, Jerry 417
family-planning programs 398
Farabundo Martí Liberation
    Front (FMLN) 146, 147, 339,
    340

fast-track authority 101,
    **158–159**, 402, 477, 479
Fatah 377
Federal Bureau of Investigation
    (FBI) 68, 104–105, 152, 153,
    **159–160,** 230, 438
Federalist Papers **160–161,** 205,
    301, 464
Federalist Party 3, 120, **161,** 205
Federalists 270
Federal Water Pollution Control
    Act (1948) 150
Federation of American Scientists
    386
Fedyaheen 273
Fellowship of Reconciliation 386
Fenians (Fenian Brotherhood)
    255
fertility rate 398
filibustering **161–162,** 338, 393
First Continental Congress (1774)
    191
first ladies and American foreign
    policy **162–164**
first-strike strategies 127–128, 357
Fish, Hamilton 109, 190
Five-Power Treaty (1922) 266,
    515
flexible response 355, 356
Florida 3–4, 16, 164, 264, 313,
    448–449, 473
fog of war 311
Food, Agriculture, Conservation,
    and Trade (FACT) 165
Food for Peace (PL 480) 9–10,
    12, **165–166,** 166–167
Foraker Act (1900) 406
Forbes, C. Cameron 204
Forbes Commission 204
Ford, Gerald 13, 19, 125, 126,
    **166,** 325, 457, 509
Ford Motor Company 309
Foreign Agriculture Service 9
foreign aid **166–168**
    economic growth and 166,
        167
    Hickenlooper amendments
        210
    humanitarian aid 166–167
    human rights and 216
    security assistance 167
    terrorism and 472
    United States Agency for
        International
        Development 494
Foreign Assistance Act (1961)
    375, 376, 494
Foreign Assistance Act (1964)
    210
foreign government and business
    interest groups 230–231
Foreign Intelligence Surveillance
    Act (1978) 105
foreign investment 480
foreign policy
    American national style *See*
        American national style
    decision-making models *See*
        decision-making models
    funding 233
    grand strategy x–xii
    idealism **221–222,** 236,
        329, 436, 437, 520–521

overview ix–xv
    past, influence of xiv
    realism 132, 221–222, 236,
        329, **413–414**
    revisionism 132, **419–420**
Foreign Service Officer Corps
    148, **168–169,** 436, 522
Formosa *See* Taiwan
Formosa Resolution (1955) 74,
    **169–170,** 512–513
Formosa Strait Resolutions 468
40 Committee 70
Four-Power Treaty (1921) 43,
    266, 515
Fourteen Points 129, **170–171,**
    174, 184–185, 214, 482–483,
    521–522, 527
Fox, Vicente 46, 209
France **171–178**
    aging population 124
    Algeria 10–11
    American Civil War 15, *15*
    American Revolution
        17–19, *18*, 171–172, 178
    Arab-Israeli conflict 22–23
    Berlin crisis (1948) 38
    Cambodia 58
    Canada 61–62, 192
    cold war 176
    European Union 154–157
    Four Power Treaty 43
    Fourteen Points 171
    French and Indian War 171,
        **179–180**
    Haiti 203
    Hawaii 207
    Iraq War 56, 177–178, 252,
        253, 348, 493, 494
    Kellogg-Briand Pact 174,
        274
    Korean War 175–176
    Laos 287
    Lebanon 290–291
    Lend-Lease Act 421
    Liberia 293
    London Naval Conference
        296–297
    Louisiana Purchase 173,
        270–271, 297–298, 299,
        448
    Madison, James 301
    Marshall Plan 305–306
    Mexico 314
    Morocco and 322
    multipolarity and 324–325
    Native Americans 334
    North American colonialism
        171
    North Atlantic Treaty
        Organization 176, 177
    nuclear testing 94, 176–177
    Operation Desert Shield 368
    Panama Canal 173
    Quasi War 2, 172–173, 206
    Suez crisis 141, 176,
        **462–463**
    Syria and 466
    Treaty of Alliance 18, 514
    Vietnam 175, 506
    Washington Conference 43,
        73, 130, 174, 214, 515
    World War I 173–174,
        482–483

World War II 174–175, *175,*
        530–531
Franco, Francisco 337, 450
Franco-American Treaty of
    Alliance 18, 514
Franklin, Benjamin 18, *18,*
    **178–179,** 258
Franks, Tommy 311
Free Cuba Political Action
    Committee 112
Freedom Flotilla 303
Free Lebanon Movement 291
Free Soil Party 519
Free Tibet Campaign 476
free trade 478–479
Frelinghuysen, Frederick **179,**
    338
French and Indian War (1756–63)
    171, **179–180,** 190–191
French Revolution 172
freshwater supplies 150
Fretilin 227
Friends Committee on National
    Legislation 386, 418
Front for the Liberation of Angola
    (FNLA) 19
Fuchs, Klaus 159–160
Fulbright, J. William 99, 121, *121,*
    **180**
Fulbright program 180, 495

**G**
gadflies 99
Gadsden, James 181
Gadsden Purchase **181,** 314
Gahagan, Helen 341
Gairy, Eric 197–198
Gaither, H. Rowan 181
Gaither Committee Report
    181–182, 453
Galarza, Ernesto 46
Gandhi, Mohandas 225
Garner, Jay M. 251, 254
Gates, William 130
GATT *See* General Agreement on
    Tariffs and Trade
Gaulle, Charles de 10, 176, 422,
    530–531
Gaza Strip 61, 260, 261, 273, 377,
    378
Geary Act (1892) 72
General Agreement on Tariffs and
    Trade (GATT) 48, 95,
    **182–183**
    Common Agricultural Policy
        155
    International Trade
        Organization 242, 243
    Kennedy Round 155, 182,
        **277–278**
    most-favored-nation
        principle and 322
    Tokyo Round 155, 182,
        **476–477**
    Uruguay Round 54, 82, 95,
        155, 158, 182, 324,
        **498–499**
General Dynamics Corporation
    317
General Motors 323, 324
*General Sherman* 445
Genet, Citizen Edmond 172, 205,
    514

genetic diversity 150
Geneva accords (1954) 506, 507
Gentleman's Agreement 266
Gephardt, Richard 226
Germany **183–188**
  Baltic states 34–35
  Berlin crisis (1948) **38–39,**
    *39,* 85, 186
  Berlin crisis (1958) **39,** 86
  Berlin crisis (1961) **39–40,**
    86
  Berlin Wall 39–40, 89, 155,
    186, 187, *187*
  China 184
  cold war overview 185–187
  Conference on Security and
    Cooperation in Europe
    95
  Coolidge, Calvin 103
  Czechoslovakia 114–115
  East and West 186–187
  European Union 154–157,
    188
  Fourteen Points 184–185
  Hughes, Charles Evans 214
  Hungary 219
  Iraq War 56, 253, 348
  Kennedy, John 186
  Marshall Plan 185–186
  Morgenthau Plan 321
  Namibia 327
  naval arms race 183–184
  North Atlantic Treat
    Organization 186
  nuclear weapons 232
  Ostpolitik 186–187
  Poland 396
  Potsdam Conference
    398–399
  Roosevelt, Theodore 184
  Samoa 183
  Soviet Union 83, 185–187
  Versailles Treaty 184–185
  Weimar era 185
  World War I 170–171, 173,
    174, 184, 482–483,
    525–527
  World War II 315, 527, 529,
    531, 538
  Zimmermann Telegram
    315, 527, 538
Gerry, Elbridge 2
Gilman, Benjamin 226
glasnost 89, 430
Glaspie, April 388
Glenn Amendment 226, 376
global interests 329
globalization **188–189**
  Agriculture, Department of
    9
  imperialism and 224
  international organization
    and 239
  multinational corporations
    324
  opposition to 188, 324, *324,*
    522
  peace movement and 387
  power resources and 400
  World Bank 522
Global Messenger 311
Global People's Forum 524
global warming 283

Golan Heights 466
Goldwater, Barry 76, 189, 271
*Goldwater et al. v. Carter* (1979)
  76, **189**
Goldwater-Nichols Defense
  Reorganization Act (1986)
  **189–190,** 272.119
Gomułka, Władysław 396–397
Gonzalez, Elian 112
Good Friday Peace Accord (1998)
  82, 352
Good Neighbor policy 215, 421,
  424
Gorbachev, Mikhail 89, *89*
  Baltic states 35
  Brezhnev Doctrine 49
  disarmament 130
  Intermediate Nuclear
    Forces Treaty 231–232,
    *232*
  New Thinking 429–430
  resignation 425
  Reykjavík Summit 93, 463
  Strategic Arms Reduction
    Treaty I 53, 458
Gore, Al 27
Grachev, Pavel *168*
grand strategies x–xii
Grant, Ulysses S. 109, 133, **190,**
  464
Great Britain **190–196**
  Adams, John 3
  Adams, John Quincy 3
  Afghanistan 4
  aging population 124
  American Civil War 14–16,
    *15,* 193, 464
  American Revolution
    17–19, 29, 171–172, 191,
    481
  Arab-Israeli conflict 22
  Atlantic Charter 422
  Berlin crisis (1948) 38
  Calhoun, John C., and 58
  Canada 61–62, 424–425,
    468
  Central Treaty Organization
    68–69
  China 71, 72, 73, 366
  Clayton-Bulwer Treaty
    80–81, 90, 192, 379–380
  cold war 195
  European Union 154–157
  Fourteen Points 171
  Franklin, Benjamin 178
  French and Indian War 171,
    **179–180,** 190–191
  Grant, Ulysses S. 190
  Hay-Pauncefote Treaty 380,
    381, 423
  India 225
  Iran 243
  Iraq War 56, 195–196, 250,
    254
  Ireland 255–256
  Israel 259
  Jay's Treaty 161, 172, 192,
    205–206, **270**
  Kuwait 282
  Latin America 192, 193
  Lend-Lease Act 292, 421
  Liberia 293
  Libya 294

Louisiana Purchase 297,
  298
Madison, James 301
Marshall Plan 305–306
Mexico 314
*Missouri v. Holland* 318
Monroe Doctrine 4, 81,
  173, **318–319,** 365–366,
  423, 502
multipolarity and 324–325
Native Americans 334
naval arms race 43,
  183–184, 296–297, 425,
  515–516
Netherlands 335
Northern Ireland 351–352
nuclear weapons 94, 195
Operation Desert Shield
  368
Opium War 71–72
Oregon Territory 371, 398
Pakistan 375
Samoa 183
Somalia 442
South Africa 443
Sudan 462
Suez crisis 141, 143, 176,
  195, 384, **462–463**
Tehran Conference
  469–470
Texas 473
Tibet 475
Truman Doctrine 485–486
ULTRA 152
United Nations 491
Venezuela boundary dispute
  81, 365–366, 502,
  **503–504**
*Ware v. Hylton* 510
War of 1812 80, 161, 192,
  264, 480–481, **510–512,**
  *511*
Washington, George, and
  514
Webster-Ashburton Treaty
  193, 488, 517–518
World War I 193–194,
  482–483, 525–526
World War II 194–195,
  528–529
Yalta Conference 49, 83,
  157, 446, **533,** 534
Zimbabwe 537
Zimmermann Telegram 538
Greece **196–197,** 398–399,
  485–486
greenhouse gasses 283
Greenpeace 343
Greenspan, Alan 30
*Greer,* USS 30
Grenada **197–198**
Grey, Edward 526
Grier, Robert 403
Griffith, Arthur 256
Grotius, Hugo 288
groupthink 38, 440–441
Guatemala **198–201**
guerrilla warfare **201**
Gulf of Tonkin Resolution 100,
  180, 271, 508, 513
Gulf Oil 372
Gulf War Syndrome **201–202,**
  368, 516–517

**H**
Habib, Philip 24, 377
Habyarimana, Juvenal 431–432
Hagel, Chuck 283
Hague Conferences 130
Haig, Alexander 146, 147, **203,**
  436
Haiti 64, 82, **203–205,** 370–371,
  416
Hale, Nathan 152
Halliburton Co. 255
Halpern, Morton 475
Hamas 262
Hamilton, Alexander 160–161,
  **205–206,** 464
Hanna, Mark 378, 381
Hanssen, Robert 152
Harbury, Jennifer 200
Harding, Warren G. 91, 206, 322,
  515
Harlan, John 36
*Harlan County,* USS 205, 371
Harris, Townsend 265
Harrison, Benjamin 70
Hassan II, King of Morocco 322
Hatch, Orrin 500
Havana Charter (1947) 182, 242,
  498
Havel, Václav 115
Hawaii 81, **207,** 365, 366, 393
hawks **207–208**
Hawley, Willis 442
Hawley-Smoot Tariff (1930) 213
Hay, John 72, 81, 90–91, **208,**
  366, 378, 380, 381
Hay-Bunau-Varilla Treaty 379,
  381
Hayes, Rutherford B. 72
Hay-Herrán Treaty 91, 208, 378,
  381
Hay-Pauncefote Treaty 380, 381,
  423
hazardous wastes 150, 151
Helms, Jesse 27, 82, 94,
  **208–209,** 234, 455, 495
Helms, Richard 129
Helms-Burton Act (1996) 111,
  140, **209–210**
Helsinki accords *See* Conference
  on Security and Cooperation in
  Europe
Heritage Foundation 475
Hernandez, General 490
Hernández Colón, Rafael 407
Herrán, Thomas 91, 381
Herzegovina *See* Bosnia and
  Herzegovina
Hickenlooper amendments 12,
  36, **210**
High Seas Convention 288
Hill and Knowlton 404
Hiroshima 57
Hispaniola *See* Dominican
  Republic; Haiti
Hiss, Alger 159–160, 307, 341
"History of U.S. Decision Making
  Process on Vietnam Policy"
  (Defense Department) *See*
  Pentagon Papers
Hitler, Adolf 174, 185
HIV/AIDS 8, 9, **210–212**
Hizb-ut-Tahrir (Hu T) 66
Hobbes, Thomas 414

Ho Chi Minh 506, 507, 508
Hodel, Donald 320
Hofstadter, Richard 308
Holmes, George 212
Holmes, Oliver Wendell 318
*Holmes v. Jennison* (1840) **212**
Holy Alliance 318
Homeland Security, Department
of **212–213,** 438, 517
Honduras 64
Hong Kong 29–30, 71
Hoover, Herbert 204, **213,**
296–297
Hoover, J. Edgar 159, 362
Hopkins, Harry 422
Hormel, Jay 13
Hot Line Agreement (1963) 26
House, Edward Mandell
("Colonel") **213–214,** 482, 526
House Foreign Affairs Committee
99
Houston, Sam 314, 473
Huerta, Victoriano 314, 315, 519
Hughes, Charles Evans **214,** 237,
515
Hughes, Harold 214
Hughes-Peynado Plan 134
Hughes-Ryan Amendment
**214–215**
Hull, Cordell **215,** 415, 442, 528
humanitarian aid 166–167
humanitarian intervention *218,*
**218–219**
human rights **215–218**
Carter, Jimmy 64, 71,
216–217, 227, 244, 446
Chile 71
China 76
Clinton, Hillary Rodham
164
Croatia 107
Indonesia 227
International Criminal Court
233
Massachusetts Burma Act
107–108
Nigeria 341
nongovernmental
organizations 343
South Korea 446
Human Rights Watch 343
human-source intelligence
(HUMINT) 79, 229
Hungary 86, **219–220,** 409–410
Huntington, Samuel 295
Hussein, King of Jordan 273, 377
Hussein, Saddam 249–251, *250*
International Criminal Court
234
Iran-Iraq War 248, 249
Iraq War 17, 56, 252, 254
Persian Gulf War 368, 388
Hutchinson, Thomas 178
Hutu 431–432
Hu Yaobang 76

**I**

ICBMs *See* intercontinental
ballistic missiles
idealism **221–222,** 236, 329, 436,
437, 520–521
ideological interest groups
230–231

illegal immigration 222–223
Illegal Immigration Reform and
Responsibility Act (1996) 223
imagery intelligence 79–80
immigration **222–223**
Chinese 72
Dominican Republic 135
illegal 222–223
Irish 255, 256
Italian 262
Japanese 266, 267
Liberia 293
Mexican 45–46, 315–316
Netherlands 335
Immigration Act (1924) 267
*Immigration and Naturalization
Service v. Chadha* (1983) 102,
**223–224**
Immigration Reform and Control
Act (1986) 222–223, 315
imperialism 135, **224–225,** 228,
437
Import Administration Office 92
India 94, 211, 222, **225–226,**
375–376
Indian Appropriation Act (1851)
334
Indian Caucus 226
Indian Friendship Council 226
Indian Removal Act (1830) 334
India-Pakistan Relief Act (1998)
226, 376
Indonesia 30, **226–228**
*Influence of Sea Power upon
History, 1660–83* (Mahan)
183–184
Inman, B. R. 332
Institute for Policy Studies (IPS)
474–475
Insular Cases **228,** 406
intellectual property 256, 447
intelligence **228–229**
CIA 67–68
code making and breaking
332
counterintelligence 104–105
director of central
intelligence 129
espionage/clandestine
collection 79–80,
**152–153,** 159, 329–330,
332, 367, 489–490
National Reconnaissance
Office 329–330
National Security Agency
**332**
Patriot Act 499
intelligence community **229–230**
Central Intelligence Agency
*See* Central Intelligence
Agency
Defense Intelligence Agency
**119–120,** 153, 228–229,
230, 349
director of central
intelligence 67, 129–130,
**129–130,** 229–230
espionage 152–153
Federal Bureau of
Investigation 68,
104–105, 152, 153,
**159–160,** 230, 438
media and 310

national intelligence
estimates 67, 229,
327–328, **327–328**
National Reconnaissance
Office 329–330
National Security Act and
330–331
National Security Agency
228–229, 230, **332**
Patriot Act 499
RAND Corporation 410
Inter-American Conference on
Problems of War and Peace
(1945) 25
Inter-American Reciprocal
Assistance and Solidarity *See*
Act of Chapultepec
inter-American relations 372
intercontinental ballistic missiles
(ICBMs) 20, 317–318, 325,
359, 367, 455, 459–460, 509
interest-group liberalism (iron
triangles) 395
interest groups xiii, **230–231,**
394–395, 417–418
intergovernmental organizations
(IGOs) 239–241
Interim Agreement on Strategic
Offensive Weapons 456
Intermediate Nuclear Forces
(INF) Treaty (1988) 130,
**231–232,** 504
intermestic issues 242
international-affairs budget **233**
International (Pan) American
Conference (1889) 25
International Atomic
Development Authority 36
International Atomic Energy
Agency (IAEA) 349
International Campaign for Tibet
476
International Campaign to Ban
Landmines 285
International Centre for
Settlement of Investment
Disputes 523
International Cooperation Agency
494
International Court of Justice
237, 491
International Criminal Court
**233–234,** 336
international crises **235,** 440
International Development
Administration 523
International Emergency
Economic Powers Act (IEEPA)
116
International Finance Corporation
523
International Geophysical Year
(IGY) 453
International Human Rights
Covenants (1966) 216
internationalism 16–17,
**235–236,** 258, 385–386,
404–405, 418
international law 233, **237–238,**
336, 415, 525
International Monetary Fund
(IMF) 30, 32, 48, 117,
**238–239,** 417

international organization
**239–241**
International Seabed Authority
289
international systems x, **241–242**
alliances and 13
bipolarity x, **41–42,** 241
collective security 89–90
economic *vs.* military x, 325
globalization and 188
imperialism and 224
multipolarity x, 241,
**324–325**
public opinion and 405
realism and 414
tripolarity **484**
unipolarity x, 241, **490–491**
International Telephone and
Telegraph Company 70
International Trade
Administration 92
International Trade Commission
233
International Trade Data System
(ITDS) 480
International Trade Organization
(ITO) 182, **242–243**
interoceanic canals 80–81, 338,
378 *See also* Panama Canal
intifada 24, 377
IOFR 117
Iran **243–245**
arms transfers to 28, 244,
246
Carter, Jimmy 64–65
Central Treaty Organization
68–69
cold war and 85
democracy in 252
drug trafficking 137
dual containment 122,
137–138, 250, 421
embassy hostage crisis
64–65, 244, **246–247,**
*247,* 501
Iran-Iraq War 244–245,
**248,** 249
Islamic revolution 244, 257
multipolarity and 325
Organization of Petroleum
Exporting Countries
364–365, 372–374
as rogue state 421
terrorism and 472
Iran-contra initiative 88,
**245–246,** 260, 340, 478
Iranian hostage crisis 64–65, 244,
**246–247,** *247,* 501
Iran-Iraq War (1980–88)
244–245, **248,** 249, 282, 465
Iran–United States Claims
Tribunal 116
Iraq **248–252** *See also* Iraq War
Arab-Israeli conflict 23
Ba'ath Party 251, 254–255
Bush, George W. 55–56
Central Treaty Organization
68–69
CIA in 106
dual containment 122,
**137–138,** 250, 325, 421
Egypt and 142
foreign aid to 168

Kurds and 106, 249, 252
multipolarity and 325
Organization of Petroleum
  Exporting Countries
  364–365, 372–374
Persian Gulf War See
  Persian Gulf War
population youth bulge 124,
  125
preemption strategy and
  401
as rogue state 420–421
terrorism and 472
United Nations 493–494
war with Iraq 244–245, **248,**
  249, 282, 465
weapons of mass destruction
  250, 505, 517
Iraq War **252–255**
  Chile 71
  China 77
  coalition of the willing 13,
    17, 253
  as collective security
    experiment 90
  France 56, 177–178, 252,
    253, 348, 493, 494
  Great Britain 56, 195–196,
    250, 254
  imperialism and 225
  media coverage 311
  moral pragmatism and 321
  North Atlantic Treaty
    Organization 348
  oil and 365
  Organization of Petroleum
    Exporting Countries 374
  public opinion 404, 405
  reconstruction 251–252
  religion and support for 418
  Russia 431
  Saudi Arabia 434
  South Korea 447
  Syria 466
  Turkey 488
  unilateralism and 17
  United Nations 493, 494
  weapons of mass destruction
    250, 505, 517
Ireland **255–256,** 351
Irish National Caucus 352
Irish Republican Army (IRA) 351,
  352
Irish Republican Brotherhood
  (IRB) 255
Ishii, Kikujiro 72
Islam, political 66, 248, 251, 254,
  **256–257,** 417–418, 462
Islamic Jihad 262
Islamic Movement of Uzbekistan
  (IMU) 66
Islamic Salvation Front (FIS) 11,
  257
isolationism **257–258**
  as American national style
    16–17
  Borah, William E., and 43
  cycles of 236
  Lindbergh and America
    First Committee 13–14
  neoisolationism 405
  neutrality legislation (1930s)
    **336–337**

Nye committee 361
  public opinion and 404–405
  Republican Party and 418
  Roosevelt, Franklin D. 421
  sectionalism and 436, 437
  Washington, George 514
Israel 209, **259–262,** 261m, 389
  See also Arab-Israeli conflict
Israel-PLO Declaration of
  Principles (1993) 302
Itaca 69
Italy **262–263**
  aging population 124
  Eritrea 151
  Ethiopia 153, 336–337
  European Union 154
  Fourteen Points and 171
  Libya 294
  London Naval Conference
    296–297
  Potsdam Conference
    398–399
  Somalia 442
  Washington Conference 515
Izetbegović, Alija 44, 116, 117

**J**

Jackson, Andrew 165, **264,** 334,
  449, 473, 518
Jackson, Henry "Scoop" 264, 265,
  347, 455, 509
Jackson, Jesse 296
Jackson, Robert 465
Jackson Amendment 455
Jackson-Vanik Amendment 99,
  126, 216, 217, **264–265**
Jamaica 64
Japan **265–270**
  Afghanistan War 269
  aging population 124, 125
  Asian financial crisis 29–30
  atomic bomb on Hiroshima
    and Nagasaki 57, 267,
    268, 531
  Bush, George H. W., and
    269
  China 72–73, 213, 265, 266,
    267, 268, 274, 366, 367,
    425, 455, 467–468,
    481–482
  Clinton, Bill 269
  Eisenhower, Dwight D.
    269
  espionage and 152
  Four Power Treaty 43
  Hawaii 207
  Hull, Cordell 215
  immigration 266, 267
  Korea 445
  London Naval Conference
    Principles 296–297
  Nixon, Richard 269
  Persian Gulf War 269
  Roosevelt, Franklin
    267–268
  Roosevelt, Theodore 266,
    423
  Russo-Japanese War 427,
    481–482
  Thailand 474
  trade issues 265, 269,
    277–278
  Vietnam 506

Washington Conference
  515, 516
  World War I 266
  World War II 268–269, 528,
    530m, 531
Jay, John 18–19, 160, 192, 270,
  448
Jay's Treaty (1794) 161, 192,
  205–206, **270**
Jefferson, Thomas **270–271**
  Barbary pirates 36
  on Cuba 108
  Democratic-Republicans
    and 120
  Florida 108, 164, 448
  Hamilton, Alexander, and
    205
  Louisiana Purchase 173,
    270–271, 297–299, 448
  vs. Federalist Party 161
  War of 1812 511
Jennison, Silas H. 212
Jerusalem 61, 273
Jiang Jieshi (Chiang Kai-shek) 73,
  86, 169, 170, 468
Jinmen (Quemoy) Island 74, 169,
  170
Johnson, Lyndon Baines 271,
  **271–272**
  Antiballistic Missile (ABM)
    Treaty 21
  ballistic missile defense 33
  covert action, use of 77
  Dominican Republic 134
  Greece 196
  McNamara, Robert 309
  National Security Council
    333
  political Islam 256
  Turkey 487
  Vietnam War 271–272, 508
Johnson-Reed Act (1924) 222
Joint Army and Navy Board 272
Joint Chiefs of Staff 118, 119,
  189, **272–273,** 331
Joint Political Military Group 259
Jones-Costigan Act (1934) 109
Jordan 22, 23, 24, 60, **273,**
  301–302, 377
Juárez, Benito 314
justification of hostilities crises 235

**K**

Kabila, Joseph 98
Kabila, Laurent 97–98
Kamal, Babrak 4, 5
Kampuchea 59
Kansas-Nebraska Act (1854) 295
Kappe, Walter 159
Karadzić, Radovan 44–45
Károly, Michael 219
Karzai, Hamid 7
Kasavubu, Joseph 96
Kashmir 225, 375
Katsura, Taro 423, 481
Kaufmann, William 410
Kazakhstan 65–67, 458, 459
Kellogg, Frank B. 174, 274
Kellogg-Briand Pact (1929) 43,
  174, 213, **274**
Kennan, George 85, 102,
  **274–275,** 352, 411
Kennedy, Jackie 163

Kennedy, John F. **275–277,** 276
  Africa 8
  Alliance for Progress 11
  arms control 27, 276–277
  arms transfers 28
  Bay of Pigs 37–38, 86, 110
  Berlin crisis (1961) 40
  brinksmanship 49
  Common Agricultural Policy
    155
  covert action, use of 77
  Cuban missile crisis 87, 110,
    **112–114,** 113, 309–310,
    487
  Dominican Republic 134,
    135
  flexible response theory
    355, 356
  General Agreement on
    Tariffs and Trade 277–278
  Germany 186, 187
  Great Britain 195
  Hickenlooper amendments
    210
  India 225
  Israel 259
  Khrushchev, Nikita 40, 429
  McNamara, Robert 309
  missile gap 317–318
  national security advisor
    331
  National Security Council
    333
  nuclear weapons 347
  Operation Mongoose
    105–106, 110
  Reciprocal Trade Agreement
    Acts 415
  South Africa 444
  United States Agency for
    International
    Development 494
  Vietnam War 87, 506, 508
Kennedy, Robert 121, 121
Kennedy, Ted 387
Kennedy Amendment 71
Kennedy Round (GATT) 155,
  182, **277–278**
Khalq 4
Khmer Empire 58
Khmer Republic 59
Khmer Rouge 58–59
Khomeini, Ayatollah Ruhollah
  244, 248, 257
Khrushchev, Nikita 86, 428–429,
  429
  Berlin crises 39, 40
  China 170
  communist ideology of 93
  Cuban missile crisis
    112–114
  Kennedy, John F. 40, 429
  Nixon, Richard 495
  Radio Free Europe/Radio
    Liberty broadcast of
    409
  Rapacki Plan 410–411
  U-2 incident 489–490
Kichiasburo Nomuro 528
Kim Dae-Jung 350, 447
Kim Jong Il 350
King, William Lyon Mackenzie
  62

Kirkpatrick, Jeane J. 65, 217, 412, 521
Kissinger, Henry **278–279,** 438
  Africa 8
  on bureaucracy 51
  Chile 70
  China 75
  Cuba 110
  détente 125–126, 265, 278
  on guerrilla warfare 201
  Iran 244
  Iranian hostage crisis 247
  as national security advisor 331
  Persian Gulf War 389
  shuttle diplomacy (Arab-Israeli conflict) 23, 259–260, 278, 377
Kissinger Commission 340
*Kitty Hawk,* USS 6
Klerk, F. W. de 444
Klingberg, Frank 258
Knox, Philander 131, 132, 339, 467
Kohl, Helmut 232
Korean War 86, **279–281,** 280*m,* 348–349, 446
  bipolarity and 41
  brinksmanship and 49
  China 74, 279–280, 446
  containment strategy and 102
  France 175–176
  land mine use 285
  MacArthur, Douglas 74, 279, 280, 300, 349, 446
  Marshall, George C. 304
  Truman, Harry 279, 280, 485
  *Youngstown Sheet and Tube Co. v. Sawyer* 533
Kosovo 218, 219, **281–282,** 345, 416, 535
Kosovo Liberation Army (KLA) 281
Kostunica, Vojislav 536
Kosygin, Alexei 21
Kun, Béla 219
Kurdish People's Republic 243
Kurds 106, 249, 252, 488
Kuwait **282–283**
  Iran-Iraq War and 245, 248, 282
  Organization of Petroleum Exporting Countries 364–365, 372–374
  Persian Gulf War 54, 249, 282, 368, 388
  public diplomacy and 404
Kyoto Protocol 140, 151, **283–284,** 329
Kyrgyzstan 65–67

**L**

La Follette, Robert 13, 418, 527
Laird rams 15
Landless People's Movement 524
land mines 107, **285–287,** 286*m*
Lansing, Robert 72–73, 482, 525, 526
Lansing-Ishii Agreement (1917) 266
Laos **287–288**

Latin America  *See also specific countries*
  Alliance for Progress 11–12
  Bipartisan Commission on United States Policy toward Central America 279
  Blaine, James 42
  Caribbean Basin Initiative 63–64
  Clayton-Bulwer Treaty 42, **80–81,** 90–91, 338, 379–380
  cold war 86, 88
  Coolidge, Calvin 103
  democratization 124
  dollar diplomacy 131–132
  Enterprise for the Americas Initiative 149–150
  filibustering 162
  Frelinghuysen, Frederick 179
  Good Neighbor policy 215, 421, 424
  Great Britain 192, 193
  Haig, Alexander 203
  Harding, Warren G. 207
  Hay, John 208
  Hoover, Herbert 213
  Hull, Cordell 215
  Monroe Doctrine  *See Monroe Doctrine*
  multinational corporations 323
  Olney, Richard 365–366
  Organization of American States  *See Organization of American States*
  Reagan, Ronald 412
  Rio Pact 2, **420**
  Tlatelolco, Treaty of 130
  unipolarity 491
  Vandenberg, Arthur 502
Latvia 34–35
Law of the Sea conferences **288–289**
*Lawry v. Reagan* 465
League of Nations 89, 170, 206, **289–290,** 482–483, 519–520
Leahy, Patrick 285, 500
Leahy, William 272
Lebanese National Movement (LNM) 291
Lebanon **290–292,** *291*
  Arab-Israeli conflict 22, 24, 260, 291–292, 301–302
  drug trafficking 137
  Eisenhower Doctrine and 144
  hostages 246
  Palestine Liberation Organization (PLO) in 377
  Reagan, Ronald 412–413
  Syria and 466
Lee, Arthur 18, 178
Lee Teng-hui 77, 469
legalism 16–17, **292**
legislative veto 98, 223–224, 513
Lend-Lease Act (1941) **292–293,** 421
Leninism 92–93, 94, 224
Lesseps, Ferdinand de 173

Letelier, Orlando 71
Levant 466
liberal internationalism 236, 405
liberalism 414
Liberation Front (FLN, Algeria) 10
liberation theology 370
Liberia 219, **293,** 415
*Liberty,* USS 259, 332
Libya 237, 256, **294,** 421, 472
Lieberman, Joseph 251
Lilienthal, David 36
Liliuokalani 207
limited international organization 240
Limited Test Ban Treaty (1963) 26
Lincoln, Abraham 14, 15, **294–295,** 403
Lindbergh, Charles A. 13–14
Lippman, Walter 295
Lippman Gap 242, **295,** 329
Lithuania 34–35
Litvinov Agreement 497
Livingston, Robert 298, 448
lobbying  *See interest groups*
Lodge, Henry Cabot 171, 290, **295–296,** *296,* 482, 483, 520
Logan, George 296
Logan Act (1799) 296
Lome, Enrique Dupuy de 449
Lomé accords 156
London Naval Conference 296–297
Lon Nol 59
López, Narciso 108, 162, *162*
Lott, Trent 94
Louisiana Purchase 3–4, 161, 173, 270–271, **297–299,** 298*m,* 448
Louverture, Toussaint 203
Loyalty Review Board 308
Lublin government (Polish Committee of National Liberation) 396
Ludlow Amendment 386, 528
Lugar, Richard 131, 164, 252
Lumumba, Patrice 96, 97
*Lusitania* 50, 213–214, 526
Luxembourg 154, 336

**M**

Maastricht Treaty (1991) 155, 156
MacArthur, Douglas 74, 268, 269, 279, 280, **300–301,** 349, 446, 485
MacDonald, Ramsey 297
Macedonia 197
Machiavelli 414
*Maddox* 272
Madero, Francisco 314
Madison, James 160, 164, **301,** 480, 512
Madrid accords 260, **301–302,** 378
MAGIC 152
Mahan, Alfred Thayer 183–184, 303
*Maine,* USS 109, 449–450, 451
Major, John 351
Makarios, Archbishop 197, 487
Malaysia 136
Manchuria 213, 267, 274, 455, 467–468

Mandela, Nelson 444
*Manhattan* 63
Manifest Destiny **302–303,** 334, 417
Mansfield, Mike 347
Mao Zedong (Mao Tse-tung) 73, 76, 86, 201
*Marbury v. Madison* 464
Marcos, Ferdinand 28
Marcy, W. L. 374
Mariel boatlift **303–304**
marijuana 137
Marines, U.S. 272, *291*
Marshall, George C. 73–74, 85, **304,** 307  *See also* Marshall Plan
Marshall, John 2, 16, 334, 464
Marshall, Thurgood 338
Marshall Plan 1–2, 85, 167, 175, 185–186, 305*m,* **305–306,** 335–336
Martin, Joseph 300–301
Marxism 92–93, 224
Marxist People's Democratic Party (Afghanistan) 4
Mas Canosa, Jorge 112
Mason, James 14
Mason, John 374
Massachusetts Burma Act (1996) 107–108
Massachusetts Peace Society 385
Mas Santos, Jorge 112
massive retaliation **306–307,** 355, 410
Matthews, George 164
Maximilian, Ferdinand 314
*Mayaguez* 166
Mazu Island 74, 170
McCarthy, Eugene 121, *121*
McCarthy, Joseph (McCarthyism) 2, 180, 280, 304, **307–308**
McCone, Jon 129
McFarlane, Robert 246
McGovern, George 121, 296
McKinley, William 109, 207, 394, 449–450, 451–453, 470
McMahon Act 37
McNamara, Robert 20, 21, 33, **308–309,** *309,* 387
measurement and signals intelligence (MASINT) 229
media and foreign policy xiii, 132, 146, **309–311**
Mexican Contract Labor Program (bracero program) **45–46**
Mexican Revolution 47, 71, 314, 364
Mexican War 181, 294–295, **311–313,** 397, 518–519
Mexico **313–316**
  Adams-Onís Treaty 4
  bracero program **45–46,** 315
  California 311–313
  cold war 315
  drug trafficking 136, 137
  El Salvador 146
  family-planning programs 398
  financial crises 30, 46–47, 117–118, 167, 316
  Gadsden Purchase 181
  immigration 222, 315–316

lands annexed by U.S. 312*m*
North American Free Trade
    Agreement (NAFTA)
    316, **343–344**
Polk, James 397
    Texas 58, 80, 311–313, 397,
        473–474, 488
    Veracruz, U.S. occupation of
        314–315
    Wilson, Woodrow 519
    Zimmermann Telegram
        315, 527, 538
Meyer, Stephen 354
MFN *See* most-favored-nation
    (MFN) status
migratory birds 318
Mikołajczyk, Stanislaw 396
milieu goals 123, 329
military *See also* Defense
    Department, U.S.; military-
    industrial complex
    civil-military relations
        **78–79**
    Federalist Papers and 160
    intelligence 228, 230
    interservice cooperation
        189–190
    Joint Chiefs of Staff 118,
        119, 189, **272–273,** 331
military assistance 167
military force, public opinion and
    405
military-industrial complex 143,
    231, **316–317,** 360–361, 419
military power 399–400
Mills, C. Wright 316–317
Milošević, Slobodan 44, 116, 117,
    281–282, 534, 535–536
Mindszenty, Cardinal 219
Mine Ban Teaty (1997) 285,
    286*m,* 287
MIRVs *See* multiple
    independently targeted reentry
    vehicles
missile gap **317–318**
*Missouri v. Holland* (1920) 49, 318
Mitchell, George 261
Mitchell, John 351
Mobil 372
Mobutu Sese Seko (Joseph
    Mobutu) 96, 97
models of foreign policy decision-
    making *See* decision-making
    models
modern diplomacy 129
Modernization Agreement (1945)
    26
Molotov-Ribbentrop
    Nonaggression Pact 34, 83, 396
Monroe, James 173, 298,
    318–319, 425, 448, 449
Monroe Doctrine **318–319**
    Adams, John Quincy, and 4
    France and 173
    Hoover, Herbert 213
    Roosevelt Corollary 133,
        423, **424**
    Venezuela boundary dispute
        81, 365–366, 502, 503
Montenegro 534, 536
Montes, Ana Belán 153
Montevideo Conference (1933)
    215

Montreal Protocol (1987) 151,
    **319–320**
Moral Majority 417
moral pragmatism 16–17,
    **320–321**
Morgenthau, Henry, Jr. 321
Morgenthau Plan **321**
Morocco 36, **321–322,** 423
Moscoso, Mireya 382
Moscow Treaty *See* Strategic
    Offense Reductions Treaty
Mossadegh, Mohammad 69, 243,
    246–247, 364
most-favored-nation (MFN) status
    76, 182, 264–265, **322–323,** 478
Mubarak, Hosni 142, 257
Mugabe, Robert 537, 538
Mujahideen 4–5, 6, 375–376, 413
multilateral diplomacy 94–95
Multilateral Implementation
    Force in Kosovo (KFOR) 345
Multilateral Investment
    Guarantee Agency 523
multinational corporations
    (MNCs) **323–324,** 363–364
multiple independently targeted
    reentry vehicles (MIRVs) 20,
    21, 359, 455, 459–460
multipolarity x, 241, **324–325**
Munich Conference (1938) 114
Murrow, Edward R. 308
Musharraf, Pervez 376
Muskie, Edmund *412*
Muslim Brotherhood 142
Mussolini, Benito 151, 153, 262
mutual assured destruction 32,
    127, 128, 355
MX missiles **325–326**

**N**
Nader, Ralph 499
NAFTA *See* North American
    Free Trade Agreement
Nagasaki 268, 531
Nagy, Imre 220
Najibullah 5
Namibia **327,** 443
Napoleon Bonaparte 173, 192,
    297–298, 299, 301, 448
Napoleon III, Emperor of France
    15, 173
narcoterrorism 471
*Nashville,* USS 91
Nasser, Gamal Abdel 8, 22–23,
    68–69, 141–142, 143, 256, 377,
    462–463
National Command Authority 118
National Greek Democratic
    League (EDES) 196
National Intelligence Authority
    67
national intelligence estimates
    (NIEs) 67, 229, 317–318,
    **327–328**
national interest 145, **328–329,**
    414, 436
National Military Establishment
    331, 333, 435
National Photographic
    Information Center (NPIC)
    229
National Reconnaissance Office
    (NRO) **329–330**

National Security Act (1947) 67,
    118, 129, 272, **330–331,** 333,
    435
national security advisor
    **331–332,** 333, 402–403, 454
National Security Agency (NSA)
    228–229, 230, **332**
National Security Council (NSC)
    **333–334**
    Central Intelligence Agency
        67
    Executive Committee
        112–114
    Iran-contra initiative
        245–246
    NSC-68 102, **352–353**
    president and 51, 333
    Tower Commission 477–478
National Security Presidential
    Directive (23) 34
National Strategy Target List
    (NSTL) 355–356
national technical means (NTMs)
    80, 504
National Trade Estimate Report
    on Foreign Trade Barriers 497
National Union for the Total
    Independence of Angola
    (UNITA) 19–20
Native Americans 171, 179–180,
    192, **334–335,** 448
NATO *See* North Atlantic Treaty
    Organization
natural law 237
natural resources, control of 363
naval arms race 183–184,
    296–297, 425, 515–516
Navigation Acts (1660) 335
Navy, U.S. 78
    cooperation among armed
        forces 272
    counterintelligence 104–105
    intelligence 230
    National Security Act 331
    naval arms race 183–184
    Puerto Rican training area
        407
    territorial sea 289
Nedzi, Lucien 77, 393
Nedzi Committee 393
Nehru, Jawaharlal 225
neo-isolationism 405
neoliberalism 414
Netanyahu, Benjamin 260–261,
    531
Netherlands 18, 154, 227,
    **335–336**
neutrality legislation (1930s) 185,
    292, 321, **336–337,** 360–361,
    421, 528
New Forum 104
New Granada 90, 91, 378
New Jewel Movement (NJM) 198
New Look 102, 143
New Thinking 429–430
New York Peace Society 385
*New York Times v. United States*
    (1971) **337–338,** 387
New Zealand 21
Ngo Dinh Diem 445, 506, 508
Nicaragua 201, **338–340**
    canal route in 338, 381
    Carter, Jimmy 64, 339

Cleveland, Grover 81
    contras 88–89, 201,
        245–246, 340
    Coolidge, Calvin 103
    dollar diplomacy and
        131–132
    Frelinghuysen, Frederick
        179
    Iran-contra initiative 88,
        245–246, 340, 478
    Pierce, Franklin 393
    Reagan, Ronald 413
    Sandinistas 64, 88–89, 146,
        339–340
    Walker, William 162, 338
Nicholson, Harold 153
Nigeria 136, 211, **340–341**
Nine-Power Treaty (1922) 266,
    515
Ninth International Conference of
    American States (1948) 371–372
Nitze, Paul 352, 457
Nixon, Pat 75, 163
Nixon, Richard **341–342**
    Angola 19
    antiballistic missile systems
        21, 33
    Arab-Israeli conflict 23,
        259–260
    arms reduction verification
        505
    arms transfers 28, 342
    Chile 70
    China 75, 75–76, 342, 469
    détente 125, 126, 264–265,
        322–323, 341, 342,
        455–457
    flexible targeting strategy
        355
    India 225
    Iran 244
    Japan 269
    Kissinger, Henry 278
    McCarthyism and 308
    national security advisor and
        331
    National Security Council
        and 333
    Pentagon Papers 387–388
    Smithsonian Agreement 441
    Soviet Union 88, 342,
        455–457, 495
    Strategic Arms Limitation
        Talks I 455–456,
        **456–457**
    territorial sea policy 289
    Venezuela 502–503
    Vietnam War 87, 341–342,
        508–509
    war powers resolution and
        101–102
Nixon Doctrine **342–343**
Nkomo, Joshua 537
nongovernmental organizations
    (NGOs) xii, **343**
Nonimportation Act (1806) 161,
    173
Non-Importation Act (1809) 511
Nonintercourse Act (1809) 301
Non-Proliferation Treaty (1968)
    26
nontariff barriers (NTBs) 140,
    477

Noriega, Manuel 53, 369–370, 379
Norris, George 527
North, Lord 191
North, Oliver 245, 246, 333
North American Aerospace Defense Command (NORAD) 62
North American Free Trade Agreement (NAFTA) 54, 63, 82, 158, 316, **343–344**, 479, 480
North Atlantic Treaty Organization (NATO) 13, **345–346**
    Baltic states 35
    burden sharing 347
    Canada 62, 63
    as collective-security organization 90
    Coordinating Committee for Mulitlateral Export Controls **103–104**
    European Union 156–157
    formation of 39, 85
    France 176, 177
    Germany 186
    Greece 196
    Hungary 220
    Intermediate Nuclear Forces Treaty 231–232
    IOFR 117
    Iraq War 253
    Italy 262
    Kosovo 281–282
    member countries 345–347, 346m
    nuclear weapons posture 347–348
    operations, scope of 347
    Partnership for Peace 383
    purpose 348
    Russia 430
    Spain 450–451
Northern Aid Committee (NORAID) 352
Northern Ireland 82, 256, **351–352**
North Korea **348–351** *See also* Korean War
    brinksmanship 49–50
    Bush, George W. 350–351
    China 74
    Clinton, Bill 349–350
    nuclear weapons 77, 82, 349–351, 376
    preemption strategy and 401
    *Pueblo*, USS, seizure of 272, 349
    as rogue state 421
    South Korea reconciliation 447
    terrorism 472
North-South Center 233
Northwest Passage 63
Novotny, Antonin 87
NSC *See* National Security Council
NSC-68 102, **352–353**
Nuclear Freeze Campaign 387
nuclear freeze movement 458
nuclear-free zones 130

Nuclear Non-Proliferation Treaty (NPT) 349
nuclear war **357–358**
nuclear weapons
    accidental use of 127, 357–358, 517
    antiballistic missiles 20–21, 33, 34, 455
    ANZUS Pact and 21
    arms control *See* arms control
    arsenals, overview **358–359**, *359*
    ballistic missile defense (BMD) 21, **32–34**, *33*, 82, 459, 461
    Baruch Plan 36–37
    bomber gap 42–43
    brinksmanship and 49
    Byrnes, James, and 57
    circular error probability 359
    climatic impact of 360
    Commerce Department and 92
    compellence strategy **353**
    Comprehensive Test Ban Treaty 26, 82, 94, 226
    cost of 359
    Cuban missile crisis 87, 110, **112–114**, *113*, 153, 309–310, 429, 487
    deterrence *See* deterrence strategies
    deterrence failures 126–127
    disarmament *See* disarmament
    doves and 135–136
    Eisenhower, Dwight D. 143, 170
    foreign aid and 375, 376
    Gaither Committee Report 181–182
    Great Britain and 195
    Hiroshima 57
    India and 225–226
    intercontinental ballistic missiles 20, 317–318, 325, 359, 367, 455, 459–460, 509
    Intermediate Nuclear Forces Treaty 130, **231–232**, 504
    Kazakhstan 66
    Kissinger, Henry 278
    manned bomber delivery 358–359
    massive retaliation 306–307, 355, 410, 439–440
    McNamara, Robert 309
    missile gap 317–318
    multiple independently targeted reentry vehicles 20, 21, 359, 455, 459–460
    MX missiles **325–326**
    North Atlantic Treaty Organization 347–348
    North Korea 77, 82, 349–351, 376
    Nunn-Lugar Act 131, 167, 459
    Open Skies proposal **367**

Pakistan and 225–226, 375, 376
Partial Nuclear Test Ban Treaty 276, *276*
peace movements and 386–387
RAND Corporation 410
Rapacki Plan 410–411
Reagan, Ronald 355, 356, 360, 412, 458
Russia 431
Stimson, Henry 455
stockpiles (1945–97) 355
Strategic Arms Limitation Talks I 126, 278, 325, 455–456, **456–457**, 505, 509
Strategic Arms Limitation Talks II 166, 325, **457–458**, 504
Strategic Arms Reduction Talks 26, 130, **458–459**
Strategic Arms Reduction Treaty I 53, **459**
Strategic Arms Reduction Treaty II 53, 458–459, **459–460**
Strategic Arms Reduction Treaty III 359, **460**
Strategic Offense Reductions Treaty 29, 31, **461–462**
submarine-launched ballistic missiles (SLBMs) 359, 459–460
tests (1945–92) *356*
verification and 504–505
*Nuclear Weapons and Foreign Policy* (Kissinger) 278
nuclear winter **360**
Nunn, Sam 131, 347
Nunn-Lugar Act (Cooperative Threat Reduction Program, 1991) 131, 167, 459
Nye, Gerald 361, 502
Nye committee 336, 337, **360–361**, 421

**O**
oceans *See* Law of the Sea conferences
October Revolutionaries 198
Office of Agriculture Export Assistance 9
Office of Global Communications 311
Office of International Affairs 479
Office of International Trade 92
Office of Nonproliferation Controls and Treaty Compliance 92
Office of Strategic Industry and Economic Security 92
Office of Strategic Services (OSS) 67, 152, 159, **362–363**
Office of Strategic Trade and Foreign Policy Controls 92
Office of Technology Assessment (OTA) 357
Office of the Special Trade Representative (OSTR) 277
Ogaden region 442
Ogdensburg Declaration 62

oil **363–365**
    crude prices (1861–2001) *364*
    debt crisis of 1980s 117
    embargo (1973) 256, 294, 373, 433
    Iran 243
    Iran-Iraq War 248
    Kuwait 282
    Libya 294
    Nigeria 341
    Organization of Petroleum Exporting Countries 117, 249, 256, 282, 294, 323, 364–365, **372–374**, 433
    Persian Gulf War 388
    Saudi Arabia 433
    Venezuela 503
Olney, Richard **365–366**, 502, 503
Olney-Pauncefote Treaty 502
O'Mahony, John 255
Omnibus Trade and Competition Act (1988) 269, 479, 480
O'Neill, John 255
open-belief system 402
Open Door policy 208, 265, 266, **366–367**, 425, 427, 481–482
Open Skies **367**
Operation Anaconda 7
Operation Bright Star 142
Operation Desert Shield 202, **367–368**
Operation Desert Storm 54, 202, **368–369**, 369m, 389
Operation Enduring Freedom *6*, 438
Operation Just Cause **369–370**, 379
Operation Market Garden 335
Operation Mongoose 105–106, 110
Operation Uphold Democracy **370–371**
Opium War (1839) 71–72
Oregon Territory 58, **371**, 398, 518
Organization of American States (OAS) 2, 12, **371–372**
    Caracas Declaration 199
    Cuba 110
    Dominican Republic 135
    Haiti 370, 372
    Helms-Burton Act 209
    Panama elections (1989) 370
Organization of Eastern Caribbean States 198
Organization of Petroleum Exporting Countries (OPEC) 364–365, **372–374**
    debt crisis of 1980s 117
    embargo (1973) 256, 294, 373, 433
    Iraq 249
    Kuwait 282
    members 372–373
    power of 323
    Saudi Arabia 433
Ortega Saavedra, Daniel 339
Ostend Manifesto (1854) 108, **374**
Ostpolitik 186–187

O'Sullivan, John L. 302–303
"Our Common Future"
  (Brundtland Commission) 139
Outer-Space Treaty (1967) 130,
  131
Owen, David 44, 501
Oxfam 343
ozone layer 319–320, 360

**P**

Pahlavi, Mohammad Reza, Shah
  of Iran 28, 243–244, 246–247
Paine, Thomas 258
Pakistan 5, 68–69, 124, 125, 137,
  225–226, **375–376**
Palestine Liberation Organization
  (PLO) 23, 24, 273, 302,
  **377–378,** 486, 531
Palestinian Authority 61
Palestinian state 261, 273, 377–378
Palmer, A. Mitchell 159
Panama 53, 91, 136, 369–370,
  **378–379,** 381
Panama Canal 378–379,
  **379–381,** 380m
    Clayton-Bulwer Treaty
      (Great Britain) 42,
      **80–81,** 90–91, 192, 338,
      379–380
    Colombia and 90–91,
      378–379, 381
    control, transfer of 382–383
    France 173
    Hay, John 208
    Hay-Bunau-Varilla Treaty
      379, 381
    Hay-Herrán Treaty 378, 381
    Roosevelt, Theodore 423
Panama Canal Treaties (1977) 64,
  382, 382–383
Panamanian Defense Forces
  (PDF) 369
paramilitary operations 106
Parcham 4
Pardo, Arvid 288
Paris, Treaty of See Treaty of Paris
  (1783)
Partial Nuclear Test Ban Treaty
  (1963) 276, 276
Partnership for Peace (PfP) 347,
  **383–384**
Pathet Lao 287
Patriot Act (2001) 160, 438,
  **499–500**
*Patterns of Global Terrorism*
  (State Department) 376, 471
Pauncefote, Julian 81, 91, 208,
  366, 380
Peace Corps 8, 233
Peace Enforcement League 386
peaceful coercion 270, 271
peacekeeping and peacemaking 8,
  218, 234, 263, **384–385,** 416,
  492, 496–497
peace movements **385–387,**
  521–522
Pearle, Richard 99
Pelton, Reichard 332
Penkovsky, Oleg 153
Pentagon Papers 337–338,
  **387–388**
People's Republic of Azerbaijan
  243

People's Republic of China (PRC)
  73–77
Peres, Shimon 302, 322
Peress, Irving 308
perestroika 89, 429
Permanent Court of International
  Justice (World Court) 290
Permanent Joint Board on
  Defense (PJBD) 62
Perón, Juan 2, 25
Perot, Ross 344
Perry, Matthew 265
Perry, William J. 168, 202, 349,
  350
Pershing, John 315, 519
Persian Gulf War **388–390,** 389
    Bush, George H. W. 54,
      249, 260, 367–369, 388,
      434, 490, 493
    Egypt 142
    Gulf War Syndrome
      201–202, 368, 516–517
    Iran 245
    Israel 260
    Japan 269
    Jordan 273
    media coverage 310
    oil and 363, 374
    Operation Desert Shield
      202, **367–368**
    Operation Desert Storm 54,
      202, **368–369,** 369m, 389
    Saudi Arabia 367–368, 434
    Turkey 487–488
    United Nations 388–389,
      493
    personality **390–391,** 402
Peru 69
Peurifoy, John 199
Philippines 28, 136, 450, 452,
  452m, 453
Pierce, Franklin 108, 133, 181,
  374, **392–393**
Pike Committee **393**
Pinckney, Charles 2
Pinckney, Thomas 448
Pinckney's Treaty (Treaty of San
  Lorenzo) 297, **393–394,** 448
Pinochet, Augusto 70, 71
Pitts, Edward 153
Plains Wars (1860s, 1870s) 334
Plan Colombia 91
Platt, Orville 394
Platt Amendment **394,** 424
pledge system 292
Plevin, André 156
Plevin plan 156
PLO See Palestine Liberation
  Organization
pluralism **394–395**
Poindexter, John 246
Point Four Program 167, **395**
Poland 89, **396–397,** 398–399,
  409, 410–411, 470, 533
policy entrepreneurs 99
Polignac Memorandum 319
Polisario 322
Polish Home Army 396
Polk, James **397–398**
    Cuba 108
    Mexican War 312–313, 314,
      518–519
    Oregon Territory 371

Texas 473–474
  vs. Whig Party 518
Pollard, Jonathan 260, 531
pollution See environment
Pol Pot 59
Pont de Nemours, Pierre-Samuel
  du 298
Popular Front for the Liberation
  of Palestine 377
Popular Movement for the
  Independence of Angola
  (MPLA) 19–20
population 124–125, 398
population policy **398**
Portsmouth, Treaty of See Treaty
  of Portsmouth
Portugal 19, 47
positivism 237
possession goals 123, 329
Potsdam Conference (1945) 83,
  **398–399,** 399, 484
Powell, Colin 68
    Bosnia and Herzegovina 44
    chairman, Joint Chiefs of
      Staff 420
    Iraq War 56, 250, 252
    national security advisor 331
    North Korea nuclear
      weapons 350
    secretary of state 436
    Strategic Offense
      Reductions Treaty 461
    World Summit on
      Sustainable Development
      523
power x, 241, **399–400,** 414
Powers, Francis Gary 152, 489
pragmatism 54
Prague Spring 87, 115
Predator unmanned aerial vehicle
  (UAV) 229
preemption 56, 252, 356, **401**
president **401–403**
    ambassadorships 101,
      401–402
    belief systems of 402
    bureaucracies and 51, 331
    Central Intelligence Agency
      and 214–215
    Congress and (overview)
      401–403
    Constitution and 101–102
    diplomatic relations,
      severing 402
    domestic influences on U.S.
      foreign policy and 132
    elections 144–145
    executive agreements 49,
      101, **157,** 344, 401,
      497–498
    fast-track authority 101,
      158–159, 402, 477, 479
    Federalist Papers and 160
    first ladies and 162–164
    *Goldwater et al. v. Carter*
      189
    Hughes-Ryan Amendment
      214–215
    International Emergency
      Economic Powers Act
      (IEEPA) 116
    legislative veto and 98, 223,
      513

Logan Act (1799) 296
    national security advisor and
      331–332, 402–403
    National Security Council
      (NSC) and 333–334
    *New York Times v. United
      States* (1971) 337–338
    personality of 390–391, 402
    summit
      conferences/diplomacy
      463–464
    Supreme Court justices 465
    trade policy 402 See also
      fast-track authority
    treaty termination 189
    *Underhill v. Hernandes*
      (1897) 490
    *United States v. Curtiss-
      Wright Export Corp.*
      (1936) **498**
    as U.S. spokesperson 402
    war-making powers of 98,
      101–102, 180, 223, 403,
      465, 512–513
    *Youngstown Sheet and Tube
      Co. v. Sawyer* **533–534**
presidential findings 214–215
Presser Amendment 226
Pressler Amendment 376
prevention vs. preemption
  strategy 401
Prize Cases (1863) **403**
Progressive Party 418
Project Air Force 410
propaganda 105
protectionism 120, 322, 479
Protestantism 417
public diplomacy **403–404**
public opinion 129, 132, 310,
  403–404, **404–406**
*Pueblo,* USS 272, 349
Puerto Rico 63–64, 228, **406–407**
Putin, Vladimir 26, 359, 430, 431,
  459, 461

**Q**

Qaddafi, Muammar al- 256, 294,
  373
al-Qaeda 6–7, 40–41, 47, 55, **408,**
  438, 473
Qassim, Abdul Karim 249
Quarles, Donald 453
Quasi War with France 2,
  172–173, 206
Quitman, John 108, 162
quotas 140–141
Qureia, Ahmed 378

**R**

Rabin, Yitzhak 260, 302, 378
racism
    atomic bomb on Hiroshima
      and Nagasaki and 267,
      268
    immigration and 222, 223
    Insular Cases and 228
    Manifest Destiny and 303
Racketeer Influenced and Corrupt
  Organizations Act (RICO) 370
Radio Free Europe 105, 409,
  **409–410**
Radio Liberty 105, 409
Radio Martí 111, 112, 495–496

railroads 181
RAND Corporation **410,** 434
Rapacki Plan (1957) **410–411**
Raskin, Marcus 474
rational-actor decision-making
    model xiii–xiv, **411–412**
Reagan, Nancy 163
Reagan, Ronald *89, 412,*
    **412–413**
    Angola 19
    Arab-Israeli conflict 24, 260,
        291, 377–378
    Arms Control and
        Disarmament Agency
        (ACDA) (arms control) 27
    arms reduction verification
        505
    arms transfers 28
    Bipartisan Commission on
        United States Policy
        toward Central America
        279
    bracero program 46
    Caribbean Basin Initiative
        63–64
    containment strategies 103
    Coordinating Committee for
        Mulitlateral Export
        Controls 104
    Cuba 111
    debt crisis (1980s) 32
    democratization 122
    disarmament 130–131
    domino theory 135
    elite decision-making theory
        146
    El Salvador 146–147
    environment 151, 320
    European Community
        (European Union) 155
    Grenada 197–198
    Haig, Alexander 203
    Haitian refugees 204, 416
    Heritage Foundation 475
    Intermediate Nuclear
        Forces Treaty 130,
        231–232, *232*
    International Emergency
        Economic Powers Act
        116
    Iran-contra initiative 88,
        245–246, **245–246,** 260,
        340, 478
    Iran-Iraq War 244–245,
        248, 465
    *Lawry v. Reagan* 465
    Libya 294
    MX missiles 326
    national security advisor and
        331
    National Security Council
        333, 477–478
    Nicaragua 339–340
    North American Free Trade
        Agreement 344
    Northern Ireland 351
    nuclear deterrence strategy
        355, 356, 360
    oil 373
    Panama 369, 370, 379, 382
    political Islam 256
    public diplomacy 404
    Republican Party 419

Reykjavík Summit 463
    South Africa 8, 444
    Strategic Arms Reduction
        Talks 26, 138, 458
    Strategic Defense Initiative
        (Star Wars) 21, 26, 33,
        131, 460–461
    Tower Commission 477–478
    UN Convention on the Law
        of the Sea 289
    Vladivostok accords 509
Reagan Doctrine 5, 103, 412, **413**
realism 132, 221–222, 236, 329,
    **413–414**
Reciprocal Trade Agreement Acts
    322, **414–415**
reconnaissance satellites 80
Red Cross 343
Red Line agreement (1928) 363
Red Scare (1919–20) 159
Refugee Act (1980) 204
refugees **415–416**
    Cuban 303–304, 416
    Dominican 135
    Haitian 204, 370, 416
    Kosovar 416
    Palestinian 61
    Rwandan 431–432
Regan, Brian 153
regionalism *See* sectionalism
Rehnquist, William 189
religion **417–418**
Republican Party 49, 99, 417,
    **418–419**
Republic of Gran Colombia 502
resulting powers, concept of 16
*Retrospect: The Tragedy and
    Lessons of Vietnam*
    (McNamara) 309
Revere Gang (Mechanics) 152
revisionism 132, **419–420**
Reykjavík Summit (1986) 93, 130,
    458
Reza Khan 243
Rice, Condoleezza 332, 522
Ridge, Tom 212–213
Ridgeway, Matthew 300
Rio Declaration (1992) 139, 523,
    524
Rio Pact (1947) 2, **420**
Rio Summit *See* Earth Summit,
    Rio de Janeiro
Roberts, Edmund 71
Robertson, Pat 417
Robinson, Randall 371
Rockefeller, David 483
Rogers, William 23, 75, 331
Rogers Act (1924) 168
Rogers Plan 23
rogue states **420–421**
Rome, Treaty of (1957) 154
Romero, Carlos Humberto 146
Roosevelt, Eleanor 163
Roosevelt, Franklin D. **421–423,**
    *422*
    Alaska boundary dispute 62
    Atlantic Charter 30, 422,
        528–529
    Bullit, William C. 50–51
    China 73
    Germany 185
    Good Neighbor policy 215,
        421, 424

Great Britain 194
    Hull, Cordell 215
    Japan 267–268
    Lend-Lease Act 292–293,
        421
    Morgenthau Plan 321
    national interest debate 329
    neutrality legislation
        336–337, 421, 528
    Office of Strategic Services
        362
    Ogdensburg Declaration
        62
    Reciprocal Trade Agreement
        Acts 415
    Soviet Union 428
    Tehran Conference *469,*
        469–470
    United Nations 491
    Yalta Conference 49, 57, 83,
        157, 446, 533, *534*
Roosevelt, Theodore **423–424**
    China 72, 367
    Dominican Republic 133,
        423
    Germany 184
    Japan 266, 423, 481–482
    Panama Canal 91, 381, 423
    Russo-Japanese War
        481–482
    Venezuela 423, 502
Roosevelt Corollary 133, 423, **424**
Root, Elihu **424–425**
Root-Takahira Agreement (1908)
    72, 266, 367, 425
Rosello, Pedro 407
Rosenberg, Julius and Ethel
    159–160
Rostow, Walt 331, 494
Royal Dutch Shell 372
Rugova, Ibrahim 281
Rumsfeld, Donald 13, 56, 78,
    177, 250, 251, 252, 253, 254,
    311, 348, 435
Rush, Richard 318, 425
Rush-Bagot Treaty (1817) 3, 192,
    **425**
Rusk, Dean 210
Russia, democratic **430–431** *See
    also* Russia, imperial; Russia,
    Soviet Union
    aging population 124, 125
    Baltic states 35
    Central Asian republics 66,
        67
    Chechnya 430
    Comprehensive Test Ban
        Treaty 26, 82, 94, 226
    foreign aid to 167
    HIV/AIDS and 211
    Iraq War 56, 253, 493, 494
    Strategic Arms Reduction
        Talks 26, 130, **458–459**
    Strategic Arms Reduction
        Treaty I 53, **459**
    Strategic Arms Reduction
        Treaty II 53, 458–459,
        **459–460**
    Strategic Arms Reduction
        Treaty III 359, **460**
    Strategic Offense
        Reductions Treaty 26,
        431, **461–462**

Russia, imperial **426–427** *See
    also* Russia, democratic; Russia,
    Soviet Union
    Alaska 10, 427, 439
    China 72, 73
    Jewish immigration 427
    Monroe Doctrine 319
    multipolarity and 324–325
    Poland 396
    Russo-Japanese War 427,
        481–482
Russia, Soviet Union **427–430**
    *See also* Russia, democratic;
    Russia, imperial
    Afghanistan 4–6, 65, 89,
        375, 408
    Angola 19
    Antibalistic Missile Treaty
        20–21, **20–21,** 33, 34, 456
    Arab-Israeli conflict 22, 23
    arms control overview 26
    Atlantic Charter 30–31
    ballistic missile defense and
        33
    Baltic states 34–35
    Baruch Plan 36–37
    Berlin crises 38–40
    bomber gap 42–43
    breakup of 425, *426*
    Brezhnev Doctrine 48–49
    brinksmanship 49
    Bullitt, William C., and 50–51
    Byrnes, James 57
    Central Treaty Organization
        68–69
    China and 74–75, 76, 87–88,
        170, 428–429
    communism in **92–94**
    Conference on Security and
        Cooperation in Europe
        95–96, 126, 216, 429
    containment of *See*
        containment
    Coordinating Committee for
        Mulitlateral Export
        Controls 103–104
    Cuba 38, 110
    Cuban missile crisis 87, 110,
        **112–114,** *113*
    Czechoslovakia 87, 115
    détente *See* détente
    disarmament overview
        130–131
    Egypt 141–142, 142
    Eisenhower, Dwight D.
        143, 144
    espionage 152–153
    Ethiopia 154
    Ford, Gerald 166
    Gaither Committee Report
        181–182
    Germany 83, 185–187
    human rights 216
    Hungary 219–220
    Indonesia 227
    Intermediate Nuclear
        Forces Treaty 130,
        231–232, 504
    Iran 243
    Iraq 248–249
    Israel 260
    Italy 262–263
    Laos 287

massive retaliation and
306–307, 355, 410
missile gap 317–318
most-favored-nation (MFN)
status 264–265, 322–323
national intelligence
estimates (NIEs) and
327–328
New Thinking 354, 429–430
Nixon, Richard, and 88,
342, 455–457, 495
nuclear deterrence strategy
of **354–355,** 357
nuclear tests (1945–92) *356*
nuclear weapon arsenal 359,
*359*
Open Skies proposal 367
Poland 396, 429, 470
Potsdam Conference 83,
**398–399,** *399,* 484
Radio Liberty 105, 409–410
Rapacki Plan 410–411
Reagan, Ronald 412, 413
Roosevelt, Franklin D. 428
Somalia 442
*Sputnik* 181, **453–454**
Strategic Arms Limitation
Talks I 126, 278, 325,
455–456, **456–457,** 505,
509
Strategic Arms Limitation
Talks II 166, 325,
**457–458,** 504
Tehran Conference
469–470
Truman, Harry 484–486,
487
U-2 incident 489–490
unipolarity and Eastern
Europe 491
United Nations 491, 533
United States Information
Agency 495
verification of arms control
504–505
Vietnam 506
Wallace, Henry, and 510
Warsaw Pact 85, 383,
**513–514**
weapons of mass destruction
516
Yalta Conference 57, 83,
446, **533,** *534*
Yugoslavia 534
Russian American Company 10,
427
Russian Revolution 83
Russo-Japanese War 427,
481–482
Rwanda 415, **431–432**
Rwandan Patriotic Front (RPF)
432
Ryan, Leo 214

**S**

Sadat, Anwar 23, 59–60, *60,* 142,
373
Sagan, Carl 360
Saint-Domingue 298
Sakhalin 481
Salassie, Haile 151
Salinas, Carlos 316, 343
Salinger, Pierre 296

Samoa 42, 81
Sandinistas 64, 88, 146, 339–340
*San Jacinto,* USS 14
Santa Anna, Antonio López de
314, 473
satellites 80, 330, 332, 410,
453–454, 489
Saudi Arabia **433–435,** *434*
arms sales to 433–434
bin Laden, Osama 40
dual containment and 138
Iraq War 250
Operation Desert Shield
367–368
Organization of Petroleum
Exporting Countries
364–365, 372–374
population youth bulge 124,
125
al-Qaeda 408
Truman, Harry, and 157
SAVAK 243, 244
Savimbi, Jonas 20, 413
Sawyer, Charles 533
Scheffer, David 234
Schlesinger, James 77, 129, 130
Schneider, René 70
Schomburgk line 503, 504
Schultz, George 246, 331
Schuman, Robert 154
Schuman Plan 154
Schwarzkopf, H. Norman 368
Scott, Winfield 313
Scowcroft, Brent 250, 326, 478
Scowcroft Commission 326
Scruggs, William 503, 504
Sebold, William 159
Second Continental Congress
(1775) 191
second-strike strategies 127–128
Secord, Richard 246
Secret Intelligence Branch (SI)
152
Secret Intelligence Service 159
sectionalism **436–437**
security assistance 167
Selassie, Haile 153–154
Seminoles 334
Senate Foreign Relations
Committee 99, 180, 209
September 11, 2001 *437,*
**437–439**
Canada 63
Central Intelligence Agency
68
collective-security response
to 90
and political Islam 257
al-Qaeda 408
Saudi Arabia 434
USA Patriot Act 160, 438,
499–500
Serbia 281, 282, 534–536
Serb National Council 107
Serb Republic of Bosnia 116
Serbs 44, 106–107, 116, 117, 281,
282, 534–535
Servan-Schreiber, Jean-Jacques
323
Service, John 308
seven sisters 323, 363, 372–373
Seven Years War *See* French and
Indian War (1756–63)

Seward, William 10, 14, 15, 72,
133, 295, **439–440**
shah of Iran *See* Pahlavi,
Mohammad Reza, Shah of Iran
Shamir, Yitzhak 302
Shanghai Communiqué (1972)
75, 126, 189
Shantung Peninsula 266, 267
Sharon, Ariel 262, 378
Shi'ite Muslims 248, 251, 254
Shine, David C. 307, 308
Shmarov, Valeriy *168*
Shotwell, James 274
Shukairy, Ahmed 377
Shultz, George 24, 320
shuttle diplomacy 23, 259–260,
278, 377
Siam *See* Thailand
Sierra Leone 293
signals intelligence (SIGINT) 79,
80, 229, 330, 332
signature intelligence (IMINT)
229
Sihanouk, Norodom 58–59
Silk Road Caucus (2001) 67
Sinai II (1975) 23
Singapore 29–30, 136
Singapore Ministerial Conference
525
Single European Act (1986) 155
single integrated operational plan
(SIOP) 307, 355–356,
**439–440**
Sinn Féin 255–256, 351, 352
Sino-Japanese War (1894–95) 72
Six-Day War (1967) 142, 377,
466
slavery 161–162, 519
Slidell, John 14, 312–313, 314
Slovakia 114–115
Slovenia 534–535
small-group decision-making
model xiv, 37–38, **440–441**
Smith, Gerald 309
Smith, H. Richardson 13
Smith, Ian 537
Smithsonian Agreement (1971)
**441**
Smoot, Reed 442
Smoot-Hawley Tariff Act (1930)
415, **441–442**
soft power 400
soil erosion 150
Solidarity trade union movement
89, 397
Somalia 8, 82, 154, 218, 219, 384,
**442–443,** *443*
Somoza Debayle, Anastasio 88,
339, 340
Somoza García, Anastasio 339
Son Ngoc Thamh 59
Souers, Sidney 221
Soule, Pierre 108, 374
"The Sources of Soviet Conduct"
(Kennan) 102, 275
Souter, David 108
South Africa 8, 125, 137, 211,
327, **443–444**
South America *See* Latin
America; *specific countries*
Southeast Asia Treaty
Organization (SEATO) 85,
225, 375, **445,** 474

South Korea 1–2, 29–30, 62, 74,
136, **445–447,** *446 See also*
Korean War
South Pacific Nuclear Free Zone
Treaty 21
South West Africa People's
Organization (SWAPO) 327
Souvanna Phouma, Prince of Laos
287
Soviet Union *See* Russia, Soviet
Union
Spain **447–451**
American Revolution
18–19, 448
Argentina 25
civil war (1936) 337
Cuba 108, 109, 374
Florida (Adams-Onís Treaty)
3–4, 164, 264, 313, 449,
473
Guatemala 198
Iraq War 56, 250, 254
Louisiana Purchase 297,
298
Mexico 313, 314
Morocco 322
multipolarity and 324–325
Pinckney's Treaty 393–394,
448
Washington, George 514
Spanish-American War 385, 394,
406, 449–450, **451–453,** *452m,*
470
spin-off crises 235
spiral of silence 310
spoilers 218
*Sputnik* 181, **453–454**
spying *See* espionage
Stalin, Joseph 48, 86, 428, 455
Atlantic Charter 31
communist ideology of 93
Greece 485, 486
Potsdam Conference
398–399, *399*
Tehran Conference *469,*
469–470
Yalta Conference 49, 533,
*534*
Yugoslavia 534
Stamp Act (1765) 180, 191
Standard Drawing Rights (SDRs)
238
Standing Consultative
Commission (SCC) 505
*Stark,* USS 248
State Department, U.S.
**454–455**
Arms Control and
Disarmament Agency **27**
as bureaucracy 51
de-mining operations 287
diplomacy 128
discrimination 522
Foreign Service Officer
Corps **168–169**
influence of 455
intelligence community
229–230
intelligence cycle 228–229
international-affairs budget
233
McCarthyism and 307, 308
responsibilities 454

State Department, U.S. *(continued)*
   secretary of 333, 390,
      **435–436**
   undersecretaries 454
   United States Information
      Agency 495–496
states rights' and federal foreign-
   policy powers 465
      *Crosby v. National Foreign
         Trade Council* (2000)
         107–108, 212
      *Holmes v. Jennison* (1840)
         212
      *Missouri v. Holland* (1920)
         49, 318
      *United States v. Belmont*
         (1934) 49, 157, 497–498
      *Ware v. Hylton* (1796) 29,
         **510**
Statute of Westminster (1931) 62
steel industry 156, 533
Stephenson, William 362
Stevens, John L. 207
Stevens, Robert 308
Stevenson, Adlai *484*
Stewart, Robert Viscount
   Castlereagh 3
Stilwell, Joseph 73
Stimson, Henry 103, 274, **455**
Stimson Doctrine 73, 213, 455
Stockholm Conference (1972)
   150–151
Stoeckl, Edouard de 10, 439
*Strangers in Our Fields* (Galarza)
   46
Strategic Air Command (SAC) 439
Strategic Arms Limitation Talks I
   (SALT I) 126, 278, 325,
   455–456, **456–457,** 505, 509
Strategic Arms Limitation Talks II
   (SALT II) 166, 325, **457–458,**
   504
Strategic Arms Reduction Talks
   (START) 26, 130, **458–459**
Strategic Arms Reduction Treaty I
   (START I) 53, **459**
Strategic Arms Reduction Treaty
   II (START II) 53, 458–459,
   **459–460**
Strategic Arms Reduction Treaty
   III (START III) 359, **460**
Strategic Defense Initiative (SDI,
   Star Wars) 21, 26, 33, 131, 412,
   **460–461**
Strategic Defense Initiative (Star
   Wars) 21, 26, 33, 131, 460–461
Strategic Offense Reductions
   Treaty (Moscow Treaty, SORT,
   2003) 26, 431, **461–462**
strategic trade 479
Stresemann, Gustav 185
Structural Impediments Initiative
   (SII) 269
Stuart, Robert Douglas, Jr. 13
Student Non-Violent Coordinating
   Committee 386
submarine-launched ballistic
   missiles (SLBMs) 359,
   459–460
Sudan **462**
Suez crisis 141, 143, 176, 195,
   384, **462–463**
Sugar Act (1764) 191

Suharto 227
Sukarno 227
Sulawesi 227
Sullivan Principles 444
Sumatra 227
summit conferences/diplomacy
   129, **463–464**
Sumner, Charles 10, 439, **464**
Sunni Muslims 248
Sun Zhongshan (Sun Yat-Sen) 73
superterrorism 471
Support for East European
   Democracy Act (SEED, 1989)
   217, 397
Supreme Court, U.S. **464–465**
   Act of State doctrine 35–36
   *American Insurance Co. v.
      Canter* (1828) **16**
   *Banco Nacional de Cuba v.
      Sabbatino* (1964) **35–36**
   *Crosby v. National Foreign
      Trade Council* (2000)
      **107–108,** 212
   *Dames & Moore v. Regan*
      (1981) **116**
   *Downs v. Bidwell* (1901) 228
   *Goldwater et al. v. Carter*
      (1979) 76, **189**
   *Holmes v. Jennison* (1840)
      **212**
   *Immigration and
      Naturalization Service v.
      Chadha* (1983) 102,
      **223–224**
   Insular Cases **228,** 406
   *Lawry v. Reagan* 465
   *Marbury v. Madison* 464
   *Missouri v. Holland* (1920)
      49, 318
   *New York Times v. United
      States* (1971) **337–338,**
      387
   Prize Cases (1863) **403**
   *Underhill v. Hernandes*
      (1897) 35–36, **490**
   *United States v. Belmont*
      (1934) 49, 157, **497–498**
   *United States v. Curtiss-
      Wright Export Corp.*
      (1936) **498**
   *Ware v. Hylton* (1796) 29,
      **510**
   *Youngstown Sheet and Tube
      Co. v. Sawyer* (1952)
      **533–534**
*Sussex* 526
sustainable development 523, 524
Sutherland, George 497–498, 498
Syria 22, 23, 141, 291, **465–466,**
   472

**T**
Tachen Islands 170
Taft, Robert 293, 395
Taft, William Howard **467–468**
   China 72
   dollar diplomacy 131, 467
   Dominican Republic 134
   Haiti 204
   Japan 423, 424, 481
   Nicaragua 338–339
   Russia 427
Taft-Hartley Act 116

Taft-Katsura Agreement (1905)
   266, 445, 467
Ta'if Agreement (1989) 291
Taiping Rebellion 366
Taiwan **468–469**
   arms sales to 469
   Asian financial crisis 29–30
   China 73–74, 76–77, 86
   drug trafficking 136
   Formosa Resolution 74,
      169–170, 512–513
   *Goldwater et al. v. Carter*
      189
   Tibet 475
Taiwan Relations Act 468
Tajikistan 65–67
Talbott, Strobe 376
Taliban 6, 376, 408, 438
Talleyrand, Charles-Maurice de
   173
Taney, Roger 212
Tanzania 97, *148*
Tariff Act (1930) 414–415
tariffs *See* trade policy and tariffs
Taylor, Charles 293
Taylor, Zachary 204, 312–313
Taylor-Rostow Report 508
Tea Act (1773) 180, 191
technical intelligence 79–80
Tehran Conference *469,*
   **469–470**
telemetry intelligence (TELINT)
   79
Teller, Henry M. 450
Teller Amendment 109, 394, 450,
   **470**
Tenet, George 68
territorial sea 288, 289
terrorism **470–473**
   attacks, numbers of *471,*
      471–472
   Bush, George W. 55
   casualties from 471–472
   chemical and biological
      weapons 516
   Cuba 472
   drug trafficking 137
   Federal Bureau of
      Investigation 159
   Homeland Security
      Department 212–213
   immigration 223
   Iran 472
   Iraq 472
   Iraq War 252
   Libya 472
   military and economic power
      resources and 400
   Morocco 322
   motives for 470–471
   Northern Ireland 351, 352
   North Korea 472
   nuclear weapons and 358
   Pakistan 376
   Palestine Liberation
      Organization 377, 378
   Patriot Act 499–500
   political Islam 257
   al-Qaeda 408, 473
   strategies for dealing with
      472
   Sudan 462
   Syria 466, 472

Texaco 372
Texas 58, 80, 311–313, 397,
   **473–474,** 488
Thailand 30, **474**
theater of power 403
think tanks 99, 132, **474–475**
Thucydides 414
Tiananmen Square 53–54, 76
Tibet **475–476**
Tito, Josip Broz, Marshal 85, 534
tobacco use, global pact on 95
Tokyo Round (GATT) 155, 182,
   **476–477**
Torricelli, Robert 111, 112, 210
Torricelli Act *See* Cuban
   Democracy Act
Toronto Group 320
Torrijos, Omar 379
Tower, John *412,* 478
Tower Commission 245–246,
   **477–478**
Trade Act (1974) 477, 497
Trade Development unit 92
Trade Expansion Act (1962) 277,
   497
trade policy and tariffs **478–479**
   Democratic Party and 120
   economic sanctions 140
   fast-track authority 101,
      **158–159,** 402, 477, 479
   General Agreement on
      Tariffs and Trade (Gatt)
      *See* General Agreement
      on Tariffs and Trade
   Hull, Cordell 215
   most-favored-nation (MFN)
      status 76, 182, 264–265,
      **322–323,** 478
   North American Free Trade
      Agreement 54, 63, 82,
      158, 316, **343–344,** 479,
      480
   president 402
   Republican Party 418
   Smoot-Hawley Tariff Act
      414–415, **441–442**
   territories and 228
   United States Trade
      Representative, Office of
      the 51, 497
   World Trade Organization
      (WTO) 156, 256, 478,
      479, 498, 499, **524–525**
Trade Reform Act (1974) 264–265
Transjordan 22, 273 *See also*
   Jordan
Treasury Department, U.S. 51,
   230, 233, **479–480**
treaties
   executive agreements and
      157
   Federalist Papers and
      160–161
   *Missouri v. Holland* (1920)
      318
   termination of 189
   Treaties for the Advancement of
      Peace 50
   Treaty of Berlin (1921) 214
   Treaty of Brest-Litovsk 427
   Treaty of Chemulpo (1882) 445
   Treaty of Ghent 192, 301,
      **480–481,** 512

Treaty of Guadalupe-Hidalgo 313, 397
Treaty of Kanagawa (1854) 265
Treaty of Mortefontaine (1800) 173
Treaty of Nanjing (1872) 71
Treaty of Paris (1763) 179–180
Treaty of Paris (1783) 3, 19, 172, 178, 191, 448, **481,** 510
Treaty of Paris (1898) 109, 453
Treaty of Portsmouth **481–482**
Treaty of San Lorenzo *See* Pinckney's Treaty
Treaty of Tlatelolco (1967) 130
Treaty of Versailles 130, 138, 170, 171, 184–185, 296, 396, **482–483,** 520
Treaty of Wangxia (Wanghia) (1844) 72, 366
Treaty of Washington (1871) 15–16, 190, 193
Treaty on European Union *See* Maastricht Treaty
Treaty on the Permanent Neutrality of the Canal (1977) 382
*Trent* affair 14
Trilateral Commission 146, 361, **483–484**
Tripartite Declaration (1950) 22
tripolarity **484**
Tripoli 36
Trist, Nicholas 313, 314
Trofimoff, George 153
Trujillo, Omar 369, 382
Trujillo, Rafael 134
Truman, Bess 163
Truman, Harry *484,* **484–485**
  Baruch Plan 36–37
  China 73–74
  containment 275, 352–353
  Dulles, John Foster 138
  freedom of the seas 288
  International Trade Organization 242–243
  Iran 85
  Israel 259
  Korean War 279, 280, 485
  Lend Lease Act (1941) 293
  MacArthur, Douglas 300
  Marshall Plan 305–306
  National Security Council 333
  North Atlantic Treaty Organization (NATO) 345
  Office of Strategic Services (OSS) 362–363
  Point Four Program 395
  Potsdam Conference 398–399, *399,* 484
  refugee policy 415–416
  Saudi Arabia 157
  Soviet Union 484–485
  Turkey 85
  Vandenberg, Arthur 502
  Vietnam War 507
  Wallace, Henry 510
  *Youngstown Sheet and Tube Co. v. Sawyer* 533
Truman Doctrine 1, 85, **485–486,** 487
Tshombe, Moise 96

TTAPS study 360
Tudjman, Franjo 44, 106, 107, 116, 117
Tunis 36
Tunisia **486**
Tunney Amendment 166
Turkey **486–488**
  arms transfers to 28
  Central Treaty Organization 68–69
  Cyprus 487
  Dardanelles 85
  drug trafficking 137
  Greece 196, 197
  Iraq War 253
  political Islam 257
  Truman Doctrine **485–486**
Turkmenistan 65–67
Turner, Stansfield 129, 330, 332
Tutsi 431–432
TV Martí 496
Tyler, John 311–312, 473–474, **488**

**U**
U-2 incident 79, 152, 367, **489–490**
Ubico Castaneda, Jorge 198
Uganda 432
Ukraine *168,* 458, 459
Ulster Defense Group 351
ULTRA 152
*Underhill v. Hernandes* (1897) 35–36, **490**
unilateralism 16–17, **490**
Union of Utrecht (1579) 335
unipolarity x, 241, **490–491**
United Arab Republic 141, 466
United Fruit Company 198, 199, 200
United Nations (UN) **491–494**
  Afghanistan 7
  Antiballistic Missile Treaty 34
  Arab-Israeli conflict 22, 23, 259
  Baruch Plan 36
  Bosnia and Herzegovina 44, 535
  Cambodia 59
  collective security and 90
  Comprehensive Test Ban Treaty 94
  Haiti 371
  humanitarian intervention 218
  human rights 215–216
  International Criminal Court 233, 234
  Iraq War 56, 177–178, 252–253, 431, 493, 494, 505
  Korean War 279, 280–281
  Namibia 327
  Netherlands 336
  organizational components of 491
  peacekeeping and peacemaking 384–385, 492
  Persian Gulf War 249, 388–389, 493
  Rwanda 432
  Somalia 442–443

Vandenberg, Arthur 502
weapons of mass destruction (WMDs) 250, 253
Yalta Conference 533
United Nations Conference on Environment and Development (UNCED) *See* Earth Summit, Rio de Janeiro
United Nations Convention on the Rights of the Child 417
United Nations Emergency Peacekeeping Force in Cyprus (UNFICYP) 384
United Nations Environment Programme (UNEP) 139, 319–320
United Nations Fourth World Conference on Women 164
United Nations High Commissioner for Refugees 415
United Nations Operation in the Congo (ONUC) 384
United Nations Population Fund 398
United Nations protection force (UNPROFOR) 117
United Nations Resolution 242 60, 259
United Nations World Summit on Social Development 164
United States Agency for International Development (USAID) 7, 66, 165, 211, 287, 486, **494–495**
United States and Foreign Commercial Service 92
United States-Baltic Charter 35
United States Border Patrol *316*
United States Catholic Conference 417
*United States Foreign Policy: Shield of the Republic* (Lippman) 295
United States Information Agency (USIA) **495–496**
United States Institute of Peace 233, **496–497**
United States-North African Economic Partnership 486
United States-North American Economic Partnership 11
United States-Northern Europe Initiative 35
United States Nuclear Weapons Cost Study Project 359
United States-South Korea Mutual Defense Treaty (1954) 446
United States Trade Representative, Office of the 51, **497**
*United States v. Belmont* (1934) 49, 157, **497–498**
*United States v. Curtiss-Wright Export Corp.* (1936) **498**
Universal Declaration of Human Rights 215–216
universal international organization 240
Universal Peace Society 385
UNPROFOR (United Nations protection force) 117

UN Resolution 242 23
Upshur-Calhoun Treaty (1844) 58
Uruguay Round (GATT) 54, 82, 95, 155, 158, 182, 324, **498–499**
USAID *See* United States Agency for International Development
USA Patriot Act (2001) 160, 438, **499–500**
USDA *See* Agriculture, U.S. Department of
Uzbekistan 65–67

**V**
Vance, Cyrus 44, 64, 247, 332, 382, 483, *501,* **501**
Vance-Owen Plan 44, 116, 501
Vandenberg, Arthur 135, 345, 361, **501–502**
Vanderbilt, Cornelius 162, 338
Vanik, Charles 264, 265
Velvet Revolution (1989) 115
Venezuela **502–503**
  Blaine, James 42
  boundary dispute with Great Britain 81, 365–366, 502, **503–504**
  debt crisis (1980s) 117
  drug trafficking 136, 503
  oil 503
  Organization of Petroleum Exporting Countries 364–365, 372–374
  Roosevelt, Theodore 423
  *Underhill v. Hernandes* (1897) 35–36, 490
Veracruz, U.S. occupation of 314–315
verification **504–506**
Versailles Treaty *See* Treaty of Versailles
Vienna Convention (1985) 320
Vietcong 506, 508
Viet Minh 506, 508
Vietnam **506–507**
  Agent Orange 516
  arms transfers 28
  bipolarity and 41
  Cambodia 58–59
  France 176, 506
  religion and 417
  Southeast Asia Treaty Organization (SEATO) 445
Vietnam Veterans Against the War 387
Vietnam War **507–509,** 508*m,* 509
  Democratic Party 121
  Ford, Gerald 166
  Fulbright, J. William 180
  guerrilla warfare 201
  hawks and 208
  Johnson, Lyndon 271–272
  land mine use 285
  McNamara, Robert 309
  Nixon, Richard 87, 341–342, 508–509
  peace movement 386–387
  Pentagon Papers 337–338, **387–388**
  Thailand and 474

Villa, Francisco "Pancho" 519
*Vincennes*, USS 245, 248
Vincent, John Carter 308
Virgin Islands 439
*Virginius* 109
Vladivostok accords **509**
Voice of America 495–496
voluntary export restriction (VER) 141
Vonsiatsky, Anastase Andreievitch 159
voter knowledge 404

**W**

Walesa, Lech 397, 429
Walker, John
Walker, William 162, 338, 393
Wallace, Henry 121, **510**
Walter-McCarran Immigration Act (1952) 315
war
    chicken hawks 250
    declaration of 100, 101–102, 180, 223, 248, 465, 512–513
    between democratic nations 121–122
    deterrence failures 126–127
    doves 136
    guerrilla warfare **201**
    hawks 208
    idealism and 221
    Jefferson, Thomas 270
    Kellogg-Briand Pact outlawing **274**
    media coverage of 311
    military-industrial complex 316–317
    peace movements **385–387**
    *vs.* crises 235
war crimes *See* International Criminal Court
*Ware v. Hylton* (1796) 29, **510**
Warner, John 407
War of 1812 61–62, 161, 192, 264, 301, 385, 480–481, **510–512,** *511*
War of the Pacific (1879–84) 69
War Powers Resolution (1973) 101–102, 180, 223, 248, **512–513**
Warsaw Pact (1955) 85, 383, **513–514**
Washington, George 12, 258, **514–515**
Washington Conference (1921–22) 43, 73, 130, 174, 214, **515–516**
Watanabe, Takeshi 483–484
Watergate burglary 77
Watkins, Arthur 308
weapons of mass destruction (WMDs) 250, 253, 505, **516–517**

Webster, Daniel 207, 371, **488, 517–518**
Webster, William 309
Webster-Ashburton Treaty (1842) 193, 371, 488
Weimar era 185
Weinberger, Caspar 147, 198, 246, 331
Weir, Benjamin 246
Welch, Richard 197
Welfare Reform Act (1996) 223
Wells, Sumner 215
West Bank 61, 260, 261, 273, 377
Western Sahara 322
West European Union 156–157, 177, 347
Westmoreland, William 309, 508
Weyler y Nicolau, Valeriano 109, 366, 451
Whig Party 313, **518**
White, Edward Douglas 228
White, Henry 482
Wilhelm II, Kaiser 183–184
Wilkes, Charles 14
Wilkinson, James 311
William II, Emperor of Germany 335
Wilmot, David 518, 519
Wilmot Proviso (1846) **518–519**
Wilson, Edith 163
Wilson, Woodrow **519–520**
    China 72
    Colombia 91
    dollar diplomacy 132
    Fourteen Points 129, **170–171,** 174, 184–185, 214, 482–483, 521–522, 527
    Haiti 204
    idealism 221, 521
    Japan 266
    League of Nations 89, 170, 206, **289–290,** 482–483, 519–520
    Lodge, Henry Cabot 296
    Mexico 314–315
    Treaty of Versailles **482–483,** 520
    World War I 50, 173, 184, 213–214, 519–520, 525, 526, 527
Wilsonianism **521–522**
Winship, Blanton 406
Wohlstetter, Albert 410
Wolfe, James W. 171
Wolfers, Arnold 329
Wolfowitz, Paul 252
women and American foreign policy 162–164, **521–522**
Women's International League for Peace and Freedom 386, 521
Women Strike for Peace 386
Wood, Leonard 394
Wood, Robert E. 13
Woods, Alan 165, 167

Woolsey, R. James 81, 475
World Bank 48, 309, 522
World Court 290
World Health Organization 95
*A World Restored* (Kissinger) 278
World Summit on Sustainable Development **523–524**
World Trade Center *437,* 437–438
World Trade Organization (WTO) 156, 256, 478, 479, 498, 499, **524–525**
World Vision 165
World War Foreign Debt Commission 206
World War I **525–528,** *527*
    Baltic states 34
    Brazil 47
    FBI 159
    Fourteen Points 129, **170–171,** 174, 184–185, 214, 482–483, 521–522, 527
    France 173–174
    Germany 170–171, 173, 174, 184, 482–483, 525–527
    Great Britain 193–194, 482–483, 525–526
    Greece 196
    House, Edward Mandell ("Colonel"), and 213–214
    Iran 243
    Italy 262
    Japan 266
    Netherlands 335
    Nye committee 360–361
    peace movement 386
    Treaty of Versailles 130, 138, 170, 171, 184–185, 296, 396, **482–483,** 520
    Wilson, Woodrow 50, 173, 184, 213–214, 519–520, 525, 526, 527
World War II **528–531,** *529m, 530m*
    America First Committee 13–14
    Argentina 25
    Atlantic Charter 30–31
    Baltic states 34–35
    Brazil 47
    Canada 62
    China 73
    cold war 83
    Committee to Defend America by Aiding the Allies 14
    Federal Bureau of Investigation 159, *160*
    France 174–175, *175,* 530–531
    Germany 185, 315, 527, 529, 531, 538

    Great Britain 194–195, 528–529
    Greece 196
    Iran 243
    Joint Chiefs of Staff in 272
    land mine use 285
    Lend-Lease Act 292–293, 421
    MacArthur, Douglas 300
    Netherlands 335
    neutrality legislation 185, 292, 321, **336–337,** 360–361, 421, 528
    Office of Strategic Services 362
    peace movement 386
    Poland in 396
    Potsdam Conference 83, 398–399, **398–399,** *399,* 484
    Rio Pact (1947) **420**
    Soviet Union 428
    summit conferences (overview) 529–531
    Tehran Conference 469–470
    Yalta Conference 49, 57, 83, 157, 446, **533,** *534*
Wriston, Harry 169
WTO *See* World Trade Organization
Wu, Harry 164
Wye River accords (1998) 260–261, **531**

**X**

XYZ affair 2–3, 173

**Y**

Yamashita, Isamu 484
Yardley, Herbert 152
Yeltsin, Boris 53, 356, 430, 459–460
Yemen 124, 125, 141–142
Yom Kippur War (1973) 23, 142, 373
*Youngstown Sheet and Tube Co. v. Sawyer* (1952) **533–534**
youth bulge 124, 125
Yugoslavia 44, 106, 116, **281–282, 534–536**

**Z**

Zahir Shah, Mohammad 4, 7
Zaire *See* Congo, Democratic Republic of the
Zelaya, José Santos 131–132, 338
zero option proposal 232
Zimbabwe (Rhodesia) 8, **537–538**
Zimmermann, Arthur 527, 538
Zimmermann Telegram 315, 527, **538**
Zionist movement 259
Zwicker, Ralph 30